Lecture Notes in Computer Science 2988
Edited by G. Goos, J. Hartmanis, and J. van Leeuwen

Springer
Berlin
Heidelberg
New York
Hong Kong
London
Milan
Paris
Tokyo

Kurt Jensen Andreas Podelski (Eds.)

Tools and Algorithms for the Construction and Analysis of Systems

10th International Conference, TACAS 2004
Held as Part of the Joint European Conferences
on Theory and Practice of Software, ETAPS 2004
Barcelona, Spain, March 29 - April 2, 2004
Proceedings

Springer

Series Editors

Gerhard Goos, Karlsruhe University, Germany
Juris Hartmanis, Cornell University, NY, USA
Jan van Leeuwen, Utrecht University, The Netherlands

Volume Editors

Kurt Jensen
University of Aarhus
Department of Computer Science
IT-parken, Aabogade 34, 8200 Århus N, Denmark
E-mail: kjensen@daimi.au.dk

Andreas Podelski
Max-Planck-Institut für Informatik
Stuhlsatzenhausweg 85, 66123 Saarbrücken, Germany
E-mail: podelski@mpi-sb.mpg.de

Cataloging-in-Publication Data applied for

A catalog record for this book is available from the Library of Congress.

Bibliographic information published by Die Deutsche Bibliothek
Die Deutsche Bibliothek lists this publication in the Deutsche Nationalbibliografie;
detailed bibliographic data is available in the Internet at <http://dnb.ddb.de>.

CR Subject Classification (1998): F.3, D.2.4, D.2.2, C.2.4, F.2.2

ISSN 0302-9743
ISBN 3-540-21299-X Springer-Verlag Berlin Heidelberg New York

Springer-Verlag is a part of Springer Science+Business Media

springeronline.com

© Springer-Verlag Berlin Heidelberg 2004
Printed in Germany

Typesetting: Camera-ready by author, data conversion by PTP-Berlin, Protago-TeX-Production GmbH
Printed on acid-free paper   SPIN: 10993156   06/3142   5 4 3 2 1 0

Foreword

ETAPS 2004 was the seventh instance of the European Joint Conferences on Theory and Practice of Software. ETAPS is an annual federated conference that was established in 1998 by combining a number of existing and new conferences. This year it comprised five conferences (FOSSACS, FASE, ESOP, CC, TACAS), 23 satellite workshops, 1 tutorial, and 7 invited lectures (not including those that are specific to the satellite events).

The events that comprise ETAPS address various aspects of the system development process, including specification, design, implementation, analysis and improvement. The languages, methodologies and tools that support these activities are all well within its scope. Different blends of theory and practice are represented, with an inclination towards theory with a practical motivation on the one hand and soundly based practice on the other. Many of the issues involved in software design apply to systems in general, including hardware systems, and the emphasis on software is not intended to be exclusive.

ETAPS is a loose confederation in which each event retains its own identity, with a separate program committee and independent proceedings. Its format is open-ended, allowing it to grow and evolve as time goes by. Contributed talks and system demonstrations are in synchronized parallel sessions, with invited lectures in plenary sessions. Two of the invited lectures are reserved for "unifying" talks on topics of interest to the whole range of ETAPS attendees. The aim of cramming all this activity into a single one-week meeting is to create a strong magnet for academic and industrial researchers working on topics within its scope, giving them the opportunity to learn about research in related areas, and thereby to foster new and existing links between work in areas that were formerly addressed in separate meetings.

ETAPS 2004 was organized by the LSI Department of the Catalonia Technical University (UPC), in cooperation with:

European Association for Theoretical Computer Science (EATCS)
European Association for Programming Languages and Systems
(EAPLS)
European Association of Software Science and Technology (EASST)
ACM SIGACT, SIGSOFT and SIGPLAN

The organizing team comprised

Jordi Cortadella (Satellite Events), Nikos Mylonakis, Robert Nieuwenhuis, Fernando Orejas (Chair), Edelmira Pasarella, Sonia Perez, Elvira Pino, Albert Rubio

and had the assistance of TILESA OPC.
ETAPS 2004 received generous sponsorship from:

UPC, Spanish Ministry of Science and Technology (MCYT), Catalan Department for Universities, Research and Information Society (DURSI), IBM, Intel.

Overall planning for ETAPS conferences is the responsibility of its Steering Committee, whose current membership is:

Ratislav Bodik (Berkeley), Maura Cerioli (Genoa), Evelyn Duesterwald (IBM, Yorktown Heights), Hartmut Ehrig (Berlin), José Fiadeiro (Leicester), Marie-Claude Gaudel (Paris), Andy Gordon (Microsoft Research, Cambridge), Roberto Gorrieri (Bologna), Nicolas Halbwachs (Grenoble), Gûrel Hedin (Lund), Kurt Jensen (Aarhus), Paul Klint (Amsterdam), Tiziana Margaria (Dortmund), Ugo Montanari (Pisa), Hanne Riis Nielson (Copenhagen), Fernando Orejas (Barcelona), Mauro Pezzè (Milan), Andreas Podelski (Saarbrücken), Mooly Sagiv (Tel Aviv), Don Sannella (Edinburgh), Vladimiro Sassone (Sussex), David Schmidt (Kansas), Bernhard Steffen (Dortmund), Perdita Stevens (Edinburgh), Andrzej Tarlecki (Warsaw), Igor Walukiewicz (Bordeaux), Michel Wermelinger (Lisbon)

I would like to express my sincere gratitude to all of these people and organizations, the program committee chairs and PC members of the ETAPS conferences, the organizers of the satellite events, the speakers themselves, and finally Springer-Verlag for agreeing to publish the ETAPS proceedings. This year, the number of submissions approached 600, making acceptance rates fall to 25%. I congratulate the authors who made it into the final program! I hope that all the other authors still found a way of participating in this exciting event and I hope you will continue submitting.

In 2005, ETAPS will be organized by Don Sannella in Edinburgh. You will be welcomed by another "local": my successor as ETAPS Steering Committee Chair – Perdita Stevens. My wish is that she will enjoy coordinating the next three editions of ETAPS as much as I have. It is not an easy job, in spite of what Don assured me when I succeeded him! But it is definitely a very rewarding one. One cannot help but feel proud of seeing submission and participation records being broken one year after the other, and that the technical program reached the levels of quality that we have been witnessing. At the same time, interacting with the organizers has been a particularly rich experience. Having organized the very first edition of ETAPS in Lisbon in 1998, I knew what they were going through, and I can tell you that each of them put his/her heart, soul, and an incredible amount of effort into the organization. The result, as we all know, was brilliant on all counts! Therefore, my last words are to thank Susanne Graf (2002), Andrzej Tarlecki and Paweł Urzyczyn (2003), and Fernando Orejas (2004) for the privilege of having worked with them.

Leicester, January 2004   José Luiz Fiadeiro
                                            ETAPS Steering Committee Chairman

Preface

This volume contains the proceedings of the 10th International Conference on Tools and Algorithms for the Construction and Analysis of Systems (TACAS 2004). TACAS 2004 took place in Barcelona, Spain, from March 29th to April 2nd, as part of the 7th European Joint Conferences on Theory and Practice of Software (ETAPS 2004), whose aims, organization, and history are detailed in a foreword by the ETAPS Steering Committee Chair, José Luiz Fiadeiro.

TACAS is a forum for researchers, developers, and users interested in rigorously based tools for the construction and analysis of systems. The conference serves to bridge the gaps between different communities including, but not limited to, those devoted to formal methods, software and hardware verification, static analysis, programming languages, software engineering, real-time systems, and communication protocols that share common interests in, and techniques for, tool development. In particular, by providing a venue for the discussion of common problems, heuristics, algorithms, data structures, and methodologies, TACAS aims to support researchers in their quest to improve the utility, reliability, flexibility, and efficiency of tools for building systems.

TACAS seeks theoretical papers with a clear link to tool construction, papers describing relevant algorithms and practical aspects of their implementation, papers giving descriptions of tools and associated methodologies, and case studies with a conceptual message.

The specific topics covered by the conference include, but are not limited to, the following:

- specification and verification techniques,
- theorem-proving and model-checking,
- system construction and transformation techniques,
- static and run-time analysis,
- compositional and refinement-based methodologies,
- testing and test-case generation,
- analytical techniques for real-time, hybrid, and safety-critical systems,
- tool environments and tool architectures,
- applications and case studies.

TACAS accepts two types of contribution: research papers and tool demonstration papers. Research papers are full-length papers covering one or more of the topics above, including tool development and case studies from the perspective of scientific research. Research papers are evaluated by the TACAS Program Committee. Tool demonstration papers are shorter papers that give an overview of a particular tool and its application. To stress the importance of tool demonstrations for TACAS, these papers are evaluated and selected by a specific member of the TACAS Program Committee who holds the title of Tool Chair.

In the years since it joined the ETAPS conference federation, TACAS has been the largest of the ETAPS member conferences in terms of number of submissions and papers accepted. TACAS 2004 received a record number of submissions: 145 research papers and 17 tool demonstration papers were submitted.

From the submitted papers, 37 research papers and 6 tool demo papers were accepted, yielding an overall acceptance ratio of 26%. Together with 2003 this represents the most competitive acceptance rate to date for TACAS (the acceptance rate has never exceeded 36% since TACAS joined ETAPS in 1999).

To carry out the difficult task of selecting a program from the large number of submissions in a fair and competent manner, we were fortunate to have highly qualified program committee members from diverse geographic and research areas. Each submission was evaluated by at least three reviewers. After a four-week reviewing process, the program selection was carried out in a two-week online program committee meeting. We believe the result of the committee deliberations was a very strong scientific program. As this year's invited speaker, the program committee selected Antti Valmari, who presented work on program verification by means of state spaces.

In conclusion, successfully organizing and implementing TACAS 2004 as represented by the proceedings recorded in this volume required significant effort by many different people during the past two years. Although it is impossible to mention everyone who contributed to TACAS 2004 by name, we would like to extend our sincere thanks to the following people: Bernhard Steffen, who served as the Tool Chair, the program committee members and additional referees, who performed admirably in spite of the high workload assigned to them, Martin Karusseit (METAFrame, Germany), for his constant and prompt support in dealing with the online conference management system, Andrey Rybalchenko (MPI für Informatik, Germany), who carried out the hard work of preparing the LNCS proceedings, Kjeld Høyer Mortensen (University of Aarhus, Denmark), for his help in preparing the TACAS 2004 website (www.daimi.au.dk/~cpn/tacas04), the TACAS Steering Committee, for inviting us to chair TACAS 2004, the ETAPS 2004 Organizing Committee, including the committee chair Fernando Orejas, and the ETAPS Steering Committee Chair José Luiz Fiadeiro for his patient guidance and prompting over the course of many months.

January 2004   Kurt Jensen and Andreas Podelski

Referees

Table of Contents

Explicite State/Petri Nets

Scheduling

Constraint Solving

Abstraction

Automata Techniques

Author Index

Revisiting Positive Equality*

Shuvendu K. Lahiri, Randal E. Bryant, Amit Goel, and Muralidhar Talupur

Carnegie Mellon University, Pittsburgh, PA
{shuvendu,agoel}@ece.cmu.edu, {randy.bryant,tmurali}@cs.cmu.edu

Abstract. This paper provides a stronger result for exploiting positive equality in the logic of Equality with Uninterpreted Functions (EUF). Positive equality analysis is used to reduce the number of interpretations required to check the validity of a formula. We remove the primary restriction of the previous approach proposed by Bryant, German and Velev [5], where positive equality could be exploited only when all the function applications for a function symbol appear in *positive* context. We show that the set of interpretations considered by our analysis of positive equality is a subset of the set of interpretations considered by the previous approach. The paper investigates the obstacles in exploiting the stronger notion of positive equality (called *robust positive equality*) in a decision procedure and provides a solution for it. We present empirical results on some verification benchmarks.

1 Introduction

Decision procedures for quantifier-free First-Order Logic (FOL) with equality have become an integral part of many formal verification tools. The importance of decision procedures lies in automatically validating (or invalidating) formulas in the logic. The ability to automatically decide formulas has been the cornerstone of several scalable verification approaches. For hardware, Burch and Dill [8] have used symbolic simulation with a decision procedure for the quantifier-free fragment of FOL to automatically verify complex microprocessor control. Bryant et al. [5] have extended their method to successfully verify superscalar processors. Recently, Lahiri, Seshia and Bryant [15] have demonstrated the use of efficient decision procedures to improve the automation for out-of-order processor verification. For software, decision procedures have been used for translation validation of compilers [19]. Decision procedures are used extensively for predicate abstraction in several software verification efforts [2,13]. They have also been used for the analysis of other concurrent infinite-state systems.

Most decision procedures for quantifier-free logic fall roughly into two categories: decision procedures based on (i) a Combination of Theories [22,17,3,18] or (ii) a validity preserving translation to a Boolean formula [5,19,21,7]. The former

---

* This research was supported in part by the Semiconductor Research Corporation, Contract RID 1029.001.

K. Jensen and A. Podelski (Eds.): TACAS 2004, LNCS 2988, pp. 1–15, 2004.

methods combine the decision procedures for individual theories using Nelson-Oppen [17] style of combination. The latter methods translate the first-order formula to a Boolean formula such that the Boolean formula is valid if and only if the first-order formula is valid. There has also been work in solving first-order formulas by using abstraction-refinement based on Boolean Satisfiability (SAT) solvers [4,9].

Among the decision procedures based on a validity preserving translation to a Boolean formula, Bryant et al. [5,5] proposed a technique to exploit the structure of equations in a formula to efficiently translate it into a Boolean formula. Their method identifies a subset of function symbols in the formula as "p-function" symbols, the function symbols which only occur in monotonically positive contexts. The method then restricts the set of interpretations for the function applications of p-function symbols for checking the validity of the formula. They have successfully used this decision procedure to automatically verify complex microprocessors. The method was initially proposed for the Logic of Equality with Uninterpreted Functions (EUF) and was later extended for the logic of Counter Arithmetic with Lambda Expressions and Uninterpreted Functions (CLU) [7, 12]. Pnueli et al. [19] use Ackermann's function elimination method [1] to remove function applications from a formula and allocate ranges for each of the variables in the resulting formula, such that the ranges are sufficient for checking validity. The technique also exploits the polarity of equations in the formula to restrict the range allocation. Rodeh et al. [21] have used the function elimination method of Bryant et al. [5] to further restrict the domain size of the variables using the algorithm in [19]. The last two decision procedures have been successfully used for validating compiler code automatically. In all the above decision procedures [5,19,21], the key idea has been to restrict the set of interpretations, by exploiting the polarity of the terms in the formula.

One of the main limitations of the *positive equality* analysis of Bryant et al. is that it is not *robust*. For a function symbol f to be a "p-function" symbol, *all* the function applications of f have to appear in monotonically positive equations. This makes it difficult to exploit positive equality, even when a small number of applications of a function appears in a *negative* context. This places stronger restrictions on the formulas to be decided efficiently and the method has not proven effective for benchmarks which display these characteristics [20].

In this paper, we present a generalization of positive equality analysis of Bryant, German and Velev [5] which allows the decision procedure to exploit positive equality in situations where the previous approach could not exploit it. This stronger version of positive equality analysis, called *robust* positive equality, restricts the interpretations to consider in deciding formulas in *EUF* to a *subset* of interpretations considered by the previous approach. We show the complexity of exploiting *robust* positive equality in a decision procedure which uses the function elimination method proposed by Bryant et al. [5]. We describe a decision procedure to exploit this stronger form of positive equality. We present verification benchmarks where this approach reduces the number of interpretations to consider by orders of magnitude compared to the previous approach.

The rest of the paper is organized as follows: In Section 2, we present Bryant et al.'s positive equality analysis. We illustrate the strengths and limitations of their approach. In Section 3, we present a generalization of the positive equality analysis called *robust* positive equality analysis. We present the *robust maximal diversity* theorem that allows us to restrict the interpretations to consider to be a subset of the interpretations considered by the previous approach. Section 4 discusses a decision procedure based on robust positive equality. We discuss the main complications in exploiting robust positive equality in a decision procedure and provide a heuristic which lets us exploit the robust positive equality. In Section 5, we compare the effectiveness of the new approach compared to the previous work on a set of verification benchmarks.

2   Background: Positive Equality and Its Limitation

In earlier work, Bryant et al. [5,5] exploited *positive equality* in the logic of EUF to give a very efficient decision procedure for this fragment. The logic of EUF is built from *terms* and *formulas*. Terms are formed by function applications (e.g. $f(x)$) or by *if-then-else (ITE)* constructs. The expression $ITE(G, T_1, T_2)$ selects T_1 when G is **true**, and T_2 otherwise. Formulas are built from predicate applications, equations between terms or using the other Boolean connectives ($\wedge$, $\vee$, $\neg$). Every function and predicate symbol has an associated arity to denote the number of arguments for the function. Function symbols of arity zero are called *symbolic constants*. Similarly, predicate symbols of arity zero are called *propositional symbolic constants*.

In positive equality analysis, the decision procedure partitions the function symbols in an EUF formula as p-function symbols and g-function symbols. A function symbol f is called a p-function symbol in an EUF formula F[1], if none of the function applications of f appear in (i) a negative equation (e.g. $f(x_1, \ldots, x_k) \neq T_1$) or (ii) in the controlling formula of an *if-then-else (ITE)* term (the controlling formula of an *ITE* is implicitly negated when choosing the *else* branch). All function symbols which are not p-function symbols are g-function symbols.

The semantics of an expression in EUF is defined relative to a non-empty domain $\mathcal{D}$ of values and an interpretation I, which assigns values to the function and predicate symbols in the formula. An interpretation I assigns a function from $\mathcal{D}^k$ to $\mathcal{D}$ for each function of arity k and a function from $\mathcal{D}^k$ to {**true**,**false**} for each predicate symbol of arity k. Given an interpretation I, the meaning of an expression E is defined as $I[E]$ inductively on the syntactic structure of E. A formula F is *valid* (also called *universally valid*), if for every interpretation I, $I[E] = $ **true**.

An interpretation I is called a *maximally-diverse* interpretation, if for any *p-function* symbol f, $I[f(U_1, \ldots, U_k)] = I[g(S_1, \ldots, S_m)]$ if and only if the following conditions hold: (i) f and g are the same function symbol and (ii) forall

---

[1] For simplicity, assume F is in negation normal form where all the negations are pushed down towards the leaves of the formula and $\neg\neg G$ is collapsed to G.

$i \in [1, \ldots, k]$, $I[U_i] = I[S_i]$. The main theorem is called the *maximal diversity theorem*[2], which is given below.

Theorem 1. Maximal Diversity Theorem. *An EUF formula F is valid iff F is true in all maximally-diverse interpretations.*

Restricting the set of interpretations to only maximally-diverse interpretations for checking validity is very efficient for EUF formulas with large number of p-function symbols. For instance, consider the formula:

$$\neg(x = y) \lor f(g(x)) = f(g(y))$$

The set of terms in the formula is $\{x, y, g(x), g(y), f(g(x)), f(g(y))\}$. Since there are 6 terms in the formula, it is sufficient to restrict the domain of each of the terms to contain at most 6 values, for checking the validity [1]. Hence, one can decide the formula by considering 6^6 interpretations. However, positive equality analysis allows us to restrict the number of combinations to search, to only 2^2 values, since only two functions x and y (of arity 0) appear in a negative equation.

However, the main bottleneck of the approach is that it is not *robust*. Positive equality can not be exploited for a function symbol f even if only one application of f appears in a negative context. For example, consider the following EUF formula:

$$F \doteq \neg(f(x) = x) \lor (f(f(f(f(x)))) = f(f(f(x)))) \tag{1}$$

After exploiting positive equality, the set of p-function symbols would be {} and the set of g-function symbols would be {x,f}. This is because both x and f appear in a negative equation, namely $\neg(f(x) = x)$ in the formula. Thus the number of interpretations to search would be $5^5 = 3125$.

However, one can see that only one application of f, namely $f(x)$, appears in a negative equation while the other applications, $f(f(x))$, $f(f(f(x)))$ and $f(f(f(f(x))))$, appear in positive equations only. In this paper, we present a generalization of the positive equality analysis which allows us to exploit the positive structure of such applications. Based on the new analysis, it is sufficient to consider only 4 interpretations to decide the validity of the formula F, instead of the 5^5 interpretations. Even for this small formula, this reduces the number of interpretations to consider $3125/4 = 781$ fold !

3   Logic of Robust Positive Equality with Uninterpreted Functions (RPEUF)

3.1   Syntax

Figure 1 gives the syntax of RPEUF[3]. The logic is essentially same as EUF or PEUF [5], but partitions the formulas (respectively, terms) into "p-formulas" and

---

[2] The definition of maximally-diverse interpretation is slightly different from the original work [5] for simplicity of presentation.

[3] We try to follow the terminology of the original paper by Bryant et al. for the rest of the paper, whenever applicable

"g-formulas" (respectively, "p-terms" and "g-terms"). Intuitively, a p-formula appears in only monotonically positive expressions, i.e. does not appear under the scope of negations ($\neg$), or in the controlling formulas of *ITE* expressions. All other formulas are g-formulas. The top-level formula can always be classified as a p-formula. The p-terms are those terms which never appear in a g-formula. More details can be found in [6]. The only difference between PEUF and RPEUF is that function symbols are not partitioned as p-function symbols and g-function symbols. Instead, each application of functions can either be a p-function application (*p-func-appl*) or a g-function application (*g-func-appl*). Let $\mathcal{T}_p(F)$ be the set of p-term function application terms in a formula F. Similarly, let $\mathcal{T}_g(F)$ be the set of g-term function application terms in a formula F.

$$
\begin{aligned}
\textit{g-term} ::=~ & \textit{ITE}(\textit{g-formula, g-term, g-term}) \\
\mid~ & \textit{g-func-appl}(\textit{p-term}, \ldots, \textit{p-term}) \\
\textit{p-term} ::=~ & \textit{g-term} \mid \textit{ITE}(\textit{g-formula, p-term, p-term}) \\
\mid~ & \textit{p-func-appl}(\textit{p-term}, \ldots, \textit{p-term}) \\
\textit{g-formula} ::=~ & \textbf{true} \mid \textbf{false} \mid \neg\textit{g-formula} \mid (\textit{g-term} = \textit{g-term}) \\
\mid~ & (\textit{g-formula} \lor \textit{g-formula}) \mid (\textit{g-formula} \land \textit{g-formula}) \\
\mid~ & \textit{predicate-symbol}(\textit{p-term}, \ldots, \textit{p-term}) \\
\textit{p-formula} ::=~ & \textit{g-formula} \mid (\textit{p-term} = \textit{p-term}) \\
\mid~ & (\textit{p-formula} \lor \textit{p-formula}) \mid (\textit{p-formula} \land \textit{p-formula})
\end{aligned}
$$

Fig. 1. Syntax for RPEUF

For any RPEUF formula F, we define $\Sigma(F)$ to be the set of function symbols in F. For a function application term T, *top-symbol*(T) returns the top-level function symbol for the term T.

3.2 Diverse Interpretations

The semantics of an expression in RPEUF is defined in a similar manner as defined in Section 2. The domain $\mathcal{D}$ is kept implicit for most of our purposes and we assume it to be the underlying domain. An interpretation defines a partitioning of the terms in the formula, where two terms belong to the same equivalence class if and only if they are assigned the same value. Interpretation I *refines* (*properly refines*) interpretation I', if I refines (properly refines) the equivalence classes induced by I'.

Given an interpretation I, function application terms $T_1 \doteq f(U_1, \ldots, .U_k)$ and $T_2 \doteq f(S_1, \ldots, S_k)$ are said to *argumentMatch* under I, if for all $j \in [1, \ldots, k]$, $I[U_j] = I[S_j]$. It is not defined when T_1 and T_2 have different top-level function symbols.

Robust Maximally Diverse Interpretation. An interpretation I is said to be *robust maximally diverse* if I satisfies the following property:

- For every term $T_1 \doteq f(U_1, \ldots, U_k) \in \mathcal{T}_p(F)$, which does not *argumentMatch* under I with any term $f(S_1 \ldots S_k) \in \mathcal{T}_g(F)$, and for any other function application term T_2, $I[T_1] = I[T_2]$, iff (i) $T_2 \doteq f(V_1, \ldots, V_k)$, and (ii) $I[U_m] = I[V_m]$, for all $m \in [1 \ldots k]$.

Example. Consider the formula in Equation 1. The interpretation Consider the formula in Equation 1. Let us assume (shown a little later in Section 4.1), the set $\mathcal{T}_p(F) \doteq \{f(f(x)), f(f(f(x))), f(f(f(f(x))))\}$, the set of positive applications. The set $\mathcal{T}_g(F)$ becomes $\{x, f(x)\}$. The interpretation $I \doteq \{x \mapsto 1, f(1) \mapsto 2, f(2) \mapsto 3, f(3) \mapsto 4\}$ is an example of a robust maximally diverse interpretation. In this interpretation, $I[f(x)] = 2, I[f(f(x))] = 3$ and $I[f(f(f(x)))] = 4$. Similarly, the interpretation $I \doteq \{x \mapsto 1, f(1) \mapsto 2, f(2) \mapsto 2\}$ is a robust maximally diverse interpretations. However, the interpretation $I \doteq \{x \mapsto 1, f(1) \mapsto 2, f(2) \mapsto 1\}$ is not a robust maximally diverse interpretation since $I[x] = I[f(f(x))] = 1$. But $f(f(x))$ is a *p-term*, whose argument $I[f(x)] = 2$ does not match the argument of the *g-term* $f(x)$, since $I[x] = 1$.

Theorem 2. Robust Maximal Diversity Theorem. *A p-formula F is universally valid iff F is true in all robust maximally diverse interpretations.*

The theorem allows us to restrict ourselves to only those interpretations which are robust maximally diverse. We will show later that in many cases, this prunes away a very large portion of the search space. The proof is very similar to the one presented for the maximal diversity theorem [6] and can be found in the extended version [14].

The following lemma establishes the correspondence between the maximally diverse interpretations and the robust maximally diverse interpretations.

Proposition 1. *If an interpretation I is a robust maximally diverse interpretation, then I is a maximally diverse interpretation.*

This follows from the fact, that for a "p-function" symbol f, a p-term $T_1 \doteq f(U_1, \ldots, U_k)$ never *argumentMatch* with a g-term $T_2 \doteq f(V_1, \ldots, V_k)$, since there are no g-terms for a "p-function" symbol f. Thus the set of robust maximally diverse interpretations is a subset of the set of maximally diverse interpretation set.

4   Decision Procedure for Robust Positive Equality

In this section, we present a decision procedure for exploiting robust positive equality. The essence of the decision procedure is similar to the decision procedure proposed by Bryant, German and Velev. But there are important differences which makes the procedure more complicated.

4.1   Extracting a RPEUF from EUF

Given a EUF formula F, one might try to label the terms and formulas as g-terms, p-terms, p-formulas, g-formulas by the syntax in Figure 1. But the choice of "promoting" g-terms and g-formulas to p-terms and p-formulas makes the grammar ambiguous. Thus the first step is to use a labeling scheme to mark the different expressions in the formula F.

For a given EUF formula F, let $\mathcal{L}_F$ be a labeling function. If $\mathcal{T}(F)$ and $\mathcal{G}(F)$ be the set of terms and formulas in F, then $\mathcal{L}_F$ satisfies the following conditions:

- If $T \in \mathcal{T}(F)$, then $\mathcal{L}_F(T) \in \{g\text{-}term, p\text{-}term\}$
- If $G \in \mathcal{G}(F)$, then $\mathcal{L}_F(G) \in \{g\text{-}formula, p\text{-}formula\}$
- This labeling is permitted by the syntax

A natural labeling function $\mathcal{L}_F^*$ [6] is to label the formulas which never appear under an odd number of negations and does not appear as a control for any ITE node, as $p\text{-}formula$. All other formulas are labeled as $g\text{-}formula$. Once the formulas are labeled, label a term as $p\text{-}term$ if it never appears in an equation labeled as $g\text{-}formula$. All other terms are marked $g\text{-}term$.

4.2   Topological Ordering of Terms

Once we have labeled all the terms in a formula F as either a p-term or a g-term, we will define a *topological order* $\preceq$, for visiting the terms. A topological order preserves the property that if T_1 is a subterm of T_2 in the formula F, then $T_1 \preceq T_2$. There can be many topological orders for the same formula.

Given a topological order $\preceq$, consider the terms that have been "labeled" by $\mathcal{L}(F)$. We will partition the terms into $\mathcal{T}_{\preceq}^+(F)$, $\mathcal{T}_{\preceq}^-(F)$ and $\mathcal{T}_{\preceq}^*(F)$ as follows: For any term $T \in \mathcal{T}(F)$:

- $T \in \mathcal{T}_{\preceq}^-(F)$ iff $\mathcal{L}(T) = g\text{-}term$
- $T \in \mathcal{T}_{\preceq}^*(F)$ iff $\mathcal{L}(T) = p\text{-}term$ and there exists $T_1 \in \mathcal{T}_{\preceq}^-(F)$ such that $T \preceq T_1$ and $top\text{-}symbol(T) = top\text{-}symbol(T_1)$.
- $T \in \mathcal{T}_{\preceq}^+(F)$ iff $T \notin \mathcal{T}_{\preceq}^-(F)$ and $T \notin \mathcal{T}_{\preceq}^*(F)$.

Intuitively, the terms in $\mathcal{T}_{\preceq}^*(F)$ are those terms which precede a negative application with the same top-level function symbol. We label some terms as members of $\mathcal{T}_{\preceq}^*(F)$ because the function elimination scheme (based on Bryant et al.'s method) eliminates function applications in a topological order. Hence we need to process all the subterms before processing a term.

For example, consider the formula in Equation 1. There are 5 terms in the formula: x, $f(x)$, $f(f(x))$, $f(f(f(x)))$, $f(f(f(f(x))))$. The labeling scheme labels the terms $x, f(x)$ as g-term and the terms $f(f(x)), f(f(f(x))), f(f(f(f(x))))$ as p-term. The only topological ordering on this set of terms is $x \preceq f(x) \preceq f(f(x)) \preceq f(f(f(x))) \preceq f(f(f(f(x))))$. Given this topological order, the partitioning results in the following sets

- $T_{\preceq}^{-}(F) = \{x, f(x)\}$, $T_{\preceq}^{*}(F) = \{\}$ and
  $T_{\preceq}^{+}(F) = \{f(f(x)), f(f(f(x))), f(f(f(f(x))))\}$.

However, consider the following formula:

$$F \doteq \neg(f(g(x)) = g(f(x))) \tag{2}$$

There are 5 terms in the formula: x, $f(x)$, $g(x)$, $f(g(x))$ and $g(f(x))$. The labeling labels $f(g(x))$, $g(f(x))$ as g-term and x, $f(x)$, $g(x)$ as p-term. Three possible topological orderings on this set of terms are:

1. $x \preceq f(x) \preceq g(x) \preceq f(g(x)) \preceq g(f(x))$, or
2. $x \preceq f(x) \preceq g(f(x)) \preceq g(x) \preceq f(g(x))$, or
3. $x \preceq g(x) \preceq f(g(x)) \preceq f(x) \preceq g(f(x))$

Given these topological order, the partitioning results in the following sets for the three orders, respectively:

1. $T_{\preceq}^{-}(F) = \{f(g(x)), g(f(x))\}$, $T_{\preceq}^{*}(F) = \{f(x), g(x)\}$ and $T_{\preceq}^{+}(F) = \{x\}$.
2. $T_{\preceq}^{-}(F) = \{f(g(x)), g(f(x))\}$, $T_{\preceq}^{*}(F) = \{f(x)\}$ and $T_{\preceq}^{+}(F) = \{x, g(x)\}$.
3. $T_{\preceq}^{-}(F) = \{f(g(x)), g(f(x))\}$, $T_{\preceq}^{*}(F) = \{g(x)\}$ and $T_{\preceq}^{+}(F) = \{x, f(x)\}$.

The example in Equation 2 illustrates several interesting points. First, even though $f(x)$ and $g(x)$ are both labeled as p-term, there is no ordering of terms such *all* the g-term with the top-level symbol f and g precede these two terms. Note that this limits us from exploiting the full power of Theorem 2. Second, the topological ordering can affect the size of the set $T_{\preceq}^{+}(F)$. The bigger the size of this set, the better the encoding is. Hence, we would like to find the topological ordering which maximizes the size of $T_{\preceq}^{+}(F)$.

4.3   Maximizing $T_{\preceq}^{+}(F)$

The problem of obtaining the optimal $\preceq$, which maximizes the size of $T_{\preceq}^{+}(F)$, turns out to be NP-complete. In this section, we reduce the problem of *maximum independent set* for an undirected graph to our problem.

Let us first pose the problem as a decision problem — is there an ordering $\preceq$ for which the number of terms in $T_{\preceq}^{+}(F)$ is at least k ? Given an ordering $\preceq$, it is easy to find out the number of terms in $T_{\preceq}^{+}(F)$ in polynomial time, hence the problem is in NP.

To show that the problem is NP-complete, consider a undirected graph $G \doteq \langle V, E \rangle$, with V as the set of vertices and E as the set of edges. Construct a *labeled and polar* directed acyclic graph (DAG) $D \doteq \langle V', E' \rangle$, where each vertex $v \in V'$ is a tuple (n_v, l_v, p_v), where n_v is the vertex identifier, l_v is a *label* of the vertex, and p_v is the *polarity* of the vertex. The label of a vertex is a function symbol, and the polarity of a vertex can either be (-) *negative* or (+) *non-negative*. It is easy to see that the vertices of D represent the *terms* in a formula, the *label* denotes the top-level function symbol associated with the term and a vertex with a *negative* polarity denotes a g-term.

The DAG D is constructed from G as follows:

- For each vertex v in V, create two vertices v^+ and v^- in V', such that $v^+ \doteq (v^1, v, +)$ and $v^- \doteq (v^2, v, -)$.
- For each edge $(v_1, v_2) \in E$, add the following pair of directed edges in E' — (v_1^+, v_2^-) and (v_2^+, v_1^-).

Finally, given an ordering $\preceq$, $\mathcal{T}_{\preceq}^+(D)$ contains a subset of those v^+ vertices which do not precede the v^- vertex with the same label v in $\preceq$. Now, we can show the following proposition (proof in [14]):

Proposition 2. *The graph G has a maximum independent set of size k if and only if the DAG D has an ordering $\preceq$ which maximizes the number of vertices in $\mathcal{T}_{\preceq}^+(D)$ to k.*

4.4   Heuristic to Maximize $\mathcal{T}_{\preceq}^+(F)$

Since the complexity of finding the optimum $\preceq$ is NP-complete, we outline a greedy strategy to maximize the number of p-terms in $\mathcal{T}_{\preceq}^+(F)$. We exploit the following proposition (proof sketch in [14]):

Proposition 3. *Given an ordering $\preceq_g$ over all the g-term of the formula, one can obtain an ordering $\preceq$ over all the terms in the formula in time linear to the size of the formula, such that the number of terms in $\mathcal{T}_{\preceq}^+(F)$ is maximum over all possible orderings consistent with the order $\preceq_g$.*

Hence, our problem has been reduced to finding the optimum ordering $\preceq_g$ among the g-terms of the formula. The algorithm has the following main steps:

1. A term $T_1 \doteq f(S_1, \dots, S_k)$ is *potentially positive* iff T_1 is a p-term and T_1 is not a subterm of any other g-term T_2, which has the same top-level function symbol f. For each function symbol f, we compute the number of *potentially positive* function applications of f in the formula.
2. Order the list of function symbols depending on the number of potentially positive terms for each function symbol. The essential idea is that if a function f has n_f potentially positive applications, and if we order all the terms of f independent of the applications of other function symbols, then the number of terms in $\mathcal{T}_{\preceq}^+(F)$ is at least n_f.
3. For each function symbol f, we order all the g-terms of f by simply traversing the formula in a depth-first manner. This ordering of g-terms is consistent with the topological order imposed by the subterm structure.
4. Finally, we obtain $\preceq_g$, by repeatedly placing all the gterms for each of the functions in the sorted function order. While placing a g-term T_1 for function f, we place all the g-terms for the other function symbols which are subterms of the g-term before T_1 in the order.

4.5   Function and Predicate Elimination

To exploit the robust positive equality, we eliminate the function and predicate applications from the RPEUF formula using Bryant et al.'s method. For a function symbol f which appears in F, we introduce symbolic constants $vf_i, \ldots, vf_k$, where k is the number of distinct application of f in the formula. Then the ith application of f (in the topological ordering $\preceq$) is replaced by the nested ITE formula, $ITE(a_i = a_1, vf_1, ITE(a_i = a_2, vf_2, \ldots ITE(a_i = a_{i-1}, vf_{i-1}, vf_i)))$. Here a_i is the argument list to the ith function application. We say that the symbolic constant vf_i is introduced while eliminating the ith application of f. The following lemma [6] describes the relationship between the original and the function-free formula. Predicate applications are eliminated similarly.

Lemma 1. *For a RPEUF formula F, the function and predicate elimination process produces a formula $\widehat{F}$ which contains only symbolic constants and propositional symbolic constants, such that F is valid iff the function-free formula $\widehat{F}$ is valid.*

Let $\mathcal{D}$ be the domain of interpretations for F. Let $V_{\preceq}$ be the set of symbolic constants introduced while eliminating the function applications and $V_{\preceq}^+ \subseteq V_{\preceq}$ be the set of symbolic constants introduced for the terms in $\mathcal{T}_{\preceq}^+(F)$. Let $\widehat{F}_p$ be the formula obtained by assigning each variable $v_i \in V_{\preceq}^+$ a value z_i, from the domain $\mathcal{D}' \doteq \mathcal{D} \cup \{z_1, \ldots, z_m\}$, where $m = |V_{\preceq}^+|$ and all z_i are distinct from values in $\mathcal{D}$. Then we can prove the following theorem:

Theorem 3. *The formula F is valid iff $\widehat{F}_p$ is true for all interpretations over $\mathcal{D}$.*

Proof. We give a very informal proof sketch in this paper. A detailed proof can be obtained very similar to the proof shown in the original paper [6].

Let us consider a robust maximally diverse interpretation I for F. Consider a symbolic constant $vf_i \in V_{\preceq}^+$, which results while eliminating the ith application of f (say T_i) in the order $\preceq$. Note that T_i is a p-term application. First, consider the case when T_i *argumentMatch* with some other term T_j, such that $T_j \preceq T_i$. In this case, the value given to vf_i does not matter, as it is never used in evaluating $\widehat{F}_p$. On the other hand, consider the case when T_i does not *argumentMatch* with any term T_j, such that $T_j \preceq T_i$. Since all the g-term for f precede T_i in $\preceq$ (by the definition of $\mathcal{T}_{\preceq}^+(F)$), it means that $I[T_i]$ is distinct from the values of other terms, unless restricted by functional consistency, i.e. $x = y \implies f(x) = f(y)$ (by Theorem 2). But the value of vf_i represents the value of $I[T_i]$, under this interpretation. Hence, we can assign vf_i a distinct value, not present in $\mathcal{D}$.

4.6   Extending Robust Positive Equality to CLU

We can extend our method to the Counter Arithmetic with Lambda Expressions and Uninterpreted Functions (CLU), in the same way proposed in UCLID [12,

7]. The only addition in the logic is the presence of inequalities ($<$) and addition by constant offsets ($+c$). In the presence of $<$, we adopt a conservative approach and say that terms T_1, T_2 appear in negative context (g-term) if they appear in an inequality ($T_1 < T_2$). Similarly, a function application term T_1 is classified as g-term if any term $T_1 + c$ (for any c) appears in negative context. Even these conservative extensions have proved beneficial for verification problems in UCLID.

5   Results

5.1   Simple Example

Let us first illustrate the working of the decision procedure on a simple formula. Consider the following formula:

$$\Psi_1 \doteq (f(f(f(y))) = f(f(y))) \vee (f(f(y)) = f(x)) \vee \neg(x = f(y)) \qquad (3)$$

The function symbols in the formula are $\Sigma(\Psi_1) = \{f, x, y\}$. Our heuristic finds the following order $\preceq$, which also happens to be the optimal order:

$$x \preceq y \preceq f(y) \preceq f(x) \preceq f(f(y)) \preceq f(f(f(y)))$$

The sets $T_{\preceq}^{-}(\Psi_1)$, $T_{\preceq}^{*}(\Psi_1)$ and $T_{\preceq}^{+}(\Psi_1)$ are:

$$T_{\preceq}^{-}(\Psi_1) = \{x, f(y)\}, T_{\preceq}^{*}(\Psi_1) = \{\}, T_{\preceq}^{+}(\Psi_1) = \{y, f(x), f(f(y)), f(f(f(y)))\}$$

The resultant formula after eliminating the function symbols using the above procedure would be

$$\widehat{\Psi}_1 \doteq (f^4 = f^3) \vee (f^3 = f^2) \vee \neg(x = f^1) \qquad (4)$$

where

$$f^1 \doteq vf_1$$
$$f^2 \doteq ITE(x = y, vf_1, vf_2)$$
$$f^3 \doteq ITE(f^1 = y, vf_1, ITE(f^1 = x, vf_2, vf_3))$$
$$f^4 \doteq ITE(f^3 = y, vf_1, ITE(f^3 = x, vf_2, ITE(f^3 = f^1, vf_3, vf_4)))$$

Thus $\widehat{\Psi}_1$ has 6 symbolic constants $\{x, y, vf_1, vf_2, vf_3, vf_4\}$. Based on robust maximal diversity theorem, we can assign *distinct* values to y, vf_2, vf_3, vf_4, since they are introduced while eliminating a function application in $T_{\preceq}^{+}(\Psi_1)$. The rest of the symbolic constants x, vf_1 have to take on 2 values each. Thus, it is sufficient to consider $2^2 = 4$ interpretations to decide the validity of the formula. In fact, it is sufficient to consider 1 value for x and 2 values for vf_1 to decide the validity, since they can either be equal or unequal. Therefore, the number of interpretations to consider is 2 for this case. Alternately, one could use a single Boolean variable to encode the equality $x = vf_1$ [10]. The final propositional formula in this case contains a single Boolean variable[4], and thus requires 2 interpretations.

The above formula was also used as a running example in previous work [19,21]. The method proposed by Pnueli [19] considers 16 interpretations to decide this formula and the method by Rodeh et al. [21] consider either 4 or 2 interpretations depending on the heuristic. In contrast, the previous positive equality work of Bryant et al. considers $5^5 = 3125$ interpretations.

5.2   Verification Benchmarks

In this section, we compare our algorithm with the original positive equality algorithm, based on a set of software verification benchmarks generated from Translation Validation of Compilers [19] and device-driver verification in BLAST [11]. Discussion on other hardware verification benchmarks can be found in an extended version of this paper [14]. All the formulas discussed in this section are valid formulas.

We have integrated the new method in the tool UCLID [7]. All the experiments are run on a 1.7GHz machine with 256MB of memory. For all these experiments, the integer variables in the formula (after function elimination) are encoded using a small-domain encoding method [7]. This method assigns each integer variable a finite but sufficiently large domain which preserves validity of the formula. The final propositional formula is checked using a Boolean Satisfiability (SAT) solver. For our case, we use mChaff [16].

Figure 2 compares the number of terms which can be assigned distinct values (i.e. the number of terms whose range contains a single value) for positive equality (*p-vars*) and the robust positive equality (*robust-p-vars*) algorithms. The column with *potential # of p-vars* denotes an upper bound on the total number of positive terms. This is obtained by simply adding the number of *potentially positive* terms for each function symbol without considering the ordering of terms across different function symbol. This is a very optimistic measure and there may not be any order $\preceq$ for which this can be achieved. The time taken by each approach is also indicated in the table.

For most of the code validation benchmarks, the number of p-terms is larger compared with the earlier work. Similar trend is also observed for the BLAST set of benchmarks. For many of the code validation benchmarks, the increase in the number of positive variables translates into an improvement of the total time taken to check the validity of the formula. This is expected as the new method reduces the number of interpretations to search. However, for a few cases, the new method is almost 10% slower than the original method, even when the number of positive variables are 10% larger. This happens because of the overhead of the robust positive equality analysis. Our current implementation requires multiple passes over the formula, which can often increase the time required to translate a

---

[4] Usually, more variables are added to express transitivity constraints, but this example does not require any, since there is a single Boolean variable

CLU formula into a Boolean formula. However, the time taken by the SAT solver (mChaff) is almost always smaller with the new method. This is particularly effective, when solving formulas for which the SAT solver time dominates the time to translate to a Boolean formula (e.g. cv46).

It is interesting to notice that for most benchmarks (except cv22) the total number of robust-p-vars is the same as the maximum possible number of p-vars possible. On one hand this suggests that the heuristic we chose is optimal for all these benchmarks. On the other hand, it shows that there are no occurrence of mutually nested function applications with alternate polarity evident in the example $\neg f(g(x)) = g(f(y))$. For this example, the maximum number of *potentially positive* terms is 4 ($\{x, y, f(y), g(x)\}$), but one can obtain at most 3 in any ordering ($\{x, y, f(y)\}$ or $\{x, y, g(x)\}$). This is because a *potentially positive* application for g appears as a subterm of a g-term for f and vice versa.

Finally, its worth pointing out some differences with the method of Rodeh et al. [21]. The paper claims that their method subsumes Bryant et al.'s positive equality. But our current method is not subsumed by the approach since the method in [21] does not exploit the topological ordering of function applications across different function symbols. However, the two approaches are complementary. Robust positive equality analysis can be used as a preprocessing step before exploiting the range-allocation scheme by Pnueli et al. and Rodeh et al.'s methods. Further, robust positive equality analysis can work with the more general logic of CLU [7], but the methods in [19,21] are restricted to EUF. It is not clear how to extend the range allocation easily in the presence of $<$ and constant offsets.

Benchmark	example	# vars	Positive Equality		Robust Positive Equality		
			#p-vars	Time taken (sec)	# p-vars	potential # p-vars	Time taken (sec)
Code Validation	cv1	17	3	1.58	7	7	1.60
	cv2	4	1	0.34	1	1	0.48
	cv20	21	6	0.40	6	6	0.47
	cv22	101	1	70.84	16	18	45.65
	cv23	101	8	23.06	22	22	15.96
	cv25	101	8	45.93	22	22	21.80
	cv37	13	4	6.40	4	4	6.32
	cv44	38	8	19.75	17	17	7.13
	cv46	70	10	> 1800	28	28	100.50
BLAST	bl7	262	109	241.27	125	125	265.38
	bl8	315	125	454.40	142	142	456.80
	blt3	268	72	11.16	94	94	11.90

Fig. 2. Comparison on Software Verification Benchmarks.

6   Conclusion and Future Work

In this work, we have presented a generalization of the positive equality analysis. The extension allows us to handle benchmarks for which the positive structure could not be exploited using the previous method. The added overhead for this generalization is negligible as demonstrated on some reasonably large benchmarks. An interesting point to observe in this paper is that most of the proofs and mathematical machineries from the previous work have been successfully reused for our extension.

There are other optimizations that can be exploited beyond the current work. We want to exploit the positive equality for the terms in $\mathcal{T}_{\underline{\ast}}^{\ast}$, which are subterms of g-terms with the same top-level function symbol. Instead of using distinct values for the symbolic constants which arise from the elimination of these terms, we are investigating the addition of extra *clauses* in the final formula, to prevent the SAT-solver from considering these interpretations. We would also like to use other range allocation methods, after exploiting robust positive equality, to further improve the decision procedure.

References

1. W. Ackermann. *Solvable Cases of the Decision Problem.* North-Holland, Amsterdam, 1954.
2. T. Ball, R. Majumdar, T. Millstein, and S. K. Rajamani. Automatic predicate abstraction of C programs. In *Programming Language Design and Implementation (PLDI '01)*, Snowbird, Utah, June, 2001. *SIGPLAN Notices*, 36(5), May 2001.
3. C. Barrett, D. Dill, and J. Levitt. Validity checking for combinations of theories with equality. In M. Srivas and A. Camilleri, editors, *Formal Methods in Computer-Aided Design (FMCAD '96)*, LNCS 1166, pages 187–201, November 1996.
4. C. W. Barrett, D. L. Dill, and A. Stump. Checking Satisfiability of First-Order Formulas by Incremental Translation to SAT. In E. Brinksma and K. G. Larsen, editors, *Proc. Computer-Aided Verification (CAV'02)*, LNCS 2404, pages 236–249, July 2002.
5. R. E. Bryant, S. German, and M. N. Velev. Exploiting positive equality in a logic of equality with uninterpreted functions. In N. Halbwachs and D. Peled, editors, *Computer-Aided Verification (CAV '99)*, LNCS 1633, pages 470–482, July 1999.
6. R. E. Bryant, S. German, and M. N. Velev. Processor verification using efficient reductions of the logic of uninterpreted functions to propositional logic. *ACM Transactions on Computational Logic*, 2(1):1–41, January 2001.
7. R. E. Bryant, S. K. Lahiri, and S. A. Seshia. Modeling and Verifying Systems using a Logic of Counter Arithmetic with Lambda Expressions and Uninterpreted Functions. In E. Brinksma and K. G. Larsen, editors, *Proc. Computer-Aided Verification (CAV'02)*, LNCS 2404, pages 78–92, July 2002.
8. J. R. Burch and D. L. Dill. Automated verification of pipelined microprocessor control. In D. Dill, editor, *Computer-Aided Verification (CAV '94)*, LNCS 818, pages 68–80, June 1994.
9. C. Flanagan, R. Joshi, X. Ou, and J. Saxe. Theorem Proving usign Lazy Proof Explication. In W. A. Hunt, Jr. and F. Somenzi, editors, *Computer-Aided Verification (CAV 2003)*, LNCS 2725, pages 355–367, 2003.
10. A. Goel, K. Sajid, H. Zhou, A. Aziz, and V. Singhal. BDD based procedures for a theory of equality with uninterpreted functions. In A. J. Hu and M. Y. Vardi, editors, *Computer-Aided Verification (CAV '98)*, LNCS 1427, pages 244–255, June 1998.

11. T. A. Henzinger, R. Jhala, R. Majumdar, and G. Sutre. Lazy Abstraction. In John Launchbury and John C. Mitchell, editors, *Proceedings of the 29th ACM SIGPLAN-SIGACT Symposium on Principles of programming languages (POPL '02)*, pages 58–70, 2002.

12. S. K. Lahiri. An efficient decision procedure for the logic of Counters, Constrained Lambda expressions, Uninterpreted Functions and Ordering. Master's thesis, ECE Department, Carnegie Mellon University, May 2001.

13. S. K. Lahiri, R. E. Bryant, and B. Cook. A symbolic approach to predicate abstraction. In W. A. Hunt, Jr. and F. Somenzi, editors, *Computer-Aided Verification (CAV 2003)*, LNCS 2725, pages 141–153, 2003.

14. S. K. Lahiri, R. E. Bryant, A. Goel, and M. Talupur. Revisiting positive equality. Technical Report CMU-CS-03-196, Carnegie Mellon University, November 2003.

15. S. K. Lahiri, S. A. Seshia, and R. E. Bryant. Modeling and verification of out-of-order microprocessors in UCLID. In J. W. O'Leary M. Aagaard, editor, *Formal Methods in Computer-Aided Design (FMCAD '02)*, LNCS 2517, pages 142–159, Nov 2002.

16. M. Moskewicz, C. Madigan, Y. Zhao, L. Zhang, and S. Malik. Chaff: Engineering an efficient SAT solver. In *38th Design Automation Conference (DAC '01)*, 2001.

17. G. Nelson and D. C. Oppen. Simplification by cooperating decision procedures. *ACM Transactions on Programming Languages and Systems (TOPLAS)*, 2(1):245–257, 1979.

18. S. Owre, J. M. Rushby, and N. Shankar. PVS: A prototype verification system. In D. Kapur, editor, *11th International Conference on Automated Deduction (CADE)*, June 1992.

19. A. Pnueli, Y. Rodeh, O. Shtrichman, and M. Siegel. Deciding equality formulas by small-domain instantiations. In N. Halbwachs and D. Peled, editors, *Computer-Aided Verification*, volume 1633 of *Lecture Notes in Computer Science*, pages 455–469. Springer-Verlag, July 1999.

20. A. Pnueli, Y. Rodeh, O. Strichman, and M. Siegel. The Small Model Property: How Small Can It Be? Information and Computation. *Information and Computation*, 178(1):279–293, 2002.

21. Y. Rodeh and O. Strichmann. Finite Instantiations in Equivalence Logic with Uninterpreted Functions. In G. Berry, H. Comon, and A. Finkel, editors, *Computer-Aided Verification (CAV '01)*, LNCS 2102, pages 144–154, 2001.

22. R. E. Shostak. Deciding Combinations of Theories. *Journal of the ACM*, 31(1):1–12, 1984.

An Interpolating Theorem Prover

K.L. McMillan

Cadence Berkeley Labs

Abstract. We present a method of deriving Craig interpolants from proofs in the quantifier-free theory of linear inequality and uninterpreted function symbols, and an interpolating theorem prover based on this method. The prover has been used for predicate refinement in the BLAST software model checker, and can also be used directly for model checking infinite-state systems, using interpolation-based image approximation.

1   Introduction

A Craig interpolant [1] for an inconsistent pair of logical formulas (A, B) is a formula ϕ that is implied by A, inconsistent with B and refers only to variables common to A and B. If A and B are propositional formulas, and we are given a refutation of $A \wedge B$ by resolution steps, we can derive an interpolant for (A, B) in linear time [5,12]. This fact has been exploited in a method of over-approximate image computation based on interpolation [7]. This provides a complete symbolic method of model checking finite-state systems with respect to linear temporal properties. The method is based entirely on a proof-generating Boolean satisfiability solver and does not rely on quantifier elimination or reduction to normal forms such as binary decision diagrams (BDD's) or conjunctive normal form. In practice it was found to be highly effective in proving localizable properties of large circuits.

Here we present a first step in expanding this approach from propositional to first-order logic, and from finite-state to infinite-state systems. We present an interpolating prover for a quantifier-free theory that includes linear inequalities over the rationals and equality with uninterpreted function symbols. As in [2] the prover combines a Boolean satisfiability solver with a proof-generating ground decision procedure. After generating a refutation for a pair of formulas (A, B), the prover derives from this refutation an interpolant ϕ for the pair. The main contribution of this work is to show how interpolants can be derived from proofs in the combined theories of linear inequality and equality with uninterpreted function symbols (LIUF). This extends earlier work that handles only linear inequalities [12]. The combination of theories is useful, for example, for applications in software model checking.

The interpolating prover has been applied in the BLAST software model checking system [3]. This system is based on predicate abstraction, and uses interpolants as a guide in generating new predicates for abstraction refinement. The approach resulted in a substantial reduction in abstract state space size

K. Jensen and A. Podelski (Eds.): TACAS 2004, LNCS 2988, pp. 16–30, 2004.

relative to earlier methods. Further, using the method of [7], the prover can be used directly to verify some infinite-state systems, such as the Fischer and "bakery" mutual exclusion protocols. In principle, it can also be applied to the model checking phase of predicate abstraction.

The paper is organized as follows. In section 2, we introduce a simple proof system for LIUF, and show how refutations in this system can be translated into interpolants. Section 3 discusses the practicalities of constructing an efficient interpolating prover using this system. Finally, section 4 discusses actual and potential applications of the interpolating prover.

2   Interpolants from Proofs

We now describe a system of rules that, given a refutation of a pair of clause sets (A, B), derive an interpolant ϕ for the pair. For the sake of simplicity, we begin with a quantifier-free logic of with linear inequalities (LI). Then we treat a logic with equality and uninterpreted functions (EUF). Finally, we combine the two theories.

2.1   Linear Inequalities

A *term* in this logic is a linear combination $c_0 + c_1 v_1 + \cdots c_n v_n$, where $v_1 \ldots v_n$ are distinct individual variables, $c_0 \ldots c_n$ are rational constants, and further $c_1 \ldots c_n$ are non-zero. When we perform arithmetic on terms, we will assume they are reduced to this normal form. That is, if x is a term and c is a non-zero constant, we will write cx to denote the term obtained by distributing the coefficient c inside x. Similarly, if x and y are terms, we will write $x + y$ to denote the term obtained by summing like terms in x and y and dropping resulting terms with zero coefficients. Thus, for example, if x is the term $1 + a$ and y is the term $b - 2a$ then $2x + y$ would denote the term $2 + b$.

An *atomic predicate* in the logic is either a propositional variable or an inequality of the form $0 \leq x$, where x is a term. A literal is either an atomic predicate or its negation. A clause is a disjunction of literals. We will write the clause containing the set of literals Γ as $\langle \Gamma \rangle$. In particular, we will distinguish syntactically between a literal l and the clause $\langle l \rangle$ containing just l. The empty clause, equivalent to false, will be written $\langle \rangle$.

A *sequent* is of the form $\Gamma \vdash \Delta$, where Γ and Δ are sets of formulas (in this case, either literals or clauses). The interpretation of $\Gamma \vdash \Delta$ is that the conjunction of the formulas in Γ entails the disjunction of the formulas in Δ. In what follows, lower case letters generally stand for formulas and upper case letters for sets of formulas. Further, a formula in a place where a set is expected should be taken as the singleton containing it, and a list of sets should be taken as their union. Thus, for example, the expression $\Gamma, \phi \vdash p, A$ should be taken as an abbreviation for $\Gamma \cup \{\phi\} \vdash \{p\} \cup A$.

Our theorem prover generates refutations for sets of clauses using the following proof rules:

$$\text{Hyp}\frac{}{\Gamma \vdash \phi}\ \phi \in \Gamma \qquad\qquad \text{Comb}\frac{\Gamma \vdash 0 \le x \quad \Gamma \vdash 0 \le y}{\Gamma \vdash 0 \le c_1 x + c_2 y}\ c_{1,2} > 0$$

$$\text{Contra}\frac{l_1, \ldots, l_n \vdash \perp}{\Gamma \vdash \langle \neg l_1, \ldots, \neg l_n \rangle} \qquad \text{Res}\frac{\Gamma \vdash \langle l, \Theta \rangle \quad \Gamma \vdash \langle \neg l, \Theta' \rangle}{\Gamma \vdash \langle \Theta, \Theta' \rangle}$$

In the above, $\perp$ is a shorthand for $0 \le -1$. All Boolean reasoning is done by the resolution rule Res. This system is complete for refutation of clause systems over the rationals. As in [10], we can obtain an incomplete system for the integers rather than the rationals by systematically translating the literal $\neg(0 \le x)$ to $0 \le -1 - x$.

We will use the notation $\phi \preceq \Gamma$ to indicate that all variables occurring in ϕ also occur in Γ. A term x is *local* with respect to a pair (A, B) if it contains a variable not occurring in B (in other words $x \npreceq B$) and global otherwise.

In order to represent the rules for deriving interpolants from proofs, we will define several classes of *interpolations*. These have the general syntactic form $(A, B) \vdash \phi\ [X]$, where the exact form of X depends on the class. Intuitively, X is a representation of an "interpolant" associated with the deduction of ϕ from A and B. In the case where ϕ is the empty clause, X should in fact be an interpolant for (A, B). For each class of interpolation, we will define a notion of validity, and introduce derivation rules that are sound, in the sense that they derive only valid interpolations from valid interpolations. To save space, we will sketch the more difficult soundness arguments here, and leave the more straightforward ones to the reader.

Definition 1. *An* inequality interpolation *has the form* $(A, B) \vdash 0 \le x\ [x', \rho, \gamma]$, *where A and B are clause sets, x and x' are terms, and ρ and γ are formulas, such that $\rho, \gamma \preceq B$ and $x', \rho, \gamma \preceq A$. It is said to be* valid *when:*

- $A, \rho \models 0 \le x' \wedge \gamma$
- $B \models \rho$ *and* $B, \gamma \models 0 \le x - x'$ *and,*
- *for all individual variables v, such that $v \npreceq B$, the coefficients of v in x and x' are equal.*

For the current system, the formulas ρ and γ are always $\top$. They will play a role later, when we combine theories. The intuition behind this definition is that $0 \le x$ is a linear combination of inequalities from A and B, where x' represents the contribution to x from A. We now begin with the interpolation rule for introduction of hypotheses. Here, we distinguish two cases, depending on whether the hypothesis is from A or B:

$$\text{HypLeq-A}\frac{}{(A, B) \vdash 0 \le x\ [x, \top, \top]}\ (0 \le x) \in A$$

$$\textsc{HypLeq-B}\frac{}{(A,B) \vdash 0 \le x \; [0, \top, \top]} \; (0 \le x) \in B$$

The soundness of these rules (*i.e.*, validity of their consequents, given the side conditions) is easily verified. The rule for combining inequalities is as follows:

$$\textsc{Comb}\frac{(A,B) \vdash 0 \le x \; [x', \rho, \gamma] \quad (A,B) \vdash 0 \le y \; [y', \rho', \gamma']}{(A,B) \vdash 0 \le c_1 x + c_2 y \; [c_1 x' + c_2 y', \rho \wedge \rho', \gamma \wedge \gamma']} \; c_{1,2} > 0$$

In effect, we derive the interpolant for a linear combination of inequalities by taking the same linear combination of the contributions from A. Again, the reader may wish to verify that the validity conditions for inequality interpolations are preserved by this rule.

Example 1. As an example, let us derive an interpolant for the case where A is $(0 \le y - x)(0 \le z - y)$ and B is $(0 \le x - z - 1)$. For clarity, we will abbreviate $(A, B) \vdash \phi \; [x, \top, \top]$ to $\vdash \phi \; [x]$. We first use the HypLeq-A rule to introduce two hypotheses from A:

$$\textsc{HypLeq-A}\frac{}{\vdash 0 \le y - x \; [y - x]} \qquad \textsc{HypLeq-A}\frac{}{\vdash 0 \le z - y \; [z - y]}$$

Now, we sum these two inequalities using the Comb rule:

$$\textsc{Comb}\frac{\vdash 0 \le y - x \; [y - x] \quad \vdash 0 \le z - y \; [z - y]}{\vdash 0 \le z - x \; [z - x]}$$

Now we introduce a hypothesis from B:

$$\textsc{HypLeq-B}\frac{}{\vdash 0 \le x - z - 1 \; [0]}$$

Finally, we sum this with our previous result, to obtain $0 \le -1$, which is false:

$$\textsc{Comb}\frac{\vdash 0 \le z - x \; [0 \le z - x] \quad \vdash 0 \le x - z - 1 \; [0 \le 0]}{\vdash 0 \le -1 \; [z - x]}$$

You may want to check that all the interpolations derived are valid. Also notice that in the last step we have derived a contradiction, and that $0 \le z - x$ is an interpolant for (A, B).

Now we introduce an interpolation syntax for clauses, to handle Boolean reasoning. If Θ is a set of literals, we will denote by $\Theta \downarrow B$ the literals of Θ occurring in B and by $\Theta \setminus B$ the literals *not* occurring in B.

Definition 2. *A* clause interpolation *has the form* $(A, B) \vdash \langle \Theta \rangle \; [\phi]$, *where A and B are clause sets, Θ is a literal set and ϕ is a formula. It is said to be* valid *when:*

- $A \models \phi \vee \langle \Theta \setminus B \rangle$, *and*
- $B, \phi \models \langle \Theta \downarrow B \rangle$, *and*
- $\phi \preceq B$ *and* $\phi \preceq A$.

Notice that if Θ is empty, ϕ is an interpolant for (A, B). Two rules are needed for introduction of clauses as hypotheses:

$$\text{HypC-A} \frac{}{(A,B) \vdash \langle \Theta \rangle \, [\langle \Theta \downarrow B \rangle]} \; \langle \Theta \rangle \in A \quad \text{HypC-B} \frac{}{(A,B) \vdash \langle \Theta \rangle \, [\top]} \; \langle \Theta \rangle \in B$$

Note that the derived interpolations are trivially valid, given the side conditions. Now, we introduce two interpolation rules for resolution of clauses. The first is for resolution on a literal *not* occurring in B:

$$\text{Res-A} \frac{\begin{array}{c} (A,B) \vdash \langle l, \Theta \rangle \, [\phi] \\ (A,B) \vdash \langle \neg l, \Theta' \rangle \, [\phi'] \end{array}}{(A,B) \vdash \langle \Theta, \Theta' \rangle \, [\phi' \vee \phi']} \; l \not\preceq B$$

Soundness. For the first condition, we know that A implies $\phi \vee l \vee \langle \Theta \setminus B \rangle$ and $\phi' \vee \neg l \vee \langle \Theta' \setminus B \rangle$. By resolution on l we have A implies $(\phi \vee \phi') \vee \langle \Theta, \Theta' \setminus B \rangle$. For the second condition, given B, we know that $\phi \implies \langle \Theta \downarrow B \rangle$ and $\phi' \implies \langle \Theta' \downarrow B \rangle$. Thus, $\phi \vee \phi'$ implies $\langle \Theta, \Theta' \downarrow B \rangle$. The third condition is trivial.

The second rule is for resolution on a literal occurring in B:

$$\text{Res-B} \frac{\begin{array}{c} (A,B) \vdash \langle l, \Theta \rangle \, [\phi] \\ (A,B) \vdash \langle \neg l, \Theta' \rangle \, [\phi'] \end{array}}{(A,B) \vdash \langle \Theta, \Theta' \rangle \, [\phi \wedge \phi']} \; l \preceq B$$

Soundness. For the first validity condition, we know that A implies $\phi \vee \langle \Theta \setminus B \rangle$ and $\phi' \vee \langle \Theta' \setminus B \rangle$. These in turn imply $(\phi \wedge \phi') \vee \langle \Theta, \Theta' \setminus B \rangle$. For the second condition, given B, we know that $\phi \implies l \vee \langle \Theta \downarrow B \rangle$ while $\phi' \implies \neg l \vee \langle \Theta' \downarrow B \rangle$. By resolution, we have that $\phi \wedge \phi'$ implies $\langle \Theta, \Theta' \downarrow B \rangle$. The third condition is trivial.

Example 2. As an example, we derive an interpolant for (A, B), where A is $\langle b \rangle, \langle \neg b \vee c \rangle$ and B is $\langle \neg c \rangle$. First, using the HypC-A rule, we introduce the two clauses from A as hypotheses:

$$\text{HypC-A} \frac{}{\vdash \langle b \rangle \, [\bot]} \qquad \text{HypC-A} \frac{}{\vdash \langle \neg b, c \rangle \, [c]}$$

We now resolve these two clauses on the variable b.

$$\text{Res-A} \frac{\vdash \langle b \rangle \, [\bot] \qquad \vdash \langle \neg b, c \rangle \, [c]}{\vdash \langle c \rangle \, [\bot \vee c]}$$

We then use the Hyp-B rule to introduce the clause from B.

$$\text{Hyp-B} \frac{}{\vdash \langle \neg c \rangle \, [\top]}$$

Finally, we resolve the last two clauses on c. We use the RES-B rule, since c occurs in B.

$$\text{RES-B}\frac{\vdash \langle c \rangle \ [c] \quad \vdash \langle \neg c \rangle \ [\top]}{\vdash \langle \rangle \ [c \wedge \top]}$$

Thus c is an interpolant for (A, B).

Finally, we introduce a rule to connect inequality reasoning to Boolean reasoning:

$$\text{CONTRA}\frac{(\{a_1, \ldots, a_k\}, \{b_1, \ldots, b_m\}) \vdash 0 \leq -1 \ [x', \rho, \gamma]}{(A, B) \vdash \langle \neg a_1, \ldots, \neg a_k, \neg b_1, \ldots, \neg b_m \rangle \ [\rho \implies (0 \leq x' \wedge \gamma)]}$$

where the b_i are literals occurring in B, and the a_i are literals *not* occurring in B.

Soundness. By the first condition of Definition 1, $\bigwedge a_i$ implies $\rho \implies (0 \leq x' \wedge \gamma)$. Moreover, $\bigvee \neg a_i$ is precisely $\langle \Theta \setminus B \rangle$ in Definition 2. This means that $\phi \vee \langle \Theta \setminus B \rangle$ is a tautology, satisfying the first validity condition. For the second condition, suppose that $\rho \implies (0 \leq x' \wedge \gamma)$ holds. From the first two conditions of Definition 1, we infer that $\bigwedge b_i$ implies $0 \leq -1$. Thus, $\langle \neg b_1, \ldots, \neg b_m \rangle$ holds. Finally, the third validity condition is guaranteed by the third condition of Definition 1.

2.2   Equality and Uninterpreted Functions

In our logic of equality and uninterpreted functions, a term is either an individual variable or a function application $f^n(x_1, \ldots, x_n)$ where f^n is a n-ary function symbol and $x_1 \ldots x_n$ are terms. An atomic predicate is a propositional variable or an equality of the form $x = y$ where x and y are terms. Refutations are generated using the following proof rules (in addition to the HYP rule):

$$\text{REFL}\frac{}{\Gamma \vdash x = x} \qquad \text{SYMM}\frac{\Gamma \vdash x = y}{\Gamma \vdash y = x}$$

$$\text{TRANS}\frac{\Gamma \vdash x = y \quad \Gamma \vdash y = z}{\Gamma \vdash x = z} \qquad \text{CONG}\frac{\Gamma \vdash x_1 = y_1 \quad \ldots \quad \Gamma \vdash x_n = y_n}{\Gamma \vdash f^n(x_1, \ldots, x_n) = f^n(y_1, \ldots, y_n)}$$

$$\text{EQNEQ}\frac{\Gamma \vdash x = y}{\Gamma \vdash \bot} \ \neg(x = y) \in \Gamma$$

Boolean reasoning can be added to the system by adding the CONTRA and RES rules of the previous system.

Definition 3. *An equality interpolation has the form* $(A, B) \vdash x = y \ [x', y', \rho, \gamma]$, *where* A *and* B *are clause sets,* x, y, x', y' *are terms, and* ρ *and* γ *are formulas, such that* $\rho, \gamma \preceq B$. *It is said to be* valid *when:*

- $A, \rho \models x = x' \wedge y = y' \wedge \gamma$,
- $B \models \rho$ and $B, \gamma, x = x', y = y' \models x = y' \wedge y = x'$,
- either $x', y' \preceq B$ or $x' = y$ and $y' = x$ *(the* degenerate *case), and*
- if $x \preceq A$ then $x' \preceq A$, else $x' = x$, and similarly for y, y'.

The intuition behind this definition is that x' and y' solutions for local terms x and y in terms of common variables (except in the degenerate case). The formula ρ is always $\top$ in the present theory. The interpolation rules for equality are as follows:

$$\text{HypEq-A} \frac{}{(A, B) \vdash x = y \; [y, x, \top, \top]} \quad (x = y) \in A$$

$$\text{HypEq-B} \frac{}{(A, B) \vdash x = y \; [x, y, \top, \top]} \quad (x = y) \in B$$

$$\text{Refl} \frac{}{(A, B) \vdash x = x \; [x, x, \top, \top]} \qquad \text{Symm} \frac{(A, B) \vdash x = y \; [x', y', \rho, \gamma]}{(A, B) \vdash y = x \; [y', x', \rho, \gamma]}$$

$$\text{Trans} \frac{\begin{array}{c} (A, B) \vdash x = y \; [x', y', \rho, \gamma] \\ (A, B) \vdash y = z \; [y'', z', \rho', \gamma'] \end{array}}{(A, B) \vdash x = z \; [x', z', \rho \wedge \rho' \wedge y' = y'', \gamma \wedge \gamma']} \quad x' \neq y, z' \neq y$$

$$\text{Trans}' \frac{\begin{array}{c} (A, B) \vdash x = y \; [x', y', \rho, \gamma] \\ (A, B) \vdash y = z \; [y'', z', \rho', \gamma'] \end{array}}{(A, B) \vdash x = z \; [x'(y''/y), z'(y'/y), \rho \wedge \rho', \gamma \wedge \gamma']} \quad x' = y \text{ or } z' = y$$

where $x(y/z)$ denotes y if $x = z$ else x. Of these, only the transitivity rules require a detailed soundness argument. The TRANS rule is the for the case when neither antecedent is degenerate. The first condition of Definition 3 is trivial. For the second, suppose B, $\rho, \rho', y' = y'', x = x'$ and $x = z'$ hold. By inductive hypothesis, we know that $x = y'$ and $z = y''$. This, since $y' = y''$, we have $x = z'$ and $z = x'$. For the third condition, the side condition of the rule ensures that $x', z' \preceq B$. The TRANS' rule handles the case when one of the two antecedents is degenerate. Suppose that $x' = y$ and $z' \neq y$. Again, the first condition is trivial. For the second condition, suppose B, $\rho \wedge \rho'$, $x = y''$ and $z = z'$. By inductive hypothesis, $z = y''$, hence $x = z'$. On the other hand, if $x' = y$ and $z' = y$, then we have immediately $x = z$ (*i.e.*, the consequent is also degenerate). The third condition is straightforward.

Now we consider the CONG rule for uninterpreted functions symbols. Suppose that from $x = y$ we deduce $f(x) = f(y)$ by the CONG rule. Except in the degenerate case, we must obtain solutions for $f(x)$ and $f(y)$ in terms of variables occurring in B. We can obtain this by simply substituting the solutions for x and y into f, as follows:

$$\text{Cong} \frac{(A, B) \vdash x = y \; [x', y', \rho, \gamma]}{(A, B) \vdash f(x) = f(y) \; [f(x'), f(y'), \rho, \gamma]}$$

Note that if the antecedent is degenerate, the consequent is also degenerate. The generalization of this rule to n-ary function is somewhat complex, and we omit it here for lack of space.

Example 3. Suppose A is $x = y$ and B is $y = z$ and we wish to derive an interpolation for $f(x) = f(z)$. After introducing our two hypotheses, we use the TRANS' rule to get $x = z$:

$$\text{TRANS}'\frac{\vdash x = y \ [y, x, \top, \top] \quad \vdash y = z \ [y, z, \top, \top]}{\vdash x = z \ [y, z, \top, \top]}$$

We then apply the CONG rule to obtain $f(x) = f(z)$:

$$\text{CONG}\frac{\vdash x = z \ [y, z, \top, \top]}{\vdash f(x) = f(z) \ [f(y), f(z), \top, \top]}$$

Finally, we deal with the EQNEQ rule, which derives false from an equality and its negation. First, we consider the case where the disequality is contained in A:

$$\text{EQNEQ-A}\frac{(A, B) \vdash x = y \ [x', y', \rho, \gamma]}{(A, B) \vdash 0 \leq -1 \ [0, \rho, \gamma \wedge (x' \neq y')]} \ (x \neq y) \in A, \ y' \neq x$$

Notice that we derive an inequality interpolation here so that we can then apply the CONTRA rule. The idea is to translate the disequality over local terms to an equivalent disequality over global terms. We handle the degenerate case separately:

$$\text{EQNEQ-A}'\frac{(A, B) \vdash x = y \ [y, x, \rho, \gamma]}{(A, B) \vdash 0 \leq -1 \ [0, \rho, \bot]} \ (x \neq y) \in A$$

The case where the disequality comes from B is handled as follows:

$$\text{EQNEQ-B}\frac{(A, B) \vdash x = y \ [x', y', \rho, \gamma]}{(A, B) \vdash 0 \leq -1 \ [0, \rho, \gamma \wedge x = x' \wedge y = y']} (x \neq y) \in B$$

In the above, if x and x' are syntactically equal, we replace $x = x'$ with $\top$, and similarly for y and y'. This fulfills the requirement that $\gamma \preceq A$, in the case when $x \npreceq A$ or $y \npreceq A$.

2.3   Combining LI and EUF

A term in the combined logic is a linear combination $c_0 + c_1 v_1 + \cdots c_n v_n$, where $v_1 \ldots v_n$ are distinct individual variables and $c_0 \ldots c_n$ are integer constants, or a function application $f^n(x_1, \ldots, x_n)$ where f^n is a n-ary function symbol and $x_1 \ldots x_n$ are terms. An atomic predicate is either a propositional variable, an inequality of the form $0 \leq x$, where x is a linear combination, or an equality of the form $x = y$ where x and y are terms.

Our proof system consists of all the previous proof rules, with the addition of the following two rules that connect equality and inequality reasoning:

$$\text{LeqEq}\frac{\Gamma \vdash x = y}{\Gamma \vdash 0 \leq x - y}$$

$$\text{EqLeq}\frac{\Gamma \vdash 0 \leq x - y \quad \Gamma \vdash 0 \leq y - x}{\Gamma \vdash x = y}$$

The LeqEq rule, inferring an inequality from an equality, can be handled by the following interpolation rule:

$$\text{LeqEq}\frac{(A, B) \vdash x = y \; [x', y', \rho, \gamma]}{(A, B) \vdash 0 \leq x - y \; [x - x' - y + y', \rho, \gamma]} \; y' \neq x$$

The idea here is that B and γ give us $x' = y'$, thus $0 \leq x - x' - y + y'$ gives $0 \leq x - y$. However, we must deal separately with the special case where the antecedent is degenerate:

$$\text{LeqEq}'\frac{(A, B) \vdash x = y \; [y, x, \rho, \gamma]}{(A, B) \vdash 0 \leq x - y \; [x - y, \rho, \gamma]}$$

We now consider the EqLeq rule, which derives an equality from a pair of inequalities. We distinguish three cases, depending on whether x and y are local or global. The first case is when both x and y are global, and is straightforward:

$$\text{EqLeq-BB}\frac{(A, B) \vdash 0 \leq x - y \; [x', \rho, \gamma]}{(A, B) \vdash 0 \leq y - x \; [y', \rho', \gamma']}{(A, B) \vdash x = y \; [x, y, \rho, 0 \leq x' \wedge 0 \leq y']} \; x \preceq B, y \preceq B$$

Note that x and y in the above rule may be arbitrary linear combinations.

The case when x is local and y is global is more problematic. Suppose, for example, that A is $(0 \leq a - x)(0 \leq z - a)$ and B is $(0 \leq b - z)(0 \leq x - b)$. From this we can infer $0 \leq b - a$ and $0 \leq a - b$, using the Comb rule. Thus, using the EqLeq rule, we infer $a = b$. To make an interpolation for this, we must have a solution for a in terms of global variables, implied by A. Unfortunately, there are no equalities that can be inferred from A alone. In fact, it is not possible in general to express interpolants in the combined theory as conjunctions of atomic predicates as we have done up to now, because the combined theory is no longer convex in the sense of [10].[1]

This is the reason the parameter ρ was introduced in the interpolation syntax. In our example, we will have

$$(A, B) \vdash a = b \; [z, 0 \leq x - z, 0 \leq z - x]$$

---

[1] Consider the atomic formulas $0 \leq a - x$, $0 \leq y - a$, $f(a) = f(q)$. These imply the disjunction $f(x) = f(q) \vee x < y$, but do not imply either disjunct by itself.

That is, A proves $a = z$, under the condition ρ that $0 \leq x - z$. This interpolation is valid, since from B we can prove $0 \leq x - z$. Using A and this fact, we can infer $a = z$. From A we can also infer $0 \leq z - x$, which, with B, gives us $z = b$, hence $a = b$. This approach can be generalized to the following rule:

$$\text{EQLEQ-AB} \frac{\begin{array}{c}(A, B) \vdash 0 \leq y - x \; [x', \rho, \gamma] \\ (A, B) \vdash 0 \leq x - y \; [x'', \rho', \gamma']\end{array}}{\begin{array}{c}(A, B) \vdash x = y \; [x + x', y, \rho \wedge \rho' \wedge 0 \leq -x' - x'', \\ \gamma \wedge \gamma' \wedge 0 \leq x' + x'']\end{array}} \quad x \not\preceq B, y \preceq B$$

The final case for the EQLEQ rule is when $x \not\preceq B$ and $y \not\preceq B$:

$$\text{EQLEQ-AA} \frac{\begin{array}{c}(A, B) \vdash 0 \leq y - x \; [\rho, x', \gamma] \\ (A, B) \vdash 0 \leq x - y \; [\rho', x'', \gamma']\end{array}}{\begin{array}{c}(A, B) \vdash x = y \; [y, x, \rho \wedge \rho' \wedge 0 \leq y - x - x' \\ \wedge 0 \leq x - y - x'', \gamma \wedge \gamma']\end{array}} \quad x \not\preceq B, y \not\preceq B$$

Soundness. Given B, we know from Definition 1 that $0 \leq y - x - x'$ and $0 \leq x - y - x''$. Note that all variables not occurring in B cancel out in these terms. Moreover, A gives us $0 \leq x'$ and $0 \leq x''$. Combining with the above, we get $x = y$.

2.4 Soundness and Completeness

The following two theorems state the soundness and completeness results for our interpolation system:

Theorem 1 (Soundness). *If a clause interpolation of the form $(A, B) \vdash \langle\rangle \; [\phi]$ is derivable, then ϕ is an interpolant for (A, B).*

Proof sketch. Validity of the interpolation is by the soundness of the individual interpolation rules and induction over the derivation length. By Definition 2 we know that A implies ϕ, that B and ϕ are inconsistent and that $\phi \preceq B$.

Theorem 2 (Completeness). *For any derivable sequent $A, B \vdash \psi$, there is a derivable interpolation of the form $(A, B) \vdash \psi \; [X]$.*

Proof sketch. We split cases on the rule used to derive the sequent, and show in each case that there is always a rule to derive an interpolation for the consequent from interpolations for the antecedents.

In effect, the proof of the completeness theorem gives us an algorithm for constructing an interpolant from a refutation proof. This algorithm is linear in the proof size, and the result is a formula (not in CNF) whose circuit size is also linear in the proof size.

3   An Interpolating Prover

Thus far we have described a proof system for a logic with linear inequalities and uninterpreted functions, and set of rules for deriving interpolants from proofs in this system. There are two further problems that we must address: constructing an efficient proof-generating decision procedure for our system, and translating interpolation problems for general formulas into interpolation problems in clause form.

3.1   Generating Proofs

The prover combines a DPLL style SAT solver, similar to Chaff [9], for propositional reasoning, with a proof-generating Nelson-Oppen style ground decision procedure[2] for theory reasoning. They are combined using the "lazy" approach of [2]. That is, the SAT solver treats all atomic predicates in a given formula f as free Boolean variables. When it finds an assignment to the atomic predicates that satisfies f propositionally, it passes this assignment to the ground decision procedure in the form of a set of literals $l_1 \ldots l_n$. The ground decision procedure then attempts to derive a refutation of this set of literals. If it succeeds, the literals used as hypotheses in the refutation are gathered (call them $m_1, \ldots, m_k$). The CONTRA rule is then used to derive the new clause $\langle \neg m_1, \ldots, \neg m_k \rangle$. This clause is added to the SAT solver's clause set. We will refer to it as a *blocking clause*. Since it is in conflict in the current assignment, the SAT solver now backtracks, continuing where it left off. On the other hand, if the ground decision procedure cannot refute the satisfying assignment, the formula f is satisfiable and the process terminates.

The SAT solver is modified in a straightforward way to generate refutation proofs by resolution (see [8] for details). When a conflict occurs in the search (*i.e.*, when all the literals in some clause are assigned to false), the solver resolves the conflicting clause with other clauses to infer a so-called "conflict clause" (a technique introduced in the GRASP solver [14] and common to most modern DPLL solvers). This inferred clause is added to the clause set, and in effect prevents the same conflict from occurring in the future. The clause set is determined to be unsatisfiable when the empty clause (false) is inferred as a conflict clause. To derive a proof of the empty clause, we have only to record the sequence of resolutions steps used to derive each conflict clause.

The SAT solver's clause set therefore consists of three classes of clauses: the original clauses of f, blocking clauses (which are tautologies proved by the ground decision procedure) and conflicts clauses (proved by resolution). When the empty clause is derived, we construct a refutation of f using the stored proofs of the blocking clauses and the conflict clauses.

---

[2] The current implementation uses the VAMPYRE proof-generating decision procedure (see http://www.eecs.berkeley.edu/~rupak/Vampyre). Proofs in its LF-style proof system are translated to the system used here.

3.2 Interpolants for Structured Formulas

Of course, the interpolation problem (A, B) is not in general given in the clause form required by our proof system. In general, A and B have arbitrary nesting of Boolean operators. We now show how to reduce the problem of finding an interpolant for arbitrary formulas (A, B) into the problem of finding an interpolant for (A_c, B_c) where A_c and B_c are in clause form.

It is well known that *satisfiability* of an arbitrary formula f can be reduced in linear time to satisfiability of a clause form formula [11]. This transformation uses a set V of fresh Boolean variables, containing a variable v_g for each non-atomic propositional subformula g of f. A small set of clauses is introduced for each occurrence of a Boolean operator in f. For example, if the formula contains $g \land h$, we add the clauses $\langle v_g, \neg v_{g \land h} \rangle$, $\langle v_h, \neg v_{g \land h} \rangle$ and $\langle \neg v_g, \neg v_h, v_{g \land h} \rangle$. These clauses constrain $v_{g \land h}$ to be the conjunction of v_g and v_h. We will refer to the collection of these clauses for all non-atomic subformulas of f as $\text{CNF}_V(f)$. We then add the clause $\langle v_f \rangle$ to require that the entire formula is true. The resulting set of clauses is satisfiable exactly when f is satisfiable.

In fact, we can show something stronger, which is that any formula implied by $CNF_V(f) \land v_f$ that does not refer the fresh variables in V is also implied by f. This gives us the following result:

Theorem 3. *Let* $A_c = \text{CNF}_U(A), \langle u_A \rangle$ *and* $B_c = \text{CNF}_V(B), \langle v_B \rangle$, *where* U, V *are disjoint sets of fresh variables, and* A, B *are arbitrary formulas. An interpolant for* (A_c, B_c) *is also an interpolant for* (A, B).

This theorem allows us to compute interpolants for structured formulas by using the standard translation to clause form.

4 Applications

The interpolating prover described above has a number of possible applications in formal verification. These include refinement in predicate abstraction, and model checking infinite-state systems, with and without predicate abstraction.

4.1 Using Interpolation for Predicate Refinement

Predicate abstraction [13] is a technique commonly used in software model checking in which the state of an infinite-state system is represented abstractly by the truth values of a chosen set of predicates. Typically, when the chosen predicates are insufficient to prove the property in question, the abstraction is refined by adding predicates. For this purpose, the BLAST software model checker uses the interpolating prover in a technique due to Ranjit Jhala [3].

The basic idea of the technique is as follows. A counterexample is a sequence of program locations (a path) that leads from the program entry point to an error location. When the model checker finds a counterexample in the abstract model, it builds a formula that is satisfiable exactly when the path is a counterexample in the concrete model. This formula consists of a set of constraints: equations that define the values of program variables in each location in the path, and predicates that must be true for execution to continue along the path from each location (these correspond to program branch conditions).

Now let us divide the path into two parts, at state k. Let A_k be the set of constraints on transitions preceding state k and let B_k be the set of constraints on transitions subsequent to state k. Note that the common variables of A and B represent the values of the program variables at state k. An interpolant for (A_k, B_k) is a fact about state k that must hold if we take the given path to state k, but is inconsistent with the remainder of the path. In fact, if we derive such interpolants for every state of the path from the same refutation of the constraint set, we can show that the interpolant for state k is sufficient to prove the interpolant for state $k + 1$. As a result, if we add the interpolants to the set of predicates defining the abstraction, we are guaranteed to rule out the given path as a counterexample in the abstract model. Alternatively, we use the set of atomic predicates occurring in the interpolants, with the same result.

This interpolation approach to predicate refinement has the advantage that it tells us which predicates are relevant to each program location in the path. By using at each program location only predicates that are relevant to that location, a substantial reduction in the number of abstract states can be achieved, resulting in greatly increased performance of the model checker [3]. The fact that the interpolating prover can handle both linear inequalities and uninterpreted functions is useful, since linear arithmetic can represent operations on index variables, while uninterpreted functions can be used to represent array lookups or pointer dereferences, or to abstract unsupported operations (such as multiplication).[3]

4.2   Model Checking with Interpolants

Image computation is the fundamental operation of symbolic model checking [4]. This requires quantifier elimination, which is generally the most computationally expensive aspect of the technique. In [7] a method of approximate image computation is described that is based on interpolation, and does not require quantifier elimination. While the method is over-approximate, it is shown that it can always be made sufficiently precise to prevent false negatives for systems of finite diameter. While [7] treats only the propositional case, the same theory applies to interpolation for first order logic. Thus, in principle the interpolating prover can be used for interpolation-based model checking of infinite-state systems whose transition relation can be expressed in LIUF.

---

[3] Unfortunately, array updates cannot be handled directly, since the theory of *store* and *select* does not have the Craig interpolation property. Suppose, for example that A is $M' = store(M, a, x)$ and B is $(b \neq c) \wedge (select(M', b) \neq select(M, b)) \wedge (select(M', c) \neq select(M, c))$. The common variables here are M and M', but no facts expressible using only these variables are implied by A (except true), thus there is no interpolant for this pair.

One potential application would be model checking with predicate abstraction. This is a case where the transition relation is expressible in first order logic and the state space is finite, guaranteeing convergence. That is, the state is defined in terms of a set of Boolean variables $v_1 \ldots v_k$ corresponding to the truth values of first-order predicates $p_1 \ldots p_k$. The abstraction relation α is characterized symbolically by the formula $\bigwedge_i v_i' \leftrightarrow p_i$. If the concrete transition relation is characterized by R, the abstract transition relation can be written as the relational composition $\alpha^{-1} \circ R \circ \alpha$. Note that the relational composition can be accomplished by a simple renaming, replacing the "internal" variables with fresh variables that are implicitly existentially quantified. That is, $R \circ S$ can be written as $R\langle U/V' \rangle \wedge S\langle U/V \rangle$ where V and V' are the current and next-state variables respectively, and U is a set of fresh variables. Thus, if the concrete transition relation can be written as a formula in LIUF, then so can the abstract transition relation.

This formula can in turn be rewritten as a satisfiability-equivalent Boolean formula, as is done in [6]. This allows the application of finite-state methods for image computation, but has the disadvantage that it introduces a large number auxiliary boolean variables, making BDD-based image computations impractical. Although SAT-based quantifier elimination techniques are more effective in this case, this approach limits the technique to a small number of predicates. On the other hand, the interpolation-based approach does not require quantifier elimination or translation of the transition relation to a Boolean formula, and thus avoids these problems.

Another possible approach would be to model check the concrete, infinite-state system directly using the interpolation method. For infinite state systems in general this process is not guaranteed to converge. However, in the special case when the model has a finite bisimulation quotient, convergence is guaranteed. This is the case, for example, for timed automata. Since the transition relation of a timed automaton can be expressed in LI, it follows that reachability for timed automata can be verified using the interpolation method. As an example, a model of Fischer's timed mutual exclusion protocol has been verified in this way. Similarly, a simple model of Lamport's "bakery" mutual exclusion, with unbounded ticket numbers, has been modeled and verified. It is possible, in principle to apply the method to software model checking. Convergence is not guaranteed, but of course, this can also be said of predicate abstraction.

5   Conclusions and Future Work

The primary contribution of this work is a method of computing Craig interpolants from refutations in a theory that includes linear inequalities and uninterpreted functions. This extends earlier results that apply only to linear inequalities. This procedure has been integrated with a proof generating decision procedure, combining a SAT solver and a Nelson Oppen style prover to create an interpolating prover.

While the motivation for this work is mainly to experiment with interpolation-based model checking of infinite-state systems, it has also been applied in a manner quite unexpected by its author, to the problem of predicate refinement in the BLAST tool.

For future work, it is hoped that the interpolating prover will be useful for direct interpolation-based software model checking, perhaps in a hybrid approach between the fully symbolic method of [7] and the explicit search method of BLAST. It is also interesting to consider what other theories might be usefully incorporated into the prover.

References

1. W. Craig. Linear reasoning: A new form of the Herbrand-Gentzen theorem. *J. Symbolic Logic*, 22(3):250–268, 1957.
2. Leonardo de Moura, Harald Rueß, and Maria Sorea. Lazy theorem proving for bounded model checking over infinite domains. In *18th Conference on Automated Deduction (CADE)*, Lecture Notes in Computer Science, Copenhagen, Denmark, July 27-30 2002. Springer Verlag.
3. T. A. Henzinger, R. Jhala, Rupak Majumdar, and K. L. McMillan. Abstractions from proofs. In *ACM Symp. on Principles of Prog. Lang. (POPL 2004)*, 2004. to appear.
4. J.R. Burch, E.M. Clarke, K.L. McMillan, D.L. Dill, and L.J. Hwang. Symbolic Model Checking: 10^{20} States and Beyond. In *Proceedings of the Fifth Annual IEEE Symposium on Logic in Computer Science*, pages 1–33, Washington, D.C., 1990. IEEE Computer Society Press.
5. J. Krajíček. Interpolation theorems, lower bounds for proof systems, and independence results for bounded arithmetic. *J. Symbolic Logic*, 62(2):457–486, June 1997.
6. S. K. Lahiri, R. E. Bryant, and B. Cook. A symbolic approach to predicate abstraction. In *Computer-Aided Verification (CAV 2003)*, pages 141–153, 2003.
7. K. L. McMillan. Interpolation and sat-based model checking. In *Computer-Aided Verification (CAV 2003)*, pages 1–13, 2003.
8. K. L. McMillan and Nina Amla. Automatic abstraction without counterexamples. To appear, TACAS'03.
9. M. W. Moskewicz, C. F. Madigan, Y. Z., L. Z., and S. Malik. Chaff: Engineering an efficient SAT solver. In *Design Automation Conference*, pages 530–535, 2001.
10. G. Nelson and D. C. Oppen. Simplification by cooperating decision procedures. *ACM Trans. on Prog. Lang. and Sys.*, 1(2):245–257, 1979.
11. D. Plaisted and S. Greenbaum. A structure preserving clause form translation. *Journal of Symbolic Computation*, 2:293–304, 1986.
12. P. Pudlák. Lower bounds for resolution and cutting plane proofs and monotone computations. *J. Symbolic Logic*, 62(2):981–998, June 1997.
13. Hassen Saïdi and Susanne Graf. Construction of abstract state graphs with PVS. In Orna Grumberg, editor, *Computer-Aided Verification, CAV '97*, volume 1254, pages 72–83, Haifa, Israel, 1997. Springer-Verlag.
14. J. P. M. Silva and K. A. Sakallah. GRASP–a new search algorithm for satisfiability. In *Proceedings of the International Conference on Computer-Aided Design, November 1996*, 1996.

Minimal Assignments for Bounded Model Checking*

Kavita Ravi[1] and Fabio Somenzi[2]

[1] Cadence Design Systems
kravi@cadence.com
[2] University of Colorado at Boulder
Fabio@Colorado.EDU

Abstract. A traditional counterexample to a linear-time safety property shows the values of all signals at all times prior to the error. However, some signals may not be critical to causing the failure. A succinct explanation may help human understanding as well as speed up algorithms that have to analyze many such traces. In Bounded Model Checking (BMC), a counterexample is constructed from a satisfying assignment to a Boolean formula, typically in CNF. Modern SAT solvers usually assign values to all variables when the input formula is satisfiable. Deriving minimal satisfying assignments from such complete assignments does not lead to concise explanations of counterexamples because of how CNF formulae are derived from the models. Hence, we formulate the extraction of a succinct counterexample as the problem of finding a minimal assignment that, together with the Boolean formula describing the model, implies an *objective*. We present a two-stage algorithm for this problem, such that the result of each stage contributes to identify the "interesting" events that cause the failure. We demonstrate the effectiveness of our approach with an example and with experimental results.

1 Introduction

The success of model checking as a verification technique for both hardware and software depends to a large extent on the counterexamples that are produced for failing properties. However, the time consuming process of devising appropriate stimuli to test a model is often replaced by the laborious interpretation of the error trace returned by the model checker. For circuits with many inputs and outputs, analyzing an execution trace—be it a counterexample or a witness—may require examination of thousands of events. Not all these events are important, as in Fig. 1, where the "full" trace produced by the model checker is shown alongside a "reduced" counterexample from which irrelevant events have been removed.

The traces of Fig. 1 describe the solution to a puzzle obtained by model checking a property claiming that no solution exists. Four children (A, B, C, and D) must cross a river over a bridge that can be passed by only two children at the time. They have only one flashlight, which is needed to pass the bridge. When two children cross the river together, they walk at the speed of the slower one. Given the speeds of the children (1, 2, 4, and 5 minutes for A, B, C, and D, respectively) one seeks the quickest way for all four to cross the river. The model of the puzzle keeps track of the location of the children

---

* This work was supported in part by SRC contract 2003-TJ-920.

K. Jensen and A. Podelski (Eds.): TACAS 2004, LNCS 2988, pp. 31–45, 2004.

	full				reduced			
time	left / right	m-t-dest	sel1	sel2	left / right	m-t-dest	sel1	sel2
0	ABCDL/	0	A	B	ABCDL/	0	A	B
1	CD/ABL	1	B	A	CD/ABL	1		
2	CD/ABL	0	B	A	CD/ABL	0	B	
3	BCDL/A	1	B	A	BCDL/A	1		
4	BCDL/A	0	C	D	BCDL/A	0	C	D
5	B/ACDL	4	A	C	B/ACDL	4		
6	B/ACDL	3	A	C	B/ACDL	3		
7	B/ACDL	2	B	A	B/ACDL	2		
8	B/ACDL	1	A	A	B/ACDL	1		
9	B/ACDL	0	A	A	B/ACDL	0	A	A or B
10	ABL/CD	0	A	B	ABL/CD	0	A	B
11	/ABCDL	1	B	A	/ABCDL	1		
12	/ABCDL	0			/ABCD	0		

Fig. 1. Two ways to present a counterexample. The values of a variable that have not changed since the previous time are shown in gray

and the light. When a child starts crossing the river, her location is immediately changed to reflect her destination, and a counter (m-t-dest) is started to keep track of how many minutes are needed to reach the destination. The model uses two inputs (sel1 and sel2) to choose one or two children who are to cross the river. A child may be chosen only if she is on the same bank as the flashlight. Moreover, the second child must be slower than the first. If, for example, sel1=B and sel2=A, as in the "full" example at time 2, then only B crosses the river.

Examination of the reduced trace shows that the selection inputs are only relevant when m-t-dest is 0. It also shows that at time 2 the value of sel2 is immaterial, given that sel1=B: Since A is faster than B, and C and D are on the opposite bank to the flashlight, B will go alone back to the left bank. At time 4, the slowest children C and D will carry the flashlight to the right bank. At time 9, C and D are slower than A and on the same bank. Hence, for A to go alone, sel2 must be neither C nor D. Finally, the position of the flashlight at time 12 is irrelevant, since the objective has been achieved. By contrast, the "full" output of the model checker shows many needless transitions, for instance, at time 5 for both sel1 and sel2. The elimination of irrelevant events can substantially simplify the designer's task, and is the subject of this paper.

In SAT-based Bounded Model Checking (BMC), the set of counterexamples to a linear-time property is the set of solutions to a satisfiability (SAT) problem. A solution to a SAT problem is an assignment of values (1 and 0, or true and false) to the variables of a Boolean formula. A partial assignment will sometimes do: for instance, $a = 1$ is sufficient to satisfy $(a \vee b) \wedge (a \vee c)$. However, modern SAT solvers usually return complete assignments. Fig. 1 witnesses that they also pay no attention to minimizing input changes over time. In both cases, the speed of the solver would likely suffer if additional concerns were added to the basic one of finding a solution. In addition, SAT solvers are not designed to produce minimal solutions. Hence, detecting and removing unnecessary values from an assignment is best done as a post-processing.

Since many problems can be cast as SAT problems, finding minimal satisfying assignments to CNF formulae may have several applications. Hence, in Sect. 3, we describe that problem in some depth. In Sect. 4, however, we show why the minimization of model checking counterexamples should not be formulated that way, and present a computation of minimal counterexamples in two steps. The one described in Sect. 4.4 provides a stepping stone to the final solution, and is guaranteed to be verifiable by three-value simulation. In Sect. 5, we discuss related work. Section 6 reports experiments, and Sect. 7 concludes with a summary and future directions.

2 Satisfiability Solvers

An assignment A for a Boolean formula F over variables V is a function from V to $\{0, 1\}$. An assignment A is *total* if the function is total; otherwise it is *partial*. An assignment A' is *compatible* with assignment A if $A' \subseteq A$. A *satisfying* assignment A for a formula F is one that causes F to evaluate to true. A minimal satisfying assignment A for a Boolean formula F is a satisfying assignment such that no $A' \subset A$ satisfies F. A minimal satisfying assignment for F corresponds to a *prime implicant* of F.

A *least-cost* assignment can be defined by assigning costs to the variables. Given an assignment A satisfying F, a least-cost (least-size) assignment compatible with A is a cheapest (smallest) subset of A that still satisfies F. Finding a least-size assignment compatible with an assignment A corresponds to finding a largest cube of F that contains A or, equivalently, a minimal *blocking clause* of F [9].

Given a Boolean formula F, the SAT problem involves finding whether a satisfying assignment for F exists. This problem is NP-complete when F is in circuit form or is in Conjunctive Normal Form (CNF). However, due to the wide variety of applications of this problem, much research has been spent in developing fast and efficient SAT solvers.

A SAT solver typically computes a total satisfying assignment for F, if one exists, otherwise returns an *UNSATISFIABLE* answer. In a SAT solver a Boolean formula F is usually represented in CNF. For instance,

$$f = (a \lor b) \land (\neg b \lor d) \ . \tag{1}$$

A CNF formula is a conjunction of *clauses*. A clause is a disjunction of *literals*. A literal is a variable or its negation. In the sequel, it is also convenient to consider the CNF formula as a set of clauses and a clause as a set of literals. The literals in f above are a, b, $\neg b$, and d; b and $\neg b$ are the positive and negative literals (or *phases*) of variable b. The clauses of the formula are $(a \lor b)$ and $(\neg b \lor d)$. A satisfying assignment for f is $\{(a, 0), (b, 1), (d, 1)\}$. It is also convenient to use literals to designate variable-value pairs. For example, the above assignment is the set of literals $\{\neg a, b, d\}$.

A literal l is true in assignment A if $l \in A$; it is false in A if $\neg l \in A$. A clause is *satisfied* by an assignment when at least one of its literals is true. A clause is *conflicting* if all of its literals are false. A clause that is neither satisfied nor conflicting is *undecided*. A *unit* clause consists of a single literal. A *pure literal* of a CNF formula F is a variable that has the same phase in all the clauses of F in which it appears.

A new family of SAT solvers [12,14,10,7] have evolved that incorporate engineering advances atop the basic DPLL algorithm [6,5] and can solve many industrial-strength problems in applications such as BMC. The optimizations include non-chronological backtracking, conflict-driven learning, and efficient Boolean constraint propagation using the two-literal watching scheme. (Refer to [15] for a survey.) We discuss our problem and solution in the context of the Zchaff solver.

Boolean Constraint Propagation: Implications in these SAT solvers are computed using Boolean Constraint Propagation (BCP). Each clause, except unit clauses, contains two literals that are marked as *watched* literals [14,10]. In computing the satisfying assignment, the SAT solver makes *decisions* or assignments by setting values to variables. As decisions are made, a clause is updated only if one of the two watched literals in the clause is rendered false by the decision. The clauses in which the false literal is watched are examined to find another literal to watch instead. If such a literal is not found, then the other watched literal is implied (*unit clause rule*). The clause then becomes the *antecedent clause* of the implication. This implied value is again propagated using BCP.

Implication Graph: Given a satisfying assignment of a CNF formula, and a subset of the assignment marked as decisions, one can construct an *implication (hyper-)graph*, $G_I = (V, E)$. The nodes of this graph V represent the literals of the assignment and the roots represent the decisions. Each *directed hyperedge* $E \subseteq 2^V \times V$ represents an implication, caused by an antecedent clause. A vertex (literal) can be the destination of multiple hyperedges, associated with multiple antecedent clauses. Equation 1 yields the following implication graph if $\neg a$ is marked as decision.

$$\neg a \longrightarrow b \longrightarrow d$$

The literal $\neg a$ is the root of this graph. The first implication is caused by the antecedent clause $(a \lor b)$ and the second implication is caused by $(\neg b \lor d)$.

3   Minimal Satisfying Assignments for CNF Formulae

When a SATISFIABLE answer is found in a SAT solver, all variables are assigned a value by either a decision or an implication, and at least one watched literal in each clause is true. The two watched-literals scheme is critical for the efficiency of BCP: It drastically reduces the number of clauses examined when a variable is updated. For efficiency, the SAT solver does not keep track of the information required to detect a partial assignment that is sufficient for the satisfaction of the formula. In any case, even the termination criteria that check for the actual satisfaction of the formula (in either CNF or circuit form), rather than checking for complete assignments, do not guarantee a minimal satisfying assignment. (The assignments made after all clauses have been satisfied are certainly redundant, but some assignments made before may also be.) It is therefore interesting to discuss how SAT algorithms may be modified to meet that requirement. It is also interesting to discuss the related issue of generating least-size assignments.

Candidate Variables: *Lifting* is the process of removing literals or, equivalently, variables from a satisfying assignment such that for each valuation of the lifted variables the formula is still satisfied. Recall that implied variables result from BCP applied to decisions. It can be easily proved that implied variables cannot be lifted: Only decision variables can be lifted. The literals in the unit clauses are considered to be implications, hence cannot be lifted; the pure literals, on the other hand, are not implications.

Negligible variables and greedy removal: The observation that when a satisfying assignment is found, at least one of the two watched literals in a clause must be true can be used to lift some literals. For each literal, the SAT solver maintains the list of clauses in which the literal is watched. The literals in the satisfying assignment that have empty lists and that do not appear in unit clauses can be removed from the satisfying assignment. All these *negligible* variables can be lifted simultaneously. Notice that none of the negligible variables are implied. Further lifting may be achieved by marking one true literal for each clause. All literals in the assignment that remain unmarked after all clauses are scanned can be lifted. Neither the negligible-variable approach nor the greedy approach yields a minimal assignment.

Brute-Force Lifting: One can check the possibility of lifting the remaining variables by flipping the value of each candidate variable while retaining the rest of the assignment, and checking satisfiability of the formula. If the formula is satisfiable, the variable can be lifted and the formula updated by dropping the literals associated with this variable (universal quantification of this variable from the formula). The resulting minimal assignment depends on the order in which the variables are considered and is not necessarily of least-cost.

Covering Approach: Least-cost assignments can be found by solving covering problems. A covering problem consists of minimizing $\sum_{1 \le i \le n} c_i \cdot x_i$, subject to constraint $\Gamma(x_1, \dots, x_n) = 1$, where Γ is a Boolean formula, and the costs c_i's are non-negative integers. We assume that Γ is in CNF. If all variables in Γ are pure literals, we talk of *unate* covering; otherwise, of *binate* covering. Unate covering is also known as *set covering*. Covering problems can be solved by generic 0-1 integer linear program solvers [11], or by dedicated algorithms based on branch and bound [3].

A unate covering problem may be solved to find a least-cost solution compatible with a starting assignment, while one independent of any particular satisfying assignment from the SAT solver can be obtained by solving a binate covering problem with one variable per literal in the CNF formula.

The above described techniques may be useful toward deriving minimal assignments that are sufficient to show the satisfiability of the given formula. The removal of negligible variables and the greedy scheme are fast and efficient. Brute-force lifting can be implemented in time quadratic in the size of the CNF formula. Finally, the covering approach is expensive, especially when seeking a globally least-cost solution.

4 Bounded Model Checking and Minimal Assignments

In this section, we first introduce Bounded Model Checking and then discuss the problem of minimal assignments for concise counterexamples.

4.1 Bounded Model Checking

Bounded model checking [1] is a technique to find bounded-length counterexamples to linear time properties. Recently, BMC has been applied with great success by formulating it as a SAT instance and solving it with the improved SAT solvers mentioned in Sect. 2. For simplicity, we only discuss invariant properties here.

We consider finite systems given as circuits composed of memory elements and combinational gates. Nondeterminism in these circuits is only due to primary inputs. Let $T(X, W, X', U)$ be the formula for the transition relation where X, W, X', and U are sets of variables representing the present states, primary inputs, next states, and gate outputs of the system. The timed version $T_i(X_i, W_i, X_{i+1}, U_i)$ represents the transitions between the i-th and the $(i + 1)$-th step of the system.

Given a system with a Boolean formula I representing the initial states, a Boolean formula $T_i(X_i, W_i, X_{i+1}, U_i)$ representing the i-step transition relation and an invariant with a Boolean formula P_k representing the failure states at step k, the length-k BMC problem is posed as a SAT instance in the following manner:

$$F = I \wedge P_k \wedge \bigwedge_{0 \le i < k} T_i(X_i, W_i, X_{i+1}, U_i) \ . \tag{2}$$

We assume that a Boolean formula is translated into CNF by introducing intermediate dependent variables in the standard fashion. If the property may fail in k transitions, the SAT solver computes a satisfying assignment that describes a counterexample to the property. If the SAT solver produces a total assignment, all variables of the system appear in the counterexample.

4.2 Motivation and Definitions

Applying the techniques described in Sect. 3 to minimize the set of variables in the counterexample to the BMC problem does not give much reduction in the number of variables. The experiments we performed using these methods yielded 2% to 7% reduction. We explain the poor performance with the following example.

Example 1. Consider a tautologous circuit with input a, output g_1, and such that $g_1 = a \vee g_0$ and $g_0 = \neg a$. Suppose that a SAT solver is given the following CNF formula to prove that g_1 can be set to 1:

$$F = (a \vee g_0) \wedge (\neg a \vee \neg g_0) \wedge (\neg g_0 \vee g_1) \wedge (\neg a \vee g_1) \wedge (a \vee g_0 \vee \neg g_1) \wedge g_1 \ .$$

Suppose the solver propagates $g_1 = 1$, decides $a = 1$, which in turn implies $g_0 = 0$. This is minimal because the satisfying assignment has to express that the inverter output is consistent with its input. Hence, it must contain both a and g_0, though $\exists g_0 . F = g_1$ does not depend on a. The intermediate variable g_0 constrains the satisfying assignment beyond what is required to justify the objective g_1.

The example shows why the methods of Sect. 3 are not appropriate for the computation of concise counterexamples: A counterexample shows a sequence of transitions from the initial states to the failure states; the most important event in the counterexample is the failure. Hence, "events" implying the failure are primary for the purpose of debugging, whereas the others convey secondary information. We want to distill the primary events out of a counterexample. Further, a user may choose to only see events related to an "interesting" set of variables. Our formulation is aimed at extracting an assignment that implies the failure with a minimal set of "interesting" events, excluding those that have no bearing on the justification of the objective.

To formalize these notions, we assume that we are given a satisfying assignment to (2) and another formula

$$\hat{F} = P_k \wedge \bigwedge_{0 \leq i < k} T_i(X_i, W_i, X_{i+1}, U_i) \ . \tag{3}$$

We want the ability to lift the initial state literals in the satisfying assignment to focus attention on those memory elements that are important to the counterexample. Hence, I is absent from (3). Sometimes, a bounded model checker will add additional constraints to (2) such as the non-existence of counterexamples of length less than k ($\bigwedge_{0 \leq i < k} \neg P_i$) to aid the SAT solver. It is important that these constraints be absent from (3) for maximal freedom in lifting variables in the satisfying assignment. Each gate in the circuit, which corresponds to a subformula, translates to a set of CNF clauses. We assume that the given CNF is such that in each clause not in P_k, we can identify the literals that correspond to the inputs and output of the gate that produced it.

We assume that we are given a set of *roots* $R \subseteq V$ that correspond to the inputs to the unrolled circuit in the BMC problem. These roots R form a set of independent variables in the formula, in the sense that $\bigwedge_{0 \leq i < k} T_i$ is satisfiable for every assignment to the variables in R. The values of the remaining variables $V \setminus R$ in $\bigwedge_{0 \leq i < k} T_i$ are determined by the valuation of R. In the BMC context, the roots are the variables representing the initial states (X_0) and the inputs (W_i, $i < k$). The user may mark some variables $S \subseteq V \setminus R$ as interesting. Typically, these are the state variables of the system and therefore, of interest in the counterexample.

An *objective* of the formula is defined as a set of clauses whose variables are non-overlapping with the set of roots R. For the sake of discussion, we assume that an objective o is represented by a unit clause (a single literal) in the formula[1]. Henceforth, we will refer to o and the literal in o interchangeably. The objective denotes conditions that *must* be implied by the minimal assignment. In the BMC problem, the objective o is a literal stating the failure of the formula at step k, P_k.

4.3   Lifting for a Minimal Assignment

In this section, we describe the lifting of literals from the given satisfying assignment A relative to the objective o. We adapt the brute-force lifting method described in Sect. 3. This is a powerful method to eliminate literals that yields a minimal assignment, albeit order-dependent. Instead of lifting a literal if the resulting assignment still satisfies the given formula, here we want to lift a literal if the resulting assignment is still sufficient to imply the objective.

The procedure is described in Fig. 2. The arguments to this procedure are the formula of (3), $\hat{F}$, the objective o, the root literals in the original assignment, A_R, and the

---

[1] There is no loss of generality in this assumption as we can augment the formula with the definition of the literal o representing the conjunction of the clauses in the objective and adding the literal itself to the formula.

interesting literals in the original assignment, A_S. The lifting of roots is tried first. For each root literal l, the negation of the objective o is asserted in place of o in $\hat{F}$. Let $\bigwedge(A_R \setminus \{l\})$ denote the conjunction of literals in A_R except l. A satisfiability check $(\text{SAT\_Solve}(F'))$ whether the literals in A_R except l together with the formula $\hat{F}$ fail to imply the objective o. If the check results in a satisfiable assignment, then l cannot be lifted; otherwise, both l and $\neg l$ imply the objective and can therefore be lifted from the existing assignment A_R. A_R is then updated by removing the lifted literal.

Once the lifting of the roots is determined, the remaining variables in A_S are checked for an implied value. If a variable in A_S can take both values due to the reduced set of roots A_R, then it is not added to the assignment A', else it is. The value of this variable in the original complete assignment is known to be possible. An additional SAT check determines whether the opposite value is consistent with the current partial assignment. Since R is an independent set, $\hat{F}$ is satisfiable for any value of the lifted roots. By contrast, since S is dependent on R, all we can say about the absent variables of S in A' is that they take different values as the values of the lifted roots are changed. Unlike the literals in A_R, those in $A_S \setminus A'$ are not really lifted according to our definition: They are simply not implied by the partial root assignment.

```
Brute_Force_Lifting($\hat{F}$, $o$, $A_R$, $A_S$)
    $F'' = $ substitute $o$ with $\neg o$ in $\hat{F}$;
    for each literal $l$ in $A_R$
        $F' = F'' \wedge \bigwedge(A_R \setminus l)$;
        if (SAT_Solve($F'$) $\neq$ SATISFIABLE) $A_R = A_R \setminus l$;
    $A' = A_R$;
    for each literal $l$ in $A_S$
        $F' = \hat{F} \wedge \neg l \wedge \bigwedge A'$;
        if (SAT_Solve($F'$) $\neq$ SATISFIABLE) $A' = A' \cup l$;
    return $A'$;
```

Fig. 2. Brute-force lifting algorithm

This method of lifting roots is effective in deriving a minimal satisfying assignment and isolating the primary events responsible for the failure of a property. Such a counterexample may help in more effective debugging as in the example of Fig. 1. Sometimes, however, the resulting counterexample may have discontinuities due to the missing values of S variables, thereby requiring some reconstruction by the user. Consider, for instance, a gate $g_2 = (g_0 \equiv g_1)$ such that, under the minimal assignment A', both $\{g_0, g_1\}$ and $\{\neg g_0, \neg g_1\}$ are possible for some values of the lifted roots, but $\{g_0, \neg g_1\}$ and $\{\neg g_0, g_1\}$ are not possible. Then A' would contain g_2, but no literal for either g_0 or g_1. In cases like these, it is useful to have an intermediate counterexample where the trace has fewer holes yet lifts to the counterexample generated by Fig. 2. Ideally, the intermediate counterexample should be three-valued simulatable (see Sect. 4.4) for easy interpretation and validation.

To prove that lifting a root does preserve the implication of the objective, the brute-force lifting algorithm goes through a sequence of unsatisfiability checks. This prevents the application of universal quantification after a successful lifting, which is what keeps the satisfiability checks trivial and ultimately gives quadratic complexity to the lifting algorithm of Sect. 3. The lifting procedure of this section requires solving one SAT instance (one SAT_Solve() call) per candidate variable. This may be expensive but it is possible to solve the multiple SAT_Solve() calls incrementally. Also, the variables of A_S implied by BCP of the reduced set of roots need not be considered for lifting. On the other hand, an intermediate assignment, if cheap to compute, can reduce the number of calls to SAT_Solve() by providing a smaller assignment to start with. This is indeed true of the intermediate assignment proposed in the following section.

4.4   Implication Graph and a Covering Solution

In three-valued logic simulation of a circuit, a signal has one of three values: 0 (false), 1 (true), and X (unknown). Boolean operators are extended to the three-valued domain in a conservative manner. For instance, $a \vee \neg a = X$ if $a = X$. As a consequence, if three-valued simulation assigns a signal in a combinational circuit value 0 or 1 for a certain input assignment, then that signal is guaranteed to have the same value under all possible replacements of X's by 0's and 1's. One easily sees that BCP in a SAT solver is closely related to three-valued simulation when "undecided" is interpreted as "unknown." In particular, three-valued simulation of a partial assignment to a CNF formula will imply the value of the objective if and only if BCP does.

An assignment that can justify the objective by pure BCP has two important advantages: On the one hand, it can be understood by a designer by a sequence of easy, local steps. On the other hand, it can be verified in linear time by widely available independent tools. The drawback of a three-valued simulatable assignment is, of course, that it may not be minimal.

We obtain a three-value simulatable partial assignment from the original assignment A produced by the SAT solver using an implication graph. Consider the implication graph where the roots are A_R, the root literals in the original assignment. We view these as decisions since they are literals of the independent set R. Note that this implication graph must contain the objective o since o is in A and is part of the dependent set. Therefore, we can use this implication graph to obtain a subset of A_R and the interesting variables A_S that transitively imply o. This is closely related to the work of [9] where a similar technique is used to enumerate a cover of the formula in terms of a defined set of roots (primary inputs and state variables). Our work is applied in a different context and is extended as explained below.

Our method is described in Fig. 3. The arguments to this procedure are the formula $\hat{F}$ from (3), A, A_R, o, and a cost function described below. First, the literals in A_R are added to the formula $\hat{F}$. The next step involves deriving the input-to-output implications. Implications where the implied literal is the output of a gate are valid input-to-output implications. (Note that the constructed CNF is such that there is only one output literal per clause.) The part of the implication graph that leads to o is traced with a backward search from o to the roots. (The input-to-output implication derivation can be combined with this backward step.) The resulting hypergraph G is a connected sub-graph of G_I

since F' is constructed from a Boolean formula representing a circuit and o is a net in the circuit.[2] Its roots are a subset of A_R and its nodes are a subset of V. The nodes of G form a lifting of the original assignment A.

Implication_Graph_Based_Lifting($\hat{F}$, A, A_R, o, $weights$)
  $F' = \hat{F} \wedge \bigwedge A_R$;
  G_I = derive input-to-output implications (F');
  G = trace graph backwards(G_I, o);
  B = formulate binate covering problem(G);
  B' = Binate Covering Solver$(B, weights)$;
  A' = map B' onto literals of A;
  return A';

Fig. 3. Binate covering-based lifting algorithm

If G is a hyper-graph with at least one set of multiple implications to a literal, it is possible to further lift literals from the assignment. For this, we use a binate covering solver with a user-defined cost function $weights$ that is $\sum_{1 \le i \le n} c_i \cdot x_i, x_i \in A_R \cup A_S$. The cost function describes the relative importance of the variables to be lifted. For example, a large c_i associated with a root variable will result in it being lifted rather than a variable with a small c_i. Our goal is to lift as many roots as possible in order to identify those roots that are critical in implying the objective.

The covering problem is formulated thus: Each node of the graph corresponds to a variable. The variable is 1 if the node is in the subgraph that is selected. A subgraph must satisfy the following constraints, which guarantee that the objective is satisfied: (1) The objective variable must be true. (2) If a variable is true, and it is not in A_R, then all the variables of at least one hyperedge into it must be true.

As a simple example, if the objective is a, and a is implied by $b \wedge c$, or by $c \wedge \neg d$ in the implication hypergraph, the constraints are

$$a \wedge (a \rightarrow c \wedge (b \vee \neg d)) = a \wedge c \wedge (b \vee \neg d) \ .$$

The optimal solution depends on the costs of b and d.

The result of the binate covering solver is mapped to a satisfying assignment A' by picking the literals corresponding to the variables in B' from A. The result of Fig. 3 is a least-cost assignment that forms a connected subset of nodes in the implication graph G from the roots to the objective.

Such an assignment is three-valued simulatable. It can be presented to the user as a series of implications that lead to the error. The counterexample is easy to understand, yet pruned of the irrelevant implications. There are fewer variables to pay attention to.

Though the restriction to three-valued simulatability means that the implication graph approach is incomplete, it may remove literals from the assignment that the lifting

---

[2] Here is where we depart from the approach of [9], which is based on a simple graph or, equivalently, a hypergraph in which the in-degree of a node is at most 1.

approach would retain. The latter never discards from A_S a literal l implied by the roots in A'. By contrast, the implication graph approach may do so when the value of l, although known, is immaterial to the objective. An example is provided by the location of the flashlight at time 12 in Fig. 1.

The implication graph in a SAT solver alone cannot exclude that a certain variable may be lifted. For instance, the implication graph for Example 1 has one root, a, and two leaves, $\neg g_0$ and g_1. Tracing back from the objective g_1 shows that $\{a\}$ is sufficient to imply g_1; however, this is not minimal. On the other hand, if we rewrote F as $g_1 \wedge (a \vee g_0) \wedge (\neg a \vee \neg g_0)$ to highlight that g_1 is implied by F, the implication graph would have no edges, and the minimal empty assignment would be found.

The implication graph derived in the SAT solver is closely linked to the representation of the circuit and to the translation of the design into the CNF formula. A redundant circuit, an inefficient translation or state encoding may mask several implications.

Example 2. An 8-state finite state machine is shown in Fig. 4. The machine has one input i. Each transition is annotated with the values of i that enable it. The three binary state variables, c, b, and a, form the state vector *state*. If one is interested in the reachability of G, the most interesting event, or *objective*, is the state vector taking value G; the primary events of interest are those that are critical to causing it. It is easily seen that all paths of length 3 from A lead to G. Hence, a minimal witness to the reachability of G in terms of initial state and primary inputs is $\{\neg c_0, \neg b_0, \neg a_0\}$. (Each subscripted variable represents the value of that variable at the time step of the subscript.)

Suppose we start with the following solution obtained by the SAT solver after quantification of the internal variables: $\{\neg c_0, \neg b_0, \neg a_0, i_0, \neg i_1, \neg i_2\}$. This corresponds to the path $A \rightarrow C \rightarrow E \rightarrow G$ in Fig. 4. We analyze the implication graph caused by this assignment in the SAT solver whose leaf is the literal representing G in the third step and whose roots are the initial states and inputs. It shows that i_2 and i_1 can be lifted. Knowing that the second state of the path is C is enough to infer that $\{c_2, \neg b_2\}$, which in turn is enough to infer that the objective is satisfied. This works because E and F have adjacent encodings. If we look at the internal nodes in the implication graph corresponding to $\{\neg c_0, \neg b_0, \neg a_0, i_0\}$ we find that a_2 is not included. That is, we have the path

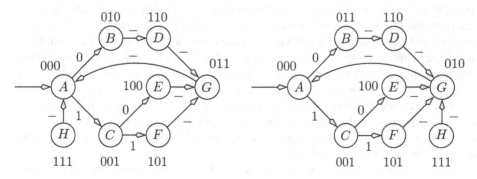

Fig. 4. State diagram for minimal error trace example

Fig. 5. Another state diagram for minimal error trace example

$$A \to C \to \{E, F\} \to G \ .$$

However, we cannot lift i_0, for we would not know b_1 and a_1, and consequently lose track of the fact that we are making progress toward G. Now let us change the implementation of Fig. 4 as shown in Fig. 5. From state $= A$ we can imply state $= \{B, C\}$ at the next time, because B and C have adjacent encodings, and from state $= \{B, C\}$ we can imply state $= \{D, E, F, H\}$ at the next time. Finally, from state $= \{D, E, F, H\}$ we can imply state $= G$ at the next time. (All without making assumptions about i.) This corresponds to the path

$$A \to \{B, C\} \to \{D, E, F, H\} \to G \ .$$

Note the importance of changing the successor of the unreachable state H.

In terms of run time, Implication_Graph_Based_Lifting() involves deriving input-output implications (cost is proportional to the size of the formula), one pass over the implication graph backwards from o, which can be combined with the formulation of the Binate Covering Problem, and one call to the Binate Covering Solver. In practice, the combination of these three steps is often cheaper than the Brute_Force_Lifting() algorithm for large CNF formulae. The assignment A' can be provided as an argument A to the Brute_Force_Lifting() algorithm. As discussed in Sect. 4.3, the expense of lifting may be mitigated by the reduction of literals by the algorithm in Implication_Graph_Based_Lifting().

The techniques of Fig. 2 and Fig. 3 complement each other. While the former is powerful, is unaffected by translation inefficiencies and is effective in finding the consequences of the primary events responsible for causing failure, the latter counterexample is three-valued simulatable, eliminates events that are implied but have no bearing on the achievement of the objective, and can serve as a guide in interpreting the result of the former by filling some holes.

5   Related Work

As mentioned in Sect. 4.4, the work of McMillan [9] is related to our lifting based on analyzing the implication graph. While his work applies this technique toward enumerating a cover, our work applies it to making traces more understandable. We extend this technique by minimizing the set of implications that justify the objective using a binate covering solver to find a minimal cover of a hypergraph. Brute-force lifting as described in Sect. 4.3 is also feasible since we only need one satisfying assignment.

In general, our problem is related to Quantified Boolean Formulae in terms of existentially quantifying the non-interesting variables but is different in that we have the notion of an objective, weights assigned to different variables, and causality between the inputs (roots) and the output (objective).

Minimization of counterexamples is addressed in [8]. The authors there distinguish between "control" and "data" signals in the counterexample and try to obtain long segments of the counterexample in which the data signals have *don't-care* values. Our work does not need the partition of control and data signals. The advantage of our method is that when segments with data signal don't-cares do not exist, different don't cares (perhaps control signals) will be extracted. On the other hand, the disadvantage is that even if long segments of data don't-cares exist, this algorithm may not find them since it has no control on which don't cares are found.

Minimization of counterexamples is useful in the context of abstraction-refinement [4]. Refinement is often more effective when it is based on the simultaneous elimination of a set of counterexamples rather than on elimination of one counterexample at a time [13]. Therefore, our technique can be applied in this context also.

6 Experimental Results

We implemented the algorithms of Sections 4.4 and 4.3 by modifying Zchaff and its interface to the model checker Vis [2]. The lifting based on the implication graph mechanism of Fig. 3 uses the binate covering solver Mincov [3]. The algorithm described in Fig. 2 is implemented in a non-incremental manner.

To enable lifting, Vis generates an auxiliary file that contains the roots R, interesting variables S, and the objective o. The R variables are the inputs of all the time frames and the initial state variables. The S variables contain the state variables over the various time frames. In case a satisfying assignment is found, this file is read by the SAT solver to perform the lifting algorithm described in Sect. 4.4. The cost of each variable in R is 1 and the cost of each variable in S is 0. The result of this algorithm is used as the starting point of the algorithm as described in Sect. 4.3.

Table 1. Experimental results of lifting based on Fig. 3 and Fig. 2

Example	Vars	CE	Original			Mincov Heuristic						Optimal		
						mincov			lift			mincov		
			R	S	Time	R	S	Time	R	S	Time	R	S	Time
s1269b	67	3	12	21	0.01	0.50	0.71	0.00	0.50	0.71	0.00	0.50	0.71	0.00
avq	388	3	30	102	0.03	0.20	0.15	0.05	0.10	0.09	0.01	0.20	0.15	0.04
min	536	3	6	15	0.03	0.67	0.87	0.01	0.50	0.53	0.03	0.67	0.87	0.01
river	1952	5	32	67	0.12	0.66	0.69	0.04	0.47	0.42	0.88	0.66	0.69	0.05
vending	4266	2	35	93	0.23	0.57	0.35	0.03	0.46	0.26	0.63	0.57	0.35	0.05
flashlight	6110	12	56	152	4.45	0.93	0.97	0.10	0.46	0.80	14.17	0.93	0.97	0.09
b10	13466	8	103	223	1.33	0.59	0.58	0.20	0.17	0.33	19.25	0.57	0.52	0.19
b13	14073	10	52	372	0.83	0.38	0.42	0.58	0.29	0.34	25.81	0.31	0.36	8.44
b05	20238	7	33	215	1.23	0.58	0.71	0.54	0.12	0.53	13.74	0.21	0.49	0.55
s1423	30212	61	1105	5253	26.66	0.49	0.35	3.94	0.28	0.29	2336.92	—	—	>2h
b09	30650	20	47	587	1.92	0.30	0.40	0.43	0.09	0.30	44.78	0.21	0.39	0.46
ns1	43756	8	184	632	14.95	0.48	0.42	0.70	0.25	0.26	562.42	0.48	0.42	0.73
b07	56456	28	57	869	5.24	0.51	0.31	2.06	0.05	0.20	208.21	0.51	0.31	2.06
usb_phy	71105	36	544	3280	19.87	0.22	0.31	1.82	0.14	0.26	1047.56	0.21	0.31	1.81
blackjack	117377	13	168	1507	54.38	0.60	0.27	1.94	0.48	0.15	861.38	0.59	0.27	1.98
Average						0.51	0.50		0.29	0.37		0.47	0.49	

All experiments were run on a Sun Fire 280R machine with 2GB of memory. The results are presented in Table 1. We ran 15 examples of varying sizes. The first column presents the name of the example, the second column contains the number of variables presented to the SAT solver, and the third column shows the length of the counterexample. Each set of three columns subsequently presents results for the original satisfying assignment, results for the three-valued simulatable counterexamples from Fig. 3 and results of further lifting based on Fig. 2, respectively. Both a heuristic and an exact solution were extracted from Mincov. The last three columns show the results of the exact solution. The three columns in each set give the number of root variables R in the resulting assignment, the number of interesting variables S, and the time in seconds taken to extract the assignments. The R and the S columns for the last three sets are presented as the fractions of the original numbers of R and S literals in the "full" set.

The results in the table show that applying the algorithm of Sect. 4.4 can provide as much as 80% reduction in the number of root literals and 85% reduction in the number of interesting literals with the average reduction being 49% and 50% of the original literals, respectively. The data for brute-force lifting are even more impressive, the average reduction in root count being 71% of the initial literals. In most cases the Mincov heuristic solutions result in reductions in literals comparable to those of the optimal solutions and can be found quickly for all examples. Further, the run time of the Implication Graph Based Lifting algorithm is often only a fraction of the original run time and the subsequent lifting phase recovers most of the differences between heuristic and exact solutions. We also compared the heuristic solution to a greedy selection of an implication graph. The two methods produce similar literal reductions, but the greedy selection puts a larger burden on the lifting algorithms, and is therefore slower.

The CPU times for the brute-force lifting of the literals are large due to the cost of one call to SAT_Solve() per candidate literal to be lifted. The performance of the brute-force lifting method may improve by the use of an incremental SAT solver. Applying BCP in the brute-force lifting algorithm to the the roots selected by binate covering may also help decrease the run time by reducing the candidate literals.

7   Conclusions

We have discussed and presented algorithms for minimal satisfying assignments for CNF formulae, both in general and in the context of Bounded Model Checking. Our experiments show that our technique is effective in terms of reduction of literals. The reduced counterexamples are often more instructive in debugging designs. Although lifting is sometimes expensive, there is room for improvement of its performance. Besides, the Implication Graph Based Lifting is quite effective in the reduction of literals.

In Example 2 of Sect. 4.4, the failing property states that G is never reached. This is a form of vacuous failure, because, in fact, G occurs along all paths from the initial state. Vacuity is related to the inputs' playing no role in the failure of the property. The precise nature of this connection remains the subject of future investigation together with the extension to full LTL model checking.

Acknowledgment. We thank Mohammad Awedh, HoonSang Jin, and Bing Li for help with Vis and Zchaff.

References

[1] A. Biere, A. Cimatti, E. Clarke, and Y. Zhu. Symbolic model checking without BDDs. In *Fifth International Conference on Tools and Algorithms for Construction and Analysis of Systems (TACAS'99)*, pages 193–207, Amsterdam, The Netherlands, Mar. 1999. LNCS 1579.

[2] R. K. Brayton et al. VIS: A system for verification and synthesis. Technical Report UCB/ERL M95/104, Electronics Research Lab, Univ. of California, Dec. 1995.

[3] R. K. Brayton and F. Somenzi. An exact minimizer for Boolean relations. In *Proceedings of the IEEE International Conference on Computer Aided Design*, pages 316–319, Santa Clara, CA, Nov. 1989.

[4] E. Clarke, A. Gupta, J. Kukula, and O. Strichman. SAT based abstraction-refinement using ILP and machine learning. In E. Brinksma and K. G. Larsen, editors, *Fourteenth Conference on Computer Aided Verification (CAV 2002)*, pages 265–279. Springer-Verlag, July 2002. LNCS 2404.

[5] M. Davis, G. Logemann, and D. Loveland. A machine program for theorem proving. *Communications of the ACM*, 5:394–397, 1962.

[6] M. Davis and H. Putnam. A computing procedure for quantification theory. *Journal of the Association for Computing Machinery*, 7(3):201–215, July 1960.

[7] E. Goldberg and Y. Novikov. BerkMin: A fast and robust SAT-solver. In *Proceedings of the Conference on Design, Automation and Test in Europe*, pages 142–149, Paris, France, Mar. 2002.

[8] H. Jin, K. Ravi, and F. Somenzi. Fate and free will in error traces. In *International Conference on Tools and Algorithms for Construction and Analysis of Systems (TACAS'02)*, pages 445–459, Grenoble, France, Apr. 2002. LNCS 2280.

[9] K. L. McMillan. Applying SAT methods in unbounded symbolic model checking. In E. Brinksma and K. G. Larsen, editors, *Fourteenth Conference on Computer Aided Verification (CAV'02)*, pages 250–264. Springer-Verlag, Berlin, July 2002. LNCS 2404.

[10] M. Moskewicz, C. F. Madigan, Y. Zhao, L. Zhang, and S. Malik. Chaff: Engineering an efficient SAT solver. In *Proceedings of the Design Automation Conference*, pages 530–535, Las Vegas, NV, June 2001.

[11] G. L. Nemhauser and L. A. Wolsey. *Integer and Combinatorial Optimization*. Wiley, New York, 1988.

[12] J. P. M. Silva and K. A. Sakallah. Grasp—a new search algorithm for satisfiability. In *Proceedings of the International Conference on Computer-Aided Design*, pages 220–227, San Jose, CA, Nov. 1996.

[13] C. Wang, B. Li, H. Jin, G. D. Hachtel, and F. Somenzi. Improving Ariadne's bundle by following multiple threads in abstraction refinement. In *Proceedings of the International Conference on Computer-Aided Design*, pages 408–415, Nov. 2003.

[14] H. Zhang. SATO: An efficient propositional prover. In *Proceedings of the International Conference on Automated Deduction*, pages 272–275, July 1997. LNAI 1249.

[15] L. Zhang and S. Malik. The quest for efficient Boolean satisfiability solvers. In *Fourteenth International Conference on Computer Aided Verification, (CAV'02)*, pages 17–36, Copenhagen, Denmark, 2002. LNCS 2404.

Numerical vs. Statistical Probabilistic Model Checking: An Empirical Study*

Håkan L.S. Younes[1], Marta Kwiatkowska[2], Gethin Norman[2], and David Parker[2]

[1] Computer Science Department, Carnegie Mellon University
Pittsburgh, PA 15213, USA
[2] School of Computer Science, University of Birmingham
Birmingham B15 2TT, United Kingdom

Abstract. Numerical analysis based on uniformisation and statistical techniques based on sampling and simulation are two distinct approaches for transient analysis of stochastic systems. We compare the two solution techniques when applied to the verification of time-bounded until formulae in the temporal stochastic logic CSL. This study differs from most previous comparisons of numerical and statistical approaches in that CSL model checking is a hypothesis testing problem rather than a parameter estimation problem. We can therefore rely on highly efficient sequential acceptance sampling tests, which enables statistical solution techniques to quickly return a result with some uncertainty. This suggests that statistical techniques can be useful as a first resort during system prototyping, rather than as a last resort as often suggested. We also propose a novel combination of the two solution techniques for verifying CSL queries with nested probabilistic operators.

1 Introduction

Continuous-time Markov chains (CTMCs) are an important class of stochastic models, widely used in performance and dependability evaluation. The temporal logic CSL (Continuous Stochastic Logic) introduced by Aziz et al. [2,3] and since extended by Baier et al. [5] provides a powerful means to specify both path-based and traditional state-based performance measures on CTMCs in a concise and flexible manner. CSL contains a time-bounded until operator, the focus of this study, that allows one to express properties such as "the probability of n servers becoming faulty within 15.07 seconds is at most 0.01".

The two dominating techniques used for analysis of stochastic systems are *numerical* methods and *statistical* methods. Numerical solution techniques can often provide a higher accuracy than statistical methods, whose results are probabilistic in nature. However, numerical methods are far more memory intensive, which often leaves statistical solution techniques as a last resort [23,7].

---

* Supported in part by DARPA and ARO under contract no. DAAD19–01–1–0485, a grant from the Royal Swedish Academy of Engineering Sciences (IVA), FORWARD and EPSRC grants GR/N22960, GR/S11107 and GR/S46727.

The verification of time-bounded CSL formulae can be reduced to transient analysis [4,5]. Efficient numerical solution techniques, such as uniformisation [14,20,18,7], for transient analysis of CTMCs have existed for decades and are well-understood. Younes and Simmons [26] have proposed a statistical approach for verifying time-bounded CSL formulae, based on acceptance sampling and discrete event simulation. The use of acceptance sampling is possible because CSL formulae only ask if a probability is above or below some threshold. Previous comparisons of numerical and statistical solution techniques have typically been based on estimation problems. This study is concerned with hypothesis testing problems, for which there exists highly efficient *sequential* acceptance sampling tests that make statistical solution techniques look more favourable than in a comparison with numerical techniques on estimation problems.

We have implemented the statistical model checking algorithm in the PRISM tool[1][16], a probabilistic model checker developed at the University of Birmingham. PRISM already implements numerical solution techniques and makes use of symbolic data representation in order to reduce memory requirements for those techniques.

Probabilistic model checking in general, and the two approaches implemented in PRISM, are described in Sect. 2. In this section we also propose a combination of numerical and statistical solution techniques to handle CSL formulae with nested probabilistic operators. The idea of combining the two techniques has been explored before [21,7], but not in the context of nested CSL queries. The mixed solution technique has also been implemented in PRISM.

In Sect. 4, we present empirical results obtained with PRISM on a number of case studies, described in Sect. 3, which serve as the comparison of the two approaches. The results demonstrate that the complexity of both the numerical and the statistical approach is typically linear in the time-bound of the property, but that the statistical approach scales better with the size of the state space. Furthermore, the statistical approach requires considerably less memory than the numerical approach, allowing us to verify models far beyond the scope of numerical solution methods. The principal advantage of numerical techniques based on uniformisation is that increased accuracy in the result comes at almost no price. The statistical solution method can very rapidly provide solutions with some uncertainty, however reducing the uncertainty is costly. This suggest that statistical techniques can be quite useful as a *first* resort during system prototyping, while numerical techniques may be more appropriate when very high accuracy in the result is required.

2 CTMCs and Probabilistic Model Checking

Probabilistic model checking refers to a range of techniques for the formal analysis of systems that exhibit stochastic behaviour. The system is usually specified as a state transition system, with probability values attached to the transitions. In this paper, we consider the case where this model is a continuous-time Markov chain (CTMC).

---

[1] PRISM web site: www.cs.bham.ac.uk/~dxp/prism

A CTMC $\mathcal{C}$ is a tuple $(S, \mathbf{R}, L)$ where S is a finite set of *states*, $\mathbf{R} : S \times S \rightarrow \mathbb{R}_{\geq 0}$ is the *rate matrix* and $L : S \rightarrow 2^{AP}$ is a *labelling function*, mapping each state to a subset of the set of atomic propositions AP. For any state $s \in S$, the probability of leaving state s within t time units is given by $1 - e^{-E(s)\cdot t}$ where $E(s) = \sum_{s' \in S} \mathbf{R}(s, s')$. $E(s)$ is known as the *exit rate*. If $\mathbf{R}(s, s') > 0$ for more than one $s' \in S$, then there is a *race* between the transitions leaving s, where the probability of moving to s' in a single step equals the probability that the delay corresponding to moving from s to s' "finishes before" the delays of any other transition leaving s. A *path* of the CTMC is a sequence of states, between each of which there is a non-zero probability of making a transition. A path of the CTMC can be seen as a single execution of the system being modelled.

In probabilistic model checking, properties of the system to be verified are specified in a temporal logic. For CTMCs, we use the temporal logic CSL [2,3, 5], an extension of CTL. The syntax of CSL is defined as

$$\Phi ::= \ true \ | \ a \ | \ \Phi \wedge \Phi \ | \ \neg \Phi \ | \ \mathcal{P}_{\bowtie p}\left(\Phi \, \mathcal{U}^{\leq t} \, \Phi\right) \ | \ \mathcal{P}_{\bowtie p}\left(\Phi \, \mathcal{U} \, \Phi\right) \ | \ \mathcal{S}_{\bowtie p}\left(\Phi\right) \ ,$$

where $p \in [0, 1]$, $t \in \mathbb{R}_{\geq 0}$, $\bowtie \in \{<, \leq, \geq, >\}$ and a is an atomic proposition from the set AP used to label states of the CTMC.

A state s of a CTMC satisfies the formula $\mathcal{P}_{\bowtie p}(\phi)$, denoted $s \models \mathcal{P}_{\bowtie p}(\phi)$, if $P(s, \phi) \bowtie p$, where $P(s, \phi)$ is the probability that a path starting in state s satisfies the path formula ϕ. Here, a path formula ϕ is either $\Phi \, \mathcal{U}^{\leq t} \, \Psi$, meaning that formula Ψ is satisfied within t time units and formula Φ is satisfied up until that point, or $\Phi \, \mathcal{U} \, \Psi$, meaning that $\Phi \, \mathcal{U}^{\leq t} \, \Psi$ holds for some $t \in \mathbb{R}_{\geq 0}$. The value $P(s, \phi)$ is defined in terms of the probability measure over paths starting in state s, as defined by Baier et al. [5]. The $\mathcal{S}_{\bowtie p}(\Phi)$ operator describes the behaviour of the CTMC in the *steady-state* or long-run. The precise semantics of this and the other CSL operators are given by Baier et al. [5]. In this paper, we focus on the *time-bounded until* operator $\mathcal{P}_{\bowtie p}\left(\Phi \, \mathcal{U}^{\leq t} \, \Psi\right)$.

2.1   Numerical Probabilistic Model Checking

The numerical model checking approach for verifying a time-bounded until formula $\mathcal{P}_{\bowtie p}\left(\Phi \, \mathcal{U}^{\leq t} \, \Psi\right)$ in a state $s \in S$ is based on first computing the probability $P(s, \Phi \, \mathcal{U}^{\leq t} \, \Psi)$, and then comparing this probability with the threshold $\bowtie p$.

First, as initially proposed by Baier et al. [4], the problem is reduced to the computation of transient probabilities on a modified CTMC. For a CTMC $\mathcal{C} = (S, \mathbf{R}, L)$, we construct the CTMC $\mathcal{C}' = (S, \mathbf{R}', L)$ by making all states satisfying $\neg \Phi \vee \Psi$ absorbing, i.e. removing all of their outgoing transitions. Hence, $\mathbf{R}'$ is obtained from $\mathbf{R}$ by removing all entries from the appropriate rows. The probability $P(s, \Phi \, \mathcal{U}^{\leq t} \, \Psi)$ in the CTMC $\mathcal{C}$ is now equal to the probability of, in the CTMC $\mathcal{C}'$, being in a state satisfying Ψ at time t having started in state s.

The computation of this probability is carried out via a process know as *uniformisation* (also known as *randomisation*), originally proposed by Jensen [14]. We construct the *uniformised* discrete-time Markov chain (DTMC) of $\mathcal{C}'$, whose probability transition matrix $\mathbf{P}$ equals $\mathbf{I} + (\mathbf{R}' - \mathbf{E}')/q$, where $\mathbf{I}$ is the identity matrix, $\mathbf{E}'$ is a diagonal matrix containing exit rates of $\mathcal{C}'$, i.e. $\mathbf{E}'(s, s')$

equals $E'(s)$ if $s = s'$ and 0 otherwise, and $q \geq \max\{E'(s) \mid s \in S\}$ is the *uniformisation constant* of the CTMC $\mathcal{C}'$.

It then follows that $P(s, \Phi \, \mathcal{U}^{\leq t} \, \Psi)$ can be computed simultaneously for all states $s \in S$ by computing the vector of probabilities

$$\underline{P}(\Phi \, \mathcal{U}^{\leq t} \, \Psi) = \sum_{k=0}^{\infty} \gamma(k, q{\cdot}t) \cdot (\mathbf{P}^k \cdot \underline{\Psi}) \ , \tag{1}$$

where $\gamma(k, q{\cdot}t)$ is the kth Poisson probability with parameter $q{\cdot}t$ (i.e. $\gamma(k, q{\cdot}t) = e^{-q{\cdot}t} \cdot (q{\cdot}t)^k / k!$), and $\underline{\Psi}$ characterises the set of states satisfying Ψ (i.e. $\underline{\Psi}(s) = 1$ if $s \models \Psi$, and 0 otherwise). If we are only interested in verifying $\mathcal{P}_{\bowtie p}(\Phi \, \mathcal{U}^{\leq t} \, \Psi)$ in a single state s, then we only need to carry out the summation in (1) for $P(s, \Phi \, \mathcal{U}^{\leq t} \, \Psi)$, which in practice can save us both memory and time. However, as pointed out by Katoen et al. [15], the asymptotic time complexity is the same when computing the entire vector $\underline{P}(\Phi \, \mathcal{U}^{\leq t} \, \Psi)$. In this paper, we only compute the entire vector for nested probabilistic formulae.

In practice, the infinite summation in (1) is truncated from the left by L_ϵ and from the right by R_ϵ by using the techniques of Fox and Glynn [8] so that the truncation error is bounded by an a priori error tolerance ϵ. This means that if $\hat{\underline{P}}(\Phi \, \mathcal{U}^{\leq t} \, \Psi)$ is the solution vector obtained with truncation, then

$$0 \leq P(s, \Phi \, \mathcal{U}^{\leq t} \, \Psi) - \hat{P}(s, \Phi \, \mathcal{U}^{\leq t} \, \Psi) \leq \epsilon \quad \forall s \in S \ . \tag{2}$$

Note that, since iterative squaring is not attractive for sparse matrices due to fill-in [22,20], the matrix products $\mathbf{P}^k$ are typically computed in an iterative fashion: $\mathbf{P}^k \cdot \underline{\Psi} = \mathbf{P} \cdot (\mathbf{P}^{k-1} \cdot \underline{\Psi})$. Also, although the left truncation point L_ϵ allows us to skip the first L_ϵ terms of (1), we still need to compute $\mathbf{P}^k \cdot \underline{\Psi}$ for $k < L_\epsilon$, so the total number of iterations required by the algorithm is R_ϵ.

Steady-State Detection. To potentially reduce the number of iterations required by the numerical model checking algorithm, we can use on-the-fly steady-state detection in conjunction with uniformisation [20,18]. If the uniformised DTMC reaches steady-state after $k_s < R_\epsilon$ iterations, then $\mathbf{P}^k \cdot \underline{\Psi} = \mathbf{P}^{k_s} \cdot \underline{\Psi}$ for all $k \geq k_s$, which means that we can compute $\hat{\underline{P}}(\Phi \, \mathcal{U}^{\leq t} \, \Psi)$ as follows using only k_s iterations:

$$\hat{\underline{P}}(\Phi \, \mathcal{U}^{\leq t} \, \Psi) = \sum_{k=L_\epsilon}^{k_s} \gamma(k, q{\cdot}t) \cdot (\mathbf{P}^k \cdot \underline{\Psi}) + (\mathbf{P}^{k_s} \cdot \underline{\Psi}) \cdot \left(1 - \sum_{k=L_\epsilon}^{k_s} \gamma(k, q{\cdot}t)\right) \ . \tag{3}$$

We can ensure that a steady-state vector actually exists by choosing q strictly greater than $\max\{E(s) \mid s \in S\}$ [20,18].

Malhotra et al. [18] derive an error bound for (3) under the assumption that the steady-state point can be detected exactly within a given error tolerance. Let $\underline{\Pi}^*$ denote the true steady-state vector. Malhotra et al. claim that if $\|\mathbf{P}^{k_s} \cdot \underline{\Psi} - \underline{\Pi}^*\| \leq \epsilon/4$ for $L_\epsilon < k_s < R_\epsilon$, then the same error bound as in (2) is guaranteed. The error analysis is flawed, however, in that it results in an error region twice as wide as the original error region. This is a result of the error due to steady-state detection being two-sided, while the truncation error is one-sided. To guarantee an error region of width ϵ instead of 2ϵ, it is necessary to bound $\|\mathbf{P}^{k_s} \cdot \underline{\Psi} - \underline{\Pi}^*\|$ by $\epsilon/8$ instead of $\epsilon/4$. This correction yields the error bounds $-\epsilon/4 \leq P(s, \Phi\, \mathcal{U}^{\leq t}\, \Psi) - \hat{P}(s, \Phi\, \mathcal{U}^{\leq t}\, \Psi) \leq 3\epsilon/4$ for all $s \in S$.

In practice, the true steady-state vector $\underline{\Pi}^*$ is not known a priori, so instead we stop when the norm of the difference between successive iterates is sufficiently small (at most $\epsilon/8$ by the above analysis), as suggested by Malhotra et al. [18].

Sequential Stopping Rule. To potentially reduce the number of iterations even further, we note that the CSL query $\mathcal{P}_{\bowtie p}\left(\Phi\, \mathcal{U}^{\leq t}\, \Psi\right)$ does not require that we compute $P(s, \Phi\, \mathcal{U}^{\leq t}\, \Psi)$ with higher accuracy than is needed to determine whether $P(s, \Phi\, \mathcal{U}^{\leq t}\, \Psi) \bowtie p$ holds. In the following analysis we restrict $\bowtie$ to $\geq$ as the other three cases are essentially the same.

Let $\hat{P}^k(s, \Phi\, \mathcal{U}^{\leq t}\, \Psi)$ denote the accumulated probability up until and including iteration k. Because each term in (1) is non-negative, we know that $\hat{P}^i(s, \Phi\, \mathcal{U}^{\leq t}\, \Psi) \geq \hat{P}^k(s, \Phi\, \mathcal{U}^{\leq t}\, \Psi)$ for all $i > k$. Therefore if $\hat{P}^k(s, \Phi\, \mathcal{U}^{\leq t}\, \Psi) \geq p$ holds for some $k < R_\epsilon$, then we can answer the query $\mathcal{P}_{\geq p}\left(\Phi\, \mathcal{U}^{\leq t}\, \Psi\right)$ affirmatively after only k iterations instead of R_ϵ (or k_s) iterations.

For early termination with a negative result, we can use the upper bound on the right Poisson tail provided by Fox and Glynn [8] for $k \geq 2 + \lfloor q \cdot t \rfloor$ to determine if $\mathcal{P}_{\geq p}\left(\Phi\, \mathcal{U}^{\leq t}\, \Psi\right)$ is false before completing R_ϵ iterations. Let $\hat{T}$ be the upper bound on the right Poisson tail. If $\hat{P}^k(s, \Phi\, \mathcal{U}^{\leq t}\, \Psi) + \hat{T} < p$, then we know already after k iterations that $\mathcal{P}_{\geq p}\left(\Phi\, \mathcal{U}^{\leq t}\, \Psi\right)$ is false.

We now have a sequential stopping rule for our algorithm, but note that the potential savings are limited by the fact that the positive part of the rule applies first after L_ϵ iterations and the negative part first after $2 + \lfloor q \cdot t \rfloor$ iterations, and both L_ϵ and R_ϵ are of the same order of magnitude as $q \cdot t$. We will see later that the sequential component of the statistical approach is much more significant.

Symbolic Representation. The PRISM tool uses binary decision diagrams (BDDs) [6] and multi-terminal BDDs (MTBDDs) [9] to construct a CTMC from a model description in the PRISM language, a variant of Alur and Henzinger's Reactive Modules formalism [1]. For numerical computation though, PRISM includes three separate *engines* making varying use of symbolic methods.

The first engine uses MTBDDs to store the model and iteration vector, while the second uses conventional data structures for numerical analysis: sparse matrices and arrays. The latter nearly always provides faster numerical computation than its MTBDD counterpart, but sacrifices the ability to conserve memory by exploiting structure. The third, *hybrid*, engine provides a compromise by storing the models in an MTBDD-like structure, which is adapted so that numerical computation can be carried out in combination with array-based storage for vectors. This hybrid approach is generally faster than MTBDDs, while handling larger systems than sparse matrices, and hence is the one used in this paper. For further details and comparisons between the engines see [17,19].

2.2   Statistical Probabilistic Model Checking

Statistical techniques, involving simulation and sampling, have been in use for decades to analyse stochastic systems. Younes and Simmons [26] show how discrete event simulation and acceptance sampling can be used to verify properties of general discrete event systems expressed as CSL formulae not including $\mathcal{P}_{\bowtie p}(\Phi \mathcal{U} \Phi)$ and $\mathcal{S}_{\bowtie p}(\Phi)$. We focus here on $\mathcal{P}_{\geq p}(\Phi \mathcal{U}^{\leq t} \Psi)$, noting that $\mathcal{P}_{\leq p}(\Phi \mathcal{U}^{\leq t} \Psi) \equiv \neg \mathcal{P}_{> 1-p}(\Phi \mathcal{U}^{\leq t} \Psi)$, and that $>$ ($<$) is practically indistinguishable from $\geq$ ($\leq$) to any acceptance sampling test (this can be said of numerical approaches as well due to the use of finite precision floating-point arithmetic).

Given a state $s \in S$ and a CSL formula $\mathcal{P}_{\geq p}(\Phi \mathcal{U}^{\leq t} \Psi)$, we wish to test whether $P(s, \Phi \mathcal{U}^{\leq t} \Psi)$ is above or below the threshold p. More specifically, we want to test the hypothesis $P(s, \Phi \mathcal{U}^{\leq t} \Psi) \geq p$ against the alternative hypothesis $P(s, \Phi \mathcal{U}^{\leq t} \Psi) < p$.

In order for acceptance sampling to be applicable, however, we first need to relax the hypotheses. For some $\delta > 0$, let H_0 be the hypothesis $P(s, \Phi \mathcal{U}^{\leq t} \Psi) \geq p + \delta$ and let H_1 be the hypothesis $P(s, \Phi \mathcal{U}^{\leq t} \Psi) \leq p - \delta$. Clearly, the formula $\mathcal{P}_{\geq p}(\Phi \mathcal{U}^{\leq t} \Psi)$ is true if H_0 holds and false if H_1 holds. An acceptance sampling test, such as Wald's *sequential probability ratio test* [24], will limit the probability of accepting H_1 when H_0 holds (false negative) to α and the probability of accepting H_0 when H_1 holds (false positive) to β. We refer to the region $I = (p - \delta, p + \delta)$ as the *indifference region*, because no guarantees regarding the error probability is given if $P(s, \Phi \mathcal{U}^{\leq t} \Psi) \in I$, and we assume that the user selects δ with this in mind. The parameters α and β determine the *strength* of the acceptance sampling test.

Wald's sequential probability ratio test is carried out as follows. Let $p_0 = p + \delta$ and $p_1 = p - \delta$, and let x_i be a sample of a Bernoulli variate X representing the result of verifying $\Phi \mathcal{U}^{\leq t} \Psi$ over a sample path starting in state s. Sample paths are generated through discrete event simulation, and we only generate as much of a sample path as is needed to determine the truth value of $\Phi \mathcal{U}^{\leq t} \Psi$. Note that we can perform simulation at the level of the PRISM language and never need to generate the underlying CTMC. At the mth stage of the test, we calculate the quantity

$$\frac{p_{1m}}{p_{0m}} = \prod_{i=1}^{m} \frac{\Pr[X = x_i \mid P(s, \Phi \mathcal{U}^{\leq t} \Psi) = p_1]}{\Pr[X = x_i \mid P(s, \Phi \mathcal{U}^{\leq t} \Psi) = p_0]} \, ,$$

where x_i is the ith sample of the Bernoulli variate X (1 if path formula holds and 0 otherwise), and $\Pr[X = x_i \mid P(s, \Phi \mathcal{U}^{\leq t} \Psi) = p_j] = p_j^{x_i}(1 - p_j)^{1-x_i}$. Hypothesis H_0 is accepted if $p_{1m}/p_{0m} \leq \beta/(1-\alpha)$, and hypothesis H_1 is accepted if $p_{1m}/p_{0m} \geq (1 - \beta)/\alpha$. Otherwise, an additional sample is required. This gives an acceptance sampling test that, for all practical purposes, has strength α and β. For further details on the test see [24].

2.3   Mixing Numerical and Statistical Techniques

Although the algorithm of Younes and Simmons [26] can handle CSL formulae with nested probabilistic operators, the way in which it is done requires in the worst case that the nested formula be verified in each state along a sample path, each time with an error inversely proportional to the length of the sample path. The numerical approach, on the other hand, can verify the nested formula for all states simultaneously at the same (asymptotic) cost as verifying the formula for a single state. This is a clear advantage when dealing with nested probabilistic operators.

We therefore propose a mixed approach, implemented in our system, where statistical sampling is used to verify the outermost probabilistic operator, while numerical techniques are used to verify the nested probabilistic operators. We can mix the numerical and statistical techniques by assuming that the result of the numerical technique holds with certainty (i.e. $\alpha = \beta = 0$ in terms of a statistical test). The nested formulae are first verified for all states using numerical methods. When verifying a path formula over a sample path we only need to read the value for each state along the path without any additional verification effort for the nested formulae. The cost for verifying the nested components of a formula is exactly the same for the mixed approach as for the numerical approach, but the use of sampling for the outermost probabilistic operator can provide a faster solution.

3   Case Studies

We now introduce three case studies, taken from the literature on performance evaluation and probabilistic model checking, on which we will base our empirical evaluation. A fourth simple case study is also introduced to illustrate the use of nested probabilistic operators in CSL.

Tandem Queueing Network. The first case study is based on a CTMC model of a tandem queueing network presented by Hermanns et al. [11]. The network consists of an $M/Cox_2/1$ queue sequentially composed with an $M/M/1$ queue. The capacity of each queue is n, and the state space is $\mathcal{O}(n^2)$. The property of interest is given by the CSL formula $\mathcal{P}_{< 0.5}\left(true\ \mathcal{U}^{\leq T}\ full\right)$ which is true in a state if there is less than a 50% chance of the queueing network becoming full within T time units, and, in the case of the sampling-based approach, we verify the correctness of this property in the state where the both queues are empty.

Symmetric Polling System. For this case study we consider an n-station symmetric polling system described by Ibe and Trivedi [12]. Each station has a single-message buffer and the stations are attended by a single server in cyclic order. The server begins polling station 1. If there is a message in the buffer of station 1, the server starts polling that station. Once station i has been polled, or if there is no message in the buffer of station i when it is being served, the server starts polling station $i + 1$ (or 1 if $i = n$). The polling and service times are exponentially distributed, as is the time from when a station has been polled until a new message fills its buffer. The fact that all rates are equal for all stations makes the system symmetric. The size of the state space for a system with n stations is $\mathcal{O}(n \cdot 2^n)$.

We will verify the property that, if station 1 is full, then it is polled within T time units with probability at least 0.5. We do so in the state where station 1 has just been polled and the buffers of all stations are full. Let $s \in \{1, \ldots, n\}$ be the station currently getting the server's attention, let $a \in \{0,1\}$ represent the activity of the server (0 for polling and 1 for serving), and let $m_i \in \{0,1\}$ be the number of messages in the buffer of station i. We can then represent the property of interest with the CSL formula $m_1{=}1 \implies \mathcal{P}_{\geq 0.5}\left(true\ \mathcal{U}^{\leq T}\ poll1\right)$ where $poll1 \equiv s{=}1 \wedge a{=}0$, and the state in which we verify the formula is given by $s{=}1 \wedge a{=}1 \wedge m_1{=}1 \wedge \ldots \wedge m_n{=}1$.

Dependable Workstation Cluster. The third case study is a dependable cluster of workstations due to Haverkort et al. [10]. The system consists of two sub-clusters each containing n workstations. Communication between the two sub-clusters is performed over a backbone connection. The workstations of each sub-cluster are connected in a star topology, with a single switch providing connectivity to the backbone. Each of the components can fail at any time, and the time to failure is exponentially distributed with different rates for different components. There is a single repair unit that can restore failed units. The repair time is assumed to be exponentially distributed. The size of the state space is $\mathcal{O}(n^2)$ for a cluster with $2n$ workstations.

The minimum quality of service (QoS) for a cluster is defined as having at least k interconnected operational workstations. This can be achieved by having at least k operational workstations in one sub-cluster with a functional switch, or by having at least k operational workstations in total with the backbone and both switches functioning properly. Let w_l and w_r denote the number of operational workstations in the left and right sub-clusters respectively. Furthermore, let b represent the atomic proposition that the backbone is working, and s_l (s_r) that the left (right) switch is up. Minimum QoS can then be defined as $minimum \equiv (w_l{\geq}k \wedge s_l) \vee (w_r{\geq}k \wedge s_r) \vee (w_l{+}w_r{\geq}k \wedge b \wedge s_l \wedge s_r)$. The property we will verify is $\mathcal{P}_{< 0.1}\left(true\ \mathcal{U}^{\leq T}\ \neg minimum\right)$, corresponding to Φ_4 of [10], that there is a less than 10% chance of the QoS dropping below minimum within T time units, and this property will be verified in the state where all units are functional.

Grid World. For the last case study we consider an $n \times n$ grid world with a robot moving from the bottom left corner to the top right corner, first along the bottom edge and then along the right edge. There is a janitor moving randomly around the grid, and the robot cannot move into a square occupied by the janitor. The objective is for the robot to reach the goal square at top right corner within T_1 time units with probability at least 0.9, while maintaining at least a 0.5 probability of periodically communicating with the base station. The CSL formula $\mathcal{P}_{\geq 0.9}\left(\mathcal{P}_{\geq 0.5}\left(true\ \mathcal{U}^{\leq T_2}\ communicate\right)\ \mathcal{U}^{\leq T_1}\ goal\right)$ expresses the given objective. The size of the state space is $\mathcal{O}(n^3)$.

4   Empirical Evaluation

We base our empirical evaluation on the case studies presented in Sect. 3. We have verified the time-bounded until formulae for the first three case studies using both the numerical and the statistical approach, varying the problem size (and thereby the size of the state space) and the time bound. Fig. 1 shows the verification time in seconds for these case studies, both as a function of the state space size and as a function of the time bound. All results, for both the numerical and the statistical approach, are for the verification of a CSL property in a *single* state. The results were generated on a 500 MHz Pentium III PC running Linux, and with a 700 MB memory limit set per process.

Memory Requirements. In the case of the numerical solution method, all experiments were run using the hybrid engine (see Sect. 2.1) which, although not necessarily the fastest engine, in general allows the analysis of larger problems than the other engines. The limiting factor in the hybrid approach is the space required to store the iteration vector: however compact the matrix representation is, memory proportional to the number of states is required for numerical solution. More precisely, the hybrid engine with steady-state detection requires storage of three double precision floating point vectors of size $|S|$, which for the memory limit of 700 MB means that systems with at most 31 million states can be analysed.[2] In practice, for the first three case studies, we were able to handle systems with about 27 million states, showing that the symbolic representation of the probability matrix is fairly compact.

The memory requirements for the statistical approach are very conservative. In principle, all that we need to store during verification is the current state, which only requires memory logarithmic in the size of the state space. We never exhausted memory during verification when using the statistical solution method.

Performance of Numerical Solution Method. For model checking time-bounded until formulae using the numerical approach, PRISM computes the Poisson probabilities (see Sect. 2.1) using the Fox-Glynn algorithm [8], which, for the hybrid engine, yields an overall time complexity of $\mathcal{O}(q{\cdot}t{\cdot}M)$, where q is the uniformisation constant of the CTMC, t is the time bound of the until formula and M is the number of non-zero entries in $\mathbf{R}$.

In all the examples considered, the number of non-zeros in the rate matrix is linear in the size of the state space. Hence, the verification time for a given time-bounded until formula is linear in the size of the state space, as can be observed in Figs. 1(a), (c), and (e). For a single model, the complexity is linear in the time bound, as demonstrated by the results in Figs. 1(b), (d), and (f). Note that Figs. 1(b) and (d) show the verification time to be constant once the time bound has become sufficiently large. This is caused by steady-state detection as described in Sect. 2.1. We can also see the effect of steady-state detection in

---

[2] We need an additional floating point vector of size $|S|$ for verifying a formula in all states simultaneously, which would make the limit 23 million states.

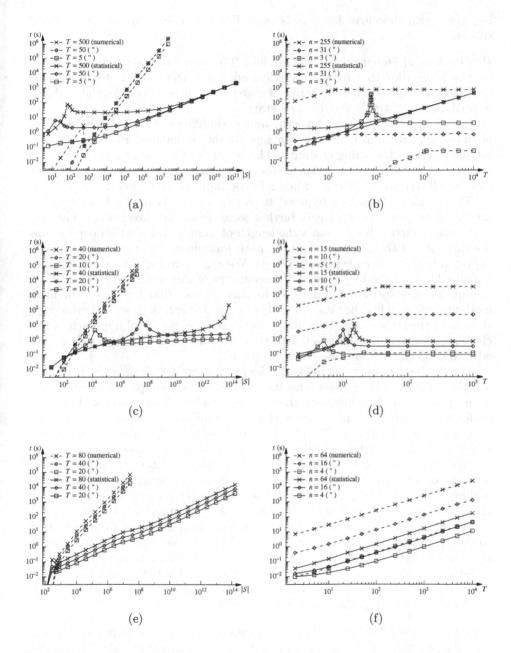

(a)

(b)

(c)

(d)

(e)

(f)

Fig. 1. The verification time, in seconds, for the tandem queueing network (top), the symmetric polling system (centre), and the dependable workstation cluster (bottom). To the left, the verification time is given as a function of the state space size, and to the right as a function of the time bound for the property that is being verified. Solid curves are for the statistical approach with $\alpha = \beta = 10^{-2}$ and $2\delta = 10^{-2}$, while dashed curves are for the numerical approach using the hybrid engine and $\epsilon = 10^{-6}$.

Fig. 1(a), with the curve for $T = 50$ and $T = 500$ coinciding for larger state spaces.

Performance of Statistical Solution Method. There are two main factors influencing the verification time for the statistical approach: the number of samples and the length of sample paths (in terms of state transitions). Consider the problem of verifying the formula $\mathcal{P}_{\geq p}(\phi)$ in a state s.

For fixed α and β (test strength) and δ (indifference region), the number of samples grows larger the closer p gets to the probability $P(s, \phi)$ that ϕ is satisfied by a path starting in state s. The results in Fig. 1 were generated using $\alpha = \beta = 10^{-2}$ and $2\delta = 10^{-2}$. The peaks in the curves for the statistical solution method all coincide with $P(s, \phi)$ being in the indifference region $[p - \delta, p + \delta]$.

The number of samples required to verify a formula of the form $\mathcal{P}_{\geq p}(\phi)$ rapidly decreases as $P(s, \phi)$ gets further away from the threshold p. The key performance factor then becomes the length of sample paths, which depends on the exit rates of the CTMC and on the path formula ϕ. An upper bound on the expected length of sample paths is $\mathcal{O}(q \cdot t)$. We can see in Fig. 1(f), where $P(s, \phi)$ remains far from the threshold and the number of samples is close to constant (about 400 samples) for all values of the time bound, that the curves for both methods have roughly the same slope. The statistical approach scales better with the size of the state space giving it the edge over the numerical approach in the cluster example, but steady-state detection gives the numerical approach a clear advantage in the tandem case study (Fig. 1(b)).

For the tandem queueing network, the arrival rate for messages is $4n$, where n is the capacity of the queues. This has as a result that sample path lengths are proportional to n. As n increases, the sample path length becomes the dominant performance factor, meaning that verification time for the statistical approach becomes proportional to n. This is to be compared with the numerical approach, whose performance is linear in the size of the state space, which is quadratic in n. Similar results can be seen for the dependable workstation cluster. In the polling example, the arrival rate λ is inversely proportional to the number of polling stations n, while the other rates remain constant for all n. This explains the levelling-off of the curves for the statistical solution method in Fig. 1(c).

Recall that we only need to generate as much of a sample path as is needed to determine the truth value of ϕ. For $\phi = \Phi \, \mathcal{U}^{\leq t} \, \Psi$, we can stop if we reach a state satisfying $\neg \Phi \vee \Psi$ (cf. the CTMC $\mathcal{C}'$ constructed in the numerical approach in Sect. 2.1). The effect of this is seen most clearly for the polling case study as we increase the time bound. Once the path formula is satisfied the average length of the sample paths does not increase (Fig. 1(d)).

Trading Accuracy for Speed. With both solution methods, it is possible to adjust the accuracy of the result. For the statistical approach, we can control the parameters α, β, and δ so as to trade accuracy for efficiency. By setting these parameters high, we can get an answer quickly. We could then gradually tighten the error bounds and/or the indifference region to obtain higher accuracy. This approach is taken by Younes et al. [25], who modify the statistical solution method for verifying CSL formulae of the form $\mathcal{P}_{\geq p}(\phi)$ without nested probabilistic operators so that it can be stopped at any time to return a result.

Figure 2 shows how the verification time for a polling system problem and a workstation cluster problem depends on the strength of the test and the width of the indifference region. We can see that the verification time is inversely proportional both to the error bounds and the width of the indifference region, and that for some parameter values the numerical approach is faster while for others the statistical approach is the fastest. Using the statistical approach with error bounds $\alpha = \beta = 10^{-10}$ and half-width of the indifference region $\delta \approx 2 \cdot 10^{-4}$, for example, we could obtain a verification result for the polling system problem ($n = 10$) in roughly the same time as is required by the numerical approach. For larger models, we would of course be able to obtain even higher accuracy with the statistical approach if allowed as much time as needed by the numerical approach to solve the problem.

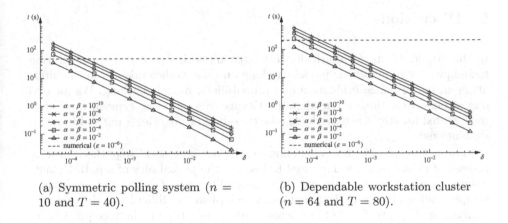

(a) Symmetric polling system ($n = 10$ and $T = 40$).

(b) Dependable workstation cluster ($n = 64$ and $T = 80$).

Fig. 2. Verification time as a function of the half-width of the indifference region for different error bounds. The dashed line in each graph represents the verification time for the numerical approach.

We can adjust the accuracy for the numerical solution method by varying the parameter ϵ, but increasing or decreasing ϵ has very little effect on the verification time as shown by Reibman and Trivedi [20] and Malhotra et al. [18]. This means that the numerical solution method can provide very high accuracy without much of a performance degradation, while the statistical solution method is well suited if a quick answer with some uncertainty is more useful. This suggest that statistical techniques can be quite useful as a *first* resort, instead of a last resort as often suggested.

Mixing Solution Techniques. Finally, we present some results for the grid world case study, where the CSL property has nested probabilistic operators. We can see in Fig. 3 that the mixed approach shares performance characteristics with both approaches, outperforming the pure numerical solution method for larger state spaces.

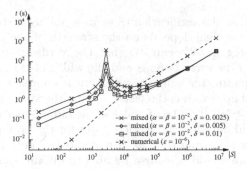

Fig. 3. Verification time as a function of state space size for the grid world example, with $T_1 = 100$ and $T_2 = 7$.

5   Discussion

In this paper, we have empirically compared numerical and statistical solution techniques for probabilistic model checking on case studies taken from the literature on performance evaluation and probabilistic model checking. We focused our attention on time-bounded properties as these are the type of properties most suited for statistical methods (the time-bound provides a natural limit for simulations).

The nature of CSL formulae allows us to use statistical hypothesis testing instead of *estimation* (we only need to know if the probability of a path formula holding is above or below some threshold). The use of sequential acceptance sampling allows the statistical approach to adapt to the difficulty of the problem: verifying a property $\mathcal{P}_{\geq p}(\phi)$ in a state s takes more time if the true probability of ϕ holding in s is close to the threshold p. This can give a clear edge for statistical methods over numerical approaches for model checking CSL formulae. Most previous assessments of statistical techniques (see, e.g., [21]) are based on parameter estimation problems, which are clearly harder in that they typically require a large number of samples. Our results show that the intuition from earlier studies does not necessarily carry over to CSL model checking. Instead of a last resort, statistical solution methods can be seen as a first resort providing a result rapidly, for example during system prototyping when high accuracy may not be a priority, while numerical techniques often remain superior when very high accuracy is required.

Our results are otherwise in line with known complexity results for the two techniques. We show a linear complexity in the time-bound for both approaches. Our results also confirm that statistical methods scale better with the size of the state space, but that high accuracy comes at a greater price than for numerical methods.

The case studies we considered in this paper were all CTMCs. For more complex models with general distributions, such as semi-Markov processes, numerical methods rely on even more elaborate techniques for verifying time-bounded properties (see e.g. [13]). A statistical approach, on the other hand, would work just as well for semi-Markov processes (assuming, of course, that samples from the distributions used in the model can be generated in roughly the same amount of time as samples from the exponential distribution).[3]

References

[1] Alur, R. and Henzinger, T. A. Reactive modules. *Formal Methods in System Design*, 15(1):7–48, 1999.

[2] Aziz, A., Sanwal, K., Singhal, V., and Brayton, R. Verifying continuous time Markov chains. In *Proc. 8th International Conference on Computer Aided Verification*, volume 1102 of *LNCS*, pages 269–276. Springer, 1996.

[3] Aziz, A., Sanwal, K., Singhal, V., and Brayton, R. Model-checking continuous-time Markov chains. *ACM Transactions on Computational Logic*, 1(1):162–170, 2000.

[4] Baier, C., Haverkort, B. R., Hermanns, H., and Katoen, J.-P. Model checking continuous-time Markov chains by transient analysis. In *Proc. 12th International Conference on Computer Aided Verification*, volume 1855 of *LNCS*, pages 358–372. Springer, 2000.

[5] Baier, C., Haverkort, B. R., Hermanns, H., and Katoen, J.-P. Model-checking algorithms for continuous-time Markov chains. *IEEE Transactions on Software Engineering*, 29(6):524–541, 2003.

[6] Bryant, R. E. Graph-based algorithms for Boolean function manipulation. *IEEE Transactions on Computers*, C-35(8):677–691, 1986.

[7] Buchholz, P. A new approach combining simulation and randomization for the analysis of large continuous time Markov chains. *ACM Transactions on Modeling and Computer Simulation*, 8(2):194–222, 1998.

[8] Fox, B. L. and Glynn, P. W. Computing Poisson probabilities. *Communications of the ACM*, 31(4):440–445, 1988.

[9] Fujita, M., McGeer, P. C., and Yang, J. C.-Y. Multi-terminal binary decision diagrams: An efficient data structure for matrix representation. *Formal Methods in System Design*, 10(2/3):149–169, 1997.

[10] Haverkort, B. R., Hermanns, H., and Katoen, J.-P. On the use of model checking techniques for dependability evaluation. In *Proc. 19th IEEE Symposium on Reliable Distributed Systems*, pages 228–237. IEEE Computer Society, 2000.

[11] Hermanns, H., Meyer-Kayser, J., and Siegle, M. Multi terminal binary decision diagrams to represent and analyse continuous time Markov chains. In *Proc. 3rd International Workshop on the Numerical Solution of Markov Chains*, pages 188–207. Prensas Universitarias de Zaragoza, 1999.

[12] Ibe, O. C. and Trivedi, K. S. Stochastic Petri net models of polling systems. *IEEE Journal on Selected Areas in Communications*, 8(9):1649–1657, 1990.

[13] Infante López, G. G., Hermanns, H., and Katoen, J.-P. Beyond memoryless distributions: Model checking semi-Markov chains. In *Proc. 1st Joint International PAPM-PROBMIV Workshop*, volume 2165 of *LNCS*, pages 57–70. Springer, 2001.

[14] Jensen, A. Markoff chains as an aid in the study of Markoff processes. *Skandinavisk Aktuarietidskrift*, 36:87–91, 1953.

---

[3] ProVer, an experimental tool for verifying time-bounded CSL properties of general discrete event systems, is available at www.cs.cmu.edu/~lorens/prover.html.

[15] Katoen, J.-P., Kwiatkowska, M., Norman, G., and Parker, D. Faster and symbolic CTMC model checking. In *Proc. 1st Joint International PAPM-PROBMIV Workshop*, volume 2165 of *LNCS*, pages 23–38. Springer, 2001.

[16] Kwiatkowska, M., Norman, G., and Parker, D. PRISM: Probabilistic symbolic model checker. In *Proc. 12th International Conference on Modelling Techniques and Tools for Computer Performance Evaluation*, volume 2324 of *LNCS*, pages 200–204. Springer, 2002.

[17] Kwiatkowska, M., Norman, G., and Parker, D. Probabilistic symbolic model checking with PRISM: A hybrid approach. In *Proc. 8th International Conference on Tools and Algorithms for the Construction and Analysis of Systems*, volume 2280 of *LNCS*, pages 52–66. Springer, 2002.

[18] Malhotra, M., Muppala, J. K., and Trivedi, K. S. Stiffness-tolerant methods for transient analysis of stiff Markov chains. *Microelectronics and Reliability*, 34(11):1825–1841, 1994.

[19] Parker, D. *Implementation of Symbolic Model Checking for Probabilistic Systems*. PhD thesis, University of Birmingham, 2002.

[20] Reibman, A. and Trivedi, K. S. Numerical transient analysis of Markov models. *Computers & Operations Research*, 15(1):19–36, 1988.

[21] Shanthikumar, J. G. and Sargent, R. G. A unifying view of hybrid simulation/analytic models and modeling. *Operations Research*, 31(6):1030–1052, 1983.

[22] Stewart, W. J. A comparison of numerical techniques in Markov modeling. *Communications of the ACM*, 21(2):144–152, 1978.

[23] Tiechroew, D. and Lubin, J. F. Computer simulation—discussion of the techniques and comparison of languages. *Communications of the ACM*, 9(10):723–741, 1966.

[24] Wald, A. Sequential tests of statistical hypotheses. *Annals of Mathematical Statistics*, 16(2):117–186, 1945.

[25] Younes, H. L. S., Musliner, D. J., and Simmons, R. G. A framework for planning in continuous-time stochastic domains. In *Proc. Thirteenth International Conference on Automated Planning and Scheduling*, pages 195–204. AAAI Press, 2003.

[26] Younes, H. L. S. and Simmons, R. G. Probabilistic verification of discrete event systems using acceptance sampling. In *Proc. 14th International Conference on Computer Aided Verification*, volume 2404 of *LNCS*, pages 223–235. Springer, 2002.

Efficient Computation of Time-Bounded Reachability Probabilities in Uniform Continuous-Time Markov Decision Processes*

Christel Baier[1], Boudewijn Haverkort[2],
Holger Hermanns[2,3], and Joost-Pieter Katoen[2]

[1] Institut für Informatik I, University of Bonn, Germany
[2] Faculty of Electrical Engineering, Mathematics and Computer Science,
University of Twente, The Netherlands
[3] Department of Computer Science, Saarland University, Germany

Abstract. A continuous-time Markov decision process (CTMDP) is a generalization of a continuous-time Markov chain in which both probabilistic and nondeterministic choices co-exist. This paper presents an efficient algorithm to compute the maximum (or minimum) probability to reach a set of goal states within a given time bound in a uniform CTMDP, i.e., a CTMDP in which the delay time distribution per state visit is the same for all states. We prove that these probabilities coincide for (time-abstract) history-dependent and Markovian schedulers that resolve nondeterminism either deterministically or in a randomized way.

1 Introduction

Why continuous-time Markov decision processes? A continuous-time Markov decision process (CTMDP) [6,14,21,24] is a generalization of a continuous-time Markov chain (CTMC) in which both probabilistic and nondeterministic choices co-exist. CTMDPs occur in many contexts, ranging from stochastic control theory [14] to dynamic power management [22]. We are particularly interested in this class of models because they can be viewed as a common semantic model for various performance and dependability modelling formalisms including generalised stochastic Petri nets [1], Markovian stochastic activity models [23], interactive Markov chains (IMC) [17] and TIPP process algebra [16].

So far, the analysis of models developed in these and related formalisms was restricted to the subset that corresponds to CTMCs, usually referred to as 'non-confused', 'well-defined', or 'well-specified' models [11,12,13,17]. All these notions are semantic notions, usually checked by an exhaustive exploration of the state space, with models being discarded if the check fails. In other words, no specification-level check is available, and the offered analysis algorithms are actually partial algorithms.

---

* This work is supported by the NWO-DFG bilateral project Validation of Stochastic Systems.

Why time-bounded reachability? Model checking of CTMCs [4] has received remarkable attention in recent years. Various model checkers exist [18,20,10], answering questions such as: *Is the probability to hop along Φ-states, until reaching a Ψ-state within 5 to 10 time units greater than 0.95?* The core algorithmic innovation allowing to answer such questions is a mapping from interval-bounded until-formulae – specified in the continuous stochastic logic CSL [2] – to time-bounded reachability problems, which in turn can be approximated efficiently using a stable numeric technique called uniformization [19]. To enable the same kind of questions being answered for models specified in any of the above mentioned formalisms, the key problem is how to compute time-bounded reachability probabilities in CTMDPs. This is the problem we address in this paper. While model checking algorithms for discrete-time Markov decision processes are well-understood [8,5], we are not aware of any model checking algorithm for continuous-time Markov decision processes.

Our contribution. Given a CTMDP, our aim is to compute the maximum (or minimum) probability to reach – under a given class of schedulers – a certain set of states within t time units, given a starting state. We consider this problem for uniform CTMDPs, a class of CTMDPs in which the delay time distribution per state visit is the same for all states, governed by a unique exit rate E. We show that an efficient greedy algorithm can be obtained using truncated Markovian deterministic (MD)-schedulers, that is, step-dependent schedulers which schedule up to a limited depth. The algorithm computes the maximum (or minimum) probabilities for timed reachability. It is then shown that these probabilities for truncated MD-schedulers coincide with the maximum (or minimum) probabilites for timed reachability for Markovian and history-dependent schedulers (both deterministic and randomized). We show that stationary Markovian schedulers – as opposed to the discrete case [8,5] – yield a smaller maximum, whereas timed history-dependent schedulers may yield a higher probability.

The main result of this paper is a computationally efficient approximation algorithm for computing maximum (or minimum) probabilities for timed reachability in uniform CTMDPs under all time-abstract schedulers. The time complexity is in $\mathcal{O}(E{\cdot}t{\cdot}N^2{\cdot}M)$ and the space complexity in $\mathcal{O}(N^2{\cdot}M)$ where t is the time bound, N is the number of states, and M is the number of actions in the CTMDP under consideration.

Organization of the paper. Section 2 introduces the necessary background. Section 3 presents the algorithm for uniform CTMDP. Section 4 places the result of the algorithm in the context of other classes of schedulers. Section 5 discusses the problem of uniformizing arbitrary CTMDPs. Section 6 concludes the paper. Proofs of all theorems can be found in [3].

2   Background and Problem Statement

2.1   Continuous-Time Markov Decision Processes

A *continuous-time Markov decision process* $\mathcal{M}$, is a tuple $(S, Act, \mathbf{R})$ with S a finite set of states, Act a finite set of actions, and $\mathbf{R} : (S \times Act \times S) \to \mathbb{R}_{\geqslant 0}$

the three-dimensional rate matrix. For each state $s \in S$ we require the existence of a pair $(\alpha, s') \in Act \times S$ with $\mathbf{R}(s, \alpha, s') > 0$. Note that this can easily be established by adding self-loops, i.e., having $\mathbf{R}(s, \alpha, s) > 0$ for some $\alpha \in Act$. If Act is a singleton, we can project $\mathbf{R}$ on an $(S \times S)$ matrix, and $\mathcal{M}$ is a CTMC.

For $B \subseteq S$, let $\mathbf{R}(s, \alpha, B)$ denote the total rate to move from state s via action α to some state in B, i.e.,

$$\mathbf{R}(s, \alpha, B) = \sum_{s' \in B} \mathbf{R}(s, \alpha, s').$$

The behavior of a CTMDP is as follows. $\mathbf{R}(s, \alpha, s') > 0$ intuitively means that there is a transition from s to s' under action α. If state s has outgoing transitions for distinct actions, one of these actions is selected nondeterministically where we assume that the nondeterminism is resolved by means of a scheduler (also called policy or adversary). Given that action α has been chosen, $1 - e^{-\mathbf{R}(s, \alpha, s') \cdot t}$ is the probability that the α-transition $s \to s'$ can be triggered within t time units. Thus, the delay of α-transition $s \to s'$ is governed by the negative exponential distribution with rate $\mathbf{R}(s, \alpha, s')$. If $\mathbf{R}(s, \alpha, s') > 0$ for more than one state s', a competition between the α-transitions originating in s exists, known as the race condition. The discrete probability of selecting α-transition $s \to s'$ is determined by the embedded discrete-time Markov decision process (DTMDP, for short) of $\mathcal{M}$, denoted $emb(\mathcal{M})$, a tuple $(S, Act, \mathbf{P})$ with S and Act as before and

$$\mathbf{P}(s, \alpha, s') = \frac{\mathbf{R}(s, \alpha, s')}{E(s, \alpha)} \text{ if } E(s, \alpha) > 0$$

and 0 otherwise. Here, $E(s, \alpha) = \mathbf{R}(s, \alpha, S)$, i.e., $E(s, \alpha)$ is the exit rate of state s via some α-transition. Note that $\mathbf{P}(s, \alpha, s')$ is the time-abstract probability for the α-transition from s to s' when action α is chosen. For $B \subseteq S$ let $\mathbf{P}(s, \alpha, B) = \sum_{s' \in B} \mathbf{P}(s, \alpha, s')$ denote the probability to move from s to some state in B via an α-transition. An alternative formulation of the requirement that in every state at least one action is enabled, can be stated using E as:

$$Act(s) = \{ \alpha \in Act \mid E(s, \alpha) > 0 \} \neq \varnothing \text{ for any state } s.$$

A CTMDP $(S, Act, \mathbf{R})$ is *uniform* if for some $E > 0$ it holds $E(s, \alpha) = E$ for any state $s \in S$ and $\alpha \in Act(s)$. Note that $E(s, \alpha) = 0$ (whence $\alpha \notin Act(s)$ follows) is possible in uniform CTMDPs. Stated in words, in a uniform CTMDP the exit rates for all states and all enabled actions are equal.

2.2   Paths

A (timed) *path* σ in CTMDP $\mathcal{M}$ is a finite or infinite sequence

$$\sigma \in (S \times Act \times \mathbb{R}_{>0})^* \times S \cup (S \times Act \times \mathbb{R}_{>0})^\omega.$$

For infinite path $\sigma = s_0, \alpha_0, t_0, s_1, \alpha_1, t_1, s_2, \alpha_2, t_2, \ldots$ we require time-divergence, i.e., $\sum t_i = \infty$. We write

$$s_0 \xrightarrow{\alpha_0, t_0} s_1 \xrightarrow{\alpha_1, t_1} s_2 \xrightarrow{\alpha_2, t_2} \cdots$$

rather than $s_0, \alpha_0, t_0, s_1, \alpha_1, t_1, s_2, \alpha_2, t_2, \ldots$. The corresponding *time-abstract* path is: $s_0 \xrightarrow{\alpha_0} s_1 \xrightarrow{\alpha_1} s_2 \xrightarrow{\alpha_2} \ldots$. We write $\sigma \to s$ for the time- and action-abstract path σ that is followed by state s. In the remainder of this paper we use the term path for timed, time-abstract, and time- and action-abstract paths whenever the kind of path is clear from the context. Let $\mathit{first}(\sigma)$ denote the state in which σ starts. For finite path σ, $\mathit{last}(\sigma)$ denotes the last state of σ.

2.3   Schedulers

Nondeterminism in a CTMDP is resolved by a *scheduler*. For deciding which of the next nondeterministic actions to take, a scheduler may have access to the current state only or to the path from the initial to the current state (either with or without timing information). Schedulers may select the next action either (i) *deterministically*, i.e., depending on the available information, the next action is chosen in a deterministic way, or (ii) in a *randomized* fashion, i.e., depending on the available information the next action is chosen probabilistically. Accordingly, the following classes of schedulers D are distinguished [21], where $Distr(Act)$ denotes the collection of all distributions on Act:

- stationary Markovian deterministic (SMD, also called simple schedulers),

$$D : S \to Act \text{ such that } D(s) \in Act(s);$$

- stationary Markovian randomized (SMR),

$$D : S \to Distr(Act) \text{ such that } D(s)(\alpha) > 0 \text{ implies } \alpha \in Act(s);$$

- Markovian deterministic (MD, also called step-dependent schedulers),

$$D : S \times I\!N \to Act \text{ such that } D(s, n) \in Act(s);$$

- Markovian randomized (MR),

$$D : S \times I\!N \to Distr(Act) \text{ such that } D(s, n)(\alpha) > 0 \text{ implies } \alpha \in Act(s);$$

- (time-abstract) history-dependent, deterministic (HD),

$$D : (S \times Act)^* \times S \to Act \text{ such that } D(\underbrace{s_0 \xrightarrow{\alpha_0} s_1 \xrightarrow{\alpha_1} \ldots \xrightarrow{\alpha_{n-1}}}_{\text{time-abstract history}}, s_n) \in Act(s_n);$$

- (time-abstract) history-dependent, randomized (HR),

$$D : (S \times Act)^* \times S \to Distr(Act)$$

such that $D(s_0 \xrightarrow{\alpha_0} s_1 \xrightarrow{\alpha_1} \ldots \xrightarrow{\alpha_{n-1}}, s_n)(\alpha) > 0$ implies $\alpha \in Act(s_n)$.

All these schedulers are time-abstract; time-dependent schedulers will be briefly discussed in Section 4. We write X to denote the class of all X-schedulers over a fixed CTMDP $\mathcal{M}$.[1]

---

[1] Strictly speaking we should write $X(\mathcal{M})$, but $\mathcal{M}$ is omitted as it should be clear from the context.

Note that for any HD-scheduler, the actions in the history can be ignored, i.e., HD-schedulers may be considered as functions $D : S^+ \rightarrow Act$, as for any sequence $s_0, s_1, \ldots, s_n$ the relevant actions α_i are given by $\alpha_i = D(s_0, s_1, \ldots, s_i)$. Hence, any state-action sequence $s_0 \xrightarrow{\alpha_0} s_1 \xrightarrow{\alpha_1} \ldots \xrightarrow{\alpha_{n-1}} s_n$ where $\alpha_i \neq D(s_0, s_1, \ldots, s_i)$ for some i, does not describe a path fragment that can be obtained from D.

The scheduler-types form a hierarchy, e.g., any SMD-scheduler can be viewed as a MD-scheduler (by ignoring parameter n) which, in turn, can be viewed as a HD-scheduler (by ignoring everything from the history except its length). A similar hierarchy exists between SMR, MR, and HR schedulers. Moreover, deterministic schedulers can be regarded as trivial versions of their corresponding randomized schedulers that assign probability 1 to the actions selected.

2.4 Induced Stochastic Process

Given a scheduler D (of arbitrary type) and a starting state, D induces a stochastic process $\mathcal{M}_D$ on CTMDP $\mathcal{M}$. For deterministic schedulers (HD, MD, and SMD), the induced process $\mathcal{M}_D$ is a continuous-time Markov chain (CTMC), referred as $\mathcal{C}_D$ in the sequel. For MD- and HD-schedulers, though, the state space of $\mathcal{C}_D$ will in general be infinitely large (but countable). Formally, HD-scheduler $D : S^+ \rightarrow Act$ on CTMDP $\mathcal{M} = (S, Act, \mathbf{R})$ induces the CTMC $\mathcal{C}_D = (S_D, \mathbf{R}_D)$ with $S_D = S^+$ as state space, $\mathbf{R}_D(\sigma, \sigma \rightarrow s) = \mathbf{R}(last(\sigma), D(\sigma), s)$ and 0 otherwise. The embedded discrete time Markov chain (DTMC) $emb(\mathcal{C}_D)$ is a tuple $(S_D, \mathbf{P}_D)$ where

$$\mathbf{P}_D(\sigma, \sigma') = \frac{\mathbf{R}_D(\sigma, \sigma')}{E_D(\sigma)} \quad \text{if } E_D(\sigma) > 0$$

and 0 otherwise. Here, $E_D(\sigma) = \sum_{\sigma' \in S_D} \mathbf{R}_D(\sigma, \sigma')$, i.e., the exit rate of σ in $\mathcal{C}_D$.

States in CTMC $\mathcal{C}_D$ are state sequences $s_0 \rightarrow s_1 \rightarrow \ldots s_{n-1} \rightarrow s_n$ corresponding to time-abstract, unlabeled path fragments in the original CTMDP $\mathcal{M}$. State s_n stands for the current state in the CTMDP whereas states s_0 through s_{n-1} describe the history. Intuitively, the stochastic process induced by HD-scheduler D on CTMDP $\mathcal{M}$ results from unfolding $\mathcal{M}$ into an (infinite) tree while resolving the nondeterministic choices according to D. For SMD-schedulers the induced CTMC is guaranteed to be finite. More precisely, for SMD-scheduler D, $\mathcal{C}_D$ can be viewed as a CTMC with the original state space S, as all sequences that end in s, say, are lumping equivalent [9].

2.5 Maximum Probability for Timed Reachability

Given CTMDP $\mathcal{M}$, our aim is to compute the maximum (or minimum) probability to reach – under a given class of schedulers – a certain set B of states within t time units, when starting from a given state s. That is, we want to calculate for time $t > 0$, $B \subseteq S$, $s \in S$ and class of X-schedulers:

$$\sup_{D \in X} \Pr_D(s, \overset{\leq t}{\leadsto} B)$$

up to some a priori given accuracy ε. Here Pr_D denotes the induced probability measure in $\mathcal{C}_D$ as formally defined by a standard cone construction in [4]. Intuitively, if B is considered as the set of "bad" states, then the value to be computed is the sharpest bound p for which it is guaranteed that the probability to reach a bad state from s in the next t time units is at most p under all "relevant" schedulers, i.e., all schedulers of type X.

3   An Algorithm for Uniform CTMDPs

In the sequel, unless otherwise stated, let $\mathcal{M}$ be uniform and E be its unique exit rate. Note that CTMC $\mathcal{C}_D$ which is obtained from the uniform CTMDP $\mathcal{M}$ by HD-scheduler D is also uniform [19].

3.1   Approximation

For HD-scheduler D, the (infinite) vector of the probabilities $\text{Pr}_D(\sigma, \overset{\leqslant t}{\rightsquigarrow} B)$ for all states σ in the CTMC $\mathcal{C}_D$ (i.e., all $\sigma \in S^+$) is given by:

$$\left(\text{Pr}_D(\sigma, \overset{\leqslant t}{\rightsquigarrow} B)\right)_{\sigma \in S^+} = \sum_{n=0}^{\infty} e^{-E \cdot t} \cdot \frac{(E \cdot t)^n}{n!} \cdot \mathbf{P}_{D,B}^n \cdot \mathbf{i}_B$$

where $\mathbf{i}_B = (\mathbf{i}_B(\sigma))_{\sigma \in S^+}$ with $\mathbf{i}_B(\sigma) = 1$ if $last(\sigma) \in B$, and 0 otherwise, and

$$\mathbf{P}_{D,B}(\sigma, \sigma') = \begin{cases} \mathbf{P}_D(\sigma, \sigma') & \text{if } last(\sigma) \in S \setminus B \\ 1 & \text{if } \sigma' = \sigma \text{ and } last(\sigma) \in B \\ 0 & \text{otherwise.} \end{cases}$$

$\mathbf{P}_{D,B}$ is the (infinite) transition probability matrix of the CTMC $\mathcal{C}_{D,B} = (S_D, \mathbf{R}_{D,B})$ that is obtained from $\mathcal{C}_D$ by equipping any B-state (i.e., any path $\sigma \in S^+$ with $last(\sigma) \in B$) with a self-loop and removing all its other outgoing transitions: $\mathbf{R}_{D,B}(\sigma, \sigma') = \mathbf{R}_D(\sigma, \sigma')$ if $last(\sigma) \notin B$, $\mathbf{R}_{D,B}(\sigma, \sigma) = E$ if $last(\sigma) \in B$, and 0 otherwise. The justification of this transformation is as follows. As the aim is to compute the probability to reach a B-state before a certain time bound, it is not of importance what happens once such a state has been visited, and therefore its outgoing transitions can be replaced by a self-loop. For the sake of brevity let

$$\psi(n) = e^{-E \cdot t} \cdot \frac{(E \cdot t)^n}{n!}$$

denote the Poisson probabilities, i.e., $\psi(n)$ is the probability of n events occurring within t time units in a Poisson process with rate E. Note that, for $s \in S$:

$$\text{Pr}_D(s, \overset{\leqslant t}{\rightsquigarrow} B) = \left(\sum_{n=0}^{\infty} \psi(n) \cdot \mathbf{P}_{D,B}^n \cdot \mathbf{i}_B\right)(s) = \psi(0) \cdot \mathbf{i}_B(s) + \left(\sum_{n=1}^{\infty} \psi(n) \cdot \mathbf{P}_{D,B}^n \cdot \mathbf{i}_B\right)(s)$$

Later we will exploit that for $s \notin B$:

$$\mathrm{Pr}_D(s, \overset{\leqslant t}{\leadsto} B) = \left(\sum_{n=1}^{\infty} \psi(n) \cdot \mathbf{P}_{D,B}^n \cdot \mathbf{i}_B \right)(s)$$

Rather than computing the precise maximum probabilities we use an approximation in the following way. For any state s, the value $\mathrm{Pr}_D(s, \overset{\leqslant t}{\leadsto} B)$ will be approximated, up to a given accuracy ε, by

$$\widetilde{\mathrm{Pr}}_D(s, \overset{\leqslant t}{\leadsto} B) = \left(\sum_{n=0}^{k} \psi(n) \cdot \mathbf{P}_{D,B}^n \cdot \mathbf{i}_B \right)(s)$$

where $k = k(\varepsilon, E, t)$ depends on ε, E and t, but neither on state s nor on scheduler D. This can be seen as follows. Let $\| \cdot \|$ denote the row-sum norm. Then, for sufficiently large $k = k(\varepsilon, E, t)$:

$$\left\| \sum_{n=0}^{\infty} \psi(n) \cdot \mathbf{P}_{D,B}^n \cdot \mathbf{i}_B - \sum_{n=0}^{k} \psi(n) \cdot \mathbf{P}_{D,B}^n \cdot \mathbf{i}_B \right\| = \left\| \sum_{n=k+1}^{\infty} \psi(n) \cdot \mathbf{P}_{D,B}^n \cdot \mathbf{i}_B \right\|$$

$$\leqslant \sum_{n=k+1}^{\infty} \psi(n) \cdot \underbrace{\|\mathbf{P}_{D,B}^n\|}_{\leqslant 1} \cdot \underbrace{\|\mathbf{i}_B\|}_{\leqslant 1} \leqslant \sum_{n=k+1}^{\infty} \psi(n) \leqslant \varepsilon$$

Note that $\sum_{n=0}^{\infty} e^{-E \cdot t} \frac{(E \cdot t)^n}{n!} = \sum_{n=0}^{\infty} \psi(n)$ converges for all E and t. Hence, for any scheduler D and state s:

$$\widetilde{\mathrm{Pr}}_D(s, \overset{\leqslant t}{\leadsto} B) = \left(\sum_{n=0}^{k} \psi(n) \cdot \mathbf{P}_{D,B}^n \cdot \mathbf{i}_B \right)(s) \leqslant \mathrm{Pr}_D(s, \overset{\leqslant t}{\leadsto} B)$$

Our strategy is to construct some HD-scheduler D_0 such that for any state $s \in S$:

$$\widetilde{\mathrm{Pr}}_{D_0}(s, \overset{\leqslant t}{\leadsto} B) \geqslant \sup_{D \in HD} \widetilde{\mathrm{Pr}}_D(s, \overset{\leqslant t}{\leadsto} B). \tag{1}$$

This yields:

$$\underbrace{\sup_{D \in HD} \mathrm{Pr}_D(s, \overset{\leqslant t}{\leadsto} B) - \varepsilon}_{\leqslant \widetilde{\mathrm{Pr}}_D(s, \overset{\leqslant t}{\leadsto} B)} \leqslant \widetilde{\mathrm{Pr}}_{D_0}(s, \overset{\leqslant t}{\leadsto} B) \leqslant \mathrm{Pr}_{D_0}(s, \overset{\leqslant t}{\leadsto} B) \leqslant \sup_{D \in HD} \mathrm{Pr}_D(s, \overset{\leqslant t}{\leadsto} B).$$

Since $\mathbf{P}_{D,B}^n(s, \sigma) = 0$ for any σ containing more than n transitions, i.e., more than $n{+}1$ states, the value

$$\widetilde{\mathrm{Pr}}_{D_0}(s, \overset{\leqslant t}{\leadsto} B) = \left(\sum_{n=0}^{k} \psi(n) \cdot \mathbf{P}_{D_0,B}^n \cdot \mathbf{i}_B \right)(s)$$

only depends on the k-th truncation of D_0, i.e., the function

$$D_0\big|_k : \bigcup_{0 < n \leqslant k} S^n \to Act, \quad D_0\big|_k(\sigma) = D_0(\sigma).$$

Intuitively speaking, only the first k decisions of D_0 are relevant (and not "later" ones) for determining the value $\widetilde{\mathrm{Pr}}_{D_0}(s, \overset{\leqslant t}{\leadsto} B)$. There are only finitely many such truncations when ranging over all HD-schedulers. The brute-force approach would consider all of them in order to determine the maximum. This technique works, but is highly inefficient because the total number of such truncations, $\prod_{s \in S} |Act(s)|^k$, grows exponentially in the number of states s with $|Act(s)| > 1$. Note that

$$\prod_{s \in S} |Act(s)|^k \geqslant 2^{|T|k} \text{ if } |Act(s)| \geqslant 2 \text{ for all } s \in T \subseteq S$$

i.e., the total number of truncations to be considered is exponential in k.

3.2   A Greedy Algorithm to Compute Scheduler D_0

Consider truncated MD-schedulers of the form $D : S \times \{1, \ldots, k\} \to Act$. (Later on, it is shown that considering such schedulers suffices.)

The actions $act(s, i) \in Act(s)$ for $0 < i \leqslant k$ will be determined such that the truncated MD-scheduler D_0 with $D_0(s, i) = act(s, i)$ fulfils equation (1). Let $\mathbf{P}_i$ denote the probability matrix of cardinality $|S| \times |S|$ where the row $\mathbf{P}_i(s, \cdot) = \mathbf{P}(s, act(s, i), \cdot)$ if $s \notin B$ and $\mathbf{P}_i(s, \cdot) = \mathbf{i}_s$ if $s \in B$, where $\mathbf{i}_s$ denotes the identity vector for state s. $\mathbf{P}_i$ thus denotes the probability matrix induced by the scheduler D_0 at step i.

For $s \notin B$, the actions $act(s, i)$ will be determined in a backward manner, i.e., starting from $i=k$. For $i=k$, the selected action $act(s, k) \in Act(s)$ satisfies:

$$\mathbf{P}_k(s, B) = \mathbf{P}(s, act(s, k), B) = \max_{\alpha \in Act(s)} \mathbf{P}(s, \alpha, B)$$

That is, $\mathbf{P}_k(s, \cdot)$ is determined such that for any state s the probability to move to a B-state within at most one step is maximized. Generalizing this strategy, for $i < k$, $act(s, i)$ is chosen such that the probability to move to a B-state within at most $k-i+1$ steps is maximal under the truncated MD-scheduler $D : S \times \{i-1, \ldots, k\} \to Act$ defined by:

$$D(s, j) = act(s, i+j-1), \text{ for } 0 < j \leqslant k-i+1.$$

That is, $\mathbf{P}_i$ is constructed such that for $i \geqslant 1$ the vector

$$q_i = \sum_{n=i}^{k} \psi(n) \cdot \mathbf{P}_i \cdot \mathbf{P}_{i+1} \cdot \ldots \cdot \mathbf{P}_n \cdot \mathbf{i}_B$$

is state-wise maximal under all vectors of the form

$$\sum_{n=i}^{k} \psi(n) \cdot \mathbf{P}_* \cdot \mathbf{P}_{i+1} \cdot \ldots \cdot \mathbf{P}_n \cdot \mathbf{i}_B$$

where $\mathbf{P}_*$ is an $|S| \times |S|$-matrix with $\mathbf{P}_*(s, \cdot) = \mathbf{P}(s, \alpha, \cdot)$ for some action $\alpha \in Act(s)$ if $s \notin B$ and $\mathbf{P}_*(s, \cdot) = \mathbf{i}_s$ if $s \in B$. In the above equations, $\mathbf{i}_B =$

$(i_B(s))_{s \in S}$ stands for the bit-vector that represents the characteristic function of B (as a subset of the original state space S). I.e., $i_B(s) = 1$ if $s \in B$ and $i_B(s) = 0$ if $s \in S \setminus B$.[2]

Informally, $q_i(s)$ is the maximum conditional probability to reach B taking i to k steps within t time units, given that state s is occupied before the i-th step. We let $q = \psi(0) \cdot i_B + q_1$, which for the $(S \setminus B)$-states agrees with the desired probability vector to reach a B-state within at most k steps when the time bound to reach B is t. For $s \in B$ we have $\Pr_D(s, \overset{\leqslant t}{\leadsto} B) = 1$. Moreover, for $s \notin B$ it holds $q(s) = \psi(0) \cdot i_B(s) + q_1(s) = q_1(s)$ (as $i_B(s) = 0$). In the sequel, we are therefore only interested in the calculation of the vector $q_1(s)$.

The main steps of our procedure are summarized in Algorithm 1. A stable and efficient algorithm to compute the Poisson probabilities $\psi(i)$ has been proposed in [15] and can be adopted here. Note that for the computation of the values $\sup_{D \in HD} \widetilde{\Pr}_D(s, \overset{\leqslant t}{\leadsto} B)$ there is no need to compute (and store) the matrices $\mathbf{P}_i$. Instead, it suffices to compute the vectors

$$q_i = \sum_{n=i}^{k} \psi(n) \cdot \mathbf{P}_i \cdot \mathbf{P}_{i+1} \cdot \ldots \cdot \mathbf{P}_n \cdot i_B$$

$$= \psi(i) \cdot \mathbf{P}_i \cdot i_B \;+\; \sum_{n=i+1}^{k} \psi(n) \cdot \mathbf{P}_i \cdot \mathbf{P}_{i+1} \cdot \ldots \cdot \mathbf{P}_n \cdot i_B$$

$$= \psi(i) \cdot \mathbf{P}_i \cdot i_B \;+\; \mathbf{P}_i \cdot \sum_{n=i+1}^{k} \psi(n) \cdot \mathbf{P}_{i+1} \cdot \ldots \cdot \mathbf{P}_n \cdot i_B$$

$$= \psi(i) \cdot \mathbf{P}_i \cdot i_B \;+\; \mathbf{P}_i \cdot q_{i+1}$$

where $q_{k+1} = \mathbf{0}$ is the 0-vector. For $s \notin B$, we have $(\mathbf{P}_i \cdot i_B)(s) = \mathbf{P}(s, \alpha, B)$ if $\alpha = act(s, i)$.

3.3   Complexity of the Algorithm

Algorithm 1 can be implemented with a space complexity in $\mathcal{O}\left(|S|^2 \cdot |Act| + |S|\right)$, where the term $|S|^2 \cdot |Act|$ stands for the representation of the uniform CTMDP $\mathcal{M}$ while the term $|S|$ stands for the vectors q_{i+1} and q_i. Note that there is no need to store q_{i+1} once q_i has been computed. The values $q_i(s, \alpha)$ are only needed temporarily, and as mentioned before, there is no need to compute and store the matrices $\mathbf{P}_i$. Inspection of the pseudo-code of Algorithm 1 reveals that the worst-case time complexity is asymptotically bounded by:

$$k \cdot \sum_{s \in S \setminus B} \sum_{\alpha \in Act(s)} \left| \{ s' \in S \mid \mathbf{R}(s, \alpha, s') > 0 \} \right|$$

---

[2] At several other places, we shall use the same notation i_B for the bit-vector $(i_B(\sigma))_{\sigma \in S^+}$ that represents the characteristic function of B viewed as subset of the state space of the CTMC induced by a HD-scheduler. Here, we identify B with the set of finite paths σ where $last(\sigma) \in B$. Whenever the notation i_B occurs in our formulae the dimension of i_B should be clear from the context.

Algorithm 1 Greedy approximation algorithm for computing $\sup\limits_{D \in HD} \Pr_D(s, \overset{\leqslant t}{\leadsto} B)$

$k := k(\varepsilon, E, t);$ (* determine number of required steps *)
for all $s \in S$ **do** $q_{k+1}(s) := 0;$ **od**   (* initialize q_{k+1} as null-vector *)
for all $i = k, k-1, \ldots, 1$ **do**
  for all $s \in S \setminus B$ **do**
    $m := -1;$
    for all $\alpha \in Act(s)$ **do**   (* search the optimal row $\mathbf{P}_i(s, \cdot)$ *)

$$m := \max\left(m, \psi(i) \cdot \mathbf{P}(s, \alpha, B) \;+\; \sum_{s' \in S} \mathbf{P}(s, \alpha, s') \cdot q_{i+1}(s') \right);$$

    od
    $q_i(s) := m;$ (* choose maximum *)
  od
  for all $s \in B$ **do** $q_i(s) := \psi(i) + q_{i+1}(s);$ **od** (* $\mathbf{P}_i(s, \cdot) := \mathbf{i}_s$ for all states $s \in B$ *)
od
for all $s \in S$ **do**
  if $s \notin B$ **then** $q(s) := q_1(s);$ **else** $q(s) := 1;$ **fi**
od
return the vector q.

---

which is in $\mathcal{O}\left(E \cdot t \cdot |S|^2 \cdot |Act|\right)$. Note that $k = k(\varepsilon, E, t)$ grows proportionally with $E \cdot t$. This bound can be improved by performing a reachability analysis (as a preprocessing phase of Algorithm 1) to determine the set T of states from which a B-state can be reached. The main iteration then only needs to be performed for all states in $T \setminus B$ rather than $S \setminus B$. For the other states we have, for any scheduler D, $\Pr_D(s, \overset{\leqslant t}{\leadsto} B) = 0$ for $s \in S \setminus T$, and $\Pr_D(s, \overset{\leqslant t}{\leadsto} B) = 1$ for $s \in B$.

3.4   Correctness of the Algorithm

Although our greedy algorithm is based on a truncated MD-scheduler – only the first k steps are memorized – it approximates the maximum probability to reach the set of states B within t time units under *all* HD-schedulers. This is shown by the following result where $q(s)$ is the s-component of the vector q as returned by Algorithm 1.

Theorem 1. $\sup\limits_{D \in HD} \Pr_D(s, \overset{\leqslant t}{\leadsto} B) - \varepsilon \;\leqslant\; q(s) \;\leqslant\; \sup\limits_{D \in HD} \Pr_D(s, \overset{\leqslant t}{\leadsto} B).$

As a result, the vector computed by Algorithm 1 is state-wise optimal under all HD-schedulers, up to the accuracy ε.

4   Other Scheduling Disciplines

By Theorem 1 it follows that our greedy algorithm computes the maximum probability for timed reachability under all HD-schedulers. In this section, we show that this also applies to any MR-, MD-, and, more importantly, to any

HR-scheduler. In addition, we will show that this does neither hold for SMD-schedulers nor for schedulers that can base their decision on the timing of actions. Finally, it is shown that adding a simple notion of fairness is invariant under these maximum probabilities for HD-schedulers.

Markovian deterministic schedulers. In the sequel, let $s \in S$ be a state, $t \geqslant 0$ a time point and $B \subseteq S$ a set of states. Theorem 1 states that the vector computed by Algorithm 1 is state-wise optimal under all HD-schedulers, up to a given accuracy ε. As Algorithm 1 calculates, in fact, a truncation of an MD-scheduler it directly follows that the suprema under MD- and HD-schedulers agree:

Theorem 2. $\displaystyle \sup_{D \in MD} \; \mathrm{Pr}_D(s, \overset{\leqslant t}{\rightsquigarrow} B) \;=\; \sup_{D \in HD} \; \mathrm{Pr}_D(s, \overset{\leqslant t}{\rightsquigarrow} B).$

History-dependent randomized schedulers. The next results yields that the supremum under HD- and HR-schedulers coincides:

Theorem 3. $\displaystyle \sup_{D \in HD} \; \mathrm{Pr}_D(s, \overset{\leqslant t}{\rightsquigarrow} B) \;=\; \sup_{D \in HR} \; \mathrm{Pr}_D(s, \overset{\leqslant t}{\rightsquigarrow} B).$

A few remarks are in order. Theorems 2 and 3 show that the suprema for the probabilities to reach a set of goal states within a given time bound under the classes of scheduler MD, HD, MR and HR coincide. (For MR-schedulers this stems from the fact that $MD \subseteq MR \subseteq HR$.) For probabilities of some other events, however, such correspondence may not be established. That is, in general, randomized schedulers can be better than deterministic schedulers. This observation was made by Beutler and Ross [7] who showed that the maximum of time-average rewards under randomized schedulers might be larger than under deterministic schedulers. In fact, the crux of the proof of Theorem 3 is the observation that the values $\mathrm{Pr}_D(s, \overset{\leqslant t}{\rightsquigarrow}_{\leqslant n} B)$ converge to $\mathrm{Pr}_D(s, \overset{\leqslant t}{\rightsquigarrow} B)$, where the subscript $\leqslant n$ denotes that B has to be reached within at most n steps. This property is not guaranteed for other events.

Stationary Markovian deterministic schedulers. Different from the discrete time setting, where SMD-schedulers suffice for maximum probabilities to reach a set of goal states within a given number of steps [8,5], this does not hold for the corresponding question – interpreting the number of steps in the discrete case as elapse of time – on CTMDPs. A counterexample is given in Fig. 1(a). Here, states are represented as circles and there is an edge between states s and s' labeled with action α if and only if $\mathbf{R}(s, \alpha, s') > 0$. Action labels and rates are indicated at each edge. Let $B = \{s_2\}$, and consider the only two relevant SMD-schedulers, D_α, selecting action α in state s_0, and D_β, selecting action β. Comparing them with $D_{\beta\alpha}$, i.e., the scheduler that after selecting β once switches to selecting α in state s_0, we find that for a certain range of time bounds t, $D_{\beta\alpha}$ outperforms both D_β and D_α. Intuitively, the chance of stuttering in state s_0 (by choosing β initially) may influence the remaining time to reach B to an extent that it becomes profitable to continue choosing α. For $t = 0.5$, for instance, $\mathrm{Pr}_{D_{\beta\alpha}}(s_0, \overset{\leqslant 0.5}{\rightsquigarrow} B) = 0.4152$, whereas for D_α and D_β these probabilities

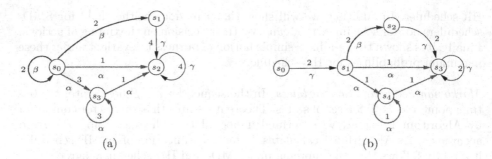

Fig. 1. Uniform CTMDPs where (a) SMD-schedulers are less powerful, and (b) where THD schedulers are more powerful than HD-schedulers.

are 0.3935 and 0.3996, respectively. Thus, SMD-schedulers are not expressive enough for maximum probabilities to reach a set of goal states within a given time bound under all HD/HR-schedulers.[3]

Timed schedulers. This paper only considers schedulers that do not take the timing information into account. It is however worth noticing that timed history-dependent (THD) schedulers are more powerful than time-abstract history dependent schedulers (class HD and HR), in the sense that it is possible that:

$$\sup_{D \in THD} \Pr_D(s, \overset{\leq t}{\leadsto} B) > \sup_{D \in HD} \Pr_D(s, \overset{\leq t}{\leadsto} B).$$

Here, *THD* refers to the class of schedulers given by functions $D : (S \times Act \times \mathbb{R}_{>0})^* \times S \to Act$ (only choosing from $Act(s)$ for any path ending in state s), i.e., THD-schedulers are able to observe the time points of state changes. To see that they may yield a higher probability, consider for example the uniform CTMDP in Fig. 1(b). In this example, it depends on the time instance of entering s_1 whether it is more profitable to continue choosing α or β. To be more precise, consider the only relevant HD-schedulers, D_α (choosing α in s_1) and D_β (choosing β). Fig. 2 plots the probability to reach B starting from state s_1 if choosing D_α, respectively D_β, given by

$$\Pr_{D_\alpha}(s_1, \overset{\leq t}{\leadsto} B) = 1 - e^{-t}, \quad \text{and} \quad \Pr_{D_\beta}(s_1, \overset{\leq t}{\leadsto} B) = 1 - e^{-2t} \cdot (1 + 2t).$$

Let t_0 be the time instance satisfying $e^{t_0} = 1 + 2t_0$, i.e., the time point where both plots cross. The THD-scheduler D defined by $D(s_0 \xrightarrow{\gamma, u} s_1) = \alpha$ if $t - u < t_0$ and β otherwise, maximizes the probability to reach $B = \{s_3\}$ from state s_0 within t time units, and obviously outperforms both D_α and D_β.

Fairness. We conclude this section by considering a simple notion of fairness for schedulers. Let $\sigma = s_0 \xrightarrow{\alpha_0, t_0} s_1 \xrightarrow{\alpha_1, t_1} \ldots$ be an infinite path. Infinite path

---

[3] For SMR-schedulers this is an open issue.

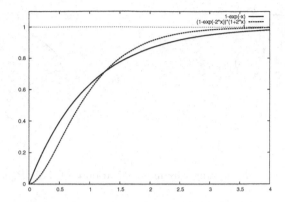

Fig. 2. Functions $1 - e^{-t}$ and $1 - e^{-2t} \cdot (1 + 2t)$ for $t \geqslant 0$

σ is called *fair* if and only if for each state s that occurs infinitely often in σ and each action $\alpha \in Act(s)$, there are infinitely many indices n such that $(s_n, \alpha_n) = (s, \alpha)$. Stated in words, for any state that is visited infinitely often, each of its outgoing actions cannot have been selected only a finite number of times. (Note that this notion of fairness is rather weak; for instance, a scheduler that finitely many times selects the same action in a state that is visited finitely often – without ever considering one of the other possibilities – is considered to be fair.) Scheduler D (of some class) is called fair if and only if

$$\Pr_D \{\sigma \in Path(s) \mid \sigma \text{ is fair } \} = 1$$

for all states $s \in S$, where $Path(s)$ denotes the set of paths that start in s. Let FHD denote the set of all fair HD-schedulers. The following result states that maximum probabilities under HD-schedulers and their fair counterparts coincide:

Theorem 4. $\sup_{D \in HD} \Pr_D(s, \overset{\leqslant t}{\leadsto} B) = \sup_{D \in FHD} \Pr_D(s, \overset{\leqslant t}{\leadsto} B)$.

5   The Uniformization Problem

Algorithm 1 assumes that the CTMDP under consideration is uniform. We now discuss the case in which the CTMDP is not uniform, i.e., the exit rates $E(s, \alpha)$ are not guaranteed to be identical for any state s and any $\alpha \in Act(s)$.

In the setting of CTMCs, uniformization [19] can be employed to transform a CTMC into a uniform one while keeping transient probabilities invariant[4]. For CTMDPs, a similar recipe might be followed. However, a simple adaptation of the uniformization approach for CTMCs (as proposed, for instance, in [6,21]) to CTMDPs is not adequate for our purpose. The problem with this approach is that the correspondence between schedulers on uniform CTMDP $\mathcal{M}'$ and its

---

[4] Although uniformization is traditionally considered as a transformation from a CTMC into a discrete-time Markov chain, it can equally well be considered as a transformation between CTMCs.

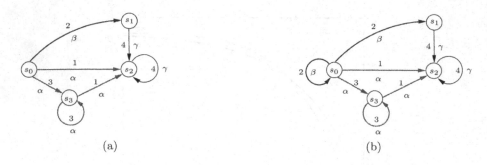

Fig. 3. An example illustrating why uniformization on CTMDPs is not obvious

original CTMDP $\mathcal{M}$ is lost. (A similar observation has been made by Beutler and Ross [7] when comparing MD- and MR-schedulers for computing time-average rewards.) This can be illustrated as follows. Applying "standard" uniformization to CTMDP $\mathcal{M} = (S, Act, \mathbf{R})$ with $E \geqslant \max_{s \in S, \alpha \in Act} E(s, \alpha)$ would yield the CTMDP $\mathcal{M}' = (S, Act, \mathbf{R}')$ with $\mathbf{R}'(s, \alpha, s') = \mathbf{R}(s, \alpha, s')$ for $s \neq s'$, and $\mathbf{R}'(s, \alpha, s) = \mathbf{R}(s, \alpha, s) + E - E(s, \alpha)$ if $\alpha \in Act(s)$ and 0 otherwise. That is, each state s is equipped with a self-loop for each action $\alpha \in Act(s)$ if E exceeds the total exit rate to take an α-transition from s. Applying this recipe to the CTMDP $\mathcal{M}$ depicted in Fig. 3(a) results in the CTMDP $\mathcal{M}'$ in Fig. 3(b). The latter has appeared in Fig. 1(a) already. It is not difficult to see that for any X-scheduler on $\mathcal{M}$ there exists a corresponding X-scheduler on $\mathcal{M}'$, as any choice in $\mathcal{M}$ can be matched by the same choice in $\mathcal{M}'$. The reverse, however, does not hold. For instance, the MD-scheduler $D_{\beta\alpha}$ on $\mathcal{M}'$ discussed in Section 4 does not correspond to any MD-scheduler D on $\mathcal{M}$, since the self-loop in state s_0 in $\mathcal{M}'$ cannot be mimicked by $\mathcal{M}$. Recall from Section 4 that $\mathrm{Pr}_{D_{\beta\alpha}}(s_0, \overset{\leqslant 0.5}{\leadsto} \{s_2\})$ is higher than the respective probabilities for D_α and D_β in $\mathcal{M}'$. The latter in turn correspond to the only relevant HD-scheduler on $\mathcal{M}$. As a consequence, the maximum probability (obtained for some MD-scheduler generated by Algorithm 1) to reach the set $\{s_2\}$ from state s_0 in 0.5 time units on $\mathcal{M}'$ is higher than the probability for any HD-scheduler in $\mathcal{M}$.

We are experimenting with other forms of uniformization to overcome this problem. As yet, it is open whether a variation of the basic concept of uniformization can be used to reduce the timed reachability problem for general CTMDPs to that of uniform CTMDPs.

6   Concluding Remarks

This paper considered the problem of computing the maximum probability to reach a set of goal states within a given time bound in a uniform CTMDP. It is shown that truncated Markovian deterministic schedulers suffice for approximating a solution to this problem in an efficient manner for (time-abstract) history-dependent and Markovian schedulers, both deterministic and randomized ones. This does neither apply to timed history-dependent schedulers nor to Markovian stationary (i.e., simple) schedulers. The question whether SMR-schedulers may yield the same optimum (or a smaller optimum) is open.

Although all results in this paper have been presented for maximum probabilities, the same results can be obtained for minimal probabilities, i.e.,

$$\inf_{D \in X} \Pr_D(s, \overset{\leq t}{\leadsto} B)$$

up to some accuracy ε.[5] Instead of a greedy policy that maximizes the probability to reach the set of goal states in each step of the computation, the algorithm in this case minimizes this quantity in each step.

The presented numerical algorithm is remarkably efficient. Its worst-case time complexity is in $\mathcal{O}(E \cdot t \cdot N^2 \cdot M)$ where E is the unique exit rate of the uniform CTMDP, t is the time bound, N is the number of states, and M is the number of actions. Thus, compared to CTMCs, the increase in computational effort is linear in the number of actions in the CTMDP, i.e., the amount of nondeterminism, but no more than that. This is the best we can hope for, since the time complexity of computing the corresponding probability in a CTMC is in $\mathcal{O}(E \cdot t \cdot N^2)$ [4].

Acknowledgments. The authors thank Luca de Alfaro (University of California at Santa Cruz) for insightful discussions. David Jansen (MPI Saarbrücken) provided various helpful comments on a draft of this paper.

References

1. M. Ajmone Marsan, G. Balbo, G. Conte, S. Donatelli, and G. Franceschinis. *Modelling with Generalized Stochastic Petri Nets*. John Wiley & Sons, 1995.
2. A. Aziz, K. Sanwal, V. Singhal and R. Brayton. Model checking continuous time Markov chains. *ACM TOCL*, 1(1): 162–170, 2000.
3. C. Baier, B. Haverkort, H. Hermanns, and J.-P. Katoen. Efficient computation of time-bounded reachability probabilities in uniform continuous-time Markov decision processes. CTIT Technical Report 03-50, University of Twente, 2003.
4. C. Baier, B. Haverkort, H. Hermanns, and J.-P. Katoen. Model-checking algorithms for continuous-time Markov chains. *IEEE Transactions on Software Engineering*, 29(6): 524–541, 2003.
5. C. Baier and M.Z. Kwiatkowska. Model checking for a probabilistic branching time logic with fairness. *Distributed Computing*, 11: 125–155, 1998.
6. D.P. Bertsekas. *Dynamic Programming and Optimal Control. Volume II*. Athena Scientific, 1995.
7. F. Beutler and K.W. Ross. Uniformization for semi-Markov decision processes under stationary policies. *Journal of Applied Probability*, 24: 644–656, 1987.
8. A. Bianco and L. de Alfaro. Model checking of probabilistic and nondeterministic systems. In *Foundations of Software Technology and Theoretical Computer Science*, LNCS 1026: 499–513, 1995.
9. P. Buchholz. Exact and ordinary lumpability in finite Markov chains. *Journal of Applied Probability*, 31: 59–75, 1994.

---

[5] Only Theorem 4 turns wrong when the supremum over all fair schedulers is replaced by the infimum over all fair schedulers. See [5] for a counterexample for DTMDPs.

10. P. Buchholz, J.-P. Katoen, P. Kemper, and C. Tepper. Model-checking large structured Markov chains. *Journal of Logic and Algebraic Programming*, 56:69–97, 2003.
11. G. Chiola, S. Donatelli, and G. Franceschinis. GSPNs versus SPNs: What is the actual role of immediate transitions? In *Petri Nets and Performance Models 1991*, IEEE CS Press, 1991.
12. G. Ciardo and R. Zijal. Well-defined stochastic Petri nets. In *Proc. 4th International Workshop on Modeling, Analysis and Simulation of Computer and Telecommunication Systems (MASCOTS'96)*, pages 278-284, 1996.
13. D.D. Deavours, and W.H. Sanders. An efficient well-specified check. In *Petri Nets and Performance Models*, IEEE CS Press, 1999.
14. E.A. Feinberg. Continuous time discounted jump Markov decision processes: a discrete-event approach. 1998.
    http://www.ams.sunysb.edu/~feinberg/public/.
15. B.L. Fox and P.W. Glynn. Computing Poisson probabilities. *Communications of the ACM*, 31(4): 440–445, 1988.
16. H. Hermanns, U. Herzog, and V. Mertsiotakis. Stochastic process algebras – Between LOTOS and Markov chains. *Computer Networks and ISDN Systems*, 30(9-10):901–924, 1998.
17. H. Hermanns. *Interactive Markov Chains and the Quest for Quantified Quality*. LNCS 2428, Springer, 2002.
18. H. Hermanns, J.-P. Katoen, J. Meyer-Kayser, and M. Siegle. A tool for model-checking Markov chains. *Int. Journal on Software Tools for Technology Transfer*, 4(2):153–172, 2003.
19. A. Jensen. Markov chains as an aid in the study of Markov processes. *Skand. Aktuarietidskrift*, 3: 87–91, 1953.
20. J.-P. Katoen, M.Z. Kwiatkowska, G. Norman and D. Parker. Faster and symbolic CTMC model checking. In *Process Algebra and Probabilistic Methods*, LNCS 2165: 23–38, Springer, 2001.
21. M.L. Puterman. *Markov Decision Processes: Discrete Stochastic Dynamic Programming*. John Wiley & Sons, 1994.
22. Q. Qiu and M. Pedram. Dynamic power managment based on continuous-time Markov decision processes. In *Design Automation Conference 99*, pp. 555–561, 1999.
23. W.H. Sanders and J.F. Meyer. Reduced base model construction methods for stochastic activity networks. *IEEE Journal on Selected Areas in Communications*, 9(1):25–36, January 1991.
24. L. Sennot. *Stochastic Dynamic Programming and the Control of Queueing Systems*. John Wiley & Sons, 1999.

Model Checking Discounted Temporal Properties[*]

Luca de Alfaro[1], Marco Faella[1,3], Thomas A. Henzinger[2], Rupak Majumdar[4], and Mariëlle Stoelinga[1]

[1] CE, Universitity of California, Santa Cruz, USA
[2] EECS, University of California, Berkeley, USA
[3] Università degli Studi di Salerno, Italy
[4] CS, University of California, Los Angeles, USA

Abstract. Temporal logic is two-valued: a property is either true or false. When applied to the analysis of stochastic systems, or systems with imprecise formal models, temporal logic is therefore fragile: even small changes in the model can lead to opposite truth values for a specification. We present a generalization of the branching-time logic CTL which achieves robustness with respect to model perturbations by giving a quantitative interpretation to predicates and logical operators, and by discounting the importance of events according to how late they occur. In every state, the value of a formula is a real number in the interval [0,1], where 1 corresponds to truth and 0 to falsehood. The boolean operators and and or are replaced by min and max, the path quantifiers ∃ and ∀ determine sup and inf over all paths from a given state, and the temporal operators ◇ and □ specify sup and inf over a given path; a new operator averages all values along a path. Furthermore, all path operators are discounted by a parameter that can be chosen to give more weight to states that are closer to the beginning of the path. We interpret the resulting logic DCTL over transition systems, Markov chains, and Markov decision processes. We present two semantics for DCTL: a *path* semantics, inspired by the standard interpretation of state and path formulas in CTL, and a *fixpoint* semantics, inspired by the μ-calculus evaluation of CTL formulas. We show that, while these semantics coincide for CTL, they differ for DCTL, and we provide model-checking algorithms for both semantics.

1 Introduction

Boolean state-transition models are useful for the representation and verification of computational systems, such as hardware and software systems. A boolean state-transition model is a labeled directed graph, whose vertices represent system states, whose edges represent state changes, and whose labels represent

---

[*] This research was supported in part by the AFOSR MURI grant F49620-00-1-0327, the ONR grant N00014-02-1-0671, and the NSF grants CCR-0132780, CCR-9988172, CCR-0225610, and CCR-0234690.

boolean observations about the system, such as the truth values of state predicates. Behavioral properties of boolean state-transition systems can be specified in temporal logic [15,4] and verified using model-checking algorithms [4].

For representing systems that are not purely computational but partly physical, such as hardware and software that interacts with a physical environment, boolean state-transition models are often inadequate. Many quantitative extensions of state-transition models have been proposed for this purpose, such as models that embed state changes into the real time line, and models that assign probabilities to state changes. These models typically contain real numbers, e.g., for representing time or probabilities. Yet previous research has focused mostly on purely boolean frameworks for the specification and verification of quantitative state-transition models, where observations are truth values of state predicates, and behavioral properties are based on such boolean observations [10,3,1,14]. These boolean specification frameworks are *fragile* with respect to imprecisions in the model: even arbitrarily small changes in a quantitative model can cause different truth values for the specification.

We submit that a proper framework for the specification and verification of quantitative state-transition models should itself be quantitative. To start with, we consider observations that do not have boolean truth values, but real values [13]. Using these quantitative observations, we build a temporal logic for specifying quantitative temporal properties. A CTL-like temporal logic has three kinds of operators. The first kind are boolean operators such as "and" and "or" for locally combining the truth values of boolean observations. These are replaced by "min" and "max" operators for combining the real values of quantitative observations. In addition, a "weighted average" ($\oplus_c$) operator is useful to generate new quantitative observations. The second kind of constructs are modal operators such as "always" ($\square$) and "eventually" ($\lozenge$) for temporally combining the truth values of all boolean observations along an infinite path. These are replaced by "inf" ("lim min") and "sup" ("lim max") operators over infinite sequences of real values. We introduce a "lim avg" ($\triangle$) operator that captures the long-run average value of a quantitative observation. For nondeterministic models, where there is a choice of future behaviors, there is a third kind of constructs: the path quantifiers "for-all-possible-futures" ($\forall$) and "for-some-possible-future" ($\exists$) turn path properties into state properties by quantifying over the paths from a given state. These are replaced by "inf-over-all-possible-futures" and "sup-over-all-possible-futures." Once boolean specifications are replaced by quantitative specifications, it becomes possible to discount the future, that is, to give more weight to the near future than to the far away future. This principle is well-understood in economics and in the theory of optimal control [2], but is equally natural in studying quantitative temporal properties of systems [7]. We call the resulting logic DCTL ("Discounted CTL"). While quantitative versions of dynamic logics [13], μ-calculi [11,16,17,7], and Hennessy-Milner logics [8] exist, DCTL is the first temporal logic in which the non-local temporal operators $\lozenge$ and $\square$, along with the new temporal operator $\triangle$ and the path quantifiers $\forall$ and $\exists$, are given a quantitative interpretation.

We propose two semantics for DCTL: a *path* semantics and a *fixpoint* semantics. In the undiscounted path semantics, the $\Diamond$ (resp. $\Box$) operator computes the sup (resp. inf) over a path, and the $\triangle$ operator computes the long-run average. The discounted versions $\Diamond_\alpha$, $\Box_\alpha$, and $\triangle_\alpha$ of these operators weigh the value of a state that occurs k steps in the future by a factor α^k, where $\alpha \leq 1$ is the discount factor. The $\forall$ and $\exists$ operators then combine these values over the paths: in transition systems, $\forall$ and $\exists$ associate with each state the inf and sup of the values for the paths that leave the state; in probabilistic systems, $\forall$ and $\exists$ associate with each state the least and greatest expectation of the value for those paths (for Markov chains, there is a single expected value at each state, but for Markov decision processes, the least and greatest expected value are generally different). Thus, the path semantics of DCTL is obtained by lifting to a quantitative setting the classical interpretation of path and state formulas in CTL.

The *fixpoint* semantics is obtained by lifting to a quantitative setting the connection between CTL and the μ-calculus [4]. In a transition system, given a set r of states, denote by $\exists\mathrm{Pre}(r)$ the set of all states that have a one-step transition to r. Then, the semantics of $\exists\Diamond r$ for a set r of states can be defined as the least fixpoint of the equation $x = r \cup \exists\mathrm{Pre}(x)$, denoted $\mu x.(r \cup \exists\mathrm{Pre}(x))$. We lift this definition to a quantitative setting by interpreting $\cup$ as pointwise maximum, and $\exists\mathrm{Pre}(x)$ as the maximal expected value of x achievable in one step [7]. The discounted semantics $\exists\Diamond_\alpha r$ is obtained by multiplying the next-step expectation with α, i.e., $\mu x.(r \cup \alpha \cdot \exists\mathrm{Pre}(x))$.

The path and fixpoint semantics coincide on transition systems, but differ on Markov chains (and consequently on Markov decision processes). This is illustrated by the Markov chain depicted at right. Consider the DCTL formula ϕ: $\exists\Diamond_\alpha q$, for $\alpha = 0.8$.

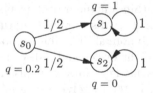

According to the path semantics, there are two paths from s_0, each followed with probability $1/2$: the first path has the discounted sup equal to 0.8, and the second has the discounted sup equal to 0.2; hence, ϕ has the value $(0.8 + 0.2)/2 = 0.5$ at s_0. According to the fixpoint semantics, $q \cup 0.8 \cdot \exists\mathrm{Pre}(q)$ has the value $\max\{0.2, 0.8 \cdot (1 + 0)/2)\} = 0.4$ at s_0, and this is also the value of ϕ at s_0. This example highlights the different perspective taken by the two semantics. The path semantics of $\exists\Diamond q$ is an "observational" semantics: if q represents, for instance, the level of water in a vessel (0 is empty, 1 is full), then $\exists\Diamond q$ is the expected value of the maximum level that occurs along a system behavior. Such a semantics is well-suited for system specification. The fixpoint semantics of $\exists\Diamond q$ is a "controlling" semantics: if q represents the retirement bonus that we receive if we decide to retire, then $\exists\Diamond q$ is the maximal expected bonus we will receive (discounting accounts for inflation). The difference is that in the fixpoint semantics we must decide when to stop: the choice of retiring, or working for one more day, corresponds to the choice between the two sides q and $\exists\mathrm{Pre}(x)$ of the $\cup$ operator (interpreted as pointwise maximum) in the fixpoint. Hence the fixpoint semantics is better suited for system control: if the goal is to reach a state with a high value of q, we must not only reach such a state, but also stop, once satisfied by a sufficiently high value of q, and move on to some subsequent control goal. In the path semantics, on the other hand, we have no control over stopping: we can only observe the value of q over infinite runs, and compute the expected value of the sup it reaches.

In DCTL, discounting serves two purposes. First, it leads to a notion of "quality" with which a specification is satisfied. For example, if we wish to reach a state with a high value of q, then the undiscounted formula $\exists\Diamond q$ is valid regardless of when the high q value is reached, whereas $\exists\Diamond_\alpha q$, for $\alpha < 1$, has a higher value if the high q value is reached earlier. Likewise, if q represents the "level of functionality" of a system, then the specification $\forall\Box_\alpha q$ will have a value that is higher the longer the system functions well, even if the system will eventually always break. Second, discounting is instrumental in achieving robustness with respect to system perturbations. Indeed, we will show that for discount factors smaller than 1, the value of DCTL formulas in both semantics is a continuous function of the values of the numerical quantities (observations, transition probabilities) of the model.

We present algorithms for model checking both semantics of DCTL over transition systems, Markov chains, and Markov decision processes (MDPs). Note that, for discount factors less than 1, DCTL is a quantitative logic even when interpreted over purely boolean state-transition systems. Over transition systems, the algorithms for $\Box_\alpha$ and $\Diamond_\alpha$ are based on iterating quantitative fixpoint expressions; the main result in this regard is that the iteration always terminates within a number of steps bounded by the diameter of the system. The algorithm for $\triangle_\alpha$ (discounted long-run average along a path) is more involved, but still polynomial: it builds on both Karp's algorithm for computing minimum mean-weight cycles and a discounted version of Bellman-Ford for computing shortest paths. For Markov chains and MDPs, we can model check the fixpoint semantics of DCTL by relying on a mix of results from optimal control [2] and the quantitative μ-calculus [7]. On the other hand, model checking the path semantics of DCTL over Markov chains and MDPs requires novel algorithms. In all cases, the model checking problem for DCTL can be solved in time polynomial in the size of the system. For transition systems, the time required is also polynomial in the size of the DCTL formula. For Markov chains and MDPs, the time required is polynomial in the size of the DCTL formula for the fixpoint semantics, and exponential for the path semantics. The latter exponential complexity is caused by the fact that, in the path semantics, the bit-wise encodings of the valuations of Markov chains and MDPs grows exponentially with respect to the number of nestings of temporal operators (in practice, of course, one would be unlikely to implement arbitrary-precision arithmetic).

2   Discounted CTL

Syntax. Let Σ be a set of propositions and let A be a set of parameters. The DCTL formulas over (Σ, A) are generated by the grammar

$$\phi ::= r \mid \mathrm{T} \mid \mathrm{F} \mid \phi \vee \phi \mid \phi \wedge \phi \mid \neg\phi \mid \phi \oplus_c \phi \mid \exists\psi \mid \forall\psi$$
$$\psi ::= \Diamond_c\phi \mid \Box_c\phi \mid \triangle_c\phi$$

where $r \in \Sigma$ is a proposition and $c \in A$ is a parameter. The formulas generated by ϕ are *state formulas*; the formulas generated by ψ are *path formulas*. The DCTL formulas are the state formulas.

2.1 Semantics for Labeled Transition Systems

We define two semantics for DCTL: the path semantics, and the fixpoint semantics. In the path semantics, the path operators $\Diamond$ and $\Box$ determine the discounted sup and inf values over a path, and the $\exists$ and $\forall$ operators determine the minimum and maximum values of the path formula over all paths from a given state. The fixpoint semantics is defined by lifting to a quantitative setting the usual connection between CTL and μ-calculus.

Discount factors. Let A be a set of parameters. A *parameter interpretation* of A is a function $\langle \cdot \rangle \colon A \to [0,1]$ that assigns to each parameter a real number between 0 and 1, called a *discount factor*. The interpretation $\langle \cdot \rangle$ is *contractive* if $\langle c \rangle < 1$ for all $c \in A$; it is *undiscounted* if $\langle c \rangle = 1$ for all $c \in A$. We write $\mathcal{I}_A$ for the set of parameter interpretations of A. We denote by $|q|_b$ the length of the binary encoding of a number $q \in \mathbb{Q}$, and we denote by $|\langle \cdot \rangle|_b = \sum_{c \in A} |\langle c \rangle|_b$ the size of the interpretation $\langle \cdot \rangle$ of A.

Valuations. Let S be a set of states. A *valuation* on S is a function $v \colon S \to [0,1]$ that assigns to each state a real between 0 and 1. The valuation v is *boolean* if $v(s) \in \{0,1\}$ for all $s \in S$. We write $\mathcal{V}_S$ for the set of valuations on S. We write $\mathbf{0}$ for the valuation that maps all states to 0, and $\mathbf{1}$ for the valuation that maps all states to 1. For two real numbers u_1, u_2 and a discount factor $\alpha \in [0,1]$, we write $u_1 \sqcup u_2$ for $\max\{u_1, u_2\}$, $u_1 \sqcap u_2$ for $\min\{u_1, u_2\}$, and $u_1 +_\alpha u_2$ for $(1 - \alpha) \cdot u_1 + \alpha \cdot u_2$. We lift operations on reals to operations on valuations in a pointwise fashion; for example, for two valuations $v_1, v_2 \in \mathcal{V}_S$, by $v_1 \sqcup v_2$ we denote the valuation that maps each state $s \in S$ to $v_1(s) \sqcup v_2(s)$.

Labeled transition systems. A *labeled transition system* (LTS) $\mathcal{S} = (S, \delta, \Sigma, [\cdot])$ consists of a set S of states, a transition relation $\delta \colon S \to 2^S \setminus \emptyset$ that assigns to each state a finite nonempty set of successor states, a set Σ of propositions, and a function $[\cdot] \colon \Sigma \to \mathcal{V}_S$ that assigns to each proposition a valuation. We denote by $|\delta|$ the value $\sum_{s \in S} |\delta(s)|$. The LTS $\mathcal{S}$ is *boolean* if for all propositions $r \in \Sigma$, the valuation $[r]$ is boolean. A *path* of $\mathcal{S}$ is an infinite sequence $s_0 s_1 s_2 \ldots$ of states such that $s_{i+1} \in \delta(s_i)$ for all $i \geq 0$. Given a state $s \in S$, we write $Traj_s$ for the set of paths that start in s.

The path semantics. The DCTL formulas over (Σ, A) are evaluated w.r.t. an LTS $\mathcal{S} = (S, \delta, \Sigma, [\cdot])$ whose propositions are Σ, and w.r.t. a parameter interpretation $\langle \cdot \rangle \in \mathcal{I}_A$. Every state formula ϕ defines a valuation $[\![\phi]\!]^{\mathrm{P}} \in \mathcal{V}_S$:

$$
\begin{aligned}
[\![r]\!]^{\mathrm{P}} &= [r] & [\![\phi_1 \vee \phi_2]\!]^{\mathrm{P}} &= [\![\phi_1]\!]^{\mathrm{P}} \sqcup [\![\phi_2]\!]^{\mathrm{P}} \\
[\![\mathrm{T}]\!]^{\mathrm{P}} &= \mathbf{1} & [\![\phi_1 \wedge \phi_2]\!]^{\mathrm{P}} &= [\![\phi_1]\!]^{\mathrm{P}} \sqcap [\![\phi_2]\!]^{\mathrm{P}} \\
[\![\mathrm{F}]\!]^{\mathrm{P}} &= \mathbf{0} & [\![\phi_1 \oplus_c \phi_2]\!]^{\mathrm{P}} &= [\![\phi_1]\!]^{\mathrm{P}} +_{\langle c \rangle} [\![\phi_2]\!]^{\mathrm{P}} \\
[\![\neg\phi]\!]^{\mathrm{P}} &= \mathbf{1} - [\![\phi]\!]^{\mathrm{P}} & [\![\exists\psi]\!]^{\mathrm{P}}(s) &= \sup\{[\![\psi]\!]^{\mathrm{P}}(\rho) \mid \rho \in Traj_s\} \\
& & [\![\forall\psi]\!]^{\mathrm{P}}(s) &= \inf\{[\![\psi]\!]^{\mathrm{P}}(\rho) \mid \rho \in Traj_s\}
\end{aligned}
$$

A path formula ψ assigns a real $[\![\psi]\!]^P(\rho) \in [0,1]$ to each path ρ of $\mathcal{S}$:

$$[\![\Diamond_c\phi]\!]^P(s_0 s_1 \ldots) = \sup\{\langle c\rangle^i \cdot [\![\phi]\!]^P(s_i) \mid i \geq 0\}$$

$$[\![\Box_c\phi]\!]^P(s_0 s_1 \ldots) = \inf\{1 - \langle c\rangle^i \cdot (1 - [\![\phi]\!]^P(s_i)) \mid i \geq 0\}$$

$$[\![\triangle_c\phi]\!]^P(s_0 s_1 \ldots) = \begin{cases} (1 - \langle c\rangle) \cdot \sum\{\langle c\rangle^i \cdot [\![\phi]\!]^P(s_i) \mid i \geq 0\} & \text{if } \langle c\rangle < 1 \\ \lim_{i \geq 0}(\frac{1}{i+1} \cdot \sum_{0 \leq j \leq i}[\![\phi]\!]^P(s_j)) & \text{if } \langle c\rangle = 1 \end{cases}$$

Notice that the limit of the first clause for $\triangle_c$ when $\langle c\rangle \to 1$ gives the second clause. If the LTS $\mathcal{S}$ is boolean and the parameter interpretation $\langle \cdot \rangle$ is undiscounted, then 1 can be interpreted as truth, 0 as falsehood, and DCTL without the operator $\triangle$ coincides with CTL.

The fixpoint semantics. In this semantics, the DCTL formulas are evaluated with respect to an LTS $\mathcal{S}$ and a *contractive* parameter interpretation $\langle \cdot \rangle \in \mathcal{I}_A$. Given a valuation $x \in \mathcal{V}_S$, we denote by $\exists \mathrm{Pre}(x) \in \mathcal{V}_S$ the valuation defined by $\exists \mathrm{Pre}(x)(s) = \max\{x(t) \mid t \in \delta(s)\}$, and we denote by $\forall \mathrm{Pre}(x) \in \mathcal{V}_S$ the valuation defined by $\forall \mathrm{Pre}(x)(s) = \min\{x(t) \mid t \in \delta(s)\}$. The fixpoint semantics $[\![\cdot]\!]^f$ for the propositions, the boolean operators, and $\oplus_c$ is similar to the path semantics, only that $[\![\cdot]\!]^P$ is replaced by $[\![\cdot]\!]^f$. The other operators are defined as follows:

$$[\![\exists\Diamond_c\phi]\!]^f = \mu x.([\![\phi]\!]^f \sqcup (\mathbf{0} +_{\langle c\rangle} \exists\mathrm{Pre}(x)))$$

$$[\![\forall\Diamond_c\phi]\!]^f = \mu x.([\![\phi]\!]^f \sqcup (\mathbf{0} +_{\langle c\rangle} \forall\mathrm{Pre}(x)))$$

$$[\![\exists\Box_c\phi]\!]^f = \mu x.([\![\phi]\!]^f \sqcap (\mathbf{1} +_{\langle c\rangle} \exists\mathrm{Pre}(x)))$$

$$[\![\forall\Box_c\phi]\!]^f = \mu x.([\![\phi]\!]^f \sqcap (\mathbf{1} +_{\langle c\rangle} \forall\mathrm{Pre}(x)))$$

$$[\![\exists\triangle_c\phi]\!]^f = \mu x.([\![\phi]\!]^f +_{\langle c\rangle} \exists\mathrm{Pre}(x))$$

$$[\![\forall\triangle_c\phi]\!]^f = \mu x.([\![\phi]\!]^f +_{\langle c\rangle} \forall\mathrm{Pre}(x))$$

Above, for a function $F: \mathcal{V}_S \to \mathcal{V}_S$, the notation $\mu x.F(x)$ indicates the unique (as $\langle c\rangle < 1$ for all $c \in A$) valuation x_* such that $x_* = F(x_*)$.

2.2 Semantics for Markov Processes

Given a finite set S, let $\mathrm{Distr}(S)$ be the set of probability distributions over S; for $a \in \mathrm{Distr}(S)$, we denote by $\mathrm{Supp}(a) = \{s \in S \mid a(s) > 0\}$ the support of a. A probability distribution a over S is *deterministic* if $a(s) \in \{0,1\}$ for all $s \in S$.

Markov decision processes. A *Markov decision process* (MDP) $\mathcal{S} = (S, \tau, \Sigma, [\cdot])$ consists of a set S of states, a probabilistic transition relation τ: $S \to 2^{\mathrm{Distr}(S)} \setminus \emptyset$, which assigns to each state a finite nonempty set of probability distributions over the successor states, a set Σ of propositions, and a function $[\cdot]: \Sigma \to \mathcal{V}_S$ that assigns to each proposition a valuation. The MDP $\mathcal{S}$ is *boolean* if for all propositions $r \in \Sigma$, the valuation $[r]$ is boolean. We denote by $|\tau|_b$ the length of the binary encoding of τ, defined by $\sum_{s \in S} \sum_{a \in \tau(s)} \sum_{t \in \mathrm{Supp}(a)} |a(t)|_b$, and we denote by $\|[\cdot]\|_b = \sum_{q \in \Sigma} \sum_{s \in S} |[q](s)|_b$ the size of the binary encoding of $[\cdot]$. Then, the binary size of $\mathcal{S}$ is given by $|\mathcal{S}|_b = |\tau|_b + \|[\cdot]\|_b$.

A finite (resp. infinite) *path* of $\mathcal{S}$ is a finite (resp. infinite) sequence $s_0 s_1 s_2 \ldots s_m$ (resp. $s_0 s_1 s_2 \ldots$) of states such that for all $i < m$ (resp. $i \in \mathbb{N}$) there is $a_i \in \tau(s_i)$ with $s_{i+1} \in \mathrm{Supp}(a_i)$. We denote by $FTraj$ and $Traj$ the sets of finite and infinite paths of S; for $s \in S$, we denote by $Traj_s$ the infinite paths starting from s. A *strategy* π for S is a mapping from $FTraj$ to $\mathrm{Distr}(\bigcup_{s \in S} \tau(s))$: once the MDP has followed the path $s_0 s_1 \ldots s_m \in FTraj$, the strategy π prescribes the probability $\pi(s_0 s_1 \ldots s_m)(a)$ of using a next-state distribution $a \in \tau(s_m)$. For all $s_0 s_1 \ldots s_m \in FTraj$, we require that $\mathrm{Supp}(\pi(s_0 s_1 \ldots s_m)) \subseteq \tau(s_m)$. Thus, under strategy π, after following a finite path $s_0 s_1 \ldots s_m$ the MDP takes a transition to state s_{m+1} with probability $\sum_{a \in \tau(s_m)} a(s_{m+1}) \cdot \pi(s_0 s_1 \ldots s_m)(a)$. We denote by Π the set of all strategies for S. The transition probabilities corresponding to a strategy π, together with an initial state s, give rise to a probability space $(Traj_s, \mathcal{B}_s, \mathrm{Pr}_s^\pi)$, where $\mathcal{B}_s$ is the set of measurable subsets of 2^{Traj_s}, and Pr_s^π is the probability measure over $\mathcal{B}_s$ induced by the next-state transition probabilities described above [12,18]. Given a random variable X over this probability space, we denote its expected value by $\mathrm{E}_s^\pi[X]$. For $i \in \mathbb{N}$, the random variable $Z_i \colon Traj_s \to S$ defined by $Z_i(s_0 s_1 \ldots) = s_i$ yields the state of the stochastic process after i steps.

Special cases of MDPs: Markov chains and transition systems. Markov chains and LTSs can be defined as special cases of MDPs. An MDP $S = (S, \tau, \Sigma, [\cdot])$ is a *Markov chain* if $|\tau(s)| = 1$ for all $s \in S$. It is customary to specify the probabilistic structure of a Markov chain via its *probability transition matrix* $P = [p_{s,t}]_{s,t \in S}$, defined for all $s, t \in S$ by $p_{s,t} = a(t)$, where a is the unique distribution $a \in \tau(s)$. An initial state $s \in S$ completely determines a probability space $(Traj_s, \mathcal{B}_s, \mathrm{Pr}_s)$, and for a random variable X over this probability space, we let $\mathrm{E}_s[X]$ denote its expectation. An MDP $S = (S, \tau, \Sigma, [\cdot])$ is an LTS if, for all $s \in S$ and all $a \in \tau(s)$, the distribution a is deterministic; in that case, we define $\delta \colon S \to 2^S$ by $\delta(s) = \{t \in S \mid \exists a \in \tau(s). \, a(t) = 1\}$.

The path semantics. The DCTL formulas over (Σ, A) are evaluated with respect to a MDP $S = (S, \tau, \Sigma, [\cdot])$ and with respect to a parameter interpretation $\langle \cdot \rangle \in \mathcal{I}_A$. The semantics $[\![\psi]\!]^\mathrm{P}$ of a path formula ψ is defined as for LTSs; we note that $[\![\psi]\!]^\mathrm{P}$ is a random variable over the probability space $(Traj_s, \mathcal{B}_s, \mathrm{Pr}_s)$. Every state formula ϕ defines a valuation $[\![\phi]\!]^\mathrm{P} \in \mathcal{V}_S$: the clauses for propositions, boolean operators, and $\oplus_c$ are as for LTSs; the clauses for $\exists$ and $\forall$ are as follows:

$$[\![\exists \psi]\!]^\mathrm{P}(s) = \sup\{\mathrm{E}_s^\pi([\![\psi]\!]^\mathrm{P}) \mid \pi \in \Pi\}, \qquad [\![\forall \psi]\!]^\mathrm{P}(s) = \inf\{\mathrm{E}_s^\pi([\![\psi]\!]^\mathrm{P}) \mid \pi \in \Pi\}.$$

The fixpoint semantics. Given a valuation $x \colon S \to [0,1]$, we denote by $\exists \mathrm{Pre}(x) \colon S \to [0,1]$ the valuation defined by $\exists \mathrm{Pre}(x)(s) = \max_{a \in \tau(s)} \sum_{t \in S} x(t) \cdot a(t)$, and we denote by $\forall \mathrm{Pre}(x) \colon S \to [0,1]$ the valuation defined by $\forall \mathrm{Pre}(x)(s) = \min_{a \in \tau(s)} \sum_{t \in S} x(t) a(t)$. With this notation, the fixpoint semantics $[\![\cdot]\!]^\mathrm{f}$ is defined by the same clauses as for LTSs.

2.3 Properties of DCTL

Duality laws. For all state formulas ϕ_1, ϕ_2 over (Σ, A), all MDPs with propositions Σ, and all contractive parameter interpretations of A and $* \in \{\mathrm{p}, \mathrm{f}\}$, we have the following equivalences: $[\![\neg\exists\Diamond_c\phi]\!]^* = [\![\forall\Box_c\neg\phi]\!]^*$, $[\![\neg\exists\Box_c\phi]\!]^* = [\![\forall\Diamond_c\neg\phi]\!]^*$, and $[\![\neg\exists\triangle_c\phi]\!]^* = [\![\forall\triangle_c\neg\phi]\!]^*$. In particular, we see that $\triangle_c$ is self-dual and that a minimalist definition of DCTL will omit one of $\{\mathrm{T}, \mathrm{F}\}$, one of $\{\vee, \wedge\}$, and one of $\{\exists, \forall, \Diamond, \Box\}$.

Comparing both semantics. We show that the path and fixpoint semantics coincide over transition systems, and over Markov systems with boolean propositions (for non-nested formulas), but do not coincide in general over (non-boolean) Markov chains. This result is surprising, as it indicates that the standard connection between CTL and μ-calculus breaks down as soon as we consider *both* probabilistic systems and quantitative valuations. Since discounting plays no role in the proof of the theorem, an analogous result holds also for the logic without the operator $\triangle$ under no discounting. On the other hand, the theorem states that the two semantics always coincide for the $\triangle_c$ operator.

Theorem 1. *The following assertions hold:*

1. *For all LTSs with propositions Σ, all contractive parameter interpretations of A, and all DCTL formulas ϕ over (Σ, A), we have $[\![\phi]\!]^{\mathrm{P}} = [\![\phi]\!]^{\mathrm{f}}$.*
2. *For all boolean MDPs with propositions Σ, all contractive parameter interpretations of A, and all DCTL formulas ϕ over (Σ, A) that contain no nesting of path quantifiers, we have $[\![\phi]\!]^{\mathrm{P}} = [\![\phi]\!]^{\mathrm{f}}$.*
3. *There is a Markov chain S with propositions Σ, a contractive parameter interpretation A, and a DCTL formula ϕ over (Σ, A) such that $[\![\phi]\!]^{\mathrm{P}} \neq [\![\phi]\!]^{\mathrm{f}}$.*
4. *For all MDPs with propositions Σ, all contractive parameter interpretations of A, and all $r \in \Sigma$, we have $[\![\exists\triangle_c r]\!]^{\mathrm{P}} = [\![\exists\triangle_c r]\!]^{\mathrm{f}}$ and $[\![\forall\triangle_c r]\!]^{\mathrm{P}} = [\![\forall\triangle_c r]\!]^{\mathrm{f}}$.*

The example for part 3 of the theorem was given in the introduction.

Robustness. Consider two MDPs $\mathcal{S} = (S, \tau, \Sigma, [\cdot])$ and $\mathcal{S}' = (S, \tau', \Sigma, [\cdot]')$ with the same state space S and the same set Σ of propositions. We define $\|\mathcal{S}, \mathcal{S}'\| = \max_{s \in S}\{\max_{r \in \Sigma} |[r](s) - [r]'(s)|, \max_{a \in \tau(s)} \min_{b \in \tau'(s)} \sum_{s' \in S} |a(s') - b(s')|, \max_{b \in \tau'(s)} \min_{a \in \tau(s)} \sum_{s' \in S} |a(s') - b(s')|\}$. It is not difficult to see that $\|\cdot, \cdot\|$ is a metric on MDPs. For an MDP $\mathcal{S}$ and a parameter interpretation $\langle\cdot\rangle$, we write $[\![\cdot]\!]^{\mathrm{f}}_{\mathcal{S}, \langle\cdot\rangle}$ and $[\![\cdot]\!]^{\mathrm{P}}_{\mathcal{S}, \langle\cdot\rangle}$ to denote the two semantics functions defined on $\mathcal{S}$ with respect to $\langle\cdot\rangle$.

Theorem 2. *Let $\mathcal{S}$ and $\mathcal{S}'$ be two MDPs with state space S, and let $\langle\cdot\rangle$ be a contractive parameter interpretation.*

1. *For all $\epsilon > 0$, there is a $\delta > 0$ such that for all DCTL formulas ϕ and all states $s \in S$, if $\|\mathcal{S}, \mathcal{S}'\| \leq \delta$, then $|[\![\phi]\!]^{\mathrm{f}}_{\mathcal{S}, \langle\cdot\rangle}(s) - [\![\phi]\!]^{\mathrm{f}}_{\mathcal{S}', \langle\cdot\rangle}(s)| \leq \epsilon$.*
2. *Let Φ be a set of DCTL formulas such that the maximum nesting depth of every formula in Φ is k. For all $\epsilon > 0$, there is a $\delta > 0$ such that for all formulas $\phi \in \Phi$ and all states $s \in S$, if $\|\mathcal{S}, \mathcal{S}'\| \leq \delta$, then $|[\![\phi]\!]^{\mathrm{P}}_{\mathcal{S}, \langle\cdot\rangle}(s) - [\![\phi]\!]^{\mathrm{P}}_{\mathcal{S}', \langle\cdot\rangle}(s)| \leq \epsilon$.*

Notice that we get the continuity statement for the path semantics only for sets of formulas with bounded nesting depth. To see this, consider the three-state

Markov chain $\mathcal{S} = (\{s_0, s_1, s_2\}, \tau, \{r\}, [\cdot])$, where $\tau(s_0)$ is the distribution that chooses s_1 with probability $1 - \epsilon$ and chooses s_2 with probability ϵ, and $\tau(s_i)$ chooses s_i with probability 1 for $i = 1, 2$. Let $[r](s_0) = [r](s_1) = 0$ and $[r](s_2) = 1$. Consider the Markov chain $\mathcal{S}'$ that differs from $\mathcal{S}$ in that $\tau(s_0)$ chooses s_1 with probability 1. Then $\|\mathcal{S}, \mathcal{S}'\| = \epsilon$. Now consider the formulas $(\exists \Diamond_c)^n r$, for $n \geq 1$. Let $x_n = [(\exists \Diamond_c)^n r]^{\mathrm{p}}_{\mathcal{S}, \langle \cdot \rangle}(s_0)$. Then $x_{n+1} = (1 - \epsilon) \cdot x_n + \langle c \rangle \cdot \epsilon$, and the limit as n goes to ∞ is $\langle c \rangle$. On the other hand, $[(\exists \Diamond_c)^n r]^{\mathrm{p}}_{\mathcal{S}', \langle \cdot \rangle}(s_0) = 0$ for all n.

3 Model Checking DCTL

The model-checking problem of a DCTL formula ϕ over an LTS, a Markov chain, or an MDP with respect to one of the two semantics $* \in \{p, f\}$ consists in computing the value $[\phi]^*(s)$ for all states s of the system under consideration. Similar to CTL model checking [4], we recursively consider one of the subformulas ψ of ϕ and compute the valuation $[\psi]^*$. Then we replace ψ in ϕ by a new proposition p_ψ with $[p_\psi] = [\psi]^*$. Because of the duality laws stated in Section 2.3, it suffices to focus on model checking formulas of the forms $\exists \Diamond_c r$, $\forall \Diamond_c r$, and $\forall \triangle_c r$, for a proposition $r \in \Sigma$. We will present the algorithms, for both semantics, over transition systems in Section 3.1, over Markov chains in Section 3.2, and over MDPs in Section 3.3.

Throughout this section, we fix a parameter interpretation $\langle \cdot \rangle$, a set of propositions Σ, a proposition $r \in \Sigma$, and a parameter c and write $[r] = q$ and $\langle c \rangle = \alpha$. We omit the superscripts p and f and just write $[\cdot]$ if the path and fixpoint semantics coincide. We restrict our attention to the case of finite-state systems and $\alpha < 1$; the case $\alpha = 1$ is treated in [6]. For complexity analyses, we assume that operations on reals (comparison, addition, and multiplication) can be performed in constant time; in other words, we provide the asymptotic complexity of each algorithm in terms of the number of arithmetic operations.

3.1 Model Checking DCTL over Transition Systems

We fix an LTS $\mathcal{S} = (S, \delta, \Sigma, [\cdot])$. As stated in Theorem 1, the two semantics of DCTL coincide over LTSs. Hence, we need only one algorithm to model check a formula in either semantics.

Model checking $\exists \Diamond$ and $\forall \Diamond$ in both semantics. The fixpoint semantics of DCTL suggests an iterative algorithm for evaluating formulas. In particular, $[\exists \Diamond_c r]^{\mathrm{f}} = \lim_{n \to \infty} v_n$, where $v_0(s) = q(s)$, and $v_{n+1}(s) = q(s) \sqcup \alpha \cdot \max\{v_n(s') \mid s' \in \delta(s)\}$ for all $n \geq 0$. Over LTSs, the fixpoint is reached in a finite number of steps, namely, $[\exists \Diamond_c r] = v_{|S|}$. To see this, observe that the value $[\exists \Diamond_c r]^{\mathrm{f}}(s)$, the maximal (discounted) maximum over all paths from s, is obtained at a state in an acyclic prefix of some path from s. The argument that $[\forall \Diamond_c r] = v_{|S|}$, where $v_{n+1}(s) = q(s) \sqcup \alpha \cdot \min\{v_n(s') \mid s' \in \delta(s)\}$, is slightly more involved. The value $[\forall \Diamond_c r]^{\mathrm{f}}(s)$, the minimal (discounted) maximum over all paths from s, is again obtained at a state s' in an acyclic prefix of some path ρ from s. This is because if some state s'' were repeated on ρ before s', then the path ρ' that results from ρ by infinitely visiting s'' (and never visiting s') would achieve a smaller (discounted) maximum than ρ.

Model checking $\forall\triangle$ in both semantics. Computing $[\![\forall\triangle_c r]\!](s)$ consists in minimizing the (discounted) average $[\![\triangle_c r]\!]$ over the paths from s. As observed by [19] for the non-discounted case, the minimal discounted average is obtained on a path ρ' from s which, after some prefix ρ keeps repeating some simple cycle ℓ. Hence ℓ contains at most $|S|$ states. To find ρ', we use two steps. In the first phase, we find for each state s the simple cycle ℓ starting at s with the minimal discounted average. In the second phase, we find the best prefix-cycle combination $\rho\ell^\omega$.

Phase 1. We need to compute $L_\alpha(s) = \min\{[\![\triangle_c r]\!]^{\mathrm{P}}(\rho) \mid \rho \in \mathit{Traj}_s$ and $\rho = (s_0 s_1 s_2 \ldots s_{n-1})^\omega$ and $n \leq |S|\}$, where the value $[\![\triangle_c r]\!]^{\mathrm{P}}(\rho)$ is given by $\frac{1-\alpha}{1-\alpha^n} \cdot \sum_{i=0}^{n-1} \alpha^i \cdot q(s_i)$. Consider the recursion $v_0(s, s') = 0$ and $v_{n+1}(s, s') = q(s) + \alpha \cdot \min\{v_n(t, s') \mid t \in \delta(s)\}$. Then $v_n(s, s')$ minimizes $\sum_{i=0}^{n-1} \alpha^i \cdot q(s_i)$ over all finite paths $s_0 s_1 \ldots s_n$ with $s_0 = s$ and $s_n = s'$. Hence

$$L_\alpha(s) = (1 - \alpha) \cdot \min\left\{ \tfrac{v_1(s,s)}{1-\alpha^1}, \tfrac{v_2(s,s)}{1-\alpha^2}, \ldots, \tfrac{v_{|S|-1}(s,s)}{1-\alpha^{|S|-1}} \right\}.$$

For a fixed state s', computing $\min\{v_n(t, s') \mid t \in \delta(s)\}$ for all $s \in S$ can be done in $O(|\delta|)$ time. Therefore, v_{n+1} is obtained from v_n in $O(|S|^2 + |S| \cdot |\delta|) = O(|S| \cdot |\delta|)$ time. Hence, the computation of $v_{|S|}$ and L_α requires $O(|S|^2 \cdot |\delta|)$ time.

Phase 2. After a prefix of length n, the cost $L_\alpha(s)$ of repeating a cycle at state s has to be discounted by α^n, which is exactly the factor by which we discount $q(s)$ after taking that prefix. Hence, we modify the original LTS $\mathcal{S}$ into an LTS $\mathcal{S}^+$, as follows. For every state $s \in S$, we add a copy $\hat{s}$ whose weight $w^+(\hat{s})$ we set to $L_\alpha(s)$; the weights $w^+(s)$ of states $s \in S$ remain $q(s)$. Moreover, for every $t \in S$ and $s \in \delta(t)$, we add $\hat{s}$ as a successor to t, that is, $\delta^+(t) = \delta(t) \cup \{\hat{s} \mid s \in \delta(t)\}$ and $\delta^+(\hat{s}) = \{\hat{s}\}$. Taking the transition from t to $\hat{s}$ corresponds to moving to s and repeating the optimal cycle from there. We find the value of the optimal prefix-cycle combination starting from s as the *discounted distance* from s to $\hat{S} = \{\hat{s} \mid s \in S\}$ in the modified graph $\mathcal{S}^+$ with weights w^+. Formally, given an LTS $\mathcal{S}$, a state s, a weight function $w \colon S \to \mathbb{R}^{\geq 0}$, a discount factor α, and a target set T, the minimal discounted distance from s to T is $d(s) = \min\{\sum_{i=0}^{n-1} \alpha^i \cdot w(s_i) \mid s_0 s_1 \ldots s_{n-1} \in \mathit{FTraj}(s)$ and $s_{n-1} \in T\}$. The value of $d(s)$ for $s \in S$ is computed by the call $DiscountedDistance(\mathcal{S}^+, w^+, \alpha, \hat{S})$ to the algorithm below, which is a discounted version of the Bellman-Ford algorithm for finding shortest paths. Our algorithm performs backward computation from the set T, because discounted shortest paths (i.e., paths whose discounted distance is minimal among all paths with the same first and last state) are closed under suffixes, but not under prefixes.

```
function DiscountedDistance(S, w, α, T) :
    for each t ∈ S do
        if t ∈ T then d(t) := w(t) else d(t) := ∞;
    for i := 1 to |S| - 1 do
        for each s ∈ S and s' ∈ δ(s) do
            if d(s) > w(s) + α · d(s') then d(s) := w(s) + α · d(s');
    return d.
```

Like the standard version, discounted Bellman-Ford runs in $O(|S| \cdot |\delta|)$ time. Thus, the complexity of computing $[\![\forall \triangle_c r]\!]$ is dominated by the first phase.

Complexity of DCTL model checking over LTSs. The overall complexity of model checking a DCTL formula is polynomial in the size of the system and the size of the formula.

Theorem 3. *Given a DCTL formula ϕ, an LTS $\mathcal{S} = (S, \delta, P, [\cdot])$, and a parameter interpretation $\langle \cdot \rangle$, the problem of model checking ϕ over $\mathcal{S}$ with respect to $\langle \cdot \rangle$ can be solved in time $O(|S|^2 \cdot |\delta| \cdot |\phi|)$.*

3.2 Model Checking DCTL over Markov Chains

As stated by Theorem 1, the path and fixpoint semantics over Markov chains coincide for the formula $\exists \triangle_c r$. Hence, we present below one algorithm for model checking this formula over Markov chains in either semantics. By contrast, the path and the fixpoint semantics over Markov chains may differ for the formulas $\exists \lozenge_c r$ and $\forall \lozenge_c r$. Hence, we need to provide algorithms for both semantics. Because of the absence of nondeterministic choice in a Markov chain, $[\![\exists \lozenge_c r]\!]^* = [\![\forall \lozenge_c r]\!]^*$ for $* \in \{f, p\}$; so giving algorithms for $\exists \lozenge_c$ suffices. This section gives the algorithm for model checking $\exists \lozenge_c r$ over a Markov chain with respect to the path semantics; the model-checking algorithm for $\exists \lozenge_c r$ in the fixpoint semantics is a special case of the algorithm for MDPs presented in Section 3.3. It is an open problem whether model checking $\exists \lozenge_c r$ in the fixpoint semantics can be improved over Markov chains. In the following, we consider a fixed Markov chain $(S, \tau, \Sigma, [\cdot])$ and its probability transition matrix P. We write I for the identity matrix.

Model checking $\exists \lozenge$ in the path semantics. When evaluating $[\![\exists \lozenge_c r]\!]^P$ in a state s, we start with the initial estimate $q(s)$. If s is the state $s_{\max}$ with the maximum value of q, the initial estimate is the correct value. If s has the second largest value for q, the estimate can only be improved if $s_{\max}$ is hit within a certain number l of steps, namely, before the discount α^l becomes smaller than $\frac{q(s)}{q(s_{\max})}$. This argument is recursively applied to all states.

Let $s_1, \ldots, s_n$ be an ordering of the states in S such that $q(s_1) \geq q(s_2) \geq \cdots \geq q(s_n)$. We use integers as matrix indices, thus writing $P(i, j)$ for p_{s_i, s_j}. For all $1 \leq j < i \leq n$ such that $q(s_i) > 0$, let $k_{i,j} = \lfloor \log_\alpha \frac{q(s_i)}{q(s_j)} \rfloor$, with the convention that $\log_\alpha 0 = \infty$. Let $v(s_i) = [\![\exists \lozenge_\alpha r]\!]^P(s_i)$. Then, $v(s_1) = q(s_1)$, and we can express the value of $v(s_i)$ in terms of the values $v(s_1), \ldots, v(s_{i-1})$. Let $K = \max\{k_{i,j} \mid k_{i,j} < \infty\}$, and for all $l > 0$, let $B_l^i = \{s_j \mid 1 \leq j < i \text{ and } 1 \leq l \leq k_{i,j}\}$. Intuitively, B_l^i contains those states that, if hit in exactly l steps from s_i, can increase the value of $v(s_i)$. For the (arbitrary) state s_i, the following holds:

$$v(s_i) = q(s_i) \cdot stay^i + \sum_{j=1}^{i-1} v(s_j) \cdot \sum_{l=1}^{k_{i,j}} \alpha^l \cdot go_{j,l}^i,$$

where $stay^i = \Pr_{s_i} \left[\bigwedge_{l>0} Z_l \notin B_l^i \right]$ and $go_{j,l}^i = \Pr_{s_i} \left[Z_l = s_j \wedge \bigwedge_{m=1}^{l-1} Z_m \notin B_m^i \right]$. It is easy to check that $stay^i + \sum_{j=1}^{i-1} \sum_{l=1}^{k_{i,j}} go_{j,l}^i = 1$. We proceed in two phases.

The first phase handles states s_i with $q(s_i) > 0$. Since the sequence $(B_l^i)_{l>0}$ is decreasing, it can have at most $|S|$ different values. It follows that there exist $m \le |S|$ and $b_1^i \le \cdots \le b_{m+1}^i \in \mathbb{N}$ and sets $X_1^i, \ldots, X_m^i \subseteq S$ such that $b_1^i = 1$, $b_{m+1}^i = K + 1$, and for all $k = 1, \ldots, m$ and all $b_k^i \le l < b_{k+1}^i$, we have $B_l^i = X_k^i$. Let P_k^i be the substochastic matrix obtained from P by disabling all transitions leading to states in X_k^i, i.e., $P_k^i(j', j) = 0$ for all j', j with $s_j \in X_k^i$. Then, for given $b_k^i \le l < b_{k+1}^i$, we have

$$go_{j,l}^i = \left((P_1^i)^{b_2^i - b_1^i} \cdot (P_2^i)^{b_3^i - b_2^i} \cdot \ldots \cdot (P_{k-1}^i)^{b_k^i - b_{k-1}^i} \cdot (P_k^i)^{l - b_k^i} \cdot P \right)(i, j).$$

Let $m_j^i = \max\{k \mid s_j \in X_k^i\}$ be the index of the last X_k^i containing s_j. We have

$$\sum_{l=1}^{k_{i,j}} \alpha^l \cdot go_{j,l}^i = \sum_{k=1}^{m_j^i} \sum_{l=b_k^i}^{b_{k+1}^i - 1} \alpha^l \cdot go_{j,l}^i =$$

$$\left(\sum_{k=1}^{m_j^i} \alpha^{b_k^i} \cdot (P_1^i)^{b_2^i - b_1^i} \cdot (P_2^i)^{b_3^i - b_2^i} \cdot \ldots \cdot (P_{k-1}^i)^{b_k^i - b_{k-1}^i} \cdot \left(\sum_{l=0}^{b_{k+1}^i - b_k^i - 1} \alpha^l \cdot (P_k^i)^l \cdot P \right) \right)(i, j) =$$

$$\left(\sum_{k=1}^{m_j^i} \alpha^{b_k^i} \cdot (P_1^i)^{b_2^i - b_1^i} \cdot (P_2^i)^{b_3^i - b_2^i} \cdot \ldots \cdot (P_{k-1}^i)^{b_k^i - b_{k-1}^i} \cdot \left(\frac{I - (\alpha P_k^i)^{b_{k+1}^i - b_k^i}}{I - \alpha P_k^i} \right) \cdot P \right)(i, j).$$

Each matrix $(P_k^i)^{b_{k+1}^i - b_k^i}$ can be computed by repeated squaring in time $O(|S|^3 \cdot \log b_k^i)$. Some further calculations show that, for a fixed i, both $\sum_{l=1}^{k_{i,j}} \alpha^l \cdot go_{j,l}^i$ and $\sum_{l=1}^{k_{i,j}} go_{j,l}^i$ can be computed in time $O(|S|^4 \cdot \log K)$. The value $stay^i$ is given by $1 - \sum_{j,l} go_{j,l}^i$. The total complexity of this phase is thus $O(|S|^5 \cdot \log K)$.

The second phase considers those states s_i with $q(s_i) = 0$. Let u be the smallest index i such that $q(s_i) = 0$. Now, $go_{j,l}^i$ is the probability of hitting s_j after exactly l steps, meanwhile avoiding all states with indices smaller than u. To compute $v(s_i)$ efficiently, we define a stochastic matrix P_0 from P by adding an absorbing state s_{n+1} and using s_{n+1} to turn all states s_j with $j < u$ into transient states (so, for all $j < u$, $P_0(j, n+1) = 1$ and $P_0(j, j') = 0$ for $j' \ne n+1$). Also, we set $\bar{v}$ to be the column vector with $\bar{v}_j = v(s_j)$ (computed in phase 1), if $j < u$, and $\bar{v}_j = 0$ otherwise. Then,

$$v(s_i) = \sum_{j=1}^{u-1} v(s_j) \cdot \sum_{l=1}^{\infty} \alpha^l \cdot (P_0)^l (i, j) = ((I - \alpha P_0)^{-1} \cdot \bar{v})(i).$$

Solving the system (3.2) takes time $O(|S|^3)$ using LUP decomposition. The time spent in the two phases amounts to $O(|S|^5 \cdot \log K)$. An alternative algorithm, which we omit for space constraints, takes time $O(|S|^3 \cdot K)$ and may thus perform better in practical applications.

Model checking $\forall \triangle$ in both semantics. Since the two semantics of the formula $\forall \triangle_c r$ coincide, a single model-checking algorithm suffices for both semantics and can be computed by the following classical equation [9]. If we let

$[\![\exists\triangle_c r]\!]$ and q denote column vectors, we have $[\![\exists\triangle_c r]\!] = (1-\alpha)\cdot\sum_{i\geq 0}\alpha^i P^i q = (1-\alpha)\cdot(I-\alpha P)^{-1}\cdot q$. Thus, we can compute the value $[\![\exists\triangle_c r]\!](s)$ for each state $s\in S$ by solving a linear system with $|S|$ variables. This takes time $O(|S|^{\log_2 7})$ using Strassen's algorithm or $O(|S|^3)$ using LUP decomposition.

Complexity of DCTL model checking over Markov chains. The overall complexity is polynomial in the size of the system. With respect to the size of the formula, the complexity is polynomial for the fixpoint semantics, and exponential for the path semantics. The latter result is due to the fact that, in the path semantics, the number of arithmetic operations is polynomial in the size of the bit-wise encoding of the valuations, and these encodings grow exponentially with respect to the number of nestings of temporal operators.

Theorem 4. *Given a DCTL formula ϕ, a Markov chain $S = (S, \tau, P, [\cdot])$, and a parameter interpretation $\langle\cdot\rangle$, the problem of model checking ϕ over S with respect to $\langle\cdot\rangle$ can be solved in time polynomial in $|S|$, $\|[\cdot]\|_b$, and $|\langle\cdot\rangle|_b$. Furthermore, the problem of model checking ϕ over S with respect to $\langle\cdot\rangle$ can be solved in time polynomial in $|\phi|$ in the fixpoint semantics, and exponential in $|\phi|$ in the path semantics.*

3.3 Model Checking DCTL over Markov Decision Processes

As it is the case for Markov chains, also for MDPs the path and fixpoint semantics do not coincide for the formulas $\exists\diamond_c r$ and $\forall\diamond_c r$, so that separate algorithms are needed. The two semantics do coincide for the formula $\forall\triangle_c r$ on MDPs, hence one algorithm suffices. We consider a fixed MDP $S = (S, \tau, \Sigma, [\cdot])$.

Model checking $\exists\diamond$ and $\forall\diamond$ in the path semantics. If $\alpha = 0$, then trivially $[\![\exists\diamond_c r]\!]^P(s) = [\![\forall\diamond_c r]\!]^P(s) = q(s)$ at all $s\in S$, so in the following we assume $0 < \alpha < 1$. The problem of computing $[\![\exists\diamond_c r]\!]^P$ on an MDP can be viewed as an optimization problem, where the goal is to maximize the expected value of the sup of q over a path. As a preliminary step to solve the problem, we note that in general the optimal strategy is *history dependent*, that is, the choice of distribution at a state depends in general on the past sequence of states visited by the path.

Example 1. Consider the system depicted on the right and assume $\alpha = 1$. The optimal choice in state s_2 depends on whether t_1 was hit or not. If it was, the current sup is 0.8 and the best choice is a_1, because with probability $\frac{1}{2}$ the sup will increase to 1. If t_1 was not hit, the best choice is a_2, because it gives a certain gain of 0.8, rather than an expected gain of 0.5. The same argument holds if α is sufficiently close to 1.

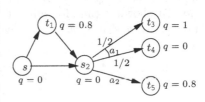

While the above example indicates that the optimal strategy is in general history-dependent, it also suggests that all a strategy needs to remember is the sup value that has occurred so far along the path. For $\pi \in \Pi$, $s \in S$, and $x \in \mathbb{R}$, we define $\mathrm{Esup}^\pi(s,x) = \mathrm{E}_s^\pi[x \sqcup \sup_{i>0} \alpha^i q(Z_i)]$; the term x corresponds to the (appropriately discounted) sup value that has occurred so far in the past of a path. Obviously, $[\![\exists\Diamond_c r]\!]^{\mathrm{P}}(s) = \sup_{\pi \in \Pi} \mathrm{Esup}^\pi(s,q(s))$ and $[\![\forall\Diamond_c r]\!]^{\mathrm{P}}(s) = \inf_{\pi \in \Pi} \mathrm{Esup}^\pi(s,q(s))$. The optimization problem to compute these quantities is phrased in terms of the variables $v(s,x)$, representing the value of $\mathrm{Esup}(s,x)$. Since we are ultimately interested in the value of $\mathrm{Esup}(s,q(s))$ for $s \in S$, and since if $x \geq 1$ we have $\mathrm{Esup}^{\pi'}(t,x) = x$ for all $t \in S$ and $\pi' \in \Pi$, it suffices to consider values for x that belong to the finite set $X = \{q(s)/\alpha^k \mid s \in S \wedge k \in \mathbb{N} \wedge q(s)/\alpha^k < 1\}$. We set up the following set of equations in the variables $\{v(s,x) \mid s \in S \wedge x \in X\}$:

$$
v(s,x) = \begin{cases} x & \text{if } x \geq \alpha \\ x \sqcup \alpha \cdot \max\limits_{a \in \tau(s)} \sum\limits_{t \in S} v(t, \frac{x}{\alpha} \sqcup q(t)) \cdot a(t) & \text{otherwise} \end{cases} \tag{1}
$$

Intuitively, the equations (1) can be understood as follows. At a state $s = s_m$ of a path $s_0 s_1 \ldots$, the quantity $v(s_m, x)$ represents the maximum over all strategies of $\sup_{i>0} \mathrm{E}_{s_m}[\alpha^i q(Z_i)]$ given that $\sup_{0 \leq i \leq m} \alpha^{-i} q(s_{m-i}) = x$. The recursion (1) then relates $v(s,x)$ to $v(t,y)$ at the successors t of s, where at t we consider the new conditioning $y = x/\alpha \sqcup q(t)$, thus discounting x by α^{-1} (as s is one step before t), and taking into account the value $q(t)$ seen at t. The following lemma relates the least fixpoint of (1) to $[\![\exists\Diamond_c r]\!]^{\mathrm{P}}$.

Lemma 1. *Let $\{v^*(s,x) \mid s \in S \wedge x \in X\}$ be the least (pointwise) fixpoint of the set of equations (1). Then, we have $[\![\exists\Diamond_c r]\!]^{\mathrm{P}}(s) = v^*(s,q(s))$ for all $s \in S$.*

Proof. Let $X' = \{q(s)/\alpha^k \mid s \in S \wedge k \in \mathbb{N}\}$ be the set that, compared to X, also includes elements greater than 1. We consider an iterative evaluation of the least fixpoint (1), given for all $s \in S$, $x \in X'$, and $k \geq 0$, by $v_0(s,x) = x$ and

$$
v_{n+1}(s,x) = \alpha \cdot \max_{a \in \tau(s)} \sum_{t \in S} v_n(t, \frac{x}{\alpha} \sqcup q(t)) \cdot a(t). \tag{2}
$$

The proof consists of two parts: (i) showing that for all $s \in S$ and $x \in X'$, there is a strategy $\pi^* \in \Pi$ such that $\mathrm{E}_s^{\pi^*}[x \sqcup \sup_{0<i\leq n} \alpha^i \cdot q(Z_i)] = v_n(s,x)$, and (ii) showing that for all $\pi \in \Pi$, $s \in S$, and $x \in X'$, we have $\mathrm{E}_s^\pi[x \sqcup \sup_{0<i\leq n} \alpha^i \cdot q(Z_i)] \leq v_n(s,x)$. Once (i) and (ii) are proved, the result follows from

$$
\lim_{n\to\infty} v_n = v^*, \qquad \lim_{n\to\infty} \mathrm{E}_s^\pi[x \sqcup \sup_{0\leq i \leq n} \alpha^i \cdot q(Z_i)] = \mathrm{E}_s^\pi[x \sqcup \sup_{i\geq 0} \alpha^i \cdot q(Z_i)].
$$

We prove only (i), since the proof of (ii) is similar. The strategy π^* is in general a function of $\langle s,x \rangle \in S \times X'$. We define it inductively: π_0^* is arbitrary; for $n \geq 0$, π_{n+1}^* first chooses a distribution $a \in \tau(s)$ that realizes the maximum in (2), and then upon a transition from s to some $t \in S$, proceeds as π_n^* from $\langle t, \frac{x}{\alpha} \sqcup q(t) \rangle$. Part (i) follows by induction, noting that for all $n \geq 0$, all $s \in S$ and all $x \in X'$

we have:

$$v_{n+1}(s,x) = \alpha \cdot \max_{a \in \tau(s)} \sum_{t \in S} v_n(t, \frac{x}{\alpha} \sqcup q(t)) \cdot a(t)$$

$$= \alpha \cdot \max_{a \in \tau(s)} \sum_{t \in S} E_t^{\pi_n^*} \left[\frac{x}{\alpha} \sqcup q(t) \sqcup \sup_{0 < i \leq n} \alpha^i \cdot q(Z_i) \right] \cdot a(t) = E_s^{\pi_{n+1}^*} \left[x \sqcup \sup_{0 < i \leq n} \alpha^i \cdot q(Z_i) \right] \blacksquare$$

To compute $[\![\forall \Diamond_c r]\!]^{\mathrm{P}}$, we simply replace $\max_{a \in \tau(s)}$ with $\min_{a \in \tau(s)}$ in (1), and again consider the least fixpoint. The least fixpoints for $[\![\exists \Diamond_c r]\!]^{\mathrm{P}}$ and $[\![\forall \Diamond_c r]\!]^{\mathrm{P}}$ can be computed by linear programming, following a standard approach. For example, to compute $[\![\exists \Diamond_c r]\!]^{\mathrm{P}}$ we consider the following linear-programming problem in the set $\{v(s,x) \mid s \in S \wedge x \in X\}$ of variables: minimize $\sum_{s \in S} \sum_{x \in X} v(s,x)$ subject to

$$v(s,x) \geq x, \qquad v(s,x) \geq \alpha \cdot \sum_{t \in S} \tilde{v}(t, \frac{x}{\alpha} \sqcup q(t)) \cdot a(t)$$

for all $s \in S$, all $x \in X$, and all $a \in \tau(s)$, where $\tilde{v}(t,x)$ is 1 if $x \geq 1$, and is $v(t,x)$ otherwise. Denoting by $\{\hat{v}(s,x) \mid s \in S \wedge x \in X\}$ an optimal solution, we have $\hat{v}(s,q(s)) = v^*(s,q(s)) = [\![\exists \Diamond_c r]\!]^{\mathrm{P}}(s)$. This linear program contains at most $2 \cdot |S| \cdot |X|$ variables. We have $|X| = -|S| \cdot \log_\alpha q_{min}$, where $q_{min} = \min\{q(s) \mid s \in S \wedge q(s) > 0\}$. Hence, if q-values are encoded in binary notation, the number of variables in the encoding is linear in the size of the input encoding of the MDP.

Model checking $\exists \Diamond$ and $\forall \Diamond$ in the fixpoint semantics. The computation of $[\![\exists \Diamond_c r]\!]^{\mathrm{f}}$ and $[\![\forall \Diamond_c r]\!]^{\mathrm{f}}$ on an MDP can be performed by transforming the fixpoints into linear-programming problems, following a standard approach. For example, for $[\![\forall \Diamond_c r]\!]^{\mathrm{f}}$ we consider the following linear programming problem in the set $\{v(s), u(s) \mid s \in S\}$ of variables: minimize $\sum_{s \in S} (v(s) - u(s))$ subject to $v(s) \geq q(s)$, $v(s) \geq u(s)$, and $u(s) \leq \alpha \cdot \sum_{t \in S} v(t) \cdot a(t)$, for all $s \in S$ and $a \in \tau(s)$. Denoting by $\{v^*(s), u^*(s) \in \mathbb{R} \mid s \in S\}$ an optimal solution, we have $[\![\forall \Diamond_c r]\!]^{\mathrm{f}}(s) = v^*(s)$ at all $s \in S$. Again, this can be solved in time polynomial in $|\mathcal{S}|_b$ and $|\alpha|_b$.

Model checking $\forall \triangle$ in both semantics. With the two semantics for $\forall \triangle_c r$ coinciding, a single algorithm suffices for model checking $\forall \triangle$ in both semantics. The fixpoint semantics of this formula immediately suggests an algorithm based on standard methods used for discounted long-run average problems [2].

Lemma 2. *Consider the following linear-programming problem in the set $\{v(s) \mid s \in S\}$ of variables: maximize $\sum_{s \in S} v(s)$ subject to $v(s) \leq (1-\alpha) \cdot q(s) + \alpha \cdot \sum_{t \in S} v(t) \cdot a(t)$, for all $s \in S$ and $a \in \tau(s)$. Denoting by $\{v^*(s) \mid s \in S\}$ an optimal solution, we have $[\![\forall \triangle_c r]\!](s) = v^*(s)$ for all states $s \in S$.*

Complexity of DCTL model checking over MDPs. As for Markov chains, also for MDPs the model checking problem can be solved in time polynomial in the size of the system, and in the fixpoint (resp. path) semantics, in time polynomial (resp. exponential) in the size of the DCTL formula.

Theorem 5. *Given a* DCTL *formula* ϕ, *an MDP* $\mathcal{S} = (S, \tau, P, [\cdot])$, *and a parameter interpretation* $\langle \cdot \rangle$, *the problem of model checking* ϕ *over* $\mathcal{S}$ *with respect to* $\langle \cdot \rangle$ *can be solved in time polynomial in* $|S|$, $|[\cdot]|_b$, *and* $|\langle \cdot \rangle|_b$. *Furthermore, the problem of model checking* ϕ *over* $\mathcal{S}$ *with respect to* $\langle \cdot \rangle$ *can be solved in time polynomial in* $|\phi|$ *in the fixpoint semantics, and exponential in* $|\phi|$ *in the path semantics.*

References

1. C. Baier, B.R. Haverkort, H. Hermanns, and J.-P. Katoen. Model checking continuous-time Markov chains by transient analysis. In *Computer-Aided Verification*, LNCS 1855, pages 358–372. Springer, 2000.
2. D.P. Bertsekas. *Dynamic Programming and Optimal Control*. Athena Scientific, 1995. Volumes I and II.
3. A. Bianco and L. de Alfaro. Model checking of probabilistic and nondeterministic systems. In *Foundations of Software Technology and Theoretical Computer Science*, LNCS 1026, pages 499–513. Springer, 1995.
4. E.M. Clarke, O. Grumberg, and D. Peled. *Model Checking*. MIT Press, 1999.
5. L. de Alfaro. *Formal Verification of Probabilistic Systems*. PhD thesis. Technical Report STAN-CS-TR-98-1601, Stanford University, 1997.
6. L. de Alfaro, M. Faella, T.A. Henzinger, R. Majumdar, and M. Stoelinga. Model checking discounted temporal properties. Technical Report UCSC-CRL-03-12, University of California, Santa Cruz, 2003.
7. L. de Alfaro, T.A. Henzinger, and R. Majumdar. Discounting the future in systems theory. In *Automata, Languages, and Programming*, LNCS 2719, pages 1022–1037. Springer, 2003.
8. J. Desharnais, A. Edalat, and P. Panangaden. Bisimulation for labeled Markov processes. *Information and Computation*, 179:163–193, 2002.
9. J. Filar and K. Vrieze. *Competitive Markov Decision Processes*. Springer, 1997.
10. H. Hansson. *Time and Probabilities in Formal Design of Distributed Systems*. Elsevier, 1994.
11. M. Huth and M.Z. Kwiatkowska. Quantitative analysis and model checking. In *Proc. Logic in Computer Science*, pages 111–122. IEEE, 1997.
12. J.G. Kemeny, J.L. Snell, and A.W. Knapp. *Denumerable Markov Chains*. Van Nostrand, 1966.
13. D. Kozen. A probabilistic PDL. In *Proc. Theory of Computing*, pages 291–297. ACM, 1983.
14. M.Z. Kwiatkowska. Model checking for probability and time: From theory to practice. In *Proc. Logic in Computer Science*, pages 351–360. IEEE, 2003.
15. Z. Manna and A. Pnueli. *The Temporal Logic of Reactive and Concurrent Systems: Specification*. Springer, 1991.
16. A. McIver. Reasoning about efficiency within a probabilistic μ-calculus. In *Proc. Probabilistic Methods in Verification*, pages 45–58. Technical Report CSR-98-4, University of Birmingham, 1998.
17. A. McIver and C. Morgan. Games, probability, and the quantitative μ-calculus. In *Logic Programming, Artificial Intelligence, and Reasoning*, LNCS 2514, pages 292–310. Springer, 2002.
18. D. Williams. *Probability with Martingales*. Cambridge University Press, 1991.
19. U. Zwick and M.S. Paterson. The complexity of mean-payoff games on graphs. *Theoretical Computer Science*, 158:343–359, 1996.

Automatic Creation of Environment Models via Training

Thomas Ball[1], Vladimir Levin[1], and Fei Xie[2]

[1] Microsoft Corporation, One Microsoft Way, Redmond, WA 98052, USA
{tball,vladlev}@microsoft.com Fax: +1 (425) 936-7329
[2] Dept. of Computer Sciences, Univ. of Texas at Austin, Austin, TX 78712, USA
feixie@cs.utexas.edu Fax: +1 (512) 471-8885

Abstract. Model checking suffers not only from the state-space explosion problem, but also from the *environment modeling* problem: how can one create an accurate enough model of the environment to enable precise yet efficient model checking? We present a novel approach to the automatic creation of environment models via *training*. The idea of training is to take several programs that use a common API and apply model checking to create abstractions of the API procedures. These abstractions then are reused on subsequent verification runs to model-check different programs (which utilize the same API). This approach has been realized in SLAM, a software model checker for C programs, and applied to the domain of Windows device drivers that utilize the Windows Driver Model API (a set of entry points into the Windows kernel). We show how the boolean abstractions of the kernel routines accessed from a device driver are extracted and merged into a boolean library that can be reused by subsequent model checking runs on new drivers. We show that the merged abstraction is a conservative extension of the boolean abstractions created by training.

1 Introduction

Recently there has been significant progress in model checking [9,21] of software programs. The technique of predicate abstraction [12] has been successfully applied to automatically create boolean program abstractions of software. In the SLAM project [7], software model checking has been applied to the domain of Windows device drivers to check that these programs are good clients of the Windows Driver Model (WDM) application programming interface (API), a direct interface to hundreds of procedures in the Windows kernel. The SLAM engine, packaged with temporal safety properties that define correct usage of the WDM API, comprises a tool called Static Driver Verifier (SDV).

As with all model checking projects, a central question that we have had to address is where a good environment model comes from. In our case, the Windows kernel is the source code we seek to model. Needless to say, this is a non-trivial piece of code, whose complexity and size are much greater than those of the device drivers that use it. We have found that highly demonic and non-deterministic over-simplified models of the driver environment often lead to SDV reporting too many false errors. To date, we have constructed models of the kernel manually and on an "as-needed" basis. These models capture the behaviors of the API that are necessary for the set of properties SDV

K. Jensen and A. Podelski (Eds.): TACAS 2004, LNCS 2988, pp. 93–107, 2004.

checks. This approach eliminates most of the false bugs while enabling model checking of reasonably large programs. However, this approach suffers from the following problems:

- Windows kernel procedures can be very complex. Manual creation of models for these procedures is a time-consuming and error-prone process.
- The Windows API evolves, which makes the maintenance of manually created environment models very difficult.
- The number of properties that SDV checks always is growing, requiring refinement of the kernel models.

Therefore, scalable software model checking requires automating the creation of environment models corresponding to the API as much as possible.

Our solution to these problems is to create environment models via *training*. That is, we leverage predicate abstraction across a large set of example drivers to automatically create models of kernel procedures. While this process can be expensive, it is only done occasionally (by the maintainers of the SDV tool).

Let us describe how training works on a single kernel procedure k (the process generalizes straightforwardly to a set of procedures). A set of drivers $\{d_1, \cdots, d_n\}$ that utilizes k is selected as the training set. SDV is run on each driver linked together with the kernel procedure k. This results in n boolean abstractions of k, which are then extracted and merged together to create a refined abstraction of the procedure, b_k. In future runs of SDV, the boolean abstraction b_k is used in the place of the kernel procedure k. That is, the boolean abstractions of a set of procedures that result from training are packaged as a boolean library which is reused in place of these C procedures in model checking on other drivers.

We have implemented this idea in the context of the SLAM project [7], in which predicate abstraction is applied to model checking of C programs, and methods for creating, extracting, merging and reusing boolean libraries are provided as extensions to the SLAM toolkit. This approach has been applied in the SDV project to automate environment modeling.

While our approach was developed in the context of the SLAM and SDV projects, we believe that the basic idea is generally applicable to programs written in other program languages and to other analysis techniques. Our approach has four basic requirements:

- **Model Creation.** An automatic method for creating abstract models of software, such as predicate abstraction, is required.
- **Model Extraction.** It must be possible to extract models at some well-defined boundary in the program, such as procedures. This means that the model checking process should preserve certain structural elements of the source program (procedures) or provide a way to extract them.
- **Model Merging.** Given a number of models for a procedure, it must be possible to conservatively merge them into a single model.
- **Model Reuse.** Given a model for a procedure, there must be a way to incorporate the model into a subsequent model checking run.

The remainder of this paper is organized as follows. Section 2 presents background on the SLAM abstraction process that creates boolean program abstractions of C programs.

Section 3 introduces the concept of boolean libraries and the algorithm for merging boolean libraries. Section 4 discusses the formal properties of our merge algorithm. Section 5 reports our experiences on applying our technique to Windows device drivers. Section 6 discusses related work. Section 7 presents future work and concludes.

2 Background

This section first gives a brief overview of the SLAM abstraction and refinement process, then introduces the basic concept of boolean programs, and finally reviews how SLAM performs predicate abstraction of C code. Detailed discussions about these topics can be found in [7,5,3,4,6].

2.1 SLAM Abstraction and Refinement Process

Given a safety property to check on a C program, the SLAM process has the following three phases: (1) abstraction, (2) model checking, and (3) refinement (predicate discovery). Three tools have been developed to support each of these phases:

- C2BP, a tool that transforms a C program P into a boolean program $\mathcal{BP}(P, E)$ with respect to a set of predicates E over the state space of P [3];
- BEBOP, a tool for model checking boolean programs [5];
- NEWTON, a tool that discovers additional predicates to refine the boolean program, by analyzing the feasibility of paths in the C program [6].

The SLAM toolkit provides a fully automatic way of checking temporal safety properties of C programs. Violations are reported by the SLAM toolkit as paths over the program P. It never reports spurious error paths. Instead, it detects spurious error paths and uses them to automatically refine the abstraction (to eliminate these paths from consideration).

2.2 Boolean Programs

Given a C program P and a set E of predicates (pure C boolean expressions containing no procedure calls), C2BP automatically creates a boolean program $\mathcal{BP}(P, E)$, which is an abstraction of P. A boolean program is essentially a C program in which the only type available is boolean. The boolean program contains $|E|$ boolean variables, each representing a predicate in E. For example, if the predicate $(x < y)$ is in E, where x and y are integer variables in P, then there is a boolean variable in $\mathcal{BP}(P, E)$ whose truth at a program point p implies that $(x < y)$ is true at p in P. For each statement s of P, C2BP automatically constructs a boolean transfer function that conservatively represents the effect of s on the predicates in E.

The syntax of boolean programs is given in Figure 1. In boolean programs, control-flow constructs such as *if-then-else* conditionals and *while* loops are represented using the non-deterministic *goto* statement and *assume* statements. For example, the statement "if (P) A else B" in a C program can be represented by:

```
goto L1, L2;
L1: assume(P); A; goto L3;
L2: assume(!P); B;
L3: skip;
```

Expressions:	e	$::=$	$T \mid F \mid x \mid !e \mid e_1\ op\ e_2 \mid choose(e, f)$
Binary operators:	op	$::=$	$\&\& \mid \|\|$
Declaration:	d	$::=$	**bool** $x_1, \cdots, x_n;$
Statements:	s	$::=$	**goto** $L_1, \cdots, L_n$
		$\mid$	$L: s$
		$\mid$	**assume**(e)
		$\mid$	**assert**(e)
		$\mid$	**return** $x_1, \cdots, x_n$
		$\mid$	$x_1, \cdots x_n := e_1, \cdots, e_n$
		$\mid$	$x_1, \cdots, x_m := f(e_1, \cdots, e_n)$
Statement sequence: $\bar{s}$		$::=$	$s_1; \cdots; s_n;$
Procedure:	p	$::=$	**bool** $id\ (f_1, \cdots, f_n)$
			begin $d\ \bar{s}$ **end**
Program:	g	$::=$	$d\ p_1 \cdots p_n$

Fig. 1. Syntax of boolean programs.

in a boolean program. The *assume* statement silently terminates execution if its expression evaluates to false, and is the dual of the *assert* statement [10]. The *assert* statement formulates a safety property. The property is violated if there exists a path in which the asserted expression evaluates to false when the *assert* statement becomes executable.

In boolean programs, variable names can be specified as an arbitrary string within curly braces, which allows us to name the boolean variable corresponding to a predicate p by "{p}". In addition to the usual boolean connectives, boolean expressions in boolean programs have a built-in function called *choose*. The semantics of the *choose(p,n)* is as follows. If p is true, then *choose* returns true. Otherwise, if n is true, then *choose* returns false. If neither p nor n is true, then *choose* non-deterministically returns true or false.

2.3   Predicate Abstraction of C Code

The SLAM abstraction algorithm handles arbitrary C programs. For each C procedure in program P, its abstraction in $\mathcal{BP}(P, E)$ is a boolean procedure. A key feature of this algorithm is modularity: each C procedure can be abstracted by C2BP given only the *signatures* of procedures that it calls. The signature of a procedure can be determined in isolation from the rest of the program given the set of predicates that are local to the procedure. C2BP operates in two passes. In the first pass, it determines the signature of each procedure. In the second pass, it uses these signatures to abstract procedure calls (along with other statements). These aspects of SLAM enable us to create, extract and reuse the boolean program models of procedures (we will deal with merging later).

We explain SLAM's modular abstraction process through an example. Figure 2(a) and (b) show two C procedures. The procedure *inc_dec* returns the increment/decrement of its first argument (x) depending on the value of its second argument (op). The procedure *main* calls *inc_dec* to increment the value of i from 1 to 2. Figure 2(c) and (d) show the boolean procedures constructed by SLAM in order to prove that the *assert* statement always succeeds. SLAM generates five predicates to prove this: in *main*, the

int inc_dec (int x, int op) {
 int t;
 	
 if (op == 0)
    t = x+1;
 else
    t = x-1;
 	
 return t;
 }
	bool inc_dec ({x==X},{op==0}) begin
	 bool {t==X+1};
	 goto L1, L2;
	
	 L1: assume({op==0});
	 {t==X+1} := choose({x==X},F); goto L3;
	
	 L2: assume(!{op==0});
	 {t==X+1} := choose(F,{x==X});
	
	 L3: return {t==X+1};
	 end

(a)	(c)

main () {
 int i = 1;
 i = inc_dec(i, 0);
 assert(i == 2);
 }
	main () begin
	 bool {i==1}, {i==2}, ret;
	 {i==1} := T;
	 ret := inc_dec(T,T);
	 {i==1},{i==2} := {i==1}&&!ret, {i==1}&&ret;
	 assert({i==2});
	 end

(b)	(d)

Fig. 2. Example C program, (a) and (b), and boolean program produced by SLAM to prove assertion, (c) and (d).

predicates i==1 and i==2; in *inc_dec*, the predicates x==X, t==X+1, and op==0, where X is a *symbolic constant* representing the value of variable x at the entry point of *inc_dec*.

Abstraction of assignments and assumes. The abstraction of assignments and *assumes* in this example is simple. Consider the assignment statement t=x+1 in the procedure *inc_dec*. If the predicate x==X is true before the execution of this statement then the predicate t==X+1 is true after. This is captured in the boolean program by the corresponding assignment statement

    {t==X+1} := choose({x==X},F);

On the other hand, the assignment statement t=x-1 translates to the boolean program statement

    {t==X+1} := choose(F,{x==X});

because it can only make the predicate t==X+1 false (when x==X is true before).

    The *assume* statements in the boolean program reflect the abstraction of the *if* conditional precisely because of the presence of the predicate op==0.

Procedure signatures. Let Q be a procedure in P, Q' be the abstraction of Q in $\mathcal{BP}(P, E)$, and E_Q be the set of predicates in E that are local to Q. The signature of procedure Q is a four-tuple (I_Q, F_Q, R_Q, M_Q), where

- I_Q is the list of formal parameters of Q.
- F_Q is the set of formal parameter predicates of Q', defined as the set of those predicates in E_Q that refer to a formal parameter of Q but do not refer to any local variable of Q.
- R_Q is the set of return predicates of Q'. They provide information to callers about the effect of Q. R_Q contains those predicates in E_Q that mention return variables of Q as well as those predicates in F_Q that reference a global variable or dereference a formal parameter of Q.
- M_Q is the modification set of procedure Q, a conservative approximation of the set of locations that Q could potentially modify.

In our example, the signature of the procedure *inc_dec* as Q is

- $I_Q = [x, op]$.
- $F_Q = \{$ x==X, op==0 $\}$. These predicates become the formal parameters of the boolean procedure corresponding to *inc_dec*.
- $R_Q = \{$ t==X+1 $\}$. This predicate becomes the return value of the boolean procedure.
- $M_Q = \{$ t $\}$.

The predicates x==X and t==X+1 deserve special mention as they contain the symbolic constant (an artificial variable) X, which represents the initial value of variable x upon entry to the procedure *inc_dec*. These predicates are said to be *polymorphic* because they do not refer to a particular value of x like 1, 4 or 12. As a result, the predicates are reusable in many different contexts.

Abstraction of procedure calls. Consider a call $y = Q(a_1 \ldots a_n)$ to procedure Q at label ℓ in a procedure R (in program P). The abstraction $\mathcal{BP}(P, E)$ contains a call to the boolean procedure Q' at label ℓ in the boolean procedure R'. Let the signature of Q be (I_Q, F_Q, R_Q, M_Q). For each formal parameter predicate $e \in F_Q$, C2BP computes a boolean expression over (boolean) variables in R' that yields the actual value of the predicate to be passed into the call.

In our example, the formal parameter predicates are x==X and op==0. The call to the procedure *inc_dec* in main is inc_dec(i,0);. Its abstraction in the boolean program is inc_dec(T,T); because the predicate x==X always is initially true (regardless of the value passed in for x at the call-site) and because the call assigns the value 0 to the formal parameter *op*, which makes the predicate op==0 true.

The return values from a call to Q' are handled as follows. Assume $R_Q = \{e_1 \ldots e_k\}$. C2BP creates k fresh local boolean variables $T = \{t_1 \ldots t_k\}$ in R' and assigns to them, in parallel, the return values of Q'. The final step is to update each local predicate of R whose value may have changed as a result of the call. Any predicate in E_R (the set of local predicates of R) that mentions variable y must be updated. In addition, we must update any predicate in E_R that could potentially be updated by Q. The modification set M_Q provides sufficient information to determine a conservative over-approximation of the set of predicates to update.

In our example, the return variable *ret* in the procedure *main* in the boolean program represents the predicate i==X+1. If the predicate i==1 is true before the call then X, the initial value of x in *inc_dec*, is equal to 1, so if i==X+1 is true on return then i==2 is true on return as well. This is captured by the assignment

Signature = ($\quad I_Q$ = [x, op], $\quad F_Q$ = { x==X, op==0 }, $\quad R_Q$ = { t==X+1 }, $\quad M_Q$ = { t })	Signature = ($\quad I_Q$ = [x, op], $\quad F_Q$ = { x==X, op==0 }, $\quad R_Q$ = { t==X-1 }, $\quad M_Q$ = { t })
bool inc_dec ({x==X},{op==0}) begin bool {t==X+1}; goto L1, L2; L1: assume({op==0}); {t==X+1} := choose({x==X},F); goto L3; L2: assume(!{op==0}); {t==X+1} := choose(F,{x==X}); L3: return {t==X+1}; end	bool inc_dec ({x==X},{op==0}) begin bool {t==X-1}; goto L1, L2; L1: assume({op==0}); {t==X-1} := choose(F,{x==X}); goto L3; L2: assume(!{op==0}); {t==X-1} := choose({x==X},F); L3: return {t==X-1}; end
(a)	(b)

Fig. 3. Two different boolean libraries of *inc_dec*

```
{i==2} := {i==1}&&ret;
```

in the boolean program (part of the parallel assignment to predicates i==1 and i==2).

3   Boolean Libraries

This section defines the structure of boolean libraries and shows how to merge two boolean libraries (of the same set of C procedures) into one.

3.1   Boolean Libraries

For a set of C procedures, a corresponding boolean library consists of two parts: the header and the body. The header contains a signature of each C procedure in the form specified in Section 2. The body contains the boolean procedures abstracted from these C procedures.

Using the procedure *inc_dec* in Figure 2(b) as an example, two different boolean libraries are shown in Figure 3. The first would be generated by running SLAM on the C program comprised of the procedure *inc_dec* and the procedure *main* in Figure 4(a). The second would be generated by running SLAM on the C program comprised of the procedure *inc_dec* and the procedure *main* in Figure 4(b).

The boolean library shown in Figure 3(a) or (b) can then be used in place of *inc_dec* when model checking a program that utilizes *inc_dec*. The SLAM abstraction process uses the signature of *inc_dec* provided in the boolean library to abstract C procedures that call *inc_dec*. SLAM directly incorporates the abstraction of *inc_dec* provided in the boolean library into the abstraction of the program.

main () {	main () {	main () {
int i = 1;	int i = 1;	int i = 1;
i = inc_dec(i, 0);	i = inc_dec(i, 1);	i = inc_dec(i, 0);
assert(i == 2);	assert(i == 0);	i = inc_dec(i, 1);
}	}	assert(i == 1);
		}
(a)	(b)	(c)

Fig. 4. Three different usages of the *inc_dec* procedure.

3.2   Merge of Boolean Libraries

For a set of C procedures, different boolean libraries may be constructed by using different sets of predicates in the abstraction process. A boolean library that contains better abstractions of these C procedures can be constructed by merging these boolean libraries. Merging boolean libraries involves construction of a new signature and a new boolean abstraction for each C procedure by merging the signatures and boolean abstractions of the procedure from these boolean libraries.

In this section, we discuss the algorithms for merging two signatures, *sig'* and *sig''*, and their corresponding boolean abstractions, Q' and Q'', of a single C procedure, Q. The algorithms can be readily generalized to the merge of an arbitrary number of boolean libraries of a C procedure or an arbitrary number of C procedures.

We will demonstrate the merge algorithms by merging the signatures and the boolean abstractions of *inc_dec* in Figure 3(a) Figure 3(b). Figure 5 shows the result of the merge.

Merge of signatures. Given the two signatures of Q, $sig' = (I_Q', F_Q', R_Q', M_Q')$ and $sig'' = (I_Q'', F_Q'', R_Q'', M_Q'')$, a new signature, $sig''' = (I_Q''', F_Q''', R_Q''', M_Q''')$, can be constructed by merging sig' and sig'' as follows:

- $I_Q''' = I_Q' = I_Q''$;
- $F_Q''' = F_Q' \cup F_Q''$;
- $R_Q''' = R_Q' \cup R_Q''$;
- $M_Q''' = M_Q' = M_Q''$.

The merge of the two signatures in Figure 3(a) and Figure 3(b) is shown in Figure 5. The basic change is that the new signature for the procedure *inc_dec* now has two return predicates (Figure 3(a) contributes the predicate t==X+1 and Figure 3(b) contributes the predicate t==X-1).

Merge of boolean procedures. A boolean procedure has a control flow structure formed by *goto* statements, *assume* statements, assignments, and procedure calls. Two boolean procedures, Q' and Q'', abstracted from Q are guaranteed to have the same control flow structure. What differentiates Q' and Q'' are the conditionals in the *assume* statements, and the variables and the expressions in the assignments and procedure calls.

Therefore, the control flow structure of the new boolean abstraction Q''' from merging Q' and Q'' is constructed by copying the control structure of either Q' or Q''. The main challenge is how to merge the expressions and variables of the corresponding *assume*, *assert*, assignment and procedure call statements in Q' and Q''.

```
Signature = (
    I_Q = [ x, op ],
    F_Q = { x==X, op==0 },
    R_Q = { t==X+1, t==X-1 },
    M_Q = { t }
)

bool inc_dec ({x==X},{op==0}) begin
    bool {t==X+1}, {t==X-1};
    goto L1, L2;

L1: assume({op==0});
    {t==X+1},{t==X-1} := choose({x==X},F), choose(F,{x==X}); goto L3;

L2: assume(!{op==0});
    {t==X-1},{t==X+1} := choose({x==X},F), choose(F,{x==X});

L3: return {t==X-1}, {t==X+1};
end
```

Fig. 5. The merged boolean library of *inc_dec*.

Merge of assignment statements. Consider an assignment statement $x=e$; at label ℓ in Q. Q' and Q'' will contain at label ℓ a parallel assignment to the boolean variables in scope at ℓ. The parallel assignment is of the following form:

$$b_1, \ldots, b_n := choose(pos_1, neg_1), \ldots, choose(pos_n, neg_n)$$

Suppose the following two parallel assignments appear at label ℓ in Q' and Q'':

$$\{p_1\}', \ldots, \{p_m\}' := choose(pos_1', neg_1'), \ldots, choose(pos_m', neg_m')$$
$$\{q_1\}'', \ldots, \{q_n\}'' := choose(pos_1'', neg_1''), \ldots, choose(pos_n'', neg_n'')$$

If for $\{p_i\}'$ there is no q_j such that $p_i = q_j$ then the assignment to $\{p_i\}$ is simply copied over from Q' to Q'''. (Symmetrically, if for $\{q_i\}''$ there is no p_j such that $q_i = p_j$ then the assignment to $\{q_i\}$ is simply copied over from Q'' to Q'''). On the other hand, if there is a q_j such that $p_i = q_j$ then $\{p_i\}'''$ is assigned in Q''' as follows:

$$\{p_i\}''' := choose(pos_i'\|pos_j'', neg_i'\|neg_j'')$$

since if either pos_i' or pos_j'' holds, $\{p_i\}$ is **true** after ℓ and if either neg_i' or neg_j'' holds, $\{p_i\}$ is **false** after ℓ. (The SLAM abstraction algorithm guarantees that pos_i' and pos_j'' do not conflict and that neg_i' and neg_j'' do not conflict.)

The boolean procedure merged from the two boolean procedures in Figure 3 is shown in Figure 5 and demonstrates how the corresponding statements are merged. The basic change is that the merged boolean procedure now updates both the predicates $t==X+1$ and $t==X-1$, based on how the predicates were updated in each input boolean procedure.

Merge of assume and assert statements. The *assume* statement is the control-flow gate statement of boolean programs. If the expression in the *assume* evaluates to true then execution proceeds past the statement. However, if the expression evaluates to false then execution (silently) halts. C2BP abstracts the *assume* statement in a sound fashion: if an *assume* in the boolean program evaluates to false then the corresponding conditional in the C program will evaluate to false.

Corresponding *assume* statements in Q' and Q'' with expressions e' and e'' are merged into the *assume* statement *assume($e'\&\&e''$)* in Q'''. That is, control in Q''' can only proceed past the *assume* if control in both Q' and Q'' can proceed past the *assume*. Conjunction of e' and e'' provides the most precise boolean abstraction of the C program possible from the merge (disjunction is sound but not as precise as conjunction).

The *assert* statement is the dual of the *assume*. The C2BP tool guarantees that if an *assert* passes in the boolean program then it passes in the C program. Thus, the merge of corresponding *assert* statements in Q' and Q'' with expressions e' and e'' is *assert($e'||e''$)* in Q'''.

Merge of procedural calls. Procedure calls in a boolean procedure are of the form:

$$t_1, \ldots, t_p := foo(e_1, \ldots, e_n);$$
$$\{\text{Assignment of variables in calling context according to } t_1, \ldots, t_p\}.$$

$e_1, \ldots, e_n$ are the actual expressions that are assigned (implicitly) to the boolean program formals (F_Q) in the signature of *foo* and $t_1, \ldots, t_p$ are temporaries corresponding to return predicates (R_Q) in the signature of *foo*.

Suppose in Q, another C procedure, R, is called. In Q' and Q'', the call to R is abstracted as shown in Figure 6. R' and R'' are two boolean procedures abstracted from

$t_1', \ldots, t_p' := R'(e_1', \ldots, e_m');$ {Assignment of variables in Q'}	$t_1'', \ldots, t_q'' := R''(e_1'', \ldots, e_n'');$ {Assignment of variables in Q''}

Fig. 6. Abstractions of the precedure call to R in Q' and Q''

R and may be different. Suppose the merge of R' and R'' is R'''. The merged procedure call in Q''' is as follows:

$$t_1''', \ldots, t_y''' := R'''(e_1''', \ldots, e_x''');$$
$$\{\text{Assignment of variables in } Q''' \text{ according to } t_1''', \ldots, t_y'''\}.$$

The expressions, $e_1''', \ldots, e_x'''$, and the temporaries, $t_1''', \ldots, t_y'''$, are created corresponding to the formal predicates and return predicates in the signature of R'''. Using the merge algorithm for assignments presented above, the expressions $e_1''', \ldots, e_x'''$ in the (implicit) assignment to the formals F_R''' are derived from the assignment of $e_1', \ldots, e_m'$ to the formals F_R' and the assignment of $e_1'', \ldots, e_n''$ to the formals F_R''. The assignment of variables in Q''' is derived from the assignment of variables in Q' and the assignment of variables in Q''.

3.3 An Open Issue: Function Pointers

The method presented above does not support construction of boolean libraries for API procedures that accept function pointers as formal parameters. Function pointers are commonly used by procedures in an API to invoke procedures defined in the client programs that utilize the API. There are several problems that function pointers introduce. First, the behavior of the API is parameterized by the client code. This makes it difficult to create a boolean library abstraction that is reusable in different contexts. Second, the modification information for the API procedure now depends on what the client code modifies (through the call to the function pointer). Thus, to support function pointers in boolean program requires a great deal of parameterization for which we do not yet have good technical solutions.

4   Properties of Merge Algorithms: Discussion and Theorems

Our approach to merging boolean libraries is sound, in other words, the boolean procedure, Q''', constructed by merging Q' and Q'' is a conservative abstraction of Q. Our approach is highly modularized and the merge of two corresponding statements from Q' and Q'' does not involve the analysis of other statements in the two procedures. Therefore, the soundness of our approach is based on the soundness of the merge algorithms for each statement. From the discussions above, it is easy to observe that for each statement in Q, our algorithms construct a conservative abstraction of the statement.

The merged abstraction Q''' also is more refined than Q' and Q'' since it combines information from the statements in both Q' and Q''. The boolean abstraction Q' of the procedure Q has only the predicates generated for the contexts in which Q was model checked. For example, the boolean library in Figure 3(a), precisely abstracts the *then* branch through the procedure, *inc_dec*, however, it abstracts the *else* branch imprecisely, because of the lack of the predicate t==X-1. If this boolean library is used in place of *inc_dec* in model checking the *main* procedure in Figure 4(b) then SLAM fails to verify the correctness of the assertion and reports a "give up case".

The above observations are supported by two formal properties of the merge algorithms. The first property, *soundness*, states that the boolean procedure, Q''', constructed by merging two boolean procedures, Q' and Q'', each being an abstraction of a C procedure, Q, is also an abstraction of Q, which means that every (feasible) execution path in Q is a (feasible) execution path in Q'''. The second property, *precision*, states that the set of execution paths allowed by Q''' is not larger than the set of execution paths shared by Q' and Q''.

Suppose E', E'', and E''' are the corresponding set of predicates for Q', Q'', and Q''', respectively. Therefore, $E''' = E' \cup E''$. Suppose e''' is a predicate where $e''' \in E'''$ and b''' is the corresponding boolean variable of e''' in Q'''. Suppose p is a feasible path in Q and Ω is the state of Q after executing p.

Theorem 1. *For any feasible p in Q, it is guaranteed that p is a feasible path in Q''' as well. Furthermore, there exists an execution of p in Q''' ending in a state Γ such that for every e''' in E''', e''' holds in Ω iff b''' is true in Γ.*

The proof of Theorem 1 is similar to the soundness proof [4] of the SLAM abstraction algorithm, where we first prove that one execution step in Q has a corresponding sequence of execution steps in its abstraction constructed by SLAM and then we prove the correctness of the algorithm using induction over execution steps. In the proof of Theorem 1, we use the same induction. The only difference is that when we prove that one execution step in Q has a corresponding sequence of execution steps in Q''', we, in addition, utilize the fact that each assignment, *assume*, *assert* or procedure call statement in Q''' is the merge of the corresponding statements in Q' and Q''.

Theorem 2. Q''' *is, at least, as precise as Q' and Q'': any execution path allowed in Q''' is also allowed by both Q' and Q''.*

From the merge algorithms, it is easy to observe that Q''' only allows a path that is feasible in both Q' and Q''.

5   Experiences with Windows Device Drivers

Windows device drivers are tightly coupled with the Windows OS. They interact with it through the Windows Driver Model (WDM) API, composed of about 1000 procedures and macros. We use Static Driver Verifier (SDV) to check the source code of a Windows device driver for possible violations of safety properties. These properties formally express WDM safety rules that describe what it means for a device driver to be a good client of the Windows kernel. The verification environment into which SDV places a device driver for model checking has two types of models: (i) scenario models (*harnesses*) that produce sequences of requests reaching a device driver through Windows OS and (ii) operation models (*stubs*) of OS procedures through which the device driver utilizes OS resources to perform requested actions with the device it controls. Presently, models of the both types are written manually in C: the scenario models have a total of 800 lines and the operation models a total of 3000 lines.

The boolean library method we propose in this paper can be used to automatically construct (train) all models of the second type, i.e. operation models. We have implemented extensions to the SLAM toolkit to realize the method. The -genlib Q option instructs SLAM to generate a boolean library for the C procedure Q after performing a verification run. The tool bpmerge takes two boolean program libraries (of the same set of procedures) and merges them as described previously. The -uselib L option instructs SLAM to perform model checking using the boolean library L in place of the corresponding OS functions whose abstractions L contains.

Using these tools, we experimented with training operation models for two WDM functions, namely, *IoAttachDeviceToDeviceStack* and *IoSetDeviceInterfaceState* [19]. The *IoAttachDeviceToDeviceStack* function whose declaration is shown in Figure 7 has 102 lines of code. It attaches the *SourceDevice* object on the top of the chain of device objects already attached over the *TargetDevice* object and returns a pointer to the device object to which the *SourceDevice* object was attached. Note that the returned device object differs from the *TargetDevice* object if there indeed exist additional drivers layered on top of the driver that controls the *TargetDevice* object. This function returns NULL if it could not perform the above action because, for example, the target device driver has been unloaded. The *IoSetDeviceInterfaceState* function whose declaration is shown in Figure 8 has 26 lines of code. It enables or disables an instance of previously registered device interface class. The *SymbolicLinkName* parameter is a pointer to a string identifying the device interface to be enabled or disabled. The *Enable* parameter

---

PDEVICE_OBJECT IoAttachDeviceToDeviceStack(IN PDEVICE_OBJECT SourceDevice,
                                            IN PDEVICE_OBJECT TargetDevice)

Fig. 7. Sample WDM procedure: IoAttachDeviceToDeviceStack

NTSTATUS IoSetDeviceInterfaceState(IN PUNICODE_STRING SymbolicLinkName,
                                    IN BOOLEAN Enable)

Fig. 8. Sample WDM procedure: IoSetDeviceInterfaceState

indicates whether the device interface is to be enabled or disabled. Depending on the value of *Enable*, the function performs different operations and returns different values.

In our experiments with these two functions, we used two real device drivers, *fdc* (9209 lines of code) and *flpydisk* (6601 lines of code), as a training set. For *IoAttachDeviceToDeviceStack*, we used an existing SDV rule from the SDV package that checks that the pointer returned by this function indeed points to the correct device object in the chain of objects. For *IoSetDeviceInterfaceState*, we constructed a new rule to check that the parameters and the return value of the function are correctly correlated.

Our experiments with the two functions described above demonstrated that boolean models of OS functions can indeed be built, trained and used with real device drivers. These two functions and the corresponding rules are rather simple. The complexity of their boolean models we automatically built appeared similar to the complexity of the original C code and therefore we did not observe radical improvement in performance when we verified drivers with boolean models instead of the original functions. We, however, observed performance improvement (about 30%) on slightly more complicated versions of these two functions we artificially constructed by introducing additional branches in their implementation bodies. A similar improvement can be observed even on the toy example we used in Sections 2 and 3. Namely, the verification of the program in Figure 4(a) takes 6 iterations when we use the C code of procedure *inc_dec* given in Figure 2(a) and 4 iterations when we use the merged boolean library of this procedure (in Figure 5). These experiments support our expectation that on a larger library of OS functions, our method will benefit not only from automation, but also from performance improvement. Further experiments with our method are in progress.

6   Related Work

Environment modeling is an indispensable part of software model checking. Many representations have been used to specify environment models. The most commonly used are program languages such as C or Java (with extensions such as non-determinism), design level specification languages such as Executable UML [18], and input languages to model checkers such as Promela [14], SMV [16], and S/R [13]. Temporal logics have also been used to specify environment models, mainly in the context of compositional reasoning [20,2,1,17]. The representations we propose for environment models are boolean libraries, which are especially suitable for environment modeling in model checking of software implementations through predicate abstraction.

Scalable application of model checking requires automation of environment modeling since manual environment modeling are time-consuming and error-prone. The importance of automating environment modeling has also been discussed in several other software model checking projects, such as Feaver [15] and Java PathFinder [8, 22]. However, there has been very limited effort on this problem. Our approach based on boolean libraries enables partial automation of environment modeling which intrinsically requires some user interactions. Our goal is to automate environment modeling as much as possible.

This paper explored the training approach for construction of boolean libraries, which, in essence, selects predicates for abstracting C procedures by selecting a typical set of programs that utilize these C procedures. There are other methods for selecting and generating predicates, such as static and dynamic analysis. For example, Ernst et al. [11] use dynamic analysis to discover "likely" program invariants that could be used support predicate selection for the purpose of constructing boolean libraries.

7 Conclusions and Future Work

Our approach has two major contributions: (1) a new representation for environment models, boolean libraries, and (2) a method to automation of environment modeling based on boolean libraries. Although the concept of boolean libraries is proposed in the context of model checking C programs through predicate abstraction, it has broader applications in other approaches to model checking such as compositional reasoning.

Our approach currently does not handle function pointers in the C procedures from which boolean libraries are to be generated. Use of function pointers is common in C libraries. Extensions that handle function pointers even in some limited fashion could broaden the application of our approach significantly. Another important future research direction is how to combine different predicate selection techniques, such as training and static analysis, to facilitate quick construction of boolean libraries that are precise enough for checking certain properties and also of minimal complexity.

Acknowledgements. We gratefully acknowledge Sriram K. Rajamani, Byron Cook, and all other members of the SLAM/SDV team for their contribution, support and feedback. We also sincerely thank James C. Browne for his help.

References

1. M. Abadi and Leslie Lamport. Conjoining specifications. *TOPLAS: Transactions on Programming Languages and Systems*, 17(3):507–535, May 1995.
2. R. Alur and T. Henzinger. Reactive modules. *Formal Methods in System Design*, 15:7–48, 1999.
3. T. Ball, R. Majumdar, T. Millstein, and S. K. Rajamani. Automatic predicate abstraction of C programs. In *PLDI 01: Programming Language Design and Implementation*, pages 203–213. ACM, 2001.
4. T. Ball, T. Millstein, and S. K. Rajamani. Polymorphic predicate abstraction. Technical Report MSR-TR-2001-10, Microsoft Research, 2001.
5. T. Ball and S. K. Rajamani. Bebop: A symbolic model checker for Boolean programs. In *SPIN 00: SPIN Workshop*, LNCS 1885, pages 113–130. Springer-Verlag, 2000.

6. T. Ball and S. K. Rajamani. Generating abstract explanations of spurious counterexamples in C programs. Technical Report MSR-TR-2002-09, Microsoft Research, January 2002.
7. T. Ball and S. K. Rajamani. The SLAM project: Debugging system software via static analysis. In *POPL 02: Principles of Programming Languages*, pages 1–3. ACM, January 2002.
8. G. Brat, K. Havelund, S. Park, and W Visser. Java PathFinder - a second generation of a Java model checker. In *Workshop on Advances in Verification*, 2000.
9. E. M. Clarke and E. A. Emerson. Design and synthesis of synchronization skeletons using branching time temporal logic. In *Workshop on Logic of Programs*, LNCS 131, pages 52–71. Springer-Verlag, 1981.
10. E. W. Dijkstra. *A Discipline of Programming*. Prentice-Hall, 1976.
11. M. D. Ernst, J. Cockrell, W. G. Griswold, and D. Notkin. Dynamically discovering likely program invariants to support program evolution. *IEEE Transactions in Software Engineering*, 27(2):1–25, February 2001.
12. S. Graf and H. Saïdi. Construction of abstract state graphs with PVS. In *CAV 97: Computer-aided Verification*, LNCS 1254, pages 72–83. Springer-Verlag, 1997.
13. R. H. Hardin, Z. Harel, and R. P. Kurshan. COSPAN. In *CAV 96: Computer-Aided Verification*, LNCS 1102, pages 421–427, 1996.
14. G. Holzmann. The Spin model checker. *IEEE Transactions on Software Engineering*, 23(5):279–295, May 1997.
15. G. J. Holzmann and M. H. Smith. An automated verification method for distributed systems software based on model extraction. *IEEE Transactions on Software Engineering*, 28(4):364–377, 2002.
16. K. L. McMillan. *Symbolic Model Checking*. Kluwer Academic Publishers, 1993.
17. K. L. McMillan. A methodology for hardware verification using compositional model checking. *Cadence TR*, 1999.
18. S. J. Mellor and M. J. Balcer. *Executable UML: A Foundation for Model Driven Architecture*. Addison Wesley, 2002.
19. W. Oney. *Programming the Microsoft Windows Driver Model*. Microsoft Press, 2003.
20. A. Pnueli. In transition from global to modular reasoning about programs. In *Logics and Models of Concurrent Systems*. NATO ASI Series, 1985.
21. J. P. Quielle and J. Sifakis. Specification and verification of concurrent systems in CESAR. In *Symposium on Programming*, LNCS 137, pages 337–351. Springer-Verlag, 1982.
22. W. Visser, K. Havelund, G. Brat, and S. J. Park. Model checking programs. In *ASE 00: Automated Software Engineering*, pages 3–12. IEEE, 2000.

Error Explanation with Distance Metrics

Alex Groce

Computer Science Department, Carnegie Mellon University
Pittsburgh, PA, 15213

Abstract. In the event that a system does not satisfy a specification, a model checker will typically automatically produce a counterexample trace that shows a particular instance of the undesirable behavior. Unfortunately, the important steps that follow the discovery of a counterexample are generally not automated. The user must first decide if the counterexample shows genuinely erroneous behavior or is an artifact of improper specification or abstraction. In the event that the error is real, there remains the difficult task of understanding the error well enough to isolate and modify the faulty aspects of the system. This paper describes an automated approach for assisting users in understanding and isolating errors in ANSI C programs. The approach is based on distance metrics for program executions. Experimental results show that the power of the model checking engine can be used to provide assistance in understanding errors and to isolate faulty portions of the source code.

1 Introduction

In an ideal world, given a trace demonstrating that a system violates a specification, a programmer or designer would always be able in short order to identify and correct the faulty portion of the code, design, or specification. In the real world, dealing with an error is often an onerous task, even with a detailed failing run in hand. This paper describes the application of a technology traditionally used for *finding* errors to the problem of *understanding and isolating* errors.

Error explanation describes automated approaches that aid users in moving from a trace of a failure to an understanding of the essence of the failure and, perhaps, to a correction for the problem. This is a psychological problem, and it is unlikely that formal proof of the superiority of any approach is possible. *Fault localization* is the more specific task of identifying the faulty core of a system.

Model checking [9] tools explore the state-space of a system to determine if it satisfies a specification. When the system disagrees with the specification, a counterexample trace [8] is produced. This paper explains how a model checker can provide error explanation and fault localization information. For a program P, the process (Figure 1) is as follows:

1. The bounded model checker CBMC uses loop unrolling and static single assignment to produce from P and its specification a SAT problem, S. The satisfying assignments of S are bounded *executions* of P that violate the specification (counterexamples).

K. Jensen and A. Podelski (Eds.): TACAS 2004, LNCS 2988, pp. 108–122, 2004.

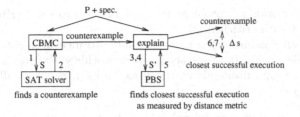

Fig. 1. Explaining an error using distance metrics.

2. CBMC uses a SAT solver to find a counterexample.
3. The `explain` tool produces a SAT problem, S'. The satisfying assignments of S' are executions of P that do *not* violate the specification.
4. `explain` uses the counterexample to add to S' an optimization problem: find a satisfying assignment that is as similar as possible to the counterexample, as measured by a *distance metric* on executions of P.
5. `explain` uses the PBS solver to find a successful execution that is as close as possible to the counterexample.
6. The differences (Δs) between the successful execution and the counterexample are computed.
7. A slicing step is applied to reduce the number of Δs the user must examine. The Δs are then presented to the user as *explanation* and *localization*.
8. If the explanation is unsatisfactory the user may add assumptions and return to step 1 (see Section 5).

There are many possible approaches to error explanation. A basic notion shared by many researchers in this area [5,12,24] and many philosophers [21] is that to explain something is to identify its causes. A second common intuition is that successful executions that closely resemble a faulty run can shed considerable light on the sources of the error (by an examination of the differences in the successful and faulty runs) [12,18,25].

David Lewis [16] has proposed a theory of causality that provides a justification for the second intuition if we assume explanation is the analysis of causal relationships. Following Hume and others, Lewis holds that a cause is something that *makes a difference*: if the cause c had not been, the effect e would not have been. Lewis equates causality to an evaluation based on distance metrics between possible worlds (*counterfactual dependence*). This provides a philosophical link between causality and distance metrics for program executions.

For Lewis, an effect e is dependent on a cause c at a world w iff at all worlds *most similar* to w in which $\neg c$, it is also the case that $\neg e$. Causality does not depend on the impossibility of $\neg c$ and e being simultaneously true of any possible world, but on what happens when we alter w *as little as possible*, other than to remove the possible cause c. This seems reasonable: when considering the question "Was Larry slipping on the banana peel causally dependent on Curly dropping it?" we do not, intuitively, take into account worlds in which another alteration (such as Moe dropping a banana peel) is introduced. Distance metrics between possible worlds are problematic, and Lewis' proposed criteria for such metrics have met with criticism [21].

Program executions are much more amenable to measurement and predication than possible worlds. If we replace possible worlds with program executions and events with propositions about those executions, a practically applicable definition emerges[1]:

Definition 1 (causal dependence). *A predicate e is* causally dependent *on a predicate c in an execution a iff:*

1. *c and e are both true for a (we abbreviate this as $c(a) \wedge e(a)$)*
2. $\exists$ *an execution b . $\neg c(b) \wedge \neg e(b) \wedge (\forall b' . (\neg c(b') \wedge e(b')) \Rightarrow (d(a,b) < d(a,b')))$*

where d is a *distance metric* for program executions (defined in Section 3). In other words, e is causally dependent on c in an execution a iff executions in which the removal of the cause also removes the effect are more like a than executions in which the effect is present without the cause.

This paper describes a distance metric that allows determination of causal dependencies and the implementation of that metric in a tool called `explain` that extends CBMC [1], a model checker for programs written in ANSI C. Note that the focus of the paper is not on computing causal dependence, which is only useful *after* forming a hypothesis about a possible cause c.

The basic approach, presented in Sections 3 and 4, is to explain an error by finding an answer to an apparently different question about an execution a: "How much of a must be changed in order for the error e *not* to occur?" `explain` answers this question by searching for an execution, b, that is as similar as possible to a, except that e is not true for b. Typically, a will be a counterexample produced by model checking, and e will be the negation of the specification. Section 3.4 provides a proof of a link between the answer to this question about changes to a and the definition of causal dependence. The guiding principle in both cases is to explore the implications of a change (in a cause or an effect) by altering as little else as possible: differences will be relevant if irrelevant differences are suppressed.

2   Related Work

Recent work has described proof-like and evidence-based counterexamples [7, 22]. Automatically generating assumptions for verification [10] can also be seen as a kind of error explanation. These approaches appear to be unlikely to result in *succinct* explanations, as they may encode the complexity of the transition system; one measure of a useful explanation lies in how much it *reduces* the information the user must consider.

Error explanation facilities are now featured in MSR's SLAM model checker [5] and NASA's JPF model checker [12]. Jin, Ravi, and Somenzi proposed a game-like explanation (directed more at hardware than software systems) in which an adversary tries to force the system into error [14]. Of these, only JPF

---

[1] Our causal dependence is actually Lewis' counterfactual dependence.

uses a (weak) notion of distance between traces, and it cannot solve for nearest successful executions.

Zeller's delta debugging [25] extrapolates between failing and successful test cases to find more similar executions, with respect to inputs only. Delta-debugging for deriving cause-effect chains [24] takes state variables into account, but requires user choice of instrumentation points and does not provide true minimality or always preserve validity of execution traces.

Renieris and Reiss [18] describe an approach that is quite similar in spirit to the one described here, with the advantages and limitations of a testing rather than model checking basis. They use a distance metric to *select* a successful test run from among a given set rather than, as in this paper, to automatically *generate* a successful run that resembles a given failing run as much as is possible. Experimental results show that this makes their fault localization highly dependent on test case quality. Section 5.1 makes use of a quantitative method for evaluating fault localization approaches proposed by Renieris and Reiss.

This paper presents a new distance metric for program executions, based on David Lewis' counterfactual analysis of causality. The other original contributions are: a method for solving the optimization problem of finding the closest successful execution to a given failing execution and a new slicing technique which can remove irrelevant code that cannot be sliced away by previous static or dynamic slicing approaches.

3   Distance Metrics for Program Executions

A distance metric [20] for program executions is a function $d(a, b)$ (where a and b are executions of the same program) that satisfies certain properties:

1. *Nonnegative property:* $\forall a . \forall b . d(a, b) \geq 0$
2. *Zero property:* $\forall a . \forall b . d(a, b) = 0 \Leftrightarrow a = b$
3. *Symmetry:* $\forall a . \forall b . d(a, b) = d(b, a)$
4. *Triangle inequality:* $\forall a . \forall b . \forall c . d(a, b) + d(b, c) \geq d(a, c)$

3.1   Representing Program Executions

In order to compute distances between program executions, we need a single, well-defined representation for those executions. Bounded model checking (BMC) [6] also relies on a representation for executions: in BMC, the model checking problem is translated into a SAT formula whose satisfying assignments represent counterexamples of a certain length.

CBMC [15] is a BMC tool for ANSI C programs. Given an ANSI C program and a set of *unwinding depths* U (the maximum number of times each loop may be executed), CBMC produces a set of constraints that encode all executions of the program in which loops have finite unwindings. CBMC uses unwinding assertions to notify the user if counterexamples with more loop executions are possible. The representation used is based on static single assignment (SSA) [3] and loop unrolling. CBMC and `explain` handle the full set of ANSI C types, structures, and pointer operations including pointer arithmetic. CBMC only checks safety properties, although in principle BMC (and the `explain` approach) can handle full LTL.

```
1  int main () {
2    int input1, input2, input3;      //input values
3    int least = input1;
4    int most = input1;
5    assume ((input1 >= 0) && (input2 >= 0) && (input3 >= 0));
6    if (most < input2)               //guard1
7      most = input2;
8    if (most < input3)               //guard2
9      most = input3;
10   if (least > input2)              //guard3
11     most = input2;                 //ERROR: should be ''least = input2''
12   if (least > input3)              //guard4
13     least = input3;
14   assert (least <= most);          //specification
15 }
```

Fig. 2. minmax.c

Given the example program minmax.c (Figure 2), CBMC produces the constraints shown in Figure 3 (U is not needed, as minmax.c is loop-free)[2]. The renamed variables describe unique assignment points: `most#2` denotes the second possible assignment to `most`. CBMC assigns uninitialized (#0) values nondeterministically — thus `input1`, `input2`, and `input3` will be unconstrained 32 bit integer values. The assumption on line 5 limits executions to those in which these values are non-negative (constraints {-15} and {-16} encode this requirement). The \guard variables encode the control flow of the program (\guard1 is the value of the conditional on line 6, etc.), and are used when presenting the counterexample to the user (and in the distance metric). Control flow is handled by using ϕ-functions, as usual in SSA: the constraint {-10}, for instance, assigns `most#3` to either `most#2` or `most#1`, depending on the conditional for the assignment to `most#2` (the syntax is that of the C conditional expression). `most#3`, therefore, is the value assigned to `most` at the point before the execution of line 8 of minmax.c. A solution to this set of constraints is an erroneous execution of minmax.c: a counterexample.

CBMC generates CNF clauses representing the conjunction of ({-1}∧{-2}∧... {-16}) with the negation of the claim (¬{1}). CBMC calls ZChaff [17], which produces a satisfying assignment in less than a second. The satisfying assignment encodes an execution of minmax.c in which the assertion is violated (Figure 4).

Figure 4 includes both an easier-to-read summary of the full counterexample generated by CBMC and the more detailed internal representation consisting of the set of all values assigned to the variables appearing in the constraints.

For given loop bounds, all executions of a program can be represented as sets of assignments to the variables appearing in the constraints. Moreover, all executions (for fixed U) are represented as assignments to the same variables.

---

[2] Output is slightly simplified for readability.

```
{-16} \guard#0 => input1#0 >= 0 && input2#0 >= 0 && input3#0 >= 0
{-15} \guard#0 == TRUE
{-14} least#1 == input1#0
{-13} most#1 == input1#0
{-12} \guard#1 == (most#1 < input2#0 && \guard#0)
{-11} most#2 == input2#0
{-10} most#3 == (\guard#1 && \guard#0 ? most#2 : most#1)
{-9}  \guard#2 == (most#3 < input3#0 && \guard#0)
{-8}  most#4 == input3#0
{-7}  most#5 == (\guard#2 && \guard#0 ? most#4 : most#3)
{-6}  \guard#3 == (least#1 > input2#0 && \guard#0)
{-5}  most#6 == input2#0
{-4}  most#7 == (\guard#3 && \guard#0 ? most#6 : most#5)
{-3}  \guard#4 == (least#1 > input3#0 && \guard#0)
{-2}  least#2 == input3#0
{-1}  least#3 == (\guard#4 && \guard#0 ? least#2 : least#1)
|--------------------------
{1}   \guard#0 => least#3 <= most#7
```

Fig. 3. Constraints generated for minmax.c

Different flow of control will simply result in differing \guard values and ϕ-function assignments.

3.2   The Distance Metric d

The distance metric d will be defined only between two executions of the same program with the same maximum bound on loop unwindings[3]. This guarantees that any two executions will be represented by constraints on the same variables. $d(a,b)$ is equal to the number of variables to which a and b assign different values.

Definition 2 (distance between two executions, $d(a,b)$). *Let a and b be executions of a program P, represented as sets of assignments, $a = \{v_0 = val_0^a, v_1 = val_1^a, \ldots, v_n = val_n^a\}$ and $b = \{v_0 = val_0^b, v_1 = val_1^b, \ldots, v_n = val_n^b\}$.*

$$d(a,b) = \sum_{i=0}^{n} \Delta(i)$$

where

$$\Delta(i) = \begin{cases} 0, val_i^a = val_i^b \\ 1, val_i^a \neq val_i^b \end{cases}$$

This definition is equivalent to the Levenshtein distance [20] if we consider executions as strings where the alphabet elements are assignments and substitution is the only allowed operation. The properties of inequality guarantee that d satisfies the four metric properties.

The representation for executions presented here has the advantage of combining precision and relative simplicity, and results in a very clean distance metric. All of the pitfalls involved in trying to align executions with different control flow for purposes of comparison are avoided by the use of SSA. Obviously, the details of the SSA encoding may need to be hidden from non-expert users (the

---

[3] Counterexamples can be extended to allow for more unwindings in the explanation.

```
Initial State
------------------------------------------------------
  input1=2147483618 (01111111111111111111111111100010)
  input2=1073741792 (00111111111111111111111111100000)
  input3=2147483615 (01111111111111111111111111011111)
State 1
------------------------------------------------------
  least=2147483618 (01111111111111111111111111100010)
State 2
------------------------------------------------------
  most=2147483618 (01111111111111111111111111100010)
State 9 file minmax.c line 11 function c::main
------------------------------------------------------
  most=1073741792 (00111111111111111111111111100000)
State 11 file minmax.c line 13 function c::main
------------------------------------------------------
  least=2147483615 (01111111111111111111111111011111)
Failed assertion: assertion file minmax.c line 14 function c::main
```

input1#0 = 2147483618	most#2 = 1073741792	most#6 = 1073741792
least#1 = 2147483618	most#3 = 2147483618	most#7 = 1073741792
most#1 = 2147483618	\guard#2 = FALSE	\guard#4 = TRUE
input2#0 = 1073741792	most#4 = 2147483615	least#2 = 2147483615
input3#0 = 2147483615	most#5 = 2147483618	least#3 = 2147483615
\guard#1 = FALSE	\guard#3 = TRUE	

Fig. 4. Counterexample for minmax.c

input1#0Δ == (input1#0 != 2147483618)	most#4Δ == (most#4 != 2147483615)
least#1Δ == (least#1 != 2147483618)	most#5Δ == (most#5 != 2147483618)
most#1Δ == (most#1 != 2147483618)	\guard#3Δ == (\guard#3 != TRUE)
input2#0Δ == (input2#0 != 1073741792)	most#6Δ == (most#6 != 1073741792)
input3#0Δ == (input3#0 != 2147483615)	most#7Δ == (most#7 != 1073741792)
\guard#1Δ == (\guard#1 != FALSE)	\guard#4Δ == (\guard#4 != TRUE)
most#2Δ == (most#2 != 1073741792)	least#2Δ == (least#2 != 2147483615)
most#3Δ == (most#3 != 2147483618)	least#3Δ == (least#3 != 2147483615)
\guard#2Δ == (\guard#2 != FALSE)	

Fig. 5. Δs for minmax.c and the counterexample in Figure 4

CBMC GUI provides this service). Any gains in the direct presentability of the representation (such as removing values for code that is not executed) are likely to be purchased with a loss of simplicity in the distance metric d.

3.3   Combining the Metric and Constraints

The next step is to consider the optimization problem of finding an execution that satisfies a constraint and is as close as possible to a given execution. The distance to a given execution (e.g. a counterexample) can be easily added to the encoding of the constraints that define the transition relation for a program. All of the Δ functions necessary to compute the distance are added as new constraints (Figure 5) by the explain tool.

These constraints do not affect satisfiability; correct values can always be assigned for the Δs. These values are used to encode the optimization problem. For a fixed a, $d(a, b) = n$ can directly be encoded as a constraint by encoding that exactly n of the Δs be set to 1 in the CNF. However, it is more efficient to use pseudo-Boolean (PB) constraints and replace ZChaff with the PB-solver PBS [2]. With PBS we can express and solve for the conditions $d(a, b) = n$,

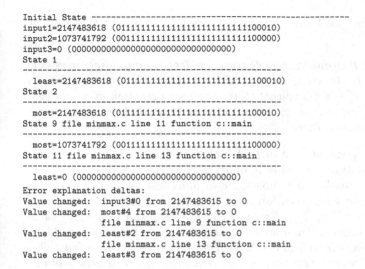

```
Initial State ------------------------------------------------------------
input1=2147483618 (01111111111111111111111111100010)
input2=1073741792 (00111111111111111111111111100000)
input3=0 (00000000000000000000000000000000)
State 1
------------------------------------------------------------------
  least=2147483618 (01111111111111111111111111100010)
State 2
------------------------------------------------------------------
  most=2147483618 (01111111111111111111111111100010)
State 9 file minmax.c line 11 function c::main
------------------------------------------------------------------
  most=1073741792 (00111111111111111111111111100000)
State 11 file minmax.c line 13 function c::main
------------------------------------------------------------------
  least=0 (00000000000000000000000000000000)
Error explanation deltas:
Value changed:  input3#0 from 2147483615 to 0
Value changed:  most#4 from 2147483615 to 0
                file minmax.c line 9 function c::main
Value changed:  least#2 from 2147483615 to 0
                file minmax.c line 13 function c::main
Value changed:  least#3 from 2147483615 to 0
```

Fig. 6. Closest successful execution and Δ values for minmax.c

$d(a, b) < n$, $d(a, b) \geq n$, etc., and, more importantly, directly solve optimization constraints, minimizing or maximizing $d(a, b)$.

From the counterexample shown in Figure 4, we can generate an execution (1) with minimal distance from the counterexample and (2) in which the assertion on line 14 is not violated. Constraints {-1}-{-16} are conjuncted with the Δ constraints (Figure 5) and the unnegated verification claim {1}. The PB constraints express an optimization problem of minimizing the sum of the Δs. The result is an execution (Figure 6) in which a change in the value of input3 results in least <= most being true at line 14. This solution is not unique. In general, there may be a very large class of executions that have the same distance from a counterexample.

The values of the Δs allow us to examine precisely the points at which the two executions differ. The first change is the different value for input3. At least one of the inputs must change in order for the assertion to hold, as the other values are all completely determined by the three inputs. The next change is in the assignment to most at line 9. Because the condition on line 8 is still not satisfied (no guards change values — control flow is the same as in the counterexample), the value of most which reaches line 10 (most#5) is not changed. The final assignment to most is also unchanged (and incorrect). The only change which reaches the assertion is the alteration to the value of least, which is now correct because input2 is no longer minimal. input2 cannot be assigned to least due to the faulty code on line 11.

3.4   Closest Successful Execution Δs and Causal Dependence

The intuition that comparison of the counterexample with minimally different successful executions provides information as to the causes of an error can be justified by showing that Δs from a (closest) successful execution are equivalent to a cause c:

Theorem 1. *Let a be the counterexample trace and let b be any closest successful execution to a. Let D be the set of Δs for which the value is not 0 (the values in which a and b differ). If δ is a predicate stating that an execution disagrees with b for at least one of these values, and e is the proposition that an error occurs, e is causally dependent on δ in a.*

Proof. e is causally dependent on δ in a iff for all of the closest executions for which $\neg\delta$ is true, $\neg e$ is also true. $\neg\delta$ only holds for executions which agree with b for all values in D. Clearly, $\neg\delta(b)$ holds. $\neg e(b)$ must also be the case, as b is defined as a closest *successful* execution to a. Assume that some trace c exists, such that $\neg\delta(c) \wedge e(c) \wedge d(a,c) \leq d(a,b)$. c must differ from b in some value (as $e(c) \wedge \neg e(b)$). c cannot differ from b for any value in D, or $\delta(c)$ would be true. However, if c differs from b in a value other than those in D, c must also differ from a in this value. Therefore, $d(a,c) > d(a,b)$, which contradicts our assumption. Therefore, e must be causally dependent on δ in a.

In the example, δ is the predicate (`input3#0 != 0`) $\vee$ (`most#4 != 0`) $\vee$ (`least#2 != 0`) $\vee$ (`least#3 != 0`). Finding the closest successful execution also produces a predicate c on which the error is causally dependent[4]. δ can be used as a starting point for hypotheses about a more general cause for the error.

4 Δ-Slicing

A successful path with minimal distance to a counterexample may include changes in values that are not actually relevant to the specification. Changes in an input value are necessarily reflected in all values dependent on that input.

Consider the program and Δ values in Figure 7. The change to c is necessary but also irrelevant to the assertion on line 10. In this case, various static or dynamic slicing techniques [23] would suffice to remove the unimportant variables. Generally, however, static slicing is of limited value as there may be some execution path other than the counterexample or successful path in which a variable *is* relevant. Dynamic slicing raises the question of whether to consider the input values for the counterexample or for the successful path.

The same approach used to generate the Δ values can be used to compute an even more aggressive "dynamic slice." In traditional slicing, the goal is to discover all assignments that are relevant to a particular value, either in any possible execution (static slicing) or in a single execution (dynamic slicing). In reporting Δ values, however, the goal is to discover precisely which *differences* in two executions are relevant to a value. Moreover, the value in question is always a predicate (the specification). A slice is an answer to the question: "What is the smallest subset of this program which always assigns the same values to this variable at this point?" Δ-slicing answers the question "What is the smallest

---

[4] Note that the proof also holds for other successful executions: minimal distance minimizes the number of terms in δ.

```
1  int main () {
2    int input1, input2;
3    int a = 1, b = 1, c = 1;
4    if (input1 > 0) {
5      a += 5; b += 6; c += 4;
6    }
7    if (input2 > 0) {
8      a += 6; b += 5; c += 4;
9    }
10   assert ((a < 10) || (b < 10));
11 }
Value changed:  input2#0 from 1073741824 to 0
Guard changed:  input2#0 > 0 && \guard#0 (\guard#2) was TRUE
                file slice.c line 7 function c::main
Value changed:  a#5 from 12 to 6
Value changed:  b#5 from 12 to 7
Value changed:  c#5 from 9 to 5
```

Fig. 7. slice.c and Δ values

subset of changes in values between these two executions that results in a change in the value of this predicate?"

To compute this "slice," we use the same Δ and pseudo-Boolean constraints as presented above. The constraints on the transition relation, however are relaxed. For every variable v_i such that $\Delta(i) = 1$ in the counterexample with constraint $v_i = expr$, and values val_i^a and val_i^b in the counterexample and closest successful execution, respectively, a new constraint is generated:

$$(v_i = val_i^a) \vee ((v_i = val_i^b) \wedge (v_i = expr))$$

That is, for every value in this new execution that changed, the value must be either the same as in the original counterexample or the same as in the closest successful run. If the latter, it must also obey the transition relation. For values that did not change ($\Delta(i) = 0$) the constant constraint $v_i = val_i^a$ is used. The "execution" generated from these constraints may not be a valid run of the program (it will not be, in any case where the slicing reduces the size of the Δs). However, no invalid state or transition will be exposed to the user: the only part of the solution that is used is the new set of Δs. These are always a subset of the original Δs. The improper execution is only used to focus attention on the truly necessary changes in a proper execution. The change in the transition relation can be thought of as encoding the notion that we allow a variable to revert to its value in the counterexample if this alteration is not observable with respect to satisfying the specification.

In slice.c, for example, the constraint c#5 == (input2#0 > 0 && \guard#0 ? c#4 : c#3) is replaced with ((c#5 == 9) || ((c#5 == 5) && (c#5 == (input2#0 > 0 && \guard#0 ? c#4 : c#3)))), and so forth. The relaxation of the transition relation allows for a better solution to the optimization problem, the Δ-slice shown in Figure 8. Another slice would replace b with a. It is only necessary to observe a change in *either* a or b to satisfy the assertion. Previous dynamic slicing techniques do not appear to provide this kind of information.

```
Value changed:   input2#0 from 1073741824 to 0
Guard changed:   input2#0 > 0 && \guard#0 (\guard#2) was TRUE
                 file slice.c line 7 function c::main
Value changed:   b#5 from 12 to 7
```

Fig. 8. Minimal observable difference set for slice.c

5   Case Study: TCAS

TCAS (Traffic Alert and Collision Avoidance System) is an aircraft conflict detection and resolution system used by all US commercial aircraft. The Georgia Tech version of the Siemens suite [19] includes an ANSI C version of the Resolution Advisory (RA) component of the TCAS system (173 lines of C code) and 41 faulty versions of the RA component.

Renieris and Reiss made use of the entire Siemens suite [18]. Their fault localization technique requires only a set of test cases (and a test oracle) for the program in question. The Siemens suite provides test cases and a correct version of the program for comparison. To apply the `explain` tool a specification must be provided for the model checker. It would be possible to hard-code values for test cases as very specific assertions, but this obviously does not reflect useful practice. "Successful" runs produced might be erroneous runs not present in the test suite. Most of the Siemens programs are difficult to specify. The TCAS component, however, is suitable for model checking with almost no modification. A previous study of the component using symbolic execution [11] provided a partial specification that was able to detect faults in 5 of the 41 versions (CBMC's automatic array bounds checking detected 2). In addition to these assertions, it was necessary to include some obvious assumptions on the inputs.

Variation #1 of the TCAS code differs from the correct version in a single line (Figure 9). A $\geq$ comparison in the correct code has been changed into a $>$ comparison on line 100. Figure 10 shows the result of applying `explain` to the counterexample generated by CBMC for this error (after Δ-slicing). The counterexample passes through 90 states before an assertion fails.

The explanation given is not particularly useful. The assertion violation has been avoided by altering an input so that the antecedent of the implication in the assertion is not satisfied. The distance metric-based technique is not fully automated; fortunately user guidance is easy to supply in this case. We are really interested in an explanation of why the second part of the implication (PrB) is true in the error trace, *given* that P1_BCond holds. To coerce `explain`

```
 100c100
// (correct version)
<        result = !(Own_Below_Threat()) || ((Own_Below_Threat()) &&
         (!(Down_Separation >= ALIM())));
---
// (faulty version #1)
>        result = !(Own_Below_Threat()) || ((Own_Below_Threat()) &&
         (!(Down_Separation > ALIM())));
```

Fig. 9. Diff of correct TCAS code and variation #1

```
Value changed:   Input_Down_Separation#0 from 400 to 159
Value changed:   P1_BCond#1 from TRUE to FALSE
                 file tcasv1.c line 255 function c::main
    P1_BCond = ((Input_Up_Separation < Layer_Positive_RA_Alt_Thresh) &&
                (Input_Down_Separation >= Layer_Positive_RA_Alt_Thresh));
    assert(!(P1_BCond && PrB)); // P1_BCond -> ! PrB
```

Fig. 10. First explanation for variation #1 (after Δ-slicing), code for violated assertion

```
Value changed:   Input_Down_Separation_1#0 from 500 to 504
Value changed:   Down_Separation#1 from 500 to 504
                 file tcasv1a.c line 215 function c::main
Value changed:   result_1#1 from TRUE to FALSE
                 file tcasv1a.c line 100 function c::Non_Crossing_Biased_Climb
Value changed:   result_1#3 from TRUE to FALSE
Value changed:   tmp#1 from TRUE to FALSE
                 file tcasv1a.c line 106 function c::Non_Crossing_Biased_Climb
Guard changed:   \guard#1 && tmp#1 (\guard#7) was TRUE
                 file tcasv1a.c line 144 function c::alt_sep_test
Value changed:   need_upward_RA_1#1 from TRUE to FALSE
                 file tcasv1a.c line 144 function c::alt_sep_test
Guard changed:   \guard#15 && need_upward_RA_1#1 (\guard#16) was TRUE
                 file tcasv1a.c line 152 function c::alt_sep_test
Guard changed:   \guard#15 && !need_upward_RA_1#1 (\guard#17) was FALSE
                 file tcasv1a.c line 152 function c::alt_sep_test
Guard changed:   \guard#17 && !need_downward_RA_1#1 (\guard#19) was FALSE
                 file tcasv1a.c line 156 function c::alt_sep_test
Value changed:   ASTUpRA#2 from TRUE to FALSE
Value changed:   ASTUpRA#3 from TRUE to FALSE
Value changed:   ASTUpRA#4 from TRUE to FALSE
Value changed:   PrB#1 from TRUE to FALSE
                 file tcasv1a.c line 230 function c::main
```

Fig. 11. Second explanation for variation #1 (after Δ-slicing)

into answering this query, we add the constraint `assume(P1_BCond);` to variation #1[5]. After model checking the program again we can reapply `explain`. The new explanation (Figure 11) is far more useful.

Observe that, as in the first explanation, only one input value has changed. The first change in a computed value is on line 100 of the program — the location of the fault! Examining the source line and the counterexample values, we see that `ALIM()` had the value 640. `Down_Separation` also had a value of 640. The subexpression `(!(Down_Separation > ALIM()))` has a value of TRUE in the counterexample and FALSE in the successful run. The fault lies in the original value of TRUE, brought about by the change in comparison operators and only exposed when `ALIM() = Down_Separation`. The rest of the explanation shows how this value propagates to result in a correct choice of RA.

For one of the five interesting[6] variations (#40), a useful explanation is produced without any added assumptions. Variations #11 and #31 also require assumptions about the antecedent of an implication in an assertion. The final variation, #41, requires an antecedent assumption and an assumption requiring that TCAS is enabled (the successful execution finally produced differs from the

---

[5] This implication antecedent solution can presumably be automated.

[6] The two errors automatically detected by CBMC are constant-valued array indexing violations that are "explained" sufficiently by a counterexample trace.

Table 1. Scores for localization techniques. Explanation execution times in seconds. Best results in boldface. FAIL indicates memory exhaustion (> 768MB used).

Var.	exp	slice	time	assm	slice	time	JPF	time	(R&R) n-c	(R&R) n-s	CBMC
#1	0.51	0.00	4	0.90	**0.91**	4	0.87	1521	0.00/0.00	0.58/0.58	0.41
#11	0.36	0.00	5	0.88	0.93	7	0.93	5673	0.00/**0.95**	0.00/**0.95**	0.51
#31	0.76	0.00	4	0.89	**0.93**	7	FAIL	-	0.00/0.00	0.00/0.00	0.46
#40	0.75	**0.88**	6	-	-	-	0.87	30,482	0.83/0.83	0.77/0.77	0.35
#41	0.68	0.00	8	0.84	0.88	5	0.30	34	0.56/0.60	**0.92/0.92**	0.38

counterexample to such an extent that changing inputs so as to disable TCAS is a closer solution).

5.1 Evaluation of Fault Localization

Renieris and Reiss[18] propose a scoring function for evaluating error localization techniques based on program dependency graphs [13]. A pdg is a graph of the structure of a program, with nodes (source code lines in this case) connected by edges based on data and control dependencies. For evaluation purposes, they assume that a correct version of a program is available. A node in the pdg is a *faulty* node if it is different than in the correct version. The score assigned to an error report (which is a set of nodes) is a number in the range 0 - 1, where higher scores are better. Scores approaching 1 are assigned to reports that contain *only faulty nodes*. Scores of 0 are assigned to reports that either include every node (and thus are useless for localization purposes) or only contain nodes that are very far from faulty nodes in the pdg. Consider a breadth-first search of the pdg starting from the set of nodes in the error report R. Call R a *layer*, BFS_0. We then define BFS_{n+1} as a set containing BFS_n and all nodes reachable in one directed step in the pdg from BFS_n. Let BFS_* be the smallest layer BFS_n containing at least one faulty node. The score for R is $1 - \frac{|BFS_*|}{|PDG|}$. This reflects how much of a program an ideal user (who recognizes faulty lines on sight) could avoid reading if performing a breadth-first search of the pdg beginning from the error report.

Table 1 shows scores for error reports generated by explain, JPF, and the approach of Renieris and Reiss. The score for the CBMC counterexample is given as a baseline. CodeSurfer [4] generated the pdgs and code provided by Manos Renieris computed the scores for the error reports. The second and third columns show scores given to reports provided by explain without using added assumptions, before and after Δ-slicing. For #1, #11, #31, and #41, a fault is included as an effect of a change in input, but removed by slicing. Columns five and six show explain results after adding appropriate assumptions, if needed. In order to produce any results (or even find a counterexample) with JPF it was necessary to constrain input values to either constants or very small ranges based on a counterexample produced by CBMC. Comparison with the JPF scores (based on subsets[7] of the full JPF reports) is therefore of dubious value. Columns

---

[7] specifically $only(pos) \cup only(neg) \cup cause(pos) \cup cause(neg) \cup (all(neg) \backslash all(pos)) \cup (all(pos) \backslash all(neg))$ for transitions and transforms [12]

eleven and twelve show minimum and maximum scores for two methods given by Renieris and Reiss [18]. After introducing assumptions and slicing, 0.88 was the lowest score for an `explain` report. Ignoring pre-assumption inclusions of faults, Δ-slicing always resulted in improved scores.

In other experiments, `explain` produced a 3 line (correct) localization of a 58 step locking-protocol counterexample for a 2991 line portion of a real-time OS microkernel in 158 seconds.

6   Future Work and Conclusions

There are a number of interesting avenues for future research. The current analysis of one failing run can be extended to the problem of "n different counterexamples with m different explanations." Another extension in progress applies the basic technique when using predicate abstraction and for LTL path+cycle counterexamples. An in-depth look at interactive explanation in practice and discussion of using `explain` to produce *maximally* different counterexamples (for comparison of similarities) are also beyond the scope of this paper.

No single "best" approach for error explanation can be formally defined, as the problem is inherently to some extent psychological. David Lewis' approach to causality is both intuitively appealing and readily translated into mathematical terms, and therefore offers a practical means for deriving concise explanations of program errors. A distance metric informed by Lewis' approach makes it possible to generate provably-most-similar successful executions by translating metric constraints into pseudo-Boolean optimality problems. Experimental results indicate that such executions are quite useful for localization and explanation.

Acknowledgments. I would like to thank Ofer Strichman, Willem Visser, Daniel Kroening, Manos Renieris, Fadi Aloul, Andreas Zeller, and Dimitra Giannakopoulou for their assistance.

References

1. http://www.cs.cmu.edu/~modelcheck/cbmc/.
2. F. Aloul, A. Ramani, I. Markov, and K. Sakallah. PBS: A backtrack search pseudo Boolean solver. In *Symposium on the theory and applications of satisfiability testing (SAT)*, pages 346–353, 2002.
3. B. Alpern, M. Wegman, and F. Zadeck. Detecting equality of variables in programs. In *Principles of Programming Languages*, pages 1–11, 1988.
4. P. Anderson and T. Teitelbaum. Software inspection using codesurfer. In *Workshop on Inspection in Software Engineering*, 2001.
5. T. Ball, M. Naik, and S. Rajamani. From symptom to cause: Localizing errors in counterexample traces. In *Principles of Programming Languages*, pages 97–105, 2003.
6. A. Biere, A. Cimatti, E. Clarke, and Y. Zhu. Symbolic model checking without BDDs. In *Tools and Algorithms for the Construction and Analysis of Systems*, pages 193–207, 1999.

7. M. Chechik and A. Gurfinkel. Proof-like counter-examples. In *Tools and Algorithms for the Construction and Analysis of Systems*, pages 160–175, 2003.
8. E. Clarke, O. Grumberg, K. McMillan, and X. Zhao. Efficient generation of counterexamples and witnesses in symbolic model checking. In *Design Automation Conference*, pages 427–432, 1995.
9. E. Clarke, O. Grumberg, and D. Peled. *Model Checking*. MIT Press, 2000.
10. J. Cobleigh, D. Giannakopoulou, and C. Păsăreanu. Learning assumptions for compositional verification. In *Tools and Algorithms for the Construction and Analysis of Systems*, pages 331–346, 2003.
11. A Coen-Porisini, G. Denaro, C. Ghezzi, and M. Pezze. Using symbolic execution for verifying safety-critical systems. In *European Software Engineering Conference/Foundations of Software Engineering*, pages 142–151, 2001.
12. A. Groce and W. Visser. What went wrong: Explaining counterexamples. In *SPIN Workshop on Model Checking of Software*, pages 121–135, 2003.
13. S. Horwitz and T. Reps. The use of program dependence graphs in software engineering. In *International Conference of Software Engineering*, pages 392–411, 1992.
14. H. Jin, K. Ravi, and F. Somenzi. Fate and free will in error traces. In *Tools and Algorithms for the Construction and Analysis of Systems*, pages 445–458, 2002.
15. D. Kroening, E. Clarke, and F. Lerda. A tool for checking ANSI-C programs. In *Tools and Algorithms for the Construction and Analysis of Systems*, 2004. To appear.
16. D. Lewis. Causation. *Journal of Philosophy*, 70:556–567, 1973.
17. M. Moskewicz, C. Madigan, Y. Zhao, L. Zhang, and S. Malik. Chaff: Engineering an Efficient SAT Solver. In *Proceedings of the 38th Design Automation Conference (DAC'01)*, pages 530–535, 2001.
18. M. Renieris and S. Reiss. Fault localization with nearest neighbor queries. In *Automated Software Engineering*, 2003.
19. G. Rothermel and M. J. Harrold. Empirical studies of a safe regression test selection technique. *Software Engineering*, 24(6):401–419, 1999.
20. D. Sankoff and J. Kruskal, editors. *Time Warps, String Edits, and Macromolecules: the Theory and Practice of Sequence Comparison*. Addison Wesley, 1983.
21. E. Sosa and M. Tooley, editors. *Causation*. Oxford University Press, 1993.
22. L. Tan and R. Cleaveland. Evidence-based model checking. In *Computer-Aided Verification*, pages 455–470, 2002.
23. F. Tip. A survey of program slicing techniques. *Journal of programming languages*, 3:121–189, 1995.
24. A. Zeller. Isolating cause-effect chains from computer programs. In *Foundations of Software Engineering*, pages 1–10, 2002.
25. A. Zeller and R. Hildebrandt. Simplifying and isolating failure-inducing input. *IEEE Transactions on Software Engineering*, 28(2):183–200, 2002.

Online Efficient Predictive Safety Analysis of Multithreaded Programs

Koushik Sen, Grigore Roşu, and Gul Agha

Department of Computer Science,
University of Illinois at Urbana-Champaign.
{ksen,grosu,agha}@cs.uiuc.edu

Abstract. An automated and configurable technique for runtime safety analysis of multithreaded programs is presented, which is able to *predict* safety violations from successful executions. Based on a user provided safety formal specification, the program is automatically instrumented to emit *relevant* state update events to an observer, which further checks them against the safety specification. The events are stamped with *dynamic vector clocks*, enabling the observer to infer a *causal partial order* on the state updates. All event traces that are consistent with this partial order, including the actual execution trace, are analyzed *on-line* and *in parallel*, and a warning is issued whenever there is a trace violating the specification. This technique can be therefore seen as a bridge between testing and model checking. To further increase scalability, a *window* in the state space can be specified, allowing the observer to infer the *most probable* runs. If the size of the window is 1 then only the received execution trace is analyzed, like in testing; if the size of the window is ∞ then all the execution traces are analyzed, such as in model checking.

1   Introduction

In multithreaded systems, threads can execute concurrently communicating with each other through a set of shared variables, yielding an inherent potential for subtle errors due to unexpected interleavings. Both heavy and lighter techniques to detect errors in multithreaded systems have been extensively investigated. The heavy techniques include traditional formal methods based approaches, such as model checking and theorem proving, guaranteeing that a formal model of the system satisfies its safety requirements by exploring, directly or indirectly, all possible thread interleavings. On the other hand, the lighter techniques include testing, that scales well and is one of the most used approaches to validate software products today.

As part of our overall effort in merging testing and formal methods, aiming at getting some of the benefits of both while avoiding the pitfalls of ad hoc testing and the complexity of full-blown model checking or theorem proving, in this paper we present a *runtime verification* technique for safety analysis of multithreaded systems, that can be tuned to analyze from one trace to all traces that are consistent with an actual execution of the program. If all traces are checked, then it becomes equivalent to online model checking of an abstract

K. Jensen and A. Podelski (Eds.): TACAS 2004, LNCS 2988, pp. 123–138, 2004.

model of the computation, called the *multithreaded computation lattice*, which is extracted from the actual execution trace of the program, like in POTA [10] or JMPaX [14]. If only one trace is considered, then our technique becomes equivalent to checking just the actual execution of the multithreaded program, like in testing or like in other runtime analysis tools like MaC [7] and PaX [5, 1]. In general, depending on the application, one can configure a window within the state space to be explored, called *causality cone*, intuitively giving a causal "distance" from the observed execution within which all traces are exhaustively verified. An appealing aspect of our technique is that all these traces can be analyzed *online*, as the events are received from the running program, and all *in parallel* at a cost which in the worst case is proportional with both the size of the window and the size of the state space of the monitor.

There are three important interrelated components of the proposed runtime verification technique namely *instrumentor*, *observer* and *monitor*. The code instrumentor, based on the safety specification, entirely automatically adds code to emit events when *relevant* state updates occur. The observer receives the events from the instrumented program as they are generated, enqueues them and then builds a configurable abstract model of the system, known as a computation lattice, on a layer-by-layer basis. As layers are completed, the monitor, which is synthesized automatically from the safety specification, checks them against the safety specification and then discards them.

The concepts and notions presented in this paper have been experimented and tested on a practical monitoring system for Java programs, JMPaX 2.0, that extends its predecessor JMPaX [12] in at least four non-trivial novel ways. First, it introduces the technical notion of *dynamic vector clock*, allowing it to properly deal with dynamic creation and destruction of threads. Second, the variables shared between threads do not need to be static anymore: an automatic instrumentation technique has been devised that detects automatically when a variable is shared. Thirdly, and perhaps most importantly, the notion of *cone heuristic*, or *global state window*, is introduced for the first time in JMPaX 2.0 to increase the runtime efficiency by analyzing the most likely states in the computation lattice. Lastly, the presented runtime prediction paradigm is safety formalism independent, in the sense that it allows the user to specify any safety property whose bad prefixes can be expressed as a non-deterministic finite automaton (NFA).

2   Monitors for Safety Properties

Safety properties are a very important, if not the most important, class of properties that one should consider in monitoring. This is because once a system violates a safety property, there is no way to continue its execution to satisfy the safety property later. Therefore, a monitor for a safety property can precisely say at runtime when the property has been violated, so that an external recovery action can be taken. From a monitoring perspective, what is needed from a safety formula is a succinct representation of its *bad prefixes*, which are finite sequences of states leading to a violation of the property. Therefore, one can abstract away safety properties by languages over finite words.

Automata are a standard means to succinctly represent languages over finite words. In what follows we define a suitable version of automata, called *monitor*, with the property that it has a "bad" state from which it never gets out:

Definition 1. *Let S be a finite or infinite set, that can be thought of as the set of states of the program to be monitored. Then an S-monitor or simply a monitor, is a tuple $\mathcal{M}on = \langle \mathcal{M}, m_0, b, \rho \rangle$, where*

- *$\mathcal{M}$ is the set of states of the monitor;*
- *$m_0 \in \mathcal{M}$ is the initial state of the monitor;*
- *$b \in \mathcal{M}$ is the* final *state of the monitor, also called* bad *state; and*
- *$\rho \colon \mathcal{M} \times S \to 2^{\mathcal{M}}$ is a non-deterministic transition relation with the property that $\rho(b, \Sigma) = \{b\}$ for any $\Sigma \in S$.*

Sequences in S^*, where ϵ is the empty one, are called (execution) traces. *A trace π is said to be a* bad prefix *in $\mathcal{M}on$ iff $b \in \rho(\{m_0\}, \pi)$, where $\rho \colon 2^{\mathcal{M}} \times S^* \to 2^{\mathcal{M}}$ is recursively defined as $\rho(M, \epsilon) = M$ and $\rho(M, \pi\Sigma) = \rho(\rho(M, \pi), \Sigma)$, where $\rho \colon 2^{\mathcal{M}} \times S \to 2^{\mathcal{M}}$ is defined as $\rho(\{m\} \cup M, \Sigma) = \rho(m, \Sigma) \cup \rho(M, \Sigma)$ and $\rho(\emptyset, \Sigma) = \emptyset$, for all finite $M \subseteq \mathcal{M}$ and $\Sigma \in S$.*

$\mathcal{M}$ is not required to be finite in the above definition, but $2^{\mathcal{M}}$ represents the set of *finite* subsets of $\mathcal{M}$. In practical situations it is often the case that the monitor is *not* explicitly provided in a mathematical form as above. For example, a monitor can be just any program whose execution is triggered by receiving events from the monitored program; its state can be given by the values of its local variables, and the bad state has some easy to detect property, such as a specific variable having a negative value.

There are fortunate situations in which monitors can be *automatically generated* from formal specifications, thus requiring the user to focus on system's formal safety requirements rather than on low level implementation details. In fact, this was the case in all the experiments that we have performed so far. We have so far experimented with requirements expressed either in extended regular expressions (ERE) or various variants of temporal logics, with both future and past time. For example, [11,13] show coinductive techniques to generate minimal static monitors from EREs and from future time linear temporal logics, respectively, and [6,1] show how to generate dynamic monitors, i.e., monitors that generate their states on-the-fly, as they receive the events, for the safety segment of temporal logic.

Example 1. Consider a reactive controller that maintains the water level of a reservoir within safe bounds. It consists of a water level reader and a valve controller. The water level reader reads the current level of the water, calculates the quantity of water in the reservoir and stores it in a shared variable w. The valve controller controls the opening of a valve by looking at the current quantity of water in the reservoir. A very simple and naive implementation of this system contains two threads: T1, the valve controller, and T2, the water level reader. The code snippet for the implementation is given in Fig. 1. Here w is in some proper units such as mega gallons and v is in percentage. The implementation is poorly synchronized and it relies on ideal thread scheduling.

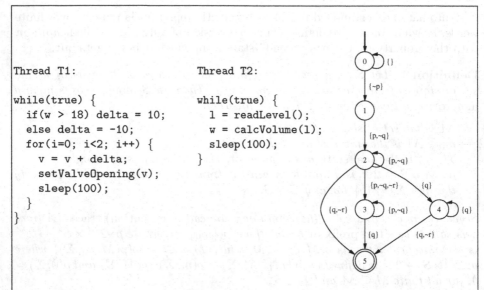

```
Thread T1:                  Thread T2:

while(true) {               while(true) {
  if(w > 18) delta = 10;      l = readLevel();
  else delta = -10;           w = calcVolume(l);
  for(i=0; i<2; i++) {        sleep(100);
    v = v + delta;          }
    setValveOpening(v);
    sleep(100);
  }
}
```

Fig. 1. Two threads (T1 controls the valve and T2 reads the water level) and a monitor.

A sample run of the system can be $\{w = 20, v = 40\}, \{w = 24\}, \{v = 50\}, \{w = 27\}, \{v = 60\}, \{w = 31\}, \{v = 70\}$. As we will see later in the paper, by a run we here mean a sequence of relevant variable writes. Suppose we are interested in a safety property that says "If the water quantity is more than 30 mega gallons, then it is the case that sometime in the past water quantity exceeded 26 mega gallons and since then the valve is open by more than 55% and the water quantity never went down below 26 mega gallon". We can express this safety property in two different formalisms: linear temporal logic (LTL) with both past-time and future-time, or extended regular expressions (EREs) for bad prefixes. The atomic propositions that we will consider are $p : (w > 26), q : (w > 30), r : (v > 55)$. The properties can be written as follows:

$$F_1 = \Box(q \rightarrow ((r \wedge p)\mathcal{S} \uparrow p)) \tag{1}$$
$$F_2 = \{\}^*\{\neg p\}\{p, \neg q\}^+(\{p, \neg q, \neg r\}\{p, \neg q\}^*\{q\} + \{q\}^*\{q, \neg r\})\{\}^* \tag{2}$$

The formula F_1 in LTL ($\uparrow p$ is a shorthand for "p and previously not p") states that "It is always the case that if $(w > 30)$ then at some time in the past $(w > 26)$ started to be true and since then $(r > 55)$ and $(w > 26)$." The formula F_2 characterizes the prefixes that make F_1 false. In F_2 we use $\{p, \neg q\}$ to denote a state where p and $\neg q$ holds and r may or may not hold. Similarly, $\{\}$ represents any state of the system. The monitor automaton for F_2 is given also in Fig. 1.

3   Multithreaded Programs

We consider multithreaded systems in which threads communicate with each other via shared variables. A crucial point is that some variable updates can causally depend on others. We will describe an efficient *dynamic vector clock* algorithm which, given an executing multithreaded program, generates appropriate messages to be sent to an external observer. Section 4 will show how the observer, in order to perform its more elaborated analysis, extracts the state update information from such messages together with the causality partial order.

3.1   Multithreaded Executions and Shared Variables

A multithreaded program consists of n threads t_1, t_2, ..., t_n that execute concurrently and communicate with each other through a set of shared variables. A *multithreaded execution* is a sequence of events $e_1 e_2 \ldots e_r$ generated by the running multithreaded program, each belonging to one of the n threads and having type *internal, read* or *write* of a shared variable. We use e_i^j to represent the j-th event generated by thread t_i since the start of its execution. When the thread or position of an event is not important we can refer to it generically, such as e, e', etc.; we may write $e \in t_i$ when event e is generated by thread t_i. Let us fix an arbitrary but fixed multithreaded execution, say $\mathcal{M}$, and let S be the set of all variables that were shared by more than one thread in the execution. There is an immediate notion of *variable access precedence* for each shared variable $x \in S$: we say e *x-precedes* e', written $e <_x e'$, iff e and e' are variable access events (reads or writes) to the same variable x, and e "happens before" e', that is, e occurs before e' in $\mathcal{M}$. This can be realized in practice by keeping a counter for each shared variable, which is incremented at each variable access.

3.2   Causality and Multithreaded Computations

Let $\mathcal{E}$ be the set of events occurring in $\mathcal{M}$ and let $\prec$ be the partial order on $\mathcal{E}$:

- $e_i^k \prec e_i^l$ if $k < l$;
- $e \prec e'$ if there is $x \in S$ with $e <_x e'$ and at least one of e, e' is a write;
- $e \prec e''$ if $e \prec e'$ and $e' \prec e''$.

We write $e || e'$ if $e \not\prec e'$ and $e' \not\prec e$. The tuple $(\mathcal{E}, \prec)$ is called the *multithreaded computation* associated with the original multithreaded execution $\mathcal{M}$. Synchronization of threads can be easily and elegantly taken into consideration by just generating dummy read/write events when synchronization objects are acquired/released, so the simple notion of multithreaded computation as defined above is as general as practically needed. A permutation of all events e_1, e_2, ..., e_r that does not violate the multithreaded computation, in the sense that the order of events in the permutation is consistent with $\prec$, is called a *consistent multithreaded run*, or simply, a *multithreaded run*.

A multithreaded computation can be thought of as the *most general assumption* that an observer of the multithreaded execution can make about the system without knowing what it is supposed to do. Indeed, an external observer simply *cannot disregard* the order in which the same variable is modified and used within the observed execution, because this order can be part of the intrinsic semantics of the multithreaded program. However, multiple consecutive reads of the same variable can be permuted, and the particular order observed in the given execution is not critical. As seen in Section 4, by allowing an observer to analyze *multithreaded computations* rather than just *multithreaded executions*, one gets the benefit of not only properly dealing with potential re-orderings of delivered messages (e.g., due to using multiple channels in order to reduce the monitoring overhead), but especially of *predicting errors* from analyzing success-ful executions, errors which can occur under a different thread scheduling.

3.3   Relevant Causality

Some of the variables in S may be of no importance at all for an external observer. For example, consider an observer whose purpose is to check the property "if $(x > 0)$ then $(y = 0)$ has been true in the past, and since then $(y > z)$ was always false"; formally, using the interval temporal logic notation in [6], this can be compactly written as $(x > 0) \rightarrow [y = 0, y > z)$. All the other variables in S except x, y and z are essentially irrelevant for this observer. To minimize the number of messages, like in [8] which suggests a similar technique but for distributed systems in which reads and writes are not distinguished, we consider a subset $\mathcal{R} \subseteq \mathcal{E}$ of *relevant events* and define the $\mathcal{R}$-*relevant causality* on $\mathcal{E}$ as the relation $\lhd := \prec \cap (\mathcal{R} \times \mathcal{R})$, so that $e \lhd e'$ iff $e, e' \in \mathcal{R}$ and $e \prec e'$. It is important to notice though that the other variables can also indirectly influence the relation $\lhd$, because they can influence the relation $\prec$. We next provide a technique based on *vector clocks* that correctly implements the relevant causality relation.

3.4   Dynamic Vector Clock Algorithm

We provide a technique based on *vector clocks* [4,9] that correctly and efficiently implements the relevant causality relation. Let $V : ThreadId \rightarrow Nat$ be a *partial* map from thread identifiers to natural numbers. We call such a map a *dynamic vector clock (DVC)* because its partiality reflects the intuition that threads are dynamically created and destroyed. To simplify the exposition and the imple-mentation, we assume that each DVC V is a total map, where $V[t] = 0$ whenever V is not defined on thread t.

We associate a DVC with every thread t_i and denote it by V_i. Moreover, we associate two DVCs V_x^a and V_x^w with every shared variable x; we call the former *access DVC* and the latter *write DVC*. All the DVCs V_i are kept empty at the beginning of the computation, so they do not consume any space. For DVCs V and V', we say that $V \leq V'$ if and only if $V[j] \leq V'[j]$ for all j, and we say that $V < V'$ iff $V \leq V'$ and there is some j such that $V[j] < V'[j]$; also, $\max\{V, V'\}$ is the DVC with $\max\{V, V'\}[j] = \max\{V[j], V'[j]\}$ for each j. Whenever a thread t_i with current DVC V_i processes event e_i^k, the following algorithm is executed:

1. if e_i^k is relevant, i.e., if $e_i^k \in \mathcal{R}$, then
    $V_i[i] \leftarrow V_i[i] + 1$
2. if e_i^k is a read of a variable x then
    $V_i \leftarrow \max\{V_i, V_x^w\}$
    $V_x^a \leftarrow \max\{V_x^a, V_i\}$

3. if e_i^k is a write of a variable x then
$$V_x^w \leftarrow V_x^a \leftarrow V_i \leftarrow \max\{V_x^a, V_i\}$$
4. if e_i^k is relevant then
    send message $\langle e_i^k, i, V_i \rangle$ to observer.

The following theorem states that the DVC algorithm correctly implements causality in multithreaded programs. This algorithm has been previously presented by the authors in [14,15] in a less general context, where the number of threads is fixed and known a priori. Its proof is similar to that in [15].

Theorem 1. *After event e_i^k is processed by thread t_i,*

- $V_i[j]$ *equals the number of relevant events of t_j that causally precede e_i^k; if $j = i$ and e_i^k is relevant then this number also includes e_i^k;*
- $V_x^a[j]$ *equals the number of relevant events of t_j that causally precede the most recent event that accessed (read or wrote) x; if $i = j$ and e_i^k is a relevant read or write of x event then this number also includes e_i^k;*
- $V_x^w[j]$ *equals the number of relevant events of t_j that causally precede the most recent write event of x; if $i = j$ and e_i^k is a relevant write of x then this number also includes e_i^k.*

Therefore, if $\langle e, i, V \rangle$ and $\langle e', j, V' \rangle$ are two messages sent by dynamic vector clock algorithm, then $e \lhd e'$ if and only if $V[i] \leq V'[i]$. Moreover, if i and j are not given, then $e \lhd e'$ if and only if $V < V'$.

4 Runtime Model Generation and Predictive Analysis

In this section we consider what happens at the observer's site. The observer receives messages of the form $\langle e, i, V \rangle$. Because of Theorem 1, the observer can infer the causal dependency between the relevant events emitted by the multithreaded system. We show how the observer can be configured to effectively analyze all possible interleavings of events that do not violate the observed causal dependency *online* and *in parallel*. Only one of these interleavings corresponds to the real execution, the others being all potential executions. Hence, the presented technique can *predict* safety violations from successful executions.

4.1 Multithreaded Computation Lattice

Inspired by related definitions in [2], we define the important notions of relevant multithreaded computation and run as follows. A *relevant multithreaded computation*, simply called *multithreaded computation* from now on, is the partial order on events that the observer can infer, which is nothing but the relation $\lhd$. A *relevant multithreaded run*, also simply called *multithreaded run* from now on, is any permutation of the received events which *does not violate* the multithreaded computation. Our major purpose in this paper is to check safety requirements against *all* (relevant) multithreaded runs of a multithreaded system.

We assume that the relevant events are only writes of shared variables that appear in the safety formulae to be monitored, and that these events contain a pair of the name of the corresponding variable and the value which was written to it. We call these variables *relevant variables*. Note that events can change the state of the multithreaded system as seen by the observer; this is formalized next. A *relevant program state*, or simply a *program state* is a map from relevant variables to concrete values. Any permutation of events generates a sequence of program states in the obvious way, however, not all permutations of events are valid multithreaded runs. A program state is called *consistent* if and only if there is a multithreaded run containing that state in its sequence of generated program states. We next formalize these concepts.

We let $\mathcal{R}$ denote the set of received relevant events. For a given permutation of events in $\mathcal{R}$, say $e_1 e_2 \ldots e_{|\mathcal{R}|}$, we let e_i^k denote the k-th event of thread t_i. Then the relevant program state after the events $e_1^{k_1}, e_2^{k_2}, ..., e_n^{k_n}$ is called a *relevant global multithreaded state*, or simply a *relevant global state* or even just *state*, and is denoted by $\Sigma^{k_1 k_2 \cdots k_n}$. A state $\Sigma^{k_1 k_2 \cdots k_n}$ is called *consistent* if and only if for any $1 \le i \le n$ and any $l_i \le k_i$, it is the case that $l_j \le k_j$ for any $1 \le j \le n$ and any l_j such that $e_j^{l_j} \lessdot e_i^{l_i}$. Let Σ^{K_0} be the *initial* global state, $\Sigma^{00 \cdots 0}$. An important observation is that $e_1 e_2 \ldots e_{|\mathcal{R}|}$ is a multithreaded run if and only if it generates a sequence of global states $\Sigma^{K_0} \Sigma^{K_1} \ldots \Sigma^{K_{|\mathcal{R}|}}$ such that each Σ^{K_r} is consistent and for any two consecutive Σ^{K_r} and $\Sigma^{K_{r+1}}$, K_r and K_{r+1} differ in exactly one index, say i, where the i-th element in K_{r+1} is larger by 1 than the i-th element in K_r. For that reason, we will identify the sequences of states $\Sigma^{K_0} \Sigma^{K_1} \ldots \Sigma^{K_{|\mathcal{R}|}}$ as above with multithreaded runs, and simply call them *runs*.

We say that Σ *leads-to* Σ', written $\Sigma \rightsquigarrow \Sigma'$, when there is some run in which Σ and Σ' are consecutive states. Let $\rightsquigarrow^*$ be the reflexive transitive closure of the relation $\rightsquigarrow$. The set of all consistent global states together with the relation $\rightsquigarrow^*$ forms a *lattice* with n mutually orthogonal axes representing each thread. For a state $\Sigma^{k_1 k_2 \cdots k_n}$, we call $k_1 + k_1 + \cdots k_n$ its *level*. A *path* in the lattice is a sequence of consistent global states on increasing level, where the level increases by 1 between any two consecutive states in the path. Therefore, a run is just a path starting with $\Sigma^{00 \cdots 0}$ and ending with $\Sigma^{r_1 r_2 \cdots r_n}$, where r_i is the total number of events of thread t_i. Note that in the above discussion we assumed a fixed number of threads n. In a program where threads can be created and destroyed dynamically, only those threads are considered that at the end of the computation have causally affected the final values of the relevant variables.

Therefore, a multithreaded computation can be seen as a lattice. This lattice, which is called *computation lattice* and referred to as $\mathcal{L}$, should be seen as an *abstract model* of the running multithreaded program, containing the relevant information needed in order to analyze the program. Supposing that one is able to *store* the computation lattice of a multithreaded program, which is a non-trivial matter because it can have an exponential number of states in the length of the execution, one can mechanically model-check it against the safety property.

Example 2. Figure 2 shows the causal partial order on relevant events extracted by the observer from the multithreaded execution in Example 1, together with the generated computation lattice. The actual execution, $\Sigma^{00} \Sigma^{01} \Sigma^{11} \Sigma^{12} \Sigma^{22} \Sigma^{23} \Sigma^{33}$, is marked with solid edges in the lattice. Besides its DVC, each global state in the lattice stores its values for the relevant vari-

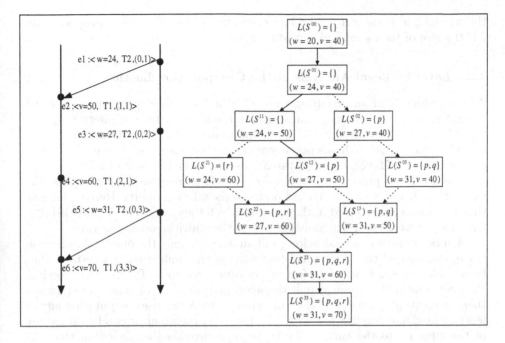

Fig. 2. Computation Lattice

ables, w and v. It can be readily seen on Fig. 2 that the LTL property F_1 defined in Example 1 holds on the sample run of the system, and also that it is not in the language of bad prefixes, F_2. However, F_1 is violated on some other consistent runs, such as $\Sigma^{00}\Sigma^{01}\Sigma^{02}\Sigma^{12}\Sigma^{13}\Sigma^{23}\Sigma^{33}$. On this particular run $\uparrow p$ holds at Σ^{02}; however, r does not hold at the next state Σ^{12}. This makes the formula F_1 false at the state Σ^{13}. The run can also be symbolically written as $\{\}\{\}\{p\}\{p\}\{p,q\}\{p,q,r\}\{p,q,r\}$. In the automaton in Fig. 1, this corresponds to a possible sequence of states 00123555. Hence, this string is accepted by F_2 as a bad prefix.

Therefore, by carefully analyzing the computation lattice extracted from a successful execution one can infer safety violations in other possible consistent executions. Such violations give informative feedback to users, such as the lack of synchronization in the example above, and may be hard to find by just ordinary testing. In what follows we propose effective techniques to analyze the computation lattice. A first important observation is that one can generate it *on-the-fly* and analyze it on a level-by-level basis, discarding the previous levels. However, even if one considers only one level, that can still contain an exponential number of states in the length of the current execution. A second important observation is that the states in the computation lattice are not all equiprobable in practice. By allowing a user configurable *window* of most likely states in the lattice centered around the observed execution trace, the presented technique becomes quite scalable, requiring $O(wm)$ space and $O(twm)$ time, where w is the size of the window, m is the size of the bad prefix monitor of the safety property, and t is the size of the monitored execution trace.

4.2   Level by Level Analysis of the Computation Lattice

A naive observer of an execution trace of a multithreaded program would just check the observed execution trace against the monitor for the safety property, say $\mathcal{M}on$ like in Definition 1, and would maintain at each moment a set of states, say $MonStates$ in $\mathcal{M}$. When a new event generating a new global state Σ arrives, it would replace $MonStates$ by $\rho(MonStates, \Sigma)$. If the bad state b will ever be in $MonStates$ then a property violation error would be reported, meaning that the current execution trace led to a bad prefix of the safety property. Here we assume that the events are received in the order in which they are emitted, and also that the monitor works over the global states of the multithreaded programs.

A smart observer, as said before, will analyze not only the observed execution trace, but also all the other consistent runs of the multithreaded system, thus being able to *predict* violations from successful executions. The observer receives the events from the running multithreaded program in real-time and enqueues them in an event queue Q. At the same time, it traverses the computation lattice level by level and checks whether the bad state of the monitor can be hit by any of the runs up to the current level. We next provide the algorithm that the observer uses to construct the lattice level by level from the sequence of events it receives from the running program.

The observer maintains a list of global states ($CurrLevel$), that are present in the current level of the lattice. For each event e in the event queue, it tries to construct a new global state from the set of states in the current level and the event e. If the global state is created successfully then it is added to the list of global states ($NextLevel$) for the next level of the lattice. The process continues until certain condition, $levelComplete?()$ holds. At that time the observer says that the level is complete and starts constructing the next level by setting $CurrLevel$ to $NextLevel$ and reallocating the space previously occupied by $CurrLevel$. Here the predicate $levelComplete?()$ is crucial for generating only those states in the level that are most likely to occur in other executions, namely those in the *window*, or the *causality cone*, that is described in the next subsection. The $levelComplete?$ predicate is also discussed and defined in the next subsection. The pseudo-code for the lattice traversal is given in Fig. 3.

Every global state Σ contains the value of all relevant shared variables in the program, a DVC $VC(\Sigma)$ to represent the latest events from each thread that resulted in that global state. Here the predicate $nextState?(\Sigma, e)$, checks if the event e can convert the state Σ to a state Σ' in the next level of the lattice, where $threadId(e)$ returns the index of the thread that generated the event e, $VC(\Sigma)$ returns the DVC of the global state Σ, and $VC(e)$ returns the DVC of the event e. It essentially says that event e can generate a consecutive state for a state Σ, if and only if Σ "knows" everything e knows about the current evolution of the multithreaded system except for the event e itself. Note that e may know less than Σ knows with respect to the evolution of other threads in the system, because Σ has global information.

```
while(not  end of computation){
  Q ← enqueue(Q, NextEvent())
  while(constructLevel()){}
}

boolean constructLevel(){
  for each e ∈ Q {
    if Σ ∈ CurrLevel and nextState?(Σ, e) {
      NextLevel ← NextLevel ⊎ createState(Σ, e)
      if levelComplete?(NextLevel, e, Q) {
        Q ← removeUselessEvents(CurrLevel, Q)
        CurrLevel ← NextLevel
        return true}}}
  return false
}
boolean nextState?(Σ, e){
  i ← threadId(e);
  if (∀j ≠ i : VC(Σ)[j] ≥ VC(e)[j] and
    VC(Σ)[i] + 1 = VC(e)[i]) return true
  return false
}
State createState(Σ, e){
  Σ' ← new copy of Σ
  j ← threadId(e);  VC(Σ')[j] ← VC(Σ)[j] + 1
  pgmState(Σ')[var(e) ← value(e)]
  MonStates(Σ') ← ρ(MonStates(Σ), Σ')
  if b ∈ MonStates(Σ') {
    output 'property may be violated'}
  return Σ'
}
```

Fig. 3. Level-by-level traversal.

The function $createState(\Sigma, e)$ creates a new global state Σ', where Σ' is a possible consistent global state that can result from Σ after the event e. Together with each state Σ in the lattice, a set of states of the monitor, $MonStates(\Sigma)$, also needs to be maintained, which keeps all the states of the monitor in which any of the partial runs ending in Σ can lead to. In the function $createState$, we set the $MonStates$ of Σ' with the set of monitor states to which any of the current states in $MonStates(\Sigma)$ can transit within the monitor when the state Σ' is observed. $pgmState(\Sigma')$ returns the value of all relevant program shared variables in state Σ', $var(e)$ returns the name of the relevant variable that is written at the time of event e, $value(e)$ is the value that is written to $var(e)$, and $pgmState(\Sigma')[var(e) \leftarrow value(e)]$ means that in $pgmState(\Sigma')$, $var(e)$ is updated with $value(e)$.

The merging operation $nextLevel \uplus \Sigma$ adds the global state Σ to the set $nextLevel$. If Σ is already present in $nextLevel$, it updates the existing state's $MonStates$ with the union of the existing state's $MonStates$ and the $Monstates$ of Σ. Two global states are same if their DVCs are equal. Because of the function $levelComplete?$, it may be often the case that the analysis procedure moves from the current level to the next one before it is exhaustively explored. That means that several events in the queue, which were waiting for other events to arrive in order to generate new states in the current level, become unnecessary so they can be discarded. The function $removeUselessEvents(CurrLevel, Q)$ removes from Q all the events that cannot contribute to the construction of any state at the next level. To do so, it creates a DVC V_{min} whose each component is the minimum of the corresponding component of the DVCs of all the global states in the set $CurrLevel$. It then removes all the events in Q whose DVCs are less than or equal to V_{min}. This function makes sure that we do not store any unnecessary events.

The observer runs in a loop till the computation ends. In the loop the observer waits for the next event from the running instrumented program and enqueues it in Q whenever it becomes available. After that the observer runs the function *constructLevel* in a loop till it returns false. If the function *constructLevel* returns false then the observer knows that the level is not completed and it needs more events to complete the level. At that point the observer again starts waiting for the next event from the running program and continues with the loop. The pseudo-code for the observer is given at the top of Fig. 3.

4.3 Causality Cone Heuristic

In a given level of a computation lattice, the number of states can be large; in fact, exponential in the length of the trace. In online analysis, generating all the states in a level may not be feasible. However, note that some states in a level can be considered more likely to occur in a consistent run than others. For example, two independent events that can possibly permute may have a huge time difference. Permuting these two events would give a consistent run, but that run may not be likely to take place in a real execution of the multithreaded program. So we can ignore such a permutation. We formalize this concept as *causality cone*, or *window*, and exploit it in restricting our attention to a small set of states in a given level.

In what follows we assume that the events are received in an order in which they happen in the computation. This is easily ensured by proper instrumentation. Note that this ordering gives the real execution of the program and it respects the partial order associated with the computation. This execution will be taken as a reference in order to compute the most probable consistent runs of the system.

If we consider all the events generated by the executing distributed program as a finite sequence of events, then a lattice formed by any prefix of this sequence is a sublattice of the computation lattice $\mathcal{L}$. This sublattice, say $\mathcal{L}'$ has the following property: if $\Sigma \in \mathcal{L}'$, then for any $\Sigma' \in \mathcal{L}$ if $\Sigma' \leadsto^* \Sigma$ then $\Sigma' \in \mathcal{L}'$. We can see this sublattice as a portion of the computation lattice $\mathcal{L}$ enclosed by a cone. The height of this cone is determined by the length of the current sequence of events. We call this *causality cone*. All the states in $\mathcal{L}$ that are outside this cone cannot be determined from the current sequence of events. Hence, they are outside the causal scope of the current sequence of events. As we get more events this cone moves down by one level.

If we compute a DVC V_{max} whose each component is the maximum of the corresponding component of the DVCs of all the events in the event queue, then this represents the DVC of the global state appearing at the tip of the cone. The tip of the cone traverses the actual execution run of the program.

To avoid the generation of possibly exponential number of states in a given level, we consider a fixed number, say w, most probable states in a given level. In a level construction we say the level is complete once we have generated w states in that level. However, a level may contain less than w states. Then the level construction algorithm gets stuck. Moreover, we cannot determine if a level has less than w states unless we see all the events in the complete computation.

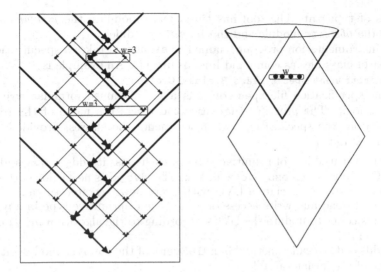

Fig. 4. Causality Cones

This is because we do not know the total number of threads that participate in the computation beforehand.

To avoid this scenario we introduce another parameter l, the length of the current event queue. We say that a level is complete if we have used all the events in the event queue for the construction of the states in the current level and the length of the queue is l and we have not crossed the limit w on the number of states. The pseudo-code for *levelComplete?* is given in Fig. 5.

```
boolean levelComplete?(NextLevel, e, Q){
  if size(NextLevel) ≥ w then
    return true;
  else if e is the last event in Q
    and size(Q) == l then
    return true;
  else return false;
}
```

Fig. 5. *levelComplete?* predicate

Note, here l corresponds to the number of levels of the sublattice that be constructed from the events in the event queue Q. On the other hand, the level of this sublattice with the largest level number and having at least w global states refers to the *CurrLevel* in the algorithm.

5   Implementation

We have implemented these new techniques, in version 2.0 of the tool Java MultiPathExplorer (JMPaX)[12], which has been designed to monitor multithreaded Java programs. The current implementation is written in Java and it removes the restriction that all the shared variables of the multithreaded program are static variables of type `int`. The tool has three main modules, the *instrumentation* module, the *observer* module and the *monitor* module.

The instrumentation program, named `instrument`, takes a specification file and a list of class files as command line arguments. An example is

`java instrument spec A.class B.class C.class`

where the specification file `spec` contains a list of named formulae written in a suitable logic. The program `instrument` extracts the name of the relevant variables from the specification and instruments the classes, provided in the argument, as follows:

i) For each variable x of primitive type in each class it adds *access* and *write* DVCs, namely `_access_dvc_x` and `_write_dvc_x`, as new fields in the class.
ii) It adds code to associate a DVC with every newly created thread;
iii) For each read and write access of a variable of primitive type in any class, it adds codes to update the DVCs according to the algorithm mentioned in Section 3.4;
iv) It adds code to call a method `handleEvent` of the *observer* module at every write of a relevant variable.

The instrumentation module uses BCEL [3] Java library to modify Java class files. We use the BCEL library to get a better handle for a Java classfile.

The *observer* module, that takes two parameters w and l, generates the lattice level by level when the instrumented program is executed. Whenever the `handleEvent` method is invoked it enqueues the event passed as argument to the method `handleEvent`. Based on the event queue and the current level of the lattice it generates the next level of the lattice. In the process it invokes `nextStates` method (corresponding to ρ in a *monitor*) of the *monitor* module.

The *monitor* module reads the specification file written either as an LTL formula or a regular expression and generates the non-deterministic automaton corresponding to the formula or the regular expression. It provides the method `nextStates` as an interface to the *observer* module. The method raises an exception if at any point the set of states returned by `nextStates` contain the "bad" state of the automaton. The system being modular, user can plug in his/her own *monitor* module for his/her logic of choice.

Since in Java synchronized blocks cannot be interleaved, so corresponding events cannot be permuted, locks are considered as shared variables and a write event is generated whenever a lock is acquired or released. This way, a causal dependency is generated between any exit and any entry of a synchronized block, namely the expected happens-before relation. Java synchronization statements are handled exactly the same way, that is, the shared variable associated to the synchronization object is written at the entrance and at the exit of the synchronized region. Condition synchronizations (wait/notify) can be handled similarly, by generating a write of a dummy shared variable by both the notifying thread before notification and by the notified thread after notification.

6   Conclusion and Future Work

A formal runtime predictive analysis technique for multithreaded systems has been presented in this paper, in which multiple threads communicating by shared variables are automatically instrumented to send relevant events, stamped by dynamic vector clocks, to an external observer which extracts a causal partial order on the global state, updates and thereby builds an abstract runtime model of the running multithreaded system. Analyzing this model on a level by level basis, the observer can infer effectively from *successful* execution of the observed system when basic safety properties can be violated by other executions. Attractive future work includes predictions of liveness violations and predictions of datarace and deadlock conditions.

Acknowledgments. The work is supported in part by the Defense Advanced Research Projects Agency (the DARPA IPTO TASK Program, contract number F30602-00-2-0586, the DARPA IXO NEST Program, contract number F33615-01-C-1907), the ONR Grant N00014-02-1-0715, the Motorola Grant MOTOROLA RPS #23 ANT, and the joint NSF/NASA grant CCR-0234524.

References

1. H. Barringer, A. Goldberg, K. Havelund, and K. Sen. Rule-Based Runtime Verification. In *Proceedings of Fifth International VMCAI conference (VMCAI'04) (To appear in LNCS)*, January 2004.
   Download: http://www.cs.man.ac.uk/cspreprints/PrePrints/cspp24.pdf.
2. H. W. Cain and M. H. Lipasti. Verifying sequential consistency using vector clocks. In *Proceedings of the 14th annual ACM Symposium on Parallel Algorithms and Architectures*, pages 153–154. ACM, 2002.
3. M. Dahm. Byte code engineering with the bcel api. Technical Report B-17-98, Freie Universit at Berlin, Institut für Informatik, April 2001.
4. C. J. Fidge. Partial orders for parallel debugging. In *Proceedings of the 1988 ACM SIGPLAN and SIGOPS workshop on Parallel and Distributed debugging*, pages 183–194. ACM, 1988.
5. K. Havelund and G. Roşu. Monitoring Java Programs with Java PathExplorer. In *Proceedings of the 1st Workshop on Runtime Verification (RV'01)*, volume 55 of *Electronic Notes in Theoretical Computer Science*. Elsevier Science, 2001.
6. K. Havelund and G. Roşu. Synthesizing monitors for safety properties. In *Tools and Algorithms for Construction and Analysis of Systems (TACAS'02)*, volume 2280 of *Lecture Notes in Computer Science*, pages 342–356. Springer, 2002.
7. M. Kim, S. Kannan, I. Lee, and O. Sokolsky. Java-MaC: a Run-time Assurance Tool for Java. In *Proceedings of the 1st Workshop on Runtime Verification (RV'01)*, volume 55 of *Electronic Notes in Theoretical Computer Science*. Elsevier Science, 2001.
8. K. Marzullo and G. Neiger. Detection of global state predicates. In *Proceedings of the 5th International Workshop on Distributed Algorithms (WADG'91)*, volume 579 of *Lecture Notes in Computer Science*, pages 254–272. Springer-Verlag, 1991.
9. F. Mattern. Virtual time and global states of distributed systems. In *Parallel and Distributed Algorithms: proceedings of the International Workshop on Parallel and Distributed Algorithms*, pages 215–226. Elsevier, 1989.
10. A. Sen and V. K. .Garg. Partial order trace analyzer (pota) for distrubted programs. In *Proceedings of the 3rd Workshop on Runtime Verification (RV'03)*, Electronic Notes in Theoretical Computer Science, 2003.

11. K. Sen and G. Roşu. Generating optimal monitors for extended regular expressions. In *Proceedings of the 3rd Workshop on* Runtime Verification (RV'03), volume 89 of *ENTCS*, pages 162–181. Elsevier Science, 2003.

12. K. Sen, G. Roşu, and G. Agha. Java MultiPathExplorer (JMPaX 2.0). Download: http://fsl.cs.uiuc.edu/jmpax.

13. K. Sen, G. Roşu, and G. Agha. Generating Optimal Linear Temporal Logic Monitors by Coinduction. In *Proceedings of 8th Asian Computing Science Conference (ASIAN'03)*, volume 2896 of *Lecture Notes in Computer Science*, pages 260–275. Springer-Verlag, December 2003.

14. K. Sen, G. Roşu, and G. Agha. Runtime safety analysis of multithreaded programs. In *Proceedings of 4th joint European Software Engineering Conference and ACM SIGSOFT Symposium on the Foundations of Software Engineering (ESEC/FSE'03)*. ACM, 2003.

15. K. Sen, G. Roşu, and G. Agha. Runtime safety analysis of multithreaded programs. Technical Report UIUCDCS-R-2003-2334, University of Illinois at Urnaba Champaign, April 2003.

Vooduu: Verification of Object-Oriented Designs Using UPPAAL

Karsten Diethers* and Michaela Huhn

Technical University of Braunschweig, D-38106 Braunschweig, Germany
{diethers,huhn}@ips.cs.tu-bs.de,
http://www.cs.tu-bs.de/ips

Abstract. The Unified Modeling Language (UML) provides sequence diagrams to specify inter-object communication in terms of scenarios. The intra-object behavior is modelled by statechart diagrams. Our tool *Vooduu* performs an automated consistency check on both views, i.e., it verifies automatically whether a family of UML statecharts modelling a system satisfies a set of communication and timing constraints given as UML sequence diagrams. The front-end of the tool is implemented as a plug-in for a commercial UML tool. For verifying, statecharts and sequence diagrams are translated to the formalism of timed automata. The tool generates temporal logic queries, which depend on an interpretation status for each sequence diagram. The verification is performed by the model checker UPPAAL. The results are retranslated into sequence diagrams. Thus the formal verification machinery is mainly hidden from the user. The tool was applied to a model of the control software of a robot prototype.

1   Introduction

Model checking has been proved to be a useful technique for the verification of complex system behavior. In a variety of case studies relevant errors were discovered and safety and correctness were improved. A number of advanced model checking tools, optimized for different tasks like the analysis of timing constraints, allow to verify systems of size and complexity that are far out of scope of manual exploration. For all success, model checking is not integrated in many system development processes so far, because it is based on a formal description for the system and the requirements, which is proprietary to the employed model checker. Although many verification tools like UPPAAL[1] provide a user friendly graphical interface, the development and maintenance of two different sets of models, one for system design and one for the verification, are considered not practicable in many industrial projects. Thus we will consequently hide the application of formal verification from the user behind a well accepted, standardized modelling language like the UML (Unified Modeling Language)[2].

---

* The work of this author was funded by the DFG

[1] http://www.uppaal.com

[2] http://www.omg.org/technology/documents/formal/uml.htm

K. Jensen and A. Podelski (Eds.): TACAS 2004, LNCS 2988, pp. 139–143, 2004.

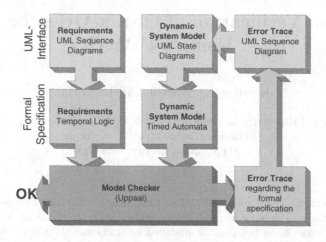

Fig. 1. Tool overview

Our tool *Vooduu* enhances a commercial UML tool by verification functionality. Within the UML, we concentrate on the dynamic view on software because unexpected error configurations caused by complex dynamic runs with timing constraints are one of the most serious problems in the field of real-time applications. These errors are not likely to be found by testing or manual exploration but can be detected by automated exhaustive search of the state space. We use UML sequence diagrams, extended by timing constraints [1], to model requirements and statecharts to model the system behavior.

We support time related constructs in sequence diagrams as well as in statecharts because the timing is crucial in our application domain, which is high speed control processes as used in robotics[3]. Consequently, we employ UPPAAL as model checker because it is tailored to the verification of time dependent systems and supports as well clock as integer variables.

The key functionalities of our tool are the proper transformation of a set of statecharts forming the system model and a set of sequence diagrams as requirements to a model checker and the reinterpretation of the verification results to the UML level in terms of sequence diagrams (Fig. 1).

Related work: Similar to us, [3] uses UPPAAL, too, to verify dynamic UML models but the semantic interpretation of several model elements (e.g. triggerless transitions) differs. In [4], an efficient transformation of statecharts to UPPAAL is implemented but it does not treat the specification of requirements by sequence diagrams. Objects do not communicate via the UML statechart event mechanism but synchronize on actions.

---

[3] SFB562 *Robotic systems for handling and assembly*
(http://www.tu-braunschweig.de/sfb562/)

2   Tool Overview

We implemented our tool as a plug-in for the UML tool *Poseidon for UML*[4] called *Vooduu*[5] (Fig. 2). As a back-end, the model checker UPPAAL is employed. Poseidon provides a graphical user interface for all UML diagrams. UPPAAL is a model checker that provides timed automata for modelling systems and temporal logic expressions for queries [5]. *Vooduu* builds the interface between them.

Figure 1 gives an overview over the tool chain which consists of four components:

- A set of UML statecharts, imported as XML-files, is interpreted as a system model. It is translated independently from the rest of the UML model into a network of timed automata [2].
- Requirements can either be added directly in the UPPAAL environment or - if one prefers to stay on the UML level - in terms of UML sequence diagrams. In the second case, a set of observer automata is generated, which register if and when relevant communication takes place. Erroneous messages and timing violations cause a transition to an error state of an observer automaton. Then the reachability of error states is checked by corresponding automatically generated queries.
- The result of the verification is visualized in the context of UML because the error traces on the UPPAAL level are hardly readable for the designer working on the UML level. If sequence diagrams are used we mark the first position at which a violation of the expected behavior occurs. Additional information for error diagnosis is provided.
- Control of the tool chain, execution of programs and translation of the internal model representation of Poseidon into XML-files are integrated as a plug-in in Poseidon.

Vooduu can handle a restricted subset of UML statecharts modelling object behavior as input: Concurrency is only permitted on the object level. A statechart consists of a hierarchy of composite and basic states with arbitrary transitions. Transitions can be triggered by explicit or timed events or they can be triggerless. For timed events, an interval for the emission can be specified. This construct is useful to model bounded execution time, e.g. if for an action not the exact but a worst case execution time is given. The statechart semantics implemented in *Vooduu* conforms to the UML standard. Most relevant for the translation to UPPAAL is the time model: time may only pass if all event queues of the statecharts, which have to be modelled explicitly at the UPPAAL level, are empty. If an event[6] occurs, it is put in the corresponding queue and the statechart reacts, possibly by emitting some additional events. As long as the system is instable, i.e. some event queues are still not empty, no time elapses. The details on the subset of UML statecharts, its semantics and the transformation to UPPAAL can be found in [2].

---

[4] For more information see http://www.gentleware.de

[5] Verification of object-oriented designs using UPPAAL

[6] which may be a time event if some timeout is reached

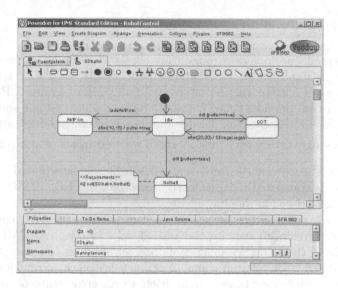

Fig. 2. *Vooduu* as plug-in for Poseidon for UML

To model requirements, we use UML sequence diagrams with some extensions necessary to specify the desired behavior precisely: each sequence diagram has a status, namely *obligatory*, which means that messages have to obey to the given interaction pattern. If the status is set to *optional* the system should allow a run, which is consistent to the sequence diagram. Moreover, a pre-chart (*if*) can be specified. If the pre-chart occurs the post-chart (*then*) becomes obligatory. Within a sequence diagram, loops can be used. A loop condition describes a set of possible iterations [1]. For messages, different modes are possible: Using synchronous messages, sending and receiving a message happen immediately. Using the asynchronous mode, the message is enqueued.

The mapping from the objects of the system model to instances in sequence diagrams can be defined in a flexible way: A set of statecharts can be mapped to one instance. The treatment of internal communication and messages not occurring in the sequence diagrams can be specified by parameters. The sending and receiving of messages can be labelled by time stamps. These time stamps can be used in timing expressions, e.g. to bound the maximal sending time of a message or the reaction time to a request. We use UML stereotypes and tagged values to model these constructs. Mainly, we verify violations of the requirements specification like:

– Incorrect message, sender, receiver
– Violation of timing conditions
– Violation of loop conditions

After modelling the dynamics of a software design using Poseidon, invoking *Vooduu* generates the necessary XML-files, starts the tool chain, performs the verification by UPPAAL and reveals the verification results.

Practical results: Our approach is limited due to the state explosion problem. In the evaluation of the tool we found that e.g. the number of states or messages in the UML diagrams does not give a good guess for the size of the state space, but crucial are the number and the interdependencies of clocks and variables and the degree of nondeterminism within the model. I.e. we could handle a medium sized rather detailed and deterministic model containing 6 processes but failed a much smaller but highly nondeterministic example.

3   Future Work

We implemented a tool that verifies whether requirements defined in terms of UML sequence diagrams are consistent with a system model in terms of UML statecharts. For future work, we intend to specialize our approach to certain application areas. E.g. for a given real-time operation system it would be useful to define a set of stereotypes which refer to its particular elements like processes, threads, channels, scheduling and communication mechanisms. This will support a more specific use of the modelling language, facilitates modelling and optimization of the translation to a model checker because non-relevant elements of the general UML can be omitted. We will integrate structural UML diagrams in the approach to support views on communication structures of software systems.

References

1. Firley, Th., Huhn, M., Diethers, K., Gehrke, Th., Goltz, U.: Timed Sequence Diagrams and Tool-Based Analysis - A Case Study. In Proc. of UML'99 - Beyond the Standard, USA, Springer, (1999) 645–660
2. Diethers, K., Goltz, U., Huhn, M.: Model Checking UML Statecharts with Time. In Proc. of UML'02, Workshop on Critical Systems Development with UML, September 2002
3. Knapp, A., Merz, S., Rauh, Ch.: Model Checking Timed UML State Machines and Collaborations. 7th Int. Symp. Formal Techniques in Real-Time and Fault Tolerant Systems (FTRTFT 2002), pp. 395–414, 2002, LNCS 2469, Springer
4. David, A., Möller, O, Yi, W.: Formal Verification of UML Statecharts with Real-Time Extensions. Fundamental Approaches to Software Engineering (FASE'2002), 2002, LNCS 2306, pp. 218–232, Springer
5. Behrman, G., David, A., Larsen, K., Möller, O., Petterson, P., Yi, W.: Uppaal - Present and Future, Proc. of the 40th IEEE Conference on Decision and Control, 2001, 2281–2286

CoPS – Checker of Persistent Security*

Carla Piazza, Enrico Pivato, and Sabina Rossi

Dipartimento di Informatica, Università Ca' Foscari di Venezia,
{piazza,epivato,srossi}@dsi.unive.it

Abstract. CoPS is an automatic checker of multilevel system security properties. CoPS can be used to check three different bisimulation-based non-interference properties for systems expressed as terms of the Security Process Algebra (SPA) language. The considered properties are persistent, in the sense that they are preserved at each execution step. Moreover, they imply the Bisimulation-based Non Deducibility on Composition (*BNDC*) property, whose decidability is still an open problem.

1 Introduction

The tool CoPS, available at http://www.dsi.unive.it/~mefisto/CoPS/, is an automatic checker of multilevel system security properties. It implements the polynomial algorithms described in [1] to check three security properties named

- *SBNDC*, i.e., *Strong Bisimulation-based Non Deducibility on Composition*,
- *P_BNDC*, i.e., *Persistent BNDC*,
- *PP_BNDC*, i.e., *Progressing Persistent BNDC*.

These are *Non-Interference* [8] properties for processes expressed as terms of the *Security Process Algebra* (SPA) [5] which is a variation of Milner's CCS [10] with actions partitioned into security levels. They imply the *Bisimulation-based Non Deducibility on Composition* (*BNDC*) property, whose decidability is still an open problem. If a system E satisfies one of the three properties checked by CoPS, then what a low level user sees of the system is not modified (in the sense of the bisimulation semantics) by composing any high level (possibly malicious) process with E, i.e., high level users cannot send confidential information down to low level users. The properties are *persistent* in the sense that if a process is *SBNDC* (resp., *P_BNDC* and *PP_BNDC*), then every reachable state is still *SBNDC* (resp., *P_BNDC* and *PP_BNDC*). As far as *P_BNDC* is concerned, in [7] persistency has been proved to be fundamental to deal with processes in dynamic contexts, i.e., contexts that can be reconfigured at runtime. Moreover, in [2] it is shown how *P_BNDC* can be used to prove properties (e.g., fairness) of cryptographic protocols. The three properties are compositional with respect to

---

* Partially supported by the MIUR Project "Modelli formali per la sicurezza", the EU Contract IST-2001-32617 "MyThS", and the FIRB project (RBAU018RCZ) "Interpretazione astratta e model checking per la verifica di sistemi embedded".

K. Jensen and A. Podelski (Eds.): TACAS 2004, LNCS 2988, pp. 144–152, 2004.

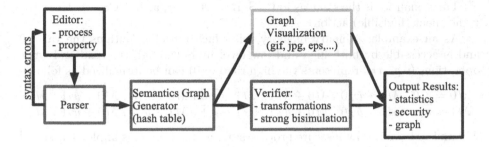

Fig. 1. CoPS Architecture

the parallel composition operator. CoPS exploits this compositionality to speed up the computation and drastically reduce the space complexity.

CoPS consists of a *graphical interface* and a *kernel module*. The graphical interface has been implemented in JAVA to get a large portability and allows to:

- *Insert the process(es)* to be checked in the editor pane. The process(es) can be either typed or loaded from a file. A tree is automatically drawn to facilitate the navigation among processes. The syntax is highlighted to get a better readability. Both fonts and colors can be changed by the user.
- *Select the security property* to be checked and start the verification. It is also possible to check whether two processes are strongly or weakly bisimilar.
- *Read the verification results.* Some time/space statistics are shown together with the security result. Moreover, syntax errors are reported.
- *View the graph* representing the semantics of the process(es). This can be also saved in a file whose type (e.g., jpg, gif, eps) can be chosen by the user.

The kernel module, whose architecture is shown in Figure 1, has been implemented in standard C to obtain good performances and consists of:

- A *parser* which checks for syntax errors and builds the syntax tree out of the SPA process.
- A *semantics graph generator* which elaborates the syntax tree to generate an adjacency-list representation of the graph associated to the process.
- A *verifier* which transforms the graph in order to use a strong bisimulation algorithm to perform the security check.

2   Persistent Security Properties

The *Security Process Algebra* (SPA) [5] is a variation of Milner's CCS [10], where the set of visible actions is partitioned into high level actions and low level ones in order to specify multilevel systems. The syntax of SPA *processes* is as follows:

$$E ::= \mathbf{0} \mid a.E \mid E + E \mid E|E \mid E \setminus v \mid E[f] \mid Z$$

The semantics is the same as in CCS. In particular, as in CCS, we denote by τ the silent (invisible) action.

As an example, a binary memory cell which initially contains the value 0 and is accessible by both high and low level users through the read and write operations (e.g., r_h0 represents the high read of 0) can be formalized as follows:

$$M0 = \overline{r_h0} \, . \, M0 + w_h0 \, . \, M0 + w_h1 \, . \, M1 + \overline{r_l0} \, . \, M0 + w_l0 \, . \, M0 + w_l1 \, . \, M1$$
$$M1 = \overline{r_h1} \, . \, M1 + w_h0 \, . \, M0 + w_h1 \, . \, M1 + \overline{r_l1} \, . \, M1 + w_l0 \, . \, M0 + w_l1 \, . \, M1$$

$M0$ and $M1$ are totally insecure processes: no access control is implemented and a high level malicious entity may write confidential information into the memory cell which can be then read by any low level user. Our security properties will aim at detecting this kind of flaws, even in more subtle and interesting situations.

The three security properties $SBNDC$, P_BNDC and PP_BNDC can be defined in terms of unwinding conditions: if a state F of a secure process performs a high level action moving to a state G, then F also performs a sequence of silent actions moving to a state K which is equivalent to G for a low level user. We denote by $(\overset{\tau}{\to})^*$ a sequence of zero or more silent actions, by $(\overset{\tau}{\to})^+$ a sequence of at least one silent action and by $(\overset{\tau}{\to})^0$ a sequence of zero actions. We also use $\approx$ for weak bisimulation (see [10]) and $\approx^p$ for progressing bisimulation (see [11]).

Definition 1 ([1]). *A process E is* SBNDC *(resp.,* P_BNDC *and* PP_BNDC*) if for all F reachable from E, if $F \overset{h}{\to} G$, then $F(\overset{\tau}{\to})^0 K$ (resp., $F(\overset{\tau}{\to})^* K$ and $F(\overset{\tau}{\to})^+ K$) and $G \setminus H \approx K \setminus H$ (resp. $G \setminus H \approx K \setminus H$ and $G \setminus H \approx^p K \setminus H$).*

The memory cell defined above does not satisfy any of the three security properties. In fact, there is a direct information flow from high to low level. We can redefine the cell by eliminating any low level read operation as follows:

$$M0 = \overline{r_h0} \, . \, M0 + w_h0 \, . \, M0 + w_h1 \, . \, M1 + w_l0 \, . \, M0 + w_l1 \, . \, M1$$
$$M1 = \overline{r_h1} \, . \, M1 + w_h0 \, . \, M0 + w_h1 \, . \, M1 + w_l0 \, . \, M0 + w_l1 \, . \, M1$$

Now the memory cell is both $SBNDC$ and P_BNDC, but not PP_BNDC.

Both $SBNDC$ and P_BNDC are compositional with respect to the parallel operator, but not with respect to the non-deterministic choice operator. On the other hand, PP_BNDC is fully compositional.

In [1] efficient polynomial algorithms to verify the three security properties are described. These algorithms are based on the reduction of the problems of checking the security properties to the problem of checking a strong bisimulation between two graphs. CoPS implements such algorithms. As far as the strong bisimulation underlying algorithm is concerned, CoPS allows the user to choose between the Paige and Tarjan's algorithm [12] and the fast bisimulation algorithm described in [4]. This choice does not affect the worst-case complexities.

3   Tool Overview and Experimental Results

A screen-shot of CoPS is shown in Figure 2: a process has been typed in the edit pane on the right (the syntactic convetions are very similar to the ones

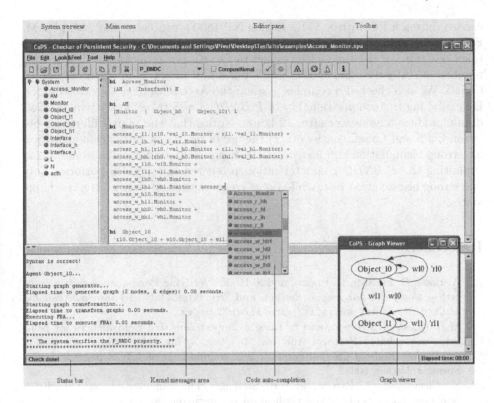

Fig. 2. A screen-shot CoPS : the process is *P_BNDC*

used on CCS processes in the Concurrency Workbench model checker [3]); the sub-processes occurring in its definition are automatically listed on the left; the verification results are shown in the bottom window. By selecting a process on the left, the editor moves on its definition and it allows one to verify it. The toolbar allows one to choose the property to be checked, stop the computation, see the graph representing the semantics of the process. The graph visualization requires the installation of GRAPHVIZ which can be downloaded at http://www.research.att.com/sw/tools/graphviz/. The SETTINGS option in the EDIT menu allows one to personalize the kernel execution by, e.g., setting the path of GRAPHVIZ and the format of the generated graph, choosing the bisimulation algorithm to be used (the Paige and Tarjan's one [12] or the one presented in [4]), avoiding the graph generation, setting the use/dimension of an hash table which speeds up the graph generation.

It is possible to avoid the use of the graphical interface and use directly the kernel via command line (`checker --help` shows the help).

CoPS has been successfully used on a number of medium-sized case studies. It has been compared with the tool CoSeC [6], which allows one to check a bisimulation-based property equivalent to *P_BNDC*. The experiments have been carried out on a PC with a AMD Athlon XP 1800+ processor and 256M RAM. For medium size processes with a number of states smaller than 2000 CoPS takes one third of the time with respect to CoSeC. For processes with a greater number of states (around 6.000) CoPS takes half of the time with respect to CoSeC. We also checked a complex system: the Access_Monitor described in [5]. By exploiting the compositionality of P_BNDC, CoPS takes 55 sec while CoSeC didn't produce any answer after 12 hours. Notice that the main differences between CoPS and CoSeC consist of: (1) the use of the Paige and Tarjan algorithm for strong bisimulation [12] instead of the Kannellakis and Smolka's one [9]; (2) exploiting the P_BNDC characterization presented in [1] CoPS performs only one strong bisimulation test, while CoSeC repeats the test over all the reachable states.

References

1. A. Bossi, R. Focardi, C. Piazza, and S. Rossi. Verifying Persistent Security Properties. *Computer Languages, Systems and Structures*, 2003. To appear. Available at http://www.dsi.unive.it/~srossi/cl03.ps.gz.
2. M. Bugliesi, A. Ceccato, and S. Rossi. Context-Sensitive Equivalences for Non-Interference based Protocol Analysis. In *Proc. of the International Symposium on Fundamentals of Computing (FCT'03)*, volume 2751 of *LNCS*, pages 364–375. Springer–Verlag, 2003.
3. R. Cleaveland, J. Parrow, and B. Steffen. The concurrency workbench: A semantics-based tool for the verification of concurrent systems. *ACM Transactions on Programming Languages and Systems (TOPLAS)*, 15(1):36–72, 1993.
4. A. Dovier, C. Piazza, and A. Policriti. A Fast Bisimulation Algorithm. In *Proc. of Int. Conference on Computer Aided Verification (CAV'01)*, volume 2102 of *LNCS*, pages 79–90. Springer-Verlag, 2001.
5. R. Focardi and R. Gorrieri. A Classification of Security Properties for Process Algebras. *Journal of Computer Security*, 3(1):5–33, 1994/1995.
6. R. Focardi and R. Gorrieri. The Compositional Security Checker: A Tool for the Verification of Information Flow Security Properties. *IEEE Transactions on Software Engineering*, 23(9):550–571, 1997.
7. R. Focardi and S. Rossi. Information Flow Security in Dynamic Contexts. In *Proc. of the 15th IEEE Computer Security Foundations Workshop (CSFW'02)*, pages 307–319. IEEE Computer Society Press, 2002.
8. J. A. Goguen and J. Meseguer. Security Policies and Security Models. In *Proc. of the IEEE Symposium on Security and Privacy (SSP'82)*, pages 11–20. IEEE Computer Society Press, 1982.
9. P. C. Kannellakis and S. A. Smolka. CCS Expressions, Finite State Processes, and Three Problems of Equivalence. *Information and Computation*, 86(1):43–68, 1990.
10. R. Milner. *Communication and Concurrency*. Prentice-Hall, 1989.
11. U. Montanari and V. Sassone. CCS Dynamic Bisimulation is Progressing. In *Proc. of the 16th International Symposium on Mathematical Foundations of Computer Science (MFCS'91)*, volume 520 of *LNCS*, pages 346–356. Springer-Verlag, 1991.
12. R. Paige and R. E. Tarjan. Three Partition Refinement Algorithms. *SIAM Journal on Computing*, 16(6):973–989, 1987.

A   Appendix

A.1   CoPS Site

CoPS is freely available at http://www.dsi.unive.it/~mefisto/CoPS/. In particular, in the site you can find:

- a short description of CoPS and its features;
- a tutorial which illustrates how to use CoPS;
- installation and configuration instructions;
- the downloadable versions together with a directory of examples;
- some references to theoretical papers on which CoPS is based;
- a form to contact us for any problem/suggestion.

CoPS, which is partially supported by the MIUR Project "Mefisto: Modelli formali per la sicurezza", the EU Contract IST-2001-32617 "MyThS", and the FIRB project (RBAU018RCZ) "Interpretazione astratta e model checking per la verifica di sistemi embedded" has been mainly tested by other participants of these projects on different case studies. Some of these case studies have been included in a directory of examples.

A.2   System Requirements and Installation Instructions

In the web pages of CoPS we put four compiled versions (for WINDOWS, LINUX, SUN, and MACOS) and a setup program for WINDOWS.

In order to use CoPS with its graphical interface it is necessary to install the JAVA RUNTIME ENVIRONMENT (JRE) version 1.3.1 or above. We recommend the use JRE version 1.4.2, because the previous versions contain a bug which can cause a malfunctioning of CoPS. However, it is possible to use the kernel, named checker, via command line (--help provides all the details).

To view a graphical representation of the semantics of the system under analysis it is necessary to install GRAPHVIZ, which can be freely downloaded at http://www.research.att.com/sw/tools/graphviz/. If you are not interested in this feature you can disable the graph generation.

The installation of CoPS only requires the download and decompression of a file containing the compiled kernel and the graphical interface. WINDOWS users can also choose to download a setup program providing a menu icon group in the program menu and an uninstall program. Files with .spa extension are automatically associated with CoPS.

The SETTINGS option in the EDIT menu allows to change the default settings, such as the GRAPHVIZ path, the underlying bisimulation algorithm, the graph generation/format, the use/dimension of an hash table, and others.

More detailed instructions and suggestions can be found in CoPS' site.

A.3   An Illustrating Example

A guided tour concerning the functionalities of CoPS and the use of its graphical interface can be found in the TUTORIAL section of our site. There we briefly recall the syntax of the SPA processes accepted by CoPS and illustrate the meaning of buttons, menus, and settings of the graphical interface through some snapshots.

Here we model a case study in order to give an intuition about the meaning of our security properties and the potentialities of CoPS .

Let us consider the E-commerce Processing System described in "Information Flow in Operating Systems: Eager Formal Methods" by J.D. Guttman, A.L. Herzog, and J.D. Ramsdell, presented at the Workshop on Issues in the Theory of Security 2003 (WITS'03). The system represents a process in which:

- an order is submitted electronically by a `Client`;
- an `E_sale` process ensures that the order is correct (e.g., the prices and discounts are correct), and, if so, passes it to the process `A_receiv` (Account Receivable);
- `A_receiv` interacts with a credit card clearing house and, if everything is ok, passes the order to the `Ship` process;
- the `Ship` process sends the order to the `Client`.

In the paper presented at WITS'03 the authors use Linear Temporal Logic to specify information flow policies for SELINUX, which can then be checked via model-checking. The `E-commerce` example is used to illustrate the technique. In particular, in this example it is important to ensure that, if the internal channels of communication are secure, then the casual chain is always the same (e.g., it is not possible that an unpaid order is shipped).

Let us model the E-commerce Processing System in the SPA language and use CoPS to check that the casual chain remains the same even in presence of a malicious attacker. To do this, all the interactions (including the ones with the client) have to be modelled as high level actions. Since we are assuming that the channels are secure these actions will be under the scope of a restriction, i.e., an attacker cannot synchronize on these actions. Then, different low level signals have to be sent out at different execution points. We have to check that also in presence of an high level attacker the low level signals are sent out in the same order, i.e., the casual chain is always the same. Hence, using the syntax[1] of CoPS we get the following processes.

```
bi E_Commerce (Client|E_sale|A_receiv|Ship)\Hc

bi Client 'sock_price_ok_and_pay_ok.shipped_order.0

bi E_sale sock_price_ok_and_pay_ok.'oklow1.'new_order_pay_ok.E_sale
        + sock_price_ok_and_pay_no.'oklow1.'new_order_pay_no.E_sale
        + sock_price_no_and_pay_ok.'nolow1.E_sale
        + sock_price_no_and_pay_no.'nolow1.E_sale
```

---

[1] In CoPS given an action `a`, `'a` stands for the output action $\bar{a}$.

Fig. 3. The process E_commerce is *P_BNDC*

```
bi A_receiv new_order_pay_ok.'oklow2.'paid_order.A_receiv
         + new_order_pay_no.'nolow2.A_receiv

bi Ship paid_order.'oklow3.'shipped_order.Ship

basi Hc sock_price_ok_and_pay_ok sock_price_ok_and_pay_no
        sock_price_no_and_pay_ok sock_price_no_and_pay_no
        new_order_pay_ok new_order_pay_no
        paid_order shipped_order

acth sock_price_ok_and_pay_ok sock_price_ok_and_pay_no
     sock_price_no_and_pay_ok sock_price_no_and_pay_no
     new_order_pay_ok new_order_pay_no
     paid_order shipped_order
```

The process E_commerce satisfies the three security properties, i.e., the casual chain order is always respected. In Figure 3 we show the positive answer of CoPS relatively to the *P_BNDC* property. Some of its sub-components (e.g., the process E_sale) are not secure. This is due to the fact that the high level channels are not locally restricted, i.e., an attacker interacting directly with a sub-component can change the casual chain. In Figure 4 we show the negative

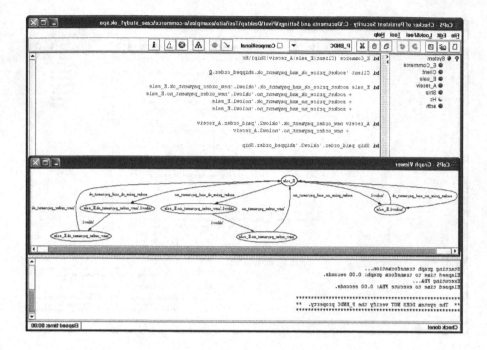

Fig. 4. The process E_sale is not *P_BNDC*

answer of CoPS relatively to *P_BNDC* for E_sale, together with its graph representation.

This example is modelled in the file case_study1_ok.spa in the subdirectory e-commerce of the directory of examples downloadable from our site. In the same directory, the files case_study2_ok_dead.spa and case_study2_ok_nodead.spa contain a variation of the E_commerce process in which the client can query the system to know the status of its order. In this case it is necessary to add timeouts to avoid that an attacker blocks the system.

Tampere Verification Tool

Heikki Virtanen, Henri Hansen, Antti Valmari, Juha Nieminen, and
Timo Erkkilä

Tampere University of Technology, Institute of Software Systems
PO Box 553, FIN-33101 Tampere, FINLAND
hansen@cs.tut.fi

Abstract. Tampere Verification Tool (TVT) is a collection of programs
for automated verification of concurrent and reactive systems. TVT has
its roots in process algebras and explicit state space exploration, but in
addition to actions, our formalism allows use of state-based information
in the form of truth-valued state propositions. Furthermore, it contains
three types of state proposition-like notions to support on-the-fly verification, and one state proposition to exploit partially defined processes.
TVT supports compositional state space construction, stubborn sets and
visual verification.

1 Introduction

The story of Tampere Verification Tool (TVT) started at the beginning of 1990's,
when CFFD semantics was first introduced [10]. CFFD describes an abstraction
of the behaviour of a system. It is the weakest congruence relation with respect
to the composition operators of process algebras that preserves both stuttering-
insensitive properties specified in linear temporal logic and deadlocks [4]. Based
on CFFD, the "Advanced Reachability Analysis" (ARA) tool [9] was developed.
ARA supports LOTOS as the modelling language, compositional construction
of a system, visual verification, and CFFD equivalence comparison. ARA was
used in the industry even a decade later [7].

Eventually, ARA became difficult to maintain, LOTOS proved ill-suited for
verification applications [6], and many new verification ideas emerged. When
Nokia offered us a contract for developing a new verification tool in 1999, we
started the development of TVT. TVT was intended to be used both in Nokia
Research Center and as a platform for developing and testing new verification
ideas in Tampere University of Technology. TVT has been made freely available
for academic use under the Nokia Open Source licence and can be downloaded
from [8].

2 Key Features

TVT is a collection of non-interactive[1] command-line programs. The programs
are used for manipulating and analysing behaviours of systems. The formalism

---

[1] The only exception is the visualisation tool which has a graphical user interface.

K. Jensen and A. Podelski (Eds.): TACAS 2004, LNCS 2988, pp. 153–157, 2004.

used as a model of the behaviour of a process is a *labelled state transition system* or an *LSTS*.

An LSTS is a labelled transition system (LTS), where the states can be labelled with truth-valued propositions. The actions of an LSTS are used to talk about how the components in a system interact with each other and the environment. In other words, the LTS-part of an LSTS describes the behaviour of the system. The propositions have been added to exploit the fact that in state-based models it is easier to express properties that depend on the global state of the system [1].

Perhaps the most important operation in TVT is the parallel composition of LSTSs. It implements a flexible parallel composition operator [6] combining parallel composition, multiple renaming, hiding and restriction. The parallel composition is controlled by a set of synchronisation rules given in a file. The file describes how actions of processes synchronise and how values of state propositions of the result are evaluated from the values of state propositions of the component processes [1]. During the construction of the state space, the program can do on-the-fly verification as discussed in [2] and in other ways, and reduction using the stubborn set method [12]. Partially defined processes, with cut states marking the pruning points [5] can also be used to further reduce the state space or to avoid the modelling of uninteresting parts of a system.

Other programs of the tool include reduction algorithms and conversions between different representations of LSTSs. Currently the tool supports reductions that preserve CFFD-semantics and strong bisimulation, but it is possible to add support for other semantics as well. The LSTS file format has been designed with that in mind.

There are programs for visualisation and comparisons of LSTS representations of systems. The theory of visual verification has been explored in [13,11].

Essentially, TVT is a framework for development of tools and methods for explicit state space exploration, with emphasis on process algebra. Real-time or hybrid methods are not included.

3   Modelling Issues

To support compositionality in full scale, TVT has two modelling languages: one for describing LSTSs and another for describing communication between LSTSs. The languages used in modelling are close to the structure of LSTSs and synchronisation rules. The only significant difference is the possibility to use local variables when defining processes. The compiler "unfolds" the variables by duplicating states and instantiating action names with data values. This resembles a lot the unfolding of a coloured Petri net into an ordinary Petri net [3].

In addition to the compositional bottom-up construction of a state space, the pre-congruence property of CFFD semantics can be used to reduce the state space even further. One can replace any component with a more deterministic one without invalidating the correctness of a correct system. In the verification phase we may use a small specification process instead of an actual component if we know that the component will be an implementation of that specification.

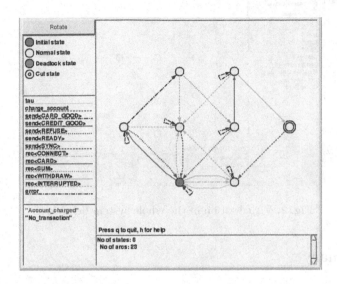

Fig. 1. Visualisation of a component behaviour

As an example of the use of TVT, consider a system consisting of a bankteller, a bank, and the communications links between them. In Figure 1 we see one component of this system, the bank. This component models the behaviour of the computer system in a bank that communicates with a bankteller machine. The actions "rec" and "send" have one parameter. In the figure, we have an explicit representation, where the values of the parameter have already been unfolded. One proposition ("Account_charged") has been selected and the state in which it is true is highlighted with a double circle.

Using the compositional approach inherent in TVT, the state space of the system that contains about 11 million states and 67 million transitions can be constructed and reduced to contain only the behaviour of the system visible to the user at the bankteller in less than a minute. The result is shown in Figure 2, drawn using the TVT visualisator.

Each program in TVT implements just one operation. This makes it possible to combine operations in various orderings, perhaps reducing intermediate results to avoid state explosion. Other programs like **make** may be used to automate the composition and include suitable reductions for different purposes, e.g., one for visualisation and another one for producing a component for use as a part of a bigger system.

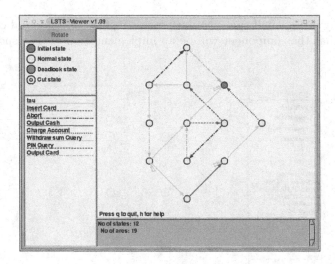

Fig. 2. Visualisation of the whole system behaviour

4   Summary

Tampere Verification Tool (TVT) is a framework for classical verification based on exhaustive and reduced state space exploration methods, on-the-fly verification, and visualisation. A key feature of TVT is compositional bottom-up construction of the state space which is an effective method to combat the state explosion problem.

The formalism used in TVT, labelled state transition system (LSTS), is derived from a pure action-based formalism, labelled transition system (LTS), by adding support for state propositions. These state propositions are used for the modelling of properties more naturally associated with states than with actions and as markers for error conditions in on-the-fly verification.

As such TVT can be used as a computer-aided software engineering tool when designing concurrent systems. In addition, TVT is a framework for implementation of software for new verification methods.

Acknowledgements. The development of TVT was supported by Nokia Research Center, The Technology Development Centre of Finland and Emil Aaltonen Foundation.

References

1. H. Hansen, H. Virtanen, and A. Valmari. Merging state-based and action-based verification. In *Proceedings of the third international conference on Application of Concurrency to System Design (ACSD 2003)*, pp. 150–156, IEEE, 2003.

2. J. Helovuo and A. Valmari. Checking for CFFD-preorder with tester processes. In *Tools and Algorithms for the Construction and Analysis of Systems, 6th International Conference, TACAS 2000*, number 1785 in Lecture Notes in Computer Science, pp. 283–298, Berlin, March 27–31 2000. Springer-Verlag.

3. K. Jensen *Coloured Petri Nets Volume 1: Basic Concepts, Analysis Methods and Practical Use*. EATCS Monographs on Theoretical Computer Science, 234 pages. Springer-Verlag, 1992.

4. R. Kaivola and A. Valmari. The weakest compositional semantic equivalence preserving nexttime-less linear temporal logic. In *Proceedings of CONCUR '92, Third International Conference on Concurrency Theory*, number 630 in Lecture Notes in Computer Science, pp. 207–221. Springer-Verlag, 1992.

5. A. Kangas and A. Valmari. Verification with the undefined: A new look. In Thomas Arts and Wan Fokkink, editors, *Proceedings of Eighth International Workshop on Formal Methods for Industrial Critical Systems (FMICS'03)*, volume 80 of *ENTCS*.

6. K. Karsisto. *A New Parallel Composition Operator for Verification Tools*. PhD thesis, Tampere University of Technology, 2003.

7. S. Leppänen and M. Luukkainen. Compositional verification of a third generation mobile communication protocol. In Ten-Hwang Lai, editor, *Proceedings of the 1st Workshop on Distributed System Validation and Verification*, pp. E118–E125, 2000.

8. Tvt-project home page. http://www.cs.tut.fi/ohj/VARG/TVT/

9. A. Valmari, J. Kemppainen, M. Clegg, and M. Levanto. Putting advanced reachability analysis techniques together: the ARA tool. In *Proceedings of Formal Methods Europe '93: Industrial-Strength Formal Methods*, number 670 in Lecture Notes in Computer Science, pp. 597–616. Springer-Verlag, 1993.

10. A. Valmari and M. Tienari. An improved failures equivalence for finite-state systems with a reduction algorithm. In *Proceedings of Protocol Specification, Testing and Verification XI*, pp. 3–18. North Holland, 1991.

11. A. Valmari, H. Virtanen, and A. Puhakka. Context-sensitive visibility. In Cleaveland R. and Garavel H., editors, *FMICS'02 7th International ERCIM Workshop on Formal Methods for Industrial Critical Systems*, volume 66 of *ENCTS*, pp. 201–217.

12. A. Valmari. Stubborn set methods for process algebras. In *Proceedings of POMIV'96, Workshop on Partial Order Methods in Verification*, volume 29 of *DIMACS Series in Discrete Mathematics and Theoretical Computer Science*, pp. 213–231. American Mathematical Society, July 1996.

13. A. Valmari and M. Setälä. Visual verification of safety and liveness. In *Proceedings of Formal Methods Europe '96: Industrial Benefit and Advances in Formal Methods*, number 1051 in Lecture Notes in Computer Science, pp. 228–247. Springer-Verlag, 1996.

SyncGen: An Aspect-Oriented Framework for Synchronization

Xianghua Deng, Matthew Dwyer, John Hatcliff, and Masaaki Mizuno

Department of Computing and Information Sciences
Manhattan, KS 66506, USA
{deng,dwyer,hatcliff,masaaki}@cis.ksu.edu

Abstract. This paper describes SyncGen – a tool for automatically synthesizing complex synchronization implementations from formal high-level specifications. In SyncGen, synchronization specifications are phrased using first-order logic or user-friendly specification patterns. From a high-level specification, a language independent synchronization solution in an intermediate guarded-command language is synthesized. Back-end translators can translate this intermediate solution into a variety of implementation frameworks including Java, C++/C with POSIX threads, and Controller Area Network message passing primitives. SyncGen has been used extensively in courses at Kansas State University. Its breadth of applicability has been demonstrated by using it to solve virtually all of the exercises given in the well-known concurrency text books of Andrews[1,2] and Hartley[4], as well as a variety of real-world problems in the embedded computing domain. The tool, along with supporting documentation and an example repository, is publicly available [6].

Concurrency is a fundamental tool for meeting the ever increasing performance demands placed on software. With improved performance, however, comes the risk of unintended interference between software components executing in parallel. Developing robust synchronization policies and implementations that assure correct component collaboration without unduly restricting parallelism is a significant challenge. Inspired by Andrews' global invariant approach to synchronization generation [1], we have developed Sync-Gen to allow application developers to synthesize customized synchronization solutions without having to concern themselves with the low-level details of their implementation. SyncGen separates the synchronzation and functional implementation of an application and provides aspect-oriented support for weaving them into a complete system. Using SyncGen, users develop sequential application code and identify regions of the application that are inter-dependent. The boundaries of those regions form the (cut) points at which synchronization policies must be enforced. Users can give a high-level formal specification of the synchronization policy which governs the collaborative execution of a group of code regions and SyncGen automatically synthesizes efficient synchronization aspect code and weaves that synchronization code into the core functional code at the appropriate region boundaries. The toolset is:

- *Useful* – the tool has been used in advanced operating systems courses extensively at Kansas State University, and students and instructors find it tremendously useful.

K. Jensen and A. Podelski (Eds.): TACAS 2004, LNCS 2988, pp. 158–162, 2004.

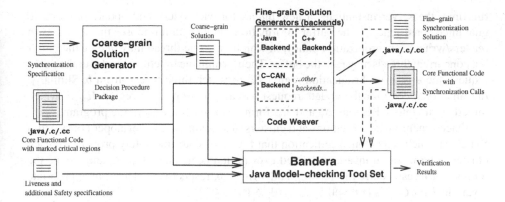

Fig. 1. SyncGen tool architecture

- *Powerful* – using a synchronization pattern system, complicated policies can be described clearly and succinctly at a very high level.
- *Expressive* – we have used the pattern system to specify solutions for almost all exercises from two well-known concurrency texts [1,2,4].
- *Automatic* – this is a push-button approach where code with very intricate semantics is automatically generated from high-level specifications. Thus, it is very easy to learn to use the tool.
- *General* – the approach is language independent and supports multiple target languages and synchronization primitives. (e.g., we currently have full tool support implemented for Java, C/C++ with POSIX threads).
- *Formal* – our aspect specification language has a rigorous semantic foundation which enables code generation techniques that use decision procedures for a quantifier-free fragment of first-order arithmetic and yields a high degree of confidence in the generated solutions.
- *Verifiable* – the structure of the generated code and associated artifacts is designed so that crucial correctness requirements can be checked automatically using existing software model-checking technology.

The tool architecture in Figure 1 depicts the main components of SyncGen, the artifacts that the user supplies (on the left), and the artifacts that the toolset synthesizes (on the right). These artifacts are discussed as we explain the operation of the tool below; for a more complete presentation see [3].

Using the SyncGen approach to developing concurrent software, a developer uses traditional methods and development environments to produce what we term the system's *core functional code*. This code realizes the behavior of each concurrent component of the system, but *does not* specify how components synchronize. Instead, the developer simply marks the *regions* of code in each component that require synchronization with syntactic tags. The developer then partitions regions into equivalence classes termed *clusters* based on which regions refer to each other. Intuitively, regions R_1 and R_2 should be in the same cluster if a thread at region R_1 waits for an event or state that is triggered or changed by a thread at R_2.

For example, consider a web server program in which a query request writes information into a shared buffer b and an update request reads the information in b. At run-time, the server instantiates a new thread for each query and update request. To guarantee consistency of the buffer information, the program imposes the well-known readers/writers synchronization policy, in which only one thread may update the buffer but concurrent threads may read the buffer. Then, within the functional code for the query request, there is a synchronization region R_r in which threads read from b. Similarly, the functional code for the update request has a synchronization region R_w in which threads write into b. Regions R_r and R_w form a sole cluster C_{rw} in the program.

Once synchronization regions and clusters are identified, the developer constructs a SyncGen synchronization specification that formally states the safety property of each cluster in terms of an invariant defined over region occupancy. Let nr and nw be the number of threads currently reading and writing b, respectively. Then, an appropriate invariant I for C_{rw} is $(nr = 0 \lor nw = 0) \land (nw \leq 1)$.

Given this high-level global invariant, SyncGen automatically generates a *coarse-grained synchronization solution* for each cluster. Notice that we must guarantee that nr and nw correctly keep track of the number of reading threads and writing threads, respectively. Therefore, before a query (update) thread enters region R_r (W_r), nr (nw) must be incremented by one. Similarly, after a query (update) thread exits R_r (R_w), nr (nw) must be decremented by one. A coarse-grained solution performs the increments so as to maintain I, using the following two high-level synchronization constructs:

1. $\langle S \rangle$: Statement S is executed atomically.
2. $\langle \textbf{await } B \rightarrow S \rangle$: Atomically check if B is true, then execute S. If B is false, the executing thread waits until B becomes true and executes S.

For the execution of $nr + +$, the following Hoare triple must hold: $\{I\}\langle\textbf{await } B \rightarrow nr + +\rangle\{I\}$; this says that if I holds in a state where B holds, then executing $nr + +$ will result in a state in which I holds. Logically B can be mechanically derived as the weakest condition such that $I \land B \Rightarrow wp(nr + +, I)$, where $wp(nr + +, I)$ denotes the weakest condition that may hold and still guarantee that if $nr + +$ executes I will hold. If B is true, $\langle S \rangle$ is used. For the web site program, the following coarse-grained solution is derived.

$$\langle\textbf{await } nw = 0 \rightarrow nr + +\rangle \qquad \langle\textbf{await } nw = 0 \land nr == 0 \rightarrow nw + +\rangle$$
$$\text{read from B} \qquad\qquad\qquad \text{write into B}$$
$$\langle nr - -\rangle \qquad\qquad\qquad\qquad \langle nw - -\rangle$$

Translation algorithms exist from a coarse-grained solution to various languages and synchronization primitives (called *fine-grained code*), including translations to Java, POSIX P-thread, CAN, active monitor, and semaphores. Each translation has been proved to maintain the global invariant; therefore, the resulting code satisfies the synchronization specification.

The functional code and fine-grained synchronization aspect code are woven by inserting, at the entries to and exits from synchronization regions in the functional code, call statements to the corresponding aspect code.

SyncGen automates the above processes (1) to generate a coarse-grained solution from a global invariant, (2) to translate the coarse-grained solution to fine-grained synchronization code, and (3) to weave the function code and the aspect code. Currently,

SyncGen implements translation algorithms to Java synchronization blocks and POSIX P-threads.

SyncGen logical specifications of invariants that capture synchronization policies. To make SyncGen more broadly usable by software developers, we have identified a large number of commonly occurring synchronization patterns and presented them to users as parameterized templates that are invoked by name. Some of the most commonly used patterns are:

- Bound(R, n): A cluster consists of a single synchronization region R. At most n threads can be in R.
- Exclusion($R_1, R_2, \cdots, R_n$): A cluster consists of n regions $R_1, R_2, \cdots, R_n$. Threads can be in at most one synchronization region out of the n synchronization regions.
- $k-$MuTex($R_1, R_2, \cdots, R_n, k$) (k-Mutual Exclusion): At most k threads can be in regions in the cluster.
- Barrier($(R_1, N_1), (R_2, N_2), \cdots, (R_n, N_n)$): N_i number of threads entering region R_i for $1 \leq i \leq n$ meet, form a group, and leave the respective synchronization regions together.

As variations of the Barrier pattern, we have

- Asymmetric Barrier: an asymmetric version of the Barrier pattern, where threads entering a subset of regions trigger the departure of threads from another subset of regions.
- Barrier with Information Exchange: An extension of the Barrier pattern where the threads forming a group exchange information before leaving together.

For example, the previous readers/writers synchronization may be specified by Bound(W, 1) $\wedge$ Exclusion(R, W). We have successfully solved most synchronization problems found in several advanced operating systems textbooks. For example, the Sleeping Barber problem may be solved by using the Barrier (for the barber and a customer to meet), k-Mutex (for customers to sit/leave chairs in the waiting room), and Asymmetric Barrier (for the barber to notify the customer of completion of the hair cut) patterns. The multiple barbers problem may be solved by simply changing the Barrier pattern to the Barrier with Information Exchange pattern so that a customer can remember which barber cuts his hair. We have also successfully applied SyncGen and the patterns to implement various event-triggered embedded control systems. In such systems, we found that the Asymmetric Barrier and Bound patterns were most used in sending/receiving events and forming critical sections, respectively.

The SyncGen web site [6] contains much more information on the usage of our tool. The complete catalog of examples, a repository of examples, a tutorial on how to use SyncGen and the implementation which synthesizes Java implementations are all available for public download.

References

1. G. R. Andrews. *Concurrent Programming: Principles and Practice.* Addison-Wesley, 1991.
2. G. R. Andrews. *Foundations of Multithreaded, Parallel, and Distributed Programming.* Addison-Wesley, 2000.
3. X. Deng, M. Dwyer, J. Hatcliff, and M. Mizuno. Invariant-based specification, synthesis, and verification of synchronization in concurrent programs. In *ICSE*, 2002.
4. S. Hartley. *Concurrent Programming - The Java Programming Language.* Oxford University Press, 1998.
5. M. Mizuno. A structured approach for developing concurrent programs in Java. *Information Processing Letters*, 69(5):233–238, Mar. 1999.
6. X.Deng, M. Dwyer, J. Hatcliff, and M. Mizuno. SyncGen. |http://syncgen.projects.cis.ksu.edu|, 2002.

MetaGame: An Animation Tool for Model-Checking Games

Markus Müller-Olm[1]* and Haiseung Yoo[2]

[1] FernUniversität in Hagen, Fachbereich Informatik, LG PI 5
Universitätsstr. 1, 58097 Hagen, Germany
mmo@ls5.informatik.uni-dortmund.de
[2] Universität Dortmund, Fachbereich Informatik, LS 5
Baroper Str. 301, 44221 Dortmund, Germany
Haiseung.Yoo@cs.uni-dortmund.de

Abstract. Failing model checking runs should be accompanied by appropriate error diagnosis information that allows the user to identify the cause of the problem. For branching time logics error diagnosis information can be given by a winning strategy in a graph game derived from the model checking instance. However, winning strategies as such are hard to grasp. In this paper we describe the MetaGame tool that computes and animates winning strategies for modal μ-calculus model checking games on finite graphs. MetaGame allows the user to play model checking games in a GUI interface thus making winning strategies more accessible.

Keywords: model checking, game, error diagnosis, branching time logic, animation

1   Introduction

Over the last two decades model checking has evolved as a useful technique that aids in the correct design of hardware and software systems. Here we are interested in checking formulas of the modal μ-calculus for small finite-state models. Such models arise, e.g., as high-level descriptions of systems as coordinated lower level components. In such scenarios, state explosion is not an issue as models typically are rather small in comparison to the models used in hardware or software model checking. Therefore, systems can be represented by explicitly given annotated graphs and global techniques can be applied.

Nowadays there is a growing awareness that model checking is most effective as an error finding technique rather than a technique for guaranteeing absolute correctness. This is partly due to the fact that specifications that can be checked automatically through model checking are necessarily partial in that they specify only certain aspects of the system behavior. Therefore, successful model checking runs while reassuring cannot guarantee full correctness. On the other hand, careful investigation of the cause for failing of model checking runs may allow

---

* On leave from Universität Dortmund.

K. Jensen and A. Podelski (Eds.): TACAS 2004, LNCS 2988, pp. 163–167, 2004.

the user to identify errors in the system. Thus, model checkers are more and more conceived as elaborate debugging tools that complement traditional testing techniques.

For model checkers being useful as debugging tools, it is important that failing model checking attempts are accompanied by appropriate *error diagnosis information* that explains why the model check has failed. Model checkers can fail *spuriously*, i.e., although the property does not hold for the investigated abstraction it may still be valid for the real system. In order to be useful it should be easy for the user to rule out spurious failures and to locate the errors in the system from the provided error diagnosis information. Therefore, it is important that error diagnosis information is easily accessible by the user.

For linear-time logics error diagnosis information is conceptually of a simple type: it is given by an (eventually cyclic) execution path of the system that violates the given property. Thus, linear-time model checkers like SPIN [3] compute and output such an *error trace* in case model checking fails. The situation is more complex for branching-time logics like the modal μ-calculus. Such logics do not just specify properties of single program executions but properties of the execution tree. Hence, meaningful error diagnosis information for branching-time logic model checking cannot be represented by linear executions, in general.

Stirling [4,5] developed a characterization of μ-calculus model checking as a *two player graph game* with a *Rabin chain winning condition* [6]. It is well-known that such games are *determined* (i.e., one of the players has a winning strategy) and that the winning player always has a *memory-less winning strategy*. Memoryless strategies can be presented as sub-graphs of the game graph.

In the game constructed from a model checking instance, Player II has a winning strategy if and only if model checking fails. Thus, we can use a winning strategy of Player II as error diagnosis information. Conversely, Player I has a winning strategy in the constructed game if and only if model checking succeeds. Thus, a winning strategy of Player I can be seen as justification for a successful model check. Thus, both successful and failing model checking runs give rise to the same type of justifying information, a nice symmetry.

However, it is not easy to interpret winning strategies as such. Therefore, we propose to *animate* winning strategies. The idea is that the user is put into the position of the losing player and plays games against the system. The system plays according to the computed winning strategy. Obviously, this implies that the user will lose all games. By this, the user increases his knowledge about the system behavior and hopefully understands the model checking result better. By the above mentioned symmetry, this idea is applicable for error diagnosis (user=Player I, system=Player II) as well as for understanding successful model checking results (user=Player II, system=Player I).

The MetaGame tool realizes this idea. It is integrated into the MetaFrame environment [2] and relies on its basic infrastructure and graph manipulation capabilities. MetaGame extends the MetaFrame environment with strategy synthesis and a GUI-based animation of μ-calculus model-checking games. A number of features are intended to allow a more informative and more easily accessible

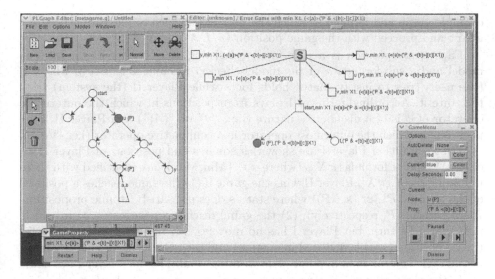

Fig. 1. A screenshot showing the main windows of MetaGame.

animation. In the next section we show an example run of MetaGame on a small illustrative example and discuss the main features.

2 Playing Games with MetaGame

As usual, system models are given by finite graphs the edges of which are labeled by actions and the nodes of which are labeled by sets of atomic propositions. System models can be created and manipulated with MetaFrame's PLGraph editor or loaded from a file. The top left window in Fig. 1 shows an example system model. The logic supported by MetaGame is a variant of the modal μ-calculus. The formula to be checked onto the system model can be typed into a text field or loaded from a file. The bottom left window in Fig. 1 shows an example formula. In standard μ-calculus syntax this formula reads $\mu X_1.(\langle a\rangle(P \wedge \langle b\rangle[c]X_1))$.

After loading or creating a system and a formula, MetaGame constructs the corresponding game graph and computes the winning regions of Player I and II and their respective winning strategies. This is done simultaneously for all positions of the game graph by a strategy synthesis algorithm that achieves essentially the same asymptotic complexity as counter-based global μ-calculus model checkers [1].

After computing the winning strategies, MetaGame offers the user to play error diagnosis games; i.e., the user is put into the position of Player I. The primary view of the played game is a designated window that shows the explored game positions in a tree-like fashion together with a "Game Menu" window that offers options for proceeding with building this tree. The big window in the right part of Fig. 1, for instance, shows a situation in an error diagnosis game for the

example graph and formula in which the user has decided to play from the state
start and proceed with the game position $(u, P \wedge \langle b \rangle [c] X_1)$.

Each game position is a pair (s, ϕ) consisting of a state s in the system
model and a sub-formula ϕ of the model-checked formula. Intuitively, Player I
(the user) tries to justify that ϕ holds for s while Player II (the system) tries
to refute it. Accordingly, Player I plays from positions in which the outermost
operator of ϕ is of a disjunctive nature (i.e., "$\vee$" or "$\langle A \rangle$") and Player II from
positions in which the outermost operator is a conjunctive operator (i.e., "$\wedge$" or
"$[A]$"). Positions of Player I are shown as squares and positions of Player II as
circles. Fixpoint formulas $\sigma X.\phi$ (where $\sigma \in \{\text{Min}, \text{Max}\}$) are identified with their
unfolding $\phi[\sigma X.\phi/X]$. Player II wins the game if (1) the game reaches a position
of the form (s, P) (or $(s, \neg P)$) where state s does not satisfy atomic proposition
P (or satisfies P, respectively); (2) the game reaches a position (s, ϕ) in which
it is Player I's turn, but Player I has no move; or (3) the game becomes cyclic
(i.e., a position (s, ϕ) is revisited in a game) and the outermost fixpoint operator
in the cycle is a minimal fixpoint. The winning conditions for Player I are dual.

In the game window, the user can choose his next move by selecting a position
in the game position tree with the mouse. After clicking the "Play" button in
the Game Menu window, the system proceeds with the game according to Player
II's winning strategy as far as possible. Afterwards it asks the user for a next
move or, if a winning situation for Player II has been reached, it informs the
user about the reason for winning. By clicking the "Fast Forward" button the
user can also instruct the system to choose some next move arbitrarily.

A number of features lead to a more informative and accessible animation.

1. As shown in Fig. 1, the *projection* of the selected game position onto the
   state and the formula component are shown in the system model and in
   the formula window by coloring the corresponding state and sub-formula,
   respectively. This allow the user to match the game position with the model
   state and the sub-formula much more easily.
2. The user can *backtrack* in a play and *multiple plays* can be in progress
   simultaneously. This is achieved by allowing the user to select his next move
   at an arbitrary place in the position tree.
3. The user can *prune* the position tree, by cutting off explored pieces he is no
   longer interested in ("Stop"-button). In addition, various *AutoDelete* options
   allow the user to automatically prune the position tree according to the place
   of the chosen next move.
4. The user can *introduce delays* into the animation of Player I's strategy and
   interrupt the animation with the "Pause" button.

Fig. 2 shows a final situation for the example graph in which the user has lost
all three possible plays. Besides error diagnosis games, MetaGame also allows
the user to play games that explain successful model checking runs.

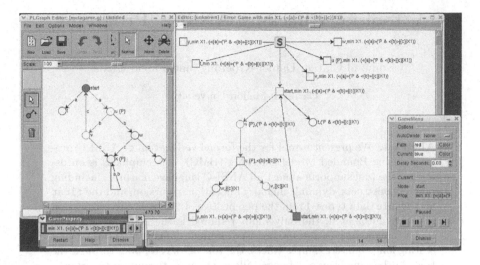

Fig. 2. A final situation.

3   Conclusion

We have described the MetaGame tool that allows the user to play model checking games in a GUI interface. As state explosion is not an issue in the intended application scenarios, we can apply global strategy synthesis and compute and store strategies for the whole game graph completely. This allows us to animate model checking games without noticeable delays and to offer the flexibility to backtrack and to have multiple plays in progress simultaneously. We consider this important factors for a wider acceptance of the idea of playing games as a means for understanding model checking results of branching time logics.

References

1. R. Cleaveland, M. Klein, and B. Steffen. Faster model checking for the modal mu-calculus. In G. v. Bochmann and D. K. Probst, editors, *Computer Aided Verification (CAV'92)*, volume 663 of *Lecture Notes in Computer Science*, pages 410–422. Springer-Verlag, June/July 1992.
2. Metaframe homepage.
   http://ls5-www.cs.uni-dortmund.de/projects/METAFrame/.
3. Spin homepage. http://spinroot.com/spin/whatispin.html.
4. C. Stirling. Local model checking games. In S. A. Smolka, editor, *Proc. 6th Intern. Conf. on Concurrency Theory (CONCUR'95)*, volume 962 of *Lecture Notes in Computer Science*, pages 1–11. Springer-Verlag, 1995.
5. C. Stirling and P. Stevens. Practical model-checking using games. In *TACAS 1998*, volume 1384 of *Lecture Notes in Computer Science*, pages 85–101, 1998.
6. W. Thomas. On the synthesis of strategies in infinite games. In E. Mayr and C. Puech, editors, *Proceedings of the 12th Annual Symposium on Theoretical Aspects of Computer Science, STACS '95*, volume 900 of *Lecture Notes in Computer Science*, pages 1–13. Springer-Verlag, 1995.

A Tool for Checking ANSI-C Programs

Edmund Clarke, Daniel Kroening, and Flavio Lerda

Carnegie Mellon University

Abstract. We present a tool for the formal verification of ANSI-C programs using Bounded Model Checking (BMC). The emphasis is on usability: the tool supports almost all ANSI-C language features, including pointer constructs, dynamic memory allocation, recursion, and the `float` and `double` data types. From the perspective of the user, the verification is highly automated: the only input required is the BMC bound. The tool is integrated into a graphical user interface. This is essential for presenting long counterexample traces: the tool allows stepping through the trace in the same way a debugger allows stepping through a program.

1 Introduction

We present a tool that uses Bounded Model Checking to reason about low-level ANSI-C programs. There are two applications of the tool: 1) the tool checks safety properties such as the correctness of pointer constructs, and 2) the tool can compare an ANSI-C program with another design, such as a circuit given in Verilog.

Many safety-critical software systems are legacy designs, i.e., written in a low level language such as ANSI-C or even assembly language, or at least contain components that are written in this manner. Furthermore, very often performance requirements enforce the use of these languages. These systems are a bigger security and safety problem than programs written in high level languages. The high level languages are usually easier to verify, as they enforce type-safety, for example. The verification of low level ANSI-C code is challenging due to the extensive use of arithmetic, pointers, pointer arithmetic, and bit-wise operators.

We describe a tool that formally verifies ANSI-C programs. The properties checked include pointer safety, array bounds, and user-provided assertions. The tool implements a technique called Bounded Model Checking (BMC) [1]. In BMC, the transition relation for a complex state machine and its specification are jointly unwound to obtain a Boolean formula that is satisfiable if there exists an error trace. The formula is then checked by using a SAT procedure. If the formula is satisfiable, a counterexample is extracted from the output of the SAT procedure. The tool checks that sufficient unwinding is done to ensure that no longer counterexample can exist by means of *unwinding assertions*.

The tool comes with a graphical user interface (GUI) that hides the implementation details from the user. It resembles tools already well-known to software engineers. If a counterexample is found, the GUI allows stepping through the trace like a debugger. We hope to make formal verification tools accessible to non-expert users this way.

K. Jensen and A. Podelski (Eds.): TACAS 2004, LNCS 2988, pp. 168–176, 2004.

Hardware Verification using ANSI-C as a Reference. A common hardware design approach employed by many companies is to first write a quick prototype that behaves like the planned circuit in a language like ANSI-C. This program is then used for extensive testing and debugging, in particular of any embedded software that will later on be shipped with the circuit. After testing and debugging the program, the actual hardware design is written using hardware description languages like Verilog. The Verilog description is then synthesized into a circuit.

Thus, there are two implementations of the same design: one written in ANSI-C, which is written for simulation, and one written in register transfer level HDL, which is the actual product. The ANSI-C implementation is usually thoroughly tested and debugged.

Due to market constraints, companies aim to sell the chip as soon as possible, i.e., shortly after the HDL implementation is designed. There is usually little time for additional debugging and testing of the HDL implementation. Thus, an automated, or nearly automated way of establishing the consistency of the HDL implementation with respect to the ANSI-C model is highly desirable.

This motivates the verification problem: we want to verify the consistency of the HDL implementation, i.e., the product, using the ANSI-C implementation as a reference [2]. Establishing the consistency does not require a formal specification. However, formal methods to verify either the hardware or software design are still desirable.

The previous work focuses on a small subset of ANSI-C that is particularly close to register transfer language. Thus, the designer is often required to rewrite the C program manually in order to comply with these constraints. Our tool supports the full set of ANSI-C language features, which makes it easier to use software written for simulation and testing as a reference model. Details of the various programming styles permitted by our tool are described in [3]. A short version is in [4].

In order to verify the consistency of the two implementations, we unwind both the C program and the circuit in tandem. The unwinding of the circuit is done as conventionally done by any Bounded Model Checker.

2   Bounded Model Checking for ANSI-C Programs

2.1   Generating the Formula

We reduce the Model Checking Problem to determining the validity of a bit vector equation. The full details of the transformation are described in [3]. The process has five steps:

1. We assume that the ANSI-C program is already preprocessed, e.g., all the `#define` directives are expanded. We then replace side effects by equivalent assignments using auxiliary variables, `break` and `continue` by equivalent `goto` statements, and `for` and `do while` loops by equivalent `while` loops.
2. The loop constructs are unwound. Loop constructs can be expressed using `while` statements, (recursive) function calls, and `goto` statements. The

while loops are unwound by duplicating the loop body n times. Each copy is guarded using an if statement that uses the same condition as the loop statement. The if statement is added for the case that the loop requires less than n iterations. After the last copy, an assertion is added that assures that the program never requires more iterations. The assertion uses the negated loop condition. We call this assertion an *unwinding assertion*.

These unwinding assertions are crucial for our approach: they assert that the unwinding bound is actually large enough. If the unwinding assertion of a loop fails for any possible execution, then we increase the bound n for that particular loop until the bound is large enough.

3. Backward goto statements are unwound in a manner similar to while loops.
4. Function calls are expanded. Recursive function calls are handled in a manner similar to while loops: the recursion is unwound up to a bound. It is then asserted that the recursion never goes deeper. The return statement is replaced by an assignment (if the function returns a value) and a goto statement to the end of the function.
5. The program resulting from the preceding steps only consists of (possibly nested) if instructions, assignments, assertions, labels, and goto instructions with branch targets that are defined after the goto instruction (forward jumps). This program is then transformed into static single assignment (SSA) form, which requires a pointer analysis. We omit the full details of this process. Here is a simple example of the transformation:

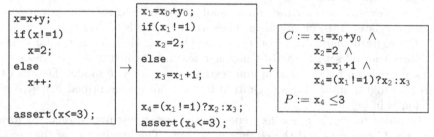

The procedure above produces two bit-vector equations: C (for the constraints) and P (for the property). In order to check the property, we convert $C \land \neg P$ into CNF by adding intermediate variables and pass it to a SAT solver such as Chaff [5]. If the equation is satisfiable, we found a violation of the property. If it is unsatisfiable, the property holds.

2.2 Converting the Formula to CNF

The conversion of most operators into CNF is straight-forward, and resembles the generation of appropriate arithmetic circuits. The tool can also output the bit-vector equation before it is flattened down to CNF, for the benefit of circuit-level SAT solvers.

CBMC allows programs that make use of dynamic memory allocation, e.g., for dynamically sized arrays or data structures such as lists or graphs. As an example, the following fragment allocates a variable number of integers using malloc, writes one value into the last array element, and then deallocates the array:

```
void f(unsigned int n) {
  int *p;

  p=malloc(sizeof(int)*n);

  p[n-1]=0;

  free(p);
}
```

While the integer n is still bounded, its maximum value requires to reserve far too many literals in order to build a CNF for the fragment above. Thus, dynamically allocated arrays are not translated into CNF by allocating literals for each potential array element. Instead, arrays with variable size are implemented by means of uninterpreted functions.

3   A Graphical User Interface

The command line version of the tool cannot be used easily by its intended users, i.e., system designers, software engineers and programmers. Such users are not likely to have a deep knowledge of formal verification tools. Therefore, to increase the usability of our tool, we have designed a user interface meant to be more familiar.

The tool has two main possible applications: the verification of properties of C programs and checking consistency of Verilog designs against a C implementation. The former is mostly addressed to software engineers and programmers, and the latter is mostly meant for hardware designers.

In order to make the tool appealing to software designers and programmers, we organized the interface in a way similar to an IDE (Integrated Development Environment). The main window allows accessing source files. Source files can be organized into projects, for which a set of options is maintained. The options allow the user to configure the parameters that are passed to CBMC on the command line. If CBMC generates an error trace, the "Watches" window, which contains the current values of the program variables, is opened. At the beginning, this window will show the initial values of the variables. Then, it is possible to step forward in the trace: the line that is "executed" is highlighted as the user steps through the trace, and the values of the variables in the Watches window are updated. This is done similarly to the way a programmer steps through a program execution during debugging. The main difference is that the trace corresponds to an erroneous execution, while during debugging this is not necessarily the case. Moreover, we allow stepping through a trace not only forward, in the way a debugger usually does, but also backward, giving the user the ability to determine more easily the causes of the error.

When trying to verify the consistency of a Verilog design and a C program, it is still possible to step through the trace generated for the C program as before, but this is not true for the Verilog design. Moreover, hardware designer are used to tools like simulators, which display waveform diagrams. In order to make our tool more suitable to hardware designers, the interface displays the traces that have been generated for a Verilog design using a waveform diagram. Therefore, while stepping through the C program, it is possible to analyze the waveform corresponding to the signals in the Verilog design.

4 Conclusion and Future Work

We described a tool that formally verifies ANSI-C programs using Bounded Model Checking (BMC). The tool supports all ANSI-C operators and pointer constructs allowed by the ANSI-C standard, including dynamic memory allocation, pointer arithmetic, and pointer type casts. The user interface is meant to appeal to system designers, software engineers, programmers and hardware designers, offering an interface that resembles the interface of tools that the users are familiar with.

When a counterexample is generated, the line number reported by CBMC is usually not pointing to the line that contains the actual bug. A version of CBMC modified by Alex Groce addresses the problem of error localization [6]: the tool displays which statements or input values are important for the fact that the property is violated.

References

1. Armin Biere, Alessandro Cimatti, Edmund M. Clarke, and Yunshan Yhu. Symbolic model checking without BDDs. In *Tools and Algorithms for Construction and Analysis of Systems*, pages 193–207, 1999.
2. Carl Pixley. Guest Editor's Introduction: Formal Verification of Commercial Integrated Circuits. *IEEE Design & Test of Computers*, 18(4):4–5, 2001.
3. E. Clarke, D. Kroening, and K. Yorav. Behavioral consistency of C and Verilog programs using Bounded Model Checking. Technical Report CMU-CS-03-126, Carnegie Mellon University, School of Computer Science, 2003.
4. Daniel Kroening, Edmund Clarke, and Karen Yorav. Behavioral consistency of C and Verilog programs using bounded model checking. In *Proceedings of DAC 2003*, pages 368–371. ACM Press, 2003.
5. Matthew W. Moskewicz, Conor F. Madigan, Ying Zhao, Lintao Zhang, and Sharad Malik. Chaff: Engineering an efficient SAT solver. In *Proceedings of the 38th Design Automation Conference (DAC'01)*, June 2001.
6. Alex Groce. Error explanation with distance metrics. In *Tools and Algorithms for the Construction and Analysis of Systems (TACAS)*, 2004.

Appendix

A Availability

The tool is available at:

> http://www.cs.cmu.edu/~modelcheck/cbmc/

The web-page provides binaries for Linux, Windows, and Solaris that are ready to install. It also offers a detailed manual with an introductory tutorial.

B   ANSI-C Language Features

The tables 1 and 2 summarize the supported ANSI-C language features and the properties that are checked automatically. A more detailed description with examples is available in the manual.

Table 1. Supported language features and implicit properties

	Supported Language Features	Properties checked
Basic Data Types	All scalar data types `float` and `double` using fixed-point arithmetic. The bit-width can be adjusted using a command line option.	
Integer Operators	All integer operators, including division and bit-wise operators Only the basic floating-point operators	Division by zero Overflow for signed data types
Type casts	All type casts, including conversion between integer and floating-point types	Overflow for signed data types
Side effects	`CBMC` allows all compound operators	Side effects are checked not to affect variables that are evaluated elsewhere, and thus, that the ordering of evaluation does not affect the result.
Function calls	Supported by inlining. The locality of parameters and non-static local variables is preserved.	1. Unwinding bound for recursive functions 2. Functions with a non-void return type must return a value by means of the return statement.
Control flow statements	`goto, return, break, continue, switch` ("fall-through" is not supported)	
Non-Determinism	User-input is modeled by means of non-deterministic choice functions	
Assumptions and Assertions	Only standard ANSI-C expressions are allowed as assertions.	Assertions are verified to be true for all possible non-deterministic choices given that any assumption executed prior to the assertion is true.
Arrays	Multi-dimensional arrays and dynamically-sized arrays are supported	Lower and upper bound of arrays, even for arrays with dynamic size

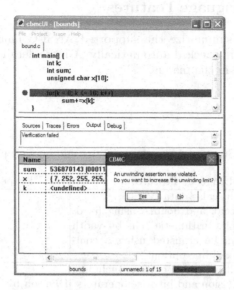

Fig. 1. The tool is able to automatically check the bound selected by the user for the unwinding of loops. If the given bound is not sufficient, the tool suggests to provide a larger bound.

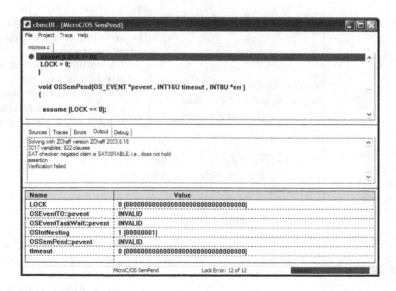

Fig. 2. The Watches windows allows keeping track of the current values of the program variables. In this case, the assertion failed because the variable LOCK has value 0.

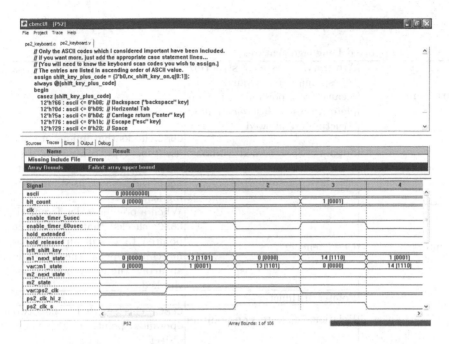

Fig. 3. The Signals window shows the values of the variables in a Verilog design using a waveform representation.

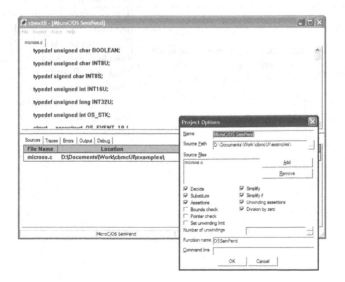

Fig. 4. The Project Options dialog allows setting up the parameters.

Table 2. Supported language features and implicit properties

Supported Language Features		Properties checked
Structures	Arbitrary, nested structure types; may be recursive by means of pointers; incomplete arrays as last element of structure are allowed	
Unions	Support for named unions, anonymous union members are currently not supported	CBMC checks that unions are not used for type conversion, i.e., that the member used for reading is the same as used for writing last time.
Pointers	Dereferencing	When a pointer is dereferenced, CBMC checks that the object pointed to is still alive and of matching type. If the object is an array, the array bounds are checked.
	Pointer arithmetic	
	Relational operators on pointers	CBMC checks that the two operands point to the same object.
	Pointer Type Casts	Upon dereferencing, the type of the object and the expression are checked to match
	Pointers to Functions	The offset within the object is checked to be zero
Dynamic Memory	`malloc` and `free` are supported. The argument of malloc may be a nondeterministically chosen, arbitrarily large value.	Upon dereferencing, the object pointed to must still be alive. The pointer passed to `free` is checked to point to an object that is still alive. CBMC can check that all dynamically allocated memory is deallocated before exiting the program ("memory leaks").

Obtaining Memory-Efficient Reachability Graph Representations Using the Sweep-Line Method

Thomas Mailund and Michael Westergaard

Department of Computer Science, University of Aarhus,
IT-parken, Aabogade 34, DK-8200 Aarhus N, Denmark,
{mailund,mw}@daimi.au.dk

Abstract. This paper is concerned with a memory-efficient representation of reachability graphs. We describe a technique that enables us to represent each reachable marking in a number of bits close to the theoretical minimum needed for explicit state enumeration. The technique maps each state vector onto a number between zero and the number of reachable states and uses the sweep-line method to delete the state vectors themselves. A prototype of the proposed technique has been implemented and experimental results are reported.

Keywords: Verification; state space methods; state space reduction; memory efficient state representation; the sweep-line method.

1 Introduction

A central problem in the application of reachability graph (also known as state-space) methods is the memory usage. Even relatively simple systems can have an astronomical number of reachable states, and when using basic exhaustive search [16], all states need to be represented in memory at the same time. Even methods that explore only parts of the reachability graph [13,33,29,2] or explore a reduced reachability graph [21,11,23], often need to store thousands or millions of states.

When storing states explicitly—as opposed to using a symbolic representation such as Binary Decision Diagrams [4,5]—the minimal number of bits needed to distinguish between N states is $\lceil \log_2 N \rceil$ bits per state. In a system with R reachable states we should therefore be able to store all reachable states using only in the order of $R \cdot \lceil \log_2 R \rceil$ bits. The number of reachable states, R, however, is usually unknown until after the reachability graph exploration; rather than knowing the number of reachable states we know the number of *syntactically possible* states S, where S is usually significantly larger than R. To distinguish between S possible states $\lceil \log_2 S \rceil$ bits are needed, so to store the R reachable states $R \cdot \lceil \log_2 S \rceil$ bits are needed. Aditional memory will be needed to store transitions.

In this paper we consider mapping the state vectors of size $\lceil \log_2 S \rceil$ bits (the full state vectors or markings) to representations of length $\lceil \log_2 R \rceil$ (the condensed representations), in such a way that full state vectors can be restored

K. Jensen and A. Podelski (Eds.): TACAS 2004, LNCS 2988, pp. 177–191, 2004.

when the reachability graph is subsequently analysed. Our approach is the following: We conduct a reachability graph exploration and assign to each new unprocessed state a new number, starting from zero and incrementing with one after each assignment. The states are in this way represented by numbers in the interval $0, \ldots, R-1$. Since the state representation obtained in this way has no relation to the information stored in the full state vector, the condensed representation cannot be used to distinguish between previously processed states and new states. To get around this problem, we keep the original (full) state vectors in a table as long as needed to recognise previously seen states. The *sweep-line method* [7,25] is used to remove the full state vectors when they are no longer needed, from memory.

In this paper we will use Place/Transition Petri nets [10] (P/T net) formalism as example to illustrate the different memory requirements needed to distinguish between the elements of the set of syntactically possible states and the set of reachable states. The use of P/T nets is only an example, the presented method applies to all formalisms where the sweep-line method can be used.

The paper is structured as follows: In Sect. 2 we summarise the notation and terminology for P/T nets and reachability graphs that we will use. In Sect. 3 we describe the condensed representation of a reachability graph, how this representation can be traversed, and how to restore enough information about the full state vectors to verify properties about the original system. In Sect. 4 we consider how the condensed representation can be calculated and in Sect. 5 we describe how the sweep-line method can be used to keep memory usage low during this construction. In Sect. 6 we report experimental results and in Sect. 7 we give our conclusions.

2   Petri Nets and Reachability Graphs

In this section we define *reachability graphs* of Place/Transition Petri nets.

Definition 1. *A **Place/Transition Petri net** is a tuple* $\mathcal{N} = (P, T, F, m_I)$ *where* P *is a set of* places, T *is a set of* transitions *such that* $P \cap T = \emptyset$, $F \subseteq P \times T \cup T \times P$ *is the* flow-relation, *and* $m_I : P \to \mathbb{N}$ *is the* initial marking.

We will use the usual notation for pre- and post-sets of nodes $x \in P \cup T$, i.e., $\bullet x = \{y \in P \cup T \mid (y, x) \in F\}$ and $x\bullet = \{y \in P \cup T \mid (x, y) \in F\}$. The state of a P/T net is given by a *marking* of the places, which is formally a multiset over the places $m : P \to \mathbb{N}$. Since sets are a special cases of multi-sets, we will use the notation $\bullet x$ to denote both the set $\bullet x$ as defined above, but also the multi-set given by $y \mapsto 1$ when $y \in \bullet x$ and $y \mapsto 0$ when $y \notin \bullet x$. We will assume that the relations $<, \leq, >$, and $\geq$, and operations $+$ and $-$, on multi-sets are defined as usual, i.e. for two multi-sets, $m_1, m_2 : P \to \mathbb{N}$, $m_1 \leq m_2 \iff \forall p \in P.m_1(p) \leq m_2(p)$, $m_1 < m_2 \iff m_1 \leq m_2 \wedge m_1 \neq m_2$, $(m_1 + m_2)(p) = m_1(p) + m_2(p)$, and $(m_1 - m_2)(p) = m_1(p) - m_2(p)$ when $m_1 \leq m_2$ and $m_1 - m_2$ is undefined when $m_1 \nleq m_2$.

Definition 2. *A transition $t \in T$ is **enabled** in marking $m : P \to \mathbb{N}$ if $m \geq \bullet t$. If t is enabled in m, it can **occur** and lead to marking m'. This is written $m\,[t\rangle\,m'$, where m' is defined by $m' = (m - \bullet t) + t\bullet$.*

We will use the common notation $m\,[\sigma\rangle\,m'$ for $\sigma = t_1 t_2 \ldots t_n \in T^*$ to mean $\exists m_i : P \to \mathbb{N}$ for $i = 0, \ldots, n$ such that $m = m_0$, $\forall i = 0, \ldots, n - 1.m_i\,[t_i\rangle\,m_{i+1}$, and $m' = m_n$. We will also write $m\,[*\rangle\,m'$ to mean $\exists \sigma \in T^*$ such that $m\,[\sigma\rangle\,m'$. We say that a marking m' is *reachable* from another marking m if $m\,[*\rangle\,m'$ and we let $[m\rangle = \{m' \mid m\,[*\rangle\,m'\}$ denote the set of markings reachable from m. When we talk about the set of *reachable markings* of a P/T net, we usually mean the set of markings reachable from the initial marking, i.e., $[m_I\rangle$. We will use R to denote the number of reachable markings, i.e., $R = |[m_I\rangle|$.

The reachability graph of a P/T net is a rooted graph that has a vertex for each reachable marking and an edge for each possible transition from one reachable marking to another.

Definition 3. *A **graph** is a tuple $(V, E, \mathsf{src}, \mathsf{trg})$ where V is a set of vertices, E is a set of edges, and $\mathsf{src}, \mathsf{trg} : E \to V$ are mappings assigning to each edge a source and a target, respectively. A **rooted graph** is a tuple $(V, E, \mathsf{src}, \mathsf{trg}, r)$ such that $(V, E, \mathsf{src}, \mathsf{trg})$ is a graph and $r \in V$ is the root.*

Definition 4. *Let $\mathcal{N} = (P, T, F, m_I)$ be a P/T net. The **reachability graph** of $\mathcal{N}$ is the rooted graph $(V, E, \mathsf{src}, \mathsf{trg}, r)$ defined by:*

- $V = [m_I\rangle$—*the set of nodes is the set of reachable markings.*
- $E = \{(m, t, m') \in V \times T \times V \mid m\,[t\rangle\,m'\}$—*the set of edges is the set of transitions from one reachable marking to another.*
- src *is given by* $\mathsf{src}(m, t, m') = m$.
- trg *is given by* $\mathsf{trg}(m, t, m') = m'$.
- $r = m_I$—*the root is the initial marking.*

We can only represent a finite reachability graph, but the reachability graph for a P/T net need not be finite, so we put some restrictions on the P/T net we consider to ensure a finite reachability graph. The first assumption we make is that the P/T net under consideration, $\mathcal{N} = (P, T, F, m_I)$, has a finite set of places, $|P| < \infty$, and a finite set of transitions, $|T| < \infty$. The second assumption is that the net is k-*bounded* for some $k \in \mathbb{N}, k > 0$, as defined below, and consider the set of possible markings to be $\mathbb{K}^P$ where $\mathbb{K} = \{0, 1, \ldots, k\}$.

Definition 5. *A P/T net (P, T, F, m_I) is k-**bounded** if and only if for all $m \in [m_I\rangle$ and for all $p \in P$: $m(p) \leq k$.*

Although the assumptions above ensure that the reachability graph is finite, it is still necessary to distinguish between $|\mathbb{K}^P|$ different states when we calculate the reachability graph. If we let S denote the number of possible states, $S = |\mathbb{K}^P|$, at least $\lceil \log_2 S \rceil$ bits are needed per state. Most likely more bits will be used since the naive representation of a state vector assigns $\lceil \log_2 (k + 1) \rceil$ bits per place using $|P| \cdot \lceil \log_2 (k + 1) \rceil$ bits per state. Our goal is to reduce this to $\lceil \log_2 R \rceil$ bits per state.

3   Condensed Graph Representation

We now turn to the problem of mapping the full markings to the condensed representation. Our approach is to assign to each reachable marking a unique integer between 0 and $R - 1$, which can be represented by $\lceil \log_2 R \rceil$ bits. In this section we describe the data structure used to represent the reachability graph $\mathcal{G} = (V, E, \mathsf{src}, \mathsf{trg}, m_I)$ in this condensed form, and how to construct it from the sets V and E as calculated by the reachability graph construction algorithm. Calculating the full reachability graph and then reducing it, defeats the purpose of using a condensed representation. We only describe the algorithm in this way to present the condensed representation in an uncomplicated setting, and we will later discuss how to construct the condensed representation on-the-fly.

3.1   Representing the Reachability Graph

We want to represent V by the numbers 0 to $R - 1$. For a marking $m \in V$ we will let $\mathsf{idx}_M(m) \in \{0, 1, \ldots, R-1\}$ denote the (unique) index of m in this range. We will represent the initial marking m_I by index 0, $\mathsf{idx}_M(m_I) = 0$. With this representation of V, we can represent the set of edges as an array, E, with R entries, where each entry, E[i], points to an array containing the edges out of the vertex v with index i. The array pointed to by E[i] consists of a header—a number, indicating the length of the array, so we can later decode the array—and the edges $\{(m, t, m') \in E \mid \mathsf{idx}_M(m) = i\}$. Each edge (m, t, m') is represented as a pair $(\mathsf{idx}_T(t), \mathsf{idx}_M(m'))$ where the first element is the index of the transition—we assume some statically defined mapping $\mathsf{idx}_T : T \to \{0, \ldots, |T|-1\}$ assigning a number to each transition—and the second element is the index of the target node of the edge. An example of this representation is shown in Fig. 1.

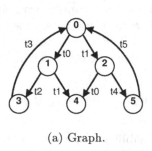

(a) Graph.

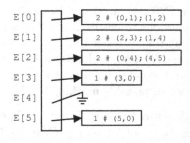

(b) Condensed representation.

Fig. 1. Representation of the reachability graph. The condensed representation of the graph in (a) is shown in (b). The edge array E[$\mathsf{idx}_M(v)$] for vertex v is written in the form $n \,\#\, (\mathsf{idx}_T(t_0), \mathsf{idx}_M(v_0) \;; \; \ldots \;; \; (\mathsf{idx}_T(t_n), \mathsf{idx}_M(v_n))$ where $n + 1$ is the length of the array and the pairs represent the edges out of v. To save memory we represent a pointer to the empty array as a grounded pointer.

Each of the pairs in the edge arrays can be represented with $\lceil \log_2 |T| \rceil + \lceil \log_2 R \rceil$ bits. In addition there is an overhead of one pointer and one number for each state in V. We assume that all edge arrays can be represented in main memory and thus that we can represent both the pointer and the number in a computer word each.[1] With this encoding, we can represent the graph $\mathcal{G} = (V, E, \mathsf{src}, \mathsf{trg}, m_I)$ using just $2wR + |E|(\lceil \log_2 |T| \rceil + \lceil \log_2 R \rceil)$ bits, where w denotes the number of bits in a computer word. Notice that this efficient representation is only possible because of our mapping $\mathsf{idx}_M : V \to \{0, \ldots, R-1\}$, which saves us from storing any of the R markings explicitly.

From the sets V and E of $\mathcal{G}$, the translation of the reachability graph to the condensed representation is as one would expect: We build the mapping idx_M as a table mapping nodes to numbers, allocate the array E and the individual edge arrays, and insert the data in the arrays.

3.2 Exploring the Condensed Reachability Graph

The condensed representation for the reachability graph explicitly contains the transition structure but does not store any information about the markings. For some applications, such as protocol consistency using language equivalence [3], this suffices; for other applications, however, we are interested in both marking and transition information. For such applications we need a method of recreating the markings from the transition information, without significant blowup in the memory requirements. The property that we will exploit for this is the marking equation, $m' = m - \bullet t + t\bullet$, from Def. 2.

When we follow an edge (i, t, i') in the condensed representation, where we know the marking of i, we calculate the marking of i' using the marking equation. If we explore the reachability graph in a depth-first manner, we can even use the rewriting of the marking equation, $m = m' - t\bullet + \bullet t$, to obtain the marking of i from the marking of i' when we return along the edge. Exploiting this, it is possible to do a depth-first graph exploration, storing only one single marking explicitly at any one time, while still having the full state vector available at each visited state. An algorithm for this is shown in Fig. 2.

By extending the algorithm in Fig. 2 with a table of sub-expressions indexed by $1, \ldots, R-1$, it can be used to check Computation Tree Logic (CTL) as in [8, Sect. 4.1], and by extending the algorithm to use nested depth-first search [17], it can be adapted to check Linear Temporal Logic (LTL).

4   Creating the Condensed Representation On-the-Fly

To calculate the condensed representation on-the-fly we want to construct the idx_M mapping as new markings are calculated, and create the edge array at $\mathsf{E[idx}_M(m)]$ as soon as the successors of m have been calculated.

---

[1] It is possible to represent both number and pointer in $\lceil \log_2 |E| \rceil$ bits, but representing both in a computer word of a fixed size independent of $|E|$ simplifies the constructions for creating the representation on-the-fly.

```
1      visited := ∅
2      m := m_I
3      DFS(0)
4
5      where proc DFS(i) is
6          if i ∈ visited return
7          /* analyse m here */
8          visited := visited ∪ {i}
9          for each (t, i') in E[i] do
10             m := m − •t + t•
11             DFS(i')
12             m := m + •t − t•
13         end for
14     end proc DFS
```

Fig. 2. Depth-first traversal of the reachability graph. A global variable m contains the current marking during the exploration. This marking is updated before and after each recursive call. The set `visited` keeps track of the visited nodes, can efficiently be implemented as a bit vector.

A few subtleties complicate the construction: we do not know the number R, and therefore we cannot immediately allocate the array E, nor can we allocate the individual edge arrays. There is also a problem with storing the numbers in the representation of the idx_M mapping, since we do not know how many bits are needed to store the numbers $\{0, \ldots, R - 1\}$. We will assume, however, that $R < 2^w$, and we can therefore represent the numbers in the table using computer words. This is potentially a waste of memory, when $\log_2 R \ll w$, but it is not likely to be a bottleneck; the majority of the memory used by the idx_M mapping (represented as a table mapping full state vectors to numbers) will be for storing the full state vectors, which will end up using $R \cdot \lceil \log_2 S \rceil$ bits. Reduction of the memory needed for storing the full state vectors in the representation of the idx_M mapping is addressed in Sect. 5.

For managing the array E note that the entries in E are all of size w bits and do not depend on the total size of $[m_I\rangle$. We can work on the *entries* of E without knowing the full size of E. For handling E itself one possibility is using a dynamically extensible array [9], expanding and relocating as needed with an amortised constant time complexity. The dynamic array approach potentially allocates an array that is too large, but will not allocate more than twice the required storage, that is, the dynamic array will use between $R \cdot w + w$ and $2 \cdot R \cdot w + w$ bits of memory (where the $+w$ is a word needed to keep track of the size of the array). To be able to relocate the dynamic array, an additional $R \cdot w$ bits of memory might be needed.

After calculating all the successors of a marking m, we can construct the edge array for m. At this point we have added all successors of m to the representation of idx_M, and since we know the number of successors, we know the size of the edge array. In the edge array we can represent each successor, m', as $\mathsf{idx}_M(m')$, using w bits. Since we have added all successors of m to the representation of idx_M, we know the maximal index, M, used in the edge array for m, so we can actually represent each successor using only $\lceil \log_2 M \rceil$ bits. With this encoding, the bits allocated per marking will now vary between the different edge arrays. To decode the arrays we must store this number with the arrays. We therefore extend the header of the edge arrays, such that it now contains both the number of edges in the array and also the number of bits allocated per marking.

5   Reducing Peak Memory Usage

When creating the condensed representation of the reachability graph as described in Sect. 4, memory is wasted because, when the algorithm terminates, the memory holds both the graph, the set of reachable markings, and the idx_M mapping. In this section we use the sweep-line method [25, 7] to keep peak memory usage small by deleting entries in the idx_M mapping.

5.1   The Sweep-Line Method

When constructing the reachability graph, it is neccesary to distinguish between new states and already visited states. For this we need to store the already visited states in memory. However, there is no need to store any states that are not reachable from the unprocessed states. Once a state is no longer reachable from the unprocessed states, it can be safely removed from memory.

The sweep-line method exploits this observation to delete states, using an approximation of the reachability relation, called a *progress measure*. The progress measure provides an ordering of the markings; states ordered less than the unprocessed states are assumed to be unreachable from the unprocessed states, and can therefore be deleted.

Definition 6 (Def. 3 in [25]). *For a P/T net (P, T, F, m_I) a **progress measure** is a tuple $\mathcal{P} = (\mathcal{V}, \sqsubseteq, \psi)$ where $\mathcal{V}$ is a set of progress values, $\sqsubseteq$ is a partial order of $\mathcal{V}$, and $\psi : \mathbb{N}^P \to \mathcal{V}$ is a mapping assigning a progress value to each marking. We say that $\mathcal{P}$ is **monotone** if $m \, [*\rangle \, m'$ implies $\psi(m) \sqsubseteq \psi(m')$.*

For monotone progress measures, the assumption that states with lower progress values are unreachable from the unprocessed states, is correct. For non-monotone progress measures, it is no longer safe just to delete states. To address this problem, we save the target nodes of edges that are not monotonic—so-called *regress edges*: (m, t, m') such that $\psi(m) \not\sqsubseteq \psi(m')$—as *persistent* markings and never delete persistent markings. The states saved as persistent in a sweep of the state space are either previously seen states or new states; there is no way for the algorithm to know which. When we see regress edges, we therefore perform another sweep, using the new persistent states as roots for the sweep. We repeat this until we no longer find new persistent states. For details of this algorithm, see [25]. A detailed example of the construction and optimisation of a progress measure can also be found in [25].

The observation used in the sweep-line method to delete states can also be used to clean up the idx_M mapping. When constructing the condensed graph representation, we only need to store the index mapping of markings we can reach from the currently unprocessed states. Using the sweep-line method for exploring the reachability graph, we can reduce the peak memory usage by deleting states in the set V and the idx_M mapping. Deleting states is only safe if the progress measure is monotone; otherwise, the condensed graph may be an unfolding of the full graph. This is treated in Sect. 5.2.

The algorithm combining the sweep-line method and the construction of the condensed graph representation is shown in Fig. 3. Like the sweep-line algorithm, this algorithm performs a number of sweeps until it no longer finds new persistent states (lines 7–9). Each sweep (lines 11–35) consists of processing unprocessed states in order of their progress measure (lines 15–18), assigning indices to their previously unseen successors (lines 21–22), and either adding the new successors to the set of unprocessed states (line 24) or to the set of persistent states and roots for the next sweep (lines 26–27). When all successors of a state are processed, the edge array is updated (line 31) using the method CREATE_EDGE_ARRAY (lines 37–43) as described in Sect. 4, and states behind the sweep-line are removed from the set V and the index mapping idx_M (lines 32–33).

By using this algorithm we only store a subset of the reachable markings explicitly while creating the condensed graph. This enables us to construct the reachability graph, in the condensed representation, in cases where storing all reachable markings in memory is impossible.

5.2   An Unfolding of the Reachability Graphs

When using a non-monotone progress measure, the reachability graph obtained from the algorithm in Fig. 3 is not the reachability graph from Def. 4; rather it is an *unfolding* of this graph [26, Chap. 13]. For poor choices of progress measures, this unfolded graph can be much larger than the original reachability graph, completely eliminating the benefits of reduction. For good choices of the progress measures, the blowup in size will be manageable and the condensed representation of nodes more than compensates for the graph unfolding. It is important to consider the relationship between the unfolded graph and the original reachability graph, to know which properties are preserved by the unfolding.

The unfolding is due to regress edges—edges along which the progress measure decreases. When following a regress edge we may reach a state which has previously been explored and since the actual marking has been deleted, we do not recognise it and explore its successor states again.

One can easily define the unfolded graph, $\mathcal{G}^u$, and show that it is bisimilar to the full reachability graph [26, Chap. 13]. This result is especially interesting in the context of model checking, since bisimulation is known to preserve CTL* in the sense of Theorem 1, which in turn implies that both CTL and LTL, the most commonly used temporal logics for model checking, are preserved.

Theorem 1 (From [8, Chap. 12]). *If $\mathcal{G}$ and $\mathcal{G}'$ are bisimilar then for every CTL* formula ϕ we have $\mathcal{G} \models \phi \Leftrightarrow \mathcal{G}' \models \phi$.*

```
1    V  := {m_I}
2    Roots := {m_I}
3    Persistent := ∅
4    idx_M (m_I) := 0
5    n := 1
6
7    while Roots ≠ ∅ do
8         SWEEP(Roots, V, Persistent, idx_M, n)
9    end while
10
11   where proc SWEEP(Roots, V, Persistent, idx_M, n) is
12        U := Roots
13        Roots := ∅
14        while U ≠ ∅ do
15             select m ∈ U s.t. ∄ m' ∈ U : ψ(m') ⊏ ψ(m)
16             U := U − {m}
17             X := {t, m' | m [t⟩ m'}
18             for all (t, m') ∈ X do
19                  if m' ∉ V then
20                       V := V ∪ {m'}
21                       idx_M (m') := n
22                       n := n + 1
23                  if ψ(m) ⊑ ψ(m') then
24                            U := U ∪ {m'}
25                       else
26                            Persistent := Persistent ∪ {m'}
27                            Roots := Roots ∪ {m'}
28                       end if
29                  end if
30             end for
31             E[idx_M (m)] := CREATE_EDGE_ARRAY(X, idx_M)
32             V := {m ∈ V | ∃ m' ∈ U : ψ(m') ⊑ ψ(m)} ∪ Persistent
33             idx_M := {m ↦ i | m ∈ V ∧ idx_M (m) = i}
34        end while
35   end proc SWEEP
36
37   where proc CREATE_EDGE_ARRAY(X, idx_M) is
38        M := max{idx_M(m') | (t, m') ∈ X|}
39        A := allocate 2·w + |X| · (⌈log_2 |T|⌉ + ⌈log_2 M⌉) bits
40        A.header := (|X|, ⌈log_2 M⌉)
41        A.edges := (idx_T(t), idx_M (m')) for each (t, m') ∈ X
42        return A
43   end proc CREATE_EDGE_ARRAY
```

Fig. 3. The sweep-line method for obtaining a condensed graph representation.

6   Experimental Results

In order to validate and evaluate the performance of the new algorithm a proof-of-concept implementation has been developed. For the theoretical presentation in the previous sections we used Place/Transition Petri nets; the techniques introduced, however, generalise to higher level net classes, such as *coloured Petri nets* (CPN) [22], in a straightforward manner. The prototype is build on top of the Design/CPN tool [1], a tool for the construction and analysis of CPNs. The prototype is implemented in the *Standard ML* (SML) programming language [32] and the progress measure is provided by the user as an SML function.

Since the Design/CPN tool is used for analysing CPN models the markings of the nets are not multi-sets over places but multi-sets over more complex data types. Consequently the markings are not integer vectors of length $|P|$, but variable-length encodings of the more complex markings. On the edges of the reachability graph it is no longer sufficient to store transitions, also the bindings are needed.

The prototype implementation of the new algorithm is slightly simpler than the algorithm described in this paper. We do not implement the variable-length numbers for node indices, but represent each index as a four byte computer word. This greatly simplifies the implementation but uses slightly more memory for smaller systems and limits the prototype to models with less than 2^{32} states, which is no serious limitation.

All experiments were conducted on a 500Mhz Pentium III Linux PC with 128 Mb of RAM.

Database Replication Protocol. The first example we consider is a database replication protocol [22, Sect. 1.3]. The protocol describes the communication between a set of database managers for maintaining consistent copies of a distributed database. When a database manager updates its local copy of the database it broadcasts an update request to all other database managers who then perform the update on their local copies and then acknowledge that the update has been performed. The progress measure for the protocol is based on the control flow of the database managers and an ordering on the database managers. See [25] for details.

Table 1 shows the performance of full reachability graph generation compared with the new algorithm. The $|D|$ column shows the number of database managers in the different configurations, the following four columns show the values for the full reachability graph, and the last four columns show the values for the new algorithm. In the full reachability graph columns the *States* column shows the number of states for each configuration, the *Avg* column shows the average number of bytes in the state vector in the different configurations, the *Memory* column shows the total memory usage in bytes for storing all states, and the *Time* column shows the time used for calculating the reachability graph in seconds. In the sweep-line columns the *States* column shows the number of states explored by the sweep-line algorithm, the *Peak* column shows the peak number of states stored during the exploration, the *Memory* column shows the number of bytes

Table 1. Database Replication Protocol.

	Full Reachability Graph				**Sweep-Line based Algorithm**					
$|D|$	States	Avg	Memory	Time	States	Peak	Memory (%)		Time (%)	
4	110	122	13,420	0	219	14	2,584	(19)	0	(-)
5	407	146	59,422	0	813	33	8,070	(14)	0	(-)
6	1,460	169	246,740	0	2,919	88	26,548	(11)	2	(-)
7	5,105	191	975,055	4	10,209	251	88,777	(9)	11	(275)
8	17,498	214	3,744,572	23	34,995	738	297,912	(8)	51	(222)
9	59,051	237	13,995,087	105	118,101	2,197	993,093	(7)	229	(218)

used for storing the states in the condensed representation plus the states in *Peak*, the number in the parentheses indicates the memory consumption of the condensed representation as a percentage of the full representation, the *Time* column shows the time used for calculating the condensed graph, and the number in parentheses shows the amount of time used for calculating the condensed representation as a percentage of the amount of time used to generate the full representation.

In the database replication protocol all states but the initial state are explored twice by the sweep-line algorithm, and consequently the condensed graph has twice as many nodes as the full graph and the time for calculating the condensed graph is roughly twice as long as the time for calculating the full reachability graph. The *Memory* in the sweep-line columns is calculated as $4 \cdot States + Avg \cdot Peak$ since one computer word (4 bytes) is used for representing each condensed state and $Avg \cdot Peak$ bytes are used for representing the states on the sweep-line. We only compare the memory usage for storing the states, as the memory usage for storing the remaining graph structure would be comparable for the two methods. Although the unfolded graph generated by the sweep-line method contains twice as many nodes as the original reachability graph the memory usage—as seen in the two Memory columns—is significantly improved. For four database managers the reduction is down to around 20%, while for nine database managers the reduction is further improved, down to around 7% of the full representation.

Stop and Wait Communication Protocol. The second example is a stop-and-wait communication protocol [24]. The protocol is parameterised with the number of packets to be sent. We use the number of packets successfully received as a monotone progress measure [7]. The performance is shown in Table 2. Here the *# packets* column shows the number of packets to be transmitted in the different configurations; the remaining columns have the same meaning as in Table 1.

For this model the peak number of states fully stored in the sweep-line method does not increase for larger configurations. As the number of packets increases the total number of states increases, but the number of states with the same progress measure does not. As for the database replication protocol, the

Table 2. Stop and Wait Communication Protocol.

# packets	Full Reachability Graph				Sweep-Line based Algorithm					
	States	Avg	Memory	Time	States	Peak	Memory	(%)	Time	(%)
20	5,286	145	766,470	17	5,286	287	62,759	(8)	24	(141)
40	10,706	146	1,563,076	35	10,706	287	84,726	(5)	50	(143)
60	16,126	146	2,354,396	53	16,126	287	106,406	(5)	77	(145)
80	21,546	146	3,145,716	71	21,546	287	128,086	(4)	103	(145)
100	26,966	146	3,937,036	89	26,966	287	149,766	(4)	129	(145)

experiments shows significant memory reduction—from around 8% for 20 packets to around 4% for 100 packets—at the cost of a slight increase in runtime—an increase about 45%–50% of the runtime of the full reachability graph algorithm in all configurations.

7   Conclusion

In this paper we have presented a condensed representation of the reachability graph of P/T nets. The condensed graph represents each marking with a number in $\{0, 1, \ldots, R - 1\}$, where $R = ||[m_I]||$, and avoids representing markings explicitly. We have developed an algorithm that constructs this representation exploiting local information about successor markings only to represent edges efficiently without knowing R, and dynamic arrays for storing edge information for each node. Using the sweep-line method we are able to reduce peak memory usage during the construction of the graph representation. When the progress measure used is monotone, the graph is isomorphic to the original reachability graph, and when the progress measure is non-monotone the graph is bi-similar to the original graph.

We have demostrated the performance of the new algorithm using two examples. The chosen examples have a quite clear notion of progress, so the sweep-line method performs well, and the amount memory used to store the reduced graphs is significaltly less than the amount of memory used to store the full graphs. The presented algorithm will not perform well on systems with little or no progress. An example of a system with little progress is the Dining Philosophers problem. If we use the number of eating philosophers as progress measure, we will at some time during the construction store nearly all states, and the memory used for storing the compact representation is overhead. Compared to the amount of memory used for storing the full state vectors, this amount is not significant, however, and the only real disadvantage is that we still use extra time for the construction. If the number of reachable states is close to the number of syntactically possible states, the amount of memory used for the condensed representation is comparable to the amount of memory used for the full representation, and little is gained from using the new algorithm.

By exploiting the marking equation of P/T nets, the ability to calculate the predecessor or successor of a state given a transition, we are able to reconstruct the markings of the reduced nodes while exploring the graph. In general, when the predecessors and successors can be deterministically determined, this approach can be used. If only successors can be calculated deterministically, the reachability graph can still be traversed and states reconstructed, by saving the current state on the depth-first stack before processing successors.

The algorithm presented here resembles the approach used in [14], where the basic sweep-line method (applicable to monotone progress measures only) was used to translate the reachability graph of a CPN model to a finite state automaton, which in turn was used to check language equivalence between a protocol specification and its service specification. In this approach the automaton is constructed by writing edge-information onto a disk before the sweep-line method garbage collects the edges, and this edge-information is the processed by another tool to translate it to an automaton. On the disk the states are represented as numbers, thus reducing memory consumption when the automaton is constructed from the file.

Using the graph construction algorithm presented in this paper, the potentially expensive step of going through a disk-representation can be avoided when constructing the language automaton. Furthermore, with the algorithm in Fig. 2 it is possible to traverse the graph reconstructing state information after the graph is constructed. The results from Sect. 5.2, relating the reachability graph to the unfolded graph, can also be used to generalise the method from [14] to non-monotone progress measures. In [14] the basic sweep-line method from [7] is used, guaranteeing that the automaton generated represents the language of the protocol being analysed. The results in Sect. 5.2 ensure that, when using non-monotone progress measures, the unfolded graph is language equivalent to the original reachability graph.

The new algorithm is designed for explicit state reachability graph analysis. For condensed state representation, such as finite automata [20], or for symbolic model checking [28, 5], where states are represented as e.g., Binary Decision Diagrams [4], the memory used for storing a set of states does not depend directly on the number of states in the set, but on regularity in the state information. Deleting states during the graph construction, as the sweep-line method does, will not necessarily reduce memory usage. On the contrary, deleting states can actually increase the memory needed to store the set of states. Combining the new algorithm with symbolic model checking, therefore, does not appear to be immediately possible.

The new technique reduces the memory usage using knowledge about the number of reachable states, and complements techniques that are aimed at efficiently representing arbitrary states from the set of syntactically possible states. The state representation in SPIN [18], Design/CPN [6], and MARIA [27], for example, exploit modularity of the system being analysed to share parts of the state vector between different states. LoLA [30] exploits invariants to avoid storing information that can be derfived from the invariant. Using one or more of these approaches one can represent sets of arbitrary states efficiently, though at least $\lceil \log_2 S \rceil$ bits are still needed per state to distinguish between S syntactically possible states. [12] considers storing sets of markings efficiently using very tight hash tables, which allows storing sets of states using less than $\lceil \log_2 S \rceil$ bits per state, but using the knowledge about the number of reachable states is not considered. Representing arbitrary states efficiently benefits the algorithm presented here as well, by reducing the memory needed for the table mapping states to indices. The reduction differs from probabilistic methods such as bitstate hashing [19,15] and hash-compaction [31,34], where all possible states are, in a sense, mapped onto a range $\{0, 1, \ldots, n\}$, for some n, but with a mapping that may not be injective on $[m_I\rangle$. The states are in this way also represented in a condensed form, but since hash collisions can occur, full coverage of the reachability graph cannot be guaranteed.

With the algorithm presented here, the sweep-line method can be used for checking more general properties than just state properties as in [25]. In particular, checking CTL* formulae, and thereby CTL and LTL formulae, now becomes possible. Future work includes using this in case studies.

References

1. Design/CPN. Online http://www.daimi.au.dk/designCPN.
2. G. Behrmann, K.G. Larsen, and R. Pelánek. To Store or Not to Store. In W.A. Hunt and F. Somenzi, editors, *Proc. of CAV 2003*, volume 2725 of *LNCS*, pages 433–445. Springer, 2003.
3. J. Billington, M.C. Wilbur-Ham, and M.Y. Bearman. Automated protocol Verification. In *Proc. of IFIP WG 6.1 5th International Workshop on Protocol Specification, Testing, and Verification*, pages 59–70. Elsevier, 1985.
4. R.E. Bryant. Graph Based Algorithms for Boolean Function Manipulation. *IEEE Transactions on Computers*, C-35(8):677–691, 1986.
5. J.R. Burch, E.M. Clarke, K.L. McMillan, D.L. Dill, and L.J. Hwang. Symbolic Model Checking: 10^{20} States and Beyond. *Information and Computation*, 98(2):142–170, 1992.
6. S. Christensen, J.B. Jørgensen, and L.M. Kristensen. Design/CPN—A Computer Tool for Coloured Petri Nets. In *Proc. of TACAS'97*, volume 1217 of *LNCS*, pages 209–223. Springer-Verlag, 1997.
7. S. Christensen, L.M. Kristensen, and T. Mailund. A Sweep-Line Method for State Space Exploration. In *Proc. of TACAS'01*, volume 2031 of *LNCS*, pages 450–464. Springer-Verlag, 2001.
8. E. Clarke, O. Grumberg, and D. Peled. *Model Checking*. The MIT Press, 1999.
9. T.H. Cormen, C.E. Leiserson, and R.L. Rivest. *Introduction to Algorithms*, chapter 18.4, pages 367–375. The MIT Press, 1990.
10. J. Desel and W. Reisig. Place/Transition Petri Nets. In *Lecture on Petri nets I: Basic Models*, volume 1491 of *LNCS*, pages 122–173. Springer-Verlag, 1998.
11. E.A. Emerson and A.P. Sistla. Symmetry and Model Checking. *Formal Methods in System Design*, 9, 1996.
12. J. Geldenhuys and A. Valmari. A Nearly Memory-Optimal Data Structure for Sets and Mappings. In T. Ball and S.K. Rajamani, editors, *Proc. of SPIN 2003*, volume 2648 of *LNCS*, pages 136–150. Springer, 2003.

13. P. Godefroid. *Partial-Order Methods for the Verification of Concurrent Systems—An Approach to the State-Explosion Problem*, volume 1032 of *LNCS*. Springer-Verlag, 1996.
14. S. Gordon, L.M. Kristensen, and J. Billington. Verification of a Revised WAP Wireless Transaction Protocol. In *Proc. of ICATPN'02*, volume 2360 of *LNCS*, pages 182–202. Springer-Verlag, 2002.
15. G.J. Holzmann. An Improved Protocol Reachability Analysis Technique. *Software, Practice and Experience*, 18(2):137–161, 1988.
16. G.J. Holzmann. Algorithms for Automated Protocol Validation. *AT&T Technical Journal*, 69(2):32–44, 1990.
17. G.J. Holzmann. *Design and Validation of Computer Protocols*. Prentice-Hall International Editions, 1991.
18. G.J. Holzmann. State Compression in SPIN: Recursive Indexing and Compression Traning Runs. In *Proc. of 3rd SPIN Workshop*, 1997.
19. G.J. Holzmann. An Analysis of Bitstate Hashing. *Formal Methods in System Design*, 13:289–307, 1998.
20. G.J. Holzmann and A. Puri. A Minimized Automaton Representation of Reachable States. *Journal on Software Tools for Technology Transfer*, 2(3):270–278, 1999.
21. C.N. Ip and D.L. Dill. Better Verification Through Symmetry. *Formal Methods in System Design*, 9, 1996.
22. K. Jensen. *Coloured Petri Nets—Basic Concepts, Analysis Methods and Practical Use. Volume 1: Basic Concepts*. Springer-Verlag, 1992.
23. K. Jensen. *Coloured Petri Nets—Basic Concepts, Analysis Methods and Practical Use. Volume 2: Analysis Methods*. Springer-Verlag, 1994.
24. L.M. Kristensen, S. Christensen, and K. Jensen. The Practitioner's Guide to Coloured Petri Nets. *Journal on Software Tools for Technology Transfer*, 2(2):98–132, 1998.
25. L.M. Kristensen and T. Mailund. A Generalised Sweep-Line Method for Safety Properties. In *Proc. of FME'02*, volume 2391 of *LNCS*, pages 549–567. Springer-Verlag, 2002.
26. T. Mailund. *Sweeping the State Space — A Sweep-Line State Space Exploration Method*. PhD thesis, Department of Computer Science, University of Aarhus, 2003.
27. M. Mäkelä. Condensed Storage of Multi-Set Sequences. In K. Jensen, editor, *Proc. of Workshop on Practical Use of High-level Petri Nets*, number DAIMI PB-547, pages 111–126. University of Aarhus, 2000.
28. K.L. McMillan. *Symbolic Model Checking*. Kluwer Academic Publishers, 1993.
29. D. Peled. All for One, One for All: On Model Checking Using Representatives. In *Proc. of CAV'93*, volume 697 of *LNCS*, pages 409–423. Springer-Verlag, 1993.
30. K. Schmidt. Using Petri Net Invariants in State Space Construction. In H. Garavel and J. Hatcliff, editors, *Proc. of TACAS 2003*, volume 2619 of *LNCS*, pages 473–488. Springer, 2003.
31. U. Stern and D.L. Dill. Improved Probabilistic Verification by Hash Compaction. In *Correct Hardware Design and Verification Methods*, volume 987 of *LNCS*, pages 206–224. Springer-Verlag, 1995.
32. J.D. Ullman. *Elements of ML Programming*. Prentice-Hall, 1998.
33. A. Valmari. Stubborn Sets for Reduced State Space Generation. In *Advances in Petri Nets '90*, volume 483 of *LNCS*, pages 491–515. Springer-Verlag, 1990.
34. P. Wolper and D. Leroy. Reliable Hashing without Collision Detection. In *Proc. of CAV'93*, volume 697 of *LNCS*, pages 59–70. Springer-Verlag, 1993.

Automated Generation of a Progress Measure for the Sweep-Line Method

Karsten Schmidt

Humboldt–Universität zu Berlin
Institut für Informatik
D–10099 Berlin

Abstract. In the context of Petri nets, we propose an automated construction of a *progress measure* which is an important pre-requisite for a state space reduction technique called the *sweep-line method*. Our construction is based on linear-algebraic considerations concerning the transition vectors of the Petri net under consideration.

1 Introduction

The sweep-line method [Mai03] is a recently proposed reduction technique for explicit state space verification. In its basic shape, it deletes previously constructed states that cannot serve as successors of states not yet explored. The key concept for this method is a so-called *progress measure* that assigns values to states which are non-decreasing w.r.t. the successor state relation. The sweep-line method was later generalized such that progress measures can be used which are non-monotonous w.r.t. the successor relation. In that case, states that have a predecessor with larger progress value are stored permanently. Thus, a good non-monotonous progress measure should be designed such that value decrease by transition occurrence happens as seldom as possible. In the original papers [CKM01,KM02], it is left to the user to provide a progress measure, assuming that the user knows about some concept of progress in the modeled system.

We propose an automated generation of a progress measure for the generalized sweep-line method. It works for place/transition Petri nets, where convenient concepts for describing progress measures cannot be found within the formalism itself (in contrast to high level nets where the language of annotations to the net can be used to formulate progress measures).

Our progress measure is not necessarily monotonous. We derive the measure from an analysis of the system's transition vectors, and their linear dependencies. We arrive at an incremental progress measure. That is, we can assign to each transition a fixed value such that the progress value of a successor state differs from the original state exactly by the value assigned to the fired transition. One advantage of this kind of progress measure is that, upon a transition occurrence, the progress value of the successor state can be computed by addition of an offset to the progress value of the predecessor, that is, in constant time. Moreover, so-called regress transitions—transitions that decrease the progress value—can be identified statically.

K. Jensen and A. Podelski (Eds.): TACAS 2004, LNCS 2988, pp. 192–204, 2004.
© Springer-Verlag Berlin Heidelberg 2004

We start with a brief description of the sweep-line method, and continue with some basics about the linear algebra of Petri nets. Then, we present our proposal to the definition of a progress measure. Finally, we propose solutions concerning the combination of the sweep-line method with well-known state space reduction techniques such as partial order reduction or symmetry reduction.

2   The Sweep-Line Method

First, we sketch the basic sweep-line method [CKM01]. At any snapshot during explicit state space exploration, we can distinguish three kinds of states. We have states already seen, and states not yet seen. Among the states already seen there are those where all enabled transitions have already been explored, and those where some successors have not yet been explored. The last kind of states is called the *front*.

Assume we assigned a progress value[1] $p(s)$ to each state s such that for all transitions t, $s \xrightarrow{t} s'$ implies $p(s) \leq p(s')$. Obviously, all states still to be tested for presence in the state space are (transitive) successors of states in the front and have thus a progress value greater or equal to the minimum progress value among the front states. Consequently, states with smaller progress values than the minimum progress value appearing in the front can be safely removed from the state space. This is exactly the reduction the sweep-line method aims at. As the front evolves forward, more and more states can be removed, leading to the intuition of a sweep-line following the front of state space exploration and removing every state behind it (cf. Fig. 1). For being able to remove as many states as possible, and as early as possible, a search strategy is recommendable where front states are explored in ascending order of their progress values. In contrast, depth first search is not recommendable as the initial state is the last one to leave the front thus making it impossible for the sweep-line to proceed forward.

For the generalized sweep line method [KM02], the monotony condition for the progress measure is dropped. Thus, the method works, at least in principle, with any assignment p of progress values to states. Now, there can be situations where a transition leads to a state with smaller progress value. Such a pair of states is called a *regress edge* in the state space.

The generalized sweep-line method complements the basic method with the following twist. Whenever a regress edge occurs during a run (as in the basic method), the target state of that edge (the state with smaller progress value) is stored and marked *persistent*. That is, it will never be removed subsequently. It is, however, not explored immediately. Due to the removal of states behind the sweep line, we cannot be sure whether or not we have already seen that state. Thus, after having finished one state space exploration, we start another state

---

[1] in general, progress values can be members of any partially ordered set. For this paper, however, it is sufficient to view progress values as integer numbers. p is not necessarily injective.

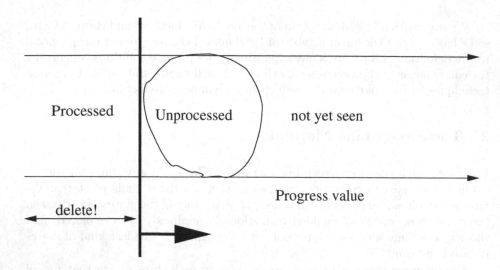

Fig. 1. A snapshot during sweep-line state space generation. States fully explored (processed) have smaller progress values than states not yet completely explored (unprocessed) and states not yet seen. States behind the sweep-line (following the unprocessed states) can be deleted.

space exploration with all states recently marked persistent as initial front. This exploration possibly re-explores parts of the state space, and can lead to further persistent states that need to be explored subsequently. It can, however, be shown that, for a finite-state system, every reachable state is visited at least once, so simple reachability queries can be verified using the method. Furthermore, the number of iterations until no additional persistent states are discovered, tends to be small.

3   Definitions

We use the notation $[P, T, F, W, m_0]$ for Petri nets, with the two finite and disjoint sets P (places) and T (transitions), the relation $F \subseteq (P \times T) \cup (T \times P)$ (arcs), the assignment $W : F \longrightarrow \mathbf{N} \setminus \{0\}$ (arc weights) and the initial marking m_0, where a marking is a mapping $m : P \longrightarrow \mathbf{N} \cup \{0\}$.

We extend W to $(P \times T) \cup (T \times P)$ by setting $W(x, y) = 0$ for $[x, y] \notin F$.

For a transition t, place vector Δt is defined by $\Delta t(p) = W(t, p) - W(p, t)$. Transition t is enabled at a marking m iff, for all $p \in P$, $m(p) \geq W(p, t)$. If t is enabled at m, t can fire at m leading to the successor state $m' = m + \Delta t$ (notation: $m \xrightarrow{t} m'$). The reachability relation $\xrightarrow{t}$ is extended to transition sequences in the canonic way, $m \xrightarrow{*} m'$ denotes reachability of m' from m by any finite transition sequence.

The incidence matrix C is a matrix with P as row index set and T as column index set, where for all transitions t, the corresponding column in C is equal to

Δt. A transition invariant is an integer solution to the system $C \cdot x = \underline{0}$ where x is a transition indexed vector of unknowns, and $\underline{0}$ is the place indexed vector of zeros.

Let $m \xrightarrow{t_1 \ldots t_n} m'$. By definition, we have $m' = m + \Delta t_1 + \cdots + \Delta t_n$. This equation can be rewritten to $m' = m + C \cdot \Psi(t_1 \ldots t_n)$ with Ψ being a vector with index set T where the entry for t is equal to the number of occurrences of t in $t_1 \ldots t_n$ (in the sequel called the *count vector* of the sequence). Equation $m' = m + C \cdot \Psi(t_1 \ldots t_n)$ is called the *state equation* for Petri nets.

A vector v is linear dependent on a set $\{v_1, \ldots, v_n\}$ of vectors if there are (rational) numbers $\lambda_1, \ldots, \lambda_n$ such that $v = \lambda_1 \cdot v_1 + \cdots + \lambda_n \cdot v_n$. A set of vectors is linear independent iff none of its members is linear dependent on the set of remaining members. For a matrix C, its rank $r(C)$ is defined as the size of the largest set of linear independent columns of C.

4   Progress Measures

A progress measure is a mapping $p : \mathbf{N}^P \longrightarrow A$, where A is an arbitrary set with a partial order $\leq$. If, for markings m, m', and a transition t, $m \xrightarrow{t} m'$ and $p(m) \not\leq p(m')$, $[m.m']$ is called a *regress edge*. A progress measure is monotonous if there are no regress edges between any two reachable markings.

Our progress measures map into the set $\mathbf{Q}$ of rational numbers, with the usual $\leq$ as its partial order. In addition, they are incremental.

A progress measure p is *incremental* if, for each $t \in T$, there is a rational number $o(t)$ (t's *offset*) such that for all m, m', $m \xrightarrow{t} m'$ implies $p(m') = p(m) + o(t)$. An incremental measure is uniquely defined by its transition offsets and the progress value of the initial marking. The progress value of the initial marking, however, does not influence the nature of the measure, so we assume $p(m_0) = 0$. Incremental progress measures have the advantage that calculation of progress values during depth first state space exploration can be done in constant time (just add the offset of the fired transition). Non-incremental measures may or may not require constant time calculations, depending on how many components of a state are considered for establishing progress.

Consider a marking m that is reached from the initial marking with two different transition sequences: $m_0 \xrightarrow{t_1 \ldots t_n} m$ and $m_0 \xrightarrow{t'_1 \ldots t'_k} m$. A consistent incremental progress measure must assign a unique progress value to m. That is, the transition offsets need to satisfy: $\sum_{i=1}^{n} o(t_i) = \sum_{j=1}^{k} o(t'_j)$.

Since the calculation of a progress measure needs to be performed prior to the state space generation, we do not have sufficient information about executable transition sequences. By the state equations $m = m_0 + C \cdot \Psi(t_1 \ldots t_n)$ and $m = m_0 + C \cdot \Psi(t'_1 \ldots t'_m)$ we know, however, that at least one of the transitions $t_1, \ldots, t_n, t'_1, \ldots, t'_k$ is linear dependent on the remaining transitions in this list. For a consistent measure, it is thus important to assign compatible values as soon as a transition is linear dependent on other ones.

Our approach works as follows. First, we determine a maximum size set U of linear independent transitions (the size of U is thus $r(C)$). This can be done in polynomial time. For each $t \in U$ we set $o(t) = 1$. Since U is of maximum size, all remaining transitions can be expressed (uniquely!) as linear combinations of transitions in U. These linear combinations determine the remaining offsets as follows. Let $U = \{t_1, ..., t_n\}$ and $t \notin U$. Then there exist $\lambda_1, \ldots, \lambda_n$ such that $\Delta t = \lambda_1 \Delta t_1 + \cdots + \lambda_n \Delta t_n$. We set $o(t) = \lambda_1 o(t_1) + \ldots \lambda_n o(t_n)$ $(= \lambda_1 + \ldots \lambda_n)$. This value can be greater than, equal to, or less than 0 (Fig. 2). Thus, among the transitions outside U, there may be regress transitions. It is obvious that our setting leads to a consistent progress measure.

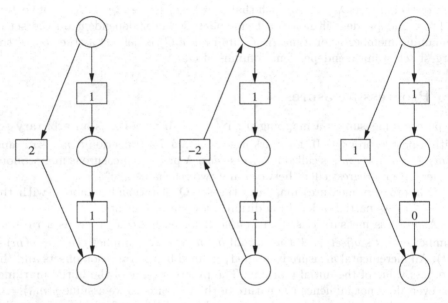

Fig. 2. The numbers in this figure are offsets. The transitions with offset 1 are members of U. The offset of the remaining transitions is determined by their linear combination from U.

Figure 3 contains a geometric interpretation of the just defined progress measure. Consider the euclidian space $Q^{|P|}$ of points with rational coordinates. Every marking defines a point in this space (with integer, even natural numbers as coordinates). The transition vectors Δt can be viewed as vectors. If $m \xrightarrow{t} m'$ then point m' is the translation of point m by vector Δt.

Linear independent vectors define a hyperplane E (the minimum size plane that contains the points defined by the translation of the point $\underline{0}$ by the respective vectors). E does not contain $\underline{0}$, so there is a unique point d in E that has minimal distance to $\underline{0}$ w.r.t. the usual euclidian metric. $\underline{0}$ and d define a line g containing both points. The progress value of a marking (a point) m is the distance of the unique intersection point i between line g and the parallel of E containing m, measured in a scale where the distance between $\underline{0}$ and d defines the unit (value 1).

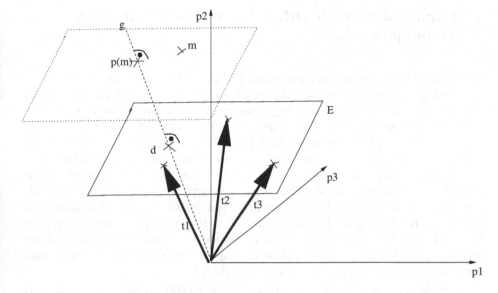

Fig. 3. Geometric interpretation of our progress measure

5   Possible Optimizations

The choice to assign offset 1 to the transitions in U is somewhat arbitrary. In fact, any assignment of offsets to transitions in U can be extended to a consistent progress measure for the whole system, following the linear combinations approach.

By changing offsets of transitions in U, the position of the plane E (and thus the direction of the progress line g) in Fig. 3 can be controlled. An optimal position would be such that as many as possible transitions point to the same side of the parallel of E through point $\underline{0}$. We tried to formulate this as an optimization problem, but did not succeed to arrive at a linear one. However, standard optimization heuristics such as simulated annealing or hill climbing may help to find close to optimal solutions. We cannot quantify the effect of such techniques at this time.

Approximating the target function (trying, for instance, to maximize the *sum* of offsets of all transitions rather than the number of transitions with positive offsets), leads to unsatisfactory results. For the sweep-line method, it is better to have many transitions with small positive offset, and few transitions with large negative offset than to have any kind of more balanced assignment.

Another source of possible optimization is the actual choice of U. While the size of U is determined by the rank of the incidence matrix C, there is some freedom left to choose its actual constituents. It might be possible to control the calculation of U such that, for instance, regress transitions do not form long chains (which would possibly lead to a large number of iterations of the sweep-line method). Results in this regard must as well be left to future work.

6 Combination with Other State Space Reduction Techniques

We consider first partial order reduction [Pel93,GW91,Val88]. Since the sweep-line method is able to investigate the set of reachable states, but not the mutual connections between states, only simple safety properties can be verified. Among them are presence of deadlocks [Val88], existence of dead transitions [Val91, Sch99b], reachability [Val91,Val93,Sch99b,KV00], and similar simple safety properties [Val93]. See [Val96,Val98] for surveys on partial order reduction methods. Partial order reduction consists of computing, in every state, a subset of the enabled transitions such that the considered property is preserved when only the transitions in the computed subset are fired. In most of the cited techniques, the subset can be determined by examining the structure of the system (here: the Petri net) and the current state. This is particularly the case for the deadlock preserving method [Val91], the methods proposed in [Sch99b] for dead transitions and reachability, and the approach in [Val93].

In [Val91], a core concept is a solution to the so-called ignorance problem. It requires detection of cycles or strongly connected components in order to avoid infinite ignorance of certain transitions. The approach of [KV00] to reachability has a similar condition. Traditionally, graph structures such as cycles or strongly connected components are detected through extensions to the depth-first search algorithm [Tar72]. Since depth first search is not available with the sweep-line method (as the initial state would be kept in the unprocessed set until the very end of state space exploration), we need a different implementation. Fortunately, a progress measure gives sufficient information, at least about cycles: every cycle contains a regress transitions (one with negative offset), or all transitions in the cycle have offset 0. While regress transitions can be immediately discovered during state space exploration, cycles containing only 0 offset transitions can as well be discovered since the involved states share the same progress value and are only deleted after having explored all of them. This means: if a property is preserved by the sweep-line method, then all existing partial order reduction approaches for that property can be combined with the sweep-line method, though not necessarily in their most efficient fashion.

Next, we consider the symmetry method [HJJJ84,CEFJ96,ES96,ID96, Sch00a,Sch00b]. Its principal compatibility to the sweep-line method was already mentioned in [Mai03]. However, there is a serious problem with the particular approach proposed in this paper. The symmetry method works by defining a suitable equivalence on the set of states, and exploring only one representative of every equivalence class. The usual implementation requires transforming every freshly computed state into a canonical representative of its class. The problem with our approach to the sweep-line method is that , ad 1, the canonical representative does not necessarily have the same progress value as the original state, and ad 2, the (incrementally determined) progress value of the canonical representative cannot be determined without having an actual transition sequence to this state. The only suitable solution to the problem is to arrange the progress measure such that equivalent states receive equal progress values.

In [Sch00a], we detect symmetries as graph automorphisms of the underlying Petri net. An automorphism is a bijection on the set of nodes (places and transitions) that respects node type, neighborhood w.r.t. the arc relation, multiplicities, and initial marking. The group of graph automorphisms defines an equivalence relation on the nodes as well as on the states of the Petri net. Two nodes are equivalent if there is a graph automorphism that maps one of them onto the other. Two states are equivalent if there is a graph automorphism that maps one of them onto the other. Thereby, for a state m and a graph automorphism σ, $\sigma(m)$ is defined by the equations $\sigma(m)(\sigma(p)) = m(p)$, for all places p. In this approach it can be proven that, if a state is reached by a sequence of transitions, equivalent states can also be reached by a sequence of equivalent transitions. Formally, $m_1 \xrightarrow{t_1 t_2 \ldots t_{n-1}} m_n$ implies $\sigma(m_1) \xrightarrow{\sigma(t_1)\sigma(t_2)\ldots\sigma(t_{n-1})} \sigma(m_n)$, for all graph automorphisms σ. Since every automorphism is expected to respect the initial state m_0, we have $\sigma(m_0) = m_0$, for all automorphisms σ.

Assume an incremental progress measure p defined by offsets $o(t_1), \ldots, o(t_n)$ to transitions $t_1, \ldots, t_n$, Let m be a state reachable from the initial state through a sequence $t_1 \ldots t_n$. Then, $p(m) = p(m_0) + o(t_1) + \cdots + o(t_n)$. For any state m' equivalent to m, we have an automorphism σ such that $m' = \sigma(m)$. Consequently, we have $p(m') = p(m_0) + o(\sigma(t_1)) + \cdots + o(\sigma(t_n))$. For achieving a symmetry respecting progress measure, it is thus sufficient to assign offsets to transitions such that equivalent transitions receive equal offsets. Then, $o(t_i) = o(\sigma(t_i))$ for all σ and all i. Unfortunately, this idea cannot be easily integrated into the approach presented so far, since the set U is not necessarily closed under the equivalence relation induced by symmetry. Furthermore, it can happen that transitions outside U, though equivalent, receive different values even if equivalent transitions inside U have equal values. It is thus necessary to compute a symmetry respecting progress measure with a more complicated approach. In the first step, we compute a generating set of all transition invariants of the Petri net, i.e. a set of invariants such that every transition invariant is a linear combination of these ones. Since we consider rational solutions, the computation can be done in polynomial time. In a second step, we calculate the offsets $(o(t_1), \ldots, o(t_n))$ of transitions $t_1, \ldots, t_n$ (where $n = card(T)$) as solutions of a homogeneous system of equations, including the following equations. First, for every generator $(a_1, \ldots, a_n)$ of the set of transition invariants, add equation $a_1 o(t_1) + \cdots + a_n o(t_n) = 0$. These equations guarantee consistency of the computed measure. Second, we add, for every pair $[t_i, t_j]$ of equivalent transitions, the equation $o(t_i) = o(t_j)$. Thus, solutions become symmetry respecting. Using a simple solution method such as Gaussian elimination, we may eventually choose some of the offset values arbitrarily. We use this opportunity to assign a positive value at least to those transitions. Every such assignment induces a positive value to a whole equivalence class (through the second kind of equations). This approach is more complicated since it requires the subsequent solution of two systems of equations. In terms of the computed progress measure, it tends, however, to yield acceptable measures, even though there exist cases where a non-trivial progress measure exists, but no non-trivial symmetry respecting progress measure (see Fig. 4).

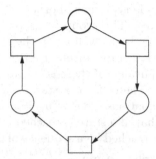

Fig. 4. This net has a progress measure where two of the transitions have offset 1 while the remaining transition has offset -2. All transitions are equivalent w.r.t. symmetry. The only symmetry respecting progress measure is thus the one assigning 0 to all transitions, and no reduction can be achieved.

Consistency of the proposed symmetry respecting progress measure can be verified as follows. Assume, one and the same state m is reached from the initial state through different transition sequences $t_1 \ldots t_k$ and $t'_1 \ldots t'_m$. The Petri net state equation yields $m = m_0 + C \cdot \Psi(t_1 \ldots t_k)$ and $m = m_0 + \Psi(t'_1 \ldots t'_m)$. Thus, $C \cdot (\Psi(t_1 \ldots t_k) - \Psi(t'_1 \ldots t'_m)) = 0$ which means that $\Psi(t_1 \ldots t_k) - \Psi(t'_1 \ldots t'_m)$ is a transition invariant. Since, through the first kind of equations introduced above, every *generator* $(a_1, \ldots, a_n)$ of the set of transition invariants satisfies $a_1 \cdot o(t_1) + \ldots a_n \cdot o(t_n) = 0$. Since every transition invariant can be expressed as a linear combination of the generators, we have that actually *all* transition invariants $(b_1, \ldots, b_n)$ satisfy $b_1 \cdot o(t_1) + \ldots b_n \cdot o(t_n) = 0$. In particular, we may conclude for the above mentioned difference of count vectors, $o(t_1) + \ldots o(t_k) - (o(t'_1) + \ldots o(t'_m)) = 0$, or, equivalently, $o(t_1) + \ldots o(t_k) = o(t'_1) + \ldots o(t'_m)$. m thus receives the same progress value, no matter which sequence is used to compute it. This means that the measure is consistent.

7 Examples

We consider first the system of dining philosophers, Fig. 5. This is a system consisting of a large number of agents where each agent performs a repeated sequence of only few actions. Thus, the state space of this system has a huge number of cycles where many of them can be performed independently. Consequently, most of the states of the system are reached by at least one regress transition (there is exactly one regress transition per philosopher). This nature of the dining philosophers system is actually an indication for *not* applying the sweep-line method which is confirmed by the results below (see the number of

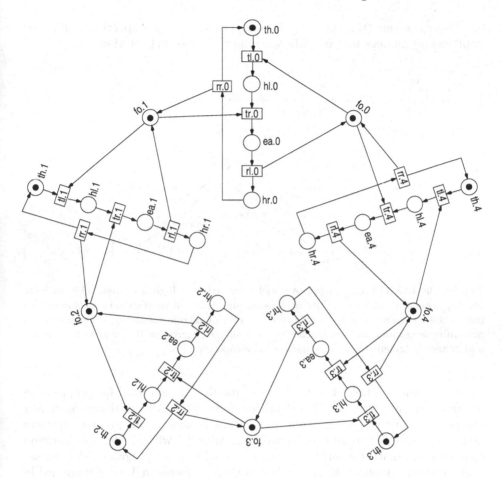

Fig. 5. The five dining philosophers system. A philosopher acts in the cycle take left fork - take right fork - release left fork - release right fork.

persistent states). We have included this system in order to show that, even for systems with no immediate concept of global progress, the sweep-line method *is* able to reduce peak memory usage. It is only necessary to combine it with partial order reduction. Partial order reduction has the effect of reducing the number of interleavings. Thus, local cycles of independent (not neighbored) philosophers are decoupled and the ratio between persistent and non-persistent states is much smaller. For realistic reactive systems, we expect an even better reduction since local cycles tend to be larger than in academic examples thus decreasing the number of regress transitions. The progress measure computed by our approach has three transitions per philosopher with offset 1, and the remaining transition with offset -3. Declaring every but one local step of a philosopher a "progress", and the remaining one as regress, appears natural even for a human generated progress measure. A person would, however, choose the same local transition to be the regress one (thus making the measure symmetry respecting) while our implementation does not compute a symmetry respecting solution.

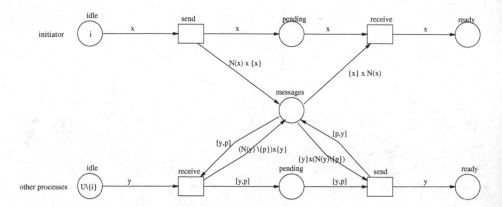

Fig. 6. The ECHO broadcasting protocol depicted as a high level net. The initiator (on top) sends messages to all its neighbors, and waits for corresponding acknowledgments. Other agents (on bottom) send (on receipt of one message), messages to all remaining neighbors, and send, after having collected corresponding acknowledgments, and acknowledgment to the originator of the message.

The second example, Fig. 6, shows a distributed algorithm for propagating information with feedback. The algorithm terminates. All transitions are linear independent. We are therefore able to compute a monotonous progress measure assigning 1 as offset to all transitions. This coincides with the human intuition that in a terminating algorithm, every executed step is "progress". We can see that in acyclic systems, the sweep-line method performs well, even if applied in isolation.

The data reported in Table 1 have been collected using the tool LoLA [Sch99a]. The implementation of the sweep-line method in LoLA is complete, including the fully automated determination of a progress measure according to the reported approach. It will be publicly available (open source) with the next release of the tool.

The numbers concerning partial order reduction concern deadlock preserving stubborn sets, but without considering the impact of on-the-fly verification. That is, state space exploration continues even after deadlocks have been found. Otherwise, numbers would be such small that no real comparison could be done.

The examples, as a few other experiments, suggest that the automatically computed progress measures are competitive to user-defined measure.

8   Conclusion

We have shown that an automated construction of a progress measure, by considering linear dependencies between transitions, leads to well-performing progress

Table 1. Experimental results: PHi = i dining philosophers, ECHOi = broadcasting algorithm for i agents in a grid-like network. Empty field = experiment not conducted; ? = out of memory. Platform: LINUX on 650 MHz Intel processor, 378 MB RAM

	PH5	PH10	PH12	PH100	PH400	ECHO3	ECHO9	ECHO25
full state space								
states	242	59048	531440	$3^{100}-1$	$3^{400}-1$	11	2628	?
trans. fired	805	393650	4251516	?	?	14	9994	?
time (sec)	0.1	5.8	71.0	?	?	0.0	0.5	?
sweep-line method								
nr. of iterations	3	3	3	?	?	1	1	1
peak nr. of states	183	54122	502378	?	?	4	634	260564
nr. persistent states	169	53299	497969	?	?	0	0	0
trans. fired	1544	720428	7710664	?	?	14	6805	1311085
time (sec)	0.1	24.3	277.8	?	?	0.1	0.1	284.7
partial order reduced state space								
states		272		29702	478802	7	1433	?
trans. fired		370		39700	638800	6	2463	?
time (sec)		0.5		2.3	115.3	0.0	0.2	?
sweep-line method plus partial order reduction								
nr. of iterations		3		11	41	1	1	1
peak nr. of states		97		9141	144936	2	340	236941
nr. persistent states		75		8929	144117	0	0	0
trans. fired		700		75800	1215204	6	2267	870495
time (sec)		0.1		17.2	1712.0	0.1	0.3	193.7

measures. For the examples discussed in the previous section, it is hard to imagine any user-defined measures that would perform significantly better. It has also become evident that a combination between the sweep-line method and partial order reduction is highly recommendable in the case of reactive systems. In the proposed fashion, the sweep-line method is well suited for the verification of low level Petri net models.

For high level models, our method can be applied in two ways. We can either unfold the high level net to a low level net and apply our method as such, or we can perform dependency analysis on the skeleton of the colored net instead. If the inscriptions of the high level net produce and consume a number of tokens that does not depend on particular transition bindings, this would lead to a sound progress measure. In the ECHO example, applied to a homogeneous network (one where all agents have the same number of neighbors), this method could be applied and would also result in a monotonous progress measure. It should be mentioned, though, that progress in high level nets does sometimes occur as a monotonous evolution of data values on certain tokens. In such cases, user defined progress measures are, without doubt, superior to automatically computed progress measures.

References

[CEFJ96] E.M. Clarke, R. Enders, T. Filkorn, and S. Jha. Exploiting symmetry in temporal logic model checking. *Formal Methods in System Design 9*, pages 77–104, 1996.

[CKM01] S. Christensen, L.M. Kristensen, and T. Mailund. A sweep-line method for state space exploration. *Proc. TACAS 01, LNCS*, 2031:450–464, 2001.

[ES96] E.A. Emerson and A.P. Sistla. Symmetry and model checking. *Formal Methods in System Design 9*, pages 105–131, 1996.

[GW91] P. Godefroid and P. Wolper. A partial approach to model checking. *6th IEEE Symp. on Logic in Computer Science, Amsterdam*, pages 406–415, 1991.

[HJJJ84] Huber, A. Jensen, Jepsen, and K. Jensen. Towards reachability trees for high–level petri nets. In *Advances in Petri Nets 1984, Lecture Notes on Computer Science 188*, pages 215–233, 1984.

[ID96] C.N. Ip and D.L. Dill. Better verification through symmetry. *Formal Methods in System Design 9*, pages 41–75, 1996.

[KM02] L.M. Kristensen and T. Mailund. A generalized sweep-line method for safety properties. *Proc. FME 02, LNCS*, 2391:549–567, 2002.

[KV00] L.M. Krisensen and A. Valmari. Improved question-guided stubborn set methods for state properties. *Proc. 21th Int. Conf. Application and Theory of Petri nets*, pages 282–302, 2000.

[Mai03] T. Mailund. *Sweeping the state space*. PhD thesis, Univerity of Aarhus, 2003.

[Pel93] D. Peled. All from one, one for all: on model–checking using representitives. *5th Int. Conf. Computer Aided Verification,Elounda, Greece, LNCS 697*, pages 409–423, 1993.

[Sch99a] K. Schmidt. Lola: A low level analyser. *Proc. Int. Conf. Application and Theory of Petri net, LNCS*, 1825:465–474, 1999.

[Sch99b] K. Schmidt. Stubborn set for standard properties. *Proc. 20th Int. Conf. Application and Theory of Petri nets, LNCS 1639*, pages 46–65, 1999.

[Sch00a] K. Schmidt. How to calculate symmetries of petri nets. *Acta Informatica 36,*, pages 545–590, 2000.

[Sch00b] K. Schmidt. Integrating low level symmetries into reachability analysis. *Proc. 6th Int. Conf. Tools and Algorithms for the Construction and Analysis of Systems, LNCS 1785*, pages 315–331, 2000.

[Tar72] R. E. Tarjan. Depth first search and linear graph algorithms. *SIAM J. Comput.*, 1:146–160, 1972.

[Val88] A. Valmari. Error detection by reduced reachability graph generation. *Proc. of the 9th European Workshop on Application and Theory of Petri Nets, Venice*, 1988.

[Val91] A. Valmari. Stubborn sets for reduced state space generation. *Advances of Petri Nets 1990, LNCS 483*, pages 491–511, 1991.

[Val93] A. Valmari. On-the-fly verification with stubborn sets. *5th Int. Conf. Computer Aided Verification,Elounda, Greece, LNCS 697*, pages 397–408, 1993.

[Val96] A. Valmari. Stubborn set methods for process algebras. *Workshop on Partial Order Methods in Verification, Princeton*, pages 192–210, 1996.

[Val98] A. Valmari. The state explosion problem. *Lectures on Petri nets I: Basic models, LNCS 1491*, pages 429–528, 1998.

Tarjan's Algorithm Makes On-the-Fly LTL Verification More Efficient

Jaco Geldenhuys and Antti Valmari

Tampere University of Technology, Institute of Software Systems
PO Box 553, FIN-33101 Tampere, FINLAND
{jaco,ava}@cs.tut.fi

Abstract. State-of-the-art algorithms for on-the-fly automata-theoretic LTL model checking make use of nested depth-first search to look for accepting cycles in the product of the system and the Büchi automaton. Here we present a new algorithm based on Tarjan's algorithm for detecting strongly connected components. We show its correctness, describe how it can be efficiently implemented, and discuss its interaction with other model checking techniques, such as bitstate hashing. The algorithm is compared to the old algorithms through experiments on both random and actual state spaces, using random and real formulas. Our measurements indicate that our algorithm investigates at most as many states as the old ones. In the case of a violation of the correctness property, the algorithm often explores significantly fewer states.

1 Introduction

Explicit-state on-the-fly automata-theoretic LTL model checking relies on two algorithms: the first for constructing an automaton that represents the negation of the correctness property, and the second for checking that the language recognized by the product of the system and the automaton is empty. This amounts to verifying that the system has no executions that violate the correctness property. An algorithm for converting LTL formulas to Büchi automata was first described in [26], and many subsequent improvements have been proposed [4,7, 10,11,19,21].

Checking the emptiness of the product automaton requires checking that none of its cycles contain any accepting states. One approach to this problem is to detect the *strongly connected components* (SCC) of the product. An SCC is a maximal set C of states such that for all $s_1, s_2 \in C$ there is a path from s_1 to s_2. An SCC is said to be *nontrivial* if it contains at least one such nonempty path, and, conversely, an SCC is *trivial* when it consists of a single state without a self-loop. The two standard methods of detecting SCCs are Tarjan's algorithm [1, 22], and the double search algorithm attributed to Kosaraju and first published in [20]. Both approaches often appear in textbooks.

Unfortunately, both algorithms have aspects that complicate their use in on-the-fly model checking. Tarjan's algorithm makes copious use of stack space,

K. Jensen and A. Podelski (Eds.): TACAS 2004, LNCS 2988, pp. 205–219, 2004.

```
     DFS(s)                              NDFS(s)
1    MARK(⟨s, 0⟩)                 10     MARK(⟨s, 1⟩)
2    for each successor t of s do 11     for each successor t of s do
3        if ¬MARKED(⟨t, 0⟩) then  12         if ¬MARKED(⟨t, 1⟩) then
4            DFS(t)               13             NDFS(t)
5        endif                    14         else if t = seed then
6    endfor                       15             report violation
7    if ACCEPTING(s) then         16         endif
8        seed := s ; NDFS(s)      17     endfor
9    endif
```

Fig. 1. The nested depth-first search algorithm of [2]

while Kosaraju's algorithm needs to explore transitions backwards. Instead, state-of-the-art algorithms perform nested depth-first searches [2,15].

In this paper, we introduce a new algorithm for detecting accepting cycles. Although it is based on Tarjan's algorithm, its time and memory requirements are often smaller than those of its competitors, because it relies on a single depth-first search, and it tends to detect violations earlier.

The rest of this paper is organized as follows: In Section 2 we describe the standard nested depth-first search algorithm, and discuss its strengths and weaknesses. Section 3 contains our proposed new algorithm and details about its implementation, correctness, and measurements with random graphs and random and actual LTL formulas. Section 4 deals with heuristics for speeding up the detection of violations. Experimental results on a real system are described in Section 5, and, finally, Section 6 presents the conclusions.

2 The CVWY Algorithm

Courcoubetis, Vardi, Wolper, and Yannakakis [2] presented the nested depth-first search algorithm for detecting accepting cycles, shown in Figure 1. (In the rest of this paper we shall refer to this algorithm by the moniker "CVWY".) The algorithm is based on a standard depth-first search. When a state has been fully explored and if the state is accepting, a second search is initiated to determine whether it is reachable from itself and in this way forms an accepting cycle.

The algorithm is clearly suited to on-the-fly verification. For each state, only two bits of information is required to record whether it has been found during the first and during the second search. Even when Holzmann's bitstate hashing technique [14] is used, hash collisions will not cause the algorithm to incorrectly report a violation.

A disadvantage of CVWY is that it does not find violations before starting to backtrack. Because depth-first search paths can grow rather long, this implies that many states may be on the stack at the time the first violation is detected, thus increasing time and memory consumption, and producing long counterexamples. It is not easy to change this behaviour, because it is important for the correctness of CVWY that, when checking an accepting state for a cycle, accepting states that are "deeper" in the depth-first search tree have already been investigated.

Tarjan's algorithm also detects completed SCCs starting with the "deepest", but it performs only a single depth-first search and can already detect states that belong to the same SCC "on its way down", which is why it needs to "remember" the states by placing them on a second stack. Such early detection of partial SCCs, and by implication, of accepting cycles, is desirable, because intuitively it seems that, not only could it reduce memory and time consumption, but could also produce smaller counterexamples.

3   Cycle Detection with Tarjan's Algorithm

Tarjan's algorithm is often mentioned but dismissed as too memory consuming to be considered useful, as, for example, in [3]. In the presentation of Tarjan's algorithm in [1] states are placed on an explicit stack in addition to being placed on the implicit *procedural* stack—that is, the runtime stack that implements procedure calls. Moreover, a state remains on the explicit stack until its entire SCC has been explored. Only when the depth-first search is about to leave a state (in other words, the state has been fully explored) and the algorithm detects that it is the root of an SCC, the state and all its SCC members are removed from the explicit stack. In consequence, the explicit stack may contain several partial SCCs—many more states than the implicit depth-first stack. In addition, each state has two associated attributes: its depth-first number and its *lowlink* value; naturally this requires extra memory.

However, we believe it is wrong to dismiss Tarjan's algorithm so quickly. Firstly, it is true that the state space of the system under investigation often forms a single, large SCC. However, the product automaton in which the accepting SCC must be detected is often broken into many smaller SCCs by the interaction of the system with the Büchi automaton. Even when the system and the Büchi automaton each consist of a single SCC it is still possible that the product will have more than one component as the Büchi transitions are enabled and disabled by the values of the atomic propositions. Secondly, and most importantly, for the automata-theoretic approach to work it is unnecessary to compute the entire SCC of a violating accepting cycle—it suffices to *detect* a nontrivial SCC that contains an accepting state. And lastly, as we show below, much of the memory requirements which at first sight may seem daunting, can be avoided by a careful implementation of the algorithm.

While these arguments do not constitute a claim that Tarjan's algorithm is necessarily viable, they do open the door to investigating its potential.

3.1   The New Algorithm

An automata-theoretic verification algorithm based on Tarjan is shown in Figure 2. We have shown a lot of detail to be able to describe how memory is used

```
      Stack = record                                    PUSH(s)
 1       state      # state stored in stack entry   28  MARK(s)
 2       lasttr     # last explored transition       29  INCR(top)
 3       lowlink    # lowlink value of this entry    30  stack[top].state := s
 4       pre            # DFS predecessor             31  stack[top].lasttr := "none"
 5       acc            # accepting state link        32  stack[top].lowlink := top
      endrecord                                       33  stack[top].pre := dftop
                                                       34  if ACCEPTING(s) then
 6  Stack stack[0...]                                  35     stack[top].acc := top
 7  int top := -1         # top of SCC stack           36  else if dftop ≥ 0 then
 8  int dftop := -1       # top of DFS stack            37     stack[top].acc := stack[dftop].acc
 9  bool violation := false                            38  else
                                                       39     stack[top].acc := -1
    MAIN()                                             40  endif
10  PUSH(initial state)                                41  dftop := top
11  while ¬violation ∧ dftop ≥ 0 do
12     s := stack[dftop].state                         POP()
13     t := next enabled transition of s
14     stack[dftop].lasttr := t                        42  p := stack[dftop].pre
15     s' := successor of s by t, if any               43  if p ≥ 0 then
16     if t = "none" then                              44     LOWLINKUPDATE(p, dftop)
17        POP()                                        45  endif
18     else if ¬MARKED(s') then                        46  if stack[dftop].lowlink = dftop then
19        PUSH(s')                                     47     top := dftop - 1
20     else if s' is on stack then                     48  endif
21        k := position of s' on stack                 49  dftop := p
22        LOWLINKUPDATE(dftop, k)
23     endif                                           LOWLINKUPDATE(f, t)
24  endwhile
25  if violation then                                  50  if stack[t].lowlink ≤ stack[f].lowlink then
26     report violation                                51     if stack[t].lowlink ≤ stack[f].acc then
27  endif                                              52        violation := true
                                                       53     endif
                                                       54     stack[f].lowlink := stack[t].lowlink
                                                       55  endif
```

Fig. 2. New algorithm for detecting accepting cycles

efficiently. Our presentation differs from the original presentation [1,22] and from the presentation of nested search algorithms in that it is iterative and not recursive. This is only a minor difference, but it avoids a small overhead associated with non-tail recursion, makes it is easier to abort in the case of a violation, and does not impede the clarity of the presentation.

However, there are other, more significant differences—so many that we chose to prove the correctness of our algorithm from scratch in Section 3.2:

1. Tarjan's algorithm uses an implicit procedural stack to manage the depth-first search, and an explicit SCC stack to store partial SCCs. That the former is a subset of the latter is easy to see: A new state is inserted into both stacks when it is first encountered. Once it is fully explored it is removed from the depth-first stack, but remains on the SCC stack until its entire SCC can be removed. This makes it possible to use only a single stack and thread the depth-first stack through it by means of the *pre* field of the *Stack* structure (line 4), and a second pointer *dftop* (line 8) to the top element of the depth-first stack. It is an invariant property of the algorithm that $top \geq dftop$, and that $stack[k].pre < k$ for any $0 \leq k \leq top$. (Other, equivalent variations are presented in [8] and [9, Appendix D].)

2. The MARKED and MARK functions in lines 18 and 28 refer to the presence of a state in the state store. Similar routines occur in Tarjan's algorithm (states

are marked as "old" or "new") and in state space construction algorithms. It is important to note that once a state has been removed from the SCC stack, its stack attributes (such as *lowlink* and *pre*) are no longer required, and the information can be discarded.

3. Line 20 omits a test made by Tarjan's algorithm to avoid the update for descendants of s that have already been investigated ("forward edges" in depth-first search terminology).

4. Tarjan's algorithm numbers states consecutively as they are found, whereas the algorithm in Figure 2 reuses the numbers of states that belong to completed SCCs.

5. When a transition from state f to state t is encountered, Tarjan's algorithm sometimes updates the *lowlink* of f with the depth-first number of t, and sometimes with the *lowlink* value of t. However, in our algorithm it is always the *lowlink* of t that is used for the update (lines 50–55). A similar change has been described in [17].

6. The most important addition to Tarjan's original algorithm is the *acc* field, defined in line 5, initialized in lines 34–40, and used in line 51. A stack entry's *acc* field keeps track of the shallowest (that is, closest to the top of the stack) accepting state on the depth-first path that leads to that stack entry.

Changes 1–4 improve the efficiency of Tarjan's algorithm. With the addition of changes 5 and 6 the new algorithm is able to tell early whether an SCC contains an accepting state.

3.2 Correctness

To show the correctness of the algorithm in Figure 2, we make use of colours. The colours are not in any way essential to the operation of the algorithm; they are simply mental tools that help us to understand that the algorithm is correct. A state can have one of the following colours:

- *White*: the state has not been found yet;
- *Grey*: the state is on the depth-first stack, in other words, it is *dftop* or *stack*[*dftop*].*pre*, or *stack*[*stack*[*dftop*].*pre*].*pre*, or ...;
- *Brown*: the state is still on the stack, but not on the depth-first stack; and
- *Black*: the state has been removed from the stack, in other words, its SCC has been completely explored.

The colour of a state can change from white to grey when it is first encountered by the depth-first search, from grey to brown when it has been fully explored but its SCC has not, and from grey or brown to black when it and its SCC have been completely explored.

The following invariants are maintained by the algorithm:

- *I1*: If a state is grey, then all stack states above it are reachable from it.
- *I2*: If a state is brown, then the topmost grey state below it on the stack exists, and is reachable from it.

- *I3*: If a state s_0 is on the stack and can reach a state below it on the stack, then there are $k > 0$ states s_1 to s_k such that $s_0 s_1 \ldots s_k$ is a path, s_1 to s_k are grey or white and the *lowlink* value of s_k is smaller than the position of s_0 on the stack.

To show that the algorithm maintains these invariants, we need the following:

Lemma 1. *Any state on the stack can reach stack[k].lowlink, where k is the position of the state on the stack.*

Proof. Via the path by which the *lowlink* value was propagated back to k.   □

We now consider the three actions the algorithm may take:

- *Forwarding* (PUSH). When the algorithm explores a transition to a new state, a white state is painted grey. Invariant *I1* is maintained because the new *dftop* becomes *top*, so no states exist above it. Other grey states can reach the old *dftop* and thus also the new state through the transition just explored. As far as *I3* is concerned: If s_0 is painted grey, the path to the state below s_0, truncated at the first non-white state after s_0, meets the requirements. If any of the s_j on s_0's path is painted grey, *I3* remains valid. Invariant *I2* is not affected.
- *Backtracking, top state becomes brown* (POP, without line 47). The state in question is in position *dftop*. To cope with *I2*, we have to show that the topmost grey state below *dftop* exists and is reachable from *dftop*. Because *dftop* is going to be painted brown instead of black, we have $stack[dftop].lowlink < dftop$. By Lemma 1, there is a path from *dftop* to some lower state s_1 on the stack. If s_1 is brown, let s_2 be the nearest grey state below it. From *I2* we know that it is reachable from s_1. If s_1 is not brown, then it is grey, in which case let $s_2 = s_1$. The topmost grey state other than *dftop* is either s_2, or, by *I1*, reachable from s_2. Therefore, *I2* also holds for the new brown state. As for *I3*: If s_0 becomes brown, the claim is not affected. If some s_j on s_0's path becomes brown, then s_{j+1} must be grey since a state is not backtracked from as long as it has white children. If s_{j+1} is below s_0 in the stack, then s_j has at most s_{j+1}'s position as its *lowlink* value, and thus qualifies as the new s_k for s_0. Otherwise, s_{j+1} is a grey state above (or at) s_0 in the stack, so following the depth-first stack from s_0 to s_{j+1} and then continuing along the earlier path constitutes a path as specified by *I3*. Invariant *I1* is not affected.
- *Backtracking, top states become black* (POP, with line 47). If any of the states that are to be painted black can reach a state below *dftop*, then, by *I1*, so can *dftop*. (Note that as most one grey state is painted black in this operation.) *I3* stays valid by the same reasoning as when the top state is painted brown. Invariants *I1* and *I2* are not affected.

Lemma 2. *Any state on the stack can reach all states above it on the stack.*

Proof. A state on the stack is either grey or brown. If the state is grey, then the lemma holds by *I1*. If it is brown, then we first invoke *I2* and then *I1*.   □

Lemma 3. *If a state is black, then all of its descendants are black.*

Proof. Since black states do not ever again change colour, it suffices to consider the case when new states are being painted black. If any of the newly painted states can reach a state below the then *dftop*, then, by *I1*, so can *dftop*. It then has a path as described by *I3*. Because all the states above *dftop* are brown, already *dftop*'s s_1 must be below it on the stack. Therefore, the condition on line 46 cannot hold, yielding a contradiction. Thus the newly painted states can reach only each other, or other black states which were painted earlier on.   □

Finally we are in a position to prove that the algorithm operates correctly:

Theorem 1. *If the algorithm announces a violation, then there is an accepting cycle.*

Proof. By Lemma 1 t can reach $stack[t].lowlink$. When a violation is reported, by Lemma 2, $stack[t].lowlink$ can reach $stack[f].acc$ which can reach f. The transition that caused the announcement is from f to t, closing the cycle.   □

Not only does the algorithm not raise false alarms, but it also has the property that it reports a violation as early as possible.

Theorem 2. *The algorithm reports a violation as soon as possible.*

Proof. Consider a nontrivial cycle with an accepting state A. If the algorithm does not terminate earlier, the following will happen. Eventually every transition of the cycle will be constructed by line 15. When the last transition of the cycle is constructed, then *dftop* is grey, and all other states in the cycle are on the stack. (They can be neither black by Lemma 3, nor white, because all transitions in the cycle are found.) Because no violation has been announced, the algorithm has never assigned to any $stack[k].lowlink$ a value smaller that $stack[k].acc$ (so no accepting state is brown). The cycle contains a transition $B \longrightarrow C$ such that B is A or above A on the stack, and C is A or below A. When the first such transition is found, the algorithm executes line 22 and announces a violation, because B's $lowlink \geq B$'s $acc \geq A$'s position $\geq C$'s position $\geq C$'s $lowlink$.   □

We have now demonstrated how an on-the-fly verification algorithm based on Tarjan can be efficiently implemented, and correctly detects accepting cycles. The question that remains is, does the extra cost of keeping backtracked states on the stack outweigh the benefit of finding errors early on?

Table 1. Comparison of the new algorithm and CVWY for random graphs and random and real LTL formulas

Edge probability	Random formulas			Formulas from literature			Combined		
0.001			*7133*			*2949*			*10082*
NEW	8.71	6.74	6.83	9.68	7.30	7.86	8.99	6.91	7.13
CVWY	41.69	30.14	37.83	36.62	26.21	31.82	40.21	28.99	36.07
0.01			*7267*			*3039*			*10306*
NEW	6.15	4.08	4.67	6.40	3.85	5.50	6.22	4.01	4.91
CVWY	25.59	15.31	21.62	24.52	13.93	20.45	25.28	14.90	21.27
0.1			*7832*			*3131*			*10963*
NEW	6.38	2.90	4.10	5.69	1.62	4.74	6.19	2.53	4.28
CVWY	78.82	32.70	72.58	65.33	24.66	58.40	74.96	30.40	68.53
0.5			*8150*			*3168*			*11318*
NEW	6.02	2.16	3.20	5.11	1.08	3.89	5.76	1.86	3.40
CVWY	92.54	47.56	84.66	80.52	35.18	70.68	89.18	44.09	80.75
0.9			*8222*			*3177*			*11399*
NEW	6.04	2.06	3.00	5.57	1.11	4.30	5.91	1.80	3.36
CVWY	88.90	47.22	80.51	81.78	35.89	71.26	86.91	44.07	77.93
Combined			*38604*			*15464*			*54068*
NEW	6.62	3.50	4.29	6.45	2.93	5.22	6.57	3.33	4.55
CVWY	66.98	35.18	60.80	58.32	27.31	51.03	64.51	32.93	58.01

3.3　Comparison with CVWY by Measurements

To investigate the impact of retaining partial SCCs on the stack, the new algorithm was compared to CVWY using random graphs and both random and actual LTL formulas. The procedure described in [23] was used to generate 360 random formulas, another 94 formulas were selected from the literature (the 12 in [7], the 27 in [21], the 55 in [5]), and a further 36 formulas were taken from a personal collection of troublesome formulas. Also the negations of these formulas were added to the list, bringing the total to 980. No attempt was made to remove duplicate LTL formulas. Each formula was converted to a Büchi automaton using the LTL2BA program [10], and the number of states in the resulting Büchi automata ranged from 1 to 177. Using another procedure from [23], 75 random 100-state graphs were generated. The graph generation algorithm selects one state as the root and ensures that every other state is reachable from it.

Every graph was checked against every LTL formula; Table 1 shows the outcome of the comparison. The three major columns contain the results for the random formulas, the human-generated formulas and the combined set, respectively. The major rows divide the results according to the connectedness of the graphs; each row describes 15 graphs that were generated with the same transition probability, while the last row contains the combined results for all 75 graphs. Within each cell, the small number in italics indicates in how many cases violations were found. For both the new and the CVWY algorithm three numbers indicate the number of unique states reached, the number of transitions explored, and the maximum size of the stack, averaged over the instances of violations, and expressed as a percentage of the total number of states or transitions in the product of the graph and the Büchi automaton. This means that every number in the last column is the sum of its counterparts in the first two columns, weighted with the number of violations.

For example, the 720 random formulas (360 randomly generated and negated) were checked against the 15 random graphs with a transition probability of 0.001. Of the 10800 products, 7133 contained violations. The new algorithm reported a violation (there may be several in each product) after exploring on average 8.71% of the states and 6.74% of the transitions of the product. During the search, the stack contained a maximum of 6.83% of the states on average. (This refers to the total number of states on the combined stack described in Section 3.1, not just the depth-first stack.) In contrast, the CVWY algorithm reports a violation after exploring on average 41.69% of the states and 30.14% of the transitions, and during the search the stack contained at most 37.83% of the states on average. (This includes the usual depth-first and the nested depth-first search stacks.)

The product automaton explored by the CVWY algorithm may, in some sense, have up to twice as many states and transitions as that explored by the new algorithm. Each state s has a depth-first version $\langle s, 0 \rangle$ and, if the state is reachable from an accepting state, a nested depth-first version $\langle s, 1 \rangle$, and the same holds for the transitions. However, in our opinion the figures as reported in the table give an accurate idea of the memory consumption of the algorithms (indicated by the percentage of states and maximum stack size) and the time consumption (indicated by the percentage of transitions). When states are stored explicitly, it is possible to represent the nested version of each state by storing only one additional bit per state. In this case, the CVWY figures for states may be divided by two before reading the table, to get a lower estimate.

The results clearly demonstrate that the new algorithm is faster (i.e., explores fewer transitions) and more memory efficient (i.e., stores fewer visited states and uses less stack space) than the CVWY algorithm, *for the formulas and random graphs investigated*. From experience we know that results on random graphs can be misleading; results for actual models and formulas are discussed in Section 5.

3.4   State Storage and Partial Orders

The new algorithm is fully compatible with bitstate hashing [14]; in fact, while the CVWY algorithm stores two bits per state, the new algorithm needs only a single bit. As we explain in the next subsection, the stack bit can be avoided if states can be searched for in the stack. The algorithm also works with state space caching [13]. Only the states on the depth-first stack need to be preserved; the other stack states are replaceable.

Partial order (or stubborn set) reduction techniques have become well-known and widely used [12,18,25]. Unfortunately, the CVWY algorithm has a drawback in this regard: Because states are visited more than once during the nested depth-first search, the reduction may cause the algorithm to ignore transitions that lead to an acceptance state. This was pointed out in [15]; the authors proposed a modification that not only corrects the problem, but also improves the performance of the algorithm slightly. (We shall refer to the modified algorithm as "HPY".) However, the modification requires extra information about transition reductions to be stored along with each state. This information can be reduced to a single bit, but at the expense of a loss in reduction. The new algorithm avoids these problems by never investigating a state more than once.

3.5   Stack Issues

While each stack element of the new algorithm carries three extra fields of information (*pre*, *lowlink*, and *acc*), the space required to store this information is small compared to the size of the states in a large system. Furthermore, since every state encountered by the algorithm is inserted in the state store (by the MARK function), the stack only needs to record a reference to the state's position in the store; it is not necessary to duplicate the state on the stack. When many partial-SCC states are retained on the stack, memory requirements can be made less severe if such lightweight stack elements are used. Note that the *lasttr* field does not count as extra information. In a recursive implementation like that in Figure 1, it is stored in a local variable on the procedural stack.

Another important implementation issue is finding states on the stack. If states are stored explicitly, there is the option of storing its stack position along with each state. As with the extra fields of the stack, the extra space required for this is usually relatively small compared to the size of states. Alternatively, a supplementary data structure such as a hash table or binary tree could help to locate states in the stack. This is necessary when bitstate hashing is used.

A significant difference between the new and the older algorithms is that CVWY/HPY can store stack information in sequential memory, which can be swapped to disk. The new algorithm, on the other hand, needs to store the *lowlink* fields of stack states in random access memory. Unfortunately, the impact of this difference depends on the structure of the model, and is difficult to judge

4   Heuristics

It is not difficult to construct a scenario where the new algorithm fares worse than the CVWY algorithm. Consider the Büchi automaton B and the system S in Figure 3. The product has exactly the same shape as S except that the state marked β is accepting, and forms the single accepting cycle.

Assuming that transitions are explored left-to-right, the CVWY algorithm detects the accepting cycle after exploring the four states of the subgraph rooted at state α. Its stack reaches a maximum depth of four and at the time of the detection, its stack contains three states (two regular states and one nested-search state). The new algorithm, on the other hand, also explores the four states of the subgraph rooted at α, but, because they form an SCC rooted at the initial state, these states remain on the stack. At the time of detecting the accepting cycle, the new algorithm's stack contains all six states of the product.

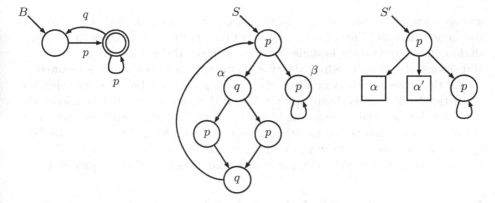

Fig. 3. A difficult case for the new algorithm

The situation is even worse if the system contains two such subgraphs, as does S' in Figure 3. In this case, CVWY explores the subgraphs at α and α', but its stack reaches a maximum size of only four. The new algorithm retains all states on the stack, so that it contains ten states when the accepting cycle is found.

If only the transition leading to β were explored first, both algorithms would detect the offending cycle after exploring just two states (plus an extra nested-search state for CVWY). This suggests the use of heuristics to guide the algorithms to detect accepting cycles more quickly. Ten heuristics were investigated, and the results are shown in Table 2. The meaning of the three columns is the same as in Table 1, as is the meaning of the three numbers (states, transitions, maximum stack size) given per experiment. Only the performance for the new algorithm is described in the table, and the first line—which agrees with the last NEW line of Table 1—shows the case where no heuristics are used.

The following heuristics were investigated: +DEPTH (−DEPTH) selects those transitions that lead to the deepest (shallowest) Büchi SCC first, +ACCEPT (−ACCEPT) selects those transitions that move closest to (furthest away from)

Table 2. Effect of heuristics on the new algorithm

Heuristic	Random formulas			Formulas from literature			Combined		
NONE	6.62	3.50	4.29	6.45	2.93	5.22	6.57	3.33	4.55
+DEPTH	6.72	3.34	4.28	7.88	3.46	6.29	7.05	3.37	4.85
−DEPTH	11.40	5.95	8.98	14.86	7.47	13.33	12.39	6.38	10.23
+ACCEPT	13.04	6.82	10.15	16.47	8.16	14.71	14.02	7.20	11.46
−ACCEPT	7.62	3.62	5.80	10.25	4.97	8.97	8.37	4.01	6.71
+STAY	12.03	6.15	9.76	16.27	8.04	14.65	13.24	6.69	11.16
−STAY	8.30	3.99	6.10	12.06	5.63	10.55	9.37	4.46	7.37
+TRUE	9.03	4.39	6.58	12.91	5.95	11.03	10.14	4.83	7.85
−TRUE	13.16	6.50	10.84	17.17	8.27	15.27	14.31	7.00	12.11

an accepting state first, +STAY (−STAY) selects those transitions that stay within the same Büchi SCC first (last), and +TRUE (−TRUE) selects those transitions that are labelled with the formula "true" first (last). If there are any ties between transitions, the order in which the transitions appear in the input is followed.

As the table shows, none of the heuristics performed better than using no heuristic at all. This is disappointing, but it does not mean that heuristics do not work. Rather, the problem might be that some heuristics work well for some Büchi automata, and poorly for others. Suggestions for heuristics search based on system transitions have been made in [13,16], and, more recently, in [6,27]. The new algorithm presented in this paper can accommodate all these suggestions.

5   Experiments with Actual Models

We have implemented a model of the echo algorithm with extinction for electing leaders in an arbitrary network, as described in [24, Chapter 7]. Three variations of the model behave in different ways:

- *Variation 1*: After a leader has been elected and acknowledged by the other nodes, the leader abdicates and a new election is held. The same node wins every election.
- *Variation 2*: A leader is elected and abdicates, as in Variation 1. However, a counter keeps track of the previous leader and gives each node a turn to win the election.
- *Variation 3*: As in Variation 2, each node gets a turn to become leader. However, one node contains an error that disrupts the cycle of elections.

Each of the variations was modelled with the SPIN system and its state space, reduced with partial orders, was converted to a graph for input by our implementation of the cycle detection algorithms. This is not the way the algorithms would be used in practice—cycle detection normally runs concurrently with the generation of the state space—but it facilitates making the experiments without having to implement the new algorithm in SPIN.

The results of our comparison are shown in Table 3. The first column contains the names of the formulas which are given explicitly below the table; a cross to the left of the formula name indicates that a violation of the property was detected. The column marked "Product" gives the number of states and transitions in the product automaton, and the columns marked "NEW", "HPY", and "CVWY" give the number of states, transitions and the maximum stack size for the new algorithm, the algorithm in [15] (HPY), and the algorithm in [2] (CVWY), respectively. As mentioned in Section 3.4, the HPY algorithm improves on the performance of the CVWY algorithm in some of the cases.

The arbitrary network specified in the model variations comprised three nodes numbered 0, 1, and 2. This explains why property B ("if ever, in the distant enough future, there is no leader, node 3 will be elected") and E ("node 3 is eventually elected once") are not satisfied by any of the models. Properties A, C, D, F, and G deal with the election of node 0, and properties H and I say

Table 3. Results of checking property ϕ for leader election in an arbitrary network

	ϕ	Product		NEW			HPY			CVWY		

Variation 1: 25714 states, 32528 transitions

	ϕ	Product		NEW			HPY			CVWY		
	A	51053	96406	51053	96406	14097	51053	128342	14097	51053	128342	14097
×	B	51849	100521	422	436	422	1159	1227	1151	1159	1227	1151
	C	12081	15198	12081	15198	199	12081	30395	199	12081	30395	199
	D	51053	96406	51053	96406	14097	51053	128342	14097	51053	128342	14097
×	E	25714	32529	389	390	389	642	657	639	692	730	639
	F	51053	96406	51053	96406	14097	51053	128342	14097	51053	128342	14097
	G	25714	32529	25714	32529	14097	25714	32529	14097	25714	32529	14097
×	H	53988	88553	610	624	610	19649	24417	1511	19649	24417	1511
×	I	53988	88553	610	624	610	19649	24417	1511	19649	24417	1511

Variation 2: 51964 states, 65701 transitions

	ϕ	Product		NEW			HPY			CVWY		
×	A	104779	204228	26742	49909	13841	35786	87539	1472	35786	87539	1472
×	B	105599	208455	886	900	886	3016	3168	3008	3016	3168	3008
	C	12081	15198	12081	15198	199	12081	30395	199	12081	30395	199
	D	103541	195893	103541	195893	40347	103541	260986	40347	103541	260986	40347
×	E	51964	65702	853	854	853	1570	1585	1567	1620	1658	1567
	F	103541	194225	103541	194225	40347	103541	259318	40347	103541	259318	40347
×	G	92140	118238	1122	1123	1122	1803	1805	1803	1803	1805	1803
×	H	293914	552899	1567	1581	1567	56254	69736	4269	56281	69777	4295
	I	132763	222806	132763	222806	40347	211890	377639	40347	211890	377639	40347

Variation 3: 40158 states, 51115 transitions

	ϕ	Product		NEW			HPY			CVWY		
×	A	81167	160470	904	906	904	2133	2222	2132	2133	2222	2132
×	B	81987	164697	904	906	904	2133	2222	2132	2133	2222	2132
	C	12081	15198	12081	15198	199	12081	30395	199	12081	30395	199
×	D	79929	152135	12777	16125	697	13239	31784	1159	13239	31784	1159
×	E	40158	51116	697	698	697	1159	1161	1159	1159	1161	1159
×	F	79929	150467	12777	16125	697	13239	31784	1159	13239	31784	1159
×	G	66450	86258	903	904	903	1365	1367	1365	1365	1367	1365
×	H	229269	435261	30917	57851	2009	142993	271769	2516	169718	315617	2896
×	I	169793	312465	37798	63689	14688	150362	281812	2292	193866	340240	2993

$$A \equiv \Diamond\Box(n \ \mathrm{U} \ \ell_0)$$
$$B \equiv \Diamond\Box(n \ \mathrm{U} \ \ell_3)$$
$$C \equiv \Diamond\ell_0$$
$$D \equiv \Box\Diamond\ell_0$$
$$E \equiv \Diamond\ell_3$$
$$F \equiv \Box(n \Rightarrow \Diamond\ell_0)$$
$$G \equiv \Box(n \vee \ell_0)$$
$$H \equiv \Diamond\Box((n \vee \ell_0 \vee \ell_1 \vee \ell_2) \wedge L(0,1) \wedge L(1,2) \wedge L(2,0))$$
$$I \equiv \Diamond\Box((n \vee \ell_0 \vee \ell_1 \vee \ell_2) \wedge L(0,2) \wedge L(1,0) \wedge L(2,1))$$

$n \equiv$ there is no leader
$\ell_x \equiv$ process x is the leader
$L(x,y) \equiv \ell_x \Rightarrow (\ell_x \ \mathrm{U} \ (n \ \mathrm{U} \ \ell_y))$

that, from some point onward, the elected leader follows the cycles 0–1–2 and 0–2–1, respectively.

In all cases the number of states and transitions explored by the new algorithm were the same as or less than those explored by the others. In three cases, variation 1 *H* and *I* and 2 *H*, the new algorithm explored more than 30 times fewer states and transitions. In two cases, 2 *A* and 3 *I*, the new algorithm required more stack entries than the other algorithms. As discussed in Section 3.5, which algorithm wins in these two cases depends on implementation details, but the new algorithm is clearly the overall winner.

6   Conclusions

We have presented an alternative to the CVWY [2] and HPY [15] algorithms for cycle detection in on-the-fly verification with Büchi automata. Our algorithm produces a counterexample as soon as an ordinary depth-first search has found every transition of the cycle. Thus it is able to find counterexamples quicker than CVWY and HPY, which need to start backtracking first. Also, it never investigates a state more than once, making it compatible with other verification techniques that rely on depth-first search. It sometimes requires a lot of stack space, but our measurements indicate that this drawback is usually outweighed by its ability to detect errors quickly.

Acknowledgments. The work of J. Geldenhuys was funded by the TISE graduate school and by the Academy of Finland.

References

1. A. V. Aho, J. E. Hopcroft, & J. D. Ullman. *The Design and Analysis of Computer Algorithms.* Addison-Wesley, 1974.
2. C. Courcoubetis, M. Y. Vardi, P. Wolper, & M. Yannakakis. Memory-efficient algorithms for the verification of temporal properties. In *Proc. 2nd Intl. Conf. Computer-Aided Verification*, LNCS #531, pp. 233–242, Jun 1990.
3. C. Courcoubetis, M. Y. Vardi, P. Wolper, & M. Yannakakis. Memory-efficient algorithms for the verification of temporal properties. *Formal Methods in System Design* 1(2/3), pp. 275–288, Oct 1992.
4. M. Daniele, F. Giunchiglia, & M. Y. Vardi. Improved automata generation for linear time temporal logic. In *Proc. 11th Intl. Conf. Computer-Aided Verification*, LNCS #1633, pp. 249–260, Jul 1999.
5. M. B. Dwyer, G. S. Avrunin, & J. C. Corbett. Property specification patterns for finite-state verification. In *Proc. 2nd ACM Workshop Formal Methods in Software Practice*, pp. 7–15, Mar 1998.
   Related site: http://www.cis.ksu.edu/santos/spec-patterns, Last updated Sept 1998.
6. S. Edelkamp, S. Leue, & A. Lluch Lafuente. Directed explicit-state model checking in the validation of communication protocols. Tech. Rep. 161, Institut für Informatik, Albert-Ludwigs-Universität Freiburg, Oct 2001.

7. K. Etessami & G. J. Holzmann. Optimizing Büchi automata. In *Proc. 11th Intl. Conf. Concurrency Theory*, LNCS #1877, pp. 154–167, Aug 2000.

8. J. Eve & R. Kurki-Suonio. On computing the transitive closure of a relation. *Acta Informatica* 8, pp. 303–314, 1977.

9. H. N. Gabow. Path-based depth-first search for strong and biconnected components. Tech. Rep. CU–CS–890–99, Dept. Computer Science, Univ. of Colorado at Boulder, Feb 2000.

10. P. Gastin & D. Oddoux. Fast LTL to Büchi automata translation. In *Proc. 13th Intl. Conf. Computer-Aided Verification*, LNCS #2102, pp. 53–65, Jul 2001.

11. R. Gerth, D. Peled, M. Y. Vardi, & P. Wolper. Simple on-the-fly automatic verification of linear temporal logic. In *Proc. 15th IFIP Symp. Protocol Specification, Testing, and Verification*, pp. 3–18, Jun 1995.

12. P. Godefroid. *Partial-order Methods for the Verification of Concurrent Systems, An Approach to the State-explosion Problem*. PhD thesis, University of Liège, Dec 1994. Also published as LNCS #1032, 1996.

13. P. Godefroid, G. J. Holzmann, & D. Pirottin. State space caching revisited. In *Proc. 4th Intl. Conf. Computer-Aided Verification*, LNCS #663, pp. 175–186, Jun 1992.

14. G. J. Holzmann. *Design and Validation of Computer Protocols*. Prentice Hall Software Series, 1991.

15. G. J. Holzmann, D. Peled, & M. Yannakakis. On nested depth first search. In *Proc. 2nd Spin Workshop*, pp. 23–32, Aug 1996.

16. F. J. Lin, P. M. Chu, & M. T. Liu. Protocol verification using reachability analysis: the state space explosion problem and relief strategies. *Computer Communication Review* 17(5), pp. 126–135, Oct 1987.

17. E. Nuutila & E. Soisalon-Soininen. On finding the strongly connected components in a directed graph. *Information Processing Letters* 49(1), pp. 9–14, Jan 1994.

18. D. Peled. All from one, one for all: On model checking using representatives. In *Proc. 5th Intl. Conf. Computer-Aided Verification*, LNCS #697, pp. 409–423, Jun 1993.

19. K. Schneider. Improving automata generation for linear temporal logic by considering the automaton hierarchy. In *Proc. Logic for Programming, Artificial Intelligence, and Reasoning*, LNCS #2250, pp. 39–54, Dec 2001.

20. M. Sharir. A strong-connectivity algorithm and its application in data flow analysis. *Computer and Mathematics with Applications* 7(1), pp. 67–72, 1981.

21. F. Somenzi & R. Bloem. Efficient Büchi automata from LTL formulae. In *Proc. 12th Intl. Conf. Computer-Aided Verification*, LNCS #1855, pp. 248–267, Jun 2000.

22. R. E. Tarjan. Depth-first search and linear graph algorithms. *SIAM Journal of Computing* 1(2), pp. 146–160, Jun 1972.

23. H. Tauriainen. A randomized testbench for algorithms translating linear temporal logic formulae into Büchi automata. In *Proc. Workshop Concurrency, Specifications, and Programming*, pp. 251–262, Sept 1999.

24. G. Tel. *Introduction to Distributed Algorithms*. Cambridge University Press, 2nd edition, 2000.

25. A. Valmari. A stubborn attack on state explosion. *Formal Methods in System Design* 1(1), pp. 297–322, 1992.

26. P. Wolper, M. Y. Vardi, & A. P. Sistla. Reasoning about infinite computation paths. In *Proc. Symp. Foundations of Computer Science*, pp. 185–194, Nov 1983.

27. C. H. Yang & D. L. Dill. Validation with guided search of the state space. In *Proc. 35th ACM/IEEE Conf. Design Automation*, pp. 599–604, Jun 1998.

Resource-Optimal Scheduling Using Priced Timed Automata

J.I. Rasmussen[1], K.G. Larsen[1], and K. Subramani[*2]

[1] Department of Computer Science, Aalborg University, Denmark,
{illum,kgl}@cs.auc.dk
[2] Department of Computer Science and Electrical Engineering, West Virginia University, USA, ksmani@csee.wvu.edu

Abstract. In this paper, we show how the simple structure of the linear programs encountered during symbolic minimum-cost reachability analysis of priced timed automata can be exploited in order to substantially improve the performance of the current algorithm. The idea is rooted in duality of linear programs and we show that each encountered linear program can be reduced to the dual problem of an instance of the min-cost flow problem. Thus, we only need to solve instances of the much simpler min-cost flow problem during minimum-cost reachability analysis. Experimental results using UPPAAL show a 70-80 percent performance gain. As a main application area, we show how to solve energy-optimal task graph scheduling problems using the framework of priced timed automata.

1 Introduction

Recently, solving real-time planning and scheduling problems using verification tools such as KRONOS, [9], and UPPAAL, [16], has shown promising results, [1, 6].

For addressing optimality constraints other than time (e.g. cost) priced timed automata (PTA) have been put forward, independently, as linearly priced timed automata in [15] and as weighted timed automata in [4]. The necessity for other optimality constraints is especially important within embedded systems where, for example, minimizing the overall energy consumption by embedded devices is imperative for their applicability.

One such problem of minimizing energy consumption is that of energy-optimal task graph scheduling (TGS). This is the problem of scheduling a number of interdependent tasks onto a number heterogeneous processors that communicate through a single bus while minimizing the overall energy requirement and meeting an overall deadline. The interdependencies state that a task cannot execute until the results of all predecessors in the graph have been computed. Moreover, the results should be available in the sense that either each of the

---

* This research was conducted in part at Aalborg University, where the author was supported by a CISS Faculty Fellowship.

K. Jensen and A. Podelski (Eds.): TACAS 2004, LNCS 2988, pp. 220–235, 2004.

predecessors have been computed on the same processor, or on a different processor and the result has been broadcasted on the bus. An example task graph taken from [12] with three tasks is depicted in Figure 1. The task t_3 cannot start executing until the results of both tasks t_1 and t_2 are available. The available resources are two processors, p_1 and p_2, and a single bus with energy consumptions $\pi_1 = 4$, $\pi_2 = 3$, and $\pi_{bus} = 10$ per time unit when operating and 1 when idle.[1] The nodes in Figure 1 are annotated with their execution times on the processors, that is, t_1 can only execute on p_1, t_2 only on p_2, and t_3 can execute on both p_1 and p_2.

The energy-optimal schedule is achieved by letting t_1 and t_2 execute on p_1 and p_2, respectively, broadcast the result of t_2 on the bus, and execute t_3 on p_1, which consumes the total of 121 energy units. On the other hand, broadcasting the result of t_1 on the bus and executing t_3 on p_2 requires 141 energy units. Both schedules are depicted as Gantt charts in Figure 2.

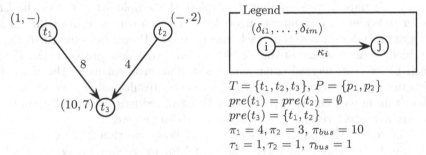

$$T = \{t_1, t_2, t_3\},\ P = \{p_1, p_2\}$$
$$pre(t_1) = pre(t_2) = \emptyset$$
$$pre(t_3) = \{t_1, t_2\}$$
$$\pi_1 = 4, \pi_2 = 3, \pi_{bus} = 10$$
$$\tau_1 = 1, \tau_2 = 1, \tau_{bus} = 1$$

Fig. 1. Example of an energy task graph with three tasks, two processors and a single bus.

Time-optimal task graph scheduling has received much attention in the research community as it is important in static, optimal scheduling of data independent algorithms onto digital signal processing architectures. For an overview of the proposed algorithms, an extensive comparison, evaluation, and benchmarks are provided in [13]. Recently, timed automata have in [1] been shown to be an efficient framework for modeling and solving TGS problems.

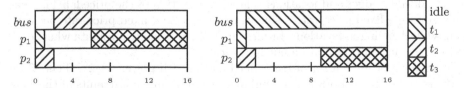

Fig. 2. a.) optimal schedule. b.) sub-optimal schedule

---

[1] We leave out units in this paper, but for real applications energy-consumption is, usually, measured in mW and execution times in ms.

For scheduling with cost extensions, timed automata are no longer sufficiently expressive. For cost-optimization problems, constraint programming, such as mixed integer linear programming (MILP), has been the preferred framework in the research community given the existence of efficient branch and bound algorithms for solving performance problems, [5,12]. Previously, the PTA approach to scheduling has shown to compete favorably with MILP for some problem instances, [15]. In this paper, we show how energy-optimal task graph problems can be modeled and solved using PTA.

The core of solving scheduling problems with PTA is symbolic minimum-cost reachability analysis. Within the reachability algorithm we frequently solve small, simple structured linear programs (LPs). As hinted in [15], reachability analysis might benefit significantly from exploiting the simple structure of these LPs since experimental results indicate that the current implementation in UP-PAAL, using the simplex method [8,11] spends 50-80 percent of the time during minimum-cost reachability, solving these LP problems.

In this paper, we show how to exploit the simple structure of the LPs in order to achieve an optimized algorithm. The idea comes from duality of linear programs and we show that each encountered LP can be reduced to the dual problem of an instance of the well-known min-cost flow problem, [2]. Thus, for each LP we can instead solve a min-cost flow problem using the much faster network simplex algorithm, [10]. Experimental results using a network simplex algorithm implementation [17] within UPPAAL reduces the overall running-time of minimum-cost reachability analysis by 70-80 percent.

The rest of this paper is organized as follows. Section 2 gives a short introduction to the theory of PTA. The model for expressing energy-optimal TGS problems as PTA is covered in Section 3. Section 4 provides symbolic semantics for PTA and gives a branch and bound algorithm for performing symbolic minimum-cost reachability analysis. In Section 5 we show how the LP encountered during minimum-cost reachability analysis are reduced to dual min-cost flow problems. Section 6 provides experimental results. Finally, we conclude the paper and reflect on future work in Section 7.

2   Priced Timed Automata

Priced timed automata, [15,7,6,4], are extensions of timed automata, [3], with prices added to edges and locations. The interpretation of the price label is, that we associate a fixed price with taking transitions and a fixed price rate per time unit while delaying in locations. Intuitively, PTA are timed automata where each finite trace has an overall accumulated price.

Formally, let $\mathbb{C}$ be a set of real-valued clocks with power set $2^{\mathbb{C}}$. Then $\mathcal{B}(\mathbb{C})$ is the set of formulae obtained as conjunctions of atomic constraints of the form $x_i \bowtie n$ and $x_i - x_j \bowtie m$, where $x_i, x_j \in \mathbb{C}$, $n \in \mathbb{N}$, $m \in \mathbb{Z}$ and $\bowtie \in \{<, \leq, =, \geq, >\}$. We refer to the elements of $\mathcal{B}(\mathbb{C})$ as clock constraints.

Definition 1 (Priced Timed Automata). *A priced timed automaton over clocks $\mathbb{C}$ and actions Act is a 5-tuple $(L, l_0, E, I, \mathcal{P})$ where L is a finite set of* *locations, l_0 is the initial location, $E \subseteq L \times \mathcal{B}(\mathbb{C}) \times Act \times 2^{\mathbb{C}} \times L$ is the set of edges, $I : L \to \mathcal{B}(\mathbb{C})$ assigns invariants to locations, and $\mathcal{P} : (L \cup E) \to \mathbb{N}$ assigns prices to edges and locations. When $(l, g, a, r, l') \in E$ we write $l \xrightarrow{g,a,r} l'$.*

Actual clock values are represented as functions from $\mathbb{C}$ to the set of non-negative reals, $\mathbb{R}_{\geq 0}$, called clock valuations. The set of all clock valuations is denoted by $\mathbb{R}^{\mathbb{C}}$, and single clock valuations are ranged over by u, u' etc.

For a clock valuation, $u \in \mathbb{R}^{\mathbb{C}}$, and a clock constraint, $g \in \mathcal{B}(\mathbb{C})$, we write $u \in g$ when u satisfies all the constraints of g. For $d \in \mathbb{R}_{\geq 0}$, we define the operation $u + d$ to be the clock valuation that assigns $u(x) + d$ to all clocks, and the operation $u[r \to 0]$ to be the clock valuation that agrees with u for all clocks in $\mathbb{C} \backslash r$ and assigns zero to all clocks in r. Furthermore, u_0 is defined to be the clock valuation that assigns zero to all clocks.

The semantics of a PTA $\mathcal{A} = (L, l_0, E, I, \mathcal{P})$ is given in terms of a labeled transition system with state set $L \times \mathbb{R}^{\mathbb{C}}$, initial state (l_0, u_0), and label set $(E \cup \{\delta\}) \times \mathbb{R}_{\geq 0}$, with the transition relation defined as:

- $(l, u) \xrightarrow{\delta, p} (l, u + d)$ if $\forall 0 \leq d' \leq d . u + d' \in I(l)$, and $p = d \cdot \mathcal{P}(l)$,
- $(l, u) \xrightarrow{e, p} (l', u')$ if $e = (l, g, a, r, l') \in E, u \in g, u' = u[r \to 0]$, and $p = \mathcal{P}(e)$.

In other words, δ-transitions correspond to delays, and e-transition correspond to edges of the automaton. The associated value, p, gives the price of the action. When performing minimum-cost reachability analysis of PTA, we are interested in finite executions of the form $\alpha = (l_0, u_0) \xrightarrow{a_1, p_1} (l_1, u_1) \xrightarrow{a_2, p_2} \cdots \xrightarrow{a_n, p_n} (l_n, p_n)$, where l_n is some goal location. The cost of the execution α is the sum of all prices on the path, $\sum_{i=1}^{n} p_i$. The minimum cost of reaching a location l is defined to be the infimum cost of all finite executions ending in a state of the form (l, u).

3   Energy-Optimal Task Graph Scheduling Using PTA

In this section we formalize the model of energy-optimal task graph scheduling and show how to translate such an instance into a PTA.

Definition 2 (Energy Task Graph). *An energy task graph is a tuple $(T, P, pre, \delta, \kappa, \pi, \tau, d)$ where $T = \{t_1, \ldots, t_n\}$ is a set of tasks, $P = \{p_1, \ldots, p_m\}$ is a set of processors, $pre : T \to 2^T$ determines the set of predecessors of every task, $\delta : T \times P \hookrightarrow \mathbb{N}$ is the execution time for tasks on processors, $\kappa : T \to \mathbb{N}$ is the bus transfer time for every task, $\pi : P \cup \{bus\} \to \mathbb{N}$ is the energy consumption rate per time unit when processing/transferring for the processors and bus, $\tau : P \cup \{bus\} \to \mathbb{N}$ is the energy consumption rate when being idle, and d is the deadline.*

We use the shorthand notations δ_{ij}, κ_i, $\{\pi, \tau\}_i$, and $\{\pi, \tau\}_{bus}$ for $\delta(t_i, p_j)$, $\kappa(t_i)$, $\{\pi, \tau\}(p_i)$, and $\{\pi, \tau\}(bus)$, respectively.

Definition 3 (Feasible Schedule). *A feasible schedule, $\mathcal{S}$, for an energy task graph $(T, P, pre, \delta, \kappa, \pi, \tau, d)$ is a function $\mathcal{S} : T \to P \times \mathbb{R}_{\geq 0} \times \mathbb{R}_{\geq 0} \cup \{\infty\}$, such that:*

1. $\forall t_i \in T . \mathcal{S}(t_i) = (p_k, s, c) \Rightarrow \delta_{ik}$ *is defined and* $c \geq s + \delta_{ik}$
2. $\forall t_i, t_j \in T$ *with* $\mathcal{S}(t_i) = (p_k, s, c), \mathcal{S}(t_j) = (p_l, s', c')$.
   a) $t_j \in pre(t_i) \wedge c = \infty \Rightarrow p_k = p_l$
   b) $t_j \in pre(t_i) \Rightarrow s \geq \begin{cases} s' + \delta_{jl} + \kappa_j : p_k \neq p_l \\ s' + \delta_{jl} : p_k = p_l \end{cases}$
   c) $p_k = p_l \wedge s' \geq s \Rightarrow s' \geq s + \delta_{ik}$
   d) $c' \geq c \Rightarrow c' \geq c + \kappa_i$
3. $len(\mathcal{S}) <= d$

where $len(\mathcal{S}) = max\{s + \delta_{ik}, c + \kappa_i \mid (t_i, p_k, s, c) \in \mathcal{S}\}$.

We will often use the notation $(t_i, p_k, s, c) \in \mathcal{S}$ when $\mathcal{S}(t_i) = (p_k, s, c)$. Given a feasible schedule, $\mathcal{S}$, the intuitive understanding of an element (t_i, p_k, s, c) is that the execution of task t_i started on processor p_k at time s and was broadcasted on the bus at time c. If $c = \infty$ the result was never broadcasted. The interpretation of the constraints are (1) tasks can only execute on allowed processors and the result cannot be broadcasted until execution has terminated. (2a) when a task depends on the result of another task, these are either executed on the same machine or the result has been broadcasted. (2b) no task can begin executing until the results of all dependent tasks are available. (2cd) each processor/bus can only execute/transfer one task/result at any time and such operations cannot be preempted. (3) the schedule should meet the deadline. The processing time, $proc(p_k)$, of a processor $p_k \in P$ is defined as $\sum_{\{i \mid (t_i, p_k, s, c) \in \mathcal{S}\}} \delta_{ik}$ and similarly for the bus. The idle time, $idle(p_k)$, is then given as $len(\mathcal{S}) - proc(p_k)$. Now, we can define the cost of schedule as:

$$\text{Cost}(\mathcal{S}) = \sum_{p_k \in P} \left(\pi_k \cdot proc(p_k) + \tau_k \cdot idle(p_k) \right) + \pi_{bus} \cdot proc(bus) + \tau_{bus} \cdot idle(bus) \quad (1)$$

A feasible schedule, $\mathcal{S}^*$, is optimal if for all feasible schedules, $\mathcal{S}$, $\text{Cost}(\mathcal{S}^*) \leq \text{Cost}(\mathcal{S})$.

Example 1. The optimal schedule (Figure 2a) for the energy task graph in Figure 1 corresponds to $\mathcal{S} = \{(t_1, p_1, 0, \infty), (t_2, p_2, 0, 2), (t_3, p_1, 6, \infty)\}$.

In the following we describe how to take any energy-optimal task graph problem instance and convert it into a network of priced timed automata. Following UPPAAL syntax, we express a timed automaton as a composition of automata synchronizing on binary channels and using shared variables that can be compared in guards and updated on transitions. Consequently, each state in the global state space is associated with a location vector, variable assignment, and clock valuation. Here, we indicate by the binary variables $fin[t_i]$ whether t_i has finished execution, by $act[p_j]$ whether p_j (or bus) is being used, and by $res[p_j][t_i]$ whether the result of t_i is available at p_j. The integer variable $d[p_j]$ expresses the time p_j (or bus) is occupied.

For a given energy task graph $(T, P, pre, \delta, \kappa, \pi, d)$ we construct a PTA for each task, processor, and the bus.

Definition 4 (Processor/Bus Automaton). *Given a processor $p_k \in P$ of an energy task graph $(T, P, pre, \delta, \kappa, \pi, d)$, the automaton for p_k has a local clock c, action $\{p_k\}$ and is defined as $(L, l_0, E, I, \mathcal{P})$ where $L = \{s_0, s_1\}$, $l_0 = s_0$, $I(s_0) = \emptyset$, $I(s_1) = c \le d[p_k]$, $\mathcal{P}(s_0) = \tau_k$, $\mathcal{P}(s_1) = \pi_k$, and $e = \{(s_0, \emptyset, \{p_k\}, \{c := 0, \text{act}[p_k] := 1\}, s_1), (s_1, c = d[p_k], \{p_k\}, \{\text{act}[p_k] := 0\}, s_0)\}$.*

The PTA for the bus is similar to the one for the processor and will not be defined explicitly. For simplicity we assign values to variables together with resetting clocks.

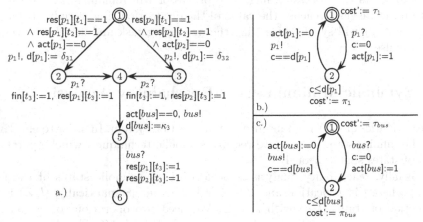

Fig. 3. Priced timed automata models for a.) task t_3 b.) processor p_1 c.) the bus.

Definition 5 (Task Automaton). *Given a task $t_i \in T$ of an energy task graph $(T, P, pre, \delta, \kappa, \pi, d)$, the automaton for t_i with $Act = \{p_k \mid \delta_{ik} \text{ is defined}\} \cup \{bus\}$ and is defined as $(L, l_0, E, I, \mathcal{P})$ where $L = \{s_0, done, bcing, bced\} \cup Act$, $l_0 = s_0$, $I(l) = \emptyset$ and $\mathcal{P}(l) = 0$ for all $l \in L$. E has the following transition for handling broadcast $(done, \text{act}[bus] = 0, \{bus\}, \{d[bus] := \kappa_i\}, bcing)$ and $(bcing, \emptyset, \{bus\}, \{\text{res}[p_k][t_i] := 1 \mid p_k \in P\}, bced)$ and for each $p_k \in Act$ we have the following two transitions:*

- *$(s_0, \text{act}[p_k] = 0 \wedge \bigwedge_{t_j \in pre(t_i)} \text{res}[p_k][t_j] = 1, \{p_k\}, \{d[p_k] := \delta_{ik}\}, p_k)$*
- *$(p_k, \emptyset, \{p_k\}, \{\text{fin}[t_i] := 1, \text{res}[p_k][t_i] := 1\}, done)$*

Now, the PTA for a energy task graph is the parallel composition of the bus automata, all task automata, and all processor automata. Furthermore, the cost of the optimal schedule is the minimum cost of reaching a location where $\bigwedge_{t_i \in T} \text{fin}[t_i] = 1$.

Example 2. Figure 3 depicts PTA models for task t_3, processor p_1, and the bus of the energy task graph of Figure 1. The two outgoing transitions from the initial state (double circle state) of Figure 3a indicates that task t_3 can execute on both machines. The guard on transition (1,2) states that the result of both

t_1 and t_2 should reside at p_1, and that p_1 should be inactive. In such case, the automaton can synchronize with p_1 and set the occupation time of p_1 to δ_{31}. When p_1 has finished execution and is ready to synchronize, the automaton will set the finish flag for t_3, update res such that the result of t_3 resides at p_1 and proceed to state 4. From here the result can be broadcasted in a similar way by synchronizing with the bus. The result of this is that res is updated such that the result of t_3 resides at all processors.

Processor p_1 of Figure 3b has price (cost) τ_1 in the initial state (1) and π_1 is the processing state (2). When p_1 synchronizes with a task, it resets the local clock and sets its processing flag. The processor will remain in the processing state until the clock reaches the value of the occupation time variable for p_1. At this point, p_1 will synchronize with the occupying task and set the processing flag to false.

4   Symbolic Minimum-Cost Reachability Analysis

The semantics of PTA is an infinite state transition system. In order to effectively handle infinite state systems we require symbolic techniques, which operate on sets of states simultaneously.

Usually, reachability analysis is performed on symbolic states of the form (l, Z) where l is a location and $Z \in \mathcal{B}(\mathbb{C})$ is a zone. Semantically, (l, Z) is the collection of states (l, u) with $u \in Z$. We need two operations on a zone, Z, delay, $Z^{\uparrow}$, and reset with respect to a set of clocks r, $\{r\}Z$. The operations are defined as $Z^{\uparrow} = \{u + d \mid u \in Z, d \in \mathbb{R}_{\geq 0}\}$ and $\{r\}Z = \{u[r \mapsto 0] \mid u \in Z\}$.

Given a symbolic state (l, Z), we define the delay successor to be $post_\delta(l, Z) = (l, (Z \wedge I(l))^{\uparrow} \wedge I(l))$ and for any edge, $e = (l, g, a, r, l') \in E$, the successor with respect to e is defined as $post_e(l, Z) = (l', \{r\}(Z \wedge g))$. Let $Post(l, Z) = \{post_\delta(l', Z') \mid (l', Z') = post_e(l, Z), e \in E\}$ be the set of successors of (l, Z) by following an edge in the automaton and delaying in that state. The symbolic semantics of a timed automaton (L, l_0, E, I, P) can then be given as a transition system with state set of the form (l, Z), initial state $post_\delta(l_0, u_0)$, and transition relation $(l, Z) \rightarrow (l', Z')$ if and only if $(l', Z') \in Post(l, Z)$.

In the core of cost-optimal reachability analysis for PTAs, we apply a symbolic semantics on a priced extension of zones, [7]. For this purpose we define the offset, $\Delta_Z \in Z$, of a zone Z as the unique clock valuation, in the closure of the zone, with $\Delta_Z(x_i) \leq u(x_i)$ for all $x_i \in \mathbb{C}$ and $u \in Z$.

Definition 6 (Priced Zone). *A priced zone, $\mathcal{Z}$, is a tuple (Z, c, r), where Z is a zone, $c \in \mathbb{N}$ is the price of the offset, Δ_Z, and $r : \mathbb{C} \rightarrow \mathbb{Z}$ assigns a cost rate, $r(x)$, to each clock, $x \in \mathbb{C}$. For any $u \in Z$, the cost of u in $\mathcal{Z}$, $\mathsf{Cost}(u, \mathcal{Z})$, is defined as $k + \sum_{x \in \mathbb{C}} r(x) \cdot u(x)$ where $k = c - \sum_{x \in \mathbb{C}} r(x) \cdot \Delta_Z(x)$.*

For a priced zone $\mathcal{Z} = (Z, c, r)$ and a clock valuation u, we write $u \in \mathcal{Z}$ when $u \in Z$.

Example 3. Figure 4 depicts a priced zone $\mathcal{Z} = (Z, 8, r)$ over clocks $\{x_1, x_2\}$, with $r(x_1) = 3$ and $r(x_2) = -2$, $\Delta_Z(x_1) = \Delta_Z(x_2) = 1$, cost function $3x_1 - 2x_2 + 7$, and constraints $x_1 - x_2 \leq 1, 1 \leq x_2 \leq 3, x_1 \geq 1$.

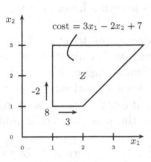

Fig. 4. A priced zone.

COST $:= \infty$; PASSED $:= \emptyset$
WAITING $:= \{post_\delta(l_0, (u_0, 0, r_0))\}$
while WAITING $\neq \emptyset$
    pick $(l, \mathcal{Z})$ from WAITING
    if $\forall (l', \mathcal{Z}') \in$ PASSED: $\neg((l', \mathcal{Z}') \sqsubseteq (l, \mathcal{Z}))$ **then**
      add $(l, \mathcal{Z})$ to PASSED
      if $l \in G$ and $mincost(\mathcal{Z}) <$ COST **then**
        COST $:= mincost(\mathcal{Z})$
      continue
      if $mincost(\mathcal{Z}) + remain(l, \mathcal{Z}) <$ COST **then**
        add $Post(l, \mathcal{Z})$ to WAITING
return COST

Fig. 5. Branch and bound algorithm.

Obviously, priced symbolic states should be pairs $(l, \mathcal{Z})$ where l is a location and $\mathcal{Z}$ is priced zone. Furthermore, we want the a-successor ($a \in \{e, \delta\}$) of a priced symbolic state $(l, \mathcal{Z})$ to be a state $(l', \mathcal{Z}')$ such that whenever $u \in \mathcal{Z}$ and $(l, u) \xrightarrow{a,p} (l', u')$ then $u' \in \mathcal{Z}'$ and $\mathsf{Cost}(u', \mathcal{Z}') = inf\{\mathsf{Cost}(u, \mathcal{Z}) + p \,|\, (l, u) \xrightarrow{a,p} (l', u')\}$.

Unfortunately, under these conditions, priced symbolic states are not directly closed under the $post_\delta$, $post_e$, and $Post$ operations. However, by applying the method outlined in [15], the above successor criteria can be met in a way such that both $post_\delta$ and $post_e$ on priced zones result in a finite union of priced zones. $Post$ on priced zones is then defined in the obvious way, $Post(l, \mathcal{Z}) = \{post_\delta(l', \mathcal{Z}') \,|\, (l', \mathcal{Z}') \in post_e(l, \mathcal{Z}), e \in E\}$.

The symbolic semantics for PTA can be stated similarly to the symbolic semantics for timed automata with $Post$ determining the transition relation and $(l_0, \mathcal{Z}_0) = post_\delta(l_0, (u_0, 0, r_0))$ as the initial state where r_0 has rate zero for all clocks.

Let $mincost(\mathcal{Z}) = inf\{\mathsf{Cost}(u, \mathcal{Z}) \,|\, u \in \mathcal{Z}\}$ denote the infimum cost over all clock valuations in $\mathcal{Z}$. The cheapest way of reaching some goal location l_g is then given as the minimum cost of all $mincost(\mathcal{Z})$ where there exists a finite path in the priced symbolic state space from the initial state to a state $(l_g, \mathcal{Z})$.

Now, we are ready to provide an algorithm for symbolic minimum-cost reachability analysis. The algorithm searches the symbolic state space based on a branch and bound approach and returns the minimum cost of reaching a location in a set of goal locations, G. The algorithm is depicted in Figure 5.

The algorithm uses a list of explored states, PASSED, and a list of states waiting to be explored, WAITING. Initially, the waiting list contains the initial state $(l_0, \mathcal{Z}_0)$. For every iteration of the while loop, we remove one element,

$(l, \mathcal{Z})$, from the list in some order. If none of the states in the passed list have the same location and are larger and cheaper ($\sqsubseteq$, defined below), we add $(l, \mathcal{Z})$ to the passed list. Then, if l is a goal locations and the minimum cost of the priced zone is the smallest encountered, we update the cheapest cost and skip to the next iteration[2]. We assume $remain(l, \mathcal{Z})$ to provide lower bound estimates on the cost of reaching a goal location from $(l, \mathcal{Z})$. We only compute the successors of $(l, \mathcal{Z})$ if there is a chance that we reach a goal location with a lower cost than previously encountered.

The algorithm terminates when there are no more states to explore and COST will hold the lowest cost of reaching a goal location. Termination of the algorithm depends on the symbolic state space being well-quasi ordered under $\sqsubseteq$, [15]. Formally, the notion of 'bigger and cheaper' between priced symbolic states is defined as follows, $(l', \mathcal{Z}') \sqsubseteq (l, \mathcal{Z})$ if and only if $l = l'$, $Z \subseteq Z'$, and for all $u \in Z$, $\mathsf{Cost}(u, \mathcal{Z}') \leq \mathsf{Cost}(u, \mathcal{Z})$ where Z and Z' are the zone parts of $\mathcal{Z}$ and $\mathcal{Z}'$, respectively.

Given two priced zones $\mathcal{Z} = (Z, c, r)$ and $\mathcal{Z}' = (Z', c', r')$ where $Z \subseteq Z'$ we can decide whether $(l, \mathcal{Z}') \sqsubseteq (l, \mathcal{Z})$ by computing $mincost(\mathcal{Z}'')$ over a priced zone $\mathcal{Z}''$ with zone part Z and $\mathsf{Cost}(u, \mathcal{Z}'') = \mathsf{Cost}(u, \mathcal{Z}) - \mathsf{Cost}(u, \mathcal{Z}')$ for all $u \in Z$. If the result is larger than zero we know that $(l, \mathcal{Z}') \sqsubseteq (l, \mathcal{Z})$.

Thus, solving $mincost(\mathcal{Z})$ becomes a central aspect of the algorithm for symbolic minimum-cost reachability and the solution corresponds to the following linear program over clock variables.

Definition 7 (*mincost* **LP**). *Given a priced zone* $\mathcal{Z} = (Z, c, r)$, *with all strong inequalities relaxed, over clock variables* $\mathbb{C}$, *the mincost LP is defined as:*

Minimize: **subject to:**

$$k + \sum_{x \in \mathbb{C}} r(x) \cdot x \qquad Z \text{ and } \forall x \in \mathbb{C} . x \in \mathbb{R}_{\geq 0}, \qquad (2)$$

Solutions to the *mincost* LP are given in terms of clock valuations and the objective function value of a given solution, u, is denoted by $z(u)$.

The *mincost* LP, when first described in [15], was solved using the simplex algorithm[3], [11]. As noted in [15], the *mincost* LP's occurring through minimum-cost reachability of practical problems are often very small, since the number of variables equals the number of clocks. Furthermore, the constraints of the LP's can be stated solely as clock difference constraints when using the difference bound matrix representation (DBM) outlined in, [14][4]. The simplex package applied, on the other hand, is tailored towards large, general LP's with up to 30000 variables and 50000 constraints, [8]. Experimental results show that, in the current implementation, 50-80 percent of the time spent during minimum-cost

---

[2] We are not concerned with the successors given the monotonicity of cost evolution.

[3] The implementation used the `lp_solve` package by Michel Berkelaar, `ftp://ftp.es.ele.tue.nl/pub/lp_solve`.

[4] By introducing a clock, x_0, whose value is always zero, any constraint of the form $x_i \bowtie n$ can be written as $x_i - x_0 \bowtie n$, $\bowtie \in \{\leq, \geq, =, <, >\}$.

reachability is used for solving *mincost* LP's. Thus, we may benefit significantly by exploiting the simple structure and/or the small size of the *mincost* LP's.

5   Minimum Cost Flow and Duality

In this section we describe a problem that is closely related to the *mincost* LP, namely the minimum cost flow problem (or min-cost flow). At the end of the section we show how the two problems relate through duality of linear programs.

Definition 8 (Min-Cost Flow Problem). *Let $G = \langle \mathcal{N}, \mathcal{A} \rangle$ be a directed graph with node set $\mathcal{N}$ and arc set $\mathcal{A} \subseteq \mathcal{N} \times \mathcal{N}$. With each node $i \in \mathcal{N}$ we associate a value $b_i \in \mathbb{N}$, such that $\sum_{i \in \mathcal{N}} b_i = 0$, with each arc $(i, j) \in \mathcal{A}$ we associate a cost c_{ij} and a variable y_{ij}. The min-cost flow problem is defined as:*

Minimize: **subject to:**

$$\sum_{(i,j) \in \mathcal{A}} c_{ij} y_{ij} \qquad \forall i \in \mathcal{N} . \sum_{\{j:(i,j) \in \mathcal{A}\}} y_{ij} - \sum_{\{j:(j,i) \in \mathcal{A}\}} y_{ji} = b_i, \qquad (3)$$

$$\forall (i, j) \in \mathcal{A} . y_{ij} \in \mathbb{R}_{\geq 0}. \qquad (4)$$

We call a node $i \in \mathcal{N}$ a supply node, demand node, or transshipment node depending on whether $b_i > 0$, $b_i < 0$, or $b_i = 0$, respectively. The intuitive interpretation of the min-cost flow problem is to find the cheapest assignment of flow to arcs, such that for each node the outflow minus the inflow equals the supply/demand of that node.

Example 4. Figure 6 depicts a min-cost flow problem with nodes $\{0, 1, 2\}$ and arcs $\{(0, 1), (0, 2), (1, 2), (2, 0)\}$. The supply/demand of the nodes are $b_0 = 1, b_2 = 2$, and $b_1 = -3$. The arc costs are $c_{01} = c_{02} = -1, c_{12} = 1$, and $c_{20} = 3$. One (non-optimal) solution that satisfies Equation 3 is to assign 4 units flow to arcs $(0, 1)$ and $(2, 0)$, and 1 to arcs $(0, 2)$ and $(1, 2)$. The cost of this solution is 8.

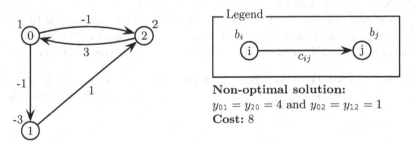

Fig. 6. Example min-cost flow problem. Node 1 is a demand node and nodes 0 and 2 are supply nodes.

For the solution of min-cost flow problems, a special and considerably faster adaptation of the general simplex algorithm, the network simplex algorithm, [10], has been proposed. Despite the worst-case exponential running-time of the network simplex algorithm it is often, in practice, faster than its polynomial time counterparts, [2].

Now, we show that instead of solving *mincost* LP's as general linear programs, we can instead solve related instances of the min-cost flow problem. The relation comes through duality of linear programming. For every linear program, called the primal, there is a closely related linear program, called the dual, and such primal/dual pairs share a number of properties. The property we exploit in this paper is the so-called strong duality theorem, [11,2]:

Theorem 1 (Strong Duality Theorem). *For every pair of primal/dual problems, if either problem has a bounded optimal solution, then so does the other and the optimal objective function values are identical.*

In other words, to obtain the optimal objective function value of a linear program, we can instead solve the dual problem since the optimal objective function values agree.

Definition 9 (Min-Cost Flow Dual). *Given a min-cost flow problem as stated in Definition 8, the dual problem is defined, over variables x_i where $i \in \mathcal{N}$, as:*

$$\textbf{Maximize:} \qquad \qquad \textbf{subject to:}$$

$$\sum_{i \in \mathcal{N}} b_i x_i \qquad \qquad \forall (i,j) \in \mathcal{A} . x_i - x_j \leq c_{ij} \qquad (5)$$

$$\forall i \in \mathcal{N} . x_i \in \mathbb{R} \qquad (6)$$

Obviously, the min-cost flow dual resembles the *mincost* LP using the DBM representation of zones. The differences are that the min-cost flow dual is a maximization problem, the decision variables range, unrestrictedly, over the reals, and the cost rates of all clocks must sum to zero. However, we can accommodate for these discrepancies by rewriting the *mincost* LP.

For this purpose we derive a linear program that is identical to the *mincost* LP in the sense, that for every solution to the *mincost* LP there is a solution in the new LP, which achieves the same objective function value, and vice versa.

Definition 10 (Relaxed *mincost* LP). *Given a priced zone $\mathcal{Z} = (Z, c, r)$ over a set of clock variables $\mathbb{C} \cup \{x_0\}$, the relaxed mincost LP is defined as[5]*

$$\textbf{Minimize:} \qquad \qquad \textbf{subject to:}$$

$$k + \sum_{x \in \mathbb{C}} r(x) \cdot (x - x_0) \qquad Z^* \text{ and } \forall x \in \mathbb{C} \cup \{x_0\} . x \in \mathbb{R} \qquad (7)$$

---

[5] Z^* denotes the representation of a zone, Z, using only difference constraints by introducing a clock, x_0. [14]. Furthermore, all strong inequalities have been relaxed.

Solutions to the relaxed *mincost* LP are given in terms of an assignment function $v : \mathbb{C} \cup \{x_0\} \rightarrow \mathbb{R}$. The objective function value of a given solution, v, is denoted by $z(v)$. The relaxed *mincost* LP has a number of interesting properties. The proofs of these properties are straight forward and can be found in, [18]

Property 1. If u is a solution to the *mincost* LP, then v is a solution to the relaxed *mincost* LP, where $v(x) = u(x)$ for all $x \in \mathbb{C}$ and $v(x_0) = 0$. Furthermore, $z(u) = z(v)$.

Property 2. If v is a solution to the relaxed *mincost* LP, then u is a solution to the *mincost* LP, where $u(x) = v(x) - v(x_0)$ for all $x \in \mathbb{C}$. Furthermore, $z(v) = z(u)$.

As a consequence of Properties 1 and 2 the optimal objective function values of the *mincost* LP and the relaxed *mincost* LP agree. In other words, when determining the lowest price of a priced zone, we can choose to solve either LP.

In order for the relaxed *mincost* LP to be a min-cost flow dual, we need to change it into a maximization problem. However, this is trivial as minimizing a function corresponds to maximizing the negated function. That is, we can negate the objective function of the relaxed *mincost* LP, solve it as a maximization problem, and negate the result.

Finally, we need to verify that the sum of all supply/demand in the primal min-cost flow problem sum to zero. This fact follows immediately from the objective function of the relaxed *mincost* LP, as the factor of x_0 is the negated sum of all cost rates of $x_i \in \mathbb{C}$.

We conclude that instead of solving the *mincost* LP, we can solve the primal min-cost flow problem of the maximization version of the relaxed *mincost* LP. This technique requires us to negate the result received from the min-cost flow problem and add the constant k in order to obtain the correct solution.

Theorem 2. *Given a priced zone $\mathcal{Z} = (Z, c, r)$, the corresponding min-cost flow problem is obtained as: For each clock $x_i \in \mathbb{C}$ create a node x_i and set $b_{x_i} = -r(x_i)$, create a node x_0 for the zero clock with $b_{x_0} = \sum_{x_i \in \mathbb{C}} r(x_i)$, and for every constraint $x_i - x_j \leq m$ in Z^* make an arc from node x_i to x_j with cost $c_{x_i x_j} = m$. The solution to the mincost LP is the negated solution to the min-cost flow problem plus k.*

Example 5. To illustrate the above technique we show that the min-cost flow problem of Figure 6 is, in fact, the primal problem of the relaxed *mincost* LP over the priced zone in Figure 4. For each of the clock variables x_0, x_1, and x_2 we have the nodes 0, 1, 2, respectively. The constraints of Z^* are $x_0 - x_1 \leq -1, x_0 - x_2 \leq -1, x_2 - x_0 \leq 3$, and $x_1 - x_2 \leq 1$, each of which corresponds to an arc with appropriate cost in the graph. The supply/demands of the nodes are given as 1, −3, and 2, respectively, which obviously equals the negated cost rates and sum to zero.

Furthermore, the optimal solution to the min-cost flow graph is $x_{20} = 2, x_{01} = 3$, and $x_{02} = x_{12} = 0$ and has cost 3. By negating the result and adding the constant $k = 7$, we obtain the optimal solution (i.e. 4) to the *mincost* LP given in Example 3.

Note that when solving the *mincost* LP, the number of variables equals the number of clocks, and when solving the dual min-cost flow problem, the number of variables equals the number of clock constraints. Thus, we are interested in reducing the number of constraints. For this purpose, we use the algorithm provided in [14] that computes a zone representation with a minimal set of constraints.

6   Experimental Results

In this section we provide the experimental results obtained for energy-optimal task graph scheduling using PTA.

For conducting the experiments we have taken the Standard Task Graph Set[6] of [19] and added communication costs, energy consumptions, and restricting task execution to a subset of the processors. The results are summarized in Table 1. The missing entries indicate that we were unable to create a problem instance that could be solved within the available memory. Simplex and Net-Simplex refer to the running-times using the standard simplex algorithm [8] and network simplex algorithm [17], respectively. The performance gain is given as Speedup and Threshold shows the time needed to compute a feasible schedule within 10 percent of the optimal.

The results in Table 1 show that the running-time of symbolic minimum-cost reachability can be improved by 70-80 percent[7] by solving the min-cost flow dual problem instead of the *mincost* LP. The results are similar when performing the same experiments on the examples reported in [15].

Given the computational complexity of (energy-optimal) task graph scheduling the, key to solving large problem instances is to guide the search towards approximate solutions as fast as possible, [13]. Unfortunately, we have been unable to find energy task graphs with known optimal solutions to use for experimenting with heuristic-based guiding techniques. However, using a random-depth first search order, Table 1 shows that even for most problems, we can obtain a solution within a 10 percent margin using only a fraction of the time need for obtaining the optimum.

Since we were unable find comparable results using other algorithms, it is hard to conclude on the competitiveness energy-optimal TGS using PTA. However, the results in [15] show that the PTA approach to cost-optimal scheduling is competitive with MILP. Furthermore, [1] provides results showing that we can efficiently find approximate solutions to TGS with timed automata using guiding heuristics. For these reasons, we are positive that using more involved

---

[6] The STG set is available at http://www.kasahara.elec.waseda.ac.jp/schedule/.

[7] We disregard the results where both algorithms terminate within one second, since there is an overhead at startup where the input is passed and converted before execution begins.

Table 1. Experimental results for 19 energy task graph instances. The results were obtained on a PentiumM 1.2GHz with 512MB RAM. Done indicates that the algorithm found the optimal and terminated within 1 sec.

Processors	Tasks	5	7	9	10	11	12
2	Simplex	0.438s	2.734s	24.889s	127.318s	15.345s	844.804s
	NetSimplex	0.205s	0.592s	4.565s	27.890s	3.041s	181.997s
	Speedup (%)	**53.2**	**78.3**	**81.7**	**78.1**	**80.1**	**78.5**
	Threshold	done	done	2.730s	0.694s	1.297s	9.663s
3	Simplex	0.466s	10.850s	27.039s	155.823s	197.141s	
	NetSimplex	0.159s	2.618s	5.235s	36.403s	56.270s	
	Speedup (%)	**65.9**	**75.9**	**80.6**	**76.6**	**71.5**	
	Threshold	done	0.392s	5.768s	1.121s	0.141s	
4	Simplex	1.827s	15.049s	31.080s	450.859s	302.062s	
	NetSimplex	0.426s	3.583s	7.006s	106.804s	87.685s	
	Speedup (%)	**76.7**	**76.2**	**77.5**	**76.3**	**71.0**	
	Threshold	done	0.593s	0.779s	4.616s	17.85s	
5	Simplex	4.122s	20.603s	44.882s			
	NetSimplex	0.896s	5.104s	10.690s			
	Speedup (%)	**78.3**	**75.2**	**76.2**			
	Threshold	done	0.476s	5.099s			

guiding heuristics together with good *remain* estimates, PTA will be a competitive approach to solving energy-optimal TGS problems.

7   Conclusions and Future Work

In this paper we have shown how to exploit the structure of the LPs solved during symbolic minimum-cost reachability through a reduction to the min-cost flow problem, thus providing an answer to the question put forward in [15]. The current implementation in UPPAAL uses a simplex algorithm to solve these LPs. Experimental results show that solving the related min-cost flow instances with a network simplex algorithm instead, reduces the overall running-time of the reachability algorithm by 70-80 percent. In particular, we have shown how to solve energy-optimal TGS problems with PTA, and through initial experimental results we believe that PTA is a competitive approach to solving such problems. Additional experiments on e.g. the aircraft landing problem, [15], indicate that the performance gain generalizes to all PTA minimum-cost reachability problems.

To improve the competitiveness of PTA in energy-optimal TGS, we need to develop more elaborate guiding heuristics and remaining estimates in order to efficiently guide the search in the direction of approximate solutions.

An interesting alternative, which can potentially provide considerable speedup, is to identify abstractions that are exact w.r.t. optimal reachability, e.g. a suitable adaption of the domination points techniques used in [1].

Another promising approach is be to develop a compositional technique for finding either approximate or exact optimal solutions. The idea is to exploit the (in)dependency structure often found in large scale real problems.

References

1. Yasmina Abdeddaim, Abdelkarim Kerbaa, and Oded Maler. Task graph scheduling using timed automata. *Proceedings of the International Parallel and Distributed Processing Symposium (IPDPS)*, 2003.
2. Ravindra K. Ahuja, Thomas L. Magnanti, and James B. Orlin. *Network Flows - Theory, Algorithms, and Applications*. Prentice Hall, 1993.
3. R. Alur and D. Dill. Automata for modelling real-time systems. In *Proc. of Int. Colloquium on Algorithms, Languages and Programming*, number 443, pages 322–335, July 1990.
4. Rajeev Alur, Salvatore La Torre, and George J. Pappas. Optimal paths in weighted timed automata. *Lecture Notes in Computer Science*, 2034:pp. 49–??, 2001.
5. J. E. Beasley, M. Krishnamoorthy, Y. M. Sharaiha, and D. Abramson. Scheduling aircraft landings - the static case. *Transportation Science*, 34(2):pp. 180–197, 2000.
6. Gerd Behrmann, Ansgar Fehnker, Thomas Hune, Kim Larsen, Paul Petterson, and Judi Romijn. Efficient guiding towards cost-optimality in UPPAAL. *Lecture Notes in Computer Science*, 2031:pp. 174+, 2001.
7. Gerd Behrmann, Ansgar Fehnker, Thomas Hune, Kim Larsen, Paul Pettersson, Judi Romijn, and Frits Vaandrager. Minimum-cost reachability for priced timed automata. *Lecture Notes in Computer Science*, 2034:pp. 147+, 2001.
8. Michel Berkelaar.
   `http://www.cs.sunysb.edu/~algorith/implement/lpsolve/implement.shtml`,
   Oct. 2003.
9. M. Bozga, C. Daws, O. Maler, A. Olivero, S. Tripakis, and S. Yovine. Kronos: A model-checking tool for real-time systems. In A. J. Hu and M. Y. Vardi, editors, *Proc. 10th International Conference on Computer Aided Verification, Vancouver, Canada*, volume 1427, pages 546–550. Springer-Verlag, 1998.
10. W. H. Cunningham. A network simplex method. *Mathematical Programming*, 11:pp. 105–106, 1976.
11. George B. Dantzig. *Linear Programming and Extensions*. Princeton University Press, Princeton, New Jersey, 1963.
12. Flavius Gruian and Krzysztof Kuchcinski. Low-energy directed architecture selection and task scheduling. *Proceedings of the 25th EuroMICRO Conference*, 1:pp. 296–302, 1999.
13. Yu-Kwong Kwok and Ishfaq Ahmad. Benchmarking and comparison of the task graph scheduling algorithms. *Journal of Parallel and Distributed Computing*, 59(3):pp. 381–422, 1999.
14. K. Larsen, F. Larsson, P. Pettersson, and W. Yi. Efficient verification of real-time systems: Compact data structure and state space reduction. In *Proc. Real-Time Systems Symposium*, pages pp. 14–24, 1997.
15. Kim Larsen, Gerd Behrmann, Ed Brinksma, Ansgar Fehnker, Thomas Hune, Paul Pettersson, and Judi Romijn. As cheap as possible: Efficient cost-optimal reachability for priced timed automata. *Lecture Notes in Computer Science*, 2102:pp. 493+, 2001.

16. Kim Guldstrand Larsen, Paul Pettersson, and Wang Yi. UPPAAL in a nutshell. *Int. Journal on Software Tools for Technology Transfer*, 1(1-2):134–152, 1997.
17. Andreas Löbel. http://www.zib.de/Optimization/Software/Mcf/, Oct. 2003.
18. Jacob Illum Rasmussen. Priced timed automata and duality - available at http://www.cs.auc.dk/~illum/pubs/ptaduality.html, 2003.
19. T. Tobita, M. Kouda, and H. Kasahara. Performance evaluation of minimum execution time multiprocessor scheduling algorithms using standard task graph set. *Proc. of PDPTA'00*, pages 745–751, 2000.

Decidable and Undecidable Problems in Schedulability Analysis Using Timed Automata*

Pavel Krčál and Wang Yi

Uppsala University
Department of Information Technology
P.O. Box 337, S-751 05 Uppsala, Sweden
{pavelk,yi}@it.uu.se

Abstract. We study schedulability problems of timed systems with non-uniformly recurring computation tasks. Assume a set of real time tasks whose best and worst execution times, and deadlines are known. We use timed automata to describe the arrival patterns (and release times) of tasks. From the literature, it is known that the schedulability problem for a large class of such systems is decidable and can be checked efficiently.

In this paper, we provide a summary on what is decidable and what is undecidable in schedulability analysis using timed automata. Our main technical contribution is that the schedulability problem will be undecidable if these three conditions hold: (1) the execution times of tasks are intervals, (2) a task can announce its completion time, and (3) a task can preempt another task. We show that if one of the above three conditions is dropped, the problem will be decidable. Thus our result can be used as an indication in identifying classes of timed systems that can be analysed efficiently.

1 Introduction

Timed automata [AD94] has been developed as a basic semantic model for real time systems. Recently it has been applied to solve scheduling problems, such as job-shop scheduling [AM01,AM02,Abd02,Feh02,HLP01] and real time scheduling [MV94,FPY02,AFM$^+$02,FMPY03,WH03]. The basic idea behind these works is to model real time tasks (or jobs) and scheduling strategies of a system as variants of timed automata and then check the reachability of pre-specified states. As the reachability problem of such automata is decidable, the scheduling problems can be solved automatically and in many cases efficiently (e.g. for fixed priority scheduling [FMPY03]) using a model-checker such as KRONOS [Yov97], UPPAAL [LPY97] or HyTECH [HHWT97]. For preemptive scheduling, stop-watch automata have been used to model preemption [MV94,CL00,Cor94,AM02]. But since the reachability problem for this class of

---

* This work has been partially supported by the Swedish Research Council and the European Research Training Network GAMES.

automata is undecidable [ACH+95] there is no guarantee for termination in the general case.

We adopt the model presented in [EWY98]. The essential idea behind the model is to use a timed automaton (*control automaton*) to describe the release (or arrival) patterns of the tasks. Tasks are released when control automaton makes a discrete transition. Each task has specified its computation (execution) time and its deadline. Released tasks are stored in a task queue and executed on a processor according to a scheduling strategy. There is a straightforward translation of such a system into a timed automaton for non-preemptive scheduling strategies. For the preemptive case, the schedulability problem was suspected to be undecidable due to the nature of preemption that may need the power of stop-watch to model.

In the original work, tasks in the queue cannot send any information back to the control automaton. The only communication between the control automaton and the task queue is the release of tasks. Once a task has been released, the control automaton has no possibility to find out any information about its execution. In particular, the control automaton does not know whether a task has finished or not. The behaviour of the control automaton is independent from the state of the queue. We say that this is a system with *one-way communication*. In this paper, we study systems where tasks can tell the control automaton that their execution has been just finished (systems with *two-way communication*). As an illustration, consider a company, where the boss assigns jobs to employees from time to time. In the model with one-way communication, the employees do not tell the boss when they finish their jobs whereas in the model with two-way communication they do.

The execution time of a task can vary within an interval – only the best and the worst execution time of each task is known. This is a natural assumption for modeling, because in many cases we cannot establish the exact computation time of a task (it depends on many circumstances from which the model abstracts), but we can establish some bounds for it. In the schedulability analysis of the systems with two-way communication we have to consider each possible finishing time, because it can influence the future behaviour of the control automaton. For instance, the boss can become too optimistic when several employees finish their jobs quickly and he can assign too many jobs to other employees. Or on the other hand, the boss can assign fewer jobs (or stop assigning new jobs at all) when the processing of some old one takes too much time (e.g. exception handling).

Recent results [FPY02,FMPY03] show that some of the schedulability problems related to preemptive scheduling are decidable. The decidability of the schedulability analysis has been proven for the following models. In [FPY02] only systems with one-way communication are considered. However, the execution times of tasks can be intervals though it is not stated clearly in this work. The best execution time is not important for the schedulability analysis of the systems with one-way communication. In [FMPY03] tasks can update data variables shared between them and the control automaton upon their completion (system with two-way communication), but the computation time should be a known constant for each task. The natural question is if schedulability analysis remains decidable for systems with two-way communication and interval execution times.

Unfortunately, the answer is negative. As the main technical contribution of this paper, we show that (1) the interval execution time of tasks, (2) the ability of the control automaton to test the exact completion time of tasks, and (3) preemption are sufficient and necessary to code the halting problem for two-counter machines. We shall also summarise previous decidability results and discuss other variants of the problem. Our goal is to identify as closely as possible the borderline between decidable and undecidable problems in schedulability analysis using timed automata. Hopefully, our result can be used as an indication in determining which classes of real-time models can be analysed efficiently.

The rest of the paper is organised as follows. In Section 2 we formally introduce our model, define the schedulability problem, and summarise previous decidability results. Section 3 contains the undecidability proof of the schedulability problem for our model. We discuss several variants of this model in Section 4. Section 5 concludes the paper with a summary and future work.

2   Preliminaries

2.1   Timed Automata with Tasks

To model two-way communication, we assume that each automaton has a distinguished clock, that is reset whenever a task finishes. This allows each task to announce its completion to the automaton. We have chosen reseting of the clock because even this simple model of two-way communication between tasks and the control automaton is sufficient for encoding of the two-counter machine. Other models of two-way communication, such as updating shared data variables upon completion are discussed later.

Syntax. Let $\mathcal{P}$ ranged over by P, Q denote a finite set of task types. A task type may have different instances that are copies of the same program with different inputs. Each task P is characterised as a pair $([B, W], D)$, where $[B, W]$ is the execution time interval and D is the deadline for P, $B \leq W \leq D \in \mathcal{N}_0$ and $W \neq 0$. The deadline D is relative, meaning that when task P is released, it should finish within D time units. We use $B(P)$, $W(P)$, and $D(P)$ to denote the best execution time, the worst execution time, and the relative deadline of the task P.

As in timed automata, assume a finite set of real-valued variables $\mathcal{C}$ for clocks. We use $\mathcal{B}(\mathcal{C})$ ranged over by g to denote the set of conjunctive formulas of atomic constraints in the form: $a \sim N$ or $a - b \sim M$ where $a, b \in \mathcal{C}$ are clocks, $\sim \in \{\leq, <, \geq, >\}$, and N, M are natural numbers. We use $\mathcal{B}_I(\mathcal{C})$ for the subset of $\mathcal{B}(\mathcal{C})$ where all atomic constraints are of the form $a \sim N$ and $\sim \in \{<, \leq\}$. The elements of $\mathcal{B}(\mathcal{C})$ are called *clock constraints* or *guards*.

Definition 1. *A timed automaton extended with tasks, over clocks C and tasks $\mathcal{P}$ is a tuple $\langle N, l_0, E, I, M, check \rangle$ where*

- $\langle N, l_0, E, I \rangle$ *is a timed automaton where*
  - N *is a finite set of locations,*
  - $l_0 \in N$ *is the initial location,*
  - $E \subseteq N \times \mathcal{B}(C) \times 2^C \times N$ *is the set of edges, and*
  - $I : N \mapsto \mathcal{B}_I(C)$ *is a function assigning each location with a clock constraint (a location invariant),*
- $M : N \hookrightarrow \mathcal{P}$ *is a partial function assigning locations with a task type,[1] and*
- $check \in C$ *is the clock which is reset whenever a task finishes.*

As a simplification we will use $l \xrightarrow{g,r} m$ to denote $(l, g, r, m) \in E$.

For convenience, in the rest of the paper we use extended timed automata (ETA) or simply automata when it is understood from the context instead of timed automata extended with tasks.

Operational Semantics. Extended timed automata may perform two types of transitions just as standard timed automata. Intuitively, a discrete transition in an automaton denotes an event triggering a task. Whenever a task is released, it will be put in a scheduling (or task) queue for execution. A delay transition corresponds to the execution of the running task with the highest priority and idling for the other tasks waiting to run.

We represent the values of clocks as functions (called clock assignments) from C to the non-negative reals. A state of an automaton is a triple (l, σ, q) where l is the current control location, σ the clock assignment, and q is the current task queue. We assume that the task queue takes the form: $[P_1(b_1, w_1, d_1), \ldots, P_n(b_n, w_n, d_n)]$ where $P_i(b_i, w_i, d_i)$ denotes a released instance of task type P_i with remaining best computing time b_i, remaining worst computing time w_i, and relative deadline d_i denoted by $b(P_i), w(P_i)$ and $d(P_i)$ respectively.

A *queue reordering function* is a sorting function which changes the ordering of the task queue elements according to the task types and parameters. It takes a task queue as an input and returns a task queue with the unmodified tasks that may be sorted in a different order. A *scheduling strategy* (Sch) is a queue reordering function which changes the ordering of task types only, but never changes the ordering of task instances of the same type. A non-preemptive strategy will never change the position of the first element in a queue, whereas a preemptive scheduling strategy may change the position of the first element in the queue (the one which is currently executed). E.g. FPS (fixed priority scheduling) or EDF (earliest deadline first) are preemptive scheduling strategies. For example, $\text{EDF}([P(3.1, 4.9, 10), Q(4, 4.5, 5.3))]) = [Q(4, 4.5, 5.3), P(3.1, 4.9, 10))]$.

---

[1] Note that M is a partial function meaning that some of the locations may have no task.

Run is a function which given a real number t and a task queue q returns the task queue after t time units of execution on a processor. The result of $\mathsf{Run}(q, t)$ for $q = [P_1(b_1, w_1, d_1), P_2(b_2, w_2, d_2), \ldots, P_n(b_n, w_n, d_n)]$ is defined as $q' = [P_1(b_1 - t, w_1 - t, d_1 - t), P_2(b_2, w_2, d_2 - t), \ldots, P_n(b_n, w_n, d_n - t)]$. For example, let $q = [Q(2, 3, 5), P(4, 7, 10)]$. Then $\mathsf{Run}(q, 3) = [Q(-1, 0, 2), P(4, 7, 7)]$ in which the first task has been executed for 3 time units (and it will be removed from the queue).

A task P in the queue may finish when $b(P) = 0$ and $w(P) \geq 0$, and it must finish when $w(P) = 0$. Finished tasks are removed from the queue.

Further, for a non-negative real number t, we use $\sigma + t$ to denote the clock assignment which maps each clock a to the value $\sigma(a) + t$, $\sigma \models g$ to denote that the clock assignment σ satisfies the constraint g and $\sigma[r]$ for $r \subseteq \mathcal{C}$ to denote the clock assignment which maps each clock in r to 0 and agrees with σ for the other clocks (i.e. $\mathcal{C} \backslash r$). We omit braces when r is a singleton.

Definition 2. *Given a scheduling strategy* Sch, *the semantics of an extended timed automaton* $\langle N, l_0, E, I, M, check \rangle$ *with initial state* (l_0, σ_0, q_0) *is a transition system defined by the following rules:*

- $(l, \sigma, q) \longmapsto_{\mathsf{Sch}} (m, \sigma[r], \mathsf{Sch}(M(m) :: q))$ *if* $l \xrightarrow{g,a,r} m$, $\sigma \models g$, *and* $\sigma[r] \models I(m)$
- $(l, \sigma, []) \xrightarrow{t}_{\mathsf{Sch}} (l, \sigma + t, [])$ *if* $(\sigma + t) \models I(l)$
- $(l, \sigma, P :: q) \xrightarrow{t}_{\mathsf{Sch}} (l, \sigma + t, \mathsf{Run}(P :: q, t))$ *if* $t \leq w(P)$ *and* $(\sigma + t) \models I(l)$
- $(l, \sigma, P :: q) \xrightarrow{0}_{\mathsf{Sch}} (l, \sigma[check], q)$ *if* $b(P) \leq 0 \leq w(P)$ *and* $\sigma[check] \models I(l)$

where $P :: q$ *denotes the queue with the process* P *inserted in* q *(at the first position), and* $[]$ *denotes the empty queue.*

2.2 Schedulability and Decidability

In this subsection we define the schedulability problem for ETA and give a summary of the previous decidability results. Undecidability is discussed in the following section. We first mention that we have the same notion of reachability as for ordinary timed automata.

Definition 3. *We shall write* $(l, \sigma, q) \longrightarrow_{\mathsf{Sch}} (l', \sigma', q')$ *if* $(l, \sigma, q) \longmapsto_{\mathsf{Sch}} (l', \sigma', q')$ *or* $(l, \sigma, q) \xrightarrow{t}_{\mathsf{Sch}} (l', \sigma', q')$ *for a delay* t. *For an automaton with initial state* (l_0, σ_0, q_0) *and for a scheduling strategy* Sch, *we say that* (l, σ, q) *is reachable iff* $(l_0, \sigma_0, q_0)(\longrightarrow_{\mathsf{Sch}})^*(l, \sigma, q)$.

Now we can formalise the notion of schedulability.

Definition 4. *(Schedulability) A state* (l, σ, q) *where* $q = [P_1(b_1, w_1, d_1), \ldots, P_n(b_n, w_n, d_n)]$ *is a failure denoted* $(l, \sigma, \mathsf{Error})$ *if there exists* i *such that* $w_i \geq 0$ *and* $d_i < 0$, *that is, a task failed in meeting its deadline. Naturally an automaton* A *with initial state* (l_0, σ_0, q_0) *is non-schedulable with* Sch *iff* $(l, \sigma, \mathsf{Error})$ *is*

reachable for some l and σ. Otherwise, we say that A is schedulable with Sch. [2]
More generally, we say that A is schedulable iff there exists a scheduling strategy
Sch *with which A is schedulable.*

The following decidability results apply to some simpler variants of the schedulability problem for extended timed automata. By this we show, that whenever preemption, clock resets, or interval execution times are not allowed, the problem becomes decidable.

Theorem 1 ([EWY98]). *The problem of checking schedulability for extended timed automata with non-preemptive scheduling strategy is decidable.*

Proof. The proof in [EWY98] handles only tasks with worst case execution time and tasks without clock resets. But it can be easily modified for our model.   □

The schedulability problem is decidable even for preemptive scheduling strategies when tasks are not allowed to communicate with an automaton (to reset clocks). Execution times of tasks can be intervals.

Theorem 2 ([FPY02]). *The problem of checking schedulability for extended timed automata with one-way communication (tasks do not reset clocks) is decidable.*

Proof. It is easy to observe that we can consider only the worst case execution time of each task and the proof is given in [FPY02].   □

The schedulability is decidable even for extended timed automata with two-way communication (tasks may reset clocks by the end of their execution) when the computation time is a known constant for each task.

Theorem 3 ([FMPY03]). *The problem of checking schedulability for extended timed automata is decidable if $B(P) = W(P)$ for all tasks P.*

Proof. The proof is given in [FMPY03].   □

When tasks have interval execution time in the system with two-way communication the computation of the control automaton can be influenced by the exact completion time of a task. The control automaton can take into consideration if a task has already finished or not and can proceed to different locations in different cases. For example, if a task does not finish in a given time the machine stops (it deadlocks, or proceeds to some idle state, i.e. no new tasks are released, just the already released tasks are computed). By this we can cut off (e.g. deadlock) branches where a task had "wrong" computation time. In fact,

---

[2] Note that the state might not be failure denoted when ETA is deadlocked and time cannot progress, even if time flow would lead to a failure denoted state. Therefore, a model where such states are reachable might still be schedulable. This is not fundamental for our proof and these states could be prohibited. But it would induce some technical difficulties making the proof less clear.

we can construct an automaton which proceeds to a certain location if and only if a task has been executed for some given exact (real) time.

Preemption enables us to sum up (accumulate) running times of tasks. Response time of the preempted task is increased by running time of each preempting task. This is sufficient to encode the two-counter machine.

3   Undecidability

Our main result in this paper is that the schedulability problem with fixed priority scheduling strategy for the automata defined in the previous section is undecidable. However, the proof does not depend on fixed priority scheduling strategy and it can be easily modified for almost all preemptive scheduling strategies (e.g. the proof holds for EDF without any modification).

Theorem 4. *The problem of checking whether extended timed automaton (defined in Definition 1) is schedulable with fixed priority scheduling strategy is undecidable.*

The proof is done by reduction of the halting problem for two-counter machine to the schedulability problem for ETA. A *two-counter machine* consists of a finite state control unit and two unbounded non-negative integer counters. Initially, both counters contain the value 0. Such a machine can execute three types of instructions: incrementation of a counter, decrementation of a counter, and branching based upon whether a specific counter contains the value 0. Note that decrementation of a counter with the value 0 leaves this counter unchanged. After execution of an instruction, a machine changes deterministically its state. One state of a two-counter machine is distinguished as *halt state*. A machine halts if and only if it reaches this state.

We present an encoding of a two-counter machine M using extended timed automaton $\mathcal{A}_M$ such that M halts if and only if $\mathcal{A}_M$ is non-schedulable, based on the undecidability proofs of [HKPV98]. In the construction, the states of M correspond to specific locations of $\mathcal{A}_M$ and each counter is encoded by a clock. We shall show how to simulate the two-counter machine operations. First, we adopt the notion of W-wrapping of [HKPV98].

Definition 5. *An extended timed automaton over set of clocks $\mathcal{C}$ is W-wrapping if for all states (l, σ, q) reachable from its initial state and for all clocks $c \in \mathcal{C}$: $\sigma \models c \leq W$. A W-wrapping edge for a clock c and a location l is an edge from l to itself that is labeled with the guard $c = W$ and which resets the clock c. A clock that is reset only by wrapping edges is called* system clock.[3] *Each time period between two consecutive time points at which any system clock contains value 0 is called* W-wrapping period.

---

[3] Note that all system clocks contain the same value.

We use wrapping to simulate discrete steps of two-counter machine. Each step is modeled by several W-wrapping periods. We define the wrapping-value of a clock to be the value of the clock when the system clock is 0. Note that a clock is carrying the same wrapping value if it is not reset by another edge than the wrapping edges. This principle is shown in Figure 1, where a is a system clock and clock t contains the same wrapping-value when the automaton takes transitions e_1 and e_3.

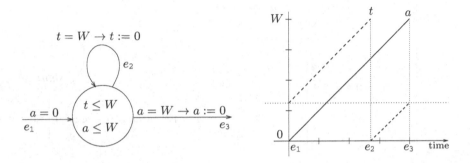

Fig. 1. The wrapping edge e_2 makes clock t carry the same wrapping-value when the transitions e_1 and e_3 are taken.

We shall encode a two-counter machine M with counters C and D using a 4-wrapping automaton $\mathcal{A}_M$ with one system clock denoted a and five other clocks c, d, h, t and $check$. In particular, we encode counters C and D of M by clocks c and d like this: counter value v corresponds to the clock wrapping-value 2^{1-v}. We use the density of the continuous domain to encode arbitrarily large values of the counters. Decrementation (incrementation) of a counter corresponds to doubling (halving) the wrapping-value of the corresponding clock. Test for zero corresponds to the check whether the clock wrapping-value equals to 2.

Now we show how to simulate the decrementation operation by doubling the wrapping-value of the clock d. To do this, we use two tasks: *short* and *long*. The task *short* has execution time within interval $[0, 1]$ and deadline 50; the task *long* has execution time within interval $[8, 8]$ and deadline 100. The tasks reset clock *check* by the end of their execution. Moreover, the priority of *short* is higher than the priority of *long*, i.e. *short* always preempts *long*. Notice that the execution time of task *short* can vary and the execution time of the task *long* is fixed.

The basic idea of doubling a wrapping-value $v \in (0, 1]$ of clock d is as follows: we assume that the current wrapping-value of d is v. We copy it to clock t (that is, to make the wrapping-value of clock t to be v). We release the task *long* non-deterministically and reset d. The idea is to use d to record the response time for *long*. We release two instances of *short* before *long* finishes, that is preempt *long* twice by *short*. We make sure that the execution time of each of these two

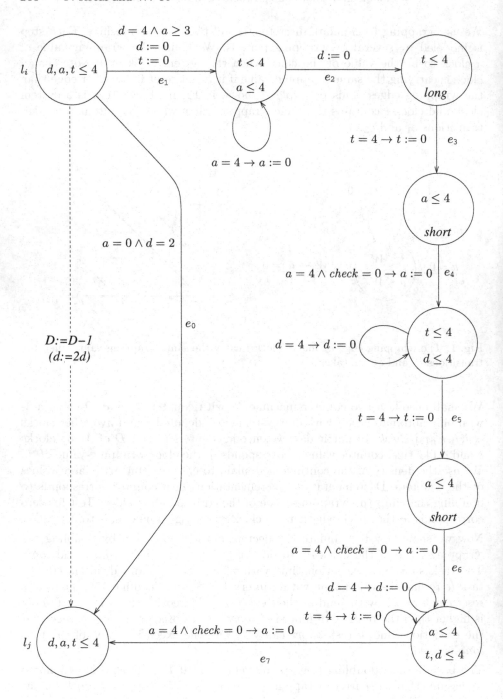

Fig. 2. A part of reduction automaton corresponding to a decrementation of D. The wrapping edges for clocks $c, h, check$, and for all clocks in locations l_i, l_j are omitted. The location invariants $c \leq 4, h \leq 4$, and $check \leq 4$ are also omitted.

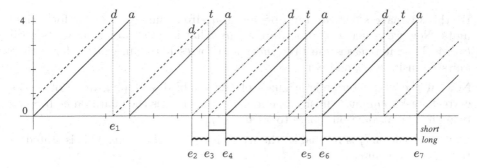

Fig. 3. Time chart of the doubling procedure.

instances of *short* is exactly v time units. Note that v can be any real number within the interval $(0, 1]$. Then the response time for *long* is exactly $8 + 2v$. Note that if *long* finishes at a time point when the system clock a is reset to 0, the wrapping-value of d is $2v$. As *long* is released non-deterministically, there will be surely one such computation.

In Figure 2, we show the part of $\mathcal{A}_M$ that doubles the wrapping-value of clock d. Figure 3 illustrates the time chart of the doubling process. Assume that a two-counter machine M is currently in state s_i and that it wants to decrease the counter D and then move to state s_j. The locations l_i and l_j of $\mathcal{A}_M$ correspond to the states s_i and s_j respectively. Note that the dashed edge shows the transition of the two-counter machine (it is not a transition of $\mathcal{A}_M$). Note also that the decrementation operation leaves a counter with value 0 unchanged; the automaton can move from l_i directly to l_j through the transition e_0 when d contains the wrapping-value 2 (which corresponds to the counter value 0). Otherwise, the following steps are taken to double the wrapping-value of d.

Firstly, the wrapping-value of d is copied to clock t (by transition e_1), that is, t carries the same wrapping-value as d. Then the automaton non-deterministically guesses the doubled wrapping-value of d (note that when d is reset, it will carry a new wrapping-value). It resets d at nondeterministically chosen time instant and at the same time it releases the task *long* (transition e_2).

The automaton waits until clock t reaches time 4, then resets t and releases *short* (transition e_3), which preempts *long*. Note that the wrapping-value of t will remain to be v and at this time point the value of the system clock a is $4 - v$. Therefore a will reach 4 in v time units.

The next transition e_4 is guarded by two constraints: $a = 4$, $check = 0$. To satisfy these constraints, the automaton has to wait in this location for v time units, and task *short* must finish at this time point, which resets the clock $check$.[4]

---

[4] We have to make sure that $check$ is not reset by a wrapping edge when it is tested by a guard of the automaton. This causes no technical difficulties and it is omitted from Figure 2.

By this we make *short* run (and prevent *long* from running) exactly for v time units. Now we repeat this procedure again. That is, the automaton waits until $t = 4$. Then it releases the task *short* and forces it to run exactly for v time units (transitions e_5 and e_6).

Now, if the non-deterministic guess of the doubled wrapping-value of d was correct, task *long* must finish when $a = 4$, which makes the guard on e_7 become true and the automaton moves to location l_j.

So if the location l_j is reachable, the wrapping-value of d is $2v$. This is stated in the following lemma.

Lemma 1. *Let (l_i, σ, q) be an arbitrary state of the automaton shown in Figure 2 where $\sigma(d) = v$ and $v \in (0, 1]$, and q is empty. Then (l_j, σ', q') is reachable for some σ' and q' and if (l_j, σ', q') is reachable, it must be the case that $q' = []$, and $\sigma'(d) = 2v$.*

Proof. The proof is obvious from the construction in Figure 2.

To increment a counter we need to halve a wrapping-value of a clock, say c. For this, we use the clock h to copy the wrapping-value of c. The new wrapping-value v of c is nondeterministically guessed and it is checked by the above doubling procedure. If the wrapping-value of h (the original wrapping-value of c) is $2v$, then the automaton can proceed to the location corresponding to the destination state in an increment instruction.

To simulate branching, we construct two transitions outgoing from a location with guards $a = 0 \wedge c = 2$ and $a = 0 \wedge c \neq 2$. The initial state of M corresponds to a location where both c and d contain the wrapping-value 2. This can be achieved by integer guards and resets.

The halt state corresponds to the location *halt* with unguarded self-loop releasing the task *long* whenever it is visited. It follows that the automaton $\mathcal{A}_M$ is schedulable if and only if the location *halt* is unreachable, i.e. the two-counter machine M does not halt.

4   Variants of the Problem

The proof can be easily modified even for some variants of the original setting. By this we want to show that the only sufficient conditions for undecidability are the following: the execution times of tasks are within intervals, an automaton can test the exact completion time of tasks, and one task can be preempted by another one.

The schedulability problem is undecidable if we use data variables to model two-way communication as described in [FMPY03] instead of a distinguished clock. Tasks can assign values to the variables shared between them and the control automaton. The automaton can use these variables in assignments and guards.

In our construction, tasks assign the value 1 to the data variable A upon completion. The edges e_4 and e_6 in the original construction are substituted by the edges e', e'' and by the location l_{int} from Figure 4. The location where the task *short* is released is left exactly after t time units, but *short* is not finished yet ($A = 0$). However, the time does not flow in the location l_{int}. Just the task *short* can finish here. When this happens the edge e'' becomes enabled and the automaton can proceed. In fact, an automaton $\mathcal{A}_M$ uses interleaving at the time instant when a task finishes to enforce and to measure correct execution time.

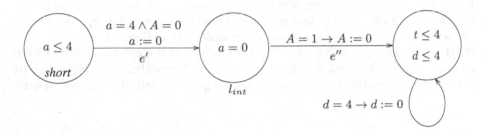

Fig. 4. Substitution of the clock resets by interleaving and data updates.

The schedulability problem is also undecidable if the tasks can only be released at integer time points. In this case, we encode a counter value v as a clock wrapping-value $4 - 2^{1-v}$. Decrementing (incrementing) of a counter does not correspond to doubling (halving) a clock wrapping-value anymore. Both instructions correspond to more complicated operations. Otherwise, the construction becomes even simpler. We do not need auxiliary clock t. Both *long* and *short* are released when $a = 0$. The task *short* should finish when $d = 0$ and we reset the clock d to obtain the doubled wrapping-value when the task *long* finishes. Synchronisation can be forced either by clock resets or by data variable updates. Figure 5 shows the time chart of the doubling procedure.

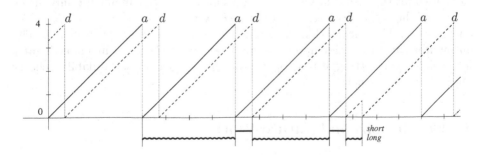

Fig. 5. The time chart of the doubling procedure for integer release points.

Schedulability will also remain undecidable if we prohibit $B(P) = W(P)$, i.e. no task is allowed to have a constant computation time. Then we use the task $long_1$ with the execution interval $[7, 8]$ instead of $long$. The guessed wrapping-value of d can be less or equal to the correctly doubled value, because the task $long$ can finish sooner. However, we repeat the whole doubling procedure with the task $long_2$ which has the execution interval $[8, 9]$. Now the automaton does not guess new wrapping-value of d, but uses the wrapping-value from the previous step. Therefore, this verifying procedure can succeed only if the wrapping-value of d was guessed correctly in the first doubling procedure.

It is sufficient to use just one preemption for doubling a clock value. Therefore, even for systems where each task can be preempted only once during its execution the schedulability problem turns out to be undecidable. Figure 6 shows the time chart of the doubling procedure. The task $short$ has the execution time within interval $[3, 4]$ and the task $long$ has the execution time within $[4, 4]$. New doubled value is nondeterministically guessed and the guess is verified by the procedure.

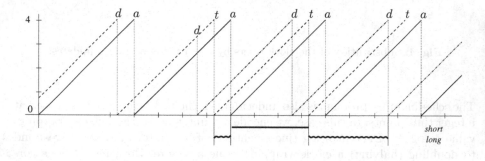

Fig. 6. Time chart of the doubling procedure using just one preemption.

Moreover, we present yet another variant of the extended timed automata for which we suspect the schedulability problem to be decidable.

Consider the extended timed automata with the following modification. The clock used for the task completion announcement ($check$) can appear only in the guards of the form $N \sim check \sim M$ or $N \sim check$ where $\sim \in \{\leq, <\}$, $N, M \in \mathcal{N}$, and $N \neq M$. This means that we prohibit equality checking for this clock. The automaton can only decide upon whether the value of $check$ lies in a non-singular interval. For this setting, it is an open problem whether the schedulability checking is decidable or not.

5   Conclusions and Future Work

We have studied timed systems where preemption can occur at any real time point. For these systems, the schedulability checking problem is decidable if either the computation time of each task is a known constant or the control automaton cannot test the exact completion time of the tasks. We have showed that the scheduling problem becomes undecidable if both of these restrictions are dropped. By comparing this result with known decidability results, we try to identify the borderline between decidable and undecidable problems in schedulability analysis for these systems.

As future work, we will try to identify a class of systems where only partial information about completion time of a task can be obtained by the control unit such that the schedulability problem will become decidable. We have presented a model of such class of systems in Section 4 as a candidate.

References

[Abd02]   Y. Abdeddaïm. *Scheduling with Timed Automata*. PhD thesis, Verimag, 2002.

[ACH⁺ 95]   R. Alur, C. Courcoubetis, N. Halbwachs, T. A. Henzinger, P.-H. Ho, X. Nicollin, A. Olivero, J. Sifakis, and S. Yovine. The algorithmic analysis of hybrid systems. *Theoretical Computer Science*, 138(1):3–34, 1995.

[AD94]   R. Alur and D. L. Dill. A theory of timed automata. *Theoretical Computer Science*, 126(2):183–235, 1994.

[AFM⁺ 02]   T. Amnell, E. Fersman, L. Mokrushin, P. Pettersson, and W. Yi. Times - a tool for modelling and implementation of embedded systems. In *Proc. TACAS'02*, volume 2280 of *LNCS*, pages 460–464. Springer, 2002.

[AM01]   Y. Abdeddaïm and O. Maler. Job-shop scheduling using timed automata. In *Proc. CAV'01*, volume 2102 of *LNCS*, pages 478–492. Springer, 2001.

[AM02]   Y. Abdeddaïm and O. Maler. Preemptive job-shop scheduling using stopwatch automata. In *Proc. TACAS'02*, volume 2280 of *LNCS*, pages 113–126. Springer, 2002.

[CL00]   F. Cassez and F. Laroussinie. Model-checking for hybrid systems by quotienting and constraints solving. In *Proc. CAV'00*, volume 1855 of *LNCS*, pages 373–388. Springer, 2000.

[Cor94]   J. Corbett. Modeling and analysis of real-time ada tasking programs. In *Proc. IEEE RTSS'94*, pages 132–141, 1994.

[EWY98]   C. Ericsson, A. Wall, and W. Yi. Timed automata as task models for event-driven systems. In *Proceedings of Nordic Workshop on Programming Theory*, 1998.

[Feh02]   A. Fehnker. *Citius, Vilius, Melius - Guiding and Cost-Optimality in Model Checking of Timed and Hybrid Systems*. PhD thesis, KU Nijmegen, 2002.

[FMPY03]   E. Fersman, L. Mokrushin, P. Pettersson, and W. Yi. Schedulability analysis using two clocks. In *Proc. TACAS 2003*, volume LNCS 2619, pages 224–239. Springer–Verlag, 2003.

[FPY02]   E. Fersman, P. Pettersson, and W. Yi. Timed automata with asynchronous processes: Schedulability and decidability. In *Proc. TACAS'02*, volume 2280 of *LNCS*, pages 67–82. Springer, 2002.

[HHWT97]   T.A. Henzinger, P.-H. Ho, and H. Wong-Toi. HYTECH: A model checker for hybrid systems. *International Journal on Software Tools for Technology Transfer*, 1(1–2):123–133, 1997.

[HKPV98] T.A. Henzinger, P.W. Kopke, A. Puri, and P. Varaiya. What's decidable about hybrid automata? *Journal of Computer and System Sciences*, 57:94–124, 1998.

[HLP01] T. Hune, K.G. Larsen, and P. Pettersson. Guided Synthesis of Control Programs using UPPAAL. *Nordic Journal of Computing*, 8(1):43–64, 2001.

[LPY97] K.G. Larsen, P. Pettersson, and W. Yi. UPPAAL in a Nutshell. *Int. Journal on Software Tools for Technology Transfer*, 1(1–2):134–152, October 1997.

[MV94] J. McManis and P. Varaiya. Suspension automata: A decidable class of hybrid automata. In *Proc. CAV'94*, volume 818, pages 105–117. Springer, 1994.

[WH03] L. Waszniowski and Z. Hanzálek. Analysis of real time operating system based applications. In *Proc. FORMATS'03*, 2003.

[Yov97] S. Yovine. Kronos: A verification tool for real-time systems. *International Journal on Software Tools for Technology Transfer*, 1(1–2):110–122, 1997.

The Succinct Solver Suite

Flemming Nielson[1], Hanne Riis Nielson[1], Hongyan Sun[1], Mikael Buchholtz[1],
René Rydhof Hansen[1], Henrik Pilegaard[1], and Helmut Seidl[2]

[1] Informatics and Mathematical Modelling
Richard Petersens Plads bldg. 321
Technical University of Denmark
DK-2800 Kongens Lyngby, Denmark
{nielson,riis,sun,mib,rrh,hepi}@imm.dtu.dk
[2] Fakultät für Informatik, I2, TU München
Boltzmannstraße 3, D-85748 Garching, Germany
seidl@in.tum.de

Abstract. The Succinct Solver Suite offers two analysis engines for solving data and control flow problems expressed in clausal form in a large fragment of first order logic. The solvers have proved to be useful for a variety of applications including security properties of Java Card bytecode, access control features of Mobile and Discretionary Ambients, and validation of protocol narrations formalised in a suitable process algebra. Both solvers operate over finite domains although they can cope with regular sets of trees by direct encoding of the tree grammars; they differ in fine details about the demands on the universe and the extent to which universal quantification is allowed. A number of transformation strategies, mainly automatic, have been studied aiming on the one hand to increase the efficiency of the solving process, and on the other hand to increase the ease with which users can develop analyses. The results from benchmarking against state-of-the-art solvers are encouraging.

1 Introduction

Ever since the pioneering work of McAllester [12] there has been a growing interest in using logical formalisms for expressing a variety of control and data flow analyses. This is facilitated by the observation that all polynomial time computable algorithms[1] can be expressed as Horn clauses, and furthermore that the worst case complexity of the specifications can easily be estimated [14]. For problems involving control flow analysis a cubic time bound is inherent although in practice better performance can be obtained in benign cases. In terms of ease of use the logical format separates implementation considerations from specification and hence increases the likelihood that a correct and useful analysis can be developed with only a limited effort. Our work over the last few years has focused on making these insights practical and in testing them on a number of analysis problems that occurred in our other research projects.

---

[1] Later work, with Ganzinger, deals with logarithmic factors as well.

K. Jensen and A. Podelski (Eds.): TACAS 2004, LNCS 2988, pp. 251–265, 2004.

To obtain easily readable formulae we quickly decided to go for the "maximal" subset of first order predicate logic that allows the appropriate theoretical results to be established. We thus arrived at Alternation-free Least Fixed Point Logic, ALFP, to be presented in Section 2, that only disallows those features of first order predicate logic that would make it impossible to ensure that a least solution always exists. This is quite in the tradition of Abstract Interpretation where the least solution is guaranteed by a Moore family result [8,13].

The Succinct Solver Suite encompasses two solver engines (dubbed V1.0 [16] and V2.0 [23]) for computing the least solution as guaranteed by the Moore family result. Additionally there are a number of frontends for clause tuning aiming at increasing performance and ease of use. Other transformations on clauses are by now part of the solvers themselves as well as mechanisms for obtaining feed-back on the internal operation of the solver in order to assist in clause tuning.

A wide variety of applications, to be presented in Section 3, have been used to validate the robustness of the specification language and to suggest the many other features to be provided by the Succinct Solver Suite [16,23] in order to be a useful tool also for the non-expert. The applications range from familiar programming languages like Java Card, over process calculi like Mobile Ambients, to the study of regular sets of solutions in the context of protocol validation.

Throughout we have focused on increasing the performance by developing a number of syntactic rearrangements of the clauses accepted; many are by now an integral part of the solvers, others are offered through separate front-ends. Equally important has been to relax the rather stringent stratification conditions imposed by the solvers so that users could more easily develop their analyses.

Finally, we have validated the performance of the Succinct Solver Suite against state-of-the-art solvers; the most challenging being XSB Prolog with tabled resolution [21]. We find the results, to be presented in Section 5, encouraging — not least the fact that the Succinct Solver Suite in optimum cases outperforms XSB Prolog by exhibiting a lower asymptotic complexity. On a few cases the Succinct Solver Suite has been able to deal with specifications for which XSB Prolog could not produce a solution.

2   Alternation-Free Least Fixed Point Logic

The Alternation-free fragment of Least Fixpoint Logic (ALFP) extends Horn clauses by allowing both existential and universal quantifications in preconditions, negative queries (subject to the notion of stratification), disjunctions of preconditions, and conjunctions of conclusions. The purest approach is to interpret the logic over a universe of unstructured constants but in the interest of flexibility we shall consider ways to allow a finite set of structured ground terms.

2.1   Syntax

Given a fixed countable set $\mathcal{X}$ of variables, a finite set $\mathcal{C}$ of constant symbols, a finite ranked alphabet $\mathcal{R}$ of predicate symbols, and a finite ranked alphabet $\mathcal{F}$

of function symbols - and let us assume that all ranks are at least 1 - we define the set of pre-ALFP clauses, cl, together with preconditions, pre, and terms, t, by the following grammar

$$
\begin{array}{lcl}
t & ::= & c \quad | \quad x \quad | \quad f\,(t_1,\ldots,t_k) \\
pre & ::= & R\,(t_1,\ldots,t_k) \quad | \quad \neg R\,(t_1,\ldots,t_k) \quad | \quad t_1 = t_2 \quad | \quad t_1 \neq t_2 \\
& & | \quad pre_1 \wedge pre_2 \quad | \quad pre_1 \vee pre_2 \quad | \quad \exists x : pre \quad | \quad \forall x : pre \\
cl & ::= & R\,(t_1,\ldots,t_k) \quad | \quad 1 \quad | \quad cl_1 \wedge cl_2 \quad | \quad \forall x : cl \quad | \quad pre \Rightarrow cl
\end{array}
$$

where $c \in \mathcal{C}$, $x \in \mathcal{X}$, $f \in \mathcal{F}$, and $R \in \mathcal{R}$. Occurrences of $R(\ldots)$ and $\neg R(\ldots)$ in preconditions are also called *queries* and *negative queries*, respectively, whereas the other occurrences are called *assertions* of the predicate R. The pre-defined predicate symbols "$=$" and "$\neq$" are infix operators for *equality* and *inequality* respectively, and we write 1 for the always true clause.

In order to ensure desirable theoretical and pragmatic properties in the presence of negation, we introduce a notion of stratification similar to the one which is known from *Datalog* [7,3]. To express this we make use of a mapping $rank : \mathcal{R} \to \mathbb{N}$ that maps predicate symbols to ranks in $\mathbb{N} = \{0, 1, \ldots\}$. We say that a clause cl is stratified (w.r.t. $rank$) if it has the form $cl = cl_0 \wedge \ldots \wedge cl_k$, and the mapping $rank : \mathcal{R} \to \mathbb{N}$ satisfies the following properties for all $i = 0, \ldots, k$ and $j_i \in \mathbb{N}$:

1. $j_0 < \cdots < j_k$;
2. $rank(R) = j_i$ for every predicate R of assertions in cl_i;
3. $rank(R) \leq j_i$ for every predicate R of queries in cl_i; and
4. $rank(R) < j_i$ for every predicate R of negative queries in cl_i.

(It is natural to choose $j_0 = 0, \ldots, j_k = k$ but the added flexibility makes it easier to make a point later on.) Intuitively, stratification ensures that a negative query is not performed until the relation queried has been fully evaluated.

2.2   Semantics

Let $\mathcal{U}$ denote the universe of ground terms, i.e. terms that do not contain variables. Given interpretations ρ and σ for predicate symbols and terms, respectively, we define the satisfaction relations

$$
(\rho, \sigma) \models pre \quad \text{and} \quad (\rho, \sigma) \models cl
$$

for preconditions and clauses in the standard way. In particular, we use $\rho(R)$ to stand for the set of k-tuples $(a_1, \ldots, a_k)$ from $\mathcal{U}^k$ associated with the k-ary predicate R and $\sigma(x)$ to stand for the element of $\mathcal{U}$ denoted by the variable x.

We shall mainly be interested in clauses cl that have no free variables. Hence the choice of the interpretation σ is immaterial, so we can fix an interpretation σ_0 with a finite range. We then call an interpretation ρ of the predicate symbols a solution to the clause cl provided $(\rho, \sigma_0) \models cl$.

Let Δ be the set of interpretations ρ of predicate symbols in $\mathcal{R}$ over $\mathcal{U}$, then $\Delta = (\Delta, \sqsubseteq)$ forms a complete lattice, where the lexicographical ordering $\sqsubseteq$ is defined by $\rho_1 \sqsubseteq \rho_2$ if and only if there is some $j \in \mathbb{N}$ such that the following properties hold:

- $\rho_1(R) = \rho_2(R)$ for all $R \in \mathcal{R}$ with $rank(R) < j$
- $\rho_1(R) \subseteq \rho_2(R)$ for all $R \in \mathcal{R}$ with $rank(R) = j$
- either j is maximal in $rank$ or $\rho_1(R) \subset \rho_2(R)$ for at least one $R \in \mathcal{R}$ with $rank(R) = j$

Proposition 1. *Assume that cl is a stratified pre-ALFP clause without free variables. Then the set $\Delta' = \{\rho \in \Delta \mid (\rho, \sigma_0) \models cl\}$ forms a Moore family, i.e. it is closed under greatest lower bounds.*

In the sequel we shall only be interested in the least solution ρ as guaranteed by the above proposition.

2.3   ALFP in Succinct Solver V1.0 vs. V2.0

The ALFP logic is defined to be the set of pre-ALFP clauses obtained by disallowing function symbols, i.e. by taking $\mathcal{F} = \emptyset$. The least solution ρ for stratified clauses, as well as the universe $\mathcal{U}$, will then be finite and may be computed using the Succinct Solver[2] V1.0 [16].

In the interest of flexibility the Succinct Solver V1.0 admits a slightly larger logic called ALFP-1.0. The rationale is to allow $\mathcal{U}$ to be a finite set of structured ground terms so that one can dispense with the coding tricks that represent k-ary function symbols using $(k + 1)$-ary predicates. Syntactically we re-allow function symbols, i.e. $\mathcal{F}$ may be non-empty, but impose the condition that only variables or ground terms may be arguments to assertions in the clauses considered. (Ground terms may still be used as arguments of queries). The universe $\mathcal{U}$ is then defined as the set of all sub-terms of ground terms occurring as arguments to assertions in the clause cl of interest. This ensures that the least solution ρ, as well as the universe $\mathcal{U}$, of a stratified clause remain finite and, hence, may be computed using the Succinct Solver[3] V1.0 [16].

The Succinct Solver V2.0 alleviates the need to precompute the finite universe $\mathcal{U}$, and to represent it using terms in the clause cl considered, at the expense of disallowing universal quantification in preconditions. To be more specific, let the "explored universe" $\mathcal{U}_\star$ be the least subset of $\mathcal{U}$ such that the range of ρ_0 is included in $\mathcal{U}_\star$ and each k-ary predicate R has $\rho(R) \subseteq \mathcal{U}_\star^k$ where ρ is the least solution. Clearly ρ is finite if and only if $\mathcal{U}_\star$ is. The logic ALFP-2.0 is obtained from pre-ALFP, by

---

[2] The succinct solvers do not syntactically distinguish between variables and constants; instead the constants are taken as the free variables in the clause considered.

[3] Actually it only allows general terms as arguments to queries of the form $x = t$.

- syntactically disallowing universal quantification in preconditions,
- adjusting the semantic interpretation of terms to only operate over $\mathcal{U}_\star$, i.e. a clause like $\forall x : pre \Rightarrow cl[t]$ really means $\forall x : \mathcal{U}_\star(x) \wedge pre \Rightarrow \mathcal{U}_\star(t) \wedge cl[t]$ where $cl[t]$ denotes a clause with a term t occurring as an argument to some assertion.

In the Succinct Solver V2.0 [23] the "explored universe" is expanded dynamically. The solver will terminate and produce the least solution ρ for those stratified clauses cl of ALFP-2.0 for which the least solution ρ (and hence $\mathcal{U}_\star$) as guaranteed by Proposition 1 is indeed finite. (It is possible to adapt termination analyses to safely indicate a set of clauses of ALFP-2.0 for which the least solution is finite but so far these have not been integrated with the Succinct Solver Suite.)

Example 1. The Succinct Solver V2.0 accepts the clause

$$R(a) \wedge \forall x : (R(x) \Rightarrow T(f(x)))$$

and upon termination produces the dynamically expanded universe $\mathcal{U}_\star = \{a, f(a)\}$.

In the Succinct Solver V1.0, this clause has to be encoded as the considerably less intuitive

$$R(a) \wedge \forall x : \forall y : (R(x) \wedge (y = f(a)) \Rightarrow T(y))$$

and the universe $\mathcal{U} = \{a, f(a)\}$ must be precomputed before solving starts.   □

Example 2. In the analysis of Java Card (to be presented in Section 3.1) we use the predicate S to abstract the run-time stack: $S(m, pc, i, a)$ is supposed to indicate that at a program point pc inside the method m, the stack may contain the element a in position i (using 0 for the top of the stack). Hence the clause

$$\forall i : \forall a : S(m, pc, i, a) \Rightarrow S(m, pc', \mathsf{suc}(i), a)$$

copies stack elements as a preparation for pushing a new element on top of the stack. This formula is directly acceptable for the Succinct Solver V2.0 whereas in V1.0 one needs to write it as

$$\forall y : \forall i : \forall a : y = \mathsf{suc}(i) \wedge S(m, pc, i, a) \Rightarrow S(m, pc', y, a)$$

and to precompute the highest stack position needed; this might take the form of adding a clause with a term

$$\mathsf{suc}(\mathsf{suc}(\ldots (\mathsf{suc}(0)) \ldots))$$

corresponding to the maximal height of a stack that can arise during execution.
   □

2.4   Relationship to Datalog and Prolog

Datalog extends propositional Horn logic with constant and variable symbols and is a commonly used core language for deductive database systems. In the CORAL system, e.g., this core language is extended with structured terms, non-floundering stratified negation and various extra features such as arithmetic and a native code interface to C++ [20]. In this respect, the ALFP approach is more "puristic". It does not aim at providing a fully fledged programming environment but instead offers a rich and convenient *logical* formalism where the least model is still efficiently computable. It is for this reason that we support explicit scoping of variables, conjunctions in conclusions etc. Accordingly, the base version ALFP-1.0 does also support universal quantification in preconditions. This feature is only meaningful in the presence of a finite universe – where it turns out to be more expressive than Datalog.

Example 3. Consider the clause [16] and an a priori defined edge relation E:

$$\forall x : (\forall y : \neg E(x, y) \lor A(y)) \Rightarrow A(x)$$

Taking $rank(E) = 1$ and $rank(A) = 2$ this ALFP formula defines a predicate A that holds on the set of all acyclic nodes in a graph given by the edge relation E, i.e., all nodes from which no cycle can be reached. Without syntactically expanding the formula to consider each element of $\mathcal{U}$, this predicate is not definable in Datalog (even if extended with stratified negation [10]).   □

Prolog extends Datalog with function symbols, negation as failure[4], and various programming constructs and is used in many logic programming systems. However, contrary to the Succinct Solver Suite many Prolog systems may loop infinitely even when only a finite subset, corresponding to $\mathcal{U}_*$, of the Herbrand universe is needed. Also, the depth-first SLD-resolution scheme, according to which Prolog programs are often evaluated, is sometimes inefficient when more than a single solution has to be computed because many subgoals are computed more than once. For these reasons Prolog systems are not in general usable as fixed point engines.

The combination of tabling and Prolog as implemented in XSB Prolog [21] solves these problems because tabling ensures that subgoals are evaluated at most once. The appropriate use of tabling both guarantees termination of programs when $\mathcal{U}_*$ is finite and greatly increases efficiency, thus allowing XSB Prolog to operate as a capable fixed point engine. In Section 5 we present the results of comparative benchmarking of XSB Prolog and the Succinct Solver Suite.

3   Applications

We have used the solver engines of the Succinct Solver Suite on a number of substantial applications as reported below. The general procedure can be outlined as follows:

---

[4] For some Prolog systems that evaluate according to two-valued semantics the existence of unique least models is only guaranteed for stratified programs.

program $\longrightarrow$ | Clause Generator | $\longrightarrow$ ALFP clause $\longrightarrow$ | Succinct Solver | $\longrightarrow$ least solution

The first phase of the application is the generation of clauses and this is clearly specific to the application at hand; the second phase is to solve the clauses using the general tool set provided by the Succinct Solver Suite and this may involve some clause tuning to increase performance (see Section 4).

3.1   Safety and Security of Java Card Byte-Code

Java Card is a variant of the Java language specifically designed for use in smart cards and other systems with limited resources.

The SecSafe project, cf. [22], has focused on using *static analysis* for verifying safety and security properties for applets written in Carmel, a dialect of the Java Card Virtual Machine Language, JCVML. The analyses developed in SecSafe cover both general features, e.g. control and data flow analyses, as well as features specific to the Java Card platform, e.g. ownership analysis for the on-card *applet firewall*.

Many of the analyses have been implemented by converting the analysis specification into a clause generator for ALFP [9] using the Succinct Solver Suite to solve the clauses. As an example the clauses generated for the control flow analysis of the "`getfield this` f" instruction are shown below, where "mid(cls, mth)" indicates the class and method of the instruction while pc gives the specific program counter of the instruction (and pc' is the program counter of the immediately following instruction):

$$\forall r: \forall a: L(\mathsf{mid}(cls, mth), pc, \mathsf{var\_0}, r) \wedge H(r, f, a) \Rightarrow$$
$$S(\mathsf{mid}(cls, mth), pc', zero, a) \wedge$$
$$\forall i: \forall a: S(\mathsf{mid}(cls, mth), pc, i, a) \Rightarrow S(\mathsf{mid}(cls, mth), pc', \mathsf{suc}(i), a) \wedge$$
$$\forall x: \forall a: L(\mathsf{mid}(cls, mth), pc, x, a) \Rightarrow L(\mathsf{mid}(cls, mth), pc', x, a)$$

This specification reflects that the instruction fetches the value of the field f, from the heap H, of the current object (a reference to which is found in local variable 0, var_0, of the local heap L) and places it on top of the stack S. Operand stacks and local heaps are computed for every instruction and therefore the current stack and local heap, both at program counter pc, are copied forward to the next instruction (located at program counter pc'). The stack contents is also moved down one position to make room at the top. Other parts of the Carmel program give rise to other clauses.

This rather naïve implementation, where no effort is made to optimise the underlying representation, is sufficient even for realistic applets as witnessed by the demonstration applet, called DeMoney, developed for the SecSafe project by Trusted Logic [11]. Solving the clauses generated for DeMoney takes on the order of 30 seconds. The benchmarks for DeMoney are discussed in more detail in Section 5.

3.2 Mobility and Access Control

Modern distributed systems such as wireless internet and mobile telephony have *mobility* of computational entities as a main characteristic. One popular model of mobility has been put forward in the calculus of *Mobile Ambients* [6]. There, computational entities (both conceptual and physical) are modelled as boundaries called *ambients*. An ambient can be inside another ambient and ambients are, thus, organised in a tree structure where mobility is represented as the capability of an ambient to move *in* and *out* of other ambients.

The ambient tree structure can be represented in ALFP as a binary predicate, I (for *inside*), describing a father-son relationship between ambients. For example, if an ambient named a contains two ambients named b and c, respectively, then it can be stated as the first two facts below:

$$I(a, b) \land I(a, c) \land I(c, in(b))$$

The third fact states that $in(b)$ is placed inside the ambient c and this represents the capability of the ambient c to move *into* the ambient b.

A control flow analysis (a so-called 0CFA) of Mobile Ambients approximates the ambient movement within the tree structure using the binary predicate I. For example, the execution of the capability to move *into* another ambient may be expressed in ALFP as [18]

$$\forall x : \forall y : \forall z : I(x, y) \land I(x, z) \land I(y, in(z)) \Rightarrow I(z, y)$$

and reads: if the ambients y and z are both inside the ambient x and, furthermore, y contains the capability to move into z then y may also be inside z as stated in the conclusion. The least solution to this clause in conjunction with the ground facts above is $\rho(I) = \{(a, b), (a, c), (c, in(b)), (b, c)\}$ describing e.g. that c may end up inside b during an execution of the ambient program.

Interestingly, the result of the analysis can also be used to ensure absence of movements. For example, the above result shows that the ambient a cannot access the ambient b. This relates to the area of *access control* as studied for example in [18] where the calculus of Discretionary Ambients is presented along with two control flow analyses. One analysis is a 0CFA as for Mobile Ambients that approximates a father-son relationship while the other is a 1CFA that approximates a grandfather-father-son relationship represented by a ternary relation. The analyses of Discretionary Ambients have been used to study mandatory access control as well as discretionary access control and have also served as the basis for extensive experiments with the Succinct Solver Suite as reported in Sections 4 and 5.

3.3 Cryptographic Protocols

There is a long and successful tradition of analysing cryptographic protocols that relies on modelling (perfect) cryptography as structured *terms*. For example, a message m encrypted under a key k can be modelled as the term $e(k, m)$, where

e is a binary constructor, and decryption can be modelled as a corresponding destructor. This is e.g. the approach taken in the Spi-calculus [2] and LySa [4] and their control flow analyses.

Consider a process, P, that repeatedly receives a message on the network in a variable x and sends $e(k, x)$ back onto the network. If it is placed in a context such that it initially receives the message m, then x will be bound to all the elements from the *infinite* set $S = \{m, e(k, m), e(k, e(k, m)), e(k, e(k, e(k, m))), \cdots \}$ during the execution of P. Hence the least solution cannot be finite.

In [4] this problem is solved by representing the infinite sets of terms using their generating tree grammars. The rules of the grammar are represented by a binary predicate R. An encoding of the grammar rules of the above set S, for example, gives rise to the facts:

$$R(l_1, e(l_2, l_1)) \quad \wedge \quad R(l_1, m) \quad \wedge \quad R(l_2, k)$$

where the first argument denotes the left-hand side of a grammar rule and the second argument denotes corresponding right-hand side. Set operations, such as membership, subset, etc., of these infinite set of terms can then be encoded in ALFP as manipulations of the grammar rules in R.

Overall, the analyses can be implemented in polynomial-time in the size of the program and in [4] the analysis is shown to be sufficiently precise to identify well-known attacks on a number of symmetric key protocols as well as showing the correctness of their amendments.

4   Program Transformations

The approach taken in the development of the succinct solvers has been to obtain a generic tool aiming at achieving the best asymptotic worst case performance reported for any analysis engine [16]. Therefore the only way to influence the operation of the solver is to perform clause tuning, which amounts to transforming the clause given as input. We have aimed at ensuring that the beneficial rearrangements can be understood at the level of inspecting the clauses themselves; this is contrary to, and in our opinion more user friendly, than the approach taken in some other systems where the user is supposed to make intelligent choices about the internal operation of the solver concerning e.g. iteration strategies.

Typically clause tuning is performed by using the clause to solve only small problems and, based on the sizes of the predicates computed, to rearrange the clause so as to be more efficient also for large problems. One additional feature has proved very helpful: one can instruct the solver to report the number of environments η (values for variables) propagated across selected implications. In Succinct Solver V2.0 [23] this is written as *pre* $\Longrightarrow cl$ and we have found that information about the number of environments gives useful information about where the solver spends its time.

The Order of Conjuncts in Preconditions. In the succinct solvers preconditions in implications are evaluated from left to right and in the context of an environment η that describes successful bindings of variables. When checking a query to a predicate P the evaluation of the remainder of the precondition is performed for all new environments η' that are obtained by unifying η with an element currently in P. The unification will fail when the binding of the variables in η does not coincide with the element of P and in this case, no further work is done. Thus, we may expect to gain efficiency by making the unification fail as early as possible in the evaluation of a precondition.

Example 4. Consider the clause $\forall x : P(x, a) \wedge P(b, x) \Rightarrow Q(x)$ Suppose that we have *a priori* knowledge that P contains few elements with b as the first component but many elements with a as the second component. Then, swapping the two conjuncts will increase efficiency since the clause

$$\forall x : P(b, x) \wedge P(x, a) \Rightarrow Q(x)$$

will have fewer environments propagated from the first query to P.   □

This observation leads to the manual optimisation strategy that queries, which restrict the variable binding most, should be put at the beginning of preconditions. Experiments with our analysis of Discretionary Ambients [5] have shown that reordering of conjuncts in preconditions may significantly improve the efficiency of solving otherwise identical clauses. As expected, the increase in efficiency varies with the structure of programs and typically ranges from a factor of ten up to a decrease in the degree of the complexity polynomial.

Memoisation. We apply *memoisation* techniques to avoid propagation of identical environments in the succinct solvers. The propagation of *completely* identical environments can only occur at disjunction and at existential quantification and hence the solver includes an automatic memoisation scheme for these constructs only.

Example 5. Consider the clause

$$\forall x : \forall y_1 : \forall y_2 : \forall y_3 : P(x, y_1) \wedge Q(y_1, y_2, y_3) \Rightarrow R(y_1, y_2, y_3)$$

where all the environments established when querying P will contain x and are propagated although x is used neither in the query to Q nor in the conclusion. If two of these environments are identical, except for the value of x, then the remainder of the clause will be evaluated twice with the exact same result.

In this case we may expect to gain efficiency by manually transforming clauses using existential quantifications or disjunctions:

$$\forall y_1 : \forall y_2 : \forall y_3 : (\exists x : P(x, y_1)) \wedge Q(y_1, y_2, y_3) \Rightarrow R(y_1, y_2, y_3)$$

Here the universal quantification of x is transformed into an existential quantification in the precondition. Thus the *memoisation* scheme ensures that no identical environments are propagated.   □

Weak Stratification. We now survey recent work [15] aiming at relaxing the rather stringent demands imposed by stratification. Somewhat informally weak stratification relaxes the restrictions imposed by stratification conditions (1) and (2) described in Section 2.1: the condition (1) is not imposed any longer and condition (2) is replaced by the requirement that $rank(R) \geq j_i$ for every predicate R of assertions in cl_i. In practice, this makes it much more convenient to write easily readable specifications.

Example 6. The clause $\forall x : R(x) \Rightarrow (S(x) \land T(x))$, where $rank(R) = 1$, $rank(S) = 2$ and $rank(T) = 3$, is weakly stratified but not stratified.   □

This transformation is available as a preprocessor in the Succinct Solver Suite.

5 Benchmarks

The use of logic based formalisms for the specification of control flow and data flow problems enables a convenient separation of concerns between specification and implementation [17]. This allows the implementation of a given analysis to be based on general purpose fixed point engines such as those of the Succinct Solver Suite.

While the worst-case complexity of, e.g., control flow analyses is inherently cubic and largely independent of the actual fixed point engine, better performance may be obtained in practice for a large family of benign programs. Hence the original solver was designed to give state-of-the-art asymptotic worst-case performance while allowing for even better performance in benign cases [16].

In [19] we compare the performance of the Succinct Solver Suite (solver V2.0) to that of XSB Prolog V2.6 [21]. The reported results are based on benchmarks obtained from control flow analyses both of Discretionary Ambient programs (Section 3.2) and of Carmel programs (Section 3.1).

When running the experiments we timed the initialisation and solve phases of the solvers separately. To do this we executed the Succinct Solver Suite in two stages (initialisation, solve) and used pre-compiled programs for XSB Prolog (compilation, solve). Where possible times were collected with and without garbage collection and the algorithm comparison is based on the times without garbage collection. We used ALFP clause generators but fed identical Normal programs[5], obtained by a syntactical expansion of ALFP clauses into logically equivalent Normal clauses, to the two solvers.

The Discretionary Ambient programs constitute abstract descriptions of a matrix-like grid of routers in which a packet has to travel from one end to the other. This structure is convenient as the complexity of the corresponding analysis problems can be adjusted by changing the connectivity of the underlying graph, i.e. increasing or decreasing the number of sites reachable in one step.

We find that problems can be divided into two types. The first type of problems induce lightly populated analyses, i.e. the order of the ratio between the

---

[5] Normal programs extend Definite (Horn) programs by allowing both positive and negative literals in clause bodies, i.e. allowing both positive and negative queries.

Running time without garbage collection and initialisation as function of program size. Logarithmic Scales.

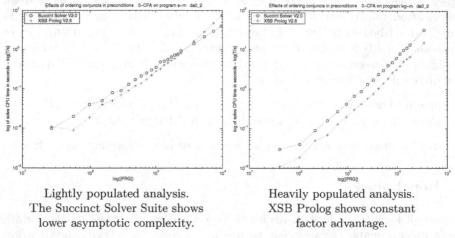

Lightly populated analysis.
The Succinct Solver Suite shows
lower asymptotic complexity.

Heavily populated analysis.
XSB Prolog shows constant
factor advantage.

Fig. 1. Benchmarks of scalable Discretionary Ambient programs.

size of the computed interpretation, $|\rho|$, and the size of the finite universe over which it is computed, $|\mathcal{U}_*|$, is $\mathcal{O}(1)$. For these problems the Succinct Solver Suite outperforms XSB Prolog by having a substantially lower asymptotic complexity on optimum clauses as depicted on the left in Figure 1.

The other type of problems induce heavily populated analyses, i.e. the order of the aforementioned ratio is more like $\mathcal{O}(\sqrt[k]{|\mathcal{U}_*|})$ for some $k \neq 0$. For these problems the Succinct Solver Suite at worst performs a small constant factor worse than XSB Prolog as depicted on the right in Figure 1.

The Carmel programs are derived from the DeMoney case study [11] provided by the industrial partner, Trusted Logic, of the EU project SecSafe. This demonstrative electronic Java Card purse was provided along with a partial Carmel implementation of V2.12 of the Java Card API. In terms of size these two programs are both small to medium programs while their combination (Applet+API) is a fairly large smart card program (about 6700 lines of code).

As seen in Table 1 the Succinct Solver Suite is slightly slower for the smallest program but twice as fast for the largest - in terms of CPU-time used for the fixed point computation. In terms of total time used the solvers perform within 10% of one another - with a marginal advantage to the Succinct Solver Suite. Interestingly, the two systems spend their time differently. XSB Prolog spends much time in the initialisation phase while the Succinct Solver Suite spends much time garbage collecting. Given that memory was never exhausted, this behaviour from the garbage collector is a bit surprising and we attribute it to the garbage collection policy of New Jersey SML, in which the Succinct Solver Suite is implemented.

Table 1. Benchmarks of Carmel based programs (2GHz Pentium 4).

Solver	Input/Mb	Sol. Size	solve CPU/s	Init/s	Total/s
Demoney Applet Stand-Alone					
Succinct Solver V2.0	1.2	4409	2.11	4.59	8.77
XSB Prolog V2.6	1.2	4409	1.78	8.27	10.41
Partial jc212 API (Trusted Logic)					
Succinct Solver V2.0	1.2	7734	2.71	4.81	11.37
XSB Prolog V2.6	1.2	7734	2.75	8.31	11.44
Combination of Applet and API					
Succinct Solver V2.0	2.4	15479	6.36	10.16	28.86
XSB Prolog V2.6	2.4	15479	13.37	16.25	30.24

6 Conclusion

The Succinct Solver Suite offers two analysis engines for solving data and control flow problems expressed in clausal form. Version 1.0 admits general clauses in a slight superset of Alternation-free Least Fixed Point Logic (ALFP) subject to a notion of stratification; intuitively ALFP is the largest fragment of first order logic that admits proving the existence of solutions over finite unstructured universes. Version 2.0 further restricts the clauses by disallowing universal quantification in preconditions; this facilitates extending the solver technology to operate over "finitely explored" structured universes.

Many applications are equally suited for versions 1.0 and 2.0 but each have applications where it is more suited than the other. In the case of version 1.0 the use of universal quantification in preconditions is indispensable when developing static analyses with mixed modalities. In the case of version 2.0 a typical example is the Java world where stack sizes are going to be finite for well-formed programs and hence one should like to avoid the a priori calculation of an upper bound.

The solvers have proved to be useful for a variety of applications. This includes analysing security properties of programs in Java Card byte-code. Variations of Mobile Ambients, in particular Safe and Discretionary Ambients, have proved useful for formulating discretionary and mandatory access control policies in the world of mobility, and the solvers have proved quite effective in solving the relevant analysis questions. Finally, we have applied the solvers to the problem of validating confidentiality and authenticity properties of protocol narrations formalised in a suitable process algebra. Ongoing work explores the use of the Succinct Solver Suite for analysing the hardware programming language VHDL as well as biologically inspired process algebras.

It is evident that the demands placed by the solver on clauses in order to achieve good efficiency, and the wishes of the user in order to develop easily readable clauses in a systematic manner, may be contradictory. To this effect we have studied and implemented a number of transformation strategies that are aimed at increasing the efficiency of the solver or at presenting a more flexible interface to the user.

The Succinct Solver Suite has been benchmarked against other solvers, mainly XSB Prolog with tabled resolution. The performance of the Succinct Solver Suite is at worst a small constant factor worse than XSB Prolog, which is hardly surprising given that the Succinct Solver Suite is written in Standard ML and spends a lot of time on garbage collection, whereas XSB Prolog is a heavily optimised C program. What is more interesting is that in optimum cases the Succinct Solver Suite outperforms XSB Prolog by having a substantially lower asymptotic complexity. On the SecSafe benchmark program, DeMoney, the two solvers exhibit the same running times (within a 10% margin). On a few cases the Succinct Solver Suite has been able to deal with specifications for which XSB Prolog could not produce a solution [1].

In future developments we hope to further assist clause tuning by incorporating the techniques for automatic estimation of the sizes of predicates [14] — something which is only feasible due to the very predictable behaviour of the solver engines. Further, we hope to provide a feature that allows users to enforce a full stop of the solver engine at the point of failure of a so-called observation predicate. The finite counter-example usually implied by such a failure is easier to recover from the partial result present at this point of computation. Finally, we hope to include the possibility of creating fresh and unique names at will during the course of computation. This would facilitate applications where the purpose of the analysis is to construct a finite automaton characterising the solution.

The Succinct Solver Suite is available from our web-pages and may be freely used for research and development.

http://www.imm.dtu.dk/cs_SuccinctSolver

Acknowledgements. This work has been supported by the EU-projects Sec-Safe (IST-1999-29075) and DEGAS (IST-2001-32072) as well as the Danish Natural Science Research Council project LoST (21-02-0507).

References

1. Personal communication with Luis Fernando P. de Castro from the XSB team. http://sourceforge.net/mailarchive/message.php?msg_id=4349555.
2. M. Abadi and A. D. Gordon. A calculus for cryptographic protocols – The Spi calculus. *Information and Computation*, 148(1):1–70, 1999.
3. K. Apt, H. Blair, and A. Walker. A theory of declarative programming. In *Foundations of Deductive Databases and Logic Programming*, pages 89–148. Morgan-Kaufman, 1988.
4. C. Bodei, M. Buchholtz, P. Degano, F. Nielson, and H. Riis Nielson. Automatic validation of protocol narration. In *Proceedings of the 16th Computer Security Foundations Workshop (CSFW 2003)*, pages 126–140. IEEE Computer Society Press, 2003.

5. M. Buchholtz, F. Nielson, and H. Riis Nielson. Experiments with Succinct Solvers. Technical Report IMM-TR-2002-4, Informatics and Mathematical Modelling, Technical University of Denmark, 2002.
6. L. Cardelli and A. D. Gordon. Mobile Ambients. *Theoretical Computer Science*, 240(1):177–213, 2000.
7. A. Chandra and D. Harel. Computable queries for relational data bases. *Journal of Computer and System Sciences*, 21(2):156–178, 1980.
8. P. Cousot and R. Cousot. Abstract interpretation: a unified lattice model for static analysis of programs by construction or approximation of fixpoints. In *POPL'97*, pages 238–252. ACM Press, New York, NY, 1977.
9. R. Rydhof Hansen. A prototype tool for JavaCard firewall analysis. In *Nordic Workshop on Secure IT-Systems, NordSec'02*, Karlstad, Sweden, November 2002. Proceedings published as Karlstad University Studies 2002:31.
10. P. G. Kolaitis. Implicit definability on finite structures and unambiguous computations (preliminary report). In *5th Annual IEEE Symposium on Logic in Computer Science (LICS)*, pages 168–180, 1990.
11. R. Marlet. DeMoney: Java Card implementation. SECSAFE-TL-008, Trusted Logic, November 2002.
12. D. McAllester. On the complexity analysis of static analyses. In *Static Analysis Symposium*, volume 1694 of *Lecture Notes in Computer Science*, pages 312–329, 1999.
13. F. Nielson, H. Riis Nielson, and C. Hankin. *Principles of Program Analysis*. Springer-Verlag, 1999.
14. F. Nielson, H. Riis Nielson, and H. Seidl. Automatic Complexity Analysis. In *European Symposium on Programming (ESOP)*, volume 2305 of *Lecture Notes in Computer Science*, pages 243–261. Springer Verlag, 2002.
15. F. Nielson, H. Riis Nielson, and H. Sun. Observation predicates in Flow Logic. Secsafe-imm-010, Informatics and Mathematical Modelling, Technical University of Denmark, September 2003.
16. F. Nielson, H. Seidl, and H. Riis Nielson. A Succinct Solver for ALFP. *Nordic Journal of Computing*, 9:335–372, 2002.
17. H. Riis Nielson and F. Nielson. Flow Logic: a multi-paradigmatic approach to static analysis. In *The Essence of Computation: Complexity, Analysis, Transformation*, volume 2566 of *Lecture Notes in Computer Science*, pages 223–244. Springer Verlag, 2002.
18. H. Riis Nielson, F. Nielson, and M. Buchholtz. Security for mobility. In *Proceedings of FOSAD 2001*, volume 2946 of *Lecture Notes in Computer Science*. Springer Verlag, 2004.
19. H. Pilegaard. A feasibility study - the Succinct Solver v.2.0, XSB Prolog v.2.6, and flow-logic based program analysis for Carmel. SECSAFE-IMM-008, Informatics and Mathematical Modelling, Technical University of Denmark, October 2003.
20. R. Ramakrishnan, D. Srivastava, S. Sudarshan, and P. Seshadri. The CORAL Deductive System. *VLDB Journal*, 3(2):161–210, 1994.
21. K. Sagonas, T. Swift, D. S. Warren, J. Freire, P. Rao, B. Cui, and E. Johnson. The XSB System. Web page: http://xsb.sourceforge.net/, 2003.
22. I. Siveroni. SecSafe. Web page: http://www.doc.ic.ac.uk/~siveroni/secsafe/, 2003.
23. H. Sun, H. Riis Nielson, and F. Nielson. Extended features in the Succinct Solver (V2.0). SECSAFE-IMM-009, Informatics and Mathematical Modelling, Technical University of Denmark, October 2003.

Binding-Time Analysis for MetaML via Type Inference and Constraint Solving

Nathan Linger and Tim Sheard

Oregon Graduate Institute at Oregon Health & Science University

Abstract. The two predominant program specialization techniques, partial evaluation and staged programming, take opposite approaches to automating binding-time analysis (BTA). Despite their common goal, there are no systems integrating both methods. Programmers must choose between the precision of manually placing staging annotations and the convenience of automating such annotation.

We present an automatic BTA algorithm for a subset of MetaML. Such an algorithm provides a basis for a system integrating staged programming and partial evaluation because it allows programmers to switch between automatic and manual staging. Our algorithm is based on typing algorithm coupled with arithmetic-constraint solving. The algorithm decorates each subexpression of both a program and its type with numeric variables representing staging-annotations and then generates simple arithmetic constraints that describe the space of all possible stagings of the original program. Benefits of our approach include expressive BTA specifications in the form of stage-annotated types as well as support for polyvariance.

1   Background

Program specialization requires a *binding-time analysis* (BTA) to divide a program into static parts that may be computed statically and dynamic parts that must be residualized. BTA can be thought of as placing *staging annotations* on a program to partition it into static and dynamic parts. The two predominant techniques for program specialization, namely *partial evaluation* and *staged programming*, differ in where they place the responsibility for BTA. Partial evaluation performs BTA automatically, while staged programming forces the programmer to place staging annotations manually. Both approaches have merit. The automatic approach is easier on the programmer, but the manual approach can be more precise. In this paper we:

1. Bridge the gap between the two kinds of systems. We show how both automatic and manual BTA can co-exist in a single system that reaps the benefits of both approaches.
2. Reemphasize the point made by Henglein[1], that BTA can be thought of as a typing problem, rather than thinking of it exclusively as a static analysis or abstract interpretation problem. This leads us to discover two new connections between BTA and types.

K. Jensen and A. Podelski (Eds.): TACAS 2004, LNCS 2988, pp. 266–279, 2004.

First, that the input to binding time analysis is really a *staged type*. Using staged types as BTA specifications is more precise, and more flexible than previous specifications, and integrates seamlessly with manual BTA.

Second, we hypothesize a new relationship between polyvariance and polymorphism: that the former is simply an instance of the latter in a richer type system.

3. Identify arithmetic constraints that describe all possible ways to correctly order the stages of a program. Rather than searching for a correct staging of a program, we can infer a set of constraints that describes the entire family of solutions. This reduces a search problem to a type inference problem that is simpler and more efficient.

1.1   Staged Programming as Manual BTA

Binding time analysis can be thought of as the placement of *staging annotations* to partition a program into static and dynamic parts. The most fundamental staging annotations are bracket ($\langle e \rangle$) and escape ($\tilde{\ }e$). These are complementary annotations that signal transitions between the static and dynamic stages. The bracket annotation delays a computation into the dynamic stage, thus producing a code fragment (similar to the backquote in LISP's quasiquote notation). Conversely, the escape annotation returns back to the static stage to calculate a code fragment, which is then spliced into a larger code fragment (similar to comma in LISP's quasiquote notation). The cognizant difference between LISP's quasiquote and staging annotations is that staging annotations respect static scoping. We assume the reader is somewhat familiar with staged languages. If not, several good sources exist [2,3,4].

A staging of an unstaged term (one without any code brackets or escapes) can be obtained by strategically placing these annotations within the term. Finding the correct locations to place these annotations can be thought of as a search problem or an inference problem.

At the type level, the bracket annotation $\langle t \rangle$ is overloaded as a type constructor for code fragments. For example, $\langle int \rangle$ (read "code of int") is the type of code fragments of type *int*. The type signature $f :: \textbf{int} \rightarrow \langle \textbf{int} \rangle \rightarrow \langle \textbf{int} \rangle$ says that f has two parameters, the first is a static integer, the second is a dynamic integer (a code fragment of type **int**), and f returns a dynamic integer as a result. This syntax comes from the staged programming language MetaML [2].

An unstaged type (one without any code brackets) can be *staged* in many ways by adding pairs of brackets around sub-terms in the type. For example the type $\textbf{int} \rightarrow \textbf{bool}$ can be staged in all of the following ways (as well as infinitely many others).

$$\textbf{int} \rightarrow \langle \textbf{bool} \rangle \qquad \langle \textbf{int} \rightarrow \textbf{bool} \rangle \qquad \langle \langle \textbf{int} \rangle \rangle \rightarrow \textbf{bool} \qquad \langle \textbf{int} \rightarrow \langle \textbf{bool} \rangle \rangle$$

The staging of a term and its type are closely related. Placing staging annotations on a term in a legal manner corresponds to staging its type as well.

1. $\langle int \to int \to int \rangle$
   a. $\langle \mu\, pow\, .\, \lambda n\, .\, \lambda x\, .$ **if** $n = 0$ **then** 1 **else** $x * pow\ (n - 1)\ x \rangle$
2. $int \to \langle int \to int \rangle$
   a. $\mu\, pow\, .\, \lambda n\, .\, \langle \lambda x\, .$ **if** $n = 0$ **then** 1 **else** $x *\ {}^{\sim}(pow\ (n - 1))\ x \rangle$
   b. $\mu\, pow\, .\, \lambda n\, .\, \langle \lambda x\, .\ {}^{\sim}($**if** $n = 0$ **then** $\langle 1 \rangle$ **else** $\langle x *\ {}^{\sim}(pow\ (n - 1))\ x \rangle) \rangle$
3. $int \to int \to \langle int \rangle$
   a. $\mu\, pow\, .\, \lambda n\, .\, \lambda x\, .\, \langle$**if** $n = 0$ **then** 1 **else** $x *\ {}^{\sim}(pow\ (n - 1)\ x) \rangle$
   b. $\mu\, pow\, .\, \lambda n\, .\, \lambda x\, .$ **if** $n = 0$ **then** $\langle 1 \rangle$ **else** $\langle x *\ {}^{\sim}(pow\ (n - 1)\ x) \rangle$
4. $int \to \langle int \rangle \to \langle int \rangle$
   a. $\mu\, pow\, .\, \lambda n\, .\, \lambda x\, .\, \langle$**if** $n = 0$ **then** 1 **else** ${}^{\sim}x *\ {}^{\sim}(pow\ (n - 1)\ x) \rangle$
   b. $\mu\, pow\, .\, \lambda n\, .\, \lambda x\, .$ **if** $n = 0$ **then** $\langle 1 \rangle$ **else** $\langle {}^{\sim}x *\ {}^{\sim}(pow\ (n - 1)\ x) \rangle$
5. $\langle int \rangle \to \langle int \to int \rangle$
   a. $\mu\, pow\, .\, \lambda n\, .\, \langle \lambda x\, .$ **if** ${}^{\sim}n = 0$ **then** 1 **else** $x *\ {}^{\sim}(pow\ \langle {}^{\sim}n - 1 \rangle)\ x \rangle$
6. $\langle int \rangle \to int \to \langle int \rangle$
   a. $\mu\, pow\, .\, \lambda n\, .\, \lambda x\, .\, \langle$**if** ${}^{\sim}n = 0$ **then** 1 **else** $x *\ {}^{\sim}(pow\ \langle {}^{\sim}n - 1 \rangle\ x) \rangle$
7. $\langle int \rangle \to \langle int \rangle \to \langle int \rangle$
   a. $\mu\, pow\, .\, \lambda n\, .\, \lambda x\, .\, \langle$**if** ${}^{\sim}n = 0$ **then** 1 **else** ${}^{\sim}x *\ {}^{\sim}(pow\ \langle {}^{\sim}n - 1 \rangle\ x) \rangle$

Fig. 1. Every possible two-stage version of the power function. (The expression form $\mu\,x\,.\,e$ is a notation for fixed points which is equivalent to **fix** $(\lambda x\,.\,e)$.) Programs types with staging annotations can be considered a *specification* of the program's staging behavior.

To illustrate this idea concretely, consider the specialization of the power function obtained by annotating its unstaged definition. We obtain such a definition by strategically placing $\langle - \rangle$ around subterms in the function's type, and $\langle - \rangle$ and ${}^{\sim}-$ around subterms in the function's body.

$$pow_1 :: \textbf{int} \to \langle \textbf{int} \rangle \to \langle \textbf{int} \rangle$$
$$pow_1\ n\ x = \textbf{if}\ n = 0\ \textbf{then}\ \langle 1 \rangle\ \textbf{else}\ \langle {}^{\sim}x *\ {}^{\sim}(pow\ (n - 1)\ x) \rangle$$

Note that this staged version of *pow* has a staged type: $\textbf{int} \to \langle \textbf{int} \rangle \to \langle \textbf{int} \rangle$ which is a staging of its original type $\textbf{int} \to \textbf{int} \to \textbf{int}$. We can use the staged power function to residualize a dynamic code fragment: $pow_1\ 3\ \langle i \rangle \hookrightarrow \langle i * i * i * 1 \rangle$.

Placing the staging annotations on the *pow* function in a different manner may lead to different staged types. Perhaps surprisingly, the staged type is an excellent specification for how to stage the term. This is illustrated in Figure 1 where we list all possible two-level stagings of the power function. Of all the staged types given in Figure 1, only a few lead to multiple valid terms. Those that do, differ only in whether the test of the conditional is static or dynamic. Of these two choices one is always "better" (more static) than the other. This leads us to consider staged types as a specification of what we want BTA to accomplish. We further discuss the expressiveness of such specifications in Section 1.4.

1.2   Automatic vs. Manual BTA

Since fully automatic methods for BTA exist, why do we bother with manual methods? Because automation often comes at the price of precision.

1. Automatic BTA can be too aggressive: Systems based upon automatic BTA may build infinite programs by indefinitely inlining recursive functions. In Figure 1, programs 2a, 3a, 4a, 5, 6, and 7 exhibit this problem. In each case, the problem is that the conditional expression's test is dynamic but the enclosed recursive call is static: so every call to *pow* results in another recursive call to *pow*.

   We see that partial evaluation of a terminating program may not terminate. This is not particularly surprising since the purpose of specialization is to change a program's evaluation order. Ensuring termination of specialization is a serious problem, and is undecidable in general.

2. Automatic BTA can be too conservative: It may fail to recognize parts of the program as static and thereby unnecessarily delay computation. In Figure 1, programs 2b, 3b, and 4b exhibit this behavior: the test in the conditional expression is made unnecessarily dynamic (a fact witnessed by the alternate stagings 2a, 3a, and 4a). In a manually staged system the programmer is responsible for avoiding these situations.

   In an automatically staged system, the expert who understands the inner workings of an automatic BTA algorithm can refactor the original program so that the BTA algorithm identifies more static computations. Such refactorings are called *binding-time improvements*. The need for binding-time improvements shows that even automatic BTA is not always so automatic.

A system combining automatic and manual BTA could reap the benefits of both worlds.

1.3 Combining Automatic and Manual BTA

One way to integrate manual and automatic BTA is to add a **stage** keyword to a staged programming language such as MetaML. The programmer could then make the following declaration:

$$\textbf{stage } pow_2 = pow \textbf{ at int} \rightarrow \langle \textbf{int} \rangle \rightarrow \langle \textbf{int} \rangle;$$

Such a declaration would instruct the compiler to calculate a staged version of *pow* (either program 4a or 4b in Figure 1) and assign that function to pow_2. For simple programs like *pow*, automatic BTA can construct the correct version. For more complex examples, the programmer can take control by manually placing the staging annotations.

Behind this declaration lies an automatic BTA algorithm that adds staging annotations to the definition of *pow* as specified by the staged type **int** $\rightarrow$ $\langle \textbf{int} \rangle \rightarrow \langle \textbf{int} \rangle$ to obtain a new function pow_2.

1.4 Staged Types as Expressive BTA Specifications

As BTA specifications, staged types are much more expressive than the standard distinction between static and dynamic. In many systems a BTA specification is nothing more than a partition of a function's arguments into static and dynamic.

There are two refinements to this basic form of BTA specifications. One refinement is partially static data. Here, some part a function's argument is statically known, but other parts are not. For example, an argument of type **list** ⟨**bool**⟩ is a list whose structure is known statically, but whose elements are dynamic. The second refinement is to allow staging a function into more than two stages. Thus a simple static vs. dynamic dichotomy is no longer sufficient. Here, a BTA specification may specify a function's argument as: ⟨⟨**int**⟩⟩, the type of an integer that will not be calculated until stage 3.

Staged types can describe both these refinements. They can also specify staging behaviors that go beyond these simple refinements. For example, consider a function of type (**int** → **list** ⟨**bool**⟩) → ⟨**int**⟩. Its argument is neither static nor dynamic, but something much more refined. Only staged types can describe this kind of higher-order partially-static data.

2   Previous Work

In earlier work [5], we developed a search based approach to BTA for a staged language. The key idea is to walk over the body of a function, considering the addition of staging annotations ⟨−⟩ and ˜− to every subterm. One can use type information to prune the search space of all annotations that lead to ill-typed programs. The search can be specified in a non-deterministic way by a set of inference rules for the judgment $\Gamma \vdash_n (e : t) \sqsubseteq (e' : t')$ whose key inference rules appear in Figure 2.

These rules are doing two typing derivations in parallel: one with annotations and one without. Doing the derivations in parallel allows the rules to ensure that all the annotated expressions and types have the same underlying structure as the corresponding unannotated ones.

The algorithm has Γ, e, t, and t' as inputs and searches for an e' such that $\Gamma \vdash_0 (e : t) \sqsubseteq (e' : t')$. However, the rules are not syntax directed on the inputs, and this leads to an implementation based upon back-tracking search. Such an algorithm works [5], but can be inefficient in many cases.

The fundamental problem is that information is flowing in the wrong direction. We want information to flow from the type to the program: deriving program annotations from type annotations. Type inference (which, for functional languages, is a sub-problem of type checking) moves information in the opposite direction, types are derived from programs. Annotation information flowing in the wrong direction means we sometimes have to guess when to add program annotations. Is there any way around this problem?

3   Annotation Variables

One way to resolve this problem of the direction of information flow is introduce *annotation variables* and generalize the type system to generate constraints on those variables. Solutions to generated constraints determine valid (concrete) staging annotations for a program. Then all the choices that forced guessing

$$[\text{INT}] \ \frac{}{\Gamma \vdash_n (i : \textbf{int}) \sqsubseteq (i : \textbf{int})} \qquad [\text{VAR}] \ \frac{\Gamma(x) = (t_2, m) \quad n \geq m}{\Gamma \vdash_n (x : t_1) \sqsubseteq (x : t_2)}$$

$$[\text{LAM}] \ \frac{\Gamma, x : (t_2, n) \vdash_n (e_1 : s_1) \sqsubseteq (e_2 : s_2) \quad t_1 \sqsubseteq t_2}{\Gamma \vdash_n ((\lambda x : t_1 . e_1) : t_1 \rightarrow s_1) \sqsubseteq ((\lambda x : t_2 . e_2) : t_2 \rightarrow s_2)}$$

$$[\text{APP}] \ \frac{\begin{array}{c} s_1 \sqsubseteq s_2 \\ \Gamma \vdash_n (e_1 : s_1 \rightarrow t_1) \sqsubseteq (e_2 : s_2 \rightarrow t_2) \\ \Gamma \vdash_n (e_1' : s_1) \sqsubseteq (e_2' : s_2) \end{array}}{\Gamma \vdash_n (e_1 \ e_1' : t_1) \sqsubseteq (e_2 \ e_2' : t_2)}$$

$$[\text{CODE}] \ \frac{\Gamma \vdash_{n+1} (e_1 : t_1) \sqsubseteq (e_2 : t_2)}{\Gamma \vdash_n (e_1 : t_1) \sqsubseteq (\langle e_2 \rangle : \langle t_2 \rangle)} \qquad [\text{ESCAPE}] \ \frac{\Gamma \vdash_n (e_1 : t_1) \sqsubseteq (e_2 : \langle t_2 \rangle)}{\Gamma \vdash_{n+1} (e_1 : t_1) \sqsubseteq (\tilde{\ } e_2 : t_2)}$$

$$[\text{LIFT}] \ \frac{\Gamma \vdash_n (e_1 : c) \sqsubseteq (e_2 : c) \quad c \in \{\textbf{int}, \textbf{bool}\}}{\Gamma \vdash_n (e_1 : c) \sqsubseteq (\textbf{lift} \ e_2 : \langle c \rangle)}$$

Fig. 2. Inference rules for type-directed BTA based on search. The meaning of the judgment $\Gamma \vdash_n (e : t) \sqsubseteq (e' : t')$ is that e' has type t' in Γ at level n, e has type t in $erase(\Gamma)$, $e = erase(e')$, and $t = erase(t')$ (where $erase$ is the operation of erasing all staging annotations).

in the search-based approach can be expressed as constraints and delayed until constraint-solving time.

What sorts of values should an annotation variable have? Any given subterm e can be annotated with an escape $\tilde{\ } e$ or brackets $\langle e \rangle$, or any combination of the two $\tilde{\ } \langle \tilde{\ } e \rangle$. However, since the two annotations cancel each other, we can normalize annotation sequences of this sort to be either all escapes or all brackets (or empty). We may encode all such annotations as integers: positive integers say how many brackets to insert; negative integers say how many escapes to insert; and zero says insert nothing. Since MetaML is a *multistage* language (it can support more than 2 program stages), annotation variables can take on values other than 1, 0, and -1. The following table shows the concrete annotations corresponding to different values of an annotation variable j that is annotating an expression e.

$$j \ \text{value} : 0 \quad 1 \quad -1 \quad 2 \quad -2 \cdots$$
$$c^j \ \text{value} : e \quad \langle e \rangle \quad \tilde{\ } e \quad \langle\langle e \rangle\rangle \quad \tilde{\ }\tilde{\ } e \cdots$$

Given a specific type with concrete annotations as a specification, matching it against the inferred type with variable annotations gives values for the annotation variables. If these values satisfy the constraints, we use them to instantiate the variable-annotated program with concrete annotations. We give a concrete example of this in Section 5.

4   Generalized Typing Rules

Figure 3 shows the subset of MetaML we will be working with and gives generalized typing rules. The superscript j represents a relative difference between levels: If e^j is at level n, then e is at level $n - j$. The main contribution of these typing rules is the [ANN] rule that generalizes both the [CODE] and [ESCAPE] rules from MetaML.

$$[\text{ANN}] \ \frac{C; \Gamma \vdash_{n+j} e : t^{j'-j}}{C \cup \{n + j \geq 0, j' \geq j\}; \Gamma \vdash_n e^j : t^{j'}}$$

$$[\text{CODE}] \ \frac{\Gamma \vdash_{n+1} e : t}{\Gamma \vdash_n \langle e \rangle : \langle t \rangle} \qquad [\text{ESCAPE}] \ \frac{\Gamma \vdash_n e : \langle t \rangle}{\Gamma \vdash_{n+1} \tilde{\ }e : t}$$

When $j = j' = 1$, the [ANN] rule instantiates to the [CODE] rule. When $j = -1$ and $j' = 0$, it instantiates to the [ESCAPE] rule. When $j = 0$, the [ANN] rule becomes vacuous.

In contrast to the previous set of inference rules, these typing rules are syntax directed. This fact is due to variable annotations. While we may not know the concrete annotations in an expression, we at least have handles for referring to them.

There are two binding constructs in the language, λ and μ. The former binds function parameters, and the latter binds fixed point values. The expression $\mu\, x\, .\, e$ is equivalent to the more familiar notations **fix** $(\lambda x\, .\, e)$ or **let** $x = e$ **in** x. Its purpose is for defining recursive functions.

The typing rules treat λ-bound and μ-bound variables differently. This is because of the MetaML feature called *cross stage persistence* that allows values bound in one stage to be used in later stages. Since this feature is not used in practice for recursive function variables, we tag this special case with a "μ" in the environment. All other variables are tagged with a "λ". The difference shows up in the rules: μ-bound variables are used only in the same stage at which they were bound, but λ-bound variables may also be used at later stages.

Each constraint in these typing rules serves a purpose. The constraint $(n \geq m)$ in the [λVAR] rule ensures that each variable is not used at an earlier stage than the one in which it is bound. The fact that this constraint is an inequality rather than an equality allows for cross stage persistence. The constraints $valid(s)$ in the [APP] rule and $(j' \geq j)$ in the [ANN] rule ensure that there are no escapes in types. The constraint $(n + j \geq 0)$ in the [ANN] rule ensures that there are no negative levels in expressions (i.e. no escapes at level zero).

An invariant guides the choice of where constraints go in the above rules. For the judgment $C; \Gamma \vdash_n e : t$, the invariant property is that the following annotations are all non-negative: the level n, all annotations in t, and all annotations in all types in Γ. It is easily checked that for every rule, if the property holds for the concluded judgment (below the line), it is also true for all the antecedent

$$s, t ::= \textbf{int} \mid \textbf{bool} \mid s \rightarrow t \mid \textbf{list } t \mid t^j$$
$$e ::= i \mid x \mid e\, e \mid \lambda x \,.\, e \mid \mu x \,.\, e \mid \textbf{if } e \textbf{ then } e \textbf{ else } e \mid e^j$$
$$\Gamma ::= \cdot \mid \Gamma, x : (t, n, \lambda) \mid \Gamma, x : (t, n, \mu)$$
$$C ::= \varnothing \mid \{n \geq m\} \mid C \cup C$$
$$n, m, j ::= 0 \mid v \mid n + m \mid n - m$$

$$[\text{INT}] \; \frac{}{\varnothing; \Gamma \vdash_n i : \textbf{int}} \qquad [\text{IF}] \; \frac{C_1; \Gamma \vdash_n e : \textbf{bool} \quad C_2; \Gamma \vdash_n e' : t \quad C_3; \Gamma \vdash_n e'' : t}{C_1 \cup C_2 \cup C_3; \Gamma \vdash_n \textbf{if } e \textbf{ then } e' \textbf{ else } e'' : t}$$

$$[\lambda\text{VAR}] \; \frac{\Gamma(x) = (t, m, \lambda)}{\{n \geq m\}; \Gamma \vdash_n x : t} \qquad [\mu\text{VAR}] \; \frac{\Gamma(x) = (t, n, \mu)}{\varnothing; \Gamma \vdash_n x : t}$$

$$[\text{LAM}] \; \frac{C; \Gamma, x : (s, n, \lambda) \vdash_n e : t}{C; \Gamma \vdash_n \lambda x \,.\, e : s \rightarrow t} \qquad [\text{FIX}] \; \frac{C; \Gamma, x : (s \rightarrow t, n, \mu) \vdash_n e : s \rightarrow t}{C; \Gamma \vdash_n \mu x \,.\, e : s \rightarrow t}$$

$$[\text{APP}] \; \frac{C_1; \Gamma \vdash_n e' : s \quad C_2; \Gamma \vdash_n e : s \rightarrow t}{C_1 \cup C_2 \cup valid(s); \Gamma \vdash_n e\, e' : t}$$

$$[\text{ANN}] \; \frac{C; \Gamma \vdash_{n+j} e : t^{j'-j}}{C \cup \{n + j \geq 0, j' \geq j\}; \Gamma \vdash_n e^j : t^{j'}}$$

$$valid(\textbf{int}) = valid(\textbf{bool}) = \varnothing \qquad valid(\textbf{list } t) = valid(t)$$

$$valid(s \rightarrow t) = valid(s) \cup valid(t) \qquad valid(t^j) = valid(t) \cup \{j \geq 0\}$$

Fig. 3.   Generalized syntax and typing rules with Constraints. The judgment $C; \Gamma \vdash_n e : t$ means "under constraints C, in typing environment Γ, at level n, expression e has type t". By convention, n and m denotes absolute levels and j denotes differences in levels.

judgments (above the line). So if a derivation tree with conclusion $C; \Gamma \vdash_n e : t$ exists, we now know $C \cup valid(t)$ guarantees that every subexpression in e has a non-negative stage and a valid type.

5 The Algorithm in Action

Here we run through the BTA algorithm for the power function. First, we do regular type inference on the unannotated program to obtain its type, which we then annotate with fresh annotation variables.

$$(\textbf{int}^a \rightarrow (\textbf{int}^b \rightarrow \textbf{int}^c)^d)^e$$

Then we annotate each sub-expression in the the original program with fresh annotation variables.

$$(\mu pow \, . \, (\lambda pow \, . \, (\lambda n \, . \, (\lambda x \, .$$
$$(\textbf{if} \, ((=^f n^g)^h 0^i)^j$$
$$\quad \textbf{then} \, 1^k$$
$$\quad \textbf{else} \, ((*^l x^m)((pow^o((-^p n^q)^r 1^s)^t)^u x^v)^w)^x$$
$$)^y)^z)^{a'})^{b'}$$

We call annotation variables placed on the body of a function *slack* variables. Then we check that the body of the function has type $(\textbf{int}^a \to (\textbf{int}^b \to \textbf{int}^c)^d)^e$. This generates constraints between the slack variables (from the body) and the variables placed on the type. The algorithm generates 31 equations and 57 in-equations. We solve the equations for as many slack variables as possible (thus eliminating them) and then simplify the remaining inequations. The following inequations are left over

$$a, b, c, d, e \geq 0 \qquad c \geq b \qquad -a + c + d \geq k \geq 0$$

along with the following annotated program

$$(\mu pow \, . \, \lambda n \, . \, (\lambda x \, .$$
$$(\textbf{if} \, n^{-a} = 0$$
$$\quad \textbf{then} \, 1^k$$
$$\quad \textbf{else} \, (x^{-b} * ((pow \, (n^{-a} - 1)^a)^{-d} \, x)^{-c})^k$$
$$)^{c-k})^d)^e$$

At this point, we are done with the first phase of our algorithm. The result is *the complete space of valid stagings of the original program and its type*. For a single function, the results of this phase are reusable across BTA calls. This approach makes polyvariance very cheap to implement.

In phase two we pick out a single program from this space by picking out a single type. For example, if we want the annotated type $int \to \langle int \rangle \to \langle int \rangle$, we match this against $(\textbf{int}^a \to (\textbf{int}^b \to \textbf{int}^c)^d)^e$, yielding the substitution $\{a, d, e \mapsto 0; b, c \mapsto 1\}$ which simplifies the constraint set to just $\{0 \leq k \leq 1\}$. Thus by picking a single (valid) staged type we have narrowed the space of possible programs down to these two

$$k = 0 : \mu \, pow \, . \, \lambda n \, . \, \lambda x \, . \, \langle \textbf{if} \, n = 0 \, \textbf{then} \, 1 \, \textbf{else} \, \tilde{} x * \tilde{} (pow \, (n - 1) \, x) \rangle$$
$$k = 1 : \mu \, pow \, . \, \lambda n \, . \, \lambda x \, . \, \textbf{if} \, n = 0 \, \textbf{then} \, \langle 1 \rangle \, \textbf{else} \, \langle \tilde{} x * \tilde{} (pow \, (n - 1) \, x) \rangle$$

We see that the "slack variable" k is not always determined by concrete annotations in the type. This happens because conditional expressions of code type sometimes have a choice between being performed statically or dynamically. If we always want the if statement to execute as soon as possible, we can maximize k symbolically by setting it to $-a + c + d$, yielding the following program

$$(\mu pow \, . \, \lambda n \, . \, (\lambda x \, .$$
$$(\textbf{if} \, n^{-a} = 0$$
$$\quad \textbf{then} \, 1^{-a+c+d}$$
$$\quad \textbf{else} \, (x^{-b} * ((pow \, (n^{-a} - 1)^a)^{-d} \, x)^{-c})^{-a+c+d}$$
$$)^{a-d})^d)^e$$

and the simpler constraint set

$$a, b, c, d, e \geq 0 \quad c \geq b \quad c + d \geq a$$

In general, there may be several upper bounds given for a slack variable s, in this case we replace s with a *max* (or *min*) operation on all of s's lower bounds (or upper bounds).

6   Polymorphism and Polyvariance

MetaML is a much richer language than the small one we have shown so far. Many features will need to be added to our language and BTA algorithm before we can handle full MetaML. The most significant extension is handling polymorphism.

In order to extend our language to handle Hindley-Milner polymorphism, we will need to extend the notion of a type scheme to include a constraint set. A type scheme would then have the form

$$\text{Type Scheme } \sigma ::= \forall \{\alpha_1, \ldots, \alpha_n\} . \forall \{j_1, \ldots, j_m\} . C \Rightarrow \tau$$
$$\text{Type } \tau ::= \textbf{int} \mid \textbf{bool} \mid \tau \to \tau \mid \textbf{list } \tau \mid \tau^a \mid \alpha$$
$$\text{Constraints } C ::= \varnothing \mid C, a \geq 0$$
$$\text{Arithmetic Expression } a ::= j \mid a + a \mid a - a$$

Instantiating a type scheme requires fresh type variables as well as fresh annotation variables. The constraint set C is instantiated to these fresh annotation variables and then asserted. This is where a constraint solver/simplifier is important. Type schemes should carry as few constraints as possible so that there is less work to do when instantiating them. We need to remove all (or most) redundant constraints.

An interesting consequence of this approach is that polyvariance collapses to qualified polymorphism. Polyvariance is an advanced BTA feature that allows a function to be used at different staging signatures in different locations. Polymorphism is a feature of type systems that allows functions to have different types at different locations. The approach outlined here handles both features with a single mechanism.

These type schemes are reminiscent of the work on qualified types [6,7]. However, the constraints C are not on types, but on annotations. The implications of this distinction are not yet clear.

7   Type Inference Implementation

We have a Haskell program that does type inference according to the generalized typing rules of the previous section. The algorithm produces many redundant inequalities so we have written an ad-hoc arithmetic inequality simplifier that eliminates many of them. This section addresses the issues that arise when moving from the typing rules to an actual algorithm.

The grammar in Figure 3 does not tell the whole story. In order to make sure we catch every possible annotation of the program, all sub-expressions of terms and types should be annotated with a fresh variable initially. Figure 4 shows Haskell datatypes for annotated and unannotated types and expressions that capture this restriction. Similar datatypes are used in the implementation. If there is no annotation possible for a certain position, the generated constraints will constrain that variable to be zero.

```
data Expr e = Lit Int | Var Name | App e e | Lam Name e | ...
data Type t = TInt | TBool | TArr t t | TList t | TVar Name
data Base s = Base (s (Base s))
data Annotated s = Ann Step (s (Annotated s))
```

annotated expressions:	Annotated Expr
annotated types:	Annotated Type
unannotated expressions:	Base Expr
unannotated types:	Base Type

Fig. 4. Haskell two-level datatypes for annotated and unannotated expressions. Values of type **Step** are linear arithmetic expressions involving annotation variables. The form of **Annotated s** ensures that every **s** sub-structure is annotated.

Constraints coming from the *valid* operator are generated on the fly by annotating every freshly generated type variable with a fresh annotation variable that is asserted to be non-negative.

The typing rules contain implicit *equality* constraints. For example, in the [μVAR] rule, there are two occurrences of the stage expression n. Each may be represented by a different arithmetic expression. In this common case, there is an implicit equality constraint generated. A similar situation occurs whenever two types are unified – corresponding annotations must be set equal to each other.

8   Future Work

Correctness Proof. A correctness theorem akin to the "minimal completion" result of Henglein [1], would say that in staged programs resulting from BTA, all work is done at the earliest possible stage. This is a more difficult result to obtain in a multistage language.

Obtaining such a result for our BTA algorithm means solving the problem of slack variables. These slack variables represent a choice between multiple valid program annotations. We believe that the algorithm places slack variables in such a way that we can always either maximize or minimize them to obtain a minimal completion of the original program. This remains to be seen.

Efficient Solver. One benefit of using a standard form of constraints is that existing efficient constraint solvers can be plugged in to replace our ad-hoc solver. What existing constraint solvers are more efficient than our ad-hoc one?

William Pugh has developed the Omega test for solving Presburger arithmetic formulas [8]. Presburger formulas are first order logical formulas with arithmetic terms built from the symbols $+$, $-$, $=$, $\leq$, and variables ranging over integers. Though the general problem is NP-Complete, the Omega test has been found to be efficient in practice (of low order polynomial time complexity).

Our form of constraints is much more restricted than Presburger formulas. Our constraints contain no quantifiers, disjunctions, or implications. For this reason, we may be able to get away with a simpler solver.

9   Related Work

In the tradition of the seminal works of Nielson and Nielson [9] and Gomard and Jones [10], Henglein builds a BTA for a two-level language based on type inference and constraint solving [1]. His main contribution is to provide the first efficient implementation of the type inference approach to BTA. Henglein is the first to separate BTA into separate type inference and constraint solving phases. As in our case, the solution of these constraints gives annotations to place in the original program. His constraints are rather ad-hoc: their form is specifically crafted for the single purpose of constraining binding times. In contrast, our much simpler constraint system arises naturally from the realization that the stage of a program is precisely captured by its type in a typed staged language. Abstracting the nesting of the code type constructor into a single integer-valued stage variable leads naturally to a type system based upon simple arithmetic constraints.

Heldman and Hughes [11] present a polychronic BTA algorithm that handles parametric polymorphism in the source language. Their approach is similar to ours in that it is based on type inference and constraint solving and they handle both polyvariance and polymorphism with the same construct. However, they only consider a two-level language and ignore partially static data. They do handle a **lift** annotation that we do not, and conversions between $\langle a \to b \rangle$ and $\langle a \rangle \to \langle b \rangle$ via a form of subtyping constraints. Also, their annotations represent stages rather than transitions between stages: an unwieldy syntactic convention for programmers.

The seminal work in multistage BTA is that of Glück and Jørgensen [12]. They generalize the constraint-based approach of Henglein to generate multistage generating extensions. Their constraints, like Henglein's, are ad-hoc. Davies [13] presents the staged language $\lambda^{\bigcirc}$ based on the $\bigcirc$ modality from linear temporal logic. He proves that $\lambda^{\bigcirc}$ is a refinement of the multistage language of Glück and Jørgensen [14].

10   Conclusions

We have developed a novel approach to BTA which is based on the well established method of type inference. We have made the following contributions:

1. The novelty of our algorithm is the expression of a program's well-stagedness in the form of simple arithmetic constraints.
2. Staged types were found to be extremely expressive as BTA specifications, much more so than anything from the partial evaluation literature. Staged types can express higher-order partially static data and arbitrarily many stages of execution.
3. Our deepest insight is that polyvariance reduces to polymorphism when stage ordering constraints are built into type schemes. This does not seem to have been addressed in the literature to date. Identifying an advanced BTA feature (polyvariance) with an advanced typing feature (polymorphism) reduces the number of concepts an algorithm must handle.
4. Our work enables a system to integrate manual staging with automatic BTA. A BTA algorithm based on our work here would enable adding the `stage` command described in Section 1.3 to MetaML.

References

1. Henglein, F.: Efficient type inference for higher-order binding-time analysis. In: Functional Programming Languages and Computer Architecture. Volume 523 of Lecture Notes in Computer Science., Springer-Verlag (1991) 448–472
2. Taha, W., Sheard, T.: Multi-stage programming with explicit annotations. In: Proceedings of the ACM SIGPLAN Symposium on Partial Evaluation and Semantics-Based Program Manipulation (PEPM), ACM Press (1997) 203–217
3. Sheard, T.: Accomplishments and research challenges in meta-programming. In: Proceedings of the Second International Workshop on Semantics, Applications, and Implementation of Program Generation (SAIG). Volume 2196 of Lecture Notes in Computer Science., Springer-Verlag (2001) 2–44
4. Sheard, T., Jones, S.P.: Template meta-programming for haskell. In: ACM SIGPLAN Workshop on Haskell, ACM Press (2002) 1–16
5. Sheard, T., Linger, N.: Search-based binding time analysis using type-directed pruning. In: Proceedings of the ACM SIGPLAN Asian Symposium on Partial Evaluation and Semantics-Based Program Manipulation (ASIA-PEPM), ACM Press (2002) 20–31
6. Jones, M.P.: Qualified Types: Theory and Practice. PhD thesis, Oxford University (1992) Also available as Programming Research Group technical report 106.
7. Odersky, M., Sulzmann, M., Wehr, M.: Type inference with constrained types. Theory and Practice of Object Systems **5** (1999) 35–55
8. Pugh, W.: The omega test: A fast and practical integer programming algorithm for dependence analysis. Communications of the ACM **38** (1992) 102–114
9. Nielson, H., Nielson, F.: Automatic binding time analysis for a typed λ-calculus. Science of Computer Programming **10** (1988) 139–176
10. Gomard, C., Jones, N.: A partial evaluator for the untyped lambda-calculus. Journal of Functional Programming **1** (1991) 21–69

11. Heldal, R., Hughes, J.: Binding-time analysis for polymorphic types. In: Andrei Ershov Fourth International Conference on Perspectives of System Informatics. Volume 2244 of Lecture Notes in Computer Science., Springer-Verlag (2001) 191–201
12. Glück, R., Jørgensen, J.: Fast binding-time analysis for multi-level specialization. In: Andrei Ershov Second International Conference on Perspectives of System Informatics. Volume 1181 of Lecture Notes in Computer Science., Springer-Verlag (1996) 261–272
13. Davies, R.: A temporal-logic approach to binding-time analysis. In: Proceedings of the 11th Annual Symposium on Logic in Computer Science. (1996) 184–195
14. Glück, R., Jørgensen, J.: Efficient multi-level generating extensions for program specialization. In: Programming Languages, Implementations, Logics, and Programs. Volume 982 of Lecture Notes in Computer Science., Springer-Verlag (1995) 259–278

A Class of Polynomially Solvable Range Constraints for Interval Analysis without Widenings and Narrowings

Zhendong Su[1] and David Wagner[2]

[1] Department of Computer Science, UC Davis, su@cs.ucdavis.edu
[2] EECS Department, UC Berkeley, daw@cs.berkeley.edu

Abstract. In this paper, we study the problem of solving integer range constraints that arise in many static program analysis problems. In particular, we present the first polynomial time algorithm for a general class of integer range constraints. In contrast with abstract interpretation techniques based on widenings and narrowings, our algorithm computes, in polynomial time, the *optimal solution* of the arising fixpoint equations. Our result implies that "precise" range analysis can be performed in polynomial time without widening and narrowing operations.

1 Introduction

Many program analysis and verification algorithms and tools have the need to solve linear integer constraints or its extensions, such as for checking array bounds to ensure memory safety [15, 38, 16, 35] and for detecting buffer overruns for security applications [36], and for array dependency analysis for parallel compilers [31, 32, 29, 33, 7, 6]. However, solving integer linear constraints is a difficult problem [22], and only very special cases have efficient algorithms [30, 3].

In this paper, we study constraints over *integer ranges*, *e.g.*, the set $\{-1, 0, 1\}$, represented as $[-1, 1]$. These constraints can be used to express many interesting program analyses [36, 10, 9]. Furthermore, we show that these constraints can be solved for their optimal solution efficiently. A key property that makes integer range constraints efficiently solvable is its simple join operation in the lattice of ranges. The join of two ranges is defined as $[l, u] \sqcup [l', u'] = [\inf\{l, l'\}, \sup\{u, u'\}]$ (where inf and sup compute the minimum and maximum of two numbers) instead of the union of the two ranges. (This does not consider $\bot$, the smallest range. See Section 2 for a complete definition of the join operator.) This use of $\sqcup$ is not as precise as the standard union. However, it is sufficient for many analysis problems [36, 10] that need lower and upper bounds information on values of integer variables.

For readers familiar with interval constraints for floating-point computation [19, 18, 4, 28] based on *interval arithmetic* [25], integer range constraints are different. Such work deals primarily with rounding errors in real numbers, and the goal is to get an approximate real interval that includes all solutions to the original constraints. Range constraints deal with integer ranges, and the goal is to find the least solution, *i.e.*, the smallest ranges that satisfy all the constraints.

Our algorithm is based on a graph formulation similar to that used by Pratt [30] and Shostak [34]. We use fixpoint computations to find the least solution. Our techniques

K. Jensen and A. Podelski (Eds.): TACAS 2004, LNCS 2988, pp. 280–295, 2004.
© Springer-Verlag Berlin Heidelberg 2004

are closely related to those used in integer programming [20], especially those targeted at program analysis and verification. We next survey some closely related work.

Tractable Linear Integer Constraints.   Pratt [30] considers the simple form of linear constraints $x \leq y + k$, where k is an integer, and gives a polynomial time algorithm based on detecting negative cycles in weighted directed graphs. The graph representation we use in this paper borrows from Pratt's method. Shostak [34] considers a slightly more general problem $ax + by \leq k$, where a, b, and k are integer constants. A worst case exponential time algorithm is given for this kind of constraints by so-called "loop residues." Nelson [26] considers the same fragment and also gives an exponential time algorithm. Aspvall and Shiloach [3] refine Shostak's "loop residue" method and give a polynomial time algorithm for the fragment with two variables. Because constraints with three variables are NP-hard [22], this may be the most general class one can hope for a polynomial time algorithm.

General Linear Integer Constraints.   General linear integer constraints are also considered in the literature. Some provers use the Fourier-Motzkin variable elimination method [31], the Sup-Inf method of Bledsoe [5], or Nelson's method based on Simplex [27]. However, all the algorithms considered for integer programming have either very high complexity or treat only special cases. In contrast, because of the special structure of the range lattice and properties of affine functions, we are able to design polynomial time algorithms for some common and rather expressive class of range constraints.

Dataflow and Fixpoint Equations.   Also related is work on dataflow equations in program analysis [21,23], and lattice constraints in abstract interpretation [10,11,13,12], and fixpoint computations in general [14, 2, 1]. There are some key differences. In this paper, the lattice we consider is an infinite height lattice. For most work in dataflow analysis, the lattices used are of finite height, in which case, termination with exact least solution is guaranteed. For abstract interpretation and general fixpoint computation, although infinite lattices are used in many cases, termination is not guaranteed, and sometimes cannot be guaranteed. Techniques such as widening and narrowing are used to control the termination of the analysis. In this work, we exploit an important property of ranges and affine functions to achieve efficient termination. For example, Cousot and Cousot's interval analysis [10] is quite efficient in practice but may lose precision due to its use of widenings (see the last part of Section 2 for an example); in comparison, our algorithm efficiently finds the *exact* least fixpoint by exploiting the structure of affine constraints, but only applies to a less general class of transfer functions. In fact, the class of constraints we consider resembles the fixpoint equations in [10]. In [36], the authors consider a simpler form of constraints than what is considered in this paper and give a worst case exponential time algorithm.

We summarize here the contributions of the paper: (i) It describes a quadratic time algorithm for solving a general class of affine range constraints (Section 3); (ii) It shows, for the first time, that precise interval analysis can be performed in polynomial time; (iii) It presents hardness and decidability results for satisfiability of some natural extensions of our constraint language (Section 4); and (iv) Our techniques might be useful for solving constraints in other lattices.

2 Preliminaries

Let $\mathbb{Z}$ denote the set of integers. The lattice of ranges is given by:

$$L \stackrel{\text{def}}{=} \{\bot\} \cup \{[l, u] \mid l \in \mathbb{Z} \cup \{-\infty\} \wedge u \in \mathbb{Z} \cup \{+\infty\} \wedge l \leq u\}$$

ordered by $\sqsubseteq$, such that $\bot \sqsubseteq r$ for any $r \in L$ and $[l_1, u_1] \sqsubseteq [l_2, u_2]$ if $l_2 \leq l_1 \leq u_1 \leq u_2$. In the lattice, $\bot$ (the empty range) is the smallest range, and $[-\infty, +\infty]$ is the largest range, also denoted by $\top$. The meet $\sqcap$ and join $\sqcup$ are defined as follows:

- $\bot \sqcap r = \bot \wedge [l_1, u_1] \sqcap [l_2, u_2] = [l = \sup\{l_1, l_2\}, u = \inf\{u_1, u_2\}]$ ($\bot$ if $l > u$);
- $\bot \sqcup r = r \wedge [l_1, u_1] \sqcup [l_2, u_2] = [\inf\{l_1, l_2\}, \sup\{u_1, u_2\}]$.

for any range $r \in L$. We select the lower bound and upper bound of a non-empty range $r = [l, u]$ by $\mathsf{lb}(r) = l$ and $\mathsf{ub}(r) = u$.

The range expressions are given by $E ::= r \mid X \mid n \times X \mid E + E$, where $r \in L$ denotes a range constant, X is a range variable, $n \times X$ denotes scalar multiplication by $n \in \mathbb{Z}$, and $E + E$ denotes range addition. A *range constraint* has the form $E \sqcap r \sqsubseteq X$. When $r = \top$, we simply write the constraint as $E \sqsubseteq X$. Notice that we require the right-hand side of a range constraint to be a variable, which is related to "definite set constraints" [17]. We give some examples using these constraints below. Readers interested in more information on the connection between range constraints and program analysis may wish to consult, for example [10, 9].

Let $\mathcal{V}$ denote the set of range variables. A *valuation* ρ is a mapping from $\mathcal{V}$ to L, the lattice of ranges. We extend ρ on variables to work on range expressions inductively, such that, $\rho([l, u]) = [l, u]$, $\rho(n \times X) = n \times \rho(X)$, and $\rho(E_1 + E_2) = \rho(E_1) + \rho(E_2)$, where $n \times [l, u] = [\inf\{nl, nu\}, \sup\{nl, nu\}]$ and $[l_1, u_1] + [l_2, u_2] = [l_1 + l_2, u_1 + u_2]$.

We say a valuation ρ *satisfies* a constraint $E \sqcap r \sqsubseteq X$ if $\rho(E) \sqcap r \sqsubseteq \rho(X)$. A valuation satisfies a set of constraints if it satisfies each one of the constraints. Such a valuation is called a *solution* of the constraints.

Proposition 1 *When* $f(X) = aX + b$ *denotes an affine function, we have* $f([l, u] \sqcap [l', u']) = f([l, u]) \sqcap f([l', u'])$ *and* $f([l, u] \sqcup [l', u']) = f([l, u]) \sqcup f([l', u'])$.

Definition 1 (Range Saturation). *A valuation* ρ *saturates a constraint* $f(X) \sqcap [c, d] \sqsubseteq Y$ *if* $[c, d] \sqsubseteq \rho(f(X))$. *It partially saturates the constraint if* $l = c$ *or* $u = d$, *where* $[l, u] = \rho(f(X)) \sqcap [c, d]$.

A set of constraints can have many solutions. For most static program analyses, we are interested in the *least solution*, if it exists, because such a solution gives us the most information. For the range constraints we consider, every set of constraints is satisfiable and has a least solution.

Proposition 2 (Existence of Least Solution) *Any set of range constraints has a least solution.*

Our goal is to compute such a least solution effectively. We denote by least_C the least solution of the constraints C. We use $\mathsf{least}(X)$ for the least solution for a range variable X if the underlying constraints are clear from the context. Next, we give some example constraint systems, which may come from an interval analysis similar to [10] of some small C program fragments. We give examples for both a flow-insensitive analysis and a flow-sensitive analysis. Notice that the interval analysis in [10] is traditionally specified as a flow-sensitive one. A constraint-based formulation sometimes can allow a more natural integration of flow-sensitivity and flow-insensitivity.

Example 1. Consider the constraints $\{[0,0] \sqsubseteq X, X+1 \sqsubseteq X\}$ (with least solution $[0,+\infty])$ from the analysis of the following C program fragment:

```
int i = 0;  /* yields the constraint [0,0] <= X */
while (i < 10) {
    ...
    i = i+1; /* yields the constraint X + 1 <= X */
}
```

Notice that this is a flow-insensitive analysis. [1]

Example 2. Consider the constraints $\{[10,10] \sqsubseteq X, (-2) \times X \sqsubseteq X\}$ (with least solution $[-\infty,+\infty])$, which come from the analysis of the following fragment:

```
int i = 10;   /* yields [10,10] <= X */
while (...) {
    ...
    i = -2*i;  /* yields (-2)*X <= X  */
}
```

Let us go back to Example 1. Notice that although the program ensures $i \leq 10$, the range we get says its value can be unbounded. To address this imprecision, we can generate more precise constraints to use non-trivial intersection constants r, in $E \sqcap r \sqsubseteq X$. This use is motivated by the goal to provide more precise analysis of ranges by modeling conditionals in while and if statements. In Example 1, we expect to say that X has the range $[0,10]$. We can model the example more precisely with the constraints $[0,0] \sqsubseteq X$ and $(X+1) \sqcap [-\infty,10] \sqsubseteq X$. Notice that the least solution of these constraints is indeed $[0,10]$ and is what we expect.

Consider another program fragment:

```
int i = 0;
while (i < n) {
    ...
    i = i+1;
}
```

---

[1] For comparison, the following constraints may be used for a flow-sensitive analysis:

$$\{[0,0] \sqsubseteq X_0, X_0 \sqsubseteq X_1, X_3 \sqsubseteq X_1, X_1 \sqcap [-\infty,9] \sqsubseteq X_2, X_2+1 \sqsubseteq X_3\}$$

where X_i's denote the variable instances at different program points. See [10] for more.

LO
   z = x − y − 3;
L1
   if(z > 0){
L2
    x = z + y + 3;
L3
    y = x − z − 3;
L4

   ...

 }

L1:	$X_0 - Y_0 - 3 \sqsubseteq Z_1$
L2:	$Z_1 \sqcap [1, +\infty] \sqsubseteq Z_2$
L3:	$Z_2 + Y_0 + 3 \sqsubseteq X_3$
L4:	$X_3 - Z_2 - 3 \sqsubseteq Y_4$

(a) Program after transformation.   (b) Constraints.

Fig. 1. An example of how to analyze relationships between variables.

We would want to express the constraints $\{[0,0] \sqsubseteq X, (X+1) \sqcap [-\infty, \mathsf{ub}(Y)] \sqsubseteq X\}$, where X and Y are the range variables for the program variables i and n respectively, and $\mathsf{ub}(Y)$ denotes the upper bound of Y. The constraint $(X+1) \sqcap [-\infty, \mathsf{ub}(Y)] \sqsubseteq X$ is equivalent to $\{[-\infty, \mathsf{ub}(Y)] \sqsubseteq Z, (X+1) \sqcap Z \sqsubseteq X\}$, where Z is a fresh range variable. In practice, we can restrict the meet operation to be with a range constant in most cases, because the range variables X and Y usually do not belong to the same strongly connected component and can be stratified (see Section 3).

Alternatively, it is sufficient to consider conditions for while and if statements of the form $x \geq 0$ (or $x > 0$) after some semantics-preserving transformations on the original code. As an example, consider the following program fragment:

```
if (x > y + 3) {
    ...
}
```

We can transform it to the code fragment in Figure 1a, where z is a temporary variable for storing intermediate results. We give labels for the few program locations. The generated constraints are given in Figure 1b. In the constraints, we use program location labels on the range variables to distinguish the instances, *i.e.*, the underlying analysis is flow-sensitive. Essentially, we use range constraints to "project" the relevant information from the condition $z \geq 0$ onto x and y. It is perhaps interesting to notice that ranges are extremely weak in relating variables.

For illustration, we provide here two simple examples to show that the standard widening and narrowing techniques [10] may not give the optimal solution even restricted to affine functions.

Example 3. Consider the following program fragment:

```
int i = 0;
while (...) {
    if (...) { i = 1; }
}
```

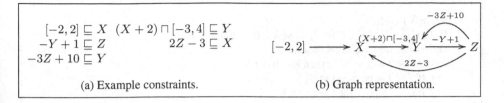

$$[-2,2] \sqsubseteq X \quad (X+2) \sqcap [-3,4] \sqsubseteq Y$$
$$-Y+1 \sqsubseteq Z \qquad\qquad 2Z-3 \sqsubseteq X$$
$$-3Z+10 \sqsubseteq Y$$

(a) Example constraints.   (b) Graph representation.

Fig. 2. Graph representation of constraints.

We obtain the constraints $\{[0,0] \sqsubseteq X, [1,1] \sqsubseteq X\}$. The optimal solution for X is $[0,1]$. However, with widenings and narrowings at program back-edges, we get $[0,+\infty]$. In general, if we have a widening operation at the variable i and if i occurs in two loops of affine constraints with different fixpoints, then widening and narrowing will give an imprecise answer.

Example 4. Consider the constraints $\{[0,0] \sqsubseteq X, (-X+1) \sqsubseteq X\}$. The optimal solution for X is $[0,1]$, however, with widenings and narrowings, we get $[0,+\infty]$.

3   An Algorithm for Solving Range Constraints

Our algorithm is based on *chaotic iteration* [11]. We start by assigning each variable $\bot$, and then iterate through the constraints using the current valuation ρ. For each constraint $E \sqcap r \sqsubseteq X$, if $\rho(E) \sqcap r \not\sqsubseteq \rho(X)$, we set $\rho(X) := (\rho(E) \sqcap r) \sqcup \rho(X)$. This process repeats until all the constraints are satisfied. Although this process always converges for any finite height lattices, it may not converge for infinite height lattices, *e.g.*, consider the constraints $X + 1 \sqsubseteq X$ and $[0,0] \sqsubseteq X$. Our approach is to extend chaotic iteration with strategies to handle this kind of cyclic constraints.

We have a natural representation of constraints as graphs. Each vertex in the graph represents a variable (or in some cases, a range constant r), and an edge from X to Y labelled $f(X) \sqcap r$ represents the constraint $f(X) \sqcap r \sqsubseteq Y$. A constraint $[l, u] \sqsubseteq X$ is represented as an edge from a node representing the range constant $[l, u]$ to the node X. Some example constraints and their graph representation are shown in Figure 2.

As mentioned above, our approach is to adapt chaotic iteration to propagate information along edges of the graph until we reach a fixpoint. This fixpoint is the least one. If the graph is acyclic, then we can simply propagate the constraints in its topologically sorted order. In the rest of the section, we consider possibly cyclic graphs. We start with a simple loop (Section 3.2), a multi-loop (Section 3.3), a strongly connected component (Section 3.4), and finally a general graph (Section 3.5).

3.1   Constraint Transformation

Although possible, it is complicated to solve directly constraints with negative coefficients. For a simpler presentation, we first describe a constraint transformation to make all constraints have positive coefficients.

---

1. Set $\rho(X) := [l, u]$.
2. If $[l', u'] = f(\rho(X)) \sqcap [c, d] \sqsubseteq \rho(X)$, then least $= \rho$.
3. Otherwise, we have a few cases:
   a) If $l' < l$ and $u' > u$, then least$(X) = [c, d]$.
   b) If $l' < l$ only, then least$(X) = [c, u]$.
   c) If $u' > u$ only, then least$(X) = [l, d]$.

Fig. 3. An algorithm for solving a simple loop.

Lemma 1. *Any system of constraints can be effectively transformed to an equivalent system where all constraints have positive coefficients.*

Proof. For each variable X in the original system, create two variables X^+ and X^-. The variable X^+ corresponds to X, and X^- corresponds to $-X$. We then apply the following transformations on the original constraints:

- Replace each *initial constraint* $[l, u] \sqsubseteq X$ with two constraints:

$$\{[l, u] \sqsubseteq X^+, [-u, -l] \sqsubseteq X^-\}$$

- Replace each constraint of the form $(aX + b) \sqcap [l, u] \sqsubseteq Y$, where $a > 0$, with two constraints:

$$\{(aX^+ + b) \sqcap [l, u] \sqsubseteq Y^+, (aX^- - b) \sqcap [-u, -l] \sqsubseteq Y^-\}$$

- Replace each constraint of the form $(aX + b) \sqcap [l, u] \sqsubseteq Y$, where $a < 0$, with two constraints:

$$\{(-aX^- + b) \sqcap [l, u] \sqsubseteq Y^+, (-aX^+ - b) \sqcap [-u, -l] \sqsubseteq Y^-\}$$

One can verify that the two systems of constraints have the same solutions on the corresponding X and X^+, and in particular, they have the same least solution. In addition, the transformation is linear time and produces a new system of constraints linear in the size of the original system.

Notice that this transformation also applies to affine functions with more than one variables. Hence, in the rest of the paper, we consider only constraints defined over positive affine functions.

3.2 A Simple Loop

Consider a loop with the constraints $[l, u] \sqsubseteq X$ and $f(X) \sqcap [c, d] = (aX + b) \sqcap [c, d] \sqsubseteq X$, where $a > 0$. We give an algorithm in Figure 3 to find its least solution. The algorithm is similar to the widening operator defined on ranges [10].

Lemma 2. *The algorithm in Figure 3 computes the least solution of a simple loop.*

---

1. Set $\rho(X) = [l, u]$.
2. Pick any constraint $f_i(X) \sqcap [c_i, d_i] \sqsubseteq X$ not satisfied by ρ, find its least solution ρ' with the initial constraint $\rho(X) \sqsubseteq X$ (cf. Figure 3).
3. Set $\rho = \rho'$.
4. Go to step 2 until all constraints are satisfied.

Fig. 4. An algorithm for solving a multi-loop.

Proof. If $[l', u'] \sqsubseteq [l, u]$, then clearly we have reached the least fixpoint, so we have least$(X) = [l, u]$. Otherwise, we have three cases to consider. (1) If $l' < l$ and $u' > u$, since $f(X) = aX + b$ is a positive affine function, lb$(f^n([l, u]))$ forms a strictly decreasing sequence and ub$(f^n([l, u]))$ forms a strictly increasing sequence. However, the lower bound can reach as low as c and the upper bound can reach as high as d. Thus, we have least$(X) = [c, d]$. The other two cases are similar.

3.3 A Multi-loop

We call constraints with more than one simple self loop a *multi-loop*. In particular, assume we have the constraints $[l, u] \sqsubseteq X$ and $f_i(X) \sqcap [c_i, d_i] \sqsubseteq X$, for $1 \leq i \leq n$. A multi-loop is considered because the solution to it hints at the basic idea for solving the more complicated cases. Basically, to solve a multi-loop, we start with X assigned the value $[l, u]$. Pick any constraint $f_i(X) \sqcap [c_i, d_i]$ not satisfied by this valuation. We find its least solution with $[l, u] \sqsubseteq X$ as the initial constraint and update the current assignment to this least solution. This process repeats until all constraints are satisfied. The algorithm is shown in Figure 4.

Lemma 3. *The algorithm in Figure 4 computes the least solution to a multi-loop in quadratic time.*

Proof. It is obvious that the algorithm outputs the least solution when it terminates. Thus, it remains to argue its time complexity. We show that step 2 is executed no more than $2n$ times, *i.e.*, the number of intersection bounds c_i and d_i. Each activation of step 2 causes the current valuation to partially saturate (cf. Definition 1) the particular constraint in question, *i.e.*, at least one lb or ub of the constraint (c_i's or d_i's) is saturated. Because a bound cannot be saturated twice, step 2 is activated at most $2n$ times. Thus, we have shown the algorithm runs in quadratic time in the size of the input constraints.

3.4 A Strongly Connected Component

In this part, we show how to handle a strongly connected component, which forms the core of our algorithm. The main observation is that one can view a strongly connected component as a mutually recursive set of equations working on the set of range variables in the component simultaneously. Let $X_1, \ldots, X_n$ be the set of variables in a component C. We view C as a set of equations working on $X_1, \ldots, X_n$ simultaneously and use the same basic idea for a multi-loop.

Multiple Initial Constraints. First, in dealing with a strongly connected component, we need to consider the case where there are multiple initial constraints $[l, u] \sqsubseteq X$ because there may be more than one incoming edges to a component, and each one corresponds to an initial constraint. To simplify our presentation, we apply another graph transformation on a strongly connected component to convert it to an equivalent one with a single initial constraint.

Lemma 4. *In a constraint graph, a strongly connected component with multiple initial constraints can be effectively transformed to an equivalent strongly connected component with a single initial constraint (in linear time and space).*

Proof. Let C be the original component. The transformation works as follows:

- Add a *fresh* range variable X^* with the initial constraint $[1, 1] \sqsubseteq X^*$.
- Replace each initial constraint $[l, u] \sqsubseteq X \in C$, where $l, u \in \mathbb{Z}$, with two constraints $\{lX^* \sqsubseteq X, uX^* \sqsubseteq X\}$.
- Replace each initial constraint $[-\infty, u] \sqsubseteq X \in C$, where $u \in \mathbb{Z}$ with two constraints $\{uX^* \sqsubseteq X, X - 1 \sqsubseteq X\}$.
- Replace each initial constraint $[l, +\infty] \sqsubseteq X \in C$, where $l \in \mathbb{Z}$ with two constraints $\{lX^* \sqsubseteq X, X + 1 \sqsubseteq X\}$.
- Replace each initial constraint $[-\infty, +\infty] \sqsubseteq X \in C$ with three constraints $\{X^* \sqsubseteq X, X + 1 \sqsubseteq X, X - 1 \sqsubseteq X\}$.
- Finally, to make the new graph strongly connected, we add the following constraint from any variable, say Y, to X^*:

$$Y \sqcap [1, 1] \sqsubseteq X^*$$

One can verify that the new strongly connected component is equivalent to the original component. The running time of the transformation is linear time, and it generates a new constraint system of size linear in $|C|$.

Non-distributivity of Ranges. One additional issue is with the non-distributivity of ranges. One can easily verify that $\sqcap$ does not distribute over $\sqcup$, *i.e.*, in general, $(r_1 \sqcup r_2) \sqcap r_3 \neq (r_1 \sqcap r_3) \sqcup (r_2 \sqcap r_3)$. For example, $[2, 2] = ([0, 1] \sqcup [3, 4]) \sqcap [2, 2] \neq ([0, 1] \sqcap [2, 2]) \sqcup ([3, 4] \sqcap [2, 2]) = \bot$. We show, however, this can be remedied to have a slightly altered lemma of distribution of $\sqcap$ over $\sqcup$.

Lemma 5 (Distributivity Lemma). *If $r_1 \sqcap r_3 \neq \bot$ and $r_2 \sqcap r_3 \neq \bot$, then $(r_1 \sqcup r_2) \sqcap r_3 = (r_1 \sqcap r_3) \sqcup (r_2 \sqcap r_3)$.*

Proof. It suffices to show that $(r_1 \sqcup r_2) \sqcap r_3 \sqsubseteq (r_1 \sqcap r_3) \sqcup (r_2 \sqcap r_3)$ because $(r_1 \sqcap r_3) \sqcup (r_2 \sqcap r_3) \sqsubseteq (r_1 \sqcup r_2) \sqcap r_3$. Consider any $a \in (r_1 \sqcup r_2) \sqcap r_3$. We have $a \in (r_1 \sqcup r_2)$ and $a \in r_3$. If $a \in r_1$ or $a \in r_2$, then $a \in (r_1 \sqcap r_3)$ or $a \in (r_2 \sqcap r_3)$. Thus, it follows that $a \in (r_1 \sqcap r_3) \sqcup (r_2 \sqcap r_3)$. Now consider the case where $a \notin r_1$ and $a \notin r_2$. Because $a \in (r_1 \sqcup r_2)$, we have $r_1 \sqcap r_2 = \bot$, and a must lie in the gap of r_1 and r_2. The conditions $r_1 \sqcap r_3 \neq \bot$ and $r_2 \sqcap r_3 \neq \bot$ then guarantees that $a \in (r_1 \sqcap r_3) \sqcup (r_2 \sqcap r_3)$.

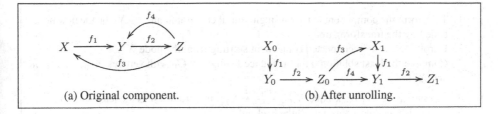

(a) Original component.   (b) After unrolling.

Fig. 5. An example of graph unrolling.

Lemma 6 (Saturation Lemma). *For any given r_1, r_2, and $r_3 = [a, b]$, either $(r_1 \sqcup r_2) \sqcap r_3 = (r_1 \sqcap r_3) \sqcup (r_2 \sqcap r_3)$ or it holds that $l = a$ or $u = b$, where $[l, u] = (r_1 \sqcup r_2) \sqcap r_3$.*

Proof. If $(r_1 \sqcup r_2) \sqcap r_3 = \bot$, then clearly $(r_1 \sqcup r_2) \sqcap r_3 = (r_1 \sqcap r_3) \sqcup (r_2 \sqcap r_3)$. Otherwise, let $[l, u] = (r_1 \sqcup r_2) \sqcap r_3) \neq \bot$. Assume that $l \neq a$ and $u \neq b$. We must have $a < l \leq u < b$. Then $(r_1 \sqcup r_2) = [l, u]$, which implies $r_1 \sqsubseteq [a, b]$ and $r_2 \sqsubseteq [a, b]$. Thus, $(r_1 \sqcup r_2) \sqcap [a, b] = (r_1 \sqcup r_2) = (r_1 \sqcap [a, b]) \sqcup (r_2 \sqcap [a, b])$.

Graph Unrolling and Constraint Paths. A strongly connected component can be viewed in the following sense as a set of functions. We unroll the component starting from X_1 with, for example, a depth first search algorithm. Each time a back-edge is encountered, we create a new instance of the target (if it has not been created). For a variable X_i in a strongly connected component, we use X_{i0} and X_{i1} to denote its first and second instances in its unrolling. We give an example in Figure 5, where Figure 5a shows the original component and Figure 5b is the result after unrolling. Essentially, we are building the depth-first tree (but we also consider the cross edges and back edges). Notice that a depth-first tree with its cross edges is a directed acyclic graph, *i.e.*, a dag. Notice also in the unrolling for a strongly connected component with variables $X_1, \cdots, X_n$, the set of back-edges are exactly those edges between the subgraph induced by $X_{10}, \cdots, X_{n0}$ and the one induced by $X_{11}, \cdots, X_{n1}$.

To solve a strongly connected component, we want to summarize all paths from X_{j_0} to X_{j_1} by $F_j(X_j) \sqsubseteq X_j$, where

$$F_j(r) \stackrel{\text{def}}{=} r \sqcup \bigsqcup_{X_{j_0} \xrightarrow{f_1} \cdots \xrightarrow{f_k} X_{j_1}} (f_k \circ \cdots \circ f_1)(r).$$

Note that, even though there may be exponentially many terms in the definition of F_j, nonetheless the output $F_j(r)$ can be computed efficiently for any input r by propagating information in topological sorted order along the edges of the unrolled graph (as done for a dag).

For a strongly connected component, we need to consider a path of constraints. We define formally its semantics.

Definition 2 (Path Constraints). *A path from X_0 to X_n is a path in the constraint graph for C. The function for a path p is the affine function obtained by composing all the functions along the edges on the path. More formally*

1. Transform the component to have a single initial constraint, and let X^* be the new node added by the transformation.
2. Unroll the strongly connected component starting from the node X^*.
3. Compute the least solution ρ for the induced subgraph G_0 with vertices $X_{10}, \cdots, X_{n0}$ and X^*_0.
4. If ρ satisfies every back-edge $X_{i0} \xrightarrow{f \sqcap [c_i, d_i]} X_{j_1}$, then return ρ as the least solution.
5. Otherwise, update ρ through all the back-edges.
   a) If there is a *new* partially saturated constraint, then go to step 1.
   b) Otherwise, an unsatisfying cyclic path can be traced to apply the algorithm for a simple loop. Update ρ and go to step 1.

Fig. 6. An algorithm for solving a strongly connected component.

- $pf(X) = id \sqcap [-\infty, +\infty]$, where id is the identity function $id(X) = X$.
- $pf(p \xrightarrow{f \sqcap [c, d]} X) = f(pf(p)) \sqcap [c, d]$.

Notice that for a path $p = X_0 \rightarrow \cdots \rightarrow X_n$, $pf(p)$ is of the form $f(X_0) \sqcap [c, d]$, where f is an affine function and $[c, d]$ is a constant range (by Proposition 1).

We apply the same basic idea as that for a multi-loop and Lemma 6 in our algorithm for solving a strongly connected component, which is shown in Figure 6.

Lemma 7. *The algorithm in Figure 6 solves a strongly connected component of the constraint graph in quadratic time in the size of the component.*

Proof. Correctness is again easy to establish since all the constraints are satisfied and every step clearly preserves the least solution. We need to argue the time complexity of the algorithm. The proof technique is similar to that for the algorithm in Figure 4. Again, we argue that the body of the loop executes at most $2n$ times, where n is the number of constraints. Lemma 6 guarantees that if step 5a is not activated, then the previous least solution computation on G_0 distributes. Thus, we can trace, in linear time, an unsatisfying path, which can be converted to a simple loop for its least solution. In that case, at least one bounds must be saturated. Because there are $2n$ bounds, the body of the loops terminates in at most $2n$ steps. Putting everything together, the total running time is quadratic in the size of the component.

3.5   A General Graph

Now it is easy to put everything together to solve an arbitrary set of affine, single-variable range constraints. The idea is to first compute the strongly connected component graph of the original graph representation of the constraints, and then process each component in their topological sorted order. The total running time is quadratic.

Theorem 1. *The least solution for a given system of range constraints can be computed in quadratic time.*

3.6   Affine Functions with More than One Variables

In this part, we consider affine functions with more than one variable. They are needed for modeling program statements such as x = y + z + 1 and for precise modeling of loops and conditionals with statements of the above form.

We first consider constraints of the form $a_0 + a_1 X_1 + \ldots + a_n X_n \sqsubseteq X$ and then extend the algorithm to the general case, where we allow intersections with constant ranges. First notice it suffices to consider constraints of the form $X + Y \sqsubseteq Z$ along with constraints of the base form, namely, $f(X) \sqsubseteq Y$ and $[l, u] \sqsubseteq X$, where $f(X) = aX + b$ is an affine function over X.

We modify our graph representation of constraints to account for this new type of constraint. The constraint $X + Y \sqsubseteq Z$ can be represented in a hyper-graph setting, with a hyper-edge from X to the node for $+$ and a hyper-edge from Y to $+$. We also have a normal directed edge from $+$ to Z labelled with the identity function. Graphically we have

$$X \cdots \to + \xrightarrow{\text{id}} Z$$
$$Y \cdots \to$$

With this modified graph representation of constraints, we again use the same framework for solving range constraints. The interesting case as before is how to handle a strongly connected component of such a graph. The basic idea for the complete algorithm is the same as before: we compute the strongly connected component graph (using both $\to$ and $\dashrightarrow$ edges) and process each component in a topological sorted order of the variables nodes.

Here is how we deal with a strongly connected component. The idea is to reduce it to a system of basic constraints (single variable affine functions). Then we apply our algorithm for solving the basic system. We first describe how we reduce a constraint $X + Y \sqsubseteq Z$ to a set of basic constraints. We assume that X and Y have non-empty initial ranges $[l_x, u_x]$ and $[l_y, u_y]$. The constraint is reduced to the following basic constraints

$$X + [l_y, u_y] \sqsubseteq Z \quad Y + [l_x, u_x] \sqsubseteq Z$$
$$[l_x, u_x] \sqsubseteq X \qquad [l_y, u_y] \sqsubseteq Y$$

For a strongly connected component in the original graph, we first need to get some initial values for all the variables in the component. This can be easily done by propagating the values in a breath-first fashion starting from the variables with initial ranges. Assume every variable has a non-empty initial value. Otherwise these variables must be the empty range and the constraints can be simplified and solved again. Then for each constraint of the form $X + Y \sqsubseteq Z$, we perform the transformation to basic constraints described above with their current initial ranges. The constraint representation of the obtained constraints is still strongly connected. We then solve for its least solution. We use that to obtain another transformed constraint system. If the current least solution satisfies these new constraints, then we have found the least solution for the original general constraints. If not, we solve for the least solution of the transformed constraints. We repeat this process until the least solution is found. The algorithm is shown in Figure 7.

---

1. Scan a strongly connected component once to compute an initial valuation ρ that is non-empty on all the variables.
2. Reduce the constraints to basic constraints, solve for the least solution ρ' of the basic constraints subject to $\rho \sqsubseteq \rho'$, and then set $\rho = \rho'$.
3. If all constraints are satisfied, return ρ. Otherwise, go to Step 2.

Fig. 7. An algorithm for solving a strongly connected component with general affine functions.

Theorem 2. *Range constraints over multivariate affine functions are solvable for their least solution in quadratic time.*

Proof. Correctness is easy. We argue that the algorithm for a strongly connected component terminates in linear time. We can simply argue that step 2 is repeated at most three times. Each time step 2 is repeated, it means for one variable, there is unsatisfied self-loop. At least one bound (either lb or ub) reaches $-\infty$ or $+\infty$. With another application of step 2, we must have either reached the least solution, or one variable reaches $[-\infty, +\infty]$, thus the least solution $[-\infty, +\infty]$ for every variable. Because the transformation to basic constraints is quadratic and produces a quadratic size system, the total running time of our algorithm for solving constraints over multivariate affine functions is quadratic.

Finally, we consider constraints with multivariate affine functions and intersections with constant ranges. The constraints are of the general form $f(X_1, \cdots, X_n) \sqcap [c, d] \sqsubseteq X$. We essentially combine the algorithms for multivariate affine functions and intersection constraints to obtain an algorithm for this class of constraints. The interesting case is, as usual, that for a strongly connected component graph. The algorithm, in this case, is exactly the same as the one shown in Figure 7, except the constraints are reduced to basic constraints with intersections. The complexity analysis is based on the same idea as that for basic intersection constraints: with a repeated invocation of Step 2, one lb or ub must be reached. The new system resulted from transformation to basic constraints has a linear number of intersection bounds. Thus we only repeat the loop a linear number of times. However, the size of the new system may be quadratic in the original system. Thus, as the main result of the paper, we obtain a cubic time algorithm for intersection constraints over multivariate affine functions.

Theorem 3 (Main). *The system of constraints $f_i(X_1, \cdots, X_m) \sqcap [c_i, d_i] \sqsubseteq Y_i$, for $1 \le i \le n$, can be solved for their least solution in cubic time.*

4   Decidability and Hardness Results

One might ask whether we can lift the restriction, made earlier, that the right-hand sides be variables. We can thus consider constraints of the form $E_1 \sqsubseteq E_2$, where E_1 and E_2 are range expressions. The interesting question is to ask whether such a system of constraints is satisfiable.

We can show that deciding satisfiability for linear range constraints is NP-hard. The proof is via a reduction from integer linear programming, which is NP-hard [22].

Theorem 4. *The satisfiability problem for general range constraints of the form $E_1 \sqsubseteq E_2$ is NP-hard.*

Proof. We reduce integer linear programming to the satisfiability of range constraints. We simply need to express that a range has to be a singleton, *i.e.*, $[n, n]$ for some integer constant n. This can be easily expressed with the constraint $-Y_i + Y_i = [0, 0]$. One can verify that Y_i is a singleton if and only if this constraint is satisfied.

Let X be an integer linear programming instance. We have m range variables $Y_1, \ldots, Y_m$. For each $(\overline{x}, b) \in X$, we create a range constraint $x_1 Y_1 + \ldots + x_m Y_m \sqsubseteq [b, +\infty]$. We also add constraints of the form $-Y_i + Y_i = [0, 0]$ to ensure that each Y_i is a singleton. It is then straightforward to verify that X has a solution if and only if the constructed range constraints have a solution.

Analogous to Presburger arithmetic, we can consider the first-order theory of range constraints, which we call *Presburger range arithmetic*. By adapting the automata-theoretic proof of the decidability of Presburger arithmetic [37, 8], we can easily demonstrate the decidability of Presburger range arithmetic.

Theorem 5. *Presburger range arithmetic is decidable.*

If non-linear range constraints are allowed, the satisfiability problem becomes undecidable via a reduction from Hilbert's 10th Problem [24].

Theorem 6. *The satisfiability problem for non-linear range constraints is undecidable.*

5   Conclusions and Future Work

We have presented the first polynomial time algorithm for finding the optimal solution of constraints for a general class of integer range constraints with applications in program analysis and verification. The algorithm is based on a graph representation of the constraints. Because of the special structure of the range lattice, we are able to guarantee termination with the optimal solution in polynomial time. It is usually difficult to reason about the efficiency and precision of abstract interpretation-based techniques in general because of widenings and narrowings. Through a specialized algorithm, this work shows, for the first time, that "precise" range analysis (w.r.t. the constraints) is achievable in polynomial time. We suspect our techniques for treating non-distributive lattices to be of independent interest and may be adapted to design efficient algorithms for other constraint problems. Future work includes the handling of non-affine functions and floating point computations, and the application of the algorithm to detect buffer overruns and runtime exceptions such as overflows and underflows. It may be also interesting to extend this work to allow symbolic constants in the constraints. Finally, it is interesting to compare the efficiency and precision of an implementation of our algorithm with those algorithms based on widenings and narrowings.

Acknowledgments. We thank the anonymous reviewers of early versions of the paper for their helpful comments.

References

1. K.R. Apt. The essence of constraint propagation. *Theoretical Computer Science*, 221(1–2):179–210, June 1999.
2. K.R. Apt. The role of commutativity in constraint propagation algorithms. *ACM Transactions on Programming Languages and Systems*, 22(6):1002–1036, 2000.
3. B. Aspvall and Y. Shiloach. A polynomial time algorithm for solving systems of linear inequalities with two variables per inequality. *SIAM Journal on Computing*, 9(4):827–845, 1980.
4. F. Benhamou and W.J. Older. Applying interval arithmetic to real, integer, and Boolean constraints. *Journal of Logic Programming*, 32(1):1–24, July 1997.
5. W.W. Bledsoe. The Sup-Inf method in Presburger arithmetic. Technical report, University of Texas Math Dept., December 1974.
6. W. Blume and R. Eigenmann. The range test: A dependence test for symbolic, non-linear expressions. In *Supercomputing '94*. IEEE Computer Society, 1994.
7. W. Blume and R. Eigenmann. Symbolic range propagation. In *Proceedings of the 9th International Symposium on Parallel Processing (IPPS'95*, pages 357–363, Los Alamitos, CA, USA, April 1995. IEEE Computer Society Press.
8. A. Boudet and H. Comon. Diophantine equations, Presburger arithmetic and finite automata. In *Proceedings of Trees in Algebra and Programming (CAAP'96)*, volume 1059 of *Lecture Notes in Computer Science*, pages 30–43. Springer-Verlag, 1996.
9. F. Bourdoncle. Abstract debugging of higher-order imperative languages. In *SIGPLAN '93 Conference on Programming Language Design and Implementation*, pages 46–55, 1993.
10. P. Cousot and R. Cousot. Static determination of dynamic properties of programs. In *Proceedings of the 2nd International Symposium on Programming*, pages 106–130, 1976.
11. P. Cousot and R. Cousot. Abstract interpretation: A unified lattice model for static analysis of programs by construction or approximation of fixpoints. In *Proceedings of the 4th ACM Symposium on Principles of Programming Languages*, pages 234–252, 1977.
12. P. Cousot and R. Cousot. Abstract interpretation frameworks. *Journal of Logic and Computation*, 2(4):511–547, 1992.
13. P. Cousot and N. Halbwachs. Automatic discovery of linear restraints among variables of a program. In *Proceedings of the 5th ACM Symposium on Principles of Programming Languages*, pages 84–97, 1978.
14. C. Fecht and H. Seidl. A faster solver for general systems of equations. *Science of Computer Programming*, 35(2–3):137–161, November 1999.
15. R. Gupta. A fresh look at optimizing array bound checking. In *Proceedings of the Conference on Programming Language Design and Implementation*, pages 272–282, 1990.
16. R. Gupta. Optimizing array bound checks using flow analysis. *ACM Letters on Programming Languages and Systems*, 1(4):135–150, March-December 1994.
17. N. Heintze and J. Jaffar. A decision procedure for a class of Herbrand set constraints. In *Proceedings of the 5th Annual IEEE Symposium on Logic in Computer Science (LICS)*, pages 42–51, June 1990.
18. T.J. Hickey. Analytic constraint solving and interval arithmetic. In *Proceedings of the 27th ACM SIGPLAN-SIGACT Symposium on Principles of Programming Languages (POLP-00)*, pages 338–351, N.Y., January 19–21 2000.

19. T.J. Hickey, M.H. van Emden, and H. Wu. A unified framework for interval constraints and interval arithmetic. In *Principles and Practice of Constraint Programming*, pages 250–264, 1998.
20. J.P. Ignizio and T.M. Cavalier. *Introduction to Linear Programming*. Prentice-Hall, 1994.
21. J.B. Kam and J.D. Ullman. Global data flow analysis and iterative algorithms. *Journal of the ACM*, 23(1):158–171, January 1976.
22. R.M. Karp. Reducibility among combinatorial problems. In R. E. Miller and J. W. Thatcher, editors, *Complexity of Computer Computations*, pages 85–103. Plenum Press, New York, 1975.
23. G.A. Kildall. A unified approach to global program optimization. In *Conference Record of the ACM Symposium on Principles of Programming Languages*, pages 194–206. ACM SIGACT and SIGPLAN, 1973.
24. Y.V. Matijasevič. On recursive unsolvability of Hilbert's Tenth Problem. In Patrick Suppes et al., editors, *Logic, Methodology and Philosophy of Science IV*, volume 74 of *Studies in Logic and the Foundations of Mathematics*, pages 89–110, Amsterdam, 1973. North-Holland.
25. R.E. Moore. *Interval Analysis*. Prentice-Hall, Englewood Cliffs, NJ, New York, 1963.
26. G. Nelson. An $n^{\log n}$ algorithm for the two-variable-per-constraint linear programming satisfiability problem. Technical Report STAN-CS-78-689, Stanford University, 1978.
27. G. Nelson. Techniques for program verification. Technical Report CSL-81-10, Xerox Palo Alto Research Center, 1981.
28. W.J. Older and A. Velino. Constraint arithmetic on real intervals. In Frédéric Benhamou and Alain Colmerauer, editors, *Constraint Logic Programming: Selected Research*, pages 175–196. MIT Press, 1993.
29. Y. Paek, J. Hoeflinger, and D.A. Padua. Efficient and precise array access analysis. *ACM Transactions on Programming Languages and Systems*, 24(1):65–109, 2002.
30. V.R. Pratt. Two easy theories whose combination is hard. Unpublished manuscript, 1977.
31. W. Pugh. The omega test: a fast and practical integer programming algorithm for dependence analysis. *Communications of the ACM*, 35(8):102–114, August 1992.
32. W. Pugh. Constraint-based array dependence analysis. *ACM Transactions on Programming Languages and Systems*, 20(3):635–678, May 1998.
33. R. Seater and D. Wonnacott. Polynomial time array dataflow analysis. In *Languages and Compilers for Parallel Computing (LCPC)*, 2001.
34. R. Shostak. Deciding linear inequalities by computing loop residues. *Journal of the ACM*, 28(4):769–779, October 1981.
35. N. Suzuki and K. Ishihata. Implementation of an array bound checker. In *Conference Record of the Fourth ACM Symposium on Principles of Programming Languages*, pages 132–143, Los Angeles, California, January 17–19, 1977. ACM SIGACT-SIGPLAN.
36. D. Wagner, J.S. Foster, E.A. Brewer, and A. Aiken. A first step towards automated detection of buffer overrun vulnerabilities. In *Symposium on Network and Distributed Systems Security (NDSS '00)*, pages 3–17, San Diego, CA, February 2000. Internet Society.
37. P. Wolper and B. Boigelot. An automata-theoretic approach to presburger arithmetic constraints. In *Static Analysis Symposium*, pages 21–32, 1995.
38. H. Xi and F. Pfenning. Eliminating array bound checking through dependent types. In *Proceedings of the ACM SIGPLAN'98 Conference on Programming Language Design and Implementation (PLDI)*, pages 249–257, Montreal, Canada, 17–19 June 1998.

A Partial Order Semantics Approach to the Clock Explosion Problem of Timed Automata

D. Lugiez, P. Niebert, and S. Zennou

Laboratoire d'Informatique Fondamentale (LIF) de Marseille
Université de Provence – CMI
39, rue Joliot-Curie / F-13453 Marseille Cedex 13
{lugiez,niebert,zennou}@cmi.univ-mrs.fr

Abstract. We propose a new approach for the symbolic exploration of timed automata that solves a particular aspect of the combinatory explosion occurring in the widely used clock zone automata, the splitting of symbolic states depending on the order of transition occurrences, even if these transitions concern unrelated components in a parallel system. Our goal is to preserve independence (commutation of transitions) from the original timed automaton to the symbolic level, thus fully avoiding state splitting, yet avoiding problems of previous similar approaches with "maximal bounds abstraction". We achieve this goal by (1) lifting the theory of Mazurkiewicz traces to timed words and symbolic state exploration, (2) examining symbolic path exploration from a formal language point of view, and (3) by splitting the concerns of (abstraction free) successor computation and zone comparison by a new abstraction related to maximal bounds. The theory results in data structures and algorithms that we have experimentally validated, finding good reductions.

1 Introduction

Timed automata [AD94] are a powerful tool for the modeling and the analysis of timed systems. They extend classical automata by *clocks*, continuous variables "measuring" the flow of time. A state of a timed automaton is a combination of its discrete control location and the *clock values* taken from the real domain. While the resulting state space is infinite, *clock constraints* have been introduced to reduce the state spaces to a finite set of equivalence classes, thus yielding a finite (although often huge) symbolic state graph on which reachability and some other verification problems can be resolved. While the theory, algorithms and tools [NSY92,LPY95] for timed automata represent a considerable achievement (and indeed impressive industrial applications have been treated), the combinatory explosion particular to this kind of modelling and analysis – sometimes referred to as "clock explosions" (at the same time similar to and different from classical "state explosion") – remains a challenge for research and practice.

Among the approaches for improve the efficiency is the transfer of "partial order reduction methods" [God96] from the discret setting (where they are known to give good reductions) to the timed setting. Partial order methods basically

K. Jensen and A. Podelski (Eds.): TACAS 2004, LNCS 2988, pp. 296–311, 2004.

try to avoid redundant research by exploiting knowledge about the structure of the reachability graph, in particular *independence* of pairs of transitions of losely related parts of a complex system. Such pairs a and b commute, i.e. a state s allowing a sequence ab of transitions to state s' also allows ba and this sequence also leads to the same state s'. However, this kind of commutation is easily lost in classical symbolic analysis algorithms for timed automata, which represent sets of possible clock values by symbolic states: Consider two "independent" transitions a resetting clock $X := 0$, and b resetting clock $Y := 0$. Executing a first and then b means that afterwards (time may have elapsed) $X \geq Y$ whereas executing b first and then a implies that afterwards $X \leq Y$. The result of this is that in the algorithms used in tools like Uppaal and Kronos, ab and ba lead to *incomparable* states.

Previous works nevertheless trying to transfer partial order methods to the timed automata setting [DGKK98,BJLY98,Min99] have have tried to overcome this problem, e.g. [BJLY98,Min99] reestablish independence of the above transitions a and b by introducing the notion of *local time semantics*. The idea is that each component in a network has its own independent time progress, only when synchronisation occurs between two components, time is synchronised. The price is that clock differences in that model arbitrarily diverge, and that in general, this reestablished commutation leads to an unavoidably *infinite* state space (where the aim was reduction!), see Proposition 8. [BJLY98] therefore restrict the class of automata in order to allow finite bounds on the state space. However, practically almost always the resulting state spaces are considerably bigger than with the classical approach.

The present work takes a completely new viewpoint on the problem of non-commutation of symbolic transitions: First of all, we clean up the theory of **timed Mazurkiewicz traces**. Where a path in a timed automaton must satisfy timing constraints, we relax a crucial assumption that transitions occur in the same order sequentially and temporally: We restrict this requirement to dependent transitions. Our formalisation generalises "local time semantics" and also the partial formalisation given in [DT98]. We believe that this formalisation is a valuable contribution as such.

The second important step is a **language theoretic view** on the verification problem of timed automata. Rather than considering immediately the problem of "symbolic states", typically representing sets of clock values, we look at the problem of possible paths through the timed automaton and the implied Myhill-Nerode right congruence (as well as a corresponding preorder notion), which is known to be equivalent to minimal automata in classical language theory. Our understanding is that all previous automata based approaches to the reachability problem in timed automata is related to this Myhill-Nerode congruence, and attempts to avoid incomparable states (by better abstractions, etc.) aim to get closer to the actual Myhill-Nerode congruence. For the framework with commutation, the Myhill-Nerode congruence is typically of infinite index (see Proposition 8), whereas the classical interleaving approaches prove its finiteness for the interleaving case.

In the third part of our contribution, **the semantical basis of a new search algorithm**, we manage to get "the best of both worlds": We compute symbolic states with respect to the infinite index Myhill-Nerode congruence for the trace semantics (but avoiding state splitting for independent transitions), but we compare states with the finite index preorder (to cut branches in the search tree), **"catchup preorder"**, which is a right congruence for the classical interleaving semantics but obviously not for the relaxed semantics. It is closely related to *zone inclusion with maximal bounds abstra ction* in the classical setting and preserves paths in the interleaving semantics. We thus preserve the worst case bounds from classical clock zone algorithms and a good number of heuristic improvements that have been applied to improve those bounds carry over to our setting. The surprising fact that this approach is actually correct (i.e. yields exactly the same set of reachable control locations of the timed automaton as the standard semantics) relies on our timed Mazurkiewicz theory, which gives us for each timed word with relaxed constraints on the temporal order an equivalent path that does respect the stronger interleaving constraints.

The paper is structured as follows: In Section 2, we introduce the formal framework of clocked and timed words and the standard semantics of timed automata. In Section 3, we introduce Clocked and Timed Mazurkiewicz traces. In Section 4, we set up a plan of the subsequent construction in language theory terms and define equivalence relations of interest. In Section 5, we develop event zones as representation of the right congruence for realisable traces. In Section 6, we define the finite index catchup preorder and combine it with the event zone automaton of Section 5 for our reachability algorithm. In Section 7, we give some experimental results, which demonstrate the potential impact of our approach. Due to lack of space, all proofs had to be omitted. A long version with all proofs is available online as technical report [LNZ04].

2   Basics

In this section, we introduce basic notions of words, languages, automata, as well as their timed counterparts.

Words and Automata. Given an alphabet Σ of actions denoted by $a, b, c \ldots$, Σ^* denotes the set of words on Σ with ϵ the empty word. Words are denoted by $u, v, w \ldots$ and a non-empty word is some finite sequence $a_1 \ldots a_n$. The length of a word w is denoted by $|w|$. As usual a Σ-automaton $\mathcal{A}$ is a quadruple $(S, s_0, \rightarrow, F)$ where S is a set of states, $s_0 \in S$ is the initial state, $F \subseteq S$ is the set of final states and $\rightarrow \subseteq Q \times \Sigma \times Q$ is a set of transitions. The set $L(\mathcal{A})$ is the set of words accepted by $\mathcal{A}$. The automaton is *deterministic* if for each state s and action a there is a at most one $s' \in S$ such that $s \xrightarrow{a} s'$.

Timed words. In real time systems, we associate to each position i of a sequence of actions $w = a_1 \ldots a_n$ a time stamp which indicates when the corresponding action takes place. More precisely, a *timed word* is a pair (w, t) with $w \in \Sigma^*$ and t is a function assigning to each position of w an element of $\mathbb{R}^+$, the set of non-negative reals. For convenience, we set $t(0) = 0$ to be an additional time stamp for the beginning. In the literature, timed words are often represented as $(a_1, t_1), (a_2, t_2) \ldots$ i.e. $t(i)$ is replaced by t_i. A timed word is *normal* if $t(i) \le t(j)$ for $i \le j$ like in $(a, 3.2)(c, 4.5)(b, 6.3)$ but not in $(a, 3.2)(c, 2.5)(b, 6.3)$. Normal timed words represent temporally ordered sequences of events and serve as standard semantics of timed automata in the literature [AD94]. Concatenation of normal words is only a partial function and the set of normal words is thus a *partial monoid* only.

Clocked words. In a timed system, events can occur only if some time constraints are satisfied. In timed automata, *clocks* belong to some finite set $\mathcal{C}$ and are used to express the time constraints between an event that resets a clock and another event that refers to the clock. This leads to the introduction of *clocked labels* which are triples (action, constraints on clocks, set of reset clocks). The constraints permitted here associate to each clock an interval (min, max) which gives the set of possible values for the clock. The interval can be left-open, right-open, left-closed, right-closed and the bounds can be finite or infinite $-\infty, +\infty$. The interval $]-\infty, +\infty[$ means that no constraint exists and such constraints will not be written explicitly. To preserve decidability, all finite bounds are assumed to be integers (or syntactically more general: rational numbers). We are interested in finite subsets Δ of the infinite set of clocked labels, called clocked alphabets. A *clocked word* over Δ, usually denoted by ω, is simply a word in Δ^*.

Normal realisations of clocked words. In a clocked word $\omega = (a_1, c_1, r_1)(a_2, c_2, r_2)$ $\cdots (a_n, c_n, r_n)$ let $last_C(\omega)$ denote the last position m where the clock C is reset, i.e. s.t. $C \in r_m$ (for $(1 \le m \le n)$). We define $last_C(\omega) = 0$ if no such position exists (i.e. we assume that all clocks are reset at time position 0).

Definition 1. *A timed word (w, t) is a* normal realisation *of a clocked word* $\omega = \alpha_1 \ldots \alpha_m$ *with* $\alpha_i = (a_i, c_i, r_i)$, *iff (i) they have the same length $(|w| = m$) and the same action sequence $w(i) = a_i$ for $i \in \{1, \ldots, m\}$, (ii) (w, t) is normal, and (iii) for all prefixes $\alpha_1 \ldots \alpha_{k-1}$ and all clocks C with $l = last_C(\alpha_1 \ldots \alpha_{k-1})$, $t(k) - t(l) \in c_k(C)$, i.e. the time elapsed since the last reset of clock C before position k meets the interval constraint at position k.*

For instance the timed word $w = (a, 3.2)(c, 4)(b, 6.2)$ is a normal realisation of $\omega = \alpha\gamma\beta$ (as defined in Figure 1). A clocked word is *realisable* iff it has a normal realisation. We say that α is a *realisable extension* of ω if $\omega\alpha$ is realisable. The set of realisable clocked words over some clocked alphabet is closed under the prefix relation. A *timed automaton* is a Δ-automaton for some clocked alphabet Δ, as in Figure 1 (where all states are final). The language of a timed automaton $\mathcal{A}$ is denoted by $L(\mathcal{A})$, and the *timed language* $L_T(\mathcal{A})$ of $\mathcal{A}$ is the set $\{(w, t) \mid (w, t)$ is a normal realisation of some $\omega \in L(\mathcal{A})\}$. On the level of clocked words, let L_N be the language of realisable clocked words accepted by $\mathcal{A}$. For instance $(a, 3.2)(c, 4)(b, 6.2) \in L_T(\mathcal{A})$ is a normal realisation of $\alpha\gamma\beta \in L_N(\mathcal{A})$.

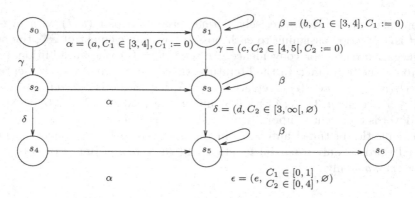

Fig. 1. A timed automaton

3   Clocked and Timed Mazurkiewicz Traces

As a representation of concurrency, we introduce an independence relation and generalise the theory of Mazurkiewicz traces to the timed setting. We first recall the basics of Mazurkiewicz trace theory in the untimed case. For an exhaustive treatment see [DR95].

Independence Relation and Traces. For an alphabet Σ, an *independence relation* is a symmetric and irreflexive relation $I_\Sigma \subseteq \Sigma \times \Sigma$. We call (Σ, I_Σ) a *partially commutative alphabet*. For convenience, we also use the dependence relation $D_\Sigma = \Sigma \times \Sigma - I_\Sigma$, which is reflexive and symmetric. As a representation of parallel systems we assume without loss of generality that $\Sigma = \bigcup_{i=1}^{l} \Sigma_i$ where $a\, D_\Sigma\, b$ iff $a, b \in \Sigma_i$ for some $i \in \{1, \dots, l\}$. We call $(\Sigma_1, \dots, \Sigma_l)$ a *distributed alphabet* of (Σ, I_Σ) and Σ_i a *component*. For convenience, we call the set $\{1, \dots, l\}$ "*Comp*" (for components). For instance $(\Sigma_1 = \{a, b, e\}, \Sigma_2 = \{c, d, e\})$ is a distributed alphabet corresponding to $\Sigma = \{a, b, c, d, e\}$ and an independence relation $I_\Sigma = \{(a, c), (c, a), (b, c), (c, b), (a, d), (d, a), (b, d), (d, b)\}$. It is well known that every partially commutative alphabet corresponds to a distributed alphabet and conversely. Intuitively, I_Σ represents concurrency between actions, whereas the distributed alphabet proposes as explanation of concurrency occurrence on distinct processes in a distributed system. In order to reference actions or locations depending on an action we define $dep(a) = \{b \in \Sigma \mid a\, D_\Sigma\, b\}$ and $loc(a) = \{i \mid a \in \Sigma_i\}$. It is obvious that $dep(a) = \bigcup_{i \in loc(a)} \Sigma_i$. In analogy to last occurrences of clock resets, we define $last_i(a_1 \dots a_n)$, the *last occurrence* of an action of the component Σ_i, as the maximal k such that $a_k \in \Sigma_i$, if such a k exists, otherwise $last_i(a_1 \dots a_n) = 0$. For instance, $last_1(acb) = 3$ and $last_2(acb) = 2$ for $(\Sigma_1 = \{a, b, e\}, \Sigma_2 = \{c, d, e\})$.

The *Mazurkiewicz trace equivalence* associated to the partially commutative alphabet (Σ, I_Σ) is the least congruence $\simeq_M$ over Σ^* such that $ab \simeq_M ba$ for any pair of independent actions $a\ I_\Sigma\ b$. A *trace* $[u]$ is the congruence class of a word $u \in \Sigma^*$. We denote by $\mathbb{M}(\Sigma, I_\Sigma)$ the set of all traces w.r.t. (Σ, I_Σ). Before adapting these notions to the timed setting, we give the connection between independence relations and automata as a condition on transition relations:

Definition 2 (asynchronous automaton). *An* asynchronous automaton *over* (Σ, I_Σ) *is a deterministic Σ-automaton such that the following two properties hold for any two letters $a, b \in \Sigma$ with $a\ I_\Sigma\ b$:*

ID: $s \xrightarrow{a} s_1 \xrightarrow{b} s_2$ *implies* $s \xrightarrow{b} s_1' \xrightarrow{a} s_2$ *for some state* s_1' [Independent Diamond]

FD: $s \xrightarrow{a} s_1$ *and* $s \xrightarrow{b} s_1'$ *implies* $s_1 \xrightarrow{b} s_2$ *for some state* s_2 [Forward Diamond]

The theoretical foundation of many partial order reduction approaches relies on the fact that the languages of asynchronous automata are closed with respect to equivalent words.Intuitively, two words are equivalent with respect to $\simeq_M$ iff they can be obtained from each other by repeatedly exchanging adjacent independent letters, as stated by the following lemma:

Lemma 3. *Let (Σ, I_Σ) be a partially commutative alphabet and $a_1 \dots a_n \simeq_M b_1 \dots b_n$ be two equivalent words. There exists a uniquely determined permutation $\pi : \{1, \dots, n\} \to \{1, \dots, n\}$, such that $a_i = b_{\pi(i)}$ and for $a_i\ D_\Sigma\ a_j$ we have $i < j$ iff $\pi(i) < \pi(j)$. Conversely, let $a_1 \dots a_n$ be a word and $\pi : \{1, \dots, n\} \to \{1, \dots, n\}$ be a permutation of indices such that for each pair i, j $a_i\ D_\Sigma\ a_j$ we have $i < j$ iff $\pi(i) < \pi(j)$. Then $a_{\pi(1)} \dots a_{\pi(n)} \simeq_M a_1 \dots a_n$. For convenience, we assume π to be defined on 0 with $\pi(0) = 0$.*

Generalisation to Clocked Words

Timed traces. The independence relation I_Σ immediately carries over to (non normal) timed words. The resulting congruence classes are called *timed traces*. Here, the exchange of two independent actions also exchanges their time stamps, e.g. $(a, 3.2)(b, 3.5)(c, 6.3) \simeq_M (a, 3.2)(c, 6.3)(b, 3.5)$ where $b\ I_\Sigma\ c$, which means that normality (temporal order of actions) is not preserved under commutation. Therefore we introduce a weaker notion of normality: a timed word (w, t) is I_Σ-*normal* iff for any two letters $a = w(i), b = w(j)$ with $i \le j$ **and additionally** $a\ D_\Sigma\ b$ we have $t(i) \le t(j)$. This relaxed normality condition is preserved under Mazurkiewicz equivalence, allowing to define normality on the level of traces: We call a timed trace $[(w, t)]$ I_Σ-*normal* iff (w, t) is I_Σ-normal.

Proposition 4. *Every I_Σ-normal timed word (w, t) is equivalent to a normal timed word (w', t').*

Independence for clocked words. To extend the independence relation I_Σ to clocked words, we define $I_\Delta \subseteq \Delta \times \Delta$ based on I_Σ as follows: $(a_1, c_1, r_1)\ I_\Delta$ (a_2, c_2, r_2) iff (i) $a\ I_\Sigma\ b$, (ii) $r_1 \cap r_2 = \emptyset$ and (iii) For all $C \in r_1$ we have $c_2(C) =]-\infty, \infty[$ and conversely for all $C \in r_2$ we have $c_1(C) =]-\infty, \infty[$.

Intuitively, conditions (ii) and (iii) arise from the view of clocks as shared variables in concurrent programming: An action resetting a clock is writing it whereas an action with a non-trivial condition on a clock is reading it. The restriction states that two actions are dependent if both are writing the same variable or one is writing a variable the other one is reading it. We call the (Δ, I_Δ) constructed in this way a *partially commutative clocked alphabet* and say that I_Δ respects I_Σ. The notion of traces and equivalence $\simeq_M$ are defined as for I_Σ.

For the rest of the paper, we will silently assume some partially commutative clocked alphabet (Δ, I_Δ). If clear from the context, we write I instead of I_Δ. Relaxing the notion of normal realisations, the following definition establishes the relation between clocked words and I-normal timed words.

Definition 5 (I_Δ-normal realisation). *Let* $\omega = \alpha_1 \ldots \alpha_n$ *with* $\alpha_j = (a_j, c_j, r_j)$ *be a clocked word over* (Δ, I_Δ). *A timed word* (w, t) I_Δ-*realises* ω *iff (i) (same length and actions)* $|\omega| = |w|$, *for* $j = 1, \ldots, |w|$ *we have* $w(j) = a_j$, *(ii) (normality)* (w, t) *is* I_Σ-*normal, (iii) (satisfaction of constraints) for all prefixes* $\alpha_1 \ldots \alpha_{k-1}$ *and all clocks* C *with* $l = last_C(\alpha_1 \ldots \alpha_{k-1})$ $t(k) - t(l) \in c_k(C)$. *In that case, we also say that* ω *is* I_Δ-*realisable and by extension that* $[(w, t)]$ *is a* I_Δ-*realisation of* ω.

For instance, the timed word $(c, 4)(a, 3.2)(b, 6.2)$ I_Δ-realises the clocked word $\gamma\alpha\beta$ (for the automaton in Figure 1, assuming α I_Δ γ). The main result of this section establishes the tight link between clocked and timed traces, in particular it shows that I-realisability is invariant under trace equivalence, allowing in principle the exploration of realisable clocked words on representatives.

Theorem 6. *Let* $\alpha_1 \ldots \alpha_n \simeq_M \beta_1 \ldots \beta_n$ *be two equivalent clocked words over* (Δ, I_Δ) *and* π *be the permutation as defined in Lemma 3. Then* $(b_1, t_1) \ldots (b_n, t_n)$ *is an* I-*normal realisation of* $\beta_1 \ldots \beta_n$ *iff* $(b_{\pi(1)}, t_{\pi(1)}) \ldots (b_{\pi(n)}, t_{\pi(n)})$ *is an* I-*normal realisation of* $\alpha_1 \ldots \alpha_n$.

Applications to the verification problem. In analogy to the definition of $L_N(\mathcal{A})$ let $L_I(\mathcal{A})$ denote the set of I-realisable clocked words accepted by $\mathcal{A}$. It is straightforward by definition that $L_T(\mathcal{A}) = \emptyset$ iff $L_N(\mathcal{A}) = \emptyset$ iff $L_I(\mathcal{A}) = \emptyset$, so that we can check this emptiness problem equivalently for either language. The important aspect of $L_I(\mathcal{A})$ is that it is closed under equivalence as expressed in the following corollary of Theorem 6:

Corollary 7. *Let* $\omega \simeq_M \omega'$ *be equivalent clocked words, then* ω *is* I-*realisable iff* ω' *is* I-*realisable and* $\omega \in L_I(\mathcal{A})$ *iff* $\omega' \in L_I(\mathcal{A})$. *If* $\omega \in L_I(\mathcal{A})$ *then there exists* $\omega' \simeq_M \omega$ *such that* $\omega' \in L_N(\mathcal{A})$.

This observation gives rise to the hope that partial order reduction techniques could be applied when checking for emptiness of $L_I(\mathcal{A})$. However, as explained in the following sections, this language cannot always be represented by a finite automaton and we need more sophisticated methods to solve this problem.

4   A Language Theoretic View

Our primary goal is to build a finite automaton for the language $L_I(\mathcal{A}) = \{\omega \mid \omega$ I-realisable and $\omega \in L(\mathcal{A})\}$, which yields an immediate way to decide the emptiness of the language. For any language, the classical way to build an automaton is to consider the Myhill-Myhill-Nerode right-congruence which yields the minimal automaton accepting the language (the states are the equivalence classes of the congruence)[1]. In our case the relevant congruence would be [2] $\omega_1 \simeq_I \omega_2$ iff $\omega_1 \lesssim_I \omega_2$ and $\omega_2 \lesssim_I \omega_1$ where $\omega_1 \lesssim_I \omega_2$ iff $\forall \omega, \omega_1 \omega$ I-realisable implies $\omega_2 \omega$ I-realisable. By definition $\simeq_M \subseteq \lesssim_I$, which justifies to write $[\omega_1] \lesssim_I [\omega_2]$. Unfortunately, this congruence is not of finite index:

Proposition 8. *There exist finite Δ for which $\lesssim_I$ and $\simeq_I$ are of infinite index.*

Proof. Let $\alpha = (a, X \in [1,1], X := 0)$, $\beta = (b, Y \in [1,1], Y := 0)$, $\gamma = (c, X \in [1,1], Y \in [1,1], Y := 0)$ with $\alpha I \beta$. Then for $i \neq j$ we have that $\alpha^i \not\lesssim_I \alpha^j$, because the extension $\omega = \beta^i \gamma$ make $\alpha^i \beta^i \gamma$ I-realisable whereas $\alpha^j \beta^i \gamma$ is not I-realisable. $\qquad\square$

This ruins our primary goal and explains why we use an indirect and complex approach to decide $L_I(\mathcal{A}) \overset{?}{=} \emptyset$. Keeping the Myhill-Nerode congruence idea in mind, we define several relations which help understanding the problems and that provide constructions similar to zones for timed automata while preserving properties of realizable traces. Again the resulting automaton is infinite but we define a relation on zones which has a finite index and allows to decide the emptiness of $L_I(\mathcal{A})$ in a finite amount of time. Given some language L, a *right-precongruence* is a relation $\lesssim_L$ such that $u \lesssim_L v$ iff $\forall w$, if $uw \in L$ implies $vw \in L$. The obvious link with $\simeq_L$ is $\simeq_L = (\lesssim_L \cap \gtrsim_L)$. The index of a preorder $\lesssim$ is by definition the index of the equivalence $\lesssim \cap \gtrsim$. We describe now all the relations that we use, apart $\lesssim_I$ and $\simeq_I$ that are already defined.

Definition 9 $(\lesssim_N, \simeq_N, \lesssim_{IN}, \simeq_{IN})$. *For clocked words ω_1, ω_2, let*

- $\omega_1 \lesssim_N \omega_2$ *iff $\forall \omega$, if $\omega_1 \omega$ has a normal realisation then $\omega_2 \omega$ has a normal realisation. In general $\simeq_M \not\subseteq \lesssim_N$, so $\lesssim_N$ cannot be lifted to traces and is given for comparisons only.*
- $\omega_1 \lesssim_{IN} \omega_2$ *iff $\forall \omega$ if there exists $\omega_1' \simeq_M \omega_1$ such that $\omega_1' \omega$ has a normal realisation, then there exists $\omega_2' \simeq_M \omega_2$ such that $\omega_2' \omega$ has a normal realisation. We define $\omega_1 \simeq_{IN} \omega_2$ by $\omega_1 \lesssim_{IN} \omega_2$ and $\omega_2 \lesssim_{IN} \omega_1$. This relation still concerns normal realization, but weakens $\lesssim_N$ by forgetting the interleaving of the past.*
- $\lesssim_{EZ}$ *(defined in section 5) is defined in terms of difference constraints sets generated by clock constraints and can be seen as an implementation of $\lesssim_I$ since $\lesssim_{EZ} \subseteq \lesssim_I$.*

---

[1] but this automaton is finite for regular languages only!
[2] for simplicity we forget momentarily the finite automaton $\mathcal{A}$

– $\lesssim_C$ is defined from $\lesssim_{EZ}$ and can be seen as an implementation of $\lesssim_{IN}$ since $\lesssim_C \subseteq \lesssim_{IN}$.

The relations $\lesssim_I, \lesssim_{EZ}$ are precongruences that are used to define automata, but they may have infinite index while $\lesssim_{IN}, \lesssim_C$ have finite index but may not be precongruences. Their properties are summarized in Figure 2

finite index not (pre)congruence	$\lesssim_C$	$\subseteq$	$\lesssim_{IN}$
	UI		UI
(pre)congruence not finite index	$\simeq_M \subseteq$ $\lesssim_{EZ}$	$\subseteq$	$\lesssim_I$

Fig. 2. Right preorders for clocked traces

The proof of Proposition 8 supports the claim that $\lesssim_{IN}$ is not a precongruence: $\alpha\alpha \simeq_{IN} \alpha\alpha\alpha$, but $\alpha\alpha\beta \not\simeq_{IN} \alpha\alpha\alpha\beta$. However, the relation $\lesssim_{IN}$ is a crucial tool for solving $L_I(\mathcal{A}) \overset{?}{=} \emptyset$ because (i) the inclusion $\lesssim_I \subseteq \lesssim_{IN}$ holds (see Proposition 17) provided some slight assumptions on the alphabet Δ, (ii) it is of finite index, (iii) it preserves the non-emptiness of $L_I(\mathcal{A})$ (in a weak sense). The relations $\lesssim_{EZ}, \lesssim_C$ represent the computational aspects of our approach and give an effective way to approximate the relations $\lesssim_I$ and $\lesssim_{IN}$.

A similar approach underlies the theory of timed automata: the language of the realisable clocked words $L_N(\mathcal{A})$ of an automaton $\mathcal{A}$ is represented by a *zone automaton* and the constructions given in the litterature can be understood as computating precongruences $\lesssim_{ZA} \subseteq \lesssim_{L_N(\mathcal{A})}$. These precongruences may have (many) more states that the ideal $\lesssim_{L_N(\mathcal{A})}$ and works for improving timed automata constructions can often be seen as tentatives to get closer to $\lesssim_{L_N(\mathcal{A})}$. But whatever the finite size of these zone automata, they prove that $\lesssim_{L_N(\mathcal{A})}$ is of finite index. The reader should notice that the bound that we get for the index of $\lesssim_C$ in Proposition 19 is remarquably close to the bound for the number of clock zones of classical timed automata.

5   Event Zones for the Representation of $\lesssim_I$

This section is devoted to the construction of $\lesssim_{EZ}$ and $\simeq_{EZ}$ with *event zones*. The aim is to obtain a right precongruence reasonably close to $\lesssim_I$ that allows efficient data structures and algorithms for the representation of congruence classes and for testing $\lesssim_{EZ}$. Difference constraint sets provide the tool needed to achieve this goal, leading to the construction of an *event zone automaton*, which specifies the set of I-realisable traces. This automaton may still be infinite and section 6 will show how to decide emptiness of the accepted language.

Difference Constraint Sets. Difference constraint sets are set of inequations of the form $x - y \leq c$ or $x - y < c$ where x and y are real valued variables and c is a numerical constant (a rational number or an integer). We represent a different constraint by a graph (the incidence matrix of which is a Difference Bounds Matrix, DBM): the variables are the vertices and there is an edge from x_i and x_j labelled by $c, \leq$ (resp. $c, <$) iff $x_i - x_j \leq c$ (resp. $x_i - x_j < c$) is one of the constraints (when several constraints relate the same variables, we choose the stricter one). The graph is completed by adding the constraints $x - x \leq 0$ for every x and $x_i - x_j < +\infty$ when no constraints $x_i - x_j \leq c$ (or $x_i - x_j < c$) exist. A solution is a valuation from the set of variables to $\mathbb{R}$ which satisfies all the constraints. Since constraints are differences there is a solution iff there is a positive solution (all variables are ≥ 0). A difference constraint set is consistent iff it has one solution. Figure 3 gives a difference constraint set corresponding to the clocked word $\alpha\beta$ of the timed automaton of Figure 1.

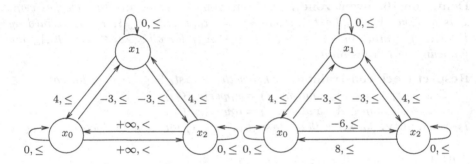

Fig. 3. A difference constraint set (left) and its closure (right).

We define $\oplus$ on pairs $(c, \prec)$ by $(c_1, \prec_1) \oplus (c_2, \prec_2) = (c_1 + c_2, \prec_1)$ if $\prec_1 = \prec_2$ and $(c_1 + c_2, <)$ otherwise. The *closure* of a difference constraint set (V, E) is the difference constraint set $(V, E') = Cl(V, E)$ such that $E'(x, y) = min\{E(x_1, x_2) \oplus \ldots \oplus E(x_{p-1}, x_p) \mid x = x_1, \ldots, x_p = y \in V\}$, i.e. the length of the shortest path from x to y if it exists, $-\infty, <$ otherwise. The closure of the previous difference constraint graph is given in Figure 3 (right part).

The closure can be computed by an all pairs shortest path algorithm such as Floyd-Warshall [CLR90]. The *projection* $\Pi_{V'}$ of (V, E) on $V' \subseteq V$ is the difference constraint set (V', E') such that $E'(x, y) = E(x, y)$ for $x, y \in V'$. The figure at right gives the projection on $\{x_0, x_2\}$ of the closure of the difference graph of Figure 3. Projection is normally only a sensible operation on closed constraint sets (i.e. such that $Cl(V, E) = (V, E)$).

Event Zones and the $\lesssim_{EZ}$ Relation. In this subsection, the link between clocked words and difference constraint sets is done in the context of I-normality via *event zones*. Then the right precongruence $\lesssim_{EZ}$ is defined and some properties of Figure 2 are proved.

Let I be an independence relation which respects I_Σ, the independence relation for some distributed alphabet $\Sigma = (\Sigma_1, \ldots, \Sigma_l)$. Let $\omega = \alpha_1 \ldots \alpha_n$ be some fixed clocked word with $\alpha_i = (a_i, c_i, r_i)$. For each position i of ω we associate an event variable x_i which corresponds to a time stamp, plus an additional x_0 for the initial stamp. Since the arrows in difference constraint graphs are couples (constant, sign), we need functions extracting from the clock constraint intervals the upper and lower (actually its opposite) bounds together with their sign:

$$upper((c_1, c_2[) = (c_2, <) \text{ and } upper((c_1, c_2]) = (c_2, \leq)$$
$$lower(]c_1, c_2)) = (-c_1, <) \text{ and } lower([c_1, c_2)) = (-c_1, \leq) \text{ (note the } - \text{ sign)}$$

Definition 10 (event zone). *The* event zone Z_ω *associated to a clocked word ω is a triple* $(V_\omega, E_\omega, Last_\omega)$ *where* $V_\omega = \{x_0, x_1, \ldots, x_{|\omega|}\}$, E_ω *is defined by* $E_\omega(x_i, x_j) = min\{(m, \prec) \mid x_i - x_j \prec m \in A_\omega\}$ *for all* $x_i, x_j \in V$ *with* A_ω *the following set of constraints:*

Respect clock constraints: *for k, l with $l = last_C(\alpha_1 \ldots \alpha_{k-1})$ for some $C \in$*
$\mathcal{C}$ $x_k - x_l \prec m \in A_\omega$ *and* $(m, \prec) = upper(c_k(C))$
    $x_l - x_k \prec m \in A_\omega$ *and* $(m, \prec) = lower(c_k(C))$
I_Σ**-normality:** *for k, l with $l = last_i(a_1 \ldots a_{k-1})$ for some $i \in loc(a_k)$ $x_l - x_k \leq$ $0 \in A_\omega$*
Totality: $x_i - x_i \leq 0 \in A_\omega$ *and* $x_i - x_j < +\infty \in A_\omega$.

and $Last_\omega : \mathcal{C} \cup Comp \rightarrow V_\omega$ *is the function which gives the last event variable occurrence of a clock C or an action of Σ_i i.e.* $Last_\omega(C) = x_i$ *such that* $i = last_C(\omega)$ *and* $Last_\omega(i) = x_j$ *such that* $j = last_i(\omega)$.

The difference constraint set associated to Z_ω is $S_\omega = (V_\omega, E_\omega)$. The closure of the zone $Z_\omega = (V_\omega, E_\omega, Last_\omega)$ is simply $Cl(Z_\omega) = (Cl(V_\omega, E_\omega), Last_\omega)$ and the projection is $\Pi_{V'}(Z_\omega) = (\Pi_{V'}(V_\omega, E_\omega), Last_\omega)$. A zone Z_ω is *consistent* iff its associated difference constraint set S_ω is consistent. By construction a zone Z_ω is consistent iff ω is I-realisable.

Definition 11 (event zone precongruence). *Let ω_1, ω_2 be two clocked words over Δ and $Cl(Z_{\omega_1}) = (V_1, E_1, Last_1), Cl(Z_{\omega_2}) = (V_2, E_2, Last_2)$ be the closure of their respective event zones. The event zone precongruence is defined in the following way: $Z_{\omega_1} \lesssim_{EZ} Z_{\omega_2}$ iff Z_{ω_1} and Z_{ω_2} are both inconsistent or Z_{ω_1} is inconsistent and Z_{ω_2} is consistent or else there are both consistent and for all $\xi_1, \xi_2 \in \mathcal{C} \cup Comp, E_1(Last_1(\xi_1), Last_1(\xi_2)) \leq E_2(Last_2(\xi_1), Last_2(\xi_2))$.*

We define $\omega_1 \lesssim_{EZ} \omega_2$ iff $Z_{\omega_1} \lesssim_{EZ} Z_{\omega_2}$ and we get the following properties:

Proposition 12. *Let ω_1, ω_2 be two clocked words. Then (i) $\omega_1 \simeq_M \omega_2$ implies $\omega_1 \lesssim_{EZ} \omega_2$, (ii) $\lesssim_{EZ}$ is a right precongruence, (iii) $\omega_1 \lesssim_{EZ} \omega_2$ implies $\omega_1 \lesssim_I \omega_2$.*

The Event Zone Automaton. For the construction of an automaton we define the notion of zone extension.

Definition 13. *An extension of an event zone* $Z_\omega = (V = \{x_0, \ldots, x_n\}, E, Last)$ *of* ω *by* $\alpha = (a, c, r) \in \Delta$, *denoted* $Z_\omega \odot \alpha$, *is the triple* $(V', E', Last')$ *such that:* (i) **The difference constraint set is extended:** $V' = V \cup \{x_{n+1}\}$ *and* E' *is defined by:*
$E'(x_i, x_j) = E(x_i, x_j)$ *for all* $x_i, x_j \neq x_{n+1}$,
$E'(x_{n+1}, x_i) = min\{(m, \prec) \mid x_{n+1} - x_i \prec m \in A_{\omega \odot \alpha}\}$
$E'(x_i, x_{n+1}) = min\{(m, \prec) \mid x_i - x_{n+1} \prec m \in A_{\omega \odot \alpha}\}$
with $A_{\omega \odot \alpha}$ *the following set of difference constraints:*

clock constraint condition: For all $x_l = Last(C)$ *with* C *a clock,*
   $x_{n+1} - x_l \prec m \in A_{\omega \odot \alpha}$ *and* $(m, \prec) = upper(c(C))$
   $x_l - x_{n+1} \prec m \in A_{\omega \odot \alpha}$ *and* $(m, \prec) = lower(c(C))$
I_Σ-*normality: For all* $x_l = Last(i)$ *with* $i \in loc(a)$ $x_l - x_{n+1} \le 0 \in A_{\omega \odot \alpha}$
totality: for all $x_i \in V$, $x_i - x_{n+1} \le +\infty, x_{n+1} - x_i \le +\infty \in A_{\omega \odot \alpha}$,
   and $x_{n+1} - x_{n+1} \le 0 \in A_{\omega \odot \alpha}$.

(ii) **Last occurrences are updated:** *if* $i \in loc(a)$ *then* $Last'(i) = x_{n+1}$, *if* $C \in r$ *then* $Last'(C) = x_{n+1}$, *otherwise* $Last'(\xi) = Last(\xi)$.

By definition, we get $Z_\omega \odot \alpha \simeq_{EZ} Z_{\omega \alpha}$. Event zones have an unbounded number of variables but only the variables representing the last occurrences of events are relevant. Let $last(Z_\omega)$ denote the projection of the closed zone $Cl(Z_\omega) = Cl(V_\omega, E_\omega, Last_\omega)$ on V_{last}, the codomain of $Last_\omega$. That is $last(Z_\omega) = \Pi_{V_{last}}(Cl(V_\omega, E_\omega), Last_\omega)$. As an example, $last(Z_{\alpha\beta})$ ($Z_{\alpha\beta}$ is depicted on the left part of Figure 3) is the projection of the closure $Cl(Z_{\alpha\beta})$ (right part of Figure 3) on the set $V_{last} = \{x_0, x_2\}$ (Figure below the Figure 3). This projection behaves well with respect to extension and $\precsim_{EZ}$:

Proposition 14. *Let* Z *be a consistent event zone and* α *be a clocked label. Then* $last(Z \odot \alpha) \simeq_{EZ} last(last(Z) \odot \alpha)$.

This justifies the use of $last(Z)$ to define the event automaton in the following construction where $\mathcal{Z}$ denotes the set of event zones over Δ and Z_ϵ is the special event zone $(V_\epsilon, E_\epsilon, Last_\epsilon)$ associated to the empty word such that $V_\epsilon = \{x_0\}$ (the initial time stamp), $E(x_0, x_0) = (0, \le)$ and $Last(\xi) = x_0$ for all $\xi \in C \cup Comp$ (everything is reset).

Definition 15 (event zone automaton). *The event zone automaton* $\mathcal{A}' = (S', s_0', \to', F')$ *associated to an asynchronous timed automaton* $\mathcal{A} = (S, s_0, \to, F)$ *is such that* $S' = S \times \mathcal{Z}/_{\simeq_{EZ}}$, *couples of discrete states and (quotients of) event zones, the initial state is* $s_0' = (s_0, [Z_0])$, *the set of final states is* $F' = \{(s, Z) \mid s \in F\}$ *and the transition relation* $\to' : S' \times \Delta \hookrightarrow S'$, *is defined by* $(s, [Z]) \overset{\alpha}{\to} (s_1, [Z_1])$ *iff* $s \overset{\alpha}{\to} s_1$ *is in* $\mathcal{A}$ *and* $Z_1 = last(Z \odot \alpha)$ *is consistent.*

Proposition 16. *The event zone automaton for an asynchronous timed automaton is an asynchronous timed automaton accepting exactly the clocked words having an I-realisation.*

6   Catchup Preorder for Language Emptiness Checking

In this section we introduce the *catchup preorder*, closely related to the maximal bounds abstraction used in classical timed automata algorithms and a very important aspect of our approach. Based on it, we then give an algorithm to decide the emptiness of timed automata languages.

Catchup preorder and equivalence. First we introduce a useful technical tool: the separator action \$. A separator \$ is an element of Δ such that the constraints are trivial (no conditions on any clocks), the reset set is empty, and for all $\alpha \in \Delta$ it holds that $\alpha \not\!\! I \$$. Any clocked alphabet Δ can be extended to a clocked alphabet Δ' containing a separator (either there is one already in Δ or we simply add one). This extension preserves the semantics: if $\omega_1 \lesssim_I \omega_2$ in Δ', then $\omega_1 \lesssim_I \omega_2$ in Δ. From now on, we assume that Δ contains such a separator \$. All previous results holds independently of the existence of \$, but it is used in the proof of the next proposition:

Proposition 17. *If Δ contains a separator \$, then $\lesssim_I \subseteq \lesssim_{IN}$.*

Definition 18 (catchup simulation of event zones). *Let ω_1, ω_2 be two clocked words and let $Z_{\omega_1\$} = (V_1, E_1, Last_1)$ and $Z_{\omega_2\$} = (V_2, E_2, Last_2)$ the event zones for $\omega_1\$, \omega_2\$$ respectively, where \$ is a separator. Moreover, for all pairs $\xi_1 \in C$, $\xi_2 \in C \cup \{1\}$ ($1 \in Comp^3$):*

- *$E_1(Last_1(\xi_1), Last_1(\xi_2)) \leq E_2(Last_2(\xi_1), Last_2(\xi_2))$; or*
- *$E_1(Last_1(\xi_1), Last_1(1))$, $E_2(Last_2(\xi_1), Last_2(1))$ (constraint between clock reset events and the separator) are both strictly smaller than $(-c, \leq)$ for the greatest non-trivial upper bound $(c, \leq)$ for ξ_1 in Δ (upper catchup); or*
- *both $E_1(Last_1(\xi_1), Last_1(\xi_2))$, $E_2(Last_2(\xi_1), Last_2(\xi_2))$ greater or equal to the opposite of the biggest lower bound for ξ_2 in Δ (lower catchup).*

Then we write that $\omega_1 \lesssim_C \omega_2$ (and say that ω_2 catchup simulates ω_1). Moreover $\omega_1 \simeq_C \omega_2$ (catchup equivalent) iff $\omega_1 \lesssim_C \omega_2$ and $\omega_2 \lesssim_C \omega_1$.

The intuition is that we abstract event zone extensions that occur in the past of already present event (e.g. events that would have occurred before the separator in the second rule). We consider such events as *late* and catching up. The second rule addresses bounds relevant to upper bounds of clocks (*upper catchup*), the third rule addresses bounds relevant to lower bounds (*lower catchup*).

Theorem 19. *$\lesssim_C \subseteq \lesssim_{IN}$ and the index of $\simeq_C$ is smaller than $(4K + 3)^{n(n+1)}$ where n is the number of clocks and K is the biggest constant mentioned in constraints.*

---

[3] This choice is arbitrary, the last action for any component is \$

An algorithm to decide the emptiness of $L_I(\mathcal{A})$. The description of the algorithm uses traces for readability, but the actual implementation relies on event zones. The set of traces is partionned into *white traces* that are not visited yet, *gray traces* that await exploration, *black traces* that have been explored, and *red traces* that have been rejected because of catchup equivalence. This last set is convenient for the correctness proof only and is useless in the implementation. The algorithm is generic and doesn't rely on the particular method used to explore traces. The key point for ensuring termination is the finite index of the relation $\lesssim_C$. The actual implementation uses several technical improvments that we do not describe because of the lack of space.

Algorithm 1 Generic exploration algorithm

Gray $\leftarrow \{[\epsilon]\}$, Black $\leftarrow \emptyset$, Red $\leftarrow \emptyset$
while Gray $\neq \emptyset$ **do**
    Choose $[\omega] \in$ Gray, Gray $\leftarrow$ Gray $\setminus \{[\omega]\}$, Black $\leftarrow$ Black $\cup \{\omega\}$
    for all $\omega' = \omega\alpha$ with $(s_\omega, \alpha, s_{\omega\alpha}) \in \to$ and $Z_{\omega\alpha}$ consistent **do**
        if $\exists[\omega''] \in$ Black $\cup$ Gray.$s_{\omega'} = s_{\omega''}$ and $\omega' \lesssim_C \omega''$ /* or weaker $\simeq_C$ */**then**
            Red $\leftarrow$ Red $\cup \{[\omega']\}$
        end if
    end for
end while
return *"empty"*

Theorem 20. *For an asynchronous timed automaton $\mathcal{A}$, Algorithm 1 terminates and yields a witness $\omega \in L_I(\mathcal{A})$ iff $L_I(\mathcal{A}) \neq \emptyset$ otherwise returns "empty".*

Comparison with clock zone automata

The zone automaton. If $I = \emptyset$, we are back to classical timed automata and $\lesssim_N = \lesssim_{IN} = \lesssim_I$. Zones and the relation $\lesssim_Z$ are the same and we can modify the algorithm to get a finite deterministic automaton for $L_N(\mathcal{A})$.

Relation of $\lesssim_{IN}$ and the convex hull overapproximation. UppAal has an option to join incomparable clock zones Z_1, Z_2 into a so-called convex hull, the least zone Z, such that containing both $Z_1, Z_2 \lesssim_N Z$. For the exploration algorithm this means replacing two state zone pairs (s, Z_i) into a single pair (s, Z). This is an overapproximation (additional states may become reachable), yet it can be used to prove language emptiness.

    Given a word $\alpha_1\alpha_2 \ldots \alpha_n$, the corresponding classical zone is $Z_{\omega_\$}$ for $\omega_\$ = \alpha_1\$\alpha_2\$ \ldots \$\alpha_n$ (the separator forbids any interleaving). We can prove that for any $\alpha_1\alpha_2 \ldots \alpha_n \in [\omega]$, if $\omega_\$ = \alpha_1\$\alpha_2\$ \ldots \$\alpha_n$ then $\omega_\$ \lesssim_I \omega$, $\omega_\$ \lesssim_{IN} \omega$ and $\omega_\$ \lesssim_C \omega$. This means that all classical zones corresponding to interleavings of the same word are included in the same event zone, i.e. the convex hull approximation is exact when applied to zones reached by equivalent interleavings only and in fact a single interleaving in our semantics already yields this convex hull!

Experiments. For practical evaluation, we have built a tool, *ELSE*, currently in prototype status. It allows both classical semantics (corresponding to clock zones) and event zones, implementing Algorithm 1. We measure reductions in terms of number of states (where feasable for the prototype) and did not compare execution times. Also, absolute comparisons with existing tools like UppAal seem not meaningful at this stage. We chose to compare the two modi of the same base implementation to estimate the potential of passing from classical semantics to event zones and catchup preorder.

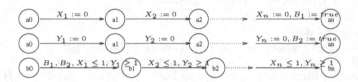

Fig. 4. The diamond example with 2n clocks

We consider three examples. The first – artificial – example is the *diamond example* of Figure 4: Two automata just reset clocks in a fixed order and when both are done, an observer tests some properties of the interleavings. The clock zone automaton has just one maximal run (trace), with a quadratic number of prefixes. Clock zone automata however have to distinguish all possible shuffles of the resets of clocks X_i and Y_j. So this artificial example gives polynomial against exponential growth. More realistic, the second example is a timed version of the dining philosophers, which yield forks taken if they do not obtain the second fork before a timeout (in order to avoid deadlocks). While both the event zone approach and the clock zone approach yield exponential blowups, the difference between the two is impressing and encouraging for applications with some distribution. The third example, popular Fischer's protocol [AL94] is a very unfavourable example, since there is hardly any independence in the models. Still, we report it to show that even in such cases, event zones may yield a fair reduction. The experimental results are summarized in Figure 5, where "EZC" stands for exploration with event zone automata and catchup preorder whereas "CZ" stands for clock zone automata. Each case concerns scalable examples with a parameter m (number of clock of each process in the diamond example, number of philosophers, number of processes Fischer protocol).

Acknowledgements. We thank Victor Braberman, Sergio Yovine, Stavros Tripakis, Oded Maler, Eugene Asarin, Yasmina Abdeddaim, Bengt Johnsson and Rom Langerak for discussions about the challenging topic. Many thanks go to Walter Vogler for his helpful constructive critique. This work was supported

process number	2	3	4	5	6	7	8	9	10	100
Diamond, EZC	19	29	41	55	71	89	109	131	155	3571
Diamond, CZ	56	198	711	2596	9607	35923	135407	–	–	–
Philosophers, EZC	13	48	153	478	1507	4791	15369	49662	161393	–
Philosophers, CZ	13	66	393	2772	23103	223052	2453967	–	–	–
Fischer, EZC	24	209	2048	21077	224536	2480277	–	–	–	–
Fischer, CZ	25	229	2393	26961	322525	4081295	–	–	–	–

Fig. 5. Experimental results

by the IST project AMETIST (Advanced Methods in Timed Systems, contract IST-2001-35304, http://ametist.cs.utwente.nl).

References

[AD94]   R. Alur and D. Dill, *A theory of timed automata*, Theoretical Computer Science **126(2)** (1994), 183–235.

[AL94]   M. Abadi and L.Lamport, *An old-fashioned recipe for real time*, ACM Transactions on Programming Languages and Systems **16** (1994), no. 5, 1543–1571.

[BJLY98]   J. Bengtsson, B. Jonsson, J. Lilius, and W. Yi, *Partial order reductions for timed systems*, Proceedings, Ninth International Conference on Concurrency Theory, LNCS, vol. 1466, Springer-Verlag, 1998, pp. 485–500.

[CLR90]   Th. Cormen, Ch. Leiserson, and R. Rivest, *Introduction to algorithms*, MIT Press, 1990.

[DGKK98]   D. Dams, R. Gerth, B. Knaack, and R. Kuiper, *Partial-order reduction techniques for real-time model checking*, Formal Methods for Industrial Critical Systems (Amsterdam), no. 10, May 1998, pp. 469–482.

[DR95]   V. Diekert and G. Rozenberg (eds.), *The book of traces*, World Scientific, 1995.

[DT98]   D. D'Souza and P.S. Thiagarajan, *Distributed interval automata: A subclass of timed automata*, 1998, Internal Report TCS-98-3.

[God96]   P. Godefroid, *Partial-order methods for the verification of concurrent systems: an approach to the state-explosion problem*, LNCS, vol. 1032, Springer-Verlag Inc., New York, NY, USA, 1996.

[LNZ04]   D. Lugiez, P. Niebert, and S. Zennou, *A Partial Order Semantics Approach to the Clock Explosion Problem of Timed Automata*, Rapport de Recherche, Laboratoire d'Informatique Fondamentale de Marseille, January 2004, available from http://www.lif.univ-mrs.fr/Rapports.

[LPY95]   K. Larsen, P. Pettersson, and W. Yi, *Model-checking for real-time systems*, Fundamentals of Computation Theory, Lecture Notes in Computer Science, August 1995, Invited talk, pp. 62–88.

[Min99]   Marius Minea, *Partial order reduction for verification of timed systems*, Ph.D. thesis, Carnegie Mellon University, 1999.

[NSY92]   X. Nicollin, J. Sifakis, and S. Yovine, *Compiling real-time specifications into extended automata*, IEE Transactions on Software Engineering, vol. 18, September 1992, pp. 794–804.

Lower and Upper Bounds in Zone Based Abstractions of Timed Automata

Gerd Behrmann[1], Patricia Bouyer[2*], Kim G. Larsen[1], and Radek Pelánek[3**]

[1] BRICS, Aalborg University, Denmark
{behrmann,kgl}@cs.auc.dk
[2] LSV, CNRS & ENS de Cachan, UMR 8643, France
bouyer@lsv.ens-cachan.fr
[3] Masaryk University Brno, Czech Republic
xpelanek@informatics.muni.cz

Abstract. Timed automata have an infinite semantics. For verification purposes, one usually uses zone based abstractions w.r.t. the maximal constants to which clocks of the timed automaton are compared. We show that by distinguishing maximal lower and upper bounds, significantly coarser abstractions can be obtained. We show soundness and completeness of the new abstractions w.r.t. reachability. We demonstrate how information about lower and upper bounds can be used to optimise the algorithm for bringing a difference bound matrix into normal form. Finally, we experimentally demonstrate that the new techniques dramatically increases the scalability of the real-time model checker UPPAAL.

1 Introduction

Since their introduction by Alur and Dill [AD90,AD94], timed automata (TA) have become one of the most well-established models for real-time systems with well-studied underlying theory and development of mature model-checking tools, *e.g.* UPPAAL [LPY97] and KRONOS [BDM+98]. By their very definition TA describe (uncountable) infinite state-spaces. Thus, algorithmic verification relies on the existence of exact finite abstractions. In the original work by Alur and Dill, the so-called region-graph construction provided a "universal" such abstraction. However, whereas well-suited for establishing decidability of problems related to TA, the region-graph construction is highly impractical from a tool-implementation point of view. Instead, most real-time verification tools apply abstractions based on so-called zones, which in practise provide much coarser (and hence smaller) abstractions.

To ensure finiteness, it is essential that the given abstraction (region as well as zone based) takes into account the actual constants with which clocks are compared. In particular, the abstraction could identify states which are identical except for the clock values which exceed the *maximum* such constants.

---

* Partially supported by ACI Cortos. Work partly done while visiting CISS, Aalborg University.
** Partially supported by GA ČR grant no. 201/03/0509.

K. Jensen and A. Podelski (Eds.): TACAS 2004, LNCS 2988, pp. 312–326, 2004.

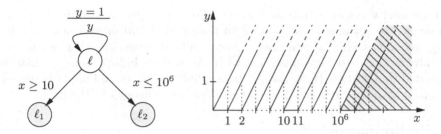

Fig. 1. A small timed automaton. The state space of the automaton when in location ℓ is shown. The area to the right is the abstraction of the last zone.

Obviously, the smaller we may choose these maximum constants, the coarser the resulting abstraction will be. Allowing clocks to be assigned different (maximum) constants is an obvious first step in this direction, and in [BBFL03] this idea has been (successfully) taken further by allowing the maximum constants not only to depend of the particular clock but also of the particular location of the TA. In all cases the *exactness* is established by proving that the abstraction respects *bisimilarity*, *i.e.* states identified by the abstraction are bisimilar.

Consider now the timed automaton of Fig. 1. Clearly 10^6 is the maximum constant for x and 1 is the maximum constant for y. Thus, abstractions based on maximum constants will distinguish all states where $x \leq 10^6$ and $y \leq 1$. In particular, a forward computation of the full state space will – regardless of the search-order – create an excessive number of abstract (symbolic) states including all abstract states of the form $(\ell, x - y = k)$ where $0 \leq k \leq 10^6$ as well as $(\ell, x - y > 10^6)$. However, assuming that we are only interested in *reachability* properties (as is often the case in UPPAAL), the application of downwards closure with respect to *simulation* will lead to an exact abstraction which could potentially be substantially coarser than closure under bisimilarity. Observing that 10^6 is an *upper* bound on the edge from ℓ to ℓ_2 in Fig. 1, it is clear that for any state where $x \geq 10$, increasing x will only lead to "smaller" states with respect to simulation preorder. In particular, applying this downward closure results in the radically smaller collection of abstract states, namely $(\ell, x - y = k)$ where $0 \leq k \leq 10$ and $(\ell, x - y > 10)$.

The fact that 10^6 is an *upper* bound in the example of Fig. 1 is crucial for the reduction we obtained above. In this paper we present new, substantially coarser yet still exact abstractions which are based on *two* maximum constants obtained by distinguishing lower and upper bounds. In all cases the exactness (w.r.t. reachability) is established by proving that the abstraction respects downwards closure w.r.t. simulation, *i.e.* for each state in the abstraction there is an original state simulating it. The variety of abstractions comes from the additional requirements to *effective* representation and *efficient* computation and manipulation. In particular we insist that zones can form the basis of our abstractions; in fact the suggested abstractions are defined in terms of low-complexity transformations of the difference bound matrix (DBM) representation of zones.

Furthermore, we demonstrate how information about lower and upper bounds can be used to optimise the algorithm for bringing a DBM into normal form. Finally, we experimentally demonstrate the significant speedups obtained by our new abstractions, to be comparable with the convex hull over-approximation supported by UPPAAL. Here, the distinction between lower and upper bounds is combined with the orthogonal idea of location-dependency of [BBFL03].

2   Preliminaries

Although we perform our experiments in UPPAAL, we describe the theory on the basic TA model. Variables, committed locations, networks, and other things supported by UPPAAL are not important with respect to presented ideas and the technique can easily be extended for these "richer" models. Let X be a set of non-negative real-valued variables called *clocks*. The set of guards $G(X)$ is defined by the grammar $g := x \bowtie c \mid g \wedge g$, where $x \in X, c \in \mathbb{N}$ and $\bowtie \in \{<, \leq, \geq, >\}$.

Definition 1 (TA Syntax). *A timed automaton is a tuple* $\mathcal{A} = (L, X, \ell_0, E, I)$, *where L is a finite set of locations, X is a finite set of clocks, $\ell_0 \in L$ is an initial location, $E \subseteq L \times G(X) \times 2^X \times L$ is a set of edges labelled by guards and a set of clocks to be reset, and $I : L \to G(X)$ assigns invariants to clocks.*

A *clock valuation* is a function $\nu : X \to \mathbb{R}_{\geq 0}$. If $\delta \in \mathbb{R}_{\geq 0}$ then $\nu + \delta$ denotes the valuation such that for each clock $x \in X$, $(\nu + \delta)(x) = \nu(x) + \delta$. If $Y \subseteq X$ then $\nu[Y := 0]$ denotes the valuation such that for each clock $x \in X \setminus Y$, $\nu[Y := 0](x) = \nu(x)$ and for each clock $x \in Y$, $\nu[Y := 0](x) = 0$. The satisfaction relation $\nu \models g$ for $g \in G(X)$ is defined in the natural way.

Definition 2 (TA Semantics). *The semantics of a timed automaton* $\mathcal{A} = (L, X, \ell_0, E, I)$ *is defined by a transition system* $S_{\mathcal{A}} = (S, s_0, \longrightarrow)$, *where $S = L \times \mathbb{R}_{\geq 0}^X$ is the set of states, $s_0 = (\ell_0, \nu_0)$ is the initial state, $\nu_0(x) = 0$ for all $x \in X$, and $\longrightarrow \subseteq S \times S$ is the set of transitions defined by:*

- $(\ell, \nu) \xrightarrow{\epsilon(\delta)} (\ell, \nu + \delta)$ *if* $\forall 0 \leq \delta' \leq \delta : (\nu + \delta') \models I(l)$
- $(\ell, \nu) \longrightarrow (\ell', \nu[Y := 0])$ *if there exists* $(\ell, g, Y, \ell') \in E$ *such that* $\nu \models g$ *and* $\nu[Y := 0] \models I(\ell')$

The *reachability problem* for an automaton $\mathcal{A}$ and a location ℓ is to decide whether there is a state (ℓ, ν) reachable from (ℓ_0, ν_0) in the transition system $S_{\mathcal{A}}$. As usual, for verification purposes, we define a symbolic semantics for TA. For universality, the definition uses arbitrary sets of clock valuations.

Definition 3 (Symbolic Semantics). *Let* $\mathcal{A} = (L, X, \ell^0, E, I)$ *be a timed automaton. The symbolic semantics of A is based on the abstract transition system* $(S, s_0, \Longrightarrow)$, *where $S = L \times 2^{\mathbb{R}_{\geq 0}^X}$, and '$\Longrightarrow$' is defined by the following two rules:*

> **Delay:** $(\ell, W) \Longrightarrow (\ell, W')$,
>   *where* $W' = \{\nu + d \mid \nu \in W \wedge d \geq 0 \wedge \forall 0 \leq d' \leq d : (\nu + d') \models I(\ell)\}$

> **Action:** $(\ell, W) \Longrightarrow (\ell', W')$ *if there exists a transition* $\ell \xrightarrow{g, Y} \ell'$ *in A, such that* $W' = \{\nu' \mid \exists \nu \in W : \nu \models g \wedge \nu' = \nu[Y := 0] \wedge \nu' \models I(\ell')\}$.

The symbolic semantics of a timed automaton may induce an infinite transition system. To obtain a finite graph one may, as suggested in [BBFL03], apply some abstraction $\mathfrak{a} : \mathcal{P}(\mathbb{R}_{\geq 0}^X) \hookrightarrow \mathcal{P}(\mathbb{R}_{\geq 0}^X)$, such that $W \subseteq \mathfrak{a}(W)$. The abstract transition system '$\Longrightarrow_\mathfrak{a}$' is then given by the following inference rule:

$$\frac{(\ell, W) \Longrightarrow (\ell', W')}{(\ell, W) \Longrightarrow_\mathfrak{a} (\ell', \mathfrak{a}(W'))} \quad \text{if } W = \mathfrak{a}(W)$$

A simple way to ensure that the reachability graph induced by '$\Longrightarrow_\mathfrak{a}$' is finite is to establish that there is only a finite number of abstractions of sets of valuations; that is, the set $\{\mathfrak{a}(W) \mid \mathfrak{a} \text{ defined on } W\}$ is finite. In this case $\mathfrak{a}$ is said to be a *finite abstraction*. Moreover, '$\Longrightarrow_\mathfrak{a}$' is said to be *sound* and *complete* (w.r.t. reachability) whenever:

Sound: $(\ell_0, \{\nu_0\}) \Longrightarrow_\mathfrak{a}^* (\ell, W)$ implies $\exists \nu \in W$ s.t. $(\ell_0, \nu_0) \longrightarrow^* (l, \nu)$

Complete: $(\ell_0, \nu_0) \longrightarrow^* (\ell, \nu)$ implies $\exists W : \nu \in W$ and $(\ell_0, \{\nu_0\}) \Longrightarrow_\mathfrak{a}^* (\ell, W)$

By language misuse, we say that an abstraction $\mathfrak{a}$ is *sound* (resp. *complete*) whenever '$\Longrightarrow_\mathfrak{a}$' is sound (resp. complete). Completeness follows trivially from the definition of abstraction. Of course, if $\mathfrak{a}$ and $\mathfrak{b}$ are two abstractions such that for any set of valuations W, $\mathfrak{a}(W) \subseteq \mathfrak{b}(W)$, we prefer to use abstraction $\mathfrak{b}$ because the graph induced by it is *a priori* smaller than the one induced by $\mathfrak{a}$. Our aim is thus to propose an abstraction which is finite, as coarse as possible, and which induces a sound abstract transition system. We also require that abstractions are *effectively* representable and may be *efficiently* computed and manipulated.

A first step in finding an effective abstraction is realising that W will always be a zone whenever $(\ell^0, \{\nu_0\}) \Longrightarrow^* (\ell, W)$. A *zone* is a conjunction of constraints of the form $x \bowtie c$ or $x - y \bowtie c$, where x and y are clocks, $c \in \mathbb{Z}$, and $\bowtie$ is one of $\{\leq, \leq, =, \geq, >\}$. Zones can be represented using *Difference Bound Matrices* (DBM). We will briefly recall the definition of DBMs, and refer to [Dil89,CGP99,Ben02,Bou02] for more details. A DBM is a square matrix $D = \langle c_{i,j}, \prec_{i,j} \rangle_{0 \leq i,j \leq n}$ such that $c_{i,j} \in \mathbb{Z}$ and $\prec_{i,j} \in \{<, \leq\}$ or $c_{i,j} = \infty$ and $\prec_{i,j} = <$. The DBM D represents the zone $\llbracket D \rrbracket$ which is defined by $\llbracket D \rrbracket = \{\nu \mid \forall 0 \leq i, j \leq n, \ \nu(x_i) - \nu(x_j) \prec_{i,j} c_{i,j}\}$, where $\{x_i \mid 1 \leq i \leq n\}$ is the set of clocks, and x_0 is a clock which is always 0, (*i.e.* for each valuation ν, $\nu(x_0) = 0$). DBMs are not a canonical representation of zones, but a normal form can be computed by considering the DBM as an adjacency matrix of a weighted directed graph and computing all shortest paths. In particular, if $D = \langle c_{i,j}, \prec_{i,j} \rangle_{0 \leq i,j \leq n}$ is a DBM in normal form, then it satisfies the *triangular inequality*, that is, for every $0 \leq i, j, k \leq n$, we have that $(c_{i,j}, \prec_{i,j}) \leq (c_{i,k}, \prec_{i,k}) + (c_{k,j}, \prec_{k,j})$, where comparisons and additions are defined in a natural way (see [Bou02]). All operations needed to compute '$\Longrightarrow$' can be implemented by manipulating the DBMs.

3   Maximum Bound Abstractions

The abstraction used in real-time model-checkers such as UPPAAL [LPY97] and KRONOS [BDM+98], is based on the idea that the behaviour of an automaton is only sensitive to changes of a clock if its value is below a certain constant. That is, for each clock there is a maximum constant such that once the value of a clock has passed this constant, its exact value is no longer relevant — only the fact that it is larger than the maximum constant matters. Transforming a DBM to reflect this idea is often referred to as *extrapolation* [Bou03,BBFL03] or *normalisation* [DT98]. In the following we will choose the term *extrapolation*.

Simulation & Bisimulation. The notion of bisimulation has so far been the semantic tool for establishing soundness of suggested abstractions. In this paper we shall exploit the more liberal notion of simulation to allow for even coarser abstractions. Let us fix a timed automaton $\mathcal{A} = (L, X, \ell_0, E, I)$. We consider a relation on $L \times \mathbb{R}_{\geq 0}^X$ satisfying the following transfer properties:

1. if $(\ell_1, \nu_1) \preccurlyeq (\ell_2, \nu_2)$ then $\ell_1 = \ell_2$
2. if $(\ell_1, \nu_1) \preccurlyeq (\ell_2, \nu_2)$ and $(\ell_1, \nu_1) \longrightarrow (\ell'_1, \nu'_1)$, then there exists (ℓ'_2, ν'_2) such that $(\ell_2, \nu_2) \longrightarrow (\ell'_2, \nu'_2)$ and $(\ell'_1, \nu'_1) \preccurlyeq (\ell'_2, \nu'_2)$
3. if $(\ell_1, \nu_1) \preccurlyeq (\ell_2, \nu_2)$ and $(\ell_1, \nu_1) \xrightarrow{\epsilon(\delta)} (\ell_1, \nu_1 + \delta)$, then there exists δ' such that $(\ell_2, \nu_2) \xrightarrow{\epsilon(\delta')} (\ell_2, \nu_2 + \delta')$ and $(\ell_1, \nu_1 + \delta) \preccurlyeq (\ell_2, \nu_2 + \delta')$

We call such a relation a (*location-based*) *simulation* relation or simply a *simulation* relation. A simulation relation $\preccurlyeq$ such that $\preccurlyeq^{-1}$ is also a simulation relation, is called a (location-based) *bisimulation relation*.

Proposition 1. *Let $\preccurlyeq$ be a simulation relation, as defined above. If $(\ell, \nu_1) \preccurlyeq (\ell, \nu_2)$ and if a discrete state ℓ' is reachable from (ℓ, ν_1), then it is also reachable from (ℓ, ν_2).*

Reachability is thus preserved by simulation as well as by bisimulation. However, in general the weaker notion of simulation preserves fewer properties than that of bisimulation. For example, deadlock properties as expressed in UPPAAL [1] are not preserved by simulation whereas it is preserved by bisimulation. In Fig. 1, $(\ell, x = 15, y = .5)$ is bisimilar to $(\ell, x = 115, y = .5)$, but not to $(\ell, x = 10^6 + 1, y = .5)$. However, $(\ell, x = 15, y = .5)$ simulates $(\ell, x = 115, y = .5)$ as well as $(\ell, x = 10^6 + 1, y = .5)$.

Classical Maximal Bounds. The classical abstraction for timed automata is based on maximal bounds, one for each clock of the automaton. Let $\mathcal{A} = (L, X, \ell_0, E, I)$ be a timed automaton. The *maximal bound* of a clock $x \in X$, denoted $M(x)$, is the maximal constant k such that there exists a guard or invariant containing $x \bowtie k$ in $\mathcal{A}$. Let ν and ν' be two valuations. We define the following relation:

$$\nu \equiv_M \nu' \stackrel{\text{def}}{\Longleftrightarrow} \forall x \in X : \text{either } \nu(x) = \nu'(x) \text{ or } (\nu(x) > M(x) \text{ and } \nu'(x) > M(x))$$

Lemma 1. *The relation $\mathcal{R} = \{((\ell, \nu), (\ell, \nu')) \mid \nu \equiv_M \nu'\}$ is a bisimulation relation.*

---

[1] There is a deadlock whenever there exists a state (ℓ, ν) such that no further discrete transition can be taken.

We can now define the abstraction $\mathfrak{a}_{\equiv_M}$ w.r.t. $\equiv_M$. Let W be a set of valuations, then $\mathfrak{a}_{\equiv_M}(W) = \{\nu \mid \exists \nu' \in W, \nu' \equiv_M \nu\}$.

Lemma 2. *The abstraction $\mathfrak{a}_{\equiv_M}$ is sound and complete.*

These two lemmas come from [BBFL03]. They will moreover be consequences of our main result.

Lower & Upper Maximal Bounds. The new abstractions introduced in the following will be substantially coarser than $\mathfrak{a}_{\equiv_M}$. It is no longer based on a single maximal bound per clock but rather on two maximal bounds per clock allowing lower and upper bounds to be distinguished.

Definition 4. *Let $\mathcal{A} = (L, X, \ell_0, E, I)$ be a timed automaton. The maximal lower bound denoted $L(x)$, (resp. maximal upper bound $U(x)$) of clock $x \in X$ is the maximal constant k such that there exists a constraint $x > k$ or $x \geq k$ (resp. $x < k$ or $x \leq k$) in a guard of some transition or in an invariant of some location of $\mathcal{A}$. If such a constant does not exist, we set $L(x)$ (resp. $U(x)$) to $-\infty$.*

Let us fix for the rest of this section a timed automaton $\mathcal{A}$ and bounds $L(x)$, $U(x)$ for each clock $x \in X$ as above. The idea of distinguishing lower and upper bounds is the following: if we know that the clock x is between 2 and 4, and if we want to check that the constraint $x \leq 5$ can be satisfied, the only relevant information is that the value of x is greater than 2, and not that $x \leq 4$. In other terms, checking the emptiness of the intersection between a non-empty interval $[c, d]$ and $]-\infty, 5]$ is equivalent to checking whether $c > 5$; the value of d is not useful. Formally, we define the LU-preorder as follows.

Definition 5 (LU-preorder $\prec_{LU}$). *Let ν and ν' be two valuations. Then, we say that*

$$\nu' \prec_{LU} \nu \xLeftrightarrow{def} \text{ for each clock } x, \begin{cases} \text{either } \nu'(x) = \nu(x) \\ \text{or } L(x) < \nu'(x) < \nu(x) \\ \text{or } U(x) < \nu(x) < \nu'(x) \end{cases}$$

Lemma 3. *The relation $\mathcal{R} = \{((\ell, \nu), (\ell, \nu')) \mid \nu' \prec_{LU} \nu\}$ is a simulation relation.*

Proof. The only non-trivial part in proving that $\mathcal{R}$ indeed satisfies the three transfer properties of a simulation relation is to establish that if g is a clock constraint, then "$\nu \models g$ implies $\nu' \models g$". Consider the constraint $x \leq c$. If $\nu(x) = \nu'(x)$, then we are done. If $L(x) < \nu'(x) < \nu(x)$, then $\nu(x) \leq c$ implies $\nu'(x) \leq c$. If $U(x) < \nu(x) < \nu'(x)$, then it is not possible that $\nu \models x \leq c$ (because $c \leq U(x)$). Consider now the constraint $x \geq c$. If $\nu(x) = \nu'(x)$, then we are done. If $U(x) < \nu(x) < \nu'(x)$, then $\nu(x) \geq c$ implies $\nu'(x) \geq c$. If $L(x) < \nu'(x) < \nu(x)$, then it is not possible that ν satisfies the constraint $x \geq c$ because $c \leq L(x)$. ∎

Using the above LU-preorder, we can now define a first abstraction based on the lower and upper bounds.

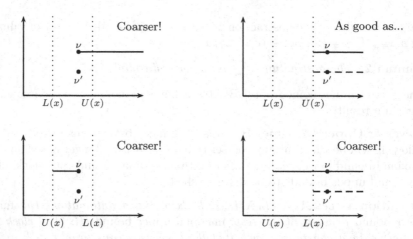

Fig. 2. Quality of $\mathfrak{a}_{\prec_{LU}}$ compared with $\mathfrak{a}_{\equiv_M}$ for $M = \max(L, U)$.

Definition 6 ($\mathfrak{a}_{\prec_{LU}}$, abstraction w.r.t. $\prec_{LU}$). *Let W be a set of valuations. We define the abstraction w.r.t. $\prec_{LU}$ as $\mathfrak{a}_{\prec_{LU}}(W) = \{\nu \mid \exists \nu' \in W,\ \nu' \prec_{LU} \nu\}$.*

Before going further, we illustrate this abstraction in Fig. 2. There are several cases, depending on the relative positions of the two values $L(x)$ and $U(x)$ and of the valuation ν we are looking at. We represent with a plain line the value of $\mathfrak{a}_{\prec_{LU}}(\{\nu\})$ and with a dashed line the value of $\mathfrak{a}_{\equiv_M}(\{\nu'\})$, where the maximal bound $M(x)$ corresponds to the maximum of $L(x)$ and $U(x)$. In each case, we indicate the "quality" of the new abstraction compared with the "old" one. We notice that the new abstraction is coarser in three cases and matches the old abstraction in the fourth case.

Lemma 4. *Let $\mathcal{A}$ be a timed automaton. Define the constants $M(x)$, $L(x)$ and $U(x)$ for each clock x as described before. The abstraction $\mathfrak{a}_{\prec LU}$ is sound, complete, and coarser or equal to $\mathfrak{a}_{\equiv_M}$.*

Proof. Completeness is obvious, and soundness comes from lemma 3. Definitions of $\mathfrak{a}_{\prec LU}$ and $\mathfrak{a}_{\equiv_M}$ give the last result because for each clock x, $M(x) = \max(L(x), U(x))$. ∎

This result could suggest to use $\mathfrak{a}_{\prec_{LU}}$ in real time model-checkers. However, we do not yet have an efficient method for computing the transition relation '$\Longrightarrow_{\mathfrak{a}_{\prec_{LU}}}$'. Indeed, even if W is a zone, it might be the case that $\mathfrak{a}_{\prec_{LU}}(W)$ is not even convex (we urge the reader to construct such an example for herself). For effectiveness and efficiency reasons we prefer abstractions which transform zones into zones because we can then use the DBM data structure. In the next section we present DBM-based extrapolation operators that will give abstractions which are sound, complete, finite and also effective.

4   Extrapolation Using Zones

The (sound and complete) symbolic transition relations induced by abstractions considered so far unfortunately do not preserve convexity of sets of valuations. In order to allow for sets of valuations to be represented *efficiently* as zones, we consider slightly finer abstractions $\mathfrak{a}_{Extra}$ such that for every zone Z, $Z \subseteq \mathfrak{a}_{Extra}(Z) \subseteq \mathfrak{a}_{\prec_{LU}}(Z)$ (resp. $Z \subseteq \mathfrak{a}_{Extra}(Z) \subseteq \mathfrak{a}_{\equiv_M}(Z)$) (this ensures correctness) and $\mathfrak{a}_{Extra}(Z)$ is a zone (this gives an effective representation). These abstractions are defined in terms of *extrapolation* operators on DBMs. If $Extra$ is an extrapolation operator, it defines an abstraction, $\mathfrak{a}_{Extra}$, on zones such that for every zone Z, $\mathfrak{a}_{Extra}(Z) = [\![Extra(D_Z)]\!]$, where D_Z is the DBM in normal form which represents the zone Z.

In the remainder, we consider a timed automaton $\mathcal{A}$ over a set of clocks $X = \{x_1, .., x_n\}$ and we suppose we are given another clock x_0 which is always zero. For all these clocks, we define the constants $M(x_i)$, $L(x_i)$, $U(x_i)$ for $i = 1, ..., n$. For x_0, we set $M(x_0) = U(x_0) = L(x_0) = 0$ (x_0 is always equal to zero, so we assume we are able to check whether x_0 is really zero). In our framework, a zone will be represented by DBMs of the form $\langle c_{i,j}, \prec_{i,j}\rangle_{i,j=0,...,n}$.

We now present several extrapolations starting from the classical one and improving it step by step. Each extrapolation will be illustrated by a small picture representing a zone (in black) and its corresponding extrapolation (dashed).

Classical extrapolation based on maximal bounds $M(x)$. Let D be a DBM $\langle c_{i,j}, \prec_{i,j}\rangle_{i,j=0...n}$. Then $Extra_M(D)$ is given by the DBM $\langle c'_{i,j}, \prec'_{i,j}\rangle_{i,j=0...n}$ defined and illustrated below:

$$(c'_{i,j}, \prec'_{i,j}) = \begin{cases} \infty & \text{if } c_{i,j} > M(x_i) \\ (-M(x_j), <) & \text{if } -c_{i,j} > M(x_j) \\ (c_{i,j}, \prec_{i,j}) & \text{otherwise} \end{cases}$$

This is the extrapolation operator used in the real-time model-checkers UPPAAL and KRONOS. This extrapolation removes bounds that are larger than the maximal constants. The correctness is based on the fact that $\mathfrak{a}_{Extra_M}(Z) \subseteq \mathfrak{a}_{\equiv_M}(Z)$ and is proved in [Bou03] and for the location-based version in [BBFL03].

In the remainder, we will propose several other extrapolations that will improve the classical one, in the sense that the zones obtained with the new extrapolations will be larger than the zones obtained with the classical extrapolation.

Diagonal extrapolation based on maximal constants $M(x)$. The first improvement consists in noticing that if the whole zone is above the maximal bound of some clock, then we can remove some of the diagonal constraints of the zones, even if they are not themselves above the maximal bound. More formally, if $D = \langle c_{i,j}, \prec_{i,j} \rangle_{i,j=0,\dots,n}$ is a DBM, $Extra_M^+(D)$ is given by $\langle c'_{i,j}, \prec'_{i,j} \rangle_{i,j=0,\dots,n}$ defined as:

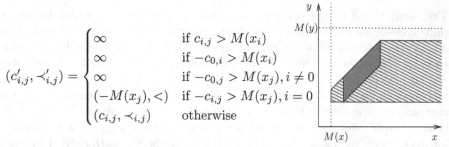

$$(c'_{i,j}, \prec'_{i,j}) = \begin{cases} \infty & \text{if } c_{i,j} > M(x_i) \\ \infty & \text{if } -c_{0,i} > M(x_i) \\ \infty & \text{if } -c_{0,j} > M(x_j), i \neq 0 \\ (-M(x_j), <) & \text{if } -c_{i,j} > M(x_j), i = 0 \\ (c_{i,j}, \prec_{i,j}) & \text{otherwise} \end{cases}$$

For every zone Z it then holds that $Z \subseteq \mathfrak{a}_{Extra_M}(Z) \subseteq \mathfrak{a}_{Extra_M^+}(Z)$.

Extrapolation based on LU-bounds $L(x)$ and $U(x)$. The second improvement uses the two bounds $L(x)$ and $U(x)$. If $D = \langle c_{i,j}, \prec_{i,j} \rangle_{i,j=0,\dots,n}$ is a DBM, $Extra_{LU}(D)$ is given by $\langle c'_{i,j}, \prec'_{i,j} \rangle_{i,j=0,\dots,n}$ defined as:

$$(c'_{i,j}, \prec'_{i,j}) = \begin{cases} \infty & \text{if } c_{i,j} > L(x_i) \\ (-U(x_j), <) & \text{if } -c_{i,j} > U(x_j) \\ (c_{i,j}, \prec_{i,j}) & \text{otherwise} \end{cases}$$

This extrapolation benefits from the properties of the two different maximal bounds. It does generalise the operator $\mathfrak{a}_{Extra_M}$. For every zone Z, it holds that $Z \subseteq \mathfrak{a}_{Extra_M}(Z) \subseteq \mathfrak{a}_{Extra_{LU}}(Z)$.

Diagonal extrapolation based on LU-bounds $L(x)$ and $U(x)$. This last extrapolation is a combination of both the extrapolation based on LU-bounds and the improved extrapolation based on maximal constants. It is the most general one. If $D = \langle c_{i,j}, \prec_{i,j} \rangle_{i,j=0,\dots,n}$ is a DBM, $Extra_{LU}^+(D)$ is given by the DBM $\langle c'_{i,j}, \prec'_{i,j} \rangle_{i,j=0,\dots,n}$ defined as:

$$(c'_{i,j}, \prec'_{i,j}) = \begin{cases} \infty & \text{if } c_{i,j} > L(x_i) \\ \infty & \text{if } -c_{0,i} > L(x_i) \\ \infty & \text{if } -c_{0,j} > U(x_j), i \neq 0 \\ (-U(x_j), <) & \text{if } -c_{0,j} > U(x_j), i = 0 \\ (c_{i,j}, \prec_{i,j}) & \text{otherwise} \end{cases}$$

Correctness of these Abstractions. We know that all the above extrapolations are complete abstractions as they transform a zone into a clearly larger one. Finiteness also comes immediately, because we can do all the computations with

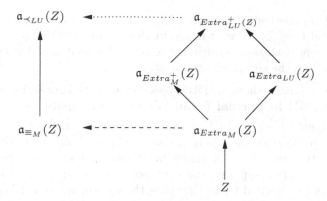

Fig. 3. For any zone Z, we have the inclusions indicated by the arrows. The sets $\mathfrak{a}_{Extra^+_M}(Z)$ and $\mathfrak{a}_{Extra_{LU}}(Z)$ are incomparable. The $\mathfrak{a}_{Extra}$ operators are DBM based abstractions whereas the other two are semantic abstractions. The dashed arrow was proved in [BBFL03] whereas the dotted arrow is the main result of this paper.

DBMs and the coefficients after extrapolation can only take a finite number of values. Effectiveness of the abstraction is obvious as extrapolation operators are directly defined on the DBM data structure. The only difficult point is to prove that the extrapolations we have presented are correct. To prove the correctness of all these abstractions, due to the inclusions shown in Fig. 3, it is sufficient to prove the correctness of the largest abstraction, *viz* $\mathfrak{a}_{Extra^+_{LU}}$.

Proposition 2. *Let Z be a zone. Then* $\mathfrak{a}_{Extra^+_{LU}}(Z) \subseteq \mathfrak{a}_{\prec_{LU}}(Z)$.

The proof of this proposition is quite technical, and is omitted here due to the page limit. Notice however that it is a key-result. Using all what precedes we are able to claim the following theorem which states that $\mathfrak{a}_{Extra^+_{LU}}$ is an abstraction which can be used in the implementation of TA.

Theorem 1. $\mathfrak{a}_{Extra^+_{LU}}$ *is sound, complete, finite and effectively computable.*

5   Acceleration of Successor Computation

In the preceding section it was shown that the abstraction based on the new extrapolation operator is coarser than the one currently used in TA model-checkers. This can result in a smaller symbolic representation of the state space of a timed automaton, but this is not the only consequence: Sometimes clocks might only have lower bounds or only have upper bounds. We say that a clock x is *lower-bounded* (resp. *upper-bounded*) if $L(x) > -\infty$ (resp. $U(x) > -\infty$). Let D be a DBM and $D' = Extra^+_{LU}(D)$. It follows directly from the definition of the extrapolation operator that for all x_i, $U(x_i) = -\infty$ implies $c'_{j,i} = +\infty$ and $L(x_i) = -\infty$ implies $c'_{i,j} = +\infty$. If we let $Low = \{i \mid x_i$ is lower bounded$\}$ and $Up = \{i \mid x_i$ is upper bounded$\}$, then it follows that D' can be represented with

$\mathcal{O}(|Low| \cdot |Up|)$ constraints (compared to $\mathcal{O}(n^2)$), since all remaining entries in the DBM will be $+\infty$. As we will see in this section, besides reducing the size of the zone representation, identifying lower and upper bounded clocks can be used to speed up the successor computation.

We will first summarise how the DBM based successor computation is performed. Let D be a DBM **in normal form**. We want to compute the successor of D w.r.t. an edge $\ell \xrightarrow{g,Y} \ell'$. In UPPAAL, this is broken down into a number of elementary DBM operations, quite similar to the symbolic semantics of TA. After applying the guard and the target invariant, the result must be checked for consistency and after applying the extrapolation operator, the DBM must be brought back into normal form. Checking the consistency of a DBM is done by computing the normal form and checking the diagonal for negative entries. In general, the normal form can be computed using the $\mathcal{O}(n^3)$-time Floyd-Warshall all-pairs-shortest-path algorithm, but when applying a guard or invariant, resetting clocks, or computing the delay successors, the normal form can be recomputed much more efficiently, see [Rok93]. The following shows the operations involved and their complexity (all DBMs except D_5 are in normal form). The last step is clearly the most expensive.

1. $D_1 = \text{INTERSECTION}(g, D) +$ detection of emptiness $\qquad \mathcal{O}(n^2 \cdot |g|)$
2. $D_2 = \text{RESET}_Y(D_1)$ $\qquad\qquad\qquad\qquad\qquad\qquad\qquad\qquad \mathcal{O}(n \cdot |Y|)$
3. $D_3 = \text{ELAPSE}(D_2)$ $\qquad\qquad\qquad\qquad\qquad\qquad\qquad\qquad\qquad \mathcal{O}(n)$
4. $D_4 = \text{INTERSECTION}(I(\ell), D_3) +$ detection of emptiness $\quad \mathcal{O}(n^2 \cdot |I(\ell)|)$
5. $D_5 = \text{EXTRAPOLATION}(D_4)$ $\qquad\qquad\qquad\qquad\qquad\qquad \mathcal{O}(n^2)$
6. $D_6 = \text{CANONIZE}(D_5)$ $\qquad\qquad\qquad\qquad\qquad\qquad\qquad\quad \mathcal{O}(n^3)$

We say that a DBM D is in *LU-form* whenever all coefficients $c_{i,j} = \infty$, except when x_i is lower bounded *and* x_j is upper bounded. As a first step we will use the fact that D_5 is in LU-form to improve the computation of D_6. CANONIZE is the Floyd-Warshall algorithm for computing the all-pairs-shortest-path closure, consisting of three nested loops over the indexes of the DBM, hence the cubic runtime. We propose to replace it with the following LU-CANONIZE operator.

proc LU-CANONIZE(D)
    for $k \in Low \cap Up$ **do**
        for $i \in Low$ **do**
            for $j \in Up$ **do**
                if $(c_{ij}, \prec_{ij}) > (c_{ik}, \prec_{ik}) + (c_{kj}, \prec_{kj})$
                    then $(c_{ij}, \prec_{ij}) = (c_{ik}, \prec_{ik}) + (c_{kj}, \prec_{kj})$ **fi**
        od od od
end

This procedure runs in $\mathcal{O}(|Low| \cdot |Up| \cdot |Low \cap Up|)$ time which in practise can be much smaller than $\mathcal{O}(n^3)$. Correctness of this change is ensured by the following lemma.

Lemma 5. *Let D be a DBM in LU-form. Then we have the following syntactic equality:* CANONIZE(D) = LU-CANONIZE(D).

As an added benefit, it follows directly from the definition of LU-CANONIZE that D_6 is also in LU-form and so is D when computing the next successor. Hence we can replace the other DBM operations (intersection, elapse, reset, etc.) by versions which work on DBMs in LU-form. The main interest would be to introduce an asymmetric DBM which only stores $\mathcal{O}(|Low| \cdot |Up|)$ entries, thus speeding up the successor computation further and reducing the memory requirements. At the moment we have implemented the LU-CANONIZE operation, but rely on the *minimal constraint form* representation of a zone described in [LLPY97], which does not store $+\infty$ entries.

6   Implementation and Experiments

We have implemented a prototype of a location based variant of the $Extra^+_{LU}$ operator in UPPAAL 3.4.2. Maximum lower and upper bounds for clocks are found for each automaton using a simple fixed point iteration. Given a location vector, the maximum lower and upper bounds are simply found by taking the maximum of the bounds in each location, similar to the approach taken in [BBFL03]. In addition, we have implemented the LU-CANONIZE operator.

As expected, experiments with the model in Fig. 1 show that the using the LU extrapolation the computation time for building the complete reachable state space does not depend on the value of the constants, whereas the computation time grows with the constant when using the classical extrapolation approach. We have also performed experiments with models of various instances of Fischer's protocol for mutual exclusion and the CSMA/CD protocol. Finally, experiments using a number of industrial case studies were made. For each model, UPPAAL was run with four different options: (-n1) classic non-location based extrapolation (without active clock reduction), (-n2) classic location based extrapolation (which gives active clock reduction as a side-effect), (-n3) LU location based extrapolation, and (-A) classic location based extrapolation with convex-hull approximation. In all experiments the minimal constraint form for zone representation was used [LLPY97] and the complete state space was generated. All experiments were performed on a 1.8GHz Pentium 4 running Linux 2.4.22, and experiments were limited to 15 minutes of CPU time and 470MB of memory. The results can be seen in Table 1.

Looking at the table, we see that for both Fischer's protocol for mutual exclusion and the CSMA/CD protocol, UPPAAL scales considerably better with the LU extrapolation operator. Comparing it with the convex hull approximation (which is an over-approximation), we see that for these models, the LU extrapolation operator comes close to the same speed, although it still generates more states. Also notice that the runs with the LU extrapolation operator use less memory than convex hull approximation, due to the fact that in the latter case DBMs are used to represent the convex hull of the zones involved (in contrast to using the minimal constraint form of [LLPY97]). For the three industrial examples, the speedup is less dramatic: These models have a more complex control structure and thus little can be gained from changing the extrapolation operator. This is supported by the fact that also the convex hull technique fails to

Table 1. Results for Fischer protocol (f), CSMA/CD (c), a model of a buscoupler, the Philips Audio protocol, and a model of a 5 task fixed-priority preemptive scheduler. -n0 is with classical maximum bounds extrapolation, -n1 is with location based maximum bounds extrapolation, -n2 is with location based LU extrapolation, and -A is with convex hull over-approximation. Times are in seconds, states are the number of generated states and memory usage is in MB.

Model	-n1			-n2			-n3			-A		
	Time	States	Mem	Time	States	Mem	Time	States	Mem	Time	States	Mem
f5	4.02	82,685	5	0.24	16,980	3	0.03	2,870	3	0.03	3,650	3
f6	597.04	1,489,230	49	6.67	158,220	7	0.11	11,484	3	0.10	14,658	3
f7				352.67	1,620,542	46	0.47	44,142	3	0.45	56,252	5
f8							2.11	164,528	6	2.08	208,744	12
f9							8.76	598,662	19	9.11	754,974	39
f10							37.26	2,136,980	68	39.13	2,676,150	143
f11							152.44	7,510,382	268			
c5	0.55	27,174	3	0.14	10,569	3	0.02	2,027	3	0.03	1,651	3
c6	19.39	287,109	11	3.63	87,977	5	0.10	6,296	3	0.06	4,986	3
c7				195.35	813,924	29	0.28	18,205	3	0.22	14,101	4
c8							0.98	50,058	5	0.66	38,060	7
c9							2.90	132,623	12	1.89	99,215	17
c10							8.42	341,452	29	5.48	251,758	49
c11							24.13	859,265	76	15.66	625,225	138
c12							68.20	2,122,286	202	43.10	1,525,536	394
bus	102.28	6,727,443	303	66.54	4,620,666	254	62.01	4,317,920	246	45.08	3,826,742	324
philips	0.16	12,823	3	0.09	6,763	3	0.09	6,599	3	0.07	5,992	3
sched	17.01	929,726	76	15.09	700,917	58	12.85	619,351	52	55.41	3,636,576	427

give any significant speedup (in the last example it even degrades performance). During our experiments we also encountered examples where the LU extrapolation operator does not make any difference: the token ring FDDI protocol and the B&O protocols found on the UPPAAL website[2] are among these. Finally, we made a few experiments on Fischer's protocol with the LU extrapolation, but without the LU-CANONIZE operator. This showed that LU-CANONIZE gives a speedup in the order of 20% compared to CANONIZE.

7   Remarks and Conclusions

In this paper we extend the *status quo* of timed automata abstractions by contributing several new abstractions. In particular, we proposed a new extrapolation operator distinguishing between guards giving an upper bound to a clock and guards giving a lower bound to a clock. The improvement of the usual extrapolation is orthogonal to the location-based one proposed in [BBFL03] in the sense that they can be easily combined. We prove that the new abstraction is sound and complete w.r.t. reachability, and is finite and effectively computable. We implemented the new extrapolation in UPPAAL and a new operator for computing the normal form of a DBM. The prototype showed significant improvements in verification speed, memory consumption and scalability for a number of models.

For further work, we suggest implementing an asymmetric DBM based on the fact that an $n \times m$ matrix, where n is the number of lower bounded clocks and m is the number of upper bounded clocks, suffices to represent the zones of the timed automaton when using the LU extrapolation. We expect this to significantly improve the successor computation for some models. We notice that when using the encoding of job shop scheduling problems given in [AM01], all clocks of the automaton are without upper bounds, with the exception of one clock (the clock measuring global time), which lacks lower bounds. Therefore an asymmetric DBM representation for this system will have a size linear in the number of clocks. This observation was already made in [AM01], but we get it as a side effect of using LU extrapolation. We also notice that when using LU extrapolation, the inclusion checking done on zones in UPPAAL turns out to be more general than the dominating point check in [AM01]. We need to investigate to what extent a generic timed automaton reachability checker using LU extrapolation can compete with the problem specific implementation in [AM01].

References

[AD90]   Rajeev Alur and David Dill.   Automata for modeling real-time systems. In *Proc. 17th International Colloquium on Automata, Languages and Programming (ICALP'90)*, volume 443 of *Lecture Notes in Computer Science*, pages 322–335. Springer, 1990.

---

[2] http://www.uppaal.com

[AD94]   Rajeev Alur and David Dill. A theory of timed automata. *Theoretical Computer Science (TCS)*, 126(2):183–235, 1994.

[AM01]   Yasmina Abdeddaim and Oded Maler. Job-shop scheduling using timed automata. In *Proc. 13th International Conference on Computer Aided Verification (CAV'01)*, volume 2102 of *Lecture Notes in Computer Science*, pages 478–492. Springer, 2001.

[BBFL03]   Gerd Behrmann, Patricia Bouyer, Emmanuel Fleury, and Kim G. Larsen. Static guard analysis in timed automata verification. In *Proc. 9th International Conference on Tools and Algorithms for the Construction and Analysis of Systems (TACAS'2003)*, volume 2619 of *Lecture Notes in Computer Science*, pages 254–277. Springer, 2003.

[BDM+98]   Marius Bozga, Conrado Daws, Oded Maler, Alfredo Olivero, Stavros Tripakis, and Sergio Yovine. KRONOS: a model-checking tool for real-time systems. In *Proc. 10th International Conference on Computer Aided Verification (CAV'98)*, volume 1427 of *Lecture Notes in Computer Science*, pages 546–550. Springer, 1998.

[Ben02]   Johan Bengtsson. *Clocks, DBMs ans States in Timed Systems*. PhD thesis, Department of Information Technology, Uppsala University, Uppsala, Sweden, 2002.

[Bou02]   Patricia Bouyer. Timed automata may cause some troubles. Research Report LSV–02–9, Laboratoire Spécification et Vérification, ENS de Cachan, France, 2002. Also Available as *BRICS Research Report RS-02-35*, Aalborg University, Denmark, 2002.

[Bou03]   Patricia Bouyer. Untameable timed automata! In *Proc. 20th Annual Symposium on Theoretical Aspects of Computer Science (STACS'03)*, volume 2607 of *Lecture Notes in Computer Science*, pages 620–631. Springer, 2003.

[CGP99]   Edmund Clarke, Orna Grumberg, and Doron Peled. *Model-Checking*. The MIT Press, Cambridge, Massachusetts, 1999.

[Dil89]   David Dill. Timing assumptions and verification of finite-state concurrent systems. In *Proc. of the Workshop on Automatic Verification Methods for Finite State Systems*, volume 407 of *Lecture Notes in Computer Science*, pages 197–212. Springer, 1989.

[DT98]   Conrado Daws and Stavros Tripakis. Model-checking of real-time reachability properties using abstractions. In *Proc. 4th International Conference on Tools and Algorithms for the Construction and Analysis of Systems (TACAS'98)*, volume 1384 of *Lecture Notes in Computer Science*, pages 313–329. Springer, 1998.

[LLPY97]   Kim G. Larsen, Fredrik Larsson, Paul Pettersson, and Wang Yi. Efficient verification of real-time systems: Compact data structure and state-space reduction. In *Proc. 18th IEEE Real-Time Systems Symposium (RTSS'97)*, pages 14–24. IEEE Computer Society Press, 1997.

[LPY97]   Kim G. Larsen, Paul Pettersson, and Wang Yi. UPPAAL in a nutshell. *Journal of Software Tools for Technology Transfer (STTT)*, 1(1–2):134–152, 1997.

[Rok93]   Tomas G. Rokicki. *Representing and Modeling Digital Circuits*. PhD thesis, Stanford University, Stanford, USA, 1993.

A Scalable Incomplete Test for the Boundedness of UML RT Models

Stefan Leue, Richard Mayr, and Wei Wei

Department of Computer Science
Albert-Ludwigs-University Freiburg
Georges-Koehler-Allee 51, D-79110 Freiburg, Germany
{leue,mayrri,wwei}@informatik.uni-freiburg.de

Abstract. We describe a scalable incomplete boundedness test for the communication buffers in UML RT models. UML RT is a variant of the UML modeling language, tailored to describing asynchronous concurrent embedded systems. We reduce UML RT models to systems of communicating finite state machines (CFSMs). We propose a series of further abstractions that leaves us with a system of linear inequalities. Those represent the message sending and receiving effect that the control flow cycles of every process have on the overall message buffer. The test tries to establish the existence of a linear combination of the effect vectors so that at least one message can occur an unbounded number of times. We discuss the complexity of this test and present experimental results using the IBOC system that we are implementing. Scalability of the test is in part due to the fact that it is polynomial for the type of sparse control flow graphs that are derived from UML RT models. Also, the analysis is local, i.e., it avoids the combinatorial state space explosion due to concurrency of the models. We also present a method to derive upper bound estimates for the maximal occupancy of each individual message buffer. While we focus on the analysis of UML RT models, the analysis can directly be applied to any type of CFSM models.

1 Introduction

The unboundedness of the communication channels in a communicating finite state machine (CFSM) model can have several negative effects. First, if the model represents a software design, the unboundedness of one or more of the communication channels hints at a possible design fault. For instance, the overflow of a communication buffer can have equally negative ramifications on the sanity of a system as, say, an overflow of the program heap due to inadequate object allocation and deallocation. Of course, unboundedness of a buffer can also be due to the environment, e.g., if it is flooded with requests from the outside. In this case, it is important to determine whether the unboundedness of certain buffers is only due to external flooding or to internal design flaws. Finally, buffers with unbounded capacity impede automated finite state analyzability since they induce an infinite state space that renders state space exploration incomplete in finite time.

In spite of the potential unboundedness of the buffers in CFSM systems one commonly observes that for many actual CFSM models the buffer occupancy is bounded by

K. Jensen and A. Podelski (Eds.): TACAS 2004, LNCS 2988, pp. 327–341, 2004.
© Springer-Verlag Berlin Heidelberg 2004

some small constant k. This is not surprising since, as we argue above, the unbounded growth of the buffers that are typically employed to implement communication channels is an undesired property of the system. If k-boundedness is proven, then one can safely replace the unbounded message buffers by k-bounded message buffers without changing the behavior of the system. Ideally, one wants to find individual bounds k_i for every buffer B_i. A system with k-bounded buffers is a finite-state system, modulo any remaining infinity due to data.

Practitioners usually notice the k-boundedness of a system either by manual inspection of the code (for small examples), or by running random simulations. Both these methods are not reliable and do no scale. The objective of our paper is to present algorithms that are capable of establishing the boundedness of CFSM models in an automated fashion. In their seminal paper [8], Brand and Zafiropulo showed that for CFSM systems with unbounded buffers many interesting properties, including reachability and boundedness, are undecidable. Consequently, the boundedness analysis that we propose in this paper is inevitably an incomplete test. We use an over-approximation of CFSMs for which boundedness is decidable and for which bounds on the buffer length can be computed. By the very nature of over-approximations, not every bounded CFSM can be detected as such by this method and the obtained bounds are not necessarily optimal. However, the computed bounds are certainly upper bounds, which is sufficient to make the system analyzable by finite-state verification methods.

While our results apply to the whole class of CFSM systems, in this paper we are interested in a particular instance of this paradigm. Variants of CFSMs form the foundation of many object-oriented modeling techniques for concurrent, reactive systems. We will focus on the modeling notation UML RT [28]. UML RT is an integral part of the current version 2.0 of the Unified Modeling Language (UML) [26]. UML RT enjoys widespread use in the design of asynchronous distributed embedded systems [16,25], and as an architectural description language [4]. Our interest in boundedness analysis for UML RT models is partly due to the availability of a commercial CASE tool supporting this modeling language. The *Rational Rose RealTime* tool suite, a direct successor to the ObjecTime Developer toolset [20], permits the graphical editing, interactive simulation and automated target platform implementation of UML RT models.

As we alluded to above, obtaining a boundedness result for a given UML RT model provides at least two benefits. First, it is an assurance of the well-formedness of the inter-object communication mechanism in the model. Second, the boundedness property of an UML RT model facilitates the translation of the model to a finite state verification tool such as the model checker SPIN [17]. SPIN requires all communication channels to have finite, compile-time known capacity limits. Having to commit to a specific channel capacity at modeling time may be undesirable. On the other hand, the fact that the boundedness of the UML RT model has been proven means that the designer can completely verify properties for models that are bounded by a sufficiently large buffer capacity limit. As we will explain later, the estimation of an actual upper bound is more intricate to obtain than the boundedness result, but we will present overapproximations that conservatively estimate buffer capacities for bounded models.

2   UML RT

UML RT has its root in the graphical modeling language ROOM [27]. ROOM has later been reconciled with the UML standard to form a UML compatible language for the modeling of real-time systems [28]. We will refer to this notation as *UML RT*. UML RT permits the description of the communication structure and the dynamic behavior of the systems. A system is decomposed into a set of concurrent active objects, called *capsules*. Capsules can be decomposed hierarchically into sub-capsules. The communication interfaces of the capsules are called *ports*. Ports can be associated with each other using *connectors* - the presence of a connector between ports indicates a communication channel. Inter-capsule communication is by message passing only, i.e., no shared variable communication is defined in UML RT.

The behavior of each capsule is described using a communicating, extended, hierarchical finite state machines (CEHFSM). These state machines are derived from ROOMCharts [27] which, in turn, are a variant of Statecharts [15]. However, as opposed to Statecharts, the CEHFSMs in UML RT are strictly sequential, i.e., the orthogonality concept of Statecharts in absent in UML RT. The operational semantics of UML RT is characterized by two salient features: state machine transitions can only be triggered by message reception, and arbitrary programming language code can be executed in the course of a transition between states. The structure of this transition code is not specifically constrained by the UML RT definition, and, in fact, the Rose RealTime tool allows arbitrary C++ or Java code to be attached to transitions.

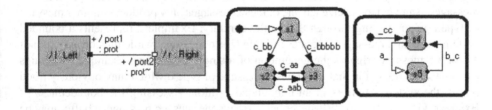

Fig. 1. The *2-Capsule* UML RT Model

Consider the simple UML RT model with two capsules given in Figure 1. It consists of two capsules, named Left and Right. Capsules represent active objects that may have state machines attached to them. Ports denote communication interfaces of capsules, and a connector between ports, such as the one between port1 and port2, represents a bi-directional communication channel. Figure 1 also illustrates the state machines associated with the two capsules. Since in UML RT the transition labels are mere names that carry no semantics, we have used speaking transition names which indicate which message sending and receiving primitives are executed in the course of the respective transition. For instance, the transition labeled with c_aab consumes a message c. It then sends two messages a and then a message b. For a more complete description of the UML RT notation we refer the reader to [28].

At the time of writing, there is no complete formal operational semantics for UML RT available in the literature that we are aware of. It turns out that the precise definition of a formal semantics is not a prerequisite for the work pursued here. We will present an approach that is taking advantage of a significant amount of abstraction in preparation of the analysis. These abstractions amount to an over-approximation of the actual system behavior so that subtle issues in the UML RT semantics, such as the ordering of message events and the treatment of message priorities, are not meaningful in the abstract system and hence for our analysis. In fact, our abstraction and the results of our algorithm are safe w.r.t. effects like message reordering and message loss in the channels. The only really necessary assumption is that no *unbounded* message duplication occurs. (Our boundedness test (YES/NO) is safe w.r.t. *finite* message duplication, but the computed upper bounds on the buffer lengths are not.)

3   Overview of the Boundedness Test

The underlying idea of our boundedness test is to determine whether at all it is possible to combine the cyclic executions of all of the processes in a UML RT model in such a way that the filling of at least one of the message buffers can be "blown up" in an unbounded way. Note that any infinite execution of the system can be understood as the combination of an infinite number of control state cycles through the CFSMs.

Consider the examples in Figure 2. All examples consist of two state machines which we assume to represent concurrent CFSMs. The state transition labels indicate message sending and receiving in the usual format. Since we are only interested in infinite execution sequences, all finite prefixes, e.g., transitions initializing the system, have been disregarded. In Example 1 it is easy to see that the system is unbounded. Any execution of the cycle through state S1 will consume a message of type a and produce two messages, b and c. However, each one of these messages only produces another message of type a when cycling through S2. To the contrary, Example 2 represents a bounded system since an a message generates a single b or c message, while the consumption of a b or a c message triggers the generation of a single a message. Example 3 contains a spontaneous transition that generates a message of type c which may obviously flood one of the system's buffers in an unbounded fashion. Assessing the boundedness of Example 4 is less obvious. Whenever the system generates a c message, a buffer may be flooded. However, if the system only ever executes the cycles in which a and b messages are exchanged, the filling of every buffer remains bounded. Whether a cycle generating a c message ever gets executed obviously depends on how the system is initialized, which is information we have already abstracted away. Since our test is conservative and only returns a boundedness result if boundedness can be proven, i.e., there is no way of combining the cycles in the CFSM in such a fashion that the buffer can be blown up, it would in this case return an "UNKNOWN" answer.

While in the above case the boundedness can be seen by manual inspection, this is not generally the case. Consider the example given in Figure 1 in which the actual boundedness of the model is far from obvious. This calls for automated methods in support of testing a system's boundedness.

4   Abstracting UML RT Models

In this section we describe a sequence of conceptual abstractions for UML RT models. Each level corresponds to a computational model for which complexity results for

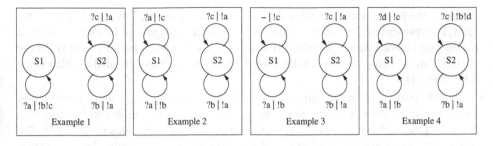

Fig. 2. Various Examples of Simple CFSM Systems

the boundedness problem are either known, or provided by our work. The abstraction is conceptual since the tool that we develop does not perform the transformations described in this section, but uses a more direct code analysis approach. The purpose of the conceptual abstraction is to reason about the complexity of our boundedness test. As mentioned above, we want to reason about the boundedness of the UML RT model in terms of summary message passing effects of simple control flow cycles. The goal of our conceptual abstraction is to arrive at a data structure that allows us to reason about these summary effects using linear combination analysis.

The abstract computational model that we obtain is an overapproximation of the original UML RT system in the following sense:

– All behavior of the original system is also possible in the overapproximation. However, there can exist some behavior that is possible in the overapproximation, but not in the original system.
– The abstraction preserves the number of messages in every communication channel (buffer) of the UML RT model. In particular, if some buffer is unbounded in the UML RT model, then it is also unbounded in the overapproximation. Furthermore, if a buffer is bounded by a constant k' in the overapproximation, then it is bounded by some constant $k \le k'$ in the original system.

The following summarizes the conceptual abstraction steps.

Level 0: UML RT. We start with the original system model described in UML RT. For the original UML RT model boundedness is, of course, undecidable, since it can contain arbitrary program code and can thus simulate Turing-machines.

Level 1: CFSMs. First, we abstract from the general program code on the transitions of the UML RT model and retain only the finite control structure of the capsules and their message passing via unbounded buffers representing the communication channels. We obtain a system of communicating finite-state machines (CFSMs), sometimes also called FIFO-channel systems [1]. For the CFSM model boundedness is also undecidable since CFSMs can still simulate Turing-machines [8].

Level 2: Parallel-Composition-VASS. In the next step we abstract from the order of the messages in the buffers and consider only the number of messages of any given type. For example, the buffer with contents abbacb would be represented by the integer vector $(2, 3, 1)$, representing 2 messages of type a, 3 messages of type b and 1 message of type c. Also we abstract from the ability to test explicitly if a given buffer is empty. In the abstraction, all actions that are enabled when the buffer is empty are also enabled when it is non-empty.

For the purpose of complexity analysis it is helpful to relate the obtained abstraction to the theory of Petri nets. The numbers of messages in any buffer can be stored on Petri net places. We then obtain a vector addition system with states (VASS) [7]. The states correspond to the control-states of the UML RT model and the Petri net places represent the buffer contents. More exactly, we obtain a *parallel-composition-VASS*. This is a VASS whose finite-control is the parallel (but unsynchronized) composition of several finite automata. Each part of this parallel composition corresponds to the finite control of some part of CFSM of level 1, and to the finite control of a capsule in the original UML RT model. Note that a parallel-composition-VASS is not exactly the same as the parallel composition of several VASS, because the places are shared by all parallel parts of the finite control. (It will be shown later that parallel-composition-VASS are in some respects more succinct that normal VASS.) The boundedness problem for parallel-composition-VASS is polynomially equivalent to the boundedness problem for Petri nets, which is $EXPSPACE$-complete [29].

Level 3: Parallel-Composition-VASS with Arbitrary Input. We now abstract from activation conditions of cycles in the control-graph of the VASS and assume instead that there are always enough messages, represented by tokens, present to start the cycle. For example, a cycle that first reads one message a from a buffer and then writes two messages a to the same buffer can be repeated infinitely often, but only if in the beginning there was at least one message a in the buffer. Any (combination of) cycles with an overall positive effect on all places has a minimal activation condition, i.e., a minimal number of tokens needed to get it started. In principle, it is decidable if there is a reachable configuration that satisfies these minimal requirements, but this involves solving the coverability problem for VASS (i.e., Petri nets). The coverability problem is the question if there exists a reachable marking which is bigger than a given marking. This problem is decidable, but at least $EXPSPACE$-hard [19,12], and thus not practical. Therefore we use this overapproximation and assume that these activation conditions can always be satisfied. More precisely, we assume that any cyclic sequence of transitions that has an overall non-negative effect on all places can be repeated arbitrarily often. As far as boundedness is concerned, we replace the problem 'Is the system bounded if starting at the given initial configuration?' by the problem 'Is the system bounded for any finite initial configuration?', also referred to as the *structural boundedness problem*. Obviously, every unbounded system is also not structurally bounded. It will be shown in Section 7 that this structural boundedness problem for parallel-composition-VASS is co-$\mathcal{NP}$-complete, unlike for standard Petri nets where it is polynomial [23,12]. (The reason for this difference is that an encoding of control-states by Petri net places does not preserve structural boundedness, because it is not assured that only one of these places is marked at any time.) Furthermore, the co-$\mathcal{NP}$-lower bound even holds if the number of simple cycles in the control-graph is only linear in the size of the system description.

Level 4: Independent Cycle System. Finally, we abstract from the fact that certain cycles in the control graph depend on each other. For example, cycles might be mutually exclusive so that executing one cycle makes another cycle unreachable, or imply each other, i.e., one cannot repeat some cycle infinitely often without repeating some other cycle infinitely often. Instead we assume that all cycles are independent and any combination of them is executable infinitely often, provided that the combined effect of this combination on all places is non-negative. It should be noted that one part of this overapproximation condition, the mutually exclusive cycles, is normally not a problem anyway. This is because in almost all practical cases the control-graph of the capsules in UML RT models is strongly connected and therefore cycles are not mutually exclusive.

The *un*boundedness problem for this abstracted model then becomes the following question: Is there any linear combination (with positive integer coefficients) of the effects of simple cycles in the control graph, such that the combined effect is non-negative on all places and strictly positive on at least one place? Since we consider an overapproximation, the original UML RT model is surely bounded if the answer to this question is 'no'. Since these effects of simple cycles can be represented by integer vectors, we get the following problem. Given a set of integer vectors, does there exist a linear combination (with positive integer coefficients) of them, such that the result is non-negative in every component and strictly positive in at least one. This problem can be solved in time polynomial in the number of vectors by using linear programming techniques. However, in the worst case the number of different simple cycles and corresponding vectors can be exponential (in the size of the control-graph), although they are not necessarily completely independent. So far, we only have an exponential-time upper bound on the *worst-case* complexity of checking boundedness at this abstraction level 4. However, the important aspect is that the time required is only polynomial in the number of simple cycles, unlike at level 3, where the problem is co-$\mathcal{NP}$-hard even for a linear number of simple cycles. This is very significant, since for instances derived from typical UML RT models, the number of simple cycles is usually small (see Section 7).

It is easy to see that the abstraction obtained at level 4 is an overapproximation of the UML RT model in the sense defined above.

5   The Concrete Abstraction

We now present the concrete abstraction of UML RT models as we are currently implementing it in the tool IBOC (*IMCOS Boundedness Checker*). Due to space limitations, the presentation only sketches the approach, a complete presentation including correctness arguments will be included in a forthcoming paper.

The objective of the concrete abstraction is to automatically transform UML RT models into a collection of *effect vectors*, each of which represents the summary message passing effect of each simple cycle in each capsule state machine. In order to obtain these vectors we extract the control flow graph of each capsule state machine from the UML RT model[1]. We annotate the edges of this graph, which we call *effect graph*, with the summary message passing effect of the UML RT model transition that it corresponds

---

[1] Note that we currently assume the transition code to only consist of linear, non-branching and non-iterating control flow structures.

to. To obtain the effect vectors we determine the simple cycles in the effect graphs using a modified depth-first search (DFS) procedure. Figure 3 presents the effect graphs that we obtain for the 2-Capsule model in Figure 1. The analysis returns the effect vectors $v_1 = (4, 1, -2)$ and $v_2 = (-1, -1, 1)$.

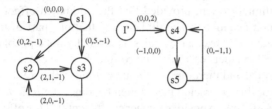 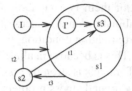

Fig. 3. Effect Graphs of the 2-Capsule Model from Figure 1

Fig. 4. Effect graph of Hierarchical State Machine

The above presentation refers to flat state machines, however, the effect graphs derived from UML RT state machines may be hierarchical as shown in Figure 4. The problem is compounded by group transitions that return to history, such as transition t2 in the example. We are adjusting the DFS algorithm to deal with composite states. If a vertex v corresponding to some state is enclosed by several composite vertices, we also collect all the successors of the enclosing vertices in addition to its own. That exactly resembles the behavior of the common edges which represent group transitions. When the target of an edge is a composite vertex, say v', a procedure is invoked to recall the latest non-composite vertex enclosed by v' in the vertex stack. The latest enclosed vertex corresponds to the last active substate when a return to history transition is taken. For the example in Figure 4, the modified DFS algorithm will determine the following cycles: $(I', t3, S2, t2, I')$, $(S2, t1, S3, t3, S2)$ and $(S3, t3, S2, t2, S3)$. Note the different targets for the return-to-history transition t2.

6   Boundedness Test

Overall Boundedness Test. We now describe the boundedness test using a linear combination analysis of the effect vectors that have been derived from the UML RT model. For every buffer and every message type there is one component in each of the effect vectors. The component can be negative if in the cycle more messages of this type were removed from a buffer than added to it. The resulting semilinear system is unbounded if and only if there exists a linear combination with positive coefficients of the effect-vectors that is positive in every component and strictly positive in at least one component. Formally, this can be described as follows: Let $v_1, \ldots, v_n \in \mathbb{Z}^k$ be the effect-vectors of all simple cycles and let v^j be the j-th component of the vector v. The question then is

$$\exists x_1, \ldots, x_n \in \mathbb{N}_0. \sum_{i=1}^{n} x_i v_i \geq \mathbf{0} \wedge \exists j. \left(\sum_{i=1}^{n} x_i v_i \right)^j > 0.$$

This can easily be transformed into a system of linear inequations and solved by standard linear programming tools. If this condition is true then our overapproximation is unbounded, but not necessarily also the UML RT model. The unboundedness could simply be due to the coarseness of the overapproximation. On the other hand, if the condition above is false, then our overapproximation is bounded, and thus our original UML-RT model is also bounded. Thus, this test yields an answer of the form "BOUNDED" in case no linear combination of the effect vectors satisfying the above constraint can be found, and "UNKNOWN" when such a linear combination exists.

Examples. Consider Example 1 from Figure 2. The effect vectors are $v_1 = (-1, 1, 1)$, $v_2 = (1, 0, -1)$ and $v_3 = (1, -1, 0)$. Obviously, $x_1 = x_2 = 1$ describes a linear combination satisfying the above constrains and we conclude "UNKNOWN". In fact, Example 1 is unbounded under any initialization of the message buffers with either a, b or c messages. For Example 2 the vectors are $v_1 = (-1, 0, 1)$, $v_2 = (-1, 1, 0)$, $v_3 = (1, 0, -1)$ and $v_4 = (1, -1, 0)$. It is easy to see that there is no linear combination of these vectors satisfying the above constraint, hence we conclude "BOUNDED". Similarly, Examples 3 and 4 lead to results "UNKNOWN". For the 2-Capsule example of Figure 1 we had obtained the effect vectors vectors $v_1 = (4, 1, -2)$ and $v_2 = (-1, -1, 1)$. To represent the > 0 condition in the linear inequation system we add a constraint $3x_1 - x_2 \geq 1$. The linear inequation solver returns infeasibility of this system of inequations, and we thus conclude a result of "BOUNDED". Note that it is not easy to see this result by manual inspection

Computing Bounds for Individual Buffers. A more refined problem is to compute upper bounds on the lengths of individual buffers in the system. In particular, some buffers might be bounded even if the whole system is unbounded. Since normally not all buffers can reach maximal length simultaneously, the analysis is done individually for each buffer B. This can be done by solving a linear programming problem that maximizes a target function f_B. f_B is a linear function whose input is our abstracted system configuration, i.e., a vector of natural numbers indicating how often which message type occurs in which buffer, and which returns the length of buffer B. Let m be the number of capsules in the system. Let C_0 be the initial configuration of the system, C_B the reachable configuration where buffer B has maximal length, and p the path from C_0 to C_B. Then p can be decomposed into m parts $p_1, \ldots, p_m$ such that p_i is the part of p that occurs in the i-th capsule. Each p_i starts at control-state s_0^i, the initial state of capsule i. Each p_i can be further decomposed into a part consisting of simple cycles and a non-cyclic part. The order of these is not important for us, since we are only interested in the effect-vectors of these paths. Let $p(s_0^i, s^i)$ be the non-cyclic part of p_i and s^i some control-state in capsule i. For any path p let $E(p)$ be its effect-vector. Then $E(p_i) = E(p(s_0^i, s^i)) + \sum_{i=1}^{n} x_i v_i$ for some x_i. It follows that $E(p) = \sum_{i=1}^{m} E(p(s_0^i, s^i)) + \sum_{i=1}^{n} y_i v_i$ for some y_i. In order to maximize our target function f_B we need to apply it to $E(p)$ and find the optimal paths to control-states $s^1, \ldots, s^m$ (note that the same control-state might be reachable via several different paths), and the optimal numbers $y_1, \ldots, y_n$. We thus need to compute $max := max(p(s_0^1, s^1), \ldots, p(s_0^m, s^m), y_1, \ldots, y_n) f_B(E(p))$.

However, the combinatorial complexity of finding the optimal paths and control-states s^i in all capsules to maximize f_B is too big for practical purposes since one would need to try out all exponentially many possible combinations. Therefore, we apply yet another overapproximation to simplify the problem. Let r_i be the minimal vector s.t.

$\forall s^i.\ r_i \geq E(p(s_0^i, s^i))$. In other words, we maximize individual components of vector $E(p(s_0^i, s^i))$ over all paths to control-states s^i. The vectors r_i can easily be computed in polynomial time by depth-first search in the individual capsules. Then we define $max' := max(y_1, \ldots, y_n) f_B \left(\sum_{i=1}^m r_i + \sum_{i=1}^n y_i v_i \right)$ which requires just one instance of a linear programming problem to be solved. It is easy to see that $max' \geq max$ and thus we have computed an upper bound. Normally, the function f_B will be the number of messages in some buffer B, but it can be any linear function. For example, one might want to count only some types of messages in a buffer and not others.

Example. Having established boundedness of the 2-Capsule example of Figure 1, we now compute the estimated upper bound for each buffer (port). First we compute the effect vectors for all non-cyclic paths. They are listed in Table 1 where $init$ and $init'$ are the initial states of the state machines. Then we take the maxima of individual components from those effect vectors and construct the overapproximated maximal effect vectors for capsule Left as $r_1 = (2, 5, 0)$ and for capsule Right as $r_2 = (0, 0, 2)$. Thus the sum is $\sum_{i=1}^n r_i = (2, 5, 2)$. We obtain the following two optimization problems (1-4 and 5-8) for the two buffers left-to-right and right-to-left:

$$
\begin{array}{ll}
max : 2 - 2x_1 + x_2 \quad (1) & \qquad max : 7 + 5x_1 - 2x_2 \quad (5) \\
2 + 4x_1 - x_2 \geq 0 \quad (2) & \qquad 2 + 4x_1 - x_2 \geq 0 \quad (6) \\
5 + x_1 - x_2 \geq 0 \quad (3) & \qquad 5 + x_1 - x_2 \geq 0 \quad (7) \\
2 - 2x_1 + x_2 \geq 0. \quad (4) & \qquad 2 - 2x_1 + x_2 \geq 0. \quad (8)
\end{array}
$$

Linear Programming returns a value of 6 for the objective function (1) and a value of 18 for the objective function (5). These values represent the estimated bounds for the communication buffers associated with port1 and port2, respectively.

Table 1. The Effect Vectors for all Non-Cyclic Paths in 2-Capsules

The non-cyclic path	The effect vectors	The non-cyclic path	The effect vectors
$< init, s1 >$	(0,0,0)	$< init, s1, s2 >$	(0,2,-1)
$< init, s1, s2, s3 >$	(2,3,-2)	$< init, s1, s3 >$	(0,5,-1)
$< init, s1, s3, s2 >$	(2,5,-2)	$< init', s4 >$	(0,0,2)
		$< init', s4, s5 >$	(-1,0,2)

7   Complexity Analysis

In this Section we analyze the complexity of the problem of checking for boundedness in general and our algorithm in particular. It has already been mentioned in Section 3 that the boundedness problem is undecidable for UML RT (level 0), undecidable for CF-SMs (level 1), $EXPSPACE$-complete for VASS (level 2), co-$\mathcal{NP}$-complete for VASS with arbitrary input (level 3), and polynomial in the number of simple cycles for Independent Cycle Systems (level 4). The only part that still needs to be shown is the $\mathcal{NP}$-completeness for parallel-combination-VASS with arbitrary input.

STRUCTURAL BOUNDEDNESS OF PARALLEL-COMPOSITION-VASS

Instance: A VASS whose finite control is given as an unsynchronized parallel composition of automata $G_1 \| \ldots \| G_n$.

Question: Is the system structurally bounded, i.e., is it bounded for every initial configuration?

Lemma 1. *Structural boundedness of parallel-composition-VASS is co-$\mathcal{NP}$-hard, even if all the control-graphs G_i are strongly connected and contain only polynomially many simple cycles.*

Proof. We reduce SAT to unboundedness of parallel-composition-VASS for some initial configuration. Let $\Phi := Q_1 \wedge \ldots \wedge Q_k$ be a boolean formula over variables $x_1, \ldots, x_n$. Each clause Q_j is a disjunction of literals and each literal is either a variable or the negation of a variable. We now construct in polynomial time a parallel-composition-VASS as follows. The system contains $k + 2$ places, $p_1, \ldots, p_k, l, g$, where the first k places each correspond to one clause, and places l, g have special functions.

For every variable x_i we define an automaton G_i with three states s_i, t_i, f_i and the following transitions. We describe the effects of these transitions on the places by vectors of integers, as usual in VASS. There are transitions from s_i to t_i, t_i to s_i, s_i to f_i and f_i to s_i that each have the following effect. They reduce place l by 1 and leave all other places unaffected. There is a transition from t_i to t_i with the following effect: For all j, if clause Q_j contains literal x_i then one token is added to p_j. Furthermore, exactly one token is removed from place g. There is a transition from f_i to f_i with the following effect. For all j, if clause Q_j contains literal $\neg x_i$ then one token is added to p_j. Furthermore, exactly one token is removed from place g.

Finally, we add another automaton T with just the state s and a transition from s to s with the effect $(-1, \ldots, -1, 0, n + 1)$. We now show that the VASS with these places and finite control $G_1 \| \ldots \| G_n \| T$ and initial control-state $(s_1, \ldots, s_n, s)$ is structurally bounded iff Φ is not satisfiable[2].

If Φ is satisfiable then there exists a variable assignment that makes all clauses Q_j true. Then there exists an unbounded run of the system of the following form. If x_i is true then go from s_i to t_i, else go to f_i. The combined effect of this is $(0, \ldots, 0, -n, 0)$. Then do each local cycle at t_i (resp. f_i) exactly once. The combined effect of this is $(e_1, \ldots, e_k, 0, -n)$, where for all j we have $e_j \geq 1$. Then we do the cycle at s exactly once. The effect of this is $(-1, \ldots, -1, 0, n + 1)$. Thus the combined effect is $\geq (0, \ldots, 0, +1)$. This combination of cycles can then be repeated infinitely often. Thus there exists an unbounded run starting at configuration $(0, \ldots, 0, n, n)$. So the system is not structurally bounded.

Now assume that Φ is not satisfiable. No infinite run from any initial configuration can change infinitely often between some s_i and t_i/f_i, because place l is decreased in these transitions and never increased anywhere else. Thus, for every i, every infinite run can only contain infinitely many loops at t_i or at f_i but not infinitely many of both. By the construction of the automata G_i, and since there is no satisfying assignment for Φ, no combination of these loops can have a strictly positive effect on all places $p_1, \ldots, p_k$. Therefore, for any initial configuration, the loop at s can only be done finitely often.

---

[2] Note also that each G_i and T are strongly connected and that the total number of simple cycles in the system is $4n + 1$.

Therefore, the local loops at states t_i/f_i can only be done finitely often, because of their effect on place g. Thus all runs from any initial configuration have finite length and the system is structurally bounded.   □

Lemma 2. *Structural boundedness of parallel-composition-VASS is in co-$\mathcal{NP}$.*

For the proof we refer the reader to the full version of the paper. We conclude the following theorem:

Theorem 3. *Structural boundedness of parallel-composition-VASS is co-$\mathcal{NP}$-complete.*

The co-$\mathcal{NP}$-hardness of the structural boundedness problem at abstraction level 3, even for small numbers of simple cycles, justifies for further abstraction to level 4, where the problem is polynomial in the number of simple cycles.

To analyze the complexity of our boundedness test algorithm for UML RT models, consider a typical input system. It consists of m capsules running in parallel and communicating with each other via buffers. Let k be the maximal size of each buffer. Thus the size of the instance is $n := \mathcal{O}(m*k)$. Note that the total number of different control-state combinations is $\mathcal{O}(k^m)$, the classical state explosion problem. However, our algorithm avoids this combinatorial explosion.

First, it extracts (the effects of) all simple cycles from the finite controls of each capsule. The time needed for this is polynomial in the number of simple cycles. Then it checks for the existence of positive linear combinations of the effects of these cycles. Again, the time required is polynomial in the number of simple cycles (by using linear programming techniques). Thus, the algorithm overall requires polynomial time in the number of simple cycles.

In the worst case, the number of simple cycles in any capsule (of size k) can be exponential in k, i.e., $\mathcal{O}(2^k)$. So the total number of simple cycles in the system is only bounded by $\mathcal{O}(m*2^k)$. Thus the worst-case complexity of the algorithm is $\mathcal{O}(poly(m*2^k))$. It should be noted that this is still normally much smaller than $\mathcal{O}(2^{m*k}) = \mathcal{O}(2^n)$. However, these worst-case complexity estimates are not very meaningful for practical problems. In typical UML RT models the finite-control graphs in the capsules are derived from programming-language-like control-flow graphs. These graphs are normally very sparse, and the number of simple cycles in them is normally polynomial, rather than exponential. Therefore, for typical UML RT models, the algorithm requires only polynomial time.

8   Experimental Results

We now report on experiments that we performed using the IBOC system. We used the 2-Capsule model of Figure 1, a UML RT model of the Alternating Bit Protocol, and the UML RT model of a telecommunications switch, called PBX. For experimentation purposes we obtained the PBX model from IBM/Rational. It is a model with a complexity comparable to that of models used in industrial development projects.

IBOC directly accesses the internal model structure inside the Rose RealTime tool and uses the LPSOLVE system for linear programming tasks. Table 2 shows the performance results of these experiments that are performed on a two processor 1GHz Pentium III PC with 2 GB memory.

The IBOC system returned "precise" boundedness results in the sense that an "UN-KNOWN" verdict in all cases corresponded to an unboundedness in the respective UML RT model. For the model of Alternating Bit protocol, for instance, IBOC returned "UN-KNOWN" and provided two counterexamples as linear combinations of cycles that potentially contribute to the unbounded growth of channels. These counterexamples indicate that two cycles in the state machine of the sender capsule may cause the unboundedness. This result is plausible since the sender injects messages into the Alternating Bit system without restraint. The PBX model is obviously of a complexity that makes it impossible to guess boundedness with manual methods. IBOC returns a "BOUNDED" result within very reasonable runtime, which proves that our analysis scales to UML RT models of realistic size. To assess the quality of the estimated buffer bounds we executed the PBX model in Rose RealTime and traced several ports. For most ports, the actual bounds are very close to the estimates. For instance, a port $configureDialPlan$ is observed to contain no more than five messages at runtime, while the estimate is seven.

Table 2. Experimental Results obtained with the IBOC System

	2-Capsule	Alternating Bit	PBX
Checked capsules	3	4	29
Checked states	30	47	736
Checked transitions	8	15	299
Checked message types	3	8	308
Checked buffers	2	4	57
Reported cycles	3	11	2030
Generated vectors	2	11	1026
Runtime for cycle detection [sec.]	0.034	0.136	24.860
Runtime for boundedness check [sec.]	0.233	1.110	28.110
Runtime for computing bounds [sec.]	0.207	-	3.250

9   Related Work

There is a vast body of literature on the problem of dealing with the unboundedness of communication queues. This includes overapproximations using lossiness assumptions for queues [1] (the boundedness problem stays undecidable for lossy queue systems [2], even under strong restrictions [21]), sufficient syntactic conditions for the unboundedness of communication channels in CFSM systems [18], the symbolic treatment of infinite queues [5,6] and the elimination of unbounded queues using structural properties of the state spaces of the CFSMs [10].

At the time of writing, no operational semantics for UML RT is available. Work described in [13] and [14] focuses on giving semantics to the structural aspects of UML RT. The translation of UML RT models into Promela was fist attempted by [24] which pointed out the tremendous problems involved in dealing with UML RT queues and their potential unboundedness. Our analysis of hierarchical UML RT CFSMs is in part based on ideas from [3].

Model Checking based on integer inequality systems has been pioneered by the INCA system [9]. Esparza and Melzer used integer linear programming to check several safety properties (e.g., mutual exclusion) for Petri nets models [22,11]. However, in most cases, the models considered were 1-safe Petri nets which are bounded by definition.

10 Conclusion

We presented an incomplete test for the boundedness of communication buffers in UML RT models. Our algorithm abstracts UML RT models such that only the communication effects of the simple control flow cycles in the capsule state machines remain. The test then tries to establish a linear combination of the resulting effect vectors that allows at least one of the system's message buffers to grow unboundedly. If such a linear combination cannot be found, the system is bounded. In addition we proposed an upper bound estimate for the maximal occupancy of individual buffers. We have argued that our analyses scale well to UML RT systems of realistic complexity, and supported this claim by experimental results using the IBOC tool.

One focus of current research is to refine the analysis, in particular when the result is "UNKNOWN". The IBOC system that we currently develop permits the identification of a sub-model to which the boundedness analysis can be limited. Another focus lies on enhancing the generation of "counterexamples", i.e., sets of cycles that lead to unboundedness. We are also interested in developing abstraction refinement procedures when the counterexamples are spurious, i.e., not executable in the original UML RT model. Future work will extend the analysis to establish boundedness results for more general types of dynamic systems, e.g., systems that dynamically generate and delete concurrent processes, or systems that dynamically allocate and deallocate objects on heap memory. Boundedness in these cases implies the absence of memory leaks due to improper memory management.

Acknowledgements. We thank John Hogg, Andreas Podelski and Bran Selic for initial discussions on the subject of this paper. IBM/Rational supported this work by providing licenses for the Rational Rose RealTime tool. The third author was supported through the DFG funded project IMCOS (grant number LE 1342/1).

References

1. P. Abdulla and B. Jonsson. Verifying Programs with Unreliable Channels. In *LICS'93*. IEEE, 1993.
2. P. Abdulla and B. Jonsson. Undecidable verification problems for programs with unreliable channels. *Information and Computation*, 130(1):71–90, 1996.
3. R. Alur, R. Grosu, and M. McDougall. Efficient reachability analysis of hierarchical reactive machines. In *Proc. of CAV'00*, volume 1855 of *LNCS*. Springer Verlag, 2000.
4. L. Bass, P. Clements, and R. Kazman. *Software Architecture in Practice*. Addison Wesley, 1998.
5. B. Boigelot and P. Goidefroid. Symbolic verification of communication protocols with infinite state spaces using qdds. In *Proc. CAV'96*, volume 1102 of *LNCS*. Springer, 1996.
6. A. Bouajjani and P. Habermehl. Symbolic reachability analysis of FIFO-channel systems with nonregular sets of configurations. In *Proc. of ICALP'97*, volume 1256 of *LNCS*, 1997.

7. A. Bouajjani and R. Mayr. Model checking lossy vector addition systems. In *Proc. of STACS'99*, volume 1563 of *LNCS*. Springer Verlag, 1999.
8. D. Brand and P. Zafiropulo. On communicating finite-state machines. *Journal of the ACM*, 2(5):323–342, April 1983.
9. James C. Corbett and George S. Avrunin. Using integer programming to verify general safety and liveness properties. *Formal Methods in System Design: An International Journal*, 6(1):97–123, January 1995.
10. W. Damm and B. Jonsson. Eliminating queues from rt uml models. In *Proc. of FTRTFT 2002*, LNCS. Springer, 2002.
11. J. Esparza and S. Melzer. Verification of safety properties using integer programming: Beyond the state equation. *Formal Methods in System Design*, 16:159–189, 2000.
12. J. Esparza and M. Nielsen. Decibility issues for Petri nets - a survey. *Journal of Informatik Processing and Cybernetics*, 30(3):143–160, 1994.
13. C. Fischer, E.-R. Olderog, and H. Wehrheim. A csp view on uml-rt structure diagrams. In *Fundamental Approaches to Software Engineering, Proc. of the 4th International Conference, FASE 2001*, volume 2029 of *LNCS*. Springer Verlag, 2001.
14. R. Grosu, M. Broy, B. Selic, and G. Stefanescu. What is behind UML-RT? *Behavioral specifications of businesses and systems*, 1999.
15. D. Harel. Statecharts: A visual formalisation for complex systems. *Science of Computer Programming*, 8:231–274, 1987.
16. D. Herzberg and A. Marburger. The use of layers and planes for architectural design of communication systems. In *Proc. of the Fourth IEEE International Symposium on Object-Oriented Real-Time Distributed Computing ISORC 2001*. IEEE Computer Society, May 2001.
17. Gerard J. Holzmann. *The Spin Model Checker - Primer and Reference Manual*. Addison-Wesley, 2004.
18. T. Jeron and C. Jard. Testing for unboundedness of fifo channels. *Theoretical Computer Science*, (113):93–117, 1993.
19. R. Lipton. The reachability problem requires exponential space. Technical Report 62, Department of Computer Science, Yale University, January 1976.
20. A. Lyons. Developing and debugging real-time software with objectime developer. available from http://www.objectime.com/otl/technical/1999q1_p017.pdf, 1999.
21. R. Mayr. Undecidable problems in unreliable computations. *TCS*, 297(1-3):337–354, 2003.
22. S. Melzer and J. Esparza. Checking system properties via integer programming. In H.R. Nielson, editor, *Proc. of ESOP'96*, volume 1058 of *Lecture Notes in Computer Science*, pages 250–264. Springer Verlag, 1996.
23. G. Memmi and G. Roucairol. Linear algebra in net theory. In *Net Theory and Applications*, volume 84 of *LNCS*, pages 213–223, 1980.
24. M. Saaltink. Generating and analysing Promela from RoseRT models. Technical Report TR-99-5537-02, ORA Canada, 1208 One Nocholas Street, Ottawa Ontario, K1N 7B7, Canada, 1999.
25. B. Selic. Turning clockwise: using UML in the real-time domain. *Comm. of the ACM*, 42(10):46–54, Oct. 1999.
26. B. Selic. An overview of uml 2.0. International Conference on Software Engineering, Tutorial Notes, May 2003.
27. B. Selic, G. Gullekson, and P.T. Ward. *Real-Time Object-Oriented Modelling*. John Wiley & Sons, Inc., 1994.
28. B. Selic and J. Rumbaugh. Using UML for modeling complex real-time systems. http://www.rational.com/media/whitepapers/umlrt.pdf, March 1998.
29. H. Yen. A unified approach for deciding the existence of certain Petri net paths. *Information and Computation*, 96(1):119–137, 1992.

Automatic Verification of Time Sensitive Cryptographic Protocols*

Giorgio Delzanno[1] and Pierre Ganty[2]

[1] Dip. di Informatica e Scienze dell'Informazione - Università di Genova
via Dodecaneso 35, 16146 Genova, Italy
giorgio@disi.unige.it
[2] Département d'Informatique - Université Libre de Bruxelles
Boulevard du Triomphe, 1050 Bruxelles, Belgium
pganty@ulb.ac.be

Abstract. We investigate the applicability of symbolic exploration to the automatic verification of secrecy and authentication properties for time sensitive cryptographic protocols. Our formal specifications are given in *multiset rewriting over first order atomic formulas* enriched with *constraints* so as to uniformly model fresh name generation and validity condition of time stamps. Our verification approach is based on data structures for symbolically representing sets of configurations of an arbitrary number of parallel protocol sessions. As a case study we discuss the verification of timed authentication for the Wide Mouth Frog protocol.

1 Introduction

Several authentication and key-establishment protocols make use of *time-stamps* to avoid possible replay attacks of malicious intruders. However, time-stamps are often abstracted away in formal models of cryptographic protocols (see e.g. [4, 6,19]). One reason for the use of this abstraction is that all known decidability results for verification of crypto-protocols are given for untimed models (see e.g. [14,18]). Powerful theorem provers like Isabelle in [2], Spass in [8], and PVS in [9] have been applied to verify timed dependent security properties.

In this paper we will present an automatic procedure for proving secrecy and authentication properties of time sensitive cryptographic protocols. Our procedure is an extension of the symbolic exploration method devised for the specification language MSR($\mathcal{L}$) of [5]. By combining multiset rewriting over first order atomic formulas [7] and linear arithmetic constraints, MSR($\mathcal{L}$) can be naturally applied to specify *unbounded* models of cryptographic protocols with *fresh name generation* and validity conditions for *time-stamps*. Our extension to the technique of [5] is based on the following points.

---

* This work was partially funded by the Information Society Technologies programme of the European Commission, Future and Emerging Technologies under the IST-2001-39252 AVISPA project.

K. Jensen and A. Podelski (Eds.): TACAS 2004, LNCS 2988, pp. 342–356, 2004.

As a first technical contribution, we will define a new *data structure* for representing infinite set of configurations of (unbounded) MSR($\mathcal{L}$) specifications. Our data structure combines two logics: the existential zones over n-ary predicates with linear arithmetic constraints of [5], and the first order term language enriched with the **sup** operator of [6]. Since existential zones are given an upward closed semantics with respect to inclusion of configurations, our data structure can be used to finitely represent snapshots of executions of an unbounded number of parallel protocol sessions. In this setting first order terms can be used to represent structured and partially specified data, whereas the special operator **sup** can be used to represent patterns occurring at arbitrary depth in a message. The term **sup**(t) represents in fact any term containing t as a subterm. Finally, linear arithmetic constraints are used to model freshness and validity conditions for nonces and time-stamps. To exploit the upward closed semantics of our symbolic representation, we incorporate the new data structure within a backward search scheme. The resulting *symbolic backward exploration* procedure is based on effective *entailment* and *pre-image* operators. These operators are defined via unification and subsumption for first order terms extended with the **sup** operator, and constraint operations like satisfiability and variable elimination.

Since verification of (control) reachability problems for unbounded cryptographic protocols is undecidable [7], termination of state exploration cannot be guaranteed in general. However, when terminating, our search procedure returns a *symbolic reachability graph* that finitely represents an infinite set of protocol traces. As a second technical contribution, we establish conditions under which the symbolic reachability graph can be used to verify security properties like *secrecy* and *authentication* in presence of validity conditions for time-stamps. The conditions we propose here can be verified by using a visit of the graph. Specifically, in order to verify that secrecy holds, we have to check that the set of nodes of the constructed graph does not contain initial protocol configurations. For authentication properties, we have to search for specific pairs of principals states along paths in the graph starting from an initial protocol configuration.

By using the term manipulation library, the graph package, and the linear constraint solver provided by Sicstus Prolog, we have extended the symbolic verification procedure defined for verification of *parametric data consistency protocols* in [5] to cope with the new class of protocols, properties, and symbolic data structures we will discuss in the present paper. As a practical contribution, we present here a detailed analysis of a timed model of the Wide Mouth Frog protocol of [3]. As shown in Section 5, using our method we have automatically proved *non-injective timed agreement* for the fixed version proposed by Lowe in [11]. Our results are obtained for an unbounded protocol model and for *parametric delays* in the validity conditions of time-stamps. In Section 6 we will compare the results of this analysis with two other methods (based on semi-automated [9] and finite-state verification [13]) applied to this protocol.

We believe that the main novelty of the resulting method with respect to existing ones is that it allows us to handle unbound parallelism, complex term structures, time-stamps, and freshness of names both at the level of specification and analysis in a uniform and effective way. Furthermore, the symbolic reachability graph allows us to verify security and authentication properties or to extract potential attacks (in form of a symbolic trace), a feature often not so easy in other verification methods based on theorem proving like TAPS [8].

2   Time Sensitive Cryptographic Protocols in MSR($\mathcal{L}$)

Let us first recall the main definitions of the language MSR($\mathcal{L}$)[5]. In this paper we will use $\cdot|\cdot$ and ϵ as multiset constructors and $\oplus$ to denote multiset union. Furthermore, we will use $Fv(t)$ to denote the set of free variables of a term or formula t. An MSR($\mathcal{L}$) specification $\mathcal{S}$ is a tuple $\langle \mathcal{P}, \Sigma, \mathcal{V}, \mathcal{I}, \mathcal{R} \rangle$, where $\mathcal{P}$ is a set of predicate symbols, Σ a first order signature, $\mathcal{V} = \mathcal{V}_t \cup \mathcal{V}_i$, $\mathcal{V}_t$ is a set of *term* variables, $\mathcal{V}_i$ is a set of *integer* variables, $\mathcal{V}_t \cap \mathcal{V}_i = \emptyset$, $\mathcal{I}$ is a set of initial configurations, and $\mathcal{R}$ is a finite set of labelled rules. A labelled rule has the form $\alpha : \mathcal{M} \longrightarrow \mathcal{N}{:}\varphi$, where α is a label, $\mathcal{M}$ and $\mathcal{N}$ are two (possibly empty) multisets of atomic formulas built on $\mathcal{P}$ and Σ, and φ is a *linear arithmetic constraint* such that $Fv(\varphi) \subseteq Fv(\mathcal{M} \oplus \mathcal{M}') \cap \mathcal{V}_i$. In this paper we will always embed *integer variables* within unary casting symbols working as *types*. For instance, in the rule $\alpha : p(ts(x), h(u)) \mid q(ts(y), h(z)) \rightarrow p(ts(y)) \mid q(ts(y), h(u, z)) : x > y$ the template $ts(\cdot)$ is used to encapsulate the integer variables x and y within a term.

The operational semantics of $\mathcal{S}$ is defined via the rewriting relation $\Rightarrow_{\mathcal{R}}$ defined over *configurations*. A configuration is a multiset of ground atomic formulas like $p(ts(3)) \mid q(ts(4), h(5))$. Given two configurations $\mathcal{M}_1$ and $\mathcal{M}_2$, $\mathcal{M}_1 \Rightarrow_{\mathcal{R}} \mathcal{M}_2$ if and only if there exists a configuration $\mathcal{Q}$ s.t. $\mathcal{M}_1 = \mathcal{N}_1 \oplus \mathcal{Q}$, $\mathcal{M}_2 = \mathcal{N}_2 \oplus \mathcal{Q}$, and $\mathcal{N}_1 \longrightarrow \mathcal{N}_2$ is a ground instance of a rule in $\mathcal{R}$. A ground instance of a rule $\alpha : \mathcal{M} \longrightarrow \mathcal{M}' : \varphi$ is obtained by extending a substitution in the set of solutions $Sol(\varphi)$ of the constraint φ to a grounding substitution (i.e. with ground terms in its range) for $Fv(\mathcal{M}, \mathcal{M}')$. Given a set of MSR($\mathcal{L}$) configurations S, the *predecessor* operator is defined as

$$Pre_{\mathcal{R}}(S) = \{\mathcal{M} \mid \exists \mathcal{M}' \in S \text{ s.t. } \mathcal{M} \Rightarrow_{\mathcal{R}} \mathcal{M}'\}.$$

A configuration $\mathcal{M}$ is *reachable* if $\mathcal{M}_0 \in Pre_{\mathcal{R}}^*(\{\mathcal{M}\})$ for some $\mathcal{M}_0 \in \mathcal{I}$. $Pre_{\mathcal{R}}^*$ represents here the transitive closure of the predecessor relation.

2.1   Time Sensitive Crypto-protocols

In the following we will assume the reader to be familiar with the use of multiset rewriting for the specification of cryptographic protocols (for more details, see e.g., [7]). Under the *perfect cryptography* assumption, time sensitive cryptographic protocols can be specified in MSR($\mathcal{L}$) as follows. Identifiers of honest principals are represented as integer numbers greater than zero. The intruder (Trudy) has the special identifier 0. The current state of honest principals is represented via atomic formulas like $r_i(id(n), \langle t_1, \ldots, t_n \rangle)$, meaning that the honest agent $n > 0$ has executed the i-th step of the protocol in the role r (and he/she is ready for next step); $t_1, \ldots, t_n$ are terms representing his/her current knowledge. Data will be represented here by means of first order terms like $id(\cdot)$ (principal identifier), $sk(\cdot)$ (secret key), $sk(\cdot, \cdot)$ (shared key), $ts(\cdot)$ (time-stamp), $enc(\cdot, \cdot)$ (encrypted message), and $\langle \cdot, \ldots, \cdot \rangle$ (tuple constructor).

The knowledge of the attacker (Trudy) is represented by a collection of atomic formulas of the shape $mem(t)$ for some term t. Trudy's behavior can be described by using a Dolev-Yao model as in [7]. We will come back to this point in Section 5. A *message* sent on a directional channel is represented by means of an atomic formula $net(sender, receiver, message)$. Encrypted data is represented as the term $enc(key, t)$, where key is a term like $sk(a, b)$ denoting a key shared between a and b, and t is a term.

To model time-stamps, we use a *global clock* whose current value is represented via an atomic formula $clock(\cdot)$. The value of the clock is non-deterministically updated via the following rule:

$$\textbf{time} : \; clock(ts(now)) \; \longrightarrow \; clock(ts(next)) \; : \; next > now$$

This rule introduces arbitrary *delays* between principals actions. Variables shared between the clock formula and a message can be used to represent generation of a time-stamp. The behavior of honest principals is defined by rule having the following shape:

$$\begin{aligned} \alpha : \; & clock(\textbf{ts}) \mid fresh(sk(y)) \mid r(id(a), \textbf{k}) \mid net(id(b), id(a), \textbf{m}) \; \longrightarrow \\ & clock(\textbf{ts}') \mid fresh(sk(y')) \mid r'(id(a), \textbf{k}') \mid net(id(a), id(b'), \textbf{m}') \; : \; \varphi \end{aligned}$$

This template represents the following transition: at instant $\textbf{ts}$ principal a receives message $\textbf{m}$ apparently from b, updates his/her state from r to r' and its knowledge from $\textbf{k}$ to $\textbf{k}'$, and, at instant $\textbf{ts}'$, he/she sends a new message $\textbf{m}'$. Freshness of a value k (key, nonce) can be ensured by adding the constraint $y' > k > y$ in the constraint φ. If we assume that a single principal step requires negligible time, then $\textbf{ts} = \textbf{ts}' = ts(now)$ for some integer variable now representing the current instant. *Parameters* in the validity conditions of time-stamps (e.g. delays) can be specified by including atomic formulas working as global memory in the initial protocol configuration as explained in the example of the next section.

2.2   The Wide Mouth Frog (WMF) Protocol

The goal of the WMF protocol [3] is to allow two principals to exchange a secret key via a trusted server. In the first step the initiator A sends to the server S the message $A, \{B, K, T_1\}_{K_{AS}}$ containing his/her identity together with a message encrypted with the key shared between A and the server S containing the identity B of the principal the initiator would like to talk to, a secret key K, and a time-stamp T_1. In the second step the server S forwards to principal B the message $\{A, K, T_2\}_{K_{BS}}$ containing A's identity, the secret key K, and an

createkey :
$clock(ts(n)) \mid fresh(sk(y)) \mid init_1(id(a))$
$\longrightarrow$
$clock(ts(n)) \mid fresh(sk(y')) \mid init_2(id(a), \langle id(b), id(s), sk(k), ts(n) \rangle)$
: $a > 0, b > 0, y' > k, k > y$

init :
$clock(ts(n)) \mid server(s) \mid init_2(id(a), \langle id(b), id(s), sk(k), ts(n) \rangle)$
$\longrightarrow$
$clock(ts(n)) \mid server(s) \mid init_3(id(a), \langle id(b), id(s), sk(k), ts(n) \rangle) \mid$
$\qquad \mid net(a, s, enc(sk(a, s), \langle r(0), id(b), sk(k), ts(n), ts(n) \rangle))$
: $a > 0, b > 0$

server :
$clock(ts(n)) \mid server(s) \mid delay(d_1, d_2) \mid$
$\qquad \mid net(a, s, enc(sk(a, s), \langle r(0), id(b), sk(k), ts(t), ts(st) \rangle))$
$\longrightarrow$
$clock(ts(n)) \mid server(s) \mid delay(d_1, d_2) \mid$
$\qquad \mid net(s, b, enc(sk(b, s), \langle r(1), id(a), sk(k), ts(n), ts(st) \rangle))$
: $a > 0, b > 0, n - d_1 \leq t, t \leq n$

resp :
$clock(ts(n)) \mid delay(d_1, d_2) \mid resp_1(id(b)) \mid server(id(s)) \mid$
$\qquad \mid net(s, b, enc(sk(b, s), \langle r(1), id(b), sk(k), ts(t), ts(st) \rangle))$
$\longrightarrow$
$clock(ts(n)) \mid delay(d_1, d_2) \mid server(id(s)) \mid resp_2(id(b), \langle id(a), sk(k), ts(n), ts(st) \rangle)$
: $a > 0, b > 0, n - d_2 \leq t, t \leq n$

Fig. 1. Wide-Mouth Frog: core protocol rules

updated time-stamp T_2. The message is encrypted with the key K_{BS} shared between B and the server. On receipt of a message the server and the responder have to check the validity of the time-stamps.

This protocol should ensure *timed-authentication*, i.e., the responder should authenticate a message coming from the initiator with a delay not greater than the (estimated a priori) network delay. In this protocol messages sent by and received from the server have the same structure. In [1] Anderson and Needham have discovered an interesting type of attacks due to this property (see also Section 5). Specifically, if Trudy repeatedly replays messages sent by the server, the server will maintain the time-stamp in the replayed message up-to-date. This way, Trudy can enforce an arbitrary delay between the time A starts the protocol and the time B receives the key, thus violating *timed authentication*. This attack can be prevented by distinguishing the two messages used in the protocol, e.g., by inserting an extra field 0/1.

2.3   Formal Specification of WMF

To specify all these aspects in a rigorous way, we specify the protocol in as in Fig. 1. In our model, at a given instant time t, the initiator a creates a new key

k (rule **createkey**) and (non-deterministically) selects a server s and a partner b. Then, a starts the protocol (rule **init**) by sending the message containing the tag $r(0)$, b, k, a time-stamp, and the message creation time (they coincide with the current time). The message is encrypted with the secret key shared between a and s represented as $sk(a, s)$. The rules **createkey** and **init** are executed within the same instant. This is achieved by storing the current time in the initiator knowledge in the former rule and by using it as a precondition in the latter. This example gives us an example of independence between state- and time-transitions in MSR($\mathcal{L}$): we can either specify several transitions within the same instant or introduce fixed/arbitrary delays within a given state transition. In rule *server* the server checks if the time-stamp is recent and then forwards the message (tagged with $r(1)$) to b. This test is modelled in a natural way by using the constraints $n - d_1 \leq t, t \leq n$, where d_1 represents a parametric delay; parameters are stored in the atomic formula $delay(d_1, d_2)$ as part of the initial configuration. In rule *resp* b performs a similar validity test for the time-stamp. Note that the *actual* creation time of the key is always copied from one message to the other. Every honest principal is allowed to play the role of both initiator and responder and to run several role instances in parallel.

In this protocol the responder should authenticate a message coming from the initiator with a delay of at most $d_1 + d_2$ time units (timed-authentication). Our goal is to show that timed-authentication holds for any $d_1, d_2 \geq 0$.

3   Verification via Symbolic Exploration

In order to define a symbolic representation of sets of configurations of multiple parallel protocol sessions we proceed in two steps. Following [6], we first introduce a special term constructor **sup**(t) that can be used to finitely represent all terms containing t as a subterm. Then, we incorporate the resulting *extended terms* in a symbolic representation of collections of protocol sessions.

3.1   Symbolic Data Structure

The set of extended terms over the variables $\mathcal{V}$ and the signature Σ is built by induction as follows: constants in Σ and variables in $\mathcal{V}$ are extended terms; if t is an extended term, **sup**(t) is an extended term; if $\boldsymbol{t}$ is a list of extended terms and f is in Σ then $f(\boldsymbol{t})$ is an extended term. Given a *ground* extended term t, its *denotation* is defined by induction as follows:

$$\llbracket c \rrbracket = \{c\} \text{ if } c \text{ is a constant;}$$
$$\llbracket \mathbf{sup}(t) \rrbracket = \{s \mid s \text{ is a ground term, } t \text{ occurs in } s\};$$
$$\llbracket f(t_1, \ldots, t_n) \rrbracket = \{f(s_1, \ldots, s_n) \mid s_1 \in \llbracket t_1 \rrbracket, \ldots, s_n \in \llbracket t_n \rrbracket\}.$$

A *symbolic configuration* is defined then as a formula $p_1(t_1) \mid \ldots \mid p_n(t_n) : \varphi$, where $p_1, \ldots, p_n$ are predicate symbols, $\boldsymbol{t}_i$ is a tuple of *extended* terms for any $i : 1, \ldots n$, and the satisfiable constraint φ is such that $Fv(\varphi) \subseteq Fv(\boldsymbol{t}_1, \ldots, \boldsymbol{t}_n)$.

In the rest of the paper we will use $M, N, \ldots$ to indicate symbolic configurations. The *ground denotation* of $M \doteq A_1 \mid \ldots \mid A_n : \varphi$ is defined as follows:

$$[\![M]\!] = \{ B_1 \mid \ldots \mid B_n \ s.t. \ \exists \ \sigma \ \text{grounding for} \ A_1 \mid \ldots \mid A_n$$
$$B_i \in [\![A_i\sigma]\!], \ i : 1, \ldots, n, \ \text{and} \ \sigma_{|Fv(\varphi)} \in Sol(\varphi) \}$$

This definition is extended to sets of symbolic configurations in the natural way. Finally, in order to reason about configurations consisting of an arbitrary number of parallel protocol sessions, we define the *upward closed denotation* of a set of symbolic configurations as follows

$$\langle\!\langle \mathbf{S} \rangle\!\rangle = \{ \mathcal{N} \mid \text{there exists} \ \mathcal{M} \in [\![\mathbf{S}]\!] \ \text{s.t.} \ \mathcal{M} \ \text{is contained in} \ \mathcal{N} \}$$

This extended semantics is particularly useful for locally representing *violations* to properties like *secrecy*, where, independently from the number of sessions and principals, disclosed secrets are shared between the intruder and a *finite* number of agents. The use of extended terms gives us a further level of parameterization, e.g., we can locally require that a piece of data occurs at some depth inside a message. As an example the upward closed denotation of the singleton with

$$p(ts(x)) \mid r(ts(y), \mathbf{sup}(f(ts(z), \mathbf{sup}(ts(x))))) \ : \ x > y, y > z$$

contains all configurations $p(ts(v_1)) \mid r(ts(v_2), \mathbf{T_1}[f(ts(v_3), \mathbf{T_2}[ts(v_1)])]) \ \oplus \ Q$ for some $v_1 > v_2 > v_3$, two ground terms with a hole $\mathbf{T_1}[\cdot]$ and $\mathbf{T_2}[\cdot]$, and some configuration Q.

The previous semantics is well-suited for a backward analysis of a protocol model in which we do not impose restrictions on the number of parallel sessions, range of time-stamps and generated nonces.

3.2   Symbolic Operations

Contrary to ordinary unification, given two extended terms t and t' the extended unification algorithm of [6] computes the *set* of *maximal general unifiers* $max.g.u.(t, t')$. The interesting case in the extension of the unification algorithm occurs when a term like $\mathbf{sup}(t)$ must be unified with t': we have to search for a subterm of t' that can be unified with t. E.g. $x \mapsto \mathbf{sup}(a)$ is a max.g.u. for $g(\mathbf{sup}(a))$ and $\mathbf{sup}(g(x))$. We can avoid bindings between integer variables and terms by restricting the unification algorithm in such a way that it cannot descend the term structure of casting terms like $ts(\cdot)$. E.g., $\sigma = \{x \mapsto a\}$ is a max.g.u. for $\mathbf{sup}(a)$ and $ts(x)$ only if ts is not a casting symbol. If ts is a casting symbol, we are forced to unify a with $ts(x)$ (we cannot select other subterms), and, thus, unification fails. When combined with constraint satisfiability and simplification, the previous operations can be used to extend the unification algorithm to symbolic configurations (i.e. multisets of atomic formulas defined over extended terms annotated with constraints). Specifically, we call the pair $\langle \sigma, \gamma \rangle$ a *maximal constrained unifier* **m.c.u.** for $M : \varphi$ and $N : \psi$, whenever $\sigma \in max.g.u.(M, N)$, and, assuming that σ' is the maximal sub-constraint of σ involving only integer variables, $\gamma \equiv \varphi, \psi, \sigma'$ is satisfiable.

Let L be a global variable, initially $= \emptyset$

$subs_t(x, t, t)$ if x is a variable and $(x \mapsto t) \in L$;

$subs_t(x, t, t)$ if x is a variable and $\not\exists s.\ (x \mapsto s) \in L$; $(x \mapsto t)$ is added to L

$subs_t(a, a, a)$ if a is a constant;

$subs_t(\mathbf{sup}(t), \mathbf{sup}(s), \mathbf{sup}(s'))$ if $subs_t(\mathbf{sup}(t), s, s')$;

$subs_t(\mathbf{sup}(t), s, \mathbf{sup}(s''))$ if $subs_t(t, s', s'')$ for some subterm s' *of* s;

$subs_t(f(t_1, \ldots, t_n), f(t'_1, \ldots, t'_n), f(s_1, \ldots, s_n))$ if $subs_t(t_1, t'_1, s_1), \ldots, subs_t(t_n, t'_n, s_n)$.

Fig. 2. Subsumption relation over symbolic configurations and extended terms.

Similarly to unification we can define a subsumption relation $subs_t$ over extended terms such that $subs_t(t, t')$ implies $[\![t']\!] \subseteq [\![t]\!]$. The algorithm is described in Fig. 2. Actually, we use a ternary relation $subs_t(t, t', s)$ that also computes a witness extended term s that is built by taking the extended subterms of t' that are needed to establish subsumption. When combined with constraint entailment, extended term subsumption allows us to define a comparison relation $\sqsubseteq$ between symbolic configurations such that $M \sqsubseteq N$ implies $\langle\!\langle N \rangle\!\rangle \subseteq \langle\!\langle M \rangle\!\rangle$. The procedure for testing $M \sqsubseteq N$ is defined as follows:

$$(M : \varphi) \sqsubseteq (N : \psi) \text{ iff } \begin{cases} subs_t(M', N, S) \text{ for some } M' = M \oplus Q \text{ for some } Q, \\ \sigma = m.g.u.(M', S), \ \sigma' = \sigma_{|V_i}, \\ \exists \boldsymbol{x}.\ (\psi, \sigma') \text{ entails } \varphi, \text{ where } \boldsymbol{x} = Fv(\psi, \sigma') \setminus Fv(S\sigma) \end{cases}$$

Intuitively, we first select a submultiset M' of M that is subsumed by N with witness S. Then, we unify S with M' (using ordinary term unification considering the symbol $\mathbf{sup}$ as any other symbol in Σ) in order to have formulas defined over the same set of variables (variables in N but not in S are projected away using existential quantification). Finally, we check entailment of the corresponding constraints.

Example 1. Consider the following symbolic configurations:

$$M_1 = p(ts(x)) \mid r(ts(y), \mathbf{sup}(f(ts(z), \mathbf{sup}(ts(x))))) : x > y, y > z$$
$$M_2 = p(ts(u)) \mid r(ts(v), f(ts(w), h(g(ts(u))))) \mid p(ts(m)) : u > v, v > w, w > m$$

Given $\sigma = \{u \mapsto x, v \mapsto y, w \mapsto z\}$ and $\gamma \equiv x > y, y > z, x = u, y = v, z = w$, $\langle \sigma, \gamma \rangle$ is an **m.c.u** for M_1 and the submultiset obtained by removing $p(ts(m))$ from M_2. Furthermore, by applying the definition, we have that $subs_t(M_1, M_2, S)$ holds with witness $S = p(ts(u)) \mid r(ts(v), \mathbf{sup}(f(ts(w), \mathbf{sup}(ts(u)))))$. The most general unifier (using ordinary first order unification) for S and M_1 is $\theta = \{x \mapsto u, y \mapsto v, z \mapsto w\}$. Thus, since $\exists u, v, w, m.u > v, v > w, w > m, x = u, y = v, z = w$ is equivalent to $x > y, y > z$, it follows that $M_1 \sqsubseteq M_2$.

3.3 Symbolic Predecessor Operator

Let **S** be a set of symbolic configurations with distinct variables each other. Symbolic backward exploration is based on the pre-image operator $\mathbf{Pre}_R$ defined over a rule R, and to its natural extension $\mathbf{Pre}_\mathcal{R}$ to a set $\mathcal{R}$ of rules. These operators take into account the upward closed semantics of symbolic configurations by applying rewriting rules as follows: submultisets of symbolic configurations are matched against submultisets of right-hand side of rules (we reason modulo any possible *context*). Namely, given $R = \alpha : \ \mathcal{A} \longrightarrow \mathcal{B} : \psi$, the operator $\mathbf{Pre}_R$ is defined as follows

$$\mathbf{Pre}_R(\mathbf{S}) = \left\{ \mathcal{A}\sigma \oplus Q\sigma \ : \ \xi \ \middle| \begin{array}{l} \exists\,(M:\varphi) \ in \ \mathbf{S}, \ M = M' \oplus Q, \ \mathcal{B} = \mathcal{B}' \oplus \mathcal{D} \\ s.t. \ \langle \sigma, \gamma \rangle \ is \ an \ \mathbf{m.c.u.} \ for \ M':\varphi \ and \ \mathcal{B}':\psi \\ \xi \equiv \exists \boldsymbol{x}.\gamma \ where \ \boldsymbol{x} = Fv(\gamma) \setminus Fv(\mathcal{A}\sigma \oplus Q\sigma) \end{array} \right\}$$

The following property holds.

Proposition 1. *Let* $\mathcal{R}$ *be a set of MSR($\mathcal{L}$) rules and* $\mathbf{S}$ *a set of symbolic configurations, then* $\langle\!\langle \mathbf{Pre}_\mathcal{R}(\mathbf{S}) \rangle\!\rangle = Pre_\mathcal{R}(\langle\!\langle \mathbf{S} \rangle\!\rangle)$.

3.4   Symbolic Backward Reachability Graph

Let $\mathbf{U}$ be a set of symbolic configurations. Our symbolic operations can be used to build a *symbolic backward reachability graph* $G = \langle \mathbf{N}, \mathbf{E} \rangle$ as follows. The set of nodes $\mathbf{N}$ is initially set to $\mathbf{U}$. At each step, for any $M \in \mathbf{N}$ and $Q \in \mathbf{Pre}_\mathcal{R}(\{M\})$ if there exists a *visited* symbolic configurations $O \in \mathbf{N}$ such that $O \sqsubseteq Q$, then we discharge Q and add an edge $O \triangleright M$ to $\mathbf{E}$. If there are no *visited* symbolic configurations that subsumes Q (i.e. Q brings new information), then Q is added to the set of nodes $\mathbf{N}$, and an edge $Q \triangleright M$ is added to the graph. If $\mathbf{Pre}_\mathcal{R}(\{M\})$ is empty, then the node M has no incoming edges. Also note that if $M \triangleright N$, then there exists R such that either $M = \mathbf{Pre}_R(\{N\})$ or $M \sqsubseteq \mathbf{Pre}_R(\{N\})$.

4   Verification of Secrecy and Authentication

Violations of secrecy properties can often be generated by only looking at one honest principal and at part of the knowledge of Trudy, they are denoted by (according to the upward closed semantics) of symbolic configurations like

$$mem(\mathbf{secret}) \mid r(id(a), \langle \ldots, \mathbf{secret}, \ldots \rangle) \ : \ true$$

Under this assumption, the following property holds.

Theorem 1 (Secrecy). *Let* $\mathcal{S}$ *be an MSR($\mathcal{L}$) protocol and attacker specification, and* $\mathbf{U}$ *be the set of symbolic configurations representing violations to a secrecy property. If the symbolic backward reachability terminates when invoked on* $\mathcal{S}$ *and* $\mathbf{U}$*, and the set* $\mathbf{N}$ *of nodes of the resulting graph does not contain initial configurations, then the protocol is not subject to secrecy attacks. The property holds for any number of nonces, principals, and parallel sessions.*

Since we work on a *concrete protocol model* and a *symbolic semantics* without approximations (unless we apply widening operators during search), our procedure with an on-the-fly check for the initial configurations can be also used for *falsification*, i.e, to extract finite-length symbolic trajectories that represent attacks.

Let us now consider authentication properties. In this section we will focus our attention on *(non-injective) agreement* [12]. A protocol guarantees *non-injective agreement*, e.g., for a responder B and for certain data d (e.g. keys/nonces), if each time the principal B completes a run of the protocol as a *responder* using data d, apparently with A, then there exists a run of the protocol with the principal A as an initiator with data d, apparently with B. *Agreement* requires a one-to-one correspondence between the runs of A and those of B. It can proved after proving non-injective agreement if freshness of part of the data in d ensures that there cannot be two different sessions with the same data.

Violations of agreement properties *cannot* be represented as upward closed sets of configurations. They are sets of *bad traces*. However, we can still exploit our symbolic search by using the following idea. We first define the two symbolic configurations

$$M_I \doteq r_i(id(a), \langle \dots, id(b), \dots \rangle) : \varphi \qquad M_R \doteq r'_f(id(b), \langle \dots, id(a), \dots \rangle) : \psi$$

M_I represents all configurations containing *at least* the initial state of the initiator a in a session, apparently with b, and M_R represents all configurations containing *at least* the final state of the responder b in a session, apparently with a. We select two generic values a and b for the identifiers of Alice and Bob, and generic nonces and keys for the data we want to observe (we will show how this can be done in practice in Section 5). Data may appear in M_I and M_R; φ and ψ can be used to define constraints over them. Our verification method is based then on the following property (formulated for the responder).

Theorem 2 (Non-injective agreement). Let S be an MSR($\mathcal{L}$) protocol and attacker specification, M_I and M_R be as described before. Suppose that the symbolic backward search terminates when invoked on $\mathbf{U} = \{M_R\}$ and S. Then, if for every path $M_0 \rhd \dots \rhd M_k \rhd M_R$ in the resulting graph going from an *initial (symbolic) configuration* M_0 to M_R, there exists i such that $M_I \sqsubseteq M_i$, then non-injective agreement property holds for any number of parallel sessions, principals, and nonces.

The previous property can be verified by checking that every *acyclic* path π going from an initial symbolic configuration to M_R *contains* at least a node N_π such that $M_I \sqsubseteq N_\pi$. Being formulated over a time sensitive specification logic, the previous properties can be used to verify time-dependent secrecy and authentication properties. In other words, we reason about time *inside* our specification logic. We will illustrate this point in Section 5.

Symbolic configurations can be used in other interesting ways. As an example, we might be interested in checking whether a key k stored in the state r_i of a principal will or will not be used to encrypt messages. This property can be used to formally justify the use of specialized theories for the intruder. We can then search for traces leading to $net(a, b, \mathbf{sup}(enc(sk(k), msg))) \mid r_j(x, \mathbf{sup}(sk(k))) : true$

Prop	Model	Description	Seed	Steps	Time	True
P_1	CoreWMF	Generated keys are never used	U_1	6	260s	Yes
P_2	CoreWMF	Nested encryption is never used	U_2	1	0.1s	Yes
P_3	WMF+Trudy	Non-injective agreement	U_3	6	24s	Yes
P_4	WMF+Trudy	Non-injective timed agreement	U_4	7	41s	Yes
P_5	WMF+Trudy	Uniqueness of gen. keys (init.)	U_5	2	0.4s	Yes
P_6	WMF+Trudy	Uniqueness of gen. keys (resp.)	U_6	11	3093s	No
P_7	OrigWMF+Trudy	Non-injective timed agreement	U_4	11	88s	No

Fig. 3. List of properties, and results of the analysis: Seeds are described in Fig. 4.

for some $j \geq i$. Furthermore, following [6], when dealing with attacker theories in which we allow arbitrary use of rules like *decryption with Trudy's key* it is often possible to apply dynamic widening operators that approximate sets of terms like $enc(sk(0), \ldots, enc(sk(0), msg) \ldots)$ with $enc(sk(0), \mathbf{sup}(msg))$. This kind of accelerations may return overapproximations.

5   Detailed Analysis of Wide Mouth Frog

In Fig. 3 we show the list of properties of WMF we have checked using our method. The *seed* U_i of symbolic exploration id described in Fig. 4, **Steps** denotes the number of iterations before reaching a fixpoint/error trace, **Time** denotes the execution time. The initial configurations of the WMF model of Fig. 1 are those containing (any number of) initial states of honest principals, servers, and auxiliary information like *fresh* and *delay*. The first two properties are related to the structure of the core protocol rules (without attacker): generated keys are never used to encrypt messages, and nested encryption is never used. We proved these two properties automatically by checking that the set of states described by the violations U_1 and U_2 are never reached via the core protocol rules. This preliminary step allows us to consider the simplified attacker theory defined in Fig. 5: we do not need rules to handle nested encryption, we assume that Trudy only uses the key she shared with the server, and that Trudy never learns new keys. This is the theory typically used for the analysis of WMF [9, 13]. In our protocol the data exchanged by the honest principals are *typed* by casting symbols. Thus, the intruder has only to deal with messages of the shape $enc(sk(a,b), \langle m_1, \ldots, m_n \rangle)$ where m_i is built using one of sk, id, ts, r. Among the typical attacker's capabilities like interception and duplication, we add the capability of *guessing* any time-stamp. This can be refined depending on the assumption taken on the intruder (e.g. guess only in the past, etc.).

Our next task is to prove *timed non-injective agreement*, i.e., non injective agreement within the maximal allowed delay of $d_1 + d_2$ time units for any value of the parameters d_1 and d_2. To prove this property, we first check *non-injective agreement* forgetting about time (property P_3), and then prove that there cannot be violations of the time-conditions (property P_4). We prove automatically P_3 starting symbolic search from the seed U_3 of Fig. 3. The atomic formula

Seed	Symbolic configurations
$\mathbf{U}_1$	$init_2(x_1, \langle x_2, sk(k), x_3, x_4\rangle) \mid net(x_5, x_6, \mathbf{sup}(enc(sk(k, x_7), x_8))) : true,$ $init_2(x_1, \langle x_2, sk(k), x_3, x_4\rangle) \mid net(x_5, x_6, \mathbf{sup}(enc(sk(x_7, k), x_8))) : true$
$\mathbf{U}_2$	$net(x_1, x_2, \mathbf{sup}(enc(x_3, \mathbf{sup}(enc(x_4, x_5))))) : true$
$\mathbf{U}_3$	$par(id(a), id(b), sk(k)) \mid resp_2(id(b), \langle id(a), sk(k), ts(e), ts(s)\rangle) \mid$ $\mid delay(ts(d_1), ts(d_2)) \; : \; e, s, d_1, d_2 \geq 0$
$\mathbf{U}_4$	$par(id(a), id(b), sk(k)) \mid resp_2(id(b), \langle id(a), sk(k), ts(e), ts(s)\rangle) \mid$ $\mid delay(ts(d_1), ts(d_2)) \; : \; e > s + d_1 + d_2$
$\mathbf{U}_5$	$init_2(x, \mathbf{sup}(sk(k))) \mid init_2(y, \mathbf{sup}(sk(k))) \; : \; true$
$\mathbf{U}_6$	$resp_2(id(a), \mathbf{sup}(sk(k))) \mid resp_2(id(b), \mathbf{sup}(sk(k))) \; : \; true$

Fig. 4. Violations/seed of symbolic exploration.

$par(id(a), id(b), sk(k))$ is used here to make the analysis parametric on principals id's (a, b, k are all variables). In the resulting fixpoint we detect only a single initial configuration. Furthermore, all paths going to the seed configuration pass through a symbolic configuration containing

$$init_2(id(a), \langle id(b), id(s), sk(k), ts(t)\rangle) \mid par(id(a), id(b), sk(k))$$

that represents the state of the *initiator* right after the creation of the key. The binding of variables a, b, and k with the parameters $par(id(a), id(b), sk(k))$ maintains the proof independent from specific identifiers and keys.

In order to check property P_4, we start our search from the violations specified by means of $\mathbf{U}_4$ (the responder terminates its part of the protocol outside the window $s + d_1 + d_2$). In the resulting fixpoint there are no initial (symbolic) configurations. Thus, there exist no path reaching the previously described violations. This proves non-injective timed-agreement for any number of parallel protocol sessions and principals, and values of d_1 and d_2.

To check agreement, we still have to check that there is a one-to-one correspondence between runs of responder and initiator. We first check if different initiators can share the same secret key. When invoked on the seed $\mathbf{U}_5$ of Fig. 3, the procedure stops without detecting error traces. Then, we try to check whether the responder can receive multiple copies of the same key by selecting the violations $\mathbf{U}_6$ of Fig. 3. Our procedure returns the following counterexample trace: Alice creates a key, starts the protocol, the server forwards the message, Trudy intercepts it, Bob receives the message, Trudy forges a copy, Bob accepts the second copy. Thus, the protocol still suffers from possible replay attacks. As suggested by Lowe in [12], this flaw can be corrected by adding an handshaking part at the end the protocol in which the principals exchange a nonce encrypted with the shared key.

Finally, in order to compare the use of our method for *falsification* with [9,13], we have considered a model (called OrigWMF in Fig 3) in which we have removed the tags distinguishing the two messages, thus going back to the original WMF

$$
\begin{aligned}
&\textbf{remove}: && net(x,y,m) \longrightarrow \epsilon && : true \\
&\textbf{intercept}: && net(x,y,m) \longrightarrow mem(m) && : true \\
&\textbf{fresh}: && fresh(sk(x)) \longrightarrow fresh(sk(y)) \mid mem(sk(n)) && : y > n, n > x \\
&\textbf{guess}: && \epsilon \longrightarrow mem(ts(t)) && : t \geq 0 \\
&\textbf{replay}: && net(x,y,m) \longrightarrow net(y,x,m) && : true \\
&\textbf{dup}: && mem(m) \longrightarrow mem(m) \mid mem(m) && : true \\
&\textbf{forge}: && mem(m) \longrightarrow net(id(a), id(b), m) && : a \geq 0, b \geq 0 \\
&\textbf{dec}: && mem(enc(sk(0,s), \langle f_1(m_1), \ldots, f_n(m_n) \rangle)) \longrightarrow && \\
&&& \quad mem(f_1(m_1)) \mid \ldots \mid mem(f_n(m_n)) && : s \geq 0 \\
&\textbf{comp}: && mem(f_1(m_1)) \mid \ldots \mid mem(f_n(m_n)) \longrightarrow && \\
&&& \quad mem(enc(sk(0,s), \langle f_1(m_1), \ldots, f_n(m_n) \rangle)) && : s \geq 0
\end{aligned}
$$

where $f_i \in \{sk/1, id/1, ts/1, r/1\}$ for $i : 1, \ldots, n$, $n \leq 5$

Fig. 5. Restricted theory of the intruder.

protocol. In this model we impose that server, initiator, and responder have different identifiers by adding constraints like $s > a, a > b$ in the core protocol rules, and we set $d_1 = d_2$. Starting from the violation U_4, we have automatically computed the following error trace: Alice sends M to the Server, the Server forwards M to Bob, time advances, Trudy impersonates Bob and replays M, the Server forwards M to Alice, time advances, Trudy impersonate Alice and replays M, the Server forwards M to Bob, time advances, Bob receives M. This trace falls in the class of attacks discovered by [1].

6   Related Work

The use of *constraint programming* combined with *symbolic exploration* over unbounded models distinguishes our approach from other methods based on theorem proving or model checking used for the analysis of protocols with time-stamps like [2,8,9,13]. In [9] Evans and Schneider perform a *semi-automated* analysis of a CSP model (with event-based time) of WMF. PVS is used to discharge proof obligations needed to find an invariant property (a rank function according to Schneider's verification method). During this process the attack with parametric validity period arises in form of a contradiction to the proof of an obligation. In [13] Lowe applies finite-state model checking to find the timed-authentication attack on finite protocol instances (an initiator, a responder, and a server), discrete time, fixed values for the validity period (namely $d_1 = d_2 = 1$) and with an upper bound on the time window observed during the state exploration. Differently from [9,13], our method can be used for both *automatic* verification and falsification in presence of parallel multiple sessions, without need of upper bounds on the time window considered during execution, and with parametric delays.

Time-stamps can be handled by the TAPS verifier [8]. The TAPS verifier generates state-dependent invariants from a protocol model. The first order theorem prover SPASS is used then to discharge the proof obligations produced by a proof system used to simplify the invariants according to the capability of the intruder. While TAPS is very fast and effective, it does not always produce readable counterexamples, an advantage of symbolic exploration methods like ours.

The uniform treatment of time-stamps and fresh name generation via constraint programming also distinguishes our method from other symbolic methods like NRLPA [16], Athena [19], and the methods of Blanchet [4], Bozga, Lakhnech and Périn [6], and Genet and Klay [10]. Furthermore, our use of the **sup** operator differs from [6]. In [6] **sup** is used to build a widening operator for computing secrecy invariants for *abstract* protocol models. On the contrary, our use of **sup** is within a symbolic representation of infinite collection of configurations of *concrete* protocol specifications. When terminating, our procedure returns accurate results that are useful for obtaining error traces. Widening operators similar to that of [6] can be included in our setting and applied to compute conservative approximations.

Our symbolic exploration method is complementary to approached based on model checking where abstractions or data independence techniques are used to extract a finite model from the original specification [13,15,18].

Finally, differently from constraint-based approaches used for*untimed* falsification of bounded number of protocol sessions [17], where *ad hoc* constraints relate a message expected by a principal to the current intruder knowledge, we use constraints for designing a symbolic *verification* method.

7 Conclusions

In this paper we have studied the applicability of symbolic exploration for the automatic verification of time sensitive cryptographic protocols. Our verification method is based on the combination of *constraint solving technology* and *first order term manipulation*. This combination provides a uniform framework for the specification of an arbitrary number of protocol sessions with fresh name generation and time-stamps.

In this paper we have described the main ideas behind this technology and discussed the analysis of the Wide Mouth Frog protocol. We have performed several other experiments on timed and untimed models (e.g. secrecy and agreement properties for Lowe's fix to the Needham-Schroeder public key protocol). The prototype procedure and the experimental results (with execution times) we obtained so far are available on the web page [20].

The verification approach presented in this paper can be coupled with a *symbolic forward exploration* method for a fixed number of sessions suitable to discover potential attacks (see [20]). Forward exploration often finds attacks faster than backward exploration. Currently, we are studying an extension of forward exploration with the lazy intruder technique of [17] to cope with MSR($\mathcal{L}$) specification and unrestricted attacker models.

References

1. R. Anderson, and R. Needham. Programming Satan's computer. Computer Science Today: 426–440, LNCS 1000, 1995.
2. G. Bella and L. C. Paulson. Kerberos version IV: inductive analysis of the secrecy goals. ESORICS '98: 361–375, 1998.
3. M. Burrows, M. Abadi, and R. Needham. A logic of authentication. *ACM Trans. on Computer Systems*, 8(1):18–36, 1990.
4. B. Blanchet. An efficient cryptographic protocol verifier based on prolog rules. CSFW '01: 82–96, 2001.
5. M. Bozzano and G. Delzanno. Beyond Parameterized Verification. TACAS '02, LNCS 2280: 221–235, 2002.
6. L. Bozga, Y. Lakhnech, and M. Périn. Pattern-based Abstraction for Verifying Secrecy in Protocols. TACAS '03, LNCS 2619: 299–314, 2003.
7. I. Cervesato, N. Durgin, P. Lincoln, J. Mitchell, and A. Scedrov. A meta-notation for Protocol Analysis. CSFW '99: 55–69, 1999.
8. E. Cohen. TAPS: A First-Order Verifier for Cryptographic Protocols. CSFW '00: 144–158, 2000.
9. N. Evans and S. Schneider. Analysing Time Dependent Security Properties in CSP Using PVS. ESORICS '00, LNCS 1895: 222–237, 2000.
10. T. Genet and F. Klay. Rewriting for Cryptographic Protocol Verification. CADE '00, LNCS 1831: 271–290, 2000.
11. G. Lowe. A Family of Attacks upon Authentication Protocols. Technical Report 1997/5, University of Leicester, 1997.
12. G. Lowe. A Hierarchy of Authentication Specifications. CSFW '97: 31-44, 1997.
13. G. Lowe. Casper: A compiler for the analysis of security protocols. CSFW '97: 18–30, 1997.
14. G. Lowe. Towards a completeness result for model checking of security protocols. *J. of Computer Security*, 7(2-3):89–146, 1998.
15. W. Marrero, E. Clarke, and S. Jha. Verifying Security Protocols with Brutus. ACM Trans. Softw. Eng. Methodol. 9(4): 443-487, 2000.
16. C. Meadows. The NRL protocol analyzer: An overview. *J. of Logic Programming*, 26(2):113–131, 1996.
17. J. Millen and V. Shmatikov. Constraint solving for bounded-process cryptographic protocol analysis. CCS '01: 166–175, 2001.
18. A. W. Roscoe and P. J. Broadfoot. Proving Security Protocols with Model Checkers by Data Independence Techniques. *J. of Computer Security*, 7(2,3):147-190, 1999.
19. D. X. Song. Athena. A New Efficient Automatic Checker for Security Protocol Analysis. CSFW '99: 192–202, 1999.
20. The MSR($\mathcal{C}$) home page: http://www.disi.unige.it/person/DelzannoG/MSR/

Simulation-Based Verification of Autonomous Controllers via Livingstone PathFinder

A.E. Lindsey[1] and Charles Pecheur[2]

[1] QSS Group, NASA Ames Research Center, Moffett Field, CA 94035, U.S.A.
`tlindsey@ptolemy.arc.nasa.gov`
[2] RIACS, NASA Ames Research Center, Moffett Field, CA 94035, U.S.A.
`pecheur@ptolemy.arc.nasa.gov`

Abstract. AI software is often used as a means for providing greater autonomy to automated systems, capable of coping with harsh and unpredictable
environments. Due in part to the enormous space of possible situations that
they aim to address, autonomous systems pose a serious challenge to traditional test-based verification approaches. Efficient verification approaches need
to be perfected before these systems can reliably control critical applications.
This publication describes *Livingstone PathFinder* (LPF), a verification tool
for autonomous control software. LPF applies state space exploration algorithms to an instrumented testbed, consisting of the controller embedded in a
simulated operating environment. Although LPF has focused on NASA's Livingstone model-based diagnosis system applications, the architecture is modular and adaptable to other systems. This article presents different facets of
LPF and experimental results from applying the software to a Livingstone
model of the main propulsion feed subsystem for a prototype space vehicle.

1 Introduction

Complex decision-making capabilities are increasingly embedded into controllers.
Robots substitute for humans in hazardous environments such as distant planets,
deep waters or battle fields. This trend is perhaps best exemplified by NASA's need
for autonomous spacecrafts, rovers, airplanes and submarines, capable of executing
in harsh and unpredictable environments. Moreover, increased autonomy can be a
significant cost saver, even in more accessible regions, by reducing the need for expensive human monitoring. An important trend in autonomous control is *model-based
autonomy*, where control is performed by a generic engine applying automated reasoning techniques to a high-level model of the system being diagnosed. This is the
case for the Livingstone diagnosis system on which the work presented here is based.
The idea behind model-based solutions is that the system, in any situation, will be
able to infer appropriate actions from the model.

While autonomous systems offer promises of improved capabilities at reduced operational costs, a serious challenge to traditional test-based verification approaches
occurs because of the enormous space of possible scenarios such systems aim to address. Several factors make testing advanced controllers particularly difficult. First,
the range of situations to be tested is significantly larger because the controller itself
is more complex and designed to operate over a broad range of unpredictable situations during a prolonged time span. The program implicitly incorporates response

K. Jensen and A. Podelski (Eds.): TACAS 2004, LNCS 2988, pp. 357–371, 2004.

scenarios to any combination of events that might occur, instead of relying on human experts to handle off-nominal cases. Second, autonomous systems close the control loops and feature concurrent interacting components. Thus, it becomes more difficult to plug in test harnesses and write test runs that drive the system through a desired behavior. Third, concurrency may introduce hard-to-detect, non-deterministic race conditions.

This paper describes a flexible framework for simulating, analyzing and verifying autonomous controllers. The proposed approach applies state space exploration algorithms to an instrumented testbed, consisting of the actual control program being analyzed embedded in a simulated operating environment. This framework forms the foundation of *Livingstone PathFinder* (LPF), a verification tool for autonomous diagnosis applications based on NASA's Livingstone model-based diagnosis system.

LPF accepts as input a Livingstone model of the physical system and a scenario script defining the class of commands and faults to be analyzed. The model is used to perform model-based diagnosis and will be used to simulate the system as well. The tool runs through all executions specified in the script, backtracking as necessary to explore alternate routes. At each step, LPF checks for error conditions, such as discrepancies between the actual simulated faults and those reported by diagnosis. If an error is detected, LPF reports the sequence of events that led to the current state.

To avoid confusion in reading what follows, it is important to clearly distinguish two similar-sounding but very different notions, that we refer to as *faults* and *errors*:

- *Faults* are physical events causing the controlled system to behave abnormally, such as a stuck valve or a sensor emitting erroneous measurements. They typically result from external degradation, and are handled by making the system fault-tolerant. Detecting and identifying faults is the goal of diagnosis systems such as Livingstone.
- *Errors* are improper behaviors of the controller, such as inaccurately identifying the current state of the controlled system. They typically result from unintended flaws in design or configuration, and need to be eliminated before the system is deployed. Detecting and identifying errors is the goal of verification techniques and tools such as LPF.

This article discusses Livingstone PathFinder on three different levels:

- As a *verification approach*, LPF applies a combination of model checking and testing principles that we refer to as *simulation-based verification*. This is the subject of Section 2.
- As a *program framework*, LPF provides an infrastructure for applying simulation-based verification to autonomous controllers. This is referred to in Section 4.5.
- As a *concrete program*, LPF currently instantiates the framework to applications based on the Livingstone diagnosis system. This constitutes the central part of the paper, mainly discussed in Section 4.

A preliminary account of this work was presented in [6]. The remainder of the paper is organized as follows: Section 2 presents the general simulation-based verification approach; Section 3 provides an overview of Livingstone; Section 4 describes the LPF software tool; Section 5 reviews some experimental results; Section 6 draws conclusions and perspectives.

2   Simulation-Based Verification

The approach we follow in the work presented is a composite between conventional testing and model checking, here referred to as *simulation-based verification*. Similar to conventional testing, it executes the real program being verified rather than an abstract model derived from the system. In order to support its interactions, the program is embedded in a testbed that simulates its *environment*. On the other hand, as in model checking the execution ranges over an entire graph of possible behaviors as opposed to a suite of linear test cases. In the optimal setting, each visited state is marked to avoid redundant explorations of the same state and can be restored for backtracking to alternate executions. Furthermore, sources of variation in the execution, such as external events, scheduling or faults, are controlled to explore all alternatives.

The rationale behind simulation-based verification is to take the advanced state space exploration algorithms and optimizations developed in the field of model checking and apply them to the testing of real code. By doing so, we avoid the need for developing a separate model for verification purposes, and more importantly for scrutinizing each reported violation to assess whether it relates to the real system or to a modeling inaccuracy. Of course, simulation-based verification will in general be significantly less efficient and scalable than model checking an abstract model of the same program. However, it should be seen as an evolutionary improvement to traditional testing approaches, with important potential gains in scalability, automation and flexibility.

To enable their controlled execution, instrumentation is introduced in both the analyzed program and its environment. To perform a true model-checking search, the tool should be capable of iterating over all alternate events at each state, backtracking to previously visited states, and detecting states that produce the same behavior. Some of these capabilities may be supported only partly or not at all, depending on the nature of the different components in the testbed and the needs and trade-offs of the analysis being performed. For example, a complex piece of software may provide checkpointing capabilities on top of which backtracking can easily be built; however, state equivalence might require an analysis of internal data structures that is either too complex, computationally expensive, or infeasible due to the proprietary nature of the software. In addition, this analysis may not be worthwhile because equivalent states will seldom be reached anyway. Even if true backtracking is not available, it can still be simulated by re-playing the sequence up to the desired state. This reduces the exploration to a suite of sequential test cases, but the additional automation and flexibility in search strategies can still be beneficial.

With these capabilities, the program and its testbed constitute a *virtual machine* that embodies a fully controllable state machine, whose state space can be explored according to different strategies, such as depth-first search, breadth-first search, heuristic-based guided search, randomized search, pattern-guided search or interactive simulation. The environment portion of the testbed is typically restricted to a well-defined range of possible scenarios in order to constrain the state space within tractable bounds.

The principle behind simulation-based verification can be traced back to Godefroid's seminal work on the VeriSoft tool [4]. VeriSoft instruments a C program with explicit stop and choice points, to allow its controlled execution over a range of traces. Verisoft makes no attempt at capturing the state of the verified program; instead, trace re-play is used to simulate backtracking. This approach is referred to as *state-less model checking*. The original contribution presented in this paper pertains to the application of that general idea to the LPF framework and tool as well as the experimental results on a real-world application. The same principle can be found in Visser and Havelund's Java PathFinder 2 [10] with a twist: a complete Java virtual machine, optimized for verification, has been built rather than merely instrumenting the Java code to be analyzed.

The models used in model-based autonomy are typically abstract and concise enough to be amenable to formal analysis. Indeed, the *Livingstone-to-SMV translator* [9] is another verification tool for Livingstone applications, focusing exclusively on the Livingstone model but allowing true exhaustive analysis through the use of symbolic model checking. Nevertheless, a good model is a necessary but insufficient condition for a suitable model-based controller. Additional factors may compromise proper operation, such as problems in the engine itself or incomplete diagnosis heuristics used to achieve desired response times. The principles and techniques we discuss here aim to supplement high-level formal analysis with efficient and flexible tools designed to scrutinize the behavior of the actual program.

3   Livingstone

As the name implies, LPF has focused on the *Livingstone model-based diagnosis system* [12]. Generally speaking, *diagnosis* involves observing the input (commands, actuators) and output (observations, sensors) of a physical system to estimate its internal state, and in particular detect and identify faulty conditions that may have occurred. In *model-based diagnosis*, this state estimate is inferred from a model of the different components of the physical plant and their interactions, both under nominal and faulty conditions. Livingstone uses a qualitative finite model. This allows the use of an efficient inference engine based on propositional logic to perform the diagnosis.

A Livingstone model defines a collection X of discrete *variables*, or *attributes*, representing the state of the various components of the physical system.[1] Each attribute $x \in X$ ranges over a finite domain D_x. A *state* s of model associates to each $x \in X$ a value $s(x) \in D_x$. The *command* and *observable* attributes $O \subset X$ capture the visible interface of the system; the *mode* attributes $M \subset X$, one for each individual component, denote the hidden state to be inferred. The domain D_m of a mode attribute m is partitioned into *nominal modes* and a (possibly empty) subset of *fault modes* $F_m \subseteq D_m$. The model also sets constraints between these attributes, both within a state and across transitions. Nominal transitions result from particular command values while fault transitions are spontaneous. Each fault mode $f \in F_m$ has a *rank* $\rho(f)$ estimating its probability (e.g. rank 4 for probability 10^{-4}).

As an example, the following Livingstone model fragments describe a valve component, extracted from the PITEX model that we used for our experiments (see Section 5). Note that Livingstone is supported by a graphical modeling environment, that generates part of this code automatically.

---

[1] The model may also cover aspects of the surrounding environment, that do not strictly belong to the controlled system but are relevant to diagnosis.

```
class ventReliefValve
  ventLine ventLineIn;
  thresholdValues pneumaticLineIn;
  ventLineTemperature ventLineOut;
  // ... more attributes
  private enum ModeType {nominal, stuckOpen, stuckClosed};
  private ModeType mode;
  stateVector [mode];
  {
    if (valvePosition = closed) {
        ventLineOut.ambient.upperBound = belowThreshold &
        ventLineOut.ambient.lowerBound = aboveThreshold &
        ventLineIn.flow.sign = zero;
    }
    // ... more constraints
    switch (mode) {
      case nominal:
        if (pneumaticLineIn = aboveThreshold) valvePosition = open;
        if (pneumaticLineIn = belowThreshold) valvePosition = closed;
      case stuckOpen:
        valvePosition = open;
      case stuckClosed:
        valvePosition = closed;
    }
  }
  failure stuckOpen(*, stuckOpen, lessLikely) { }
  failure stuckClosed(*, stuckClosed, likely) { }
```

Livingstone performs diagnosis by receiving observations (that is, values of commands and observables) and searching for mode values (possibly including faults) that are consistent with these observations. The result is a list of *candidates* $(c_1, \ldots, c_n)$, where each candidate c assigns a value $c(m)$ to every mode attribute $m \in M$ and has a rank $\rho(c)$ resulting from the faults leading to that candidate. For verification purposes, we will say that a candidate c *matches* a state s, written $c \approx s$, if they have the same mode values, and that c *subsumes* s, written $c \sqsubseteq s$, if faults of c are also faults of s. Formally, $c \approx s$ iff $\forall m \in M \; c(m) = s(m)$, and $c \sqsubseteq s$ iff $\forall m \in M. c(m) \in F_m \Rightarrow c(m) = s(m)$.

Livingstone's best-first search algorithm returns more likely, lower ranked candidates first $(\rho(c_i) \leq \rho(c_{i+1}))$. In particular, when the nominal case is consistent with Livingstone's observations, the empty (i.e. fault-free) candidate (of rank 0) is generated. The search is not necessarily complete: to tune response time, Livingstone has configurable parameters that limit its search in various ways, such as the maximum number of rank of candidates returned.

The first generation of Livingstone (in Lisp) flew in space as part of the Remote Agent Experiment (RAX) demonstration on Deep Space 1 [7]. Livingstone 2 (or L2) has been re-written in C++ and adds temporal trajectory tracking. A utility program, l2test, provides a command line interface to perform all L2 operations interactively. l2test commands can be stored in *L2 scenario* files for batch replay. A third generation supporting more general constraint types (hybrid discrete/continuous models) is under development.

4   Livingstone PathFinder

The *Livingstone PathFinder* (LPF) program is a simulation-based verification tool for analyzing and verifying Livingstone-based diagnosis applications. LPF executes a Livingstone diagnosis engine, embedded into a simulated environment, and runs that assembly through all executions described by a user-provided scenario script, while checking for various selectable error conditions after each step.

The architecture of the LPF tool is depicted in Figure 1. The testbed under analysis consists of the following three components:

- *Diagnosis*: the diagnosis system being analyzed, based on the Livingstone diagnosis *engine*, interpreting a *model* of the physical system.
- *Simulator*: the simulator for the physical system on which diagnosis is performed. Currently this is a second Livingstone engine interpreting a model of the physical system. The models used in the Diagnosis and the Simulator are the same by default but can be different.
- *Driver*: the simulation driver that generates commands and faults according to a user-provided scenario script. The scenario file is essentially a non-deterministic test case whose elementary steps are commands and faults.

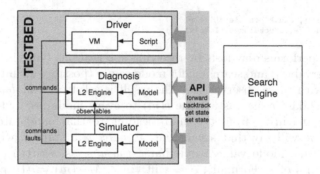

Fig. 1. Livingstone PathFinder Architecture

From a testing standpoint, the Diagnosis is the *implementation under test* (IUT), while the Driver and Simulator constitute the *test harness*. All three components are instrumented so that their execution can be single-stepped in both forward and backward directions. Together, these three elements constitute a non-deterministic state machine, where the non-determinism comes mainly from the scenario script interpreted by the Driver.[2] The *Search Engine* controls the order in which the tree of possible executions of that state machine is explored. In each forward step, LPF performs the following cycle of operations:

```
event := get next step from the Driver
apply event to the Simulator
if      event is a command
then    notify event to the Diagnosis
else    do nothing (Faults are not directly visible to Diagnosis)
obs := get updated observations from the Simulator
notify obs to the Diagnosis
ask Diagnosis to update its candidates
```

---

[2] LPF can also deal with non-determinism in the Simulator.

This cycle is repeated along all steps covered by the scenario, according to the chosen search strategy. Before each cycle, the current state is saved (using Livingstone's built-in checkpointing capability) so it can be later restored to explore alternate routes. User-selectable error conditions, such as consistency between the diagnosis results and the actual state of the Simulator, are checked at the end of each cycle, and a trace is reported if an error is detected. Since the cycle needs to be repeatedly rolled and unrolled by the backtracking search, it cannot simply be implemented as a program iteration, but instead needs to be simulated using non-trivial bookkeeping of the search trajectory.

LPF bears some resemblance to *conformance testing*, in that it checks whether the Diagnosis, seen as an implementation, "conforms" to the Simulator, seen as a specification. The "conformance" relation, however, is quite different from classical conformance relations that require the implementation to behave similarly (in some specific precise sense) to the specification (see e.g. [2]). Here, the relation is one of observability, i.e. that the implementation (Diagnosis) can *track* the state of the specification (Simulator). Even if Simulator and Diagnosis are "equivalent", in the sense that they operate on identical models of the controlled system, Diagnosis may still fail to "conform", because the observation it receives or its own computing limitations prevent accurate tracking. This is indeed the situation we consider by using the same model in both the Simulator and the Diagnosis.

4.1   Scenario Scripts

The driver constrains the possible executions to a user-provided combination of commands and faults, defined in a *scenario script*. This is essential to reduce the state space to a tractable size: the state space of the PITEX Livingstone *model*, used in the experiments reported later in this paper, is on the order of 10^{55} states. Although model states do not necessarily map into simulator or diagnosis states, this still gives a fair estimate of the orders of magnitude.

The scenario script is essentially a non-deterministic program whose elementary instructions are commands and faults. It can be viewed as an extended test case (or test suite) representing a tree of executions rather than a single sequence (or a set thereof). Scenarios are built from individual commands and faults using sequential, concurrent (interleaved) and choice statements, according to the following syntax:

$$stmt ::= \text{"}event\text{"} \; ; \; | \; \{ \; stmt^* \; \} \; | \; \textbf{mix} \; stmt \; (\textbf{and} \; stmt)^* \; | \; \textbf{choose} \; stmt \; (\textbf{or} \; stmt)^*$$

These operators have their classical semantics from process algebras such as CSP [5], that we will not repeat here. For example, the following scenario defines a sequence of three commands, with one fault chosen among three occurring at some point in the sequence. LPF provides a way to automatically generate a scenario combining all commands and faults of a model following this sequence/choice pattern. More configurable ways to generate scenarios from models or other external sources is an interesting direction for further work.

```
mix {
    "command test.breaker.cmdIn = on" ;
    "command test.breaker.cmdIn = off" ;
    "command test.breaker.cmdIn = on" ;
} and
```

```
choose "fault test.bulb.mode = blown" ;
or "fault test.bulb.mode = short" ;
or "fault test.meter.mode = broken" ;
```

4.2   Error Conditions

In each state along its exploration, LPF can check one or several *error conditions* among a user-selectable set. In addition to simple consistency checks, LPF supports the following error conditions: given a list of candidates $(c_1, \ldots, c_n)$ and a simulator state s,

- *Mode comparison* checks that the best (lowest-ranked) candidate matches the Simulator state, i.e. $c_1 \approx s$,
- *Candidate matching* checks that at least one candidate matches the Simulator state, i.e. $\exists k.c_k \approx s$, and
- *Candidate subsumption* checks that at least one candidate subsumes the Simulator state, i.e. $\exists k.c_k \sqsubseteq s$.

where $\approx$ and $\sqsubseteq$ were defined in Section 3. These conditions constitute three successive refinement steps with the notion that diagnosis should properly track the state of the (simulated) system. *Mode comparison* only considers the most likely candidate and reports errors even if another reported candidate matches the state, which is overly restrictive in practice since the injected fault may not be the most likely one. Alternatively, *candidate matching* considers all candidates. Even so, a fault may often remain unnoticed without causing immediate harm, as long as its component is not activated: for example a stuck valve will not be detected until one tries to change its position. Experience reveals this to be a frequent occurrence, causing a large proportion of spurious error reports. In contrast, *candidate subsumption* only reports cases where none of the diagnosed fault sets are *included* in the actual fault set. For example, the empty candidate is subsumed by any fault set and thus never produces an error using this condition. While this will not detect cases where diagnosis misses harmful faults, it will catch cases where the wrong faults are reported by the diagnosis engine. This condition has provided the best results thus far, as further discussed in Section 5.

4.3   Simulators in LPF

The modular design of LPF accommodates the use of different simulators through a generic application programming interface (API). As a first step, we have been using a second Livingstone engine instance for the Simulator (used in a different way: simulation infers outputs from inputs and injected faults, whereas diagnosis infers faults given inputs and outputs).

Using the same model for simulation and diagnosis may appear to be circular reasoning but has its own merits. It provides a methodological separation of concerns: by doing so, we validate operation of the diagnostic system under the assumption that the diagnosis model is a perfect model of the physical system, thus concentrating on proper operation of the diagnosis algorithm itself. Incidentally, it also provides a cheap and easy way to set up a verification testbed, even in the absence of an independent simulator.

On the other hand, using the same model for the simulation ignores the issues due to inaccuracies of the diagnosis model w.r.t. the physical system, which is a main source of problems in developing model-based applications. In order to address this concern, we have already been studying integration of NASA Johnson Space Center's CONFIG simulator system [3]. Note that higher fidelity simulators are likely to be less flexible and efficient; for example, they may not have backtracking or checkpointing.

4.4   Search Strategies

LPF currently supports two alternative state space exploration algorithms. The first is a straightforward depth-first search. The second performs a *heuristic (or guided) search*. Heuristic search uses a *heuristic* (or *fitness function*) to rank different states according to a given criterion and explores them in that order. Provided that a good heuristic can be found, heuristic search can be used to automatically orient the search over a very large state space towards the most critical, suspicious, or otherwise interesting states. This offers two advantages: The first is that errors are likely to be found earlier on and the second is the production of shorter counterexample paths.

The first heuristic uses the execution depth, i.e. the number of steps to that state. This heuristic results in performing a *breadth-first search*. Although this exploration strategy does not use any application knowledge to improve the search, its main benefit over depth-first search is in providing the shortest counter-examples.

The second heuristic, called *candidate count*, uses the number of candidates generated by Diagnosis. The intuition is that executions with a low number of diagnosis candidates are more likely to lead to cases where no correct candidate is reported.

4.5   Implementation Notes

Backtracking of the Diagnosis and Simulator take advantage of checkpointing capabilities present in Livingstone. Using built-in checkpointing capabilities provide better performance than extracting and later re-installing all relevant data through the API of Livingstone engine.

LPF also offers a number of useful auxiliary capabilities, such as generating an expanded scenario tree, counting scenario states, exploring the simulator in isolation (no diagnosis), generating a default scenario, and producing a wide array of diagnostic and debugging information, including traces that can be replayed using the l2test command-line interface or in Livingstone simulation tools. LPF is written in Java and makes extensive use of Java interfaces to support its modular architecture. The core source base consists of 47 classes totaling 7.4K lines. It has been successfully run on Solaris, Linux and Windows operating systems.

Livingstone PathFinder is built in a modular way, using generic interfaces as its main components. The Simulator and Diagnosis components implement generic interfaces, that capture generic simulation and diagnosis capabilities but remain independent of Livingstone-specific references. The top-level class that encompasses all three components of the testbed and implements the main simulation loop discussed in Section 4 only uses the generic abstractions provided by these interfaces.

This provides a flexible, extensible framework for simulation-based verification of diagnosis applications beyond the purely Livingstone-based setup (both for diagnosis and simulation) shown in Figure 1. Both the Simulator and Diagnosis modules are replaceable by alternative implementations, not necessarily model-based, provided those implementations readily provide the corresponding generic interfaces.

Livingstone PathFinder is not available for download but can be obtained free of charge under a NASA licensing agreement. Please contact the authors if interested.

5   Experimental Results

The Livingstone diagnosis system is being considered for Integrated Vehicle Health Maintenance (IVHM) to be deployed on NASA's next-generation space vehicles. In that context, the PITEX experiment has demonstrated the application of Livingstone-based diagnosis to the main propulsion feed subsystem of the X-34 space vehicle [1,8], and LPF has been successfully applied to the PITEX model of X-34. This particular Livingstone model consists of 535 components and 823 attributes, 250 transitions, compiling to 2022 propositional clauses.

Two different scenarios have been used to analyze the X-34 model:

- The *PITEX baseline scenario* combines one nominal and 29 failure scenarios, derived from those used by the PITEX team for testing Livingstone, as documented in [8]. This scenario covers 89 states.
- The *random scenario* covers a set of commands and faults combined according to the sequence/choice pattern illustrated in Section 4.1. This scenario is an abbreviated version of the one automatically generated by LPF, and covers 10216 states.

We will first discuss scalability and compare different error conditions using depth-first search, then discuss the benefits of heuristic search and finally illustrate two different errors found during the experiments.

5.1   Depth-First Search

Our initial experiments involved searching the entire state space, letting the search proceed normally after detecting an error, and reporting any additional errors. We used the depth-first algorithm in this case, since heuristic search offers no advantage when searching through all states of the scenario. Table 1 summarizes our depth-first search statistics. It shows that LPF covered the *PITEX baseline* and *random* scenario at an average rate of 51 states per minute (on a 500MHz Sun workstation).

When searching for *candidate matching*, LPF reported an excessive number of errors, most of which were *trivial*, in the following sense: when a fault produces no immediately observable effect, Livingstone diagnosis does not infer any abnormal behavior and reports the empty candidate. For example, although a valve may be stuck, the fault will stay unnoticed until a command to that valve fail to produce the desired change of position. While these errors are indeed missed diagnoses, experience shows that they are in most cases expected and do not constitute significant diagnosis flaws. In particular, while searching for *candidate matching* error condition violations

Table 1. Depth-first search statistics

scenario	search[1]	condition[2]	errors	non-trivial	states	states/min
baseline	all	CM	27	4	89	44
baseline	all	CS	0	0	89	67
random	all	CM	9621	137	10216	51
random	all	CS	5	5	10216	52
random	one	CS	1	1	8648	49
random	min	CS	2	2	8838	44

[1] all=search all errors, one=stop at first error, min=search for minimal trace
[2] CM=candidate matching, CS=candidate subsumption

the *baseline* scenario produced 27 errors of which only 4 were not trivial. The same search over the *random* scenario resulted in 9621 errors of which 137 were non-trivial.

In contrast, verification over the *random* scenario using the *candidate subsumption* error condition reported a total of 5 errors, all of which were non-trivial (the *baseline* scenario reported no errors). Indeed, the *candidate subsumption* error condition will only activate if all candidates report some incorrect fault, but not when faults are missed. In particular, the empty candidate subsumes all cases and will, by definition, never prompt an error.

For illustration purposes, the last two rows in Table 1 show results using two alternative termination criteria: either stopping at the first error (*one*), or continue searching only for shorter error traces (*min*). *Search one* finds the first error (at depth 16) only after 8648 states, i.e. after it has already covered a large part of the state space. As a result, the benefit of using *search min* is rather marginal in this case; it finds a second error, at depth 3, by exploring only 190 additional states.

5.2   Heuristic Search

In this section, we illustrate the benefits of using heuristic search, using the large *random* scenario. In this case, we are interested in how quickly the search can detect an error, and thus stop at the first error found. The fitness function types used were *breadth-first search* and *candidate count*, both described in Section 4.4. We tried both the *candidate subsumption* and *candidate matching* error conditions.

The results are summarized in Table 2, including depth-first search for comparison purposes. They show that, using breadth-first search, LPF mapped through only 154 states before detecting a candidate subsumption error at depth 3, compared to 8648 states to depth 16 using depth-first search. The candidate-count heuristic also explores 154 states, although it goes a little deeper to depth 5. For the less selective candidate-matching error condition, LPF finds an error after just 4 states using candidate-count or breadth-first search, compared to 17 states with depth-first search. As expected, heuristic search (both breadth-first search and the candidate-count heuristic) detected the error significantly faster than depth-first search. These results illustrate that heuristic search can save a great deal of time by skipping large parts of the search space where errors are less likely to be found.

Table 2. Comparison of Heuristic vs. depth-first search

strategy	max. depth	condition[1]	time	states	states/min
DFS	16	CS	02:55:38	8648	49
BFS	3	CS	00:03:56	154	38
CC	5	CS	00:03:42	154	38
DFS	16	CM	00:00:15	17	68
BFS	2	CM	00:00:13	4	20
CC	1	CM	00:00:11	4	24

[1] See Table 1

5.3   Example Scenario 1

Our first example involves the *PITEX baseline* scenario, and was performed with an earlier version of L2 in which, as it turns out, the checkpointing functionality used by LPF was flawed. The scenario involves a double fault, where a valve sv31 (on a liquid oxygen venting line) gets stuck and a micro-switch sensing the position of that valve fails at the same time. The sequence of events is as follows:

1. A command open is issued to sv31.
2. A command close is issued to sv31.
3. The open microswitch of sv31 breaks.
4. sv31 fails in stuck-open position.

The microswitch fault remains undetected (Livingstone still reports the empty candidate after event 3), however the stuck valve causes a fault diagnosis: after event 4, Livingstone reports the following candidates (the number before the # sign is the time of occurrence of the presumed fault):

```
Candidate 0)
  5#test.vr01.modeTransition=stuckOpen:2
Candidate 1)
  -#test.vr01.modeTransition=stuckClosed:2
Candidate 2)
  -#test.sv31.modeTransition=stuckClosed:3
Candidate 3)
  -#test.vr01.modeTransition=stuckOpen:2
  3#test.vr01.modeTransition=stuckClosed:2
Candidate 4)
  5#test.forwardLo2.rp1sv.modeTransition=unknownFault:5
Candidate 5)
  -#test.forwardLo2.rp1sv.modeTransition=unknownFault:5
Candidate 6)
  3#test.forwardLo2.rp1sv.modeTransition=unknownFault:5
Candidate 7)
  5#test.sv31.modeTransition=stuckOpen:5
Candidate 8)
  -#test.sv03.sv.modeTransition=stuckClosed:3
  3#test.sv03.openMs.modeTransition=faulty:3
Candidate 9)
  -#test.sv03.sv.modeTransition=stuckClosed:3
  -#test.sv03.openMs.modeTransition=faulty:3
```

At this point, LPF reports a candidate-matching error, indicating that none of the Livingstone candidates match the modes from the simulator. The fault is detected (otherwise no faulty candidates would be generated), but incorrectly diagnosed (note that candidate 7 *subsumes*, but does not *match*, the actual faults). At this point the data seems to suggest that Livingstone is not properly generating all valid candidates.

To further interpret and confirm the results reported by LPF, we ran l2test on the L2 scenario associated with this error. The following list of candidates were generated, which differs from those obtained above via LPF:

```
Candidate 0)
  5#test.vr01.modeTransition=stuckOpen:2
Candidate 1)
  4#test.vr01.modeTransition=stuckOpen:2
Candidate 2)
  4#test.forwardLo2.modeTransition=unknownFault:5
Candidate 3)
  3#test.forwardLo2.modeTransition=unknownFault:5
Candidate 4)
  4#test.sv31.sv.modeTransition=stuckOpen:5
Candidate 5)
  5#test.forwardLo2.modeTransition=unknownFault:5
Candidate 6)
  -#test.forwardLo2.modeTransition=unknownFault:5
Candidate 7)
  5#test.sv31.sv.modeTransition=stuckOpen:5
```

Although none of these match the actual faults either (i.e. there is indeed a candidate-matching error in this state), the difference also shows that the results from LPF were flawed. Further analysis revealed that the discrepancy originated from a checkpointing bug. In particular, Livingstone did not properly restore its internal constraint network when restoring checkpoints, resulting in a corrupted internal state and incorrect diagnosis results. With our assistance, the error was localized and resolved in a new release of the Livingstone program.

5.4   Example Scenario 2

The second example considers one of the five errors reported using Candidate subsumption on the Random scenario. It involves a solenoid valve, sv02, which sends pressurized helium into a propellant tank. A command close is issued to the valve, but the valve fails and remains open—in LPF terms, a fault is injected in the simulator. The following sample output lists the candidates reported by Livingstone after the fault occurs in sv02:

```
Candidate 0)
  4#test.sv02.openMs.modeTransition=faulty:3
Candidate 1)
  3#test.sv02.openMs.modeTransition=faulty:3
Candidate 2)
  2#test.sv02.openMs.modeTransition=faulty:3
Candidate 3)
  -#test.sv02.openMs.modeTransition=faulty:3
Candidate 4)
  -#test.sv02.rp1sv.modeTransition=unknown:4
```

The injected fault, test.sv02.rp1sv.mode=stuckOpen, is detected (otherwise no faulty candidates would be generated) but incorrectly diagnosed: none of these candidates matches or subsumes the correct fault. The first four candidates consist of a faulty open microswitch sensor at different time steps (microswitches report the valve's position). The last candidate consists of an unknown fault mode. The L2 scenario corresponding to this error was replayed in l2test and produced identical results, confirming the validity of the results from LPF. Further analysis by application specialists revealed that fault ranks in the X-34 model needed re-tuning, which resolved the problem.

6   Conclusions and Perspectives

Livingstone PathFinder (LPF) is a software tool for automatically analyzing model-based diagnosis applications across a wide range of scenarios. *Livingstone* is its current target diagnosis system, however the architecture is modular and adaptable to other systems. LPF has been successfully demonstrated on a real-size example taken from a space vehicle application.

Although the experiments have so far been performed only by the LPF development team, Livingstone specialists from the PITEX project have shown great interest in the results we obtained. In comparison, their verification approach is based on running a fixed, limited set of test cases, as detailed in [8]. LPF shows great potential for radically expanding the number of tested behaviors, with a modest additional effort from the users. Our next stage is to put the tools in the hands of the developers. In this perspective, we have also been adding a graphical user interface and integrating LPF into the Livingstone modeling and simulation tool.

LPF is under active development, in close collaboration with Livingstone application developers at NASA Ames. After considerable efforts resolving technical issues in both LPF and relevant parts of Livingstone, we are now contributing useful results to application specialists, who in turn reciprocate much needed feedback and suggestions on further improvements. The *candidate subsumption* error condition is the latest benefit from this interaction. Directions for further work include new search strategies and heuristics, additional error conditions including capture of application-specific criteria, improved post-treatment and display of the large amount of data that is typically produced.

Future work includes support for determining state equivalence, to allow pruning the search when reaching a state equivalent to an already visited one. The potential benefits from this approach remain to be assessed: as Livingstone retains data not only about the current step but previous ones as well, cases where equivalent states are reached through different executions may be very infrequent. As an alternative, experiments with weaker or approximate equivalences may be performed to reduce the search space, at the risk of inadvertently missing relevant traces.

We are also currently adapting LPF to MIT's Titan model-based executive [11], which offers a more comprehensive diagnosis capability as well as a reactive controller. This extends the verification capabilities to involve the remediation actions taken by the controller when faults are diagnosed. In this regard, LPF can be considered as evolving towards a versatile system-level verification tool for model-based controllers.

Acknowledgments. This research is funded by NASA under ECS Project 2.2.1.1, *Validation of Model-Based IVHM Architectures*. The authors would like to thank Livingstone application developers at NASA Ames, especially Sandra Hayden and Adam Sweet, for their active cooperation, and Livingstone lead developer Lee Brownston for his responsive support. We are also grateful to reviewers of previous versions of this article for their helpful comments. All trademarks used are properties of their respective owners.

References

1. A. Bajwa and A. Sweet. The Livingstone Model of a Main Propulsion System. In *Proceedings of the IEEE Aerospace Conference*, March 2003.
2. E. Brinksma. A Theory for the Derivation of Tests. In: S. Aggarwal, K. Sabnani, eds., *Protocol Specification, Testing and Verification, VIII*. North-Holland, Amsterdam, 1988, ISBN 0-444-70542-2, 63–74.
3. L. Fleming, T. Hatfield and J. Malin. Simulation-Based Test of Gas Transfer Control Software: CONFIG Model of Product Gas Transfer System. *Automation, Robotics and Simulation Division Report*, AR&SD-98-017, (Houston, TX:NASA Johnson Space Center Center, 1998).
4. P. Godefroid. Model Checking for Programming Languages using VeriSoft. In *Proceedings of the 24th ACM Symposium on Principles of Programming Languages*, pages 174-186, Paris, January 1997.
5. C. A. R. Hoare. *Communicating Sequential Processes*. Prentice-Hall, 1985.
6. A.E. Lindsey and C. Pecheur, Simulation-Based Verification of Livingstone Applications. *Workshop on Model-Checking for Dependable Software-Intensive Systems*, San Francisco, June 2003.
7. N. Muscettola, P. Nayak, B. Pell and B. Williams. Remote Agent: To Boldly Go Where No AI System Has Gone Before. *Artificial Intelligence*, vol. 103, pp. 5-47, 1998.
8. C. Meyer, H. Cannon, Propulsion IVHM Technology Experiment Overview, In *Proceedings of the IEEE Aerospace Conference*, March 8-15, 2003.
9. C. Pecheur, R. Simmons. From Livingstone to SMV: Formal Verification for Autonomous Spacecrafts. In *Proceedings of First Goddard Workshop on Formal Approaches to Agent-Based Systems*, NASA Goddard, April 5-7, 2000. Lecture Notes in Computer Science, vol. 1871, Springer Verlag.
10. W. Visser, K. Havelund, G. Brat and S. Park. Model Checking Programs. In *Proceedings of the IEEE International Conference on Automated Software Engineering*, pages 3-12, September 2000.
11. B. Williams, M. Ingham, S. Chung and P. Elliot, Model-based Programming of Intelligent Embedded Systems and Robotic Space Explorers. In *Proceedings of the IEEE Modelings and Design of Embedded Software Conference*, vol. 9, no.1 pp. 212-237, 2003.
12. B. Williams and P. Nayak, A Model-based Approach to Reactive Self-Configuring Systems. In *Proceedings of the National Conference on Artificial Intelligence*, vol. 2, pp. 971-978, August 1996.

Automatic Parametric Verification of a Root Contention Protocol Based on Abstract State Machines and First Order Timed Logic

Danièle Beauquier, Tristan Crolard, and Evguenia Prokofieva

Laboratory of Algorithmics, Complexity and Logic
University Paris 12 – Val de Marne*(France)
{beauquier, crolard, prokofieva}@univ-paris12.fr

Abstract. The paper presents a verification of the IEEE Root Contention Protocol as an illustration of a new and innovative approach for the verification of real-time distributed systems. Systems are modeled with basic Gurevich abstract state machines (ASMs), and requirements are expressed in a first order timed logic (FOTL). FOTL is undecidable, however the protocol we study is in a decidable class of practical interest. Advantages of this framework are twofold: on the one hand, a great expressive power which permits in particular an easy treatment of parameters, on the other hand the modeling task is simplified by an adequat choice of tools.

Keywords: Parametric verification, real-time distributed systems, predicate logic, IEEE 1394a standard, root contention protocol, Gurevich abstract state machines.

1 Introduction

The IEEE 1394 serial bus protocol (also called "FireWire") is a standard that enables fast transfer of digital information between PCs and peripheral devices such as video recorders, music systems, and so on. The IEEE Root Contention Protocol (RCP), a part of the IEEE 1394 standard, has become a popular case study for investigating the feasibility of formal specification and verification techniques. Its purpose is to elect a leader among two processes, and its correctness depends on the use of randomization and timing delays. The challenge is to synthesize automatically necessary and sufficient conditions on timing parameters for the protocol's correctness.

We apply to this case study a new and innovative approach for the verification of real-time distributed systems which offers some advantages compared to existing frameworks. Our methodology consists in embedding of the whole problem in a first order timed logic (FOTL) and in reducing the problem to the validity of a closed formula in this logic. The process comprises three steps:

---

* 61, Av. du Général de Gaulle, 94010 Créteil Cedex France

K. Jensen and A. Podelski (Eds.): TACAS 2004, LNCS 2988, pp. 372–387, 2004.

- *Step 1.* the system under consideration is specified as a Gurevich Abstract State Machine (ASM) and this machine is translated in an automatic way in a formula Φ_{Syst} of FOTL.
- *Step 2.* The requirements specification is written down as a FOTL formula Φ_{Spec}.
- *Step 3.* An automatic verification of the validity of $\Phi_{Syst} \rightarrow \Phi_{Spec}$ is applied.

Since validity is undecidable for FOTL, step 3 is not always realizable. In [BS02] decidable classes of this logic with practical interest are described. The fundamental idea which prevails and sustains the philosophy hidden behind these classes is the following observation: in "practical systems" the algorithm which governs the behavior of the system and the requirements to verify are not very complicated, in other words, if there is a counter-model to $\Phi_{Syst} \rightarrow \Phi_{Spec}$, there must exist a "simple" one, i.e. a counter-model of bounded complexity. Roughly speaking, the complexity is given by the number of intervals of time where the system has a "constant" behavior.

In [BS02] sufficient semantic conditions for Φ_{Syst} and Φ_{Spec} are given which ensure that if $\Phi_{Syst} \rightarrow \Phi_{Spec}$ has a counter-model, then it has a counter-model of a fixed known complexity. The cornerstone is that one can decide whether a FOTL formula has a (counter-)model of a given complexity. The algorithm consists of an elimination of abstract function symbols, which leads to a first order formula of the decidable theory of real addition and multiplication, for which we have to check the satisfiability. At this point, we use a quantifier elimination algorithm implemented in the tool Reduce [Hea99].

In the case of the RCP, we prove (in a simple way) that all the runs of the ASM modeling a cycle of the protocol have a complexity bounded by some constant. So clearly, if the protocol does not satisfy the requirements, there is a run with a bounded complexity which is a counter-model. Then the sufficient conditions given in [BS02] do not need to be proved.

What are the advantages of our approach? A first one is that modeling the system and the requirements does not need much effort and the models we get are very close to the initial specification. As a result, there are less sources of errors in the modeling process. A second advantage is the expressive power of the chosen formalism. FOTL contains arithmetic operations over reals and is much more expressive than classical temporal logics and classical timed automata. Moreover, treatment of parameters is not a difficulty in this framework. Thirdly, for a large class of practical verification problems, the sufficient conditions which lead to a decidable class are satisfied and easy to prove. At last, in case of failure, an efficient description of all the counter-models of a given complexity is provided, which is very important for practical detection of errors.

What are the limits of this method? The limits are in the complexity of *Step 3* in the verification process. The quantifier elimination algorithm has a rather "high" practical complexity and the method can only be applied if the number of quantifiers to eliminate is not too large. To overcome this obstacle we decompose the ASM into smaller ones.

The rest of this paper is organised as follows. Section 2 gives a short description of the Root Contention Protocol. Section 3 presents our logical framework for verification of real-time systems: FOTL syntax and semantics are described as well as basic Gurevich abstract state machines; the notion of finite complexity of a model is introduced. Section 4 is devoted to our modeling of the RCP and to the obtained verification results. In the last section, we compare our techniques to the existing ones and we draw some conclusions.

2   The Root Contention Protocol

The IEEE 1394 standard specifies a high performance serial bus that enables fast data transfer within networks of multimedia systems and devices. It is defined as a multi-layered system using different protocols for different phases. Components connected to the bus are referred to as nodes. Each node has ports for bidirectional connection to some other nodes. The Root Contention Protocol is a sub-protocol of the Initialization phase. The Initialization phase takes place after bus resets. That may occur if a component was added or removed from the network or an error was detected. This phase attemps to find a spanning tree out of the network and then to elect a leader to act as a bus manager. Informally, the leader election works as follows. At initial state, a node waits for a "be my parent" request (parent notification, PN signal) from its neighbors in the spanning tree. When it receives such a request from a neighbor node it replies with a CN signal (Child Notification) as acknowledgement and adds this node to its list of children. When a node has received from all of its ports except one a PN signal, it sends to the remaining neighbor a PN signal. The leaf nodes start to send a PN signal to their only neighbor at the initial state. The tree is constructed bottom-up and at the end, either a leader is elected (the node which has received PN signals from all its neighbors becomes the root), or two nodes are in contention, i.e. each node wants the other one to be a root. Contention is detected independently by each node when a PN request arrives while waiting for a CN acknowledgement.

At this moment the Root Contention Protocol starts. The node sends an Idle signal to its partner and picks a random bit. If the bit 1 comes up, then the node waits for a short time (*fast*) in the interval [*fast_min*, *fast_max*]. If the bit 0 comes up, then the node waits for a long time (*slow*) in the interval [*slow_min*, *slow_max*]. Of course, $0 < fast\_min \leq fast\_max < slow\_min \leq slow\_max$ holds. When this time is over, the node looks for a message from the contender node. If there is a PN signal, it sends a CN signal and becomes a leader. If there is no message (Idle), it sends a PN signal and waits for acknowledgment. In this case a root contention may reoccur.

The communication between two nodes has a delay with an upper bound *delay*. The choice of timing parameters plays an important role. For the protocol to work correctly constraints on the timing parameters are essential. Figure 1 gives two examples of scenario depending on parameters values.

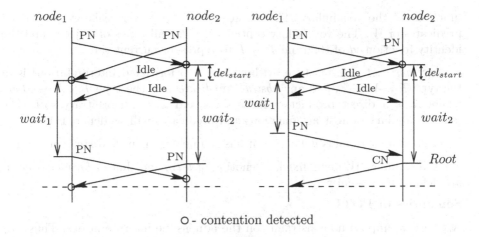

O - contention detected

Fig. 1. Two among possible scenarios of the RCP

The aim of verification is to derive automatically necessary and sufficient conditions on timing parameters for a correct protocol behavior, namely eventually, the protocols ends with one and only one node elected as root.

3   First Order Timed Logic (FOTL)

In this section we briefly present the first order logic framework for real-time verification from [BS97], [BS02] and the notion of basic Gurevich ASM [GH96].

3.1   Syntax and Semantics of FOTL

A First Order Timed Logic used in this framework is constructed in two steps. Firstly, we choose a simple, if possible decidable theory to deal with concrete mathematical objects (the underlying theory), like reals, and secondly, we extend it in a 'minimal' way by abstract functions to deal with our specifications. Here we take as the underlying theory the theory of real addition and multiplication, and extend it by functions with at most one time argument and with other arguments being of finite abstract sorts. More details are given below.

Syntax of FOTL

The vocabulary W of a FOTL consists of a finite set of *sorts*, a finite set of *function symbols* and a finite set of *predicate symbols*. To each sort there is attributed a set of variables. Some sorts are predefined, i. e. have fixed interpretations. Here the predefined sorts are the real numbers $\mathbb{R}$, time $\mathcal{T} =_{df} \mathbb{R}_{\geq 0}$ treated as a subsort of $\mathbb{R}$ and $Bool = \{True, False\}$. The other sorts are finite.

Some functions and predicates are also predefined. As predefined constants we take all rational numbers. Addition and multiplication of reals are predefined functions of the vocabulary. The predicates $=$, $\leq$, $<$ over reals are predefined predicates of W. The vocabulary contains $' ='$ for all types of objects, and the identity function id of the type $\mathcal{T} \to \mathcal{T}$ to represent current time.

Any *abstract function* (i. e. without any a priori fixed interpretation) is of the type $\mathcal{T} \times \mathcal{X} \to \mathcal{Z}$, and any *abstract predicate* is of the type $\mathcal{T} \times \mathcal{X} \to Bool$, where $\mathcal{X}$ is a direct product of finite sorts and $\mathcal{Z}$ is an arbitrary sort. The (sub)vocabulary of abstract functions and predicates will be denoted V.

A function symbol is *dynamic* if it has a time argument and *static* otherwise.

A vocabulary W being fixed, the notion of *term* and that of *formula* over W are defined in a usual way.

Semantics of FOTL

A priori we impose no constraints on the admissible interpretations. Thus, the notions of interpretation, model, satisfiability and validity are treated as in first order predicate logic modulo the predefined part of the vocabulary.

3.2   Gurevich Basic Abstract State Machines (ASM)

To represent the algorithms we use Gurevich Abstract State Machine (ASM) [Gur95]. This formalism is powerful, gives a clear vision of semantics of timed algorithms and permits to change easily the level of abstraction. A basic ASM is a program with one external loop consisting of simultaneously executed **If-Then**-operators. In principle, Gurevich ASMs may serve as an intermediate language between user's languages for algorithm specification and a logic framework. (This claim is supported by numerous applications of Gurevich ASM, see http://www.eecs.umich.edu/gasm/.)

A *basic ASM* is a tuple of the form $(W, Init, Prog)$, where W is a vocabulary, $Init$ is a closed formula describing the initial state and $Prog$ is a program.

Sorts, variables and functions are like in subsection 3.1 except that *time cannot be an argument of functions*. We classify the functions using the same terms as in subsection 3.1, namely *abstract* or *predefined* on the one hand and *static* or *dynamic* on the other hand. Dynamic functions are classified into *external* and *internal*.

External functions are not changed by the ASM, internal functions, on the contrary, are computed by the ASM and are obviously abstract and dynamic. Predefined static functions have a fixed interpretation valid for every $t \in \mathcal{T}$. The interpretation of a predefined dynamic function, though changing with time, does not depend on the functioning of the machine. We assume that any ASM vocabulary contains a predefined external dynamic function CT of type $\to \mathcal{T}$ which gives the current time.

The program $Prog$ has the following syntax:

> **Repeat**
> **ForAll** $\omega \in \Omega$
>   **InParallelDo**
>   **If** $G_1(\omega)$ **Then** $A_1(\omega)$ **EndIf**
>   **If** $G_2(\omega)$ **Then** $A_2(\omega)$ **EndIf**
>   ....
>   **If** $G_m(\omega)$ **Then** $A_m(\omega)$ **EndIf**
>   **EndInParallelDo**
> **EndForAll**
> **EndRepeat**

Ω is an abstract sort which permits to parametrize the ASM. We will not use it in the paper. Each G_i is a *guard*, i. e. a formula over the vocabulary W, not having free variables except ω, and each A_i is a list of assignments (called *updates*) whose terms also do not have free variables except ω. Each assignment is of the form $f(T) := \theta$, where f is an internal function, θ is a term and T is a list of terms of the type corresponding to the type of f.

Informally all guards are checked simultaneously and instantaneously, and all the updates of rules with true guards are executed also simultaneously and instantaneously. To save the space we will not write **Repeat** and **InParallelDo**.

Semantics of an ASM

Precise semantics is given in [BS02] and follows [GH96]. We give here just an intuitive description. For a given interpretation of abstract sorts we define the semantics of the program in terms of runs (executions). Informally, given an input, that is an interpretation of external functions for each moment of time, the machine computes a run which is an interpretation of internal functions for each moment of time or at least, for an initial segment of $\mathcal{T}$. Notice that external functions which are classified as static have the same interpretation for every moment of time.

The behavior of the machine is deterministic. All the **If-Then**-operators are executed simultaneously in parallel and instantaneously as well as all the assignments in any **Then**-part if the corresponding guard is true. Of course, whenever the assignments are inconsistent, the execution is interrupted, and the run of the algorithm becomes undefined thereafter. Notice that the effect of an assignment executed at time t takes place *after* time t but not *at* time t.

We consider only *total runs*, i.e. those defined on whole $\mathcal{T}$. Below "run" means "total run".

3.3   Translation of an ASM into a FOTL Formula

In order to reason about the behavior of an ASM we are to embed the functions of the vocabulary of the machine into FOTL. And at this moment, time becomes explicit to represent our vision of the functioning of the machine. To 'time' the dynamic functions of an ASM we proceed as follows.

If f is a dynamic function of type $\mathcal{X} \to Z$ in the vocabulary of an ASM, the corresponding logical function is denoted by f° and is of type $\mathcal{T} \times \mathcal{X} \to Z$. Thus the predefined dynamic function CT becomes CT° in the logic, that is the identity: $CT^\circ(t) = t$.

It turns out that one can characterize the set of total runs of a basic ASM by an FOTL formula ([BS02]). We generate automatically this formula using the translator that we developed for this purpose[1].

3.4   Finite Complexity

Complexity of finite partial interpretations

A general definition of this notion is given in [BS02]. To treat our case study, we need only abstract functions of type $\mathcal{T} \to Z$ where Z is a predefined sort. For this reason the definition we give below is limited to this case. The general definition given in [BS02] needs more technical details.

A partial interpretation f^* of an abstract function f over $\mathcal{T}' \subset \mathcal{T}$ is a finite partial interpretation (FPI) with complexity k if $\mathcal{T}'$ is a union of k disjoint intervals and f^* is constant on each interval.

A finite partial interpretation (FPI) of V with complexity k is a collection of FPIs with complexity k, one for each abstract function.

Complexity of interpretations

An interpretation f^* of f has complexity k if $\mathcal{T}$ is a union of k disjoint intervals and f^* is constant on each interval (intervals are arbitrary, in particular they can be reduced to a single point).

An interpretation of V has complexity k if the interpretation of each abstract function from V has complexity k.

3.5   Decision Procedure

In [BS02], the following result is proved and the corresponding algorithm is described:

Theorem 1 *Given an integer $k > 0$, one can decide whether a closed FOTL formula has a (counter)-model with complexity k.*

On the other hand, there exist some semantic sufficient conditions ([BS02]) on formulas Φ and Ψ which ensure that if $\Phi \to \Psi$ has a counter-model, it has a counter-model of bounded complexity. Formula Φ must be "finitely satisfiable", and formula Ψ must be "finitely refutable". As a matter of fact, it turns out that these conditions are verified by a large class of verification problems. We mention it to underline that our framework is general enough. But we do not need to use these conditions here, because we prove directly that the runs of the ASM modeling the protocol have a complexity equal to 3, so we have only to apply the decision procedure of Theorem 1. This decision procedure works as follows. Given a closed FOTL-formula G and an integer k, there exists a formula G_0 of the decidable theory of real addition and multiplication which is valid iff G has a model of complexity k. The formula G_0 is obtained by an elimination

---

[1] Available at http://www.univ-paris12.fr/lacl/crolard.

of abstract function symbols using the fact that models of complexity k can be described by a finite set of real parameters. Notice that G_0 depends on G and k. In [BS02] the following result is proved:

Proposition 1 *A closed FOTL formula G has a model of complexity k if and only if G_0 is valid (interpreted over $\mathbb{R}$ with its usual relations, addition and multiplication).*

Thus, starting with a FOTL formula G (of the form $\Phi_{syst} \to \Phi_{spec}$ in our case), we build the formula G_0 of the theory of real addition and multiplication and we check its validity using an algorithm of elimination of real quantifiers. We use for this elimination the tool Reduce [Hea99]. If the formula G is not closed and contains free parameters, the elimination procedure applied to G_0 gives a quantifier free formula to be satisfied by parameters in order that G is satisfied.

4 Modeling and Verification of RCP

This section falls in three parts. Firstly we present how we use ASMs to model the behavior of the protocol. Secondly we express the requirements in FOTL. Thirdly, we give a report on the results of our model checking experiment.

4.1 The RCP Model as an ASM

Our model describes the behavior of contented nodes during one RCP cycle. First we give below an ASM A which corresponds to the behavior of a node from the moment it enters a contention state. The arrival of signals is modeled by an update of variables representing ports. The probabilistic choice is replaced by a non deterministic one which is modeled by an external boolean function.

The vocabulary of the ASM A consists of

Predefined sorts:

- $Signal = \{$PN, CN, Idle$\}$.

There are three possible signals: Idle, PN which is a Parent Notification signal and CN which is a Child Notification signal.

Static functions:

- $delay$ is the (maximal) communication delay.
- $fast\_min$, $fast\_max$ are minimal and maximal values of short waiting time.
- $slow\_min$, $slow\_max$ are minimal and maximal values of long waiting time.
All these functions have type $\to \mathcal{T}$.

External dynamic functions:

- $fast : \to \mathcal{T}$ and $slow : \to \mathcal{T}$ are respectively fast and slow waiting times.
- $Alea : \to Bool$ is a random bit.
- $Port_{rcpt} : \to Signal$ is the receipt port of the node, the node reads the signals he receives on this port.

Internal dynamic functions:
- $WaitEnd : \to \mathcal{T}$ is the time when the waiting period of the node stops
- $Port_{snd} : \to Signal$ is used by the node to send signals to its contention partner. If the node sends a signal at time t, it arrives to its contender node at time $t + delay$. This event is modeled by an update of function $Port_{snd}$ at time $t + delay$.
- $State : \to Signal$ is the value of the last signal sent by the node.
- $Root : \to Bool$ is equal to $True$ when the node knows it is root.

Static and external timed functions are subject to the following axiom:

Axiom:
$delay > 0 \ \wedge \ (\forall t \geq 0$
$(0 < fast\_min \leq fast°(t) \leq fast\_max < slow\_min \leq slow°(t) \leq slow\_max)).$

When a contention phase starts for a node, its state is Idle, and the content of its $Port_{snd}$ is PN (Initial Conditions). Then the behavior of the node in the machine is as follows. It picks (here at time 0) a random bit, this is done by a test on the value of the external function $Alea$. According to the value of the random bit, the value of $Wait$ is put equal to $slow$ or to $fast$ (rules (1) and (1')). The values $slow$ and $fast$ satisfy the constraints $slow\_min \leq slow \leq slow\_max$ and $fast\_min \leq fast \leq fast\_max$ respectively. At the same time, the node sends an Idle signal, which arrives at time $delay$ (rule(2)). When the node ends its waiting period, according to the value of the receipt port ($Port_{rcpt}$), it changes its state (rules (3), (3')). Rules (4) and (4') correspond to the arrival of the signal sent at the end of the waiting period (PN or CN). Later a new contention situation will be detected by the node if it is in a PN state (which means that the last signal it sent is a PN signal), and it receives a PN signal from its partner. Initial conditions of the machine A are:

Init:

$State = \text{Idle} \wedge Port_{snd} = \text{PN} \wedge Port_{rcpt} = \text{PN} \wedge Root = false.$

---

(1) **If** $Alea = \text{true} \wedge CT = 0$ **Then** $WaitEnd := CT + fast$ **EndIf**
(1') **If** $Alea = \text{false} \wedge CT = 0$ **Then** $WaitEnd := CT + slow$ **EndIf**
(2) **If** $State = \text{Idle} \wedge CT = delay$ **Then** $Port_{snd} := \text{Idle}$ **EndIf**
(3) **If** $State = \text{Idle} \wedge Port_{rcpt} = \text{Idle} \wedge CT = WaitEnd$
    Then $State := \text{PN}$ **EndIf**
(3') **If** $State = \text{Idle} \wedge Port_{rcpt} = \text{PN} \wedge CT = WaitEnd$
    Then $State := \text{CN}; Root := \text{true}$ **EndIf**
(4) **If** $State = \text{PN} \wedge CT = WaitEnd + delay$ **Then** $Port_{snd} = \text{PN}$ **EndIf**
(4') **If** $State = \text{CN} \wedge CT = WaitEnd + delay$ **Then** $Port_{snd} = \text{CN}$ **EndIf**

ASM A modeling one cycle of a node

The two nodes which are in contention phase are not synchronized, for this reason they do not start contention at the same time (the difference between starting times is at most equal to $delay$). Machine A describes the behavior of one node during a cycle which starts at time zero. To describe the process the two contender nodes we need two processes which start asynchronously. Let n_i, $i \in \{1,2\}$ be the two contender nodes. For $i \in \{1,2\}$, $\bar{i}$ denotes the value in $\{1,2\}$ different from i. Since the receipt port for one process is the sending port for the other one, we denote by $Port_{i,\bar{i}}$ the sending port of node i and so $Port_{\bar{i},i}$ is its receipt one. Without loss of generality, we can skip step (1-1') and start at step (2) with initial conditions: for $i \in \{1,2\}$ $State_i =$ Idle, $Port_{\bar{i},i} =$ PN, $Root_i = false$ and the waiting period $wait_i$ of node n_i satisfies $fast\_min \leq wait_i \leq fast\_max \vee slow\_min \leq wait_i \leq slow\_max$. Machine B describes the behavior of the two nodes during one cycle, where at time zero node n_1 starts its contention ($delay\_start_1 = 0$) and node n_2 is in contention for a duration $delay\_start_2$ where $0 \leq delay\_start_2 \leq delay$.

In this machine, $wait_i$ and $delay\_start_i$ are static functions of type $\rightarrow \mathcal{T}$. For $i \in \{1,2\}$, function $delay\_start_i$ satisfies $0 \leq delay\_start_i \leq delay$.

$\underline{Init}$:

$\forall i \in \{1,2\}$
$State_i =$ Idle $\wedge Port_{i,\bar{i}} =$ PN $\wedge Root_i = false \wedge delay\_start_1 = 0$

ForAll $i \in \{1,2\}$
  (1) **If** $State_i =$ Idle $\wedge CT = delay - delay\_start_i$
      Then $Port_i :=$ Idle **EndIf**
  (2) **If** $State_i =$ Idle $\wedge Port_{\bar{i},i} =$ Idle $\wedge CT = wait_i - delay\_start_i$
      Then $State_i :=$ PN **EndIf**
  (2') **If** $State_i =$ Idle $\wedge Port_{\bar{i},i} =$ PN $\wedge CT = wait_i - delay\_start_i$
      Then $State_i :=$ CN **EndIf**
  (3) **If** $State_i =$ PN $\wedge CT = wait_i - delay\_start_i + delay$
      Then $Port_i =$ PN **EndIf**
  (3') **If** $State_i =$ CN $\wedge CT = wait_i - delay\_start_i + delay$
      Then $Port_i =$ CN; $Root_i =$ true **EndIf**

ASM B modeling one cycle of the two contender nodes

4.2   The Requirements in FOTL

The aim is to synthesize necessary and sufficient conditions on values of parameters $delay$, $fast\_min$, $fast\_max$, $slow\_min$, $slow\_max$ for which the following statement S holds:

    Eventually, the protocol ends up with one (and only one) node elected as root.
We will denote by $\mathcal{P}$ the list of parameters:

$$delay, \; fast\_min, \; fast\_max, \; slow\_min, \; slow\_max.$$

We consider three properties related to one cycle of the protocol.

    Safety: No two roots are elected
    Liveness: At least one root is elected

Content: A new contention appears.

The translation of these properties in FOTL is as follows:

$$\text{Safety:} \quad \neg \, (\exists t \; IsRoot_1(t) \; \wedge \; \exists t \; IsRoot_2(t))$$

where $IsRoot_i(t) =_{def} Root_i^{\circ}(t) \; \wedge \; Port_{i,\bar{i}}^{\circ}(t) = \text{CN} \; \wedge \; State_i^{\circ}(t) = \text{PN}$.

Actually when a node i becomes root, the other one $\bar{i}$ knows it only when he receives the acknowledgment (the CN signal), moreover, to be sure that this aknowledgment concerns its last PN request and not the previous one, $\bar{i}$ must be in state PN.

$$\text{Liveness:} \quad \exists t \; (IsRoot_1(t) \; \vee \; IsRoot_2(t)).$$
$$\text{Content:} \quad \exists t \; Contention_1(t) \; \wedge \exists t \; Contention_2(t)$$

where $Contention_i(t) =_{def} State_i^{\circ}(t) = \text{PN} \; \wedge \; Port_{\bar{i},i}^{\circ}(t) = \text{PN}$.

Actually, a node detects a new contention if it is in state PN and it receives a signal PN.

The machine B is splitted into two cases according to whether random bits have the same value or not.

Case 1 : the two random bits are different. We look for a necessary and sufficient condition C_1 on values of parameters from $\mathcal{P}$ that turn true *Safety* and *Liveness*.

Case 2 : the two random bits are equal. We look for a necessary and sufficient condition C_2 on values of parameters from $\mathcal{P}$ that turn true *Safety* and (*Liveness* or *Content*).

Notice that in Case 2, whatever are the values of parameters in $\mathcal{P}$, there is a chance of root contention at the end of the cycle.

Clearly $C_1 \wedge C_2$ is a necessary and sufficient condition on parameters $\mathcal{P}$ such that whatever are values of $wait_i$ and $delay\_start_i$ for $i = 1, 2$, eventually the protocol ends up with one (and only one) node elected as root. Actually if $C_1 \wedge C_2$ is satisfied then while the random bits are equal, due to property *Safety* and (*Liveness* or *Content*) either there is again contention or one and exactly one node is root and the process stops. Moreover if it happens that the random bits are different, then, again due to *Safety* and *Liveness* the process stops since one single node is root. As eventually one has different random bits (the probability to never get different random bits is equal to zero) the protocol satisfies the requirement S.

Conversely, if $C_1 \wedge C_2$ is not satisfied, then if in a cycle the random bits are different three cases occur:
- the two nodes are root and the protocol is not correct
- no node is root and there is no new contention, the protocol stops and fails
- no node is root and there is a new contention.

Moreover for each cycle with equal random bits, a new contention can occur.

So if $C_1 \wedge C_2$ is not satisfied, either two roots are elected, either the protocol stops and fails because no root is elected, or the process can run infinitely entering infinitely often in contention.

We have proved that $C_1 \wedge C_2$ is a necessary and sufficient condition for protocol correctness. The next section describes how we get $C_1 \wedge C_2$.

4.3   Model-Checking Results

Let Φ_B be the FOTL formula which characterizes the set of runs of machine B. The first step is to prove that every run of machine B has complexity 3. Notice that machine B does not have external dynamic functions. So we have only to look at internal ones. Every guard has an atom of the form $CT = f$, where f is an external static function. So every guard can be true only once: at moment f. Moreover guards with the same $CT = f$ atom, like (2) and (2') for example, "are not true together". Then no more than one guard is true at any moment of time. We have three internal functions whose interpretations are computed by the ASM. Function $State_i$ can be changed by executing rules (2) or (2') at moment $delay$. So no more than one assignment will take place for $State_i$ and the maximal complexity of its interpretations is 2. Function $Root_i$ can be changed by rule (2') at $CT = wait_i - delay\_start_i$, and its complexity is also 2. At last $Port_i$ can be changed by rule (1) at time $delay$, and by rule (3) or (3') at time $wait_i + delay$, so its complexity is 3. The maximal complexity of interpretations is 3, and every model of Φ_B is a model of complexity 3.

As a consequence, for every FOTL formulas Φ, Ψ, the formula $\Phi \wedge \Phi_B \to \Psi$ has a counter-model iff it has a counter-model of complexity 3.

One can observe that the requirements depend on the equality or no equality of the random bits got by the two contender nodes. Consider the following formulas:

$A_1 : (fast\_min \le wait_1 \le fast\_max \wedge slow\_min \le wait_2 \le slow\_max)$

$A_2 : (fast\_min \le wait_2 \le fast\_max \wedge slow\_min \le wait_1 \le slow\_max)$

$A_3 : (slow\_min \le wait_1 \le slow\_max \wedge slow\_min \le wait_2 \le slow\_max)$

$A_4 : (fast\_min \le wait_1 \le fast\_max \wedge fast\_min \le wait_2 \le fast\_max)$

We split the machine B in two machines, one with the axiom $A_1 \vee A_2$ which corresponds to the case when the two bits are different, and a second one with the axiom $A_3 \vee A_4$ which corresponds to the case when the two bits are equal.

Let

$R_1 : Safety$

$R_2 : Liveness$

$R_3 : Liveness \vee Content$

where $Safety$, $Liveness$, and $Content$ are requirements defined as in subsection 4.2.

The formula $(A_1 \vee A_2) \wedge \Phi_B$ describes the runs with different random bits and the formula $(A_3 \vee A_4) \wedge \Phi_B$ with equal ones. The verification problem of RCP is reduced to compute for what values of parameters from $\mathcal{P}$ the following formulas are valid

$$\forall delay\_start \le delay \; \forall wait_1 \; \forall wait_2 (((A_1 \vee A_2) \wedge \Phi_B) \to (R_1 \wedge R_2)) \qquad (1)$$

$$\forall delay\_start \le delay \; \forall wait_1 \; \forall wait_2 (((A_3 \vee A_4) \wedge \Phi_B) \to (R_1 \wedge R_3)) \qquad (2)$$

From the remark made before, we have to compute what values of parameters ensure the existence of counter-models of complexity 3.

The next step is to generate automatically (using our FOTL2REDUCE tool) formulas $\mathcal{C}_j^i$ of the theory of real addition (here we do not need multiplication) for $i = 1, 2$, $j = 1, 2$ or $i = 3, 4$, $j = 1, 3$ such that $\mathcal{C}_j^i$ is valid iff FOTL formula $A_i \wedge \Phi_B \to R_j$ has a counter-model of complexity 3. It is done by applying to formula $\neg(A_i \wedge \Phi_B \to R_j)$ our abstract symbol elimination algorithm. It turns out that the formula $\mathcal{C}_1^i$ returned by the elimination for $i = 1, 2$ is $False$.

The last step is to apply a quantifier elimination algorithm to formulas:

$\forall delay\_start \le delay \ \forall wait_1 \ \forall wait_2 (\neg \mathcal{C}_j^i)$.

We denote the result of this quantifiers elimination by $\widetilde{\mathcal{C}}_j^i$. The conditions $\mathcal{C}_1$ and $\mathcal{C}_2$ can be now written:

$\mathcal{C}_1 = \wedge_{i=1,2,\ j=1,2} \widetilde{\mathcal{C}}_j^i$ and $\mathcal{C}_2 = \wedge_{i=3,4,\ j=1,3} \widetilde{\mathcal{C}}_j^i$

So $\mathcal{C}_1 = \widetilde{\mathcal{C}}_2^1 \wedge \widetilde{\mathcal{C}}_2^2$ and $\mathcal{C}_2 = \widetilde{\mathcal{C}}_2^1 \wedge \widetilde{\mathcal{C}}_2^3$. Thus formula (1) is valid iff $\mathcal{C}_1$ is true and formula (2) is valid iff $\mathcal{C}_2$ is true.

But it is not enough to get "nice" necessary and sufficient conditions. The obtained results are too big to be easily interpreted. So we experimented with different techniques of simplification realized in Reduce and obtained suitable results by applying iteratively a "tableau simplifier" method. The result we get is a small formula compared to the initial one, nevertheless it is not completely simplified, and we did not succeed to achieve the simplification with Reduce. So the last simplification is done by hand, but it is easy to perform. We get:

$\mathcal{C}_1 : \ 2 * delay < fast\_min \wedge 2 * delay < slow\_min - fast\_max$.

$\mathcal{C}_2 : \ 2 * delay < fast\_min$.

The table below summarizes the performance of our experiments.

property	parameters	time	memory	processor
$Safety$	5	0m6	750M	UltraSparc II (64bits) 440mhg
$Liveness$	5	17m03	3G	UltraSparc III (64bits)[2] (2×)900mhg
$Liveness \vee Content$	5	75m36	3G	UltraSparc III (64bits) (2×)900mhg

The entire process of verification is summarized in Figure 2. The inputs are the ASM which models the system, the complexity k, and the requirements written in FOTL. The ASM2FOTL tool transforms an ASM into an FOTL formula. The FOTL2REDUCE tool proceeds to the elimination of abstract symbol functions and gives the result with the help of Reduce.

---

[2] We would like to thank J.-M. Moreno from the Computer Science Department of Paris 7 University for allowing us to experiment with this server.

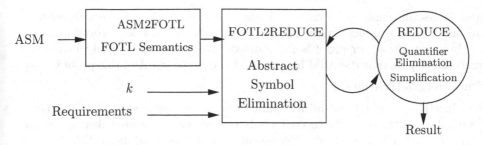

Fig. 2.

5 Comparison with Other Methods – Conclusion

The paper [Sto02] contains a comparative study of formal verification methods applied to the IEEE 1394 RCP. Case studies are divided into three classes: papers that study the functional behaviour of the protocol, papers that employ parametric model checking to synthesize the parameters constraints needed for protocol correctness, and at last papers that focus on the performance analysis of RCP. Our paper belongs to the second class, so we restrict our comparaison to this class [BLSdRT00,TSB00,CAS01,HRSV02].

The modeling

First of all, since the values of probabilities of random bits are not relevant for the analysed properties of Safety and Liveness, the probabilistic part is replaced by a non deterministic one in all the papers.

The four papers use linear parametric timed automata to model the protocol and choose different model checking tools.

The processes which represent the nodes and the wires communicate via synchronization. The abstraction which is done is rather far from the initial specification and it is not always clear whether this modeling is correct, because the behavior of the whole system is not easy to apprehend.

The use of ASMs widely reduces the efforts to accomplish in order to model the protocol. The description of the useful part of the protocol is given by a basic ASM with 5 rules and the properties to verify are very easy to write down in FOTL logic.

Another important aspect is the expressiveness of the models. The tools used in [BLSdRT00,TSB00,HRSV02] can treat only linear constraints, which is enough for RCP, but is a limitation for more general cases. ASMs with the FOTL logic used in the present paper and the TReX tool used in [CAS01] permit non linear arithmetical constraints. Nevertheless, TReX overapproximates the constraints for which a property does not hold, so several runs of the tool with different initial constraints are needed to derive the exact contraints. It is not entirely automatic.

The analysis made in [CAS01] is based on results of [SV99]. In this latter paper, in order to demonstrate that *Impl* (the parallel composition of Nodes and Wires automata) is a correct implementation of *Spec* three intermediate automata are introduced with a laborious stepwise abstraction procedure.

In comparison, our proof is more direct. We have just to verify before the mechanical part that the ASM has a bounded complexity. And this proof is easy.

Parameters treatment

In [BLSdRT00,TSB00] not all five parameters are considered at the same time. Depending on the property to verify, only one or two values are taken as parameters, the other values are fixed constants. In our method, as in [CAS01], the five values are parameters at the same time; a restriction for us is that the delay is always taken as its maximal value.

As a conclusion, we are convinced that our approach to the problem verification is a promising one as it is demonstrated by this case study, and by a previous one, namely the Generalized RailRoad Crossing Problem [BTE03]. The modeling process of the system with ASMs is direct and easy, FOTL is a powerful logic with which requirements are very easy to write down. Our algorithm provides directly necessary and sufficient conditions for the correctness of the system. We hope to improve the time and the space necessary to the computation by using for quantifiers elimination not a general algorithm but a specific one which should be more efficient.

We do not have for the moment an achieved tool, with a user friendly interface, it is a first experiment. But, in view of these first encouraging and competitive results, we intend to develop this tool and to make more experiments.

References

[BLSdRT00] G. Bandini, R.L. Lutje Spelberg, R.C.H. de Rooij, and W.J. Toetenel. Application of parametric model checking - the root contention protocol. In *Sixth Annual Conference of the Advanced School for Computing and Imaging(ASCI 2000)*, Lommel, Belgium, June 2000.

[BS97]   D. Beauquier and A. Slissenko. On semantics of algorithms with continuous time. Technical Report 97–15, Revised version., University Paris 12, Department of Informatics, 1997. Available at http://www.eecs.umich.edu/gasm/ and at http://www.univ-paris12.fr/lacl/.

[BS02]   D. Beauquier and A. Slissenko. A first order logic for specification of timed algorithms: Basic properties and a decidable class. *Annals of Pure and Applied Logic*, 113(1–3):13–52, 2002.

[BTE03]   D. Beauquier, Crolard T., and Prokofieva E. Automatic verification of real time systems: A case study. In *Third Workshop on Automated Verification of Critical Systems (AVoCS'2003)*, Technical Report of the University of Southampton, pages 98–108, Southampton (UK), April 2003.

[CAS01]   A. Collomb-Annichini and M. Sighireanu. Parametrized reachability analysis of the IEEE 1394 root contention protocol using TReX. In *Proceedings of the Workshop on Real-Time Tools (RT-TOOLS'2001)*, 2001.

[GH96]   Y. Gurevich and J. Huggins. The railroad crossing problem: an ex-
            periment with instantaneous actions and immediate reactions. In H. K.
            Buening, editor, *Computer Science Logics, Selected papers from CSL'95*,
            pages 266–290. Springer-Verlag, 1996. Lect. Notes in Comput. Sci.,
            vol. 1092.

[Gur95]   Y. Gurevich. Evolving algebra 1993: Lipari guide. In E. Börger, edi-
            tor, *Specification and Validation Methods*, pages 9–93. Oxford University
            Press, 1995.

[Hea99]   Anthony C. Hearn. Reduce user's and contributed packages manual, ver-
            sion 3.7. Available from Konrad-Zuse-Zentrum Berlin, Germany, Febru-
            ary 1999. http://www.uni-koeln.de/REDUCE/.

[HRSV02]   T.S. Hune, J.M.T. Romijn, M.I.A. Stoelinga, and F.W. Vaandrager.
            Linear parametric model checking of timed automata. *Journal of Logic
            and Algebraic Programming*, 2002.

[Sto02]   M.I.A. Stoelinga. Fun with FireWire: Experiments with verifying the
            IEEE 1394 root contention protocol. In J.M.T. Romijn S. Maharaj,
            C. Shankland, editor, *Formal Aspects of Computing*, 2002. accepted for
            publication.

[SV99]   M.I.A. Stoelinga and F.W. Vaandrager. Root contention in IEEE 1394.
            pages 53–75, Bamberg, Germany, May 1999.

[TSB00]   H. Toetenel, R.L. Spelberg, and G. Bandini. Parametric verification
            of the IEEE 1394a root contention protocol using LPMC. In *Sev-
            enth International Conference on Real-Time Systems and Applications
            (RTCSA'00)*, Cheju Island, South Korea, December 2000.

Refining Approximations in Software Predicate Abstraction

Thomas Ball[1], Byron Cook[1], Satyaki Das[2], and Sriram K. Rajamani[1]

[1] Microsoft Corporation
[2] Stanford University

Abstract. Predicate abstraction is an automatic technique that can be used to find abstract models of large or infinite-state systems. In tools like SLAM, where predicate abstraction is applied to software model checking, a number of heuristic approximations must be used to improve the performance of computing an abstraction from a set of predicates. For this reason, SLAM can sometimes reach a state in which it is not able to further refine the abstraction.

In this paper we report on an application of Das & Dill's algorithm for predicate abstraction refinement. SLAM now uses this strategy lazily to recover precision in cases where the abstractions generated are too coarse. We describe how we have extended Das & Dill's original algorithm for use in software model checking. Our extension supports procedures, threads, and potential pointer aliasing. We also present results from experiments with SLAM on device driver sources from the Windows operating system.

1 Introduction

Automatic iterative abstraction refinement strategies allow us to apply model checking to large or infinite-state systems. When applying iterative abstraction refinement, we must strike a delicate balance between the accuracy of the abstraction that is produced and the speed at which it is generated. Therefore, in practice, a number of coarse approximations are typically employed. SLAM [1], for example, uses the *Cartesian approximation* [2] and the *maximum cube length approximation* [3]. In addition, SLAM's abstraction module uses a special purpose symbolic theorem prover which is similar to the work of Lahiri, Bryant & Cook [4] but optimized for speed and not precision. For this reason SLAM can run into the following situation:

- The abstract program has an error trace t.
- The trace t is found to be infeasible in the concrete program, and a set of predicates S are generated to rule out t in the abstraction.
- Even after abstracting the program with respect to S, since the abstraction is imprecise, t is still feasible in the abstraction.

As a result, iterative refinement is unable to make further progress. This situation, which we call an NDF-state (for "No Difference Found" in the error traces

K. Jensen and A. Podelski (Eds.): TACAS 2004, LNCS 2988, pp. 388–403, 2004.

seen in two successive iterations of iterative refinement), is not merely a theoretical concern. Users of predicate abstraction based tools do encounter it in practice.

```
1)              void main()
2)              {
3)                  int x = *;
4)                  int y = *;
5)                  int z = *;
6)                  if (x<y) {
7)                      if (y<z) {
8)                          if (!(x<z)) {
9)                              error();
10)                         }
11)                     }
12)                 }
13)             }
```

Fig. 1. Example program

As an example, consider the small C program in Fig. 1, where * models nondeterministic value introduction. This program calls the procedure error() if x is not less than z after first checking that x is less than y and that y is less than z. By the transitivity of <, we know that error() will never be called. Without using the technique described in this paper, SLAM's standard predicate abstraction algorithm can not prove that the call to error() is unreachable. In this case, the incompleteness is due to SLAM's use of the Cartesian approximation, in which the update of each predicate is modeled independently.

To see why the property cannot be proved, consider the abstraction in Fig. 2. This is what SLAM would produce when given the following predicates: $\{b1 \triangleq x < y, b2 \triangleq y < z, b3 \triangleq x < z\}$.

Notice how the abstraction models the update of the Boolean variables independently. For example, when modeling the effect of the instruction at line 5, SLAM determines that both b2 and b3 could be affected. It therefore assigns nondeterministically chosen values to the Boolean variables. In this example the approximation causes the abstraction to lose the transitivity correlation between b1, b2 and b3. For this reason we cannot rule out the trace to the call to error() in the abstraction. A more precise modeling of the assignment would not lose this information. The more accurate translation might be as follows:

```
b2 = *;
if (b1 && b2) { b3 = 1; } else { b3 = *; }
```

Frequently, the style of approximation used in Fig. 2 is good enough to prove properties correct. In fact: it is often better — as argued by Ball, Podelski & Rajamani [2] — because the more precise abstraction comes with an unnecessary

```
1)          void main()
2)          {
)               bool b1, b2, b3;
3)              b1,b3 = *,*;
4)              b1,b2 = *,*;
5)              b2,b3 = *,*;
6)              if (b1) {
7)                  if (b2) {
8)                      if (!b3) {
9)                          error();
10)                     }
11)                 }
12)             }
13)         }
```

Fig. 2. Abstraction of the program in Fig. 1 with respect to the predicates $\{b1 \triangleq x < y, b2 \triangleq y < z, b3 \triangleq x < z\}$. Note that $b1, b2$ = e,g; represents parallel assignment.

performance cost in cases where it is not needed. But, as we see in this case, the approximation can be too coarse at times.

The tension is that, if we model all possible correlations, the performance of computing the abstraction becomes intractable. However, for every correlation that we drop, there will inevitably be an example that requires it. What we need is a technique that refines these correlations only in the unusual cases in which they are important.

In this paper we describe such a technique. It is based on Das & Dill's algorithm for abstraction-refinement [5]. In the example described above, the technique would examine the trace to the call to error() and then, as a result of its analysis, refine the abstraction of the assignment to z as:

```
b2,b3 = *,* constrain (!(b1 && b2' && !b3'));
```

where the **constrain** keyword in the abstraction will cause SLAM's symbolic reachability module to ignore transitions that do not maintain the invariant. Notice that we're using b3' to represent the value of b3 after the transition. With this refinement on the transition relation of the abstraction, a symbolic reachability engine can then be used to prove that the abstraction does not call error().

This paper makes two novel contributions:

- We provide details on our extension to Das & Dill's original technique that allows for its application in software model checking. The extension that we describe supports procedures, threads and potential pointer aliasing.
- We demonstrate the technique's effectiveness on real-world industrial benchmarks. We report on the results of experiments run on the source code of a number of device drivers written for the Windows operating system. We demonstrate that the technique's impact on SLAM's accuracy is large, while its tax on performance is modest.

The paper is organized as follows: Section 2 describes SLAM's implementation of predicate abstraction with iterative refinement for software. In Section 3 we introduce CONSTRAIN, which is our extension to Das & Dill's algorithm. Section 4 describes the results of our experiments with CONSTRAIN and the checking of Windows operating system device drivers. We then relate our work to the literature in Section 5, discuss ideas for future work in Section 6, and make several concluding observations in Section 7.

2   Predicate Abstraction and Software Model Checking

Predicate abstraction is a technique proposed by Graf & Saïdi [6] and Colón & Uribe [7]. The idea is to find a set of predicates that must be maintained when proving a property of a transition system. The predicates are then used to compute an abstraction of the original transition system that is more amenable to algorithmic verification techniques such as model checking. Counter-example guided refinement is a technique that can be used to automate the search for these predicates.

SLAM is an implementation of counter-example driven refinement for the C language, using predicate abstraction. SLAM combines three modules to automatically compute an abstraction of a C program based on counter-examples encountered during the abstraction process. The modules are called C2BP [2,3], BEBOP [8,9] and NEWTON [10]

C2BP is used within SLAM to abstract C programs. C2BP takes as input a program P and a set of predicates $\{e_1, \cdots, e_n\}$, which are expressions with Boolean type that may contain relational and arithmetical sub-expressions, and produces an abstraction. The abstraction is represented as a *Boolean program*— a form much like a C program in which all variables have type **bool**. C2BP operates by abstracting each statement s in P into a corresponding statement s_b in the abstraction. The statement s_b conservatively maintains the value of each predicate e_i using a representative Boolean variable.

SLAM performs symbolic model checking on the Boolean program produced by C2BP with BEBOP. If BEBOP can prove that the Boolean program does not call **error()** then the C program also can not call **error()**. We know this is true because the Boolean program is an abstraction of the C program. If BEBOP finds a failing trace in the abstraction that corresponds to a real error in the original C program then SLAM terminates after providing information to the user about the trace. Otherwise, the spurious counter-example found by BEBOP is used to compute additional predicates. The tasks of determining if found traces are real and the generation of new predicates is performed by the module NEWTON.

In the case that the counter-example is spurious and additional predicates are found, then C2BP is called again. This loop is repeated until the program is proved correct, a real trace to **error()** is found, or a state is reached in which a spurious trace cannot be ruled out via additional predicates. As mentioned in Section 1, this final case is an NDF-state.

3 Extending Das and Dill's Abstraction Refinement for Software Model Checking

Das & Dill's algorithm [5] refines an abstract transition relation by looking for spurious transitions in traces and ruling them out in the abstraction using only the predicates already available. Our adaptation of Das & Dill's algorithm to software model checking is called CONSTRAIN. CONSTRAIN takes, as arguments, the original C program and a trace through the abstraction that includes the valuation of the predicates at each step. CONSTRAIN then returns a set of constraints to be added to the abstraction. In pseudo ML-syntax, CONSTRAIN has the following type:

$$\text{CONSTRAIN} : (\text{pgm} \times \text{abstr} \times \text{trace}) \rightarrow \text{constraint list}$$

CONSTRAIN analyzes each abstract transition in the trace using a function called SPURIOUS, which has the following ML-like type:

$$\text{SPURIOUS} : (\text{inst} \times \text{absState} \times \text{absState} \times (\text{absState option})) \rightarrow \text{query}$$

In the invocation $\text{SPURIOUS}(i, a_0, a_1, \text{Some}(a_c))$, the first parameter ($i$) is the transition's instruction in the C program. The second and third parameters (a_0 and a_1) are the transition's pre-state and post-state. The fourth parameter a_c is optional, and is used only for processing procedure return instructions. For a return instruction from procedure R, a_c is the state that the abstraction was in just before calling the procedure R. For other instructions, the fourth parameter is passed the value None. CONSTRAIN maintains a stack on which the abstract state is pushed when a trace crosses into a procedure call, and is popped when a trace crosses a procedure return transition, so as to supply the fourth parameter for SPURIOUS for processing return instructions.

The type query is a logic expression that CONSTRAIN can then pass to an automatic theorem prover such as Simplify [11], Verifun [12] or CVC [13]. If the query is provably valid then the abstract transition at instruction i is spurious and can be constrained.

3.1 Discovering Spurious Transitions

SLAM represents C programs in an intermediate nondeterministic control-flow-graph representation where all instructions are either assignment statements, assume statements, procedure calls or procedure returns. We define SPURIOUS for each of these instruction types. Let $\mathcal{E}$ be the concretization function from abstract states to sets of concrete states, and let $\text{Pre}(i, \Theta)$ be the pre-image of states Θ with respect to instruction i. More precisely,

$$\text{Pre}(i, \Theta) \triangleq \{c \mid \exists c' \in \Theta \text{ such that } c \text{ can transition to } c' \text{ via instruction } i\}$$

For deterministic instructions, Pre can be computed using WP, the weakest precondition [14]. Within WP we use Morris's general axiom of assignment [15] to conservatively model possible pointer aliasing relationships.

Assignment and Assume statements. If i is an assignment statement or an assume statement, then SPURIOUS is defined as:

$$\text{SPURIOUS}(i, a_0, a_1, \text{None}) \triangleq (\mathcal{E}(a_0) \implies \neg\text{Pre}(i, \mathcal{E}(a_1)))$$

If $\text{SPURIOUS}(i, a_0, a_1, \text{None})$ is a valid query then a constraint $\neg(a_0 \wedge a_1')$ can be added to the abstraction to rule out the spurious abstract transition. Here a_1' denotes the state a_1 expressed in terms of primed or next-state variables.

Consider the example from Figs. 1 and 2 from Section 1. Suppose that we call SPURIOUS with the abstract transition

$$\text{b1} \wedge \text{b2} \wedge \text{b3} \quad \overset{5}{\cdots\cdots\!\!>} \quad \text{b1} \wedge \text{b2} \wedge \neg\text{b3}$$

That is, we are asking SPURIOUS the question: "Should the abstraction's state be allowed to change from ($\text{b1} \wedge \text{b2} \wedge \text{b3}$) to ($\text{b1} \wedge \text{b2} \wedge \neg\text{b3}$) by executing the statement at line 5?"

More precisely, we are interested in the value of:

$$\text{SPURIOUS}(5, \;\text{b1} \wedge \text{b2} \wedge \text{b3}, \;\text{b1} \wedge \text{b2} \wedge \neg\text{b3}, \;\text{None})$$

Note that $\mathcal{E}(\text{b1}) \triangleq \text{x} < \text{y}$, $\mathcal{E}(\text{b2}) \triangleq \text{y} < \text{z}$, and $\mathcal{E}(\text{b3}) \triangleq \text{x} < \text{z}$. Let us use α to denote the nondeterministically chosen value that was introduced by *. After unfolding Pre and $\mathcal{E}$, $\text{SPURIOUS}(5, \;\text{b1} \wedge \text{b2} \wedge \text{b3}, \;\text{b1} \wedge \text{b2} \wedge \neg\text{b3}, \;\text{None})$ equals

$$((\text{x} < \text{y}) \wedge (\text{y} < \text{z}) \wedge (\text{x} < \text{z})) \Rightarrow (\neg((\text{x} < \text{y}) \wedge (\text{y} < \alpha) \wedge \neg(\text{x} < \alpha)))$$

Since this query can be proved valid by a theorem prover, CONSTRAIN then produces the following constraint which rules out this transition:

```
constrain (!(b1 && b2 && b3 && b1' && b2' & !b3'));
```

Notice that this constraint is not quite the same as the constraint from Section 1. Later, we will describe an optimization that produces that constraint.

Procedure calls and returns. Let instruction i be a call to procedure R from some procedure Q of the C program:

$$x = R(e_1, e_2, \ldots, e_N)$$

For convenience, we will make the procedure call and the assignment of the return value explicit in the intermediate representation of the C program with the introduction of a fresh variable x_{ret}:

$$x_{ret} = R(e_1, e_2, \ldots, e_N);$$
$$x = x_{ret};$$

The abstraction of this call is divided into three parts: (1) the computation of actual parameters, (2) the corresponding call in the Boolean program, and (3) computation of the side effects of the call. The computation of the actual parameters in the Boolean program takes the form: $p_1, p_2, \ldots, p_j = c_1, c_2, \ldots, c_j$, as defined by Ball *et al.* [3], where j is the number of formal parameters for function R in the Boolean program (note that j could be different from N, the number of formal parameters for R in the C program), and $\{p_1, p_2, \ldots p_j\}$ are temporary variables introduced in the Boolean program. The actual call to R in the Boolean program takes the form:

$$ret_1, ret_2, \ldots, ret_k = R(p_1, p_2, \ldots, p_j)$$

where k is the number of predicates in R that are return predicates, and the variables $\{ret_1, ret_2, \ldots, ret_k\}$ are temporaries used to hold values of the return predicates in Q. Immediately following the call, all local predicates that could be modified by the call are updated.

Let a_0 be the abstract state immediately before execution of i, and let a_1 be the abstract state just after the call is made. Let the formal parameters of f be $f_1, f_2, \ldots f_n$. Let i^p denote the special parallel assignment instruction $f_1, f_2, \ldots f_n = e_1, e_2, \ldots e_n$. SPURIOUS is defined as:

$$\text{SPURIOUS}(i, a_0, a_1, \text{None}) \triangleq \mathcal{E}(a_0) \implies \neg\text{Pre}(i^p, \mathcal{E}(a_1))$$

Assume that CONSTRAIN uses a function δ to map formal parameter predicates of R to the corresponding parameter temporaries in $\{p_1, p_2, \ldots p_j\}$, If SPURIOUS$(i, a_0, a_1, \text{None})$ is valid, then CONSTRAIN will add $\neg(a_0 \wedge \delta(a_1'))$, to the computation of actual parameters for the call in the abstraction.

We will now define SPURIOUS for procedure return instructions. Let i be the statement **return r** in R. Recall that the call to R in Q assigns the return value to variable x. We first define two auxiliary functions: ρ over the variables in scope at Q, and γ over variables in scope at R. The function ρ is defined as follows:

$$\rho(v) = \begin{cases} v & \text{if } v \text{ is a local variable or formal parameter of } Q \\ v_o & \text{if } v \text{ is a global variable, where } v_o \text{ is a fresh variable} \end{cases}$$

Conceptually, we can think of v_o as caching the value of global v in Q just before the call to R. The function γ is defined as follows:

$$\gamma(v) = \begin{cases} v & \text{if } v \text{ is global} \\ x_{ret} & \text{if } v \text{ is } r \\ \rho(e_i) & \text{if } v \text{ is a symbolic value of the parameter } f_i \text{ to } R \end{cases}$$

Let i^r denote the assignment statement in the intermediate form $x = x_{ret}$. Let a_0 be an abstract state just before execution of the return statement, and let a_1 be an abstract state just after execution of the return statement, and let a_c be the state just before execution of the call to R. In this case we define SPURIOUS as:

$$\text{SPURIOUS}(i, a_0, a_1, \text{Some}(a_c)) \triangleq (\gamma(\mathcal{E}(a_0)) \wedge \rho(\mathcal{E}(a_c))) \implies \neg\text{Pre}(i^r, \mathcal{E}(a_1))$$

If SPURIOUS$(i, a_0, a_1, \text{Some}(a_c))$ is valid, then CONSTRAIN will add $\neg(a_0 \wedge \omega(a_c) \wedge a_1')$ to the return transition in the abstraction, where ω maps each predicate in R to the corresponding return temporary from $\{ret_1, ret_2, \ldots, ret_k\}$, is added for the instruction that computes the side-effects of the call.

```
1)   int foo(int a)              11)     void main()
2)   {                           12)     {
3)       int b = *;              13)         int x = *;
4)       if (a<b) {              14)         int y = *;
5)           return b;           15)         int z = *;
6)       } else {                16)         if (x<y) {
7)           exit();             17)             z = foo(y);
8)       }                       18)             if (!(x<z)) {
9)   }                           19)                 error();
10)                              20)             }
                                 21)     }
```

Fig. 3. Example program with procedure calls and returns

3.2 Example of Return Processing

As an example of how CONSTRAIN and SPURIOUS handle procedure returns, consider the program in Fig. 3. When modeling the return from foo we must consider three states: (1) The state of the program just before the call to foo, (2) the state of the program just before the return from foo, and (3) the state of the program just after the return from foo.

Imagine that SLAM is tracking the following predicates (where α is used to represent the symbolic initial value of the argument to foo):

$$\text{main} : \{b1 \triangleq x < y, b2 \triangleq y < z, b3 \triangleq x < z\}$$
$$\text{foo} : \{a1 \triangleq \alpha < b\}$$

The following is part of a spurious trace that BEBOP might find while model checking the abstraction:

$$b1 \wedge \neg b2 \wedge \neg b3 \quad \xdashrightarrow{17} \quad \cdots \quad \dashrightarrow \quad a1 \quad \xdashrightarrow{5} \quad b1 \wedge \neg b2 \wedge \neg b3$$

At the procedure call transition at line 17, CONSTRAIN will push the state $b1 \wedge b2 \wedge b3$ onto the stack. Then, when processing the return instruction at line 5, CONSTRAIN will pop the stack and call SPURIOUS with this popped state as the optional parameter:

$$\text{SPURIOUS}(17, \text{ a1, } b1 \wedge \neg b2 \wedge \neg b3, \text{ Some}(b1 \wedge \neg b2 \wedge \neg b3))$$

which we can evaluate by unfolding the definitions of $\mathcal{E}$, γ, ρ and SPURIOUS:

$$(\gamma(\mathcal{E}(a1)) \wedge \rho(\mathcal{E}(b1 \wedge \neg b2 \wedge \neg b3))) \Longrightarrow \neg\text{Pre}(17^r, \mathcal{E}(b1 \wedge \neg b2 \wedge \neg b3))$$

$$\Leftrightarrow_\mathcal{E} \quad \gamma((\alpha < b)) \wedge \rho((x < y) \wedge \neg(y < z) \wedge \neg(x < z)) \Longrightarrow \neg\text{Pre}(17^r, (x < y) \wedge \neg(y < z) \wedge \neg(x < z))$$

$$\Leftrightarrow_\rho \quad \gamma((\alpha < b)) \wedge (x < y) \wedge \neg(y < z) \wedge \neg(x < z) \Longrightarrow \neg\text{Pre}(17^r, (x < y) \wedge \neg(y < z) \wedge \neg(x < z))$$

$$\Leftrightarrow_{\text{Pre\&}\gamma} \quad (y < z_{\text{ret}}) \wedge (x < y) \wedge \neg(y < z) \wedge \neg(x < z) \Longrightarrow \neg((x < y) \wedge \neg(y < z_{\text{ret}}) \wedge \neg(x < z_{\text{ret}}))$$

Since the last expression is provably valid[1] CONSTRAIN will add the constraint

```
constrain ( !(b1 && !b2 && b3 && ret1 && b1' && !b2' & !b3'));
```

(where `ret1` is the return temporary corresponding to `a1`) to the instruction that computes the side effects of the call.

3.3   Optimizations and Additional Extensions

In the example from Section 3.1 we were not able to compute the constraint promised in Section 1. However, by iteratively dropping predicates from the abstract states and re-evaluating SPURIOUS we can find this strengthened constraint. After searching for the necessary predicates we will find that

$$\text{SPURIOUS}(5,\ \texttt{b1},\ \texttt{b2} \wedge \neg \texttt{b3},\ \texttt{None})$$

is valid, which gives us the following stronger constraint `!(b1 && b2' && !b3')`. This is an important optimization because it allows CONSTRAIN to eliminate more spurious transitions than the weaker constraint does. However, the approach that we currently use to compute this strengthening is not optimal. We will discuss this further in Section 6.

As another optimization consider the fact that, although it is not always true, the constraint that we found in Section 1 can be encoded as something that holds for all time. That is, in this case, transitivity is true regardless of the transition at line 5. For this reason, the constraint could be expressed in such a way that the reachability engine ignores all transitions that violate the invariant whenever the invariant is in scope. As an optimization, BEBOP provides exactly this construct through the keyword **enforce**. When performing reachability analysis on this abstraction, BEBOP will then prune states from consideration in which the **enforce** constraint is not true.

CONSTRAIN can potentially find and rule out spurious transitions at multiple points along a given trace. Through experimentation we have found that, when CONSTRAIN is used lazily, the overall performance of SLAM is at its best when CONSTRAIN is allowed to return only up to the first five constraints found during a single pass. We have also found that, when an **enforce** constraint is found, it is best to return immediately.

CONSTRAIN can also find multiple constraints if it is executed multiple times using the same set of predicates, but different traces. That is, if CONSTRAIN and BEBOP are alternated without the addition of new predicates via NEWTON. We have found that, when used lazily, it is most efficient to allow up to four alternations of BEBOP and CONSTRAIN before running NEWTON again in order to find additional predicates. Beyond these four calls, few of the constraints that are found and instrumented into the abstraction seem to contribute to SLAM's overall accuracy or performance.

---

[1] By the transitivity of $<$ over x, y and z_{ret}

CONSTRAIN can easily be extended to support thread-switches in the traces that are passed to it. For this purpose CONSTRAIN maintains a set of call-stacks—one for each thread. The traces contain information about when threads are switched. CONSTRAIN then switches between the stacks during the analysis.

4   Experimental Results

In Section 1 we conjectured that Das & Dill's algorithm [5] could be used to improve SLAM's precision while not significantly degrading performance. In this section we attempt to measure this with experimental findings. We also demonstrate how several of C2BP's approximations effect SLAM's performance and accuracy.

4.1   Improving Accuracy with Das and Dill's Algorithm

To determine the effectiveness of CONSTRAIN, we have executed SLAM on software model checking benchmarks using the following three configurations:

No Constrain: SLAM without support from CONSTRAIN.

Lazy mode: SLAM using CONSTRAIN, in which CONSTRAIN is used simply as an NDF-state recovery method. Each call to CONSTRAIN is allowed to generate up to five constraints, and CONSTRAIN is called up to four times before returning to the standard SLAM loop.

Eager mode: SLAM with CONSTRAIN in which C2BP is configured to be maximally imprecise, leaving CONSTRAIN as the only working abstraction mechanism. In this configuration, because CONSTRAIN is doing all of the reasoning during the abstraction computation, each call to CONSTRAIN is allowed to add up to 200 new constraints, and CONSTRAIN can be executed up to 200 times before new predicates are sought out.

For each of these three configurations, SLAM was then used to check 35 safety properties of 26 Windows device drivers (910 checks in total, 644 of which require SLAM's analysis). The timeout threshold was set to 1200 seconds. The memory threshold was set to 500 megabytes. The sizes of the device drivers used in these experiments ranged from 10,000 to 40,000 lines of C code. The results are in Fig. 4.

The most important aspect of this figure is the first row, which represents the number of cases in which SLAM terminated in an NDF-state. In the **No Constrain** column we can see that in 170 out of the 910 checks (or nearly one in five checks if we ignore the 266 cases where a property did not apply to a driver) SLAM became stuck in an NDF-state. This was the result that SLAM's users experienced before we implemented CONSTRAIN: 170 cases where SLAM was not able to produce a useful result due to incompleteness.

The **Lazy mode** column represents the result of running SLAM with CONSTRAIN as an NDF-state recovery method. In 167 out of 170 NDF-state cases, CONSTRAIN provided accuracy enough that SLAM was able to make further

Result	No Constrain	Lazy mode	Eager mode
Termination in NDF-state	170	3	3
Property passes found	470	554	544
Time/memory threshold exceeded	59	107	122
Property violations found	19	50	45
Property not applicable to driver	266	266	266

Fig. 4. Results from experiments with CONSTRAIN on 26 device drivers and 35 safety properties. Of the 910 checks, only 644 require SLAM's analysis. The time threshold was set to 1200 seconds. The memory threshold was set to 500 megabytes.

progress. The three cases in which SLAM still reached an NDF-state are due to some subtle problems that occur when refining abstractions in the presence of some special heap-based data structures.

The **Eager** column displays the result from running SLAM using a disabled C2BP module: The functional result is largely the same, but the performance is less impressive than the **Lazy mode**. In this configuration, 15 additional checks exceed the 20 minute timeout.

4.2 Impact on Performance

In order to measure CONSTRAIN's effect on SLAM's performance we first recorded the total CONSTRAIN runtime required to compute the results of the **Lazy mode** column of Fig. 4 and compared it the total runtime of SLAM. We found that ten percent of SLAM's overall runtime was spent in the CONSTRAIN module.

Then, in order to determine the impact on SLAM's performance in just the cases where CONSTRAIN is actually used, we collected a number of averages while running SLAM in the default (lazy) configuration on 126 benchmarks that required at least one call to CONSTRAIN in order to recover from an NDF-state. The statistical averages are displayed in Fig. 5.

Description	Average
SLAM runtime	354.31s
Amount of runtime spent in CONSTRAIN	81.24s
Calls to CONSTRAIN	4.40
CONSTRAIN refinement iterations	1.74
Constraints generated	6.17

Fig. 5. Averages collected when applying SLAM to 126 device-driver based benchmarks in which CONSTRAIN is required to recover from an NDF-state.

We can see that, even when we limit the averages to those cases in which CONSTRAIN is called, its impact on SLAM's overall runtime is not overwhelming.

In these cases, 23 percent of SLAM's overall runtime was spent computing constraints. On average, CONSTRAIN was called about five times per model-checking run. And, on average, the refinement loop using CONSTRAIN and BEBOP was called in less than two iterations of SLAM's main loop. Finally, employing CONSTRAIN resulted in, on average, less than seven constraints to the final Boolean abstraction found.

4.3   Tuning the Approximations

In order to understand how the calls to CONSTRAIN are affected by C2BP's approximations we ran SLAM in various configurations on four drivers with six properties. In one case SLAM's analysis is not required.

Unfortunately, the Cartesian abstraction cannot be turned off in C2BP. However, we can adjust the use of the maximum cube length approximation and our fast but imprecise symbolic theorem prover.

Description	S/3	S/5	S/∞	C/3	C/5	C/∞
Total calls to CONSTRAIN	99	112	408	10	7	5
Total constraints generated	145	160	705	7	5	3
Termination in NDF-state	0	0	0	0	0	0
Property passes found	15	14	13	6	5	4
Time/memory threshold exceeded	7	8	9	17	18	19
Property violations found	1	1	1	0	0	0
Property not applicable to driver	1	1	1	1	1	1

Fig. 6. Totals collected while checking six properties on four drivers with SLAM using 6 different configurations. **S** = use of our symbolic theorem prover; **C** = use of a standard concrete theorem prover; **3** = maximum cube length set to three; **5** = maximum cube length set to five; ∞ = maximum cube length not set. The timeout threshold was set to 1200 seconds. The space threshold was set to 500 megabytes.

Fig. 6 displays the results from running SLAM in the following six configurations: **S/3** is SLAM's default configuration, in which the symbolic theorem prover is used and the cubes are limited to a maximum of three. **S/5** uses the symbolic theorem prover with cubes limited to five. **S/∞** uses the symbolic theorem prover and does not limit the cubes. **C/3** uses a more accurate concrete theorem prover and limits the cubes to three. **C/5** uses the concrete theorem prover and limits the cubes to five. **C/∞** uses the concrete theorem prover and does not limit the cubes.

In Fig. 6 **S/3** provides the best performance and accuracy because it maximizes the property violations and passes found, and minimizes the cases in which SLAM's execution exceeded the time or memory threshold. An interesting side-effect of enlarging the cube sizes when the symbolic theorem prover is used is that the precision actually goes down. The reason is that this prover only implements a subset of first-order logic and larger cube sizes increase the chances of unsupported symbols.

Fig. 6 demonstrates that, rather than shutting off C2BP's approximations, it is best to leave them on for the common cases. In the uncommon cases that require more precision, CONSTRAIN can patch up the result.

5   Related Work

The use of counter-examples to automatically guide refinement in model checking has been described in many papers, including those by Alur *et al.* [16], Balarin & Sangiovanni-Vincentelli [17] and Clarke *et al.* [18]. Predicate abstraction combined with counter-example driven refinement has been since widely adopted for the verification of software-like systems. Examples of tools that use this strategy include InVeSt [19], SLAM [10], BOOP [20], CALVIN [21] Murφ– [22], BLAST [21] and MAGIC [23]. However, in all of these tools, refinement has traditionally consisted of adding additional predicates.

Rather than simply adding more predicates, more recent research work has focused on improving the abstractions produced in predicate abstraction. The work in this area can be categorized as follows:

Removing corner-case problems: As an example consider the Cartesian abstraction. This approximation essentially causes invariants involving disjunctions of predicates to be lost. CONSTRAIN deals with this as it does with all other approximations: it explicitly restricts transitions one-by-one that violate the disjunctions. Another way of avoiding this is to add predicates which explicitly contain these disjunctions. In the context of BLAST, recent work by Henzinger, Jhala & McMillan [24] does precisely this.

Better abstraction algorithms: For example, Lahiri, Bryant & Cook [4] describe a technique that uses a symbolic theorem prover to avoid the necessity of the *maximum cube length approximation*. In principle, by using this theorem prover, C2BP could improve the quality of the abstractions generated. Because our symbolic prover supports such a limited subset of logic we have found (in Fig. 6) that the maximum cube length approximation is *still* a good thing to do.

Making better use of the predicates: Our work falls into this category. Another strategy in this category is the work on removing redundant predicates [25,23]. For example, during the predicate discovery phase, Chaki *et al.* [23] analyze many counter-example traces instead of one. They find predicates that can eliminate each of the spurious traces. Then they find a minimal set of these predicates so that each of the spurious traces can be removed and add those predicates.

6   Future Work

In Section 3.3 we alluded to the fact that CONSTRAIN attempts to strengthen the constraints that it finds. To compute this strengthening CONSTRAIN speculatively throws out predicates one-by-one from the calls to SPURIOUS until the minimal set that is required is found. This results in an algorithm that makes a linear number of calls to the theorem prover for each constraint generated. However, many automatic theorem provers compute something that is close to the strengthening that CONSTRAIN is searching for. Examples include CVC [13] and Verifun [12]. In the future we should investigate using this information provided by the theorem prover to strengthen constraints.

NDF-states are currently the only trigger that cause SLAM to invoke CONSTRAIN. It is possible that there are additional good triggers. For example: if a large majority of predicates are being added to rule out transitions through a small segment of code, CONSTRAIN might be better able to refine the abstraction than NEWTON and C2BP. Adding additional triggers is something that we hope to investigate further.

The `enforce` constraints mentioned in Section 3.3 are extremely strong and can, in theory, require the reachability engine to perform lots of unnecessary work. In the future we should explore other options. For example, we could simply add a standard constraint at the beginning of the function body where today we place an `enforce` constraint. This would mean that the constraint would not be maintained as an invariant by the reachability module, but would in many cases be maintained by the abstraction instead. Another alternative would be to add the time-invariant as a constraint at each transition along the trace passed to CONSTRAIN.

CONSTRAIN currently only supports forward passes through traces. However, in principle, CONSTRAIN could be run backwards along a trace. It could then quickly return only a small subset of constraints generated from the last spurious transitions. We have not yet investigated this approach. One complication to this method is that a backwards analysis of a trace by CONSTRAIN will have to handle procedure calls and returns in a special way. The problem is that, at the point where the return is being analyzed, we must know the state of the abstraction at which the procedure was called. In the forward-based analysis this is natural to track. But, in order to support a backwards-based analysis, we would need to add a forward pre-pass of the trace in which the states of the program just before procedure calls are recorded.

7   Conclusion

Predicate-abstraction tools do not scale without the use of some approximations. However, with increased imprecision, predicate-abstraction based refinement loops are not always able to make progress. In this paper we have described an application of and extension to Das & Dill's method, called CONSTRAIN, which selectively recovers precision in cases where it is needed. CONSTRAIN handles the characteristics of software, including procedures, threads, and pointer aliasing. Our experimental results demonstrate that with CONSTRAIN, SLAM benefits from C2BP's fast approximations in the cases where they work, and recovers precision in the cases where the precision is needed to make progress. In practice, this strategy has tremendously improved the usability of SLAM, making it a predictable and usable tool for the validation of device driver correctness.

Acknowledgments. The authors would like to thank David Dill, Ranjit Jhala, Shuvendu Lahiri, Vladimir Levin, Ken McMillan, and Shaz Qadeer for their ideas and comments related to this work

References

1. Ball, T., Rajamani, S.K.: Automatically validating temporal safety properties of interfaces. In: SPIN 00: SPIN Workshop. LNCS 1885. Springer-Verlag (2000) 113–130
2. Ball, T., Podelski, A., Rajamani, S.K.: Boolean and Cartesian abstractions for model checking C programs. In: TACAS 01: Tools and Algorithms for Construction and Analysis of Systems. LNCS 2031, Springer-Verlag (2001) 268–283
3. Ball, T., Majumdar, R., Millstein, T., Rajamani, S.K.: Automatic predicate abstraction of C programs. In: PLDI 01: Programming Language Design and Implementation, ACM (2001) 203–213
4. Lahiri, S.K., Bryant, R.E., Cook, B.: A symbolic approach to predicate abstraction. In: CAV 03: International Conference on Computer-Aided Verification. (2003) 141–153
5. Das, S., Dill, D.L.: Successive approximation of abstract transition relations. In: Proceedings of the Sixteenth Annual IEEE Symposium on Logic in Computer Science. (2001) June 2001, Boston, USA.
6. Graf, S., Saïdi, H.: Construction of abstract state graphs with PVS. In Grumberg, O., ed.: CAV 97: Conference on Computer Aided Verification. Volume 1254 of Lecture notes in Computer Science., Springer-Verlag (1997) 72–83 June 1997, Haifa, Israel.
7. Colón, M.A., Uribe, T.E.: Generating finite-state abstractions of reactive systems using decision procedures. In: CAV 98: Conference on Computer-Aided Verification. Volume 1427 of Lecture Notes in Computer Science., Springer-Verlag (1998) 293–304
8. Ball, T., Rajamani, S.K.: Bebop: A symbolic model checker for Boolean programs. In: SPIN 00: SPIN Workshop. LNCS 1885. Springer-Verlag (2000) 113–130
9. Ball, T., Rajamani, S.K.: Bebop: A path-sensitive interprocedural dataflow engine. In: PASTE 01: Workshop on Program Analysis for Software Tools and Engineering, ACM (2001) 97–103
10. Ball, T., Rajamani, S.K.: Generating abstract explanations of spurious counterexamples in C programs. Technical Report MSR-TR-2002-09, Microsoft Research (2002)
11. Detlefs, D., Nelson, G., , Saxe, J.B.: Simplify: A theorem prover for program checking. Technical Report HPL-2003-148, HP Labs (2003)
12. Flanagan, C., Joshi, R., Ou, X., Saxe, J.B.: Theorem proving using lazy proof explication. In: CAV 03: International Conference on Computer-Aided Verification. (2003) 355–367

13. Stump, A., Barrett, C., Dill, D.: CVC: a cooperating validity checker. In: CAV 02: International Conference on Computer-Aided Verification. (2002) 87–105
14. Dijkstra, E.: A Discipline of Programming. Prentice-Hall (1976)
15. Morris, J.M.: A general axiom of assignment. In: Theoretical Foundations of Programming Methodology. Lecture Notes of an International Summer School. D. Reidel Publishing Company (1982) 25–34
16. Alur, R., Itai, A., Kurshan, R., Yannakakis, M.: Timing verification by successive approximation. Information and Computation 118(1) (1995) 142–157
17. Balarin, F., Sangiovanni-Vincentelli, A.L.: An iterative approach to language containment. In: CAV 93: International Conference on Computer-Aided Verification. (1993) 29–40
18. Clarke, E.M., Grumberg, O., Jha, S., Lu, Y., Veith, H.: Counterexample-guided abstraction refinement. In: CAV 00: International Conference on Computer-Aided Verification. (2000) 154–169
19. Lakhnech, Y., Bensalem, S., Berezin, S., Owre, S.: Incremental verification by abstraction. In: TACAS 01: Tools and Algorithms for the Construction and Analysis of Systems. (2001)
20. Weissenbacher, G.: An abstraction/refinement scheme for model checking C programs. Master's thesis, Graz University of Technology, Graz, Austria (2003)
21. Henzinger, T.A., Jhala, R., Majumdar, R., Qadeer, S.: Thread modular abstraction refinement. In: CAV 03: International Conference on Computer-Aided Verification, Springer Verlag (2003) 262–274
22. Das, S., Dill, D.L.: Counter-example based predicate discovery in predicate abstraction. In: FMCAD 02: Formal Methods in Computer-Aided Design, Springer-Verlag (2002)
23. Chaki, S., Clarke, E., Groce, A., Strichman, O.: Predicate abstraction with minimum predicates. In: CHARME 03: Advanced Research Working Conference on Correct Hardware Design and Verification Methods. (2003)
24. Thomas A. Henzinger, Ranjit Jhala, R.M., McMillan, K.L.: Abstractions from proofs. In: POPL 04: Symposium on Principles of Programming Languages, ACM Press (2004)
25. Clarke, E., Grumberg, O., Talupur, M., Wang, D.: Making predicate abstraction efficient: How to eliminate redundant predicates. In: CAV 03: International Conference on Computer-Aided Verification. (2003) 355–367

Checking Strong Specifications Using an Extensible Software Model Checking Framework*

Robby, Edwin Rodríguez, Matthew B. Dwyer, and John Hatcliff

Department of Computing and Information Sciences Kansas State University **

Abstract. The use of assertions to express correctness properties of programs is growing in practice. Assertions provide a form of checkable redundancy that can be very effective in finding defects in programs and in guiding developers to the cause of a defect. A wide variety of assertion languages and associated validation techniques have been developed, but run-time monitoring is commonly thought to be the only practical solution.

In this paper, we describe how specifications written in the Java Modeling Language (JML), a general purpose behavioral specification language for Java, can be validated using a customized model checking framework. Our experience illustrates the need for customized state-space representations and reduction strategies in model checking frameworks in order to effectively check the kind of strong behavioral specifications that can be written in JML. We discuss the advantages of model checking relative to other specification validation techniques and present data that suggest that the cost of model checking strong program specifications is practical for several real programs.

1 Introduction

The idea of interspersing specifications of the intended behavior of a program directly in the source code is nearly as old as programming itself [6]. Those foundational ideas inspired the development of more elaborate design practices and methodologies, for example, design-by-contract [15]. The use of assertional specifications has long been regarded as a means for improving software quality, but only recently have studies demonstrated support for this conjecture [21]. The increasing numbers of modern languages (e.g., Java, C#, PHP) and implementation frameworks (e.g., .NET, MFC) that include simple assertion mechanisms suggests that they are poised to finally having the practical impact that was predicted decades ago.

To fulfill this promise, there is a need for program assertion checking mechanisms that are cost-effective, automatic, and thorough in considering both specification and program behavior. Run-time monitoring of assertions during program execution is the only mechanism that is widely used in practice today. It is both cost-effective and automatic, but only reasons about the individual program behaviors that are executed. This

---

* This work was supported in part by the U.S. Army Research Office (DAAD190110564), by DARPA/IXO's PCES program (AFRL Contract F33615-00-C-3044), by NSF (CCR-0306607) by Lockheed Martin, and by Rockwell-Collins.
** 234 Nichols Hall, Manhattan, KS 66506, USA.
   {robby,edwin,dwyer,hatcliff}@cis.ksu.edu

K. Jensen and A. Podelski (Eds.): TACAS 2004, LNCS 2988, pp. 404–420, 2004.
© Springer-Verlag Berlin Heidelberg 2004

lack of coverage of program behavior is a significant weakness of run-time methods, especially for concurrent programs where subtle errors may depend on the order in which threads execute. To address the program behavior coverage problem, a variety of static analysis approaches have been proposed to thoroughly check a program's possible behaviors with respect to certain lightweight specifications, such as, pointer null-ness and array bounds [5] and propositional temporal properties [25]. These methods gain program coverage by sacrificing the expressiveness of their specification language.

Building on a long-line of work on formal methods for manual reasoning about complete behavioral specifications of programs, several recent languages have emerged that balance the desire for completeness and the pragmatics of checkability. The Java Modeling Language (JML) is one such language [13]. With JML one can specify properties of varying strength from lightweight assertions about pointer null-ness to complete functional correctness of program components; the latter we refer to as a *strong* property. JML is a *behavioral interface specification language* that allows developers to specify both the syntactic and behavioral interface of a portion of Java code. It supports the "design by contract" paradigm by including notation for pre/post-conditions and invariants. JML uses Java's expression syntax and adds, for example, constructs for quantification over object instances and for expressing detailed properties of heap allocated data. This allows developers to create very natural and compact statements of strong specifications of the behavior of Java programs.

In this paper, we describe how we have adapted a flexible model checking framework called Bogor [18] to check JML specifications of sequential and concurrent Java programs. Model checking adds a new and complementary approach to the existing run-time and theorem-proving technologies for reasoning about JML. While tools based on those technologies have proven effective in supporting certain kinds of Java validation and verification activities, there is currently no *automatic* technique for *thoroughly* checking a wide-range of *strong* JML specifications especially in the presence of *concurrency*. Our checking tool is automatic and exhaustive in its reasoning about general JML properties up to user-defined bounds on the space consumed by a program run.

Previous work on using model checking to verify stronger specification has achieved only limited success for several reasons. First, existing model checkers, such as Spin [9], do not provide direct support for modeling dynamically allocated objects and heap structures making it difficult to even represent the program's behavior; Bogor maintains an explicit, yet compact, representation of the dynamic program heap [20]. Second, even if one could encode the behavior in the input language of such a model checker, the underlying checking algorithms would not exploit the semantic properties of the original language to optimize the state space search; Bogor incorporates novel partial order reductions that exploit the semantics of a program's heap and locking structure to achieve efficiency [3]. Finally, existing model checking frameworks support temporal properties but do not provide direct support for expressing rich data or heap-related functional properties; Bogor supports extension via user-defined atomic expressions that can be evaluated over the full extent of a program state including the heap [18].

The contributions of this paper are as follows:

- we demonstrate that with a sufficiently feature-rich model checking framework one can check strong behavioral specifications;

Table 1. JML Reasoning Tools and Technologies

Tool (technology)	Automation Usability	JML Coverage	Behavior Coverage	Scalability
LOOP[24] (semi-automated theorem proving)	fair (straight line code), poor (otherwise)	very high	complete (for sequential)	poor
ESC[5] (automated decision procedures)	good (annotations usually needed)	low	high (for sequential), moderate (otherwise)	excellent (modular treatment of methods)
JMLC[2] (run-time monitoring)	excellent	moderate	low (determined by test harness)	excellent
Bogor[18] (model checking)	excellent	very high	moderate (determined by test harness)	good (for unit-level reasoning)

- we describe how Bogor's extension facilities can be applied to implement checking of JML specifications, including specifications that have proven difficult to check by other means such as run-time checking or theorem-proving; and
- we demonstrate that the overhead of checking JML specifications can, in most cases, be eliminated through the use of sophisticated state-space reductions.

In the next section, we survey existing technologies and tools for reasoning about JML specifications; we also discuss non-JML based approaches. Section 3 introduces a JML annotated Java example that will be used to illustrate the analysis techniques we have developed. Section 4 details our strategy for efficiently reasoning about JML specifications on-the-fly during state-space exploration of a concurrent Java program. In Section 5, we detail the analysis of a collection of JML annotated Java programs and report on the cost and effectiveness of checking them with Bogor and then conclude.

2   Background

JML is emerging as a popular assertion definition language for Java. It is a rich speci-fication language that can support a range of uses from simple assertions about method parameters and local data to a complete design-by-contract methodology with abstract behavioral interface specifications. Burdy et. al. [1] survey the steadily growing body of tool support for reasoning about JML specifications. Broadly speaking, there are three underlying technologies used in these tools: semi-automated theorem proving, automated decision procedures (a restricted form of theorem proving), and run-time monitoring. These technologies have different advantages and disadvantages which we assess along four dimensions:

Automation/Usability. How much effort is needed to use the technology or tool?
JML Coverage. How much of the JML language is supported?
Behavior Coverage. How much of a program's behavior is considered in reasoning?
Scalability. How does reasoning cost grow with system size and complexity?

Table 1 summarizes the strengths and weaknesses of the basic technologies in terms of these dimensions. We cite specific tools that implement JML reasoning with those technologies, but the strengths and weaknesses mentioned are, for the most part, characteristics of the underlying technology. We note that despite their weaknesses each of these tools is *useful* in that they have been used to find errors in real Java programs.

LOOP [24] is the most mature theorem-prover-based JML reasoning system. It translates JML specifications and Java source code into proof obligations for the theorem prover PVS [16]. The semantics of the code and specifications are represented as PVS theories, and users verify specifications against the code by interacting with the PVS command-line interface to discharge the generated proof obligations. LOOP is difficult for novices to use since it requires detailed knowledge of logical representation of Java semantics. While recent advances in LOOP's calculus allow nearly automatic verification of methods with straight-line code performing integer calculations, for general Java applications, LOOP scales poorly due to the complexities of its logical treatment of aliasing. With sufficient expertise, however, LOOP allows very strong correctness properties to be established with the highest possible degree of confidence.

ESC/Java is another theorem-prover-based tool for a subset of JML. ESC/Java allows the user to work at the Java level by encapsulating the translation of verification conditions to an underlying theorem prover. It gains a high degree of automation by treating a small subset of JML and by sacrificing precision in the results of its analysis. ESC/Java targets the efficient, automatic checking of null references and simple integer properties (e.g., array bounds violations), but does not support richer properties, for example, those that require quantification over class instances or any of JML's heap related primitives. ESC/Java is fully automatic and its modular checking approach allows it to scale to large programs (e.g., up to 50K lines of code).

Cheon and Leavens [2] have developed a run-time checker (jmlc) which compiles JML-annotated programs into bytecode that includes run-time assertions to check JML specifications. As with other run-time analysis methods, reasoning using jmlc requires a complete Java program, thus if a single class or method is to be analyzed an appropriate test harness must be constructed. Aside from this, using jmlc is fully automatic for a good portion of the JML language; notably lacking are general support for class instance domains and access to pre-condition state values in post-conditions. jmlc implements run-time checking on top of existing JVMs and consequently it provides no direct support for multi-threaded programs.

2.1   Other Related Work

There have been an enormous number of efforts to define languages for specifying and reasoning about program behavior. We are interested in providing automated reasoning support for strong properties of modern concurrent object-oriented languages, thus most of the existing work on simple assertion languages and manual formal methods is lacking. Recent work on OCL (Object Constraint Language) and Alloy are aimed at supporting at least some of our goals.

Space constraints do not permit a detailed discussion of the different checking mechanisms that have been proposed for OCL. One line of work (cf. [10]) is similar to jmlc in that it generates run-time assertions for checking Java. Another direction is to compare

OCL specifications with other UML models (cf. [17]) rather than program source code. However, a number of the issues regarding reasoning about heap-allocated program data are not considered in that work.

The Alloy Annotation Language (AAL) [11] is a language for annotating Java code with a syntax that is similar to JML. AAL supports analysis, via bounded satisfiability checking, of loop-free code sequences that may have method invocations. AAL targets the verification of small methods that maintain invariants on complex heap structures (e.g., red-black trees). The Java heap is modeled in Alloy using relations, and checking is carried out automatically by generating all possible heap-structures that can be constructed from a user-bounded set of objects. AAL does not support reasoning about concurrent programs.

2.2 JML Model Checking

The work described in this paper complements existing JML tools by model checking. As summarized in Table 1, our tool targets developers who are interested in automated methods for finding bugs by checking rich JML specifications against program modules written in full-featured multi-threaded Java where the modules being checked are of the size typically considered in unit testing.

3 An Example

Figure 1 presents a concurrent linked-list-based queue from [12] with some JML specification that we have added to describe its behavior. Instances of the LinkedNode class implement the nodes of the linked list representing the queue. The LinkedQueue class provides put and get (not shown) methods that implement a fine-grain locking protocol, through the use of protected methods insert and extract, to maximize concurrent access to the queue. This design leads to functional code that is nested inside synchronized statements and conditionals in those protected methods. In order to specify the pre/post-condition behavior of that functional code we have re-factored it into additional protected methods, for example insert2.

When a new queue is created, an object that is used to guarantee mutual exclusion of put operations is created and assigned to the putLock field, and a new node is created and assigned to the head and tail instance fields (this node forms the head of every list). Whenever a thread attempts to get an object from an empty queue, the thread is blocked (the code is not shown). If the queue is not empty, then only the head is locked, and its stored value is returned. The dequeueing is done in the extract method. Whenever an object is enqueued, the tail is locked, a new node is created to store the object and one of the threads waiting to dequeue is notified.

JML specifications are written in Java comments with special tags such as //@. Pre-conditions and post-conditions for non-exceptional return are written using the JML keywords [requires] and [ensures] respectively. The [non_null] annotation on a reference-type field of an object o is an invariant that the field never has a null value. General invariants on instance data are stated using [instance invariant] clauses. The instance invariants for a class C (as well as invariant short-hands such as [non_null])

```
public class LinkedQueue {                          synchronized Object extract() {
  final /*@ non_null @*/ Object putLock;              synchronized (head) return extract2();
  /*@ non_null @*/ LinkedNode head;                 }
  /*@ non_null @*/ LinkedNode last;                 /*@ behavior
  int waitingForTake = 0; ...                        @   assignable head, head.next.value;
  //@ invariant waitingForTake >= 0;                 @   ensures \result == null
  //@ invariant \reach(head).has(last);              @      || (\exists LinkedNode n;
  /*@ behavior                                        @         \old(\reach(head)).has(n);
   @   assignable head, last, putLock,               @         n.value == \result
   @              waitingForTake;                     @         && !(\reach(head).has(n))); @*/
   @   ensures \fresh(head, putLock) &&            Object extract2() {
   @           head.next == null; @*/                 Object x = null;
  public LinkedQueue() {                              LinkedNode first = head.next;
    putLock = new Object();                           if (first != null) {
    last = head = new LinkedNode(null);                 x = first.value;
  }                                                     first.value = null;
  /*@ behavior                                          head = first;
   @   ensures \result <==>                           }
   @           head.next == null; @*/                  return x;
  public boolean isEmpty() {                         }
    synchronized (head)                              /*@ behavior
      return head.next == null;                       @   requires x != null;
  }                                                    @   ensures last.value == x
  /*@ behavior                                         @        && \fresh(last); @*/
   @     requires n != null;                        void insert(Object x) {
   @     assignable last, last.next; @*/              synchronized (putLock) {
  void insert2(LinkedNode n) {                          LinkedNode p = new LinkedNode(x);
    last.next = n;                                      synchronized (last) insert2(p);
    last = n;                                           if (waitingForTake > 0)
  }                                                       putLock.notify();
  /*@ behavior                                           return;
   @   requires x != null;                          } }
   @   ensures true;                                }
   @ also behavior                                  class LinkedNode {
   @   requires x == null;                            public Object value;
   @   signals (Exception e) e instanceof            public LinkedNode next; ...
   @   IllegalArgumentException; @*/                 /*@ behavior ensures value == x &&
  public void put(Object x) {                         @              next == null; @*/
    if (x == null)                                    public LinkedNode(Object x) {
      throw new IllegalArgumentException();             value = x;
    insert(x);                                        }
  }                                                 }
}
```

Fig. 1. A Concurrent Linked-list-based Queue Example (excerpts)

are required to hold true in special states that JML defines as *visible states*. The actual definition is somewhat involved, but the basic idea is that the invariant is not required to hold before the object is initialized nor during intermediate steps that occur in methods of C.

The [assignable] clauses state a form of *frame condition* for a method: only the variables listed in [assignable] are allowed to be assigned to. However, locations that are local to the method (or methods it calls) and locations that are created during the method's execution are not subject to this restriction.

The isEmpty method's post-condition states that the method returns true if and only if there is only one node in the list (i.e., the list header). For the extract2 method, the post-condition states that the result is null (when the list is empty) or that there exists a node n such that n is in the list in the pre-state of the method, n is returned as the method result, and n is not in the list in the post-state of the method. The construct [\old(e)] refers to the value that the expression e had in the pre-state of a method, and [\reach(x)] gives the set of objects reachable by following reference chains originating from x. The put method illustrates a *heavyweight* specification where all possible invocations are treated by one of the [behavior] clauses. For the insert method, a pre-condition requires that the argument giving the object to be inserted is not null, and the post-condition ensures that the last list node holds the object supplied for insertion. The [\fresh($x_1, \ldots, x_n$)] construct specifies that x_i is non-null, and the object pointed to by x_i was not allocated in the pre-state of m.

JML is a large and complex specification language and space constraints make it impossible to detail all of the language features. In the subsequent presentation, we focus on those features that are problematic to check with existing technologies or that raised particular issues in the implementation of our model checking support. A complete discussion of our support for JML features is given at [19].

4   Checking JML Specifications with Bogor

All the JML checking tools of Table 1 have a two-phase implementation strategy. In the first phase, JML specifications along with the associated Java code are translated to a lower-level representation. In the second phase, the lower-level representations are checked using the corresponding verification technologies.

A significant portion of the effort in implementing JML checking is associated with the translation phase. This is non-trivial, since it is this phase that captures the JML semantics associated with class inheritance, method overriding, etc. For example, the "effective precondition" (i.e., the condition that should actually be checked as compared to the one that is written in JML comments) of a method that overrides a previously defined method, is a combination of all the pre-conditions listed in the current method conjoined with all preconditions defined in the method of the same signature above the present one in the inheritance hierarchy. Specifications for implemented interfaces must also be taken into account. In addition, since invariants are checked at method entry/exit, invariants are conjoined with pre/post-conditions to form the effective pre/post-conditions. Fortunately, the JML definition is reasonably clear about the rules for forming the structure of effective pre/post-conditions [13]. Of the JML tools described earlier, our implementation architecture is most closely related to that of jmlc since it and jmlc both translate to executable representations (bytecode and Bogor models, respectively).

The contrasts that we draw with jmlc stem from the fact that using Bogor as a verification engine provides significant flexibility. The target representations produced by jmlc have a fixed granularity of actions (bytecode plus assertions), and jmlc has no control over the execution of those actions (they are simply executed by a normal JVM). On the other hand, one can think of Bogor as an extensible interpreter where richer verification primitives (e.g., quantification over heap structures) can be implemented directly using Bogor's extension mechanisms, and where direct control over action execution (e.g., scheduling of thread actions) can be obtained using Bogor's pluggable state-space exploration engine modules.

In the rest of this section, we give an overview of how we use the flexibility of Bogor to implement almost all of the JML language. We do not discuss the details of the translation process to Bogor, since general strategies for translating JML have already been described in other work [2]. Our support for JML is made possible by several novel capabilities of the Bogor model checking framework.

Richer verification primitives: jmlc must represent all verification requirements as regular Java bytecode. With Bogor, we add primitives to the modeling language to directly represent almost all JML constructs such as quantification, [\reach], [\old], etc. Many of these constructs are very difficult to represent using Java bytecode/assertions and almost impossible to represent correctly in the presence of concurrency. For example, the general form of universal quantification in jmlc involves instrumenting the Java code to build extra data structures that hold references to all allocated objects of a particular type. For correctness in the presence of concurrency, all these objects should be locked in a single atomic step to prevent other threads with direct access to those objects from modifying them during the evaluation of the quantification expression, but this is impossible with Java bytecodes.

Direct access to underlying data structures representing the heap: When one adds extensions to Bogor's modeling language, the semantics of extensions is implemented by plugging in code to the Bogor interpretive engine. This code has full access to Bogor's internal representations, including its representation of the heap. Thus, constructs such as universal quantification and [\reach] are easily implemented by traversing the Bogor representation of the current state.

Direct access to state history: Fully implementing [\old] using only byte-code/assertions is virtually impossible since in general the state of all objects reachable from the argument of [\old] must be preserved (this is addressed in detail below). Since model checkers naturally save a compact representation of each encountered state, [\old] can be easily implemented by calling the state-space management facilities in Bogor to retrieve relevant portions of the pre-state.

Control of interleaving: In the presence of concurrency, it is difficult to implement checking of almost all JML pre/post-conditions or invariants using bytecode/assertions since, conceptually, evaluations of these expressions should happen in a single atomic step (i.e., there should be no interference from other threads). There are a number of problems in trying to achieve this by locking individual objects occurring in the expressions (e.g, undesirable interference can still occur unless all the objects are locked in a single step). In Bogor, since extension implementations have complete control of the Bogor scheduler, and other threads can simply be suspended during the evaluation of a specification expression – this effectively allows the expression to be evaluated in a single atomic step in relation to other thread actions. Furthermore, it is the direct control of interleaving that allows the model checking engine to explore all possible schedules for the program, giving the relatively high behavior coverage referenced in Table 1.

4.1 Lightweight versus Heavyweight Specifications

One can write partial JML specifications that capture correctness properties of a fragment of code in a manner similar to the use of assertion facilities. JML also allows users to enrich the specification of parts of a program even to the point of giving a complete specification of total correctness for a method or class. These heavyweight specifications are distinguished in JML by the use of the [behavior] keyword. Users specify the different cases of a method's intended behavior using separate [behavior] clauses.

A heavyweight specification should be *complete* (i.e., each possible invocation context satisfies the [requires] part of a [behavior] clause) and *deterministic* (i.e., no invocation context satisfies the [requires] part of more than one [behavior] clauses). Given the expressiveness of JML it is not always easy to determine whether these constraints are met, so our model checking framework checks for completeness and determinism of heavyweight JML specifications.

4.2   Pre/Post-conditions and Invariants

The JML constructs [requires,ensures,signals] are used to specify pre-conditions, normal post-conditions, and exceptional post-conditions, respectively. Normal post-conditions are checked on method exits caused by executing a return bytecode in Java, and exceptional post-conditions are checked on exits caused by an uncaught exception. As described earlier, we check pre-conditions for a thread t entering a method m when t's PC (program counter) is at (before executing) the first bytecode instruction of m. The Bogor representation of the pre-condition is wrapped together with the representation of the first bytecode of the method in a Bogor atomic block, which guarantees that no interleavings can occur between the start of the checking

and the completion of the first bytecode. For normal post-conditions the following actions are wrapped in a Bogor atomic block: the return expression (if it exists) is evaluated and the resulting value is assigned to a temporary variable, the post-condition is evaluated (occurrences of \return yield the value held in the temporary variable), and the return control action is executed. Without such support (e.g., [2]), spurious errors might be reported, for example, if a put call is interleaved after a call to isEmpty (in Figure 1) returns true, but before the post-condition is evaluated. For exceptional post-conditions, we take advantage of Bogor's built-in exception tables (following the same structure as Java bytecode). In a single atomic block in the exception handler, the exception is caught, the assertion is checked, and then the exception is re-thrown.

A JML [invariant] is checked in "visible states" as described in Section 3. This means that the notion of invariant in JML is weaker than the notion of invariant used in model checking where invariants are required to hold in *every* state.

4.3   Referencing Pre-states

[\old(e)] yields the value of the expression e evaluated in the pre-state of a method m. We will discuss the evaluation of this construct in detail; the issues encountered are representative of the interesting challenges that one faces when trying to implement the semantics of a number of JML constructs. Run-time checking of [\old] appearing in a post-condition p can be implemented by (a) storing the value of e in a special local variable v_e when entering m and then (b) replacing \old(e) with v_e in p [2]. When [\old] expressions involve object references, especially comparisons between method pre- and post-state references, this approach may require storage of large portions of the pre-state heap. Despite the potential costs involved, supporting reference values in [\old] is necessary if one aims to express strong properties about heap data. In a concurrent setting, an additional complication arises if there are *multiple* pre-states associated with a particular post-state of m. For example, when a thread t is ready to execute method

m, but before t enters m, one or more actions from other threads may be interleaved — yielding a succession of states where entrance of t into m could occur from any one of these. A model checker explores all interleavings of threads, and therefore it can naturally check a post-condition with respect to all associated pre-states.

Since an explicit-state model checker such as Bogor stores all states, one would think that we can simply retrieve appropriate pre-states from the model checker's depth-first-stack of visited states when evaluating [\old]. Unfortunately, this straightforward strategy may miss some error states because the model checker may end up hitting a state stored in the cache (and thus backtrack) before it reaches the exit points of a method (and this may happen even though the pre-states are different).

Figure 2 presents a fragment of Java with a simple post-condition and the state-space constructed by Bogor using a depth-first search state exploration with two instances of the Race thread. For simplicity, a state is denoted by a vector comprising four integers: (1) the value of the static variable x, (2) the PC of the main thread, (3) the PC of the first instance of Race, and (4) the second instance of Race. We use • to denote a thread that has died or has not been created yet. We denote the PC of threads at loc$X$ by the integer X. The first location of the main thread is loc0. A straight arrow denotes an atomic step in the model checker, and a dotted arrow denotes an atomic step that causes the model checker to backtrack because it has seen the resulting state (i.e., the resulting state is stored in the model checker's cache). In order to reduce the state-space, we use the thread symmetry reduction presented in [20]. This causes, for example, the state $\langle 0, •, 1, 2 \rangle$ to be considered as observationally equivalent to the state $\langle 0, •, 2, 1 \rangle$. We also use the partial-order reduction presented in [3]. This causes all the transitions of the main thread (not shown – it simply creates the two instances of Race) to execute without any interleavings of the newly created Race instances. The reductions do not affect the result of checking the post-condition; the problem that we are presenting also occurs in the unreduced state-space. Also note that the post-condition is checked whenever loc4 is executed. That is, the execution of the return statement is aggregated with the transition that checks the post-condition in an atomic transition.

As can be observed, there exists a trace through the state-space of Figure 2 that violates the post-condition:

$$\langle 0, 0, •, • \rangle \to \langle 0, •, 1, 1 \rangle \to \langle 0, •, 2, 1 \rangle \to \langle 0, •, 3, 1 \rangle \to \langle 0, •, 3, 2 \rangle \to$$
$$\langle 0, •, 3, 3 \rangle \dashrightarrow \langle 0, •, 4, 3 \rangle \dashrightarrow \langle 1, •, •, 3 \rangle \dashrightarrow \langle 1, •, •, 4 \rangle \dashrightarrow \langle 1, •, •, • \rangle$$

Specifically, at step $\langle 1, •, •, 4 \rangle \dashrightarrow \langle 1, •, •, • \rangle$ the post-condition will fail because the value of x at one of the pre-states of the second instance of Race (i.e., $\langle 1, •, 4, 3 \rangle$) is non-zero. However, this violating trace is not found by the state space exploration because the atomic step $\langle 0, •, 3, 3 \rangle \dashrightarrow \langle 1, •, 4, 3 \rangle$ causes Bogor to backtrack because it has seen the state $\langle 1, •, 4, 3 \rangle$ from a different trace. Thus, the subsequent steps (including the post-condition check) in the error trace are not encountered in the state-space exploration.

We solve this problem by identifying a portion of the pre-state that can be used to distinguish the post-states; it suffices to consider the set of objects reachable from references that are visible in the pre-state. This calculation can be performed efficiently in Bogor because: (1) Bogor employs state-of-the-art collapse compression that reuses parts of previous states when storing a new state [20], and (2) we can augment the thread state that will execute the post-conditions containing [\old(e)] by the collapsed state

```
class Race extends Thread {
  private static int x;

  public void run () {
    loc1 : x = 0;
    loc2 : foo ();
  }

  /*@ ensures
    @  \old(x) == 0;
    @*/
  private void foo () {
    loc3 : x = 1;
    loc4 : return;
  }
}
```

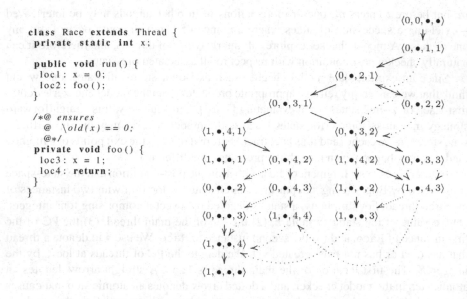

Fig. 2. Race Example and its DFS state-space

encoding the relevant pre-state objects. The result is similar to adding the collapsed pre-state as a local variable of the method, for example,

```
private void foo () {
  int collapseState = Bogor.getCollapsedState(e);
  loc3 : x = 1;
  loc4 : return;
}
```

where method `Bogor.getCollapsedState(e)` returns the unique collapsed state id of the object referred to by *e* (and all objects reachable from *e*). Intuitively, this makes post-states with different pre-states distinguishable from each other (i.e., observationally inequivalent). In general, this addition to the state space might cause significant increase in checking time and space, but as we show in Section 5, this can be mitigated through the use of reduction techniques that detect and exploit atomic method execution as determined by partial order reduction [8].

4.4   Methods in JML Expressions

JML specification expressions can invoke Java methods as "helper expressions". Semantically, this is only sound if the method does not change the observable state. The method annotation [pure] declares that a method *m* is side-effect free. The JML definition of *pure* is that *m* does not diverge and its assignable clause (described below) is empty. Under this definition, synchronized methods, such as `isEmpty` in Figure 1, are not pure since they require modification of an object's lock state; it would be useful to consider them as pure as discussed in [14]. To address this, users can configure the model checker to require only that annotated methods are *weakly pure*. A weakly pure method can contain assignments (e.g., to local variables)

if the state observed by other threads does not change. In other words, in a context in which the method is executed without any interleavings, the post-state of the method should be identical to its pre-state (modulo differences in the PC for the executing thread). Using this definition, the isEmpty method can be considered as weakly pure. This condition can be checked in Bogor by comparing the pre-states and post-states of methods as they are called.

4.5   Object Operations

The [assignable $ap_1, \ldots, ap_n$] annotation for a method m specifies that the field/-variable given by the access path ap_i can be assigned during the execution of m. In JML, each access path ap_i must have the form $x.f_1 \ldots f_k$, where f_i is either a field or an array access, and where $k > 0$; access paths with null-prefixes are ignored.

The assignable clause is difficult to check precisely due to the presence of aliasing, and consequently many tools simply avoid this check. Bogor's explicit representation of the heap can be used to exactly determine variable aliasing and to decide precisely whether an assignment satisfies the assignable clause. When an assignable clause is specified for an access path $x.f_1 \ldots f_k$, we extend Bogor so that it records that the field f_k of the object represented by $x.f_1 \ldots f_{k-1}$ (when entering m) may be assigned during the execution of m; any assignment to the heap in the body of the method that has not been recorded is flagged as an error. In addition, for nested method calls the semantics of [assignable] requires that the sets of assignable locations of a nested method are a subset of those for any enclosing method. Bogor can easily check this on-the-fly since its explicit heap representation keeps precise alias information.

[\reach(x)] gives the objects reachable by following reference chains originating from x. JML also includes variants of [\reach] that filter the objects based on their types and field navigations [13]. Heap reachability is used in Bogor for partial-order reductions [3] and thread symmetry reduction [20]. Given this existing functionality in Bogor, [\reach(x)] is easily evaluated by calling the appropriate Bogor libraries.

[\lockset] gives all the objects locked by the current thread. The notion of lock set is already used in Bogor's partial order reductions as well [3], and

it can be implemented by calling the existing Bogor libraries, just as with [\reach(x)].

[\fresh($x_1, \ldots, x_n$)] requires that, at the post-states of a method m, variables x_i are non-null and the objects bound to x_i are not present in any of the pre-states of m. [\fresh] implicitly accesses the pre-state of a method, thus, we adapt the strategy of storing additional data to distinguish pre-states that was developed for [\old]. For [\fresh], however, we explicitly store newly allocated object references in a local variable to minimize the stored state information, since the number of allocated objects in a method activation is usually smaller than the set of all objects in the pre-state.

4.6 Logic Operations

The universal quantification expression [\forall(τ X; $R(X)$; $C(X)$)] holds true when $C(X)$ is satisfied by all values of quantified variables $X = x_1, \ldots, x_n$ of type τ that satisfy the range predicate $R(X)$. Bogor supports bounded (finite) quantifications over integer types and quantifications over reference types. Quantifications over reference types are implemented by collecting reachable τ objects from any global variables or threads. The existential quantification expression [\exists(τ X; $R(X)$; $C(X)$)] is supported similarly as [\forall].

The set comprehension notation expression [new JMLObjectSet { τ x | $P(x)$ }] gives the set of values of type τ that satisfies the predicate P. We model the abstract set using the generic set type extension described in [18]. The set construction is done using a similar approach as [\forall].

5   Evaluation

Support for JML features has been added to Bogor through its language extension facilities [18]. We extended Bogor's input language syntax with JML's primitive operations and implemented their semantics by using Bogor's APIs [19] to access the full program state and the trace of states leading to the current state.

We used Bogor to reason about six real Java programs, five of which are multi-threaded and manipulate non-trivial heap-allocated data structures. Table 2 reports several measures of program size: **loc** is the number of control points in the source text, **threads** is the number of threads of control in the instance of the program, and **objects** is the maximum number of allocated objects on any program execution. All programs were annotated with JML invariants, pre- and post-conditions and assignable clauses; the table highlights the challenging features used in the specifications for each program. We report the number of states visited during model checking as well as machine dependent measures, the run-time in seconds (s) and memory in mega-bytes; data was gathered running Bogor under JDK 1.4.1 on a 2 GHz Opteron (32-bit mode) with maximum heap of 1 GB running Linux (64-bit mode).

For each program version, we ran model checks for each of the four combinations of object-sharing based partial order reductions (POR) and JML checking features. By comparing runs with and without JML checking, one can determine the overhead of JML checking. For half of the examples, regardless of the use of reductions, the use of potentially problematic features like [\old] and [\fresh] yields no significant overhead for JML checking. Without POR, however, there is non-trivial overhead for three of the six programs; in the worst-case, LinkedQueue, space consumption increased by a factor of three and time by a factor of six. This is not unexpected since the JML specifications for LinkedQueue contain [\reach] expressions within a [\old]; consequently nearly all of the pre-state heap must be used to distinguish post-states. Comparing runs with and without POR reveals the significant benefit of sophisticated POR; it yields between 2 and 4 orders of magnitude reductions in the size of the state space on our set of example programs. Furthermore, the use of POR significantly mitigates JML checking overhead. For the worst-case example, run-time overhead is reduced from a factor of six

Table 2. Checking time/space for JML Annotated Java Programs

Program	POR and JML	no JML	no POR	no JML and no POR
BoundedBuffer[7]	164 loc	`\fresh, \old, signals`		
3 threads	69 states	69 states	2647 states	2647 states
10 objects	1 s/0.8 MB	1 s/0.6 MB	4 s/1.2 MB	3 s/1.0 MB
7 threads	1098 states	1098 states	1601745 states	1601745 states
18 objects	26 s/1.2 MB	23 s/1.0 MB	8936 s/180.2 MB	8458 s/167.7 MB
DiningPhilosopers[7]	193 loc	`\forall, \fresh`		
4 threads	38 states	38 states	12514 states	12514 states
6 objects	1 s/1.1 MB	1 s/0.7 MB	27 s/2.5 MB	20 s/2.0 MB
6 threads	1712 states	1712 states	1939794 states	1939794 states
8 objects	32 s/2.3 MB	24 s/1.8 MB	9571 s/159.9 MB	8719 s/157.6 MB
LinkedQueue[12]	228 loc	`\fresh, \reach, \old, signals, \exists`		
3 threads	2833 states	1533 states	17064 states	11594 states
22 objects	10 s/1.6 MB	5 s/1.0 MB	38 s/3.7 MB	21 s/2.3 MB
5 threads	39050 states	12807 states	1364007 states	423538 states
32 objects	144 s/5.9 MB	72 s/2.5 MB	14557 s/140.5 MB	2415 s/46.4 MB
RWVSN[12]	227 loc	`\old`		
4 threads	183 states	183 states	2621 states	2255 states
5 objects	1 s/1.0 MB	1 s/0.8 MB	2 s/1.5 MB	2 s/1.0 MB
7 threads	18398 states	18398 states	4995560 states	4204332 states
9 objects	185 s/6.8 MB	144 s/3.0 MB	34804 s/463.7 MB	26153 s/366.3 MB
ReplicatedWorkers[4]	543 loc	`\fresh, \old, \reach`		
4 threads	1751 states	1751 states	322016 states	269593 states
19 objects	14 s/2.1 MB	13 s/1.9 MB	897 s/29.8 MB	716 s/26.6 MB
6 threads	10154 states	10154 states	12347415 states	10016554 states
21 objects	99 s/3.3 MB	92 s/2.8 MB	30191 s/391.8 MB	21734 s/282.5 MB
Arrays.sort(Object[])	151 loc	`\forall, \exists, \old`		
1 thread	2 states	2 states	21597 states	21597 states
502 objects	82 s/2.0 MB	7 s/1.9 MB	391 s/49.5 MB	343 s/48.8 MB

to a factor of two. For the RWVSN and ReplicatedWorkers, the fact that these programs have methods with atomic execution behavior allows our POR to eliminate nearly all of the JML checking overhead. Only when methods are not atomic does JML checking suffer significant overhead.

5.1 Discussion

The increase in complexity of JML brings an increase in the possibility of making errors in writing specifications. In the presence of concurrency, it is not uncommon to make subtle errors in defining the intended behavior of a class or method. We experienced this in annotating several of the examples used in our study. As has been observed by others, we found that the generation of counter-examples proved to be extremely useful in debugging erroneous specifications. The exhaustive nature of the search in model checking makes it a much more effective *specification debugging* tool than run-time checking.

We included a standard comparison sorting program in our set of examples to demonstrate Bogor's behavior on a declarative JML specification of rich behavioral properties (i.e., the post-state is an ordered permutation of the pre-state). Despite the richness of this specification, due to the single-threaded nature of the program the method trivially executes atomically, and there is no overhead for JML checking. Our partial order reduction dramatically reduces the number of states, memory and time required for analysis since it defers the storage of a global state until the *current* thread reaches a point where it modifies data that can be observed by another thread. Since there are no other threads, this only happens at the final program state, hence the second state.

6   Conclusion

For model checking to become useful as a software validation technique it must become *more efficient* (so that it provides feedback on fragments of real code in a matter of minutes), *more expressive* (so that it can reason about a broad range of functional properties of interest to software developers), and *more standardized* (so that developer investment in writing specifications can be leveraged for multiple forms of validation and documentation). In this paper, we have presented an approach to customizing a model checking framework to meet these goals by incorporating novel state-space reductions and support for reasoning about behavioral properties written in JML. Our initial data suggests that the combination of these techniques can provide cost-effective reasoning about non-trivial properties of real multi-threaded Java programs.

Bogor supports nearly all of JML, but there are a few features that we are still working to support. Chief among these are JML's *model programs* which we are implementing as Bogor type extensions that directly encode the model abstract data types (ADTs) as first-class types in the Bogor input language. We believe this alternative will be more efficient than [2] because we can apply various reduction algorithms to those ADTs, as shown in [18].

In this paper, we considered complete Java programs, but we plan to support the analysis of partial programs as well.

Ongoing work [23] is exploring techniques for synthesizing test harnesses for unit level reasoning. An important consideration in this process is the selection of input values to achieve thorough coverage of the behavior of both the program and the specification, and we are extending recent work by Stoller [22] towards that end.

References

1. L. Burdy, Y. Cheon, D. Cok, M. Ernst, J. Kiniry, G. T. Leavens, K. R. M. Leino, and E. Poll. An overview of JML tools and applications. In *Proceedings of the Eighth International Workshop on Formal Methods for Industrial Critical Systems*, 2003.
2. Y. Cheon and G. T. Leavens. A runtime assertion checker for the java modeling language. In *Proceedings of the International Conference on Software Engineering Research and Practice*, 2002.

3. M. B. Dwyer, J. Hatcliff, V. R. Prasad, and Robby. Exploiting object escape and locking information in partial order reductions for concurrent object-oriented programs. *Formal Methods in System Designs*, 2004. (to appear).

4. M. B. Dwyer and V. Wallentine. A framework for parallel adaptive grid simulations. *Concurrency : Practice and Experience*, 9(11):1293–1310, Nov. 1997.

5. C. Flanagan, K. R. M. Leino, M. Lillibridge, G. Nelson, J. B. Saxe, and R. Stata. Extended static checking for Java. In *Proceedings of the ACM SIGPLAN 2002 Conference on Programming language design and implementation*, 2002.

6. R. Floyd. Assigning meaning to programs. In *Proceedings of the Symposium on Applied Mathematics*, 1967.

7. S. Hartley. *Concurrent Programming - The Java Programming Language*. Oxford University Press, 1998.

8. J. Hatcliff, Robby, and M. B. Dwyer. Verifying atomicity specifications for concurrent object-oriented software using model checking. In *Proceedings of the Fifth International Conference on Verification, Model Checking and Abstract Interpretation*, Jan. 2004.

9. G. J. Holzmann. The model checker SPIN. *IEEE Transactions on Software Engineering*, 23(5):279–294, May 1997.

10. H. Hussmann, B. Demuth, and F. Finger. Modular architecture for a toolset supporting OCL. In *The Third International Conference on The Unified Modeling Language (LNCS 1939)*, 2000.

11. S. Khurshid, D. Marinov, and D. Jackson. An analyzable annotation language. In *Proceedings of the 17th ACM conference on Object-oriented programming, systems, languages, and applications*, 2002.

12. D. Lea. *Concurrent Programming in Java: Second Edition*. Addison-Wesley, 2000.

13. G. T. Leavens, A. L. Baker, and C. Ruby. JML: a Java modeling language. In *Formal Underpinnings of Java Workshop*, Oct. 1998.

14. G. T. Leavens, Y. Cheon, C. Clifton, and C. Ruby. How the design of JML accommodates both runtime assertion checking and formal verification. In *Proceedings of the 1st International Symposium on Formal Methods for Components and Objects*, Nov. 2002.

15. B. Meyer. *Object-oriented Software Construction*. Prentice-Hall, 1988.

16. S. Owre, J. M. Rushby, and N. Shankar. PVS: A prototype verification system. In *Proceedings of the 11th International Conference on Automated Deduction (LNCS 607)*, 1992.

17. M. Richters and M. Gogolla. Validating UML models and OCL constraints. In *The Third International Conference on The Unified Modeling Language (LNCS 1939)*, 2000.

18. Robby, M. B. Dwyer, and J. Hatcliff. Bogor: An extensible and highly-modular model checking framework. In *Proceedings of the 9th European Software Engineering Conference held jointly with the 11th ACM SIGSOFT Symposium on the Foundations of Software Engineering*, 2003.

19. Robby, M. B. Dwyer, and J. Hatcliff. Bogor Website. |http://bogor.projects.cis.ksu.edu|, 2003.

20. Robby, M. B. Dwyer, J. Hatcliff, and R. Iosif. Space-reduction strategies for model checking dynamic systems. In *Proceedings of the 2003 Workshop on Software Model Checking*, July 2003.

21. D. S. Rosenblum. A practical approach to programming with assertions. *IEEE Transactions on Software Engineering*, 21(1):19–31, Jan. 1995.

22. S. D. Stoller. Domain partitioning for open reactive systems. In *Proceedings of the International Symposium on Software Testing and Analysis*, 2002.

23. O. Tkachuk, M. Dwyer, and C. Pasareanu. Automated environment generation for software model checking. In *Proceedings of the 18th International Conference on Automated Software Engineering*, Oct. 2003.

24. J. van den Berg and B. Jacobs. The LOOP compiler for Java and JML. In *Proceedings of the 7th International Conference on Tools and Algorithms for the Construction and Analysis of Systems (LNCS 2031)*, 2001.

25. W. Visser, K. Havelund, G. Brat, , and S. Park. Model checking programs. In *Proceedings of the 15th IEEE Conference on Automated Software Engineering*, Sept. 2000.

Applying Game Semantics to Compositional Software Modeling and Verification[*]

Samson Abramsky, Dan R. Ghica, Andrzej S. Murawski, and C.-H. Luke Ong

Oxford University Computing Laboratory
Parks Road, Oxford, OX1 3QD, U. K.

Abstract. We describe a software model checking tool founded on game semantics, highlight the underpinning theoretical results and discuss several case studies. The tool is based on an interpretation algorithm defined compositionally on syntax and thus can also handle open programs. Moreover, the models it produces are equationally fully abstract. These features are essential in the modeling and verification of software components such as modules and turn out to lead to very compact models of programs.

1 Introduction and Background

Game Semantics has emerged as a powerful paradigm for giving semantics to a variety of programming languages and logical systems. It has been used to construct the first syntax-independent fully abstract models for a spectrum of programming languages ranging from purely functional languages to languages with non-functional features such as control operators and locally-scoped references [1,2,3,4,5,6].

We are currently developing Game Semantics in a new, algorithmic direction, with a view to applications in computer-assisted verification and program analysis. Some promising steps have already been taken in this direction. Hankin and Malacaria have applied Game Semantics to program analysis, e.g. to certifying secure information flows in programs [7,8]. A particularly striking development was the work by Ghica and McCusker [9] which captures the game semantics of a procedural language in a remarkably simple form, as regular expressions. This leads to a decision procedure for observational equivalence on this fragment. Ghica has subsequently extended the approach to a call-by-value language with arrays [10], to model checking Hoare-style program correctness assertions [11] and to a more general model-checking friendly specification framework [12].

Game Semantics has several features which make it very promising from this point of view. It provides a very *concrete* way of building *fully abstract* models. It has a clear operational content, while admitting *compositional methods* in the style of denotational semantics. The basic objects studied in Game

---

[*] The authors gratefully acknowledge the support of UK EPSRC, Canadian NSERC and St. John's College, Oxford University.

Semantics are games, and strategies on games. Strategies can be seen as certain kinds of highly-constrained processes, hence they admit the same kind of automata-theoretic representations central to model checking and allied methods in computer-assisted verification. Moreover, games and strategies naturally form themselves into rich mathematical structures which yield very accurate models of advanced high-level programming languages, as the various full abstraction results show. Thus the promise of this approach is to carry over the methods of model checking (see e.g. [13]), which has been so effective in the analysis of circuit designs and communications protocols, to much more *structured* programming situations, in which data-types as well as control flow are important.

A further benefit of the algorithmic approach is that by embodying game semantics in tools, and making it concrete and algorithmic, it should become more accessible and meaningful to practitioners. We see Game Semantics as having the potential to fill the role of a "Popular Formal Semantics," called for in an eloquent paper by Schmidt [14], which can help to bridge the gap between the semantics and programming language communities. Game Semantics has been successful in its own terms as a semantic theory; we aim to make it useful to and usable by a wider community.

Model checking for state machines is a well-studied problem (e.g. Murϕ [15], Spin [16] and Mocha [17] to name a few systems). Software model checking is a relatively new direction (see e.g. [18]); the leading projects (e.g. SLAM [19], and *Bandera* [20]) excel in tool constructions. The closest to ours in terms of target applications is the SLAM project, which is able to check safety properties of C programs. This task is reduced in stages to the problem of checking if a given statement in an instrumented version of the program in question is reachable, using ideas from data-flow and inter-procedural analysis and abstract interpretation.

In relation to the extensive current activity in model checking and computer assisted verification, our approach is distinctive, being founded on a highly-structured *compositional* semantic model. This means that we can directly apply our methods to *open program phrases* (i.e. terms-in-context with free variables) in a high-level language with procedures, local variables and data types. This ability is essential in analyzing properties of software components. The soundness of our methods is guaranteed by the properties of the semantic models on which they are based. By contrast, most current model checking applies to relatively "flat" unstructured situations.

Our semantics-driven approach has some other additional benefits: it is generic and fully automated. The prototype tool we have implemented has the level of automation of a compiler. The input is a program fragment, with very little instrumentation required, and the output is a finite-state (FS) model. The resulting model itself can be analyzed using third-party model-checking tools, or our tool can automatically extract traces with certain properties, e.g. error traces.

Software model checking is a fast-developing area of study, driven by needs of the industry as much as, if not more than, theoretical results. Often, tool development runs well ahead of rigorous considerations of soundness of the methods being developed. Our aim is to build on the tools and methods which have been developed in the verification community, while exploring the advantages offered by our semantics-directed approach.

2   A Procedural Programming Language

Our prototypical procedural language is a simply-typed call-by-name lambda calculus with basic types of booleans (**bool**), integers (**exp**), assignable variables (**var**) and commands (**comm**). We denote the basic types by σ and the function types by θ. *Assignable* variables, storing integers, form the state while commands change the state. In addition to abstraction $(\lambda x : \sigma.M)$ and application (FA), other terms of the language are conditionals, uniformly applied to any type, (**if** B **then** M **else** N), recursion (**fix** $x : \sigma.M$), constants (integers, booleans) and arithmetic-logic operators $(M * N)$; we also have command-type terms which are the standard imperative operators: dereferencing (explicit in the syntax, !V), assignment $(V := N)$, sequencing $(C; M$, note that we allow, by sequencing, expressions with side-effects), no-op (**skip**) and local variable block (**new** x **in** M). We write $M : \sigma$ to indicate that term M has type σ.

This language, which elegantly combines state-based procedural and higher-order functional programming, is due to Reynolds [21] and its semantic properties have been the object of extensive research [22].

If the programming language is restricted to first-order procedures, (more precisely, we restrict types to $\theta ::= \sigma \mid \sigma \to \theta$) tail recursion (iteration) and finite data-types then the Abramsky-McCusker fully abstract game model for this language [3] has a very simple regular-language representation [9]. The formulation of the regular-language model in loc. cit. is very well suited for proving equivalences "by hand," but we will prefer a slightly different but equivalent presentation [23] because it is more uniform and more compact. The referenced work gives motivation and numerous examples for the model presented below.

2.1   Extended Regular Expressions

This section describes the representation of the game model using a language of extended regular expressions. Due to space constraints, a basic understanding of game semantics must be assumed as background. Otherwise, the reader is encouraged to refer to the literature mentioned in the Introduction.

Terms are interpreted by languages over alphabets of moves $\mathcal{A}$. The languages, denoted by $\mathcal{L}(R)$, are specified using extended regular expressions R. They include the standard regular expressions consisting of the empty language $\emptyset$, the empty sequence ϵ, concatenation $R \cdot S$, union $R + S$, Kleene star R^*, and the elements of the alphabet taken as sequences of unit length. We also use the additional constructs of intersection $R \cap S$, direct image under homomorphism ϕR and inverse image $\phi^{-1} R$. The languages defined by these extensions are the obvious ones.

It is a standard result that any extended regular expression constructed from the operations described above denotes a regular language, which can be recognized by a finite automaton which can be effectively constructed from the regular expression [24].

We will often use the disjoint union of two alphabets to create a larger alphabet: $\mathcal{A}_1 + \mathcal{A}_2 = \{a^{\langle 1 \rangle} \mid a \in \mathcal{A}_1\} \cup \{b^{\langle 2 \rangle} \mid b \in \mathcal{A}_2\} = \mathcal{A}_1^{\langle 1 \rangle} \cup \mathcal{A}_2^{\langle 2 \rangle}$. The tags $-^{\langle i \rangle}$ are used on a lexical level, resulting in new and distinct symbols belonging to the larger alphabet. The disjoint union gives rise to the canonical maps: $\mathcal{A}_1 \xrightleftharpoons[\text{outl}]{\text{inl}} \mathcal{A}_1 + \mathcal{A}_2 \xleftrightarrow[\text{outr}]{\text{inr}} \mathcal{A}_2$. The definition of the maps is:

$$\text{inl}\, a = a^{\langle 1 \rangle} \qquad\qquad \text{outl}\, a^{\langle 1 \rangle} = a \qquad\qquad \text{outr}\, a^{\langle 1 \rangle} = \epsilon$$
$$\text{inr}\, b = b^{\langle 2 \rangle} \qquad\qquad \text{outl}\, b^{\langle 2 \rangle} = \epsilon \qquad\qquad \text{outr}\, b^{\langle 2 \rangle} = b$$

If $\phi : \mathcal{A} \to \mathcal{B}^*$ and $\phi' : \mathcal{C} \to \mathcal{D}^*$ are homomorphisms then we define their sum $\phi + \phi' : \mathcal{A} + \mathcal{C} \to (\mathcal{B} + \mathcal{D})^*$ as $(\phi + \phi')(a^{\langle 1 \rangle}) = (\phi a)^{\langle 1 \rangle}$, respectively $(\phi + \phi')(c^{\langle 2 \rangle}) = (\phi' c)^{\langle 2 \rangle}$.

Definition 1 (Composition). *If R is a regular expression over alphabet $\mathcal{A} + \mathcal{B}$ and S a regular expression over alphabet $\mathcal{B} + \mathcal{C}$ we define the* composition $R \circ S$ *as the regular expression $R \circ S = out(out_1^{-1}(R) \cap out_2^{-1}(S))$, over alphabet $\mathcal{A} + \mathcal{C}$, with maps $\mathcal{A} + \mathcal{B} \xrightleftharpoons[out_1]{in_1} \mathcal{A} + \mathcal{B} + \mathcal{C} \xleftrightarrow[out_2]{in_2} \mathcal{B} + \mathcal{C}$ and $\mathcal{A} + \mathcal{C} \xrightleftharpoons[out]{in} \mathcal{A} + \mathcal{B} + \mathcal{C}$.*

Regular expression composition is very similar to composition of finite state transducers [25]. Sets $\mathcal{A}$ and $\mathcal{B}$ represent, respectively, the input and the output of the first transducer; sets $\mathcal{B}$ and $\mathcal{C}$ represent, respectively, the input and the output of the second transducer. The result is a transducer of inputs $\mathcal{A}$ and output $\mathcal{C}$. For example, let $\mathcal{A} = \{a\}$, $\mathcal{B} = \{b\}$, $\mathcal{C} = \{c\}$; then $(ab)^* \circ (bcc)^* = (acc)^*$.

2.2   Alphabets

We interpret each type θ by a language over an alphabet $\mathcal{A}[\![\theta]\!]$, containing the *moves* from the game model. For basic types σ it is helpful to define alphabets of questions $\mathcal{Q}[\![\sigma]\!]$ and answers $\mathcal{A}_q[\![\sigma]\!]$ for each $q \in \mathcal{Q}[\![\sigma]\!]$. The alphabet of type σ is then defined as $\mathcal{A}[\![\sigma]\!] = \mathcal{Q}[\![\sigma]\!] \cup \bigcup_{q \in \mathcal{Q}[\![\sigma]\!]} \mathcal{A}_q[\![\sigma]\!]$. The basic type alphabets are:

$$\mathcal{Q}[\![\text{exp}]\!] = \{q\}, \ \mathcal{A}_q[\![\text{exp}]\!] = \mathsf{N} \qquad\qquad \mathcal{Q}[\![\text{bool}]\!] = \{q\}, \ \mathcal{A}_q[\![\text{bool}]\!] = \{t, f\}$$
$$\mathcal{Q}[\![\text{var}]\!] = \{q\} \cup \{w(n) \mid n \in \mathsf{N}\}, \qquad \mathcal{A}_q[\![\text{var}]\!] = \mathsf{N}, \mathcal{A}_{w(n)} = \{\star\}$$
$$\mathcal{Q}[\![\text{comm}]\!] = \{q\}, \ \mathcal{A}_q[\![\text{comm}]\!] = \{\star\}.$$

where $\mathsf{N} = \{-n, \cdots, -1, 0, 1, \cdots, n\}$.

Alphabets of function types are defined by $\mathcal{A}[\![\sigma \to \theta]\!] = \mathcal{A}[\![\sigma]\!] + \mathcal{A}[\![\theta]\!]$.

A typing judgement $\Gamma \vdash M : \theta$ is interpreted by a regular expression $R = [\![\Gamma \vdash M : \theta]\!]$ over alphabet $\sum_{x_i : \theta_i \in \Gamma} \mathcal{A}[\![\theta_i]\!] + \mathcal{A}[\![\theta]\!]$.

For any type $\theta = \sigma_1 \to \cdots \to \sigma_k \to \sigma$, it is convenient to define the regular language K_θ over alphabet $\mathcal{A}[\![\theta]\!] + \mathcal{A}[\![\theta]\!]$, called the *copy-cat* language:

$$K_\theta = \sum_{q \in \mathcal{Q}[\![\sigma]\!]} q^{\langle 2 \rangle} \cdot q^{\langle 1 \rangle} \cdot \left(\sum_{i=1,k} R_i \right)^* \cdot \sum_{a \in \mathcal{A}_q[\![\sigma]\!]} a^{\langle 1 \rangle} \cdot a^{\langle 2 \rangle},$$

where $R_i = \sum_{q \in \mathcal{Q}[\![\sigma_i]\!]} q^{\langle 2 \rangle} \cdot q^{\langle 1 \rangle} \cdot \sum_{a \in \mathcal{A}_q[\![\sigma_i]\!]} a^{\langle 1 \rangle} \cdot a^{\langle 2 \rangle}$. This regular expression represents the so-called copy-cat strategy of game semantics, and it describes the generic behaviour of a sequential procedure. At second-order [26] and above [2] this behaviour is far more complicated.

2.3   Regular-Language Semantics

We interpret terms using an evaluation function $[\![-]\!]$ mapping a term $\Gamma \vdash M : \theta$ and an environment u into a regular language R. The environment is a function, with the same domain as Γ, mapping identifiers of type θ to regular languages over $\mathcal{A}[\![\Gamma]\!] + \mathcal{A}[\![\theta]\!]$. The evaluation function is defined by recursion on the syntax.

Identifiers. Identifiers are read from the environment: $[\![\Gamma, x : \theta \vdash x : \theta]\!]u = u(x)$.

Let. $[\![\Gamma \vdash \mathbf{let}\, x\, \mathbf{be}\, M\, \mathbf{in}\, N]\!]u = [\![\Gamma, x : \theta \vdash N]\!](u \mid x \mapsto [\![\Gamma \vdash M]\!]u)$.

Abstraction. $[\![\Gamma \vdash \lambda x : \sigma.M : \sigma \to \theta]\!]u = \phi([\![\Gamma, x : \sigma \vdash M : \theta]\!](u \mid x \mapsto K_\sigma))$, where ϕ is the (trivial) associativity isomorphism.

Linear application and contraction. $[\![\Gamma, \Delta \vdash MN]\!]u = [\![\Gamma \vdash M]\!]u \circ ([\![\Delta \vdash N]\!]u)^*$, with composition $- \circ -$ defined as before. Contraction is

$$[\![\Gamma, z : \theta \vdash M[z/x, z/x'] : \theta]\!]u = (\mathrm{id}_1 + \delta + \mathrm{id}_2)([\![\Gamma, x : \theta, x' : \theta \vdash M : \theta]\!]u),$$

where id_1 and id_2 are identities on $\mathcal{A}[\![\Gamma]\!]$ and, respectively, $\mathcal{A}[\![\theta]\!]$. It is well known that application can be harmlessly decomposed in linear application and contraction. The homomorphism $\delta : \mathcal{A}[\![\theta]\!] + \mathcal{A}[\![\theta]\!] \to \mathcal{A}[\![\theta]\!]$ only removes tags from moves. Note that this interpretation is specific to first-order types. In higher-order types this interpretation of contraction by un-tagging can result in ambiguities.

Block Variables. Consider the following regular expression over alphabet $\mathcal{A}[\![\mathbf{var}]\!]$: $\mathrm{cell} = \left(\sum_{n \in \mathbb{N}} \mathsf{w}(n) \cdot \star \cdot (\mathsf{q} \cdot n)^* \right)^*$. Intuitively, this regular expression describes the sequential behaviour of a memory cell: if a value n is written, then the same value is read back until the next write, and so on. We define block variables as $[\![\Gamma \vdash \mathbf{new}\, x\, \mathbf{in}\, M : \sigma]\!]u = [\![\Gamma, x : \mathbf{var} \vdash M : \sigma]\!]u \circ \mathrm{cell}$,

Constants. Finally, the interpretation of constants is:

$$[\![n : \mathbf{exp}]\!] = \mathsf{q} \cdot \mathsf{n}, \quad [\![\mathbf{true} : \mathbf{bool}]\!] = \mathsf{q} \cdot \mathsf{t}, \quad [\![\mathbf{false} : \mathbf{bool}]\!] = \mathsf{q} \cdot \mathsf{f}$$

$$[\![-\mathbf{op}- : \sigma \to \sigma \to \sigma']\!] = \sum_{p \in \mathbb{N}} \sum_{\substack{m, n \in \mathbb{N} \\ p = m\, op\, n}} \mathsf{q}^{\langle 3 \rangle} \cdot \mathsf{q}^{\langle 1 \rangle} \cdot \mathsf{m}^{\langle 1 \rangle} \cdot \mathsf{q}^{\langle 2 \rangle} \cdot \mathsf{n}^{\langle 2 \rangle} \cdot \mathsf{p}^{\langle 3 \rangle}$$

$$[\![- := - : \mathbf{var} \to \mathbf{exp} \to \mathbf{comm}]\!] = \sum_{n \in \mathbb{N}} \mathsf{q}^{\langle 3 \rangle} \cdot \mathsf{q}^{\langle 2 \rangle} \cdot \mathsf{n}^{\langle 2 \rangle} \cdot \mathsf{w}(n)^{\langle 1 \rangle} \cdot \star^{\langle 1 \rangle} \cdot \star^{\langle 3 \rangle}$$

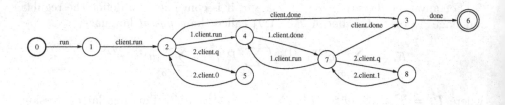

Fig. 1. A simple switch

$$\llbracket \textbf{if} - \textbf{then} - \textbf{else} - : \textbf{bool} \to \sigma \to \sigma \to \sigma \rrbracket$$

$$= \sum_{q \in \mathcal{Q}\llbracket \sigma \rrbracket} q^{\langle 4 \rangle} \cdot \mathsf{q}^{\langle 1 \rangle} \cdot \mathsf{t}^{\langle 1 \rangle} \cdot q^{\langle 2 \rangle} \cdot \sum_{a \in \mathcal{A}_q \llbracket \sigma \rrbracket} a^{\langle 2 \rangle} \cdot a^{\langle 4 \rangle}$$

$$+ \sum_{q \in \mathcal{Q}\llbracket \sigma \rrbracket} q^{\langle 4 \rangle} \cdot \mathsf{q}^{\langle 1 \rangle} \cdot \mathsf{f}^{\langle 1 \rangle} \cdot q^{\langle 3 \rangle} \cdot \sum_{a \in \mathcal{A}_q \llbracket \sigma \rrbracket} a^{\langle 3 \rangle} \cdot a^{\langle 4 \rangle}$$

$$\llbracket -;- : \textbf{comm} \to \sigma \to \sigma \rrbracket = \sum_{q \in \mathcal{Q}\llbracket \sigma \rrbracket} q^{\langle 3 \rangle} \cdot \mathsf{q}^{\langle 1 \rangle} \cdot \star^{\langle 1 \rangle} \cdot q^{\langle 2 \rangle} \cdot \sum_{a \in \mathcal{A}_q \llbracket \sigma \rrbracket} a^{\langle 2 \rangle} \cdot a^{\langle 3 \rangle}$$

$$\llbracket \textbf{while} - \textbf{do} - : \textbf{bool} \to \textbf{comm} \to \textbf{comm} \rrbracket$$

$$= \mathsf{q}^{\langle 3 \rangle} \cdot \left(\mathsf{q}^{\langle 1 \rangle} \cdot \mathsf{t}^{\langle 1 \rangle} \cdot q^{\langle 2 \rangle} \cdot \star^{\langle 2 \rangle} \right)^{*} \cdot \mathsf{q}^{\langle 1 \rangle} \cdot \mathsf{f}^{\langle 1 \rangle} \cdot \star^{\langle 3 \rangle}$$

$$\llbracket \textbf{div} : \textbf{comm} \rrbracket = \emptyset, \qquad \llbracket \textbf{ skip} : \textbf{comm} \rrbracket = \mathsf{q} \cdot \star.$$

The operator **op** ranges over the usual arithmetic-logic operators, and *op* is its obvious interpretation.

2.4   A Warm-up Example

This simple example illustrates quite well the way the game-based model works. It is a toy abstract data type (ADT): a switch that can be flicked on, with implementation:

```
client : com -> exp -> com |-
    new var v:= 0 in
    let set be v := 1 in
    let get be !v in
    client (set, get) : com.
```

The code consists of local integer variable v, storing the state of the switch, together with functions set, to flick the switch on, and get, to get the state of the switch. The initial state of the switch is *off*. The non-local, undefined, identifier client is declared at the left of the turnstile |-. It takes a command

and an expression-returning functions as arguments. It represents, intuitively, "the most general context" in which this ADT can be used.

A key observation about the model is that the *internal state* of the program is abstracted away, and only the observable actions, of the *nonlocal* entity client, are represented, insofar as they contribute to terminating computations. The output of the modeling tool is given in Fig. 1.

Notice that no references to v, set, or get appear in the model! The model is only that of the possible behaviours of the client: whenever the client is executed, if it evaluates its second argument (get the state of the switch) it will receive the value 0 as a result; if it evaluates the first argument (set the switch on), one or more times, then the second argument (get the state of the switch) will always evaluate to 1. The model does not, however, assume that client uses its arguments, or how many times or in what order.

2.5   Full Abstraction

Full abstraction results are crucial in semantics, as they are a strong qualitative measure of the semantic model. Full abstraction is defined with respect to observational equivalence: two terms are equivalent if and only if they can be substituted in all program contexts without any observable difference in the outcome of computation. This choice of observables is therefore canonical, and arises naturally from the programming language itself. In practice, fully abstract models are important because they identify all and only those programs which are observationally equivalent.

Formally, terms M and N are defined to be observationally equivalent, written $M \equiv N$, if and only if for any context $C[-]$ such that both $C[M]$ and $C[N]$ are closed terms of type **comm**, $C[M]$ converges if and only if $C[N]$ converges. The theory of observational equivalence, which is very rich (see e.g. [9] for a discussion), has been the subject of much research [22].

Theorem 1 (Full abstraction [3,9]). $\Gamma \vdash M \equiv N$ iff $\mathcal{L}(\llbracket \Gamma \vdash M : \theta \rrbracket u_0) = \mathcal{L}(\llbracket \Gamma \vdash N : \theta \rrbracket u_0)$, where $u_0(x) = K_\theta$ for all $x : \theta$ in Γ.

As an immediate consequence, observational equivalence for the finitary fragment discussed here is decidable. It can be shown that the full abstraction result holds relative to contexts drawn from either the restricted fragment or the full programming language [27].

3   Applications to Analysis and Verification

The game model is *algorithmic, fully abstract* and *compositional*, therefore it provides excellent support for compositional program analysis and verification.

The initial decidability result of the previous section was extended to higher-order (recursion and iteration-free) call-by-name procedural programming by Ong [26] and, for call-by-value, by Murawski [28]. This required the use of deterministic pushdown automata [29,30], since the associated sets of complete

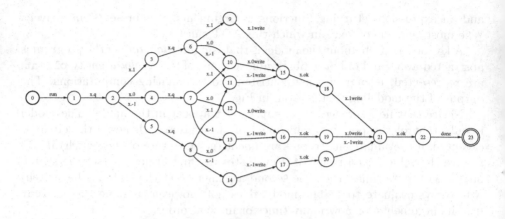

Fig. 2. A model of sorting

plays in the game semantics are no longer regular. Various other extensions of the programming fragment, e.g. by introducing unrestricted recursion [26] or further increasing the order of the fragment [31], lead to undecidability. The game-theoretic approach seems to offer a useful and powerful tool for investigating the algorithmic properties of programming language fragments, e.g. the complexity of program equivalence [32].

A different direction of research is the development of game-based, model-checking friendly specification languages. Such specification languages are necessary in order to fully exploit the compositionality of the game-based approach. It is of little use to reason about program fragments if properties of the whole program cannot be then compositionally inferred, without requiring further model-checking. The first steps in this direction are taken in [12].

3.1   Tool Support and Case Studies

The theoretical applications of game semantics have been very successful. However, since the complexity of the regular-language algorithms involved in the generation of the finite-state machines representing the game models is exponential (both in time and in space), it was unclear whether the technique was practicable. This is in fact a common situation in software model checking: the asymptotic complexity of the algorithms involved is high, but it turns out that the worst-case scenario only happens in pathological cases. Many programs can be in fact verified. But the only way to make such pragmatic assessments is to implement and experiment. We have implemented a prototype tool, and the results are very positive.

Our tool converts an open procedural program into the finite-state machine representation of the regular-language game model. Very little user instrumentation of the source code is required. The data-abstraction schemes (i.e. what finite sets of integers will be used to model integer variables) for integer-typed variables need to be supplied, using simple code annotations. The tool is implemented in CAML; most of the back-end heavy duty finite-state machine processing is done using the AT&T FSM library [33]. A more complete description of the tool is available in [34].

In the following we will present two case studies which best illustrate the distinctive features of our model: a sorting program and an abstract data type implementation.

3.2 Sorting

In this section we will discuss the modeling of a sorting program, a pathological problem for model checking because of the connection between data and control flow. We will focus on *bubble-sort*, not for its algorithmic virtues but because it is one of the most straightforward non-recursive sorting algorithms. The implementation we will analyze is the one in Fig. 3. Meta-variable n, representing the size of the array, will be instantiated to several different values. Observe that the program communicates with its environment using non-local **var**-typed identifier x:**var** only. Therefore, the model will only represent the actions of x. Since we are in a call-by-name setting, x can represent any **var**-typed procedure, for example interfacing with an input/output channel. Notice that the array being effectively sorted, a[], is not visible from the outside of the program because it is locally defined.

We first generate the model for $n = 2$, i.e. an array of only 2 elements, in order to obtain a model which is small enough to display and discuss. The type of stored data is integers in the interval $[-1, 1]$, i.e. 3 distinct values. The resulting model is as in Fig. 2. It reflects the dynamic behaviour of the program in the following way: every trace in the model is formed from the actions of reading all $3 \times 3 = 9$ possible combinations of values from x, followed by writing out the same values, but in sorted order. Fig. 4 gives a snapshot of the model for $n = 20$.

The output is a FS machine, which can be analyzed using standard FS-based model checking tools. Moreover, this model is an *extensional* model of sorting: all sorting programs on an array of size n will have isomorphic models. Therefore, a straightforward method of verification is to compare the model of a sorting program with the model of another implementation which is known to be correct. In the case of our finite-state models, this is a decidable operation.

Increases in the array lead to (asymptotically exponential) increases in the time and space of the verification algorithm. In the table below we give several benchmark results for running the tool on our development machine (SunBlade 100, 2GB RAM). We give the execution time, the size of the largest automaton generated in the process, and the size of the final automaton. For reference, we also include the size of the state space of the program, i.e. the number of states representable by the array and the other variables in the program.

```
x:var |-                                                     1
  array a[n] in                                              2
  new var i:=0 in                                            3
  while !i < n do a[!i]:=!x; i:=!i+1 od;                     4
  new var flag:=1 in                                         5
  while !flag do                                             6
    new var i:=0 in                                          7
    flag:=0;                                                 8
    while !i < n - 1 do                                      9
      if !a[!i] > !a[!i+1] then                             10
        flag:=1;                                            11
        new var temp:=!a[!i] in                            12
          a[!i]:=!a[!i+1];                                 13
          a[!i+1]:=!temp                                   14
      else skip fi;                                        15
      i:=!i+1                                              16
    od                                                     17
  od;                                                      18
  new var i:=0 in                                          19
  while !i < n do x:=!a[!i]; i:=!i+1 od : com.             20
```

Fig. 3. An implementation of sorting

n	Time (mins.)	State space (Max.)	State space (Model)	State space (Program)
5	5	3,376	163	60,750
10	10	64,776	948	3,542,940
15	120	352,448	2,858	96,855,122,250
20	240	1,153,240	6,393	55,788,550,416,000

For arrays larger than 30 the memory requirements could not be handled.

We can see that models have very compact sizes. Moreover, the maximum size of the work space is significantly less than that used by a (naive) state exploration algorithm. The key observation is the following: the fact that the state of the array is *internalized* and only a purely behavioural, observationally fully abstract model is presented leads to significant savings in required memory space. Moreover, the compositional nature of our construction ensures that all intermediate models are observationally fully abstract, and allows us to perform local minimizations at every step.

This kind of "observational" abstraction, which comes for free with our fully abstract model, is fundamentally different than other, syntactic and "stateful," abstraction techniques such as slicing [35].

3.3 ADT Invariants

We define an assertion as a function which takes as argument a boolean, the condition to be asserted. It does nothing if the condition is true and calls an

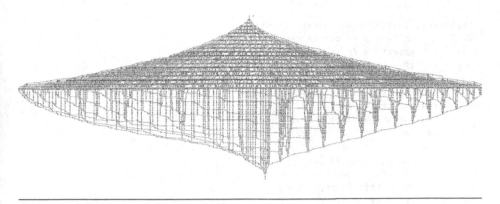

Fig. 4. A model of sorting: 20 element-array

(nonlocal) **error** procedure if the condition is false. In the resulting model, any trace containing the actions **error.run, error.done** will represent a usage of the ADT which violates the invariant, i.e. an *error trace*.

The encoding of safety properties using code-level assertions is quite standard in SMC, e.g. [19], and it is also known that every safety property can be encoded in a regular language [36]. Using the assertion mechanism in conjunction with modeling open programs, such as modules, offers an elegant solution to the problem of checking equational properties or invariants of ADTs.

For example, consider an implementation of a finite-size stack, using a fixed-size array. The interface of the stack is through functions **push(n)** and **pop**. Their implementation is the obvious one (see Fig. 5). In addition, the stack component assumes the existence of functions **overflow** and **empty** to call if a **push** is attempted on a full stack, respectively a **pop** is attempted on an empty stack. These functions need not be implemented.

Suppose that we want to check, for a size 2 stack, whether it is the case that the last value pushed onto the stack is the value at the top of the stack. We do this by using the assertion **invariant** on lines 21–24 of Fig. 5. Notice the undefined component **VERIFY** of this program: it stands for *all* possible uses of the stack module and the assertion to be checked. The idea of providing such a generic closure of an open program can be traced back to [37], and several game-like solutions have been already proposed [38,39]. The game model which we use provides this closure, correct and complete, directly at the level of the concrete programming language.

The tool automatically builds the model for the above and extracts its shortest failure trace (see Fig. 6).

Action **1.VERIFY** represents a **push** action. So the simplest possible error is caused by pushing 3 times the value 1 onto the 2-element stack. Indeed, if the stack is already full, pushing a new element will cause an overflow error. The

```
empty:com, overflow:com, m:exp, error:com,                     1
VERIFY : com -> exp -> com -> com |-                           2
    let assert be fun a : exp.                                 3
        if a then skip else error fi in                        4
    array buffer[n] in                                         5
    let size be n in                                           6
    new var crt:=0 in                                          7
    let isempty be !crt = 0 in                                 8
    let isfull be !crt = size in                               9
    let push be fun x : exp.                                    10
        new var temp:=x in                                     11
        if isfull then overflow                                12
        else buffer[!crt]:=!temp;                              13
        crt:=!crt+1 fi                                         14
        in                                                     15
    let pop be                                                 16
        if isempty then empty; 0                               17
        else crt:=!crt - 1;                                    18
             !buffer[!crt] fi                                  19
        in                                                     20
    let invariant be                                           21
        new var x:=m in                                        22
        push(!x); pop = !x                                     23
        in                                                     24
    VERIFY(push(m), pop, assert(invariant))                    25
: com.                                                         26
```

Fig. 5. A stack module

failure of the assertion in this case should have been expected since the stack is finite size.

4   Limitations and Further Research

The initial results of our effort to model and verify programs using Game Semantics are very encouraging: this approach proves to give compact, practicable representations of many common programs, while the ability to model open programs allows us to verify software components, such as ADT implementations.

We are considering several further directions:

Language extensions: the procedural language fragment we are currently handling only includes basic imperative and functional features. We are considering several ways to extend it, and the principal emphasis is on adding concurrency features. A game semantic model for shared-variable parallelism has been recently developed by our group [40]. We are also considering a version of this tool which would handle call-by-value languages.

```
0     1        run
1     2        VERIFY.run
2     3        1.VERIFY.run
3     4        m.q
4     5        m.1
5     6        1.VERIFY.done
6     7        1.VERIFY.run
7     8        m.q
8     9        m.1
9     10       1.VERIFY.done
10    11       3.VERIFY.run
11    12       m.q
12    13       m.0
13    14       overflow.run
14    15       overflow.done
15    16       error.run
16    17       error.done
17    18       3.VERIFY.done
18    19       VERIFY.done
19    20       done
20
```

Fig. 6. Shortest failure trace of stack component

Specifications: in order to truly support compositional verification we intend
to expand the tool to model *specifications* of open programs, rather than
just open programs. A theoretical basis for that is already provided in [12],
which is in turn inspired by the game-like ideas of *interface automata* [38].

Tools and methodology: enriching the features of the tool and making it
more robust and user friendly. For example, the definability result in [3]
guarantees that any trace in the model can be mapped back into a program.
Using this, we can give the user *code* rather than *trace* counterexamples to
failed assertions. We would also like to investigate applying the tool to the
modeling and verification of a larger, more realistic case study.

Scalable model checking: our methods so far apply only to *finite* data and
store. Verifying a program operating on finite data and store is an excellent
method for bug detection and provides a fairly high measure of confidence
in the correctness of the code, but it does not represent a *proof*. There is, in
general, no guarantee that the properties of a program of given size generalize. But we hope that recent results in *data independence* [41,42] can help
overcome such limitations.

We are actively engaged in investigating the above topics, and we are grateful to
the Engineering and Physical Sciences Research Council of the United Kingdom
for financial support in the form of the research grant *Algorithmic Game Se-*

mantics and its Applications; there is also a related project on *Scalable Software Model Checking based on Game Semantics* by Ranko Lazic of the University of Warwick.

References

1. Abramsky, S., Jagadeesan, R., Malacaria, P.: Full abstraction for PCF. Information and Computation **163** (2000)
2. Hyland, J.M.E., Ong, C.H.L.: On full abstraction for PCF: I, II and III. Information and Computation **163** (2000)
3. Abramsky, S., McCusker, G.: Linearity, sharing and state: a fully abstract game semantics for Idealized Algol with active expressions. In: Proc. of 1996 Workshop on Linear Logic. ENTCS **3**, Elsevier (1996) Also [22, Chap. 20].
4. Abramsky, S., McCusker, G.: Full abstraction for Idealized Algol with passive expressions. Theoretical Computer Science **227** (1999) 3–42
5. Abramsky, S., Honda, K., McCusker, G.: A fully abstract game semantics for general references. In: Proc. of LICS'98 (1998)
6. Laird, J.: Full abstraction for functional languages with control. In: Proc. of LICS'97 (1997) 58–67
7. Hankin, C., Malacaria, P.: Generalised flowcharts and games. LNCS **1443** (1998)
8. Hankin, C., Malacaria, P.: Non-deterministic games and program analysis: an application to security. In: Proc. of LICS'99 (1999) 443–452
9. Ghica, D.R., McCusker, G.: Reasoning about Idealized ALGOL using regular languages. In: Proc. of 27th ICALP. LNCS **1853**, Springer-Verlag (2000)
10. Ghica, D.R.: Regular language semantics for a call-by-value programming language. In: 17th MFPS. ENTCS **45**, Aarhus, Denmark, Elsevier (2001) 85–98
11. Ghica, D.R.: A regular-language model for Hoare-style correctness statements. In: Proc. of the Verification and Computational Logic 2001, Florence, Italy (2001)
12. Ghica, D.R.: A Games-based Foundation for Compositional Software Model Checking. PhD thesis, Queen's University School of Computing, Kingston, Ontario, Canada (2002)
13. Clarke, E.M., Grumberg, O., Peled, D.A.: Model Checking. The MIT Press, Cambridge, Massachusetts (1999)
14. Schmidt, D.A.: On the need for a popular formal semantics. ACM SIGPLAN Notices **32** (1997) 115–116
15. Dill, D.L.: The Murϕ verfication system. In: Proc. of CAV'96. LNCS **1102**, Springer-Verlag (1996) 390–393
16. Holzmann, G.J., Peled, D.A.: The state of SPIN. In: Proc. of CAV'96. LNCS **1102**, Springer-Verlag (1996) 385–389
17. Alur, R., Henzinger, T.A., Mang, F.Y.C., Qadeer, S.: MOCHA: Modularity in model checking. In: Proc. of CAV'98, Springer-Verlag (1998) 521–525
18. Henzinger, T.A., Jhala, R., Majumdar, R., Sutre, G.: Lazy abstraction. In: Proc. of 29th POPL, ACM Press (2002) pp. 58–70
19. Ball, T., Rajamani, S.K.: The SLAM toolkit. In: Proc. of CAV'01. (2001) 260–275
20. Corbett, J.C., Dwyer, M.B., Hatcliff, J., Laubach, S., Păsăreanu, C.S., Zheng, H.: Bandera. In: Proc. of the 22nd International Conference on Software Engineering, ACM Press (2000) 439–448

21. Reynolds, J.C.: The essence of ALGOL. In de Bakker, J.W., van Vliet, J.C., eds.: Algorithmic Languages, Proc. of the International Symposium on Algorithmic Languages, Amsterdam, North-Holland, Amsterdam (1981) 345–372 Also [22, Chap. 3].
22. O'Hearn, P.W., Tennent, R.D., eds.: ALGOL-like Languages. Progress in Theoretical Computer Science. Birkhäuser, Boston (1997) Two volumes.
23. Abramsky, S.: Algorithmic game semantics: A tutorial introduction. Lecture notes, Marktoberdorf International Summer School 2001. (2001)
24. Hopcroft, J.E., Ullman, J.D.: Introduction to Automata Theory, Languages, and Computation. Addidon Wesley (1979)
25. Reape, M., Thompson, H.S.: Parallel intersection and serial composition of finite state transducers. COLING-88 (1988) 535–539
26. Ong, C.H.L.: Observational equivalence of third-order Idealized Algol is decidable. In: Proc. of LICS'02. (2002) 245–256
27. Ghica, D.R., McCusker, G.: The regular-language semantics of first-order Idealized ALGOL. Theoretical Computer Science (to appear)
28. Murawski, A.S.: Variable scope and call-by-value program equivalence. in preparation (2003)
29. Senizergues: L(A) = L(B)? decidability results from complete formal systems. TCS: Theoretical Computer Science **251** (2001)
30. Stirling, C.: Deciding DPDA equivalence is primitive recursive. LNCS **2380** (2002) 821–865
31. Murawski, A.S.: On program equivalence in languages with ground-type references. In: Proc. of LICS'03, IEEE Computer Society Press (2003)
32. Murawski, A.S.: Complexity of first-order call-by-name program equivalence. submitted for publication (2003)
33. — AT&T FSM Library^{tm} – general-purpose finite-state machine software tools http://www.research.att.com/sw/tools/fsm/.
34. Ghica, D.R.: Game-based software model checking: Case studies and methodological considerations. Technical Report PRG-RR-03-11, Oxford University Computing Laboratory (2003)
35. Hatcliff, J., Dwyer, M.B., Zheng, H.: Slicing software for model construction. Higher-Order and Symbolic Computation **13** (2000) 315–353
36. Manna, Z., Pnueli, A.: A hierarchy of temporal properties. In Dwork, C., ed.: Proc. of the 9th Annual ACM Symposium on Principles of Distributed Computing, Québec City, Québec, Canada, ACM Press (1990) 377–408
37. Colby, C., Godefroid, P., Jagadeesan, L.: Automatically closing open reactive programs. In: Proc. of PLDI'98, Montreal, Canada (1998) 345–357
38. de Alfaro, L., Henzinger, T.A.: Interface automata. In Gruhn, V., ed.: Proc. of the 9th ESEC/FSE-01. Software Engineering Notes **26, 5**, New York, ACM Press (2001) 109–120
39. Alur, R., Henzinger, T.A., Kupferman, O.: Alternating-time temporal logic. J. of the ACM **49** (2002) 672–713
40. Ghica, D.R., Murawski, A.S.: Angelic semantics of fine-grained concurrency. In Proc. of FOSSACS'04 (2004) To appear.
41. Lazic, R.S.: A Semantic Study of Data Independence with Applications to Model Checking. PhD thesis, University of Oxford (1999)
42. Lazic, R., Nowak, D.: A unifying approach to data-independence. LNCS **1877** (2000)

Solving Disjunctive/Conjunctive Boolean Equation Systems with Alternating Fixed Points

Jan Friso Groote[2,3] and Misa Keinänen[1,3]

[1] Dept. of Computer Science and Engineering, Lab. for Theoretical Comp. Science
Helsinki University of Technology, P.O. Box 5400, FIN-02015 HUT, Finland
`Misa.Keinanen@hut.fi`
[2] Departement of Mathematics and Computer Science, Eindhoven University
of Technology, P.O. Box 513, 5600 MB Eindhoven, The Netherlands
[3] CWI, P.O. Box 94079, 1090 GB Amsterdam, The Netherlands `J.F.Groote@tue.nl`,

Abstract. This paper presents a technique for the resolution of alternating disjunctive/conjunctive boolean equation systems. The technique can be used to solve various verification problems on finite-state concurrent systems, by encoding the problems as boolean equation systems and determining their local solutions. The main contribution of this paper is that a recent resolution technique from [13] for disjunctive/conjunctive boolean equation systems is extended to the more general disjunctive/conjunctive forms with alternation. Our technique has the time complexity $O(m + n^2)$, where m is the number of alternation free variables occurring in the equation system and n the number of alternating variables. We found that many μ-calculus formulas with alternating fixed points occurring in the literature can be encoded as boolean equation systems of disjunctive/conjunctive forms. Practical experiments show that we can verify alternating formulas on state spaces that are orders of magnitudes larger than reported up till now.

1 Introduction

Modal μ-calculus [10] is an expressive logic for system verification, and most model checking logics can be encoded in the μ-calculus. Many important features of system models, like equivalence/preorder relations and fairness constraints, can be expressed with the logic, also. For these reasons, μ-calculus is a logic widely studied in the recent systems verification literature.

It is well-known that the μ-calculus model checking problem is in the complexity class NP ∩ co-NP. Emerson, Jutla, and Sistla [7,8] showed the problem can be reduced to determining the winner in a parity game, and thus is in NP (and also by symmetry in co-NP). More recently, Jurdzinsky [9] showed that the problem is even in UP ∩ co-UP. Yet the complexity of μ-calculus model checking problem for the unrestricted logic is an open problem; no polynomial algorithm has been discovered.

Nevertheless, various effective model checking algorithms exist for expressive subsets. Arnold and Crubille [2] presented an algorithm for checking alternation depth 1 formulas of μ-calculus, which is linear in the size of the model and

K. Jensen and A. Podelski (Eds.): TACAS 2004, LNCS 2988, pp. 436–450, 2004.
© Springer-Verlag Berlin Heidelberg 2004

quadratic in the size of the formula. Cleaveland and Steffen [6] improved the result by making the algorithm linear also in the size of the formula. Andersen [1], and similarly Vergauwen and Lewi [16], showed how model checking alternation depth 1 formulas amounts to the evaluation of *boolean graphs*, resulting also in linear time techniques for model checking alternation depth 1 formulas. Even more expressive subsets of μ-calculus were investigated by Bhat and Cleaveland [5] as well as Emerson et al. [7,8]. They presented polynomial time model checking algorithms for fragments L1 and L2, which may contain alternating fixed point formulas.

In this paper, instead of treating μ-calculus expressions together with their semantics, we prefer to work with the more flexible formalism of boolean equation systems [1,12,13,17]. Boolean equation systems provide a useful framework for studying verification problems of finite-state concurrent systems, because μ-calculus expressions can easily be translated into this simple formalism (see e.g. [3,12,13] for such translations).

We restrict the attention to boolean equation systems, which are either in disjunctive or in conjunctive form. We found that many practically relevant μ-calculus formulas (actually virtually all of them) can be encoded as boolean equation systems that are disjunctive, conjunctive, or disjunctive/conjunctive straight (see definition 3). For instance, the model checking problems for Hennessy-Milner logic (HML), Computation Tree Logic (CTL), and many equivalence/preorder checking problems result in alternation-free boolean equation systems in disjunctive/conjunctive forms (see for instance [13]). Moreover, encoding the L1 and L2 fragments of the μ-calculus (and similar subsets) or many fairness constraints as boolean equation systems result in alternating systems which are in disjunctive/conjunctive form.

Hence, the problem of solving disjunctive/conjunctive boolean equation systems with alternating fixed points is so important that developing special purpose solution techniques for these classes is worthwhile. Recently, the question has been addressed by Mateescu [13], who presented a resolution algorithm for disjunctive/conjunctive boolean equation systems. But, this approach is restricted to alternation-free systems. We are only aware of one sketch of an algorithm that is directed to alternating disjunctive/conjunctive boolean equation systems (proposition 6.5 and 6.6 of [12]). Here a $O(n^3)$ time and $O(n^2)$ space algorithm is provided where n is the number of variables[1]. Our algorithm is a substantial improvement over this.

In this paper, we address the problem of solving alternating disjunctive/conjunctive straight boolean equation systems. The algorithm for the resolution of such equation systems is quite straightforward comparable to the alternation-free case presented in [13]. Essentially, the idea consists of computing simple kinds of dependencies between certain variables occurring in the equation sys-

---

[1] The paper [12] claims an $O(n^2)$ time algorithm, assuming the existence of an algorithm which allows union of (large) sets, and finding and deletion of elements in these in constant time. To our knowledge for this only a linear and most certainly no constant time algorithm exists.

tems. Our technique is such that it ensures linear-time worst case complexity of solving alternation-free boolean equation systems, and quadratic for the alternating systems. More precisely, we present resolution algorithms for the disjunctive/conjunctive classes which are of complexity $O(m + n^2)$, where m is the number of alternation-free variables and n the number of alternating variables occurring in the system. Hence, our approach preserves the best known worst case time complexity of model checking of many restricted but expressive fragments of the μ-calculus.

The paper is organized as follows. Section 2 introduces basic notions concerning boolean equation systems. Section 3 introduces the subclasses of disjunctive, conjunctive and disjunctive/conjunctive straight boolean equation systems and illustrates that many formulas with alternating fixed points fall into these classes. Section 4 presents the algorithm and section 5 provides some initial experimental results. In section 6 we wrap up and provide an open problem that we were unable to solve, but which – if solved – would eliminate the quadratic factor in the time complexity of our algorithm.

2   Boolean Equation Systems

We give here a short introduction into boolean equation systems. A boolean equation system is an ordered sequence of fixed point equations like

$$(\sigma_1 x_1 = \alpha_1)(\sigma_2 x_2 = \alpha_2) \ldots (\sigma_n x_n = \alpha_n)$$

where all x_i are different. We generally use the letter $\mathcal{E}$ to represent a boolean equation system, and let ϵ stand for the empty boolean equation system. The symbol σ_i specifies the polarity of the fixed points. The symbol σ_i is μ if the i-th equation is a least fixed point equation and ν if it is a greatest fixed point equation. The order of equations in a boolean equation system is very important, and we keep the order on variables and their indices in strict synchrony. We write $\mathcal{X} = \{x_1, x_2, \ldots, x_n\}$ for the set of all boolean variables. For each $1 \leq i \leq n$ we allow α_i to be a formula over boolean variables and constants *false* and *true* and operators $\wedge$ and $\vee$, summarized by the grammar:

$$\alpha ::= \quad true \mid false \mid x \in \mathcal{X} \mid \alpha_1 \wedge \alpha_2 \mid \alpha_1 \vee \alpha_2.$$

We write $x_i \in \alpha_j$ if x_i is a subterm of α_j.

The semantics of boolean equation systems provides a uniquely determined *solution*, to each boolean equation system $\mathcal{E}$. A solution is a valuation assigning a constant value in $\{0, 1\}$ (with 0 standing for *false* and 1 for *true*) to all variables occurring in $\mathcal{E}$. Let $v, v_1, \ldots$ range over valuations, where each v is a function $v : \mathcal{X} \to \{0, 1\}$. We extend the definition of valuations to terms in the standard way. So, $v(\alpha)$ is the value of the term α after substituting each free variable x in α by $v(x)$. Let $v[x:=a]$ denote the valuation that coincides with v for all variables except x, which has the value a. We suppose that $[x:=a]$ has priority over all operations and $v[x:=a]$ stands for $(v[x:=a])$. Similarly, we apply $[x:=a]$ to terms;

$\alpha[x:=a]$ indicates the term α where all occurrences of x have been replaced by a.

Definition 1 (The solution of a boolean equation system). *The solution of a boolean equation system $\mathcal{E}$ relative to a valuation v, denoted by $[\![\mathcal{E}]\!]v$, is an assignment inductively defined by*

$$[\![\epsilon]\!]v = v$$
$$[\![(\sigma_i x_i = \alpha_i)\mathcal{E}]\!]v = \begin{cases} [\![\mathcal{E}]\!]v[x_i:=\mu x_i.\alpha_i([\![\mathcal{E}]\!]v)] & \text{if } \sigma_i = \mu \\ [\![\mathcal{E}]\!]v[x_i:=\nu x_i.\alpha_i([\![\mathcal{E}]\!]v)] & \text{if } \sigma_i = \nu \end{cases}$$

where $\mu x_i.\alpha([\![\mathcal{E}]\!]v) = \bigwedge\{a | \alpha_i([\![\mathcal{E}]\!]v[x:=a]) \Rightarrow a\}$ *and* $\nu x_i.\alpha([\![\mathcal{E}]\!]v) = \bigvee\{a | a \Rightarrow \alpha_i([\![\mathcal{E}]\!]v[x:=a])\}$.

It is said that a variable x_i *depends on* variable x_j, if α_i contains a reference to x_j, or to a variable x_k such that x_k depends on x_j. Two variables x_i and x_j are mutually dependent if x_i depends on x_j and vice versa.

A boolean equation system $\mathcal{E}$ is *alternation free* if, for any two variables x_i and x_j occurring in $\mathcal{E}$, x_i and x_j are mutually dependent implies $\sigma_i = \sigma_j$. Otherwise, system $\mathcal{E}$ is said to be *alternating* and it contains *alternating fixed points*.

Example 1. Let $\mathcal{X}$ be the set $\{x_1, x_2, x_3\}$ and assume we are given a boolean equation system

$$\mathcal{E}_1 \equiv ((\mu x_1 = x_1 \wedge x_2)(\mu x_2 = x_1 \vee x_2)(\nu x_3 = x_2 \wedge x_3)).$$

The system $\mathcal{E}_1$ is alternation-free, because it does not contain mutually dependent variables with different signs. Yet, note that variable x_3 with sign $\sigma_3 = \nu$ depends on variables x_1 and x_2 with different sign. A solution of $\mathcal{E}_1$ is given by the valuation $v : \mathcal{X} \to \{0, 1\}$ defined by $v(x_i) = 0$ for $i = 1, 2, 3$.

Example 2. Let $\mathcal{X}$ be the set $\{x_1, x_2, x_3\}$ and assume we are given a boolean equation system

$$\mathcal{E}_2 \equiv ((\nu x_1 = x_2 \wedge x_1)(\mu x_2 = x_1 \wedge x_3)(\nu x_3 = x_3 \vee true)).$$

The system $\mathcal{E}_2$ is alternating, because it contains mutually dependent variables with different signs, like x_1 and x_2 with $\sigma_1 \neq \sigma_2$. A solution of $\mathcal{E}_2$ is given by the valuation $v : \mathcal{X} \to \{0, 1\}$ defined by $v(x_i) = 1$ for $i = 1, 2, 3$.

In Mader [12] there are two lemmas that allow to solve boolean equation systems. As our proofs are based on these, we restate these here.

Lemma 1 (Lemma 6.2 of [12]). *Let $\mathcal{E}_1$ and $\mathcal{E}_2$ be boolean equation systems and let $\sigma x = \alpha$ and $\sigma x = \alpha'$ be boolean equations where*

$$\alpha' = \begin{cases} \alpha[x:=true] & \text{if } \sigma = \nu, \\ \alpha[x:=false] & \text{if } \sigma = \mu. \end{cases}$$

Then $[\![\mathcal{E}_1(\sigma x = \alpha)\mathcal{E}_2]\!]v = [\![\mathcal{E}_1(\sigma x = \alpha')\mathcal{E}_2]\!]v$.

Lemma 2 (Lemma 6.3 of [12]). *Let $\mathcal{E}_1$, $\mathcal{E}_2$ and $\mathcal{E}_3$ be boolean equation systems and let $\sigma_1 x_1 = \alpha$, $\sigma_1 x_1 = \alpha'$ and $\sigma_2 x_2 = \beta$ be boolean equations where $\alpha' = \alpha[x_2{:=}\beta]$. Then*

$$\llbracket \mathcal{E}_1(\sigma_1 x_1 = \alpha)\mathcal{E}_2(\sigma_2 x_2 = \beta)\mathcal{E}_3 \rrbracket v = \llbracket \mathcal{E}_1(\sigma_1 x_1 = \alpha')\mathcal{E}_2(\sigma_2 x_2 = \beta)\mathcal{E}_3 \rrbracket v.$$

3   Disjunctive/Conjunctive Boolean Equation Systems

We introduce disjunctive/conjunctive form boolean equation systems in their most elementary form

Definition 2. *Let $\sigma x = \alpha$ be a fixed point equation. We call this equation disjunctive if no conjunction symbol ($\wedge$) appears in α, and we call it conjunctive if no disjunction ($\vee$) symbol appears in α. Let $\mathcal{E}$ be a boolean equation system. We call $\mathcal{E}$ conjunctive (respectively disjunctive) iff each equation in $\mathcal{E}$ is conjunctive (respectively disjunctive).*

But our algorithm applies to a much wider class of equation systems, namely those where the conjunction and disjunction symbol are not used in a nested way

Definition 3. *Let $\mathcal{E}$ be a boolean equation system. We call $\mathcal{E}$ disjunction/conjunction straight (DCS) iff for all variables x_i and x_j in $\mathcal{E}$ that are mutually dependent, the equations $\sigma_i x_i = \alpha_i$ and $\sigma_j x_j = \alpha_j$ in $\mathcal{E}$ are both conjunctive or both disjunctive.*

Observation I. The problem of solving disjunction/conjunctive straight boolean equation systems can be reduced to iteratively dealing with disjuntive or conjuntive boolean equation systems as follows. In a DCS boolean equation system the variables can be partitioned in blocks such that variables that mutually depend on each other belong to the same block. The dependency relation among variables can be extended to blocks in the sense that block B_i depends on block B_j if some variable $x_i \in B_i$ depends on some variable $x_j \in B_j$. This dependency relation is an ordering. We can start to find solutions for the variables in the last block, setting them to *true* or *false*. Using lemma 2 we can substitute the solutions for variables in blocks higher up in the ordering.

The following simplification rules can be used to simplify the equations

- $(\phi \wedge true) \mapsto \phi$
- $(\phi \wedge false) \mapsto false$
- $(\phi \vee true) \mapsto true$
- $(\phi \vee false) \mapsto \phi$

and the resulting equation system has the same solution. The rules allow to remove each occurrence of *true* and *false* in the right hand side of equations, except if the right hand side becomes equal to *true* or *false*, in which case yet another equation has been solved. By recursively applying these steps all non trivial occurrences of *true* and *false* can be removed from the equations and we call the resulting equations *purely disjunctive* or *purely conjunctive*.

Note that each substitution and simplification step reduces the number of occurrences of variables or the size of a right hand side, and therefore, only a linear number of such reductions are applicable.

After solving all equations in a block, and simplifying subsequent blocks the algorithm can be applied to the blocks higher up in the ordering iteratively solving them all.

Note that this allows us to restrict our attention to algorithms to solve purely disjunctive/conjunctive straight systems.

Example 3. Consider the boolean equation system $\mathcal{E}_2$ of example 2. The system $\mathcal{E}_2$ is not in conjunctive form. An equivalent conjunctive equation system $\mathcal{E}_3$ is obtained by replacing α_3 of $\mathcal{E}_2$ with *true* and propagating $x_3 = true$ throughout the formula using lemma 2. This results in the following sequence

$$\mathcal{E}_3 = ((\nu x_1 = x_2 \wedge x_1)(\mu x_2 = x_1)(\nu x_3 = true))$$

within which no disjunctions occur in right-hand sides of equations.

Observation II. We found that many formulas with apparently alternating fixed points lead to boolean equation systems that are disjunction/conjunction straight and therefore can be solved efficiently with our techniques.

Consider for instance the examples in section 3.5 in [4]. All formulas applied to any labelled transition systems yield disjunction/conjunction straight boolean equation systems, except for the modal formula

$$\mu Y.\nu Z.(P \wedge [a]Y) \vee (\neg P \wedge [a]Z).$$

But this formula is equivalent to the formula

$$\mu Y.(([a]Y \vee \nu Z.(\neg P \wedge [a]Z))).$$

which does lead to DCS equation systems.

As an illustration we explain the transformation of the last formula in the example section of [4]:

$$\nu X.\mu Y.\nu Z.[a]X \wedge (\langle a \rangle true \Rightarrow [-a]Y) \wedge [-a]Z.$$

If we consider a labeled transition system $M = (S, A, \longrightarrow)$ then the boolean equation system looks like:

$$\left.\begin{array}{l} \nu\, x_s = y_s \\ \mu\, y_s = z_s \\ \nu\, z_s = \bigwedge\limits_{s' \in \nabla(a,s)} x_{s'} \wedge (\bigwedge\limits_{s' \in \nabla(a,s)} false \vee \bigwedge\limits_{s' \in \nabla(\neg a,s)} y_{s'}) \wedge \bigwedge\limits_{s' \in \nabla(\neg a,s)} z_{s'} \end{array}\right\} \text{ for all } s \in S.$$

Here, $\nabla(a, s) := \{s' | s \xrightarrow{a} s'\}$ and $\nabla(\neg a, s) := \{s' | s \xrightarrow{b} s'$ and $b \neq a\}$. On first sight these equations do not appear to be a conjunctive boolean equation system, as in the third group of equations a disjunction occurs. However, for each concrete labelled transition system the left side of this disjunction will either become true or false for each state $s \in S$. By applying the simplification rules the formula quickly becomes conjunctive.

4   The Algorithm

We develop our resolution algorithm in terms of a *variable dependency graph* similar to those of *boolean graphs* [1], which provide a representation of the dependencies between variables occurring in equation systems.

Definition 4 (Variable dependency graph). *Let* $\mathcal{E} = ((\sigma_1 x_1 = \alpha_1)(\sigma_2 x_2 = \alpha_2) \ldots (\sigma_n x_n = \alpha_n))$ *be a disjunctive/conjunctive boolean equation system. The dependency graph of* $\mathcal{E}$ *is a triple* $G_{\mathcal{E}} = (V, E, L)$ *where*

- $V = \{i \mid 1 \leq i \leq n\} \cup \{\bot, \top\}$ *is the set of nodes*
- $E \subseteq V \times V$ *is the set of edges such that for all equations* $\sigma_i\, x_i = \alpha_i$
  - $(i, j) \in E$, *if a variable* $x_j \in \alpha_i$
  - $(i, \bot) \in E$, *if false occurs in* α_i
  - $(i, \top) \in E$, *if true occurs in* α_i
  - $(\bot, \bot), (\top, \top) \in E$
- $L : V \rightarrow \{\mu, \nu\}$ *is the node labeling defined by* $L(i) = \sigma_i$ *for* $1 \leq i \leq n$, $L(\bot) = \mu$, *and* $L(\top) = \nu$.

Observe that in the definition above the sink nodes with self-loops, $\bot$ and $\top$, represent the constants *false* and *true*. The ordering on nodes (given by their sequence number) is extended to $\bot$ and $\top$ by putting them highest in the ordering.

The key idea of our technique is based on the following observation that to obtain local solutions of variables in disjunctive/conjunctive equation systems, it suffices to compute the existence of a cycle in the dependency graph with certain properties.

Lemma 3. *Let* $G_{\mathcal{E}} = (V, E, L)$ *be the dependency graph of a disjunctive (respectively conjunctive) boolean equation system* $\mathcal{E}$. *Let* x_i *be any variable in* $\mathcal{E}$ *and let valuation* v *be the solution of* $\mathcal{E}$. *Then the following are equivalent:*

1. $v(x_i) = 1$ *(respectively* $v(x_i) = 0$)
2. $\exists j \in V$ *with* $L(j) = \nu$ *(respectively* $L(j) = \mu$) *such that:*
   a) *j is reachable from i, and*
   b) $G_{\mathcal{E}}$ *contains a cycle of which the lowest index of a node on this cycle is* j.

Proof. We only prove this lemma for disjunctive boolean equation systems. The case for conjunctive equation systems is dual and goes in the same way. First we show that (2) implies (1). If j lies on a cycle with all nodes with numbers larger than j, there are two possibilities. Either j equals $\top$ or $1 \leq j \leq n$. In the last case, there is a sub-equation system of $\mathcal{E}$ that looks as follows:

$$\nu x_j \quad = \alpha_j$$
$$\vdots$$
$$\sigma_{k_1} y_{k_1} = \alpha_{k_1}$$
$$\sigma_{k_2} y_{k_2} = \alpha_{k_2}$$
$$\vdots$$
$$\sigma_{k_n} y_{k_n} = \alpha_{k_n}$$

where $x_j \in \alpha_j[y_{k_1} := \alpha_{k_1}][y_{k_2} := \alpha_{k_2}][y_{k_3} := \alpha_{k_3}] \ldots [y_n := \alpha_{k_n}]$. Using lemma 2 we can rewrite the boolean equation system $\mathcal{E}$ to an equivalent one by replacing the equation $\nu x_j = \alpha_j$ by:

$$\nu x_j = \alpha_j[y_{k_1} := \alpha_{k_1}][y_{k_2} := \alpha_{k_2}][y_{k_3} := \alpha_{k_3}] \ldots [y_n := \alpha_{k_n}].$$

Now note that the right hand side contains only disjunctions and the variable x_j at least once. Hence, by lemma 2 the equation reduces to

$$\nu x_j = true.$$

Now, as x_j is reachable from x_i, the equation $\sigma_i x_i = \alpha_i$ can similarly be replaced by $\sigma_i x_i = true$. Hence, for any solution v of $\mathcal{E}$, it holds that $v(x_i) = 1$. In case j equals $\top$, the term $true$ is reachable from x_i. In a similar way using lemma 2 we can replace $\sigma_i x_i = \alpha_i$ by $\sigma_i x_i = true$.

Now we prove that (1) implies (2) by contraposition. So, assume that there is no j with $L(j) = v$ that is reachable from i such that j is on a cycle with only higher numbered nodes.

We prove with induction on $n - k$ that $\mathcal{E}$ is equivalent to the same boolean equation system where equations $\sigma_{k+1} x_{k+1} = \alpha_{k+1}, \ldots, \sigma_n x_n = \alpha_n$ that are reachable from x_i, have been replaced by $\sigma_{k+1} x_{k+1} = \beta_{k+1}, \ldots, \sigma_n x_n = \beta_n$ where all β_l are disjunctions of $false$ and variables that stem from $x_1, \ldots, x_k$. If the inductive proof is finished, the lemma is also proven: consider the case where $n - k = n$. This says that $\mathcal{E}$ is equivalent to a boolean equation system where all right hand sides of equations reachable from x_i are equal to $false$. So, in particular $x_i = false$, or in other words, for every solution v of $\mathcal{E}$ it holds that $v(x_i) = 0$.

For $n - k = 0$ the induction hypothesis obviously holds. In particular $true$ cannot occur in the right hand side of any equation reachable from x_i. So, consider some $n - k$ for which the induction hypothesis holds. We show that it also holds for $n - k + 1$. So, we must show if equation $\sigma_k x_k = \alpha_k$ is reachable from x_i, it can be replaced by an equation $\sigma_k x_k = \beta_k$ where in β_k only variables chosen from $x_1, \ldots, x_{k-1}$ and $false$ can occur.

As x_k is reachable from x_i, all variables x_l occuring in α_k are also reachable from x_i. By the induction hypothesis the equations $\sigma_l x_l = \alpha_l$ for $l > k$ have been replaced by $\sigma_l x_l = \beta_l$ where in β_l only $false$ and variables from $x_1, \ldots, x_k$

occur. Using lemma 2 such variables x_l can be replaced by β_l and hence, α_k is replaced by γ_k in which *false* and variables from $x_1, \ldots, x_k$ can occur.

What remains to be done is to remove x_k from γ_k assuming $x_k \in \gamma_k$. This can be done as follows. Suppose σ_k equals ν, then, as x_k occurs in γ_k, there must be a path in the dependency graph to a node $x_{l'}$ with $l' > k$ such that $x_k \in \alpha_{l'}$. But this means that the dependency graph has a cycle on which k is the lowest value. This contradicts the assumption. So, it cannot be that $\sigma_k = \nu$, so, $\sigma_k = \mu$. Now using lemma 1 the variable x_k in α_k can be replaced by *false* and subsequently be eliminated. This finalizes the induction step of the proof. $\square$

Now consider a disjunctive/conjunctive straight boolean equation system $\mathcal{E}$. In order to find a solution for $\mathcal{E}$ we first partition the set of variables $\mathcal{X}$ into blocks such that variables are in the same block iff these are mutually dependent. As $\mathcal{E}$ is disjunctive/conjunctive straight, all variables in each block have defining equations that are either disjunctive or conjunctive. Using the well known algorithm [15] for the detection of strongly connected components, the partition can be constructed in linear time on the basis of the variable dependency graph. As argued earlier, the equations belonging to the variables in each block can be solved iteratively. If the variables in a block do not depend on unsolved variables, the equations in this block can be solved. So, we only have to concentrate on solving disjunctive or conjunctive equations belonging to variables in a single block.

So, we present here an algorithm to solve a disjunctive boolean equation system. The conjunctive case is dual and goes along exactly the same lines. Our algorithm is an extension of Tarjan's [15] algorithm to detect strongly connected components. It is given in figure 1 and explained below.

We assume that the boolean equation system has already been transformed into a variable dependency graph $G = (V, E, L)$. There are two main functions *solve* and *find*. The function *solve* takes the index i of a variable x_i of interest and solves it by reporting it to be either 0 or 1. The procedure *find*(k) constructs all the strongly connected components from node k and applies lemma 3 to them.

We use a standard adjacency-list representation and keep an array of lists of nodes. We assume that an array *sign* is given that indicates the label for each node. I.e. *sign*$[i] = \nu$ if the label of node i is $L(i) = \nu$, and *sign*$[i] = \mu$ if the label of node i is $L(i) = \mu$.

We keep an integer array *value*, initially set to all zeros, containing numbers indicating the order in which nodes have been visited. If *value*$[i] = 0$, this indicates that node i has not yet been visited. In addition, we keep a stack of integers, *stack*, represented as an array of size $|V|$ with a stack pointer p initially set to zero. We have integers *id* (initially zero), *min*, and *m* for the detection of SCCs, which occur in a similar vein in the algorithm for the detection of SCCs in [15]. The variable *id* is used to number the nodes with consecutive numbers in the sequence they are visited by the algorithm. The variable *min* refers to an earlier visited node, reachable from node k. If no such node exists, *min* = *value*$[k]$ at the end of the first **for** loop and node k is the root of a strongly connected component that includes all higher numbered nodes residing on the stack. The

```
int find(int k)
    if (sign[k] = ν ∧ adjacency list of k contains k)
        report xᵢ gets value 1; stop;
    id := id + 1;  value[k] := id;
    min := id;
    stack[p] := k;  p := p + 1;
    for (all nodes t in the adjacency list of k) do
        if (value[t] = 0)
            m := find(t);
        else m := value[t];
        if (m < min)
            min := m;
    od
    if (min = value[k])
        mu := false;  nu := false;
        S := ∅;
        while (stack[p] ≠ k) do
            p := p - 1;  n := stack[p];
            if (sign[n] = ν)
                nu := true;
            else mu := true;
            S := S ∪ {n};
        od
        if (|S| > 1 ∧ mu = false)
            report xᵢ gets value 1; stop;
        if (|S| > 1 ∧ mu = true ∧ nu = true)
            for (all nodes j in S with sign[j] = ν) do
                if (cycle(G, S, j) = true) report xᵢ gets value 1; stop;
            od
    return min;


void solve(int i)
    p := 0; id := 0;
    for ( l := 0 to |V| ) do
        value[l] := 0;
    od
    find(i);
    if (xᵢ is not yet reported 1)
        report xᵢ gets value 0;
```

Fig. 1. An algorithm for alternating, disjunctive boolean equation systems.

variable m plays the role of a simple auxiliary store. Finally, we keep also a set S, integer n, and booleans mu and nu for processing the SCCs, explained below.

The procedure *solve* invokes the recursive procedure *find*. The procedure *find* first checks whether the node k being visited is labelled with ν and has a self-loop. If these hold, we have found a node that trivially satisfies conditions (2a) and (2b) of lemma 3, and the solution $v(x_i) = 1$ can be reported and the execution of the algorithm is terminated. Otherwise, *find* pushes the nodes onto a stack, and recursively searches for strongly connected components. If such a component is found (when $min = value[k]$), *find* puts all nodes in the component that reside on the stack in a set S. While doing so, it is checked whether all nodes in the component have the same label. If a label is ν, corresponding to the fixed point operator ν, the variable nu is set to *true*, and if a label is μ, corresponding to polarity μ, the variable mu is set to true. If $mu = false$ on a SCC with more than one node, all nodes have label ν and so, conditions (2a) and (2b) of lemma 3 are trivially satisfied, and solution of x_i can be reported to 1.

If both variables nu and mu are true, the component is alternating. In this case it must be checked whether the SCC contains a cycle of which the smallest numbered node j has label $L(j) = \nu$, according to lemma 3 to justify x_i to be set to 1. This is simply checked by applying a procedure $cycle(G_{\mathcal{E}}, S, j)$ to all nodes $j \in S$ with $sign[j] = \nu$. The procedure *cycle* consists of a simple linear depth first search and is not given in detail here.

Finally, if no node j with $L(j) = \nu$ satisfying conditions (2a) and (2b) of lemma 3 was found, we can report at the end of the procedure *solve* the solution v of $\mathcal{E}$ be such that $v(x_i) = 0$.

We find that the algorithm is correct and works in polynomial time and space.

Theorem 1. *The algorithm for local resolution works correctly on any purely disjunctive/conjunctive system of boolean equations.*

In order to formally estimate the computational costs, denote the set of alternating variables in a system $\mathcal{E}$ with variables in $\mathcal{X}$ by $alt(\mathcal{E})$, and define it as a set $\{x_i \mid x_i \in \mathcal{X}$ and x_i is mutually dependent with some $x_j \in \mathcal{X}$ such that $\sigma_i \neq \sigma_j\}$. The set of alternation free variables is denoted by $af(\mathcal{E})$ and is defined as $af(\mathcal{E}) = \mathcal{X} - alt(\mathcal{E})$. Note that for alternation-free boolean equation systems it holds that $alt(\mathcal{E}) = \emptyset$, because there are no ocurrences of mutually dependent variables with different signs. Then, it is easy to see that:

Theorem 2. *The algorithm for local resolution of disjunctive/conjunctive boolean equation systems requires time $O(af(\mathcal{E}) + alt(\mathcal{E})^2)$ and space $O(|\mathcal{E}|)$.*

5   Some Experiments

In this section, we describe an implementation of the resolution algorithm presented in the previous section. This prototype solver for alternating disjunctive/conjunctive boolean equation systems is implemented in C. To give an

impression of the performance, we report experimental results on solving two
verification problems using the tool.

As benchmarks we used two sets of μ-calculus model checking problems taken
from [11] and [14], converted to boolean equation systems. We do not take exactly
the same formulas because our algorithm solves these in constant time, which
would not give interesting results. The verification problems consist of checking
μ-calculus formulas of alternation depth 2, on a sequence of regular labelled
transition systems M_k of increasing size (see figure 2).

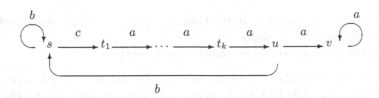

Fig. 2. Process M_k for model checking the properties ϕ_1 and ϕ_2.

Suppose we want to check, at initial state s of process M_k, the property
that transitions labeled b occur infinitely often along every infinite path of the
process. This is expressed with alternating fixed-point formula:

$$\phi_1 \equiv \nu X.\mu Y.([b]X \wedge [-b]Y) \tag{1}$$

The property is false at state s and we use the solver to find a counter-example
for the formula. In second series of examples, we check the property that there is
an execution in M_k starting from state s, where action a occurs infinitely often.
This is expressed with the alternating fixed point formula

$$\phi_2 \equiv \nu X.\mu Y.(\langle a \rangle X \vee \langle -a \rangle Y) \tag{2}$$

which is true at initial state s of the process M_k.

The problems of determining whether the system M_k satisfies the specifications ϕ_1 and ϕ_2 can be directly encoded as problems of solving the corresponding
alternating boolean equation systems, which are in conjunctive and disjunctive
forms. We report the times for the solver to find the local solutions corresponding
to the local model checking problems of the formulas at state s.

The experimental results are given in table 1. The columns are explained
below:

- Problem:
  - the process M_k, with $k + 3$ states
  - ϕ_1 the formula $\nu X.\mu Y.([b]X \wedge [-b]Y)$ to be checked
  - ϕ_2 the formula $\nu X.\mu Y.(\langle a \rangle X \vee \langle \neg a \rangle Y)$ to be checked

Table 1. Summary of execution times.

Problem		n	Time (sec)
$M_{5000000}$	ϕ_1	10 000 006	2.6
	ϕ_2	10 000 006	3.0
$M_{10000000}$	ϕ_1	20 000 006	5.5
	ϕ_2	20 000 006	6.4
$M_{15000000}$	ϕ_1	30 000 006	7.5
	ϕ_2	30 000 006	9.0

- n: the number of equations in the boolean equation system corresponding to the model checking problem
- Time: the time in seconds to find the local solution

The times reported are the time for the solver to find the local solutions measured as system time, on a 2.4Ghz Intel Xeon running linux (i.e. the times for the solver to read the equation systems from disk and build the internal data structure are excluded).

In the problem with the property ϕ_1, the solver found local solutions (and counterexamples) even without executing the quadratic part of the algorithm. In the problem with property ϕ_2, the quadratic computation needed to be performed only on very small portions of the equation systems. These facts are reflected in the performance of the solver, which exhibits linear growth in the execution times with increase in the size of the systems to be verified, in all of the experiments.

The benchmarks in [11] and [14] are essentially the only benchmarks in the literature for alternating boolean equation systems of which we are aware. These benchmarks have a quite simple structure, and therefore we must be careful in drawing general results from them. A more involved practical evaluation is desireable here and benchmarking on real world protocols and systems is left for future work.

6   Discussion and Conclusion

We argued that the verification of many formulas in the modal mu-calculus with alternating fixed points amounts to the verification of disjunctive/conjunctive straight boolean equation systems. Subsequently we provided an algorithm to solve these and showed that the performance of this algorithm on the standard benchmarks from the literature yield an improvement of many orders of magnitude. We believe that this makes the verification of a large class of formulas with alternating fixed points tractable, even for large, practical systems.

The algorithm that we obtain is for the large part linear, but contains an unpleasant quadratic factor. Despite several efforts, we have not been able to eliminate this. In essence this is due to the fact that we were not able to find a sub-quadratic algorithm for the following problem:

Open problem. Given a directed labelled graph $G = (V, E, L)$ of which the set of nodes is totally ordered. The labeling $L : V \to \{0, 1\}$ assigns to each node a value. Determine whether there exist a cycle in G of which the highest node has label 1.

As we believe that this problem has some interest by itself we provide it here.

Acknowledgements. We thank Michel Reniers for commenting a draft of this paper. The work of second author was supported by Academy of Finland (project 53695), Emil Aaltonen foundation and Helsinki Graduate School in Computer Science and Engineering.

References

1. H.R. Andersen. Model checking and boolean graphs. Theoretical Computer Science, 126:3-30, 1994.
2. A. Arnold and P. Crubille. A linear time algorithm to solve fixed-point equations on transition systems. Information Processing Letters, 29:57-66, 1988.
3. A. Arnold and D. Niwinski. Rudiments of μ-calculus. Studies in Logic and the foundations of mathematics. Volume 146, Elsevier, 2001.
4. J. Bradfield and C. Stirling. Modal Logics and mu-Calculi: An introduction. Chapter 4 of Handbook of Process Algebra. J.A. Bergstra, A. Ponse and S.A. Smolka, editors. Elsevier, 2001.
5. G. Bhat and R. Cleaveland. Efficient local model-checking for fragments of the modal μ-calculus. In Proceedings of the Int. Conf. on Tools and Algorithms for the Construction and Analysis of Systems, Lecture Notes in Computer Science 1055, pages 107-126, Springer Verlag 1996.
6. R. Cleaveland and B. Steffen. Computing Behavioural relations logically. In proceedings of the 18 International Colloquium on Automata, Languages and Programming, Lecture Notes Computer Science 510, pages 127-138, Springer Verlag, 1991.
7. E.A. Emerson, C. Jutla and A.P. Sistla. On model checking for fragments of the μ-calculus. In C. Courcoubetis, editor, Fifth Internat. Conf. on Computer Aided Verification, Elounda, Greece, Lecture Notes in Computer Science 697, pages 385-396, Springer Verlag, 1993.
8. E.A. Emerson, C. Jutla, and A.P. Sistla. On model checking for the μ-calculus and its fragments. Theoretical Computer Science 258:491-522, 2001.
9. M. Jurdzinski. Deciding the winner in parity games is in $UP \cap co-UP$. Information Processing Letters, 68:119-124, 1998.
10. D. Kozen. Results on the propositional μ-calculus. Theoretical computer Science 27:333-354, 1983.
11. X. Liu, X, C.R. Ramakrishnan and S.A. Smolka. Fully Local and Efficient Evaluation of Alternating Fixed Points. In B. Steffen, editor, Proceedings of TACAS'98, Lecture Notes in Computer Science 1384, Springer Verlag, 1988.
12. A. Mader. Verification of Modal Properties using Boolean Equation Systems. PhD thesis, Technical University of Munich, 1997.

13. R. Mateescu. A Generic On-the-Fly Solver for Alternation-Free Boolean Equation Systems. Proceedings of the 9th International Conference on Tools and Algorithms for the Construction and Analysis of Systems TACAS'2003 (Warsaw, Poland), volume 2619 of Lecture Notes in Computer Science, pages 81-96. Springer Verlag, April 2003.
14. B. Steffen, A. Classen, M. Klein, J. Knoop and T. Margaria. The fixpoint analysis machine. In I. Lee and S.A. Smolka, editors, Proceedings of the Sixth International Conference on Concurrency Theory (CONCUR '95), Lecture Notes in Computer Science 962, pages 72-87. Springer Verlag, 1995.
15. R. Tarjan. Depth-First Search and Linear Graph Algorithms. SIAM J. Computing, Vol. 1, No. 2, June 1972.
16. B. Vergauwen and J. Lewi. A linear algorithm for solving fixed-point equations on transition systems. In J.-C. Raoult, editor, CAAP'92, Lecture Notes Computer Science 581, pages 321-341, Springer Verlag, 1992.
17. B. Vergauwen and J. Lewi. Efficient Local Correctness Checking for Single and Alternating Boolean Equation Systems. In proc. of ICALP'94.

How Vacuous Is Vacuous?

Arie Gurfinkel and Marsha Chechik

Department of Computer Science, University of Toronto,
Toronto, ON M5S 3G4, Canada.
{arie,chechik}@cs.toronto.edu

Abstract. Model-checking gained wide popularity for analyzing software and hardware systems. However, even when the desired property holds, the property or the model may still require fixing. For example, a property φ: "on all paths, a request is followed by an acknowledgment", may hold because no requests have been generated. *Vacuity detection* has been proposed to address the above problem. This technique is able to determine that the above property φ is *satisfied vacuously* in systems where requests are never sent. Recent work in this area enabled the computation of *interesting witnesses* for the satisfaction of properties (in our case, those that satisfy φ and contain a request) and vacuity detection with respect to subformulas with single and multiple subformula occurrences.

Often, the answer "vacuous" or "not vacuous", provided by existing techniques, is insufficient. Instead, we want to identify all subformulas of a given CTL formula that cause its vacuity, or better, identify all maximal such subformulas. Further, these subformulas may be mutually vacuous. In this paper, we propose a framework for identifying a variety of degrees of vacuity, including mutual vacuity between different subformulas. We also cast vacuity detection as a multi-valued model-checking problem.

1 Introduction

Model-checking gained wide popularity for analyzing software and hardware systems. However, even when the desired property φ holds, the property or the model may still require fixing. Early work on "suspecting a positive answer" addressed the fact that temporal logic formulas can suffer from antecedent failure [2]. For example, the property $p = AG(req \Rightarrow AFack)$ ("on all paths, a request is followed by an acknowledgment") may hold because no requests have been generated, and thus model-checkers should distinguish between *vacuous satisfaction* of φ, in systems where requests are never generated, and non-vacuous satisfaction, in which at least one request is generated.

Industrial experience [3] convinced researchers that vacuous satisfaction of problems presents a serious problem. Based on this experience, Beer et al. [3] proposed the following definition of vacuity: a formula φ is vacuous in a subformula ψ on a given model if ψ does not influence the value of φ on this model. For example, for models where requests are not generated, property p is vacuous in ack. Vacuity detection has been an active area of research [23,24,25,14,1,4]. Work in this area enabled computation of *interesting witnesses* [3] for the satisfaction of properties (for our property p, it is a computation that satisfies it and contains a request), vacuity detection with multiple occurrences of a subformula [1], extensions to different temporal logics [14,23], etc.

K. Jensen and A. Podelski (Eds.): TACAS 2004, LNCS 2988, pp. 451–466, 2004.
© Springer-Verlag Berlin Heidelberg 2004

We feel that vacuity detection should always accompany a model-checking run. If the model-checker does not yield a witness or a counterexample (as is the case in CTL [12] for true universal properties, false existential properties, and all mixed properties), then a vacuity check is essential for accepting the answer, since it can point to a mismatch between the model and the property. Clearly, if vacuity detection can determine not only whether a property φ is vacuous, but also whether it is true or false, then the interesting witness to non-vacuity can be used to inspect either answer. Information about vacuity is useful even in cases when the model-checker *can* generate a counterexample – knowing that a formula is vacuous helps understand the generated evidence or skip it completely (e.g., when vacuity resulted from a typo).

Let us look at checking whether a propositional formula φ is vacuous in a subformula b: (1) b is non-vacuous in b; (2) if φ is non-vacuous in b, then so is $\neg\varphi$; (3) $a \vee b$ is non-vacuous in b if a is false; (4) $a \wedge b$ is vacuous in b if a is false. These examples lead us to constructing the truth table shown in Figure 1(a). That is, to check whether a propositional formula φ is vacuous in b, we can replace b with the value "matters" (M) and evaluate the resulting propositional formula according to the rules of the truth table. If the result is M, then the value of b matters, and φ is non-vacuous in b; otherwise, φ is vacuous, and we know whether it is true or false. For example, the first row of Figure 1(a) specifies that when a is true, then $a \wedge b$ is non-vacuous in b, $a \vee b$ is vacuously true, $\neg a$ is vacuously false, and $\neg b$ is non-vacuous. So, to check whether $(a \wedge \neg b) \vee c$ is vacuous in b when a is true and c is false, we substitute M for b and evaluate the resulting expression: $(\text{true} \wedge \neg M) \vee \text{false} = (\text{true} \wedge M) \vee \text{false} = M \vee \text{false} = M$. Therefore, the formula is non-vacuous in b.

The same idea can be used for checking vacuity of temporal properties. Note that Figure 1(a) is just the truth table for the 3-valued Kleene logic [20]. Thus, simple vacuity detection, or reasoning with the value "matters", is exactly the 3-valued model-checking problem [9,6,19]!

As we show in this paper, a variety of generalizations of the simple vacuity problem can be solved by reducing them to multi-valued model-checking problems [9] over some logic $\mathcal{L}$, where the values of $\mathcal{L}$ are used to keep track of *how* the formula depends on its subformulas. For example, we can determine whether φ is non-vacuous *and* true or non-vacuous *and* false by refining the value "matters" into "non-vacuously true" and "non-vacuously false", resulting in a four-valued logic and thus four-valued model-checking. We also show that witnesses and counterexamples computed by multi-valued model-checking can be used to produce interesting witnesses for arbitrary CTL formulas. We discuss vacuity detection with respect to a single subformula in Section 3, after giving the necessary background in Section 2.

The idea of using multi-valued logic for encoding different degrees of vacuity is also applicable to cases where we want to check vacuity of a formula φ with respect to several subformulas. In those cases, we are interested in determining all maximal subformulas of φ in which it is vacuous, and gracefully deal with multiple occurrences of the same subformula. To solve this problem, we introduce the notion of *mutual vacuity* between different subformulas. We then cast mutual vacuity detection as a multi-valued model-checking problem, where logic values encode different degrees of vacuity, such as "φ is mutually vacuously true in a and b, vacuous in c and d independently, and non-vacuous in e". As in the case of checking vacuity for a single subformula, witnesses and counterexamples provided by multi-valued model-checking give sufficient information

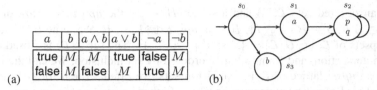

	a	b	$a \wedge b$	$a \vee b$	$\neg a$	$\neg b$
	true	M	M	true	false	M
	false	M	false	M	true	M

(a)

(b)

Fig. 1. (a) Truth table for checking vacuity in b. (b) A simple Kripke structure.

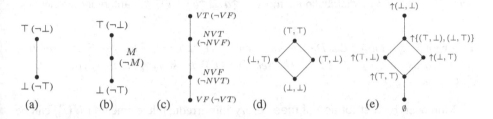

Fig. 2. Examples of De Morgan algebras. $\ell_1(\neg \ell_2)$ means that $\ell_1 = \neg \ell_2$. (a) Classical logic **2**. (b) Kleene logic **3**; (c) A 4-valued algebra **4**; (d) Cross-product 2×2; (e) Upset algebra $U(2 \times 2)$.

to explain the answer given by the vacuity algorithm. Vacuity detection with respect to several subformulas is discussed in Section 4. In Section 5, we address complexity issues, and Section 6 concludes the paper.

2 Background

In this section, we give the necessary background on lattice theory and model-checking.

Lattice Theory. A finite *lattice* is a partial order $(\mathcal{L}, \sqsubseteq)$, where every finite subset $B \subseteq \mathcal{L}$ has a least upper bound (called "join" and written as $\sqcup B$) and a greatest lower bound (called "meet" and written $\sqcap B$). The maximum and the minimum elements of the lattice are denoted by $\top$ and $\bot$, respectively. If $(\mathcal{L}, \sqsubseteq)$ is a lattice and its ordering $\sqsubseteq$ is clear from the context, we refer to it as $\mathcal{L}$. A lattice is *distributive* if meet and join distribute over each other. A lattice is *De Morgan* [5] if it is distributive and there exists a function $\neg : \mathcal{L} \to \mathcal{L}$ such that for all $a, b \in \mathcal{L}$,

$\neg\neg a = a$	involution	$a \sqsubseteq b = \neg a \sqsupseteq \neg b$	anti-monotonicity
$a \sqcap b = \neg(\neg a \sqcup \neg b)$	De Morgan 1	$a \sqcup b = \neg(\neg a \sqcap \neg b)$	De Morgan 2

We refer to a De Morgan lattice $\mathcal{L}$ with a given $\neg$ as De Morgan algebra. Examples of some De Morgan algebras are given in Figure 2. Note that the algebra **2**, corresponding to classical two-valued logic, is a subalgebra of any De Morgan algebra. We often use symbols true and false to denote the top and bottom elements of **2**.

An element j of a lattice $\mathcal{L}$ is *join-irreducible* [13] iff $j \neq \bot$ and for any x and y in $\mathcal{L}$, $j = x \sqcup y$ implies $j = x$ or $j = y$. In other words, j is join-irreducible if it cannot be further decomposed into a join of other elements in the lattice. We denote the set of all join-irreducible elements of a lattice $\mathcal{L}$ by $\mathcal{J}(\mathcal{L})$. Every element ℓ of a finite lattice $\mathcal{L}$ can be uniquely decomposed as a join of all join-irreducible elements below it, i.e. $\ell = \sqcup\{j \in \mathcal{J}(\mathcal{L}) \mid j \sqsubseteq \ell\}$ [13].

Given an ordered set $(\mathcal{L}, \sqsubseteq)$ and a subset $B \subseteq \mathcal{L}$, the *upward closure* of B is $\uparrow B \triangleq \{\ell \in \mathcal{L} \mid \exists b \in B \cdot b \sqsubseteq \ell\}$. B is an *upset* if $\uparrow B = B$. We write $U(\mathcal{L})$ for the set of all upsets of $\mathcal{L}$, i.e. $U(\mathcal{L}) = \{A \subseteq \mathcal{L} \mid \uparrow A = A\}$. The set $U(\mathcal{L})$ is closed under union and intersection, and forms a lattice ordered by set inclusion. We call the lattice $(U(\mathcal{L}), \subseteq)$ an *upset* lattice of $\mathcal{L}$. For singleton sets, we often write a for $\{a\}$, and $\uparrow a$ instead of $\uparrow\{a\}$. Let a, b be elements of a lattice $\mathcal{L}$, then

$$\uparrow a \sqcap \uparrow b = \uparrow(a \sqcup b) \quad \text{distribution of meet} \qquad \uparrow a \sqsupseteq \uparrow b = a \sqsubseteq b \quad \text{anti-monotonicity of } \uparrow$$

Theorem 1. *If a lattice $\mathcal{L}$ is De Morgan, then so is $U(\mathcal{L})$, where for $j \in \mathcal{J}(\mathcal{L})$, negation is defined as $\neg_U \uparrow j \triangleq \mathcal{L} \setminus \downarrow \neg j$. The set $\mathcal{J}(U(\mathcal{L}))$ is isomorphic to $\mathcal{L}$ via $\uparrow : \mathcal{L} \rightarrow \mathcal{J}(U(\mathcal{L}))$.*

Moreover, by **distribution of meet**, every join-irreducible element of $U(\mathcal{L})$ can be uniquely decomposed as a meet of upsets of join-irreducible elements of $\mathcal{L}$.

Theorem 2. *If $\mathcal{L}_1$ and $\mathcal{L}_2$ are De Morgan algebras, then so is their cross-product $\mathcal{L}_1 \times \mathcal{L}_2$ where meet, join and negation are extended point-wise. Furthermore, $\mathcal{J}(\mathcal{L}_1 \times \mathcal{L}_2) = (\mathcal{J}(\mathcal{L}_1) \times \bot) \cup (\bot \times \mathcal{J}(\mathcal{L}_2))$.*

For example, the algebra in Figure 2(d), denoted $\mathbf{2} \times \mathbf{2}$, is a cross-product of two algebras $\mathbf{2}$. Its upset lattice is shown in Figure 2(e). In the rest of this paper, we often use $\wedge$ and $\vee$ for lattice operations $\sqcap$ and $\sqcup$, respectively.

Model Checking. A model is a Kripke structure $K = (S, R, s_0, A, I)$, where S is a finite set of states, $R : S \times S \rightarrow \mathbf{2}$ is a (total) transition relation, $s_0 \in S$ is a designated initial state, A is a set of atomic propositions, and $I : S \times A \rightarrow \mathbf{2}$ is a labeling function, assigning a value to each $a \in A$ in each state. We assume that any subset of $B \subseteq S$ can be represented by a propositional formula over A, i.e. 2^S is isomorphic to $PF(A)$ the set of propositional formulas over A. An example of a Kripke structure is given in Figure 1(b), where $A = \{a, b, p, q\}$. Note that only reachable states are shown, and in each state, only true atomic propositions are shown.

$\mathcal{X}$CTL$(\mathcal{L})$ [9] is an extension of *Computation Tree Logic* (CTL) [12] to De Morgan algebras. Its syntax is defined with respect to a set A of atomic propositions and a De Morgan algebra $\mathcal{L}$:

$$\varphi = \ell \mid p \mid \varphi \vee \varphi \mid \varphi \wedge \varphi \mid \neg\varphi \mid EX\varphi \mid AX\varphi \mid EF\varphi \mid AF\varphi$$
$$\mid EG\varphi \mid AG\varphi \mid E[\varphi \, U \, \varphi] \mid A[\varphi \, U \, \varphi],$$

where $p \in A$ is an atomic proposition and $\ell \in \mathcal{L}$ is a constant. Informally, the meaning of the temporal operators is: given a state and all paths emanating from it, φ holds in one (EX) or all (AX) next states; φ holds in some future state along one (EF) or all (AF) paths; φ holds globally along one (EG) or all (AG) paths, and φ holds until a point where ψ holds along one (EU) or all (AU) paths.

We write $\llbracket \varphi \rrbracket^K(s)$ to indicate the value of φ in the state s of K, and $\llbracket \varphi \rrbracket(s)$ when K is clear from the context. Temporal operators EX, EG, and EU together with the propositional connectives form an adequate set [11] (i.e. all other operators can be defined from them). The formal semantics of $\mathcal{X}$CTL$(\mathcal{L})$ is given in Figure 3. In what follows, we refer to $\mathcal{X}$CTL$(\mathcal{L})$ as multi-valued CTL, and to model-checking problem of $\mathcal{X}$CTL$(\mathcal{L})$

$$
\begin{aligned}
[\![\ell]\!](s) &\triangleq \ell & [\![p]\!](s) &\triangleq I(s,p) \\
[\![\varphi \wedge \psi]\!](s) &\triangleq [\![\varphi]\!](s) \sqcap [\![\psi]\!](s) & [\![\varphi \vee \psi]\!](s) &\triangleq [\![\varphi]\!](s) \sqcup [\![\psi]\!](s) \\
[\![\neg\varphi]\!](s) &\triangleq \neg[\![\varphi]\!](s) & [\![EX\varphi]\!](s) &\triangleq \bigsqcup_{t \in S}(R(s,t) \sqcap [\![\varphi]\!](t)) \\
[\![EG\varphi]\!](s) &\triangleq [\![\nu Z \cdot \varphi \wedge EXZ]\!](s) & [\![E[\varphi U\psi]]\!](s) &\triangleq [\![\mu Z \cdot \psi \vee \varphi \wedge EXZ]\!](s)
\end{aligned}
$$

Fig. 3. Semantics of XCTL($\mathcal{L}$).

as multi-valued model-checking. Note that model-checking of XCTL(2) is exactly the classical CTL model-checking problem.

Multi-valued model-checking is reducible to several classical model-checking problems [17]. Since each element of a lattice can be decomposed using join-irreducible elements, model-checking a XCTL($\mathcal{L}$) formula φ is reduced to solving $[\![\varphi]\!](s) \sqsupseteq j$ for every join-irreducible element of the lattice, and composing the results.

Theorem 3. *[17] For every De Morgan algebra $\mathcal{L}$, every XCTL($\mathcal{L}$) formula φ and a join-irreducible j, there exists a XCTL(2) formula $\varphi \Uparrow j$, called the j-cut of φ, such that $[\![\varphi \Uparrow j]\!] = ([\![\varphi]\!] \sqsupseteq j)$.*

In our case, the formula $\varphi \Uparrow j$ is obtained from φ as follows: (a) for every $\ell \in \mathcal{L}$ that occurs positively in φ, replace it by the value of $\ell \sqsupseteq j$, (b) for every $\ell \in \mathcal{L}$ that occurs negatively in φ, replace it by the value of $\ell \sqsupseteq \sqcup(\mathcal{L} \setminus \downarrow\neg j)$. Furthermore, since every XCTL(2) formula φ is in XCTL($\mathcal{L}$) for any $\mathcal{L}$, a cut of φ is itself ($\varphi \Uparrow j = \varphi$). For example, $(AG((a \wedge M) \Rightarrow AF(q \wedge M)) \Uparrow M$ is $AG((a \wedge \bot) \Rightarrow (AF(q \wedge \top)))$. Theorem 4 shows how to combine the results of the cuts to obtain the solution to the multi-valued model-checking problem.

Theorem 4. *[17] Let $\mathcal{L}$ be a De Morgan algebra and φ be a XCTL($\mathcal{L}$) formula. Then, $[\![\varphi]\!] = \bigsqcup_{j_i \in \mathcal{J}(\mathcal{L})}(j_i \wedge [\![\varphi \Uparrow j_i]\!])$.*

We write $\varphi[\psi]$ to indicate that the formula φ may contain an occurrence of ψ. An occurrence of ψ in $\varphi[\psi]$ is *positive* (or of positive polarity) if it occurs under the scope of even number of negations, and is *negative* otherwise. A subformula ψ is pure in φ if all of its occurrences have the same polarity. We write $\varphi[\psi \leftarrow q]$ for a formula obtained from φ by replacing ψ with q. A formula φ is *universal* (or in ACTL) if all of its temporal operators are universal, and is *existential* (or in ECTL) if all they are existential. In both cases, negation is restricted to the level of atomic propositions.

Quantified CTL (QCTL) is an extension of CTL with quantification over propositional formulas [22]. QCTL extends the syntax of CTL by allowing free variables and universal and existential quantifiers over them to occur in the formula. Let $\varphi[Y]$ be a QCTL formula with a free variable Y. The semantics of universal and existential quantifiers is:

$$
\begin{aligned}
[\![\forall Y \cdot \varphi[Y]]\!](s) &\triangleq \forall p \in PF(A) \cdot [\![\varphi[Y \leftarrow p]]\!](s) \\
[\![\exists Y \cdot \varphi[Y]]\!](s) &\triangleq \exists p \in PF(A) \cdot [\![\varphi[Y \leftarrow p]]\!](s)
\end{aligned}
$$

A QCTL formula $\varphi[X]$ in which X is the only free variable can be seen as a function $\lambda x \cdot \varphi[X \leftarrow x]$ from CTL to CTL. If X is positive in φ, then $\varphi[X]$ is monotonically increasing, i.e. $(p \Rightarrow q) \Rightarrow (\varphi[X \leftarrow p] \Rightarrow \varphi[X \leftarrow q])$; if X is negative, $\varphi[X]$ is monotonically decreasing. Since false and true are the smallest and the largest elements of CTL, respectively, we get the following theorem:

Theorem 5. *Let* $\varphi[X]$ *be a QCTL formula in which all occurrences of X are positive. Then* $(\forall X \cdot \varphi[X]) = \varphi[X \leftarrow \text{false}]$, *and* $(\exists X \cdot \varphi[X]) = \varphi[X \leftarrow \text{true}]$.

Vacuity. We define vacuity of a CTL formula φ using quantified CTL as suggested in [1].

Definition 1. *[1] A formula φ is vacuously* true *in ψ at state s iff* $[\![\forall Y \cdot \varphi[\psi \leftarrow Y]]\!](s)$, *it is vacuously* false *iff* $[\![\neg \exists Y \cdot \varphi[\psi \leftarrow Y]]\!](s)$. *A formula φ is vacuous if it contains a subformula ψ such that φ is vacuous in ψ.*

Note that according to our definition, if ψ is not a subformula of φ, then φ is trivially vacuous in ψ. In this paper, we do not consider vacuity with respect to a subformula that occurs both positively and negatively; instead, we treat the two occurrences as independent subformulas. Under this assumption, all definitions given in [1], including Definition 1, referred to by the authors as *structure vacuity*, are equivalent.

3   Vacuity in a Single Subformula

In this section, we look at checking whether a formula φ is vacuous with respect to a single subformula ψ.

3.1   Vacuity Detection Using 3-Valued Logic

As we have shown in Section 1, detecting vacuity of a propositional formula φ with respect to a formula b that is pure in φ can be accomplished by (a) replacing all of the occurrences of b by M, and (b) interpreting the result in 3-valued Kleene logic. This approach can be easily extended to CTL since according to its semantics, CTL is just an interpretation of propositional logic over Kripke structures. For example, the meaning of $EX(a \vee b)$ evaluated in state s is $[\![EX(a \vee b)]\!](s) = \bigvee_{t \in S} R(s,t) \wedge ([\![a]\!](t) \vee [\![b]\!])(t)$, and it is vacuous in b if and only if the propositional formula denoting its meaning is vacuous in b. If we replace b by M, we obtain that $[\![EX(a \vee b)]\!](s)$ is vacuous in b iff $\bigvee_{t \in S}(R(s,t) \wedge ([\![a]\!](t) \vee [\![M]\!](t))) = [\![EX(a \vee M)]\!](s)$ evaluates to either $\top$ or $\bot$, and is non-vacuous otherwise. This leads to a simple vacuity detection algorithm for checking whether φ is vacuous in ψ on a Kripke structure K:

function Vacuous (φ, ψ, K) : **boolean**
  $\ell =$ ModelCheck $(\varphi[\psi \leftarrow M], K)$
  return $(\ell \neq M)$

Proof of correctness of this algorithm is given by the following theorem:

Theorem 6. *Let $\varphi[\psi]$ be a CTL formula, and ψ is pure in φ. Then,*

$$[\![\varphi[\psi \leftarrow M]]\!](s) = \begin{cases} \top & \text{iff } \varphi \text{ is vacuously true in } \psi \\ M & \text{iff } \varphi \text{ is non-vacuous in } \psi \\ \bot & \text{iff } \varphi \text{ is vacuously false in } \psi. \end{cases}$$

Table 1. A few examples of vacuity checking of φ with respect to b.

Formula	Condition	Answer	Comment
$\varphi = b$	$b = \text{true}$	(true, {})	φ is true iff b is true
$\varphi = a$	$a = \text{true}$	(true, $\{b\}$)	φ does not depend on b and is therefore
	$a = \text{false}$	(false, $\{b\}$)	vacuously true in b iff a is true
$\varphi = a \wedge b$	$a = \text{false}$	(false, $\{b\}$)	φ does not depend on b
	$a = \text{true}, b = \text{true}$	(true, {})	φ depends on b
$\neg\varphi$	φ is (true, $\{b\}$)	(false, $\{b\}$)	negation changes the answer but preserves vacuity

Now consider the case where a subformula b occurs both positively *and* negatively in φ. In this case, the 3-valued vacuity detection algorithm is no longer complete. For example, $\varphi = AG(b \Rightarrow b)$ is clearly vacuous in b; however, $\varphi[b \leftarrow M] = AG(M \Rightarrow M) = AG(M) = M$. Thus, non-vacuity of a formula cannot be trusted. Yet, the algorithm remains sound. For example, $AG(q \Rightarrow AF(p \Rightarrow AXp))$ is vacuous in p on any model where a state in which q holds is unreachable, and in those models, $AG(q \Rightarrow AF(M \Rightarrow AXM))$ evaluates to $\top$ as well. We summarize this in the following theorem:

Theorem 7. *Let $\varphi[\psi]$ be a CTL formula with a subformula ψ. If $[\![\varphi[\psi \leftarrow M]]\!](s)$ is $\top$, then φ is vacuously* true *in ψ; if $[\![\varphi[\psi \leftarrow M]]\!](s)$ is $\bot$, then φ is vacuously* false *in ψ.*

In the rest of the paper, we only check vacuity of φ with respect to pure subformulas.

3.2   True and False Non-vacuity

The 3-valued model-checking approach to vacuity detection can determine whether a subformula is non-vacuous, but it does not tell us whether a non-vacuous formula evaluates to true or false. That is, this approach keeps track of whether a given subformula matters for the evaluation of the formula, but not *how* it influences the final result. In this section, we show that the flavor of vacuity detection that can determine the truth and falsity of a given formula as well as vacuity of a subformula is equivalent to a 4-valued model-checking problem.

Once again, we start with a series of examples and use the notation $(\ell, \text{Vacuity})$, where ℓ is the value of the formula φ and Vacuity is the set of vacuous subformulas of φ. In examples in Table 1, we look at the vacuity of φ with respect to a subformula b. After examining all combinations and building a truth table for the propositional connectives, it becomes evident that the truth table corresponds to meet, join, and negation of a 4-valued De Morgan algebra **4**, shown in Figure 2(c). The values of the algebra are interpreted as follows: VT, VF are vacuously true and false, and NVT, NVF are non-vacuously true and false, respectively.

Thus, checking whether φ is vacuous in b is equivalent to model-checking the formula φ' obtained from φ by replacing all occurrences of b with an expression $(b \wedge NVT) \vee (\neg b \wedge NVF)$, or equivalently, since b is boolean, $\varphi' = \varphi[b \leftarrow b \wedge NVT \vee NVF]$. Note that this corresponds to $\varphi[b \leftarrow M] = \varphi[b \leftarrow b \wedge M \vee M]$ for the case addressed in Section 3.1. For example, if $\varphi = a \wedge b$, then $\varphi' = a \wedge (b \wedge NVT \vee NVF)$, and if a is true (i.e. VT), the expression simplifies to $VT \wedge (b \wedge NVT \vee NVF) = b \wedge NVT \vee NVF$. That is, the answer is NVT iff b is true, as desired. The correctness of our analysis is captured by the following theorem.

Theorem 8. *Let* $\varphi[\psi]$ *be a CTL formula, and* ψ *is pure in* φ. *Then,*

$$[\![\varphi[\psi \leftarrow \psi \wedge NVT \vee NVF]]\!](s) = \begin{cases} VT & \textit{iff } \varphi \textit{ is vacuously } \mathsf{true} \textit{ in } \psi; \\ NVT & \textit{iff } \varphi \textit{ is non-vacuously } \mathsf{true} \textit{ in } \psi; \\ NVF & \textit{iff } \varphi \textit{ is non-vacuously } \mathsf{false} \textit{ in } \psi; \\ VF & \textit{iff } \varphi \textit{ is vacuously } \mathsf{false} \textit{ in } \psi. \end{cases}$$

The algebra 4 has three join-irreducible elements: VT, NVT, and NVF. Thus, by Theorem 4, model-checking the formula $\varphi[b \leftarrow b \wedge NVT \vee NVF]$ is reducible to three classical model-checking problems. In particular, if b occurs positively in φ, then

$$[\![\varphi[b \leftarrow b \wedge NVT \vee NVF]]\!] \sqsupseteq VT \ \ = [\![\varphi[b \leftarrow \mathsf{false}]]\!]$$
$$[\![\varphi[b \leftarrow b \wedge NVT \vee NVF]]\!] \sqsupseteq NVT = [\![\varphi[b \leftarrow b]]\!]$$
$$[\![\varphi[b \leftarrow b \wedge NVT \vee NVF]]\!] \sqsupseteq NVF = [\![\varphi[b \leftarrow \mathsf{true}]]\!]$$

This is exactly the vacuity checking algorithm of Kupferman and Vardi [24,23].

Alternatively, we can view the vacuity detection problem as follows: given a QCTL formula $\varphi[X]$ with a free variable X, find which of the substitutions $[X \leftarrow \mathsf{false}]$, $[X \leftarrow b]$, and $[X \leftarrow \mathsf{true}]$ lead to φ being true. The set of substitutions forms a 3-valued De Morgan algebra isomorphic to **3** via the mapping (true $\rightarrow \top$, false $\rightarrow \bot, \varphi \rightarrow M$). If X occurs positively in φ, then if substituting false for X makes φ true, then so does substituting b and true. Further, if substituting b for X makes φ true, then so does true. That is, the set of all possible solutions is the set of upsets of $\mathbf{3} - U(\mathbf{3})$. Since **3** is a De Morgan algebra, by Theorem 1, $U(\mathbf{3})$ is De Morgan as well, and is isomorphic to 4 via the mapping ($\uparrow$false $\rightarrow VT, \uparrow\varphi \rightarrow NVT, \uparrow$true $\rightarrow NVF, \uparrow\emptyset \rightarrow VF$). So, using either intuition, this type of vacuity detection is a multi-valued model-checking problem over the algebra 4.

3.3   Witnesses to Non-vacuity

Beer et al. [4] pointed out that it is essential not only to tell the user that his/her formula is not vacuous, but also to give an interesting witness explaining *why* it is the case. For example, to show non-vacuity of $AG(p \Rightarrow q)$, we need to exhibit a path starting from the initial state that goes through the state where both p and q hold. Yet, the approach of Beer et al can only produce witnesses for non-vacuity of properties expressed in ACTL. We now show how to use our framework to compute witnesses to non-vacuity of arbitrary CTL formulas.

Definition 2. *[16] Let* φ *be a* $\chi CTL(\mathcal{L})$ *formula,* ℓ *be an element of* $\mathcal{L}$, *s be a state of a Kripke structure* K, *and assume that the value of* φ *in state* s *is* ℓ, *i.e.* $[\![\varphi]\!](s) = \ell$. *Then, a* witness *to* φ *is an evidence that justifies that* $[\![\varphi]\!](s) \sqsupseteq \ell$, *and its* counterexample *is an evidence for* $[\![\varphi]\!](s) \sqsubseteq \ell$.

As described in [16], a value of a universal formula φ in a model K is an infimum (or meet) over values of φ on all paths of K. Thus, a counterexample to $[\![\varphi]\!](s) = \ell$ is a minimal subtree of the computational tree of K on which φ evaluates to ℓ. For example, the path s_0, s_1, s_2 in the model in Figure 1(b) is a counterexample to $[\![AG\neg p]\!](s_0)$.

Dually, a witness to an existential formula $[\![\varphi]\!](s) = \ell$ is also a minimal subtree of the computational tree of K on which φ evaluates to ℓ. Note that "minimal" does not mean "linear" (unlike [23,24]), but only that all paths are necessary for the explanation.

We now apply multi-valued witnesses and counterexamples to compute explanations why an arbitrary CTL formula is non-vacuous. Let $\varphi[b]$ be a universal CTL formula with a subformula b, and let $\varphi' = \varphi[b \leftarrow b \wedge NVT \vee NVF]$ be a corresponding χCTL(4) formula that is used to check the vacuity of φ with respect to b. If $[\![\varphi']\!](s)$ evaluates to NVT, then its counterexample is a subtree of the computational tree on which φ evaluates to true, and its value depends on b. That is, the counterexample is a witness to non-vacuity of φ with respect to b, exactly as computed by [4]. Similarly, a counterexample to $[\![\varphi']\!](s) = NVF$ is both an execution of the system that violates φ and a witness to non-vacuity of φ. Dualizing the examples yields that if $\varphi[b]$ is existential, then a witness to φ' is also a witness to non-vacuity of φ. Combining witnesses and counterexamples allows us to give evidence to non-vacuity of an arbitrary CTL formula.

For example, consider a formula $\varphi = AXEX(p \Rightarrow q)$ evaluated in the state s_0 of the model in Figure 1(b). To check whether φ is vacuous in q, we model-check $\varphi' = \varphi[q \leftarrow q \wedge NVT \vee NVF]$ and obtain the result NVT, i.e. φ is true and is non-vacuous in q. The path s_0, s_1 is a counterexample to AX, provided that $[\![EXp \Rightarrow (q \wedge NVT \vee NVF)]\!](s_1) = NVT$, i.e., this path explains why the value of AX cannot be more than NVT. The path s_1, s_2 is the witness to the EX operator, i.e., it explains why this EX cannot be less than NVT. The combination of these is a path s_0, s_1, s_2 which is a witness to non-vacuity of φ with respect to q.

If φ is vacuous, then a witness to its vacuity is just the classical counterexample (or witness) to φ. For example, if φ is universal and $[\![\varphi']\!](s) = VF$, then a counterexample to φ' is a computation of the model in which φ is false independently of b. Further, if $[\![\varphi']\!](s) = VT$, then φ is true independently of b in any computation of the model, i.e. every computation is a witness.

4   Vacuity in Many Subformulas

In this section, we look at the problem of detecting maximal vacuous subformulas and vacuity with respect to several occurrences of a subformula.

4.1   Towards Mutual Vacuity

Vacuity checking can be seen as a check of correctness, or well-formedness, of the property. A negative result, i.e., that the property is vacuous, indicates a problem that should be brought to the user's attention. Thus, a simple binary answer is not sufficient, since it only indicates an existence of the problem, but does not provide any information on how to locate and solve it. In addition to determining that the formula φ is vacuous and producing witnesses and counterexamples explaining the answer, we expect the vacuity detection algorithm to yield the following information:

1. **Vacuous subformulas of** φ. Since φ can be vacuous in many subformulas, e.g., $\varphi = a \vee b$ when a and b are true, the algorithm should return *all* vacuous subformulas of φ. When φ is complex, it is more useful to receive information just about *maximal* (w.r.t. subformula ordering) subformulas. For example, if q and r are the *only* maximal

vacuous subformulas in $AG(p \Rightarrow (q \vee r))$, then a state in which p is true is reachable, and q or r hold in it; on the other hand, if $q \vee r$ is the maximal vacuous subformula, then there are no reachable states in which p is true. Clearly, it is useful to differentiate between these two cases.

2. **Dealing with multiple occurrences of the same subformula.** The algorithm should check vacuity of φ not only with respect to each subformula ψ, but also for each occurrence of ψ separately. For example, suppose p occurs in φ twice. Then φ can be vacuous in p, e.g., when $\varphi = AG(q \Rightarrow AF(p \wedge AXp))$ and q never happens; φ can be vacuous in some occurrences of p but not in others, e.g., when $\varphi = p \wedge AG(q \Rightarrow AFp)$; φ can be vacuous in each occurrence of p separately, but not be vacuous in p, e.g., $\varphi = (AFp) \vee (A[qUp])$ and both disjuncts are true.

In this section, we introduce a notion of *mutual* vacuity and show that an algorithm that can detect all maximal subsets of atomic propositions of φ in which it is mutually vacuous is sufficient for detecting vacuity in many subformulas, while satisfying the above requirements. Note that our results hold only for subformulas of pure polarity.

Definition 3. *A formula* $\varphi[\psi_1, \ldots, \psi_n]$ *is* mutually vacuously true *in* $\psi_1, \ldots, \psi_n$ *in state* s *iff* $[\![\forall Y_1, \ldots Y_n \cdot \varphi[\psi_1 \leftarrow Y_1, \ldots, \psi_n \leftarrow Y_n]]\!](s)$ *is* true; *it is* mutually vacuously false *iff* $[\![\neg \exists Y_1, \ldots Y_n \cdot \varphi[\psi_1 \leftarrow Y_1, \ldots, \psi_n \leftarrow Y_n]]\!](s)$ *is* true.

We say that φ is mutually vacuous in $\psi_1, \ldots \psi_n$ if it is mutually vacuously true or mutually vacuously false in $\psi_1, \ldots, \psi_n$, denoted (true, $\{\psi_1, \ldots, \psi_n\}$) and (false, $\{\psi_1, \ldots, \psi_n\}$), respectively. Let Atomic(ψ, φ) be the set of all occurrences in φ of atomic propositions occurring in ψ, e.g. Atomic($EFp, (EFp) \wedge (AGp)$) is the first occurrence of p. Using mutual vacuity, we can reduce the vacuity checking problem to the level of atomic propositions:

Theorem 9. *A formula* $\varphi[\psi]$ *is vacuously* true *(false) in* ψ *iff it is mutually vacuously* true *(false) in* Atomic(ψ, φ).

Detecting mutual vacuity with respect to atomic propositions is also sufficient for detecting mutual vacuity with respect to arbitrary subformulas.

Theorem 10. *Let* $\Psi = \{\psi_1, \ldots, \psi_n\}$. *A formula* $\varphi[\Psi]$ *is mutually vacuously* true *(false) in* Ψ *iff it is mutually vacuously* true *(false) in* $\bigcup_{\psi \in \Psi}$ Atomic(ψ, φ).

From Theorem 10, mutual vacuity checking can be used to determine vacuity w.r.t. different occurrences of the same subformula.

Theorem 11. *Let* $\varphi[\psi]$ *be a formula with multiple occurrences of* ψ *of the same polarity, and let* $\Psi = \{\psi_1, \ldots, \psi_n\}$ *be the set of these occurrences. Then,* φ *is vacuously* true *(false) in the subformula* ψ *iff it is mutually vacuously* true *(false) in* Ψ.

Consider the algorithm that receives a formula φ and detects all maximal subsets of Atomic(φ, φ) in which φ is mutually vacuous. By Theorems 9-11, such an algorithm satisfies all of the requirements set earlier in this section. In the rest of this section, we show how to construct such an algorithm by casting mutual vacuity into a multi-valued model-checking problem.

Table 2. A few examples of vacuity checking of $\varphi[a, b]$.

Formula	Condition	Answer	Comment
$\varphi = a$	$a = \text{true}$	$(\text{true}, \{b\})$	true iff a is true
	$a = \text{false}$	$(\text{false}, \{b\})$	
$\varphi = b$	$b = \text{true}$	$(\text{true}\{a\})$	true iff b is true
$\varphi = \varphi_1[a] \wedge \varphi_2[b]$	$\varphi_1[a]$ is $(\text{true}, \{a, b\})$ and $\varphi_2[b]$ is $(\text{true}, \{a\})$	$(\text{true}, \{a\})$	true, non-vacuous in b, and vacuous in a
	$\varphi_1[a]$ is $(\text{true}, \{a, b\})$ and $\varphi_2[b]$ is $(\text{false}, \{a, b\})$	$(\text{false}, \{a, b\})$	false, mutually vacuous in $\{a, b\}$
	$\varphi_1[a]$ is $(\text{false}, \{b\})$ and $\varphi_2[b]$ is $(\text{false}, \{a\})$	$(\text{false}, \{\{a\}, \{b\}\})$	false, vacuous in a and in b
$\varphi = \neg\varphi_1[a, b]$	$\varphi_1[a, b]$ is $(\text{true}, \{a\})$	$(\text{false}, \{a\})$	$\neg$ does not affect vacuity

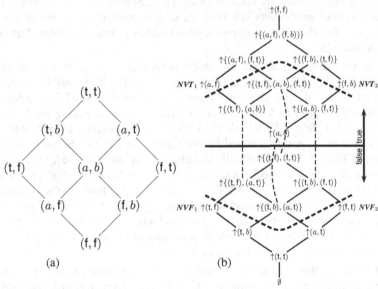

Fig. 4. De Morgan algebras for vacuity detection: (a) 3×3; (b) $U(3 \times 3)$.

4.2 Detecting Mutual Vacuity

Assume that we have a formula $\varphi[a, b]$, and we want to check whether it is vacuous in a, b, or both. A few examples of φ are given in Table 2. For example, if $\varphi = a$, then it is vacuous in b, and it is true iff a is true.

The result of exploring all combinations and building the vacuity tables for the propositional connectives is isomorphic to the De Morgan algebra given in Figure 4(b). In this figure, we use t and f to stand for true and false, respectively. Further, both thin dashed and solid lines indicate lattice ordering – the differentiation was made only to enhance the visual presentation. Values $\uparrow(a, \text{false})$ and $\uparrow(\text{true}, \text{false})$ correspond to non-vacuously true (NVT_1) and non-vacuously false (NVF_1) in a, respectively. Similarly, $\uparrow(\text{false}, b)$ and $\uparrow(\text{false}, \text{true})$ correspond to NVT_2 and NVF_2 in b, as indicated in the figure.

Table 3. Correspondence between values of ℓ and vacuity of φ.

Value of ℓ	$\uparrow$(false, false)	$\uparrow\emptyset$	$\uparrow(a, b)$	$NVF_1 \vee NVF_2$	NVF_1	NVT_2
Vacuity of φ	(true, $\{a, b\}$)	(false, $\{a, b\}$)	(true, $\{\}$)	(false, $\{\}$)	(false, $\{b\}$)	(true, $\{a\}$)

Alternatively, we can view mutual vacuity detection of $\varphi[a, b]$ as follows: given a QCTL formula $\varphi' = \varphi[a \leftarrow X, b \leftarrow Y]$ with free variables X and Y, find which substitutions from $L = \{$true, a, false$\} \times \{$true, b, false$\}$ for (X, Y) make φ' true. The set L forms a De Morgan algebra isomorphic to $\mathbf{3} \times \mathbf{3}$, given in Figure 4(a). Assuming that φ' is positive in both X and Y, then if substituting (false, b) for (X, Y) makes φ' true, then so does any pair in $\{$true, a, false$\} \times b$. This means that φ is vacuously true in a; in other words, its value is (true, $\{a\}$). Similarly, if (false, false) makes φ' true, then so does every other substitution, so φ is mutually vacuous in a and b, i.e., (true, $\{a, b\}$). Finally, if substituting (a, false) makes φ' true, but (false, true) does not, then φ is (true, $\{b\}$).

As illustrated above, the set of substitutions that make φ' true is an element of $U(L)$. Since L is a De Morgan algebra, so is $U(L)$ (by Theorem 1); moreover, it is isomorphic to the algebra given in Figure 4(b). As in Section 3.2, checking vacuity of $\varphi[a, b]$ with respect to a and b is equivalent to model-checking the formula $\varphi' = \varphi[a \leftarrow a \wedge NVT_1 \vee NVF_1, b \leftarrow b \wedge NVT_2 \vee NVF_2]$. Vacuity of φ in state s of some Kripke structure is then determined by the value $\ell = [\![\varphi']\!](s)$. Some of the examples are given in Table 3. For example, if the value of ℓ is $\uparrow$(false, false), then φ is true and is mutually vacuous in a and b. In this algebra, any value above $\uparrow(a, b)$ and any value below $\uparrow\{(\mathsf{t}, \mathsf{f}), (\mathsf{f}, \mathsf{t})\}$ ($NVF_1 \vee NVF_2$) indicate that φ is true or false, respectively, as shown in Figure 4(b) by thick solid lines. Also, any value above NVT_1 means that φ is vacuous in b (it may also be vacuous in a), and any value above NVT_2 means that φ is vacuous in a, as indicated by thick dashed lines in Figure 4(b). False vacuity is also guaranteed for values below NVF_1 and NVF_2.

Before giving the general algorithm for detecting mutual vacuity of a formula, we introduce some additional notation. Let $V = U(\Pi_{i=1}^n \mathbf{3})$ be a De Morgan algebra, and $\{a_1, \ldots, a_n\}$ be n atomic propositions occurring in φ. Let $\kappa_i : \mathbf{3} \to V$ be an embedding of $\mathbf{3}$ into V such that $\kappa_1(\ell) = \uparrow(\ell, \mathsf{false}, \ldots)$, $\kappa_2(\ell) = \uparrow(\mathsf{false}, \ell, \mathsf{false}, \ldots)$, etc. In particular, if $V = U(\mathbf{3})$, as in Section 3.2, then $\kappa_1(\ell) = \uparrow\ell$. Thus, if we interpret the values of $\mathbf{3}$ as $\{$true, a, false$\}$, then $\kappa_1(a) = NVT$, $\kappa_1(\mathsf{true}) = NVF$ and $\kappa_1(\mathsf{false}) = VT$. Similarly, if $V = U(\mathbf{3} \times \mathbf{3})$, as in the example of checking $\varphi[a, b]$, $\kappa_1(a) = NVT_1$, $\kappa_1(\mathsf{true}) = NVF_1$, $\kappa_2(b) = NVT_2$, and $\kappa_2(\mathsf{true}) = NVF_2$. For $A \subseteq \{a_1, \ldots, a_n\}$, we define $f(A) \triangleq \uparrow(x_1, \ldots, x_n)$ and $g(A) \triangleq \uparrow(y_1, \ldots, y_n)$, where

$$x_i = \begin{cases} \mathsf{false} & \text{if } a_i \in A \\ a_i & \text{otherwise} \end{cases} \qquad y_i = \begin{cases} \mathsf{false} & \text{if } a_i \in A \\ \mathsf{true} & \text{otherwise} \end{cases}$$

Theorem 12. *Let φ' be a $\chi CTL(V)$ formula obtained from φ by replacing each a_i by $(a_i \wedge \kappa_i(a_i)) \vee \kappa_i(\mathsf{true})$. Then, φ is mutually vacuously true in $A \subseteq \{a_1, \ldots, a_n\}$ in state s of a Kripke structure K iff $[\![\varphi']\!](s) \sqsupseteq f(A)$; and φ is mutually vacuously false iff $[\![\varphi']\!](s) \sqsubseteq g(A)$.*

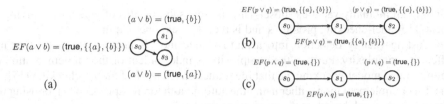

Fig. 5. Proof-like witnesses for non-vacuity of (a) $EF(a \vee b)$, (b) $EF(p \vee q)$, and (c) $EF(p \wedge q)$.

Moreover, the largest mutually vacuous subset can be extracted directly from the result of model-checking φ'. For example, if $[\![\varphi']\!](s) \sqsupseteq \uparrow(\mathsf{false}, \mathsf{false}, a_3)$, then φ is $(\mathsf{true}, \{a_1, a_2\})$; and if the result is equal to $\uparrow(\mathsf{false}, \mathsf{false}, a_3)$, then we also know that φ is definitely not vacuous in a_3.

4.3 Witnesses and Counterexamples

Multi-valued witnesses and counterexamples provide witnesses for mutual non-vacuity, just as they do for vacuity detection with respect to a single subformula. Let K be a Kripke structure, φ be a universal formula whose atomic subformulas are a, b, and c, and φ' be the multi-valued formula used to check mutual vacuity of φ. If φ in state s is $(\mathsf{true}, \{a, b\})$, then (a) it is non-vacuous in c, and (b) a counterexample to $[\![\varphi']\!](s) = \uparrow(\mathsf{false}, \mathsf{false}, c)$ is a minimal subset of the computational tree of K on which φ evaluates to true, and is mutually vacuous in a and b, and non-vacuous in c. This allows us to generate witnesses for mutual non-vacuity for arbitrary CTL formulas.

In the case of mutual vacuity, a witness even for a single temporal operator may contain more than one path. Consider formulas evaluated in state s_0 of the model in Figure 1(b). The formula $EF(a \vee b)$ is $(\mathsf{true}, \{\{a\}, \{b\}\})$, corresponding to the value $NVT_1 \vee NVT_2$, and its witness for non-vacuity consists of two paths: s_0, s_1 (explaining non-vacuity in a) and s_0, s_3 (explaining non-vacuity in b), as shown in Figure 5(a). The number of paths in a witness does not necessarily correspond to the number of ways a formula is vacuous. For example, $EF(p \vee q)$ is also $(\mathsf{true}, \{\{p\}, \{q\}\})$; however, its witness for non-vacuity is a single path s_0, s_1, s_2, shown in Figure 5(b). The formula $EF(p \wedge q)$ is non-vacuous, i.e., it evaluates to $(\mathsf{true}, \{\})$, but its witness for non-vacuity, shown in Figure 5(c), is the same as the one for $EF(p \vee q)$.

Proof-like witness presentation was introduced in [16] to disambiguate between the different paths in a multi-valued witness. In this approach, each state of the witness is labeled with the part of the formula that it explains. For example, in Figure 5(a), state s_1 is labeled with $(\mathsf{true}, \{b\})$ indicating that it explains non-vacuity in a (and vacuity in b). Similarly, state s_0 of the witness in Figure 5(c) is labeled with $(\mathsf{true}, \{\})$, indicating that it is a witness for non-vacuity, etc.

5 Complexity

In this section, we look at the complexity of vacuity detection of a formula φ.

To determine vacuity of φ with respect to a single subformula requires solving two model-checking problems and therefore has the same complexity as model-checking φ.

Finding all mutually vacuous subsets of n atomic subformulas of φ requires solving at most 3^n model-checking problems and is therefore exponential in n.

Casting vacuity detection into a multi-valued model-checking problem does not affect its complexity. Further, the complexity is independent of the implementation of multi-valued model-checking, be that the reduction to classical model-checking [17], or the direct implementation, either using the automata-theoretic approach [7], or using the symbolic approach based on decision diagrams [9].

A symbolic approach to checking a χCTL($\mathcal{L}$) formula φ over a De Morgan algebra $\mathcal{L}$ in a Kripke structure $K = (S, R, s_0, A, I)$ is a fixpoint computation of a monotone function over the lattice $\mathcal{L}^S$ of functions from the statespace S to $\mathcal{L}$. The computation of the fixpoint converges in at most $O(|S|)$ iterations [15], i.e. it is linear in the size of the statespace, just as classical model-checking. Each iteration consists of a symbolic pre-image computation, i.e. computing $[\![EX\psi]\!]$ for some ψ, which is polynomial in the size of the transition relation and the size of the symbolic representation of $[\![\psi]\!]$, and is linear in the complexity of meet and join operations on $\mathcal{L}$. Finally, the complexity of meet and join operations is in the worst case linear in $|\mathcal{J}(\mathcal{L})|$ [18].

The algebra used for mutual vacuity detection with respect to n atomic subformulas has 3^n join-irreducibles, leading to a symbolic algorithm that is exponential in n. However, in practice, various heuristics can be used to implement meet and join much more efficiently. For example, if $\mathcal{L}$ is relatively small, we can pre-compute its meet and join tables, reducing their complexity to $O(1)$. Alternatively, elements of $\mathcal{L}$ can be represented in a way that allows the implementation of meet and join using logical bitwise operations [10], taking advantage of the ability of modern hardware to perform logical operations on several bits in parallel. Furthermore, only some of the algebra values are used in the computation of vacuity detection for any given problem. Thus, even if the algebra is large, it is still possible to precompute the relevant portions of meet and join tables dynamically, again reducing their complexity to $O(1)$.

Direct automata-theoretic approach to multi-valued model-checking yields similar results [7,8]. Guided by our experience [18], we conjecture that the vacuity detection problem is feasible if implemented on top of a direct multi-valued model-checker, even when a naive reduction to several classical model-checking problems is not.

6   Conclusion

In this paper, we have shown that the vacuity checking problem [3] is an instance of a multi-valued model-checking over a De Morgan algebra $\mathcal{L}$ [9], where the values of $\mathcal{L}$ are used to keep track of how a formula depends on its subformulas. In the process, we have introduced a more general notion of vacuity, *mutual vacuity*, that captures truth or falsity of a property, its vacuity with respect to subformulas, and vacuity with respect to different occurrences of the same subformula. In addition, we have shown that witnesses and counterexamples for multi-valued model-checking coincide with the notion of an interesting witness [3], and give users all the necessary information for debugging vacuous properties. Note that all results of this paper trivially extend to (multi-valued) μ-calculus [21,17], and thus to CTL* and LTL.

In the future, we plan to address vacuity detection for subformulas with mixed polarity [1]. Further, this paper addressed two extremes of the vacuity detection problem: vacuity with respect to a single subformula, and mutual vacuity with respect to all subformulas. Other vacuity detection problems, such as only detecting vacuity with respect to all (atomic) subformulas, but not their mutual vacuity, reduce to multi-valued model-checking over a subalgebra of the algebra used for mutual vacuity detection. Exploring this is left for future work.

Acknowledgment. We thank Shiva Nejati for her comments on an earlier draft of this paper. Financial support for this research has been provided by NSERC.

References

1. R. Armoni, L. Fix, A. Flaisher, O. Grumberg, N. Piterman, A. Tiemeyer, and M. Vardi. "Enhanced Vacuity Detection in Linear Temporal Logic ". In *CAV'03*, volume 2725 of *LNCS*, pages 368–380, July 2003.
2. D. Beaty and R. Bryant. "Formally Verifying a Microprocessor Using a Simulation Methodology". In *Proceedings of DAC'94*, pages 596–602, 1994.
3. I. Beer, S. Ben-David, C. Eisner, and Y. Rodeh. "Efficient Detection of Vacuity in ACTL Formulas". In *CAV'97*, volume 1254 of *LNCS*, 1997.
4. I. Beer, S. Ben-David, C. Eisner, and Y. Rodeh. "Efficient Detection of Vacuity in Temporal Model Checking". *FMSD*, 18(2):141–163, March 2001.
5. G. Birkhoff. *Lattice Theory*. Americal Mathematical Society, 3 edition, 1967.
6. G. Bruns and P. Godefroid. "Model Checking Partial State Spaces with 3-Valued Temporal Logics". In *CAV'99*, volume 1633 of *LNCS*, pages 274–287, 1999.
7. G. Bruns and P. Godefroid. "Temporal Logic Query-Checking". In *LICS'01*, pages 409–417, June 2001.
8. G. Bruns and P. Godefroid. "Model Checking with Multi-Valued Logics". Tech. Memorandum ITD-03-44535H, Bell Labs, May 2003.
9. M. Chechik, B. Devereux, S. Easterbrook, and A. Gurfinkel. "Multi-Valued Symbolic Model-Checking". *ACM Trans. on Soft. Eng. and Method.*, 2003. (In press.).
10. M. Chechik, B. Devereux, S. Easterbrook, A. Lai, and V. Petrovykh. "Efficient Multiple-Valued Model-Checking Using Lattice Representations". In *CONCUR'01*, volume 2154 of *LNCS*, pages 451–465, August 2001.
11. E. Clarke, O. Grumberg, and D. Peled. *Model Checking*. MIT Press, 1999.
12. E.M. Clarke, E.A. Emerson, and A.P. Sistla. "Automatic Verification of Finite-State Concurrent Systems Using Temporal Logic Specifications". *ACM Trans. on Prog. Lang. and Sys.*, 8(2):244–263, April 1986.
13. B.A. Davey and H.A. Priestley. *Introduction to Lattices and Order*. 1990.
14. Y. Dong, B. Sarna-Starosta, C.R. Ramakrishnan, and S. A. Smolka. "Vacuity Checking in the Modal Mu-Calculus". In *Proceedings of AMAST'02*, volume 2422 of *LNCS*, pages 147–162, September 2002.
15. A. Gurfinkel. "Multi-Valued Symbolic Model-Checking: Fairness, Counter-Examples, Running Time". Master's thesis, University of Toronto, October 2002.
16. A. Gurfinkel and M. Chechik. "Generating Counterexamples for Multi-Valued Model-Checking". In *FME'03*, volume 2805 of *LNCS*, September 2003.
17. A. Gurfinkel and M. Chechik. "Multi-Valued Model-Checking via Classical Model-Checking". In *CONCUR'03*, volume 2761 of *LNCS*, September 2003.
18. A. Gurfinkel, M. Chechik, and B. Devereux. "Temporal Logic Query Checking: A Tool for Model Exploration". *IEEE Tran. on Soft. Eng.*, 29(10):898–914, 2003.
19. M. Huth, R. Jagadeesan, and D. A. Schmidt. "Modal Transition Systems: A Foundation for Three-Valued Program Analysis". In *ESOP'01*, volume 2028 of *LNCS*, pages 155–169, 2001.

20. S. C. Kleene. *Introduction to Metamathematics*. New York: Van Nostrand, 1952.
21. D Kozen. "Results on Propositional μ-calculus". *Theor. Comp. Sci.*, 27:334–354, 1983.
22. O. Kupferman. "Augmenting Branching Temporal Logics with Existential Quantification over Atomic Propositions". *J. Logic and Computation*, 7:1–14, 1997.
23. O. Kupferman and M. Vardi. "Vacuity Detection in Temporal Model Checking". In *CHARME'99*, volume 1703 of *LNCS*, pages 82–96, 1999.
24. O. Kupferman and M. Vardi. "Vacuity Detection in Temporal Model Checking". *STTT*, 4(2):224–233, February 2003.
25. M. Purandare and F. Somenzi. "Vacuum Cleaning CTL Formulae". In *CAV'02*, volume 2404 of *LNCS*, pages 485–499. Springer-Verlag, July 2002.

A Temporal Logic of Nested Calls and Returns*

Rajeev Alur[1], Kousha Etessami[2], and P. Madhusudan[1]

[1] University of Pennsylvania
[2] University of Edinburgh

Abstract. Model checking of linear temporal logic (LTL) specifications with respect to pushdown systems has been shown to be a useful tool for analysis of programs with potentially recursive procedures. LTL, however, can specify only regular properties, and properties such as correctness of procedures with respect to pre and post conditions, that require matching of calls and returns, are not regular. We introduce a *temporal logic of calls and returns* (CARET) for specification and algorithmic verification of correctness requirements of structured programs. The formulas of CARET are interpreted over sequences of propositional valuations tagged with special symbols *call* and *ret*. Besides the standard global temporal modalities, CARET admits the *abstract-next operator* that allows a path to jump from a call to the *matching* return. This operator can be used to specify a variety of non-regular properties such as partial and total correctness of program blocks with respect to pre and post conditions. The abstract versions of the other temporal modalities can be used to specify regular properties of *local* paths within a procedure that skip over calls to other procedures. CARET also admits the *caller* modality that jumps to the most recent pending call, and such caller modalities allow specification of a variety of security properties that involve inspection of the call-stack. Even though verifying context-free properties of pushdown systems is undecidable, we show that model checking CARET formulas against a pushdown model is decidable. We present a tableau construction that reduces our model checking problem to the emptiness problem for a Büchi pushdown system. The complexity of model checking CARET formulas is the same as that of checking LTL formulas, namely, polynomial in the model and singly exponential in the size of the specification.

1 Introduction

Propositional linear temporal logic (LTL) is a popular choice for specifying correctness requirements of reactive systems [23,22]. LTL formulas are built from atomic propositions using temporal modalities such as "next," "always," and "until," and are interpreted over infinite sequences of states that assign values to atomic propositions. The LTL model checking problem is to determine whether all the computations of a system satisfy a given LTL specification. In

---

* Supported in part by ARO URI award DAAD19-01-1-0473 and NSF award CCR-0306382.

K. Jensen and A. Podelski (Eds.): TACAS 2004, LNCS 2988, pp. 467–481, 2004.

traditional model checking [11,21,16], the model is a finite state machine whose vertices correspond to system states and whose edges correspond to system transitions. However, model checking is also feasible when the model is a *recursive state machine* (or equivalently, a *pushdown system*), in which vertices can either be ordinary states or can correspond to invocations of other state machines in a potentially recursive manner. Recursive state machines (RSMs) can model the control flow in typical sequential imperative programming languages with recursive procedure calls. Model checking of LTL specifications with respect to RSMs can be solved in time polynomial in the size of the model and exponential in the size of the specification [7,5,12,1,3,20]. This problem has been well studied over the last few years leading to efficient implementations and applications to program analysis as well as model checking of C or Java programs [24,2,13,10].

While LTL is an attractive specification language for capturing regular sequencing requirements such as "between successive write operations to a variable, a read operation should occur," it cannot express requirements such as "if the pre-condition p holds when a module is invoked, the post-condition q should hold when the module returns." This requires matching of calls and returns, and is a context-free property if calls are nested (recall that the language $\{a^n b^n \mid n \in \mathbb{N}\}$ is a non-regular context-free language [17]). Correctness of program blocks with respect to *pre* and *post* conditions has been emphasized in the verification literature since the early days of logics for structured programs [15], and also forms an integral part of modern interface specification languages for object oriented programming such as JML [6]. In this paper, we introduce CARET —a temporal logic that can express requirements about matching calls and returns, along with the necessary tools for algorithmic reasoning. Algorithmic verification of nonregular specifications have been considered previously [4,14,19], but to the best of our knowledge, this is the first specification language that allows specification of partial and total correctness with respect to pre and post conditions, and has a decidable model checking problem with respect to boolean abstractions of recursive sequential programs.

The formulas of our logic are interpreted over *structured computations*. A structured computation is an infinite sequence of states, where each state assigns values to atomic propositions, and can be additionally tagged with *call* or *ret* symbols. A call denotes invocation of a (sequential) program module, and the matching return denotes the exit from this module, where a module may correspond to a procedure or a function in structured imperative languages such as C, or methods in object-oriented languages such as Java, or remote invocations of components in a distributed environment. Given a structured computation, the *abstract-successor* of the i-state is defined to be the matching return position if the i-th state is a call, and $i + 1$ otherwise. Besides the global temporal modalities, CARET admits their *abstract* counterparts. For example, $\bigcirc^a \varphi$ holds at a position if φ holds at its abstract-successor position. Consequently, if the state formula $call_A$ denotes the invocation of a module A, then the CARET formula $\Box(call_A \wedge p \rightarrow \bigcirc^a q)$ specifies the total correctness with respect to the pre-condition p and post-condition q. An abstract path is obtained by applying the abstract-successor operation repeatedly, and captures the *local* computation within a module that removes computation fragments corresponding to calls to other blocks. The abstract-versions of operators such as *always* and *until* can be used to specify regular requirements about such local paths.

In a structured computation, for every position, besides the global and abstract successors, there is also a natural notion of the *caller* position which gives the most recent unmatched call position. The caller path, obtained by repeated applications of the *caller* operator can be interpreted as the contents of the call-stack at a position. Our logic admits the *caller* counterparts of all the temporal modalities. These modalities allow specification of properties that require inspection of the call-stack such as "a module A should be invoked only if the module B belongs to the call-stack," or "the number of interrupt-handlers in the call-stack should never exceed 10." It is worth noting that the relevance of stack inspection for specifying correctness of security properties and calling sequences of interrupt handlers has been identified by many researchers, and decision procedures for checking specific properties already exist [18,10,13,9]. In particular, [13] uses LTL on pushdown systems but allows the atomic propositions of the LTL formula to correspond to any regular language evaluated over the call stack. Our logic mixes global, abstract, and temporal modalities allowing integrated specifications, and is more expressive allowing specification of properties such as "variable x remains unchanged after the current call returns."

Given an RSM (or a pushdown system) whose vertices are labeled with atomic propositions, there is a natural way to associate a set of structured computations by tagging invocations and returns with *call* and *ret* symbols. The model checking problem, then, is to check whether all computations of an RSM S satisfy a CARET specification φ. Note that both S and φ define context-free languages, and problems such as inclusion and emptiness of intersection are undecidable for context-free languages [17]. However, in our setting, the model and the specification are synchronized on the *call* and *ret* symbols, and as a result we show that the model checking problem becomes decidable. Our decision procedure generalizes the tableau-based construction for LTL model checking: given an RSM S and a specification φ, we show how to construct another RSM S_φ with generalized Büchi conditions such that S_φ has an accepting run iff S has a computation that violates φ. The time complexity of the decision procedure is polynomial in the size of S and exponential in the size of φ. This is identical to the time complexity of model checking of LTL specifications with respect to RSMs, and the model complexity is exactly the same as that of the reachability problem for RSMs (cubic in general, and linear if the number of entries denoting the inputs to a module, or the number of exits denoting the outputs of a module, is bounded). As in the case of LTL, model checking of CARET with respect to RSMs is EXPTIME-complete, and its model complexity is PTIME-complete.

Related Work: In [4], the authors show a restricted but decidable temporal logic which allows variables to count the number of occurrences of states in intervals which then can be compared using Presburger constraints. The work in [19] deals with model checking regular systems against pushdown tree-automata specifications. Propositional dynamic logic can be augmented with some restricted classes of context-free languages (those accepted by simple-minded PDAs) such that validity is decidable [14]. Stack inspection is considered in [18] where the authors propose a logic that can specify properties of the stack at any point using temporal operators; in [13] a more general way of accessing the stack is provided using propositions that are interpreted using automata that run over the stack.

2   Computation Model

2.1   Structured Computations

Let us fix a finite set Γ of symbols. The augmented alphabet of Γ is the alphabet: $\hat{\Gamma} = \Gamma \times \{call, ret, int\}$. The symbol *call* denotes the invocation of a module, *ret* denotes the exit or the return from a module and *int* stands for internal actions of the current module. For $\sigma \in \Gamma$, we call the symbols of the form $(\sigma, call)$, (σ, ret) and (σ, int), *calls*, *returns* and *internal symbols*, respectively.

For an infinite word α and an integer $i \geq 0$, we use α_i to denote the i-th symbol in α and α^i to denote the suffix of α starting at the i-th symbol.

For a word α over $\hat{\Gamma}$, there is a natural notion of a matching between calls and returns: if $\alpha_i = (\sigma, call)$ and $\alpha_j = (\sigma', ret)$, we say that j is the *matching return* for i if j is the return corresponding to the call at i. Formally, we define a more general partial function R_α that maps any $i \in \mathbb{N}$ to the first unmatched return after i: if there is a j' such that j' is greater than i and j' is a return and the number of calls and returns in $\alpha_{i+1} \ldots \alpha_{j'-1}$ are equal, then $R_\alpha(i) = j$, where j is the smallest such j'; else $R_\alpha(i) = \bot$. If α_i is a call, then $R_\alpha(i)$ will be its corresponding return.

In the logic we define we have three notions of successor:

- The global-successor ($succ^g$) is the usual successor function. The global-successor of i in α, denoted $succ^g_\alpha(i)$, is $i + 1$.
- The abstract-successor ($succ^a$) points to the next "local" successor. If the current symbol is a call, then it skips the entire computation within the call and moves to the matching return. Otherwise, it is the global-successor provided the global-successor is not a return. If the global successor is a return, then the abstract-successor is defined as $\bot$. Formally, if α_i is an internal symbol or a return, then: if α_{i+1} is not a return, then $succ^a_\alpha(i)$ is $i + 1$, otherwise it $\bot$. If α_i is a call, then $succ^a_\alpha(i) = R_\alpha(i)$. Note that if α_i is a call that has no matching return, then $succ^a_\alpha(i)$ is $\bot$.
- The caller ($succ^-$) is a "past" modality that points to the innermost call within which the current action is executed. If there is a $j' < i$ such that $\alpha_{j'}$ is a call and $R_\alpha(j') > i$ or $R_\alpha(j') = \bot$, then $succ^-_\alpha(i) = j$, where j is the greatest such j'. Otherwise, $succ^-_\alpha(i) = \bot$.

Notice that we do not demand that calls have matching returns, or even that returns have matching calls. In the models of programs that we consider, it is true that every return has a matching call (but calls to a module may never return). However, since our logic does not require this assumption, we have chosen to present it in this general framework.

2.2   Recursive State Machines

Recursive state machines (RSMs) were introduced in [1], and independently in [3] under a different name, to model the interprocedural control flow in recursive programs. RSMs are expressively equivalent to pushdown systems, but they more tightly capture the control flow graphs of procedural programs and enable us to more directly reason about them. We therefore adopt RSMs as system models in this paper.

Syntax. A *recursive state machine* (RSM) S over a set of propositions AP is a tuple $(M, \{S_m\}_{m \in M}, start)$, where M is a finite set of module names, for every $m \in M$, S_m is a *module* $S_m = (N_m, B_m, Y_m, En_m, Ex_m, \delta_m, \eta_m)$, and $start \subseteq \bigcup_{m \in M} N_m$, is a set of start nodes. Each module S_m consists of the following components:

- A finite nonempty set of *nodes* N_m and a finite set of *boxes* B_m.
- A labeling $Y_m : B_m \to M$ that assigns to every box a module name.
- A nonempty set of *entry* nodes $En_m \subseteq N_m$ and a nonempty set of *exit* nodes $Ex_m \subseteq N_m$.
- Let $Calls_m = \{(b, e) \mid b \in B_m, e \in En_{Y_m(b)}\}$ denote the set of *calls* of m and let $Retns_m = \{(b, x) \mid b \in B_m, x \in Ex_{Y_m(b)}\}$ denote the set of *returns* in m. Then, $\delta_m : N_m \cup Retns_m \to 2^{N_m \cup Calls_m}$ is a *transition function*.
- Let $V_m = (N_m \cup Calls_m \cup Retns_m)$. We refer to V_m as the set of *vertices* of S_m. η_m is a labeling function $\eta_m : V_m \to 2^{AP}$ that associates a set of propositions to each vertex, i.e., to nodes, calls and returns.

We let $V = \bigcup_{m \in M} V_m$ denote the set of all vertices of S and let $\eta : V \to 2^{AP}$ be the extension of all the functions η_m, $m \in M$. Also, let $B = \bigcup_{m \in M} B_m$ and let $Y : B \to M$ denote the function that extends all the functions Y_m ($m \in M$).

Figure 1 depicts an example RSM in which there are two modules, S_1 and S_2. The calls and returns have been identified explicitly by labeling them with c and r, respectively. Module S_1, for example, has two entries labeled by p and by q, only one exit, labeled x, and two boxes b_1 and b_2. Note that calls and returns can also have other propositions labeling them, and these may differ from the labels of the corresponding entries and exits. For example the call of box $b2$ has label t, and this differs from the label z of the entry to S_2, which box $b2$ maps to. Assume that the entry of S_1 labeled q is the unique start node. In such a case, a sample computation of the RSM, annotated with call and return information, consists of the sequence of labels:

$(\{q\}, int)\ (\{d\}, int)\ (\{t\}, call)\ (\{z\}, int)\ (\{t\}, int)\ (\{y\}, int)\ (\{w\}, ret) \ldots$.

Semantics. From an RSM S we define a (infinite) global Kripke structure $K_S = (Q, Init, \kappa, \delta)$. The (global) *states*, denoted Q, are elements $(\gamma, u) \in B^* \times V$ such that either

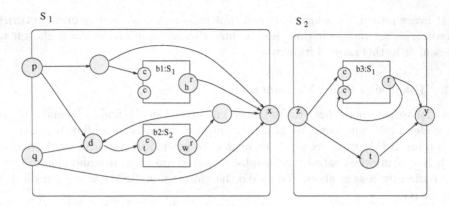

Fig. 1. A sample RSM

- $\gamma = \epsilon$ and $u \in V$, or,
- $\gamma = b_1 \ldots b_k$ (with $k \geq 1$) and $\forall i \in [1, k-1]$, $b_{i+1} \in B_{Y(b_i)}$ and $u \in V_{Y(b_k)}$.

The initial states are $Init = \{(\epsilon, u) \in Q \mid u \in start\}$. The labeling function is $\kappa((\gamma, u)) = (\eta(u), z)$, where $z = int$ if u is a node, $z = call$ if u is a call, and $z = ret$ if u is a return.

The global transition relation $\delta : Q \to 2^Q$, is defined as follows. For $s = (\gamma, u)$ and $s' = (\gamma', u')$, $s' \in \delta(s)$ if and only if one of the following holds:

- **Internal move:** $u \in (N_m \cup Retns_m) \setminus Ex_m$, $u' \in \delta_m(u)$, and $\gamma' = \gamma$
- **Call a module:** $u = (b, e) \in Calls_m$, $u' = e$ and $\gamma' = \gamma.b$
- **Return from a call:** $u \in Ex_m$, $\gamma = \gamma'.b$, and $u' = (b, u)$

Let $\Gamma = 2^{AP}$ and $\hat{\Gamma} = \Gamma \times \{call, ret, int\}$. For a word $\alpha = \alpha_0 \alpha_1 \ldots \in \hat{\Gamma}^\omega$, a *run* of K_S on α is a sequence of states $\pi = s_0, s_1, \ldots$ where $\kappa(s_i) = \alpha_i$, for all $i \in \mathbb{N}$, and such that $s_0 \in Init$ and for every $i \in \mathbb{N}$, $s_{i+1} \in \delta(s_i)$.
For an RSM S, let $\mathcal{L}(S) = \{\alpha \in \hat{\Gamma}^\omega \mid$ there is a run of K_S on $\alpha\}$.

3   Linear Temporal Logic of Calls and Returns

3.1   Syntax and Semantics

Let $\Gamma = 2^{AP}$, where AP is a finite set of *atomic propositions*. Let the augmented alphabet of Γ be $\hat{\Gamma} = \Gamma \times \{call, ret, int\}$. Let P denote the set $AP \cup \{call, ret, int\}$. The models of our logic are the words in $\hat{\Gamma}^\omega$.

The *Propositional Linear Temporal Logic of Calls and Returns* (CARET) over AP is the set of formulas defined by:

$$\varphi := \ p \mid \varphi \vee \varphi \mid \neg\varphi \mid \bigcirc^g \varphi \mid \varphi \mathcal{U}^g \varphi \mid \bigcirc^a \varphi \mid \varphi \mathcal{U}^a \varphi \mid \bigcirc^- \varphi \mid \varphi \mathcal{U}^- \varphi$$

where $p \in P$.

For a word $\alpha \in \hat{\Gamma}^\omega$, we define the semantics by inductively defining when (α, n) satisfies a formula φ, where $n \in \mathbb{N}$. A word α satisfies φ iff $(\alpha, 0)$ satisfies φ. For a word α over $\hat{\Gamma}$, $n \in \mathbb{N}$, the semantics is defined as:

- $(\alpha, n) \models p$ iff $\alpha_0 = (X, d)$ and $p \in X$ or $p = d$ (where $p \in P$)
- $(\alpha, n) \models \varphi_1 \vee \varphi_2$ iff $(\alpha, n) \models \varphi_1$ or $(\alpha, n) \models \varphi_2$
- $(\alpha, n) \models \neg\varphi$ iff $(\alpha, n) \not\models \varphi$
- $(\alpha, n) \models \bigcirc^g\varphi$ iff $(\alpha, succ_\alpha^g(n)) \models \varphi$, i.e., iff $(\alpha, n+1) \models \varphi$.
- $(\alpha, n) \models \bigcirc^a\varphi$ iff $succ_\alpha^a(n) \neq \bot$ and $(\alpha, succ_\alpha^a(n)) \models \varphi$.
- $(\alpha, n) \models \bigcirc^-\varphi$ iff $succ_\alpha^-(n) \neq \bot$ and $(\alpha, succ_\alpha^-(n)) \models \varphi$.
- $(\alpha, n) \models \varphi_1 \mathcal{U}^b \varphi_2$ (for any $b \in \{g, a, -\}$) iff there is a sequence of positions $i_0, i_1, \ldots, i_k$, where $i_0 = n$, $(\alpha, i_k) \models \varphi_2$ and for every $0 \leq j \leq k - 1$, $i_{j+1} = succ_\alpha^b(i_j)$ and $(\alpha, i_j) \models \varphi_1$.

The operators $\bigcirc^g$ and $\mathcal{U}^g$ are the usual global-next and global-until operators of LTL. The $\bigcirc^a$ and $\mathcal{U}^a$ operators are the abstract versions of the next and until operators— $\bigcirc^a\varphi$ demands that the abstract successor state satisfy φ while $\varphi_1 \mathcal{U}^a \varphi_2$ demands that the abstract path from the current position (i.e. the path formed by successive abstract successors) satisfy $\varphi_1 \mathcal{U} \varphi_2$.

The formula $\bigcirc^-\varphi$ demands that the caller of the current position satisfies φ while $\varphi_1 \mathcal{U}^- \varphi_2$ demands that the backward path of successive caller states (which is always finite) satisfies $\varphi_1 \mathcal{U} \varphi_2$.

As in standard linear temporal logic, we will use $\lozenge^b\varphi$ as an abbreviation for $True\,\mathcal{U}^b\varphi$, and $\square^b\varphi$ for $\neg\lozenge^b\neg\varphi$, for $b \in \{a, g, -\}$. While writing specifications, we will omit the superscript g as the global scope coincides with the classical interpretation of temporal operators, and we will also use logical connectives such as conjunction and implication freely.

Given an RSM S and a formula φ of CARET, both over AP, define $S \models \varphi$ to mean that for every $\alpha \in \mathcal{L}(S)$, $\alpha \models \varphi$. We are ready to define the model-checking question we are interested in:

Model-checking problem:

  Given an RSM S and a formula φ of CARET, does $S \models \varphi$?

Consider the RSM S, of Figure 1. Assume $start = En_1$, then $S \models \square^g(d \rightarrow \lozenge^g z)$ because every global path starting at the vertex labelled d leads to the entry of S_2, which is labeled z (assuming there are no other vertices labeled d). However, $S \not\models \square^g(d \rightarrow \lozenge^a z)$ because abstract runs starting in S_1 stay only within S_1 and do not go inside a box to visit the entry of S_2, and hence do not encounter the label z. Also note that $S \models \square^g(y \rightarrow \bigcirc^- t)$ because if we are at the exit of the module S_2, then the last call (which must exist because executions begin in S_1) must have occured from the call of box b_2 (the only box labeled by S_2).

3.2   Specifying Requirements

Pre and Post Conditions: In the classical verification formalisms such as Hoare logic, correctness of procedures is expressed using pre and post conditions [15]. Partial correctness of a procedure A specifies that if the pre-condition

p holds when the procedure A is invoked, then if the procedure terminates, the post-condition q is satisfied upon return. Total correctness, in addition, requires the procedure to terminate. Assume that all calls to the procedure A are characterized by the proposition p_A. Then, the requirement

$$\varphi_{total} : \ \Box \, [\, (call \wedge p \wedge p_A) \ \rightarrow \ \bigcirc^a q \,]$$

expresses the total correctness, while

$$\varphi_{partial} : \ \Box \, [\, (call \wedge p \wedge p_A) \ \rightarrow \ \neg \bigcirc^a \neg q \,]$$

expresses the partial correctness.

Boundedness: The number of unmatched calls at a position in a word corresponds to the height of the stack at that position. The requirement that "every call must return," or equivalently, "the stack should be empty infinitely often", is expressed by the specification

$$\varphi_{empty} : \ \Box \, (\, call \rightarrow \bigcirc^a ret \,)$$

A weaker requirement is that the stack should be repeatedly bounded, that is, there exists a natural number n such that infinitely often the stack is of height at most n. These kinds of specifications have been studied for pushdown games [8]. This property can be specified in CARET by the formula:

$$\varphi_{rep\text{-}bounded} : \ \Diamond\Box \, (\, call \rightarrow \bigcirc^a ret \,)$$

Even though this specification does not rule out the possibility that the stack grows unboundedly, an RSM S satisfies the requirement $\varphi_{rep\text{-}bounded}$ iff there exists a natural number n such that the number of pending calls at any position is at most n. The boundedness requirement itself is not expressible in our logic.

Local Properties: The abstract path starting at a node inside a module A is obtained by successive applications of $\bigcirc^a$ operator, and skips over invocations of other modules called from A. CARET formulas can specify properties of such abstract paths. For example, if the proposition t_A denotes that the control is within a module A, then the formula

$$\varphi_{local\text{-}response} : \ \Box \, [(t_A \ \wedge \ p) \ \rightarrow \ \Diamond^a q]$$

specifies the *local* version of the response property "every request p is followed by a response q." In general, any LTL expressible local property can be specified in CARET.

Stack Inspection Properties: The caller path starting at a node inside a module A is obtained by successive applications of $\bigcirc^-$ operator, and encodes the stack at that position. As shown in [18,13], stack inspection can specify a variety of security properties. For instance, the requirement that a module A should be invoked only within the context of a module B, with no intervening call to an overriding module C, is expressed by the formula

$$\varphi_{stack} : \ \Box \, (call \wedge p_A \rightarrow (\neg p_C)\,\mathcal{U}^- p_B\,).$$

In general, any property that can be formulated as a star-free regular property of the stack content can be expressed in CARET. For example, when a critical procedure is invoked, one can require that all the procedures in the call stack have the necessary privilege. We refer the reader to [18,13] for the relevance of such specifications for capturing security domains, authority delegation, and stack inspection policies in modern programming languages such as Java. Since CARET can state properties of the stack as well as the global evolution, it can express dynamic security policy constraints, where the permissions change depending upon what privileges have been used thus far (see [18] where such constraints are motivated but cannot be expressed in their logic).

It is worth noting that CARET allows nesting of different types of modalities. The requirement that a temporal property φ holds when the current module returns is expressed by the formula

$$\varphi_{upon\text{-}return} : \bigcirc^- \bigcirc^a \varphi$$

This property is not expressible in existing approaches such as augmenting LTL with regular stack valuations [13].

Interrupt-driven sequences: Interrupt-driven software are prevalent in the embedded software domain where the stack-size is very limited. In this setting, while the system is handling an interrupt, the same interrupt could occur, causing the stack to get large. Estimating the maximum stack content is thus a relevant question (see for example [9]). The property that states that "in computations where an interrupt is not interrupted by itself, the formula φ holds" can be expressed in CARET as:

$$\varphi_{no\text{-}rec\text{-}int} : \Box \left((call \wedge p_{int}) \to \neg \bigcirc^- \Diamond^- p_{int} \right) \to \varphi$$

We can also write CARET formulas that are true only where the stack depth reaches n, for some constant n.

RSM Encoding: Our logic is rich enough to encode the computations of an RSM in a manner similar to the encoding of finite-state machines in LTL. For an RSM S, we write the formula φ_S by introducing a proposition for every vertex of S and ensuring local rules of the evolution of S using the global-next modalities. To ensure that a call at (b, e) returns to some return of the form (b, x), we can assert the following: whenever $p_{(b,e)}$ holds (where $p_{(b,e)}$ is the proposition for (b, e)), either $\neg \bigcirc^a$ *true* holds or for precisely one return of the form (b, x), both $\bigcirc^a p_{(b,x)}$ and $\bigcirc^g \Diamond^a p_x$ hold. Then for any S, φ_S is such that for any formula φ, $S \models \varphi$ iff $\varphi_S \to \varphi$ is valid.

It is worth noting that if S and S' are RSMs (or pushdown automata) then $\varphi_S \wedge \varphi_{S'}$ does not represent the intersection of their languages in the usual sense due to the shared *call* and *ret* tags; it represents the synchronized product where the two are required to synchronize on when to call (i.e. push) and when to return (i.e. pop).

4   Model Checking

In this section we show how to solve the model checking problem for RSMs against CARET specifications. We first define the notion of recursive generalized Büchi automata which our decision procedure will use.

4.1   Recursive Generalized Büchi Automata

Our automata-based algorithms will use RSMs augmented with acceptance conditions: both ordinary and generalized Büchi conditions. A *recursive generalized Büchi automaton* (RGBA) $S = (M, \{S_m\}_{m \in M}, start, \mathcal{F})$ consists of an RSM together with a family $\mathcal{F} = \{F_1, \ldots, F_r\}$ of accepting sets of vertices of S where $F_j \subseteq V$, for $j \in \{1, \ldots, r\}$. When there is only one accepting set, $\mathcal{F} = \{F\}$, we have a *Recursive Büchi Automaton* (RBA).

For an RGBA S, the acceptance condition $\mathcal{F} = \{F_1, \ldots, F_r\}$, induces an acceptance condition on the Kripke structure K_S: $\mathcal{F}^\# = \{F_1^\#, \ldots, F_r^\#\}$, where $F_i^\# = \{(\gamma, u) \in Q \mid u \in F_i\}$. We say a run π of K_S is an *accepting* run iff for all $F \in \mathcal{F}$, for infinitely many $i \in \mathbb{N}$, $s_i \in F^\#$. For an RGBA S, let $\mathcal{L}(S) = \{\alpha \in \hat{\Gamma}^\omega \mid$ there is an accepting run of K_S on $\alpha\}$. Note that when there is no acceptance condition, i.e., when $\mathcal{F}$ is the empty set, every run is accepting, and thus such RGBAs correspond to ordinary RSMs.

An important parameter of the size of an RSM S, introduced in [1], is $\theta_S = \max_{m \in M} \min\{|En_m|, |Ex_m|\}$, that is, each module has at most θ_S entries or θ_S exits. It was shown in [1] that reachability analysis for RSMs and language emptiness for RBAs can be performed in time $O(|S|\theta_S^2)$ and space $O(|S|\theta_S)$. This construction can be generalized to obtain the following:

Proposition 1. *Given an RGBA S, with acceptance condition $\mathcal{F} = \{F_1, \ldots, F_r\}$, checking $\mathcal{L}(S) = \emptyset$ can be solved in time $O(r|S|\theta_S^2)$ and space $O(r|S|\theta_S)$.*

To see why the proposition holds, let us recall the algorithm of [1] for the analysis of RBAs with one acceptance condition F. That algorithm proceeds in two phases. In the first phase, for each component S_m, we compute for every entry en and every exit ex of S_m whether there is a path from (ϵ, en) to (ϵ, ex) in the global Kripke structure K_S, and if so, whether there is a path that goes through an accepting state in $F^\#$. This involves solving reachability in an And-Or graph and takes time $O(|S|\theta_S^2)$ and space $O(|S|\theta_S)$. We then augment the RSM with "summary edges" between calls and returns of boxes, to indicate reachability from entries to exits, and we label these summary edges as "accepting edges" if it is possible to get from the entry to the exit via an accepting state. In addition, we also add edges from a call to the corresponding entry of the component that labels the call's box. Once all these edges are added, we are left with an ordinary (flat) Büchi automaton of size $O(|S|\theta_S)$, in which we must detect the existence of a reachable accepting cycle (which we can in linear time).

To generalize this construction to RGBAs with acceptance condition $\mathcal{F} = \{F_1, \ldots, F_r\}$, we first observe that we can do the first phase of "summary edge" calculation separately with respect to every accepting set $F_i \in \mathcal{F}$. We then label each summary edge from a call to a return with the set $C \subseteq \{1, \ldots, r\}$ of "colors" corresponding to those accepting sets which can be visited on some path from the respective entry to the exit. The computation takes time $O(r|S|\theta_S^2)$, and the resulting flat generalized Büchi automaton H has $O(|S|\theta_S)$ edges, but summary edges can each be labeled with $O(r)$ colors. To check that $\mathcal{L}(H) = \emptyset$, we can use a slightly modified version of the standard algorithm for conversion of the generalized Büchi automaton H to a Büchi automaton, to produce a Büchi automaton H' of size $O(r|S|\theta_S)$ that accepts the same language as H. We then run a linear time emptiness test on this Büchi automaton.

4.2   The Decision Procedure

The main construction here will show how to build, for any RSM S and a formula φ over AP, a recursive generalized Büchi automata (RGBA) that accepts exactly the set of words in $\mathcal{L}(S)$ that satisfy φ. For simplifying the proof, we assume without loss of generality that in the RSMs we consider, entries have no incoming transitions, exits have no outgoing transitions and there are no transitions from returns to calls nor exits.

Let φ be a formula over AP. The closure of φ, $Cl(\varphi)$, is the smallest set that contains φ, contains $call$, ret and int, and satisfies the following properties:

- If $\neg\varphi' \in Cl(\varphi)$ or $\bigcirc^b\varphi' \in Cl(\varphi)$ (for some $b \in \{g, a, -\}$), then $\varphi' \in Cl(\varphi)$.
- If $\varphi' \vee \varphi'' \in Cl(\varphi)$, then $\varphi', \varphi'' \in Cl(\varphi)$.
- If $\varphi'\mathcal{U}^b\varphi'' \in Cl(\varphi)$, where $b \in \{g, a, -\}$, then φ', φ'', and $\bigcirc^b(\varphi'\mathcal{U}^b\varphi'')$ are in $Cl(\varphi)$.
- If $\varphi' \in Cl(\varphi)$ and φ' is not of the form $\neg\varphi''$ (for any φ''), then $\neg\varphi' \in Cl(\varphi)$.

It is straightforward to see that the size of $Cl(\varphi)$ is only linear in the size of φ. Henceforth, we identify $\neg\neg\varphi$ with the formula φ.

An *atom* of φ is a set $Y \subseteq Cl(\varphi)$ that satisfies the following properties:

- For every $\varphi' \in Cl(\varphi)$, $\varphi' \in Y$ iff $\neg\varphi' \notin Y$.
- For every formula $\varphi' \vee \varphi'' \in Cl(\varphi)$, $\varphi' \vee \varphi'' \in Y$ iff ($\varphi' \in Y$ or $\varphi'' \in Y$).
- For every formula $\varphi'\mathcal{U}^b\varphi'' \in Cl(\varphi)$, where $b \in \{a, g, -\}$, $\varphi'\mathcal{U}^b\varphi'' \in Y$ iff either $\varphi'' \in Y$ or ($\varphi' \in Y$ and $\bigcirc^b(\varphi'\mathcal{U}^b\varphi'') \in Y$).
- Y contains exactly one of the elements in the set $\{call, ret, int\}$.

Let $Atoms(\varphi)$ denote the set of atoms of φ; note that there are $2^{O(|\varphi|)}$ atoms of φ. To handle formulas in LTL, we can build a pushdown automaton whose states are of the form (u, A), where u is the current node of the RSM that is being simulated and A is an atom that represents the set of formulas true at u. We can use the stack for storing the names of the boxes, pushing in the box name at a call and popping it at the return.

The main difference in the construction for CARET formulas is that at a call, the atom A true at the call is also pushed onto the stack along with the box b. When the call returns, we pop b and A and make sure that the abstract-next requirements in A get satisfied at the return-node. Note that we cannot keep track of A using the finite-state control because recursive calls will make the set of atoms to be remembered unbounded.

The caller modality is easier to handle. If we are at a call (b, e) where the set of formulas A is true, then a formula $\bigcirc^-\varphi'$ is true in the module being called only if $\varphi' \in A$. The caller formulas are hence passed down from the caller to the called module. The above two ideas are the crux of the construction.

There are several other technical issues to be handled. When an until-formula $\varphi_1\, \mathcal{U}^b \varphi_2$ is asserted at a node, we must make sure the liveness requirement φ_2 is eventually satisfied. This is done (as for LTL) using a generalized Büchi condition, one for each until formula. Caller-until formulas do not even require such a condition as the caller-path from any node is finite.

If an abstract-until formula $\varphi_1\, \mathcal{U}^a \varphi_2$ is asserted at a node u in a module, its liveness requirement φ_2 must be met in the abstract path from u and not in a node belonging to an invocation from the current module. In order to handle this we also keep track in the state whether the current node belongs to an invocation that will eventually return or not. For an abstract-until formula, the Büchi condition corresponding it has only states that correspond to invocations that do not return.

Let us now describe the construction formally. Let the given RSM be $(M, \{S_m\}_{m \in M}, start)$. Let $M' = \{m' \mid m \in M\}$ be a new set of module names, one for each module $m \in M$. The recursive generalized Büchi automaton we construct is $(M', \{S_{m'}\}_{m \in M'}, start', \mathcal{F})$ which is defined below.

Let $Tag = \{inf, fin\}$. For every node $u \in N_m$ that is not an exit there are nodes of the form (u, A, t) in $S_{m'}$, where A is an atom that represents the set of formulas that hold at u and $t \in Tag$ is a tag that signifies whether the run in the current module is infinite (inf–will never exit) or is finite (fin–will exit eventually). Similarly, for every $b \in B_m$, there are boxes of the form (b, A, t) in $S_{m'}$ where t is a tag and A is an atom containing formulas true at entries (b, e).

For any vertex v of S, we say an atom A is propositionally consistent with v if $\eta(v) \cap AP = A \cap AP$ and, further, if v is a node, then $int \in A$, if v is a call, then $call \in A$ and if v is a return then $ret \in A$.

For every $m \in M$, if $S_m = (N_m, B_m, Y_m, En_m, Ex_m, \delta_m, \eta_m)$, then $S'_m = (N_{m'}, B_{m'}, Y_{m'}, En_{m'}, Ex_{m'}, \delta_{m'}, \eta_{m'})$ where

- $N_{m'} = \{\, (u, A, t) \mid u \in N_m \setminus Ex_m, A \in Atoms(\varphi), t \in Tag$ and A is propositionally consistent with $u\,\} \cup$
  $\{\, (x, A, R) \mid x \in Ex_m, A, R \in Atoms(\varphi),$ and A is propositionally consistent with $x\,\}$
- $B_{m'} = B_m \times Atoms(\varphi) \times Tag; \quad Y_{m'}(b, A, t) = (Y_m(b))'$
- $En_{m'} = \{(e, A, t) \mid e \in En_m, A \in Atoms(\varphi), t \in Tag\}$
- $Ex_{m'} = \{(x, A, R) \mid x \in Ex_m, A, R \in Atoms(\varphi)\}$
- $\eta_{m'}((u, A, t)) = \eta_m(u), \quad \eta_{m'}(((b, A, t), (e, A', t'))) = \eta_m((b, e))$, and
  $\eta_{m'}(((b, A, t), (x, A', R))) = \eta_m((b, x))$

Notice that calls are of the form $((b, A, t), (e, A', t'))$. In this A is the set of formulas true at this call and A' is the set of formulas true at the next vertex which will be the entry e. Hence, since the box-name (b, A, t) is pushed on the stack, the formulas A true at the call is remembered across the invocation.

Exits are of the form (x, A, R); here A denotes the formulas that are true at the exit x while R denotes the formulas true when the control returns to the called module. At a return $((b, A, t), (x, A', R))$, since the set of formulas true at the call was A and the set of formulas true at return is R, we will require that the abstract-next requirements in A are met in R.

For atoms A and A', we define a relation $AbsNextReq(A, A')$ that is true iff the abstract-next requirements in A are exactly the ones that hold in A', i.e. for each $\bigcirc^a \varphi' \in Cl(\varphi)$, $\bigcirc^a \varphi' \in A$ iff $\varphi' \in A'$. Similarly, we define a relation $GlNextReq(A, A')$ that is true iff the global-next requirements in A are exactly the ones that hold in A', i.e. for each $\bigcirc^g \varphi' \in Cl(\varphi)$, $\bigcirc^g \varphi' \in A$ iff $\varphi' \in A'$.

Also, let the caller formulas in A be denoted by $CallerFormulas(A) = \{\bigcirc^- \varphi' \mid \bigcirc^- \varphi' \in A\}$. The transition relation $\delta_{m'}$ is defined as follows:

(T1) From nodes to non-exit nodes: $\delta_{m'}((u, A, t))$ contains (u', A', t') iff:
- $u' \in \delta_m(u)$; $t = t'$
- $GlNextReq(A, A')$ and $AbsNextReq(A, A')$
- $CallerFormulas(A) = CallerFormulas(A')$

(T2) From nodes to calls: $\delta_{m'}((u, A, t))$ contains $((b, A', t'), (e, A'', t''))$ iff:
- $(b, e) \in \delta_m(u)$; $t' = t$
- A' is propositionally consistent with (b, e).
- $GlNextReq(A, A')$ and $AbsNextReq(A, A')$
- $CallerFormulas(A) = CallerFormulas(A')$
- $GlNextReq(A', A'')$; $CallerFormulas(A'') = \{\bigcirc^- \varphi' \in Cl(\varphi) \mid \varphi' \in A'\}$
- If $t'' = inf$, then $t = inf$ and there is no formula of the kind $\bigcirc^a \varphi$ in A'.

(T3) From nodes to exits:
$\delta_{m'}((u, A, t))$ contains (x, A', R), where $x \in Ex_m$, iff:
- $x \in \delta_m(u)$; $t = fin$
- $GlNextReq(A, A')$; $AbsNextReq(A, A')$; $GlNextReq(A', R)$
- $CallerFormulas(A) = CallerFormulas(A')$
- There is no formula of the kind $\bigcirc^a \varphi$ in A'.

(T4) From returns to nodes: $\delta_{m'}((b, A, t), (x, A', R))$ contains (u, A'', t'') iff
- $u \in \delta_m((b, x))$; $t'' = t$
- $AbsNextReq(A, R)$; $CallerFormulas(A) = CallerFormulas(R)$
- R is propositionally consistent with (b, x).
- $GlNextReq(R, A'')$ and $AbsNextReq(R, A'')$
- $CallerFormulas(R) = CallerFormulas(A'')$

The set of initial nodes is the set $start' = \{(u, A, t) \mid u \in start, \varphi \in A, A \text{ does not contain any formulas of the form } \bigcirc^- \varphi', t = inf\}$.

We say an atom A *momentarily satisfies* an abstract or global until formula $\varphi_1 \mathcal{U}^b \varphi_2$ (where $b = g$ or $b = a$) if either $\varphi_2 \in A$ or $\varphi_1 \mathcal{U}^b \varphi_2 \notin A$.
The generalized Büchi condition $\mathcal{F}$ is given by the following sets:
- A set containing all vertices of the form (u, A, t), where $t = inf$.
- For every global-until formula $\varphi_1 \mathcal{U}^g \varphi_2$ in $Cl(\varphi)$, there is a set in $\mathcal{F}$ containing all vertices of the form (u, A, t) or (x, A, R) or $((b, A, t, R), (e, A', t'))$ or $((b, A', t, A), (x, A'', A))$ where A momentarily satisfies $\varphi_1 \mathcal{U}^g \varphi_2$.
- For every abstract-until formula $\varphi_1 \mathcal{U}^a \varphi_2$ in $Cl(\varphi)$, there is a set in $\mathcal{F}$ containing all vertices of the form (u, A, t), $((b, A, t, R), (e, A', t'))$ or $((b, A', t, A), (x, A'', A))$ where A momentarily satisfies $\varphi_1 \mathcal{U}^a \varphi_2$ and $t = inf$.

The first set ensures that the tags were guessed correctly. The second class of states ensure that global-until formulas get satisfied eventually. For abstract-until formulas that get asserted at nodes where the abstract-path is infinite, the third class of sets ensure that they get eventually satisfied. Hence:

Theorem 1. *Given an RSM S and a formula φ, the model-checking problem for S against φ can be solved in time $|S| \cdot \theta_S^2 \cdot 2^{O(|\varphi|)}$, i.e., in time polynomial in S and exponential in the size of the formula. The problem is* EXPTIME-*complete (even when the RSM is fixed).*

Proof: Given RSM S and a formula φ, construct the RGBA $S_{\neg\varphi}$ for the RSM S and the negation of the formula φ. This RGBA generates exactly the runs of S that do not satisfy φ. Note that for every vertex/edge in S, we have $2^{O(|\varphi|)}$ vertices/edges in the RGBA; similarly $\theta_{S_{\neg\varphi}}$ is $\theta_S \cdot 2^{O(|\varphi|)}$. Also, the number of generalized Büchi sets is at most $|\varphi|+1$. By Proposition 1, the complexity follows and the problem is in EXPTIME. It is known that checking RSMs against LTL is already EXPTIME-hard, even when the RSM is fixed (this follows from the proof in [5]). Hence the problem is EXPTIME-complete.   □

5   Conclusions

We have proposed a notion of structured computations that abstractly captures reactive computations with nested calls and returns of program modules. We have introduced a temporal logic that allows specification of requirements of such computations, and a decision procedure to model check such specifications with respect to recursive state machines. This leads to a rich and unified framework for algorithmic reasoning about temporal requirements, stack inspection properties, and classical correctness requirements of structured programs. While our technical focus has been on model checking, CARET can be used in other applications such as simulation and runtime monitoring where LTL has been established to be fruitful.

The temporal modalities presented in this paper are natural for structured computations, but are not exhaustive. For example, one can define *global-predecessor*, *abstract-predecessor*, and *next-return* as the temporal duals of the global-successor, abstract-successor, and last-caller modalities, respectively. These can be added to the logic at no extra cost. On the other hand, consider the *within* modality I: $I\varphi$ holds at a call position i iff the computation fragment from position i to j, where j is the matching return, satisfies the temporal formula φ. Adding this modality raises the complexity of model checking to 2EXPTIME. A related question concerns the *expressive completeness* of the logic. We are currently studying the problem of characterizing the subclass of context-free properties that can be algorithmically checked against an RSM model.

Acknowledgement. We thank Mihalis Yannakakis for fruitful discussions.

References

1. R. Alur, K. Etessami, and M. Yannakakis. Analysis of recursive state machines. In *Proc. of CAV'01*, LNCS 2102, pages 207–220. Springer, 2001.
2. T. Ball and S. Rajamani. Bebop: A symbolic model checker for boolean programs. *SPIN Workshop on Model Checking of Software*, LNCS 1885, pages 113–130, 2000.

3. M. Benedikt, P. Godefroid, and T. Reps. Model checking of unrestricted hierarchical state machines. In Proc. ICALP, volume LNCS 2076, pages 652–666. 2001.
4. A. Bouajjani, R. Echahed, and P. Habermehl. On the verification problem of nonregular properties for nonregular processes. In *Proc., 10th Annual IEEE Symp. on Logic in Computer Science*, pages 123–133. IEEE, 1995.
5. A. Bouajjani, J. Esparza, and O. Maler. Reachability analysis of pushdown automata: Applications to model checking. In *CONCUR'97: Concurrency Theory, Eighth International Conference*, LNCS 1243, pages 135–150. Springer, 1997.
6. L. Burdy, Y. Cheon, D. Cok, M. Ernst, J. Kiniry, G.T. Leavens, R. Leino, and E. Poll. An overview of JML tools and applications. In *Proc. 8th International Workshop on Formal Methods for Industrial Critical Systems*, pages 75–89, 2003.
7. O. Burkart and B. Steffen. Model checking for context-free processes. In *CONCUR'92: Concurrency Theory*, LNCS 630, pages 123–137. Springer, 1992.
8. T. Cachat, J. Duparc, and W. Thomas. Solving pushdown games with a Σ_3 winning condition. In *Proc. of CSL 2002*, LNCS 2471, 322–336. Springer, 2002.
9. K. Chatterjee, D. Ma, R. Majumdar, T. Zhao, T.A. Henzinger, and J. Palsberg. Stack size analysis for interrupt driven programs. In *Proceedings of the 10th International Symposium on Static Analysis*, volume LNCS 2694, pages 109–126, 2003.
10. H. Chen and D. Wagner. Mops: an infrastructure for examining security properties of software. In *Proceedings of ACM Conference on Computer and Communications Security*, pages 235–244, 2002.
11. E.M. Clarke and E.A. Emerson. Design and synthesis of synchronization skeletons using branching time temporal logic. In *Proc. Workshop on Logic of Programs*, LNCS 131, pages 52–71. Springer-Verlag, 1981.
12. J. Esparza, D. Hansel, P. Rossmanith, and S. Schwoon. Efficient algorithms for model checking pushdown systems. In *Computer Aided Verification, 12th International Conference*, LNCS 1855, pages 232–247. Springer, 2000.
13. J. Esparza, A. Kucera, and S. S. Schwoon. Model-checking LTL with regular valuations for pushdown systems. *Information and Computation*, 186(2):355–376, 2003.
14. D. Harel, D. Kozen and J. Tiuryn. *Dynamic Logic*. MIT Press, 2000.
15. C.A.R. Hoare. An axiomatic basis for computer programming. *Communications of the ACM*, 12(10):576–580, 1969.
16. G.J. Holzmann. The model checker SPIN. *IEEE Transactions on Software Engineering*, 23(5):279–295, 1997.
17. J.E. Hopcroft and J.D. Ullman. *Introduction to Automata Theory, Languages, and Computation*. Addison-Wesley, 1979.
18. T. Jensen, D. Le Metayer, and T. Thorn. Verification of control flow based security properties. In *Proc. of the IEEE Symp. on Security and Privacy*, 89–103, 1999.
19. O. Kupferman, N. Piterman, and M.Y. Vardi. Pushdown Specifications. In *Proc. of LPAR 02*, LNCS 2514, pages 262–277. Springer, 2002.
20. O. Kupferman, N. Piterman, and M.Y. Vardi. Model checking linear properties of prefix-recognizable systems. In Proc. of *CAV 02*, LNCS 2404, 371–385, 2002.
21. O. Lichtenstein and A. Pnueli. Checking that finite-state concurrent programs satisfy their linear specification. In *Proc., 12th ACM POPL*, pages 97–107, 1985.
22. Z. Manna and A. Pnueli. *The temporal logic of reactive and concurrent systems: Specification*. Springer-verlag, 1991.
23. A. Pnueli. The temporal logic of programs. In *Proceedings of the 18th IEEE Symposium on Foundations of Computer Science*, pages 46–77, 1977.
24. T. Reps, S. Horwitz, and S. Sagiv. Precise interprocedural dataflow analysis via graph reachability. In *Proc. ACM POPL*, pages 49–61, 1995.

Liveness with Incomprehensible Ranking[*]

Yi Fang[1], Nir Piterman[2], Amir Pnueli[1,2], and Lenore Zuck[1]

[1] New York University, New York, {yifang,amir,zuck}@cs.nyu.edu
[2] Weizmann Institute, Rehovot, Israel Nir.Piterman@weizmann.ac.il
Amir.Pnueli@weizmann.ac.il

Abstract. The methods of Invisible Invariants and Invisible Ranking were developed originally in order to verify temporal properties of parameterized systems in a fully automatic manner. These methods are based on an instantiate-project-and-generalize heuristic for the automatic generation of auxiliary constructs and a *small model property* implying that it is sufficient to check validity of a deductive rule premises using these constructs on small instantiations of the system. The previous version of the method of Invisible Ranking was restricted to cases where the helpful assertions and ranking functions for a process depended only on the local state of this process and not on any neighboring process, which seriously restricted the applicability of the method, and often required the introduction of auxiliary variables.

In this paper we extend the method of Invisible Ranking to cases where the helpful assertions and ranking functions of a process may also refer to other processes. We first develop an enhanced version of the small model property, making it applicable to assertions that refer both to processes and their immediate neighbors. This enables us to apply the Invisible Ranking method to parameterized systems with ring topologies. For cases where the auxiliary assertions refer to all processes, we develop a novel proof rule which simplifies the selection of the next helpful transition, and enables the validation of the premises possible under the (old) small model theorem.

1 Introduction

Uniform verification of parameterized systems is one of the most challenging problems in verification today. Given a parameterized system $S(N) : P[1]\| \cdots \|P[N]$ and a property p, uniform verification attempts to verify $S(N) \models p$ for every $N > 1$. One of the most powerful approaches to verification which is not restricted to finite-state systems is *deductive verification*. This approach is based on a set of proof rules in which the user has to establish the validity of a list of premises in order to validate a given property of the system. The two tasks that the user has to perform are:

1. Identify some auxiliary constructs which appear in the premises of the rule;
2. Use the auxiliary constructs to establish the logical validity of the premises.

---

[*] This research was supported in part by NSF grant CCR-0205571, ONR grant N000140310916, the Minerva Center for Verification of Reactive Systems, the European Community IST project "Advance", and the Israel Science Foundation grant 106/02-1.

K. Jensen and A. Podelski (Eds.): TACAS 2004, LNCS 2988, pp. 482–496, 2004.
© Springer-Verlag Berlin Heidelberg 2004

When performing manual deductive verification, the first task is usually the more difficult, requiring ingenuity, expertise, and a good understanding of the behavior of the program and the techniques for formalizing these insights. The second task is often performed using theorem provers such as PVS [OSR93] or STEP [BBC$^+$95], which require user guidance and interaction, and place additional burden on the user. The difficulties in the execution of these two tasks are the main reason why deductive verification is not used more widely.

A representative case is the verification of invariance properties using the *invariance rule* of [MP95]. In order to prove that assertion r is an invariant of program P, the rule requires coming up with an auxiliary assertion φ which is *inductive* (i.e. is implied by the initial condition and is preserved under every computation step) and which strengthens (implies) r.

In [PRZ01,APR$^+$01] we introduced the method of *invisible invariants*, which proposes a method for automatic generation of the auxiliary assertion φ for parameterized systems, as well as an efficient algorithm for checking the validity of the premises of the invariance rule. In [FPPZ04] we extended the method of invisible invariants to *invisible ranking*, by applying the method for automatic generation of auxiliary assertions to general assertions (not necessarily invariant), and proposing a rule for proving liveness properties of the form $\Box(p \rightarrow \Diamond q)$ (i.e, *progress properties*) that embeds the generated assertions in its premises, and efficiently checks for their validity.

The generation of invisible auxiliary constructs is based on the following idea: It is often the case that an auxiliary assertion φ for a parameterized system has the form $q(i)$, $\forall i.q(i)$ or, more generally, $\forall i \neq j.q(i,j)$. We construct an instance of the parameterized system taking a fixed value N_0 for the parameter N. For the finite-state instantiation $S(N_0)$, we compute, using BDD-techniques, some assertion ψ, which we wish to generalize to an assertion in the required form. Let r_1 be the projection of ψ on process index 1, obtained by discarding references to all variables which are local to all processes other than $P[1]$. We take $q(i)$ to be the generalization of r_1 obtained by replacing each reference to a local variable $P[1].x$ by a reference to $P[i].x$. The obtained $q(i)$ is our candidate for the body of the inductive assertion $\varphi : \forall i.q(i)$. We refer to this part of the process as *project&generalize*. For example, when computing invisible invariants, ψ is the set of reachable states of $S(N_0)$. The process can be easily generalized to generate assertions of the type $\forall i_1, \ldots, i_k.p(\vec{i})$.

Having obtained a candidate for the assertion φ, we still have to check the validity of the premises of the proof rule we wish to employ. Under the assumption that our assertional language is restricted to the predicates of equality and inequality between bounded range integer variables (which is adequate for many of the parameterized systems we considered), we proved a *small model* theorem, according to which, for a certain type of assertions, there exists a (small) bound N_0 such that such an assertion is valid for every N iff it is valid for all $N \leq N_0$. This enables using BDD techniques to check the validity of such an assertion. The assertions covered by the theorem are those that can be written in the form $\forall \vec{i} \exists \vec{j}.\psi(\vec{i}, \vec{j})$, where $\psi(\vec{i}, \vec{j})$ is a quantifier-free assertion which may refer only to the global variables and the local variables of $P[i]$ and $P[j]$.

Being able to validate the premises on $S[N_0]$ has the additional important advantage that the user never sees the automatically generated auxiliary assertion φ. This assertion is produced as part of the procedure and is immediately consumed in order to validate the premises of the rule. Being generated by symbolic BDD techniques, the representation of the auxiliary assertions is often extremely unreadable and non-intuitive, and will usually not contribute to a better understanding of the program or its proof. Because the user never gets to see it, we refer to this method as the "method of *invisible invariants*."

As shown in [PRZ01,APR⁺01], embedding a $\forall \vec{i}.q(\vec{i})$ candidate inductive invariant in the main proof rule used for safety properties results in premises that fall under the small model theorem. In [FPPZ04], the proof rule used for proving progress properties requires that some auxiliary constructs have no quantifiers in order to result in $\forall \exists$-premises. In particular, it requires the "helpful assertions", describing when a transition is helpful (thus, leads to a lower ranked state), to be quantifier-free. This is the case for many simple protocols. In fact, many parameterized protocols that have been studied in the literature can be transformed into protocols that have unquantified helpful transitions by adding some auxiliary variables that allow, in each state, to determine the helpful assertions.

In this paper, we extend the method of invisible ranking and make it applicable to a much wider set of protocols in two directions:

- The first extension allows expression such as $i \pm 1$ to appear both in the transition relation as well as the auxiliary constructs. This extension is especially important for ring algorithms, where many of the assertion have a $p(i, i + 1)$ or $p(i, i - 1)$ component.
- The second extension, allows helpful assertions (and ranking functions) for, say process i, to be of the form $h(i) = \forall j.H(i, j)$, where $H(i, j)$ is a quantifier-free assertion. Such helpful assertions are common in "unstructured" systems where whether a transition of one process is helpful depends on the states of all its neighbors. Substituted in the standard proof rules for progress properties, such helpful assertions lead to premises which do not conform to the required $\forall \exists$ form, and therefore cannot be validated using the small model theorem.

To handle the first extension, we establish a new small model theorem, to which we refer as the *modest model theorem* (introduced in Subsection 3.1). This theorem shows that, similarly to the small model theorem of [PRZ01] and [FPPZ04], $\forall \exists$-premises, containing $i \pm 1$ sub-expressions, can be validated on relatively small models. The size of the models, however, is larger compared to the previous small model theorem.

To handle the second extension, we introduce a novel proof rule: The main difficulty with helpful assertions of the form $h(i) = \forall j.H(i, j)$ is in the premise (D4 of rule DISTRANK of Section 2) which claims that every "pending" state has some helpful transitions enabled on it. Identifying the particular helpful transition for each pending state is the hardest step when applying the rule. The new rule, PRERANK (introduced in Section 4), implements a new mechanism for selecting the helpful transitions based on the installment of a *pre-order* among the helpful transitions in each state. The "helpful" transition is identified as any transition which is minimal according to this pre-order.

We emphasize that the two extensions are part of the same method, so that we can handle systems that both use ± 1 and require universal helpful assertions. For simplicity of exposition, we separate the extensions here.

We show the applicability of the extensions on two algorithms, a solution to the Dining Philosophers problems that uses ± 1 (but does not require quantified helpful assertions), and the Bakery algorithm that requires quantified helpful assertions (but does not use ± 1).

The paper is organized as follows: In Section 2 we present the general computational model of FDS and the restrictions which enable the application of the invisible auxiliary constructs methods. We also review the small model property which enables automatic validation of the premises of the various proof rules. In addition, we outline a procedure that replaces compassion by justice requirements, describe the DISTRANK proof rule, and explain how we automatically generate ranking and helpful assertions for the parameterized case. In Section 3 we describe the modest model theorem which allows handling of $i \pm 1$ expressions within assertions, and demonstrate these techniques on the Dining Philosopher problem. In Section 4 we present the new PRERANK proof rule that uses pre-order among transitions, discuss how to automatically obtain the pre-order, and demonstrate the techniques on the Bakery algorithm. All our examples have been run on TLV [Sha00]. The interested reader may find the code, proof files, and output of all our examples in *cs.nyu.edu/acsys/Tlv/assertions*.

Related Work. The problem of uniform verification of parameterized systems is, in general, undecidable [AK86]. One approach to remedy this situation, pursued, e.g., in [EK00], is to look for restricted families of parameterized systems for which the problem becomes decidable. Unfortunately, the proposed restrictions are very severe and exclude many useful systems such as asynchronous systems where processes communicate by shared variables.

Another approach is to look for sound but incomplete methods. Representative works of this approach include methods based on: explicit induction ([EN95]), network invariants that can be viewed as implicit induction ([LHR97]), abstraction and approximation of network invariants ([CGJ95]), and other methods based on abstraction ([GZ98]). Other methods include those relying on "regular model-checking" (e.g., [JN00]) that overcome some of the complexity issues by employing *acceleration* procedures, methods based on symmetry reduction (e.g., [GS97]), or compositional methods (e.g., ([McM98]) that combine automatic abstraction with finite-instantiation due to symmetry. Some of these approaches (such as the "regular model checking" approach) are restricted to particular architectures and may, occasionally, fail to terminate. Others, require the user to provide auxiliary constructs and thus do not provide for fully automatic verification of parameterized systems.

Most of the mentioned methods only deal with safety properties. Among the methods dealing with liveness properties, we mention [CS02] which handles termination of sequential programs, network invariants [LHR97], and *counter abstraction* [PXZ02].

2 Preliminaries

In this section we present our computation model, the small model theorem, and the proof rule we use for the verification of progress properties.

2.1 Fair Discrete Systems

As our computational model, we take a *fair discrete system* (FDS) $S = \langle V, \Theta, \rho, \mathcal{J}, \mathcal{C} \rangle$, where

- V — A set of *system variables*. A *state* of S provides a type-consistent interpretation of the variables V. For a state s and a system variable $v \in V$, we denote by $s[v]$ the value assigned to v by the state s. Let Σ denote the set of all states over V.
- Θ — The *initial condition*: An assertion (state formula) characterizing the initial states.
- $\rho(V, V')$ — The *transition relation*: An assertion, relating the values V of the variables in state $s \in \Sigma$ to the values V' in an S-successor state $s' \in \Sigma$.
- $\mathcal{J}$ — A set of *justice (weak fairness)* requirements (assertions); A computation must include infinitely many states satisfying each of the justice requirements.
- $\mathcal{C}$ — A set of *compassion (strong fairness)* requirements: Each compassion requirement is a pair $\langle p, q \rangle$ of state assertions; A computation should include either only finitely many p-states, or infinitely many q-states.

For an assertion ψ, we say that $s \in \Sigma$ is a ψ-state if $s \models \psi$. A *computation* of an FDS S is an infinite sequence of states $\sigma : s_0, s_1, s_2, \dots$, satisfying the requirements:

- *Initiality* — s_0 is initial, i.e., $s_0 \models \Theta$.
- *Consecution* — For each $\ell = 0, 1, \dots$, the state $s_{\ell+1}$ is an S-successor of s_ℓ. That is, $\langle s_\ell, s_{\ell+1} \rangle \models \rho(V, V')$ where, for each $v \in V$, we interpret v as $s_\ell[v]$ and v' as $s_{\ell+1}[v]$.
- *Justice* — for every $J \in \mathcal{J}$, σ contains infinitely many occurrences of J-states.
- *Compassion* – for every $\langle p, q \rangle \in \mathcal{C}$, either σ contains only finitely many occurrences of p-states, or σ contains infinitely many occurrences of q-states.

2.2   Bounded Fair Discrete Systems

To allow the application of the invisible constructs methods, we place further restrictions on the systems we study, leading to the model of *fair bounded discrete systems* (FBDS), that is essentially the model of bounded discrete systems of [APR+01] augmented with fairness. For brevity, we describe here a simplified two-type model; the extension for the general multi-type case is straightforward.

Let $N \in \mathbb{N}^+$ be the *system's parameter*. We allow the following data types:

1. **bool**: the set of boolean and finite-range scalars;
2. **index**: a scalar data type that includes integers in the range $[1..N]$;
3. **data**: a scalar data type that includes integers in the range $[0..N]$; and
4. arrays of the types **index** $\mapsto$ **bool** and **index** $\mapsto$ **data**.

Atomic formulas may compare two variables of the same type. E.g., if y and y' are **index** variables, and z is a **index** $\mapsto$ **data**, then $y = y'$ and $z[y] < z[y']$ are both atomic formulas. For $z :$ **index** $\mapsto$ **data** and $y :$ **index**, we also allow the special atomic formula $z[y] > 0$. We refer to quantifier-free formulas obtained by boolean combinations of such atomic formulas as *restricted assertions*.

As the initial condition Θ, we allow assertions of the form $\forall i.u(i)$, where $u(i)$ is a restricted assertion.

As the transition relation ρ, as well as the justice requirements $\mathcal{J}$, we allow assertions of the form $\exists \vec{i} \forall \vec{j}.\psi(\vec{i}, \vec{j})$ for a restricted assertion $\psi(\vec{i}, \vec{j})$. For simplicity, we assume that all quantified variables, free variables, and index constants are of type **index**.

$$\prod_{i=1}^{N} P[i] :: \begin{array}{l} \textbf{in} \quad N : \textbf{natural where } N > 1 \\ \textbf{local} \ y \ : \textbf{array } [1..N] \textbf{ of } [0..N] \textbf{ where } y = 0 \\ \left[\begin{array}{l} \textbf{loop forever do} \\ \left[\begin{array}{l} 0 : \textbf{NonCritical} \\ 1 : y := \text{maximal value to } y[i] \text{ while preserving order of elements} \\ 2 : \textbf{await } \forall j \neq i : (y[j] = 0 \ \vee \ y[j] > y[i]) \\ 3 : \textbf{Critical} \\ 4 : y[i] := 0 \end{array}\right] \end{array}\right] \end{array}$$

Fig. 1. Program BAKERY

Example 1 (The Bakery Algorithm).
Consider program BAKERY in Fig. 1, which is a variant of Lamport's original Bakery Algorithm that offers a solution of the mutual exclusion problem for any N processes. In this version of the algorithm, location ℓ_0 constitutes the non-critical section which may non-deterministically exit to the trying section at location ℓ_1. Location ℓ_1 is the ticket assignment location. Location ℓ_2 is the waiting phase, where a process waits until it holds the minimal ticket. Location ℓ_3 is the critical section, and location ℓ_4 is the exit section. Note that y, the ticket array, is of type **index** $\mapsto$ **data**, and the program location array (which we denote by π) is of type **index** $\mapsto$ **bool**. Note also that the ticket assignment statement at ℓ_1 is non-deterministic and may modify the values of all tickets. Fig. 2 describes the FBDS corresponding to program BAKERY.

$$V : \begin{cases} y : \textbf{array}[1..N] \textbf{ of } [0..N] \\ \pi : \textbf{array}[1..N] \textbf{ of } [0..4] \end{cases}$$

$\Theta : \forall i : \pi[i] = 0 \ \wedge \ y[i] = 0$

$\rho : \exists i : \forall j, k \neq i : (\pi'[j] = \pi[j]) \wedge$
$$\left[\begin{array}{l} \pi[i] = \pi'[i] \ \wedge \ y'[i] = y[i] \ \wedge \ y'[j] = y[j] \\ \vee \ \pi[i] = 0 \ \wedge \ \pi'[i] \in \{0,1\} \ \wedge \ y'[i] = y[i] \ \wedge \ y'[j] = y[j] \\ \vee \ \pi[i] = 1 \ \wedge \ \pi'[i] = 2 \ \wedge \ y'[j] < y'[i] \ \wedge \\ \qquad (y[j] = 0 \leftrightarrow y'[j] = 0) \ \wedge \ (y[j] < y[k] \leftrightarrow y'[j] < y'[k]) \\ \vee \ \pi[i] = 2 \ \wedge \ (y[j] = 0 \vee y[j] > y[i]) \ \wedge \ \pi'[i] = 3 \ \wedge \ y'[i] = y[i] \ \wedge \ y'[j] = y[j] \\ \vee \ \pi[i] = 3 \ \wedge \ \pi'[i] = 4 \ \wedge \ y'[i] = y[i] \ \wedge \ y'[j] = y[j] \\ \vee \ \pi[i] = 4 \ \wedge \ \pi'[i] = 0 \ \wedge \ y'[i] = 0 \ \wedge \ y'[j] = y[j] \end{array}\right]$$

$$\mathcal{J} : \begin{cases} \{J_1[i] : \pi[i] \neq 1 \ | \ i \in [1..N]\} & \cup \\ \{J_2[i] : \neg(\pi[i] = 2 \ \wedge \ \forall j \neq i \ (y[j] = 0 \vee y[j] > y[i]) \ | \ i \in [1..N]\} \cup \\ \{J_3[i] : \pi[i] \neq 3 \ | \ i \in [1..N]\} & \cup \\ \{J_4[i] : \pi[i] \neq 4 \ | \ i \in [1..N]\} \end{cases}$$

$\mathcal{C} : \emptyset$

Fig. 2. FBDS for Program BAKERY

Let α be an assertion over V, and R be an assertion over $V \cup V'$, which can be viewed as a transition relation. We denote by $\alpha \circ R$ the assertion characterizing all state which are R-successors of α-states. We denote by $\alpha \circ R^*$ the states reachable by an R-path of length zero or more from an α-state.

2.3 The Small Model Theorem

Let $\varphi : \forall \vec{i} \exists \vec{j}. R(\vec{i}, \vec{j})$ be an AE-formula, where $R(\vec{i}, \vec{j})$ is a restricted assertion which refers to the state variables of a parameterized FBDS $S(N)$ and to the quantified (**index**) variables $\vec{i}$ and $\vec{j}$. Let N_0 be the number of universally quantified and free **index** variables appearing in R. The claim below (stated in [PRZ01] and extended in [APR$^+$01]) provides the basis for automatic validation of the premises in the proof rules:

Theorem 1 (Small model property).
Formula φ is valid iff it is valid over all instances $S(N)$ for $N \leq N_0 + 2$.

The small model theorem allows to check validity of AE-assertions on small model. In [PRZ01,APR$^+$01] we obtain, using *project&generalize*, candidate inductive assertions for the set of reachable states that are A-formulae, checking their inductiveness required checking validity of AE-formulae, which can be accomplished, using BDD techniques. In [FPPZ04] we obtain, using *project&generalize*, candidate assertions for various assertions (pending, helpful, ranking), all A- or E-formulae and, using these assertions, the premises of the progress proof rule are again AE-formulae, which can be checked using the theorem.

2.4 Removing Compassion

The proof rule we are employing to prove progress properties assumes a compassionless system. As was outlined in [KPP03], every FDS S can be converted into an FDS $S_J = \langle V_J, \Theta_J, \rho_J, \mathcal{J}_J, \emptyset \rangle$ with no compassion, where

$$V_J : V \cup \{nvr_p : \textbf{boolean} \mid \langle p, q \rangle \in \mathcal{C}\} \qquad \Theta_J : \Theta \wedge \bigwedge_{\langle p,q \rangle \in \mathcal{C}} \neg nvr_p$$

$$\rho_J : \rho \wedge \left(\bigwedge_{\langle p,q \rangle \in \mathcal{C}} nvr_p \rightarrow nvr'_p \right) \qquad \mathcal{J}_J : \mathcal{J} \cup \{nvr_p \vee q \mid \langle p, q \rangle \in \mathcal{C}\}$$

This transformation adds to the system variables a new boolean variable nvr_p for each compassion requirement $\langle p, q \rangle \in \mathcal{C}$. The intended role of these variables is to identify, nondeterministically, a point in the computation, beyond which p will never be true again. The initial value of all these variables is 0 (*false*). The transition relation allows nondeterministically to change the value of any nvr_p variable from 0 to 1 but not vice versa. Finally, to the justice requirements we add a new justice requirement $nvr_p \vee q$ requiring that there are infinitely many states in which either nvr_p or q is true. Let *Err* denote the assertion $\bigvee_{\langle p,q \rangle \in \mathcal{C}} p \wedge nvr_p$, describing states where both p and nvr_p hold, which indicates that the prediction that p will never occur has been premature. For σ_J, a computations of S_J, we denote by $\sigma_J \Downarrow_V$ the sequence obtained from σ_J by projecting each state on the variables of S. The relation between S and its compassion-free version S_J can be stated as follows:

> Sequence σ is a computation of S iff there exists σ_J an *err*-free computation of S_J such that $\sigma_J \Downarrow_V = \sigma$.

It follows that

$$S \models q \Rightarrow \Diamond r \quad \text{iff} \quad S_J \models (q \wedge \neg Err) \Rightarrow \Diamond(r \vee Err)$$

Which allows us to assume that FBDSS we consider here have an empty compassion set.

2.5 The DISTRANK Proof Rule

In [FPPZ04] we presented a proof rule for progress properties that exploits the structure of parameterized systems, by associating helpful assertions and ranking functions with each transition. The proof rule is presented in Fig. 3.

For a parameterized system with a transition domain $\mathcal{T} = \mathcal{T}(N)$
  set of states $\Sigma(N)$,
  justice requirements $\{J_\tau \mid \tau \in \mathcal{T}\}$,
  invariant assertion φ,
  assertions $q, r, pend$ and $\{h_\tau \mid \tau \in \mathcal{T}\}$,
  and ranking functions $\{\delta_\tau \colon \Sigma \to \{0, 1\} \mid \tau \in \mathcal{T}\}$

D1. $q \wedge \varphi$ $\to$ $r \vee pend$

D2. $pend \wedge \rho$ $\to$ $r' \vee pend'$

D3. $pend \wedge \rho$ $\to$ $r' \vee \bigwedge_{\tau \in \mathcal{T}} \delta_\tau \geq \delta'_\tau$

D4. $pend$ $\to$ $\bigvee_{\tau \in \mathcal{T}} h_\tau$

For every $\tau \in \mathcal{T}$

D5. $h_\tau \wedge \rho$ $\to$ $r' \vee h'_\tau \vee \delta_\tau > \delta'_\tau$

D6. h_τ $\to$ $\neg J_\tau$

$$q \Rightarrow \Diamond r$$

Fig. 3. The liveness rule DISTRANK

The rule is configured to deal directly with parameterized systems. Typically, the parameter domain provides a unique identification for each transition, and will have the form $\mathcal{T}(N) = [0..k] \times N$ for some fixed k. For example, in program BAKERY, $\mathcal{T}(N) = [0..4] \times N$, where each justice transition can be identified as $J_m[i]$ for $m \in [0..4]$ (corresponding to the various locations in each process), and $i \in [1..N]$. In the rule, assertion φ is an invariant assertion characterizing all the reachable states[1]. Assertion $pend$ characterizes the states which can be reached from a reachable q-state by an r-free path. For each transition τ, assertion h_τ characterizes the states at which this transition is *helpful*. That is, these are the states whose every J_τ-satisfying successor leads to a progress towards the goal, which is expressed by immediately reaching the goal or a decrease in the ranking function δ_τ, as stated in premise D5. The ranking functions δ_τ are used in order to measure progress towards the goal. See [FPPZ04] for justification of the rule.

Thus, in order to prove a progress property we need to identify the assertions φ, $pend$, and δ_τ, h_τ for every $\tau \in \mathcal{T}$. For a parameterized system, the progress properties we are considering are of the form $\forall z.q(z) \Rightarrow \Diamond r(z)$. We instantiate the system to a small number of processes, fix some process z, use *project&generalize* to obtain candidates

---

[1] Note that a precondition for the application of the invisible ranking method is the successful application of invisible invariants [PRZ01,APR$^+$01].

for $pend$ and δ_τ, h_τ, and use the small model theorem to check the premises D1–D6, as well as the inductiveness of φ. However, in order for this to succeed, the generated assertions should adhere to some strict syntactic form. Most notably, h_τ can either be a restricted or an E-assertion in order to prove the validity of D4, since when h_τ has an A-fragment, D4 is no longer an AE-assertion.

Unfortunately, the success of this approach depends on the helpful assertions referring only the the process they "belong" to, without mention of any other process. In many cases, this cannot be the case – helpful transitions need to refer to neighboring processes. We study two such main cases: One in which processes are arranged in a ring. and a process can access some variables of its immediate neighbors, and the other where a process can access variables of all other processes.

3   Protocols with $p(i, i + 1)$ Assertions

In many algorithms, particularly those based on ring architectures, the auxiliary assertions depend only on a process and its immediate neighbors. Consider such an algorithm for a ring of size N. For every $j = 1, .., N$, define $j \oplus 1 = (j \bmod N) + 1$ and $j \ominus 1 = ((j - 2) \bmod N) + 1$. We are interested in assertions of the type $p(i, i \oplus 1)$ and $p(i, i \ominus 1)$. Having the ± 1 operator, these assertions do not fall into our small model theorem that restricts the operators to comparisons (and, expressing ± 1 using comparisons requires additional quantification.) However, as we show here, there is a small model theorem that allows proving validity of $\forall \exists p(i, i \pm 1)$ assertions. The size of the model, however, is larger than the previous one, which is why we refer to it as "modest".

3.1   Modest Model Theorem and Incomprehensible Assertions

Theorem 2 (Modest Model Theorem). *Let S be a parameterized* FBDS *with no* **data** *variables[2]. Let $\varphi \colon \vec{\forall i} \exists \vec{j}.R(\vec{i}, \vec{j})$ be such that $\vec{i}$ and $\vec{j}$ are* **index** *variables, and $R(\vec{i}, \vec{j})$ is a restricted assertion augmented by operators $\oplus 1$ and $\ominus 1$. Let K be the number of universally quantified, index constants (including 1 and N), and free variables in φ. Assume there are L* **index** $\mapsto$ **bool** *arrays in S. Define $N_0 = (K - 1)2^L + K$. Then:*

$$\varphi \text{ is valid over } S(N) \text{ for every } N \geq 2 \quad \text{iff} \quad \varphi \text{ is valid over } S(N) \text{ for every } N \leq N_0$$

Proof Outline: Let $\psi = \neg \varphi$, i.e.. $\psi = \exists \vec{i} \forall \vec{j}.\neg R(\vec{i}, \vec{j})$. It suffices to show that if ψ is satisfiable, then it is satisfiable in an instantiation $S(N)$ for some $N \leq N_0$.

Assume that ψ is satisfiable in some state s of $S(N_1)$ and that $N_1 > N_0$. Let $u_1, u_2, \ldots, u_k$ be the values of **index**-variables (or constants) which appear existentially quantified or free in ψ. Without loss of generality, assume $1 = u_1 < u_2 < \ldots < u_k = N$. Since there are at most K such values, $k \leq K$. Since $N_1 > N_0$, there exist some u_i and u_{i+1} such that $u_{i+1} - u_i - 1 > 2^L$ (i.e. the number of indices between u_i and u_{i+1} is greater than 2^L). We construct a state s', in an instantiation $N_1' < N_1$, such that $s' \models \psi$. This process is repeated, until all u_j's are at most 2^L apart.

Since $u_{i+1} - u_i - 1 > 2^L$, there exist two indices, m and n, such that $u_i < m < n < u_{i+1}$ and $a[n] = a[m]$ for every **index** $\mapsto$ **bool** array a. Intuitively, removing the

---

[2] This assumption is here for simplicity. It can be removed at the cost of increasing the bound.

processes whose indices are $m + 1, \ldots, n$ does not impact any of the other processes u_j's, since the **index** $\mapsto$ **bool** values of their immediate neighbors remain the same. After the removal, the remaining processes are renumbered, to reflect the removal.

Thus, we construct from s a new state s', leaving the **index** variables in the range $1..m$ intact, and reducing the **index** indices larger than n by $n - m$, maintaining the assignments of their **index** $\mapsto$ **bool** variables. Obviously, s' is a state of $S(N_1 - (n-m))$ that satisfies ψ. □

Remarks: The (outline of the) proof of the theorem implies that:

1. If there are **index** $\mapsto$ **bool** variables in the system, for some non-boolean finite **bool**, then 2^L in the bound should be replaced by the product of the sizes of ranges of all **index** $\mapsto$ **bool** variables.
2. When the system has either $p(i, i \oplus 1)$ or $p(i, i \ominus 1)$ assertions, but not both, then the bound computed in the theorem can be reduced by $K - 1$ to $N_0 = (K - 1)2^L + 1$.
3. If the free variables in the system are consecutive, then the bound computed can be reduced accordingly. E.g., if in addition to 1 and N also $N - 1$ is in R, then $(K - 1)2^L + K$ can be replaced by $(K-2)2^L + K$, since there are at most $K-2$ "gaps" to collapse.

The generation of all assertions is completely invisible; so is the checking of the premises on the instantiated model. However, the instantiation of the modest model requires feeding the assertions into the larger model. This can be done completely automatically, or with some user intervention. Whichever it is, while the user may see the assertions, there is no need for the user to comprehend them. In fact, being generated using BDD techniques, they are often incomprehensible.

3.2   Example: Dining Philosophers

We demonstrate the use of the modest model theory on validating DISTRANK on a classical solution to the dining philosophers problem.

Consider program DINE that offers a solution to the dining philosophers problem for any N philosophers. The program uses semaphores for forks. In this program, $N-1$ philosophers, $P[1], \ldots, P[N-1]$, reach first for their left forks and then for their right forks, while $P[N]$ reaches first for its right fork and only then for its left fork.

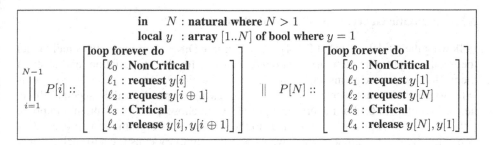

Fig. 4. Program DINE: Solution to the Dining Philosophers Problem

The semaphore instructions "**request** x" and "**release** x" appearing in the program stand, respectively, for "⟨**when** $x = 1$ **do** $x := 0$⟩" and "$x := 1$". Consequently, we have a compassion requirement for each "**request** x", indicating that if a process is requesting a semaphore that is available infinitely often, it obtains it infinitely often.

As outlined in Subsection 2.4, we transform the FBDS into a compassion-free FBDS by adding two new boolean arrays, nvr_1 and nvr_2, each $nvr_\ell[i]$ corresponding to the request of process i at location ℓ. Fig. 5 describes the variables, initial conditions, and justice requirements of the FBDS we associate with Program DINE.

$$V : \begin{cases} y, nvr_1, nvr_2 : \textbf{array } [1..N] \textbf{ of bool} \\ \pi : \qquad\qquad \textbf{array } [1..N] \textbf{ of } [0..4] \end{cases}$$

$$\Theta : \forall i. \, (\pi[i] = 0 \,\wedge\, y[i] \,\wedge\, \neg nvr_1[i] \,\wedge\, \neg nvr_2[i])$$

$$\mathcal{J} : \begin{cases} \{J_1[i] : nvr_1[i] \,\vee\, \pi[i] \neq 1 \mid i \in [1..N]\} \,\cup \\ \{J_2[i] : nvr_2[i] \,\vee\, \pi[i] \neq 2 \mid i \in [1..N]\} \,\cup \\ \{J_3[i] : \pi[i] \neq 3 \mid i \in [1..N]\} \qquad\qquad \cup \\ \{J_4[i] : \pi[i] \neq 4 \mid i \in [1..N]\} \end{cases}$$

Fig. 5. FBDS for Program DINE

The progress property of the original system is $(\pi[z] = 1) \Rightarrow \Diamond(\pi[z] = 3)$, which is proven in two steps, the first establishing that $(\pi[z] = 1) \Rightarrow \Diamond(\pi[z] = 2)$ and the second establishing that $(\pi[z] = 2) \Rightarrow \Diamond(\pi[z] = 3)$. For simplicity of presentation, we restrict discussion to the latter progress property.

Since $P[N]$ differs from $P[1], \ldots, P[N-1]$, and since it accesses $y[1]$, which is also accessed by $P[1]$, and $y[N]$, which is also accessed by $P[N-1]$, we choose some z in the range $2, \ldots, N-2$ and prove progress of $P[z]$. The progress property of the other three processes can be established separately (and similarly.) Taking into account the translation into a compassion-less system, the property we attempt to prove is

$$(\pi[z] = 2) \;\Rightarrow\; \Diamond(\pi[z] = 3 \vee Err) \qquad (2 \leq z \leq N - 2)$$

where

$$Err = \bigvee_{i=1}^{N-1} \begin{array}{l} (\pi[i] = 1 \,\wedge\, y[i] \,\wedge\, nvr_1[i]) \;\vee\; (\pi[i] = 2 \,\wedge\, y[i+1] \,\wedge\, nvr_2[i]) \\ \vee \quad (\pi[N] = 1 \,\wedge\, y[1] \,\wedge\, nvr_1[N]) \vee (\pi[N] = 2 \,\wedge\, y[N] \,\wedge\, nvr_2[N]) \end{array}$$

3.3 Automatic Generation of Symbolic Assertions

Following the guidelines in [FPPZ04], we instantiate DINE according to the small model theorem, compute the auxiliary *concrete* constructs for the instantiation, and abstract them. Here, we chose an instantiation of $N_0 = 6$ (obviously, we need $N_0 \geq 4$; it seems safer to allow at least a chain of three that does not depend on the "special" three, hence we obtained 6.) For the progress property, we chose $z = 3$, and attempt to prove $(\pi[3] = 2) \Rightarrow \Diamond(\pi[3] = 3 \vee Err)$. Due to the structure of Program DINE, process $P[i]$ depends only on it neighbors, thus, we expect the auxiliary constructs to include only assertions that refer to two neighboring process at the time. We chose to focus on pairs of the form $(i, i \ominus 1)$.

We first compute $\varphi^a(i, i \ominus 1)$, which is the abstraction of the set of reachable states. We distinguish between three cases, $i = 1$, $i = N$, and $i = 2, \ldots, N-1$. For the first, we project the concrete φ on 1 and 6 (and generalize to 1 and N), for the second, we project the concrete φ on 6 and 5 (and generalize to N and $N-1$), and for the third we project the concrete φ on 3 and 2 (and generalize to i and $i-1$). Thus, for the general $i \notin \{1, N\}$ case we obtain:

$$\varphi^a(i, i-1) = \begin{pmatrix} (y[i-1] \to \pi[i-1] < 2) \wedge (\pi[i-1] > 2 \to \pi[i] < 2) \\ \wedge (y[i] \leftrightarrow (\pi[i-1] < 3 \wedge \pi[i] < 2)) \end{pmatrix}$$

We then take : $\varphi^a = \varphi^a(1, N) \wedge \varphi^a(N, N-1) \wedge \forall i \neq 1, N.\varphi^a(i, i-1)$ and define $pend^a = reach^a \wedge \neg Err \wedge \pi[3] = 2$.

For the helpful sets, and the δ's, we obtain, as expected, assertions of the type $p(i, i \ominus 1)$. E.g., for every $j = z + 1, \ldots, N-1$, we get

$$h_2^a[j] : \pi[j-1] = 2 \wedge nvr_2[j-1] \wedge \pi[j] = 2 \wedge \neg nvr_2[j]$$
$$\delta_2[j] : \neg nvr_2[j] \wedge (\pi[j-1] = 2 \wedge nvr_2[j-1] \to \pi[j] < 3)$$

Thus, the proof of inductiveness of φ, as well as all premises of DISTRANK are now of the form covered by the modest model theorem.

To compute the size of the instantiation needed, note that the product of ranges of **index $\mapsto$ bool** variables is 40 (5 locations, and 2 each for the fork and two nvr's). There are three free variables in the system, 1, N, and $N-1$. (The reason we include $N-1$ is, e.g., its explicit mention in φ^a). Following the remarks on the modest model theorem, since the three variables are consecutive, and since in all constructs we have only $i \ominus 1$, the size of the (modest) model we need to take is $40(u + 1) + u$, where u is the number of universally quantified variables. Since $u \leq 2$ for each of D1–D6 (it is 0 for D4, 1 for D1, and 2 for D2, D3, and D5), we choose an instantiation of 122.

Construct	BDD nodes
φ	1,779
$pend$	3,024
ρ	10,778
h_p's	< 10
δ	$\leq$ 10

Premise	Time to Validate
φ (inductiveness)	0.39 seconds
D1, D4, D6	< 0.02 seconds
D2	0.42 seconds
D3	163.74 seconds
D5	138.59 seconds

Fig. 6. Run-time Results for Verifying Liveness of Program DINE

Fig. 6 shows the number of BDD nodes computed for each auxiliary construct and the time it took to validate the inductiveness of φ and each of the premises D1–D6 on the largest instantiation (122 philosophers). Checking all instantiations (2–122) took about 8 hours.

4   Imposing Ordering on Transitions

In this section we study helpful assertions that are "truly" universal. Such helpful assertions are quite frequent. In fact, most helpful assertions are of the type $h(i) : \forall j.p(i, j)$ where i is the index of the process that can take a helpful step, and all other processes

(j) satisfy some supporting conditions. Incorporating such helpful assertions in Premise D4 of rule DISTRANK results in an EA-disjunct which is out of the scope of the small model theorem. We present a new proof rule for progress that allows to order the helpful assertions in terms of the precedence of their helpfulness, so that "the helpful" assertion is the minimal in the ordering, thus avoiding the disjunction in the r-h-s of Premise D4.

4.1 Pre-ordering Transitions

A binary relation $\preceq$ is a pre-order over domain $\mathcal{D}$ if it is reflexive, transitive, and total. Let S be an FBDS with set of transitions $\mathcal{T}(N) = [0..k] \times N$ (as in Section 2). For every state in $S(N)$, define a pre-order $\preceq$ over $\mathcal{T}$. From totality of $\preceq$, every $S(N)$-state has minimal $\tau_\ell[i] \in \mathcal{T}$ according to $\preceq$. We replace D4 in DISTRANK with a premise stating that for every pending state s, the minimal transition in s is also helpful at s. The new rule PRERANK appears in Fig. 7. To avoid confusion we name its premises R1–R9. PRERANK is exactly like DISTRANK, with the addition of a pre-order $\preceq : \Sigma \to 2^{\mathcal{T} \times \mathcal{T}}$, rules checking that it is a pre-order (R7–R9), and replacement of D4 by R4.

For a parameterized system with a transition domain $\mathcal{T} = \mathcal{T}(N)$
  set of states $\Sigma(N)$,
  justice requirements $\{J_\tau \mid \tau \in \mathcal{T}\}$,
  invariant assertion φ,
  assertions $q, r, pend$ and $\{h_\tau \mid \tau \in \mathcal{T}\}$,
  ranking functions $\{\delta_\tau : \Sigma \to \{0,1\} \mid \tau \in \mathcal{T}\}$,
  and a pre-order $\preceq : \Sigma \mapsto 2^{\mathcal{T} \times \mathcal{T}}$

R1. $q \wedge \varphi$	$\to$	$r \vee pend$
R2. $pend \wedge \rho$	$\to$	$r' \vee pend'$
R3. $pend \wedge \rho$	$\to$	$r' \vee \bigwedge_{\tau \in \mathcal{T}} \delta_\tau \geq \delta'_\tau$

For every $\tau \in \mathcal{T}$

R4. $pend \wedge \left(\bigwedge_{\tau_1 \in \mathcal{T}} \tau \preceq \tau_1 \right)$	$\to$	h_τ
R5. $h_\tau \wedge \rho$	$\to$	$r' \vee h'_\tau \vee \delta_\tau > \delta'_\tau$
R6. h_τ	$\to$	$\neg J_\tau$
R7. $pend$	$\to$	$\tau \preceq \tau$

For every $\tau_1, \tau_2 \in \mathcal{T}$

R8. $pend \wedge \tau \preceq \tau_1 \wedge \tau_1 \preceq \tau_2$	$\to$	$\tau \preceq \tau_2$
R9. $pend$	$\to$	$\tau \preceq \tau_1 \vee \tau_1 \preceq \tau$

$$q \Rightarrow \Diamond r$$

Fig. 7. The liveness rule PRERANK

In order apply PRERANK automatically, we have to generate $\preceq$. We instantiate $S(N_0)$, compute concrete $\preceq$, and then *project&generalize* to compute an abstract $\preceq^a$. The main problem is the computation of the concrete $\preceq$. We define $s \models \tau_1 \preceq \tau_2$ if:

$$s \models ((\neg h_{\tau_2} \wedge pend) \, \mathcal{W} \, (h_{\tau_1} \wedge pend)) \vee \neg((\neg h_{\tau_1} \wedge pend) \, \mathcal{W} \, (h_{\tau_2} \wedge pend)) \tag{1}$$

where $\mathcal{W}$ is the *weak-until* or *unless* operator.

	$\tau_1[j]$	$\tau_2[j]$	$\tau_3[j]$	$\tau_4[j]$
$\tau_1[i]$	$i = j$ $\lor\ j \neq z$ $\lor\ \pi[z] = 2$	$j \neq z \land \pi[z] = 2 \land \alpha$ $\lor$ $i = j = z \land \pi[z] = 1$	$j = z$ $\lor\ (\pi[z] = 2 \land \alpha$ $\land \pi[j] \neq 3)$	$j = z$ $\lor\ \pi[z] = 2 \land \alpha$ $\land \pi[j] < 3$
$\tau_2[i]$	$j \neq z$ $\lor\ \pi[z] = 2$	$i = j$ $\lor\ \beta$ $\lor\ \pi[j] \neq 2$ $\lor\ j \neq z \land y[z] < y[j]$	$j = z \lor \pi[z] = 1$ $\lor\ i = j \land \pi[j] \neq 3$ $\lor\ i \neq j \land (\pi[j] \notin \{2,3\}\lor$ $\beta \lor y[z] < y[j])$	$j = z \lor \pi[z] = 1$ $\lor\ i = j \land \pi[j] < 3$ $\lor\ i \neq j \land (\pi[j] < 2$ $\lor\ \beta\ \lor y[z] < y[j])$
$\tau_3[i]$	$j \neq z$ $\lor\ \pi[z] = 2$	$\neg(i = j = z)\land$ $(\pi[z] = 1 \lor \beta$ $\lor \pi[i] = 3 \lor \alpha)$	$i = j \lor j = z$ $\lor\ \beta \lor \pi[i] = 3$ $\lor\ \gamma(2,3)$	$(i = j \land \pi[i] = 2)$ $\lor\ \beta \lor \pi[i] = 3$ $\lor\ \gamma(2..4)$ $\lor\ \pi[z] = 1 \lor j = z$
$\tau_4[i]$	$j \neq z$ $\lor\ \pi[z] = 2$	$\neg(i = j = z)\land$ $(\pi[z] = 1 \lor \beta$ $\lor \pi[i] > 2 \lor \alpha)$	$j = z \lor \beta$ $\lor\ i \neq j \land \pi[i] > 2$ $\lor\ \gamma(2,3)$	$i = j \lor j = z$ $\lor\ \beta \lor \pi[i] > 2$ $\lor\ \gamma(2..4)$

Fig. 8. The pre-order, where $\alpha\colon \pi[j] = 2 \rightarrow y[z] < y[j]$, $\beta\colon \pi[i] = 2 \land y[i] < y[j]$, and $\gamma(L)\colon \pi[j] \in L \rightarrow y[z] < y[j]$.

The intuition behind the first disjunct is that for a state s, h_{τ_1} is "helpful earlier" than h_{τ_2} if every path leading from s that reaches h_{τ_1} doesn't reach h_{τ_2} before. The role of the second disjunct is to guarantee the totality of $\preceq$, so that when h_{τ_1} precedes h_{τ_2} in some computations, and h_{τ_2} precedes h_{τ_1} in others, we obtain both $\tau_1 \preceq \tau_2$ and $\tau_2 \preceq \tau_1$. To abstract a formula $\varphi(\tau_{\ell_1}[i])\ \mathcal{W}\ \varphi(\tau_{\ell_2}[j])$, we use *project&generalize*, projecting onto processes i and j. To abstract the negation of such a formula, we first abstract the formula, and then negate the result. Therefore, to abstract Formula (1), we abstract each disjunct separately, and then take the disjunction of the abstract disjuncts.

4.2   Case Study: Bakery

Consider program BAKERY of Example 1. Suppose we want to verify $(\pi[z] = 1) \Rightarrow \Diamond(\pi[z] = 3)$. We instantiate the system to $N_0 = 3$, and obtain the auxiliary assertions φ, *pend*, the h's and δ's[3]. After applying *project&generalize*, we obtain for $h_\ell[i]$, two type of assertions. One is for the case that $i = z$, and then, as expected, $h_2[z]$ is the most interesting one, having an A-construct claiming that z's ticket is the minimal among ticket holders. The other case is for $j \neq z$, and there we have a similar A-construct (for j's ticket minimality) for $\ell = 2, 3, 4$. For the pre-order, one must consider $\tau_{\ell_1}[i] \preceq \tau_{\ell_2}[j]$ for every $\ell_1, \ell_2 = 1, ..., 4$ and $i = z \neq j, i = j \neq z, i, j \neq z$ for $(\ell_1, i) \neq (\ell_2, j)$. The results for $\tau_{\ell_1}[i] \preceq \tau_{\ell_2}[j]$ for $i \neq z$ that are not trivially ⊤ are listed in Fig. 8.

Using the above pre-order, we succeeded in validating Premises R1–R9 of PRERANK, thus establishing the liveness property of program BAKERY.

---

[3] *cs.nyu.edu/acsys/Tlv/assertions* contains full list of assertions and pre-order definitions

References

[AK86]   K. R. Apt and D. Kozen. Limits for automatic program verification of finite-state concurrent systems. *IPL*, 22(6), 1986.

[APR+01]   T. Arons, A. Pnueli, S. Ruah, J. Xu, and L. Zuck. Parameterized verification with automatically computed inductive assertions. In 13th *CAV*, LNCS 2102, 2001.

[BBC+95]   N. Bjørner, I.A. Browne, E. Chang, M. Colón, A. Kapur, Z. Manna, H.B. Sipma, and T.E. Uribe. STeP: The Stanford Temporal Prover, User's Manual. Technical Report STAN-CS-TR-95-1562, CS Department, Stanford University, Nov. 1995.

[CGJ95]   E.M. Clarke, O. Grumberg, and S. Jha. Verifying parametrized networks using abstraction and regular languages. In 6th *CONCUR*, LNCS 962, 395–407, 1995.

[CS02]   M. Colon and H. Sipma. Practical methods for proving program termination. In 14th *CAV*, LNCS 2404, 442–454, 2002.

[EK00]   E.A. Emerson and V. Kahlon. Reducing model checking of the many to the few. In 17th *CADE*, pages 236–255, 2000.

[EN95]   E. A. Emerson and K. S. Namjoshi. Reasoning about rings. In 22nd *POPL*, 1995.

[FPPZ04]   Y. Fang, N. Piterman, A. Pnueli, and L. Zuck. Liveness with invisible ranking. In 5th *VMCAI*, LNCS, 2004.

[GS97]   V. Gyuris and A. P. Sistla. On-the-fly model checking under fairness that exploits symmetry. In 4th *TACAS*, LNCS 1384, 424–438, 1998.

[GZ98]   E.P. Gribomont and G. Zenner. Automated verification of szymanski's algorithm. In 9th *CAV*, LNCS 1254, 1997.

[JN00]   B. Jonsson and M. Nilsson. Transitive closures of regular relations for verifying infinite-state systems. In 6th *TACAS*, LNCS 1785,2000.

[KPP03]   Y. Kesten, N. Piterman, and A. Pnueli. Bridging the gap between fair simulation and trace inclusion. In 15th *CAV*, LNCS 2725, 381–392. 2003.

[LHR97]   D. Lesens, N. Halbwachs, and P. Raymond. Automatic verification of parameterized linear networks of processes. In 24th *POPL*, 1997.

[McM98]   K.L. McMillan. Verification of an implementation of Tomasulo's algorithm by compositional model checking. In10th *CAV*, LNCS 1427, 110–121, 1998.

[MP95]   Z. Manna and A. Pnueli. *Temporal Verification of Reactive Systems: Safety.* 1995.

[OSR93]   S. Owre, N. Shankar, and J.M. Rushby. User guide for the PVS specification and verification system (draft). Tech. report, CS Lab., SRI International, CA, 1993.

[PRZ01]   A. Pnueli, S. Ruah, and L. Zuck. Automatic deductive verification with invisible invariants. In 7th *TACAS*, LNCS 2031, 82–97, 2001.

[PXZ02]   A. Pnueli, J. Xu, and L. Zuck. Liveness with $(0, 1, \infty)$-counter abstraction, In 14th *CAV*, LNCS 2404, 107–122. 2002.

[Sha00]   E. Shahar. *The TLV Manual*, 2000. http://www.wisdom.weizmann.ac.il/~verify/tlv.

Guided Invariant Model Checking Based on Abstraction and Symbolic Pattern Databases

Kairong Qian and Albert Nymeyer

School of Computer Science
The University of New South Wales
UNSW Sydney 2052 Australia
{kairongq, anymeyer}@cse.unsw.edu.au

Abstract Arguably the two most important techniques that are used in model checking to counter the combinatorial explosion in the number of states are abstraction and guidance. In this work we combine these techniques in a natural way by using (homomorphic) abstractions that reveal an error in the model to guide the model checker in searching for the error state in the original system. The mechanism used to achieve this is based on *pattern databases*, commonly used in artificial intelligence. A pattern database represents an abstraction and is used as a heuristic to guide the search. In essence, therefore, the same abstraction is used to reduce the size of the model and guide a search algorithm. We implement this approach in NuSMV and evaluate it using 2 well-known circuit benchmarks. The results show that this method can outperform the original model checker by several orders of magnitude, in both time and space.

1 Introduction

In the past decade, model checking has become the formal method of choice to verify reactive systems [1]. While it is an automated method, model checking inherently suffers from the well-known "state explosion" problem, where the complexity of the model is exponential in the number of components that comprise the system. Not surprisingly, most research in model checking is focused on ways to minimise the impact of state explosion. Symbolic model checking [2, 3,4] and on-the-fly, memory-efficient model checking [5,6] have had some quite dramatic successes in the field. Although these methods have been successfully used to verify some industrial strength systems, they are still unable to cope with large systems in general. In [7], Clarke et. al. have developed a method for using abstract interpretation of the system to reduce the complexity of (CTL) model checking. This is based on the observation that irrelevant information can be abstracted away from the concrete system to significantly reduce the size of the model, while preserving the properties to be verified. The drawback of this method is that it induces false negative results, namely, if this method reports a counterexample that shows the property in the abstract system is violated, then the counterexample may not be valid in the concrete system (called a *spurious*

K. Jensen and A. Podelski (Eds.): TACAS 2004, LNCS 2988, pp. 497–511, 2004.

counterexample). If a spurious counterexample is found, one has to refine the model and repeat the verification again. This is called the *abstraction-refinement* model checking paradigm [8,9].

More recently, inspired by heuristic search in artificial intelligence, many researchers have investigated the applicability of heuristic search techniques to model checking. This can be referred to as the *guided* model checking paradigm [10,11,12,13,14,15,16]. The effectiveness of this approach, however, depends strongly on the informedness of the search heuristics. Generally, only intuitive heuristics can be invented by humans. More informative heuristics can be very application-dependent and complex to derive.

In artificial intelligence, an application-independent heuristic, called *pattern databases*, has been successfully employed to solve hard search problems such as the N-puzzle and Rubik's cube [17,18]. To define a pattern database, we refer to a fixed part of a given state as a pattern. The set of all such patterns forms the domain of the database. Given any state, the pattern can be looked up in the pattern database to find the minimum path length from a state containing the pattern to a goal state. In essence, a pattern contains the subgoals that must be achieved to solve the problem [17].

For example, in a puzzle, we can consider a subset of tiles to be a pattern. A pattern database is then based on the retrograde analysis of the pattern starting at the goal state. Because we only consider the pattern during the course of pattern database construction, many original states may become indistinguishable from the pattern (i.e. if we mask out non-pattern information, two states result in the same configuration). Note that a pattern database is essentially an abstraction of a system.

In [19,20], Holte et. al. extend the notion of "pattern" to homomorphic abstraction in an attempt to automatically create application-independent heuristics. Generally, we can abstract a system using two methods: *homomorphic* abstraction and *embedded* abstraction. Homomorphic abstraction can be achieved by merging groups of states and all transitions within the group are therefore not observable in the abstract system, whereas embedded abstraction can be achieved by adding more transitions to the system. In the abstraction-refinement paradigm of model checking, to preserve the temporal properties of the system, one often uses data abstraction [7]. In essence, data abstraction is a homomorphic abstraction. We focus on safety properties in this work, all properties can be expressed using ACTL* of form $\mathbf{AG}\varphi$, where φ is a Boolean expression of atomic propositions.

Effective and intuitive heuristics are hard to find in guided model checking because of the high complexity. The lack of good heuristics hinders the ability of the guided search to reduce the size of the state space. As well, the refinement of an abstract system can be computationally expensive. In this work, we combine the abstraction and guided approach, using pattern databases that are derived from homomorphic abstractions of the system. These patterns guide the model checking algorithm towards a goal (error) state.

The rest of paper is structured as follows. We formally define homomorphic abstractions in Section 2 and symbolic pattern databases in Section 3. Our approach and experimental evaluation are described in Section 4 and 5 respectively. Finally we conclude the paper and propose some possible future research.

2   Homomorphic Abstractions

In this work we are only interested in finite-state transition systems that can be formalised in the following way.

Definition 1 (Transition systems). *A finite state transition system is a 3-tuple $M = (S, T, S_0)$, where*

- *S is a finite set of states*
- *$T \subseteq S \times S$ is a transition relation*
- *$S_0 \subseteq S$ is a set of initial states*

The set of states of a transition system can be described by a non-empty set of state variables $X = (x_0, x_1, ..., x_n)$, where each variable x_i ranges over a finite domain D_i. A homomorphic abstraction of a transition system is denoted by a set of surjections $H = (h_1, h_2, ..., h_n)$, where each h_i maps a finite domain D_i to another finite domain $\hat{D}_i$ with $|\hat{D}_i| \leq |D_i|$. If we apply H to all states of a transition system, denoted by $H(S)$, we will generate an abstract version of the original, concrete system.

Definition 2 (Homomorphic abstraction). *Given a transition system $M = (S, T, S_0)$ and a set of surjective mapping functions $H = (h_1, h_2, ..., h_n)$, a homomorphic abstraction of M is also a transition system and denoted $\hat{M} = (\hat{S}, \hat{T}, \hat{S}_0)$, where*

- *$\hat{S} = H(S)$ is a set of states with $|\hat{S}| \leq |S|$*
- *$\hat{T} \subseteq \hat{S} \times \hat{S}$ is a transition relation, where $(\hat{s}_1, \hat{s}_2) \in \hat{T}$ iff $\hat{s}_1 = H(s_1) \wedge \hat{s}_2 = H(s_2) \wedge \exists s_1 \exists s_2 (s_1, s_2) \in T$*
- *$\hat{S}_0 = \{\hat{s} | \hat{s} \in \hat{S} \wedge \hat{s} = H(s) \wedge s \in S_0\}$*

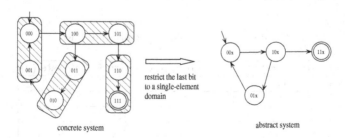

Fig. 1. A homomorphic abstraction of a transition system

Intuitively, a homomorphic abstraction is a kind of relaxation of the concrete transition system in the sense that we deliberately eliminate some information by merging groups of states. In [7], Clarke et. al. prove that a homomorphic abstraction preserves a class of temporal properties (ACTL*): in other words, the concrete and abstract system satisfy the same set of formulae. Note however that if the abstract system does not satisfy the property, we cannot conclude that the concrete system violates the property: the model needs to be further refined and model-checked again. Refinements however can be computationally expensive. Instead, we use the homomorphic abstraction to construct a pattern database to guide the search towards an error state in the concrete system.

3   Symbolic Pattern Databases

In the guided model checking paradigm, one must provide heuristics (or hints) to steer the model checking algorithm. In practice most heuristics are application dependent, so there is a strong need to discover a systematic way of relaxing the system. Pattern databases provides a systematic way of deriving heuristics. In essence, a pattern is a subgoal of the goal state. In this work we are interested in searching for a given goal state in a transition system rather than in verifying the system as a whole. We therefore need to add another element, a goal state G, to the 3-tuple M. Without loss of generality, we define G to be a single state [1]. If we have a transition system $M = (S, T, S_0, G)$, then a homomorphic abstraction will map the goal state to the subgoal state, i.e. $\hat{G} = H(G)$. By applying this mapping to the entire set of states of the system, we will have an abstract system $\hat{M} = (\hat{S}, \hat{T}, \hat{S}_0, \hat{G})$, where $\hat{T}$ and $\hat{S}_0$ are defined in the same manner as in Definition 2.

For example in Figure 1 we show a transition system and a homomorphic abstraction that restricts the right-most bit to a single-element domain. By applying this abstraction to every state of the system, we generate the abstract system shown in Figure 1 as well. A pattern database can be constructed based on this abstract system. An item in the pattern database is a 2-tuple $(\hat{s}, n)$, where $\hat{s} \in \hat{S}$ is an abstract state and n is the number of transitions required to reach $\hat{s}$ from the abstract goal. A simple example of a pattern database for the abstract system in Figure 1 is shown in Table 1.

Table 1. An example of pattern database

abstract state ($\hat{s}$)	transitions from abstract goal state (n)
11	0
10	1
00	2
01	3

---

[1] Multiple goals can be handled quite easily by removing the detected goal state from the goal set and running the algorithm until the goal set is empty.

A pattern database is based on the breadth-first backward traversal of the abstract system $\hat{M}$. While traversing backward in the abstract system, we label each abstract state $\hat{s}$ with the number of transitions starting at state $\hat{G}$. Note that there can be more than one path from $\hat{G}$ to a state $\hat{s}$, but we keep the shortest one. (When the breadth-first traversal encounters a state that has been labelled before, it is simply ignored.) Since we are interested in finite systems, the breadth-first traversal will eventually expand all states backward-reachable from $\hat{G}$ in $\hat{M}$. This is called the fixed point. Once we reach this fixed point, we collect all states (with labels) and put them into a table similar to Table 1. This is the pattern database of the system M with respect to the homomorphic abstraction H. Note that many states will be labelled with the same number because they are the same distance from the abstract goal state.

In symbolic model checking, sets of states can be encoded as binary decision diagrams (BDDs) [2,21]. Since our approach is also based on symbolic model checking, we represent the entire pattern database using BDDs as well. Note that symbolic pattern databases have been used in planning problems and can represent very large pattern databases, and often uses relatively less memory than explicit representations [22]. This is mainly because of the compactness nature of BDDs [21]. We represent those states in explicit pattern databases that have the same label (the same number of transitions starting at $\hat{G}$) with a single BDD, denoted b_i, where i is the label of that set of states. Because the pattern database is derived using the backward breadth-first traversal in the abstract system, i should range over $\{0, 1, 2, \ldots, N\}$ where N is the maximum depth of the traversal. In the worst case, N would be $|\hat{S}| - 1$.

Definition 3 (Symbolic Pattern Database). *Given a transition system* $M = (S, T, S_0, G)$ *and a homomorphic abstraction H, the symbolic pattern database of M with respect to H is a set of BDDs $P = \{b_0, b_1, \ldots, b_N\}$, where b_0 is the BDD representing the abstract goals $\hat{G} = H(G)$, and b_i is the BDD representing all states at depth i in a breadth-first backward traversal in the abstract system starting at $\hat{G}$. The depth of P, denoted $|P|$, is defined to be the maximum depth N of the backward traversal, i.e. $|P| = N$.*

In Figure 2 we show the BDDs representing the symbolic pattern database of the example in Table 1. We use a Boolean vector $X = (x_0, x_1, x_2)$ to represent a state in the concrete system, so an abstract state can be represented by $\hat{X} = (x_0, x_1)$. The symbolic pattern database contains 4 BDDs representing the characteristic Boolean functions of the corresponding abstract states: $b_0 = x_0 \wedge x_1, b_1 = x_0 \wedge \overline{x_1}, b_2 = \overline{x_0} \wedge \overline{x_1}, b_3 = \overline{x_0} \wedge x_1$.

Intuitively, because the homomorphic abstraction clusters a set of states of the concrete system as a single state of the abstract system, the path in the concrete system can be short-circuited. In the extreme case, 2 states that are not reachable from each other in the concrete system can become reachable when mapping them to the abstract system. For a transition system $M = (S, T, S_0, G)$, we define the cost of any state s to be the minimum number of transitions using backward breadth-first traversal starting at G, denoted c_s. The following lemma

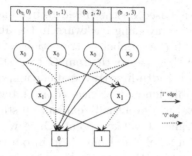

Fig. 2. An example of symbolic pattern database

shows that the cost of the state $\hat{s}$ in the abstract system is a lower bound of the cost of its corresponding concrete state s.

Lemma 1. *Given 2 transition systems $M = (S, T, S_0, G)$ and $\hat{M} = (\hat{S}, \hat{T}, \hat{S}_0, \hat{G})$, if $\hat{M}$ is a homomorphic abstraction of M, i.e. $\hat{M} = H(M)$, then for any state $s \in S$ and $\hat{s} \in \hat{S}$, $c_s \geq c_{\hat{s}}$ where $\hat{s} = H(s)$.*

Proof. Suppose $\pi = s_1, s_2, s_3, \ldots, s_n$ is an arbitrary path in M with $s_n = G$. If all states along the path are distinct, then $c_{s_1} = n$. If all the states $H(s_1), H(s_2), \ldots, H(s_n)$ are also distinct, then following the definition of a homomorphic abstraction, there exists a path $\hat{\pi} = H(s_1), H(s_2), \ldots, H(s_n)$. Thus, $c_{s_1} = c_{\hat{s}_1}$. If all states in $H(s_1), H(s_2), \ldots, H(s_n)$ are not distinct, say $H(s_i) = H(s_j), i < j$, then all states between them will be short-circuited in the abstract path, since a traversal from $H(s_{i-1})$ to $H(s_{j+1})$ only needs 2 transitions. Thus, $c_{s_1} > c_{\hat{s}_1}$.

4   The Guided Invariant Model Checking Algorithm

4.1   Standard Invariant Model Checking Algorithm

In computational tree logic (CTL), an invariant of a transition system can be expressed as $AG\varphi$. In symbolic model checking, we can use two methods, namely pre-image and image computation, to check the correctness of this class of properties. Given a set of states F and transition relation T, pre-image and image are computed as follows: $pre\text{-}image(T, F) = \{s | (r \in F) \wedge ((s, r) \in T)\}$ and $image(T, F) = \{s | (r \in F) \wedge ((r, s) \in T)\}$. The pre-image invariant checking is based on a greatest fixed point calculation algorithm [2,1] as characterised by $\mathbf{AG}\varphi = \nu Z.\varphi \wedge \mathbf{AX}Z$, where νZ is the greatest fixed point operator. In practice, this algorithm corresponds to a backward breadth-first search and may be inefficient because some states generated by the backward search may not be reachable from the initial state of the system (and hence need not have been computed).

Another method, image computation, is based on forward breadth-first search. This algorithm requires two inputs: the transition system (S, T, S_0) and the error state $\overline{\varphi}$, where φ is the invariant that holds in any state along all paths. For convenience, we use the transition system with a goal element $G = \overline{\varphi}$ as an input, where $G \notin S_0$. The algorithm is shown in Figure 3. In each iteration, a set of new reachable states R_{new} and the difference between R_{old} and R_{new}, F (frontier), are computed. To check whether the invariant has been violated, F is intersected with the error state in each iteration as well. If the intersection is

Procedure InvarCheck (S, T, S_0, G)
1    $R_{old} \leftarrow False$
2    $R_{new} \leftarrow S_0$
3   **while**$(R_{old} \neq R_{new})$
4        $F \leftarrow R_{new} \wedge \overline{R_{old}}$
5        $R_{old} \leftarrow R_{new}$
6        $F \leftarrow Image(T, F)$
7   **if** $(F \wedge G \neq False)$
8   **return** $ErrorFound$
9        $R_{new} \leftarrow R_{old} \vee F$
10   **return** $NoErrorFound$

Fig. 3. Symbolic invariant checking algorithm

not empty, we terminate the algorithm and report the error. If the intersection remains empty and the set of reachable states does not change (a fixed point), then we can claim that invariant φ is never violated in this model. Note that we test the existence of an error state in each iteration (on-the-fly), whereas some model checkers compute the entire set of reachable states and then intersect it with error states. For large transition systems, computing all reachable states may not be feasible as the BDD representing the reachable states is too large. In this work, we use an on-the-fly technique to test for error states.

4.2   An Example

Before formally introducing our guided model checking algorithm, we illustrate the technique on the transition system that we saw in Figure 1. We use a Boolean vector $X = (x_0, x_1, x_2)$ to represent a state, and the invariant we are interested in is that all three Boolean variables cannot be true simultaneously in any state. This property can be expressed in CTL as $\mathbf{AG}(\overline{\alpha})$, where $\alpha = \overline{x_0} \vee \overline{x_1} \vee \overline{x_2}$. Hence, our search goal (error state) is the complement of the property α. To construct the pattern database, we define a homomorphic abstraction H that abstract the third Boolean variable, x_2, to a single-element domain. So the abstract system can be constructed as shown in Figure 1. We then apply standard model checking (the **InvarCheck** algorithm shown in Figure 3) to the abstract system. In this example, **InvarCheck** will report an error because there is a path leading from $\hat{S}_0 = (0, 0)$ to $\hat{G} = (1, 1)$ in the abstract system. At this point, instead of

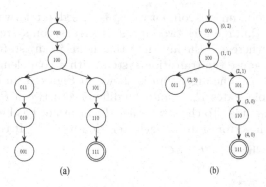

Fig. 4. The search trees generated by the (a) **InvarCheck**, and (b) **GuidedInvarCheck** algorithms for the example in Section 4.2

refining the abstract system and checking it again, we use the abstract system to construct a symbolic pattern database as shown in Table 1 and Figure 2.

The essence of the guided algorithm is that each state (set of states) is associated with an estimated distance to the goal as well as the actual distance from the initial state. We use the symbolic pattern database constructed from the homomorphic abstraction to assign to each state an estimated value (Figure 1 and Table 1). We map a state in the concrete system to an abstract state and look up its estimated value in the database. For example, for the state $(0, 1, 1)$, the corresponding abstract state is $(0, 1, x)$ and the estimated value is 3 (see Table 1). In a symbolic pattern database, each item is a BDD representing a set of abstract states, so the database look-up can be accomplished by calculating the conjunction of two BDDs. For example, to look for the estimated distance for state $(1, 0, 0)$, we iteratively compute $(x_0 \wedge \overline{x_1} \wedge \overline{x_2}) \wedge b_i$ for i from N to 0. If the resulting BDD is not constant $False$, we assign i to $(1, 0, 0)$ as the estimated distance. In this particular case, $(x_0 \wedge \overline{x_1} \wedge \overline{x_2}) \wedge b_1$ is not constant $False$, so we assign the estimated value 1 to that state. Thus, the symbolic pattern database will partition a set of states according to their estimated value. Our invariant model checking algorithm is therefore guided by the symbolic pattern database in its search for an error in the concrete system. In Figure 4, we show the difference in the search tree with and without heuristic guiding. In this figure we label the states in the guided algorithm by a pair consisting of the number of actual and estimated transitions (resp.).

4.3   Guided Invariant Model Checking Algorithm

The guided algorithm is shown in Figure 5. In contrast to the standard algorithm **InvarCheck**, the guided algorithm takes a homomorphic abstraction function H as input in addition to the concrete transition system.

Procedure GuidedInvarCheck $((S, T, S_0, G), H)$
1   **if** (**InvarCheck**$((H(S), H(T), H(S_0), H(G)) = NoErrorFound)$
2   **return** $NoErrorFound$
3    $P \leftarrow construct(H(S), H(T), H(S_0), H(G))$
4    $SearchQueue \leftarrow (0, 0, S_0)$
5    $Closed \leftarrow False$
6   **while** $(SearchQueue \neq \phi)$
7      $(g, h, F) \leftarrow SearchQueue.pop()$
8   **if** $(F \wedge G \neq False)$
9   **return** $ErrorFound$
10     $Closed \leftarrow Closed \vee F$
11     $F \leftarrow Image(T, F) \wedge \overline{Closed}$
12     $QueueImage(P, F, g + 1)$
13   **return** $NoErrorFound$

Procedure QueueImage $(P, Img, Cost)$
1    $n \leftarrow |P|$
2   **while** $(n > 0)$
3      $I \leftarrow b_n \wedge Img$
4   **if** $(I \neq \phi)$
5        $SearchQueue \leftarrow (Cost, n, I)$
6        $Img \leftarrow Img \wedge \overline{I}$
7   **if** $(Img = \phi)$ **return**
8      $n \leftarrow n - 1$
9    $SearchQueue \leftarrow (Cost, \infty, I)$

Fig. 5. The guided invariant checking algorithm that uses a pattern database.

In line 1, an abstract model is constructed using the abstraction function H and standard **InvarCheck** is called to prove the invariant. If this succeeds, then the invariant is true in the concrete system (as discussed in Section 2). If this fails, the algorithm then constructs a symbolic pattern database (line 3) according to the abstract function H (as discussed in Section 3). $SearchQueue$ in line 4 is a priority queue used to determine which state(s) should be explored first. The element of the queue is a 3-tuple, (g, h, S) where g is the actual number of transitions to S from the initial state, h is estimated number of transitions to a goal (error) state and S is a BDD representing a set of states. When determining which element should be dequeued for further exploration, $SearchQueue$ considers $f = g + h$ as the priority key and pops the element with minimum f. In lines 5-13, the heuristic search algorithm A* [23,24] is adapted to symbolically explore the state space in the concrete model.

The difference between the guided algorithm and **InvarCheck** is that whenever the image of the frontier, F, is computed, we employ the symbolic pattern database to partition this image and assign each sub-image with a heuristic evaluation before we push it back to the search queue. This is shown in procedure

QueueImage in Figure 5. Given a set of states, Img, this procedure iterates through every item b_i in P, and checks whether there exists a subset I of Img, such that $H(G)$ can be reached from $H(I)$ in the abstract system (line 3 of procedure **QueueImage**). Note that if the Img cannot be partitioned by P, we simply push it back to the search queue with heuristic evaluation ∞ (line 9).

We prove that the guided algorithm **GuidedInvarCheck** is both correct and optimal.

Theorem 1 (Correctness). *Given a transition system (S, T, S_0, G) and a homomorphic abstraction H, and let R_g and R_i be the indication returned from* **GuidedInvarCheck**$((S, T, S_0, G), H)$ *and* **InvarCheck**(S, T, S_0, G) *respectively. Then $R_g \Leftrightarrow R_i$.*

Proof. As **InvarCheck** and **GuidedInvarCheck** both use state space exploration, if **GuidedInvarCheck** detects an error, so will **InvarCheck**, and vice versa. If there is no error in the system, **InvarCheck** will explore all reachable states (the fixed point) and report *NoErrorFound*. In this case, we have to prove **GuidedInvarCheck** also explores all reachable states. This is detected by the *Closed* set that stores all states explored by **GuidedInvarCheck**. When all reachable states have been explored, $Image(T, F) \wedge \overline{Closed}$ (line 11) will be an empty set, so nothing is pushed into the search queue. Hence, the search queue will eventually become empty and *NoErrorFound* will be returned. Thus, in all cases the two algorithms will return the same result, i.e. $R_g \Leftrightarrow R_i$.

An important outcome of the model checking technique is that it can provide the counterexamples (or witnesses in the case of existential properties), showing why the property is violated. A counterexample, or error trace, is a path starting at the initial state of the concrete system and leading to an error state. Given a transition system $M = (S, T, S_0, G)$, we define an error trace as follows.

Definition 4. *An error trace is a finite path, $\pi = s_0, s_1, \ldots, s_n$, in M, where $s_0 \in S_0$, $s_n = G$ and $(s_i, s_{i+1}) \in T$ $(i \in [0, n-1])$. The length of this path, denoted $L(\pi)$, is the number of states along the path, i.e. $L(\pi) = n + 1$.*

Generally, the shorter the length of the error trace, the easier it is for human beings to interpret it. Because **InvarCheck** corresponds to a breadth-first forward search, it will determine the minimum-length error trace. The following theorem ensures that **GuidedInvarCheck** detects the minimum error trace as well.

Theorem 2 (Optimality). *Let $M = (S, T, S_0, G)$ be a transition system and H be a homomorphic abstraction. Let π_i and π_g be the error traces detected by* **InvarCheck** *and* **GuidedInvarCheck** *respectively. Then $L(\pi_g) = L(\pi_i)$.*

Proof. The proof of the theorem can be established by proving that **GuidedInvarCheck** detects the shortest path from the initial state s_0 to a goal state $s_g = G$. Note that the state space exploration algorithm in **GuidedInvarCheck** is adapted from the heuristic search algorithm A*. If the lower bound heuristic is used, the algorithm guarantees the path is shortest (minimum cost) [23,24].

So we need to prove the symbolic pattern database heuristic is a lower bound. According to lemma 1, for any path $\pi = s_0, s_1, \ldots, s_n$ in the concrete system and its corresponding path $\hat{\pi} = \hat{s}_0, \hat{s}_1, \ldots, \hat{s}_n$ in the abstract system, $c_{s_0} \geq c_{\hat{s}_0}$. Thus the symbolic pattern database heuristic is a lower bound and $L(\pi_g) = L(\pi_i)$.

We could of course use more than one symbolic pattern database to guide the algorithm. Let $M = (S, T, S_0, G)$ be a transition system and $H_0, H_1, \ldots, H_{k-1}$ be homomorphic abstractions. We hence can construct k symbolic pattern databases. When partitioning the image in the procedure **QueueImage**, we search all symbolic pattern databases to find the largest heuristic estimated value for the sub-image. This will make the heuristic estimation more accurate and guide the search more efficiently, but it also increases the computation complexity. Because all H_i are homomorphic abstractions, every symbolic pattern database is still a lower bound heuristic. Using multiple symbolic pattern database will therefore preserve the optimality of the algorithm. Note that if multiple pattern databases are used, the error trace will have the same length as the trace detected by using a single pattern database. Using multiple pattern databases instead of a single pattern database would involve a straightforward extension to the **GuidedInvarCheck** algorithm.

5   Experimental Evaluation

To determine the effectiveness of guiding, we have implemented our algorithm in the model checker, NuSMV [4]. For the purpose of comparison, we modify the so-called ad hoc algorithm in NuSMV [2] to test for the existence of an error, as shown in Figure 3. Experiments are carried out in a machine running Linux with an Intel 933Hz CPU and 512MB RAM.

In this work, we did not use any input variable ordering. The abstraction method we use is to make some Boolean variables invisible. Note that because our approach does not involve any refinements, we require that the abstraction not to be too coarse. In general, the criteria to select an abstraction granularity is that it should be feasible to construct the symbolic pattern database in a small amount of time with maximum depth. The relation between the granularity ("abstractness") of the abstraction and the accuracy of the resulting heuristic has been studied by Prieditis and Davis in 1995 [25]. In this work, we set the threshold for the construction to be 60 seconds. If the construction cannot finish within 60 seconds, we have to abandon the abstraction and choose another more abstract system.

The two benchmark circuits we use in this paper were published in David L. Dill's thesis [26]. Since we focus on error detection, we use two "buggy" designs for our evaluation. The first circuit family is called a tree arbiter circuit, which is used to enforce mutual exclusion among users accessing shared resources.

---

[2] In NuSMV, safety properties can be checked by using either standard fixed point evaluation algorithm, or an "ad hoc" algorithm which computes the set of reachable states and intersects it with the set of error states.

The basic element of this circuit family is the arbiter cell, which implements
the mutual exclusion between two users. For more than two users, cells can be
connected to form a tree-like structure. The bottom level cells are connected
to users and the top cell to the shared resource. The request signal from a
user propagates upwards from the bottom level of the tree, and if the shared
resource is granted to the user, the acknowledgement propagates downwards
only to the user who requested it. The second circuit family, distributed mutual
exclusion ring (DME), is used to implement mutual exclusion as well. Instead of
forming a tree-like structures, DME cells are connect as a ring. Mutual exclusion
is implemented by passing a token in the cell ring. In this work, we construct
interleaving finite models for these circuits and check the invariant that no two
users receive an acknowledgement simultaneously. The results of our experiment
is shown in Table 2.

Table 2. Experimental Results for the tree arbiter and DME

			InvarCheck		GuidedInvarCheck	
Circuits	Depth	BDD vars	Total nodes	CPU time (s)	Total nodes	CPU time (s)
tree-arb 7	20	50	322,452	1.340	47,778	2.357
tree-arb 9	20	64	483,286	2.300	634,783	3.120
tree-arb 11	21	78	1,249,438	6.360	560,439	2.440
tree-arb 13	21	92	5,593,886	13.590	450,156	2.520
tree-arb 15	24	106	161,297,839	4759.000	4,262,998	19.290
tree-arb 17	24	120	—	> 6 hours	7,323,386	35.260
tree-arb 19	24	134	—	> 6 hours	7,922,396	34.930
dme 06	26	114	—	> 6 hours	3,316,858	18.240
dme 08	30	152	—	> 6 hours	93,794,232	1137.000

Note that all error traces detected by our method have exactly the same
length as detected by standard **InvarCheck** in NuSMV. For each circuit, we
experimented with a few invariants and only report those errors with depth more
than 20, because short error traces can be easily detected by both algorithms
regardless of model size. We also report the number of BDD variables used to
encode each model to reflect the size of the system. The memory use of the two
algorithms is reflected in the total nodes allocated by the BDD engine that is
contained in NuSMV. The hyphens in the table are for those experiments that
did not terminate within (a randomly chosen) 6 hours.

For the tree arbiter circuits, **GuidedInvarCheck** can easily handle up to
19 cells, whereas **InvarCheck** cannot handle more than 15 cells in less than 6
hours. Note that there is a time-line cross-over in the table between 9 and 11
cells. For smaller circuits, **InvarCheck** can detect errors faster than **Guided-
InvarCheck**. For larger circuits, the performance of **InvarCheck** deteriorates
rapidly, while the time taken by **GuidedInvarCheck** remains quite constant.
This occurs because in systems with a low level of concurrency, BDD-based

breadth-first search is more efficient than guided search. As described in Section 4.3, **GuidedInvarCheck** also needs to partition the image (BDD slicing) and this introduces some overhead as well. For systems with a high level of concurrency, BDD-based breadth-first search is dominated by huge BDD computations, whereas guided search partitions large BDDs into smaller ones, and only explores promising states, thereby avoiding the exponential growth in the size of the BDDs.

We only experimented with 2 of the circuits in the DME family as **InvarCheck** could not cope with circuits that had more than 6 cells in the available time. **GuidedInvarCheck** could however handle up to 8 cells with an error depth of 30. For larger circuits, we need to resort to manipulating the variable ordering to improve the performance.

The experimental results indicate that the guided approach can outperform standard model checking by several orders of magnitude, in both time and required memory. As expected, **GuidedInvarCheck** not only detects the errors much quicker than **InvarCheck**, but also found the shortest error traces.

6   Conclusions and Future Work

In this paper, we have presented a symbolic model checking algorithm that combines homomorphic abstraction and guided search techniques. We introduce a mechanism called symbolic pattern databases to provide a heuristic to guide the model checker. The pattern databases represent the relaxed system and associate each state of the system with a heuristic value (i.e., the estimated number of transitions to an error state). This is required by the underlying heuristic search algorithm to partition the states and guide the search.

The guided search is of course only used when an error is detected in the abstract system. In essence we double-dip on the abstraction: the abstraction reduces the size of the state space directly, but also indirectly as a result of the guided search. There is no need for further abstraction refinements in this work, although embedding guided search in an iterative abstraction-refinement approach would make interesting further work.

It is important to note that guided model checking algorithms like ours are designed for debugging, and not verification. For systems that have no errors, the guided approach does not have any conceptual advantage over conventional model checking algorithms. However, the guided method does slice large BDDs, which reduces the sizes of the BDDs substantially. Although pattern databases are memory-based heuristics, the use of BDDs to represent them also helps to counter any potential size problem, and make a seamless integration with symbolic model checking possible. In this work, we only use BDDs to store symbolic pattern database (the abstracted state space). An interesting next step would be to determine whether other alternative data structures, such as algebraic decision diagrams (ADDs) and multi terminal BDDs (MTBDDs), have better performances than BDDs.

While the guided algorithm is fully automated, we still require human inter-action to determine the level of abstraction. In this work, we only implement one method of constructing an abstraction. The improvement that we have found using guided model checking is of course expected: what sets this work apart is the way we have derived the heuristic. Using our approach, the quality of the heuristic will be dependent on the quality of the user-constructed abstraction rather than the application domain. Our next step is to investigate how the way that the abstraction is constructed affect efficiency of the guidance algorithm in practice.

References

1. Clarke, E.M., Grumberg, O., Peled, D.: Model Checking. MIT Press (1999)
2. McMillan, K.: Symbolic model checking. Kluwer Academic Publishers, Boston, MA (1993)
3. Burch, J., Clarke, E., McMillan, K., Dill, D., Hwang, L.: Symbolic model checking: 10^{20} states and beyond. In: Proceedings of the Fifth Annual IEEE Symposium on Logic in Computer Science, Washington, D.C., IEEE Computer Society Press (1990) 1–33
4. Cimatti, A., Clarke, E.M., Giunchiglia, F., Roveri, M.: NuSMV: A new symbolic model verifier. In: Proceedings of the 11th International Conference on Computer Aided Verification, Trento, Italy, July 6-10. Volume 1633 of Lecture Notes in Computer Science., Springer (1999) 495–499
5. Courcoubetis, C., Vardi, M.Y., Wolper, P., Yannakakis, M.: Memory-efficient al-gorithms for the verification of temporal properties. Formal Methods in System Design 1 (1992) 275–288
6. Holzmann, G.J.: The model checker SPIN. Software Engineering 23 (1997) 279–295
7. Clarke, E.M., Grumberg, O., Long, D.E.: Model checking and abstraction. ACM Transactions on Programming Languages and Systems 16 (1994) 1512–1542
8. Clarke, E.M., Grumberg, O., Jha, S., Lu, Y., Veith, H.: Counterexample-guided abstraction refinement. In: Proceedings the 12th International Conference on Com-puter Aided Verification, Chicago, IL, July 15-19. Volume 1855 of Lecture Notes in Computer Science., Springer (2000) 154–169
9. Clarke, E., Gupta, A., Kukula, J., Strichman, O.: SAT based abstraction-refinement using ILP and machine learning techniques. In: Proceedings of the 14th International Conference on Computer Aided Verification, Copenhagen, Den-mark, July 27-31. Volume 2404 of Lecture Notes in Computer Science., Springer (2002) 265–279
10. Yang, C.H., Dill, D.L.: Validation with guided search of the state space. In: Proceedings of the 35th Conference on Design Automation, Moscone center, San Francico, California, USA, June 15-19, ACM Press (1998) 599–604
11. Alur, R., Wang, B.Y.: "Next" heuristic for on-the-fly model checking. In: Proceed-ings of the 10th International Conference on Concurrency Theory,, Eindhoven, The Netherlands, August 24-27. Volume 1664 of Lecture Notes in Computer Science., Springer (1999) 98–113
12. Bloem, R., Ravi, K., Somenzi, F.: Symbolic guided search for CTL model checking. In: Proceedings of the 37th Conference on Design Automation, Los Angeles, CA, June 5-9, ACM (2000) 29–34

13. Edelkamp, S., Lafuente, A.L., Leue, S.: Directed explicit model checking with HSF–SPIN. In: Model Checking Software, 8th International SPIN Workshop, Toronto, Canada, May 19-20, Proceedings. Volume 2057 of Lecture Notes in Computer Science., Springer (2001) 57–79

14. Reffel, F., Edelkamp, S.: Error detection with directed symbolic model checking. In: FM'99 - Formal Methods, World Congress on Formal Methods in the Development of Computing Systems, Toulouse, France, September 20-24, Proceedings, Volume I. Volume 1708 of Lecture Notes in Computer Science., Springer (1999) 195–211

15. Cabodi, G., Nocco, S., Quer, S.: Mixing forward and backward traversals in guided-prioritized bdd-based verification. In: Proceedings of the 14th International Conference Computer Aided Verification, Copenhagen, Denmark, July 27-31. Volume 2404 of Lecture Notes in Computer Science., Springer (2002) 471–484

16. Santone, A.: Heuristic search + local model checking in selective mu-calculus. IEEE Transactions on Software Engineering **29** (2003) 510–523

17. Culberson, J.C., Schaeffer, J.: Searching with pattern databases. In: Proceedings of the 11th Biennial Conference of the Canadian Society for Computational Studies of Intelligence, Toronto, Ontario, Canada, May 21-24. Volume 1081 of Lecture Notes in Computer Science., Springer (1996) 402–416

18. Korf, R.: Finding optimal solutions to to Rubik's cube using pattern databases. In: Proceedings of the Fourteenth National Conference on Artificial Intelligence and Ninth Innovative Applications of Artificial Intelligence Conference, July 27-31, Providence, Rhode Island, AAAI Press / The MIT Press (1997) 700–705

19. Holte, R.C., Mkadmi, T., Zimmer, R.M., MacDonald, A.J.: Speeding up problem solving by abstraction: A graph oriented approach. Artificial Intelligence **85** (1996) 321–361

20. Holte, R., Hernadvolgyi, I.: Experiments with automatically created memory-based heuristics. In: Proceedings of the 4th International Symposium on Abstraction, Reformulation, and Approximation, Horseshoe Bay, Texas, USA, July 26-29. Volume 1864 of Lecture Notes in Computer Science., Springer (2000) 281–290

21. Bryant, R.E.: Graph-based algorithms for Boolean function manipulation. IEEE Transactions on Computers **C-35** (1986) 677–691

22. Edelkamp, S.: Symbolic pattern databases in heuristic search planning. In: Proceedings of the Sixth International Conference on Artificial Intelligence Planning Systems, April 23-27, Toulouse, France, AAAI (2002) 274–283

23. Pearl, J.: Heuristics: Intelligent Search Strategies for Computer Problem Solving. Addison-Wesley, USA (1984)

24. Nymeyer, A., Qian, K.: Heuristic search algorithm based on symbolic data structures. In: Proceedings of the 16th Australian Joint Conference in Artificial Intelligence, Perth, Australia, 3-5 December. Volume 2903 of Lecture Notes in Artificial Intelligence., Springer (2003) 966–979

25. Prieditis, A., Davis, R.: Quantitatively relating abstractness to the accuracy of admissible heuristics. Artificial Intelligence **74** (1995) 165–175

26. Dill, D.L.: Trace Theory for Automatic Hierarchical Verification of Speed-Independent Circuits. The MIT Press, MA (1988)

Numeric Domains with Summarized Dimensions

Denis Gopan[1], Frank DiMaio[1], Nurit Dor[2], Thomas Reps[1], and Mooly Sagiv[2]

[1] Comp. Sci. Dept., University of Wisconsin; {gopan,dimaio,reps}@cs.wisc.edu
[2] School of Comp. Sci., Tel-Aviv University; {nurr,msagiv}@post.tau.ac.il

Abstract. We introduce a systematic approach to designing *summarizing abstract numeric domains* from existing numeric domains. Summarizing domains use *summary* dimensions to represent potentially unbounded collections of numeric objects. Such domains are of benefit to analyses that verify properties of systems with an unbounded number of numeric objects, such as shape analysis, or systems in which the number of numeric objects is bounded, but large.

1 Introduction

Verifying the correctness of complex software systems requires reasoning about numeric quantities. In particular, an analysis technique may have to discover certain relationships among values of *numeric objects*, such as numeric variables, numeric array elements, or numeric-valued fields of heap-allocated structures [2]. For example, to verify that there are no buffer overruns in a particular C program, an analysis needs to make sure that the value of an index variable does not exceed the length of the buffer at each program point where the buffer is accessed [16].

Numeric analyses have been a research topic for several decades, and a number of numeric domains that allow to approximate numeric state of a system have been designed over the years. These domains exhibit varying precision/cost tradeoffs, and target different types of numeric properties. The list of existing numeric domains includes: **non-relational domains**: intervals [7,15], congruences [5]; **weakly relational domains**: difference constraints [4], octagons [11]; **relational domains**: polyhedra [2, 6], trapezoidal congruences [10].

Existing numeric domains are able to keep track of only a fixed number of numeric objects. Traditionaly, a finite set of stack-allocated numeric variables deemed *important* for the property to be verified is identified for the analysis. The remaining numeric objects, e.g., numeric array elements or heap-allocated numeric objects, are modeled conservatively.

Two problems that plague existing numeric domains are:

- It may be impossible to verify certain numeric properties by considering only a fixed number of the numeric objects in the system. For example, in programs that use collections (or, in general, dynamic memory allocation), it is impossible to determine statically the set of memory locations used by a program.
- The resources required for higher-precision relational numeric domains, such as polyhedra, are subject to combinatorial explosion. This is due to the representation of elements of the numeric domain; for instance, the number of elements in the frame

K. Jensen and A. Podelski (Eds.): TACAS 2004, LNCS 2988, pp. 512–529, 2004.
© Springer-Verlag Berlin Heidelberg 2004

```
(1)  for(i = 0; i < n; i++) {
(2)     t = 0;
(3)     for(k = ia[i]; k < ia[i+1]; k++) {
(4)        j = ja[k];
(5)        t += a[k] * x[j];
(6)     }
(7)     y[i] = t;
(8)  }
```

$$0 \leq ja[\cdot] < n$$
$$0 \leq ia[\cdot] \leq nnz$$

(b)

$$0 \leq ja[\cdot] < n$$
$$0 \leq ia[\cdot] \leq nnz$$
$$0 \leq k < nnz$$
$$0 \leq i < n$$
$$0 \leq j < n$$

(c)

(a)

Fig. 1. Multiplication of a sparse matrix by a vector: (a) multiplication code; (b) initial constraints, imposed by *CSR* format; (c) constraints that represent the abstract numeric state at line 5.

representation of a polyhedron grows exponentially with the number of tracked objects.

The typical approach to reasoning about an unbounded number of objects (or simply a very large number of objects) is by employing abstraction. The set of objects is divided into a fixed number of groups based on certain criteria. Each group is then represented (*summarized*) by a single abstract object. The groups themselves need not be of bounded size. As an example, consider TVLA, a framework for shape analysis, which concerns the problem of determining "shape invariants" for programs that perform destructive updating on dynamically allocated storage. TVLA uses so-called "canonical abstraction" to create bounded-size representations of memory states [14,9]. To reason about numeric properties in such a *summarizing* framework, an analysis needs to be able to capture the relationships among values of *groups* of numeric objects, rather than relationships among values of *individual* numeric objects. Moreover, what appears to be a natural way of applying existing techniques is, in fact, unsound.

In this paper, we define a systematic approach for extending existing numeric domains to support arbitrary summarization. The domain to be extended must support four extra operations: *expand, fold, add,* and *drop* which will be disccused in detail in later sections. The extended numeric domain exposes a standard numeric-domain interface. For purposes of this paper, we assume that a client analysis has the responsibility of indicating which abstract objects are summary ones. At one extreme, if the analysis does not do any summarization, the extended domain operates exactly as the original domain. In the presence of summarization, the extended domain produces safe answers, with minimal loss of precision.

The program in Fig. 1(a) multiplies an $(n \times n)$ sparse matrix stored in the *compressed sparse row (CSR)* format [13] by a vector x of size n. In the *CSR* format, a sparse matrix is represented using three arrays:

- the array a, of size nnz, stores the matrix elements row by row (nnz is the number of non-zero elements in the matrix);
- the array ja, of size nnz, stores the column indices for the elements in a; thus, *CSR* format imposes the constraint $0 \leq ja[\cdot] < n$ on each element of the array ja;

– the array ia, of size $n + 1$, stores the offsets to the beginning of each row in the arrays a and ja; thus, *CSR* format imposes the constraint $0 \le ia[\cdot] \le nnz$ on each element of the array ia.

Note that, if the matrix is properly represented in *CSR* format, both array acceses on line 5 (shown in bold) will never be out of bounds. Yet, most existing analyses are not able to verify this property because array indices k and j are computed through the use of *indirection* arrays, ia and ja.

We used the summarizing extension of the polyhedral numeric domain [2,6] to verify that both array accesses in line 5 are, indeed, always in bounds, if the constraints imposed by *CSR* format hold initially. We used two *summary* dimensions to represent all elements of the arrays ia and ja, respectively. Such summarization allowed us to represent the abstract numeric states of the program as 7-dimensional polyhedra. It follows directly from the constraints shown in Fig. 1(c) that the values of both indices j and k at line 5 are within the bounds of the corresponding arrays.

The contributions this paper makes are

– The extended numeric domains constructed using our technique support arbitrary summarization, which makes them suitable for a wide range of client analyses: on the one hand, the analysis could be as simple as summarizing the values of all elements of an array; on the other hand, it could be as involved as using canonical abstraction for summarization (which would allow multiple, dynamically changing segments of an array to be summarized separately—see Sect. 7).
– The requirements that we place on the numeric domain to be extended are minimal: a safe implementation of four operations must be provided. Because of this flexibility, the numeric domain that is most suitable for a problem can be employed by a client analysis.
– When coupled with a suitable client, such as TVLA, our extended numeric domains are able to operate on unbounded collections of numeric objects.
– For large fixed-size collections of numeric objects, our extended numeric domains allow trading some precision for analysis efficiency (in terms of both memory usage and running time).

As will be illustrated in Ex. 1, what looks like a natural approach to performing operations over values in an extended numeric domain is actually unsound. The formalization of a sound approach is the major technical contribution of this paper.

The remainder of the paper is organized as follows: Sect. 2 discusses concrete semantics. Sect. 3 introduces the concept of reducing dimensionality via summarization. Sect. 4 describes what is involved in extending a standard numeric domain (i.e., as long as it meets certain assumptions about various primitive operations). Sect. 5 describes how to perform safe computations on values of extended numeric domains. Sect. 6 discusses related work. Sect. 7 sketches the application of this technique to a situation in which multiple, dynamically changing segments of an array are summarized separately.

2   Concrete Semantics

Our goal is to perform static analysis of systems in which the number of numeric objects (i) may change as the system operates, and (ii) cannot be bounded statically. A concrete numeric state of the system, denoted $S^\natural$, is an assignment of a value to each numeric object. In each particular state the number of numeric objects is finite, and will be denoted as $N^{S^\natural}$, or N when $S^\natural$ is clear from context. We denote the set of objects in state $S^\natural$ by $Obj^{S^\natural} = \{v_1, ..., v_N\}$. Following the traditional numeric analysis approach, we associate each numeric object with a dimension of an N-dimensional space, and encode a concrete numeric state of the system as an N-dimensional point. We use a function $dim^{S^\natural} : Obj^{S^\natural} \to \{1, ..., N\}$ to map numeric objects to corresponding dimensions.

Let $\mathbb{V}$ denote a set of possible numeric values (such as $\mathbb{Z}$ or $\mathbb{Q}$). Because the number of numeric objects, and hence the number of dimensions, is not bounded a priori, a concrete numeric state may be a point in a space of arbitrary (finite) dimension:

$$S^\natural \in \mathbb{V}^+, \quad \text{where } \mathbb{V}^+ = \bigcup_{k=1}^{\infty} \mathbb{V}^k$$

Given an expression $e(w_1, ..., w_k)$, where $w_i \in Obj^{S^\natural}$, we evaluate it at a concrete numeric state $S^\natural$ as follows: let $x[i]$ denote the i-th component of a vector $x \in \mathbb{V}^N$; we define

$$[\![e(w_1, ..., w_k)]\!]_\natural(S^\natural) = e(S^\natural[dim^{S^\natural}(w_1)], ..., S^\natural[dim^{S^\natural}(w_k)]).$$

To each program point we attach a set of concrete states $D^\natural \subseteq \mathbb{V}^+$. We define the program's concrete collecting semantics using the following transformers:

- **Numeric tests** filter the set of concrete states:

$$[\![e(w_1, ..., w_k)?]\!]_\natural(D^\natural) = \{S^\natural \in D^\natural : [\![e(w_1, ..., w_k)]\!]_\natural(S^\natural) = true\}$$

- **Assignments** change the value of a single numeric object (in each concrete state):

$$[\![v_i \leftarrow e(w_1, ..., w_k)]\!]_\natural(D^\natural) =$$
$$= \left\{ \bar{S}^\natural : \exists S^\natural \in D^\natural \text{ s.t. } \left[\begin{array}{c} Obj^{\bar{S}^\natural} = Obj^{S^\natural}, \ dim^{\bar{S}^\natural} \equiv dim^{S^\natural} \\ \bar{S}^\natural[dim^{S^\natural}(v_i)] = [\![e(w_1, ..., w_k)]\!]_\natural(S^\natural), \\ \bar{S}^\natural[j] = S^\natural[j] \text{ for } j \neq dim^{S^\natural}(v_i) \end{array} \right] \right\}$$

- **Union** collects the sets at control flow merge points.

Determining the exact sets of concrete states at each program point is, in general, undecidable. The goal of static analysis is to collect at each program point an overapproximation of the set of concrete states that may arise there. We use the framework of abstract interpretation to formalize such analyses.

Existing numeric analyses identify overapproximations of the sets of concrete states that arise at program points using a set representation that can be easily stored and manipulated in a computer. Such value spaces are called *numeric domains*. The assumption that existing numeric domains make is that the number of numeric objects is fixed throughout the analysis, thus allowing sets of concrete states to be represented as subsets of a space with a fixed number of dimensions.

In the semantics formulated above, however, the concrete numeric states arising at a given program point belong to spaces of possibly different numbers of dimensions.

Therefore, existing numeric domains cannot be used directly. In the next section, we show how a set of points in spaces of different dimensionalities can be abstracted by a subset of a space with a fixed, smaller number of dimensions.

3   Summarizing Numeric Domains

In this section, we introduce a numeric domain that uses a subset of a space with a fixed number of dimensions to overapproximate a set of points in spaces of different dimensionalities. The idea behind the abstraction is that some dimensions of the fixed-dimensional space will represent the values of potentially unbounded collections of numeric objects, rather than the values of individual objects. The numeric domain is not able to differentiate between the individual objects that are members of such collections, and preserves only overall properties of the collection, e.g., lower and upper bounds on the values of its members.

We call the process of grouping numeric objects into a collection *summarization*. In this paper, for the sake of simplifying the presentation, we assume that each client analysis that uses one of our summarizing numeric domains is responsible for defining which numeric objects are to be summarized, and which collections are to be formed. In the simplest case, as illustrated in the introduction, all elements of an array may be summarized by a single dimension. Ultimately, our goal is to implement more complicated summarizations, including canonical abstraction [14], which would allow parts of an array to be summarized, and would let the summarization partition on array elements change during the course of the analysis; see Sect. 7 for more on combining a client analysis that uses canonical abstraction with a summarizing numeric domain.

Formally, we assume that the concrete numeric objects are separated into M groups, where M is determined by the client analysis. Some groups may contain just one numeric object, while others may contain a set of objects of a priori unbounded size. In the abstract numeric state S, each group is represented by an abstract numeric object. We denote the set of abstract numeric objects by $Obj^S = \{u_1, ... u_M\}$. The abstract objects that represent groups with more than one element are called *summary* objects. For describing and justifying our techniques, we will refer to (conceptual) mappings that map numeric objects of a concrete state $S^\natural$, to the corresponding numeric objects of an abstract state S; such a mapping is called a *summarization* function, e.g., $F_{sum} : Obj^{S^\natural} \to Obj^S$.

A *summarizing abstract numeric domain* represents an abstract numeric state S as a subset of M-dimensional space, where each dimension corresponds to an abstract numeric object. Function $dim^S : Obj^S \to \{1, ..., M\}$ maps an abstract object to its corresponding dimension.

The *abstraction* of a concrete numeric state is an M-dimensional subset constructed by *folding* together the *summarized* dimensions. For example, as illustrated in Fig. 2, if $S^\natural = (1, 2, 3, 4) \in \mathbb{V}^4$ and the summarization function is defined as

$$F_{sum} = [v_1 \mapsto u_1, v_2 \mapsto u_2, v_3 \mapsto u_2, v_4 \mapsto u_2]$$

the abstraction of $S^\natural$ is $S = \{(1, 2), (1, 3), (1, 4)\} \subseteq \mathbb{V}^2$. Note that the abstraction loses the distinction between the values of summarized numeric objects; e.g., under the above

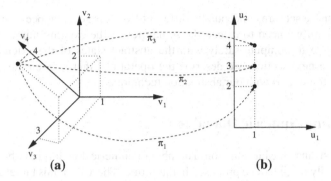

Fig. 2. Abstraction example: (a) concrete numeric state $S^\natural$; (b) abstraction of $S^\natural$. $F_{sum} = [v_1 \mapsto u_1, v_2 \mapsto u_2, v_3 \mapsto u_2, v_4 \mapsto u_2]$ and $\Pi_{F_{sum}} = \{\pi_1, \pi_2, \pi_3\}$.

summarization function, S is also an abstraction for the concrete states $(1, 3, 2, 4)$ and $(1, 4, 3, 2)$.

Let $S^\natural \in \mathbb{V}^N$ be a concrete numeric state, whose abstraction is $S \subseteq \mathbb{V}^M$. Each point $x \in S$ is constructed by taking an *orthogonal projection* $\pi : \mathbb{V}^N \to \mathbb{V}^M$ of $S^\natural$, such that

$$x[dim^S(u)] = \pi(S^\natural)[dim^S(u)] = S^\natural[dim^{S^\natural}(v)]$$

where $u \in Obj^S, v \in Obj^{S^\natural}$ and $u = F_{sum}(v)$. We denote the set of all such projections as $\Pi_{F_{sum}}$. As shown in Fig. 2, given the above summarization function, the set $\Pi_{F_{sum}}$ contains three projections: π_1 projects the dimensions corresponding to v_1 and v_2, π_2 projects the dimensions corresponding to v_1 and v_3, and π_3 projects the dimensions corresponding to v_1 and v_4.

Formally, given a summarization function F_{sum}, we say that an abstract state $S \subseteq \mathbb{V}^M$ *represents* a concrete state $S^\natural$ (denoted by $S^\natural \sqsubseteq^{F_{sum}} S$) iff:

$$S \supseteq \{x \in \mathbb{V}^M : x = \pi(S^\natural) \text{ for some } \pi \in \Pi_{F_{sum}}\}$$

Sometimes, when F_{sum} is not important for the discussion, we will omit it from the notation and write $S^\natural \sqsubseteq S$. It is easy to see that abstract states form an infinite-height lattice ordered by set inclusion, where the *bottom* element is the empty set, and the *join* and the *meet* operations correspond to set union and set intersection, respectively.

Given a set of concrete states $D^\natural \subseteq \mathbb{V}^+$, and an abstract state $S \subseteq \mathbb{V}^M$, we say that $D^\natural \sqsubseteq S$ if S abstracts every element in $D^\natural$, i.e., $S^\natural \sqsubseteq S$ for all $S^\natural \in D^\natural$.

We use existing numeric domains to store and manipulate M-dimensional subsets that correspond to abstract states. Numeric domains impose certain restrictions on the subsets they are able to represent; therefore, it may be impossible to represent an abstract numeric state precisely. In such cases, an overapproximation of that abstract state is represented. For example, the abstract state $\{(1, 2), (1, 3), (1, 4)\} \subseteq \mathbb{V}^2$ cannot be represented as a polyhedron directly, but can be approximated by the polyhedron

$$\{x \in \mathbb{V}^2 : x[1] = 1 \text{ and } 2 \le x[2] \le 4\}.$$

Because these sets are conceptually different from the sets that occur in the existing numeric domain, we need to extend the semantics of the existing numeric domain in order to be able to compute safely with the abstract states of the extended numeric domain. In the next section, we describe the operations that a given numeric domain must support to be used with our abstraction technique.

4   Extending Numeric Domains

As was pointed out in the introduction, a number of numeric domains have been designed, and undoubtedly more will be proposed in the future. These domains target different numeric properties, and exhibit different precision/cost tradeoffs. What is common among all of them is that they use a compact representation for a subset of a multidimensional space, and define a number of operations that allow a client analysis to (i) evaluate certain kinds of numeric conditions, and (ii) transform an underlying subset according to the semantics of a program statement.

The assumption that all existing numeric domains make is that each point within the represented subset corresponds to a concrete numeric state of the system, and vice versa. This assumption is relied on when proving the correctness of the implementations of operations for transforming the set, and for evaluating conditions. In contrast, in our abstraction a concrete state corresponds to a *collection* of points within the subset represented by a numeric domain, and each individual point within the represented subset may belong to the abstraction of *multiple* concrete states.

To provide for sound evaluation of conditions and set transformations induced by program statements, the numeric domain needs to be extended with several extra operations that map between subsets of spaces of different dimensionality. In this section, we give a detailed description of these operations, and show how they can be implemented for several existing numeric domains.

4.1   Standard Semantics of a Numeric Domain

Let us define the standard *interface* of a numeric domain. The operations that the numeric domain exposes are abstract state transformers that manipulate subsets of N-dimensional space. As mentioned above, the semantics of the state transformers is defined under the assumption that each concrete numeric state corresponds to a single point within the abstract state and vice versa.

Let d_i denote the i-th dimension of $\mathbb{V}^N$. Let formula $e(w_1, ..., w_k)$, where $w_i \in \{d_1, ..., d_N\}$, denote either a numeric condition or a numeric computation. We will use the following notation to denote the standard numeric domain operations

- **Numeric tests:** $[\![e(w_1, ..., w_k)?]\!]_{std}$
- **Assignments:** $[\![d_i \leftarrow e(w_1, ..., w_k)]\!]_{std}$
- **Join:** $\sqcup_{std}$
- **Widening operator:** ∇_{std}

The detailed definitions of the abstract state transformers can be found in the corresponding papers [7,15,4,11,5,2,10].

The operations defined below insert and remove arbitrary dimensions of the multidimensional space. After each such operation, dimensions with indices above that of the inserted or removed dimension have to be renumbered. To somewhat simplify the presentation by avoiding recomputation of dimension indices within the operation definitions, we introduce a function $[\cdot]'$ that maps the dimensions of the original space to the corresponding dimensions of the resulting space after the j-th dimension has been removed (used by operations *fold* and *drop*). Similarly, we introduce a dimension mapping $[\cdot]''$ for inserting the new dimension j (used by operations *expand* and *add*).

$$k' = \begin{cases} k-1 & \text{if } k > j \\ k & \text{if } k < j \\ \text{undefined} & \text{if } k = j \end{cases} \qquad k'' = \begin{cases} k+1 & \text{if } k \geq j \\ k & \text{if } k < j \end{cases}$$

4.2 The *fold* Operation

The *fold* operation formalizes the concept of folding dimensions together. Let $S \subseteq \mathbb{V}^N$. The $fold_{i,j}$ transforms S into a subset of $\mathbb{V}^{N-1}$ by folding dimension j into dimension i. For an arbitrary subset of $\mathbb{V}^N$, $fold_{i,j}$ is defined as follows:

$$fold_{i,j}(S) = \left\{ x \in \mathbb{V}^{N-1} : \exists y \in S \text{ s.t. } \begin{bmatrix} (x[i'] = y[i]) \vee (x[i'] = y[j]) \\ \wedge \, \forall k \neq i, j \, [x[k'] = y[k]] \end{bmatrix} \right\}$$

If multiple dimensions need to be folded together, we construct the corresponding transformation by composing several *fold* operations.

Note that the *fold* operation as defined above is not closed in most existing numeric domains. For example, consider a two-dimensional polyhedron

$$P = \left\{ x \in \mathbb{V}^2 : 1 \leq x[1] \leq 3 \text{ and } 7 \leq x[2] \leq 12 \right\}$$

Clearly, $fold_{1,2}(P) = \{ x \in \mathbb{V} : (1 \leq x \leq 3) \vee (7 \leq x \leq 12) \}$ is not a polyhedron. For such domains, we define $[\![fold_{i,j}]\!]_{std}(S)$ to be an overapproximation of the set $fold_{i,j}(S)$ that is representable in that domain, e.g., for polyhedral domain, $[\![fold_{1,2}]\!]_{std}(P) = \{ x \in \mathbb{V} : 1 \leq x \leq 12 \}$.

4.3 The *expand* Operation

The *expand* operation is essentially the opposite of the *fold* operation. Let $S \subseteq \mathbb{V}^N$. The $expand_{i,j}$ transforms S into a subset of $\mathbb{V}^{N+1}$ by creating an exact copy of the i-th dimension and inserting it as a new dimension j. For an arbitrary subset of $\mathbb{V}^N$, the $expand_{i,j}$ operation is defined as follows:

$$expand_{i,j}(S) = \left\{ x \in \mathbb{V}^{N+1} : \exists y, z \in S \text{ s.t. } \begin{bmatrix} x[i''] = y[i] \wedge x[j] = z[i] \\ \wedge \, \forall k \neq i \, [x[k''] = y[k] = z[k]] \end{bmatrix} \right\}$$

For instance, for the example from Sect. 3, $expand_{2,3}(\{(1,2),(1,3),(1,4)\})$ is equal to $\{(1,2,2),(1,2,3),(1,2,4),(1,3,2),(1,3,3),(1,3,4),(1,4,2),(1,4,3),(1,4,4)\}$. More complex expansions can be constructed by composing several $expand_{i,j}$ operations.

Let $S \subseteq \mathbb{V}^N$. Note that the $expand_{i,j}(S)$ constructs the *maximal* subset $S' \subseteq \mathbb{V}^{N+1}$, such that $fold_{i,j}(S')$ is S. In fact, *fold* and *expand* form a Galois insertion:

$$expand_{i,j} \circ fold_{i,j}(S) \supseteq S \quad \text{and} \quad fold_{i,j} \circ expand_{i,j}(S) = S$$

Unlike *fold*, the *expand* operation is closed on all of the existing numeric domains we have experimented with so far, and is likely to be closed for any numeric domain. Our conviction is based on the fact that the values along the i-th dimension of the original subset are precisely represented by the numeric domain. Therefore, the values along the newly introduced j-th dimension can also be precisely represented in that domain.

4.4 The *add* and *drop* Operations

The *add* and *drop* are two auxiliary operations that add new dimensions and remove specified dimensions from a multidimensional space. Let $S \subseteq \mathbb{V}^N$. The $add_j(S)$ embeds S into $\mathbb{V}^{N+1}$ after inserting a new dimension, j, into $\mathbb{V}^N$.

$$add_j(S) = \left\{ x \in \mathbb{V}^{N+1} : \exists y \in S \text{ s.t. } x[j] \in \mathbb{V} \text{ and } \forall k \left[x[k''] = y[k] \right] \right\}$$

The $drop_j(S)$ computes the projection of S onto $\mathbb{V}^{N-1}$, removing the dimension j, from $\mathbb{V}^N$.

$$drop_j(S) = \left\{ x \in \mathbb{V}^{N-1} : \exists y \in S \text{ s.t. } \forall k \neq j \left[x[k'] = y[k] \right] \right\}$$

The add_j operation is closed in all numeric domains and can be implemented precisely. The $drop_j$ operation is closed in the numeric domains that we have experimented with; furthermore, we were able to design precise implementations of $[\![drop_j]\!]_{std}$ for those domains. Thus, for the sake of the minimality arguments given in Sect. 5, we assume that the numeric domain to be extended must furnish a precise implementation of the *drop* operation.

4.5 Implementation Examples

In this section, we show how to implement the above operations for several existing numeric domains. For this discussion we have chosen numeric domains that use a diverse set of representations: the non-relational *interval* domain [7,15], the fully relational *polyhedral* domain [2,6], and a family of *weakly-relational* domains constructed in [12].

In the *interval* domain, the subset of a multidimensional space is represented by maintaining upper and lower bounds for values along each dimension, i.e., an N-dimensional subset is represented by an ordered set I of N intervals. The $[\![add_j]\!]_{int}(I)$ operation is defined by inserting interval $[-\infty, \infty]$ as the new j-th interval into I. The $[\![drop_j]\!]_{int}(I)$ operation removes the j-th interval from I. The operation $expand_{i,j}$ is defined as follows:

$$[\![expand_{i,j}]\!]_{int}(I) = J \quad \text{where} \quad J[j] = I[i] \quad \text{and} \quad \forall k \left[J[k''] = I[k] \right]$$

The $fold_{i,j}$ operation is not closed on the interval domain, hence we define $[\![fold_{i,j}]\!]_{int}(I)$ to overapproximate the resulting set as follows:

$$[\![fold_{i,j}]\!]_{int}(I) = J \quad \text{where} \quad J[i'] = I[i] \sqcup_{int} I[j] \quad \text{and} \quad \forall k \neq i, j [J[k'] = I[k]]$$

In the *polyhedral* domain, the subset of the multidimensional space is represented as an intersection of a finite set of linear constraints, i.e., by a polyhedron. Most polyhedral libraries, such as Parma [1], provide routines for adding and removing dimensions. The operation $[\![add_j]\!]_{poly}$ and $[\![drop_j]\!]_{poly}$ may be implemented by direct invocation of those routines. A little extra care may be necessary to maintain the proper numbering of the dimensions. Also, note that the operation $[\![drop_j]\!]_{poly}$ directly corresponds to *Fourier-Motzkin elimination* [3] of dimension j.

The $[\![expand_{i,j}]\!]_{poly}(P)$ operations is implemented by augmenting the set of constraints that represent P: for each linear constraint involving dimension i, we add a similar constraint with dimension j substituted for dimension i (and all constraints are remapped according to $[\cdot]''$). The $fold_{i,j}$ operation is not closed for polyhedra, therefore we define $[\![fold_{i,j}]\!]_{poly}(P)$ to compute an overapproximation of the set $fold_{i,j}(P)$ as follows:

$$[\![fold_{i,j}]\!]_{poly}(P) = [\![drop_j]\!]_{poly}(P \sqcup_{poly} [\![d_i \leftarrow d_j]\!]_{poly}(P))$$

In *weakly-relational* domains, a subset of $\mathbb{V}^N$ is represented by a set of constraints of the form $d_j - d_i \in C$, where d_j and d_i refer to the dimensions j and i, respectively. C is an element of a non-relational *base* numeric domain, such as the interval domain. A weakly-relational domain maintains an $N \times N$ matrix m, where each element $m_{ij} \in C$ encodes a constraint $d_j - d_i \in m_{ij}$. A *closure* operation $[\cdot]^*$ that propagates the constraints through the matrix is defined. For more details, see [12].

The $[\![add_j]\!]_{wr}$ operation is implemented by inserting the j-th row and j-th column into the matrix m. The elements of the inserted row and column are initialized to the $\top$ element of the corresponding non-relational base domain. The $[\![drop_j]\!]_{wr}$ operation is implemented by removing the j-th row and j-th column from the *closed* matrix m^*. The operation $[\![expand_{i,j}]\!]_{wr}$ is implemented by inserting copies of the i-th row and i-th column into matrix m^* as the (new) j-th row and j-th column, respectively; the elements m_{ij}, m_{ji}, and m_{jj} are set to $\top$. The operation $[\![fold_{i,j}]\!]_{wr}$ is implemented by using m^* and recomputing the elements of its i-th row and i-th column by taking the join of their value with the value of the corresponding elements in the j-th row and j-th column. The $[\![drop_j]\!]_{wr}$ operation is applied to the resulting matrix.

5 Abstract Semantics

In existing numeric domains, each point in the abstract state corresponds to a unique concrete state. Therefore, each point in the abstract state contains enough information to compute how the corresponding concrete state is transformed; consequently it can be transformed independently of other points in the abstract space. Hence, using appropriate finite representations for subsets of N-dimensional space (e.g., polyhedra), the abstract state transformer can be defined as an operation that is applied to all points in the subset simultaneously (e.g., a linear transform) to produce the resulting abstract state. In our case, there is no such correspondence between the concrete states and individual points in the abstract state. Instead, each concrete state corresponds, in general, to a subset of the abstract state, and each point in the abstract state belongs to the abstractions of a (possibly infinite) set of concrete states. Hence, the points within the abstract state cannot be used independently when applying a transformation. However, we will now show that by making appropriate calls to *expand* and *fold*, it is possible to use existing numeric domains to compute the results of transformations safely and precisely.

In general, a transformation consists of two steps. First, for each point in the abstract state we compute the values to which the transformation formula evaluates in the concrete states corresponding to this point. Second, given the values computed in the first step, we update each point. Ordinarily, the standard semantics of a numeric domain is able to combine the two steps, because each point in the abstract state corresponds to a single concrete state and vice versa, i.e., (i) a transformation formula evaluates to a single value for each point in the abstract state, (ii) each point in the original abstract state corresponds to a single point in the transformed abstract state.

In our situation, each point within the abstract state corresponds to the *projections* of one or more concrete states, rather than to a single concrete state, and may not contain all the values necessary to evaluate the transformation formula. Therefore, applying the standard semantics of the numeric domain may produce an *unsound* result. We illustrate this situation with the following example.

Example 1. Consider a concrete state $S^\natural$ with four numeric objects x, y_1, y_2, and y_3. Let $S^\natural = (1, 2, 3, 4)$. Consider an abstraction S in which y_1, y_2, and y_3 are folded into a summary numeric object y: $S = \{(1, 2), (1, 3), (1, 4)\}$. Let the transformation formula be $x \leftarrow y_2$. Evaluating this formula by binding y_2 to the summary dimension corresponding to y and treating each point in S independently, results in $S' = \{(2, 2), (3, 3), (4, 4)\}$. Now, applying the transformation to $S^\natural$ yields a concrete numeric state $(3, 2, 3, 4)$ whose abstraction $\{(3, 2), (3, 3), (3, 4)\}$ is clearly not a subset of S'.

Intuitively, the problem occurs because for a given point x in S, we failed to compute the set of *all* values to which the transformation formula evaluates in concrete states that have x as a projection. Hence, to be able to treat the points within the abstract state independently, we need to overcome the following problems:

- **The evaluation problem.** For each point in the abstract state S, we need to compute the set of all values to which the transformation formula evaluates, across all of the concrete states $S^\natural \sqsubseteq S$ whose abstraction includes that point. The problem is that to compute these values we may need information from other points within the abstract state.
- **The update problem.** Given the above set of values for a particular point in the abstract state, we need to define how to update that point. The problem is that the point needs to be updated differently for each value in the set. Therefore, a single point in the initial abstract state may produce a potentially infinite number of points within the transformed abstract state.

Example 2. Assume the same situation as in Ex. 1. Concrete numeric object y_2 is represented by a summary numeric object in the abstract domain. Therefore, for each point in S, the values that y_2 can take on are $\{2, 3, 4\}$. Transforming each point according to each value of y_2, we get the transformed abstract state $S' = \{(\alpha, \beta) : \alpha, \beta = 2, 3, \text{ or } 4\}$. It is easy to see that S' abstracts all possible concrete states that may arise as a result of the transformation of concrete states abstracted by S.

In the following discussion, we will often refer to concrete states whose abstraction includes a particular point within the abstract state. We introduce a concise notation to simplify the presentation: suppose that $S \subseteq \mathbb{V}^M$ is an abstract state; let x be a point in S, and let $S^\natural \sqsubseteq S$ be a concrete state whose abstraction contains x. We denote this relationship as $S^\natural \sqsubseteq_x S$.

5.1   General Overview of the Approach

Let $e(w_1, ..., w_k)$ be a numeric formula, where each w_i denotes a concrete numeric object. Each concrete numeric object w_i in the formula corresponds to either a summary or non-summary abstract numeric object. Without loss of generality, we assume that first $\hat{k}$ of the w_i's, where $0 \leq \hat{k} \leq k$, correspond to summary numeric objects.

Let $S \subseteq \mathbb{V}^M$ be an abstract numeric state, and let x be a point in S. We denote the set of values that $e(w_1, ..., w_k)$ evaluates to in all concrete numeric states $S^\natural \sqsubseteq_x S$ as

$$Values_e^S(x) = \{[\![e(w_1, ..., w_k)]\!]_\natural(S^\natural) : S^\natural \sqsubseteq_x S\}$$

Given a test $e(w_1, ..., w_k)?$, or an assignment $v_i \leftarrow e(w_1, ..., w_k)$, we transform an abstract numeric state S in three steps:

- **Preparation step.** First, we construct a set $S_e \subseteq \mathbb{V}^{M+\hat{k}}$, which allows us to compute the set $Values_e^S(x)$ for each point $x \in S$ by using the standard semantics associated with the numeric domain. We construct S_e by creating exact copies of the dimensions of S that correspond to the summary abstract numeric objects $F_{sum}(w_1), ..., F_{sum}(w_{\hat{k}})$. The detailed description of this construction is given in Sect. 5.2.

- **Transformation step.** Next, we use the standard semantics of the numeric domain to perform the transformation of S_e. Certain care is necessary to handle the assignments to summary numeric objects, because these objects also represent the concrete numeric objects whose value is not changed by the assignment. For such assignments, we introduce an extra dimension to capture the new values that are assigned to the numeric object, and then combine the new values with the old values by folding this extra dimension into the dimension that corresponds to the object. The details are covered in Sects. 5.3, 5.4, and 5.5.

- **Clean-up step.** Finally, we remove from S_e the dimensions introduced in the preparation step to produce an M-dimensional subset that corresponds to the updated abstract state, S'.

Because the clean-up step returns us to a situation in which $\Pi_{F_{sum}}$ defines a mapping from concrete states in $\mathbb{V}^N$ to abstract states (subsets of $\mathbb{V}^M$), the standard numeric domain join operation, $\sqcup_{std}$, can be used to combine numeric states at control flow merge points. The standard semantics of a widening operator, ∇_{std}, is safe with respect to the abstraction. Thus, for brevity, we will not discuss widening in this paper.

5.2 Evaluation of Numeric Formulas

Let $S \in \mathbb{V}^M$ be an abstract state, and let $e(w_1, ..., w_k)$ be a numeric formula. We will show how to construct the set S_e, so that it is possible to compute $Values_e^S(x)$ for all $x \in S$ by applying standard numeric domain operations to S_e.

Let $S^\natural \sqsubseteq S$. The value $[\![e(w_1, ..., w_k)]\!]_\natural(S^\natural)$ is completely determined by the values that the w_i's have in $S^\natural$. Thus, to be able to use the standard semantics of the numeric domain, we will extend S by adding k extra dimensions, and put all combinations of values w_i's have in $S^\natural \sqsubseteq_x S$ into the new dimensions for each $x \in S$,

$$S_e = \left\{ y \in \mathbb{V}^{M+k} : \begin{array}{l} x = (y[1], ..., y[M]) \in S,\ S^\natural \sqsubseteq_x S,\ \text{and} \\ y[M+j] = S^\natural[dim^{S^\natural}(w_j)]\ \text{for}\ j = \{1, ..., k\} \end{array} \right\}$$

Now we can compute $Values_e^S(x)$ for all points $x \in S$ in parallel by evaluating the formula $e(d_{M+1}, ..., d_{M+k})$ on S_e using the standard semantics of the $(M+k)$-dimensional numeric domain.

We can simplify the set S_e somewhat. Let $x \in S$. It follows from the abstraction that if $F_{sum}(w_i)$ is a non-summary abstract numeric object, then for all $S^\natural \sqsubseteq_x S$,

$$S^\natural[dim^{S^\natural}(w_i)] = x[dim^S(F_{sum}(w_i))]$$

Therefore, we do not need to create extra dimensions for w_i that correspond to non-summary abstract objects (i.e., $i > \hat{k}$). The simplified definition of S_e is

$$S_e = \left\{ y \in \mathbb{V}^{M+\hat{k}} : \begin{array}{l} x = (y[1], ..., y[M]) \in S,\ S^\natural \sqsubseteq_x S\ \text{and} \\ y[M+j] = S^\natural[dim^{S^\natural}(w_j)]\ \text{for}\ j \in \{1, ..., \hat{k}\} \end{array} \right\}$$

This definition of S_e allows us to compute the set $Values_e^S(x)$ for all points $x \in S$ by evaluating the formula $e(d_{M+1}, ..., d_{M+\hat{k}}, d_{dim^S(F_{sum}(w_{\hat{k}+1}))}, ..., d_{dim^S(F_{sum}(w_k))})$ on S_e using the standard semantics of the $(M + \hat{k})$-dimensional numeric domain. For brevity, we will refer to the above formula as $e(\bar{d})$ in the remainder of the paper.

The dimensions $M+j$ of S_e, where $j \in \{1, ..., \hat{k}\}$, are constructed by creating exact copies of dimensions $dim^S(F_{sum}(w_j))$. We use a composition of *expand* operations, denoted *expand$_e$*, to construct them:

$$S_e = [\![expand_e]\!]_{std}(S)$$
$$= [\![expand_{dim^S(F_{sum}(w_{\hat{k}})), M+\hat{k}}]\!]_{std} \circ ... \circ [\![expand_{dim^S(F_{sum}(w_1)), M+1}]\!]_{std}(S)$$

After the transformation is applied to the set S_e, we need to project the transformed set S'_e back into M-dimensional space. We define the operation *drop$_e$* as a composition of *drop* operations to remove the dimensions $d_{M+1}, ..., d_{M+\hat{k}}$,

$$S' = [\![drop_e]\!]_{std}(S'_e) = [\![drop_{M+1}]\!]_{std} \circ ... \circ [\![drop_{M+\hat{k}}]\!]_{std}(S'_e)$$

5.3   Numeric Tests

Let $S \in \mathbb{V}^M$ be an abstract state and let $e(w_1, ..., w_k)$ be a numeric condition. We want to construct the most-precise abstract state S', such that for any concrete state $S^\natural \sqsubseteq S$ in which $e(w_1, ..., w_k)$ holds, $S^\natural \sqsubseteq S'$. Let $Obj^{S'} = Obj^S$ and $dim^{S'} \equiv dim^S$. We define the abstract transformer as follows:

$$S' = [\![e(w_1, ..., w_k)?]\!](S) = \{x : x \in S \text{ and } true \in Values_e^S(x)\}$$
$$= [\![drop_e]\!]_{std} \circ [\![e(\bar{d})?]\!]_{std} \circ [\![expand_e]\!]_{std}(S)$$

We argue that the above transformation is sound. Let $S^\natural \sqsubseteq S$ be an arbitrary concrete numeric state such that the condition $e(w_1, ..., w_k)$ holds in $S^\natural$. By the definition of set $Values_e^S(x)$, it follows that $true \in Values_e^S(x)$ for all points x in the abstraction of $S^\natural$. Hence, by the definition of the transformation, the entire abstraction of $S^\natural$ is in S'. Therefore, $S^\natural \sqsubseteq S'$. The equality on the second line of the definition is justified by the discussion of how to compute set $Values_e^S(x)$ in Sect. 5.2.

Also, we argue that the result of the transformation is minimal in the sense that no points can be excluded from S'. Note that, by construction, for all points $x \in S'$, the set $Values_e^S(x)$ contains the value $true$. Hence there exists at least one concrete state $S^\natural \sqsubseteq S$ in which the condition holds and whose abstraction contains x.

5.4   Assignments to Non-summary Objects

Let $S \in \mathbb{V}^M$ be an abstract state and let $v_i \leftarrow e(w_1, ..., w_k)$ be an assignment, such that $F_{sum}(v_i)$ is a non-summary abstract object. We want to construct the most precise abstract state $S' \in \mathbb{V}^M$, such that for any concrete state $S^\natural \sqsubseteq S$,

$$[\![v_i \leftarrow e(w_1, ..., w_k)]\!]_\natural(S^\natural) \sqsubseteq S'$$

Let $Obj^{S'} = Obj^S$ and $dim^{S'} \equiv dim^S$. Also let $m = dim^S(F_{sum}(v_i))$. We define the abstract transformer as follows:

$$S' = [\![v_i \leftarrow e(w_1, ..., w_k)]\!](S)$$
$$= \{y : \exists x \in S \text{ s.t. } y[m] \in Values_e^S(x) \text{ and } y[j] = x[j] \text{ for } j \neq m\}$$
$$= [\![drop_e]\!]_{std} \circ [\![d_m \leftarrow e(\bar{d})]\!]_{std} \circ [\![expand_e]\!]_{std}(S)$$

Let us show that this transformation is sound. Let $S^\natural \sqsubseteq^{F_{sum}} S$ be an arbitrary concrete numeric state, such that $[\![e(w_1, ..., w_k)]\!]_\natural(S^\natural) = \alpha$. We denote the concrete state, to which $S^\natural$ is transformed as the result of the assignment, by $\hat{S}^\natural$, where:

$$\hat{S}^\natural = [\![v_i \leftarrow e(w_1, ..., w_k)]\!]_\natural(S^\natural)$$

Both $S^\natural$ and $\hat{S}^\natural$ are points in N-dimensional space. By the definition of the concrete semantics, $S^\natural$ and $\hat{S}^\natural$ are equal component-wise, except for component v_i which is equal to α in $\hat{S}^\natural$. Let us pick an arbitrary projection $\pi \in \Pi_{F_{sum}}$. Let $x = \pi(S^\natural)$ and $\hat{x} = \pi(\hat{S}^\natural)$. Since $F_{sum}(v_i)$ is a non-summary abstract numeric object, the m-th component of $\hat{x}$ is equal to α, whereas other components are equal to corresponding components of x. Now, since $x \in S$ and $\alpha \in Values_e^S(x)$, it follows by construction that $\hat{x} \in S'$. Therefore, $\hat{S}^\natural \sqsubseteq^{F_{sum}} S'$. The equality on the third line of the definition is justified by the discussion of how to compute set $Values_e^S(x)$ in Sect. 5.2.

Also, the transformation is minimal in the sense that for every point $x' \in S'$, there exists a concrete state $S^\natural \sqsubseteq S$, such that x' is in the abstraction of a concrete state $\hat{S}^\natural$, where

$$\hat{S}^\natural = [\![v_i \leftarrow e(w_1, ..., w_k)]\!]_\natural(S^\natural)$$

By construction, the point x' is in S' if there exists a point $x \in S$, which is equal to x' component-wise with the exception of component $x'[m]$, whose value is in $Values_e^S(x)$. By definition of the set $Values_e^S(x)$, there exists a concrete state $S^\natural \sqsubseteq S$, such that its abstraction contains point x and $[\![e(w_1, ..., w_k)]\!]_\natural(S^\natural) = x'[m]$. Then, from the concrete semantics and the abstraction mechanism, it follows that x' is in the abstraction of concrete state $\hat{S}^\natural$.

5.5 Assignments to Summary Objects

Let $S \in \mathbb{V}^M$ be an abstract state and let $v_i \leftarrow e(w_1, ..., w_k)$ be an assignment, such that $F_{sum}(v_i)$ is a summary abstract object. We want to construct the most precise abstract state $S' \in \mathbb{V}^M$, such that for any concrete state $S^\natural \sqsubseteq S$,

$$[\![v_i \leftarrow e(w_1, ..., w_k)]\!]_\natural(S^\natural) \sqsubseteq S'$$

Let $Obj^{S'} = Obj^S$ and $dim^{S'} \equiv dim^S$. Also let $m = dim^S(F_{sum}(v_i))$. We define the abstract transformer as follows:

$$\begin{aligned}
S' &= [\![v_i \leftarrow e(w_1, ..., w_k)]\!](S) \\
&= \{y : \exists x \in S \text{ s.t. } y[m] \in Values_e^S(x) \cup \{x[m]\} \text{ and } y[j] = x[j] \text{ for } j \neq m\} \\
&\sqsupseteq [\![drop_e]\!]_{std} \circ [\![fold_{d_m, d_n}]\!]_{std} \circ [\![d_n \leftarrow e(\bar{d})]\!]_{std} \circ [\![add_{d_n}]\!]_{std} \circ [\![expand_e]\!]_{std}(S)
\end{aligned}$$

The soundness and minimality arguments are the same as in the Sect. 5.4. The only difference is that the abstract object $F_{sum}(v_i)$ corresponds to a collection of concrete numeric objects, only one of which is updated. Hence, for each point $x \in S$, the component $x[m]$ may preserve its old value. Note, that $\sqsupseteq$ in the third line of the equation is due to the implementation $[\![fold]\!]_{std}$, which computes an overapproximation of *fold* in most numeric domains.

6   Related Work

The introduction already mentioned several numeric domains that have been investigated, including *non-relational domains*, such as intervals [7,15] and congruences [5]; *weakly relational domains*, such as difference constraints [4] and octagons [11]; and *relational domains*, such as polyhedra [2,6] and trapezoidal congruences [10]. In all of this work, the assumption is made that there are a fixed number of numeric objects to track, where the number is known in advance. In contrast, our work provides techniques for

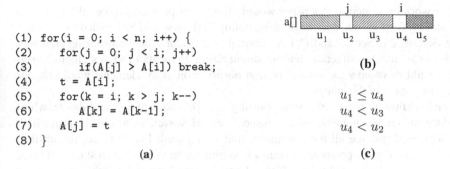

```
(1)  for(i = 0; i < n; i++) {
(2)      for(j = 0; j < i; j++)
(3)          if(A[j] > A[i]) break;
(4)      t = A[i];
(5)      for(k = i; k > j; k--)
(6)          A[k] = A[k-1];
(7)      A[j] = t
(8)  }
```

(a)

(b)

$$u_1 \leq u_4$$
$$u_4 < u_3$$
$$u_4 < u_2$$

(c)

Fig. 3. Insertion sort: (a) code for insertion sort; (b) array partitioning: abstract objects u_i represent array segments; (c) invariants captured by the abstract state at line 4.

performing static analysis in the presence of an unbounded number of concrete numeric objects (which are then collapsed into some number of summary objects).

Yavuz-Kahveci and Bultan present an algorithm for shape analysis in which numeric information is attached to summary nodes; the information on a summary node u of a shape-graph S bounds the number of concrete nodes that are mapped to u from any concrete memory configuration that S represents [17]. This represents a different approach to combining a collection of numeric quantities from the one pursued in our work: in [17], each combined object contributes 1 to a *sum* that labels the summary object; in our approach, when objects are combined together, the effect is to create a *set* of values.

7 Future Work

In this section, we sketch how the techniques developed in the paper could be applied in a situation in which multiple, dynamically changing segments of an array are summarized separately.

The goal would be to use static analysis to prove the correctness of an array-sorting program, such as the insertion-sort program shown in Fig. 3(a). The idea would be to use summary numeric objects to represent segments of the array. Fig. 3(b) depicts a situation that occurs during the execution of insertion sort. This would be represented using three summary numeric objects: u_1, u_3, and u_5. As the sort progresses, u_1, u_3, and u_5 must be associated with different segments of the array. In other words, the dimensionalities of the spaces that they represent have to vary.

To actually carry this out in a static-analysis algorithm, the main difficulty would be to find which dimensions/segments to merge, and when to adjust the pattern of merging during the course of the analysis. Fortunately, this is addressed by canonical abstraction [14]. The verification of sorting algorithms by means of shape analysis (using the TVLA system [9]) was described in [8]. However, TVLA does not provide a facility to describe numeric values directly; thus, in [8] it was necessary to introduce a "work-around"—an artificial binary predicate *dle* (for "data less-than or equal"), to record whether the value of one element is less than or equal to the value of another element.

The work presented in this paper would allow such problems to be addressed in a more straightforward manner: the numeric manipulations would be handled by the operations described in Sect. 5, and TVLA's normal mechanisms for summarizing elements, based on canonical abstraction, and unsummarizing elements (TVLA's "focus" operation) would drive how the summarization partition on array elements would change during the course of the analysis.

Some additional issues arise in supporting the operations of *new* and *delete*, which introduce and remove numeric objects, respectively. However, the mechanisms that have been presented provide all the machinery that is required. For instance, the abstract semantics for the *new* operation is to *add* a new dimension to an abstract state initialized to a range of possible initial values. If the client analysis indicates that the added object is to be summarized by one of the existing abstract objects, the new dimension is then *folded* into the corresponding existing dimension. *Deleting* a non-summary numeric object *drops* the corresponding dimension from the abstract state.

Space limitation precludes giving a full treatment of the remaining issues involved in using summarizing abstract numeric domains in conjunction with canonical abstraction.

References

1. R. Bagnara, E. Ricci, E. Zaffanella, and P. M. Hill. Possibly not closed convex polyhedra and the parma polyhedra library. In *Static Analysis Symp.*, volume 2477, pages 213–229, 2002.
2. P. Cousot and N. Halbwachs. Automatic discovery of linear constraints among variables of a program. In *Symp. on Princ. of Prog. Lang.*, 1978.
3. G. B. Dantzig and B. C. Eaves. Fourier-motzkin elimination and its dual. *Journal of Combinatorial Theory (A)*, 14:288–297, 1973.
4. D.L. Dill. Timing assumptions and verification of finite-state concurrent systems. In *Automatic Verification Methods for Finite State Systems*, pages 197–212, 1989.
5. P. Granger. *Analyses Semantiques de Congruence*. PhD thesis, Ecole Polytechnique, 1991.
6. N. Halbwachs, Y.-E. Proy, and P. Roumanoff. Verification of real-time systems using linear relation analysis. *Formal Methods in System Design*, 11(2):157–185, 1997.
7. W.H. Harrison. Compiler analysis of the value ranges for variables. *Trans. on Softw. Eng.*, 3(3):243–250, 1977.
8. T. Lev-Ami, T. Reps, M. Sagiv, and R. Wilhelm. Putting static analysis to work for verification: A case study. In *Int. Symp. on Software Testing and Analysis*, pages 26–38, 2000.
9. T. Lev-Ami and M. Sagiv. TVLA: A system for implementing static analyses. In *Static Analysis Symp.*, pages 280–301, 2000.
10. F. Masdupuy. *Array Indices Relational Semantic Analysis using Rational Cosets and Trapezoids*. PhD thesis, Ecole Polytechnique, 1993.
11. A. Mine. The octagon abstract domain. In *Proc. Eighth Working Conf. on Rev. Eng.*, pages 310–322, 2001.
12. A. Mine. A few graph-based relational numerical abstract domains. In *Static Analysis Symp.*, pages 117–132, 2002.
13. Y. Saad. Sparsekit: A basic tool kit for sparse matrix computations, version 2. Tech. rep., Comp. Sci. Dept. Univ. of Minnesota, June 1994.
14. M. Sagiv, T. Reps, and R. Wilhelm. Parametric shape analysis via 3-valued logic. *Trans. on Prog. Lang. and Syst.*, 24(3):217–298, 2002.
15. C. Verbrugge, P. Co, and L.J. Hendren. Generalized constant propagation: A study in C. In *Int. Conf. on Comp. Construct.*, volume 1060 of *Lec. Notes in Comp. Sci.*, pages 74–90, 1996.

16. D. Wagner, J. Foster, E. Brewer, and A. Aiken. A first step towards automated detection of buffer overrun vulnerabilities. In *Symp. on Network and Distributed Systems Security (NDSS)*, February 2000.
17. T. Yavuz-Kahveci and T. Bultan. Automated verification of concurrent linked lists with counters. In *Static Analysis Symp.*, pages 69–84, 2002.

Symbolically Computing Most-Precise Abstract Operations for Shape Analysis*

G. Yorsh[1]**, T. Reps[2], and M. Sagiv[1]

[1] School of Comp. Sci., Tel-Aviv Univ., {gretay, msagiv}@post.tau.ac.il
[2] Comp. Sci. Dept., Univ. of Wisconsin, reps@cs.wisc.edu

Abstract. Shape analysis concerns the problem of determining "shape invariants" for programs that perform destructive updating on dynamically allocated storage. This paper presents a new algorithm that takes as input an abstract value (a 3-valued logical structure describing some set of concrete stores X) and a precondition p, and computes the most-precise abstract value for the stores in X that satisfy p. This algorithm solves several open problems in shape analysis: (i) computing the most-precise abstract value of a set of concrete stores specified by a logical formula; (ii) computing best transformers for atomic program statements and conditions; (iii) computing best transformers for loop-free code fragments (i.e., blocks of atomic program statements and conditions); (iv) performing interprocedural shape analysis using procedure specifications and assume-guarantee reasoning; and (v) computing the most-precise overapproximation of the meet of two abstract values. The algorithm employs a decision procedure for the logic used to express properties of data structures. A decidable logic for expressing such properties is described in [5]. The algorithm can also be used with an undecidable logic and a theorem prover; termination can be assured by using standard techniques (e.g., having the theorem prover return a safe answer if a time-out threshold is exceeded) at the cost of losing the ability to guarantee that a most-precise result is obtained. A prototype has been implemented in TVLA, using the SPASS theorem prover.

1   Introduction

Shape-analysis algorithms (e.g., [11]) are capable of establishing that certain invariants hold for (imperative) programs that perform destructive updating on dynamically allocated storage. For example, they have been used to establish that a program preserves treeness properties, as well as that a program satisfies certain correctness criteria [8]. The TVLA system [8] automatically constructs shape-analysis algorithms from a description of the operational semantics of a given programming language, and the shape abstraction to be used.

---

* Supported by ONR contract N00014-01-1-0796.
** Supported in part by the Israel Science Foundation founded by the Academy of Sciences and Humanities.

K. Jensen and A. Podelski (Eds.): TACAS 2004, LNCS 2988, pp. 530–545, 2004.
© Springer-Verlag Berlin Heidelberg 2004

The methodology of abstract interpretation has been used to show that the shape-analysis algorithms generated by TVLA are *sound* (conservative). Technically, for a given program, TVLA uses a finite set of abstract values L, which forms a join semi-lattice, and an adjoined pair of functions (α, γ), which form a Galois connection [2]. The abstraction function α maps potentially infinite sets of concrete stores to the *most-precise* abstract value in L. The concretization function γ maps an abstract value to the set of concrete stores that the abstract value represents. Thus, soundness means that the set of concrete stores $\gamma(a)$ represented by the abstract values a computed by TVLA includes all of the stores that could ever arise, but may also include superfluous stores (which may produce false alarms).

1.1 Main Results

The overall goal of our work is to improve the precision and scalability of TVLA by employing decision procedures. In [15], we show that the concretization of an abstract value can be expressed using a logical formula. Specifically, [15] gives an algorithm that converts an abstract value a into a formula $\widehat{\gamma}(a)$ that exactly characterizes $\gamma(a)$—i.e., the set of concrete stores that a represents.[1] This is used in this paper to develop algorithms for the following operations on shape abstractions:

- Computing the most-precise abstract value that represents the (potentially infinite) set of stores defined by a formula. We call this algorithm $\widehat{\alpha}(\varphi)$ because it is a constructive version of the algebraic operation α.
- Computing the operation $assume[\varphi](a)$, which returns the most-precise abstraction of the set of stores represented by a for which a precondition φ holds. Thus, when applied to the most general abstract value $\top$, the procedure $\widehat{assume}[\varphi]$ computes $\widehat{\alpha}(\varphi)$. However, when applied to some other abstract value a, $\widehat{assume}[\varphi]$ refines a according to precondition φ. This is perhaps the most exciting application of the method described in the paper, because it would permit TVLA to be applied to large programs by using procedure specifications.
- Computing *best abstract transformers* for atomic program statements and conditions [2]. The current transformers in TVLA are conservative, but are not necessarily the best. Technically, the best abstract transformer of a statement described by a transformer τ amounts to $assume[\tau](a)$, where τ is a formula over the input and output states and a is the input abstract value. The method can also be used to compute best transformers for loop-free code fragments (i.e., blocks of atomic program statements and conditions).
- Computing the most-precise overapproximation of the meet of two abstract values. Such an operation is useful for combining forward and backward shape analysis to establish temporal properties, and when performing interprocedural analysis in the Sharir and Pnueli functional style [12]. Technically, the meet of abstract values a_1 and a_2 is computed by $\widehat{\alpha}(\widehat{\gamma}(a_1) \wedge \widehat{\gamma}(a_2))$.

---

[1] As a convention, a name of an operation marked with a "hat" ($\widehat{}$) denotes the algorithm that computes that operation.

The *assume* **Operation** can be used to perform interprocedural shape analysis using procedure specifications and assume-guarantee reasoning. Here the problem is to interpret a procedure's pre- and post-conditions in the most precise way (for a given abstraction). For every procedure invocation, we check if the current abstract value potentially violates the precondition; if it does, a warning is produced. At the point immediately after the call, we can assume that the post-condition holds. Similarly, when a procedure is analyzed, the pre-condition is assumed to hold on entry, and at end of the procedure the post-condition is checked.

The core algorithm $\widehat{assume}$ presented in the paper computes $assume[\varphi](a)$, the refinement of an abstract value a according to precondition φ. In [16] we prove the correctness of the algorithm, i.e., $\widehat{assume}[\varphi](a) = assume[\varphi](a) = \alpha(\llbracket\varphi\rrbracket \cap \gamma(a))$. Fig. 1 depicts the idea behind the algorithm. It shows the the concrete and abstract value-spaces as the rectangle on the left and the oval on the right. The points in the right oval represent abstract values with the corresponding sets of concrete values (defined by γ) shown as ovals on the left. The algorithm works its way down in the right oval, which on the left corresponds to progressing from the outer oval towards the inner region, labeled X. The algorithm repeatedly refines abstract value a by eliminating the ability to represent concrete stores that do not satisfy φ. It produces an abstract value that represents the tightest set of stores in $\gamma(a)$ that satisfy φ. Of course, because of the inherent loss of information due to abstraction, the result can also describe stores in which φ does not hold. However, the result is as precise as possible for the given abstraction, i.e., it is the tightest possible overapproximation to $\llbracket\varphi\rrbracket \cap \gamma(a)$ expressible in the abstract domain.

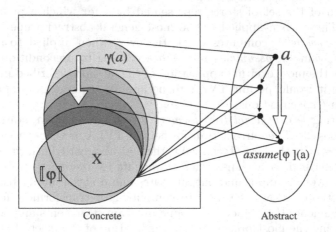

Fig. 1. The $\widehat{assume}[\varphi](a)$ algorithm. The set $X = \llbracket\varphi\rrbracket \cap \gamma(a)$ describes all stores that are represented by a and satisfy φ.

The $\widehat{assume}$ algorithm employs a decision procedure for the logic used to express properties of data structures. In [5], a logic named $\exists\forall^{DTC(E)}$ is described, which is both *decidable* and *useful* for reasoning about shape invariants. Its main features are sketched in Section 3.1. However, the $\widehat{assume}$ algorithm can also be used with an undecidable logic and a theorem prover; termination can be assured by using standard techniques (e.g., having the theorem prover return a safe answer if a time-out threshold is exceeded) at the cost of losing the ability to guarantee that a most-precise result is obtained.

Prototype Implementation. To study the feasibility of our method, we have implemented a prototype of the $\widehat{assume}$ algorithm using the first-order theorem prover SPASS [14]. Because SPASS does not support transitive closure, the prototype implementation is applicable to shape-analysis algorithms that do not use transitive closure [6,13]. So far, we tried three simple examples: two cases of $\widehat{assume}$, one of which is the running example of this paper, and one case of best transformer. On all queries posed by these examples, the theorem prover terminated. The number of calls to SPASS in the running example is 158, and the overall running time was approximately 27 seconds.

2   Overview of the Framework

This section provides an overview of the framework and the results reported in the paper. The formal description of the $\widehat{assume}$ algorithm appears in Section 3.

As an example, consider the following precondition, expressed in C notation as: (x -> n == y) && (y != null) (which will be abbreviated in this section as p), where x and y are program variables of the linked-list data-type defined in Fig. 2(a). The precondition p can be defined by a closed formula in first-order logic: $\varphi_0 \stackrel{\text{def}}{=} \exists v_1, v_2 : x(v_1) \wedge n(v_1, v_2) \wedge y(v_2)$. The operation $assume[p](a)$ enforces precondition p on an abstract value a. Typically, a represents a set of concrete stores that may arise at the program point in which p is evaluated. The abstract value a used in the running example is depicted by the graph in Fig. 2(S). This graph is an abstraction of all concrete stores that contain a non-empty linked list pointed to by x, as explained below.

2.1   3-Valued Structures

In this paper, abstract values that are used to represent concrete stores are sets of 3-valued logical structures over a vocabulary $\mathcal{P}$ of predicate symbols. Each structure has a universe U of individuals and a mapping ι from k-tuples of individuals in U to values $1, 0$, or $1/2$ for each k-ary predicate in $\mathcal{P}$. We say that the values 0 and 1 are **definite values** and that $1/2$ is an **indefinite value**, meaning "either 0 or 1 possible"; a value l_1 is **consistent** with l_2 (denoted by $l_1 \sqsubseteq l_2$) when $l_1 = l_2$ or $l_2 = 1/2$; $\bigsqcup W$ denotes the least upper bound of the values in the set W.

A 3-valued structure provides a representation of stores: individuals are abstractions of heap-allocated objects; unary predicates represent pointer variables that point from the stack into the heap; binary predicates represent pointer-valued fields of data structures; and additional predicates in $\mathcal{P}$ describe certain properties of the heap. A special predicate eq has the intended meaning of equality between locations. When the value of eq is $1/2$ on the pair $\langle u, u \rangle$ for some node u, then u is called a "summary" node and it may represent more than one linked-list element. Table 1 describes the predicates required for a program with

Table 1. The set of predicates for representing the stores manipulated by programs that use the `List` data-type from Fig. 2(a) and two pointer variables x, y.

Predicate	Intended Meaning
$x(v)$	Does pointer variable x point to element v?
$y(v)$	Does pointer variable y point to element v?
$n(v_1, v_2)$	Does the n field of v_1 point to v_2?
$eq(v_1, v_2)$	Do v_1 and v_2 denote the same element?
$is(v)$	Is v pointed to by more than one field ?

pointer variables x and y, that manipulates the linked-list data-type defined in Fig. 2(a). 3-valued structures are depicted as directed graphs, with individuals as graph nodes. A predicate with value 1 is represented by a solid arrow; with value $1/2$ by a dotted arrow; and with value 0 by the absence of an arrow.

In Fig. 2(S), the solid arrow from x to the node u_1 indicates that predicate x has the value 1 for the individual u_1 in the 3-valued structure S. This means that any concrete store represented by S contains a linked-list element pointed to by program variable x. Moreover, it **must** contain additional elements (represented by the summary node u_2, drawn as a dotted circle), some of which **may** be reachable from the head of the linked-list (as indicated by the dotted arrow from u_1 to u_2, which corresponds to the value $1/2$ of predicate $n(u_1, u_2)$), and some of which **may** be linked to others (as indicated by the dotted self-arrow on u_2). The dotted arrows from y to u_1 and u_2 indicate that program variable y **may** point to any linked-list element. The absence of an arrow from u_2 to u_1 means that there is **no** n-pointer to the head of the list. Also, the unary predicate is is 0 on all nodes and thus not shown in the graph, indicating that every element of a concrete store represented by this structure may be pointed to by at most one n-field.

We next introduce the subclass of bounded structures [10]. Towards this end, we define **abstraction predicates** to be a designated subset of unary predicates, denoted by $\mathcal{A}$. In the running example, all unary predicates are defined as abstraction predicates. A **bounded structure** is a 3-valued structure in which for every pair of distinct nodes u_1, u_2, there exists an abstraction predicate q such that q evaluates to different definite values for u_1 and u_2. All 3-valued structures used throughout the paper are bounded structures. Bounded structures are used in shape analysis to guarantee that the analysis is carried out w.r.t. a finite set of abstract structures, and hence will always terminate.

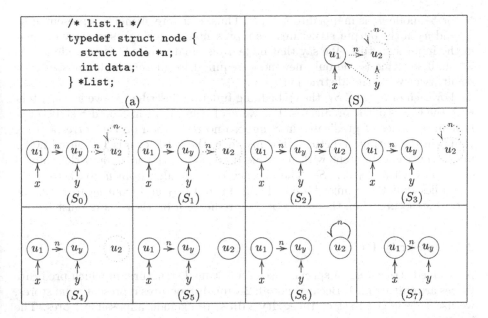

Fig. 2. (a) A declaration of a linked-list data-type in C. (S) The input abstract value $a = \{S\}$ represents all concrete stores that contain a non-empty linked list pointed to by the program variable x, where the program variable y may point to some element. $(S_0$–$S_7)$ The result of computing $assume[p](a)$: the abstract value $a' = \{S_0, \ldots, S_7\}$ represents all concrete stores that contain a linked-list of length 2 or more that is pointed to by x, in which the second element is pointed to by y.

2.2   Embedding Order on 3-Valued Structures

3-valued structures are ordered by the **embedding order** ($\sqsubseteq$), defined below. $S \sqsubseteq S'$ guarantees that the set of concrete stores represented by S is a subset of those represented by S'.

Let S and S' be two 3-valued structures, and let f be a surjective function that maps nodes of S onto nodes of S'. We say that f **embeds** S in S' (denoted by $S \sqsubseteq_f S'$) if for every predicate $q \in \mathcal{P}$ of arity k and all k-tuples $\langle u_1, \ldots, u_k \rangle$ in S, the value of q over $\langle u_1, \ldots, u_k \rangle$ is consistent with, but may be more specific than, the value of q over $\langle f(u_1), \ldots, f(u_k) \rangle$: $\iota^S(q)(u_1, \ldots, u_k) \sqsubseteq \iota^{S'}(q)(f(u_1), \ldots, f(u_k))$. We say that S **can be embedded into** S' (denoted by $S \sqsubseteq S'$) if there exists a function f such that $S \sqsubseteq_f S'$.

In fact, the requirement of $assume[p](a)$ can be rephrased using embedding: generate the most-precise abstract value a' such that all concrete stores that can be embedded into a' (i) can be embedded into a, and (ii) satisfy the precondition p. Indeed, the result of $assume[p](a)$, shown in Fig. 2(S_0–S_7), consists of 8 structures, each of which can be embedded into the input structure Fig. 2(S). The embedding function maps u_1 in the output structure to the same node u_1 in each of S_0–S_7 output structures. Each one of the output structures S_0–S_6 contains nodes u_y and u_2, both of which are mapped by the embedding to u_2 in

S; for S_7, node u_y is mapped to u_2 in S. Thus, concrete elements represented by u_y and u_2 in the output structures are represented by a single summary node u_2 in the input structure. We say that node u_y is "materialized" from node u_2. As we shall see, this is the only new node required to guarantee the most-precise result, relative to the abstraction.

For each of $S_0, \ldots, S_7$, the embedding function described above is consistent with the values of the predicates. The value of x on u_1 is 1 in S_i and S structures. Indefinite values of predicates in S impose no restriction on the corresponding values in the output structures. For instance, the value of y is $1/2$ on all nodes in S, which is consistent with its value 0 on nodes u_1 and u_2 and the value 1 on u_y in each of $S_0, \ldots, S_7$. The absence of an n-edge from u_2 back to u_1 in S implies that there must be no edge from u_y to u_1 and from u_2 to u_1 in the output structures, i.e., the values of the predicate n on these pairs must be 0.

2.3   Integrity Rules

A 2-valued structure is a special case of a 3-valued structure, in which predicate values are only 0 and 1. Because not all 2-valued structures represent valid stores, we use a designated set of **integrity rules**, to exclude impossible stores. The integrity rules are fixed for each particular analysis and defined by a conjunction of closed formulas over the vocabulary $\mathcal{P}$, that must be satisfied by all concrete structures. For the linked-list data-type in Fig. 2(a), the following conditions define the admissible stores: (i) each program variable can point to at most one heap node, (ii) the n-field of an element can point to at most one element, (iii) $is(v)$ holds if and only if there exist two distinct elements with n-fields pointing to v. Finally, eq is given the interpretation of equality: $eq(v_1, v_2)$ holds if and only if v_1 and v_2 denote the same element.

2.4   Canonical Abstraction

The abstraction we use throughout this paper is **canonical abstraction**, as defined in [11]. The surjective function β takes a 2-valued structure and returns a 3-valued structure with the following properties:

- β maps concrete nodes into abstract nodes according to **canonical names** of the nodes, constructed from the values of the abstraction predicates.
- β is a **tight** embedding [11], i.e., the value of the predicate q on an abstract node-tuple is $1/2$ only when there exist two corresponding concrete node-tuples with different values.

A 3-valued structure S is an ICA (Image of Canonical Abstraction) if there exists a 2-valued structure $S^{\natural}$ such that $S = \beta(S^{\natural})$. Note that every ICA is a bounded structure.

For example, all structures in Fig. 2(S_0–S_7) produced by $assume[p](a)$ operation are ICAs, whereas the structure in Fig. 2(S) is not an ICA. The structure in Fig. 2(S_1) is a canonical abstraction of the concrete structure in Fig. 3(a) and also the one in Fig. 3(b).

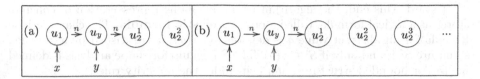

Fig. 3. Concrete stores represented by the structure S_1 from Fig. 2. (a) The concrete nodes u_2^1 and u_2^2 are mapped to the abstract node u_2. (b) The concrete nodes u_2^1, u_2^2 and u_2^3 are mapped to the abstract node u_2. More concrete structures can be generated in the same manner, by adding more isolated nodes that map to the summary node u_2.

The abstraction function α is defined by extending β pointwise, i.e., $\alpha(W) = \{\beta(S^\natural) \mid S^\natural \in W\}$ where W is a set of 2-valued structures. The concretization function γ takes a set of 3-valued structures W and returns a potentially infinite set of 2-valued structures $\gamma(W)$ where $S^\natural \in \gamma(W)$ iff $S^\natural$ satisfies the integrity rules and there exists $S \in W$ such that $\beta(S^\natural) \sqsubseteq S$.

The requirement of $assume[p](a)$ to produce the most-precise abstract value amounts to producing $\alpha(X)$, where X is the set of concrete structures that embed into a and satisfy p. Indeed, the result of $assume[p](a)$ in Fig. 2(S_0–S_7) satisfies this requirement, because S_0–S_7 are the canonical abstractions of all structures in X.

For example, structure S_1 from Fig. 2 is a canonical abstraction of each of the structures in Fig. 3. However, S_1 is not a canonical abstraction of S_2 from Fig. 2,[2] because the value $1/2$ of n for $\langle u_y, u_2 \rangle$ requires that a concrete structure abstracted by S_1 have two pairs of nodes with the same canonical names as $\langle u_y, u_2 \rangle$ and with different values of n. This requirement does not hold in S_2, because it contains only one pair $\langle u_1, u_2 \rangle$ with those canonical names. Without S_2, the result would not include the canonical abstractions of all concrete structures in X, but it would be semantically equivalent (because S_2 can be embedded into S_1). The version of the $\widehat{assume}[p](a)$ algorithm that we describe does include S_2 in the output. It is straightforward to generalize the algorithm to produce the smallest semantically equivalent set of structures.

It is non-trivial to produce the most-precise result for $assume[p](a)$. For instance, in each of S_0–S_6 there is no back-edge from u_2 to u_y even though both nodes embed into the node u_2 of the input structure, which has a self-loop with n evaluating to $1/2$. It is a consequence of the integrity rules that no back-edge can exist from any u_2^j to u_y in any concrete structure that satisfies p: precondition p implies the existence of an n-pointer from u_1 to u_y, but u_y cannot have a second incoming n-edge (because the value of the predicate is on u_y is 0).

Consequently, to determine predicate values in the output structure, each concrete structure that it represents must be accounted for. Because the number of such concrete structures is potentially infinite, they cannot be examined explicitly. The algorithm described in this paper uses a decision procedure to perform this task symbolically.

---

[2] S_2 is a 2-valued structure, and is a canonical abstraction of itself.

Towards this end, the algorithm uses a symbolic representation of concrete stores as a logical formula, called a **characteristic formula**. The characteristic formula for an abstract value a is denoted by $\hat{\gamma}(a)$; it is satisfied by a 2-valued structure $S^\natural$ if and only if $S^\natural \in \gamma(a)$. The $\hat{\gamma}$ formula for shape analysis is defined in [15] for bounded structures, and it includes the integrity rules.

In addition, a necessary requirement for the output of $\widehat{assume}$ to be a set of ICAs is imposed by the formula $\varphi_{q,u_1,\dots,u_k}$, defined in Eq. (1) below; this is used to check whether the value of a predicate q can be $1/2$ on a node-tuple $\langle u_1, \dots, u_k \rangle$ in a structure S. Intuitively, the formula is satisfiable when there exists a concrete structure represented by S that contains two tuples of nodes, both mapped to the abstract tuple $\langle u_1, \dots, u_k \rangle$, such that q evaluates to different values on these tuples. If the formula is not satisfiable, S is not a result of canonical abstraction, because the value of q on $\langle u_1, \dots, u_k \rangle$ is not as precise as possible, compared to the value of q on the corresponding concrete nodes.

3   The $\widehat{assume}$ Algorithm

The $\widehat{assume}$ algorithm is shown in Fig. 4. Section 3.1 explains the role of the decision procedure and the queries posed by our algorithm. The algorithm is explained in Section 3.2 (phase 1) and Section 3.3 (phase 2). Finally, the properties of the algorithm are discussed in Section 3.4.

procedure $\widehat{assume}(\varphi$: Formula, a: a set of bounded structures): Set of ICA structures
    $result := a$
    // Phase 1
    $result := bif\,(\varphi, result)$
    // Phase 2
    while there exists $S \in result, q \in \mathcal{P}$ of arity k, and $u_1, \dots, u_k \in U^S$ such that
        $\iota^S(q)(u_1, \dots, u_k) = 1/2$ and $done(S, q, u_1, \dots, u_k) = false$ do
            $done(S, q, u_1, \dots, u_k) := true$
            if $\hat{\gamma}(S) \wedge \varphi \wedge \varphi_{q,u_1,\dots,u_k}$ is **not** satisfiable then $result := result \setminus \{S\}$
            $S_0 := S[q(u_1, \dots, u_k) \mapsto 0]$
            if $\hat{\gamma}(S_0) \wedge \varphi$ is satisfiable then $result := result \cup \{S_0\}$
            $S_1 := S[q(u_1, \dots, u_k) \mapsto 1]$
            if $\hat{\gamma}(S_1) \wedge \varphi$ is satisfiable then $result := result \cup \{S_1\}$
    return $result$

Fig. 4. The $\widehat{assume}$ procedure takes a formula φ over the vocabulary $\mathcal{P}$ and computes the set of ICA structures $result$. $\hat{\gamma}$ includes the integrity rules in order to eliminate infeasible concrete structures. The formula $\varphi_{q,u_1,\dots,u_k}$ is defined in Eq. (1). The procedure $bif\,(\varphi, result)$ is shown in Fig. 5. The flag $done(S, q, u_1, \dots, u_k)$ marks processed q-tuples; initially, $done$ is $false$ for all predicate tuples.)

procedure *bif* (φ: Formula, W: Set of bounded structures): Set of bounded structures
for all $S \in W$
  if $\widehat{\gamma}(S) \wedge \varphi$ is **not** satisfiable then $W := W \setminus \{S\}$
while there exists $S \in W, q \in \mathcal{A}$ and $u \in U^S$ such that $\iota^S(q)(u) = 1/2$
  $W := W \setminus \{S\}$
  if $\widehat{\gamma}(S) \wedge \varphi \wedge \varphi_{q,u}$ is satisfiable then $W := W \cup S[u \mapsto u.0, u.1][q(u.0) \mapsto 0, q(u.1) \mapsto 1]$
  $S_0 := S[q(u) \mapsto 0]$
  if $\widehat{\gamma}(S_0) \wedge \varphi$ is satisfiable then $W := W \cup \{S_0\}$
  $S_1 := S[q(u) \mapsto 1]$
  if $\widehat{\gamma}(S_1) \wedge \varphi$ is satisfiable then $W := W \cup \{S_1\}$
return W

Fig. 5. The procedure takes a set of structures and a formula φ over the vocabulary $\mathcal{P}$, and computes the bifurcation of each structure in the input set, w.r.t. the input formula. Note that at the beginning of the procedure, it ensures that each structure in the working set W represents at least one concrete structure that satisfies φ. The formula $\varphi_{q,u}$ is defined in Eq. (1). The operation $S[u \mapsto u.0, u.1]$ performs a bifurcation of the node u in S, setting the values of all predicates on $u.0$ and $u.1$ to the values they had on u.

3.1 The Use of the Decision Procedure

The formula $\varphi_{q,u_1,\ldots,u_k}$ guarantees that a concrete structure must contain two tuples of nodes, both mapped to the abstract tuple $\langle u_1, \ldots, u_k \rangle$, on which q evaluates to different values. This is captured by the formula

$$\varphi_{q,u_1,\ldots,u_k} \stackrel{\text{def}}{=} \exists w_1^1, \ldots, w_k^1, w_1^2, \ldots, w_k^2 : \bigwedge_{i=1}^{k} \text{node}_{u_i}^S(w_i^1) \wedge \bigwedge_{i=1}^{k} \text{node}_{u_i}^S(w_i^2)$$
$$\wedge \neg \bigwedge_{i=1}^{k} eq(w_i^1, w_i^2) \wedge q(w_1^1, \ldots, w_k^1) \wedge \neg q(w_1^2, \ldots, w_k^2)$$
$$(1)$$

$\varphi_{q,u_1,\ldots,u_k}$ uses the *node* formula, also defined in [15], which uniquely identifies the mapping of concrete nodes into abstract nodes. For a bounded structure S, $\text{node}_u^S(v)$ simply asserts that u and v agree on all abstraction predicates.

The function **isSatisfiable**(ψ) invokes a decision procedure that returns **true** when ψ is satisfiable, i.e., the set of 2-valued structures that satisfy ψ is non-empty. This function guides the refinement of predicate values. In particular, the satisfiability checks on a formula ψ are used to make the following decisions:

- Discard a 3-valued structure S that does not represent any concrete store in X by taking $\psi \stackrel{\text{def}}{=} \widehat{\gamma}(S) \wedge \varphi$.
- Materialize a new node from node u w.r.t. the value of $q \in \mathcal{A}$ in S (phase 1) by taking $\psi \stackrel{\text{def}}{=} \widehat{\gamma}(S) \wedge \varphi \wedge \varphi_{q,u}$.
- Retain the indefinite value for predicate q on node-tuple $\langle u_1, \ldots, u_k \rangle$ in S (in phase 2) by taking $\psi \stackrel{\text{def}}{=} \widehat{\gamma}(S) \wedge \varphi \wedge \varphi_{q,u_1,\ldots,u_k}$.

This requires a decision procedure for the logic that expresses φ, $\varphi_{q,u}$ and $\widehat{\gamma}$, including the integrity rules.

A Decidable Logic for Shape Analysis [5] describes the logic $\exists \forall^{DTC(E)}$, defined by formulas of the form $\exists v_1, \ldots, v_n \forall v_{n+1}, \ldots, v_m : \varphi(v_1, \ldots, v_m)$, where $\varphi(v_1, \ldots, v_m)$ is a quantifier-free formula over an arbitrary number of unary predicates and a single binary predicate $E(v_i, v_j)$. Instead of general transitive closure, $\exists \forall^{DTC(E)}$ only allows $E^*(v_i, v_j)$, which denotes the *deterministic transitive closure* [4] of E: E-paths that pass through an individual that has two or more successors are ignored in E^*. In [5], $\exists \forall^{DTC(E)}$ is shown to be useful for reasoning about shape invariants of data structures, such as singly and doubly linked lists, (shared) trees, and graph types [7]. Also, the satisfiability of $\exists \forall^{DTC(E)}$ formulas is decidable and NEXPTIME-complete, hence the $\exists \forall^{DTC(E)}$ decision procedure is a candidate implementation for the *isSatifiable* function. [3]

To sidestep the limitations of this logic, [5] introduces the notion of *structure simulation*, and shows that structure simulations can often be automatically maintained for the mutation operations that commonly occur in procedures that manipulate heap-allocated data structures. The simulation is defined via translation of FO^{TC} formulas to equivalent $\exists \forall^{DTC(E)}$ formulas.

Undecidable Logic. The $\widehat{assume}$ algorithm can also be used with an undecidable logic and a theorem prover. The termination of the function isSatisfiable can be assured by using standard techniques (e.g., having the theorem prover return a safe answer if a time-out threshold is exceeded) at the cost of losing the ability to guarantee that a most-precise result is obtained.

If the timeout occurs in the first call to a theorem prover made by phase 2, the structure S is not removed from *result*. If a timeout occurs in any other satisfiability call made by *bif* or by phase 2, the structure examined by this call is added to the output set. Using this technique, $\widehat{assume}$ always terminates while producing sound results.

3.2 Materialization

Phase 1 of the algorithm performs node "materialization" by invoking the procedure *bif*. The name *bif* comes from its main purpose: whenever a structure has an indefinite value of an abstraction predicate q on some abstract node, supported by different values on corresponding concrete nodes, the node is *bifurcated* into two nodes and q is set to different definite values on the new nodes. The *bif* procedure produces a set of 3-valued structures that have the same set of canonical names as the concrete stores that satisfy φ and embed into a. The *bif* procedure first filters out potentially unsatisfiable structures, and then iterates over all structures $S \in W$ that have an indefinite value for an abstraction predicate $q \in \mathcal{A}$ on some node u. It replaces S by other structures. As a result of this phase, all abstraction predicates have definite values for all nodes in each of the structures. Because the output structures are bounded structures, the number of different structures that can be produced is finite, which guarantees that *bif* procedure terminates.

---

[3] Another candidate is the decision procedure for monadic 2-nd order logic over trees [3], MONA, which has non-elementary complexity.

In the body of the loop in *bif*, we check if there exists a concrete structure represented by S that satisfies φ in which q has different values on concrete nodes represented by u (the query is performed using the formula $\varphi_{q,u}$). In this case, a new structure S' is added to W, created from S by duplicating the node u in S into two instances and setting the value of q to 0 for one node instance, and to 1 for another instance. All other predicate values on the new node instances are the same as their values on u.

In addition, two copies of S are created with 0 and 1, respectively, for the value of $q(u)$. To guarantee that each copy represents a concrete structure in X an appropriate query is posed to the decision procedure. Omitting this query will produce a sound, but potentially overly-conservative result.

Fig. 6 shows a computation tree for the algorithm on the running example. A node in the tree is labeled by a 3-valued structure, sketched by showing its nodes. Its children are labeled by the result of refining the 3-valued structure w.r.t. the predicate and the node-tuple on the right, by the values shown on the outgoing edges.

The order in which predicate values are examined affects the complexity (in terms of the number of calls to a decision procedure, the size of the query formulas in each call and the maximal number of explored structures), but it does not affect the result, provided that all calls terminate. The order in Fig. 6 was chosen for convenience of presentation. The root of the tree contains the sketch of the input structure S from Fig. 2(S); u_1 is the left circle and u_2 is the right circle. Fig. 6 shows the steps performed by *bif* on the input $\{S\}$ in

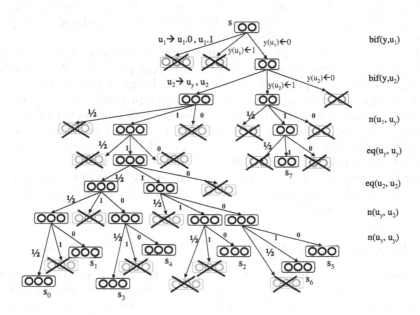

Fig. 6. A computation tree for $\widehat{assume}[p](a)$ for a shown in Fig. 2(a).

Fig. 2. *bif* examines the abstraction predicate y, which has indefinite values on the nodes u_1 and u_2. The algorithm attempts to replace S by T', T_1, and T_0, shown as the children of S in Fig. 6. The structures T' and T_1 are discarded because all of the concrete structures they represent violate integrity rule (i) for x (Section 2.3) and the precondition p, respectively. The remaining structure T_0 is further modified w.r.t. the value of $y(u_2)$. However, setting $y(u_2)$ to 0 results in a structure that does not satisfy p, and hence it is discarded.

3.3   Refining Predicate Values

The second phase of the $\widehat{assume}$ algorithm refines the structures by lowering predicate values from $1/2$ to 0 and 1, and throwing away structure S when the structure has a predicate q that has the value $1/2$ for some tuple $q(u_1, \ldots, u_k)$, but the structure does not represent any 2-valued structure with corresponding tuples $q(u'_1, \ldots, u'_k) = 0$ and $q(u''_1, \ldots, u''_k) = 1$.

For each structure S and an indefinite value of a predicate $q \in \mathcal{P}$ on a tuple of abstract nodes, we eliminate structures in which the predicate has the same values on all corresponding tuples in all concrete structures that are represented by S and satisfy φ. (This query is performed using the formula in Eq. (1).) In addition, two copies of S are created with the values 0 and 1 for q, respectively. To guarantee that each copy represents a concrete structure in X, an appropriate query is posed to a decision procedure. The *done* flag is used to guarantee that each predicate tuple is processed only once.

The bulk of Fig. 6 (everything below the top two rows) shows the refinement of each predicate value in the running example. Phase 2 starts with two structures, T'_2 and T'_3, of size 2 and 3, produced by *bif*. Consider the refinement of T'_2 w.r.t. $n(u_1, u_y)$, where u_1 is pointed to by x and u_y is pointed to by y (the same node names as in Fig. 2).

The predicate tuple $n(u_1, u_y)$ cannot be set to $1/2$, because it requires the existence of a concrete structure with two different pairs of nodes mapped to $\langle u_1, u_y \rangle$; however, integrity rule (i) in Section 2.3 implies that there is exactly one node represented by u_1 and exactly one node represented by u_y. Intuitively, this stems from the fact that the (one) concrete node represented by $u_1(u_y)$ is pointed to by x(y). The predicate tuple $n(u_1, u_y)$ cannot be set to 0, because this violates the precondition p, according to which the element pointed to by y (represented by u_y) must also be pointed to by the n-field of the element pointed to by x (represented by u_1). Guided by the computation tree in Fig. 6, the reader can verify that the structures in Fig. 2(S_0–S_7) are generated by $\widehat{assume}[p](a)$. (The final answer is read out at the leaves).

3.4   Properties of the Algorithm

We determine the complexity of the algorithm in terms of (i) the size of each structure, i.e., the number of nodes and definite values, (ii) the number of structures, and (iii) the number of the calls to the decision procedure. The size of each query formula passed to the decision procedure is linear in the size of the examined structure, because $\widehat{\gamma}(S)$ is linear in S, φ is usually small, and the size of $\varphi_{q,u}$ is fixed for a given $\mathcal{P}$. The complexity in terms of (ii) and (iii) is linear in the height of the abstract domain of sets of ICA structures defined over $\mathcal{P}$, which is doubly-exponential in the size of $\mathcal{P}$. Nevertheless, it is exponentially more efficient than the naive **enumerate-and-eliminate** algorithm over the abstract domain. The reason is that the algorithm described in this paper examines only one descending chain in this abstract domain, as shown in Fig. 1.

To prove the correctness of the algorithm, it is sufficient to establish the following properties (the proofs appear in [16]):

1. All the structures explored by the algorithm are bounded structures.
2. $result \sqsupseteq \alpha(\llbracket \varphi \rrbracket \cap \gamma(a))$. This requirement ensures that the result is **sound**, i.e., $result$ contains canonical abstractions of all concrete structures in X. This is a global invariant throughout the algorithm.
3. $result \sqsubseteq \alpha(\llbracket \varphi \rrbracket \cap \gamma(a))$. This requirement ensures that $result$ does not contain abstract structures that are not ICAs of any concrete store in X. This holds upon the termination of the algorithm.

4   Computing the Best Transformer

The BT algorithm manipulates the two-store vocabulary $\mathcal{P} \cup \mathcal{P}'$, which includes two copies of each predicate — the original unprimed one, as well as a primed version of the predicate. The original version of the predicate contains the values before the transformer is applied, and the primed version contains the new values.

The best-transformer algorithm $BT(\tau, a)$ takes a set of bounded structures a over a vocabulary $\mathcal{P}$, and a transformer formula τ over the two-store vocabulary $\mathcal{P} \cup \mathcal{P}'$. It returns a set of ICA structures over the two-store vocabulary that is the canonical abstraction of all pairs of concrete structures $\langle S_1^{\natural}, S_2^{\natural} \rangle$ such that $S_2^{\natural}$ is the result of applying the transformer τ to $S_1^{\natural}$. $BT(\tau, a)$ is computed by $\widehat{assume}(\tau, extend(a))$ that operates over the two-store vocabulary, where $extend(a)$ extends each structure in $S \in a$ into one over a two-store vocabulary by setting the values of all primed predicates to $1/2$.

The two-store vocabulary allows us to maintain the relationship between the values of the predicates before and after the transformer. Also, τ is an arbitrary formula over the two-store vocabulary; in particular, it may contain a precondition that involves unprimed versions of the predicates, together with primed predicates in the "update" part. The result of the transformer can be obtained from the primed version of the predicates in the output structure.

5   Related Work and Conclusions

In [9], we have presented a different technique to compute best transformers in a more general setting of finite-height, but possibly infinite-size lattices. The technique presented in [9] handles infinite domains by requiring that a decision procedure produce a concrete counter-example for invalid formulas, which is not required in the present paper.

Compared to [9], an advantage of the approach taken in the present paper is that it iterates from above: it always holds a legitimate value (although not the best). If the logic is undecidable, a timeout can be used to terminate the computation and return the current value. Because the technique described in [9] starts from $\bot$, an intermediate result cannot be used as a safe approximation of the desired answer. For this reason, the procedures discussed in [9] must be based on decision procedures. Another potential advantage of the approach in this paper is that the size of formulas in the algorithm reported here is linear in the size of structures (counting 0 and 1 values), and does not depend on the height of the domain.

This paper is also closely related to past work on predicate abstraction, which also uses decision procedures to implement most-precise versions of the basic abstract-interpretation operations. Predicate abstraction is a special case of canonical abstraction, when only nullary predicates are used. Interestingly, when applied to a vocabulary with only nullary predicates, the algorithm in Fig. 4 is similar to the algorithm used in SLAM [1]. It starts with 1/2 for all of the nullary predicates and then repeatedly refines instances of 1/2 into 0 and 1. The more general setting of canonical abstraction requires us to use the formula $\varphi_{q,u_1,u_2,\dots,u_k}$ to identify the appropriate values of non-nullary predicates. Also, we need the first phase (procedure *bif*) to identify what node materializations need to be carried out.

This paper was inspired by the Focus[4] operation in TVLA, which is similar in spirit to the *assume* operation. The input of Focus is a set of 3-valued structures and a formula φ. Focus returns a semantically equivalent set of 3-valued structures in which φ evaluates to a definite value, according to the Kleene semantics for 3-valued logic [11]. The $\widehat{assume}$ algorithm reported in this paper has the following advantages: (i) it guarantees that the number of resultant structures is finite. The Focus algorithm in TVLA generates a runtime exception when this cannot be achieved. This make Focus a partial function, which was sometimes criticized by the TVLA user community. (ii) The number of structures generated by $\widehat{assume}$ is optimal in the sense that it never returns a 3-valued structure unless it is the canonical abstraction of some required store.

The latter property is achieved by using a decision procedure; in the prototype implementation, a theorem prover is used instead, which makes $\widehat{assume}$ currently slower than Focus. In the future, we plan to develop a specialized decision procedure for the logic $\exists\forall^{DTC(E)}$, which we hope will give us the benefits of $\widehat{assume}$ while maintaining the efficiency of Focus on those formulas for which Focus is defined.

To summarize, for shape-analysis problems, the methods described in this paper are more automatic and more precise than the ones used in TVLA, and allow modular analysis with assume-guarantee reasoning, although they are currently much slower. This work also provides a nice example of how abstract-interpretation techniques can exploit decision-procedures/theorem-provers. Methods to speed up these techniques are the subject of ongoing work.

---

[4] In Russian, Focus means "trick" like "Hocus Pocus".

References

1. T. Ball and S.K. Rajamani. The SLAM toolkit. In *Proc. Computer-Aided Verif.*, Lec. Notes in Comp. Sci., pages 260–264, 2001.
2. P. Cousot and R. Cousot. Systematic design of program analysis frameworks. In *Symp. on Princ. of Prog. Lang.*, pages 269–282, New York, NY, 1979. ACM Press.
3. J.G. Henriksen, J. Jensen, M. Jørgensen, N. Klarlund, B. Paige, T. Rauhe, and A. Sandholm. Mona: Monadic second-order logic in practice. In *Tools and Algorithms for the Construction and Analysis of Systems, First International Workshop, TACAS '95, LNCS 1019*, 1995.
4. N. Immerman. *Descriptive Complexity*. Springer-Verlag, 1999.
5. N. Immerman, A. Rabinovich, T. Reps, M. Sagiv, and G. Yorsh. Decidable logics for expressing heap connectivity. In preparation, 2003.
6. N.D. Jones and S.S. Muchnick. Flow analysis and optimization of Lisp-like structures. In S.S. Muchnick and N.D. Jones, editors, *Program Flow Analysis: Theory and Applications*, chapter 4, pages 102–131. Prentice-Hall, Englewood Cliffs, NJ, 1981.
7. N. Klarlund and M. Schwartzbach. Graph types. In *Symp. on Princ. of Prog. Lang.*, New York, NY, January 1993. ACM Press.
8. T. Lev-Ami and M. Sagiv. TVLA: A system for implementing static analyses. In *Static Analysis Symp.*, pages 280–301, 2000.
9. T. Reps, M. Sagiv, and G. Yorsh. Symbolic implementation of the best transformer. In *Proc. VMCAI*, 2004. To appear.
10. M. Sagiv, T. Reps, and R. Wilhelm. Parametric shape analysis via 3-valued logic. In *Symp. on Princ. of Prog. Lang.*, pages 105–118, New York, NY, January 1999. ACM Press.
11. M. Sagiv, T. Reps, and R. Wilhelm. Parametric shape analysis via 3-valued logic. *Trans. on Prog. Lang. and Syst.*, 2002.
12. M. Sharir and A. Pnueli. Two approaches to interprocedural data flow analysis. In S.S. Muchnick and N.D. Jones, editors, *Program Flow Analysis: Theory and Applications*, chapter 7, pages 189–234. Prentice-Hall, Englewood Cliffs, NJ, 1981.
13. E. Y.-B. Wang. *Analysis of Recursive Types in an Imperative Language*. PhD thesis, Univ. of Calif., Berkeley, CA, 1994.
14. C. Weidenbach. SPASS: An automated theorem prover for first-order logic with equality. Available at "http://spass.mpi-sb.mpg.de/index.html".
15. G. Yorsh. Logical characterizations of heap abstractions. Master's thesis, Tel-Aviv University, Tel-Aviv, Israel, 2003. Available at "http://www.math.tau.ac.il/∼ gretay".
16. G. Yorsh, T. Reps, and M. Sagiv. Symbolically computing most-precise abstract operations for shape analysis. Technical report, TAU, 2003. Available at "http://www.cs.tau.ac.il/∼gretay".

Monotonic Abstraction-Refinement for CTL

Sharon Shoham and Orna Grumberg

Computer Science Department, Technion, Haifa, Israel,
{sharonsh,orna}@cs.technion.ac.il

Abstract. The goal of this work is to improve the efficiency and effectiveness of the abstraction-refinement framework for CTL over the 3-valued semantics. We start by proposing a symbolic (BDD-based) approach for this framework. Next, we generalize the definition of abstract models in order to provide a *monotonic* abstraction-refinement framework. To do so, we introduce the notion of *hyper-transitions*. For a given set of abstract states, this results in a more precise abstract model in which more CTL formulae can be proved or disproved.

We suggest an automatic construction of an initial abstract model and its successive refined models. We complete the framework by adjusting the BDD-based approach to the new monotonic framework. Thus, we obtain a monotonic, symbolic framework that is suitable for both verification and falsification of full CTL.

1   Introduction

The goal of this work is to improve the efficiency and effectiveness of the abstraction-refinement framework for CTL over the 3-valued semantics. We first suggest a symbolic (BDD-based) approach for this framework. Next, we generalize the definition of abstract models in order to provide a *monotonic* abstraction-refinement framework. The new definition results in more precise abstract models in which more CTL formulae can be proved or disproved. Finally, we adjust the BDD-based approach to the new monotonic framework.

Abstraction is one of the most successful techniques for fighting the state explosion problem in model checking [5]. Abstractions hide some of the details of the verified system, thus result in a smaller model. Usually, they are designed to be *conservative* for *true*, meaning that if a formula is true of the abstract model then it is also true of the concrete (precise) model of the system.

The branching-time logic CTL [5] is widely used in model checking. In the context of abstraction, often only the universal fragment of CTL, ACTL, is considered. Over-approximated abstract models are used for verification of ACTL formulae while under-approximated abstract models are used for their refutation.

Abstractions designed for full CTL have the advantage of handling both verification and refutation on the same abstract model. A greater advantage is obtained if CTL is interpreted w.r.t. the 3-valued semantics [11]. This semantics evaluates a formula to either *true*, *false* or *indefinite*. Abstract models can then be designed to be conservative for both *true* and *false*. Only if the value of a formula in the abstract model is indefinite,

K. Jensen and A. Podelski (Eds.): TACAS 2004, LNCS 2988, pp. 546–560, 2004.

its value in the concrete model is unknown. In this case, a refinement is needed in order to make the abstract model more precise.

The first result of this paper is a BDD-based approach for this framework. We use a symbolic model checking for CTL with the 3-valued semantics [3]. If the model checking results in an indefinite value, we find a cause for this result and derive from it a criterion for refinement. Previous works [15,18,19] suggested abstraction-refinement mechanisms for various branching time logics over *2-valued* semantics, for *specific* abstractions. In [20] the 3-valued semantics is considered. Yet, their abstraction-refinement is based on games and is not suitable for a symbolic evaluation.

In order to motivate our next result we need a more detailed description of abstract models for CTL. Typically, each state of an abstract model represents a set of states of the concrete model. In order to be conservative for CTL the abstract model should contain both *may* transitions ($\xrightarrow{\text{may}}$) which over-approximate transitions of the concrete model, and *must* transitions ($\xrightarrow{\text{must}}$), which under-approximate the concrete transitions [14,8]. In our work we use abstract models which are called *Kripke Modal Transition Systems* (KMTS) [12,10]. In KMTSs, for every abstract states s_a and s_a', $s_a \xrightarrow{\text{may}} s_a'$ iff there *exists* a concrete state s_c represented by s_a and there *exists* a concrete state s_c' represented by s_a' such that $s_c \to s_c'$ ($\exists\exists$-condition). $s_a \xrightarrow{\text{must}} s_a'$ iff for *all* s_c represented by s_a there *exists* s_c' represented by s_a' such that $s_c \to s_c'$ ($\forall\exists$-condition).

Refinements "split" abstract states so that the new, refined states represent smaller subsets of concrete states. Several abstraction-refinement frameworks have been suggested for ACTL and LTL with the 2-valued semantics, where abstractions are conservative for *true* [13,4,1,6,2]. There, the refined model obtained from splitting abstract states has less (may) transitions and is therefore *more precise* in the sense that it satisfies more properties of the concrete model. We call such a refinement *monotonic*.

For full CTL with the 3-valued semantics, an abstraction-refinement framework has been suggested in [20]. For such a framework, one would expect that after splitting, the number of must transitions will increase as the number of may transitions decreases. Unfortunately, this is not the case. Once a state s_a' is split, the $\forall\exists$-condition that allowed $s_a \xrightarrow{\text{must}} s_a'$ might not hold any more. As a result, the refinement is not monotonic since CTL formulae that had a definite value in the unrefined model may become indefinite.

In [9] this problem has been addressed. They suggest to keep copies of the unrefined states in the refined model together with the refined ones. This avoids the loss of must transitions and guarantees monotonicity. Yet, this solution is not sufficient because the *old* information is still expressed w.r.t. the "unrefined" states and the *new* information (achieved by the refinement) is expressed w.r.t. the refined states. As a result the additional precision that the refinement provides cannot be combined with the old information. This is discussed extensively in Section 4.1.

In this work we suggest a different monotonic abstraction-refinement framework which overcomes this problem. For a given set of abstract states, our approach results in a more precise abstract model in which more CTL formulae have a definite value. Moreover, our approach avoids the need to hold copies of the unrefined states.

Inspired by [17], we define a *generalized KMTS* (GKMTS) in which must transitions are replaced by *must hyper-transitions*, which connect a single state s_a to a set of states A. A GKMTS includes $s_a \xrightarrow{\text{must}} A$ iff for *all* s_c represented by s_a there *exists* s_c' represented by some $s'_a \in A$ such that $s_c \rightarrow s'_c$. This weakens the $\forall\exists$-condition by allowing the resulting states s'_c to be "scattered" in several abstract states.

In general, the number of must hyper-transitions might be exponential in the number of states in the abstract model. In practice, optimizations can be applied in order to reduce their number. We suggest an automatic construction of an initial GKMTS and its successive refined models in a way that in many cases avoids the exponential blowup.

In order to complete our framework, we also adjust for GKMTSs the 3-valued symbolic model checking and the refinement suggested above for KMTSs. Thus, we obtain a monotonic, symbolic framework that is suitable for both verification and falsification of full CTL.

Organization. In Section 2 we give some background for abstractions and the 3-valued semantics. We also present a symbolic 3-valued model checking algorithm. In Section 3 we suggest a refinement mechanism that fits the symbolic 3-valued model checker. In Section 4 we present *generalized* KMTSs and their use as abstract models. Finally, we present our monotonic abstraction-refinement framework in Section 5.

2   Preliminaries

Let AP be a finite set of atomic propositions. In this paper we consider the logic CTL, defined as follows: $\varphi ::= \text{tt} \mid p \mid \neg\varphi \mid \varphi \wedge \varphi \mid A\psi$ where $p \in AP$, and ψ is a *path formula* defined by $\psi ::= X\varphi \mid \varphi U\varphi \mid \varphi V\varphi$. Other operators can be expressed in the usual manner [5]. Let $Lit = AP \cup \{\neg p : p \in AP\}$. The (concrete) semantics of CTL formulae is defined w.r.t. a *Kripke structure* $M = (S, S_0, \rightarrow, L)$, where S is a finite set of states, $S_0 \subseteq S$ is a set of initial states, $\rightarrow \subseteq S \times S$ is a transition relation, which must be *total* and $L : S \rightarrow 2^{Lit}$ is a labeling function, such that for every state s and every $p \in AP$, $p \in L(s)$ iff $\neg p \notin L(s)$. A *path* in M from s is an infinite sequence of states, $\pi = s_0, s_1, \ldots$ such that $s = s_0$ and $\forall i \geq 0, s_i \rightarrow s_{i+1}$.

$[(M, s) \models \varphi] = \text{tt}$ ($= \text{ff}$) means that the CTL formula φ is true (false) in the state s of the Kripke structure M. $[(M, \pi) \models \psi] = \text{tt}$ ($= \text{ff}$) has the same meaning for path formulae over paths (see [5]). M *satisfies* φ, denoted $[M \models \varphi] = \text{tt}$, if $\forall s_0 \in S_0$: $[(M, s_0) \models \varphi] = \text{tt}$. Otherwise, M *refutes* φ, denoted $[M \models \varphi] = \text{ff}$.

2.1   Abstraction

We use *Kripke Modal Transition Systems* [12,10] as abstract models that preserve CTL.

Definition 1. *A* Kripke Modal Transition System *(KMTS) is a tuple* $M = (S, S_0, \overset{must}{\longrightarrow}, \overset{may}{\longrightarrow}, L)$, *where* S, S_0 *are defined as before,* $\overset{must}{\longrightarrow} \subseteq S \times S$ *and* $\overset{may}{\longrightarrow} \subseteq S \times S$ *are transition relations such that* $\overset{may}{\longrightarrow}$ *is total and* $\overset{must}{\longrightarrow} \subseteq \overset{may}{\longrightarrow}$[1], *and* $L : S \rightarrow 2^{Lit}$ *is a labeling function such that for every state* s *and* $p \in AP$, *at most* one of p and $\neg p$ is in $L(s)$.

A finite or infinite sequence of states $\pi = s_0, s_1, \ldots$ is a *path* in M from s if $s = s_0$ and for every two consecutive states s_i, s_{i+1} in the sequence, $s_i \overset{may}{\longrightarrow} s_{i+1}$. π is a *must (may)* path if it is *maximal* and for every s_i, s_{i+1} we have that $s_i \overset{must}{\longrightarrow} s_{i+1}$ ($s_i \overset{may}{\longrightarrow} s_{i+1}$). The maximality is in the sense that π cannot be extended by any transition of the same type.

---

[1] The requirement that $\overset{must}{\longrightarrow} \subseteq \overset{may}{\longrightarrow}$ is not essential for the purposes of this paper.

Note, that a Kripke structure can be viewed as a KMTS where $\rightarrow = \xrightarrow{must} = \xrightarrow{may}$, and for each state s and $p \in AP$, we have that exactly one of p and $\neg p$ is in $L(s)$.

Construction of an Abstract KMTS. Let $M_C = (S_C, S_{0C}, \rightarrow, L_C)$ be a (concrete) Kripke structure. Let S_A be a set of *abstract states* and $\gamma : S_A \rightarrow 2^{S_C}$ a total *concretization function* that maps each abstract state to the set of concrete states it represents.

An abstract model, in the form of a KMTS $M_A = (S_A, S_{0A}, \xrightarrow{must}, \xrightarrow{may}, L_A)$, can then be defined as follows. The set of initial abstract states S_{0A} is built such that $s_{0a} \in S_{0A}$ iff $\exists s_{0c} \in S_{0C} : s_c \in \gamma(s_{0a})$. The "if" is needed in order to preserve truth from M_A to M_C, while "only if" is needed to preserve falsity.

The labeling of an abstract state is defined in accord with the labeling of all the concrete states it represents. For $l \in Lit : l \in L_A(s_a)$ only if $\forall s_c \in \gamma(s_a) : l \in L_C(s_c)$. It is thus possible that neither p nor $\neg p$ are in $L_A(s_a)$. If the "only if" is replaced by "iff", then we say that the abstract labeling function is *exact*.

The *may*-transitions in an abstract model are computed such that every concrete transition between two states is represented by them: if $\exists s_c \in \gamma(s_a)$ and $\exists s'_c \in \gamma(s'_a)$ such that $s_c \rightarrow s'_c$, then there exists a may transition $s_a \xrightarrow{may} s'_a$. Note that it is possible that there are additional may transitions as well. The *must*-transitions, on the other hand, represent concrete transitions that are common to all the concrete states that are represented by the source abstract state: a must transition $s_a \xrightarrow{must} s'_a$ exists only if $\forall s_c \in \gamma(s_a) \exists s'_c \in \gamma(s'_a)$ such that $s_c \rightarrow s'_c$. Note that it is possible that there are less must transitions than allowed by this rule. That is, the may and must transitions do not have to be *exact*, as long as they maintain these conditions.

Other constructions of abstract models can be used as well. For example, if γ is a part of a *Galois Connection* [7] $(\gamma : S_A \rightarrow 2^{S_C}, \alpha : 2^{S_C} \rightarrow S_A)$ from $(2^{S_C}, \subseteq)$ to $(S_A, \sqsubseteq)$, then an abstract model can be constructed as described in [8] within the framework of *Abstract Interpretation* [7,16,8]. It is then not guaranteed that $\xrightarrow{must} \subseteq \xrightarrow{may}$.

3-Valued Semantics. [12] defines the *3-valued* semantics $[(M, s) \overset{3}{\models} \varphi]$ of CTL over KMTSs, and similarly $[(M, \pi) \overset{3}{\models} \psi]$ for path formulae, preserving both satisfaction (tt) and refutation (ff) from the abstract to the concrete model. Yet, a new truth value, $\bot$, is introduced, meaning that the truth value over the concrete model is unknown and can be either tt or ff. Intuitively, in order to preseve CTL, we examine *truth* of a formula of the form $A\psi$ along all the *may paths*. Its *falsity* is shown by a single *must path*.

Definition 2 (Precision Preorder). *Let M_1, M_2 be two KMTSs over states S_1, S_2 and let $s_1 \in S_1$ and $s_2 \in S_2$. We say that (M_1, s_1) is more precise than (M_2, s_2), denoted $(M_1, s_1) \leq_{crt} (M_2, s_2)$, if for every φ in CTL: $[(M_2, s_2) \overset{3}{\models} \varphi] \neq \bot \Rightarrow \quad [(M_1, s_1) \overset{3}{\models} \varphi] = [(M_2, s_2) \overset{3}{\models} \varphi]$. Similarly, we say that M_1 is more precise than M_2, denoted $M_1 \leq_{crt} M_2$, if for every φ in CTL: $[M_2 \overset{3}{\models} \varphi] \neq \bot \Rightarrow [M_1 \overset{3}{\models} \varphi] = [M_2 \overset{3}{\models} \varphi]$.*

The following definition formalizes the relation between two KMTSs that guarantees preservation of CTL formulae w.r.t. the 3-valued semantics.

Definition 3 (Mixed Simulation). *[8,10] Let $M_1 = (S_1, S_{01}, \xrightarrow{must}_1, \xrightarrow{may}_1, L_1)$ and $M_2 = (S_2, S_{02}, \xrightarrow{must}_2, \xrightarrow{may}_2, L_2)$ be two KMTSs. We say that $H \subseteq S_1 \times S_2$ is a mixed simulation from M_1 to M_2 if $(s_1, s_2) \in H$ implies the following:*

1. $L_2(s_2) \subseteq L_1(s_1)$.
2. if $s_1 \xrightarrow{may}_1 s_1'$, then there is some $s_2' \in S_2$ s.t. $s_2 \xrightarrow{may}_2 s_2'$ and $(s_1', s_2') \in H$.
3. if $s_2 \xrightarrow{must}_2 s_2'$, then there is some $s_1' \in S_1$ s.t. $s_1 \xrightarrow{must}_1 s_1'$ and $(s_1', s_2') \in H$.

If there is a mixed simulation H such that $\forall s_1 \in S_{01} \exists s_2 \in S_{02} : (s_1, s_2) \in H$, and $\forall s_2 \in S_{02} \exists s_1 \in S_{01} : (s_1, s_2) \in H$, then M_2 is greater by the mixed simulation relation than M_1, denoted $M_1 \preceq M_2$.

In particular, Definition 3 can be applied to a (concrete) Kripke structure M_C and an (abstract) KMTS M_A constructed based on S_A, γ as described above. By doing so, we get that M_A is greater by the mixed simulation relation than M_C. The mixed simulation $H \subseteq S_C \times S_A$ can be induced by γ as follows: $(s_c, s_a) \in H$ iff $s_c \in \gamma(s_a)$. Preservation of CTL formulae is then guaranteed by the following theorem.

Theorem 1. *[10] Let $H \subseteq S_1 \times S_2$ be the mixed simulation relation from a KMTS M_1 to a KMTS M_2. Then for every $(s_1, s_2) \in H$ we have that $(M_1, s_1) \leq_{CTL} (M_2, s_2)$. We conclude that $M_1 \leq_{CTL} M_2$.*

Note that if the KMTS M is in fact a Kripke structure, then for every CTL formula we have that $[(M, s) \overset{3}{\models} \varphi] = [(M, s) \models \varphi]$. Therefore, Theorem 1 also describes the relation between the 3-valued semantics over an abstract KMTS and the concrete semantics over the corresponding concrete model.

Exact KMTS. If the labeling function and transitions of the constructed abstract model M_A are *exact*, then we get the *exact* abstract model. This model is *most precise* compared to all the KMTSs that are constructed as described above w.r.t. the given S_A, γ.

2.2 Symbolic 3-Valued Model Checking

[3] suggests a symbolic multi-valued model checking algorithm for CTL. We rephrase their algorithm for the special case of the 3-valued semantics, discussed in our work.

Let M be a KMTS and φ a CTL formula. For $v \in \{tt, ff, \bot\}$ we denote by $\lfloor\varphi\rfloor_v$ the set of states in M for which the truth value of φ is v. That is, $s \in \lfloor\varphi\rfloor_v$ iff $[(M, s) \overset{3}{\models} \varphi] = v$. Model checking is done by computing these sets for the desired property φ. If all the initial states of M are in $\lfloor\varphi\rfloor_{tt}$, then $[M \overset{3}{\models} \varphi] = tt$. If at least one initial state is in $\lfloor\varphi\rfloor_{ff}$, then $[M \overset{3}{\models} \varphi] = ff$, and otherwise $[M \overset{3}{\models} \varphi] = \bot$.

The algorithm that computes the sets $\lfloor\varphi\rfloor_{tt}$ and $\lfloor\varphi\rfloor_{ff}$ uses the following notation. For $Z \subseteq S : ax(Z) = \{s \mid \forall s' : s \xrightarrow{may} s' \Rightarrow Z(s')\}$ and $ex(Z) = \{s \mid \exists s' : s \xrightarrow{must} s' \wedge Z(s')\}$. The algorithm is as follows.

$$
\begin{array}{ll}
\lfloor tt \rfloor_{tt} = S & \lfloor tt \rfloor_{ff} = \emptyset \\
\lfloor p \rfloor_{tt} = \{s \in S : p \in L(s)\} & \lfloor p \rfloor_{ff} = \{s \in S : \neg p \in L(s)\} \quad \text{for } p \in AP \\
\lfloor \neg\varphi_1 \rfloor_{tt} = \lfloor\varphi_1\rfloor_{ff} & \lfloor \neg\varphi_1 \rfloor_{ff} = \lfloor\varphi_1\rfloor_{tt} \\
\lfloor \varphi_1 \wedge \varphi_2 \rfloor_{tt} = \lfloor\varphi_1\rfloor_{tt} \cap \lfloor\varphi_2\rfloor_{tt} & \lfloor \varphi_1 \wedge \varphi_2 \rfloor_{ff} = \lfloor\varphi_1\rfloor_{ff} \cup \lfloor\varphi_2\rfloor_{ff} \\
\lfloor AX\varphi_1 \rfloor_{tt} = ax(\lfloor\varphi_1\rfloor_{tt}) & \lfloor AX\varphi_1 \rfloor_{ff} = ex(\lfloor\varphi_1\rfloor_{ff}) \\
\lfloor A(\varphi_1 U \varphi_2) \rfloor_{tt} = \mu Z.\lfloor\varphi_2\rfloor_{tt} \cup (\lfloor\varphi_1\rfloor_{tt} \cap ax(Z)) \\
\lfloor A(\varphi_1 U \varphi_2) \rfloor_{ff} = \nu Z.\lfloor\varphi_2\rfloor_{ff} \cap (\lfloor\varphi_1\rfloor_{ff} \cup ex(Z)) \\
\lfloor A(\varphi_1 V \varphi_2) \rfloor_{tt} = \nu Z.\lfloor\varphi_2\rfloor_{tt} \cap (\lfloor\varphi_1\rfloor_{tt} \cup ax(Z)) \\
\lfloor A(\varphi_1 V \varphi_2) \rfloor_{ff} = \mu Z.\lfloor\varphi_2\rfloor_{ff} \cup (\lfloor\varphi_1\rfloor_{ff} \cap ex(Z))
\end{array}
$$

Furthermore, for every CTL formula φ, $\lfloor\varphi\rfloor_\bot$ is computed as $S \setminus (\lfloor\varphi\rfloor_{tt} \cup \lfloor\varphi\rfloor_{ff})$.

The fixpoint operators $\mu Z.\tau(Z)$ and $\nu Z.\tau(Z)$ are computed as follows. For $Z \subseteq S$ we define $\tau^i(Z)$ to be the ith application of τ to Z. Formally, $\tau^0(Z) = Z$ and for every $i > 0$: $\tau^{i+1}(Z) = \tau(\tau^i(Z))$. Since the transformers (τ's) used in the fixpoint definitions of AU and AV are monotonic and continuous (similarly to [5]), then they have a least fixpoint (μ) and a greatest fixpoint (ν) [21]. Furthermore, $\mu Z.\tau(Z)$ can be computed by $\bigcup_i \tau^i(\emptyset)$ and $\nu Z.\tau(Z)$ can be computed by $\bigcap_i \tau^i(S)$.

3 3-Valued Refinement

Model checking of an abstract KMTS w.r.t. the 3-valued semantics may end with an indefinite result, raising the need for a refinement of the abstract model. In this section we suggest a refinement mechanism that fits the use of the symbolic 3-valued model checking algorithm presented above. This results in a symbolic 3-valued abstraction-refinement algorithm for CTL. The suggested refinement follows similar lines as the refinement of [20], where a game-based model checking was used.

We start with some definitions and observations regarding the symbolic 3-valued model checking algorithm. For $\varphi \in \{A(\varphi_1 U \varphi_2), A(\varphi_1 V \varphi_2)\}$ and for $v \in \{\text{tt}, \text{ff}\}$ we denote by $\lfloor\varphi\rfloor_v^i$ the set of states at the beginning of the ith iteration of the fixpoint computation of $\lfloor\varphi\rfloor_v$ ($i \geq 0$). Furthermore, for $\bot$, we define $\lfloor\varphi\rfloor_\bot^i$ to be the set $S \setminus (\lfloor\varphi\rfloor_{\text{tt}}^i \cup \lfloor\varphi\rfloor_{\text{ff}}^i)$. Note that the sets $\lfloor\varphi\rfloor_\bot^i$ are *not* necessarily monotonic and that $\lfloor\varphi\rfloor_\bot$ is *not* computed by a fixpoint computation.

For every state $s \in \lfloor\varphi\rfloor_\bot$ we define $en(s)$ to be the number of the iteration where s was first added to $\lfloor\varphi\rfloor_\bot^i$. Note that $\lfloor\varphi\rfloor_\bot^0 = \emptyset$, therefore $en(s)$ is always ≥ 1. Also note that $en(s)$ can be computed from the intermediate results of the fixpoint computation when needed, without having to remember it for every state. We also have the following.

Lemma 1. *If* $s \in \lfloor\varphi\rfloor_\bot$ *then* $\forall i \geq en(s)$: $s \in \lfloor\varphi\rfloor_\bot^i$. *Furthermore, if* $\varphi = A(\varphi_1 U \varphi_2)$ *then* $\forall i < en(s)$: $s \in \lfloor\varphi\rfloor_{\text{ff}}^i$ *and if* $\varphi = A(\varphi_1 V \varphi_2)$ *then* $\forall i < en(s)$: $s \in \lfloor\varphi\rfloor_{\text{tt}}^i$.

We now describe our refinement. As in most cases, our refinement consists of two parts. First, we choose a criterion that tells us how to split the abstract states. We then construct the refined abstract model, using the refined abstract state space.

Suppose the model checking result is $\bot$ and refinement is needed. This means that there exists at least one initial state s_0 for which the truth value of φ is $\bot$, i.e. $s_0 \in \lfloor\varphi\rfloor_\bot$. Our goal is to find and eliminate at least one of the causes of the indefinite result. We first search for a *failure state*. This is a state s such that (1) the truth value of some subformula φ' of φ in s is $\bot$; (2) the indefinite truth value of φ' in s *affects* the indefinite value of φ in s_0; and (3) the indefinite value of φ' in s can be *discarded* by splitting s. The latter requirement means that the state s *itself* is responsible for introducing (some) uncertainty. The other requirements demand that this uncertainty is relevant to the model checking result. A failure state is found by applying the following recursive algorithm on s_0 and φ (where $s_0 \in \lfloor\varphi\rfloor_\bot$).

Given a state s and a formula φ' s.t. $s \in \lfloor\varphi'\rfloor_\bot$, algorithm FindFailure returns a failure state and either an atomic proposition or a may transition as the *cause* for failure.

Algorithm FindFailure (s, φ')

- If $\varphi' = p \in AP$: return s and p as the cause.
- If $\varphi' = \neg\varphi_1$: call FindFailure on s and φ_1 (we know that $s \in \lfloor\varphi_1\rfloor_\bot$).

- If $\varphi' = \varphi_1 \wedge \varphi_2$: call FindFailure on s and φ_i for some $i \in \{1, 2\}$ such that $s \in \lfloor\varphi_i\rfloor_\perp$ (such i must exist).
- If $\varphi' = AX\varphi_1$:
  - If there exists $s_1 \in S$ such that $s \xrightarrow{\text{may}} s_1$ and $s_1 \in \lfloor\varphi_1\rfloor_{\text{ff}}$ then return s and $s \xrightarrow{\text{may}} s_1$ as the cause.
  - Otherwise, call FindFailure on s_1 and φ_1 such that $s \xrightarrow{\text{may}} s_1$ and $s_1 \in \lfloor\varphi_1\rfloor_\perp$ (such s_1 must exist).
- If $\varphi' = A(\varphi_1 U \varphi_2)$ or $A(\varphi_1 V \varphi_2)$:
  - If $s \in \lfloor\varphi_2\rfloor_\perp$ then call FindFailure on s and φ_2.
  - Otherwise, if $s \in \lfloor\varphi_1\rfloor_\perp$ then call FindFailure on s and φ_1.
  - Otherwise, if there exists $s_1 \in S$ such that $s \xrightarrow{\text{may}} s_1$ and $s_1 \in \lfloor\varphi'\rfloor_{\text{ff}}$ then return s and $s \xrightarrow{\text{may}} s_1$ as the cause.
  - Otherwise, if there exists $s_1 \in S$ such that $s \xrightarrow{\text{may}} s_1$ and $s_1 \in \lfloor\varphi'\rfloor_\perp$ and $en(s_1) < en(s)$ then call FindFailure on s_1 and φ.
  - Otherwise, choose $s_1 \in S$ such that $s \xrightarrow{\text{may}} s_1$ and $s_1 \in \lfloor\varphi'\rfloor_\perp$ (and $en(s_1) \geq en(s)$) and return s and $s \xrightarrow{\text{may}} s_1$ as the cause (such s_1 must exist).

Note that the order of the "if" statements in the algorithm determines the failure state returned by the algorithm. Different heuristics can be applied regarding their order.

Theorem 2. *The algorithm is well defined, meaning that all the possible cases are handled and the algorithm can always proceed. Furthermore, it always terminates.*

Intuitively, at every moment FindFailure looks for a reason for the indefinite value of the current formula φ' in the current state s. If s itself is not responsible for introducing the indefinite value, then the algorithm greedily continues with a state and formula that *affect* the indefinite value of φ' in s. This continues until a failure state is reached.

Theorem 3. *Let s be the failure state returned by FindFailure. Then the cause returned by the algorithm is either (1) $p \in AP$ such that neither p nor $\neg p$ label s; or (2) an outgoing may transition of s which is not a must transition.*

In the first possibility described by Theorem 3, the labeling of s causes it to be in $\lfloor p \rfloor_\perp$, thus it introduces an uncertainty and is considered the cause for failure. To demonstrate why the second case is viewed as a cause for failure, consider a formula $A\varphi_1$ which is indefinite in a state s. If s has an outgoing may transition to a state s_1 where the value of φ_1 is ff, then s is considered a failure state with the may transition (which is *not* a must transition, by Theorem 3) being the cause. This is because changing the may transition to a must transition will make the value of $AX\varphi_1$ in s definite (ff). Alternatively, if all such transitions are eliminated, it will also make the value of $AX\varphi_1$ in s definite (tt).

A more complicated example of a may transition being the cause for the failure is when φ' is either $A(\varphi_1 U \varphi_2)$ or $A(\varphi_1 V \varphi_2)$ and (1) $s \notin \lfloor\varphi_2\rfloor_\perp$, (2) $s \notin \lfloor\varphi_1\rfloor_\perp$, (3) there is no $s_1 \in S$ such that $s \xrightarrow{\text{may}} s_1$ and $s_1 \in \lfloor\varphi'\rfloor_{\text{ff}}$ and (4) there is no $s_1 \in S$ such that $s \xrightarrow{\text{may}} s_1$ and $s_1 \in \lfloor\varphi'\rfloor_\perp$ and $en(s_1) < en(s)$. In this case the algorithm considers s to be a failure state and the cause is a may transition (which is *not* a must transition, by Theorem 3) to a state s_1 such that $s_1 \in \lfloor\varphi'\rfloor_\perp$ and $en(s_1) \geq en(s)$. To understand why this is a failure state, we focus on the case where $\varphi' = A(\varphi_1 U \varphi_2)$. By Lemma 1, at iteration $en(s)$ (≥ 1), s moved from $\lfloor\varphi'\rfloor_{\text{ff}}^{en(s)-1}$ to $\lfloor\varphi'\rfloor_\perp^{en(s)}$. By the description of the fixpoint computation of $\lfloor\varphi'\rfloor_{\text{ff}}$ we conclude that $s \notin \lfloor\varphi_2\rfloor_{\text{ff}} \cap (\lfloor\varphi_1\rfloor_{\text{ff}} \cup ex(\lfloor\varphi'\rfloor_{\text{ff}}^{en(s)-1}))$.

Yet, by (1), $s \notin \lfloor \varphi_2 \rfloor_\perp$ and thus $s \in \lfloor \varphi_2 \rfloor_{ff}$ (otherwise it would be in $\lfloor \varphi_2 \rfloor_{tt}$ and thus also in $\lfloor \varphi' \rfloor_{tt}$, in contradiction). Moreover, since s_1 is not yet in $\lfloor \varphi' \rfloor_\perp^{en(s)-1}$, then by Lemma 1 it must be at $\lfloor \varphi' \rfloor_{ff}^{en(s)-1}$ at that time. We consider $s \xrightarrow{may} s_1$ to be the cause for failure because if it was a must transition rather than a may transition then s would be in the set $ex(\lfloor \varphi' \rfloor_{ff}^{en(s)-1})$ and therefore would remain in the set $\lfloor \varphi' \rfloor_{ff}^{en(s)}$ for at least one more iteration. Thus it would have a better chance to remain in the set $\lfloor \varphi' \rfloor_{ff}$ until fixpoint is reached, changing the indefinite value of φ' in s to a definite one.

Once we are given a failure state s and a corresponding cause for failure, we guide the refinement to discard the cause for failure in the hope for changing the model checking result to a definite one. This is done as in [20], where the failure information is analyzed and used to determine how the set of concrete states represented by s should be split. A criterion for splitting *all* abstract states can then be found by known techniques, depending on the abstraction used (e.g. [6,4]).

Having defined the refinement, we now have a symbolic abstraction-refinement algorithm for CTL that uses the 3-valued semantics. In the next sections we will show how this algorithm can be improved, by using a new notion of abstract models.

4   Generalized Abstract Models

In this section we suggest the notion of a generalized KMTS and its use as an abstract model which preserves CTL. This notion allows better precision of the abstraction.

4.1   Motivation

The main flaw of using KMTSs as abstract models is in the must transitions, which make the refinement not necessarily *monotonic* w.r.t. the precision preorder. The following example demonstrates the problem. We consider the traditional refinement that is based on splitting the states of the (abstract) model.

Example 1. Consider the following program P.

P::   input: $x > 0$
      pc=1: if $x > 5$ then $x := x + 1$ else $x := x + 2$ fi
      pc=2: while *true* do if $odd(x)$ then $x := -1$ else $x := x + 1$ fi od

Suppose we are interested in checking the property $\varphi = EF(x \leq 0)$, which is clearly satisfied by this program. The concrete model of the program is an infinite state model. Suppose we start with an abstract model where concrete states that "agree" on the predicate $(x \leq 0)$ (taken form the checked property φ) are collapsed into a single abstract state. Then we get the abstract model M described in Fig. 1(a), where the truth value of φ is indefinite. Now, suppose we refine the model by adding the predicate $odd(x)$. Then we get the model M' described in Fig. 1(b), where we still cannot verify φ. Moreover, we "lose" the must transition $s_0 \xrightarrow{must} s_1$ of M. This transition has no corresponding must transition in the refined model M'. This loss causes the formula $EX(x > 0)$ which is true in M to become indefinite in M'. Thus $M' \not\leq_{CTL} M$.

The source of the problem is that when dealing with KMTSs as abstract models, we are *not* guaranteed to have a mixed simulation between the refined abstract model

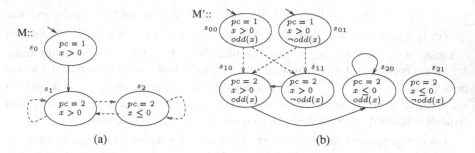

Fig. 1. (a) An abstract model M describing the program P; (b) The abstract model M' resulting from its refinement. Outgoing transitions of s_{21} are omitted since they are irrelevant.

and the unrefined one, even if both are exact. This means that the refined abstract model is not necessarily more precise than the unrefined one, even though each of its states represents less concrete states. This is again demonstrated by Example 1. There, both the initial states of M' cannot be matched with the (only) initial state s_0 of M in a way that fulfills the requirements of mixed simulation. This is because s_0 has an outgoing must transition whereas the initial states of M' have none. Consequently, $M' \not\preceq M$.

[9] suggests a refinement where the refined model *is* smaller by the mixed simulation than the unrefined one. The solution there is basically to use both the new refined abstract states and the old (unrefined) abstract states. This is a way of overcoming the problem that the destination states of must transitions are being split, causing an undesired removal of such transitions. This indeed prevents the loss of precision. Yet, this solution is not sufficient, as demonstrated by the following example.

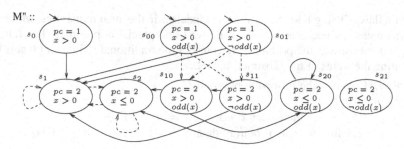

Fig. 2. The model M'' achieved by applying refinement as suggested in [9] on M from Fig. 1(a). Outgoing transitions of s_{21} are omitted since they are irrelevant, and so are additional outgoing may transitions of the unrefined states (there are no additional outgoing must transitions for the unrefined states).

Example 2. Fig. 2 presents the refined model M'' achieved by applying refinement as suggested in [9] on the model M from Fig. 1(a). Indeed, we now have a mixed simulation relation from the refined model M'' to the unrefined model M, by simply matching each state with itself or with its super-state, and the loss of precision is prevented. In particular, the truth value of $EX(x > 0)$ in M'' (unlike M' from Fig. 1(b)) is tt, since there are must transitions from the initial states of M'' to the *old* unrefined state s_1. Yet, in order to verify the desired property $\varphi = EF(x \leq 0)$, we need a must transition to (at least one of) the *new* refined states s_{10} and s_{11} from which a state satisfying $x \leq 0$ is definitely reachable (this information was added by the refinement). However, the $\forall\exists$ condition is still *not* fulfilled between these states. As a result we cannot benefit from the additional precision that the refinement provides and φ is *still* indefinite.

This example demonstrates that even when using the refinement suggested in [9], must transitions may still be removed in the "refined" part of the model, containing the new refined states. As a result the additional precision that the refinement provides cannot necessarily be combined with the old information.

4.2   Generalized KMTSs

Having understood the problems that result from the use of must transitions in their current form, our goal here is to suggest an alternative that will allow to weaken the $\forall\exists$ condition. Following the idea presented in [17] (in a slightly different context), we suggest the use of *hyper-transitions* to describe must transitions.

Definition 4 (Hyper-Transition). *Given a set of states S, a* hyper-transition *is a pair (s, A) where $s \in S$ and $A \subseteq S$ is a nonempty set of states. Alternatively, a* hyper-transition *from a state s is a nonempty set of (regular) transitions from s.*

A (regular) transition (s, s') can be viewed as a hyper-transition (s, A) where $A = \{s'\}$.

Recall that a (regular) must transition exists from s_a to s'_a in an abstract model only if *every* state represented by s_a has a (concrete) transition to *some* state represented by s'_a. The purpose of the generalization is to allow such a concrete transition to exist to *some* state represented by *some* (abstract) state in a set A_a (which plays the role of s'_a). This can be achieved by using a hyper-transition. The hyper-transition will still perform as a must transition in the sense that it will represent at least one concrete transition of each concrete state represented by s_a (maintaining the $\forall\exists$ meaning).

Definition 5. *A* Generalized Kripke Modal Transition System *(GKMTS) $M = (S, S_0, \xrightarrow{must}, \xrightarrow{may}, L)$ is a KMTS except that $\xrightarrow{must} \subseteq S \times 2^S$ and for every $(s, A) \in \xrightarrow{must}$ and $s' \in A$, we have that $(s, s') \in \xrightarrow{may}$ holds. Alternatively, viewing a hyper-transition (s, A) as a set of (regular) transitions $\{(s, s') : s' \in A\}$, we require that $(s, A) \subseteq \xrightarrow{may}$.*

The latter requirement replaces the requirement that $\xrightarrow{must} \subseteq \xrightarrow{may}$ in a KMTS. A KMTS can be viewed as a GKMTS where every must hyper-transition is a regular transition.

As before, a *may path* in M is an *infinite* path in M. However, instead of a *must path* we now have a *must hyper-path*. To formally define it we use the following notation.

Definition 6. *Let Π be a set of paths, then $pref_i(\Pi)$ denotes the set of all the prefixes of length i of the paths in Π.*

Definition 7 (Must Hyper-Path). *A* must hyper-path *from a state s is a nonempty set Π of paths from s, such that for every $i \geq 0$:*

$$pref_{i+1}(\Pi) = \bigcup_{\pi_i \in pref_i(\Pi)} \{\pi_i \cdot s : s \in A_{\pi_i}\}$$

where for $\pi_i = s_0, s_1, \ldots, s_i \in pref_i(\Pi)$, the set $A_{\pi_i} \in 2^S$ is either (1) the target set of some must hyper-transition (s_i, A_{π_i}), or (2) the empty set, $\emptyset$, if there is no must hyper-transition exiting s_i.

Recall that our intention is to use GKMTSs as abstract models. Considering this goal, Definition 7 is aimed at maintaining the desired property that if there is a must hyper-path Π from the abstract state s_a then every concrete state represented by s_a has a corresponding concrete path, i.e. a path that is represented by *some* path in Π.

Note that a must hyper-path can include finite paths since A_{π_i} can be empty.

3-Valued Semantics. We generalize the 3-valued semantics of CTL for GKMTSs. The semantics is defined similarly to the (regular) 3-valued semantics, except that the use of must paths is replaced by must hyper-paths. In addition, for a (path) formula ψ of the form $X\varphi$, $\varphi_1 U\varphi_2$, or $\varphi_1 V\varphi_2$ and a must hyper-path Π, we define

- $[(M, \Pi) \models^{3} \psi] = \text{tt (ff)}$, iff for every $\pi \in \Pi$ we have that $[(M, \pi) \models^{3} \psi] = \text{tt (ff)}$
- Otherwise, $[(M, \Pi) \models^{3} \psi] = \perp$.

Note that the (regular) 3-valued semantics handles finite must paths as well.

The notion of a mixed simulation relation, that guaranteed preservation of CTL formulae between two KMTSs, is generalized as well when dealing with GKMTSs.

Definition 8 (Generalized Mixed Simulation). *Let* $M_1 = (S_1, S_{01}, \overset{must}{\longrightarrow}_1, \overset{may}{\longrightarrow}_1, L_1)$ *and* $M_2 = (S_2, S_{02}, \overset{must}{\longrightarrow}_2, \overset{may}{\longrightarrow}_2, L_2)$, *be two GKMTSs. We say that* $H \subseteq S_1 \times S_2$ *is a generalized mixed simulation from* M_1 *to* M_2 *if* $(s_1, s_2) \in H$ *implies the following:*

1. $L_2(s_2) \subseteq L_1(s_1)$.
2. *if* $s_1 \overset{may}{\longrightarrow}_1 s_1'$, *then there is some* $s_2' \in S_2$ *s.t.* $s_2 \overset{may}{\longrightarrow}_2 s_2'$ *and* $(s_1', s_2') \in H$.
3. *if* $s_2 \overset{must}{\longrightarrow}_2 A_2$, *then there is some* $A_1 \subseteq S_1$ *s.t.* $s_1 \overset{must}{\longrightarrow}_1 A_1$ *and* $(A_1, A_2) \in \tilde{H}$, *where* $(A_1, A_2) \in \tilde{H} \Leftrightarrow \forall s_1' \in A_1 \exists s_2' \in A_2 : (s_1', s_2') \in H$.

If there is a generalized mixed simulation H *such that* $\forall s_1 \in S_{01} \exists s_2 \in S_{02} : (s_1, s_2) \in H$, *and* $\forall s_2 \in S_{02} \exists s_1 \in S_{01} : (s_1, s_2) \in H$, *then* M_2 *is greater by the generalized mixed simulation relation than* M_1, *denoted* $M_1 \preceq M_2$.

Theorem 4. *Let* $H \subseteq S_1 \times S_2$ *be a generalized mixed simulation relation from a GKMTS* M_1 *to a GKMTS* M_2. *Then for every* $(s_1, s_2) \in H$ *we have that* $(M_1, s_1) \leq_{cn} (M_2, s_2)$. *We conclude that* $M_1 \leq_{cn} M_2$.

Construction of an Abstract GKMTS. Given a concrete Kripke structure M_C, a set S_A of abstract states and a concretization function γ, an abstract GKMTS M_A is constructed similarly to an abstract KMTS with the following difference: a must hyper-transition $s_a \overset{must}{\longrightarrow} A_a$ exists only if $\forall s_c \in \gamma(s_a) \exists s_c' \in \left(\bigcup_{s_a' \in A_a} \gamma(s_a') \right) : s_c \rightarrow s_c'$.

This construction assures us that $M_C \preceq M_A$ w.r.t. the generalized mixed simulation. Therefore, Theorem 4 guarantees preservation of CTL from M_A to M_C.

The use of GKMTSs allows construction of abstract models that are more precise than abstract models described as KMTSs, when using the same abstract state space and the same concretization function. This is demonstrated by the following example.

Example 3. Consider the *exact* KMTS M described in Fig. 1(a) for the program P from Example 1. The state s_1 has no outgoing must transition. Therefore, even verification of the simple formula $EXEX(true)$ fails, although this formula holds in every concrete model where the transition relation is total. Using a GKMTS (rather than a KMTS) as an abstract model allows us to have a must hyper-transition from s_1 to the set $\{s_1, s_2\}$. Therefore we are now able to verify the tautological formula $EXEX(true)$.

Exact GKMTS. As with KMTSs, the must hyper-transitions of a GKMTS do not have to be *exact*, as long as they maintain the new $\forall\exists$ condition. That is, it is possible to have less must hyper-transitions than allowed by the $\forall\exists$ rule. If all the components of the GKMTS are exact, then we get the *exact* GKMTS, which is *most precise* compared to all the GKMTSs that are constructed by the same rules based on the given S_A, γ.

Any abstract GKMTS and in particular the exact GKMTS can be reduced without damaging its precision, based on the following observation. Given two must hyper-transitions $s_a \xrightarrow{\text{must}} A_a$ and $s_a \xrightarrow{\text{must}} A'_a$, where $A_a \subset A'_a$, the transition $s_a \xrightarrow{\text{must}} A'_a$ can be discarded without sacrificing the precision of the GKMTS. Therefore, a possible optimization would be to use only *minimal* must hyper-transitions where A_a is minimal. This is similar to the approach of [8], where the destination state of a (regular) must transition is chosen to be the smallest state w.r.t. a given partial order on S_A.

In general, even when applying the suggested optimization, the number of must hyper-transitions in the exact GKMTS might be exponential in the number of states. In practice, computing *all* of them is computationally expensive and unreasonable. Later on, we will suggest how to choose an initial set of must hyper-transitions and increase it gradually in a way that in many cases avoids the exponential blowup.

5   Monotonic Abstraction-Refinement Framework

In this section our goal is to show how GKMTSs can be used in practice within an abstraction-refinement framework designed for full CTL. We also show that using the suggested framework allows us to achieve the important advantage of a *monotonic* refinement when dealing with full CTL and not just a universal fragment of it.

We start by pointing out that using *exact* GKMTSs as abstract models solves the problem of the non-monotonic refinement, described in Section 4.1.

Definition 9 (Split). *Let S_C be a set of concrete states, let S_A and S'_A be two sets of abstract states and let $\gamma : S_A \to 2^{S_C}$, $\gamma' : S'_A \to 2^{S_C}$ be the corresponding concretization functions. We say that (S'_A, γ') is a split of (S_A, γ) iff there exists a (total) function $\rho : S'_A \to S_A$ such that for every $s_a \in S_A$: $\left(\bigcup_{\rho(s'_a)=s_a} \gamma'(s'_a) \right) = \gamma(s_a)$.*

Theorem 5. *Let M_C be a (concrete) Kripke structure and let M_A, M'_A be two exact GKMTSs defined based on (S_A, γ), (S'_A, γ') respectively, such that $M_C \preceq M_A$ and $M_C \preceq M'_A$. If (S'_A, γ') is a split of (S_A, γ), then $M'_A \preceq M_A$.*

Theorem 5 claims that for exact GKMTSs, refinement that is based on splitting abstract states is monotonic. This is true without the need to hold "copies" of the unrefined abstract states. Yet, as claimed before, constructing the exact GKMTS is not practical. Therefore, we suggest a compromise that fits well into the framework of abstraction-refinement. We show how to construct an initial abstract GKMTS and how to construct a refined abstract GKMTS (based on splitting abstract states). The construction is done in a way that is on the one hand computationally efficient and on the other hand maintains a monotonic refinement. The basic idea is as follows. In each iteration of the abstraction-refinement we first construct an abstract KMTS, including its may transitions and its (regular) must transitions. We then compute additional must *hyper-transitions* as described below.

Construction of an Initial Abstract Model M_0:
Given an initial set of abstract states S_0 and a concretization function γ_0:

1. construct an abstract KMTS based on (S_0, γ_0).
2. for every abstract state, add a must hyper-transition which is the set of all its outgoing may transitions.

Note that the set of all the outgoing may transitions of a state indeed fulfills the $\forall\exists$ condition and thus can be added as a must hyper-transition. This results from the totality of the concrete transition relation along with the property that every concrete transition is represented by some may transition. We call such must hyper-transitions *trivial*.

Construction of a Refined Model M_{i+1}:
Suppose that model checking of the abstract model M_i resulted in an indefinite result and refinement is needed. Let (S_{i+1}, γ_{i+1}) be the split of (S_i, γ_i), computed by some kind of a refinement mechanism. Construct M_{i+1} as follows.

1. construct an abstract KMTS based on (S_{i+1}, γ_{i+1}).
2. for every must hyper-transition (including regular must transitions) $s_i \xrightarrow{\text{must}} A_i$ in M_i and for every state $s_{i+1} \in S_{i+1}$ that is a sub-state of $s_i \in S_i$, add to M_{i+1} the must hyper-transition $\bigcup_{s'_i \in A_i} \{s_{i+1} \xrightarrow{\text{may}} s'_{i+1} : s'_{i+1} \text{ is a sub-state of } s'_i\}$.
3. [optional] discard from M_{i+1} any must hyper-transition $s_{i+1} \xrightarrow{\text{must}} A_{i+1}$ that is not *minimal*, which means that there is $s_{i+1} \xrightarrow{\text{must}} A'_{i+1}$ in M_{i+1} where $A'_{i+1} \subset A_{i+1}$.

The purpose of step 2 above is to avoid the loss of information from the previous iteration, without paying an additional cost. To do so, we derive must hyper-transitions in M_{i+1} from must hyper-transitions in M_i, while avoiding the recomputation of the $\forall\exists$ rule. Namely, if there is a must hyper-transition from s_i to A_i in M_i, then for every state s_{i+1} in M_{i+1} that is a sub-state of s_i we add an outgoing must hyper-transition to the set of all sub-states of states in A_i, excluding states to which s_{i+1} does not have a may transition. Clearly, given that $s_i \xrightarrow{\text{must}} A_i$, we are guaranteed that the $\forall\exists$ condition holds for the corresponding hyper-transitions in M_{i+1} as well. Note that this is not damaged by excluding from the destination set states to which s_{i+1} does not have a may transition. This is because the lack of a may transition shows that the $\exists\exists$ condition does not hold between s_{i+1} and the relevant states. Therefore they cannot contribute to the satisfaction of the $\forall\exists$ condition anyway and can be removed. By using this scheme, the construction of the GKMTS requires no additional computational cost, compared to the construction of a (regular) KMTS.

The purpose of step 3 is to reduce the GKMTS without sacrificing its precision. Note that the reduction done in this step can be performed *during* step 2.

Theorem 6. *Let M_C be a concrete Kripke structure and let $M_0, M_1, \ldots M_i, \ldots$ be the abstract GKMTSs constructed as described above. Then*
(1) for every $i \geq 0$: $M_C \preceq M_i$; and   (2) for every $i \geq 0$: $M_{i+1} \preceq M_i$.

Theorem 6 first ensures that the construction of the initial and the refined GKMTSs described above yields abstract models which are greater by the generalized mixed simulation relation than the concrete model. Moreover, it ensures that although we do not use the exact GKMTSs, we still have a generalized mixed simulation relation between GKMTSs from different iterations in a monotonic fashion. This means that we do not lose information during the refinement and we get "closer" to the concrete model.

Example 4. To demonstrate these ideas we return to the program P from Example 1 and see how the use of GKMTSs as described above affects it. The initial GKMTS M_0 is similar to the KMTS M from Fig. 1(a), with two additional *trivial* must hyper-transitions from s_1 and from s_2 to $\{s_1, s_2\}$. Yet, the truth value of $\varphi = EF(x \leq 0)$ remains indefinite in this model. When we construct the refined model M_1 (based on the addition of the predicate $odd(x)$), we get a GKMTS that is similar to the KMTS M' from Fig. 1(b), but M_1 also has additional must hyper-transitions. In particular, it has two trivial must hyper-transitions from both of its initial states to the set $\{s_{10}, s_{11}\}$. These must hyper-transitions are the refined version of the (regular) must transition from s_0 to s_1 in M_0: They exist because the initial states of M_1 are sub-states of the initial state s_0 of M_0 and the set $\{s_{10}, s_{11}\}$ consists of all the sub-states of s_1. Their existence in M_1 allows to verify φ, since due to them each of the initial states now has an outgoing must hyper-path in which all the paths reach s_{20} where $x \leq 0$.

Example 4 also demonstrates our advantage over [9] which stems from the fact that our refinement does not use "copies" of the unrefined abstract states, unlike [9]. This example shows that in our approach the *old* information (from the unrefined model) is expressed with respect to the *new* refined states. Consequently, the old information and the new information, for which refinement was needed, can be combined, resulting in a better precision.

To conclude this section and make the suggested ideas complete, it remains to provide (1) a model checking algorithm that evaluates CTL formulae over GKMTSs, using the generalized 3-valued semantics; and (2) a suitable refinement mechanism to be applied when the model checking result is indefinite. Using these two components within the general framework suggested above, results in an actual abstraction-refinement framework where the refinement is monotonic.

Model Checking. As a model checking algorithm we suggest a simple generalization of the symbolic 3-valued algorithm presented in Section 2.2. The only change is in the definition of the operator $ex(Z)$, which is now defined to be

$$ex(Z) = \{s \mid \exists s_1', \ldots s_n' : s \xrightarrow{\text{must}} \{s_1', \ldots, s_n'\} \wedge \bigwedge_{i=1}^{n} Z(s_i')\}$$

Refinement. As for the refinement mechanism, we can use the algorithm suggested in Section 3 in order to find a failure state, analyze the failure and decide how to split the abstract states. To be convinced of that, one needs to notice that the refinement is based on may transitions only. Therefore no change is needed.

Moreover, the construction of a refined model M_{i+1} can be improved when this refinement mechanism is used. Namely, during the failure analysis it is possible to learn about additional must hyper-transitions that can be added to M_{i+1}. This is because if the cause for failure is a may transition $s_i \xrightarrow{\text{may}} s_i'$ (in M_i) then the split is done by separating the set S_C' of all the concrete states represented by s_i that have a corresponding outgoing transition, from the rest (see [20]). In this case, we are guaranteed that after the split, the $\forall \exists$ condition holds between the sub-state of s_i representing the concrete set S_C' and the set containing all the sub-states of s_i'. Therefore, we can add such a must hyper-transition to M_{i+1} without additional computational cost.

Other extensions of the refinement mechanism, which are more GKMTS-oriented and further exploit the use of must hyper-transitions, are omitted due to space limitations.

Theorem 7. *For finite concrete models, iterating the suggested abstraction-refinement process is guaranteed to terminate with a definite answer.*

References

1. S. Barner, D. Geist, and A. Gringauze. Symbolic localization reduction with reconstruction layering and backtracking. In *Computer-Aided Verification (CAV)*, Denmark, July 2002.
2. P. Chauhan, E.M. Clarke, J. Kukula, S. Sapra, H. Veith, and D.Wang. Automated abstraction refinement for model checking large state spaces using sat based conflict analysis. In *Formal Methods in Computer Aided Design (FMCAD)*, November 2002.
3. M. Chechik, B. Devereux, A. Gurfinkel, and S. Easterbrook. Multi-valued symbolic model-checking. Technical Report CSRG-448, University of Toronto, April 2002.
4. E.M. Clarke, O. Grumberg, S. Jha, Y. Lu, and H. Veith. Counterexample-guided abstraction refinement. In *Computer Aided Verification (CAV)*, LNCS, Chicago, USA, July 2000.
5. E.M. Clarke, O. Grumberg, and D.A. Peled. *Model Checking*. MIT press, December 1999.
6. E.M. Clarke, A. Gupta, J. Kukula, and O. Strichman. SAT based abstraction-refinement using ILP and machine leraning techniques. In *Computer Aided Verification (CAV)*, 2002.
7. P. Cousot and R. Cousot. Abstract interpretation: A unified lattice model for static analysis of programs by construction or approximation of fixpoints. In *popl4*, pages 238–252, 1977.
8. D. Dams, R. Gerth, and O. Grumberg. Abstract interpretation of reactive systems. *ACM Transactions on Programming Languages and Systems (TOPLAS)*, 19(2), March 1997.
9. P. Godefroid, M. Huth, and R. Jagadeesan. Abstraction-based model checking using modal transition systems. In *CONCUR*, 2001.
10. P. Godefroid and R. Jagadeesan. Automatic abstraction using generalized model checking. In *Computer Aided Verification (CAV)*, LNCS, Copenhagen, Denmark, July 2002.
11. P. Godefroid and R. Jagadeesan. On the expressiveness of 3-valued models. In *Verification, Model Checking and Abstract Interpretation (VMCAI)*, LNCS, January 2003.
12. M. Huth, R. Jagadeesan, and D. Schmidt. Modal transition systems: A foundation for three-valued program analysis. *LNCS*, 2028:155–169, 2001.
13. R.P. Kurshan. *Computer-Aided-Verification of Coordinating Processes*. Princeton University Press, 1994.
14. K.G. Larsen and B. Thomsen. A modal process logic. In *LICS*, July 1988.
15. W. Lee, A. Pardo, J. Jang, G. D. Hachtel, and F. Somenzi. Tearing based automatic abstraction for CTL model checking. In *ICCAD*, pages 76–81, 1996.
16. C. Loiseaux, S. Graf, J. Sifakis, A. Bouajjani, and S. Bensalem. Property preserving abstractions for the verification of concurrent systems. *Formal Methods in System Design*, 1995.
17. K. S. Namjoshi. Abstraction for branching time properties. In *CAV*, Boulder, CO, July 2003.
18. A. Pardo and G. D. Hachtel. Automatic abstraction techniques for propositional mu-calculus model checking. In *Computer Aided Verification (CAV)*, pages 12–23, 1997.
19. A. Pardo and G. D. Hachtel. Incremental CTL model checking using BDD subsetting. In *Design Automation Conference*, pages 457–462, 1998.
20. S. Shoham and O. Grumberg. A game-based framework for CTL counterexamples and 3-valued abstraction-refinement. In *Computer Aided Verification*, Boulder, CO, July 2003.
21. A. Tarski. A lattice-theoretical fixpoint theorem and its applications. *Pacific J. Math*, 1955.

Omega-Regular Model Checking*

Bernard Boigelot, Axel Legay, and Pierre Wolper

Université de Liège,
Institut Montefiore, B28,
4000 Liège, Belgium
{boigelot,legay,pw}@montefiore.ulg.ac.be,
http://www.montefiore.ulg.ac.be/~{boigelot,legay,pw}/

Abstract. "Regular model checking" is the name of a family of techniques for analyzing infinite-state systems in which states are represented by words or trees, sets of states by finite automata on these objects, and transitions by finite automata operating on pairs of state encodings, i.e. finite-state transducers. In this context, the central problem is then to compute the iterative closure of a finite-state transducer. This paper addresses the use of regular model-checking like techniques for systems whose states are represented by infinite (omega) words. Its main motivation is to show the feasibility and usefulness of this approach through a combination of the necessary theoretical developments, implementation, and experimentation. The iteration technique that is used is adapted from recent work of the authors on the iteration of finite-word transducers. It proceeds by comparing successive elements of a sequence of approximations of the iteration, detecting an "increment" that is added to move from one approximation to the next, and extrapolating the sequence by allowing arbitrary repetitions of this increment. By restricting oneself to weak deterministic Büchi automata, and using a number of implementation optimizations, examples of significant size can be handled. The proposed transducer iteration technique can just as well be exploited to compute the closure of a given set of states by the transducer iteration, which has proven to be a very effective way of using the technique. Examples such as a leaking gas burner in which time is modeled by real variables have been handled completely within the automata-theoretic setting.

1 Introduction

At the heart of all the techniques that have been proposed for exploring infinite state spaces, is a symbolic representation that can finitely represent infinite sets of states. In early work on the subject, this representation was domain specific, for example linear constraints for sets of real vectors. For several years now, the idea that a generic finite-automaton based representation could be used in

---

* This work was partially funded by a grant of the "Communauté française de Belgique - Direction de la recherche scientifique - Actions de recherche concertées" and by the European IST-FET project ADVANCE (IST-1999-29082).

K. Jensen and A. Podelski (Eds.): TACAS 2004, LNCS 2988, pp. 561–575, 2004.

many settings has gained ground, starting with systems manipulating queues and integers [WB95,BGWW97,WB98,BRW98], then moving to parametric systems [KMM$^+$97], and, recently, reaching systems using real variables [BBR97, BJW01,BHJ03].

Beyond the necessary symbolic representation, there is also a need to "accelerate" the search through the state space in order to reach, in a finite amount of time, states at unbounded depths. In acceleration techniques, the move has again been from the specific to the generic, the latter approach being often referred to as regular model checking. In regular model checking (see e.g. [BJNT00, DLS01]), the transition relation is represented by a finite-state transducer and acceleration techniques aim at computing the iterative closure of this transducer algorithmically, though necessarily foregoing totality or preciseness, or even both. The advantages of using a generic technique are of course that there is only one method to implement independently of the domain considered, that multidomain situations can potentially be handled transparently, and that the scope of the technique can include cases not handled by specific approaches. Beyond these concrete arguments, one should not forget the elegance of the generic approach, which can be viewed as an indication of its potential, thus justifying a thorough investigation.

So far, generic acceleration techniques have been developed and mostly used for parametric systems, though in [JN00,BLW03] it is shown that they can also be applied to systems with integer variables. Quite naturally, in these cases system states are described by finite words or, for some parametric systems, by finite trees ([AJMd02,BT02]), and the corresponding types of automata are used. On the other hand, the regular model checking approach has not been developed for infinite words, though these are used to represent reals in [BJW01] and [BHJ03], but with domain-specific accelerations. Besides reals, using infinite words to describe states can be useful while checking liveness properties of parametric systems since behaviors violating such properties are necessarily infinite and thus might involve an infinite number of processes.

This paper addresses the problem of using regular model-checking like techniques for systems whose states are represented by infinite (omega) words, hence its title. Its main motivation is to show the feasibility of the approach through a combination of the necessary theoretical developments, implementation, and experimentation. The main features of the techniques developed in this paper are the following. First, to avoid the hard to implement algorithms needed for some operations on infinite-word automata, only omega-regular sets that can be defined by weak deterministic Büchi automata will be considered. This is of course restrictive, but as is shown in [BJW01], it is sufficient to handle sets of reals defined in the first-order theory of linear constraints, leads to algorithms that are very similar to the ones used in the finite-word case, and allows us to work with reduced deterministic automata as a normal form.

Second, taking advantage of this, we lift to weak deterministic Büchi automata the techniques developed in [BLW03], but consider the problem of extrapolating an arbitrary sequence of automata, not just the iterations of a transducer.

This generalization is immediate and moving to omega-words involves only minor technical problems, but has been an opportunity to fine-tune the method. Basically, a sequence of automata is extrapolated by comparing its successive elements, and attempting to identify an "increment" that keeps being added when moving from one element to the next. The acceleration is then obtained by allowing arbitrary repetitions of this increment. The issue of the preciseness of this acceleration is handled with an adapted version of the criterion presented in [BLW03].

Third, we turn to the pragmatics of computing reachable states. Taking advantage of the fact that our extrapolation technique works on automata, not just on transducers, we consider computing reachable states both by computing the closure of the transducer representing the transition relation, and by repeatedly applying the transducer to a set of initial states. The first approach yields a more general object and is essential if one wishes to extend the method to the verification of liveness properties ([BJNT00]), but the second is often less demanding from a computational point of view and can handle cases that are out of reach for the first. Preciseness is not always possible to check when working with state sets rather than transducers, but this just amounts to saying that what is computed is possibly an overapproximation of the set of reachable states, a situation which is known to be pragmatically unproblematic.

Fourth, by implementing and working with examples, we have tuned our approach so that it can handle transducers of substantial size. The most costly step in the computations that are performed is the combination of a transducer with itself, or with an automaton representing a set of states, and the determinization step that is needed after projecting out the intermediate variables. Two tactics have been used to improve the efficiency of this step: using a dominance relation between states as described in [BLW03] and simply doing a bisimulation reduction before applying determinization. The effect of theses tactics can be very substantial. Finally, even though we technically need to work with the reflexive closure of the transducers, some steps can be computed with the nonreflexive transducer. By considering various strategies that exploit this, substantial performance improvements have also been obtained.

Our case studies and experiments include simple linear relations defined over the reals as well as models of hybrid systems (see e.g. [ACH$^+$95]), including a leaking gas burner and an alternating bit protocol with timers. The transducers that are handled contain up to over a thousand states.

2   Preliminaries

An *infinite word* (or ω-*word*) w over an alphabet Σ is a mapping from the natural numbers to Σ. The set of infinite words over Σ is denoted Σ^ω. A *Büchi automaton* is a tuple $(Q, \Sigma, \delta, q_0, F)$, where Q is a set of *states*, $q_0 \in Q$ is the *initial state*, $\delta : Q \times \Sigma \to 2^Q$ is the *transition function* ($\delta : Q \times \Sigma \to Q$ if the automaton is deterministic), and $F \subseteq Q$ is the set of *accepting* states.

A *run* π of a Büchi automaton $A = (Q, \Sigma, \delta, q_0, F)$ on an ω-word w is a mapping $\pi : \mathbb{N} \to Q$ such that $\pi(0) = q_0$, and for all $i \geq 0$, $\pi(i+1) \in \delta(\pi(i), w(i))$ (nondeterministic automaton) or $\pi(i+1) = \delta(\pi(i), w(i))$ (deterministic automaton).

Let $inf(\pi)$ denote the set of states that occur infinitely often in a run π. A run π is said to be *accepting* if $inf(\pi) \cap F \neq \emptyset$. An ω-word w is *accepted* by a Büchi automaton if that automaton admits at least one accepting run on w. The language $L_\omega(A)$ *accepted* by a Büchi automaton A is the set of ω-words it accepts. A language $L \subseteq \Sigma^\omega$ is *omega-regular* if it can be accepted by a Büchi automaton. It is well known that the union and intersection of Büchi automata can be computed efficiently. However, the complement operation requires intricate algorithms that not only are worst-case exponential, but are also hard to implement and optimize.

We now introduce the notion of *weak* automaton [MSS86]. For a Büchi automaton $A = (Q, \Sigma, \delta, q_0, F)$ to be weak, there has to be partition of its state set Q into disjoint subsets $Q_1, \ldots, Q_m$ such that for each of the Q_i, either $Q_i \subseteq F$, or $Q_i \cap F = \emptyset$, and there is a partial order $\leq$ on the sets $Q_1, \ldots, Q_m$ such that for every $q \in Q_i$ and $q' \in Q_j$ for which, for some $a \in \Sigma$, $q' \in \delta(q, a)$ ($q' = \delta(q, a)$ in the deterministic case), $Q_j \leq Q_i$. A weak automaton is thus a Büchi automaton such that each of the strongly connected components of its graph contains either only accepting or only non-accepting states, and transitions leaving a component always move to a lower one.

Not all omega-regular languages can be accepted by weak deterministic Büchi automata, nor even by weak nondeterministic automata. However, there are algorithmic advantages to working with weak automata: weak deterministic automata can be complemented simply by inverting their accepting and non-accepting states; and there exists a simple determinization procedure for weak automata [Saf92], which produces Büchi automata that are deterministic, but generally not weak. Nevertheless, if the represented language can be accepted by a weak deterministic automaton, the result of the determinization procedure will be *inherently weak* according to the definition below [BJW01] and thus easily transformed into a weak automaton.

Definition 1. *A Büchi automaton is* inherently weak *if none of the reachable strongly connected components of its transition graph contain both accepting (visiting at least one accepting state) and non-accepting (not visiting any accepting state) cycles.*

This gives us a pragmatic way of staying within the realm of weak deterministic Büchi automata. We start with sets represented by such automata. This is preserved by union, intersection and complementation operations. If a projection is needed, the result is determinized by the known simple procedure. Then, either the result is inherently weak and we can proceed, or it is not and we are forced to stop. The latter cases might never occur, for instance if we are working with automata representing sets of reals definable in the first-order theory of linear constraints [BJW01]. A final advantage of weak deterministic Büchi automata is that they admit a normal form, which is unique up to isomorphism [Löd01].

3   The Omega Regular Model Checking Framework

We use the following modeling framework:

Definition 2. *A program is a triple $P = (\Sigma, \phi_I, R)$ where*

- *Σ is a finite alphabet, over which the program configurations are encoded as infinite words;*
- *ϕ_I is a set of initial configurations represented by a weak deterministic automaton over Σ;*
- *R is a transition relation represented by a weak deterministic transducer over Σ (i.e., a weak automaton over $\Sigma \times \Sigma$).*

Using the encoding of reals by infinite words presented in [BBR97,BJW01], this class of programs includes systems using variables ranging over $\mathbb{R}$ and $\mathbb{Z}$ and for which the data operations involving these variables are definable in $\langle \mathbb{R}, \mathbb{Z}, +, \leq \rangle$. Note that, in particular, linear hybrid systems [ACH+95] fall within this category.

Given a program (Σ, ϕ_I, R), we consider two verification problems:

- *Computing the transitive closure of R:* The goal is to compute a infinite-word transducer representing the reflexive and transitive closure R^* of R. Such a closure can be used for computing the reachability set $R^*(\phi_I)$ of the program, or for finding cycles between reachable program configurations [BJNT00].
- *Computing the reachable states:* The goal is to compute a Büchi automaton representing $R^*(\phi_I)$, which can be used for checking omega-regular safety properties of the program.

In this paper, we tackle both of these problems by the same approach, which consists in constructing successive approximations of R^* or $R^*(\phi_I)$, and trying to algorithmically construct an approximation of their limit. In certain cases, we will be able to prove that our approximation is exact. In order to show that the approximations to be considered can be selected quite freely, we need the following lemma [BLW03].

Lemma 1. *Let R be a relation, and $R_0 = R \cup Id$, where Id is the identity relation. If $s_1, s_2, \ldots$ is an infinite subsequence of the natural numbers, then $R^* = \bigcup_{k \geq 0}(R_0)^{s_k}$ and, similarly, $R^*(\phi_I) = \bigcup_{k \geq 0}(R_0)^{s_k}(\phi_I)$.*

Thus, given a program (Σ, ϕ_I, R), we compute a transducer T_0 representing $R \cup Id$, and select a *sampling sequence* $s = s_1, s_2, \ldots$ as discussed in [BLW03]. Computing R^* (resp. $R^*(\phi_I)$) then amounts to computing the limit of the sequence of automata $(T_0)^{s_1}$, $(T_0)^{s_2}$, $(T_0)^{s_3}$, $\ldots$ (resp. $(T_0)^{s_1}(A_{\phi_I})$, $(T_0)^{s_2}(A_{\phi_I})$, $(T_0)^{s_3}(A_{\phi_I})$, $\ldots$, where A_{ϕ_I} is an automaton representing ϕ_I). The problem of computing the limit of a sequence of automata is addressed in the next section.

4   Detecting Increments

Consider a sequence $A^1, A^2, A^3, \ldots$ of infinite-word automata, which are assumed to be weak and deterministic. Our goal is to determine whether, for sufficiently large i, the automaton A^{i+1} differs from A^i by some additional constant finite-state structure. Our strategy, borrowed from [BLW03,Leg03], consists in comparing a finite number of successive automata until a suitable increment can be detected.

For each $i > 0$, let $A^i = (Q^i, \Sigma, q_0^i, \delta^i, F^i)$. In order to identify common parts between A^i and A^{i+1}, we consider two equivalence relations between their states:

- The *forward equivalence relation* $E_f^i \subseteq Q^i \times Q^{i+1}$ is such that $(q, q') \in E_f^i$ iff the language accepted from q in A^i is identical to the language accepted from q' in A^{i+1};
- The *backward equivalence relation* $E_b^i \subseteq Q^i \times Q^{i+1}$ is such that $(q, q') \in E_b^i$ iff the finite-word language accepted by A^i with q as final state is identical to the finite-word language accepted by A^{i+1} with q' as final state.

The relations E_f^i and E_b^i can be computed by procedures similar to those developed for finite-word transducers in [BLW03,Leg03], replacing Hopcroft's minimization algorithm for finite-word automata [Hop71] by a variant suited for weak deterministic automata [Löd01].

The relations E_f^i and E_b^i enable us to define our notion of finite-state "increment" between two successive automata.

Definition 3. *The automaton A^{i+1} is* incrementally larger *than A^i if the relations E_f^i and E_b^i cover all the states of A^i. In other words, for each $q \in Q^i$, there must exist $q' \in Q^{i+1}$ such that $(q, q') \in E_f^i \cup E_b^i$.*

Definition 4. *If A^{i+1} is incrementally larger than A^i, then the set Q^i can be partitioned into $\{Q_b^i, Q_f^i\}$, such that*

- *The set Q_f^i contains the states q covered by E_f^i, i.e., for which there exists q' such that $(q, q') \in E_f^i$;*
- *The set Q_b^i contains the remaining states.*

The set Q^{i+1} can now be partitioned into $\{Q_H^{i+1}, Q_{I_0}^{i+1}, Q_T^{i+1}\}$, where

- *The head part Q_H^{i+1} is the image by E_b^i of the set Q_b^i;*
- *The tail part Q_T^{i+1} is the image by E_f^i of the set Q_f^i, dismissing the states that belong to Q_H^{i+1} (the intention is to have an unmodified head part);*
- *The increment $Q_{I_0}^{i+1}$ contains the states that do not belong to either Q_H^{i+1} or Q_T^{i+1}.*

It is worth mentioning that, according to these definitions, the strongly connected components of A^{i+1} are each fully contained in either its head part, tail part, or increment.

Our expectation is that, when moving from one automaton to the next in the sequence, the detected increment will always be the same. We formalize this property by the following definition.

Definition 5. *The sequence of automata A^i, A^{i+1}, ..., A^{i+k} grows incrementally if*

- *for each $j \in [0, k-1]$, A^{i+j+1} is incrementally larger than A^{i+j};*
- *for each $j \in [1, k-1]$, the increment $Q_{I_0}^{i+j+1}$ is the image by E_b^{i+j} of the increment $Q_{I_0}^{i+j}$.*

Consider a sequence A^i, A^{i+1}, ..., A^{i+k} that grows incrementally. The tail part Q_T^{i+j} of A^{i+j}, $j \in [2, \ldots, k]$, will then consist of $j-1$ copies of the increment plus a part that we will name the *tail-end part*. Precisely, Q_T^{i+j} can be partitioned into $\{Q_{I_1}^{i+j}, Q_{I_2}^{i+k}, \ldots, Q_{I_{j-1}}^{i+j}, Q_{T_f}^{i+j}\}$, where

- for each $\ell \in [1, \ldots, j-1]$, the *tail increment* $Q_{I_\ell}^{i+j}$ is the image by the relation $E_f^{i+j-1} \circ E_f^{i+j-2} \circ \cdots \circ E_f^{i+j-\ell}$ of the "head" increment $Q_{I_0}^{i+j-\ell}$, where "$\circ$" denotes the composition of relations;
- the *tail-end set* $Q_{T_f}^{i+j}$ contains the remaining elements of Q_T^{i+j}.

Our intention is to extrapolate the automaton A^{i+k} by adding more increments, following the same regular pattern as the one detected in the incrementally growing sequence. In order to do this, we need to compare the transitions leaving different increments. We use the following definition [BLW03,Leg03].

Definition 6. *Let A^{i+k} be the last automaton of an incrementally growing sequence, let $Q_{I_0}^{i+k}, \ldots, Q_{I_{k-1}}^{i+k}$ be the isomorphic increments detected within T_0^{i+k}, and let $Q_{T_f}^{i+k}$ be its "tail end" set. Then, an increment $Q_{I_\alpha}^{i+k}$ is said to be communication equivalent to an increment $Q_{I_\beta}^{i+k}$ iff, for each pair of corresponding states (q, q'), $q \in Q_{I_\alpha}^{i+k}$ and $q' \in Q_{I_\beta}^{i+k}$, and $a \in \Sigma$, we have that, either*

- *$\delta(q, a) \in Q_{I_\alpha}^{i+k}$ and $\delta(q', a) \in Q_{I_\beta}^{i+k}$, hence leading to corresponding states by the existing isomorphism,*
- *$\delta(q, a)$ and $\delta(q', a)$ are both undefined,*
- *$\delta(q, a)$ and $\delta(q', a)$ both lead to the same state of the tail end $Q_{T_f}^{i+k}$, or*
- *there exists some γ such that $\delta(q, a)$ and $\delta(q', a)$ lead to corresponding states of respectively $Q_{I_{\alpha+\gamma}}^{i+k}$ and $Q_{I_{\beta+\gamma}}^{i+k}$.*

In order to extrapolate A^{i+k}, i.e., to guess the value of A^{i+k+1}, we simply insert an extra increment $Q_{I_{e_1}}^{i+k}$ between the head part of A^{i+k} and its head increment $Q_{I_0}^{i+k}$ and define the transitions leaving it in order to make it communication equivalent to $Q_{I_0}^{i+k}$. Of course, before doing so, it is heuristically sound to check that a sufficiently long prefix of the increments of A^{i+k} are communication equivalent with each other.

5   An Acceleration Step for Sequences of Weak Automata

Given a sequence of automata, consider an automaton A^{e_0} of this sequence to which the extrapolation step described at the end of the last section can be applied. Its state set Q can be decomposed into a head part Q_H, a series of k increments $Q_{I_0}, \ldots, Q_{I_{k-1}}$, and a tail end part Q_{T_f}. Repeatedly applying the extrapolation step yields a series of extrapolated automata $A^{e_1}, A^{e_2}, \ldots$. Our goal is to build a single automaton that accepts all the words accepted by these automata, i.e., an automaton $A^{e_*} = \bigcup_{i \geq 0} A^{e_i}$. The automaton A^{e_*} can be built from A^{e_0} by the following algorithm.

1. Build an isomorphic copy $A_{I_0 copy}$ of the automaton formed by the states in Q_{I_0}, the transitions between them, and the outgoing transitions from these states to states in $Q_{I_1}, Q_{I_2}, \ldots, Q_{I_{k-1}}$, and Q_{T_f}.
2. Make all the states of $A_{I_0 copy}$ non-accepting;
3. For each state $q \in Q_{I_0} \cup Q_H$ and $a \in \Sigma$, if $\delta(q, a)$ leads to a state q' in an increment Q_{I_j}, $1 \leq j \leq k - 1$, then
   a) Add transitions labeled by a from q to the state corresponding to q' (by the increment isomorphism) in every increment Q_{I_ℓ} with $1 \leq \ell < j$, as well as to the state corresponding to q' in $A_{I_0 copy}$;
   b) If $q \in Q_{I_0}$, then let q_{copy} be the state corresponding to q in $A_{I_0 copy}$. Add transitions labeled by a from q_{copy} to the state corresponding to q' in every increment Q_{I_ℓ} with $1 \leq \ell < j$, as well as to the state corresponding to q' in $A_{I_0 copy}$.

These construction rules allow A^{e_*} to simulate the computations of any of the A^{e_i}, $i \geq 0$. Notice that the transitions added at the last step may introduce new cycles from states of $A_{I_0 copy}$ to themselves (following these cycles amounts to visiting some additional number of increments). Since the accepting runs of the A^{e_i} can only go through a finite number of increments, it is essential to make these cycles non-accepting, which is the reason behind the duplication of the first increment into $A_{I_0 copy}$.

6   Safety and Preciseness

After having constructed the acceleration A^{e_*} of a sequence $A^1, A^2, \ldots$ of automata, it remains to check whether it accurately corresponds to what we really intend to compute, i.e., $\bigcup_{i>0} A^i$. This is done by first checking that the acceleration is *safe*, in the sense that it captures all behaviors of $\bigcup_{i>0} A^i$, and then checking that it is *precise*, i.e. that it has no more behaviors than $\bigcup_{i>0} A^i$. We check both properties using sufficient conditions. We develop separately these conditions for the two problems outlined in Section 3.

6.1   Transitive Closure of a Relation

Let T_0 be a reflexive infinite-word transducer over the alphabet $\Sigma \times \Sigma$, and let T_0^{e*} be the result of applying the acceleration algorithm described in Section 5 to a sequence $(T_0)^{s_1}, (T_0)^{s_2}, (T_0)^{s_3}, \ldots$ of suitably sampled powers of T_0.

Lemma 2. *The transducer T_0^{e*} is a safe acceleration if $L_\omega(T_0^{e*} \circ T_0^{e*}) \subseteq L_\omega(T_0^{e*})$.*

Indeed, we have $L_\omega(T_0) \subseteq L_\omega(T_0^{e*})$ and thus, by induction, $L_\omega((T_0)^i) \subseteq L_\omega(T_0^{e*})$ (since T_0 is reflexive).

In practice, checking the condition expressed by Lemma 2 requires to complement T_0^{e*}. By construction (see Section 5), this transducer is weak but generally not deterministic. Our approach consists in determinizing T_0^{e*}, and then checking whether the resulting transducer is inherently weak. In the positive case, this transducer can be turned into a weak deterministic one and easily complemented. Otherwise, the test cannot be completed.

We now turn to determining whether the acceleration is precise. This amounts to checking that any word accepted by T_0^{e*} or, equivalently, by some $T_0^{e_i}$, is also accepted by some sampled power $(T_0)^{s_j}$ of the transducer T_0. The idea, borrowed from the procedure developed for finite-word transducers [Leg03,BLW03], is to check that this property can be proved inductively. Our sufficient condition is formalized by the following definition.

Definition 7. *A sequence $T_0^{e_1}, T_0^{e_2}, \ldots$ of extrapolated transducers is inductively precise if, for all $i > 1$ and words $w \in L_\omega(T_0^{e_i})$, there exist $0 < j, j' < i$ such that $w \in L_\omega(T_0^{e_j} \circ T_0^{e_{j'}})$.*

To check inductive preciseness, we use weak automata with counters. It is possible to add a counter c to T_0^{e*} in such a way that, when a word $w \in \Sigma \times \Sigma$ is accepted, the value of c stabilizes before reaching the final accepting strongly connected component, and gives the index i of an extrapolated transducer $T_0^{e_i}$ that accepts w (the construction is similar to the one proposed in [Leg03]). The resulting counter automaton is denoted T_c^{e*}. Furthermore, we write $T_{c=i}^{e*}$ (resp. $T_{c<i}^{e*}$) to denote the automaton T_c^{e*} in which the final value of the counter is required to be equal (resp. less than) i in order to accept a word.

Using three copies $T_{c_1}^{e*}$, $T_{c_2}^{e*}$ and $T_{c_3}^{e*}$ of T_0^{e*}, the inductive preciseness criterion can be expressed as

$$\forall w \in (\Sigma \times \Sigma)^\omega, \, \forall i > 1 \, [w \in L_\omega(T_{c_1=i}^{e*}) \supset w \in L_\omega(T_{c_2<i}^{e*} \circ T_{c_3<i}^{e*})]. \tag{1}$$

This condition can be checked in the following way. It can be shown that, for any word $w \in (\Sigma \times \Sigma)^\omega$ and counter value $i > 0$, w can at most be accepted by one run of $T_{c_1=i}^{e*}$. Moreover, the transitions of $T_{c_1}^{e*}$ are labeled by symbols in $\Sigma \times \Sigma$ and by a counter incrementing operation $+i$, where i is in a finite range $0 \leq i \leq d$. The automaton $T_{c_1}^{e*}$ is, by construction, weak and deterministic with respect to the alphabet $\Sigma \times \Sigma \times [0, d]$ (we denote by $Ta_{c_1}^{e*}$ the automaton $T_{c_1}^{e*}$

considered over this augmented alphabet). Thanks to these properties, deciding Condition (1) reduces to checking

$$L_\omega(Ta^{e_*}_{c_1} \cap (T^{e_*}_{c_2 < c_1} \circ T^{e_*}_{c_3 < c_1})) = L_\omega(Ta^{e_*}_{c_1}). \tag{2}$$

Since it is sufficient to consider the differences $c_1 - c_2$ and $c_1 - c_3$, we are left with the problem of checking equality of accepted languages between a two-counter weak automaton and a weak deterministic automaton. Following the strategy described in [Leg03,BLW03], we impose synchronization conditions on the pairs of counters (c_1, c_2) and (c_1, c_3) so as to reduce the problem to a finite-state one. It is worth mentioning that, since $Ta^{e_*}_{c_1}$ is weak and deterministic, the automaton accepting the left-hand side of (2) must be inherently weak in order to satisfy the condition. This makes it possible to check easily (2), by first computing minimized deterministic automata accepting both sides [Löd01], and then checking whether their transition graphs are isomorphic.

6.2   Limit of a Sequence of Reachable Sets

Let T_0 be a reflexive infinite-word transducer over the alphabet $\Sigma \times \Sigma$ and let A be an automaton over Σ. Let $A^{e_0}, A^{e_1}, \ldots$ be automata extrapolated from a finite sampled subsequence of A, $T_0(A)$, $(T_0)^2(A)$, $(T_0)^3(A)$, $\ldots$. Let A^{e_*} be the result produced by the acceleration algorithm described in Section 5 (we thus have $L_\omega(A^{e_*}) = \bigcup_{i \geq 0} L_\omega(A^{e_i})$).

Lemma 3. *The automaton A^{e_*} is a safe acceleration if $L_\omega(T_0(A^{e_*})) \subseteq L_\omega(A^{e_*})$.*

Like in the case of Lemma 2, this condition can be checked provided that determinizing $T_0(A^{e_*})$ produces an inherently weak automaton.

Determining whether the acceleration is precise is a more difficult problem, for which we provide only a partial solution. Our sufficient precision criterion is formalized by the following definition.

Definition 8. *Let $k > 0$. The sequence A^{e_0}, A^{e_1}, $\ldots$ is k-inductively precise if for all $i > 0$ and words $w \in L_\omega(A^{e_i})$, there exists $j < i$ such that $w \in L_\omega(T^k_0(A^{e_j}))$.*

To check k-inductive preciseness, one can use the same strategy as the one outlined in Section 6.1, checking here only the value of the difference between two counters.

In practical applications, the condition expressed by Definition 8 is usually only satisfied when the sequence A, $T_0(A)$, $(T_0)^2(A)$, $(T_0)^3(A)$, $\ldots$ can be sampled at periodic points (the value of k then corresponds to the chosen period). In other situations, when we are able to assess safety but not preciseness, the accelerated automaton A^{e_*} provides an overapproximation of $\bigcup_{i \geq 0}(T_0)^i(A)$. This can be seen as the result of *widening* the transition relation modeled by the transducer T_0, and is often sufficient for validating the property of interest.

7   Implementation Issues

Implementing the techniques presented in this paper requires potentially costly composition and determinization procedures. In this section, we describe three algorithmic improvements that, in many practical cases, decrease substantially the cost of these procedures.

Dominance. The determinization algorithm for weak automata is derived from the classical subset construction for finite-word automata. As it has been observed in [BLW03], the sets of states that are manipulated during determinization may contain a large number of states that do not influence the behavior of the resulting automaton, because they are *dominated* by other states. Adapting the dominance detection method proposed in [BLW03] to weak deterministic automata is direct and requires only minor algorithmic modifications.

Bisimulation reduction. Consider a transducer T_0 and an exponential sampling sequence $s_i = 2^i$ for all $i > 0$. Any transducer $(T_0)^{s_j}$, with $j > 1$, can easily be computed as the sequential composition of $(T_0)^{s_{j-1}}$ with itself. This composition produces, in general, an automaton with $O(N^2)$ states, with $N = |(T_0)^{s_j}|$, which is costly to determinize. In many experiments, it has been observed that applying a bisimulation reduction to the result of the composition before determinizing it reduces dramatically the cost of computing $(T_0)^{s_j}$.

Nonreflexive composition. Let T be a transducer and $T_0 = T \cup Id$. Consider again an exponential sampling $s_i = 2^i$ for $i > 0$. In experiments, one observes that computing the deterministic form of $(T_0)^{s_j}(A)$, where $j > 1$ and A is some given automaton, is usually much more costly than computing $(T)^{s_j}(A)$. The computation of $(T_0)^{s_j}$ can then be made more efficient by using the formula $(T_0)^{s_j} = ((T_0)^{s_{j-1}} \circ (T)^{s_{j-1}}) \cup (T_0)^{s_{j-1}}$ instead of $(T_0)^{s_j} = (T_0)^{s_{j-1}} \circ (T_0)^{s_{j-1}}$.

8   Experiments

The techniques presented in this paper have been tested on several case studies, using a prototype implementation that relies on the LASH package [LASH] for handling automata. The transition relations that have been considered are all defined over real variables, and represented by *Real Vector Automata* [BBR97], i.e., Büchi automata operating over the binary encoding of numbers.

The first series of test cases consisted of computing the reflexive and transitive closure of relations of the form $(x, x + (1/k))$ for several values of k. In each case, our detection algorithm was able to identify a suitable increment, and applying the acceleration step produced an exact representation of the expected result. The next batch of experiments concerned relations with both discrete and continuous features, such as those of Timed Petri Nets [Bow96]. It is worth mentioning that the disjunctive nature of such relations prevents the use of specific acceleration techniques like those proposed in [BBR97,BHJ03]. For all these case studies, the sampling sequence consisted of the powers of 2. In Table 1, we give the number of states of the minimal and deterministic form of the transducers that were iterated, of the computed closure, and of the largest power of the transducer that had to be constructed in order to detect an increment.

Table 1. Examples of transducers modeling relations and their iteration.

Relation	$\|T_0\|$	$\|T_0^*\|$	Max $\|T_0^n\|$
$(x, x + (1/2))$	9	15	38
$(x, x + (1/4))$	11	18	42
$(x, x + (1/3))$	8	22	53
$(x, x + (1/7))$	10	40	87
$(x, x + (1/17))$	30	84	197
$(x, x + (1/8192))$	33	51	86
$(x, x + (1/65536))$	39	60	98
$\{((x,y),(x+\alpha,y+\alpha)) \mid \alpha \in [0,0.5], x \geq 0, y \geq 0\}$ $\cup \{((x,y),(x,y+1)) \mid x \geq 0, 0 \leq y \leq x-1\}$	184	309	3500
$[\{((x,y),(x+1,y-1))\} \cup \{((x,y),(x-1,y+1))\} \cup$ $\{((x,0),(x+1+\alpha,0)) \mid \alpha\in[0,0.5]\}$ $\cup \{((0,y),(0,y+1+\alpha)) \mid \alpha\in[0,0.5]\}]$ $\cap \mathbb{R}_{\geq 0}^2 \times \mathbb{R}_{\geq 0}^2$	82	84	507
$\{((x,y),(x+2+\alpha,y-1-\alpha)) \mid \alpha\in[0,0.5]\} \cap \mathbb{R}_{\geq 0}^2 \times \mathbb{R}_{\geq 0}^2$	108	596	3944
$[\{((x,y),(x+(1/3),y-(1/2)))\} \cup$ $\{((x,y),(x-(1/2),y+(1/3)))\}] \cap \mathbb{R}_{\geq 0}^2 \times \mathbb{R}_{\geq 0}^2$	336	229	958
$\{((x,y,z),(x+1+\alpha,y+2,z+\alpha)) \mid \alpha\in[0,0.5]\}$	220	421	44621

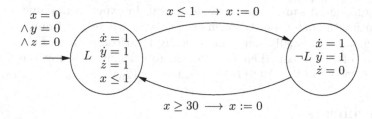

Fig. 1. Hybrid automaton modeling the leaking gas burner.

We also used our prototype for computing reachable sets. For the disjunctive relation $[\{((x,y),(x+2+\alpha,y-1-\alpha)) \mid \alpha\in[0,0.3]\} \cup \{((x,y),(x-1-\alpha,y+2+\alpha)) \mid \alpha\in[0,0.3]\}] \cap \mathbb{R}_{\geq 0}^2 \times \mathbb{R}_{\geq 0}^2$, the computation of its transitive closure had to be stopped after generating transducers with more than one million states. On the other hand, computing the set of configurations reachable from the state $(1,1)$ resulted in a transducer with only 234 states, which was swiftly produced, the largest automaton build during the procedure having 635 states.

We also applied our method to the more challenging problem of analyzing a linear hybrid automaton. The case study consisted of computing the closure of the transition relation of the *leaking gas burner* described in [ACH+95]. This system consists in a gas burner that leaks during periods of less than one time unit (t.u.), these periods being separated by at least 30 t.u. A linear hybrid automaton modeling the leaking gas burner is given in Figure 1. The states L and $\neg L$ correspond respectively to the leaking and non-leaking situations, x measures the leaking periods and the interval between them, y is absolute time, and z keeps track of the cumulated leaking duration. With our implementation, we were able to compute a superset of its reachable set of configurations. We then compared this set with the one produced by the technique described in [BHJ03] (which is specific to linear hybrid automata), from which it turned out that our computed set was actually exact. For this case study, the minimal and deterministic form of the transition relation is a transducer with 2406 states, and the representation of the reachability set has 524 states. The largest automaton considered by the increment detection procedure had 1892 states.

Our prototype was also applied to several other case studies. Those include an alternating bit protocol with unreliable channels and a timer [BSW69], as well as other disjunctive relations.

9 Conclusions

Attempting to verify infinite-state systems while working exclusively with automata-theoretic representations and algorithms can appear as a somewhat quixotic endeavor. Indeed, working with domain-specific representations will in most cases be more efficient. But, this efficiency is gained at the price of limited applicability, sometimes even within the chosen domain, for instance restricting oneself to convex sets while dealing with constraints. This is to be contrasted with the fact that the automaton-based representation used in this paper has, for instance, the unique capability of algorithmically handling arbitrary combinations of linear constraints involving both reals and integers. Also, a single representation makes the handling of multiple domains direct and, for some domains such as parametric systems, words and automata are the only available representation.

Furthermore, the results of this paper show that accelerating sequences of weak Büchi automata can be done without any specific attention to what the automata actually represent or any, a priori, restriction on their structure. To some extent, this possibility is already present in earlier work, in particular [Tou01], but making it available for infinite-word automata is unique and very useful from the point of view of the applications that can be handled. Finally, exploiting rather basic algorithmic and implementation optimizations makes it possible to handle automata of significant size. There is certainly room for further improvement and lack of efficiency might, after all, not be a real issue for automata-based approaches.

The leaking gas burner example that has been handled is small, but has long been a challenge for algorithmic approaches and was handled without any specific tailoring of our fairly simple approach. What is really exciting about this direction of work is that so much could be achieved with so little.

References

[ACH⁺95]   R. Alur, C. Courcoubetis, N. Halbwachs, T. A. Henzinger, P.-H. Ho, X. Nicollin, A. Olivero, J. Sifakis, and S. Yovine. The algorithmic analysis of hybrid systems. *Theoretical Computer Science*, 138(1):3–34, 1995.

[AJMd02]   P. A. Abdulla, B. Jonsson, P. Mahata, and J. d'Orso. Regular tree model checking. In *Proc. 14th Int. Conf. on Computer Aided Verification*, Lecture Notes in Computer Science. Springer-Verlag, July 2002.

[BBR97]   B. Boigelot, L. Bronne, and S. Rassart. An improved reachability analysis method for strongly linear hybrid systems. In *Proceedings of the 9th International Conference on Computer-Aided Verification*, number 1254 in Lecture Notes in Computer Science, pages 167–177, Haifa, Israel, June 1997. Springer-Verlag.

[BGWW97]   Bernard Boigelot, Patrice Godefroid, Bernard Willems, and Pierre Wolper. The power of QDDs. In *Proc. of Int. Static Analysis Symposium*, volume 1302 of *Lecture Notes in Computer Science*, pages 172–186, Paris, September 1997. Springer-Verlag.

[BHJ03]   B. Boigelot, F. Herbreteau, and S. Jodogne. Hybrid acceleration using real vector automata. In *Proceedings 15th International Conference on Computer Aided Verification (CAV)*, volume 2725 of *Lecture Notes in Computer Science*, pages 193–205, Boulder, USA, 2003. Springer-Verlag.

[BJNT00]   A. Bouajjani, B. Jonsson, M. Nilsson, and Tayssir Touili. Regular model checking. In E. A. Emerson and A. P. Sistla, editors, *Proceedings of the 12th International Conference on Computer-Aided Verification (CAV'00)*, volume 1855 of *Lecture Notes in Computer Science*, pages 403–418. Springer-Verlag, 2000.

[BJW01]   Bernard Boigelot, Sébastien Jodogne, and Pierre Wolper. On the use of weak automata for deciding linear arithmetic with integer and real variables. In *Proc. International Joint Conference on Automated Reasoning (IJCAR)*, volume 2083 of *Lecture Notes in Computer Science*, pages 611–625, Siena, Italy, June 2001. Springer-Verlag.

[BLW03]   Bernard Boigelot, Axel Legay, and Pierre Wolper. Iterating transducers in the large. In *Proc. 15th Int. Conf. on Computer Aided Verification*, volume 2725 of *Lecture Notes in Computer Science*, pages 223–235, Boulder, USA, July 2003. Springer-Verlag.

[Bow96]   F. D. J. Bowden. Modelling time in Petri nets. In *Proceedings of the second Australia-Japan Workshop on Stochastic Models in Engineering, Technology and Management*, Gold Coast, Australia, July 1996.

[BRW98]   Bernard Boigelot, Stéphane Rassart, and Pierre Wolper. On the expressiveness of real and integer arithmetic automata. In *Proc. 25th Colloq. on Automata, Programming, and Languages (ICALP)*, volume 1443 of *Lecture Notes in Computer Science*, pages 152–163. Springer-Verlag, July 1998.

[BSW69]   Bartlett, K. A., Scantlebury, R. A., and Wilkinson, P. T. A note on reliable full–duplex transmission over half–duplex links. *Communications of the ACM*, 12(5):260–261, May 1969.

[BT02]   A. Bouajjani and T. Touili. Extrapolating tree transformations. In *Proc. 14th Int. Conf. on Computer Aided Verification*, Lecture Notes in Computer Science. Springer-Verlag, July 2002.

[DLS01]   D. Dams, Y. Lakhnech, and M. Steffen. Iterating transducers. In *Proceedings 13th International Conference on Computer Aided Verification (CAV)*, volume 2102 of *Lecture Notes in Computer Science*, pages 286–297, Paris, France, 2001. Springer.

[Hop71]   J. E. Hopcroft. An $n \log n$ algorithm for minimizing states in a finite automaton. *Theory of Machines and Computation*, pages 189–196, 1971.

[JN00]   B. Jonsson and M. Nilson. Transitive closures of regular relations for verifying infinite-state systems. In S. Graf and M. Schwartzbach, editors, *Proceeding of the 6th International conference on Tools and Algorithms for the Construction and Analysis of Systems (TACAS'00)*, volume 1875 of *Lecture Notes in Computer Science*, pages 220–234. Springer, 2000.

[KMM$^+$97]   Y. Kesten, O. Maler, M. Marcus, A. Pnueli, and E. Shahar. Symbolic model checking with rich assertional languages. In *Proceedings of 9th International Conference on Computer-Aided Verification (CAV'97)*, volume 1254 of *Lecture Notes in Computer Science*, pages 424–435. Springer, 1997.

[LASH]   The Liège Automata-based Symbolic Handler (LASH). Available at http://www.montefiore.ulg.ac.be/~boigelot/research/lash/.

[Leg03]   A. Legay. Iterating transducers: from experiments to concepts and algorithms. Master's thesis, University of Liège, 2003.

[Löd01]   C. Löding. Efficient minimization of deterministic weak ω−automata. *Information Processing Letters*, 79(3):105–109, 2001.

[MSS86]   D. E. Muller, A. Saoudi, and P. E. Schupp. Alternating automata, the weak monadic theory of the tree and its complexity. In *Proc. 13th Int. Colloquium on Automata, Languages and Programming*, pages 275–283, Rennes, 1986. Springer-Verlag.

[Saf92]   S. Safra. Exponential determinization for ω-automata with strong-fairness acceptance condition. In *Proceedings of the 24th ACM Symposium on Theory of Computing*, Victoria, May 1992.

[Tou01]   T. Touili. Regular model checking using widening techniques. In *Proceeding of Workshop on Verification of Parametrized Systems (VEPAS'01)*, volume 50 of *Electronic Notes in Theoretical Computer Science*, 2001.

[WB95]   Pierre Wolper and Bernard Boigelot. An automata-theoretic approach to Presburger arithmetic constraints. In *Proc. Static Analysis Symposium*, volume 983 of *Lecture Notes in Computer Science*, pages 21–32, Glasgow, September 1995. Springer-Verlag.

[WB98]   Pierre Wolper and Bernard Boigelot. Verifying systems with infinite but regular state spaces. In *Proc. 10th Int. Conf. on Computer Aided Verification*, volume 1427 of *Lecture Notes in Computer Science*, pages 88–97, Vancouver, July 1998. Springer-Verlag.

FASTer Acceleration of Counter Automata in Practice

Sébastien Bardin, Alain Finkel, and Jérôme Leroux

LSV, CNRS UMR 8643
ENS de Cachan
61 avenue du président Wilson
F-94235 CACHAN Cedex
FRANCE
{bardin,finkel,leroux}@lsv.ens-cachan.fr

Abstract. We compute reachability sets of counter automata. Even if the reachability set is not necessarily recursive, we use symbolic representation and acceleration to increase convergence. For functions defined by translations over a polyhedral domain, we give a new acceleration algorithm which is polynomial in the size of the function and exponential in its dimension, while the more generic algorithm is exponential in both the size of the function and its dimension. This algorithm has been implemented in the tool FAST. We apply it to a complex industrial protocol, the TTP membership algorithm. This protocol has been widely studied. For the first time, the protocol is automatically proved to be correct for 1 fault and N stations, and using abstraction we prove the correctness for 2 faults and N stations also.

Keywords: acceleration, counter automata, reachability set, convex translation, TTP protocol.

1 Introduction

Context. Many real systems are infinite, because of parameters or unbounded data structures, such as counters, queues or stacks. We focus here on systems modelled by *counter systems*, i.e. automata extended with unbounded integer variables. Counter systems are a valuable abstraction since they allow to model a large range of complex systems, from communication protocols to multithreaded JAVA programs [Del]. Moreover many well-known models, reset/transfert Petri nets [DFS98], Broadcast protocols [EFM99] are subcases of counter systems. In general, reachability properties are undecidable for counter systems.

Counter systems. Let us recall that Presburger arithmetics is the first order additive theory $< \mathbb{N}^m, \leq, + >$. This theory is decidable, and Presburger sets (i.e. sets defined by a Presburger formula) can be represented symbolically by means of automata [BC96,WB00,Ler03b]. This representation is closed under common operations and both emptiness and inclusion are decidable. Moreover,

K. Jensen and A. Podelski (Eds.): TACAS 2004, LNCS 2988, pp. 576–590, 2004.

the successor and predecessor of a Presburger set by an affine function are still Presburger sets. Thus the automata representation provides an efficient way to perform model-checking (or at least to check safety properties) on counter systems, building the reachability set of the system and testing for the inclusion with Presburger sets representing the property to verify. Several symbolic model-checkers use this framework [ALV,LAS,FAS].

State of the art. However, for a general counter system, the reachability set is not necessarily a Presburger set nor a recursive set. The classical fixpoint computation algorithm, consisting in firing one by one the transitions of the system until all the reachable states have been computed, may not terminate. A solution to help convergence is to use *acceleration*. Acceleration allows to compute in one step the exact effect of iterating an arbitrary number of times a control loop of the counter system. Acceleration is also called *meta-transition* [BW94] or *exact widening* in abstract interpretation. In [BW94,Boi98], it is proved that, given a convex polyhedral set S, under some algebraic conditions on the affine function σ, $post^*_\sigma(S)$ and $pre^*_\sigma(S)$ are also computable Presburger sets. Actually, we can even compute the transition relation as a Presburger formula. In [FL02], this result is extended to all Presburger sets.

The problem comes down to finding the good cycles whose accelerations will lead to the reachability set computation. An important step is the *reduction result* given in [FL02], which allows to replace a set C of cycles of length k ($|C|$ is exponential in k) by another equivalent set of cycles C', such that $|C'|$ is polynomial in k.

Tools for acceleration. To the best of our knowledge, three symbolic model-checkers (LASH,FAST,TREX) with acceleration are available for counter systems. LASH and FAST use the automata representation for Presburger sets. LASH is limited to convex guards and the user has to provide cycles to accelerate. FAST has full Presburger guards and can find automatically cycles to acccelerate. TREX [TRE] is designed to verify timed counter systems. TREX uses Constrained Parametric DBMs [AAB00] instead of automata to represent symbolic sets. Untimed models of TREX are restrictive counter systems, because guards and actions are strictly included in those of FAST and LASH. In the other hand, dense clocks are allowed and in particular cases, non linear sets may be computed.

Our results. In this paper, we focus on applying effectively acceleration techniques on counter systems. We investigate the specific case of *counter automata*, where functions are translations over convex polyhedral domains.

1. We give a 3-EXPTIME bound in the size of the domain for the generic Presburger acceleration. For counter automata, we give a simpler acceleration formula (*polyhedral acceleration*), which is proved to be *at most quadratic in the size of the domain*. [BW94,Boi98] also investigate functions with convex domains, but they are not restricted to translations. Thus their acceleration

cannot be expressed so easily than ours, and even if the resulting automata are the same, the intermediate computations are likely to be smaller with our formula. No complexity result is given in [BW94,Boi98].

2. The polyhedral acceleration is implemented in the tool FAST and applied to a non-trivial case study, the membership algorithm of the TTP protocol. This protocol was proved manually to be correct for k faults and N stations in [BM02] and a non-automatic verification with LASH and ALV is performed for 1 fault and N stations. In this paper, *the protocol is verified fully automatically for 1 fault and N stations, and using abstraction it is verified for 2 faults and N stations.*

Outline. Section 2 gives basic definitions and an overview of the main results on acceleration for counter systems. Section 3 investigates the specific case of counter automata, and gives the polyhedral acceleration algorithm. Finally in section 4, FAST is used to verify the complex industrial TTP protocol.

2   Acceleration of Counter Systems

2.1   Counter Systems

We are interested in accelerating transitions for counter systems whose transitions are guarded affine functions. Firstly we introduce Presburger arithmetics, which is the first order theory $< \mathbb{N}^m, \leq, + >$. Then we describe counter systems.

Definition 1 (Presburger logic). *Consider a finite set X of free variables x. The set of Presburger formulas ϕ over X is defined by the grammar:*

$$t ::= 0|1|x|t - t|t + t$$
$$\phi ::= t \leq t|\neg\phi|\phi \vee \phi|\exists y; \phi|true$$

Definition 2 (Presburger-linear function [FL02]). *A Presburger-linear function f over m counters is a tuple $f = (M, v, D)$ such that $\forall x \in D, f(x) = M.x + v$, with M a square matrix, v a vector and $D \subseteq \mathbb{N}^m$ a Presburger set called the guard of f.*

Definition 3 (Counter systems). *A counter system over m counters L is a tuple $L = (\Sigma, f_\Sigma)$ where Σ is a finite alphabet of actions and $f_\Sigma = \{f_a; a \in \Sigma\}$ is a set of Presburger-linear functions over m counters.*

Remark 1. We can add a control structure to a counter system without changing the expressibility of the models, encoding control states as a variable.

Definition 4 (The monoid of a counter system). *We call the monoid of a counter system L the multiplicative monoid generated by the set of square matrices $\{M_a; a \in \Sigma\}$ of L. When L is composed of a unique function $f(s) = M.s + v$, then this monoid is simply written $< M >$.*

Counter systems with a finite monoid have nice acceleration properties and appear to be well-spread in practice. For example all transfer/reset/inhibitors Petri Nets and all Broadcast protocols are counter systems with a finite monoid.

2.2   Unambiguous Binary Automata

The automata approach is very fruitful to represent Presburger sets. An integer is represented by its encoding into a basis r. Then a set of integers is represented by an automaton whose associated language is exactly this set [BC96]. Number Decision Diagrams (NDDs) [Boi98,WB00] are usually used to represent any Presburger set of $\mathbb{N}^m$. Unambiguous Binary Automata [Ler03b,Ler03a] (UBA) is a similar approach, but they are proved to be smaller than NDDs [Ler03a].

Let $|\mathcal{A}|$ be the number of states of the automaton $\mathcal{A}$. Recall these results useful to bound the size of the UBA $\mathcal{A}(X)$ when X is defined by a first order formula (these results are deduced from results on NDDs summarized in [BB02]):

- the UBA $\mathcal{A}(X)$ where $X = \{x \in \mathbb{N}^m;\ \sum_{i=1}^{m} \alpha_i.x_i \# c\}$ with $\alpha_i, c \in \mathbb{Z}$ and $\# \in \{\leq, \geq, =\}$ can be computed in time and space bounded by $m.(\sum_{i=1}^{m} |\alpha_i| + |c|) + 1$.
- the UBA $\mathcal{A}(X)$ where $X = \{x \in \mathbb{N}^m;\ \sum_{i=1}^{m} \alpha_i.x_i = c[k]\}$ with $\alpha_i, c, k \in \mathbb{Z}$ and $c[k]$ denotes c *modulo* k, can be computed in time and space bounded by $2.m.|k| + 1$.
- the UBA $\mathcal{A}(X \cap Y)$ can be computed in time and space bounded by $|\mathcal{A}(X)|.|\mathcal{A}(Y)|$.
- the UBA $\mathcal{A}(\Pi(X))$ where Π is a projection function (removing some components) can be computed in time and space bounded by $m.2^{|\mathcal{A}(X)|}$.
- the UBA $\mathcal{A}(\mathbb{N}^m \backslash X)$ can be computed in time and space bounded by $|\mathcal{A}(X)|$.

2.3   Main Results on Acceleration

Let f be a function, and S a set, we define the acceleration of f, denoted f^*, by $f^*(S) = \bigcup_{i \in \mathbb{N}} f^i(S)$. R_f^* is the relation associated with f^*. The results on acceleration are summarised in this section. We denote by $||v||_\infty$ the infinite norm of the vector v, and by F the function f with no guard.

Acceleration of a cycle. In [FL02] it is proved that for a Presburger-linear function $f = (M, v, D)$ with a finite monoid, the transition relation R_f^* can be computed as a Presburger formula, of the form

$$R_f^* = \{(x, x') | x \in D \land (\exists k \geq 0; x' = F^k(x) \land (\forall i; 0 \leq i < k, F^i(x) \in D))\}\ (1)$$

This result extends the one of [Boi98] which is restricted to affine functions over convex guards. No complexity result is given in the literature for this construction. We propose an upper-bound of the complexity.

Proposition 1. *Let $f = (M, v, D)$ be a Presburger linear function with a finite monoid. An UBA that represents the relation R_f^* can be computed in 3-EXPTIME in $|\mathcal{A}(D)|$, $||v||_\infty$ and $||M||_\infty$ and 5-EXPTIME in m.*

Remark 2. Getting an exponential lower-bound is an open problem. However it seems that this bound can be reached in the worst case.

Remark 3. In practice m, $||v||_\infty$ and $||M||_\infty$ are small (≤ 100), while $|\mathcal{A}(D)|$ can be very large (from 100 up to several millions, see section 3).

Finding the good cycles. Acceleration allows to help the convergence of the reachability set computation. Now the problem is to find the sequence of *good cycles* to accelerate, i.e. cycles whose acceleration will lead to the reachability set computation. But for a finite counter system $L = (\Sigma, f_\Sigma)$, the number of Presburger-linear functions in the set $C_k = \{f_\sigma;\ \sigma \in \Sigma^{\leq k}\}$ may be exponential in k. However, this exponential number of functions can be *reduced* to a set of Presburger-linear functions $[C_k]$ with a polynomial size in k [FL02].

2.4   The Tool FAST and Its Heuristic

FAST [BFLP03] is a tool dedicated to the analysis of counter systems, using symbolic representation with automata and acceleration. To find the cycles to accelerate, FAST provides an automatic search, which is often sufficient (all the examples on the FAST Web page [FAS] have been verified fully automatically).

We present the heuristic used in FAST to compute the reachability set of an initial set S_0, given a finite counter system L. The semi-algorithm we propose can be seen as an extension of the semi-algorithm presented in [Boi98]. The basic idea is to add cycles to the initial set of linear transitions, and to accelerate them. These cycles are called *meta-transitions*. In [Boi98] cycles to be accelerated are provided by the user. Here we want these cycles to be found automatically.

Our problem is divided into two separate steps: the computation of the interesting cycles from a set of transitions, and the search heuristic given a set of cycles. For *the cycles computation*, the main problem is *the potentially exponential number of cycles*. For *the search heuristic*, the problem is *the automata explosion problem*. Because there is no relationship between the size of the set which is represented and the size of the automaton which represents it, choosing a bad function can lead to a set whose representation by automata is very large, and thus, the subsequent operations will take too much time.

The cycle computation. We make the assumption that, *in pratical cases, good cycles have a small length*. So we do not try to consider all the cycles at once, but only all the cycles of length less or equal to a constant k. We compute the cycles in a *static and incremental way*. *Static* because the set of cycles we use is fixed during the search. *Incremental* because if the search fails (according to a *stop criterion*), the length of cycles is increased and a new search is done. To efficiently compute the cycles, we use the reduction result from section 2.

(0) $k \leftarrow 1$
(1) *Compute C_k, the reduced set of cycles of length $\leq k$*
(2) *Use the search algorithm with S_0 and $L \cup C_k$*
(3) *if a fixpoint S is found then return S*
    else (the stop criterion is met) do $k \leftarrow k + 1, goto$ (1)

The search heuristic. The main point is to overcome the automata explosion problem. For this purpose, we introduce in the classic fixpoint algorithm a *minimization* step where we only try to reduce the size of the automaton computed so far. Thus our heuristic can be seen as two nested greedy algorithms. The first one tries to build new states (*new states first*). Once it is done we enter the minimization step (*smaller automaton first*), where transitions are chosen if they lead to smaller automaton. When it is not possible anymore, we come back to the first part. The search finishes when a fixpoint is found or when the stop criterion is met. Moreover, we choose the transitions to be fired with *fairness* assumptions, in order to avoid choosing always the same.

$S \leftarrow S_0$
while there exists f *such that* $f^*(S)$ *reaches new states do*
    $S \leftarrow f^*(S)$
    while there exists f *such that* $|\mathcal{A}(f^*(S))| < |\mathcal{A}(S)|$ *do*
        $S \leftarrow f^*(S)$
    end while
end while
return S

The stop criterion. Building a good stop criterion is not easy. After lots of experiments, we distinguish two simple and relevant factors to know when to increase cycle length. The first factor is the *size of the automaton built*. When it becomes too large, computation cannot be managed anymore and so the semi-algorithm will certainly not terminate within reasonable time. The second factor is *the depth of the search*. After lots of experiments, it seems that when the heuristic finishes, it ends rather quickly. So if the search is going too deep, the cycle length is probably too small.

In FAST, the user can define the maximal depth and the maximal size of the automaton. In practice, it is not very difficult to use, because the default setup (no limit on the size, 100 for the maximal depth) is often sufficient.

3 Acceleration of Counter Automata

3.1 The Generic Acceleration May Be too Complex

The generic acceleration technique we use may be very expensive and lead to very large automata. In practice it works well, but there are few examples where FAST cannot compute an accelerated transition relation because the automata manipulated are too large.

For example, considering the transition in figure 1, when FAST tries to compute the acceleration of the transition relation, the size of the internal automata explodes and the tool stops. This is due to the fact that we use MONA [MON] as an automata library. In this library, the number of states of the automata is limited (to 2^{24}), and during the computation this limit is exceeded. This example is taken from the TTP protocol (see section 4). It is the only practical example we found which brings MONA, and thus FAST, out of its limits.

$$Cp_1 \geq N \wedge Cp_2 < N \wedge d_{11} < C_{11} \wedge$$
$$d_1 + d_{11} - dA_{11} - dF_{11} - dA_{10} + dF_{10} - d_0 - d_{10} - d_{00} + dA_{00} + dF_{00} \leq 0$$
$$\rightarrow dF' := dF + 1, Cp_1' := Cp_1 + 1, Cp_2' := Cp_2 + 1, dF_{11}' := dF_{11} + 1, C_{11}' := C_{11} + 1$$

Fig. 1. A transition which brings FAST out of its limits

3.2   A Simpler Acceleration for Counter Automata

We can notice that the example above belongs to a particular case: functions are translations over a (convex) polyhedral domain.

Definition 5 (convex translation). *A convex translation f is a Presburger-linear function $f = (I, v, D)$ where I is the identity matrix and D is a polyhedron.*

Definition 6 (counter automaton). *A counter automaton L is a counter system whose functions are all convex translations.*

In such a case we can use a simpler acceleration formula, because we do not need to test if all the successors are in the guard. As long as the first element and the last element are in the guard, the intermediate elements are in the guard as well. The transition relation can be computed as

$$R_f^* = \{(x, x') | x \in D \wedge (\exists k \geq 0; x' = F^k(x) \wedge k > 0 \Rightarrow F^{k-1}(x) \in D)\} \quad (2)$$

[BW94,Boi98] study functions over convex domains, but because these functions are not restricted to translations they cannot use the above argument. We will present in the following an acceleration formula based on ideas from (2) which is proved to be quadratic in the domain of the function.

Proposition 2. *Let $f = (I, v, D)$ be a convex translation. The accelerated transition relation of f is equal to:*

$$R_f^* = I \cup \{(x, x') \in D \times (D + v); \ x' - x \in \mathbb{N}.v\} \quad (3)$$

Proof. Let $R = \{(x, x') \in D \times (D + v); \ x - x' \in \mathbb{N}.v\}$. Consider $(x, x') \in R_f^*$ and let us prove that $(x, x') \in I \cup R$. There exists $n \geq 0$ such that $x' = f^n(x) = x + n.v$. If $n = 0$ then $(x, x') = (x, x) \in I \cup R$. Otherwise, we have $n \geq 1$. From $f^{n-1}(x) \in D$, we deduce $f^n(x) \in f(D) = D + v$. Therefore $(x, x') \in I \cup R$. Let us prove the converse by considering $(x, x') \in I \cup R$. Remark that if $(x, x') \in I$, then $(x, x') \in R_f^*$. So we can assume that $(x, x') \notin I$. In this case, $(x, x') \in D \times (D + v)$

and there exists $n \geq 1$ such that $x' = x + n.v$. As $x + n.v \in D + v$, we have $x + (n-1).v \in D$. As D is a convex set and x and $x + (n-1).v \in D$, for any $k \in \{0, \ldots, n-1\}$, we have $F^k(x) = x + k.v \in D$. Therefore $x' = f^n(x)$ and we have proved $(x, x') \in R_f^*$. □

Theorem 1. *Let $f = (I, v, D)$ be a convex translation. An UBA $\mathcal{A}(R_f^*)$ representing the relation R_f^* can be computed in time and space bounded by*

$$|\mathcal{A}(R_f^*)| \leq |\mathcal{A}(D)|^2.4.(4.m.\,||v||_\infty + 1)^{3.m}$$

Proof. Let us consider the relation $R = \{(x, x') \in \mathbb{N} \times \mathbb{N};\ x' - x \in \mathbb{N}.v\}$ and let $I_0 = \{i \in \{1, \ldots, m\};\ v_i \neq 0\}$ and $I = \{i \in \{1, \ldots, m\};\ v_i = 0\}$. Remark that if $I_0 = \emptyset$ then $R_f^* = I$ and in this case $|\mathcal{A}(R_f^*)| = 4$. So, we can assume that there exists an index $i_0 \in I_0$. We denote by ϕ the Presburger fomula $\phi := (x'_{i_0} - x_{i_0} \geq 0)$ if $v_{i_0} > 0$ and $\phi := (x'_{i_0} - x_{i_0} \leq 0)$ otherwise.

Let $a[b]$ denote the value a modulo b. We now prove that R is defined by the following Presburger formula:

$$\phi \bigwedge_{i \in I} (x'_i = x_i) \bigwedge_{i \in I_0 \setminus \{i_0\}} ((x'_i - x_i).v_{i_0} = (x'_{i_0} - x_{i_0}).v_i) \bigwedge_{i \in I_0} (x'_i - x_i = 0[v_i])$$

Let $(x, x') \in R$. There exists $n \geq 0$ such that $x' - x = n.v$. For every $i \in I$, we have $x'_i = x_i$. Moreover, for every $i \in I_0$, we have $x'_i - x_i = n.v_i$ and $x'_{i_0} - x_{i_0} = n.v_{i_0}$. Hence $(x'_i - x_i).v_{i_0} = (x'_{i_0} - x_{i_0}).v_i$ and $x'_i - x_i = 0[v_i]$. From $x'_{i_0} - x_{i_0} = n_{i_0}.v_{i_0}$, we deduce that ϕ is true. Let us prove the converse by considering a tuple (x, x') such that ϕ is true and for every $i \in I$, we have $x'_i = x_i$ and for every $i \in I_0$ we have $(x'_i - x_i).v_{i_0} = (x'_{i_0} - x_{i_0}).v_i$ and $x'_i - x_i = 0[v_i]$. As $x'_i - x_i = 0[v_i]$, there exists $n_i \in \mathbb{Z}$ such that $x'_i - x_i = n_i.v_i$. From the equality $(x'_i - x_i).v_{i_0} = (x'_{i_0} - x_{i_0}).v_i$, we deduce $n_i.v_i.v_{i_0} = n_{i_0}.v_{i_0}.v_i$. As $v_i.v_{i_0} \neq 0$, we have $n_i = n_{i_0}$ for every $i \in I_0$. In particular, we have $x' = x + n_{i_0}.v$. As ϕ is true, we deduce $n_{i_0} \geq 0$ from $x'_{i_0} - x_{i_0} = n_{i_0}.v_{i_0}$. So $(x, x') \in R$.

An UBA that represents ϕ or $(x'_i = x_i)$ can be computed in time and space bounded by $2.m+1$. We can also compute an UBA that represents $(x'_i - x_i).v_{i_0} = (x'_{i_0} - x_{i_0}).v_i$ in time and space bounded by $m.(2.|v_{i_0}|+2.|v_i|)+1 \leq 4.m.\,||v||_\infty+1$. Moreover, we can compute an UBA that represents $x'_i - x_i = 0[v_i]$ in time and space bounded by $2.m.|v_i| + 1 \leq 2.m.\,||v||_\infty + 1$. Therefore, we can compute an UBA that represents R in time and space bounded by $(4.m.\,||v||_\infty + 1)^{2.m}$.

From the equality $R_f^* = I \cup ((D \times (D + v)) \cap R)$, we deduce that R_f^* is computable in time and space bounded by $|\mathcal{A}(I)|.|\mathcal{A}(D)|.|\mathcal{A}(D+v)|.|\mathcal{A}(R)|$. From [BB03], we deduce that an UBA that represents $D + v$ can be computed in time and space bounded by $|\mathcal{A}(D)|.(m.\,||v||_\infty + 1)^m$. Moreover, recall that $|\mathcal{A}(I)| = 4$.

We have proved that R_f^* can be computed in time and space bounded by:

$$|\mathcal{A}(D)|^2.4.(4.m.\,||v||_\infty + 1)^{2.m}.(m.\,||v||_\infty + 1)^m$$
$$\leq |\mathcal{A}(D)|^2.4.(4.m.\,||v||_\infty + 1)^{3.m}$$

□

Remark 4. For the polyhedral acceleration, the complexity is quadratic in the size of the automaton representing the guard D, polynomial in $||v||_\infty$ and exponential in the number of counters m. This is a major improvement compared to the generic case (section 2), where the complexity is 3-EXPTIME in the size of the automaton representing the guard D, 3-EXPTIME in $||v||_\infty$ and 5-EXPTIME in m. Note that the resulting automaton is the same (the representation is canonical), the difference is on the intermediate automata.

Results. With this simpler acceleration formula, the acceleration relation of the transition of figure 1 can be computed, avoiding the automata explosion problem. The computation takes 18 seconds, 260 Mbytes (!). The resulting automaton has 413,447 states. For comparison, automata representing accelerations of transitions in [FAS] have roughly 300 states.

4   FAST in Practice: The TTP/C

This section describes the verification of the TTP/C protocol with FAST. In previous work, the protocol has been semi-automatically verified by the tools ALV and LASH for N stations (microprocessors) and 1 fault, but the tools fail for 2 faults. Here FAST verifies the protocol fully automatically for N stations and 1 fault, and using abstraction the protocol is verified for N stations and 2 faults.

4.1   Presentation of the TTP Protocol

The TTP [KG94] is used in car industry to manage embedded microprocessors. We focus here on the *group membership algorithm* of the TTP. It is a *fault-tolerant algorithm*. It ensures that if a fault occurs, after a certain amount of time the embedded microprocessors which are still valid keep on communicating with each other, without any partition among the microprocessors. We were interested in verifying such a protocol since it is a complex industrial case study which needs a very expressive model, with two causes of infinity: the number of stations and the number of faults.

The time is divided into rounds. Each round is divided into as many slots of communication as the number of stations (microprocessors). Each station s_i has a *membership list* stating which stations s_j are considered as invalid. During a slot, only one station sends a message, the others are listening. A sender sends its membership list to all listeners. A listener which receives a list different from its own list considers the message as invalid (and updates its own list). When a station receives in a round more invalid messages than valid ones, *the station considers itself as invalid*. It becomes inactive (it listens but does not send anymore). The goal of the membership algorithm is to ensure that after a certain amount of time following a fault, the system reaches a configuration where the active stations are all corresponding with each other, i.e. they have all the same membership list. For a more complete description, one can refer to [KG94,BM02].

4.2   Previous Non-automatic Verification of the TTP

There have been lots of studies on the TTP protocol in general, and on its membership algorithm in particular. We start from the work of Merceron and Bouajjani. In [BM02] they propose a family of counter systems abstractions, depending on the number of faults considered. They prove manually that the algorithm is valid for any number of stations N and any number of faults k. Actually they prove more: the algorithm stabilizes within two rounds after the k-ieth fault occurs.

They also try to prove automatically with different tools (LASH and ALV) the correctness of the protocol. For 1 fault and N stations, they verify it in a "user-guided way": they divide the protocol in two submodules. They compute the reachability set of the first submodule and prove automatically a nice property on it (true only for 1 fault). Then they use this property to simplify the computation of the second submodule. For N stations and more than 1 fault, the computation does not terminate.

4.3   Automatic Verification for 1 Fault and N Stations

The model. The abstraction we use was proposed by Merceron and Bouajjani in [BM02]. The corresponding counter system is given in figure 2. N is the number of stations. C_W (resp. C_F) is the number of working (resp. faulty) stations. A fault splits stations into two cliques C_1 and C_0 of stations which only communicate within the same clique. C_p is the number of elapsed slots in the round. It is reseted to 0 when $C_p = N$ (and a new round begins). Variable d (resp. d_0, d_1, d_F) is the number of working stations (resp. in clique 0, in clique 1, faulty) which have emitted a message during the round. The control node **normal** represents the normal behaviour of the system. When a failure occurs, the system moves into the control node **Round1**, and then this round is finished, the system moves into the control node **later**. The property to check is that, two rounds after the failure occurs, valid stations are all communicating with each other, which is expressed by:

$$(P_1)\ \ state = later \wedge C_p = N \Rightarrow (C_1 = 0 \vee C_0 = 0)$$

The translation of this abstraction in counter systems is not direct, because of the nondeterministic affectations from control node **normal** to control node **round1**. The transition from **later** to **normal** indicates that the protocol comes back to the normal behaviour, and that another failure can occur. Fortunately, it is not relevant for our property because we are interested in what happens in control node **later**. Thus we can remove this transition. Then the nondeterministic affectation will happen only once, hence it will be encoded in the initial configuration.

Results. FAST checks *fully automatically* that property P_1 is verified. Tests have been performed on an Intel Pentium 4 at 2.4 GHz with 1 Gbyte of RAM.

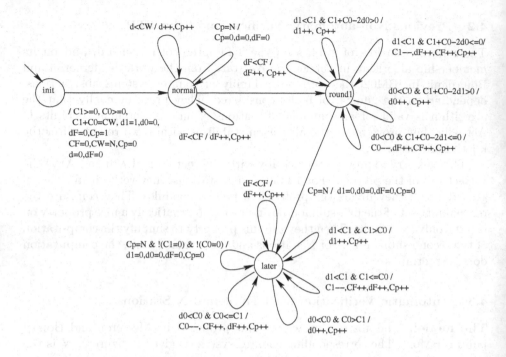

Fig. 2. Counter system for the TTP/C protocol, 1 fault and N stations

Computing the reachability set only requires cycles of length 1. It takes 940 seconds and 73 Mbytes. The reachability set has 27,932 states.

4.4 Abstraction and Automatic Verification for 2 Faults and N Stations

The model. The abstraction proposed in [BM02] for 2 faults is converted into a counter system as in the 1-fault case. The counter system is presented in figure 3. Differences with the 1-fault case are mainly because there are now three different cliques. Moreover the behaviour during the end of $Round_0$, the round where the first failure occurs (this round starts with the first failure) has to be separated from the round $Round_1$ starting with the second failure. The first failure splits stations in cliques C_1 and C_0, then the second failure occurs in C_1 which is split into C_{11} and C_{10}. C_0 becomes C_{00} and C_{01} does not exists. Variables d_0 and d_1 are the number of stations of C_0 and C_1 which have emitted after the first failure and before the second. C_{p1} (resp. C_{p2}) is the number of elapsed slots since the first failure (resp. second failure) occured. Variable d_{00} (resp. d_{10}, d_{11}, d_F) is the number of stations in clique C_{00} (resp. in clique C_{10}, in clique C_{11}, faulty stations) which have emitted a message during the round following the second failure. Variable dA_{00} (resp. dA_{11}, dA_{10}) is the number of stations in clique C_{00} (resp. C_{11}, C_{10}) which have emitted after the end of $Round_0$ and before the end of $Round_1$. Variable dF_{00} (resp. dF_{11}, dF_{10}) is the number of faulty stations in clique C_{00} (resp. C_{11}, C_{10}) whose time slot is elapsed after the end of $Round_0$ and before the end of $Round_1$. The property to check is still the absence of clique, which is expressed by P_2 as follows:

$$(P_2)\ state = later \wedge C_{p2} = N \Rightarrow ((C_{11} \neq 0 \wedge C_{10} = 0 \wedge C_{00} = 0) \vee$$
$$(C_{11} = 0 \wedge C_{10} \neq 0 \wedge C_{00} = 0) \vee (C_{11} = 0 \wedge C_{10} = 0 \wedge C_{00} \neq 0))$$

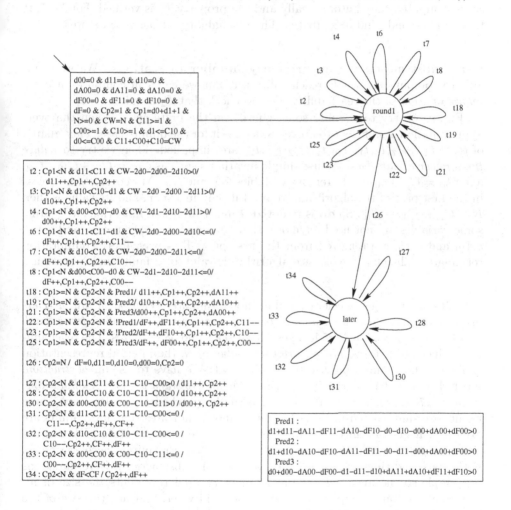

Fig. 3. Counter system for the TTP/C protocol, 2 faults and N stations

Presburger acceleration fails. When accelerating the transitions, the size of the internal automata manipulated by FAST explodes and the tool stops (see section 3). It highlights the complexity of this protocol.

Using polyhedral acceleration for a small number of stations. All the transitions except t_{26} are convex translations. Moreover t_{26} does not need to be accelerated because it is not a loop. Hence polyhedral acceleration can be used instead of the Presburger acceleration technique. FAST manages to compute accelerations of the transitions. Unfortunately, with an arbitrary number of stations, the MONA size limit is exceeded during the reachability set computation and FAST stops. However, when fixing the value of N to 5, the reachability set is computed fully automatically and the property P_2 is verified. For N=5, it takes 446 seconds and 588 Mbytes. The reachability set has 5,684 states.

Using abstraction for an arbitrary number of stations. We were unable to compute the whole reachability set, but we can still compute an *over-approximation* of the reachability set and check that P_2 is valid.

Firstly we try to simplify some guards on the finite case. When the over-approximation is sufficient to prove P_2, we use it for the infinite case. Thus guards of $t_2, t_3, t_4, t_6, t_7, t_8, t_{18}, t_{19}, t_{21}, t_{22}, t_{23}, t_{25}$ are simplified. Then we try to *reduce the number of variables*. We use simple invariants such as $C_W = C_{11} + C_{10} + C_{00}$ and $C_{p1} = C_{p2} + d_0 + d_1$ to remove variables C_W and C_{p1}. Moreover, d_F is useless in the first part of the algorithm, we need it only in `later`, and its value is then $N - C_{11} - C_{00} - C_{10}$. So d_F is removed. Finally after simplifications in guards, some variables are not used anymore. Hence, d_0 and d_1 are removed, and dA_{11}, dA_{10} and dA_{00} are removed from the first part. This way, FAST computation terminates. The clique avoidance algorithm is valid for 2 faults and N stations.

Results. Presburger acceleration does not terminate. With *polyhedral acceleration*, FAST checks *fully automatically* that property P_2 is verified *for a small number of stations*. For N=5 it takes 446 seconds and 588 Mbytes. The reachability set has 5,684 states. For *an arbitrary value of N*, the internal representation explodes when computing the reachability set. We have to use an *abstraction*. FAST checks that property P_2 is verified *for an arbitrary number N of stations*. It takes 175 seconds and 210 Mbytes with the polyhedral acceleration. These results are summarized in table 1. The symbol ↑ indicates that FAST limits are exceeded, hence intermediate automata have more than 2^{24} states. We can notice that polyhedral acceleration works better than Presburger acceleration, in both space and time, except for the last case (the abstraction). Here, functions are simple so the maximal amount of memory used represents the size of intermediate automata representing the reachability set, and not the size of the acceleration relations like in the other examples.

5   Conclusion and Future Work

The polyhedral acceleration appears to be very interesting since it allows to compute acceleration relations for which the Presburger acceleration takes too

Table 1. Benchmark for the verification of the TTP/C with FAST

	Presburger acceleration		polyhedral acceleration		
	time1 seconds	memory1 Mbytes	time2 seconds	memory2 Mbytes	number of states
1 fault, N stations	940	73	600	63	27,932
2 faults, 5 stations	↑	↑	446	588	5,684
2 faults, 10 stations	↑	↑	12,365	588	273,427
2 faults, 15 stations	↑	↑	↑	↑	↑
2 faults, N stations	↑	↑	↑	↑	↑
2 faults, N stations (abstraction)	210	200	175	200	11,036

much memory. We can probably define other acceleration algorithms, more restrictive than Presburger acceleration but more efficient. Another direction is to find a generic acceleration more efficient than the one described here, using smart intermediate computations. Finally, the TTP protocol is a really challenging case-study. Even when the reachability set is computed by FAST, we are never far from the limits of the tool. More efficient Presburger automata libraries, using for example cache systems or modular computation, are necessary to scale up acceleration to wider systems.

References

[AAB00]   A. Annichini, E. Asarin, and A. Bouajjani. Symbolic techniques for parametric reasoning about counter and clock systems. volume 1855, pages 419–434, 2000.
[ALV]   ALV homepage. http://www.cs.ucsb.edu/~bultan/composite/.
[BB02]   C. Bartzis and T. Bultan. Efficient symbolic representations for arithmetic constraints in verification. Technical Report ucsb cs:TR-2002-16, University of California, Santa Barbara, Computer Science, 2002.
[BB03]   C. Bartzis and T. Bultan. Efficient image computation in infinite state model checking. volume 2725, pages 249–261, 2003.
[BC96]   A. Boudet and H. Comon. Diophantine equations, Presburger arithmetic and finite automata. In H. Kirchner, editor, *Proc. Coll. on Trees in Algebra and Programming (CAAP'96)*, volume 1059, pages 30–43, 1996.
[BFLP03] S. Bardin, A. Finkel, J. Leroux, and L. Petrucci. FAST: Fast Acceleration of Symbolic Transition systems. volume 2725, pages 118–121, 2003.
[BM02]   A. Bouajjani and A. Merceron. Parametric verification of a group membership algorithm. volume 2469, pages 311–330, 2002.
[Boi98]   B. Boigelot. *Symbolic Methods for Exploring Infinite State Spaces*. PhD thesis, Université de Liège, 1998.

[BW94]   B. Boigelot and P. Wolper. Symbolic verification with periodic sets. volume 2725, pages 55–67, 1994.

[Del]   G. Delzanno. *Home Page – Giorgio Delzanno.*
            http://www.disi.unige.it/person/DelzannoG/.

[DFS98]   C. Dufourd, A. Finkel, and P. Schnoebelen. Reset nets between decidability and undecidability. In *Proc. 25th Int. Coll. Automata, Languages, and Programming (ICALP'98), Aalborg, Denmark, July 1998*, volume 1443, pages 103–115, 1998.

[EFM99]   J. Esparza, A. Finkel, and R. Mayr. On the verification of broadcast protocols. In *Proc. 14th IEEE Symp. Logic in Computer Science (LICS'99), Trento, Italy, July 1999*, pages 352–359. IEEE Comp. Soc. Press, 1999.

[FAS]   FAST *homepage.* http://www.lsv.ens-cachan.fr/fast/.

[FL02]   A. Finkel and J. Leroux. How to compose Presburger-accelerations: Applications to broadcast protocols. volume 2556, pages 145–156, 2002.

[KG94]   H. Kopetz and G. Grünsteidl. A time trigerred protocol for fault-tolerant real-time systems. In *IEEE computer*, volume January, pages 14–23, 1994.

[LAS]   LASH *homepage.*
            http://www.montefiore.ulg.ac.be/~boigelot/research/lash/.

[Ler03a]   J. Leroux. *Algorithmique de la vérification des systèmes à compteurs. Approximation et accélération. Implémentation de l'outil* FAST. PhD thesis, École Normale Supérieure de Cachan, 12th december 2003.

[Ler03b]   J. Leroux. The affine hull of a binary automaton is computable in polynomial time. 2003.

[MON]   *The* MONA *project.* http://www.brics.dk/mona/.

[TRE]   TREX *homepage.* http://www.liafa.jussieu.fr/~sighirea/trex/.

[WB00]   P. Wolper and B. Boigelot. On the construction of automata from linear arithmetic constraints. volume 1785, pages 1–19, 2000.

From Complementation to Certification

Orna Kupferman[1]* and Moshe Y. Vardi[2]**

[1] Hebrew University, School of Engineering and Computer Science, Jerusalem 91904, Israel
orna@cs.huji.ac.il, http://www.cs.huji.ac.il/~orna
[2] Rice University, Department of Computer Science, Houston, TX 77251-1892, U.S.A.
vardi@cs.rice.edu, http://www.cs.rice.edu/~vardi

Abstract. In the automata-theoretic approach to model checking we check the emptiness of the product of a system S with an automaton $\mathcal{A}_{\neg\psi}$ for the complemented specification. This gives rise to two automata-theoretic problems: *complementation* of word automata, which is used in order to generate $\mathcal{A}_{\neg\psi}$, and the *emptiness* problem, to which model checking is reduced. Both problems have numerous other applications, and have been extensively studied for nondeterministic Büchi word automata (NBW). Nondeterministic *generalized* Büchi word automata (NGBW) have become popular in specification and verification and are now used in applications traditionally assigned to NBW. This is due to their richer acceptance condition, which leads to automata with fewer states and a simpler underlying structure.

In this paper we analyze runs of NGBW and use the analysis in order to describe a new complementation construction and a symbolic emptiness algorithm for NGBW. The complementation construction exponentially improves the best known construction for NGBW and is easy to implement. The emptiness algorithm is almost identical to a known variant of the Emerson-Lei algorithm, and our contribution is the strong relation we draw between the complementation construction and the emptiness algorithm – both naturally follow from the analysis of the runs, which easily implies their correctness. This relation leads to a new *certified* model-checking procedure, where a positive answer to the model-checking query is accompanied by a certificate whose correctness can be checked by methods independent of the model checker. Unlike certificates generated in previous works on certified model checking, our analysis enables us to generate a certificate that can be checked automatically and symbolically.

1 Introduction

In *model checking*, we check whether all the computations of a given system S satisfy a specification ψ. The system is usually given as a labeled state-transition graph and ψ is a formula in LTL or a word automaton. In the automata-theoretic approach to model checking [Kur94b,VW94], one constructs an automaton $\mathcal{A}_{\neg\psi}$ for the negation of ψ and takes its product with S. The system S is correct with respect to ψ if this product is empty.

---

* Supported in part by BSF grant 9800096, and by a grant from Minerva.
** Supported in part by NSF grants CCR-9988322, CCR-0124077, CCR-0311326, IIS-9908435, and IIS-9978135, by BSF grant 9800096, and by a grant from the Intel Corporation.

K. Jensen and A. Podelski (Eds.): TACAS 2004, LNCS 2988, pp. 591–606, 2004.
© Springer-Verlag Berlin Heidelberg 2004

When ψ is given as an LTL formula, the construction of $\mathcal{A}_{\neg\psi}$ is relatively straight-forward, we first negate ψ and then apply on $\neg\psi$ one of the many known translations of LTL formulas to word automata (cf. [VW94,GPVW95,SB00]). When the specification is given as an automaton $\mathcal{A}_{\psi}$, the task is harder and one needs to complement the automaton. The product of $\mathcal{A}_{\neg\psi}$ and S can be viewed as a word automaton $\mathcal{A}_{S \times \neg\psi}$, and it is empty iff no computation of S violates ψ. Thus, the model-checking problem gives rise to two automata-theoretic problems: *complementation* of word automata, which is used in order to generate $\mathcal{A}_{\neg\psi}$ from $\mathcal{A}_{\psi}$, and the *emptiness* problem, to which model checking is reduced. Both problems have numerous other applications. First, refinement and optimization techniques that are based on language containment rather than simulation involve complementation and emptiness [Kur94a]. In addition, complementation is used in specification formalisms like ETL [Wol83,VW94], which have automata within the logic, and emptiness is used for satisfiability, planning and synthesis [Büc62,GV00, MW84].

Complementation and emptiness have been extensively studied for *nondeterministic Büchi word automata* (NBW, for short). The Büchi acceptance condition consists of a subset F of the state space, and a run of the automaton is accepting iff it visits F infinitely often. Consider an NBW $\mathcal{A}$ with n states. In [Büc62], Büchi described a doubly-exponential complementation construction, which was improved in [SVW87] to a construction with $2^{O(n^2)}$ states. Only in [Saf88], Safra introduced an asymptotically optimal determinization construction, which also enabled a $2^{O(n \log n)}$ complementation construction, matching the known lower bound [Mic88]. Another $2^{O(n \log n)}$ construction was suggested in [Kla91], which circumvents the need for determinization. The optimal constructions in [Saf88,Kla91] are complicated, making their implementation very difficult [THB95]. In [KV01b], we suggested an optimal complementation construction that is based on alternating automata. This construction is considerably simpler, making it the first construction to be implemented [Mer00,GKSV03]. The emptiness problem for NBW can be easily solved in linear time and NLOGSPACE [VW94]. The easy algorithms, however, are based on depth-first search, and cannot be implemented symbolically, which is very desirable in practice. Emerson and Lei's algorithm for evaluation of μ-calculus formulas suggests a quadratic symbolic algorithm for the problem [EL86], and many variants of it have been suggested and studied (cf. [HTKB92,HKSV97, KPR98]). More involved algorithms with only $O(n \log n)$ [BGS00] and $O(n)$ [GPP03] symbolic steps are known too, but it is not clear that these algorithms are better in practice then the Emerson-Lei algorithm [RBS00].

The *generalized Büchi* acceptance condition consists of a set $\{F_1, \ldots, F_k\}$ of subsets of the state space, and a run of the automaton is accepting iff it visits F_i infinitely often, for all $1 \le i \le k$. The number k of sets is the *index* of the automaton. The richer acceptance condition leads to automata with fewer states and simpler underlying structure. For example, the traditional translation of an LTL formula ψ to an NBW results in an automaton with state space $2^{cl(\psi)} \times 2^{cl(\psi)}$ [VW94]; the set $cl(\psi)$ is the set of ψ's subformulas and each state consists of a "local component", which checks satisfaction of local requirements and an "eventuality component", which checks satisfaction of eventualities. Using the generalized Büchi condition, it is easier to handle the different eventuality requirements, there is no need to the eventuality component, and the state space of the automaton is $2^{cl(\psi)}$ [GPVW95]. Nondeterministic generalized Büchi word automata (NGBW, for short) have become popular in specification and verification and are now used in applications traditionally assigned to NBW [Kur94b]. Once the NGBW is constructed, it is easy to translate it to an equivalent NBW, and then apply the known algorithms for NBW. For an NGBW with n states and index k, the constructed NBW has $O(nk)$ states [Cho74].

In this paper we analyze runs of NGBW, and use the analysis in order to suggest a new complementation construction and a symbolic emptiness algorithm for them. Recall that an NGBW $\mathcal{A}$ rejects a word w if every run of $\mathcal{A}$ has a set F_i in the acceptance condition that is visited only finitely often. The runs of $\mathcal{A}$ can be arranged in a DAG (directed acyclic graph). We show that $\mathcal{A}$ rejects w iff it is possible to label the vertices of the DAG by ranks so that some local conditions on the ranks of vertices and their successors are met. Intuitively, the ranks measure the distance from a position from which no states in F_i are visited.

The complementation construction that follows from the analysis results in an NBW with $2^{O(n \log nk)}$ states. This exponentially improves current complementation constructions, which first translate the NGBW into an NBW with $O(nk)$ states, and ends up in an NBW with $2^{O(nk \log nk)}$ states. Like the construction in [KV01b], our construction is simple and easy to implement. The extension of the reasoning in [KV01b] to NGBW is not trivial and was left open in [GKSV03]. (A trivial extension of [KV01b] to NGBW does exists, but results in an NBW with $2^{O(nk \log nk)}$ states. The technical achievement of the construction here is a simultaneous handling of all the sets in the acceptance condition, which is the key to the improved complexity.) The emptiness algorithm that follows from the analysis is almost identical to the OWCTY algorithm of [FFK+01] for symbolic detection of bad cycles. Our contribution is the strong relation we draw between the complementation construction and the emptiness algorithm – both naturally follow from the analysis of the runs, which easily implies their correctness.

Beyond the theoretical contribution of the relation between complementation and emptiness, it gives rise to a new *certified* model-checking procedure. As discussed in [Nam01,PPZ01,PZ01], it is desirable to accompany a positive answer of a model checker by a proof whose correctness can be verified by methods that are independent of the model checker. As in the case of proof-carrying codes (cf. [Nec97]), such a proof certifies that the systems was verified, and checking the certificate is much easier than the original verification task. In addition, as in the case of a counterexample that is returned to the user when model checking fails, the proof explains why model checking succeeds and leads to a better understanding of the system. For a discussion of other applications of certificates, see [Nam01].

Recall that model checking is reduced to checking the emptiness of the product $\mathcal{A}_{S \times \neg \psi}$ of the system S and the complemented specification $\mathcal{A}_{\neg \psi}$. We show that the ranks we associate with the vertices in the run DAG of $\mathcal{A}_{S \times \neg \psi}$ constitute a certificate that the product of S and $\mathcal{A}_{\neg \psi}$ is indeed empty. Moreover, by adding to our symbolic emptiness algorithm an algebraic decision diagram (ADD) that maintains the ranks, the certificate is generated symbolically (ADDs extend OBDDs by allowing the leaves to have values from arbitrary domains, thus they maintain functions that are not necessarily Boolean. Thus, while OBDDs represent Boolean functions, ADDs represent pseudo-

Boolean functions [BFG+97].) Once the certificate is generated, it can be easily checked, automatically and symbolically, or manually, and it involves only local checks and no fixed points. Unlike the certificates in [Nam01,PPZ01,PZ01], whose goal is to provide the user with a deductive proof to ponder, our goal is to generate a compact certificate that can be verified automatically. Since a deductive proof usually consists of a long list of assertions, we believe that machine-checkable certificates are more appropriate in the verification of large systems. The generation of certificates that can be checked automatically is possible thanks to the analysis of runs, which bounds the domain of the well-founded sets that are used in the deductive certificates generated in previous works. As explained in Section 6, our method can generate, for users that are interested in a manual check, also "list-based" proofs.

2   Preliminaries

A *word automaton* is $\mathcal{A} = \langle \Sigma, Q, \delta, Q_{in}, \alpha \rangle$, where Σ is the input alphabet, Q is a finite set of states, $\delta : Q \times \Sigma \to 2^Q$ is a transition function, $Q_{in} \subseteq Q$ is a set of initial states, and α is an acceptance condition that defines a subset of Q^ω. Given an input word $w = \sigma_0 \cdot \sigma_1 \cdots$ in Σ^ω, a *run* of $\mathcal{A}$ on w is a word $r = q_0, q_1, \ldots$ in Q^ω such that $q_0 \in Q_{in}$ and for every $i \geq 0$, we have $q_{i+1} \in \delta(q_i, \sigma_i)$. Since the transition function may specify many possible transitions for each state and letter, $\mathcal{A}$ may have several runs on w. A run is accepting iff it satisfies the acceptance condition α. We consider here the *generalized Büchi* acceptance condition, where $\alpha = \{F_1, \ldots, F_k\}$ is a set of subsets of Q. The number k of sets is the *index* of α) (or $\mathcal{A}$). For a run r, let $inf(r)$ denote the set of states that r visits infinitely often. That is, $inf(r) = \{q \in Q : q_i = q \text{ for infinitely many } i \geq 0\}$. As Q is finite, it is guaranteed that $inf(r) \neq \emptyset$. A run r is accepting iff $inf(r) \cap F_j \neq \emptyset$ for all $1 \leq j \leq k$. That is, r is accepting if every set in α is visited infinitely often. The *generalized co-Büchi* acceptance condition dualizes the generalized Büchi condition. Thus, again $\alpha = \{F_1, F_2, \ldots, F_k\}$ is a set of subsets of Q, but a run r is accepting if $inf(r) \cap F_j = \emptyset$ for some $1 \leq j \leq k$. Thus, r visits some set in α only finitely often.

If the automaton $\mathcal{A}$ is *nondeterministic*, then it accepts an input word w iff it has an accepting run on w. If $\mathcal{A}$ is *universal*, then it accepts w iff all its runs on w are accepting. The *language* of $\mathcal{A}$, denoted $\mathcal{L}(\mathcal{A})$ is the set of words that $\mathcal{A}$ accepts. Dualizing a nondeterministic generalized Büchi automaton (NGBW) amounts to viewing it as a universal generalized co-Büchi automaton (UGCW). It is easy to see that by dualizing $\mathcal{A}$, we get an automaton that accepts its complementary language. Note that nondeterministic Büchi automata (NBW) are a special case of NGBW, with $k = 1$.

In the linear-time approach to model checking, we check whether all the computations of a given system S satisfy a specification ψ. The system is usually given as a labeled state-transition graph and ψ is either a formula in LTL or a word automaton (traditionally, NBW or NGBW). LTL formulas can be translated to word automata. The original translation in [VW94] uses NBW. More recent translations use NGBW. For example, it is shown in [GPVW95] that an LTL formula ψ of length m can be translated to an NGBW $\mathcal{A}_\psi$ that accepts exactly all the words that satisfy ψ. The automaton $\mathcal{A}_\psi$ has $2^{O(m)}$ states and index m.

3   Ranks for UGCW

Let $\mathcal{A} = \langle \Sigma, Q, Q_{in}, \delta, \alpha \rangle$ be a universal co-Büchi automaton with $\alpha = \{F_1, \ldots, F_k\}$. Let $|Q| = n$. The runs of $\mathcal{A}$ on a word $w = \sigma_0 \cdot \sigma_1 \cdots$ can be arranged in an infinite DAG (directed acyclic graph) $G_r = \langle V, E \rangle$, where

- $V \subseteq Q \times \mathbb{N}$ is such that $\langle q, l \rangle \in V$ iff some run of $\mathcal{A}$ on w has $q_l = q$. For example, the first level of G_r contains the vertices $Q_{in} \times \{0\}$.
- $E \subseteq \bigcup_{l \geq 0}(Q \times \{l\}) \times (Q \times \{l+1\})$ is such that $E(\langle q, l \rangle, \langle q', l+1 \rangle)$ iff $\langle q, l \rangle \in V$ and $q' \in \delta(q, \sigma_l)$.

Thus, G_r embodies exactly all the runs of $\mathcal{A}$ on w. We call G_r the *run* DAG of $\mathcal{A}$ on w. For a set $F \subseteq Q$, we say that a vertex $\langle q, l \rangle$ in G_r is an *F-vertex* iff $q \in F$. We say that G_r is *accepting* if each path π in G_r has an index $1 \leq j \leq k$ such that π contains only finitely many F_j-vertices. It is easy to see that $\mathcal{A}$ accepts w iff G_r is accepting.

Let $[2n]$ denote the set $\{0, 1, \ldots, 2n\}$, and let $[2n]^{odd}$ and $[2n]^{even}$ denote the set of odd and even members of $[2n]$, respectively. Also, let $R = [2n]^{even} \cup ([2n]^{odd} \times \{1, \ldots, k\})$, and $\leq$ be the lexicographical order on the elements of R. We refer to the members of R in $[2n]^{even}$ as *even ranks* and refer to the members of R in $[2n]^{odd} \times \{j\}$ as *odd ranks with index j*.

A *ranking* for G_r is a function $f : V \to R$ that satisfies the following conditions:

1. For all vertices $\langle q, l \rangle \in V$, if $f(\langle q, l \rangle) = \langle 2i+1, j \rangle$, then $q \notin F_j$.
2. For all edges $\langle \langle q, l \rangle, \langle q', l+1 \rangle \rangle \in E$, we have $f(\langle q', l+1 \rangle) \leq f(\langle q, l \rangle)$.

Thus, a ranking associates with each vertex in G_r a rank in R so that ranks along paths decrease monotonically, and F_j-vertices cannot get an odd rank with index j. Note that each path in G_r eventually gets trapped in some rank. We say that the ranking f is an *odd ranking* if all the paths of G_r eventually get trapped in an odd rank. Formally, f is odd iff for all paths $\langle q_0, 0 \rangle, \langle q_1, 1 \rangle, \langle q_2, 2 \rangle, \ldots$ in G_r, there is $l \geq 0$ such that $f(\langle q_l, l \rangle)$ is odd, and for all $l' \geq l$, we have $f(\langle q_{l'}, l' \rangle) = f(\langle q_l, l \rangle)$. Note that, equivalently, f is odd if every path of G_r has infinitely many vertices with odd ranks.

In the rest of this section we prove that G_r is accepting iff it has an odd ranking. Consider a (possibly finite) DAG $G \subseteq G_r$. We say that a vertex $\langle q, l \rangle$ is *finite* in G iff only finitely many vertices in G are reachable from $\langle q, l \rangle$. For a set $F \subseteq Q$, we say that a vertex $\langle q, l \rangle$ is *F-free* in G iff all the vertices in G that are reachable from $\langle q, l \rangle$ are not F-vertices. Note that, in particular, $\langle q, l \rangle$ is not an F-vertex.

We define an infinite sequence of DAGs $G_0 \supseteq G_1 \supseteq G_1^1 \supseteq \ldots G_1^k \supseteq G_3 \supseteq G_3^1 \supseteq \ldots G_3^k \supseteq G_5 \ldots$ as follows. To simplify notations, we sometimes refer to G_{2i+1}^{k+1} as G_{2i+2} and refer to G_{2i+1} as G_{2i+1}^1. Thus, $G_1^1 = G_1$, $G_2 = G_1^{k+1}$, $G_3^1 = G_3$, $G_4 = G_3^{k+1}$, and so on.

- $G_0 = G_r$.
- $G_{2i+1} = G_{2i} \setminus \{\langle q, l \rangle \mid \langle q, l \rangle$ is finite in $G_{2i}\}$.
- $G_{2i+1}^{j+1} = G_{2i+1}^j \setminus \{\langle q, l \rangle \mid \langle q, l \rangle$ is F_j-free in $G_{2i+1}^j\}$, for $1 \leq j \leq k$.

Lemma 1. *For every $i \geq 0$, there exists l_i such that for all $l \geq l_i$, there are at most $n - i$ vertices of the form $\langle q, l \rangle$ in G_{2i}.*

Proof: We prove the lemma by an induction on i. The case where $i = 0$ follows from the definition of G_0. Indeed, in G_r all levels $l \geq 0$ have at most n vertices of the form $\langle q, l \rangle$. Assume that the lemma's requirement holds for i, we prove it for $i+1$. Consider the DAG G_{2i}. We distinguish between two cases. First, if G_{2i} is finite, then G_{2i+1} is empty, G_{2i+2} is empty as well, and we are done. Otherwise, we claim that there must be some F_j-free vertex in G_{2i+1}^j, for some $1 \leq j \leq k$. To see this, assume, by way of contradiction, that G_{2i} is infinite and all the vertices in G_{2i+1}^j are not F_j-free, for all $1 \leq j \leq k$. Note that then $G_{2i+1}^j = G_{2i+1}$ for all $1 \leq j \leq k$. Thus, all the vertices in G_{2i+1} are not F_j-free, for all $1 \leq j \leq k$. Since G_{2i} is infinite, G_{2i+1} is also infinite. Also, each vertex in G_{2i+1} has at least one successor. Consider some vertex $\langle q_0, l_0 \rangle$ in G_{2i+1}. Since, by the assumption, it is not F_1-free, there exists an F_1-vertex $\langle q_0', l_0' \rangle$ reachable from $\langle q_0, l_0 \rangle$. Let $\langle q_1, l_1 \rangle$ be a successor of $\langle q_0', l_0' \rangle$. By the assumption, $\langle q_1, l_1 \rangle$ is not F_2-free. Hence, there exists an F_2-vertex $\langle q_1', l_1' \rangle$ reachable from $\langle q_1, l_1 \rangle$. Let $\langle q_2, q_2 \rangle$ be a successor of $\langle q_1', l_1' \rangle$. By the assumption, $\langle q_2, l_2 \rangle$ is not F_3-free. Thus, we can continue similarly and construct an infinite sequence of vertices $\langle q_h, l_h \rangle$ and $\langle q_h', l_h' \rangle$ such that for all h, the vertex $\langle q_h', l_h' \rangle$ is a $F_{(h \bmod k)+1}$-vertex reachable from $\langle q_h, l_h \rangle$, and $\langle q_{h+1}, l_{h+1} \rangle$ is a successor of $\langle q_h', l_h' \rangle$. Such a sequence, however, corresponds to a path in G_r that visits F_j infinitely often, for all $1 \leq j \leq k$, contradicting the assumption that G_r is accepting.

So, let j be the minimal index for which there is an F_j-free vertex in G_{2i+1}^j, and let $\langle q, l \rangle$ be such a vertex. By the minimality of j, we have that G_{2i+1}^j is equal to G_{2i+1}, and it contains no finite vertices. Hence, every F_j-free vertex in G_{2i+1}^j has a successor, which is also F_j-free, thus we can assume without loss of generality that $l \geq l_i$. We claim that taking $l_{i+1} = l$ satisfies the lemma's requirement. That is, we claim that for all $x \geq l$, there are at most $n - (i+1)$ vertices of the form $\langle q, x \rangle$ in G_{2i+2}. Recall that $\langle q, l \rangle$ is not finite in G_{2i}. Thus, there are infinitely many vertices in G_{2i} that are reachable from $\langle q, l \rangle$. Hence, by König's Lemma, G_{2i} contains an infinite path $\langle q, l \rangle, \langle q_1, l+1 \rangle, \langle q_2, l+2 \rangle, \ldots$. For all $x \geq 1$, the vertex $\langle q_x, l+x \rangle$ has infinitely many vertices reachable from it in G_{2i} and thus, it is not finite in G_{2i}. Therefore, the path $\langle q, l \rangle, \langle q_1, l+1 \rangle, \langle q_2, l+2 \rangle, \ldots$ exists also in G_{2i+1}. Recall that $\langle q, l \rangle$ is F_j-free in G_{2i+1}^j. Hence, being reachable from $\langle q, l \rangle$, all the vertices $\langle q_x, l+x \rangle$ on the path are F_j-free as well. Therefore, they are not in G_{2i+1}^{j+1}. It follows that for all $x \geq l$, the number of vertices of the form $\langle q, x \rangle$ in G_{2i+1}^{j+1} (and hence also in G_{2i+2}) is strictly smaller than their number in G_{2i}. Hence, by the induction hypothesis, we are done.   □

Lemma 1 implies that G_{2n} is finite, and G_{2n+1} is empty.

Each vertex $\langle q, l \rangle$ in G_r has a unique $i \geq 1$ such that $\langle q, l \rangle$ is either finite in G_{2i} or F_j-free in G_{2i+1}^j, for some $1 \leq j \leq k$. This induces a function $f : V \to R$ defined as follows.

$$f(\langle q, l \rangle) = \begin{bmatrix} 2i & \text{If } \langle q, l \rangle \text{ is finite in } G_{2i}. \\ \langle 2i+1, j \rangle & \text{If } \langle q, l \rangle \text{ is } F_j\text{-free in } G_{2i+1}^j. \end{bmatrix}$$

For an odd rank $\eta = \langle 2i+1, j \rangle$, we refer to G_{2i+1}^j as G_η.

Lemma 2. *For every vertex $\langle q, l \rangle$ in G_r and $\eta \in R$, if $\langle q, l \rangle \notin G_\eta$, then $f(\langle q, l \rangle) < r$.*

Lemma 3. *For every two vertices $\langle q, l \rangle$ and $\langle q', l' \rangle$ in G_r, if $\langle q', l' \rangle$ is reachable from $\langle q, l \rangle$, then $f(\langle q', l' \rangle) \leq f(\langle q, l \rangle)$.*

Lemma 4. *For every infinite path in G_r, there exists an index $1 \leq j \leq k$ and a vertex $\langle q, l \rangle$ with an odd rank with index j such that all the vertices $\langle q', l' \rangle$ on the path that are reachable from $\langle q, l \rangle$ have $f(\langle q', l' \rangle) = f(\langle q, l \rangle)$.*

The proofs of Lemmas 2, 3, and 4 appear in the full version. We can now conclude with Theorem 1 below.

Theorem 1. G_r *is accepting iff it has an odd ranking.*

Proof: Assume first that there is an odd ranking for G_r. Then, every path in G_r eventually gets trapped in some odd rank $\langle 2i + 1, j \rangle$. Hence, as F_j-vertices cannot get this rank, the path visits F_j only finitely often, and we are done.

For the other direction, note that Lemma 3, together with the fact that a vertex gets an odd rank with index j only if it is F_j-free, imply that the function f described above is a ranking. Lemma 4 then implies that the ranking is odd.   □

We note that the reasoning above is similar to the one described for co-Büchi automata in [KV01b]. The extension to the case of generalized co-Büchi is not trivial and involves a refinement of the DAG G_{2i+2}. In particular, the minimality of j in the proof of Lemma 1 is crucial for its correctness.

4   Complementation of NGBW

Theorem 1 implies that a UGCW $\mathcal{A}$ accepts a word w iff there is an odd ranking for the run DAG G_r of $\mathcal{A}$ on w – a ranking in which every infinite path in G_r has infinitely many vertices with an odd rank. Intuitively, the theorem suggests that the requirements imposed by the generalized co-Büchi condition (finitely often, for some set in α) can be reduced to a new condition of a simpler type (infinitely often, for vertices with an odd rank). Recall that by dualizing an NGBW, we get a UGCW for the complementary language. Theorem 1 enables us to translate this UGCW to an NBW, resulting in the complementation construction described below.

Theorem 2. *Let $\mathcal{A}$ be an NGBW with n states and index k. There is an NBW $\mathcal{A}'$ with $2^{O(n \log kn)}$ states such that $\mathcal{L}(\mathcal{A}') = \Sigma^\omega \setminus \mathcal{L}(\mathcal{A})$.*

Proof: Let $\tilde{A}$ be the UGCW that dualizes $\mathcal{A}$. The UGCW $\tilde{A}$ accepts exactly all words rejected by $\mathcal{A}$. We obtain $\mathcal{A}'$ by translating $\tilde{A}$ to an NBW. When $\mathcal{A}'$ reads a word w, it guesses a ranking for the run DAG G_r of $\tilde{A}$ on w. At a given point of a run of $\mathcal{A}'$, it keeps in its memory a whole level of G_r and a guess for the ranks of the vertices at this level. In order to check that the ranking is odd, $\mathcal{A}'$ keeps track of states that owe a visit to vertices with odd ranks.

Before we define $\mathcal{A}'$, we first need some notations. A *level ranking* for $\mathcal{A}$ is a function $g : Q \rightarrow R$, such that if $g(q)$ is odd with index j, then $q \notin F_j$. Let $\mathcal{R}$ be the set of all level rankings[1]. For $S \subseteq Q$ and a letter σ, let $\delta(S, \sigma) = \bigcup_{s \in S} \delta(s, \sigma)$. Note that if level $l - 1$ in G_r contains the states in S, and the l-th letter in w is σ, then level l of G_r contains the states in $\delta(S, \sigma)$. For two level rankings g and g' in $\mathcal{R}$ and a letter σ, we say that g' *covers* $\langle g, \sigma \rangle$ if for all q and q' in Q, if $q' \in \delta(q, \sigma)$, then $g'(q') \leq g(q)$. Thus, if g describes the ranks of the vertices of level $l - 1$, and the l-th letter in w is σ, then g' is a possible level ranking for level l. Finally, for $g \in \mathcal{R}$, let $odd(g) = \{q : g(q) \in [2n]^{odd} \times \{1, \dots, k\}\}$. Thus, $odd(g)$ contains states to which g gives an odd rank.

Let $\mathcal{A} = \langle \Sigma, Q, q_{in}, \delta, \alpha \rangle$. Then $\mathcal{A}' = \langle \Sigma, Q', q'_{in}, \delta', \alpha' \rangle$, where

- $Q' = 2^Q \times 2^Q \times \mathcal{R}$. A state $\langle S, O, g \rangle \in Q'$ indicates that the current level of the DAG contains the states in S and the guessed level ranking for the current level is g. The set $O \subseteq S$ contains states along paths that have not visited a vertex with an odd rank since the last time O has been empty.
- $q'_{in} = \langle \{q_{in}\}, \emptyset, f_{in} \rangle$, where $f_{in}(q) = 2n$ for all $q \in Q$.
- δ' is defined, for all $\langle S, O, g \rangle \in Q'$ and $\sigma \in \Sigma$, as follows.
  - If $O \neq \emptyset$, then $\delta'(\langle S, O, g \rangle, \sigma) = \{\langle \delta(S, \sigma), \delta(O, \sigma) \setminus odd(g'), g' \rangle : g' \text{ covers } \langle g, \sigma \rangle\}$.
  - If $O = \emptyset$, then $\delta'(\langle S, O, g \rangle, \sigma) = \{\langle \delta(S, \sigma), \delta(S, \sigma) \setminus odd(g'), g' \rangle : g' \text{ covers } \langle g, \sigma \rangle\}$.
- $\alpha' = 2^Q \times \{\emptyset\} \times \mathcal{R}$.

Thus, when $\mathcal{A}'$ reads the l-th letter in the input, it guesses the level ranking for level l in the run DAG. This level ranking should cover the level ranking of level $l - 1$. In addition, in the O component, $\mathcal{A}'$ keeps track of states along paths that owe a visit to a vertex with an odd rank. When all the paths of the DAG have visited a vertex with an odd rank, the set O becomes empty, and is initiated according to the states in the current level and its ranking. The acceptance condition then checks that there are infinitely many levels in which O become empty.

Since there are at most $(k(2n + 1))^n$ level rankings, the number of states in $\mathcal{A}'$ is at most $2^{2n} \cdot (k(2n + 1))^n = 2^{O(n \log kn)}$. □

Note that the previous complementation construction for NGBW involves a $2^{O(nk \log nk)}$ blow up, as they first translate the NGBW into an NBW with $O(nk)$ states, and complementing an NBW with m states results in an NBW with $2^{O(m \log m)}$ states [Saf88,Mic88]. Thus, our construction exponentially improves the previous construction.

5   Model Checking

Recall that the model-checking problem is reduced to the emptiness problem of an NGBW $\mathcal{A}_{S \times \neg \psi}$ over a single-letter alphabet. Equivalently, we can check the nonemptiness of the UGCW $\tilde{\mathcal{A}}_{S \times \neg \psi}$ that dualizes $\mathcal{A}_{S \times \neg \psi}$. Indeed, since $\mathcal{A}_{S \times \neg \psi}$ has a single-letter alphabet, it is empty iff $\tilde{\mathcal{A}}_{S \times \neg \psi}$ is not empty (see also [MP87]).

---

[1] When we refer to level rankings, we only care for the ranks of a subset of Q (the set of states that appear in the corresponding level). For technical convenience, we let g range on all states.

In this section we describe a symbolic algorithm for UGCW non-emptiness. The algorithm is induced by the analysis in Section 3, and its correctness follows immediately from Theorem 1. The algorithm is a variant of Emerson-Lei algorithm and is similar to the OWCTY algorithm of [FFK$^+$01] for detecting bad-cycles (see also [HTKB92, KPR98]). The tight relation between the complementation construction and the emptiness procedure is very interesting, as it shows that progress in the emptiness procedure can be measured by means of the ranks that are used in the construction of the complementary automaton. As we describe in the next section, this observation gives rise to a new *certified* model-checking procedure.

Consider a single-letter UGCW $\mathcal{A} = \langle \{a\}, Q, \delta, Q_{in}, \alpha \rangle$. The analysis in Section 3 associates ranks with members of the infinite set $Q \times \mathbb{N}$. On the other hand, nonemptiness algorithms handle the finite state set Q. Accordingly, we first associate ranks with states:

Lemma 5. *Consider a UGCW $\mathcal{A}$ over a single-letter alphabet. Then, for every state q of $\mathcal{A}$, all the vertices in $\{q\} \times \mathbb{N}$ have the same rank.*

Proof: Consider a state q and two levels l_1 and l_2 such that $\langle q, l_1 \rangle$ and $\langle q, l_2 \rangle$ are vertices in G_r. Recall that the DAG G_r embodies all the runs of $\mathcal{A}$ on the input word. Since $\mathcal{A}$ is a single-letter UGCW, the sub-DAG with root $\langle q, l_1 \rangle$ coincides with the sub-DAG with root $\langle q, l_2 \rangle$. Indeed, both embody exactly all the runs of $\mathcal{A}$ with initial state q on a^ω. Thus, all the sub-DAGs of G_r with roots in $\{q\} \times \mathbb{N}$ coincide. Hence, it is easy to prove by an induction on $r \in R$ that for all states q and $r \in R$, either all vertices in $\{q\} \times \mathbb{N}$ get rank r, or no vertex in $\{q\} \times \mathbb{N}$ gets rank r. $\qquad\square$

For a state q of $\mathcal{A}$, the *rank of q*, denoted $rank(q)$, is the rank of the vertices $\{q\} \times \mathbb{N}$ in G_r. We are now ready to describe the nonemptiness procedure that follows. The procedure, described in Figure 1, gets as input the UGCW $\mathcal{A}$ and calculates the set b of all the states q such that $\mathcal{A}$ with initial state q is empty. The UGCW $\mathcal{A}$ is then not empty iff $Q_{in} \cap b = \emptyset$. The algorithm uses the following set-based operations (all easily implemented by means of OBDDs).

- The operator $pre : 2^Q \rightarrow 2^Q$. Given a set of states γ, the set $pre(\gamma)$ contains all states that have an immediate successor in γ. Formally, $q \in pre(\gamma)$ iff $\delta(q, a) \cap \gamma \neq \emptyset$ (in temporal logic, $q \models EX\gamma$).
- The operator $until : 2^Q \times 2^Q \rightarrow 2^Q$. Given two sets of states η and γ, the set $until(\eta, \gamma)$ contains all states that reach a state in $\gamma \cap \eta$ via states in η. Formally, $q \in until(\eta, \gamma)$ iff there are $q_0, \ldots, q_l$ such that $q_0 = q$, for all $0 \leq i < l$, we have that $q_{i+1} \in \delta(q_i, a)$ and $q_i \in \eta$, and $q_l \in \eta \cap \gamma$ (in temporal logic, $q \models E\eta U(\eta \wedge \gamma)$). Note that the operator $until$ can be implemented by repeatedly applying the pre and intersection operators, until a fixpoint is reached.

Note that the set b is monotonically decreasing during the execution of the procedure NonEmpty. Intuitively, b contains all states that have not yet been ranked. At initialization, b contains all the states, and in each iteration it is intersected with some set. We say that a state q is removed from b in iteration $i[0]$ if q is removed from b during the internal while loop of the i-th external while loop. We say that q is removed from b in iteration $(i[1], j)$ if q is removed from b during the j-th internal for loop of the i-th external while loop. Lemma 6 then follows directly from the definition of ranks.

---

procedure NonEmpty($\mathcal{A}$)
  $b := Q$;
  while b changes **do**
    while b changes **do** $b := b \cap pre(b)$;
    for $j = 1 \ldots k$ **do** $b := b \cap until(b, F_j)$;
  if $Q_{in} \cap b = \emptyset$ **then return**("not empty") **else return**("empty");

Fig. 1. A nonemptiness procedure.

Lemma 6. *Consider a state q in $\mathcal{A}$.*

– *The state q is removed from b in iteration $i[0]$ iff $rank(q) = 2i$.*
– *The state q is removed from b in iteration $(i[1], j)$ iff $rank(q) = \langle 2i + 1, j \rangle$.*

By Lemma 6, a state q is removed from b during the execution of the procedure if it has a well-defined rank, which holds, by Theorem 1, if $\mathcal{A}$ with initial state q is not empty. Thus, Lemma 6, together with the analysis in Section 3, naturally induce the algorithm and immediately imply its correctness. (The only, minor, difference between our algorithm and the OWCTY algorithm [FFK$^+$01], is that in our algorithm the internal while loop precedes the internal for loop, rather than the other way around. Since the purpose of the internal while loop is to eliminates quickly states that cannot be on a cycle, it makes sense to apply it as soon as possible.)

Remark 1. When ψ is a safety property, the automaton $\mathcal{A}_\psi$ is a looping automaton (all infinite runs are accepting), and the automaton $\mathcal{A}_{\neg\psi}$ can be defined as a nondeterministic automaton on finite words [Sis94,KV01a]. Thus, a runs of $\mathcal{A}_{\neg\psi}$ is accepting iff it reaches a set F of accepting states. Accordingly (assuming that the system has no fairness conditions), the automaton $\tilde{A}_{S \times \neg\psi}$ is a universal automaton in which all runs except these that reach F are accepting. As a result, we need a much simpler nonemptiness procedure, which corresponds to backwards traversal. Thus, it initializes b with $Q \setminus F$, follows with the single while loop **while** b changes **do** $b := b \cap pre(b)$, and returns "not empty" when $Q_{in} \subseteq b$.

6   Certified Model Checking

Recall that $\tilde{A}_{S \times \neg\psi}$ with initial state q is not empty iff $rank(q)$ is well defined, and hence belongs to R. Thus, beyond a correctness proof, the analysis in Section 3 can be used in order to accompany the output of the procedure described in Figure 1 by a certificate, namely the odd ranking, that $\tilde{A}_{S \times \neg\psi}$ is indeed not empty, and S satisfies ψ. In this section we describe how to generate and check such a certificate.

As we showed, a function $f : V \to R$ is an odd ranking if F_j-vertices do not get an odd rank with index j, ranks along paths decrease monotonically, and all the paths of G_r eventually get trapped in an odd rank. The number of vertices along a path that get an even rank depends on the input word and is in general unbounded. Accordingly, checking whether a given function f is an odd ranking involves, in addition to local checks, also a check for eventualities, which involves a fixed-point computation. We now show that when $\mathcal{A}$ is a single-letter automaton, as is the case with $\tilde{A}_{S \times \neg \psi}$, it is possible to bound the number of vertices that get even ranks. Let $\mathcal{A} = \langle \{a\}, Q, \delta, Q_{in}, \alpha \rangle$ be a single-letter UGCW. Consider a vertex $\langle q, l \rangle$ that is finite in G_{2i}. Let $height(q, l)$ be the length of the longest path from $\langle q, l \rangle$ to a leaf of G_{2i}.

Lemma 7. *For all vertices $\langle q, l \rangle$, we have that $height(q, l) \in \{0, \ldots, n - 1\}$.*

Proof: Assume by way of contradiction that G_{2i} contains a vertex $\langle q, l \rangle$ such that $height(q, l) \geq n$. Then, the longest path from $\langle q, l \rangle$ to a leaf of G_{2i} contains at least one state q' that repeats at least twice. Thus, there is a path in G_{2i} that starts in $\langle q, l \rangle$, reaches a vertex $\langle q', l_1 \rangle$ with $l_1 \geq l$ and continues to a vertex $\langle q', l_2 \rangle$ with $l_2 > l_1$. As argued in the proof of Lemma 5, the sub-DAG with root $\langle q', l_1 \rangle$ coincides with the sub-DAG with root $\langle q', l_2 \rangle$. Hence, there is a path in G_{2i} that starts in $\langle q', l_2 \rangle$ and reaches a vertex $\langle q', l_3 \rangle$ with $l_3 > l_2$. By repeating this argument, we obtain an infinite path in G_{2i} that starts in $\langle q, l \rangle$, contradicting the fact that $\langle q, l \rangle$ is finite. $\square$

Following Lemma 7, we refine our set of ranks to $R = ([2n]^{even} \times \{1, \ldots, n\}) \cup ([2n]^{odd} \times \{1, \ldots, k\})$. We say that a function $f : V \to R$ is a *bounded odd ranking* if the following hold.

1. For all vertices $\langle q, l \rangle \in V$, if $f(\langle q, l \rangle) = \langle 2i + 1, j \rangle$, then $q \notin F_j$.
2. Consider an edge $\langle \langle q, l \rangle, \langle q', l + 1 \rangle \rangle \in E$.
   a) If $f(\langle q, l \rangle)$ is odd, then $f(\langle q', l + 1 \rangle) \leq f(\langle q, l \rangle)$.
   b) If $f(\langle q, l \rangle)$ is even, then $f(\langle q', l + 1 \rangle) < f(\langle q, l \rangle)$.

Thus, in a bounded odd ranking, the rank of successors of a vertex $\langle q, l \rangle$ with an even rank must be strictly smaller than the rank of $\langle q, l \rangle$.

Theorem 3. *Let $\mathcal{A}$ be a single-letter automaton. Then, G_r is accepting iff it has a bounded odd ranking.*

Proof: Each bounded odd ranking is also an odd ranking (with the height component being ignored). Thus, the direction from right to left follows from Theorem 1. For the other direction, we refine the function $rank : V \to R$ to account for heights of vertices. Thus, $rank(q, l)$, for $\langle q, l \rangle$ that is finite with height h in G_{2i} is $\langle 2i, h \rangle$. It is easy to see that, as with odd ranking, the first two conditions on rank being a bounded odd ranking hold. For the third condition, consider a vertex $\langle q, l \rangle$ with rank $\langle 2i, h \rangle$. By the definition of height, the successors of $\langle q, l \rangle$ in G_{2i} have heights that are strictly smaller than h. By Lemma 2, the successors of $\langle q, l \rangle$ that are not in G_{2i} have rank that is strictly smaller than $2i$. Thus, all the successors of $\langle q, l \rangle$ have ranks that are strictly smaller than $\langle 2i, h \rangle$, and we are done. $\square$

It turns out that the nonemptiness procedure actually accounts for heights too: we say that a state q is removed from b in iteration $(i[0], h)$ if q is removed from b during the i-th external while loop and its h-th internal while loop (we start to count iterations from 0). Lemma 8 then follows directly from the definition of ranks.

Lemma 8. *Consider a state q in $\mathcal{A}$.*

- *The state q is removed from b in iteration $(i[0], h)$ iff $rank(q) = \langle 2i, h \rangle$.*
- *The state q is removed from b in iteration $(i[1], j)$ iff $rank(q) = \langle 2i + 1, j \rangle$.*

In a symbolic implementation of the procedure NonEmpty, we maintain b in an OBDD. By maintaining in addition an ADD that maps states to ranks, we generate a certificate that can be used the certify the model-checking procedure. Let $f : Q \to R$ be a partial function from Q to R. The procedure Certified_Nonempty described in Figure 2 gets as input a single-letter UGCW $\mathcal{A}$ and calculates, in addition to the set b, also a function f that describes the odd ranking, which is returned in case no state of Q_{in} is in b^2. The procedure uses the operator $assign$, which given a set $\gamma \subseteq Q$ and a rank $r \in R$, returns a function in which all the states in γ are assigned r. In addition, initializing f to $\emptyset$ corresponds to an empty function, and $\cup$ between two functions with disjoint domains returns their union.

> **procedure** Certified_NonEmpty($\mathcal{A}$)
> $b := Q; f := \emptyset; i := 0;$
>   **while** b changes **do**
> $i := i + 1;$
> $h := 0;$
>   **while** b changes **do**
> $b := b \cap pre(b);$
> $f := f \cup assign(b \setminus pre(b), (2i, h));$
> $h := h + 1;$
>   **for** $j = 1 \ldots k$ **do**
> $b := b \cap until(b, F_j);$
> $f := f \cup assign(b \setminus until(b, F_j), (2i + 1, j));$
>   **if** $Q_{in} \cap b = \emptyset$ **then return**("not empty with certificate" f) **else return** ("empty");

Fig. 2. A nonemptiness procedure that generates a certificate.

The procedure can be easily implemented symbolically, with f being maintained in an ADD. Note that R consists of pairs, thus in some ADD implementations, where the domain of the ADD is restricted to single values, we have to encode R, which is easy.

Once the procedure Certified_Nonempty terminates and f is returned to the user, she can check that f represent a bounded odd ranking and that all the states in Q_{in} have a rank. Note how the use of heights, which enables us to consider bounded odd rankings, is essential here, as checking f involves only local checks (a comparison of a rank of vertices and their successors) and no fixed points. As described in the procedure Check_Certificate in Figure 3, the check can be done automatically and symbolically. The procedure uses the following Boolean functions.

---

[2] In case the intersection of Q_{in} and b is not empty, it is possible to enhance the procedure to return an evidence to the emptiness of $\mathcal{A}$; this is similar to the known generation of counterexamples and we do not discuss it here.

- $undef : 2^Q \to \{\textbf{true}, \textbf{false}\}$. Given a set γ of states, $undef(\gamma)$ is true iff f does not assign a rank to some state in γ; i.e., $\gamma \cap comp(f^{-1}(R)) \neq \emptyset$.
- $oops : \{1, \ldots, k\} \times 2^Q \to \{\textbf{true}, \textbf{false}\}$. Given an index $1 \leq j \leq k$ and a set γ of states, $oops(j, \gamma)$ is true iff there is $q \in \gamma$ with an odd rank with index j; i.e., $f(q) \in [2n]^{odd} \times \{j\}$. The symbolic implementation of $oops$ checks whether the intersection of $f^{-1}([2n]^{odd} \times \{j\})$ and b is empty.

The correctness of the procedure Check_Certificate follows immediately from Theorem 3.

---

procedure Check_Certificate($\mathcal{A}, f$)
  if $undef(Q_{in})$ **then return**("incorrect certificate");
  for $j = 1 \ldots k$ **do**
    if $oops(j, F_j)$ **then return**("incorrect certificate");
  for all $q \in Q$ and $q' \in \delta(q, a)$ **do**
    if $f(q)$ is odd and $f(q') > f(q)$ **then return** ("incorrect certificate");
    if $f(q)$ is even and $f(q') \geq f(q)$ **then return** ("incorrect certificate");
  return("correct certificate");

Fig. 3. Verifying that a certificate is correct.

In the case of LTL model checking, the automaton $\mathcal{A}$ is $\tilde{\mathcal{A}}_{S \times \neg \psi}$ and its state space consists of pairs $\langle s, P \rangle$, where s is a state of S and $P \subseteq cl(\psi)$ is a set of LTL formulas. The automaton $\tilde{\mathcal{A}}_{S \times \neg \psi}$ with initial state $\langle s, P \rangle$ is not empty if each path that starts in s violates at least one formula in P. Each set in the generalized Büchi acceptance condition corresponds to a formula of the form $\varphi U \theta$ and consists of all the states $\langle s, P \rangle$ in which P contains θ or does not contain $\varphi U \theta$. The rank of a state $\langle s, P \rangle$ explains how one of the formulas in P is not satisfied. If the rank is even, the explanation is transfered, via local conditions, to the successors of s. If the rank is odd, the particular formula that is not satisfied is recorded (by means of the index of the odd rank). Hence, for users that prefer to get a certificate that is similar to deductive proofs generated by proof-theoretic approaches to verification [MP92] (as in [PPZ01,PZ01]), it is possible to present the certificate as a list of states and how they satisfy (that is, do not satisfy the negation of) relevant subformulas of ψ.

Remark 2. As discussed in Remark 1, when ψ is a safety property, nonemptiness of $\tilde{\mathcal{A}}_{S \times \neg \psi}$ can be checked by backwards traversal and the nonemptiness procedure consists of the single loop **while** b changes **do** $b := b \cap pre(b)$. In this case, we can take b itself as the certificate, and there is no need to compute ranks. To check that b is a correct certificate, one has to check that $Q_{in} \subseteq b$, $b \cap F = \emptyset$, and $b = b \cap pre(b)$. Thus, while the computation of b involves a fixed-point, checking that it is indeed a fixed-point involves only local checks.

7 Discussion

We suggested a new complementation construction for NGBW. The analysis behind the construction led to a symbolic certified model-checking procedure. For an NGBW with n states and index k, our complementation results in an NBW with $2^{O(n \log nk)}$ states. This exponentially improves current complementation construction that first translate the NGBW into an NBW with $O(nk)$ states, and end up in an complementary automaton with $2^{O(nk \log nk)}$ states. Using our analysis it can also be shown that an alternating generalized co-Büchi word automaton with n states and index k can be translated to an alternating weak word automaton with $O(n^2 k)$ states, rather than $O(n^2 k^2)$, which would be the result of a translation that first translates the automaton into an alternating co-Büchi automaton. These improvements suggest that when it is possible to use both NGBW and NBW, one should prefer an NGBW with fewer states, even if its index is large. The above give rise to the following problem:

Given an NBW, find an equivalent NGBW with fewer states.

In particular, it'd be interesting to look for a variant of the translation in [MH84], of an alternating Büchi word automaton with state space Q into an NBW with state space $2^Q \times 2^Q$, that will end up in an NGBW with state space 2^Q.

Another open problem refers to the particular nonemptiness algorithm we were able to relate to the complementation construction and to augment with a certificate. Recall that our algorithm is similar to the OWCTY algorithm, which is a variant of the quadratic Emerson-Lei algorithm. As discussed in Section 1, more recent algorithms solve the nonemptiness problem with a sub-quadratic number of symbolic steps [BGS00, GPP03]. It'd be interesting to consider whether these algorithms can be related to complementation as well.

References

[BFG+97]   R. Bahar, E. Frohm, C. Gaona, G. Hachtel, E. Macii, A. Pardo, and F. Somenzi", Algebraic decision diagrams and their applications. FMSD 10(2/3):171–206, 1997.

[BGS00]   R. Bloem, H.N. Gabow, and F. Somenzi. An algorithm for strongly connected component analysis in $n \log n$ symbolic steps. In Proc. *FMCAD*, LNCS 1954, pages 37–54, 2000.

[Büc62]   J.R. Büchi. On a decision method in restricted second order arithmetic. In Proc. *Internat. Congr. Logic, Method. and Philos. Sci. 1960*, pages 1–12, Stanford, 1962. Stanford University Press.

[Cho74]   Y. Choueka. Theories of automata on ω-tapes: A simplified approach. *Journal of Computer and System Sciences*, 8:117–141, 1974.

[EL86]   E.A. Emerson and C.-L. Lei. Efficient model checking in fragments of the propositional μ-calculus. In Proc. *1st LICS*, pages 267–278, 1986.

[FFK+01]   K. Fisler, R. Fraer, G. Kamhi, M.Y. Vardi, and Z. Yang. Is there a best symbolic cycle-detection algorithm? In Proc. *7th TACAS*, LNCS 2031, pages 420–434, 2001.

[GKSV03]   S. Gurumurthy, O. Kupferman, F. Somenzi, and M.Y. Vardi. On complementing nondeterministic Büchi automata. In Proc. *12th CHARME*, LNCS, 2003.

[GPP03]   R. Gentilini, C. Piazza, and A. Policriti. Computing strongly connected components in a linear number of symbolic steps. In Proc. *14th SODA*, pages 573–582, 2003.

[GPVW95] R. Gerth, D. Peled, M.Y. Vardi, and P. Wolper. Simple on-the-fly automatic verification of linear temporal logic. In *Protocol Specification, Testing, and Verification*, pages 3–18. Chapman & Hall, August 1995.

[GV00] G. De Giacomo and M.Y. Vardi. Automata-theoretic approach to planning for temporally extended goals. In Proc. *5th ECP*, LNAI 1809, pages 226–238, 2000.

[HKSV97] R.H. Hardin, R.P. Kurshan, S.K. Shukla, and M.Y. Vardi. A new heuristic for bad cycle detection using BDDs. In Proc. *9th CAV*, LNCS 1254, pages 268–278, 1997.

[HTKB92] R. Hojati, H. Touati, R. Kurshan, and R. Brayton. Efficient ω-regula language containment. In Proc. *4th CAV*, LNCS 663, 1992.

[Kla91] N. Klarlund. Progress measures for complementation of ω-automata with applications to temporal logic. In Proc. *32nd FOCS*, pages 358–367, 1991.

[KPR98] Y. Kesten, A. Pnueli, and L. Raviv. Algorithmic verification of linear temporal logic specifications. In Proc. *25th ICALP*, LNCS 1443, pages 1–16, 1998.

[Kur94a] R.P. Kurshan. The complexity of verification. In *26th STOC*, pages 365–371, 1994.

[Kur94b] R.P. Kurshan. *Computer Aided Verification of Coordinating Processes*. Princeton Univ. Press, 1994.

[KV01a] O. Kupferman and M.Y. Vardi. Model checking of safety properties. *Formal methods in System Design*, 19(3):291–314, November 2001.

[KV01b] O. Kupferman and M.Y. Vardi. Weak alternating automata are not that weak. *ACM Trans. on Computational Logic*, 2001(2):408–429, July 2001.

[Mer00] S. Merz. Weak alternating automata in Isabelle/HOL. In *Theorem Proving in Higher Order Logics: 13th International Conference*, LNCS 1869, pages 423–440, 2000.

[MH84] S. Miyano and T. Hayashi. Alternating finite automata on ω-words. *Theoretical Computer Science*, 32:321–330, 1984.

[Mic88] M. Michel. Complementation is more difficult with automata on infinite words. CNET, Paris, 1988.

[MP87] Z. Manna and A. Pnueli. Specification and verification of concurrent programs by ∀-automata. In Proc. *Proc. 14th POPL*, pages 1–12, 1987.

[MP92] Z. Manna and A. Pnueli. *The Temporal Logic of Reactive and Concurrent Systems: Specification*. Berlin, January 1992.

[MW84] Z. Manna and P. Wolper. Synthesis of communicating processes from temporal logic specifications. *ACM TOPLAS*, 6(1):68–93, January 1984.

[Nam01] K.S. Namjoshi. Certifying model checkers. In Proc. *13th CAV*, LNCS 2102, pages 2–13, 2001.

[Nec97] G.C. Necula. Proof-carrying code. In Proc. *24th POPL*, pages 106–119, 1997.

[PPZ01] D. Peled, A. Pnueli, and L.D. Zuck. From falsification to verification. In Proc. *21th FST&TCS*, LNCS 2245, pages 292–304, 2001.

[PZ01] D. Peled and L.D. Zuck. From model checking to a temporal proof. In *Proc. 8th SPIN Workshop on Model Checking of Software*, LNCS 2057, pages 1–14, 2001.

[RBS00] K. Ravi, R. Bloem, and F. Somenzi. A comparative study of symbolic algorithms for the computation of fair cycles. In Proc. *FMCAD*, LNCS 1954, pages 143–160, 2000.

[Saf88] S. Safra. On the complexity of ω-automata. In *29th FOCS*, pages 319–327, 1988.

[SB00] F. Somenzi and R. Bloem. Efficient Büchi automata from LTL formulae. In Proc. *12th CAV*, LNCS 1855, pages 248–263. 2000.

[Sis94] A.P. Sistla. Satefy, liveness and fairness in temporal logic. *Formal Aspects of Computing*, 6:495–511, 1994.

[SVW87] A.P. Sistla, M.Y. Vardi, and P. Wolper. The complementation problem for Büchi automata with applications to temporal logic. *TCS*, 49:217–237, 1987.

[THB95] S. Tasiran, R. Hojati, and R.K. Brayton. Language containment using nondeterministic ω-automata. In Proc. *8th CHARME*, LNCS 987, pages 261–277, 1995.

[VW94]   M.Y. Vardi and P. Wolper. Reasoning about infinite computations. *Information and Computation*, 115(1):1–37, November 1994.

[Wol83]   P. Wolper. Temporal logic can be more expressive. *Information and Control*, 56(1–2):72–99, 1983.

Author Index

Lecture Notes in Computer Science

For information about Vols. 1–2871

please contact your bookseller or Springer-Verlag

Vol. 2926: L. van Elst, V. Dignum, A. Abecker (Eds.), Agent-Mediated Knowledge Management. XI, 428 pages. 2004. (Subseries LNAI).

Vol. 2923: V. Lifschitz, I. Niemelä (Eds.), Logic Programming and Nonmonotonic Reasoning. IX, 365 pages. 2004. (Subseries LNAI).

Vol. 2919: E. Giunchiglia, A. Tacchella (Eds.), Theory and Applications of Satisfiability Testing. XI, 530 pages. 2004.

Vol. 2917: E. Quintarelli, Model-Checking Based Data Retrieval. XVI, 134 pages. 2004.

Vol. 2916: C. Palamidessi (Ed.), Logic Programming. XII, 520 pages. 2003.

Vol. 2915: A. Camurri, G. Volpe (Eds.), Gesture-Based Communication in Human-Computer Interaction. XIII, 558 pages. 2004. (Subseries LNAI).

Vol. 2914: P.K. Pandya, J. Radhakrishnan (Eds.), FST TCS 2003: Foundations of Software Technology and Theoretical Computer Science. XIII, 446 pages. 2003.

Vol. 2913: T.M. Pinkston, V.K. Prasanna (Eds.), High Performance Computing - HiPC 2003. XX, 512 pages. 2003. (Subseries LNAI).

Vol. 2911: T.M.T. Sembok, H.B. Zaman, H. Chen, S.R. Urs, S.H. Myaeng (Eds.), Digital Libraries: Technology and Management of Indigenous Knowledge for Global Access. XX, 703 pages. 2003.

Vol. 2910: M.E. Orlowska, S. Weerawarana, M.M.P. Papazoglou, J. Yang (Eds.), Service-Oriented Computing - ICSOC 2003. XIV, 576 pages. 2003.

Vol. 2909: R. Solis-Oba, K. Jansen (Eds.), Approximation and Online Algorithms. VIII, 269 pages. 2004.

Vol. 2909: K. Jansen, R. Solis-Oba (Eds.), Approximation and Online Algorithms. VIII, 269 pages. 2004.

Vol. 2908: K. Chae, M. Yung (Eds.), Information Security Applications. XII, 506 pages. 2004.

Vol. 2907: I. Lirkov, S. Margenov, J. Wasniewski, P. Yalamov (Eds.), Large-Scale Scientific Computing. XI, 490 pages. 2004.

Vol. 2906: T. Ibaraki, N. Katoh, H. Ono (Eds.), Algorithms and Computation. XVII, 748 pages. 2003.

Vol. 2905: A. Sanfeliu, J. Ruiz-Shulcloper (Eds.), Progress in Pattern Recognition, Speech and Image Analysis. XVII, 693 pages. 2003.

Vol. 2904: T. Johansson, S. Maitra (Eds.), Progress in Cryptology - INDOCRYPT 2003. XI, 431 pages. 2003.

Vol. 2903: T.D. Gedeon, L.C.C. Fung (Eds.), AI 2003: Advances in Artificial Intelligence. XVI, 1075 pages. 2003. (Subseries LNAI).

Vol. 2902: F.M. Pires, S.P. Abreu (Eds.), Progress in Artificial Intelligence. XV, 504 pages. 2003. (Subseries LNAI).

Vol. 2901: F. Bry, N. Henze, J. Ma luszyński (Eds.), Principles and Practice of Semantic Web Reasoning. X, 209 pages. 2003.

Vol. 2900: M. Bidoit, P.D. Mosses (Eds.), Casl User Manual. XIII, 240 pages. 2004.

Vol. 2899: G. Ventre, R. Canonico (Eds.), Interactive Multimedia on Next Generation Networks. XIV, 420 pages. 2003.

Vol. 2898: K.G. Paterson (Ed.), Cryptography and Coding. IX, 385 pages. 2003.

Vol. 2897: O. Balet, G. Subsol, P. Torguet (Eds.), Virtual Storytelling. XI, 240 pages. 2003.

Vol. 2896: V.A. Saraswat (Ed.), Advances in Computing Science – ASIAN 2003. VIII, 305 pages. 2003.

Vol. 2895: A. Ohori (Ed.), Programming Languages and Systems. XIII, 427 pages. 2003.

Vol. 2894: C.S. Laih (Ed.), Advances in Cryptology - ASIACRYPT 2003. XIII, 543 pages. 2003.

Vol. 2893: J.-B. Stefani, I. Demeure, D. Hagimont (Eds.), Distributed Applications and Interoperable Systems. XIII, 311 pages. 2003.

Vol. 2892: F. Dau, The Logic System of Concept Graphs with Negation. XI, 213 pages. 2003. (Subseries LNAI).

Vol. 2891: J. Lee, M. Barley (Eds.), Intelligent Agents and Multi-Agent Systems. X, 215 pages. 2003. (Subseries LNAI).

Vol. 2890: M. Broy, A.V. Zamulin (Eds.), Perspectives of System Informatics. XV, 572 pages. 2003.

Vol. 2889: R. Meersman, Z. Tari (Eds.), On The Move to Meaningful Internet Systems 2003: OTM 2003 Workshops. XIX, 1071 pages. 2003.

Vol. 2888: R. Meersman, Z. Tari, D.C. Schmidt (Eds.), On The Move to Meaningful Internet Systems 2003: CoopIS, DOA, and ODBASE. XXI, 1546 pages. 2003.

Vol. 2887: T. Johansson (Ed.), Fast Software Encryption. IX, 397 pages. 2003.

Vol. 2886: I. Nyström, G. Sanniti di Baja, S. Svensson (Eds.), Discrete Geometry for Computer Imagery. XII, 556 pages. 2003.

Vol. 2885: J.S. Dong, J. Woodcock (Eds.), Formal Methods and Software Engineering. XI, 683 pages. 2003.

Vol. 2884: E. Najm, U. Nestmann, P. Stevens (Eds.), Formal Methods for Open Object-Based Distributed Systems. X, 293 pages. 2003.

Vol. 2883: J. Schaeffer, M. Müller, Y. Björnsson (Eds.), Computers and Games. XI, 431 pages. 2003.

Vol. 2882: D. Veit, Matchmaking in Electronic Markets. XV, 180 pages. 2003. (Subseries LNAI).

Vol. 2881: E. Horlait, T. Magedanz, R.H. Glitho (Eds.), Mobile Agents for Telecommunication Applications. IX, 297 pages. 2003.

Vol. 2880: H.L. Bodlaender (Ed.), Graph-Theoretic Concepts in Computer Science. XI, 386 pages. 2003.

Vol. 2879: R.E. Ellis, T.M. Peters (Eds.), Medical Image Computing and Computer-Assisted Intervention - MICCAI 2003. XXXIV, 1003 pages. 2003.

Vol. 2878: R.E. Ellis, T.M. Peters (Eds.), Medical Image Computing and Computer-Assisted Intervention - MICCAI 2003. XXXIII, 819 pages. 2003.

Vol. 2877: T. Böhme, G. Heyer, H. Unger (Eds.), Innovative Internet Community Systems. VIII, 263 pages. 2003.

Vol. 2876: M. Schroeder, G. Wagner (Eds.), Rules and Rule Markup Languages for the Semantic Web. VII, 173 pages. 2003.

Vol. 2875: E. Aarts, R. Collier, E.v. Loenen, B.d. Ruyter (Eds.), Ambient Intelligence. XI, 432 pages. 2003.

Vol. 2874: C. Priami (Ed.), Global Computing. XIX, 255 pages. 2003.